CGMA

全球特许管理会计师考试综合案例与解析［运营级］

CGMA CASE STUDY
EXAMINATION AND ANALYSIS
(Operational Level)

上

国际注册专业会计师公会◎编著

中信出版集团·北京

图书在版编目（CIP）数据

CGMA 全球特许管理会计师考试综合案例与解析：运营级：全 2 册 / 国际注册专业会计师公会编著．-- 北京：中信出版社，2019.1
ISBN 978-7-5086-9810-6

Ⅰ．①C… Ⅱ．①国… Ⅲ．①管理会计－资格考试－自学参考资料 Ⅳ．① F234.3

中国版本图书馆 CIP 数据核字（2018）第 265639 号

CGMA 全球特许管理会计师考试综合案例与解析（运营级）

编　　著：国际注册专业会计师公会
出版发行：中信出版集团股份有限公司
（北京市朝阳区惠新东街甲 4 号富盛大厦 2 座　邮编　100029）
承 印 者：北京诚信伟业印刷有限公司

开　　本：787mm×1092mm　1/16　　印　张：82.5　　字　数：1112 千字
版　　次：2019 年 1 月第 1 版　　印　次：2019 年 1 月第 1 次印刷
广告经营许可证：京朝工商广字第 8087 号
书　　号：ISBN 978-7-5086-9810-6
定　　价：249.00 元（全 2 册）

编委会

主　编　（以姓氏拼音为序）

顾朝阳　郭　飞　李　宁　李　颖
林　涛　钱　苹　邵　军　孙　健
孙　毅　谈多娇　田高良　杨　霞

编　者　（以姓氏拼音为序）

毕可佳　董士钧　郭晓梅　吉伟莉
季玉华　李　飞　梁耀荣　熊雪妍
唐　艳　王凌华　徐国栋　杨琬君
原盼盼　张桂玲　仲子昀

Preface

From the ancient times to the present, the change of every era is closely connected with innovation of tools and technologies. Since the 21st century, the rapid rise of information technology and AI(artificial intelligence) is promoting a new technological revolution. The rapid development of AI will profoundly change human social life and the world as well. On July 20, 2017, the State Council of China officially released a notice for the development of a new generation AI development plan. The overall development of disciplines, theoretical modeling, technological innovation, hardware and software upgrades etc. associated with the new generation AI, is leading to chain-style breakthroughs, promoting and accelerating all sectors of the economy and society shifting from digitization and networking to intelligentization.

With the rapid development of AI, many standardized practices in the finance area are being handled by systems. In the era of big data, the digital electronic operation model has resulted in huge surplus of entry level accounting personnel. Meanwhile, as to the large scale enterprises, the rise of financial shared service centers enables them to process accounting transactions in a large-scale and standardized way, therefore, the structure and size of the financial team will face substantial adjustments. The rapid development of science and technology is an important factor in promoting the transformation of financial personnel.

The CIMA(Chartered Institute of Management Accountants) has been dedicated to the management accounting education in China for more than 10 years, and in 2017, it formally established the Association of International Certified Professional Accountants (AICPA | CIMA) with the AICPA(American Institute of Certified Public Accountants). CIMA, the professional qualifications of accountants has also evolved to the professional qualifications of the CGMA(Chartered Global Management Accountants). The Association aims to promote the credibility of professional accountants, advance personal career development and professional success, create more business opportunities for enterprises, and facilitate global economic development. In the era of big data, it is one of our growth missions in China to help China's financial personnel to transform themselves successfully, to educate the next generation of financial talents, to meet the urgent needs of companies and government for management accountants in the new era, and to help promote China's economic development.

With the cooperation and support of enterprises, universities and the market, the Association has grown to a certain scale in China, with more than ten thousand students and members. The number of candidates who take the CGMA exam increase rapidly every year. The most classic part of the CGMA exam is the case study exam which is very realistic, providing practical guidance and a practical and effective learning path to the financial personnel for their ability transformation. The case teaching method has been introduced to China relatively late, with few application in management accounting teaching. The teachers and students are extremely lack of high-quality case teaching resources in this area, especially lack of cases and assessment systems that use multidisciplinary knowledge to solve practical problems. The educational features of CGMA have greatly filled this gap.

In "the Outline of the 13th Five-Year Plan for Accounting Reform and Development" released in 2016, the Ministry of Finance of China clearly stated that the construction of a management accounting guidance system should be strengthened, the application of management accounting should be popularized, and the management efficiency of accounting should be improved. It is also stated that to accelerate the training of management accounting talents, by 2020, to achieve the goal of 30,000 management accounting talents who are proficient in wealth management, or good at management and decision making. With the help of this book, the Association of International Certified Professional Accountants expects to promote the overall bilingual teaching of CGMA management accounting, and to contribute to the development of management accounting and talent training in China.

CGMA Case Study Examination and Analysis (*Operational Level*) is based on the *CGMA Management Accounting Competency Framework*, aiming to develop candidates' abilities of management accounting application and help them understand the business (including the business models) and its operating environment, identify risks and opportunities faced by organizations, through risk management and appropriate responses, help organizations seize the opportunity to create value for stakeholders at all times.

CGMA Case Study Examination and Analysis (*Operational Level*) covers five selected cases of CGMA operational level in the previous CGMA exam seasons, with examination techniques, key answers and expert commentary. This book can solve the issue of lacking teaching resources of management accounting cases in China, also help finance professionals learn management accounting knowledge and form relative mindset in an easier and faster way and successfully transform themselves in the era of AI. At the same time, as a tutorial book, this book will also help candidates who will participate in the operational level test to become familiar with the test pattern and prepare for the test better.

We are honored to invite prestigious teachers from 11 famous universities in North Asia to participate in the compilation of this bilingual tutorial book, they are Tsinghua University, Hong Kong Chinese University, Xi'an Jiaotong University, Xiamen University, Zhongnan University of Economics and Law, Central University of Finance and Economics, Jiangxi University of Finance and Economics, Tianjin University of Finance and Economics, Xi'an International Studies University, Shanghai Lixin University of Accounting and Finance, Hubei University of Economics. The completion of this book is a breakthrough. Hereby, we would like to express our sincere gratitude to the eleven universities for their support and contribution to China's management accounting education.

We hope to take this book as a starting point. Together with our colleagues in the management accounting education sector in China, we will keep working on the localization of CGMA tutorial cases, and we will continue to update and publish case resources to meet the needs of reader at different levels.

The Association of International Certified Professional Accountants

CEO Barry C. Melancon

North Asia Regional VP Vicky Li

March, 2018

序

从古到今，每个时代的改变都离不开工具和技术的革新。21 世纪以来，信息技术和人工智能的迅速崛起正在酝酿掀起新一轮科技革命。人工智能的迅速发展将深刻地改变人类社会的生活，改变世界。2017 年 7 月 20 日，国务院正式发布和印发了新一代人工智能发展规划的通知。与新一代人工智能相关的学科发展、理论建模、技术创新、软硬件升级等的整体推进，正在引发链式突破，推动经济社会各领域从数字化、网络化向智能化加速跃升。

随着人工智能的快速发展，财务领域中许多标准化的业务正在被电子系统所取代，大数据时代下数字化的电子操作模式造成了大量初级会计人员的过剩。同时，对于大型企业来说，财务共享中心的兴起使他们能够以一种规模化、标准化的方式处理会计核算业务，因此财务团队的结构和规模将面临重大调整。科技的快速发展是推动财务人员转型的重要因素。

在中国从事管理会计教育 10 余载的 CIMA（英国皇家特许管理会计师公会），于 2017 年与 AICPA（美国注册会计师协会）一起正式创立了国际注册专业会计师公会（AICPA | CIMA）。CIMA，英国皇家特许管理会计师职业资格也随之进一步演化升级为 CGMA（全球特许管理会计师职业资格）。新公会旨在提升专业会计师的公信力，促进个人的职业发展和职业成功，拓展企业商务机遇，推动全球经济发展。在大数据时代，如何帮助中国的财务人员成功转型，培养下一代的财务精英人才，满足新时代的企业和政府对于管理会计师的急切需求，推动中国经济的发展，是我们在中国的成长使命之一。

在企业、高校、市场的通力合作和支持下，国际注册专业会计师公会在中国已发展至一定规模，拥有上万名学员和会员，参加 CGMA 考试的考生每年都在迅速增加。CGMA考试体系中最经典的是案例分析考试，其案例拟真度很高，不仅具有实践指导意义，也为财务人员的能力转型提供了切实有效的学习路径。案例教学法进入我国的时间较晚，在管理会计教学中的应用也较少，广大师生极度缺乏这方面优质的案例教学资源，特别是综合运用多学科知识解决实际问题的案例及考核体系。CGMA 的教育特色大大填补了这一空白。

财政部在2016年发布的《会计改革与发展“十三五”规划纲要》中明确提出，要加强管理会计指引体系的建设，推进管理会计的广泛应用，提升会计工作的管理效率。它还提到要加快推进管理会计人才的培养，力争到2020年培养出3万名精于理财、善于管理和决策的管理会计人才。国际注册专业会计师公会期望通过本书，全面推进CGMA管理会计的双语教学，为中国的管理会计事业发展及人才培养略尽绵力。

《CGMA全球特许管理会计师考试综合案例与解析（运营级）》基于《CGMA管理会计能力框架》，旨在培养学习者的管理会计应用能力，帮助学习者了解商业（包括商业模式）及其运营环境，识别组织的风险和机会。通过对风险进行管理并做出适当反应，组织可以把握机会，在各个时期为利益相关人创造价值。

《CGMA全球特许管理会计师考试综合案例与解析（运营级）》涵盖了CGMA过往考季的5篇运营级精选案例，并附有考试技巧、考点解答，以及专家点评等全方面内容，可以在解决国内管理会计案例教学资源匮乏问题的同时，帮助财务专业人员更好更快地学习管理会计知识，形成特定的思维，让其在人工智能时代成功转型。同时，作为教学辅导书，本书也有助于参加运营级考试的考生熟悉考试模式，更好地为考试做准备。

本书很荣幸地邀请到了清华大学、香港中文大学、西安交通大学、厦门大学、中南财经政法大学、中央财经大学、江西财经大学、天津财经大学、西安外国语大学、上海立信会计金融学院、湖北经济学院十一所北亚区知名高校的名师参与汇编，开创性地完成了这本中英双语教学著作。在此，我们对这十一所高校对中国管理会计教育事业的倾力支持和贡献表示由衷的感谢！

我们希望以本书作为起点，与国内管理会计教育界的诸位同人一道，将CGMA教学案例的本地化开发变成一项持续的工作，不断推陈出新，出版适用于不同层级人员学习需求的案例资源，以飨读者。

国际注册专业会计师公会

首席执行官　Barry C. Melancon

北亚区总裁　李颖

2018年3月

总　目

上　册

下　册

目 录（上册）

第一部分

PART 1

CGMA考试简介

THE INTRODUCTION OF

CGMA EXAM

CGMA Exams and Its Operational Case Study Exam

CGMA is the most widely management accounting designation in the world. It distingvishes more than 150,000 accounting and finance professionals who have advanced proficiency in finance, operation, strategy and management.

People with the CGMA designation drive business decisions in companies, preserving value, protecting assets and chasing new opportunities. They're the ones on the inside, keeping track of monthly performance and everyday trends. They can combine numbers, smarts and creativity to uncover unseen problems, and give a fresh spin on solutions.

The CGMA professional qualification comprises three pillars of domain knowledge divided into three levels of achievement. The pillars are enterprise, performance and financial. The levels are operational, management and strategic. When combined with the required practical experience, the CGMA qualification ensures that members are business ready. The syllabus and related assessment will ensure that CGMA qualified finance professionals are competent in their accounting, finance and other skills, and confident in using them to add value to the many organisations in which they work.

To complete the CGMA qualification, and be able to use the CGMA® designation, students need to do some thing.

(1) Meet the entry requirements of the professional level qualification.

(2) Study for and complete the relevant professional level assessments, culminating in the strategic case study exam.

(3) Complete three years of relevant practical experience, which can be gained before, during and/or after studies.

CGMA Syllabus

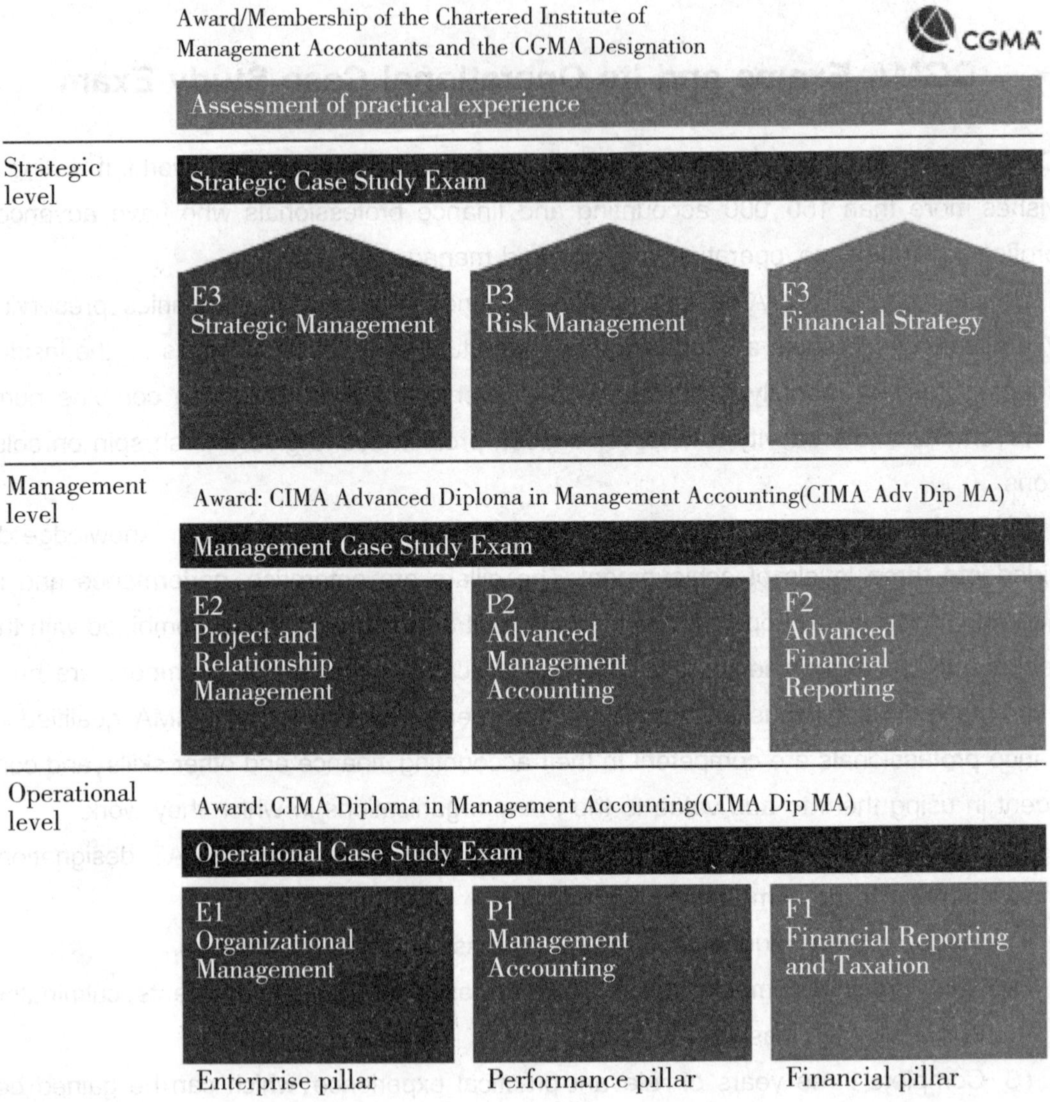

The Pillars

The three pillars represent specific areas of knowledge. The content of each pillar develops as students move up the qualification. The three pillars are interlinked to provide a coherent body of knowledge that will equip successful students with the competencies they require.

The enterprise pillar deals with the formulation of strategy, as well as its effective implementation. It emphasizes how change management, project management, relationship management and the structuring of organisations can help to successfully implement strategy.

The performance pillar uses the tools and techniques of management accounting and risk management to ensure that strategy is realistic and to monitor its implementation. It shows students how to use their understanding of costs to construct budgets, make decisions about prices and capital expenditure, manage costs and manage performance. It develops the ability of students to progressively identify, classify, evaluate and manage risk.

The financial pillar focus on the financial accounting and reporting obligations of the organisation. This includes an understanding of the regulatory framework and external reporting requirements, and the ability to construct and evaluate complex financial statements to show the financial position and performance of the organisation. The fundamentals of business tax are covered, as are the tax implications of financing decisions. It also looks at formulating financial strategy, which is linked to the formulation of organizational strategy in the enterprise pillar and assessing risk in the performance pillar.

The subjects in each learning pillar are designed to be sequential, from operational level to strategic level, encouraging the progressive development of knowledge, techniques and skills.

The Levels

The syllabus is also divided into three levels of achievement. The students' progress from the operational level to the management level and finally to the strategic level. At each level students study subjects across the three pillars.

The operational level covers the implementation of strategy, as well as reporting on the implementation of strategy. Its focus is the short-term.

The management level translates the strategy decided at higher levels, and communicates it to lower levels for implementation. It monitors and reports on the implementation of strategy, and ensures corrective action is taken when required. It has a medium-term focus.

The strategic level concentrates on making strategic decisions and providing the context for which those decisions will be implemented. Its focus is the long-term.

Syllabus Topic Weightings

Each subject is divided into a number of broad syllabus topics. A percentage weighting is shown against each syllabus topic and is intended as a guide to the proportion of study time each topic requires.

It is essential that all topics in the syllabus are studied, as all topics will be examined. The weightings do not specify the number of marks that will be allocated to topics in the examination.

	ENTERPRISE PILLAR	PERFORMANCE PILLAR	FINANCIAL PILLAR
STRATEGIC (DECIDE) MAKE STRATEGIC DECISIONS PROVIDE OVERALL CONTEXT FOR EFFECTIVE IMPLEMENTATION OF STRATEGY	**E3 Strategic Management** A Interacting with the organisation's environment 20% B Evaluating strategic position and strategic options 30% C Leading change 20% D Implementing strategy 15% E The role of information systems in organisational strategy 15%	**P3 Risk Management** A Identification, classification and evaluation of risk 20% B Responses to strategic risk 20% C Internal controls to manage risk 20% D Managing risks associated with cash flows 20% E Managing risks associated with capital investment decisions 20%	**F3 Financial Strategy** A Formulation of financial strategy 25% B Financing and dividend decisions 35% C Corporate finance 40%
MANAGEMENT (MONITOR) MONITOR IMPLEMENTATION OF STRATEGY ENSURE CORRECTIVE ACTION IS TAKEN	**E2 Project and Relationship Management** A Introduction to strategic management and assessing the global environment 30% B The human aspects of the organisation 20% C Managing relationships 20% D Managing change through projects 30%	**P2 Advanced Management Accounting** A Cost planning and analysis for competitive advantage 25% B Control and performance management of responsibility centres 30% C Long-term decision making 30% D Management control and risk 15%	**F2 Advanced Financial Reporting** A Sources of long-term finance 15% B Financial reporting 60% C Analysis of financial performance and position 25%
OPERATIONAL (IMPLEMENT) IMPLEMENT STRATEGY REPORT ON IMPLEMENTATION OF STRATEGY	**E1 Organisational Management** A Introduction to organisations 25% B Managing the finance function 15% C Managing technology and information 15% D Operations management 15% E Marketing 15% F Managing human resources 15%	**P1 Management Accounting** A Cost accounting systems 30% B Budgeting 25% C Short-term decision making 30% D Dealing with risk and uncertainty 15%	**F1 Financial Reporting and Taxation** A Regulatory environment for financial reporting and corporate governance 10% B Financial accounting and reporting 45% C Management of working capital, cash and sources of short-term finance 20% D Fundamentals of business taxation 25%
	Articulate a vision *How do we develop strategy?* *How do we plan for its effective implementation?*	**Ground the vision in reality** *How do we ensure our strategy is realistic?* *How do we monitor activity to ensure strategy is being implemented effectively?*	**Report attainment of the vision** *How do we prepare financial statements?* *How do we interpret financial statements to understand our performance and to help us make decisions?*

Lead Learning Outcomes

Each syllabus topic contains one or more lead learning outcomes, related component learning outcomes and indicative syllabus content.

Each lead learning outcome has several characteristics.

- Defines the skill or ability that a well-prepared candidate should be able to exhibit in an examination.
- Is examinable and demonstrates the approach likely to be taken in examination questions.

The lead learning outcomes are a part of hierarchy learning objectives. The verbs used at the beginning of each learning outcome relate to a specific learning objective e. g. evaluate performance using fixed and flexible budget reports.

The verb "evaluate" indicates a high-level learning objective (level 5). Because learning objectives are hierarchical, it is expected that at this level, students will have knowledge of fixed and flexible budget techniques, be able to apply them and assess performance using relevant reports.

The table lists the learning objectives and the verbs that appear in the syllabus learning outcomes.

Learning objective	Verbs used	Definition
EVALUATION How you are expected to use your learning to evaluate, make decisions or recommendations	Advise	Counsel, inform or notify
	Evaluate	Appraise or assess the value of
	Recommend	Propose a course of action
ANALYSIS How you are expected to analyse the detail of what you have learned	Analyse	Examine in detail the structure of
	Categorise	Place into a defined class or division
	Compare and contrast	Show the similarities and/or differences between
	Construct	Build up or compile
	Discuss	Examine in detail by argument
	Interpret	Translate into intelligible or familiar terms
	Prioritise	Place in order of priority or sequence for action
	Produce	Create or bring into existence

APPLICATION How you are expected to apply your knowledge	Apply	Put to practical use
	Calculate	Ascertain or reckon mathematically
	Demonstrate	Exhibit by practical means
	Prepare	Make or get ready for use
	Reconcile	Make or prove consistent/compatible
	Solve	Find an answer to/prove with certainty
	Tabulate	Arrange in a table
COMPREHENSION What you are expected to understand	Describe	Communicate the key features of
	Distinguish	Highlight the differences between
	Explain	Make clear or intelligible/state the meaning or purpose of
	Identify	Recognise, establish or select after consideration
	Illustrate	Use an example to describe or explain something
KNOWLEDGE What you are expected to know	List	Make a list of
	State	Express, fully or clearly, the details/facts of
	Define	Give the exact meaning of

Structure of the Assessments

CGMA's computerized assessments support the competency-based syllabus and respond to the changing needs of students and employers. The abandoned paper-based examinations reflects the wider use of technology, both within education, and in the workplace. These methods of assessment also ensure the learning outcomes tested will be those that demonstrate the knowledge, skill and abilities required for businesses today.

Two types of examinations will be used for the CGMA professional fixed and flexible—nine objective tests and three integrated case studies. Each of the nine subjects will be assessed by an objective test.

The case study exams will be used for each level of the CGMA syllabus (operational, management and strategic) integrating knowledge across the three pillars.

Objective Tests

The objective tests will focus on levels one, two and three of the CGMA hierarchy of learning objectives. However, they will also test levels four and five, especially at the management and strategic levels. Therefore, candidates can be tested on knowledge, comprehension, application, analysis and evaluation, in these examinations.

The objective tests are 90 minutes long. The results will be available shortly after sitting an objective test, and will provide candidates with specific feedback. Where a student has not passed, this feedback will provide information to help and guide them in revising, prior to re-sitting. Within each level, candidates are able to sit the objective tests in any order. However, they must complete (or receive an exemption from) the three objective tests at each level, prior to attempting that level's integrated case study tests. Each level's case study must be completed before progressing to the next level's objective tests.

Integrated Case Study Exams

The integrated case study exams combine the knowledge and learning across the three pillars, and are set within a simulated business context relating to one or more fictionalized organisations.

The integrated case studies are three hours long. They include both pre-seen material (including a database of related information) and unseen material, made available during the assessment.

The case studies incorporate long and short responses, supported by analysis of both financial and non-financial information. Their focus is: application, analysis and evaluation which are levels three, four and five of the CGMA hierarchy of verbs. The case studies will be marked by examiners.

Simulated business issues in the integrated case studies provide candidates with the opportunity to demonstrate their familiarity with the context and interrelationships of that level's subjects. This reflects the cross-functional working required in the workplace. Skills will include research and analysis, presentation of both financial and non-financial information, and communication skills.

Feedback will be provided to candidates with their results. Exam sittings for the case study exams will occur every three months. Candidates must have completed (or have been exempted from) the three objective tests at a particular level, before attempting that level's integrated case study.

An Example of Integrated Case Study Content

The integrated case study exams combine the knowledge and learning across the three pillars, and are set within a simulated business context relating to one or more fictionalized organisations—based on a real business or industry.

	YOUR ROLE	YOUR AUDIENCE	QUESTION TYPES	SAMPLE CASE STUDY SCENARIOS	
STRATEGIC	Senior manager	CFO and rest of senior management team	Long responses supported by analysis of both financial and non-financial information	E3	Analysis of strategic options, leading to recommendations and justification
				P3	Risks associated with this need to be scrutinised
				F3	A financial strategy needs to be formulated, ensuring the strategy is adequately funded
MANAGEMENT	Manager	CFO and senior business managers	Long and short responses supported by analysis of both financial and non-financial information	E2	Consideration of key stakeholders, and implementation via projects
				P2	Product and pricing decision, and/or the performance evaluation of division(s)/component parts
				F2	Impact on the financial statements and the performance of the organisation
OPERATIONAL	Finance officer	Manager and product owners	Short responses, supported by analysis of both financial and non-financial information	E1	Analysis of the structure of the organisation, as well as cross-functional communication
				P1	Costing and/or budgeting issues
				F1	Impact on the preparation of financial statements and tax implications

Exam Information and Timetable

Exams	Availability	Type of assessment	Length of assessment	Location
Objective tests				
E3 P3 F3 E2 P2 F2 E1 P1 F1	On-demand (Year round)	Computerised objective tests	90 minutes	Can be sat globally at Pearson VUE test centres
Integrated case studies				Locations of Pearson VUE test centres can be found via the CIMA website
Strategic Level Management Level Operational Level	Four sittings per year (February, May, August and November)	Computerised integrated case study	3 hours	

The Operational Case Study Exam

The case study exams are intended to demonstrate that students can apply the technical, business, people and leadership skills from the learning outcomes in the three subjects at the operational level (E1, P1 and F1) in a business context. There is no separate syllabus content for the operational case study exam.

The technical content and theory for the three subjects at a level will have already been tested thoroughly in the objective tests. The operational case study exam aims to test the application of this knowledge to real life business scenarios and, in doing so, tests the higher level skills of application, analysis and evaluation.

Recapping the Knowledge

- You may have been exempted from some subjects or passed the exams a few years ago. It will therefore be important for you to revise/recap the theory in these subjects and ensure you are familiar with the content.
- Remember that the case study will focus on the higher level skills, therefore it's important to master the ability to understand, evaluate and apply what you know to a real business context. Past exam questions which focus on providing this type of answer will help you to master these skills and also to recap any gaps in theoretical knowledge.
- It is still important to be aware of the level of the verb within each component learning outcome. This shows the skill level which you can expect to be examined in the case study exam. CIMA official website has past questions linked to component learning outcomes within the resources section of each subject and is therefore a good study resource to use in practicing past exam questions.
- Most technical calculations will be examined in the objective test exams, therefore there will be minimal focus on this skill in the case study exam. However, interpretation of results and understanding of financial statements remains vital, as this will help to provide a more comprehensive answer in the exam.

How to Recap Theory for Each Subject?

- If you need to revise the theory, you can buy the *CIMA-Kaplan Practice & Revision Kit* and revise the theory through question practice.
- If you think you need to learn from the beginning, you can buy the *CIMA-Kaplan Study Text* or if you prefer online learning, you can use cimastudy. com to learn by yourself. Self-study guides are available in CIMA official website and they can be help you organise your studies.

It is useful to familiarize yourself with the terminology we are using to describe our case study exams.

Pre-seen material—introductory overview information about a fictitious organization which is based upon a real life business or industry—published 7 weeks in advance of the exam date.

Additional information—new material introduced during the exam, may be in the form of documents (reports, articles) or emails from work colleagues.

Scene setting—the presentation of the scenario for the case which gives context to the triggers.

Triggers—something that changes the thinking required around the case study and requires you to take some action within the context of the case study. This could take a number of forms, such as: new information about the company or market (e. g. set of accounts or media article; an opinion that provides a different perspective on existing information) or a change in the priority of a task.

Tasks—essentially the "question requirements", what you have to do in response to the triggers.

Business skills, leadership skills, technology skills, and people skills—the competencies tested via the case study exams.

Pre-seen Material and Its Purpose

Pre-seen material will be published on CIMA official website seven weeks prior to the exam. It consists of introductory overview information and a number of other documents to set the scene or provide additional background data on the (fictitious) organisation, its competitors, markets etc. The same organisation and pre-seen materials will feature in all of the examinations in a particular exam window.

The purpose of the pre-seen material is to allow you to familiarise yourself with the (fictitious) organisation, its business/industry, market, competitors and so on. Although fictitious, the organisation in the case study will be modeled on real life business examples so that you can demonstrate your competence in applying theoretical skills to more or less real business scenarios. There is no need for you to over-research "real life" facts and statistics on the business or industry on which the case may be modelled. Your time will be better spent immersing yourself in the pre-seen material and getting up to speed with all aspects of the organisation and business portrayed in it.

Although the pre-seen material will be available to you in the exam room, the time pressures within the exam mean you will not have time to read it in depth but simply have it there as a reference point to check a detail or figure. This means you must be totally familiar with the material, and have analysed it in detail before entering the exam. However, you will not specifically be examined on background facts and data; it is how you use this information in your answers that will count.

It will be useful for you to refer the pre-seen material for the operational case study exam.

Scene Setting and Trigger

Once in the exam, the scene will be set by.

- The introduction of a scenario in which your role within the organisation will be introduced (note: the role may have already been introduced in the pre-seen).
- Additional information presented, for example, the market, competitors, key employees, financial highlights. Your role will reflect the level of the exam. E. g. at operational level, the role might be a finance officer whose job is quite internally focused and the tasks will reflect that.

Robyn (a typical finance officer)

At the operational level, Robyn is responsible for implementing strategy. Her focus is on the short-term. She needs to understand costs and cost accounting, in order for her to start preparing budgets, and to advise about short-term changes in products, volume and prices. Putting budgets together for the business also requires an understanding of how the business is structured. Robyn will need to communicate aspects of the budget, during both preparation and delivery, to non-finance staff.

Robyn prepares financial reports to show how the business is performing. She'll need to know about the regulatory environment, financial reporting, and business taxation. She may make decisions on working capital, cash and short-term finance.

Then, you will be presented with a "trigger", which sets the context for the actual tasks to be undertaken. The task would be about responding to the trigger but might have more than one element within it. E. g. an analysis and a written report may be required.

Specified Time for Each Section

As the case studies are designed to simulate real business scenarios, there is a "real time" element built in. Each new trigger gives rise to one or more tasks which are contained in a defined time frame within the exam. Tasks will appear in the form of a request or an instruction from a colleague to provide information, analysis or advice in response to issues arising from the triggers. Therefore, the tasks will not be structured in the same way as the current traditional exam "question requirements" and the CGMA verb hierarchy will not be used explicitly. As you move up through the qualification, the requirements in the case studies will become less structured and you will need to identify and prioritize issues, make judgements, consider potential solutions and so on, just as you would lie in an actual business situation.

The timings for each section are clearly shown on screen and give an indication of the marks available. So, for instance, a section allocated 45 minutes would be worth 25% of the marks in total (which may be spread across more than one requirement). You are moved on automatically after the time allocated to each section runs out and you cannot go back and check or amend your responses. This ensures that you get a sense of urgency to complete a task or respond to a request from a senior manager, just as you would lie in a real life work situation. It is in this way that you are able to demonstrate the competencies which are core to this assessment concept.

Time Management

During the time available for a section, you are expected to do some thing.

- Read the material provided in or around the unseen trigger.
- Identify the task or tasks, distinguishing separate components within each task.
- Plan an answer which covers all the required issues.
- Produce the answer.
- Check the answer.

Identify and Interpret the Task

This requires careful reading. You will need to identify all separate components within a task.

For instance, task four of the operational case study practice exam asks for two distinct areas to be covered in an email.

- Concerns about the cash position.
- Business to business marketing.

The first of these can be divided in two based on the instructions ("Firstly, why is the position so bad? Secondly, is there anything that we can do to improve the cash position so that the overdraft limit isn't breached?"). You would need to identify these separate requirements and address them in answers to cover all the points required.

Plan the Answer

As a rough rule, planning an answer should take up one third of the available time. There are three tools you can use to create your answer plan.

- The on-screen scratch pad—this can be accessed at any time during the exam, minimized, moved across the screen and resized. What is typed on to the scratch pad cannot be copy-pasted onto the main answer.
- The wipe clean note pad given out at the test center. If you fill up this white board, you can ask for another.
- The space available for presenting your answers on screen. Once you complete typing the full answer, please make sure you delete your answer plan to avoid con-

fusion to the marker.

In preparing the plan, you need to ensure that you have addressed the competencies expected at each level. It won't be enough to provide technically perfect definitions of terms requiring discussion, you will have to apply them to the organisation in the scenario.

The weightings for the competencies can be found in the syllabus and you should be aware of these when preparing your answers. Depending on the nature of the task and the weightings of the competencies, there may not be marks for each of the four competencies in each task. First and foremost you need to make sure that you address the task at hand and all aspects of it. If you do that correctly then you will be gaining marks across the competencies.

You shouldn't try to shoehorn, say leadership, into every task—at the operational level it is only worth 6% and therefore wouldn't be in more than 1 or 2 of the tasks.

Produce the Answer

You must appreciate that a good answer is not necessarily a long answer and, in all probability, a long answer is not necessarily a good answer. It is far more important to focus on quality rather than quantity.

Communication is going to be important in many of the tasks, appreciating who the audience is in each task, what they want to know, in what depth and in what level of technical detail is an important skill which needs to be practiced. Targeted communications which provide appropriate information with a clear commentary (if required) will earn most marks.

These assessments are not tests of typing speed. A typing speed of 20 words per minute, a rate achieved or bettered by 90% of office workers, will be sufficient in the exam. Basic formatting tools are available to candidates, such as bold, italic, underline, cut, copy and paste.

Check the Answer

You will receive a warning when there are five minutes of a section remaining. At that point, you should review your answer to check it.

- Covers the points in the plan.
- Presents a logical discussion.

■ Prioritizes issues according to what you understand the concerns of the organisation to be.

Conclusion

These case study exams are quite different to what you have encountered so far but by introducing them from operational level onwards, CGMA aims to help you develop the business skills required to apply knowledge to real world scenarios. Doing this under "real time" time constraints will help you demonstrate to your employer your competence and "business readiness".

The exams will be marked by CGMA's highly experienced markers and results delivered to you within a number of weeks, in time to allow you to enter and prepare for the next sitting if unsuccessful.

As with the objective tests, feedback on areas of strengths and weaknesses will be provided to both successful and unsuccessful candidates.

Operational Case Study Exam Grade Descriptions

	Fail	Moderate	Strong
Competencies	The learning outcomes/assessment criteria have not been met An unsatisfactory response to the tasks. The work may display some strengths but these are insufficient to demonstrate the standard expected of a minimally competent candidate A fail grade can generally be described using some or all of the following characteristics:	The learning outcomes/assessment criteria have been met to an acceptable standard A satisfactory response to the tasks. The work achieves the standard expected of a minimally competent candidate. There is scope for improvement beyond this level A moderate grade can generally be described using some or all of the following characteristics:	The learning outcomes/assessment criteria have been met fully, at a good or very good standard A good response to the tasks. The work exceeds the standard expected of a minimally competent candidate. A strong response does not necessarily imply perfection, so there may still be some scope for improvement beyond this level A strong grade can generally be described using some or all of the following characteristics:

（续表）

	Fail	Moderate	Strong
Technical skills	■ Demonstrates basic knowledge of the techniques and technical knowledge required across all three pillars, but some clear gaps across core syllabus areas ■ Limited understanding and/or exploration of key accounting issues/core topics ■ Little or no meaningful description of the application of techniques ■ Discussion of the results obtained from techniques and decision models is generally invalid ■ Significant and/or frequent errors in application of technical knowledge and interpretation of presented data/information	■ Demonstrates adequate knowledge of the techniques and technical knowledge required across all three pillars, although there may be some gaps ■ A general understanding and/or exploration of key accounting issues/core topics ■ Describes the application of techniques in a way that implies competence ■ Discusses the results obtained from techniques and decision models in a way that implies sufficient understanding ■ Minimal technical errors in application of technical knowledge and interpretation of presented data/information	■ Demonstrates good knowledge and understanding of the techniques and technical knowledge required across all three pillars ■ Good understanding and exploration of key accounting issues/core topics; supported by accurate and relevant arguments/examples ■ Discusses the application of techniques in a way that implies competence ■ Discusses the results obtained from techniques and decision models in a way that implies good understanding ■ No significant technical errors in application of technical knowledge and interpretation of presented data/information
Business skills	■ Demonstrates insufficient familiarity with the scenario described in the pre-seen and unseen materials by presenting responses that do not address the case study context ■ An inadequate understanding of the business under review. Limited understanding and application of relevant principles and techniques to the business context. ■ Limited understanding of business relationships, business models and the market environment. Over use of irrelevant learned business models with little or no application to the case study context.	■ Demonstrates adequate familiarity with the scenario described in the pre-seen and unseen materials by presenting responses that address the case study context ■ An adequate understanding of the business under review. Recognises and applies relevant principles and techniques to the business context ■ Adequate understanding of business relationships, business models and market environment, supported by relevant application to the case study context	■ Demonstrates strong familiarity with the scenario described in the pre-seen and unseen materials by presenting responses that address the case study context ■ A strong understanding of the business under review. Good understanding of current techniques and practices relevant to the specific business context ■ Good understanding of business relationships, business models and market environment, supported by relevant application to the case study context ■ Makes good use of new information from the unseen material and

（续表）

	Fail	Moderate	Strong
Business skills	■ Makes limited or no use of new information from the unseen material or pre-seen material to support explanations or discussions relating to business issues ■ Unsupported impractical and/or illogical suggestions without sound and reasoned explanations. Simple lists or generic comments/examples provided	■ Makes use of new information from the unseen material and the pre-seen material to support explanations or discussions relating to business issues, but not always in the most appropriate or relevant manner ■ Some practical and logical suggestions are offered Examples are given within the context of the business	the pre-seen material to support explanations or discussions relating to business issues. Good assessment of the relevance and value of new information evident ■ Substantiated suggestions which are generally accurate, practical and logical; supported by relevant examples. Arguments are fully developed and explained within the context of the business
People skills	■ Presentation and structure of responses are not in an appropriate format for the task requirements/character(s) in the task scenarios ■ An inadequate understanding of the issues that might affect the responses of the characters under review ■ Tasks are not approached in a way that demonstrates an adequate understanding of human behaviour ■ Little or no consideration given to the impact of an organization's management and their decisions on business stakeholders, including personnel ■ Standard of communication is poor: responses are disorganized and lack a coherent structure	■ Presentation and structure of responses are appropriate to the task requirements/character(s) in the task scenarios ■ An adequate understanding of the issues that might affect the responses of the characters under review ■ Where appropriate, tasks are approached in a way that demonstrates an adequate understanding of human behaviour ■ Some consideration given to the impact of an organisation's management and their decisions on business stakeholders, including personnel ■ Standard of communication is satisfactory: although responses are generally coherent there is some lack of clarity of thought or expression	■ Presentation and structure of responses meets the task requirements to a good standard and is tailored to suit different personalities and motivations of characters in the task scenarios ■ A strong understanding of the issues that might affect the responses of the characters under review ■ Where appropriate, tasks are approached in a way that demonstrates a good understanding of human behaviour ■ Full consideration given to the impact of an organisation's management and their decisions on business stakeholders, including personnel. This is evident throughout the decision-making process and proposed solutions ■ Standard of communication is good. Concepts expressed in a clear and systematic manner

（续表）

	Fail	Moderate	Strong
Leadership skills	Any marks earned against leadership skills will have contributed to your overall score. However, the pass/ fail decision does not depend on your performance in the area due to the low(6%) competency weighting		
	■ Limited understanding of coaching and mentoring skills associated with leading and motivating the characters described in the pre-seen and unseen materials, and/or a limited understanding of motivational factors within the organisation ■ There are many impractical or illogical suggestions	■ An adequate understanding of coaching and mentoring skills associated with leading and motivating the characters described in the pre-seen and unseen materials and/or an adequate understanding of motivational factors within the organisation ■ Some practical and logical suggestions	■ Full consideration given to coaching and mentoring skills associated with leading and motivating the characters described in the pre-seen and unseen materials and/or a good understanding of motivational factors within the organisation ■ Suggestions are generally practical, logical and innovative
Integration skills	Any marks earned against integration skills will have contributed to your overall score. However, the pass/ fail decision does not depend on your performance in this area due to the low total mark allocation		
	■ Little or no evidence of integration across the pillars	■ Some integration within and across the pillars, but potential for further development	■ Good knowledge and understanding across all the competencies and awareness of the connections and interactions within and across pillars

CGMA 考试及运营级案例分析考试

CGMA 是全球广泛持有的管理会计师头衔。全球已有 150 000 名精通财务、运营、战略与管理的会计和财务专业人士荣获此头衔。

持有 CGMA 头衔的员工，在企业中主要负责驱动企业决策，维护企业价值，保护企业资产并寻找新机会。他们会通过跟踪每月绩效，掌握日常趋势，从而对各项数据了如指掌。他们能够将数据、智慧和创造力三者完美融合，从而发现隐藏的问题，并对既有解决方案提出新的洞见。

CGMA 专业资格考试由 3 个主要的知识板块构成，每个板块又可进一步分为 3 个层级。3 个板块分别是企业板块、绩效板块、财务板块，而层级分别是运营级、管理级和战略级。当与实际经验相结合时，拥有 CGMA 职业资格能确保那些员工具备相应的商业能力。课程大纲和相应的评估则能保证经过 CGMA 认证的专业人员可以胜任公司的会计、财务和其他工作，并有信心利用这些技能给他们所在的公司带来价值。

要想通过 CGMA 的资格考试并使用 CGMA 头衔，考生需要做到以下几点。

（1）符合职业资格的入门要求。

（2）学习并完成相关的专业考试，最终通过战略级案例分析考试。

（3）拥有 3 年以上的相关工作经验，其可以是在学习之前、之间和/或之后获得的。

CGMA 大纲

授予/CIMA皇家特许管理会计师公会会员资格及CGMA全球特许管理会计师头衔

CGMA

实践经验评估

战略级

战略案例分析考试

E3 战略管理	P3 风险管理	F3 财务战略

管理级

授予/CIMA管理会计高级文凭

管理案例分析考试

E2 项目与关系管理	P2 高级管理会计	F2 高级财务报告

运营级

授予/CIMA管理会计文凭

运营案例分析考试

E1 组织管理	P1 管理会计	F1 财务报告与税务
企业板块	绩效板块	财务板块

知识板块

3 个板块代表着 3 个知识领域，且每个板块的内容难度随着考生学习的深入而加大。这 3 个板块相互关联，提供的是一个连贯的知识体系，以便让成功通过 CGMA 考试的学员具备他们所需的能力。

企业板块关注的是战略的形成和有效的实施。它强调如何进行变革管理、项目管理、人际管理和能推动公司战略成功实施的公司架构。

绩效板块注重使用管理会计与风险管理的工具和方法，确保战略具有可行性并监督其实施过程。它向学生展示了如何利用他们对预算成本的理解，如何控制成本和管理绩效，让学员逐步学会识别、分类、评估和控制风险。

财务板块注重财务会计和对组织的报告责任。它包括对监管框架和对外出具财务报告的要求的理解，以及构建和评估复杂财务报表的能力，以显示该组织的财务状况和业绩。财务板块还涵盖营业税的基本原理以及融资决策的税务影响，同时，它还关注与企业板块中组织战略形成和绩效板块中风险评估相关的财务战略的形成过程。

每一个学习板块的内容是有先后顺序的，从运营级到战略级，以帮助学员逐步获得知识、技巧和能力。

层级

课程大纲同样也分为 3 个层级，学员从运营级开始学习，再到管理级，最终到战略级。在每一个层级，学员都需要完成与 3 个板块相关的内容的学习。

运营级涵盖战略的实施和实施进程的报告，关注的是短期。

管理级要求对更高层级的战略决策进行分析和讨论，以便基层员工实施。它还要监督和汇报战略的实施效果，并保证在正确的时间点有正确的行动，关注的是中期。

战略级注重战略决策的制定，以及为决策推行提供必要的环境，关注的是长期。

课程大纲中各个主题的权重

每个科目都会有数个大纲主题。每一个大纲主题都会对应一个百分比，表示学习该主题所需要花费的时间比例。

所有课程大纲中的主题都需要学习，因为所有的都将被考查，但是这个比例并不等同考试中分配分数的比例。

战略级（决策）	E3战略管理	P3风险管理	F3财务战略
进行战略决策，为战略有效执行提供全方位的便利条件	A 与组织所处的环境相互影响 20% B 评估战略定位和战略选择 30% C 领导变革 20% D 实施战略 15% E 信息系统在公司战略中的作用 15%	A 识别、分类和评估风险 20% B 对战略风险做出响应 20% C 内部控制和风险管理 20% D 管理与现金流相关的风险 20% E 管理与资本投资决策相关的风险 20%	A 制定财务战略 25% B 融资和股息决策 35% C 公司财务 40%
管理级（监管）	E2项目管理与关系管理	P2高级管理会计	F2高级财务报告
监督战略的实施状况，确保已经采取正确的行动	A 引入战略管理，评估全球环境 30% B 组织的人力资源管理 20% C 关系管理 20% D 通过项目实现管理变革 30%	A 为获取竞争优势而进行的成本规划和分析 25% B 责任中心的控制和业绩管理 30% C 制定长期决策 30% D 管理控制与风险 15%	A 长期资金来源 15% B 财务报告 60% C 财务业绩和财务状况分析 25%
运营级（执行）	E1组织管理	P1管理会计	F1财务报告和税务
实施战略，对实施的进度进行汇报	A 组织导论 25% B 财务职能管理 15% C 技术和信息管理 15% D 运营管理 15% E 市场营销 15% F 人力资源管理 15%	A 成本核算系统 30% B 预算 25% C 制定短期决策 30% D 应对风险与不确定性 15%	A 财务报告和公司治理的监管环境 10% B 财务会计和报告 45% C 营运资金管理，现金和短期资金来源管理 20% D 企业税收基础 25%
	企业板块	绩效板块	财务板块
	阐明愿景	证明愿景是可行的	报告愿景的完成情况
	我们如何形成战略？ 我们怎么制订和实施有效的计划？	如何保证我们的战略是可行的？ 我们如何监管以确保战略有效地实施？	我们如何准备财务报告？ 我们如何使用财务报表来解释公司的财务状况并帮助制定决策？

学习成果

每个大纲主题都包括一个或者多个学习成果，其与学习内容和大纲详解相关。

每一个学习成果都具备两个特征。

- 明确准备充分的学员应该在考试中展现的技能或能力。
- 是可考查的，并说明了在考试试题中可能采用的考查方法。

学习成果是多级学习目标结构中的一部分。每个学习成果开头使用的动词都与特定的学习目标有关，例如，使用固定和弹性的预算报告来评估绩效。

动词“评估”表示一个较高层次的学习目标（5 级）。因为学习目标是分层级的，在该级别，学员将会了解固定预算和弹性预算，并能使用它们以及用相关报告评估绩效。

下表列出了学习目标以及会在大纲学习成果中出现的动词。

学习目标	关键词	定义
评估 你觉得你应该如何使用你学到的知识去评价、制定决策或者是提出建议	建议	建议、告知或通知
	评价	评估或评价某事或某物的价值
	推荐	建议采取一系列的行动
分析 你如何分析你所学到的具体内容	分析	仔细检验某组织的结构
	归类	放入定义好的层级或部门
	比较和对比	指出两者间的相似和/或不同
	构建、创立	构建或编制
	讨论	详细探讨
	解释	转换成更易懂或更熟悉的术语
	排序	将要执行的任务按顺序排列
	创造	建立或者付诸实践
应用 你将如何利用你的知识	应用	投入实际使用
	计算	数据方面的估计或测算
	证明	通过实际情况说明
	准备	达到可以使用的状态
	调整	证明一致/兼容
	解决	找到答案/确切地证明
	列表	编写表格
理解 你想要明白什么	描述	描述某物的关键特点
	区分	强调两者的不同
	解释	明确或理解/说明意义或目的
	识别	在思考后发现、建立或者选择
	举例说明	利用例子描述或者解释某事
了解 你想知道什么	列示	列出清单
	陈述	充分清楚地表述某事的细节/真实内容
	定义	给出确切的意义

考试框架

CGMA 的计算机考试能有效支撑以能力为基础的课程大纲，并能根据学员和求职者的需求变化随时做出调整，而且纸质考试的日渐消亡，也反映了科技在教育领域和职场中的广泛应用。这些评估方法同样也能确保这些经过测试的学习成果是当下企业需要员工具备的知识、技能和能力。

既统一又灵活的 CGMA 专业考试会使用两种考试形式——9 场客观题考试和 3 场综合案例分析考试。9 个科目都将通过客观题考试进行评估。

3 场综合案例分析考试分别对应 CGMA 大纲框架的每一层级（运营级、管理级和战略级），并整合了 3 个板块的知识。

客观题考试

客观题考试偏重测试 CGMA“动词”等级图中的前 3 个学习等级。当然，第 4 和第 5 等级也会被测试，尤其是当它们涉及管理级和战略级的内容时。因此，在这些考试中，我们会测试学员的知识、理解、应用、分析和评估能力。

客观题考试时间为 90 分钟。考试结果将在进行客观考试不久后公布，并会向考生提供具体的反馈。如果有学生没有通过考试，这个反馈将提供信息以帮助和指导他们在下次参加考试前重新进行复习。在每一个等级中，学员都能随机参加 3 场客观题考试，但他们必须在每个级别完成（或获得免试）3 场客观题考试，才能进行这个级别的综合案例分析考试。只有通过上一个级别的案例分析考试后，才能进行下一级别的客观题考试。

综合案例分析考试

综合案例分析考试将 3 个板块的学习内容进行了整合，并设置了逼真的虚拟商业场景——基于真实的一个或者多个公司。

综合案例分析考试时间为 3 个小时。考试材料包括事先看过的材料（包括相关信息的数据）和未看过的材料。

案例分析是基于对财务和非财务信息的分析，给予长期和短期的反馈，侧重于 CGMA“动词”等级图中的第 3 个、第 4 个和第 5 个，即应用、分析和评估。案例分析将由考官进行评分。

综合案例分析考试中的模拟商业问题给学员提供了展示他们对于内容和该级别科目

内在关系的了解的机会，也反映了工作场所中所需要的跨职能工作能力。其技能包含对财务和非财务信息的研究、分析和展示能力，以及交流能力。

考试成绩和结果反馈将会提供给学员。综合案例分析考试每 3 个月举行一次，学员必须完成（或已经被准予免试）某一等级的 3 次客观题考试之后，才能参加该等级的综合案例分析考试。

综合案例分析的内容示例

综合案例分析考试将 3 个板块的学习内容联系在一起，并将之放入包括一个或多个虚构组织所模拟的商业背景中，其中的这些虚构组织是基于一个真实的企业或行业的情况建立的。

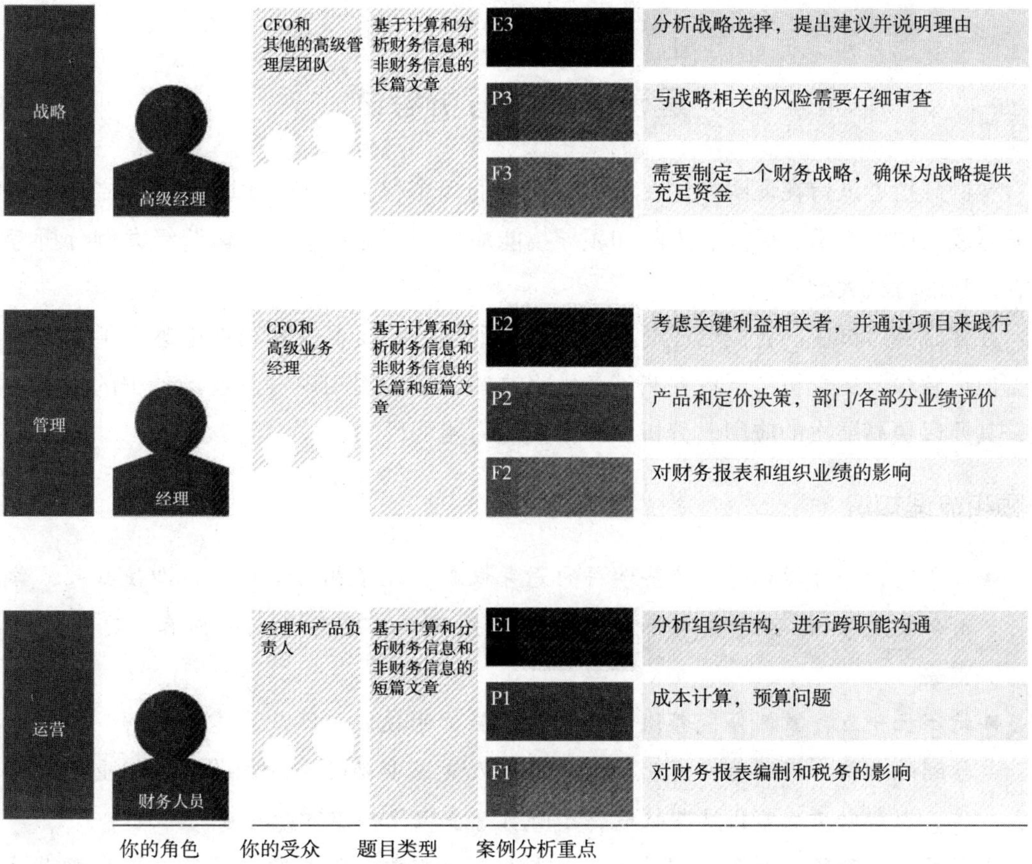

考试信息和时间表

考试	考试时间	考试类型	考试时长	考点
客观题考试				
E3 P3 F3 E2 P2 F2 E1 P1 F1	根据需求	机考客观题	90 分钟	可以在全球的Pearson VUE考试中心进行
综合案例分析考试				
战略级 管理级 运营级	每年4次报名考试（2、5、8、11月）	机考综合案例分析	3小时	在CIMA的网站能找到PearsonVUE考试中心的位置

运营级案例分析考试

案例分析考试旨在证明考生在学习运营级的 3 个科目（E1、P1 和 F1）之后，可以将学习成果中的技术、商业、人际和领导技能应用到商业环境中。运营级案例分析考试没有单独的考试大纲。

在客观题考试中，我们已经对这一层级 3 个科目的技术内容和理论进行了全面的测试。但运营级案例分析考试旨在测试考生将这些知识应用到现实商业场景中的情况，为此，其要以更高层次的应用、分析和评估技能为测试目标。

回顾和梳理知识

- 几年前，你可能获得了某些学科的免考权或通过了相关考试。但即使如此，你仍有必要复习/梳理这些学科涉及的理论并确保自己熟悉相关内容，这一点非常重要。
- 请牢记一点，案例分析考试侧重于更高层次的技能，因此，掌握理解、评估和将学到的知识应用到现实商业场景中的能力是很重要的。以往的考题侧重于提供答案，以帮助考生掌握这些技能，了解自身在理论知识方面存在的不足。
- 了解每一阶段学习成果中的动词水平也十分重要，因为它揭示了案例分析考试中考生希望被测试的技能水平。CIMA 官网列出了过去的考题并将它们与每个科目资源部分的阶段学习成果对应了起来，因此，这是一个很好的学习资源，考生可以用它练习过去的考题。

- 绝大多数技术性计算将在客观题考试中进行测试，因此，案例分析考试很少涉及这项技能。然而，阐释结果以及理解财务报表仍然至关重要，因为这将有助于考生更为全面地回答考题。

如何梳理每个科目的理论?

- 如果需要复习理论知识，考生可以购买 *CIMA–Kaplan Practice & Revision Kit*，通过回答问题来复习理论知识。
- 如果考生认为自己需要从头开始学习，则可以购买 *CIMA–Kaplan Study Text*；如果考生更喜欢在线学习方式，就可以通过“cimastudy. com”网站进行自学。CIMA官网提供了自学指南，可以帮助考生安排自己的学习内容。

熟悉我们在案例分析考试中会用到的术语，是非常有用的。

背景材料——以真实业务或行业为基础的虚构组织的介绍性概述信息。考前资料会在考试前 7 周发布。

附加信息——考试期间所补充的新材料，它可能是文件（报告、文章）或同事发来的电子邮件。

场景设置——案例的场景陈述，为触发事项提供背景。

触发事项——会改变案例分析所需的思考，并要求考生在案例的既定情景下采取一些行动。触发事项可有多种表现形式，如有关公司或市场的新信息（例如账目或媒体文章，从不同视角来看待现有信息的某个观点），抑或任务优先级别的改变。

任务——实质上是“答题要求”，是为应对触发事项，考生必须采取的举措。

商业技能、领导技能、技术技能、人际技能——是案例分析考试所测试的能力。

背景材料及其用途

考试前 7 周我们会在 CIMA 官网上发布背景材料，它包括介绍性的概述信息和其他一些文件，目的是设置情景或者提供（虚构）组织及其竞争对手、市场等附加背景数据。在特定的考试窗口期，同一个组织和相同的背景材料将出现在所有考试中。

我们提供背景材料的目的是让考生熟悉（虚构）组织及其业务/行业、市场、竞争对手等情况。虽然案例分析所涉及的组织是虚构的，但它是以现实商业为基础构造的，因此，考生能够在一定程度上展示自身将理论技能应用于真实业务场景中的能力。考生无须过多研究案例可能涉及的业务或行业在“现实生活”中的实际情况和统计数据，最好将时间用于深入研究背景材料，快速掌握案例所涉及的组织和业务的所有方面。

尽管在考试过程中，考生仍然有机会翻看背景材料，但考试的时间限制会让考生没有时间来深入阅读背景材料，只能将其作为检查某个细节或数字的参考。这意味着考生必须完全熟悉这些材料，并在考前加以详细分析。但是，考试不会专门考查背景事实和数据，而是考查考生如何应用这些信息来回答考题并覆盖得分要点。

对于运营级案例分析考试而言，考生参考背景材料是很有用的。

场景设置和触发事项

一旦开始考试，考生将会看到以下场景设置。

- 介绍考生在组织中所担当的角色将面临的场景（注意：背景材料可能会对角色做预先介绍）。
- 给出附加信息，例如市场、竞争对手、关键员工、财务要点等。考生担当的角色将反映考试级别，例如，在运营层面，这个角色可能是一个财务人员，他的工作侧重于内部，其任务也将反映这一点。

Robyn（一名具有代表性的财务主管）

在运营级，Robyn 负责战略的实施，其工作侧重于短期。她需要了解成本和成本核算，以便着手准备预算，并针对产品、数量和价格的短期变化提出建议。将为企业制定预算的工作聚集在一起，这就要求 Robyn 了解企业的架构。在编写和提交预算期间，Robyn 还需要与非财务人员就预算的各个方面进行沟通。

Robyn 要编写财务报告以说明企业的经营情况，因此，她需要了解监管环境、财务报告要求和企业税费。她可能还需要对营运资金、现金和短期融资做出决定。

然后，考生会接触到一个“触发事项”，它为需要执行的实际任务设定了背景。这个任务是对触发事项的回应，但可能涉及多个元素，例如可能需要进行分析和做出书面报告。

考试各个部分的特定时间

案例分析旨在模拟真实的业务情景，因此，其中内置了一个“实时”元素。每个新的触发事项都会形成一项或多项任务，而这些任务都处在考试所界定的时间范围内。任务将以同事发出请求或指示的形式出现，为触发事项所引发的问题提供信息、分析或建议。因此，这些任务不会采用现有传统考试“答题要求”那样的结构，而且也不会明确使用 CGMA 的动词层次结构。随着资质级别的提高，案例分析考试的要求将不再那么结构化，考生需要确定问题及其优先顺序，做出判断，考虑潜在的解决方案等，就像现实业务中的实际操作一样。

每个部分的考试时间都清晰地显示在电脑屏幕上，也指明了该部分被赋予的分值。例如，某个部分被分配了 45 分钟的答题时间，那么，它将占到总分值的 25%（分值可能分散在多个要求中）。在分配给每个部分的考试时间结束之后，考试内容将自动向后切换，考生不能返回前一个部分进行检查或修改答案。这样做可以确保考生能够感受到完成任务或响应高管人员要求的紧迫感，就像现实生活中的工作场景一样。通过这种方式，考生能够展示自身是否具备这一评估概念下的核心能力。

时间管理

在各个部分规定的考试时间内，考生需要做以下事情。

- 阅读提供的材料或隐含的触发事项。
- 确定一项或多项任务，区分各项任务的单独要素。
- 构思答案，其内容需涵盖所有要求作答的问题。
- 书写答案。
- 检查答案。

识别和阐释任务

该项任务要求考生仔细阅读考试材料，从中识别出该任务涉及的所有单独要素。

例如，在运营级案例分析练习考试中，第 4 项任务要求考生书写的电子邮件涵盖两个不同的领域。

- 对现金状况的关注和担忧。
- 企业之间的营销。

根据指示，第一项内容可分为两部分。（“首先，为什么现金状况如此糟糕？其次，我们是否可以采取一些举措来改善现金状况，以确保不会‘超出’透支额度?”）考生需要明确这些单独要求，并在答案中加以说明，以涵盖所有答题要点。

构思答案

一个大概的规则是，构思答案所花的时间应占考试时间的1/3。考生可以利用以下3种工具来构思自己的答案。

- 屏幕上的便笺本。在考试期间，考生可在任何时候访问便笺本，将其最小化，在电脑屏幕上移动或调整大小，但录入便笺本中的内容不能直接复制粘贴到主体答案中。
- 考试中心发放的空白便笺纸。如果一张用完了，考生可以再要一张。
- 电脑屏幕上用于书写答案的空间。在输入完整的答案之后，考生应确保删除了答案草稿，以避免评卷人产生混淆。

在构思答案时，考生需要确保自己已经展现出了各个级别考试所考查的能力。仅在技术上对需要讨论的术语进行完美的定义是不够的，考生务必要将这些术语应用到具体的组织场景中去。

考生可通过考试大纲了解能力方面的分值分配，在准备答案时应考虑到这些权重。根据任务的性质以及所考查能力的分值分配，可以得知，在每个任务所涉及的4项能力中，有些能力可能没有对应的分值。首先，考生需要确保自己处理了手头的任务且覆盖了所有方面。如果完全做到这一点的话，考生将获得能力方面的分值。

考生不应将有关内容，如领导力等，生硬地体现在每个任务中——在运营级的考试中，领导力只占6%的分值，因此，它所涉及的任务最多为1项或2项。

书写答案

考生必须明白，答得好并不一定非要答得长，冗长的答案十之八九不是好答案，注重质量要远胜于注重数量。

在很多任务中，交流都是非常重要的事项。考生要弄清楚每个任务对应的人员，他们希望了解什么，需要了解到何种程度以及达到哪种技术细节层面，这是一项重要的技能，需要加以练习。如果有针对性地进行沟通，并提供恰当的信息和清晰的评论（如有需要），那么，考生将获得最高的分数。

这些评估并不是测试考生的打字速度。每分钟20个单词的打字速度，90%的办公室人员都能达到或超过这一打字速度，而这用来应付考试已经足够了。考生能够获取基本的格式工具，如加粗、斜体、下划线、剪切、复制和粘贴。

检查答案

在各个部分的考试时间仅剩下 5 分钟的时候，考生将收到警示信号。此时，考生应该检查自己的答案并查看其是否符合以下要求。

- 涵盖了答案草稿中的要点。
- 进行了符合逻辑的讨论。
- 根据自己对组织所关注的事项的理解来安排了处理问题的优先顺序。

总结

这些案例分析考试与考生之前所接触过的考试完全不同，但是 CGMA 从运营级开始引入这类考试，旨在帮助考生提升所需的业务技能，以便其将知识应用到现实场景中。考试时设置的“实时”形式的时间限制，有助于考生向雇主展示自己的能力和“业务熟练度”。

CGMA 会聘请经验丰富的阅卷人来进行人工打分，考试结果也将在数周之内反馈给考生。这样，如果未能通过本次考试，考生也有足够的时间来报考和准备下一次的考试。

与客观题考试一样，无论考生是否通过考试，CGMA 都会向每名考生提供反馈信息，说明他们的优点以及不足。

运营级案例分析考试成绩描述

	不合格	合格	优秀
能力	考生未能实现学习成果/未达到评估标准。 对任务的回答不够理想。考生在这项工作中可能展示了某些优点，但这些还不足以证明考生具备考试所要求的最低能力 未能通过考试的考生通常具有如下所述的部分或全部特征：	考生在一定程度上实现了学习成果/达到了评估标准 对任务的回答令人满意。考生在这项工作中达到了考试所考查的最低能力标准，但在这个水平之上有提升空间 达到合格标准的考生通常具有如下所述的部分或全部特征：	考生完全实现了学习目标/达到了评估标准，且展现了良好或优秀的水准。 对任务做出了很好的回答。考生在这项工作中所展现的能力超过了考试所考查的最低能力标准。做出了很好的回答并不意味着回答堪称完美，考生在这个水平之上仍有一些提升空间 达到优秀标准的考生通常具有如下所述的部分或全部特征：

（续表）

	不合格	合格	优秀
技术技能	■ 已经掌握了3个板块所要求的技术基础知识以及科技知识，但与考试大纲核心领域的要求还存在明显的差距 ■ 对关键会计问题/核心议题的理解和/或探索有限 ■ 对技术应用的描述很少或根本没有意义 ■ 未能有效讨论应用技术和决策模型所取得的结果 ■ 在应用技术性知识以及阐述所列示的数据/信息时出现了重大和/或频繁的错误	■ 已经充分掌握了3个板块所要求的技术知识以及科技知识，但存在一些差距 ■ 对关键会计问题/核心议题有一定的理解和/或探索 ■ 对技术应用的描述展示了自身的能力 ■ 对应用技术和决策模型所取得的结果进行了讨论并展示了自身充分的理解 ■ 在应用技术性知识以及阐述所列示的数据/信息时存在较小的技术错误	■ 已经很好地掌握和理解了3个板块所要求的技术以及科技知识 ■ 对关键会计问题/核心议题有充分的理解和探索，并能运用准确及相关的论点/例子加以佐证 ■ 对技术应用进行了讨论并展示了自身的能力 ■ 对应用技术和决策模型所取得的结果进行了讨论并展示了自身出色的理解 ■ 在应用技术性知识以及阐述所列示的数据/信息时不存在明显的技术错误
商业技能	■ 对考前资料和现场资料所描述的场景不够熟悉，未能针对案例的背景来答题 ■ 对需要审查的业务理解不足。对相关原则和技术的理解不够，未能结合业务环境加以有效应用 ■ 对业务关系、商业模式和市场环境的理解不足。滥用所知但不相关的商业模式，且很少或根本没有应用案例中给出的条件 ■ 未能充分利用或根本没有利用现场资料或考前资料所提供的新信息来为相关业务问题的阐释或讨论提供支持 ■ 提出的建议不切实际和/或不符合逻辑，且没有做出有效和合理的解释。只提供了简单的列表或泛泛而谈的评论/常见例子	■ 很好地熟悉了考前资料和现场资料所描述的场景，做出的回答契合案例分析的背景 ■ 充分理解了需要审查的业务，梳理出了相关原则和技术并结合业务环境加以应用 ■ 充分了解了业务关系、商业模式和市场环境，并结合案例分析的背景加以正确应用。 ■ 利用现场资料和考前资料提供的新信息来为相关业务问题的阐释或讨论提供支持，但所采用的方式并非最为恰当或最为相关的 ■ 提出了一些切合实际且合乎常理的建议。根据业务所处的环境给出了一些例子	■ 非常熟悉考前资料和现场资料所描述的场景，做出的回答契合案例分析的背景 ■ 深入了解了需要审查的业务，对与特定业务环境相关的现有技术和实践有充分的了解 ■ 深入了解了业务关系、商业模式和市场环境，并结合了案例分析的背景加以正确应用 ■ 充分利用现场资料和考前资料所提供的新信息来为相关业务问题的解释或讨论提供支持。很好地评估了新信息的相关性和价值 ■ 提出的实质性建议是准确、切合实际且合乎逻辑的，并运用了相关例子加以佐证。根据业务所处环境，展开了充分的论证和阐释

（续表）

	不合格	合格	优秀
人际技能	■ 未能结合任务所处的场景，根据任务要求/所涉及人员，以适当的形式来表述和组织答案 ■ 未能充分理解那些可能影响到当事人及其反应的问题 ■ 任务的处理方式未能展示出对人类行为的充分了解 ■ 很少或根本没有考虑到组织管理层及其决策对业务利益相关方（其中包括人员）的影响 ■ 糟糕的沟通：答案混乱无序，缺乏连贯的结构	■ 答案的表述和组织形式恰当，结合了任务所处的场景，契合任务要求/所涉及人员 ■ 充分理解了那些可能影响到当事人及其反应的问题 ■ 在适当的情况下，以适当的方式来处理任务，展示了对人类行为的充分了解 ■ 对组织管理层及其决策对业务利益相关方（其中包括人员）的影响做了一定的考虑 ■ 沟通水平令人满意：虽然答案在总体上连贯一致，但想法或表述还存在一些不甚清晰的地方	■ 答案的表述和组织很好地契合了任务要求，并能结合任务所处的场景，根据所涉及人员的不同性格和动机做出具体的阐述 ■ 深入认识了那些可能影响到当事人及其反应的问题 ■ 在适当的情况下，以适当的方式来处理任务，展示了对人类行为的深入了解 ■ 充分考虑了组织管理层及其决策对包括全体人员在内的业务利益相关方的影响，这一点在整个决策制定过程以及所提出的解决方案中体现得非常明显。 ■ 良好的沟通：概念以清晰和系统的方式被表述
领导技能	任何与领导技能相关的得分都有助于提高考生的总分。但是否能通过考试并不取决于考生在这一方面的表现，因为领导能力的分值权重很低（6%）		
	■ 对于如何领导和激励考前资料和现场资料中所描述的人员，未能充分掌握与之相关的指导和辅导技能，并且/或者未能充分了解组织内部的激励因素 ■ 提出了许多不切实际或不符合逻辑的建议	■ 对于如何领导和激励考前资料和现场资料中所描述的人员，充分掌握了与之相关的指导和辅导技能，并且/或者充分了解了组织内部的激励因素 ■提出了一些切合实际且合乎常理的建议	■ 对于如何领导和激励考前资料和现场资料中所描述的人员，全面考虑了与之相关的指导和辅导技能，并且/或者深入了解了组织内部的激励因素 ■ 就总体而言，所提出的建议切合实际、合乎常理并具有创新性
综合技能	任何与综合技能相关的得分都有助于提高考生的总分。但是否能通过考试并不取决于考生在这一方面的表现，因为其在总分值中的占比很低		
	■ 很少或根本没有证据可以证明考生具备跨科目的整合能力	■ 具备一定的科目内和跨科目综合能力，但有进一步的发展空间	■ 良好地掌握和理解了各项能力所涉及的知识，对科目内部和科目之间的联系和相互影响有了充分的认识

第二部分

PART 2

CGMA运营级案例

THE CGMA'S OPERATIONAL
LEVEL CASE

案例一

CASE 1

至臻糕点公司

FIRST CLASS BAKERY

Background Materials

Introduction

First Class Bakery manufactures cakes and desserts which are packaged and sold directly to food retailers. All production is carried out on a single site in the west of Beeland, a country that has B$ as its currency.

Most of the cakes are manufactured for large food retailers who sell the cakes with their own brand. First Class Bakery packages the cakes using the brand required by each retailer.

Some cakes and desserts are sold to small independent food retailers under First Class Bakery's own brand. All sales are made in Beeland, in B$.

First Class Bakery was established over 30 years ago by three brothers: John, James, and Frank Mitchell. The three brothers owned and ran the business until recently when 80% of its equity shares were sold to Universal Foods, a large group quoted on Beeland's stock market. The two older brothers John and James retired from the business altogether. Frank Mitchell, who is 62, has remained with the business with a 20% equity stake and now is the managing director. Frank has until now always worked in the production side of the business.

Since the acquisition, Universal Foods has brought in a number of key directors and managers from other parts of the group to work exclusively in First Class Bakery. These people include Rajiv Patel, the new finance director, and Fred Knight, the new sales and marketing director.

First Class Bakery is situated on the outskirts of a major town. There are two sites: a production site and a garage site. The garage site houses First Class Bakery's distribution fleet. The production site is large, with a single large building to deal with the main production and several separate buildings for stores and offices.

Products

First Class Bakery manufactures a range of cakes and desserts at its production site. This range is split into three product lines: slab cakes, special occasion cakes and desserts.

Slab Cakes

Slab cakes are cakes which have no frosting or decoration. They are made in the following flavours: lemon, banana, ginger, vanilla, cherry, walnut, chocolate and coffee.

The ingredients for slab cakes are mixed in one flavour at a time and are baked in long deep tins. Once cooled and removed from the tins, the cakes are cut to size and then packaged in a clear wrapping with the appropriate food retailer or First Class Bakery label affixed.

Slab cakes are sold predominately to large food retailers under their own brands, although some are sold to small independent retailers under the First Class Bakery brand. Slab cakes sales account for approximately 60% of First Class Bakery's revenue.

Special Occasion Cakes

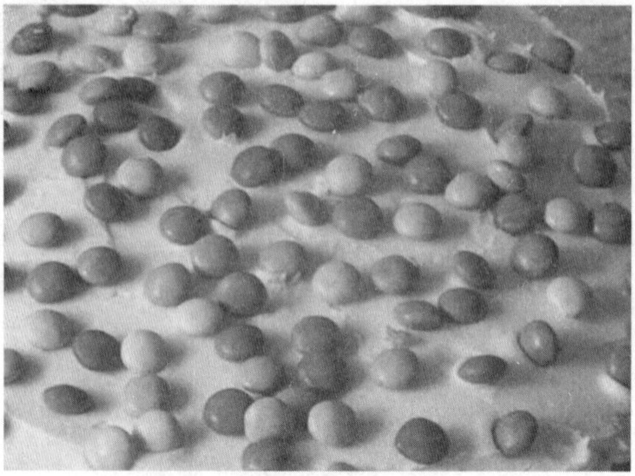

Special occasion cakes have frosting and decoration. The base cake's flavour is vanilla or chocolate, which is mixed and then baked in individual shallow foil tins. Once cooled, special occasion cakes are topped with frosting and embellished with decorations. A variety of frosting colours and decorations are used depending upon customers' requirements, although most special occasion cakes are topped with sprinkles and small sweets. Seasonally appropriate decorations are also used depending on the customers' requirements.

All special occasion cakes are sold under the food retailer's own label, and these account for approximately 35% of First Class Bakery's revenue.

Desserts

The desserts made by First Class Bakery are cake based. This is a relatively new product line and has its own designated small production line within the production facility. Currently three flavours of desserts are made：chocolate，toffee and treacle.

The dessert is sold in a plastic pot. Each pot includes a layer of sauce below the cake. The desserts are designed so that people can warm it up before eating it and then turn the pot upside down.

Desserts currently account for approximately 5% of First Class Bakery's revenue and are all sold with First Class Bakery labels to small independent food retailers.

Shelf-life

First Class Bakery's products have a shelf life of 8 to 12 weeks，depending on the fruit and sugar content. The packaging that First Class Bakery uses ensures that the freshness is maintained，so that the quality of the product is maintained.

Product Development

Other than dealing with customer specification's changes in flavour and decoration，there has been little product development at First Class Bakery in respect of slab cakes and special occasion cakes for a number of years.

The focus over the past three years has been on the design and launch of the dessert range. As yet the dessert range has not secured a major customer base.

Universal Foods recently brought in a new product development manager，Tony Swift，who now works exclusively within First Class Bakery. His role is to：

- focus on expanding the dessert range；
- introduce a range of products which cater to the latest consumer's preference for healthier cakes，using unrefined sugar and organic ingredients；
- develop a new range of gluten free cakes.

Production

Production can be broken down into 3 main processes for all product ranges.

- Ingredient preparation.
- Mixing and baking.

■ Finishing.

Slab cakes and special occasion cakes are manufactured on the main production line, whilst desserts are manufactured on a small self-contained line.

Slab cakes and Special Occasion Cakes

Ingredient Preparation

Production is carried out on a batch basis. Each flavour of slab cake and special occasion cake is mixed in a batch which will make 500 units of finished product. Each type of product uses the same basic recipe for the cake mixture, which includes butter, sugar, flour and eggs. However, different flavours are used and nuts and/or fruits may be added.

At the ingredient preparation stage, the dry ingredients (flour and sugar) are measured out and placed in 12. 5kg bags. A batch of cake mixture requires 62. 5kg of both flour and sugar and hence 5 bags of each are placed in a wheeled bin ready for mixing. Each wheeled bin will ultimately include the ingredients for one batch of cakes.

Butter and eggs are stored in a large refrigerated unit. Butter is purchased in 5kg blocks. Each batch requires 62. 5kg of butter and hence 12. 5 blocks are used for each batch of cakes. Within the refrigerated unit, butter is stored in piles of 12. 5 blocks so that it is easy to complete the ingredients for each batch. Eggs are also stored within the unit in trays of 25 (which is how they are received from the supplier). Four trays of eggs (that is 100 eggs) are needed for each batch.

The blocks of butter and trays of eggs are placed in the wheeled bins shortly before mixing. Most of the employees in the ingredient preparation area are unskilled.

Mixing and Baking

Mixing is carried out by large industrial mixers. The butter and sugar are initially mixed together until they are light and fluffy and then the flour and eggs are gradually added and beaten into the mixture. Flavourings and any fruit and nuts are added at the end of the mixing process.

The mixers are manually controlled by employees who are skilled at knowing when to start adding the flour and eggs and when to add the flavourings. When employees are satisfied with the mixture consistency, they will pour the mixture into a vat.

If the batch is for slab cakes, pour the mixture from the vat into long deep tins, which have been placed by hand onto a conveyor belt. The pouring process itself is automated. When full, the tins move on the conveyor belt to the ovens.

If the batch is for special occasion cakes, 10 individual foil trays will be placed by hand on baking trays side by side. These baking trays are then placed on a conveyor belt and pass through the pouring process to the ovens.

All cakes are baked in 3 industrial ovens, with the baking trays placed in to or out of the oven by hand. Each industrial oven is capable of baking 5 trays of special occasion cakes (based on 5 shelves in the oven) or 12 tins of slab cake (based on 4 shelves in the oven). One type of cake is baked at a time in each oven.

The ovens are computer controlled with a set baking time programmed for each type of cake, although the experienced and skilled employees do have a manual override facility if they feel that a batch needs slightly longer baking. After this, the tins or trays of cake are left to cool in large stacking trolleys.

Finishing

When they are cool, the stacking trolleys will be moved by hand to separate sections on the main line: one section for slab cakes and one section for special occasion cakes.

Slab cakes are taken out of the tin by hand and then placed on a conveyor belt. The rest of the process is mostly automated: the long cake is cut into the appropriate number of individual cakes by machine and wrapped in a clear cellophane wrapper. The corresponding labels will have been placed into the machine according to the batch and be attached automatically. At the end of the line, the cakes are packaged into boxes by hand.

Special occasion cakes (in their foil tins) are placed by hand onto a conveyor belt individually. The rest line is semi-automated: each cake will have frosting piped onto the top of it by machine. Frosting is made in chocolate and vanilla flavours by a small team of bakers who continually fill the frosting to the vats within the machine. A significant amount of time is therefore taken to set up machinery to ensure that the correct frosting is used.

Then the cakes are decorated with the appropriate decorations according to the customers' requirements. This is done by hand because their requirements are constantly changing and experience has shown that manual decoration is more efficient. It also ensures that the end product can be sold as handiwork. This work is typically undertaken by semi-skilled employees but only after they have proved their ability to do the task.

Because of the nature of special occasion cakes, more inspections are carried out compared to slab cakes; typically three times as many special occasion cakes are inspected than slab cakes.

After decoration, each special occasion cake will be placed by hand into the appropriate customer box. These individually boxed cakes are then placed into large boxes which are ready for the distribution to customers.

Boxes of finished product are taken by forklift to the despatch warehouse.

Desserts

The production process for desserts is similar to cakes, although it is carried out on its own line. The desserts production line is only two years old and it is mostly automated.

Ingredient Preparation

The ingredients for desserts are stored in their own storage area. The procedures of measuring ingredients for a batch are the same as for cakes.

Mixing, Baking and Finishing

The mixing of the dessert mixture is carried out in the same way as cakes. The sauce that is included in the desserts is made in large industrial pans because it involves the appropriate heating of butter and sugar to create the sauce. Cakes and sauce mixtures are poured into the appropriate vats respectively at the start of the production line.

The rest of the process is automated with a facility for the production employees to halt the production line, if for example they believe that the desserts need to be baked for longer or if there is a problem with the operation of the line. Each flavour of desserts requires a slightly different programme on the production line and hence there is a period of setting-up time required to ensure that the correct programme is selected. Typically, because the vats also need to be cleaned out for each change of flavour, only one flavour a day is produced and hence the programme setting-up occurs at the start of each day.

The production line starts with sauce and then cake mixture being poured into the individual dessert pots which then pass along the production line straightly into ovens. The desserts are baked for a set time and passed through a cooling phase before being packaged. All of this is automated.

As with the slab cakes and special occasion cakes, a mix of unskilled, semi-skilled and skilled employees is used in the manufacture of desserts. The skilled employees are used in the mixing process for both the cakes and sauces and to supervise the production line. The cleaning of vats and ensuring that the production line is stocked with empty desserts pots and the appropriate packaging for each flavour is carried out by semi-skilled and unskilled employees.

First Class Bakery Customers

Slab Cakes

Approximately 85% of slab cakes manufactured are sold to three national food retailers under their own labels. Each of these major retailers purchases different flavours, although the lemon and coffee slab cakes are common to all three.

The other 15% of slab cakes manufactured are sold with a First Class Bakery label to small independent food retailers. At any time there are approximately 30 small independent retailers, although this does fluctuate, as customers come and go.

Special Occasion Cakes

All of the special occasion cakes manufactured are sold to three national food retailers under their own labels. Two of these three retailers also purchase slab cakes from First Class Bakery, although one does not. Therefore across slab cakes and special occasion cakes there are four national food retail customers.

Each retailer has its own specifications for special occasion cakes in terms of frosting colours and decorations. These specifications regularly change due to the time of year.

Desserts

All of the desserts manufactured are sold as First Class Bakery branded products. Currently these desserts are only sold to small independent retailers, although one of the large national retailer customers did order a trial amount a few months ago. This large retailer has not yet placed a larger order.

Customer Relationships

First Class Bakery has close relationships with its large food retailer customers through personal contact, but due to resource constraints it has not been able to develop such links with smaller retailers. As a result, sales to smaller retailers have achieved very little growth. The competitors of First Class Bakery all use up to date information systems to assist the management of customer relations and other areas of business.

Credit Terms

First Class Bakery offers 30 days credit terms to all its customers. Two of the national retailers pay promptly, although the other two national retailers often delay payment for the smallest discrepancy in paper-work. The small independent customers often pay late.

Customer Perception

First Class Bakery is regarded by its national and independent food retail customers as a manufacturer of high-quality cakes and desserts. Whilst occasionally cakes and desserts have to be returned as a result of damage in transit, a customer has never returned any products due to the poor manufacturing quality.

In a recent survey to all customers, First Class Bakery scored highly in respect of product quality and value for money, although it was marked down in respect of promptness of delivery. This survey also showed customer's increasing concerns about environmental issues and the notion of responsible sourcing of ingredients.

The First Class Bakery brand currently has a limited presence in the market. The launch of the desserts range two years ago has made a start in terms of building the brand, although First Class Bakery branded products are still only available in small independent food retailers. Universal Foods has brought in a marketing expert, Fred Knight, to be the sales and marketing director to improve its brand perception. Fred Knight now solely works for First Class Bakery.

Distribution

First Class Bakery has a fleet of ageing delivery vehicles which are used to transport products to customers. These vehicles only just comply with current legislation regarding emissions. When not in use, the fleet is kept at the garage site five kilometres from the main production site.

This site includes a fully functioning garage facility which is used to maintain and repair the trucks when needed. The garage has on occasion been unable to cope with the demands of vehicle repairs, which has caused delays in scheduled deliveries, particularly to the smaller customers.

The distribution site is in what has recently become a residential area, and it is surrounded by new housing developments.

There are a number of qualified mechanics and 15 drivers who work at the garage site.

Suppliers

First Class Bakery sources most of its ingredients from a single supplier. To date, the directors of First Class Bakery have believed that single sourcing ensures better quality of both product and service.

Flour is purchased directly from a single flour mill which is located near to the First Class Bakery production site. The directors have always considered that to create the best quality products, flour should be as fresh as possible to ensure that the rising agents in the flour work to the optimum. Hence they have always been keen that the flour supplier is reasonably close-by so that deliveries can be small and often.

Sugar is sourced from a major importer and distributor of sugar and sugar products. This supplier has warehouses and a distribution network all over Beeland.

Butter is purchased from a national dairy products supplier.

Eggs are usually purchased from a nearby supplier. Occasionally an additional supplier is used for eggs, if the local supplier is unable to fulfil the order.

Flavourings and decorations used in the cakes and desserts are sourced from a total of seven different suppliers, some of which are located in other countries. Each of these suppliers supplies a different type of flavouring or decoration.

Recycling and Environmental Policy

First Class Bakery seeks as far as possible to recycle packaging for ingredients. Sacks used to transport flour and sugar and egg trays are usually given back to suppliers for further use. The majority of production waste is sold to local farms as pig feed. A small amount of waste is disposed at a cost to the business.

Employees

First Class Bakery's Four Directors

- Frank Mitchell as managing director (MD).
- Rajiv Patel as finance director (FD).
- Nisha Sanders as production director (PD).
- Fred Knight as sales and marketing director (SMD).

There are also a number of senior managers within the business. The key senior managers are detailed in the following.

Total Employees Number

	Number
Production	325
Administration	23
Distribution	30
Total	378

Production Employees Number

	Departments				Total
	Ingredient preparation	Mixing and baking	Finishing	Warehouse and general factory support	
Production operative	30	120	130	0	280
Supervisor	2	10	10	10	32
Management				10	10
R&D personnel				3	3
Total	32	130	140	23	325

Administration Employees Number

	Number
Director (MD, FD and SMD)	3
Finance①	4
Sales and marketing	6
Purchasing administration support	2
Production scheduling and stores administration support	3
Human resources and payroll	3
Information technology support	2
Total	23

①Finance includes the finance manager, Tim Walker, who is a qualified accountant, a senior accountant and two junior accountants. You are one of the junior accountants. None of the finance employees are qualified in credit control.

Key People

The key members of management and the chain of command are shown in the following organisational chart.

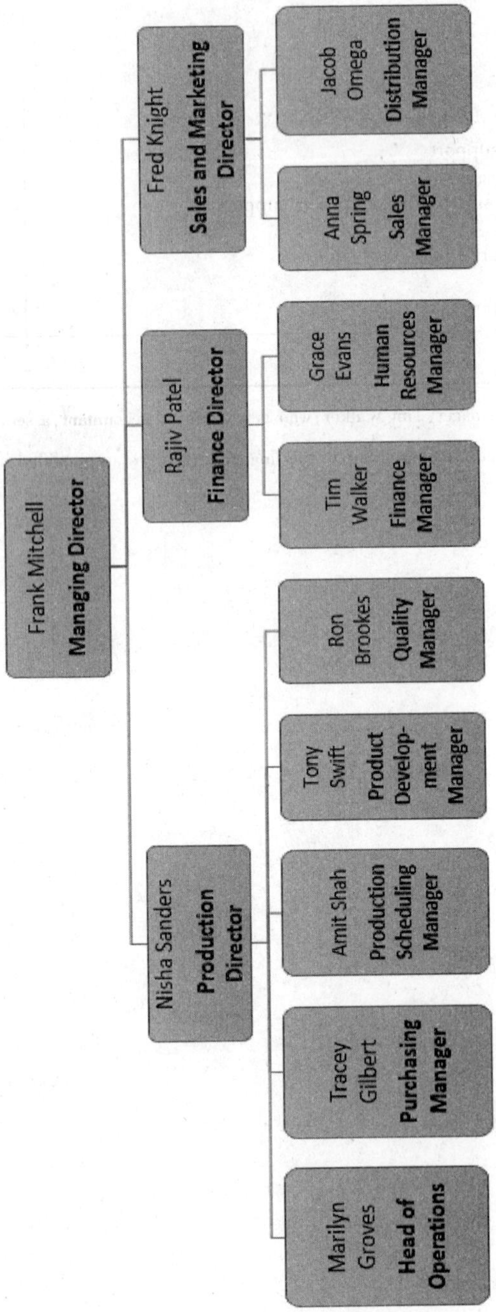

Financial Statements for 2015

First Class Bakery's Statement of Profit or Loss for the Year Ended 31 December 2015

	2015 (B$000)	2014 (B$000)
Revenue	56,125	58,243
Cost of sales	(39,849)	(40,188)
Gross profit	16,276	18,055
Distribution costs	(2,578)	(2,160)
Administrative expenses	(11,964)	(11,358)
Finance costs	(191)	(183)
Profit before tax	1,543	4,354
Tax	(465)	(1,304)
Profit for the year	1,078	3,050

First Class Bakery's Statement of Financial Position for the Year Ended 31 December 2015

	2015 (B$000)	2015 (B$000)	2014 (B$000)	2014 (B$000)
Assets				
Non-current assets				
Property, plant and equipment		5,463		6,146
Current assets				
Inventories	1,814		1,672	
Trade and other receivables	5,620		5,146	
Cash and cash equivalents	—		870	
		7,434		7,688
Total assets		12,897		13,834

（续表）

	2015 (B$000)	2015 (B$000)	2014 (B$000)	2014 (B$000)
Equity and Liabilities				
Ordinary share capital issued		1		1
Retained earnings		5,934		5 356
Total equity		5,935		5,357
Non-current liabilities				
Bank loan		1,800		2,500
Current liabilities				
Bank overdraft	385		—	
Trade and other payables	4,312		4,673	
Tax payable	465		1,304	
		5,162		5,977
Total equity and liabilities		12,897		13,834

First Class Bakery's Statement of Cash Flows for the Year Ended 31 December 2015

	B$000	B$000
Cash flows from operating activities		
Profit before tax		1,543
Adjustments		
Depreciation	1,083	
Finance costs	191	
		1,274
Movements in working capital		
Increase in inventories	(142)	
Increase in trade and other receivables	(474)	
Decrease in trade payables	(361)	
		(977)
Cash generated from operations		1,840
Tax paid	(1,304)	
Finance costs paid	(191)	
		(1,495)
Net cash from operating activities		345

（续表）

	B$000	B$000
Cash flows from investing activities		
Purchase of property, plant and equipment	(400)	
Net cash from investing activities		(400)
Cash flows from financing activities		
Dividend paid	(500)	
Loan repayment	(700)	
Net cash from financing activities		(1,200)
Net decrease in cash and cash equivalents		(1,255)
Cash and cash equivalents at the beginning of the year		870
Cash and cash equivalents at the end of the year		(385)

Budget Information

Summary budget information for the year ended 31 December 2016 is summarized as follows.

Average Selling Price and Gross Margin for Each Product Line

	Slab cake (B$)	Special occasion cake (B$)	Desserts (B$)
Average selling price per unit	1.17	3.35	1.50
Average gross profit per unit	0.34	0.96	0.57

Budgeted Sales Volume

	Slab cake	Special occasion cake	Desserts
Budgeted sales volume in units	28,500,000	5,800,000	2,090,000

Budgeted Gross Profit (Based on Average Selling Prices and Gross Margins)

	Slab cake (B$000)	Special occasion cake (B$000)	Desserts (B$000)	Total (B$000)
Total budgeted sales	33,345	19,430	3,135	55,910
Total budgeted cost of sales	(23,655)	(13,862)	(1,944)	(39,461)
Gross profit	9,690	5,568	1,191	16,449

Information Systems

The current management information system within First Class Bakery is outdated and only provides basic day-to-day information for management. The system is unable to meet the increasing needs of management such as the information about environment and quality related costs.

Costing System

First Class Bakery uses a traditional absorption costing system. The management methods of production overheads are as follows.

- Production overheads are allocated across five departments: three production and two service. The three production departments are ingredients preparation, mixing and baking and finishing. The two service departments are stores and general factory support. Allocation bases include the carrying value of machinery, employee numbers and the area of factory space utilised.
- The production overhead allocated to the service departments is reallocated to the production departments on a pre-determined basis that has remained the same for the last two years.
- Each of the three production departments has its own overhead allocation rate which is based on direct labour hours.

Budgeting and Standards

Up until now First Class Bakery has used an incremental approach to budgeting. Each year the finance team prepares the new budget based on the previous year's data, updates it for known changes in volumes, prices, wages rates and overhead costs. Standards for time and usage of ingredients have not been updated for two years. This is justified by the finance team on the grounds that the production process and the recipes used have not changed in that period. Each month a variance report is produced by the finance team which typically will be distributed to all key managers and then discussed in management meetings.

Industry

The Market

Beeland is a developed country with a population of 35 million. Demand for pre-packaged cakes and desserts saw significant growth from the early 1970s through until 1995. This growth in pre-packaged cakes and desserts coincided with the growth in supermarkets and consumers' demand for convenience foods.

Since 1995, as people become more health-conscious, there has been a small but steady decline in demand. Indeed, in the past few years, with the increasing popularity of home baking, this decline in demand has speeded up.

In 2014, the retail value of pre-packaged cakes and desserts sold in Beeland was B$ 1,680 million compared to an equivalent value (based on 2014 prices) of B$ 2,016 million in 1994. In 2015, this retail value has fallen further to B$ 1,650 million.

The market for pre-packaged cakes and desserts has two elements: branded products and food retailer own-label products. Branded products account for approximately 65% of all sales and food retailer own-label for 35%.

The branded market is dominated by three brands, which collectively account for 80% of the branded market. The other 20% of this market is made up of over 100 separate brands.

The Manufacturers

There are 150 facilities manufacturing pre-packaged cakes and desserts in Beeland. Over half of these are owned by large corporations, either directly or as a subsidiary. The rest operate as independent companies, many of which are family run.

Five years ago, there were 175 such facilities and ten years ago there were 250.

There are three large corporations which dominate much of the packaged food production in Beeland. They are Universal Foods, Southern Foods and Hallett Foods. Each of these corporations operates as a large group with a number of subsidiaries which manufacture a range of pre-packaged foods either as a branded product or a food retailer own-label product.

Universal Foods is the largest of these groups and manufactures 20% of all pre-packaged food in Beeland. Universal Foods owns a number of well-known brands.

Daily News

16 December 2015 | No. 7823 | B$1.00

The Rise of Gluten Free

Ahmed Shah , Lifestyle Correspondent

It used to be the case not that long ago, that the mere mention of the word “gluten free”, would conjure up an image of dry and uninspiring bread and pasta substitutes. To be diagnosed as gluten intolerant means a life time of uninteresting alternatives and little in the way of sweet treats. Not anymore!

The past 5 years has seen a relative explosion in the numbers of people in Beeland being diagnosed as gluten intolerant, with a report showing that there are 600 new people a month joining the GFSB (Gluten Free Society of Beeland). Indeed the chairperson of the society Claire Higgins, said that eating a gluten free diet is no longer just about having to. Many people are now choosing to do so for health and lifestyle reasons.

This growth in demand for gluten free products such as bread, pasta and bakery items has pushed manufacturers to look at ways to make gluten free versions of their products.

The bread industry was the first to really grasp the issue and it is now a common place to find specialist gluten free bread on our supermarket shelf.

The cake and bakery manufacturers are finally starting to catch up. Just last week Mr. Smarty cakes launched two new gluten free cakes, which not only look great, but taste great as well. We’re told that an expansion of the range will come in the next 6 months.

Being gluten intolerant myself, I can finally say that I can have my cake and eat it!

Environmental Business Weekly

16 May 2015 | B$2.50

Pollution from Food Processing Plants and Environmental Protection

Mark Lewis, Business Correspondent

The food industry is now facing increasing pressure to ensure that its activities are environmentally sensitive, but there is also increased internal pressure to maintain or increase profitability in the face of fierce competition. The food-processing industry has special concerns about the health and safety of the consumer.

Key resources used by the food processing industry include water, raw materials and energy. Traditionally water is used as an ingredient, an initial and intermediate cleaning source, an efficient transportation conveyor of raw materials and the principal agent used in sanitising the machinery and plant areas.

The Environaware Pressure Group has recently voiced its concerns regarding the need to take all possible steps to ensure the health and safety of consumers.

A number of organisations have incurred fines for non-compliance with legislation aimed at ensuring the health and safety of consumers.

At Arminster Crown Court,the Foods R Us Manufacturing Group was recently fined B$250,000 for failing to comply with legislation concerning Advanced Wastewater Practices. It was known that they immediately lost contracts with two of their major customers when this became public knowledge.

A spokesman for the Foods R Us Manufacturing Group told me that procedures had been in place which should ensure that such failures would not occur in the future.

The Environaware Pressure Group has also raised concerns about heavy-duty trucks being a source of environmental pollution and are now lobbying the government to pass legislation that would impose stricter controls over vehicle emissions.

If the government passes legislation then this will have a widespread cost implications for a large number of businesses within Beeland.

Tax Regime in Beeland

Corporate Profits

- The corporate tax to be applied to taxable profits is 30%.
- Unless otherwise stated below accounting rules on recognition and measurement are follows for tax purposes.
- The following expenses are not allowable for tax purposes.

  —Accounting depreciation.

  —Amortisation.

  —Entertaining expenditure.

  —Donations to political parties.

  —Taxes paid to other public bodies.
- Tax depreciation allowances are available on items of plant and machinery (including vehicles used for business purposes) at a rate of 25% per year on a reducing balance basis.
- Tax losses can be carried forward to offset against future taxable profits from the same business.

背景材料

介绍

“至臻糕点公司”生产蛋糕和甜点，再将它们包装好直接销售给食品零售商。所有产品均在该公司位于 Beeland（比兰迪）西部的工厂进行生产，该国货币是 B$ ①。

至臻糕点公司生产的大部分蛋糕都出售给大型食品零售商，后者以自有品牌对外销售，该公司按照每个零售商所要求的品牌包装蛋糕。另一些蛋糕和甜点则出售给独立的小型食品零售商，并以至臻糕点公司的品牌对外销售。所有销售业务都在 Beeland 国内进行，交易货币为 B$ 。

至臻糕点公司是由 John（约翰）、James（詹姆斯）和 Frank Mitchell（弗兰克·米切尔）三兄弟在 30 多年前创立的，且一直由三兄弟共同拥有和经营。直到最近，他们将至臻糕点公司 80% 的股份卖给了通用食品公司，后者是一家在 Beeland 上市的大型公司。自此以后，John 和 James 完全退出至臻糕点公司，而 62 岁的 Frank 仍然持有 20% 的股权，现担任该公司的总经理。此前，Frank 一直负责该公司的生产业务。

在完成收购之后，通用食品从内部的其他部门调用了一些人员到至臻糕点公司专职担任重要董事和管理者工作，其中包括新任财务总监 Rajiv Patel（雷基弗·帕特尔）和新任销售和市场营销总监 Fred Knight（弗雷德·奈特）。

至臻糕点公司位于 Beeland 一个主要城镇的郊区，拥有两个基地：一个生产基地和一个车库。车库用于停放至臻糕点公司的配送车辆。生产基地规模很大，包括一个大型生产厂房还有用作仓库和办公室的几个独立建筑。

产品

至臻糕点公司生产多种蛋糕和甜点，共有 3 条产品线：普通切片蛋糕、特殊场合蛋

---

① 此处及以下所称“B$ ”，均指 Beeland 当地货币，该货币为虚拟货币。

糕和甜点。

普通切片蛋糕

普通切片蛋糕上没有任何糖霜和装饰，共有以下几种口味：柠檬、香蕉、生姜、香草、樱桃、核桃、巧克力和咖啡。

普通切片蛋糕的配料一次按一种口味进行混合，然后放到一个又长又深的金属烤盘里烘焙，冷却后取出并切割，而后加以包装，贴上相应食品零售商或至臻糕点公司的标签。

普通切片蛋糕主要出售给大型食品零售商并以其自有品牌对外销售，还有一些则出售给独立的小型零售商并以至臻糕点公司的品牌对外销售。普通切片蛋糕业务约占至臻糕点公司收入的60% 。

特殊场合蛋糕

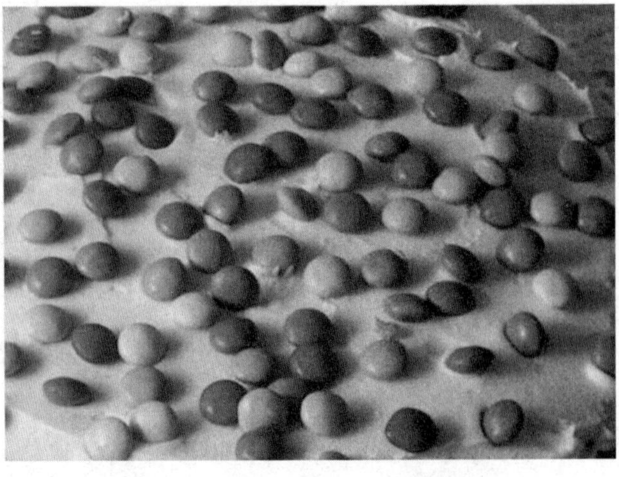

特殊场合蛋糕会有糖霜和装饰，其蛋糕胚是香草或巧克力味的。按照口味混合配料后，将其放进独立的铝箔浅盘里进行烘焙，冷却后在顶部用糖霜和装饰加以点缀。虽然大多数特殊场合蛋糕上都有裱花和小糖果，但也可以根据客户的要求定制各种糖霜颜色和装饰种类。此外，还可根据客户的要求使用时令性装饰物。

所有的特殊场合蛋糕都是以食品零售商的自有品牌对外出售的，这类业务约占至臻糕点公司收入的 35% 。

甜点

至臻糕点公司的甜点都是以蛋糕为胚子的。这是一个相对较新的产品线，在生产基地中拥有一条专用的小型生产线。目前，该公司共生产三种口味的甜点：巧克力、太妃糖和蜜糖。

甜点放在塑料小盒里出售，并且在蛋糕下面铺有一层调味酱。这样包装是为了方便人们在食用之前将其加热，然后将小盒子倒置过来。

目前，甜点业务约占至臻糕点公司收入的 5% ，全部出售给独立的小型食品零售商并以至臻糕点公司的品牌对外出售。

保质期

至臻糕点公司烘焙产品的保质期为 8 ~ 12 周，这取决于产品中水果和糖分的含量。至臻糕点公司所使用的包装能够确保产品的新鲜度，进而使得产品质量得到保证。

产品开发

除了应对客户在口味和装饰方面的变化以外，多年以来，至臻糕点公司在普通切片蛋糕和特殊场合蛋糕的产品开发方面鲜有作为。

在过去三年中，至臻糕点公司一直把重点放在设计和推出甜点系列上，因为该公司在这一业务领域还未能获得主要客户。

最近，通用食品调来了新的产品开发经理 Tony Swift（托尼·斯威夫特），他现在专门为至臻糕点公司工作，其工作职责如下。

- 专注于扩大甜点系列。
- 引入一系列新产品，迎合消费者新的消费偏好——更健康的蛋糕，使用精制糖和有机材料。
- 开发新的无麸质蛋糕系列。

生产

所有系列产品的生产过程都可以分为 3 个主要流程。

- 原料准备。
- 搅拌和烘焙。
- 包装。

普通切片蛋糕和特殊场合蛋糕在主要生产线上生产，而甜点则在一个独立的小型生产线上生产。

普通切片蛋糕和特殊场合蛋糕

原料准备

生产采用批量方式进行。普通切片蛋糕和特殊场合蛋糕按照不同口味以批量方式混合原料，每批次可生产 500 份成品。每种产品使用相同的基本原料，其中包括黄油、糖、面粉和鸡蛋，但会根据不同口味进行调整并添加坚果和（或）水果。

在原料准备阶段，将干性材料（面粉和糖）的用量称出来并放入承重 12.5 千克的袋子中。每批次蛋糕分别需要 62.5 千克的面粉和糖，因此可以将 5 袋面粉和 5 袋糖放入一个轮式搅拌器中等待混合。最终，搅拌器所混合的原料足够生产一个批次的蛋糕。

黄油和鸡蛋储存在一个大型的冷藏库中。黄油是按 5 千克一块的规格采购的。每一批次的蛋糕需要 62.5 千克黄油，即 12.5 块。因此在冷藏库内，黄油每 12.5 块堆放在一起，这样可以方便地完成批次生产的配料工作。鸡蛋在冷藏库中按 1 个托盘 25 个鸡蛋的规格进行存放（供应商就是按此规格供货的）。每批次蛋糕需要 4 个托盘的鸡蛋（100 个鸡蛋）。

在搅拌工作即将开始前，才将黄油和鸡蛋放入轮式搅拌器中。原料准备工序上的大部分员工属于非熟练人员。

搅拌和烘焙

搅拌是通过大型工业搅拌器完成的。首先将黄油和糖混合在一起，一直搅拌直到它们变得轻薄和蓬松，然后将面粉和鸡蛋分批加到混合物中拌匀；在搅拌流程的最后，再加入调味品、水果和坚果。

搅拌器是由员工手动控制的，这些员工技术娴熟，知道何时该添加面粉和鸡蛋，何时该加入调味品。当员工觉得混合物搅拌适度后，再将它们倒进大桶中。

如果是生产普通切片蛋糕，则将混合物从大桶倒入又深又长的烤盘中。先由员工手动将烤盘放置到传送带上，而后机器自动完成灌注工作，在烤盘装好之后，通过传送带运送到烤箱。

如果是生产特殊场合蛋糕，先由员工手动将 10 个铝箔托盘并排放到烤盘上，而后将烤盘放到传送带上，完成灌注工序并传送到烤箱。

所有蛋糕都是在 3 个工业烤箱中烤制的，由员工手动将烤盘放入或移出烤箱。每个工业烤箱可以烤制 5 盘特殊场合蛋糕（烤箱有 5 层烤架）或 12 盘普通切片蛋糕（烤箱有 4 层烤架）。烤箱每次只烤制一种类型的蛋糕。

尽管烤箱是由计算机控制的，可设定每种类型蛋糕的烤制时间，但烤箱同时具备人工操作功能。经验丰富、技术娴熟的员工可以根据他们的感觉来适当延长烘烤时间。烘烤完成之后，烤盘内的蛋糕会移到大型堆装车上进行冷却。

包装

经过冷却之后，员工会将堆装车推到主要生产线的不同位置：一部分用于普通切片蛋糕，另一部分用于特殊场合蛋糕。

员工手动将普通切片蛋糕从烤盘中取出并放到传送带上，剩下的流程几乎全部自动完成：用机器将长条蛋糕切成合适的数量并用透明玻璃纸包装；事先按照生产批次放入相应的标签，用机器将标签贴到外包装上；最后，由员工将蛋糕分装到盒子里。

员工将（铝箔烤盘中的）特殊场合蛋糕手动取出并逐个放到传送带上。剩下的工序是半自动化操作的：由机器将糖霜挤到蛋糕的顶部，而糖霜则是由一小组烘焙师制作成巧克力和香草口味，而后不断填充到机器的装料桶之中。因此，员工需要花大量的时间来设置机器，以确保其使用了正确的糖霜。

然后，根据客户的要求对蛋糕进行适当的装饰。这部分工作是由手工完成的，因为客户的要求总是不断变化，而经验表明，手工装饰更具效率。此外，这也能确保最终产品可以按照手工产品的价位进行出售。这项工作通常由半熟练的员工完成，前提是他们能证明自己具备这项能力。

鉴于特殊场合蛋糕的性质，它需要更多的检查，工作量通常是普通切片蛋糕的3倍。

完成装饰工作之后，每个特殊场合蛋糕都由员工放入合适的包装盒中，而后再将这些单独装盒的蛋糕放到大包装箱中邮寄给客户。

每盒成品都由叉车运送到发货仓库。

甜点

甜点的制作工艺与蛋糕类似，但在单独的生产线上完成。甜点的生产线才开发两年，主要是自动化操作。

原料准备

甜点的原料储存在专门的存放区域，其一个生产批次的配比称量流程与蛋糕的一样。

搅拌、烘焙和包装

原料按照与蛋糕制作相同的方式进行混合和搅拌。甜点中的调味酱是在工业大锅中制作的，因为需要适度加热黄油和糖。在生产线的开始，把蛋糕和调味酱的混合物分别倒入适当的装料桶中。

剩下的工序将全部自动完成，但生产线也设有员工手动中止功能。例如，如果生产人员认为甜点需要烘烤更长时间，或者生产线的运转出现了问题，就会启动这种功能。每种口味的甜点对生产线程序的要求稍有不同，因此员工需要一些设置时间以确保选择了正确的程序。通常，每次调整口味都需要对装混合物的大桶进行彻底清洗，而生产线每天只生产一种口味，因此在每天工作伊始，员工需要对生产线的程序进行重新设置。

生产时首先制作调味酱，然后将蛋糕混合物倒入甜点烤杯，而后经过生产线各个环节直至进入烤箱。甜点按照预设时间进行烘焙，而后冷却，最后加以包装，所有这些工序都是自动完成的。

在制作普通切片蛋糕和特殊场合蛋糕时，整个生产过程需要非熟练、半熟练和熟练的操作人员。在蛋糕和调味酱的混合过程中，需要熟练员工对生产线进行监控；而装料桶的清洁工作、确保在生产线上放置空的甜点烤杯、确保各种口味得到相应的包装，这些工作则是由半熟练和非熟练员工完成的。

至臻糕点公司的客户

普通切片蛋糕

大约 85% 的普通切片蛋糕销售给了三家全国性的食品零售商，并以它们各自的自有品牌对外出售。虽然这三家主要零售商采购的蛋糕口味不尽相同，但柠檬和咖啡这两种最为普遍。

其他 15% 的普通切片蛋糕则销售给了独立的小型食品零售商，并以至臻糕点公司的品牌对外出售。因为客户的去留，这部分零售商的数量的确会有波动，但无论何时都有 30 家左右。

特殊场合蛋糕

所有的特殊场合蛋糕都销售给了三家全国性的食品零售商，并以各自的自有品牌对外出售。其中两家零售商还从至臻糕点公司采购普通切片蛋糕，因此，共有四家全国性的食品零售商从至臻糕点公司购买普通切片蛋糕和特殊场合蛋糕。

在糖霜颜色和装饰方面，每家零售商都对特殊场合蛋糕提出了自己的规格要求，这些规格要求每年都会定期修改。

甜点

所有甜点都以至臻糕点公司的自有品牌对外销售。尽管在几个月之前，上述大型全国性零售商的其中一家尝试性地下了一个订单，但当前，这些甜点只销售给独立的小型零售商。截至目前，这家大型零售商没有再下更大的订单。

客户关系

至臻糕点公司与其大型食品零售商客户保持着密切的人员联系，但由于资源有限，一直未能与较小的零售商进行密切联系。因此，面向较小零售商的销售量未见增长。至臻糕点公司的竞争对手都采用了最新的信息系统以协助管理客户关系和其他业务领域。

信用期限

至臻糕点公司为所有客户提供了 30 天的信用期。有两家全国性零售商会及时付款，但另外两家往往会因为书面资料上的小小出入而延付货款。独立的小型客户经常延付货款。

顾客印象

独立的和全国性的食品零售商客户都将至臻糕点公司视为一家高品质蛋糕和甜点的生产厂商。虽然偶尔会有一些产品因运输过程造成的损坏而被退回，但从未发生过顾客因产品质量问题而退货的情况。

最近，针对所有客户开展的调查显示，虽然交货速度有所下降，但至臻糕点公司在质量和价值方面都获得了很高的评价。这项调查还表明，客户越来越关注环境问题和负责任的原料采购理念。

目前，至臻糕点公司自有品牌的市场覆盖率有限。虽然早在两年之前，至臻糕点公司就以自有品牌向市场推出了甜点系列，启动了品牌创建工作，但其销售仍然只限于独立的小型食品零售商。通用食品公司引入了市场营销专家 Fred Knight，让他担任至臻糕点公司的销售和市场营销总监以强化该公司的品牌意识。目前，Fred Knight 只为至臻糕点公司工作。

配送

至臻糕点公司拥有一支车队以便将产品运送给客户，但这些车辆已经比较老旧，只符合现行的废气排放法规。无运输任务时，车辆会停放在主要生产基地 5 公里以外的车库。

这个车库配有齐全的维修设施，可对车辆进行所需的维护和修理。但有时候，也会由于设施无法满足车辆的维修需求，导致预定交货的延误，尤其是与小型客户最为常见。

配送站点所在的地区最近被开发成了住宅区，周围都在开发和建设新房。

车库如今拥有若干名合格的修理技工和 15 名司机。

供应商

至臻糕点公司的大部分原料都采购自一家供应商。到目前为止，至臻糕点公司的董事们都认为单一来源的采购能确保公司获得更高质量的产品和服务。

面粉直接采购自一家面粉加工厂，该厂距离至臻糕点公司生产基地较近。董事们一直认为要生产出质量上乘的产品，面粉就应尽量新鲜，以确保面粉中的发酵物质能发挥出最佳效果。因此，他们一直希望面粉供应商尽可能地靠近生产基地，以便供应商能以小批量的方式频繁发货。

糖采购自一家主要的糖及糖制品进口分销商。该供应商的仓库和配送网点遍布Beeland全境。

黄油采购自一家全国性的乳制品供应商。

鸡蛋通常采购自附近的供应商。如果当地的供应商偶尔无法满足订单需求，则从另一个供应商处采购鸡蛋。

用于制作蛋糕和甜点的调味品与装饰品共采购自七家不同的供应商，其中一些供应商位于境外。每家供应商提供的调味品或装饰品各不相同。

回收利用和环境政策

至臻糕点公司尽可能地回收利用原料的包装材料，用于运输面粉和糖的袋子以及装运鸡蛋的托盘通常都会返还给供应商以重复使用。大部分生产废料会出售给当地农场用作猪饲料，少量废料需出资处理。

员工

至臻糕点公司的四名总监

- Frank Mitchell，常务总监。
- Rajiv Patel，财务总监。
- Nisha Sanders（妮莎·桑德斯），生产总监。
- Fred Knight，销售和市场营销总监。

该公司还有几名高管。其中的关键人员将在下文进行详细说明。

员工人数

	数量
生产	325
行政	23
配送	30
员工总数	378

生产员工人数

	部门				员工总数
	原料准备	搅拌与烘焙	包装	仓库和工厂支持	
生产操作人员	30	120	130	0	280
监督人员	2	10	10	10	32
管理人员				10	10
研发人员				3	3
员工总数	32	130	140	23	325

行政人员人数

	数量
总监（常务、财务、销售和市场营销）	3
财务[①]	4
销售和市场营销	6
采购行政支持	2
生产调度和仓库行政支持	3
人力资源和工资管理	3
信息技术支持	2
员工总数	23

①财务人员包括财务经理 Tim Walker（蒂姆·沃克），他是一名优秀的会计师，此外还有一名高级会计师和两名初级会计师。你是其中一名初级会计师。没有任何一名财务人员取得了信用控制资格。

关键人员

关键管理人员和职权结构情况如下面的组织图所示。

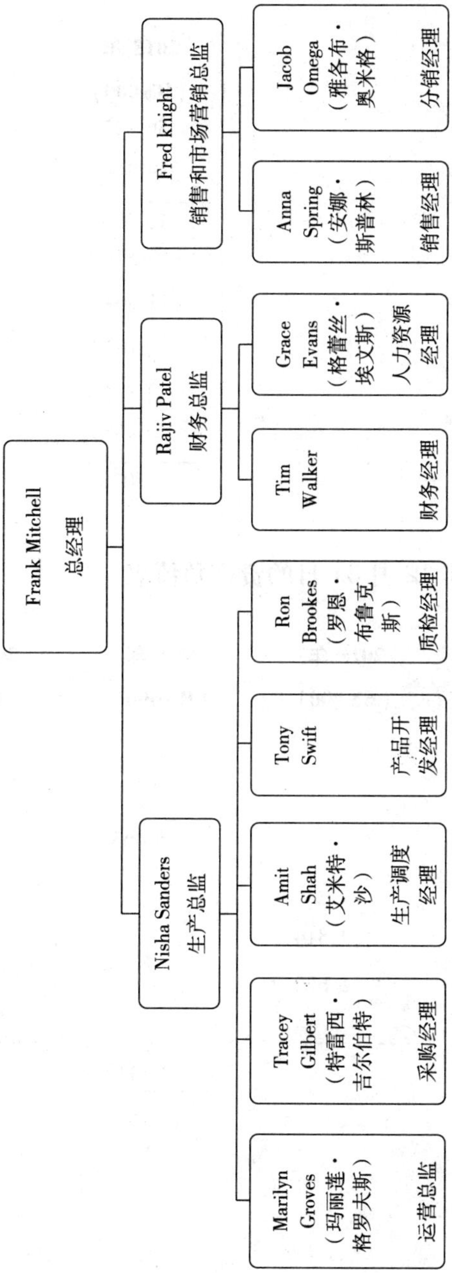

至臻糕点公司2015 年年度财务报表

至臻糕点公司截至2015 年12 月31 日的年度利润表

	2015 年 (B$000)	2014 年 (B$000)
收入	56 125	58 243
销售成本	(39 849)	(40 188)
毛利润	16 276	18 055
配送成本	(2 578)	(2 160)
行政支出	(11 964)	(11 358)
财务成本	(191)	(183)
税前利润	1 543	4 354
税费	(465)	(1 304)
全年利润	1 078	3 050

至臻糕点公司截至2015 年12 月31 日的资产负债表

	2015 年 (B$000)	2015 年 (B$000)	2014 年 (B$000)	2014 年 (B$000)
资产				
非流动资产				
不动产、厂房和设备		5 463		6 146
流动资产				
存货	1 814		1 672	
应收账款	5 620		5 146	
现金及现金等价物	—		870	
		7 434		7 688
总资产		12 897		13 834
所有者权益及负债				
发行的普通股本		1		1
留存收益		5 934		5 356
所有者权益总额		5 935		5 357

（续表）

	2015 年 (B$000)	2015 年 (B$000)	2014 年 (B$000)	2014 年 (B$000)
非流动负债				
银行贷款		1 800		2 500
流动负债				
银行透支款	385		—	
应付账款	4 312		4 673	
应交税费	465		1 304	
		5 162		5 977
所有者权益及负债总额		12 897		13 834

至臻糕点公司截至 2015 年 12 月 31 日的现金流量表

	B$000	B$000
经营活动现金流		
税前利润		1 543
调整		
折旧	1 083	
财务费用	191	
		1 274
运营资本变动		
库存的增加	(142)	
应收款项的增加	(474)	
应付账款的减少	(361)	
		(977)
经营活动产生的现金流		1 840
已付税款	(1 304)	
已付财务费用	(191)	
		(1 495)
经营活动的净现金流		345
投资活动的现金流		
购置不动产、厂房和设备	(400)	
投资活动的净现金流		(400)
筹资活动的现金流		

（续表）

	B$000	B$000
本期已支付股息	（500）	
偿还贷款	（700）	
筹资活动的净现金流		（1 200）
现金及现金等价的净减少		（1 255）
期初现金及现金等价物		870
期末现金及现金等价物		（385）

预算信息

截至2016年12月31日的年度预算信息汇总如下。

每个产品线的平均售价与平均毛利统计表

	普通切片蛋糕（B$）	特殊场合蛋糕（B$）	甜点（B$）
单位产品平均售价	1.17	3.35	1.50
单位产品平均毛利	0.34	0.96	0.57

预算销量

	普通切片蛋糕	特殊场合蛋糕	甜点
每个产品线的预算销量	28 500 000	5 800 000	2 090 000

按平均售价和平均毛利计算得出的毛利润预算统计表

	普通切片蛋糕（B$000）	特殊场合蛋糕（B$000）	甜点（B$000）	总计（B$000）
总销售额预算	33 345	19 430	3 135	55 910
总销售成本预算	（23 655）	（13 862）	（1 944）	（39 461）
毛利润	9 690	5 568	1 191	16 449

信息系统

至臻糕点公司现在使用的管理信息系统已经过时，只能为管理层提供基本的日常信息。该系统提供的信息无法满足日益增长的管理需要，例如缺少环境和质量等相关的成本信息。

成本核算系统

至臻糕点公司使用传统的完全成本（又称“吸收成本”）核算系统，其管理生产费用的方法有如下几种。

- 首先，将生产费用分配给五个部门：三个生产部门和两个服务部门。三个生产部门分别是原料准备、搅拌与烘烤、包装部门；两个服务部门分别是仓库和工厂支持部门。分配基础包括机器设备的账面价值、员工人数和工厂场地的使用面积等。
- 分配给服务部门的生产费用而后再按照预先确定的基础分配给生产部门，这一分配基础在过去两年中一直未变。
- 每个生产部门都有各自基于直接劳动时间的生产费用分配率。

预算和标准

到目前为止，至臻糕点公司一直使用增量方法来制定预算。每年，财务团队都会根据上一年的数据编制新的预算，根据数量、价格、工资水平和间接成本等方面的已知变化进行相应调整。时间和用料标准这两年以来并无更新，财务团队给出的理由是生产过程和所用食谱在这一期间没有任何变化。每个月，财务团队都会编写差异报告，通常会将它们发送给所有主管，然后在管理会议上进行讨论。

产业

市场

Beeland 这个国家属于发达国家，人口为 3 500 万。从 20 世纪 70 年代初到 1995 年，包装蛋糕和甜点的需求量显著增长，而在同一时期，超市不断涌现，消费者对方便食品的需求也不断增长。

自 1995 年以来，随着人们健康意识的增强，人们对包装蛋糕和甜点的需求量出现了小幅且稳步的下降。事实上，在过去几年里，随着家庭烘焙的日益普及，这一需求呈加速下降的态势。

2014 年，Beeland 国内包装蛋糕和甜点的零售总值为 B$ 16. 80 亿，与之相比，1994 年的零售总值（基于 2014 年的价格）为 B$ 20. 16 亿。而在 2015 年，这一数值已经下降至 B$ 16. 50 亿。

包装蛋糕和甜点市场分为两部分：品牌产品和食品零售商自有品牌产品。品牌产品约占所有销售的65%，而食品零售商自有品牌产品约占35%。

品牌产品市场主要由三大品牌占据，共占市场份额的80%，另外20%则是由100多个不同品牌分享。

生产商

Beeland境内共有150家公司生产包装蛋糕和甜点，其中一半以上作为直属企业或子公司为大型企业所有；余下的则是独立经营的公司，其中很多为家族经营企业。

5年前，这类生产公司有175家；而10年前，这类生产公司有250家。

在Beeland境内，三家大型企业占据了包装食品生产的大部分份额，它们分别是通用食品、南方食品和哈利特食品。这些公司都是大型集团企业，旗下各个子公司生产一系列品牌食品和食品零售商自有品牌食品。

通用食品是最大的食品生产商，其生产的包装食品占Beeland市场的20%。通用食品拥有一批知名品牌。

每日新闻

2015年12月16日 | 7823号 |B$1.00

无麸质食品的兴起

生活方式记者 Ahmed Shah（阿曼德·沙）

就在不久之前，“无麸质食品”一词让人联想到的还是干燥无味的面包和面食替代品。如果被诊断为麸质食品不耐受体制，那么，这意味着此人终生都要食用让人毫无食欲的替代食品，基本不能享受“甜蜜”的生活方式。但现在，情况不再如此。

过去5年里，Beeland国内被诊断为麸质食品不耐受体质的人数呈爆炸式增长，据报道，每个月都会有大约600个人加入“Beeland无麸质食品社团”。该社团的主席Claire Higgins（克莱尔·希金斯）表示，事实上，食用无麸质食品不再是迫不得已的行为。现在，许多人都是出于健康问题和生活方式的考虑而选择食用无麸质食品。

面包、面食和烘焙糕点等无麸质食品的需求日益增长，这推动生产商开始研究和生产无麸质产品。

面包行业是第一个真正直击问题、抢占先机的行业。现在，在超市的货架上，无麸质面包的身影随处可见。

蛋糕和烘焙食品生产商终于开始奋起直追。上周，Mr. Smarty（斯玛特先生）蛋糕公司推出了两款无麸质蛋糕，不仅外形美观，口味也极佳。我们得知未来6个月内，厂家还会继续扩大无麸质蛋糕的种类。

我本人就属于麸质食品过敏体质，现在我终于可以说——我能够吃到属于自己的蛋糕了！

环境商业周刊

2015年5月16日 | B$2.50

食品加工业造成的污染与环境保护

商业记者Mark Lewis（马克·刘易斯）

当前，在确保自身活动的环境问题敏感性方面，食品加工业正面临着越来越大的压力。而与此同时，面对激烈的竞争，企业保持或提高盈利水平的内在压力也在不断加大。食品加工业需要特别关注消费者的健康和安全问题。

食品加工业所用的主要资源包括水、生鲜材料和能源。水的传统用途包括：构成食品成分、生产初始和中间的清洁资源、生鲜传送的有效介质、机器和厂房的主要消毒物质。

近日，环境保护组织表达了它的担忧，它认为社会组织需要采取所有可能的举措以确保顾客的健康和安全。

一些组织因未能遵循确保顾客健康和安全的相关立法而遭受罚款。

最近，美国食品制造集团因未能遵守废水深度处理的相关规定而被Arminster（阿明斯特）刑事法庭处以B$250 000的罚款。据我们所知，当这一处罚消息被外界获知以后，该集团立刻失去了两名主要客户。

美国食品制造集团的发言人告诉我，该集团的整改措施目前已经落实到位，应该能够确保未来不再发生此类状况。

此外，环境保护组织对重型卡车造成的环境污染十分忧心，现在，他们正游说政府通过立法对汽车尾气排放进行更为严格的控制。

如果Beeland政府通过立法，那么，这将对该国境内诸多企业的成本管理产生巨大的影响。

Beeland 的税收体制

企业利润

- 企业所得税为应税利润的 30%。
- 除非另有规定，否则在税务方面，应遵守下列关于确认和计量的会计准则。
- 以下费用不得税前扣除：

  ——会计折旧；

  ——摊销；

  ——文娱开支；

  ——政党捐款；

  ——缴纳给其他公共机构的税款。
- 厂房和机器设备（包括商用车辆）的折旧可以抵税，年抵扣率为 25%，以其递减余额为基础。
- 可抵税损失可以结转，以抵减同一企业未来的应税利润。

Variant 1

This examination is structured as follows：

Section number	Number of tasks	Time for section(minutes)
1	1	45
2	1	45
3	1	45
4	2	45

The time available for each section is for reading,planning and writing your answer(s).

Please note section 4 consists of two tasks. Please leave enough time to complete both parts.

Section 1

You receive the following email from Rajiv Patel.

From: Rajiv Patel, Finance Director
To: Junior Accountant
Subject: ABC (activity-based costing) system

Yesterday I received an email from David Spencer, finance director of Universal Foods (our parent company).

He is really pleased with the way that the business is now operating after the acquisition. In particular he is excited about the new products that our product development team are working on and is looking forward to some of these being launched in the next year.

He is keen though that we should look at how we cost our products. Most of the production subsidiaries within the Universal Foods Group use an ABC system as the means of cost management. He believes that our business would benefit from the implementation of ABC system and has asked me to prepare a briefing paper for our other directors regarding the introduction of ABC system within First Class Bakery.

I have already made a start on the briefing paper and have written a general introduction for the other directors about what ABC system is. However, David has asked that the briefing paper also contains the following three sections.

- The potential benefits from using an ABC system that specifically relate to First Class Bakery.
- The steps involved in the design of an ABC system for First Class Bakery, taking into account the potential problems that may occur.
- Recommendations with justifications of three cost drivers we could use.

Please prepare the first draft of the above three sections of the briefing paper for me.

Many thanks.

Rajiv Patel
Finance Director
First Class Bakery

Write the draft briefing paper sections requested by Rajiv Patel.

Section 2

A few weeks later, Tim Walker forwards you an email from Frank Mitchell. He asks you to draft a response that he can then forward to Frank.

Forwarded email：

From：Frank Mitchell, Managing Director
To：Tim Walker, Finance Manager
Subject：CRM(customer relationship management) system and accounting queries

There are two issues that I need your help with please.

Firstly, the sales and marketing director, Fred Knight, has requested that we invest in a new CRM system. He believes that, given the new products currently being developed, we could greatly expand our customer base in the independent food retail sector and also potentially launch an online service to sell our cakes directly to consumers.

Fred is obviously very keen and can only say positive things about it, but I would like a more balanced view of the potential benefits and drawbacks to us arising from investment in a CRM system.

My second issue relates to the financial statements. I recently had a conversation with David Spencer, the finance director at Universal Foods who said that 100% of our income, expenses, assets and liabilities would be included within the group financial statements. He also said that we would need to change our policy in respect of our property to a revaluation one, as this is group policy.

This has left me with a couple of queries：

(1) Why will 100% of our income, expenses, assets and liabilities be included in the group financial statements? Surely my 20% investment means that First Class Bakery is partly mine and therefore I don't see why Universal Foods needs to include it in their financial statements at all.

(2) Why do we need to change to a revaluation policy and what are the implications of doing so on our financial statements this year and in future years?

I look forward to your response.

Frank Mitchell

Managing Director

First Class Bakery

Write the email requested by Tim Walker.

Section 3

Six months later, you receive the following email from Tim Walker.

From: Tim Walker, Finance Manager

To: Junior Accountant

Subject: New IT system and budgeting approach

After the successful implementation of the new CRM system, the directors are considering replacing other IT systems. The directors have asked for a report for their next meeting on the benefits that could arise within our business as a consequence of an investment in new IT systems.

Rajiv has suggested that if the investment in the new IT systems goes ahead, it would be a good time to consider changing the current system of incremental budgeting to a system based on either ABB (activity-based budgeting) or ZBB (zero-based budgeting). We will soon be launching two new product types on our main production line (sandwich cakes and swiss rolls) and Rajiv believes that we need better costing information. He has requested a report on ABB and ZBB that can be circulated to all of the directors. The directors have already been briefed on ABC and therefore Rajiv has said that the report does not need to cover these principles. He has also told me that there is no need to explain what ABB and ZBB are because he has already done this.

Please could you prepare the following two sections for a report that I will send to the directors regarding the above.

- An explanation of the benefits that First Class Bakery might gain from investing in new IT systems. Please include examples of strategic, operational and intangible benefits to First Class Bakery.

■ An explanation of the potential advantages to First Class Bakery of an ABB and ZBB approach to budgeting compared with the current approach.

Thank you!

Tim Walker

Finance Manager

First Class Bakery

Write the report sections requested by Tim Walker.

Section 4

A month later, you receive the following email from Tim Walker.

From: Tim Walker, Finance Manager

To: Junior Accountant

Subject: Marketing campaign decision and new credit controller

We are soon to launch our new cake ranges. Fred Knight, the sales and marketing director, and his team have been working hard and have secured a number of potential new customers for both our existing cake ranges and the new cake ranges under our First Class Bakery label. These customers are mostly small independent food retail businesses, although a large chain of coffee shops is amongst them.

I'm just in the process of appointing a new person to our finance team, whose sole responsibility will be credit control and the management of balances owed from customers. We will need a briefing note for this person in respect of his role, which I would like you to prepare.

Fred Knight has also engaged Futuristic Consulting to undertake market research on the level of sales that we could expect. They have evaluated three different marketing campaign options for the promotion of our First Class Bakery branded products, taking into account the possible outcomes which could result from each campaign.

Futuristic Consulting have sent through a schedule of their results with the comment: "... that the choice of marketing campaign may be dependent on the 'attitude to risk and uncertainty' of the directors." The schedule is attached to this email, although there is no further explanation. I know that the directors will need an explanation of the schedule and also the comment made by Futuristic Consulting. Therefore, I would like you to do two things for me please.

(1) Prepare a briefing paper for the new credit controller, which outlines the procedures for:

- assessing the creditworthiness of new customers;
- setting credit limits for new and existing customers.

(2) Prepare a briefing paper which can be circulated ahead of the next directors meeting that explains:

- the meaning of the data contained in the schedule from Futuristic Consulting;
- how different "attitudes to risk and uncertainty" may affect the decision to be made by the directors of which campaign to undertake.

Thank you.

Tim Walker

Finance Manager

First Class Bakery

Schedule Attached to the Email

Campaign A:

Predicted additional profit in B$	**Probability**	**Expected value in B$**
200,000	0.3	60,000
500,000	0.6	300,000
1,000,000	0.1	100,000
		460,000
Standard deviation		224,499
Coefficient of variation		48.80%

Campaign B：

Predicted additional profit in B$	Probability	Expected value in B$
100,000	0.2	20,000
600,000	0.6	360,000
700,000	0.2	140,000
		520,000
Standard deviation		213,541
Coefficient of variation		41.07%

Campaign C：

Predicted additional profit in B$	Probability	Expected value in B$
350,000	0.3	105,000
400,000	0.4	160,000
450,000	0.3	135,000
		400,000
Standard deviation		37,730
Coefficient of variation		9.68%

Write the briefing paper for the new credit controller.

Write the briefing paper for the directors regarding Futuristic Consulting's schedule.

试卷一

本次考试的结构如下：

序号	任务数	时间（分钟）
1	1	45
2	1	45
3	1	45
4	2	45

每个部分规定的时间可用于读题、组织和书写答案。

请注意任务四包括两项子任务，需留足时间。

任务一

你收到了来自财务总监 Rajiv Patel 的邮件。

发件人：财务总监 Rajiv Patel
收件人：初级会计
主题：作业成本法（ABC）系统

昨天，我收到母公司通用食品的财务总监 David Spencer（大卫·斯宾塞）发来的邮件。

他对我们公司在并购后的经营感到非常满意。他特别提到了我们的产品开发部正在研发的新产品，并希望其中有一部分能在来年推向市场。

不过，他希望我们检视一下我们的产品成本核算方法。通用食品公司采用作业成本法对旗下绝大部分的产品系列实施成本管理。他相信如果我们公司实施作业成本法，一定也能从中获益，他要求我就在至臻糕点公司内部实施作业成本法准备一份简报，并向其他董事做报告。

简报的内容我已经开了一个头，并就作业成本法向其他董事写了一个一般性介绍。不过，David 希望简报还包括下面这些内容。

- 至臻糕点公司实施作业成本法的潜在收益。
- 至臻糕点公司实施作业成本法的步骤，以及可能遇到的潜在问题。
- 提出我们将采用的三个成本动因，并说明原因。

请你帮我准备一下简报中上述三个部分的初稿。

多谢！

至臻糕点公司
财务总监
Rajiv Patel

请写出 Rajiv Patel 要求的简报相关部分内容。

任务二

几周之后，Tim Walker 转发给你一封来自 Frank Mitchell 的邮件。他要求你写一封回邮，以便他再转发给 Frank。

转发的邮件如下。

发件人：总经理 Frank Mitchell

收件人：财务经理 Tim Walker

主题：客户关系管理（CRM）系统与会计疑问

在如下两个问题上，我希望得到你的帮助。

第一个问题是，负责销售和市场营销的总监 Fred Knight，提出我们应引进全新的客户关系管理系统。他确信，在目前正在开发新产品的情况下，我们将有可能极大地扩展我们的独立食品零售商客户群，并有可能通过网上直销方式把我们的蛋糕直接出售给消费者。

很显然，Fred 的感觉是很敏锐的，但他往往只会说好的那一面，而我希望更加全面地权衡我们投资客户关系管理系统的潜在优缺点。

我的第二个问题与财务报表有关。我最近和通用食品的财务总监 David Spencer 有过一次交谈，他说我们的收入、费用、资产和负债将被 100% 地并入集团的财务报表。他还说我们需要根据集团的会计政策对我们的资产价值进行重估。

对此，我有一些疑问：

（1）为什么我们的收入、费用、资产和负债要 100% 并入集团的财务报表？我还持有 20% 的股份，这说明至臻糕点公司中有我的一份，因此我完全不明白为什么通用食品要把我们合并进它们的财务报表。

（2）为什么我们需要变更为资产价值重估政策，这么做对我们今年和未来的财务报表会产生什么影响？

期待你的回复。

至臻糕点公司

总经理

Frank Mitchell

请根据 Tim Walker 的要求回复邮件。

任务三

6 个月后，你收到 Tim Walker 发来的邮件，内容如下。

发件人：财务经理 Tim Walker

收件人：初级会计

主题：新 IT 系统和预算方法

在新的客户关系管理系统成功运行之后，董事们正在考虑更新其他的 IT 系统。董事们希望我们提供一份报告，分析在我们公司内部投资新的 IT 系统的好处，以供下次会议使用。

Rajiv 建议，如果公司决定投资 IT 系统，那么当下是一个很好的时机，我们可以把现行的增量预算系统改变为作业预算（ABB）或者零基预算（ZBB）系统。我们很快将推出两种新的产品（夹层蛋糕和瑞士卷）以丰富我们的主产品线，Rajiv 确信我们需要更好的成本信息。他要求就作业预算和零基预算提交一份报告以供董事们传阅。Rajiv 说董事们对作业成本系统已经有了初步了解，因此报告中不需要对这些内容再做论述。他还说我也不必解释什么是作业预算和零基预算，这部分的内容他已经做了。

我需要针对上述问题向董事们提交一份报告，请你帮我准备一下下面这两个部分的内容。

- 阐明至臻糕点公司将从新 IT 系统投资上获得的好处，请从战略、运营和无形收益等方面举例说明。
- 相比现行预算方法，说明作业预算和零基预算对至臻糕点公司的潜在好处。

谢谢！

至臻糕点公司
财务经理
Tim Walker

请根据 Tim Walker 的要求写一份报告。

任务四

一个月后，你收到了 Tim Walker 发来的邮件，内容如下。

发件人：财务经理 Tim Walker
收件人：初级会计
主题：营销活动决策与新信用管理员

我们马上就要推出新的蛋糕系列产品了。负责销售和市场营销的总监 Fred Knight 和他的团队已经奋战了一段时间，并为现有的蛋糕产品线和我们至臻糕点公司自有品牌的新蛋糕产品线都争取了一大批潜在的新客户。其中虽然包括一家大型的咖啡连锁店，但绝大多数仍旧是小型的独立食品零售商。

我正在为我们的财务团队招聘一个新人，他将专门负责信用控制和客户应收款余额管理。我们需要对其岗位职责做一份简要的说明，希望你帮我准备一下。

Fred Knight 还请 Futuristic（未来）咨询公司就我们预期的销售水平进行了市场调研。针对至臻糕点公司自有品牌产品的推销情况，他们估算了三种不同营销方案所可能产生的收益。

Futuristic 咨询公司以表格形式发来他们的调研结果，同时提出："……对营销活动的选择将取决于董事们'对风险和不确定性的态度'。"我把表格作为附件一并发给你，但是文件中未做任何说明。我听说董事们需要一份关于表格和 Futuristic 咨询公司反馈意见的详细解读，因此，希望你可以替我做这样两件事。

（1）给新的信用管理员做一份简报，说明下面两项工作的程序。

- 评估新客户的信用价值。
- 对新老客户设置信用限额。

（2）做一份简报以供董事们在下一次董事会前传阅，说明以下内容。

- Futuristic 咨询公司反馈的表格中数据的意思。
- 董事们不同的"对风险和不确定性的态度"将会如何影响他们对即将展开的营销活动的决策。

谢谢！

至臻糕点公司
财务经理
Tim Walker

本邮件附件中的表格

方案 A：

预期增量利润（B$）	概率	期望值（B$）
200 000	0.3	60 000
500 000	0.6	300 000
1 000 000	0.1	100 000
		460 000
标准差		224 499
变异系数		48.80%

方案 B：

预期增量利润（B$）	概率	期望值（B$）
100 000	0.2	20 000
600 000	0.6	360 000
700 000	0.2	140 000
		520 000
标准差		213 541
变异系数		41.07%

方案 C：

预期增量利润（B$）	概率	期望值（B$）
350 000	0. 3	105 000
400 000	0. 4	160 000
450 000	0. 3	135 000
		400 000
标准差		37 730
变异系数		9. 68%

请为信用管理员撰写工作说明简报。

请为董事们就 Futuristic 咨询公司的表格撰写解读简报。

Variant 1 Suggested Answers

Section 1

The Report on Using ABC System

The Potential Benefits for Us to Use the ABC System

More Accurate Costing Information

The application of ABC principles would assist in the provision of more realistic assessments of product profitability since ABC would give management a better understanding of what drives overhead costs within First Class Bakery. The application of ABC can be used in conjunction with customer profitability analysis to give a more accurate view of the profit or loss earned by servicing individual customers within First Class Bakery.

Management Better Placed to Control Overhead Costs

Management can focus on controlling the incidence of the chosen cost drivers and this will assist in control of the level of costs incurred. An example would be the fall in the number of sales orders processed within our sales administration team. In an ABC system, the fall in the number of sales orders processed would be immediately apparent because the cost driver rate would be applied to fewer orders and this might lead to a decision to reduce resources in this area.

ABC Is Concerned with All Overhead Costs

ABC recognises that overhead costs are not all related to production and sales volume. Our overheads relate to other activities such as product development, production planning, quality control and customer service. Since ABC focuses on all overhead costs, it would provide a much better insight into what drives our overhead costs.

The costs of activities not included in the costs of the products made by First Class Bakery may be considered to be not contributing to the value of those products. The following questions could then be asked.

- What are the purposes of these activities?
- How does First Class Bakery benefit from these activities?
- Could the number of employees involved in these activities be reduced?

The Steps Involved in the Design of the ABC System for First Class Bakery

Identification of Activities

The implementation of ABC within First Class Bakery would require the identification of the major activities that take place within our business. For example, the purchasing of ingredients might be identified as a major activity.

Level of Aggregation of Activities

We would need to decide what constitutes a reasonable level of aggregation as regards the activities which are to be measured by the ABC system. It would be important to determine this level of aggregation using cost versus benefits criteria. For example, the purchasing of ingredients includes receiving purchase requisitions, identification and selection of suppliers, raising of purchase orders, sending purchase orders, and progressing purchase orders.

Allocation of Costs to Cost Centres

After the activities have been identified, the cost of resources consumed within First Class Bakery must be assigned to each activity. The aim of this exercise is to determine how much we are spending on each of the major activities. Many resources will be directly attributable to specific activity centres but others, for example production labour and lighting and heating, may be indirect and jointly shared by several activities. These costs should be assigned to activities on the basis of cause and effect cost drivers. It is important that arbitrary allocations should not be made.

Identification of Cost Drivers

Of critical importance to the successful implementation of ABC system is the identification of relevant cost drivers which are needed in order to assign the costs to each activity cost centre. Please see next section for examples of possible cost drivers.

Measurement of Cost Drivers

The final stage in designing the ABC system for First Class Bakery would involve the application of cost driver rates to products. In this respect, it is vital that the selected cost driver is measurable in such a way that enables it to be identified with individual cakes. A factor that must be considered in the selection of appropriate cost drivers is the ease and cost of obtaining data on cost driver consumption by products.

Recommendations Regarding Three Appropriate Cost Drivers We Should Use

Number of Ingredients Required

Within First Class Bakery, the number of ingredients required vary significantly between slab cake and special occasion cake production, given the different number of ingredients used in each type of cake. The number of ingredients or even the number of purchase orders could be a cost driver for procurement costs.

Number of Production Set-ups

The number of production set-ups required by slab cakes are much fewer than special occasion cakes which require frequent changes to be made to automated decorating equipment each time the production changes. The number of production set-ups could be a cost driver for material handling costs and production scheduling costs.

Number of Inspections

Another such transaction driver which is highly relevant to our business is the number of inspections performed. Special occasion cakes are subject to three times more inspections per batch than slab cakes. The number of inspections could be a cost driver for quality inspection costs.

Section 2

From: Assistant Management Accountant

To: Tim Walker, Finance Manager

Subject: CRM system and accounting queries

Potential Benefits and Potential Problems Arising from an Investment in a CRM System

Potential Benefits

Better Relationships with Customers

Successful implementation of a CRM system will enable us to get closer to our customers and to use improved knowledge of our customers to know them better, which in turn could boost sales.

We already have close relationships with our large food retailer customers through personal contact, but due to resource constraints have not been able to develop these links with the smaller retailers. As a result, sales to smaller retailers have stagnated and indeed customers seem to come and go regularly. With a CRM system we would be well placed to manage all customer relationships centrally via the storage of both existing and potential customer contact information.

Better Processing of Information

The CRM system can organise and synchronise business processes, sales, marketing, customer service and technical support. These will have two effects: the releasing of employees' time and the enhancement of our customers experience.

The investment in CRM system would help us to identify, attract and gain new customers whilst retaining existing customers. It might also enable us to persuade past customers to buy our products again.

More Efficient Marketing

The CRM system will provide us with more efficient marketing communications with our customers by holding mail and e-mail addresses for a mass distribution of promotions and new products, thereby building and maintaining good customer relationships.

An investment in CRM system will supply our marketers and operational managers with the information to control, develop and manage the marketing activities in a more effective manner.

The successful implementation of the CRM system will remove competitive disadvantages that we might have assumed that our major competitors already have such systems in place.

Potential Problems

Cost of the Investment

The cost of the CRM system will depend on what we require the system to do and the degree of fit we wish to achieve with the needs of the business. Bespoke software packages are much more expensive than "off the shelf" packages. There are associated costs with the implementation of CRM system such as the hardware platform required to run the CRM system. There would also be an opportunity cost attaching to a CRM system investment insofar as there might be other potential projects competing for budget approval by our parent.

Change the Existing Operations

There may be a need to adjust existing business processes, workflows and responsibilities to fit the software. This might impact upon production and will require careful planning.

Staff Training Required
Inevitably the implementation of any new system will involve the staff training to help them use that system. We will almost certainly need the services of an external consultant company since we lack the in-house expertise to manage the job. There is also an unavoidable cost of our staff having to take time away from their normal activities such as dealing with customer enquiries.

Accounting Issues

Consolidation Query
As a result of the acquisition, First Class Bakery has become a subsidiary of Universal Foods, which means that its income, expenses, assets and liabilities need to be consolidated with the rest of the group within a single set of group financial statements. It is exactly what David Spencer is referring to.

First Class Bakery has become a subsidiary because Universal Foods now owns 80% of the equity share capital (with you owning the remaining 20%), which gives it the power to control the operating and financial policies of our business. Your investment of 20% can not stop First Class Bakery from being a subsidiary of Universal Foods and therefore can not stop the need for our business to be consolidated with the rest of the group. Your investment of 20% will be reflected in the group financial statements as a non-controlling interest in a subsidiary.

The group financial statements are an aggregation of the income, expenses, assets and liabilities of all the entities controlled by Universal Foods. They are prepared to give the shareholders of Universal Foods a complete view of the profitability and financial position of the group as a whole.

Whilst the income, expenses, assets and liabilities of our business will be included in the group's financial statements, we will still need to prepare financial statements for First Class Bakery in its own right because it is still a separate entity from a legal point of view. Therefore there is still a statutory responsibility of the directors to prepare financial statements for First Class Bakery.

Revaluation Query
Where there is a group of entities preparing group financial statements, reporting standards require each entity consolidated to use consistent accounting policies. That is the reason why David Spencer has stated that he wanted us to change our policy to the re-

valuation of property. Clearly the group policy must be to revalue property assets.

It should be noted that there are two ways to achieve consistent accounting policies for group companies. Either each group company uses the same policy in their own financial statements or do some adjustments when the consolidated financial statements are prepared. In our case, David Spencer has requested that we change our policy, obviously he adopts the former approach.

The implication of changing the policy is that we will need to have the property that we own valued at 31 December 2016 by an independent valuation expert. This value is the amount that will be included in our financial statements for property.

It is likely that the property value will be considerably higher than the carrying value due to the fact that the property was purchased a number of years ago. This means that there will be a revaluation gain at the year-end. This gain however does not affect profit as it will be credited to a revaluation reserve and be shown within other comprehensive income.

In future years, depreciation for property will be based on its revalued amount. This means the depreciation charge will be higher which will affect profits. We will also need to regularly revalue the property and amend its carrying value accordingly.

If our property has declined in value, then it should be noted that there will be a revaluation loss. This would directly impact profit, unless it reverses the previous surplus in which case it will be debited to the revaluation surplus and certainly will impact other comprehensive income.

Thanks.

Assistant Management Accountant
First Class Bakery

Section 3

New IT System and Budgeting Report

Benefits of a New IT System

The principal benefits that might be gained from a new IT system investment are detailed below.

Strategic Benefits

Strategic benefits relate to company's long-term aims; they are concerned with the company as a whole and related to its environment. The investment should make First Class Bakery more flexible and reactive to its environment. It will almost certainly give more up-to-date information to our managers thereby enabling quicker decisions to be made. Our long-term aims relate to profitability and stability and these in turn are driven by growth. This growth is in terms of both revenue and product range.

New products is the key to growth, it is essential that products should be both desirable to customers and profitable to us. Internally improved costing from the new system would provide accurate data to underpin launch decisions and to monitor the success of products that have been launched. Externally the new system might be capable of recording data on customer taste, competitor actions and economic and social trends. The data for determining what product characteristics are needed could feed into the product development process.

More sophisticated planning tools might be available from the new system, enabling detailed, accurate and frequent forecasts to feed into the whole of our operations, perhaps via the use of an EIS (executive information system).

We could use an extranet to link up our chosen suppliers with customers, which will greatly improve our supply chain management. IT system plays an important role in the provision, storage, management and consultation of the information management which is a part of supply chain management. IT system can also provide for all areas of our business through systems such as e-procurement and customer relationship management.

If we have the same e-business capability as our business partners who are our suppliers and customers, the management of our supply chain will be more easily achievable. Selling, delivering, ordering, designing and manufacturing can all be linked which means that we could achieve cost reduction, time saving, faster innovation, better marketing and better quality levels.

Other areas of our value chain such as human resource management, marketing and service would benefit from the implementation of a new IT system via the availability of more accurate information.

Operational Benefits

Operational benefits are concerned with day-to-day activities and there are many possible examples. Real-time information from the factory floor could assist with monitoring quality and enable short-term planning decisions to be made more effectively. The investment probably makes day-to-day operations more efficient or removes non-value adding activities from our value chain in order to increase the overall productivity of the business.

Improved inventory management might assist in the reduction of the inventory volume whilst preventing the occurrences of stock outs. These reductions in inventory levels, with the assistance of a new IT system for supply chain planning and scheduling can lead to cost reductions. Sales forecasting software fed into manufacturing resources planning can be used in shop floor planning and scheduling more efficiently. These initiatives may be linked to the strategic benefit such as the achievement of cost leadership.

Intangible Benefits

Intangible benefits tend to have longer-term consequences for an organisation and they can prove to be very important. It should be acknowledged that intangible benefits can only be measured in a subjective manner. That said, a benefit of a new IT system investment may be that staff morale within our business will improve as staff might perceive that "state of the art" tools are being made available to them in order to assist their effectiveness within their roles.

Another significant benefit of this type is that customer satisfaction levels may be well increased as a result of improved information flows to and from First Class Bakery. This would enhance our customers' perception to First Class Bakery, which would improve our competitive position.

ABB or ZBB As Alternatives to the Current System of Incremental Budgeting

ABB

ABB is a method of budgeting based on an activity framework, utilising cost driver data in the budget setting and variance feedback processes. ABB, as the name suggests, utilises activity-based thinking. In fact, ABC needs to be in place for ABB to work. All of the tasks and costs that we discussed some months ago would be required to implement ABC, but once that was done it would be logical to consider the implementation of ABB within First Class Bakery.

The arguments in favour of ABB are much the same as for ABC. Activities arise costs. The more times an activity is performed, the greater will be the total cost of that activity. Different products use different activities in different quantities. It follows that with accurate activity data, accurate and detailed budgets are a clear possibility.

Since we produce many different types of product using different combinations of activities, ABB could provide management with more meaningful information for budgetary control. ABB provides useful control information by emphasising that activity costs might be controllable if the activity volume can be controlled.

First Class Bakery is focused on improving quality levels. The use of ABB can provide useful information for a quality assessment programme by relating the cost of an activity to the level of service provided, for example, stores requisitions processed by our stores department. Such information would enable the user departments to assess whether or not they are getting a cost-effective service.

It is worth considering that ZBB and ABB are not necessarily mutually exclusive. Although ZBB challenges how we currently do things, once new approaches are determined they can be evaluated using activity based thinking. Different activity levels provide the base for the base packages and incremental packages of ZBB. Thus it is possible to use ZBB and ABB in tandem.

ZBB

The adoption of ZBB would encourage our managers to question what is currently done and to seek alternatives which are better and lower-cost. This would lead to the identification of non-essential costs relating to inefficient or obsolete operations and their removal from the budget for the forthcoming period. Our present system of incremental budgeting cannot remove such inefficiencies.

ZBB is extremely future focused, unlike the current system of incremental budgeting which is backward looking and bases next year's budget on what has happened in the past.

ZBB would require a higher level of involvement of all levels of our staff since significantly more information would be required to complete our budget. Preparation of the decision packages will normally require the involvement of many employees and therefore creating an opportunity for their views to be considered. The involvement of more employees into the budgetary process would not only raise levels of both "budget awareness" and "budget acceptance" but also might generate useful ideas and promote job satisfaction across the wider staff.

The adoption of ZBB within First Class Bakery will assist in the creation of an organisational environment in which change is more readily accepted and also lead to enhanced knowledge and understanding of our cost behaviour patterns. If ZBB were to be implemented then our resources should be allocated more efficiently and economically.

Section 4

The Brief Report on Sales Activities and Credit Controller

Assessing the Creditworthiness of New Customers

Before any new customer is taken on it is important to ensure that they will be able to pay for the goods sold to it on credit. As a credit controller, one of your responsibilities is to make an assessment on a potential customer's creditworthiness, in other words, their ability to pay.

The majority of new customers that you will need to assess will be small independent food retailers, where cash flow is often a concern. Therefore it is vital that this assessment is carried out.

In order to make the assessment as a credit controller, there are a number of steps that need to happen. The assessment itself will be undertaken by the credit controller and the finance manager jointly. The credit controller will be responsible for collecting data about the customer which will be discussed with the finance manager at each of the following steps, so that potential customers who clearly are a significant credit risk will not be progressed further.

The first step is to collect information about the potential customer. This information will come from:

- the financial statements of the customer, which will give you an indication of their financial stability, cash position, outstanding commitments and an idea of how long they take to pay their current suppliers;
- an internet search on the business to see if there are any indications of problems paying in the past (such as legal proceedings).

The second step will then be to secure references from independent third parties involved with the potential customer. The customer will need to give authority for such references, which will include:

- a reference from the potential customer's bank;
- references from the potential customer's suppliers.

The last step is to obtain a credit agency reference for the customer.

Setting Credit Limits

There are two aspects to setting credit limits:

- the amount of credit that is given (the maximum amount a customer can owe at any one time);
- the time limit for payment (how long a customer has to pay from the date of the invoice).

Given the nature of our customers, there is no standard credit limit either in terms of amount or time, each customer is judged on its own basis.

For a new customer, this judgement will be based on the information obtained in the assessment of creditworthiness and it will be undertaken by the credit controller and the finance manager jointly. Typically new customers will get a low credit amount and shorter time frame initially, which will be increased once they prove themselves to be good payers.

It is important that the credit limits of existing customers are reviewed regularly as well. This review will involve:

- looking at the past payment record to see if they have paid in time;
- assessing whether any new information has come to light which affects their ability to pay.

If there has been a change in circumstances or indeed a new customer has proved their ability to pay then credit limits can be changed accordingly.

This review should happen every two months for each customer. Although, if there is evidence of a change in risk profile before the review, actions should be taken immediately.

The Data in the Table

The table prepared by Futuristic Consulting shows the expected value of each of the marketing campaigns A, B and C.

The data in the table indicates that there are three possible outcomes for each campaign. The first column indicates predicted additional profit. These are all different numbers and represent the net effect of additional sales less additional costs (including marketing costs).

The probabilities are the likelihood of each outcome arising based on Futuristic's estimates. The expected value is the sum of each outcome multiplied by its associated probability. Thus the expected value is the weighted average of all outcomes where the weighting is by probability.

In general, a higher expected value is more attractive than a lower one but please see my comments on attitudes to risk below.

In the case of the attached schedule, campaign B has the highest expected value and campaign C has the lowest.

The expected value alone gives no indication of the range of possible outcomes. The expected value is not the most likely result, it even might not be one of the possible outcomes as can be seen from the possible outcomes of the three campaigns. The expected value is the long-run average outcome if the same event is to be repeated over and over again.

Care should be exercised when using expected values in "one off decisions" as it is simply a weighted average.

It should also be borne in mind that the probabilities used in the calculation of the expected value of each of the three campaigns might be very subjective in nature.

Risk Attitudes

It is highly probable that all decision makers will not have the same attitude to risk. In this regard, a director within First Class Bakery may be a "Risk Seeker", "Risk Neutral" or "Risk Averse".

A "Risk Seeker" is a decision maker who is interested in the best outcomes no matter how small the likelihood is. Campaign A has the highest standard deviation and also the highest coefficient of variation. This indicates high upside potential as evidenced by the possible outcome of B$1,000,000. For these reasons, the risk seeker would be attracted to campaign A.

A "Risk Neutral" decision maker will consider all possible outcomes and will select the strategy that maximises the expected value or benefit. In the case of First Class Bakery, a risk neutral decision maker would select campaign B which has the highest expected value of the three campaigns under consideration. This type of decision maker would ignore both standard deviation and coefficient of variation.

A "Risk Averse" decision maker acts on the assumption that the worst conditions might occur and tries to avoid risk. Campaign C has the lowest standard deviation and also the lowest coefficient of variation. This indicates that campaign C is most likely to result in an outcome which is closed to the expected value and therefore has a low downside risk. For these reasons, this type of decision maker would be attracted to campaign C.

As regards the final decision, the choice of marketing campaign would be influenced by the "collective" risk attitude of the directors of First Class Bakery.

试卷一　参考答案

任务一

关于采用作业成本法的简报

采用作业成本法的好处

更准确的成本核算信息

由于作业成本法可以帮助至臻糕点公司的管理层更好地理解到底是什么导致了间接成本的产生，因此对产品盈利性的评估会更切合实际。作业成本系统与客户盈利性分析结合运用，将会提高至臻糕点公司对其所服务的每个单独客户盈亏分析的准确度。

更好地实施间接成本管理

作业成本系统可以使管理层把精力集中在控制选定的成本动因上，而这将有助于控制成本费用水平。我们以公司销售管理团队处理的销售订单数减少为例做说明。在作业成本系统中，销售订单数的下降可以实时呈现，因为成本动因分配率会被应用到更少的订单上，而这可能会促使管理层做出减少在该领域配置资源的决策。

作业成本法关注所有的间接成本

作业成本法的设计者明白，并非所有的间接成本都与生产和销售量相关。我们的间接费用也与其他作业相关，如产品开发、生产计划、质量控制和客户服务等。由于作业成本法关注所有的间接成本，它会帮助我们更好地理解到底是什么驱动了间接成本的产生。

在至臻糕点公司内部已产生但未计入产品成本的作业成本有可能被认为是对产品价值没有贡献。于是，接下来就要问这样几个问题：

- 实施这些作业的目的是什么？
- 至臻糕点公司如何从这些作业中获益？
- 是否可以减少参与这些作业的员工数？

设计至臻糕点公司实施作业成本法的步骤

确认作业

实施作业成本法要求至臻糕点公司确认其经营过程中发生的主要作业。例如，原料采购就可能被确认为一项主要作业。

归集作业水平

为了通过作业成本法计量作业，我们需要确定什么是合理的归集水平。成本效益原则是确定归集水平的重要考量因素。例如，原料采购包括接收请购单、甄别和选择供应商、提交采购订单、发送采购订单和处理采购订单。

将成本分配到成本中心

作业确认之后，至臻糕点公司内部消耗的资源成本应被分配给各个作业，其目的是确定我们在主要作业上的资源消耗量。许多资源将被直接追踪到特定的作业，但其他的比如人工、照明和供热，可能同时服务于几个作业，是间接的。这些成本将通过以因果关系为基础的作业动因进行分配，同时必须避免被武断地分配。

确认成本动因

要成功实施作业成本法，确认相关的成本动因尤其重要，这是把成本分配到各作业成本中心的过程所必需的。可能的成本动因参见后文。

计量成本动因

设计至臻糕点公司作业成本法的最后一个步骤是用成本动因分配率分配产品成本。从这点看，选择可以计量的、可以把成本明确分配到每一块蛋糕的成本动因十分关键。选择恰当的成本动因要考虑的一个因素是可以很方便、低成本地取得产品消耗的成本动因数据。

建议采用的三个成本动因

原料需求数量

在至臻糕点公司，生产普通切片蛋糕和特殊场合蛋糕所需的物料变化很大，不同类型的蛋糕需要的原料数量不同。原料数量甚至是订单数量都可以考虑作为采购成本的成本动因。

生产整备次数

特殊场合蛋糕的生产每变化一次都需要变更自动装配设备，相比之下生产普通切片蛋糕需要的生产整备次数少得多。生产设备的调整次数可以考虑作为材料处理成本和生产计划成本的成本动因。

检验次数

与公司业务高度相关的另一个交易动因是检验次数。特殊场合蛋糕要求的批量检验次数是普通切片蛋糕的三倍。因此检验次数可以考虑作为质量监控成本的成本动因。

任务二

发件人：管理会计助理

收件人：财务经理 Tim Walker

主题：客户关系管理系统与会计疑问

投资客户关系管理系统的潜在优缺点

客户关系管理潜在优点

优化客户关系

客户关系管理系统若能成功实施将有助于我们更加贴近客户，并通过改进后的知识增进我们对客户的了解，这反过来将会促进销售。

通过个人私交的方式我们已经和大型零售商客户建立了紧密的联系，但受资源的限制，我们尚未能与那些小型的零售商建立类似的联系。结果就是，面向小型零售商的销售陷入停滞，客户看起来总是来来往往的。有了客户关系管理系统，我们就可以通过对既有和潜在客户的联系信息的存储，在总部管理所有的客户关系。

优化信息流程

客户关系管理系统可以组织和同步业务流程、销售、营销、客户服务和技术支持。这会产生两个结果：解放员工时间，强化客户体验。

在客户关系管理系统上的投资将有助于我们在维护老客户的同时甄别、吸引、获得新客户。它还可能促使我们过去的客户再次购买我们的产品。

更高效地营销

客户关系管理系统将使我们可以通过邮件或电子邮件的方式向客户大量发布促销信息和新产品通告，从而更为高效地进行营销传播，这也有利于建立并维持良好的客户关系。

在客户关系管理系统上的投资将为我们的营销人员和业务经理提供所需的信息，让他们以更为高效的方式控制、开发和管理营销活动。

客户关系管理系统若能成功运行将消除我们与那些已经实施了类似系统的主要竞争对手之间的相对劣势。

潜在缺点

投资成本

客户关系管理系统的成本取决于我们所将采用的系统以及要求其在多大程度上切合

我们的业务需求。相比通用软件，定制软件要贵得多。在实施客户关系管理系统的过程中还会产生一些附带成本，例如运行客户关系管理系统所需的硬件平台。此外，由于可能还有其他潜在的项目需要向母公司申请预算，因此还要考虑投资客户关系管理系统的机会成本。

改变现有的业务操作

为了适应软件的要求，可能需要调整现有的业务流程、工作程序和职责分配。这可能会对生产产生影响，因此需要认真规划。

需要培训员工

实施任何新系统都不可避免地需要员工培训以帮助他们学会使用。由于公司内部没有这方面的专家可以完成这项工作，因此毋庸置疑地需要借助外部咨询公司的服务。此外，还有一项无法规避的成本，就是这肯定要挤占我们的员工花在处理客户疑问等日常工作上的时间。

会计疑问

合并报表问题

作为并购的结果之一，至臻糕点公司已经变成通用食品集团的一个子公司，这意味着它的收入、费用、资产和负债需要与集团的其他子公司一起被合并进集团的财务报表，也就是 David Spencer 所说的财务报表。

除了你所保留的 20% 股份外，通用食品集团现在持有我们 80% 的股份，因此至臻糕点公司已经成为它的一个子公司，这使得它有权控制我们的经营和财务政策。你拥有的 20% 股份并不能阻止至臻糕点公司变成通用食品集团子公司这样一个事实，因此也就不能阻止通用食品集团对我们进行并表。你的 20% 的股权投资将被反映在集团财务报表的少数股权项下。

集团财务报表综合反映了通用食品集团所控制的所有主体的收入、费用、资产和负债。这些报表是为了方便集团股东从总体上把握集团的盈利性和财务状况。

由于从法律角度看，至臻糕点公司仍旧是一个独立的法律主体，因此在把我们的收入、费用、资产和负债合并进集团财务报表的同时，我们仍旧需要编制独立的财务报表。因此，董事们仍旧负有编制至臻糕点公司财务报表的法律责任。

资产价值重估问题

只要涉及集团财务报表的编制，财务报告准则就会要求并表的各个会计主体都采用一致的会计政策。这也就是为什么 David Spencer 要求我们变更为资产价值重估政策。很显然，集团的财务政策一定要求对资产进行价值重估。对于集团来说，有两种方法可以实现会计政策的一致。要么各个子公司在编制各自报表时采用相同的会计政策，要么集团在编制合并报表时进行调整。就目前来看，David Spencer 已经要求我们变更会计政策，显然他选择的是前者。

会计政策变更意味着我们需要聘请一位独立的估价师对我们 2016 年 12 月 31 日记录在册的资产进行估价。估价的结果将作为我们的资产在财务报表上的入账金额。

公司资产都是在几年前购置的，其实际价值可能要比账面价值高出许多，所以在年末会实现重估值收益。这种收益会被贷记入重估值准备账户，并反映在其他整体收益当中，并不会对年度利润产生影响。

在未来的几年中，我们将以重估值为基础计算资产的折旧。这意味着计提的折旧费用将会上升，并影响当期利润。我们需要定期对资产进行价值重估并修正它的账面价值。

如果我们的资产出现减值，就会导致重估值失败。这会直接影响利润，除非前期计提的准备可以完全覆盖，这种情况下我们将借记重估值准备账户，当然，这也会对其他整体收益产生影响。

感谢！

至臻糕点公司
管理会计助理

任务三

新 IT 系统和预算方法报告

新 IT 系统的好处

下面阐述投资新 IT 系统可能获得的主要利益。

战略利益

战略利益与企业的长期目标相关，它们关注企业整体并与所处环境相关联。投资将赋予至臻糕点公司更大的弹性并提高我们对环境的反应能力。几乎可以肯定的是，它会为管理者提供更多最新的信息，这也将使决策过程更为迅速。我们的长期目标与盈利性和稳定性有关，而反过来这些又都是由增长驱动的。这里所谓的增长既包括收入提高也包括产品线开发。

新产品是实现增长的关键，这些新产品必须既能满足客户需求又能为公司带来利润。对内来说，新系统提供的改进版成本计算方法可以为我们的新产品开发决策提供准确的数据支持，也可以对已经成功推向市场的产品实施监控。对外来说，新系统可能具备记录客户品味、竞争者行动以及经济和社会趋势等数据的能力。在产品开发过程中，可以依靠这些数据来确定新产品所应具备的特性。

新系统还可能提供更为复杂的规划工具，诸如通过经理信息系统（EIS）对企业整体的经营进行细节、精确、高频的预测。

通过外部网，我们可以把经过挑选的供应商和客户连接起来，这将会极大地提高我们的供应链管理水平。在供应、仓储、管理和咨询等供应链管理的信息管理方面，IT 系统扮演着重要的角色。通过诸如电子采购和客户关系管理等系统，IT 系统可以服务于企业经营的各个方面。

如果我们和我们的供应商、客户等商业伙伴一样都具备了电子商务能力，供应链管理就将变得轻而易举。销售、发货、采购、设计和制造等环节就可以联系在一起，而这意味着成本降低、时间节省、创新加快、高效营销和质量水平提升。

新 IT 系统运行之后，价值链的其他方面，如人力资源管理、市场营销和客户服务等，也将因为有了更为准确的信息而获益。

经营利益

经营利益与日常活动相关，对此有许多例子。工厂的实时信息将有助于质量监控，它可以使短期规划的制订更为高效。该项投资可以使日常经营更富效率，或者剔除价值链上那些非增值作业，这也将有助于提高企业的整体生产力。

改善存货管理将有助于在降低库存的同时规避缺货风险。新 IT 系统对供应链的规划和安排能够减少存货量，而这必将导致成本的下降。通过与制造资源计划相连接，销售预测软件规划和安排商店现场的效率将会提升。这些举措还可能和战略利益挂钩，如实现成本领先。

无形利益

无形利益可对一个组织产生较长期的影响，它的重要性不言而喻。但与此同时，无形利益只能通过主观方法进行衡量。也就是说，投资新 IT 系统可能会使员工意识到为了提高他们的工作效率，公司为他们提供了“最先进”的工具，这有利于提升员工的士气。

另一个重要的无形利益是，由于流通于至臻糕点公司的信息流得以优化，客户满意水平可能会大幅度提升。这会改善客户对至臻糕点公司的印象，并提高我们的竞争地位。

以作业预算或零基预算替代现行增量预算体系

作业预算

作业预算是一种建立在作业基础上的预算方法，它利用成本动因数据进行预算编制和差异反馈。作业预算，就像它的名字所暗示的那样，它运用的是作业基础思维。实际上，要使作业预算发挥作用就要求企业实施作业成本法。几个月之前，我们讨论过实施作业成本法所要完成的任务和承担的成本，而一旦这些工作都完成了，那么顺理成章地就要考虑在至臻糕点公司内部实施作业预算了。

支持作业预算的理由和支持作业成本法的理由很相像。作业产生成本，一项作业发生的次数越多，该作业的总成本就越高。不同的产品，使用不同数量的不同作业。有了准确的作业数据，做出严谨、详细的预算就不在话下了。

由于我们通过不同作业的组合生产许多种类的产品，作业预算可以为管理层实施预算控制提供更有意义的信息。如果作业的数量可控，那么作业的成本也应该可控，基于此，作业预算提供了有用的控制信息。

至臻糕点公司关注的焦点在于提升质量水平。通过作业成本与所提供的服务水平相挂钩，作业预算可以为质量评估项目提供有用的信息，例如，材料部门处理的领料申请。这类信息可以帮助用料部门评估他们得到的服务是否划算。

要知道，零基预算和作业预算未必是互相排斥的。零基预算挑战的是我们现行的做事方法，一旦决定采用新方法，就可以利用作业思维进行评估。不同的作业水平提供了零基预算的基础决策包和增量决策包的基础。因此零基预算和作业预算是有可能协同使用的。

零基预算

采用零基预算将会促使管理者去审视我们目前在做的事，并寻求更好、更便宜的替代方案。这将帮助我们识别那些消耗在无效或过气业务上的不必要的成本，并将其从下一阶段的预算中剔除。我们现行的增量预算并不会消除这类低效作业和成本。

零基预算是极其未来导向的，不同于我们现行的增量预算，增量预算是过去导向的，它以过去发生的事情为基础来制定下一年度的预算。

零基预算在更大程度上要求各个层级的员工都参与到制定预算的过程中来，因为它需要多得多的信息才能完成预算。它通常需要大量的员工加入预算的准备工作中，这样就有机会了解不同的意见。让更多员工参与预算过程不但会提升“预算意识”和“预算接受度”，而且可能会产生更好的意见和建议并在更大范围内提升员工的职业满意度。

采用零基预算将有助于至臻糕点公司创建一种更容易接受改变的组织环境，并能够强化对我们成本行为模式的认识和理解。如果实施了零基预算，我们的资源配置将会变得更高效、更经济。

任务四

关于信用管理员与营销方案的简报

评估新客户的信用价值

在获取新客户之前，很重要的一点是要确保赊销客户具备为其所购买的商品付款的能力。作为信用管理员，你的一项职责是评估潜在客户的信用价值，换句话说，就是他们的付款能力。

大多数你需要评估的新客户将会是小型的独立食品零售商，他们经常现金流吃紧，因此信用评估就显得很重要。

作为信用管理员，评估工作要分为几个步骤开展。评估由信用管理员和财务经理共同完成。信用管理员的职责是在每一个步骤的工作中收集与财务经理讨论所需的客户数据，从而保证信用风险明显的客户不会被进一步开发。

第一步，收集潜在客户的信息。信息来源包括：

- 客户的财务报表，这将让你从整体上了解它们的财务稳健性、现金状况、对外债务，以及它们偿付供应商货款的时长；
- 借助互联网查看是否有任何迹象显示它们过往在支付方面出过问题，例如是否涉及法律诉讼。

第二步，从与潜在客户有关的第三方处取得对他们的评价。取得评价前要获得客户的授权，评价包括：

- 银行对潜在客户的评价；
- 供应商对潜在客户的评价。

最后一步，取得征信机构对客户的评价。

设置信用限额

设定信用额度包括如下两个方面：

- 给定的信用金额，也就是一个客户一次的最大负债额；
- 支付期限，也就是客户需要在发票日之后多长时间内付款。

考虑到客户的性质，我们没有给信用金额和时间设置固定标准，而是根据每个客户的情况一案一定。

对新客户的信用价值判断建立在信息评估的基础上，判断由信用管理员和财务经理共同完成。典型情况下，新客户最开始只能获得金额小、期限相对较短的信用限额，而一旦他们有了良好的付款记录，就可以提高限额。

定期检查既有客户的信用条件也很重要。检查包括如下内容：

- 翻看过往的付款记录，看看他们是否按期付款；
- 评估是否存在对他们的付款能力产生影响的新信息。

如果经营环境发生变化或者一个新客户已经证实了他们的付款能力，那么就可以据此变更信用条件。

针对各个客户的检查，每两个月进行一次。当然，在检查之前一旦有证据表明风险有所变化，就应该立即采取行动。

表格中的数据

Futuristic 咨询公司提供的表格展示了营销方案 A、B 和 C 的预期价值。

表格中的数据说明，每种方案都有三种可能的结果。第一列数字说的是各种方案的预期增量利润。这些数字各不相同，它们是销售收入增量扣减成本（包括营销成本）增量后的净额。

概率是指 Futuristic 咨询公司预估的各种结果发生的可能性。期望值是各栏的预期增量利润乘以各自概率的乘积之和。因此，期望值是各种情况下预期增量利润以概率为权重的加权平均数。

一般来说，期望值高的方案比期望值低的方案更有吸引力，但要考虑风险，这一点我在下面会谈到。

就附件资料来看，方案 B 的期望值最高，方案 C 的期望值最低。

期望值本身没有说明其出现的可能范围。它并不是最可能出现的结果，从三种营销活动的方案中我们可以看到，它甚至不是一个可能出现的结果。期望值说明的是长期平均情况，也就是说我们不断重复同样的事情，我们才会得到这样的结果。

由于只是一个加权平均数，因此运用期望值进行一次性决策时需要格外谨慎。

还必须注意，计算三个营销方案的期望值时所用的概率具有主观性。

风险态度

决策制定者很有可能并不具有相同的风险态度，而这意味着，至臻糕点公司的董事们有可能分属“风险偏好者”、“风险中性者” 或者是“风险厌恶者”。

一个“风险偏好” 的决策者感兴趣的是那个产出结果最好的方案，而不管这个结果实现的可能性有多小。方案 A 的标准差最大，变异系数也最大。这表明可能出现较高收益，而我们也确实看到这个方案有实现 B$ 1 000 000 收益的可能。基于这些理由，风险偏好者将会倾向于方案 A。

一个“风险中性” 的决策者将会考虑各种可能的结果并选择期望值最大的方案。在至臻糕点公司案例中，一个风险中性者将会选择方案 B，该方案的期望值是三个方案中最高的。这类决策者决策时会忽略掉标准差和变异系数。

一个“风险厌恶” 的决策者会假设最坏的情况来行动并试图规避风险。方案 C 的标准差和变异系数都最小，这说明方案 C 的实际结果会最接近期望值，因此下行的风险也最小。基于这些理由，这种类型的决策者会选择方案 C。

对于营销方案的最终选择将取决于至臻糕点公司董事会整体的风险态度。

Variant 1　Marking Guidance

Section	Technical skills		Business skills		People skills		Leadership skills		Integration	Total
1	Potential benefits and the implementation of ABC system with examples of appropriate cost drivers	18	Potential benefits of ABC system	4					3	25
2	Accounting queries in respect of consolidation and revaluation reserve	12			Benefits and drawbacks of the investment in a CRM system	13				25
3	Advantages of an ABB and ZBB approach to budgeting compared to an incremental approach	13	Strategic, operational and intangible benefits of the investment in new IT systems	12						25
4	Procedures for setting credit limits for new and existing customers Decision making under conditions of uncertainty	6 13					Assessment of creditworthiness of potential customers	6		25
Total marks available for each competency		62		16		13		6	3	100

试卷一　评分指南

部分	技术技能		商业技能		人际技能		领导技能		综合能力	总计
1	作业成本法的潜在收益及其实施步骤，合适的成本动因举例	18	作业成本法的潜在优点	4					3	25
2	合并会计报表及资产价值重估准备的相关疑问	12			投资客户关系管理系统的利弊分析	13				25
3	对比增量预算，作业预算和零基预算这两种预算方法的优点	13	投资新 IT 系统的战略利益、经营利益、无形利益	12						25
4	针对新老客户设定信用限额的程序 不确定性条件下的决策	6 13					评估潜在客户的信用价值	6		25
各技能评分合计		62		16		13		6	3	100

厦门大学名师解惑

本套题目的案例主体是至臻糕点公司，试卷一共有四项任务，考查了 E1、P1、F1 三门课程的知识点，具体包括作业成本法、客户关系管理系统、合并报表和会计政策变更、资产价值重估准备、新 IT 系统和预算方法、信用管理员职责和不确定性决策。其中 P1（48）的知识点分数比重最高，其次是 E1（25），最后则是 F1（24）。这和 OCS 的考纲要求基本一致。该试卷考核了考生的四项能力，其中技术技能的分值占 64%，商业技能的分值占 15%，人际技能的分值占 12%，领导技能的分值占 6%，与 CGMA 管理会计能力框架的技能要求一致。考生在备考时应根据考试重点有所侧重。另外的 3 分是考查综合能力的，可能是对不同模块或不同能力的整合。这些得分点嵌在任务里，完成任务时满足要求就能得分。

该试卷的每项任务涉及以下知识点：

任务	问题	科目	知识点
任务一	实施作业成本法的潜在收益	P1	作业成本法（ABC）
	实施作业成本法的步骤，可能遇到的潜在问题		
	选择成本动因		
任务二	客户关系管理	E1	客户关系管理（CRM）
	合并报表范围	F1	合并报表（consolidated financial statements）
	资产重估及其对财务报表的影响	F1	资产价值重估（revaluation）
任务三	投资 IT 系统的好处	E1	IT 系统（IT system）
	作业预算和零基预算的优点	P1	作业预算（ABB）、零基预算（ZBB）
任务四	不确定性条件下营销活动决策	P1	不确定性及风险态度（attitudes to risk and uncertainty）、期望值（expected value）
	如何评估新客户信用价值，设置客户信用限额	F1	评估信用价值（assess creditworthiness）、信用限额（credit limits）

上述各项任务要求以邮件、报告或工作笔记等形式来呈现答案，对问题的描述非常明确，答题时既要注意内容的针对性，也要注意形式的规范性。

对应知识点深度剖析

作业成本法的潜在收益及其实施步骤，合适的成本动因举例

考生需要掌握作业成本法的专业知识，并回答出所有问题。

关于作业成本法的优点，基本上可以利用P1大纲中的知识点来阐述，而如何利用作业成本的信息为公司管理服务，则需要结合案例来分析。关于作业成本法的实施步骤，要根据大纲的知识点按顺序列出，建议标题鲜明，并结合案例简单举例说明。成本动因的选择，需要根据案例的实际情景做出解释。

投资客户关系管理系统的优缺点

考核考生对于E1相关知识点“客户关系管理系统支持组织的战略和经营”的掌握程度，需逐项列出，并尽可能结合案例背景适当分析。

合并报表问题

需要讨论公司被合并后控制权发生转移的状况，以及编制合并报表的条件。同时，结合案例背景，阐述针对少数股东权益的处理方式。

资产重估

需要阐述母公司、子公司在编制合并报表时保持会计政策一致性的方法，同时讨论会计政策变更对财务的影响，包括升值和减值。

投资IT系统的主要利益、经营利益和无形利益

背景材料提到现有系统已经过时，而本题的情景是讨论投资新系统的好处。根据题目要求，完整阐述战略利益。

作业成本法和零基预算的好处

背景材料提到当前的预算方式是传统的增量预算，本题考查其他的替代方式，要能对其分别做出评价。

不确定性条件下的决策

考生需要理解风险态度对决策的影响，同时，要结合所给表格中的数据，对期望值、标准差的含义以及该结果对决策可能产生的影响做出分析。

评估新客户信用价值及设置客户信用限额

此题考查F1中的知识点。考生需要针对新老客户分别提出不同的方法，可能的话，也可以参考竞争对手的做法。

考生注意事项

背景资料是提前下发的，考生在阅读时，可以根据相关资料对考核范围做一些猜测。比如，从资料上看，该企业有两大类顾客。两大类产品在生产的复杂性上存在着较大的差异，而两大类顾客也存在着比较大的差异。因此，基于这些资料，可以合理推测，作业成本法应该是考核的一个主要内容。此外，由于资料中提到了该食品厂近期被一家大型上市公司收购了，因此也可以合理推测将会有涉及并表的会计问题出现。资料还提到现有财务人员没有信用控制资格，而顾客的付款也并不是很及时，所以有可能会做这方面的考核。其他可能的考点，则只限于推测，例如信息系统、环保与安全问题等。在备考时，要对这些内容重点复习，特别是技能部分。

在答题的时候，要避免只是简单复述教科书的知识点，而要结合案例公司的实际情况，例如，具体到两个产品线的产品差异、两大类客户的差异来做分析。特别是陈述成本动因的选择时，更应该结合企业的实际业务来阐述。当然，也可以略施技巧，例如，反复强调至臻糕点公司应如何做等。此外，还要注意避免出现过多对背景或任务的阐述，要把时间用于解决任务中的问题。

最后，注意回答时的措辞、格式、论述的结构完整性和论点的鲜明整体性等。例如，在回答优缺点时，应使用鲜明的标题，分点分行明确地列举，这个是综合分的得分点。

Variant 2

This examination is structured as follows：

Section number	Number of tasks	Time for section(minutes)
1	1	45
2	1	45
3	2	45
4	1	45

The time available for each section is for reading,planning and writing your answer(s).

Please note section 3 consists of two tasks. Please leave enough time to complete both parts.

Section 1

Rajiv Patel sends the following on-line article to his team.

Wheat Prices to Soar

15 February 2016 **By: James Fredricks**

World wheat prices are at an all-time high as a result of poor harvests in many key wheat growing regions of the world.

In particular, growers in Beeland and its neighbouring country Geeland are reporting yields 40% lower than normal due to consistent bad weather and storms. Other major growing countries such as Deeland and Reeland are reporting yields 15% lower as a result of crop disease. Only Jeeland is reporting above average yields.

Flour mills are already reporting a lack of supply and are warning that prices are likely to rise even further. This is expected to affect bread producers the most, although other bakery related manufacturers are also expected to be affected. Ultimately it will be us, the consumer, who will be hit the hardest as prices increase!

Six weeks later, Rajiv Patel sends you the following email.

From：Rajiv Patel, Finance Director
To：Management Accountant Assistant
Subject：Variance reporting

Before Tim, the finance manager, went on his annual leave, he calculated the ingredients and labour variances for last month in respect of slab cakes. His schedule for these variances is attached, although he has not produced any commentary.

In terms of the variances themselves, I'm concerned about the size of them. We switched our flour supplier at the start of this period in an attempt to limit the impact of the price rises, although I know that this has led to some production issues. A number of batches of cake were scrapped, due to their not rising properly. We've also changed our egg supplier.

I'm also concerned about employee morale which seems on the low side at the moment, partly as a result of these production issues but also because of some uncertainty around our future given that we are now owned by Universal Foods.

Frank Mitchell has been asking me about our variance reports and whether there is any further detail that could be given. I very briefly mentioned mix and yield variances to him and he has asked for a report for the directors, which looks at whether such variances would indeed give us useful information.

Please prepare a report that I can give to the directors which includes:

- possible reasons for the ingredients and labour variances for slab cakes which are shown in the attached schedule;
- an explanation of whether calculating mix and yield variances for ingredients, labour and also sales variances would give us more useful information.

Many thanks.

Rajiv Patel
Finance Director
First Class Bakery

Summary of ingredients variances for slab cakes for the month:

	Flour	Butter	Eggs	Sugar	Total
Variance:	B$	B$	B$	B$	B$
Price	69,300A	6,100F	24,960F	5,800A	44,040A
Usage	26,500A	18,420A	28,100A	18,820A	91,840A

Summary of production labour variances for slab cakes for the month:

	Skilled	Semi-skilled	Unskilled	Total
Variance:	B$	B$	B$	B$
Rate	Nil	1,500A	9,500A	13,300A
Efficiency	2,235F	7,800A	10,355A	15,900A

Notes:

For the characteristic of variance reporting, all ingredients are measured in kilograms. The quantity of eggs is converted into a kilogram measure. Each batch of slab cake requires equal kilograms of flour, butter and sugar. The amount of eggs in kilograms is half that of the other ingredients.

Write the report requested by Rajiv Patel.

Section 2

A month later, Tim Walker sends you the following email.

From: Tim Walker, Finance Manager

To: Management Accountant Assistant

Subject: New flour suppliers

The directors met yesterday and decided, because of the production issues, to look at alternative flour suppliers. They are uncertain whether to just use one supplier (like we have in the past) or to use a number of different suppliers.

I've started looking at three potential new flour suppliers, who for ease of reference I've called A, B and C. So far, I've gathered information about each supplier's working capital position. This is attached to this email.

I am now working on a report for the directors to include both an evaluation of the suitability of each supplier and an explanation of the relative benefits of multi-sourcing rather than single-sourcing our flour supply.

Please prepare draft sections to go into this report to the directors on the following:

- an analysis of working capital positions of suppliers A,B and C,based on the information in the attached schedule, together with an explanation of any potential implications of this analysis for our business;
- an explanation of the relative benefits and drawbacks of multi-sourcing rather than single-sourcing our flour requirements.

Many thanks.

Tim Walker

Finance Manager

First Class Bakery

Schedule Attached to the Email

Information about flour suppliers A,B and C:

	Supplier A	Supplier B	Supplier C
Inventory days (day)	25	25	40
Trade receivables days(day)	35	15	60
Trade payables days(day)	40	70	80

Further information:

- The above ratios are calculated from information in the latest financial statements for each supplier.
- Each supplier has a 31 December year end.
- Each supplier has advised that normal credit terms are 30 days for both sales and purchases.
- Each supplier mills their own flour from wheat sourced directly from farms in their own country.
- Suppliers A and B are based in Beeland and sell all of their flour within Beeland.
- Supplier C is based in Jeeland and sells 50% of its flour outside of Jeeland.

■ Jeeland is situated across a sea from Beeland. The currency of Jeeland is J$.

Write the report sections requested by Tim Walker.

Section 3

A few months later, Tim Walker sends you the following email.

From: *Tim Walker, Finance Manager*
To: *Management Accountant Assistant*
Subject: 2017 *budgets and employee morale*

It's coming up to budget setting time again. As you know, in the past, we've taken a fairly simple incremental approach to setting our budget. Certainly in the past two years, all we've done is to adjust expected sales volumes and to increase the ingredient unit costs, labour rates and the overheads by an inflationary amount each year. We've not changed any labour time measurements, nor involved any production staff in budget setting. After the finance team has prepared the budget, it has usually been audited by the other directors on the recommendation of the finance director.

Rajiv has suggested that we take a participative ZBB approach to setting the budget for 2017 rather than an imposed incremental approach. However, Frank remains unconvinced that such a change would be beneficial to First Class Bakery and has asked for a briefing paper, to be discussed at the next directors' meeting, which explains the difference in these approaches and the suitability of a participative ZBB approach within First Class Bakery.

In addition, Rajiv has asked for a separate briefing paper on the actions we could take and the factors that need to be considered in order to raise the motivation levels of our employees. The drop in employee morale is worrying him and he would like to take the briefing paper to the next directors' meeting so that they can discuss how to address the issue.

Please could you draft both briefing papers.

Many thanks.

Tim Walker

Finance Manager

First Class Bakery

Write a briefing paper regarding a participative ZBB approach to setting the budget for 2017.

Write a briefing paper regarding the actions to take and the factors to consider to raise the motivation levels of our production employees.

Section 4

A month later, Tim Walker sends you the following email.

From: Tim Walker, Finance Manager

To: Management Accountant Assistant

Subject: Falling sales for First Class Bakery label slab cakes

I've been working closely with Anna Spring, sales manager, concerning the declining sales of our First Class Bakery label slab cakes.

There are currently two main options being considered in the short term.

- Accept a six month contract to sell these cakes to a large discount food retailer under an exclusivity clause. This would mean that we could not continue to sell the First Bakery label slab cakes to our existing independent retailers.
- Undertake a six-month marketing campaign for the First Class Bakery label slab cakes, either at a spend of B$ 50,000 or B$ 20,000.

I've already drawn up a decision tree for the above decision but please can you prepare an explanation of what each branch of the tree represents, what the values at points A, B, C and D represent and an explanation of the optimum decision based on the diagram. I've attached the decision tree diagram to this email. There is no need to prepare any further calculations regarding the decision tree.

In the longer term, there is a concern about our overall level of sales. Since 2013, revenue has fallen and 2016 is set to continue the trend. Revenue as reported in our financial statements is one of the key performance measures that Universal Foods reviews us and thus it's important that we change this trend and start to increase revenue.

There is an opportunity to acquire an interest in Home Style Bakery, a bespoke cake manufacturer 10 kilometres away. Home Style Bakery is currently family owned, with five shareholders, each with 20% of the equity shares. Each of the shareholders is a director and each equity share carries equal voting rights. At the moment, I'm not sure how many of the shareholders are willing to sell; it could be anything from one to all of them.

Given that we could potentially purchase anything from 20% to 100% of Home Style Bakery, Frank Mitchell has asked to be briefed on the factors that need to be considered when determining whether the investment in Home Style Bakery will be a trade investment, associate or subsidiary. He would also like to know how this classification would then impact our statement of profit or loss, assuming that we do prepare group financial statements. He is particularly keen to understand the impact on revenue. Please prepare a response to Frank's queries that I can send on to him.

Many thanks.

Tim Walker

Finance Manager

First Class Bakery

Decision tree:

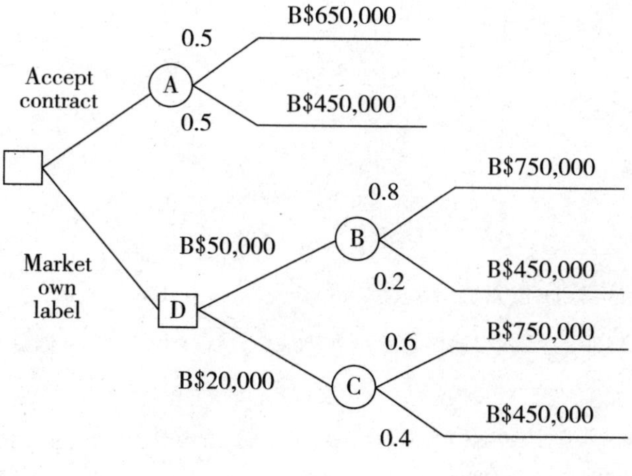

Notes:

(1) The monetary values included above relate to contribution earned for a six-month period.

(2) The monetary values at points A, B, C and D are as follows:

A = B$ 550,000

B = B$ 690,000

C = B$ 630,000

D = B$ 640,000

Write the email requested by Tim Walker.

试卷二

本次考试的结构如下：

序号	任务数	时间（分钟）
1	1	45
2	1	45
3	2	45
4	1	45

每个部分规定的时间可用于读题、组织和书写答案。
请注意任务三包括两项子任务，需留足时间。

任务一

Rajiv Patel 把下面这一篇网络文章发给了他的团队。

小麦价格将飙升

2016 年 2 月 15 日　　作者：James Fredricks（詹姆斯·弗雷德里克斯）

由于全球多个小麦主产区歉收，小麦价格处于历史高位。

最为严重的是 Beeland 及其邻国 Geeland（吉兰迪），这两国的小麦受持续的恶劣天气和风暴的影响，较往年减产 40%。其他的小麦主产国，如 Deeland（笛兰迪）和 Reeland（瑞兰迪）由于作物病害也减产了 15%。据报道，只有 Jeeland（基兰迪）实现了增收。

多家面粉厂已经宣告供应短缺，并警示价格可能还将进一步攀升。预期这对面包厂商将会产生最为严重的影响，同时其他与烘焙相关的食品制造业也会受到影响。但最后，受涨价影响最大的竟然是我们——消费者！

6 个星期之后，Rajiv Patel 发给你一封邮件。

发件人：财务总监 Rajiv Patel
收件人：管理会计助理
主题：差异分析报告

财务经理Tim在年假之前，计算了普通切片蛋糕上个月的原材料差异和人工差异。我把这些表格附在邮件后面了，不过他没有对这些表格做任何说明。

就差异本身而言，我关心的是它们的规模。为了减轻价格上涨的影响，我们在年初更换了面粉供应商，我知道这已经带来了一些生产上的问题。由于发酵不当，相当数量的蛋糕报废了。我们也更换了鸡蛋供应商。

我还关注到，这段时间员工的士气低落，其中有一部分是由生产问题产生的，但也有一部分是因为我们被通用食品收购，员工对公司的未来感到不确定。

这段时间以来，Frank Mitchell一直在要有关差异的分析报告，问我能不能提供一些深度分析的材料。我简单地向他解释了什么是组合差异和产出差异，他希望我们向董事提交一份报告，看看这些差异能否给我们一些有用的信息。

请你准备一份报告以便我提交给董事们，其中应包括以下内容。

- 说明造成表格中普通切片蛋糕原材料差异和人工差异的可能原因。
- 解释一下，如果计算出原材料、人工和销售差异中的组合差异和产出差异，这些数据能否给我们提供一些有用的信息。

多谢！

至臻糕点公司

财务总监

Rajiv Patel

普通切片蛋糕的原材料月度差异：

	面粉	奶油	鸡蛋	砂糖	合计
差异	B$	B$	B$	B$	B$
价格差异	69 300A	6 100F	24 960F	5 800A	44 040A
数量差异	26 500A	18 420A	28 100A	18 820A	91 840A

普通切片蛋糕的人工月度差异：

	熟练	半熟练	非熟练	合计
差异	B$	B$	B$	B$
工资率差异	0	1 500A	9 500A	13 300A
效率差异	2 235F	7 800A	10 335A	15 900A

注：

基于差异分析报告的特点，所有的原材料均以千克为计量单位进行统计。鸡蛋数量也转换为千克计量。每批次的普通切片蛋糕需要相等重量的面粉、奶油和砂糖。所需鸡蛋的千克数是其他原材料的一半。

请根据 Rajiv Patel 的要求撰写报告。

任务二

一个月后，Tim Walker 发给你如下邮件。

发件人：财务经理 Tim Walker
收件人：管理会计助理
主题：新的面粉供应商

董事们昨天开会并决定更换面粉供应商，解决生产中出现的问题。但他们不确定是延续我们过去只用一家供应商的做法，还是改用几家不同的供应商。

我考察了三家新的面粉供应商，为了方便讨论，不妨称之为 A、B 和 C。到目前为止，我已经收集了这三家供应商的运营资本信息。这些信息作为附件附在本邮件后。

我现在正在准备一份提交给董事会的报告，其中包括对各家供应商是否合适的评估，以及对我们选择多家供应商比独家供应商更合理的解释。

请帮我准备下面这些部分，以便我补充提供给董事会的报告：

- 利用附件中的资料，分析供应商 A、B 和 C 的运营资本情况，同时结合它们对我们公司的潜在影响进行分析。
- 相比独家供应商，说明多家供应商的优缺点。

多谢！

至臻糕点公司
财务经理
Tim Walker

邮件附表

面粉供应商 A、B 和 C 的相关信息：

	供应商 A	供应商 B	供应商 C
存货周转天数（天）	25	25	40
应收款周转天数（天）	35	15	60
应付款周转天数（天）	40	70	80

补充资料：

- 上述数据是根据各供应商最新一期的财务报表计算出来的。
- 各供应商都是在每年 12 月 31 日结账。
- 通常情况下，各供应商采购与销售的信用期都是 30 天。
- 各面粉供应商都从自己国家的农场直接采购小麦加工成面粉。
- 供应商 A 和 B 的基地在 Beeland，其生产的所有面粉只在 Beeland 境内销售。
- 供应商 C 是 Jeeland 的公司，生产的面粉有 50% 销售到 Jeeland 之外。
- Jeeland 与 Beeland 一海相隔。Jeeland 的货币是 J$ 。

请根据 Tim Walker 的要求撰写报告相应内容。

任务三

几个月之后，Tim Walker 发给你如下邮件。

发件人：财务经理 Tim Walker
收件人：管理会计助理
主题：2017 年预算和员工士气

又到制定预算的时候了。如你所知，过去我们采用相当简单的增量预算法编制预算。当然，在过去两年，我们只是调整了预期销售量，根据通货膨胀率调高了单位材料成本、人工成本率和间接费用。我们没有改变人工时间的计量，也没有吸收任何员工进入预算的编制过程。在财务部门准备好之后，预算通常由财务总监作为议案提出并报给其他董事审核。

Rajiv 在 2017 年编制预算时建议以参与式的零基预算取代强制性的增量预算。不过，Frank 对于这样的改变对至臻糕点公司是否有利仍持怀疑态度，他要求我们提交一份简报，解释这些预算方法的差异，以及在至臻糕点公司推行参与式零基预算的合理性，以供下次董事会讨论。

此外，Rajiv 还要我们单独再提交一份简报，分析我们应该采取哪些行动、考虑哪些因素才能提升各级员工的士气。他为员工士气的低落感到担忧，他也希望把这份简报提交给下次董事会，以便他们讨论这一议题。

请你草拟一下这两份简报。

多谢！

至臻糕点公司
财务经理
Tim Walker

请针对 2017 年实施参与式零基预算的相关事项撰写简报。
请列举出提升员工士气所应采取的行动和考虑的因素。

任务四

一个月之后，Tim Walker 发给你如下邮件。

发件人：财务经理 Tim Walker
收件人：管理会计助理
主题：至臻糕点公司自有品牌的普通切片蛋糕销量下降

最近，我和销售经理 Anna Spring 合作密切，我们在共同处理至臻糕点公司自有品牌的普通切片蛋糕销量下降的问题。

就短期来看，我们想出两个主要的备选方案。

- 接受一家大型食品折扣零售商为期六个月的独占合同。这意味着我们将不能再把自有品牌的产品卖给现有的独立零售商客户。
- 针对至臻糕点公司自有品牌的普通切片蛋糕，开展一场为期 6 个月的营销活动，费用预算为 B$ 50 000 或 B$ 20 000。

针对上述决策，我已经画了一张决策树，你能否准备一份报告，对决策树各个分支的含义，以及 A、B、C 和 D 四个点的含义进行解读，并利用该图说明一下什么是最优决策？我把决策树作为附件一并发给你。你不需要针对决策树做更多的计算。

就长期来看，我们的整体销售水平令人担忧。2013 年销售开始下滑，2016 年仍旧延续了这种趋势。财务报表反映的销售收入是通用食品公司考核我们的关键指标之一，因此扭转下滑趋势、实现增长非常重要。

现在我们有一个收购 Home Style Bakery（如家糕点）的机会，这是一家距离我们 10 公里之外的定制蛋糕生产商。Home Style Bakery 是一个家族企业，共有 5 个股东，每个人持有 20% 的股份。每个股东都是公司董事，大家拥有相同的投票权。目前我不清楚会有多少股东愿意出售他们的股份，从一个到全部都有可能。

考虑到我们有可能买入 Home Style Bakery20% 到 100% 的股份，Frank Mitchell 要我们报告一下，把对 Home Style Bakery 的投资确定为一般商业投资、关联企业还是子公司应该考虑哪些因素。他还想知道，站在准备集团报表的角度考虑，不同的选择对我们报告的盈亏会产生什么影响。他尤其关心对损益表的影响。请针对 Frank 的疑问准备一份解答，我好发给他。

多谢！

至臻糕点公司
财务经理
Tim Walker

决策树：

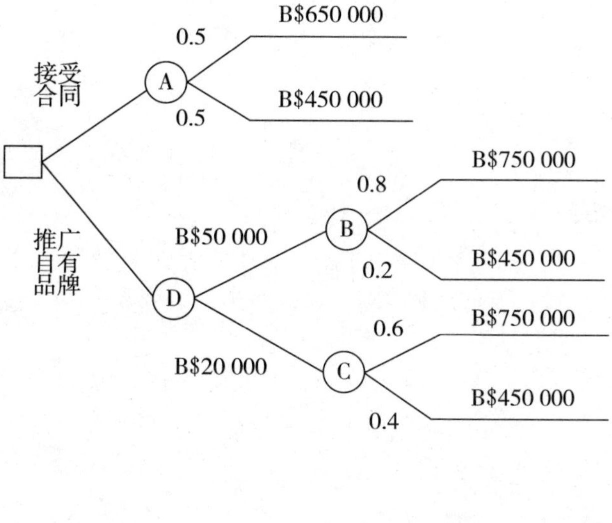

注：

（1）上面反映的是6个月内可赚取的以货币计量的价值。

（2）A、B、C和D点代表的以货币计量的价值分别是：

A = B$ 550 000

B = B$ 690 000

C = B$ 630 000

D = B$ 640 000

请根据 Tim Walker 的要求回复邮件。

Variant 2　Suggested Answers

Section 1

Variance Analysis Report

Possible Reasons for Variances

Ingredients Price Variance

The price variance measures the difference between the actual price per kilogram of ingredient and the standard price per kilogram. An adverse variance means that the actual cost per kilogram is more than the standard price, whilst a favourable variance means that the actual cost per kilogram is less than the standard price.

The price variances show that we have paid less for our butter and eggs than our anticipation. Possibly because that we have been able to negotiate a discount with our suppliers for the butter. The egg price could be a direct result of changing egg supplier.

The price variances also show that we have paid more for our flour and sugar than anticipated. Clearly the adverse flour variance is the result of the global price increase and is very significant at a value of B$ 69,300 for the month. This represents nearly half of the total ingredients cost variance for last month. The sugar variance is small in comparison, but perhaps indicates that the weather issues affecting wheat production have also had an impact on sugar production.

Ingredients Usage Variances

The starting point for calculating the material usage variance is to compare the standard quantity of ingredients that should have been used with the actual quantity which has been used. The adverse ingredients usage variances in respect of flour, butter, eggs and sugar may be due to careless handing of those ingredients by production employees.

Other possible causes of this adverse variance are errors in the blending mix of ingredients and baking errors leading to under-baking or over-baking of products. It is also possible that there have been quality issues with some of our ingredients. Maybe the new flour and egg suppliers are supplying inferior quality ingredients. This has perhaps led to increased usage as a result of wasted production.

Labour Rate Variances

The labour rate variance is calculated by comparing the standard rate per hour with the actual rate paid per hour. The labour rate variance of nil in respect of skilled labour implies that the actual rate paid to skilled employees was equal to the standard rate. The adverse labour rate variances in respect of semi-skilled and unskilled employees may be due to a negotiated increase in wage rates that has not yet been reflected in the standard wage rate for these employees.

It might be the case that these labour rate variances have occurred because a standard is used which represents a single average rate for some of our operations which have been performed by employees who are paid at several different rates. It is also possible that the appropriate grade of labour has not been matched to activities and this has caused part or even all of the adverse labour rate variances.

Labour Efficiency Variances

The labour efficiency variance represents the quantity variance for direct labour. As such, it indicates the standard labour cost of any change from the standard level of labour efficiency. The favourable variance in respect of skilled labour is a consequence of using less labour hours per unit than expected. This might be due to improved efficiency resulted from a high level of training. The adverse labour efficiency variances in respect of semi-skilled and unskilled labour could be attributable to not adhering to our planned maintenance schedule, which has led to more downtime during the period. It is also possible that these adverse labour efficiency variances are attributable to the loss of morale and the need to redo batches of production.

Usefulness of Mix Variances and Yield Variances

Mix variances and yield variances can be calculated where there are a number of inputs into a process (such as ingredients of labour type) or where there are a number of different products sold.

Mix variances and yield variances could therefore potentially be calculated for ingredients usage variance, labour efficiency variance and sales volume variance.

Ingredients Variance

The ingredients mix variance if calculated would be a measure of whether a change in the mix proportion of the ingredients is more or less expensive than expected. It would potentially give management an indication of whether changing the mix of ingredients has a positive or detrimental impact on profit. If a greater proportion of a cheaper ingredient is used then the mix variance will be favourable (that is profit will increase) and if a greater proportion of a more expensive ingredient is used then it will be adverse (that is profit will decrease).

The ingredients yield variance if calculated would tell us the effect of varying the level of overall input into the production process on the output and as its name suggests, it gives management an indication of whether the yield or output from our production process is more or less than it should be. This in essence therefore is a measure of the impact of changing the mix on the level of output.

Mix variances and yield variances are often calculated where a business has a number of inputs into the production process and it is possible to vary the mix of those inputs. In our case, using slab cakes as our example, there are four base ingredients (flour, butter, eggs and sugar) and then flavourings. Our cakes are made by a set recipe and there is little scope to change it without damaging the quality of the cake. Therefore the calculation of ingredients mix variances and yield variances is going to be of limited value to our business because we cannot significantly change the mix of the ingredients; our ingredients cannot be substituted for each other.

Labour Efficiency Variance

Within First Class Bakery we use different grades of labour throughout our production process and we set our standard labour cost for each product type based on a pre-determined mix of these grades of labour.

It is possible therefore that we could decide to change the mix of labour grades. A labour mix variance will allow us to see the impact of this on profit. If we were to use a greater proportion of skilled labour than the original budget then we would expect this to generate an adverse mix variance. If we were to use more unskilled labour then we would expect a favourable mix variance. Thus the labour mix variance will show the monetary impact of changing the mix of labour used in production, in isolation from the impact of this change on overall yield.

Conversely, a labour yield variance will measure the effect on cost of any difference between the actual labour working hours and the hours justified by the output produced. The labour yield variance may be viewed as being the labour output variance or the team productivity variance. It measures the efficiency of the production team as a whole, excluding the monetary impact of the change in mix in terms of how much the workers are paid.

Clearly, the two variances will need to be viewed together. We would expect an adverse mix variance (hence a greater use of skilled labour) to lead to a favourable yield variance.

Sales Volume Variance

The sales volume variance can be split into a sales mix variance and a sales quantity variance. The sales mix variance will indicate the impact of changing the relative mix of products sold on our profit and the sales quantity variance will show the impact of the change in the overall quantity sold (assuming that these are sold in the same proportion as originally budgeted).

This is useful information because it could indicate whether a particular product is declining, even if sales overall are increasing. This in turn would allow management to focus on those products to boost sales. Clearly with only three product types at present this variance might be of limited value, but if we increase our product types then this variance will become more beneficial.

Section 2

From: Management Accountant Assistant
To: Tim Walker, Finance Manager
Subject: New flour supplier

Analysis of Each Supplier's Working Capital Position and Potential Implications for First Class Bakery

Inventory Days

Both suppliers A and B keep inventory for an average of 25 days, compared to 40 days for supplier C.

Wheat and the resultant flour produced by each mill have a limited shelf life (albeit a few months) and therefore we would expect inventory days to be relatively low. Therefore holding inventory for approximately 25 days seems reasonable; the fact that they are the same indicates that this is perhaps the industry norm.

Supplier C is based in Jeeland, which could be one of the reasons why it holds inventory for longer (possibly wheat is in transit for longer as Jeeland is a larger country or bussiness practices are different). In addition, supplier C sells 50% of its flour to other countries and hence flour has to be shipped abroad, again increasing the time of transportation.

From First Class Bakery's perspective, there is a greater risk that flour will be infected with pests or deteriorated in quality if supplier C is used due to its longer holding period.

Trade Receivables Days

From the trade receivables days, it would appear that supplier B takes an aggressive approach to the management of receivables as the days are only 15 compared to its advised credit period of 30 days. It's possible that supplier B offers a generous prompt payment discount to its customers. This could therefore be beneficial to our business as this would have a direct impact on profit, although to achieve any discount we would need to have the cash available to make the early payment. Indeed, as we had an overdraft at the end of 2015, it is highly unlikely that we would be in a position to take advantage of this.

Supplier A's trade receivables days is largely in line with its credit period, whilst supplier C's is double its credit period. For supplier C it's possible that extended credit terms are given to overseas customers. Again this is something that First Class Bakery might benefit from to manage our cash flows.

Trade Payables Days

Supplier B and supplier C would appear to take an aggressive approach to the management of payables, at 70 and 80 days respectively. All of the flour mills obtain wheat directly from farmers in their respective countries and hence their payables will relate to these farmers. Taking excessive time to pay these farmers could indicate an ethical issue, which we are best not to be associated with.

Benefits and Drawbacks of Multi-sourcing

Greater Security of Supply

If we were reliant on a single supplier then if there were problems with that supplier (perhaps as a result of a fire disaster), it could seriously disrupt production. We need a constant supply of flour and cannot make any products without it; hence it is important that supply is consistent.

By having a number of suppliers, if there were a problem with one supplier, we can easily switch to another one to ensure the continuity of production.

Greater Pressure on Suppliers to be Competitive

If suppliers are aware that they are one of a number of suppliers, then there is an incentive for them to be competitive in terms of price, delivery lead times, quality and credit terms. A single supplier maybe less incentivised to perform well.

There are also a number of drawbacks from multi-sourcing compared to single-sourcing, as follows:

Not Easy to Develop and Maintain Relationships

It is important that there are good relationships with suppliers to ensure price, quality and continuity of supply. If there is only one supplier, it is relatively easy to develop and maintain a good relationship. The greater the number of suppliers, though, the harder and more time consuming this becomes.

Possible Economies of Scale Lost

Economies of scale will only arise from buying flour in bulk. By using multiple suppliers we will spread the volumes required across the supplier base, which means that the opportunities for bulk purchasing discounts are reduced.

Thanks.

Management Accountant Assistant

First Class Bakery

Section 3

Participative ZBB Report

A Participative ZBB Approach to Budget Setting

Difference in Approach

Currently we use an imposed incremental approach to setting the budget for the year.

- The budget is prepared centrally by the finance team, with little involvement from production and other employees. This budget is then approved by senior management, with seemingly little questioning.
- The budget for each year is based on the budget from the year before and adjusted for anticipated changes in prices and usage.

A participate ZBB approach to setting the budget for 2017 will mean that：

- The budget is set collaboratively, with input from all managers and employees with budget responsibility.
- The budget for 2017 will start from a zero position. This means that all elements of the budget will need to be reassessed from scratch including：the quantities of ingredients to be used in each batch, the time taken in all elements of the production process and the overhead costs.

Suitability of a Participative ZBB Approach for First Class Bakery

There are a number of ways in which a participative ZBB approach might be beneficial for First Class Bakery.

Employee Morale Improved

Allowing production managers and budget holders to have an input into the budget should improve morale, because they will feel that they are listened to.

Involving managers and employees in setting the budget should lead to greater acceptance of the targets and hence motivates them to achieve the budget. They will feel more invested in the process at a personal level. Employee morale is currently on the low side and therefore setting the budget in this way could help to counter that.

Greater Level of Knowledge

Junior managers and production employees will have more detailed knowledge of the operations within First Class Bakery and may be best placed to advise what is feasible in the budget, which means that the budgets should be more realistic. This could be of great help in revising our out-of-date standards.

More Accurate Standards

Because each standard is being reassessed, it means that the costing information will be more accurate. This means that pricing decisions will be improved as there will be a better understanding of the cost of each cake. It also means that variances are more meaningful because differences from the standard will be the result of factors that can be looked at rather than just the result of incorrect or out of date standards.

It Focuses on the Future

An incremental approach to budgeting is by its nature backward looking because it starts with what has happened before and adjusts for any known changes. This means that inefficiencies that are inherent in the budget are rolled forward and there is no incentive to change behaviour or focus.

However, whilst there are potential benefits to changing the approach, we need to balance up the cost of making this change against these benefits. Involving a greater number of employees and starting from a zero base will undoubtedly take considerable time and hence will generate a significant cost to the business. Indeed many businesses, when implementing ZBB, will carry it out on a rolling basis of a department at a time, for this very reason.

In our case, the benefits to be gained from the change might not be enough to support the cost. Ultimately we produce cakes to a set recipe, any change in which will potentially affect the quality of production and therefore sales. As a result, our standards for usage of ingredients must already be at a sensible position. There may be benefits though in terms of looking more closely at labour time standards (as this could potentially result in more efficient practices) and the motivational benefits will also be worthwhile.

Motivation of Our Production Employees

Reward System

We should review our reward system since a well-designed reward system can certainly assist in keeping staff highly motivated in order to deliver high performance.

The purpose of the reward system is to improve performance by linking it to rewards in a clearly defined manner. Performance incentives may result in our staff focusing their efforts and attention on improving their own performance which in turn, should lead to improved organisational performance. It might be the case that these levels increase upon the introduction of a well-constructed reward system.

The reward system should cover all staff. In particular the system should encourage desirable behaviour and recognise that different employees will be motivated by different factors.

Job Redesign

We should strengthen job redesign which aims to improve performance by increasing the level of understanding and motivation of our production employees. Another aim of job redesign is to ensure that the motivation varies from each individual and satisfies their need for personal growth and development.

Job Enrichment

Hertzberg suggests that job enrichment could be an effective way of motivating employees. Job enrichment is a deliberate planned process to increase the responsibility, challenge and creativity of a job. It involves giving a higher level of responsibility and autonomy to the jobholder.

Job Enlargement

Job enlargement represents an attempt to widen the job by adding extra, usually related tasks thereby increasing an employee's workload. It does not involve a higher level but simply more of the existing work that the employee does. Some employees may view the increased scope of their work as raising their status within the organisation and hence their level of motivation might increase.

Job Rotation

Job rotation involves the planned rotation of employees between jobs in an attempt to alleviate the monotony resulted from the repetitive nature of a given job. It therefore allows for a degree of variety by moving employees from one job to another. In this regard, job rotation can provide a fresh, challenging job.

Working Arrangements

The ways in which management allows employees to work will affect their motivation and performance. We should consider providing flexible working arrangements to our employees, which might lead them to realize that we are catering to their needs and their motivation may increase as a consequence of this.

Section 4

From: Management Accountant Assistant

To: Tim Walker, Finance Manager

Subject: Falling sales for First Class Bakery label slab cakes

Decision Tree

The Branches of the Decision Tree

A decision tree is used in situations where there are multiple decisions to be made which follow on from each other. This is exactly the situation here: the first decision is whether to accept the exclusivity contract with the new customer or to undertake a marketing campaign instead and the second is the budget of the marketing campaign at B$ 50,000 or B$ 20,000.

Each branch of the tree considers each of these decisions. The top branch relates to the first decision. The branch shows that if the contract is accepted there is a 50% chance of making profit of B$ 650,000 and a 50% chance that it will be B$ 450,000.

The bottom branch considers the second decision assuming that the first decision is to undertake a marketing campaign rather than accept the contract. This branch shows that if marketing spend is B$ 50,000 then there is an 80% chance of profit of B$ 750,000 and a 20% chance of B$ 450,000. If the marketing spend is only B$ 20,000 then the chance of making the higher profit of B$ 750,000 falls to 60%.

Points A,B,C and D and the Overall Optimum Decision

The value at point A of B$ 550,000 is the expected value of the decision to accept the contract, calculated as the sum of each possible outcome multiplied by its probability of occurrence.

Point B is the expected value of the decision to spend B$ 50,000 on a marketing campaign. Point C is the expected value of the decision to spend B$ 20,000 on a marketing campaign.

Point D represents the optimum position relating to the second decision. From point B when we deduct the marketing spend of B$ 50,000, this gives an expected value of B$ 640,000. From point C when we deduct the marketing spend of B$ 20,000, this gives an expected value of B$ 610,000. The optimum decision if a marketing campaign is chosen is therefore to spend B$ 50,000 as it has the higher expected value.

Move to the left of the diagram, we can see comparing points A and D, that the optimum decision on an expected value basis is therefore the marketing campaign, because this gives the higher value.

Possible Acquisition of Home Style Bakery

Determining whether the Investment Is a Subsidiary, Associate or Trade Investment

When determining the type of investment for consolidation purposes, the key consideration is whether we will have control over the operating and financing decisions that Home Style Bakery makes. If First Class Bakery has control over these decisions or the power to control these decisions, the investment will be a subsidiary.

If instead First Class Bakery has significant influence over the decisions of Home

Style Bakery then the investment will be an associate.

If there is neither the power to control nor significant influence over decisions then this will be a simple trade investment.

Whether there is control or significant influence depends on the following factors.

- The percentage investment in the equity shares of Home Style Bakery and the proportion of voting rights held. In this instance, we know that each equity share carries equal voting rights. Typically control will be gained where more than 50% of these rights are held and significant influence where 20% are held. In our case, there is some uncertainty over the level of investment — it could be 20%, 40%, 60%, 80% or 100%.
- The representation on the board of directors. In the case of Home Style Bakery, each director has a 20% stake, and therefore it seems sensible to assume that each 20% block acquired will result in a director's post. At a 60% investment and 3 out of 5 of the directors, this would give us the power to control and hence at 60% or above the investment is likely to be a subsidiary.
- The power or influence of other shareholders. If we have a 20% stake, given there will still be four of the original directors then it is likely that we won't even have significant influence. However, at 40% with two out of five directors, it is more likely to be significant influence and hence an associate.

Impact on Statement of Profit or Loss

If a subsidiary, then acquisition accounting will apply. This means that 100% of Home Style Bakery's income and expenses will be included within First Class Bakery. Any inter-company trade would then be eliminated. If less than 100% of Home Style Bakery is acquired, the share of profit that relates to the non-controlling interests will be shown underneath the statement of profit or loss.

If an associate, then equity accounting will apply. This means that our share of Home Style Bakery's profit for the year will be shown on one line in the statement of profit or loss. This is called share of profit of associate.

If a trade investment, then only the dividends received will be included in the statement of profit or loss.

In respect of revenue, only a subsidiary will increase this figure because we will include all of the subsidiaries revenue with ours. None of the other category of investment will affect the revenue.

Thanks!

Management Accountant Assistant
First Class Bakery

试卷二　参考答案

任务一

差异分析报告

差异产生的可能原因

原材料价格差异

价格差异计算的是每千克原材料实际价格与标准价格之间的差异。不利差异指的是每千克原材料的实际成本高于标准价格，而有利差异指的是低于标准价格。

价格差异分析显示，我们在奶油和鸡蛋上支付的成本比预期的要少。这很可能是因为我们在和奶油供应商的谈判中取得了价格折扣，而鸡蛋的价格变动可能是更换了鸡蛋供应商的直接结果。

价格差异分析同时显示，我们在面粉和砂糖上支付的成本高于预期。很显然，面粉的不利差异是全球价格上涨的结果。差异十分显著，上个月就达到了 B$ 69 300，这几乎占上个月原材料成本差异的一半。相比之下，砂糖的价格差异就要小得多了，但这也许说明影响小麦生产的天气同样也影响了砂糖的生产。

原材料数量差异

计算物料数量差异的第一步是比较原材料的标准耗用量与实际耗用量。在面粉、奶油、鸡蛋和砂糖上出现了不利的数量差异，原因或许要归结为生产工人没有认真控制这些原材料的使用。

造成不利差异的其他原因可能还包括原材料配料出错，以及烘焙操作失误导致的产品烘焙不足或过头。此外，还可能是因为部分原材料的质量出了问题，抑或是新的面粉和鸡蛋供应商提供了低质量的原材料。由于出现了废品，消耗量也增加了。

工资率差异

工资率差异可以通过比较标准小时工资率和实际小时工资率计算而得。熟练工人的工资率差异为 0，表示实际支付给熟练工人的工资率和标准工资率相等。半熟练工人和非熟练工人产生不利工资率差异的原因，或许应该归结为通过谈判提高了工资率，而这种调整尚未反映到这些工人的标准工资率当中。

产生工资率差异的原因还可能包括这样一种情况，即有些操作由分属不同工资水平的工人完成，但是我们只用一个单一的平均工资率来统一表示。也有可能是因为不同工资等级的工人没有安排在合适的作业流程上，这也会造成一部分甚至是全部的不利工资率差异。

人工效率差异

人工效率差异表示所耗用的直接人工的数量差异。同样，它表明的是任何偏离标准人工效率的标准人工成本差异。熟练工人的人工效率有利差异表示生产单位产品所耗用的熟练工人工时数少于预期。效率的提升或许是高水平培训的结果。半熟练和非熟练工人的人工效率不利差异产生的原因可以归结为没有坚持执行事先规划好的维修计划，导致这段时间内机器故障增多。这些不利人工效率差异还有可能是士气低落、需要重新批量生产产品的缘故。

组合差异与产出差异的用处

一旦一个生产流程需要消耗不同的投入物（如不同类别的工人），或者出售不同种类的产品，就可以计算组合差异与产出差异。

计算组合差异与产出差异可以应用在原材料数量差异、人工效率差异和销售量差异的分析上。

原材料差异

如果计算原材料组合差异，那它计量的就是投入物的组合构成是否发生变化，比预期贵了或便宜了。这有可能给管理层一个提示，说明改变投入物组合会对利润带来怎样的影响。如果使用了更多便宜的投入物，那么组合差异就是有利的，也就是说利润将会上升；而如果使用了较多较贵的投入物，那么它就是不利的，也就是说利润会下降。

计算原材料产出差异将告诉我们改变生产投入物的水平会对产出带来什么样的影响，顾名思义，它也为管理层提供了一个说明生产产出是高于还是低于应有水平的指标。它本质上是对产出组合变化的影响的计量。

当一个企业的生产业务需要消耗一系列的投入物，而且有可能改变这些投入物的组合时，就要计算组合差异与产出差异。就我们公司来看，以普通切片蛋糕为例，生产过程需要四种基本原材料（面粉、奶油、鸡蛋和砂糖）以及香料。我们的蛋糕是按照设定的配方生产的，在不改变蛋糕品质的前提下，配方可调整的空间很小。因此，计算投入物的组合差异和产出差异对我们价值不大，因为我们没有办法大幅度改变投入物组合，也没有办法实现投入物之间的互相替代。

人工效率差异

至臻糕点公司的生产使用了不同等级的工人，公司也根据事先设定的人工等级的组合确定各个产品的标准人工成本。

这就存在改变不同人工等级组合的可能性，人工组合差异将帮助我们看清这种改变对利润的影响。如果我们使用了比最初预算比例要高的熟练工人，那么这将会给我们带来不利的组合差异。而如果我们使用了比预期要多的非熟练工人，那么这将会实现有利的组合差异。因此，如果不考虑这种变化对总产量的影响，人工组合差异将揭示改变生产过程中的人工组合所带来的货币性影响。

反过来，人工的产出差异计量的是实际工时与根据实际产量调整的工时之间的差异对成本的影响。人工产出差异可以看作是劳动力产出差异或是团队生产力差异。它计量的是剔除了改变人工组合所带来的货币性影响之后的整个生产团队的效率。

很显然，这两种差异需要综合起来分析。我们可以看到，不利的组合差异（如使用更多的熟练工人）通常会导致有利的产出差异。

销售量差异

销售量差异可以区分为销售组合差异和销售数量差异。销售组合差异揭示的是改变销售产品的组合对我们利润的影响，而销售数量差异说明的是在不改变预算设定的产品组合的情况下，销售总量变动的影响。

这些信息非常有用，因为它将揭示即便在总销量上升的情况下，某个特定产品的销量是否出现了下降。这反过来将使得管理层可以重点关注这些产品并开展促销。很显然，由于我们目前只有三个品种的产品，这种差异分析对我们的价值有限，但一旦我们增加了产品种类，那么进行这种差异分析就很有必要了。

任务二

发件人：管理会计助理
收件人：财务经理 Tim Walker
主题：新的面粉供应商

各供应商运营资本状况及其对至臻糕点公司的潜在影响分析

存货周转天数

供应商 A 和供应商 B 的平均存货周转天数都是 25 天，而相比之下供应商 C 为 40 天。

各工厂生产的小麦及合成面粉都有保质期，虽然是几个月的时间，但我们也希望存货天数相对短一些。就此看来，25 天的存货周转期是合理的。供应商的存货周期相对一致表明这或许是行业的正常水平。

供应商 C 位于 Jeeland，这可能是造成他们存货周期比较长的一个理由（或许是因为

Jeeland 国土面积较大需要较长的运输时间，抑或是商业习惯有差异）。此外，供应商 C 有一半的产品销售到国外，面粉需要用船运出境，这也增加了运输的时间。

从至臻糕点公司的角度看，如果选用供应商 C，由于存货持有时间较长，将有可能面临较大的病虫害或变质风险。

应收款周转天数

从应收款周转天数来看，供应商 B 采取的是激进的应收款管理，它的周转天数只有 15 天而其制定的信用期是 30 天。这可能是因为供应商 B 向它的客户提供了较大的即时付款折扣。这或许会有利于我们的业务，它会直接影响企业利润，不过为了获得折扣，我们需要有可用的现金才能做到提前付款。事实上，考虑到公司在 2015 年年底出现了透支，看起来我们不太可能获得这种好处。

供应商 A 的应收款天数与其信用期非常一致，而供应商 C 的应收款天数则几乎是信用期的两倍，他们可能是延长了境外客户的信用期。这可能会给我们的现金流管理带来一些好处。

应付款周转天数

看起来，供应商 B 和供应商 C 都采取了激进的应付款管理策略，周转期分别是70 天和 80 天。所有的面粉加工厂都是从其各自所在国家的农户那里直接获得小麦，他们的应付款管理对这些农户影响较大。延长向农户的付款期可能存在一定的道德问题，我们最好不要卷入其中。

多供应商的优缺点分析

供应更有保障

如果我们依赖单一的供应商，那么一旦该供应商出了问题（如受到火灾等灾难的影响），就将给我们的生产带来严重的破坏。我们需要源源不断的面粉供应，每一样产品都离不开面粉，因此持续的供应非常重要。

如果有了多家供应商，那么万一其中一家出了问题，我们可以很轻易地转向其他的供应商，进而保证生产的连续性。

增加供应商之间的竞争压力

如果供应商意识到他们只是诸多供应商之中的一家，那么他们就有动力通过改善价格、交货期、质量和信用条件等来提高自身的竞争力。而独家供应商或许会缺乏这种激励。

相比独家供应商，采用多供应商也有一些缺点。

发展和维护关系的难度较大

为了保证低价、优质并维持供应的连续性，与供应商维持良好的关系就很重要。如果只有一家供应商，那么建立与维护良好的关系就相对简单。供应商数量越多，难度就越大，需要消耗的时间也越多。

可能会丧失规模经济效益

只有大批量采购才有可能形成规模经济。采用多供应商，我们的采购量分配在多家供应商之间，那么获得团购折扣的机会就降低了。

感谢！

至臻糕点公司

管理会计助理

任务三

参与式零基预算法报告

运用参与式零基预算法编制预算

方法上的差异

目前，我们采用增量预算法编制年度预算。

- 预算由财务部门集中编制，很少有生产及其他部门的员工参与，预算编制后报经高级管理层批准实施。目前来看，在这个过程中很少有人对预算提出质疑。
- 每年的预算都以上一年度的预算为基础，再根据预期的价格和数量变化进行调整。

采用参与式零基预算法编制2017年年度预算，意味着：

- 预算的编制需要集体协作，所有负有预算责任的经理和员工都要参与；
- 2017年的预算编制将从零出发，这意味着需要从头开始评估预算的所有要素，包括每批产品耗用的投入物、各生产过程消耗的时间和制造费用。

至臻糕点公司实施参与式零基预算的可行性分析

运用参与式零基预算法编制预算将给至臻糕点公司带来许多好处。

提升员工士气

允许生产经理及预算执行人员参与预算的编制可以提升士气，因为他们会感觉他们的意见得到了倾听。

参与预算编制的经理和员工会更容易接受目标，因此也会激励他们努力实现预算。在个人层面上，他们会对这个过程寄予更多希望。目前公司的员工士气低落，用这种方法编制预算可能有助于扭转局面。

吸收更广泛的知识

低阶经理和生产员工对至臻糕点公司的经营过程有更为详细的了解，想让他们派上用场，最好的地方或许就是预算，这样编制出来的预算也更符合实际情况。他们在我们修订那些已经过时的标准时将发挥巨大的作用。

更精确的标准

由于每一个标准都将被重新评估，成本核算信息将变得更为精确。对每一块蛋糕成本的更好的理解，将提高我们定价决策的水平。这也意味着差异分析将更有意义，因为我们将可以看清到底是什么因素导致偏离标准的差异发生，而不是只有出了错的结果或过时的标准。

聚焦未来

增量预算方法本质上是历史导向的，因为它以过去的事为起点并根据已知的变化进行调整。这意味着过去无效率的行为将通过预算被固化并向后延续，同时还缺乏改变行为或工作重点的动力。

改变预算的编制方法会带来一些潜在的好处，但与此同时我们需要权衡改变的成本与获得的利益。由于涉及更多员工，而且是从零开始编制，因此毫无疑问需要消耗很多时间，这也会给企业带来相当高的成本。也是因为这个原因，许多企业在实施零基预算的时候采用一次一个部门的滚动开发模式。

就我们公司来看，改变预算方法可以获得的利益恐怕不足以弥补成本。我们按照既定配方生产蛋糕，任何变动都可能影响产品的质量进而影响销售。因此，我们的原材料耗用量标准早已合理设定。或许仔细分析人工时间标准会有一些收获（例如更高效率的操作），在激励员工方面也有一定价值。

生产员工的激励

报酬体系

考虑到设计合理的报酬体系有助于员工保持高昂的士气并做出良好的业绩，我们有必要审视一下我们的报酬体系。

报酬体系的目标是通过清晰的定义将业绩的改善与员工报酬挂钩。奖励机制促使员工追求个人效益、关注个人业绩，从而提升组织业绩。结果可能是这样的：在导入并建构良好的报酬体系的基础上，各方面的水平都会有所提升。

报酬体系应涵盖所有员工。尤其是，方案应该能够激励出令人满意的行为，同时还要认识到不同的员工受不同因素的激励。

工作再设计

我们应该加强工作再设计。工作再设计的目的在于通过提升认知、激励生产员工以改善业绩。它的另一个目的是确保激励要因人而异，满足员工成长和发展的需要。

工作丰富化

赫兹伯格认为，丰富工作内容是激励员工的有效途径。工作丰富化是一个经过规划的深思熟虑的过程，它将提升员工工作的责任心、挑战欲和创造力，包括赋予员工更大的责任和自治权。

职责扩大化

职责扩大化试图通过增加额外的（通常是相关的）任务拓宽职责内容，以此增加员工的工作量。通常它不包括更高层级的工作，而只是增加员工的现有工作。部分员工会把这种工作量的增加看作是他们在组织内部地位的提高，因此也可能提高他们的工作积极性。

工作轮换

工作轮换涉及员工在不同岗位之间有计划的轮换，其目的是减少千篇一律的重复所带来的单调性。因此，它允许在一定程度上将员工从一个岗位转移到另一个岗位。从这个角度看，工作轮换可以使工作变得更有新鲜感、更富挑战性。

工作安排

管理层规定的工作方式会影响员工的士气和表现。我们应该向员工提供有弹性的工作安排，这可能会让他们意识到我们在配合他们的需要，这样做可能会提升员工士气。

任务四

发件人：管理会计助理

收件人：财务经理 Tim Walker

主题：至臻糕点公司自有品牌的普通切片蛋糕销量下降

决策树

决策树的分支

如果碰到多级决策且后续决策以前期决策为基础的情况，就可以运用决策树。这里的情况就很典型：第一步是选择接受新客户的排他性合同，还是启动营销活动作为替代；第二步是决定营销活动的预算是 B$ 50 000 还是 B$ 20 000。

决策树的各个分支分别代表这些决策内容。上部的分支代表第一步决策。该分支显示，如果接受合同，那么有50%的可能获利B$650 000，有50%的可能只能获利B$450 000。

下部的分支代表第二步决策，也就是假设第一步决策已经确定要启动营销活动而非接受合同。这个分支显示，如果营销活动投入B$50 000，那么有80%的可能将获利B$750 000，有20%的可能获利B$450 000。如果营销活动投入B$20 000，那么获利B$750 000的可能性就降低到60%。

A、B、C、D点和总体最优决策

A点的价值B$550 000说明的是接受合同期望值，是通过加总各种可能实现的收益与其概率的乘积的结果。

B点是投入B$50 000进行营销活动的期望值。

C点是投入B$20 000进行营销活动的期望值。

D点表示第二种决策的最佳状态。从B点出发，可知扣除B$50 000的营销活动成本后可实现的期望值是B$640 000。从C点出发，可知扣除B$20 000的营销活动成本后可实现的期望值是B$610 000。那么，如果确定选择营销活动的话，投入B$50 000营销活动费的方案要更优一些，因为它的期望值更大。

转到图表的左边，我们可以比较A点和D点。如果依据期望值进行最优决策的话，那应该选择营销活动，因为该方案提供的期望值更大。

收购Home Style Bakery的可能性分析

确定投资类型是子公司、关联企业还是一般商业投资

如果从合并报表角度考虑投资类型，那么核心问题是我们能否控制Home Style Bakery的经营和财务决策。如果至臻糕点公司已经能控制Home Style Bakery的决策，或具备控制其决策的能力，那么该投资就属于子公司。

如果至臻糕点公司对Home Style Bakery的决策具有重大影响力，那么说明该投资属于关联企业。

如果我们既不能控制决策也不具有重大影响力，那这就只是一般的商业投资。

是否具备控制力或重大影响力取决于如下因素。

- 所占的Home Style Bakery股权比重以及所持有的投票权比例。本案中，我们知道该公司相同的股份比例持有的投票权是相同的。一些典型的决策控制要求决策人所持有的股权比例超过50%，而持有股权超过20%就可被认为拥有重大影响力。就我们的案子来看，我们的投资存在一定的不确定性——可能是20%、40%、

60%、80% 或者 100%。

- 在董事会中的表决权。在 Home Style Bakery 的案子中，每个董事持有 20% 的份额，因此有理由推论每 20% 的股权对应一个董事席位。如果投资比例达到或超过 60%，取代 5 个董事席位中的 3 个，那么我们将获得控制权，因此投资占 60% 或以上的情况下，该投资将属于子公司。
- 其他股东的权力或影响力。如果我们持有 20% 的股份，也就是说仍留有 4 位创始股东，那么很可能我们甚至都不具有重大影响力。因此，更大的可能是购买 40% 的股份，取代 5 个董事席位中的 2 个，才是具有重大影响力的标准，这样的投资才属于关联企业。

对损益表的影响

如果是子公司，就要运用收购合并的会计政策。这意味着 Home Style Bakery 100% 的收入和费用都将会合并进至臻糕点公司的财务报表，并且需要剔除所有公司间的交易。如果收购的股权比例少于 100%，那么非控制权益相对应比例的利润将被反映在损益表的底部。

如果是关联公司，就要运用权益法。这意味着我们在 Home Style Bakery 的持股比例相对应的年度利润将被反映在损益表中。这就是所谓的关联公司利润。

如果属于一般商业投资，那么只有收到的股利会被反映进利润表。

从收入的角度看，只有子公司会增加公司收入，因为我们会把所有子公司的收入并入公司收入。其他投资类型不会影响收入。

感谢！

至臻糕点公司
管理会计助理

Variant 2　Marking Guidance

Section	Technical skills		Business skills		People skills		Leadership skills		Integration	Total
1	Reasons for ingredients variances and labour variances Usefulness of mix variances and yield variances	11 7	Usefulness of mix variances and yield variances	4					3	25
2	Analysis of the working capital position of potential suppliers	13	Benefits and drawbacks of multi-sourcing	12						25
3	Suitability of a participative ZBB approach to budgeting	13			Improving motivation levels	12				25
4	Decision tree Factors to consider when deciding whether an investment in another entity is a subsidiary, associate or trade investment	13 6					Impact of different investments types on the statement of profit or loss	6		25
Total marks available for each competency		63		16		12		6	3	100

试卷二　评分指南

部分	技术技能		商业技能		人际技能		领导技能		综合能力	总计
1	产生原材料差异和人工差异的原因 组合差异与产出差异的用处	11 7	组合差异与产出差异的用处	4					3	25
2	分析潜在供应商的营运资本状况	13	多供应商的优缺点分析	12						25
3	运用参与式零基预算编制预算的可行性	13			提升士气水平	12				25
4	决策树 考虑对另一公司的收购到底是属于子公司、关联企业还是一般商业投资	13 6					不同投资类型对损益表的影响	6		25
各技能评分合计		63		16		12		6	3	100

厦门大学名师解惑

本套题目的案例主体是至臻糕点公司，试卷一共有四项任务，考查了 E1、P1、F1 三门课程的知识点，具体包括成本差异分析、强制性预算与参与式预算、增量预算与零基预算、运营资本分析、供应商的数量选择、员工激励和不确定性决策。其中 P1（48）的知识点分数比重最高，其次是 E1（24），最后则是 F1（25）。这和 OCS 的考纲要求基本一致。该试卷考核了考生的四项能力，其中技术技能的分值占 63%，商业技能的分值占 16%，人际技能的分值占 12%，领导技能的分值占 6%，与 CGMA 管理会计能力框架的技能要求一致。考生在备考时应根据考试重点有所侧重。另外的 3 分是考查综合能力的，可能是对不同模块或不同能力的整合。这些得分点嵌在任务里，完成任务时能满足要求，就能得分。

该试卷的每项任务涉及以下知识点：

任务	问题	科目	知识点
任务一	产生原材料差异和人工差异的原因	P1	差异原因（reasons for variances）
	组合差异与产出差异的有效性	P1	组合和产出差异（mix and yield variances）
任务二	分析备选供应商的运营资金状况	F1	运营资金状况（working capital position）
	分析多供应商对比单一供应商的优缺点	E1	多供应商与单一供应商（multi-sourcing vs single-sourcing）
任务三	参与式零基预算的可行性	P1	参与式零基预算（participative ZBB）
	员工激励的影响因素	E1	员工激励（motivation levels of staff）
任务四	决策树	P1	决策树（decision tree）
	投资类型分析及对损益表的影响	F1	投资类型：子公司，关联公司，商业投资（subsidiary，associate or trade investment）

上述各项任务要求以邮件、报告或工作笔记等形式来呈现答案，对问题的描述非常明确，答题时既要注意内容的针对性，也要注意形式的规范性。

对应知识点深度剖析

产生原材料差异和人工差异的原因

考生需要理解并能应用差异产生的原因。除了能阐述差异原因外，考生要结合案例公司的产品特点和生产工艺，并根据表格中的实际差异结果来分析。例如面粉价格的上涨与新闻中的全球性原料价格上涨有关。另外，数量差异也可能和质量或是生产操作有关。在人工差异上，要特别注意熟练人工的工资率不存在差异，效率差异是有利的，并做出解释。

组合差异和产出差异的作用

要说明组合差异和产出差异可以用在原料数量差异、人工效率差异和销售量差异的进一步分析中。本题特别要注意到，尽管了解组合差异可以帮助管理层通过改变投入的组合来调整成本，从而调整利润，但是本案例公司的蛋糕是按照设定的配方生产的，要调整配方而不改变其口感或质量的可能性很小。所以，原料的组合差异和产出差异对于公司的管理决策作用不大。人工的组合差异和产出差异则可能影响到管理决策。另外，销售组合差异和产出差异也可以为经营管理提供有用的信息。

供应商的运营资本状况分析

可以就每个供应商的运营资本状况分别讨论，或是对不同的运营资本内容就不同供应商展开对比讨论。如果是分不同运营资本内容展开讨论，最终还需要对供应商的整体状况做出分析。表面上看，供应商B的存货占用周期和应收款周期合计短于其应付款的周转期，但是，可能会存在运营资金不足的问题，另外还有延迟付款的道德问题等。

多供应商与单一供应商的对比分析

本题要求考生能结合案例公司的情况来分析优缺点。例如，多个供应商情况下，遇到意外情况（如产区自然灾害）时能保证面粉供应不受影响等。

应用参与式零基预算的可行性

除了解释概念以外，要把重点放在改变预算模式对于公司的好处上。另外，阐述参与式零基预算的优点时，可以和强制性预算做对比。

员工激励

该题考查考生对激励手段的了解程度。除了陈述考纲的知识点外，更重要的是要结合案例公司的背景来阐述。

利用决策树进行决策

结合给定的决策树和问题展开描述，并解释各种可能结果（A, B, C）的期望值含义，同时做出最优决策的判断。考生要注意把握问题点，回答全部问题，避免因漏答而失分。

投资类型及其对报表的影响

本题中收购的股份数不确定，因此需要根据各种可能的情况来判断不同的投资类型。同时需要关注的是投票表决权的取得，这是影响投资类型的两个主要标准。另外，还要完整回答收购对于损益表的潜在影响，这个问题容易被遗漏。

考生注意事项

1. 考生在阅读背景材料时，可以对可能的考核范围做一些猜测。比如，资料提到企业实施了预算，可以预测将会涉及预算的内容。另外，可能会有差异分析的内容，这是和预算紧密联系的知识点。当然，本套题的难点在于解释组合差异和产出差异的作用。与P1的考查不同的是，考生不需要完成计算，但必须能解释其应用。另外，可以事先对企业的财务报表做简单的财务分析，以便对当前的财务状况有基本的了解。本套题的第四个任务，出现了背景资料中没有的一个新收购项目，看似不好准备，但是，如果考生注意到原来资料里有提到被收购的事项，并且事先就收购会计做好复习的话，应对此题就不难了。考生在备考时，要对这些内容重点复习，特别是技能部分的练习。

2. 要花时间阅读任务内容，把其中的具体要求逐项列出，在作答时完整地完成。例如任务四的决策树问题，其中包含了三个要求，就需要完整地一一回答。而收购Home Style Bakery的问题，包含了投资类型判断和不同类型对损益表的影响这两问。如果审题不够细致，可能漏答失分。

3. 在考试的时候，要避免只是就教科书的知识点简单复述，而要结合案例公司的实际情况作答。例如在评价供应商的时候，要结合公司的实际情况判断是否合适，提出相应建议等。差异分析更是要结合公司当前状况，例如产品组合、工艺流程等来解释其可能存在的原因。

4. 注意回答时的措辞、格式、论述的结构完整性和论点的鲜明整体性等。例如在回答时，使用鲜明的标题，分点分行明确地列举，这个是综合分得分点。

Variant 3

This examination is structured as follows:

Section number	Number of tasks	Time for section(minutes)
1	1	45
2	1	45
3	1	30
4	1	60

The time available for each section is for reading, planning and writing your answer(s).

Section 1

You arrive at work to find the following email from Frank Mitchell, managing director, which has been distributed to all employees.

From: Frank Mitchell, Managing Director
To: All Employees
Subject: New gluten free range

I am pleased to announce that, after considerable work undertaken by our product development team, we will be launching a new range of gluten free cakes.

The range is to be called GA (Gluten Absent) and will be manufactured in a new facility based two kilometres from here, with financial support from our new parent company, Universal Foods.

The GA range will launch with three products to start with:

- a plain lemon slab cake;
- a carrot cake with a lemon flavoured frosting;
- a coffee and walnut sandwich cake with coffee flavoured icing in the middle and coffee flavoured frosting on the top.

The plan is to launch this new range to the market under a "GA" brand and to sell to our existing customer base as well as establishing an online facility for consumers to purchase directly from us.

So, exciting times ahead!

Frank Mitchell
Managing Director
First Class Bakery

A few weeks later, you receive the following email from Tim Walker.

From: Tim Walker, Finance Manager
To: Management Accountant Assistant
Subject: GA product costings

I've been having various discussions about how we are going to cost our new GA range of products that will be manufactured in the new production facility. It has already been decided that the new facility will have its own costing system and Rajiv in particular is keen that we implement ABC, because this is what other Universal Foods production facilities use.

I've managed to find out the following about the new production process.

- The ingredient preparation and mixing process will be largely the same as we currently use, although there is one key difference. Each of the cakes will use different ingredients, there will be no common ingredients. Each lemon cake will need 5 ingredients, each carrot cake 10 ingredients and each coffee cake 12 ingredients. In total, 27 different ingredients will need to be purchased from 10 different suppliers, with some suppliers able to deliver in bulk and others not being able to do so.
- After the mixture is poured into the vat at the start of the production line, the process of pouring into tins, baking, cooling and placing the icing and frosting on the carrot and coffee cakes will be automated. The lemon cake will be baked in long trays and cut after it has cooled before quality checking and packaging. Each carrot cake will be baked in an individual square tin. A finished coffee cake will require two individual round coffee cakes, each of which will be baked in individual tins.
- Assembly of the coffee cake and packaging of all cakes into boxes will be done manually. Prior to packaging, each production run of cakes will require quality checks, and it is anticipated that twice as many coffee and carrot cakes will be checked compared to lemon cakes.
- The production line will only be able to make one type of cake at a time and each time the type changes there will need to be a period of time to clean out the vat, pour lines of mixture, and to reset the production line for the correct size of baking tins, and the correct process regarding the frosting. We expect to sell roughly the same amount of each cake but due to their different shelf lives (lemon will have the longest and coffee the shortest), it is

anticipated that each cake will have a different production run size.

Please send me an email.

- Your suggestions for three cost drivers that could be used to both attribute overhead costs to products and control costs within the new production facility. Please explain why each of your suggested cost drivers would be appropriate.
- An explanation of the potential benefits and drawbacks associated with using ABC as the costing system in the new facility.

Many thanks.

Tim Walker
Finance Manager
First Class Bakery

Write a response to the email from Tim Walker.

Section 2

A month later, Tim Walker comes to your desk and says:

I've just come out of a finance meeting with the directors where we discussed two separate issues relating to the new GA production facility which is still under construction.

Firstly, the directors are keen to implement a JIT (just in time) approach to inventory management for both raw materials and finished goods. They would like a report on the requirements for the successful operation of such an approach as well as the barriers that there might be to the new GA production facility, with specific reference to suppliers and the production process itself.

Secondly, Tony Swift, the product development manager, presented a schedule showing the expenditure he expects to incur relating to the project to develop the recipes and baking process for the GA products. Frank has asked for an explanation of how the expected expenditure shown in the schedule should be treated in the financial statements in accordance with relevant IFRS (International Financial Reporting Standards). This is the first of many development projects we expect in the future and Frank is keen to understand the principles.

Please send me an email which addresses both of these issues as this will help me to respond to Frank and the other directors.

After the conversation, Tim hands you the schedule from Tony Swift.

Schedule from Product Development Manager

GA project expected project expenditures and costs:

Project	Expected costs(B$)
Purchase of new equipment	50,000
Initial research reports on GA products ingredients	20,000
Salaries for development employees	35,000
Ingredients purchased for testing	30,000
Share of energy costs associated with the new kitchen	10,000
Share of product development manager's salary	10,000
Share of general factory overhead	30,000

Notes:

(1) The new equipment is for the new product kitchen. To date, this kitchen has only been used to develop the new GA range. After the project is completed, this kitchen will be used to develop other new products in separate projects.

(2) The share of my salary included is based on the time I will have spent on the project. The salaries for development employees also relate solely to time on this project.

Draft the email requested by Tim Walker.

Section 3

From: Tim Walker, Finance Manager
To: Management Accountant Assistant
Subject: GA marketing mix

I've just come out of our latest management meeting regarding the launch of the GA range. Product trials and research indicate that the range is going to be well received; both consumers and retailers alike feel that the packaging is innovative and better than any of our competitors. It would appear that the GA is being perceived as a quality brand. There is also an indication that, because of the unrefined sugars and many organic nature of the ingredients, that the GA range is being perceived as a healthier cake brand, compared to other gluten free cake brands.

Fred Knight, the sales and marketing director, was in the meeting talking about the marketing mix for the new range. He mentioned the introduction of electronic marketing regarding sales of GA products and the online sales directly to consumers.

So that I'm prepared for the next meeting, it would be really helpful if you were able to draft a briefing report which discusses the elements of the marketing mix that should be given consideration regarding the introduction of online sales of GA products.

Thank you.

Tim Walker
Finance Manager
First Class Bakery

Write the briefing report requested by Tim Walker.

Section 4

A month later, you receive the following email from Tim Walker.

From: Tim Walker, Finance Manager
To: Management Accountant Assistant
Subject: New production facility

Break-even Position

I have been asked to look at the break-even position with regard to the three new GA products and to provide a report for the directors on this.

Early indications are that there is already considerable interest in the new products from a number of new customers and hence it is anticipated that sales will be at an acceptable level. However, the directors are concerned as to whether the level of sales will be sufficient to break-even, given the high fixed costs associated with the new facility.

We anticipate that, after about six months, sales will increase as a result of the marketing campaign and hence any lack of profitability and cash flow from the new facility will be short term. The other management accountant assistant has prepared a multi-product break-even chart. I've had a brief look but don't have time to review this in detail at present. However, I know the directors will want an explanation of this chart.

Cash Flow Management

The other issue that the directors are concerned about at the moment is the short-term working capital position of the new facility. Clearly there are going to be new customers and new suppliers and certainly in the short-term profitability is going to be low.

Rajiv has suggested that an aggressive approach to the investment in working capital should be implemented for the new facility. He has asked me to brief the directors on what this means to the business and how we might implement such an approach. He said there is no need to reference the JIT approach to inventory management as the directors have already discussed this at length.

Please send me an email that I can forward on to the directors which explains the following matters.

- What the points A, B, C, D and E on the break-even chart represent and the difference between the two lines shown on the chart?
- The usefulness of this break-even chart to us.
- What is meant by an aggressive approach to working capital management and how we might implement this? Please focus on the implementation of the approach rather than any risks arising from the approach.

Tim Walker
Finance Manager
First Class Bakery

Multi-product break-even chart from the management accountant assistant:

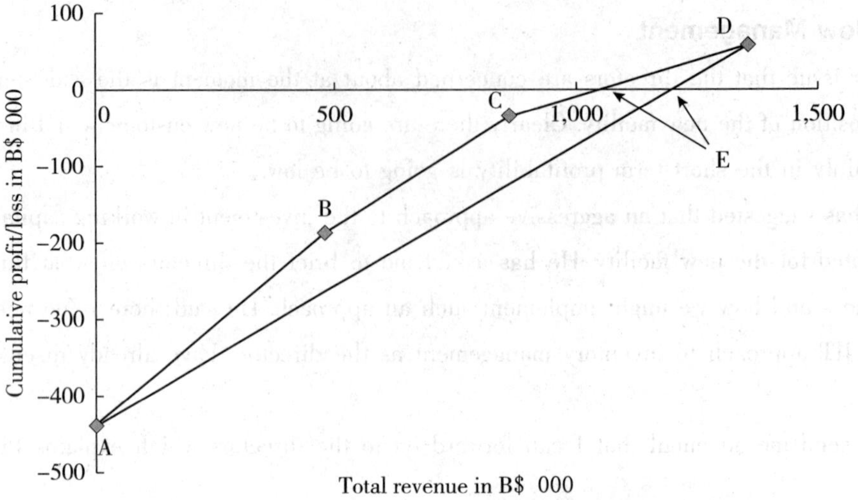

Base data used in the preparation of the above chart:

	Lemon	Carrot	Coffee
Selling price per cake (B$)	1.60	4.00	4.75
Variable costs per cake(B$)	1.30	1.90	2.85
Contribution per cake(B$)	0.30	2.10	1.90
C/S ratio	19%	53%	40%

Notes:

(1) The chart is based on the expected sales volumes, contribution levels and fixed costs for October which will be the second month of production in the new GA facility.

(2) The total revenue that is expected for October is comprised as follows: lemon 37%, carrot 34% and coffee 29%. The total revenue is expected to be B$1,356,000 for the month.

Draft your response to Tim Walker.

试卷三

本次考试的结构如下：

序号	任务数	时间（分钟）
1	1	45
2	1	45
3	1	30
4	1	60

每个部分规定的时间可用于读题、组织和书写答案。

任务一

上班时，你收到总经理 Frank Mitchell 发给公司全体员工的如下邮件。

发件人：总经理 Frank Mitchell
收件人：全体员工
主题：无麸质新产品

我很高兴地向大家宣布，在我们的产品开发团队的不懈努力下，公司将推出一系列全新的无麸质蛋糕。

我们将该系列产品命名为 GA（麸质不再），它将在距此两公里之外的全新设备上生产，我们的新东家——通用食品公司将为设备建设提供财务支持。

最开始，我们会先推出三种 GA 产品：

- 普通柠檬切片蛋糕；
- 带有柠檬风味糖霜的胡萝卜蛋糕；
- 咖啡和胡桃三明治蛋糕，中间夹有咖啡酥皮，上面覆盖咖啡糖衣。

该系列产品计划以 GA 品牌推向市场，在向我们现有客户销售的同时，将建立网络平台以便客户直接购买。

让我们共同期待这一激动人心的时刻！

至臻糕点公司
总经理
Frank Mitchell

几周之后，你收到了来自 Tim Walker 的邮件。

发件人：财务经理 Tim Walker
收件人：管理会计助理
主题：GA 产品的成本核算

最近我一直在参加有关如何核算 GA 系列新产品成本的各种讨论，这些产品将在新的设备上生产。刚刚确定下来，新生产线将采用独立的成本核算体系，Rajiv 特别希望我们采用作业成本法，这也是通用食品公司其他生产线所使用的成本核算方法。

我设法找到了一些有关新产品生产流程的资料。

- 除了一个重要区别外，原料准备和搅拌过程同我们现在的做法基本一致。不同的蛋糕需要不同的原材料，彼此之间截然不同。生产柠檬蛋糕需要 5 种原料，胡萝卜蛋糕需要 10 种，而咖啡蛋糕需要 12 种。总的来说，我们需要从 10 个不同的供应商处采购 27 种不同的原材料，其中一些供应商可以批量供货，而另一些则做不到。
- 生产线的第一步是将混合料倒入大桶，之后再注入马口铁托盘，烘焙，冷却，在胡萝卜蛋糕和咖啡蛋糕上添加糖霜和糖衣，这些步骤都是自动化完成的。柠檬蛋糕在长托盘上烘焙，待冷却后切片，再进行质量检验和包装。每一块胡萝卜蛋糕都需要单独放在方形马口铁托盘中烘焙。完成一块咖啡蛋糕需要两片圆形的咖啡蛋糕，每一片都需要在单独的马口铁托盘中烘焙。
- 咖啡蛋糕的贴合成型以及各类蛋糕的包装都要依靠手工操作。在包装之前，要求按批次对蛋糕进行质量检验，胡萝卜蛋糕和咖啡蛋糕的检验频次是柠檬蛋糕的两倍。
- 生产线每次只能生产一种蛋糕，每一次生产品种的变动都需要一段时间来清理大桶、浇注混合料、重设生产线、放置合适尺寸的烤盘以及根据结霜需要调整生产流程。我们希望每种蛋糕都可以按大致相同的数量进行销售，但考虑到它们的货架期各不相同（柠檬蛋糕最长，咖啡蛋糕最短），每种蛋糕的单批产量都有所不同。

请给我写一封回邮，回答以下内容。

- 提出你建议的三个成本动因，所选择的成本动因既要有助于把间接费用归集于产品，还要有助于新生产线的成本控制。请分别解释你选择的成本动因的合理性。
- 解释一下在新生产线上采用作业成本法进行成本核算的优缺点。

多谢！

至臻糕点公司

财务经理

Tim Walker

请根据 Tim Walker 的要求回复邮件。

任务二

一个月之后，Tim Walker 到办公室找到你，并对你说：

我刚和董事们开完一个财务会议，会上我们讨论了关于目前仍在建设中的 GA 新生产线的两个独立的问题。

第一，董事们希望采用适时制（JIT）管理原材料和产成品库存。他们要求我们提交一份报告，具体分析一下在新生产线成功实施适时制有什么要求、会遇到什么障碍，重点从供应商和生产流程角度来谈。

第二，生产开发经理 Tony Swift 提供了一份表格，具体列示了他所预计的有关 GA 产品配方和烘焙流程开发的费用开支。Frank 要求我们从国际财务报告准则的角度解释一下，表格中列示的费用开支会对财务报表产生怎样的影响。这是我们预期未来会开发的诸多项目中的第一个，因此 Frank 希望对准则有所了解。

请你针对上述两个问题写一封邮件发给我，我好回复 Frank 和其他董事。

说完之后，Tim 把 Tony Swift 做的表格递给了你。

生产开发经理做的表格

GA 项目开支和成本预估：

项　目	预计成本（B$）
新设备购置成本	50 000
GA 产品原料的初始研究报告	20 000
开发部员工薪水	35 000
购买试验用材料	30 000
新厨房能源成本分摊	10 000
生产开发经理薪水分摊	10 000
工厂管理费用分摊	30 000

注：

（1）新设备是为新生产厨房添置的。截至目前，该厨房仅用于新的 GA 产品开发。项目完成后，该厨房可用于开发其他项目的新产品。

（2）我的工资根据我在该项目上投入的时间进行分摊。开发部员工的工资也与他们在该项目上投入的时间挂钩。

请根据 Tim Walker 的要求回复邮件。

任务三

发件人：财务经理 Tim Walker
收件人：管理会计助理
主题：GA 产品的组合营销

我刚参加完 GA 系列产品发布前的最后一次管理会议。产品测试和相关研究结果显示，该系列产品有很高的市场接受度，消费者和零售商都觉得我们的包装很有新意，比竞争对手要好得多。看起来 GA 已被认定为优质品牌。还有结果显示，由于使用了非精炼砂糖和大量的有机食材，GA 被看作是一种有别于其他无麸质蛋糕的健康蛋糕品牌。

销售和市场营销总监 Fred Knight 在会议上谈到了新产品的组合营销问题。他提出，把电子化营销手段引入 GA 产品的销售，并通过线上销售直接把产品卖给消费者。

我需要为此准备一份报告以供下次会议使用，请你以“为 GA 导入线上销售并开展组合营销的过程中需要考虑哪些因素”为主题写一份简报给我。

谢谢！

至臻糕点公司
财务经理
Tim Walker

请根据 Tim Walker 的要求写一份简报。

任务四

一个月之后，你收到了 Tim Walker 发来的如下邮件。

发件人：财务经理 Tim Walker
收件人：管理会计助理
主题：新生产线

盈亏平衡状况

最近，我被问及三种 GA 产品的盈亏平衡状况，并被要求就此向董事们提交一份报告。

初期情况显示，有大批新客户对新产品表现出极大的兴趣，因此可以预期，销售将达到一个可接受的水平。由于新的生产设备会带来较高的固定成本，董事们担心这样的销售水平是否足以实现盈亏平衡。

考虑到营销活动的效果，我们预期销售收入会在6个月之后开始上升，因此新生产线的盈利性和现金流的短缺现象是短期的。另一个管理会计助理已经准备了一份多品种产品的盈亏分析图。我粗略看了一下，但目前没有时间仔细分析。不过，我想董事们应该希望该图表能附有一个详细说明。

现金流管理

当下，董事们还关心新生产线的短期运营资金水平。很显然，由于顾客和供应商都是新的，短期的盈利性将会比较低。

Rajiv 建议我们采用激进的方法管理新生产线的运营资金，他要求我简要地向董事们说明这对企业经营意味着什么，以及我们将如何实施这样的方法。他说我们不需要解释什么是存货的适时制方法，董事们已经很详细地讨论过这个问题。

请给我写一封邮件，我好转给董事们，邮件应说明如下几个问题。

- 盈亏平衡图上的A、B、C、D和E点分别代表什么？图中的两条线有什么区别？
- 这张盈亏平衡图对我们有什么用？
- 什么是运营资金管理的激进方法？我们应如何实施？请集中于方法的实施，不必过于纠缠于相关的风险问题。

至臻糕点公司

财务经理

Tim Walker

管理会计助理所做的多产品盈亏平衡图：

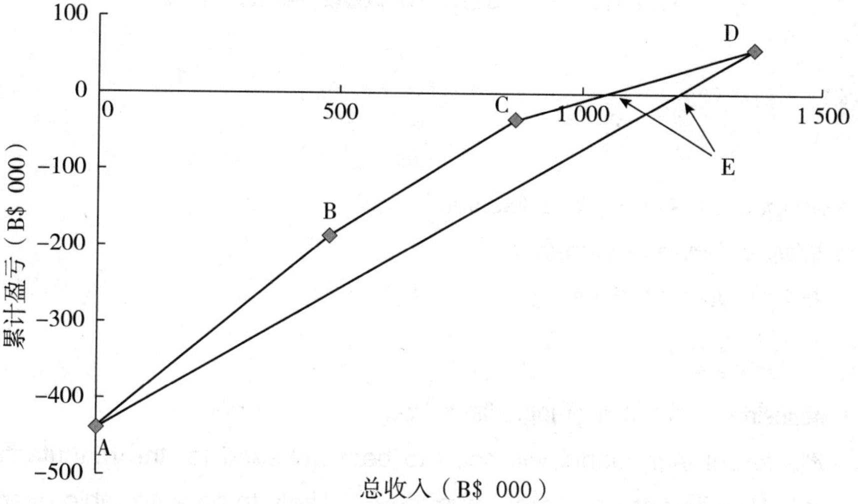

绘制上图所采用的基础数据：

	柠檬	胡萝卜	咖啡
单位产品售价（B$）	1.60	4.00	4.75
单位产品变动成本（B$）	1.30	1.90	2.85
单位产品边际贡献（B$）	0.30	2.10	1.90
边际贡献率（%）	19	53	40

注：

（1）该图以 GA 新生产线上线的第二个月，也就是 10 月的预期销售量、边际贡献水平和固定成本数据为基础绘制。

（2）预期 10 月的月度总收入为 B$1 356 000，产品构成分别是：柠檬蛋糕 37%，胡萝卜蛋糕 34%，咖啡蛋糕 29%。

请根据 Tim Walker 的要求回复邮件。

Variant 3　Suggested Answers

Section 1

From：Management Accountant Assistant

To：Tim Walker, Finance Manager

Subject：GA product costings

Activity Cost Drivers

Ingredient Purchasing — Number of Ingredients Used

A total of 27 different ingredients will need to be purchased for the manufacture of the GA cakes from 10 different suppliers. Thus there is likely to be a sizeable overhead cost attached to the ingredients purchasing, which will warrant a separate activity cost centre.

Different GA cakes requires a different number of ingredients：lemon cake only 5 ingredients, carrot 10 ingredients and coffee 12 ingredients. It would not be fair for the costing of each cake to simply take an equal share of this purchasing cost or indeed for an arbitrary measure such as direct labour hours to be used, because each cake will use this activity to a different degree. Further, each ingredient is specific to a type of GA cake and we know that some suppliers will be able to deliver in bulk but others will not. This means that the number of purchase orders required to purchase the appropriate ingredients for each cake will differ, which compounds the issue of a fair allocation of the purchasing costs across each GA cake.

An appropriate cost driver here would be the number of different ingredients used.

Production Line Set-up — Number of Set-up

Each time that a different cake is produced, there will need to be a period of setting-uptime, which will involve cleaning out the vat, pouring lines and setting up the machinery. Clearly the greater the number of set-ups required the greater the cost will be and hence there is a clear link between the activity（which is the set-up）and its cost driver（which will be the number of set-ups）.

In our case, we expect our production runs for each of the three GA cakes to be of different sizes, despite the fact that we expect to sell roughly the same number of each cake. Thus each type of cake will require a different number of set-ups during the course of the year. Therefore it would seem appropriate to reflect this in the product costing of each type of cake.

An appropriate cost driver here would be the number of set-ups required.

Quality Control — Number of Quality Inspections

Given the nature of our products as foodstuffs, the process of quality control is very important because we do not want to be selling cakes which either do not taste as they should or are damaged in anyway. Therefore the process of quality control will incur significant overhead cost. If we were to quality check each type of cake in exactly the same way, then allocating this cost on the basis of a volume driven measure would be appropriate. However, we expect that coffee and carrot cakes will be quality checked more often than lemon cake and therefore it would be unfair to treat each cake the same.

An appropriate cost driver here would be the number of quality inspections.

Potential Benefits and Problems Associated with Using ABC

Potential Benefits

An ABC system will give us a better understanding of how costs are generated in terms of what drives the cost because there is a focus on the activity and the driver of the cost incurred for that activity. A better understanding of how costs arise could lead to better cost control. Take production line set-up costs as an example. By having set-up costs as an activity means that the amount of cost incurred each time there is a set-up is known and visible. Given this awareness then it will mean greater focus on production scheduling to ensure that the minimum number of set-ups is undertaken as this would minimise the overall cost. This would be especially important if in the future new GA cake products were introduced while production scheduling became more complex.

ABC leads to more accurate costing information because the cost per unit is derived from the usage of the activity rather than the overhead being shared on an arbitrary basis. This helps to ensure that pricing decisions are sensible in light of anticipated margins. This is especially important where the products are new to the market as in the case of GA.

ABC is particularly beneficial where there are a large number of products which are different in nature. If the GA range expands into desserts or other forms of product, having a better understanding of how the costs are driven will help in the making of more informed pricing decisions.

Potential Drawbacks

The main issue is that it can be costly to implement. Significant management time will need to be invested to establish the activity cost centres and associated cost drivers. In addition, there will need an investment in technology so that appropriate data can be captured in respect of cost drivers. This information gathering of course becomes more complex the greater the number of products. You mention that Patrick has suggested 20 activity cost centres. That level of detail will require significant time in terms of setting up the system as well as significant time monitoring it once implemented.

Another issue is that there will still be some overhead costs for which it is hard to identify a cost driver other than a volume related measure such as machine time or direct production labour. Therefore some overhead will still need to be arbitrarily absorbed into product costings.

Thanks!

Management Accountant Assistant
First Class Bakery

Section 2

From: Management Accountant Assistant
To: Tim Walker, Finance Manager
Subject: Gluten absent project

JIT

The aim of a JIT approach to inventory management is to minimise inventory levels as far as possible, both for goods inwards and goods outwards.

For First Class Bakery and the new GA facility, the idea would be to only schedule production for firm orders from customers who would be despatched as soon as production was completed. In addition, ingredients would only be received when required for production.

There are many potential benefits to us of doing this, including the reduction of inventory holding costs and wastage for ingredients and cakes which have gone beyond their best before dates. However, these benefits do not automatically accrue simply as a consequence of the adoption of a JIT to inventory management approach. Indeed, there are a number of requirements for success, which will be considered here in respect of suppliers and the production process itself.

Suppliers

We need to be confident in our suppliers of ingredients both in terms of their ability to deliver what we need in time and ensure the quality of ingredients so that the production process is smooth. There will be a number of new suppliers for the GA facility and therefore it is vital that before we commit to them that we assess their ability to deliver quality ingredients when required, if we are to follow a JIT approach.

The suppliers also need to be flexible in terms of when they deliver and therefore it is important that whenever possible, we source from suppliers within a close proximity to us. This not only helps for a more flexible approach to delivery but is also something that we can use positively in our branding and advertising of GA, because we will be able to label the cakes as "sourced locally".

Clearly the ability to develop these relationships with suppliers is unknown at the moment. Many of the ingredients that we will need are specialised and therefore it is possible that suppliers are limited and hence we will be limited in their selection. This could mean that we will have less scope to request delivery on demand and therefore this could limit our ability to operate a JIT approach.

Production Process

We also need to have confidence in our production process. It will be important to use appropriately skilled employees at the ingredient preparation and mixing stages of production to ensure that the quality is high. If a JIT approach is being used then there is little room for error; production needs to be completed "right first time". This is less of an issue than supplier selection because we already have highly experienced and skilled employees who we can transfer.

We need to ensure that the production line to be installed is fit for purpose and that once up and running it is appropriately maintained. Any stoppage time on the line will ultimately mean that customer orders are not being satisfied in a timely manner and therefore customer relationships might be damaged. Again the ability to manage the production process is within our control.

There also needs to be flexibility in the production process. Employees need to be able to adapt to changes quickly and the production line needs to be able to switch from one product to another quickly. Whilst I'm confident that we could train employees to be flexible, the flexibility of the production line itself is more of an issue. We can only make one type of cake at a time and each time this changes requires significant set-up time. We will need to look at ways in which this could be managed.

Financial Reporting

In respect of the accounting management of the expenditure incurred in the development of the GA range of cakes, there are three main questions that need to be addressed.

- Is the expenditure linked to a research project or a development project?
- If the project is a development project, do we met the conditions to capitalise the expenditure?
- What expenditure can be capitalised?

Research Expenditure or Development Expenditure?

The distinction between research expenditure and development expenditure is important because it determines whether the expenditure might be capitalised (development expenditure) or whether it must be expensed to profit or loss straight away (research expenditure).

In our case, this is development expenditure because the result of the project is a new range of gluten free products which it is intended to bring to the market as soon as the production facility is built. There is a potential intangible asset, in the form of the knowledge gained in the development of the recipes for the GA cakes, which is expected to generate future economic benefit.

Conditions for Capitalising Development Expenditure?

Development expenditure can only be capitalised as an intangible asset if a number of criteria have been met. Indeed it is only that expenditure incurred after all of the criteria have been met that can be capitalised. The criteria are as follows.

- It is technically feasible to complete the intangible asset so that it can be used. In our case, the recipes and baking process that we are developing are the intangible asset and it is likely that from early in the project this criteria will have been met because we will have had the expertise and experience within the team to create the end recipes.
- It is intended to complete the intangible asset so that it can be used. It is likely that this intention was satisfied at the start of the project.
- The business has the ability to use the intangible asset. Again this will have been met at the start of the project because the development work has been carried out in-house.
- The intangible asset is expected to generate future economic benefit. The whole purpose of the project has been to develop the GA recipes so that a new range of cakes could be launched. Gluten free cakes are already in the market and the end product is itself a product that customers want to purchase. Hence early in the project, it is likely that this criteria would have been satisfied.
- The resources exist to complete the intangible asset. Again from the start of the project, there was always an intention to develop products which would be sold and therefore resources would have been made available.
- The expenditure attributable to the intangible asset can be reliably measured. Again given the nature of the costs and the fact that there was a dedicated team working on the development of the recipes and baking processes, this will have been satisfied from the start of the project.

So, it is likely that all of these criteria have been met at some point during the progress of the project. The key thing to establish is the point at which all of these criteria were satisfied, because from that date, development expenditure incurred should be capitalised.

What Expenditure Can Be Capitalised?

There are two items on the schedule provided by Tony Swift which are not development expenditure.

- B$ 50,000 has been spent on new equipment within the new product development kitchen. These are tangible assets of the business which will be used on future development projects and as such are not part of the development expenditure. Instead B$50,000 will be included as an addition to PPE(property, plant and equipment) in the statement of financial position.

- As with any other PPE, these assets will need to be depreciated over their useful economic life. The depreciation charge will reduce the carrying value of the assets in the statement of financial position. Usually the depreciation charge will also reduce profit, however in this instance, it is possible that some of this depreciation charge can be included as part of development costs.
- There is B$30,000 of general overhead included. This cannot be included as part of development expenditure in accordance with IAS 38 because this is an allocation of the general overhead and not a cost directly incurred as a result of the development. It should be expensed to profit and loss.

To conclude, we will be able to capitalise that development expenditure (excluding the B$50,000 of PPE and the general overheads) which has occurred when we will have met all of the criteria discussed above. Both the intangible asset and the PPE will need to be amortised or depreciated over the useful economic life, with this charge reducing profit each year.

Thanks!

Management Accountant Assistant
First Class Bakery

Section 3

GA Marketing Mix Report

The Elements of the Marketing Mix that Should Be Given Consideration in Respect of On-line Sales

Our marketing mix could be viewed as being the set of controllable variables and their levels that we use to influence our target market. We could base our marketing action plan around our marketing mix under the heading of 7Ps, as follows:

Product

Our product development team has placed a major focus upon the healthier eating quality of the GA product range. Initial product surveys have gained widespread approval. The results from these surveys have indicated that our packaging is regarded by both retailers and individuals, as being innovative and better than that used by our competitors. There is already a perception of this product range as quality. The product also, because of its gluten free properties, means that it is particularly attractive to customers who are wheat intolerant.

Price

There are a number of factors that have an influence on the price that we can charge for our products. Of course we will need to ensure that we cover all of our costs and make a profit in the long term. We need to be mindful that a number of our competitors have developed gluten free product offerings which are similar to our GA products. There is a high level of branding in the market and whilst initial surveys have been very favourable, we must be careful not to over-price our products especially given the fact that our GA brand is relatively new to the market place.

We also need to recognise that our customers can influence the price that we charge for our GA products. The supermarkets have tremendous purchasing power and so we need to take this into account when pricing our products. As far as individual on-line customers are concerned, we need to give consideration to their perceptions of "value for money" or whether they would pay a premium price for a premium product.

Promotion

It will be vital that our marketing department selects the right combination of promotional tools in order to promote the GA products to both existing and new customers. Probably, non-personal, mass-media communications that are aimed at the whole market, such as advertising, would be appropriate to our circumstances. We could also use sales promotion initiatives such as, for example, discounts for first orders and on-line coupons. We must also consider how to integrate the website for the on-line sales into this part of the promotional mix.

Place

Place is concerned with where to sell the goods. We already have well established distribution channels providing good geographical coverage with major supermarkets. It would be a benefit to our business if these supermarkets adopt our GA products. This will give the range a presence in the market and improve the speed at which consumers who might buy on-line become aware.

As regards on-line sales, speed of delivery will assume critical significance to potential customers. In this regard, we should give consideration to our choice to store GA products on site to ensure the speedy delivery and the processes that we have for dealing with orders in a timely manner.

People

We would need to ensure that we have adequately trained staff and support services to deal with on-line enquiries and sales. Customers will soon look elsewhere if their on-line orders are not dealt with in a timely or accurate manner.

Processes

This concerns the processes used to support the customer's interaction with First Class Bakery. We would need to ensure that, for example, payment and delivery processes are robust and reliable.

Physical Evidence

Website design would be of critical importance to the success of our on-line sales activities. Attention should be paid to the enhancement of the website in terms of its user friendliness. For example, ease of navigation would be critical to the successful establishment of on-line sales.

Section 4

From: Management Accountant Assistant

To: Tim Walker, Finance Manager

Subject: New production facility

Interpretation of the Multi-product Break-even Chart

Point A

Point A is the point at which there is no revenue, where sales volumes are nil. At this point, fixed costs will still be incurred because by their very nature that these costs are incurred regardless of production or activity levels. This means that where revenue is nil, a loss will be generated equal to the amount of fixed costs. From the chart therefore we can see that the level of fixed costs for October is approximately B$ 440,000. These are the costs that need to be covered by contribution before a profit can be made.

Point D

At the other extreme, point D represents the total revenue and profit that is expected for the month based on the expected sales volumes for each cake type, the contribution per cake and the fixed costs of approximately B$440,000. The chart indicates that sales revenue of approximately B$1,340,000 is expected which would generate a profit of approximately B$80,000.

Points B and C

Points B and C are at sales volumes between zero (point A) and the total expected sales of point D. Each of these points is plotted on the assumption that we will sell our products in order of profitability where profitability is measured on the basis of the C/S ratio. The C/S ratio is essentially the margin of contribution per cake to sales price per cake and indicates for every B$1 of revenue generated, how much that cake will contribute towards the fixed costs of the business.

Clearly, if we sell the cake with the highest C/S ratio first and then the rest in order of C/S ratio, then it means that we will cover the fixed costs more quickly than if we were to sell the cakes in the planned proportions. From the information under the chart we can see that carrot cake has the highest C/S ratio, followed by coffee cake and lemon cake. This means that the line has been constructed so that we sell all of our volume of carrot cakes first, then coffee cakes and lastly lemon cakes.

Point B on the chart is therefore the point at which we will have sold all of our carrot cakes (but none of the other cakes). Point C is the cumulative position where all of the carrot cakes and coffee cakes are sold.

Point E

Point E is the break-even point on each line.

Looking at the chart, one can see that the break-even point (the point at which neither a profit nor a loss is expected to be made) on the straight line is where revenue is approximately B$1,225,000. This means that revenue can fall to this level from the expected level of B$1,356,000 before we reach the point where fixed costs are not covered by contribution.

The line ABCD has a different break-even point to the straight line. Here the break-even position is where revenue is approximately B$1,050,000. This means that revenue could fall to this from the expected total of B$1,356,000 before a loss starts to be made.

The Difference between the Two Lines

The line between points A and D represents the expected profit or loss at different revenue levels assuming that the mix of sales that we expect is kept the same regardless of the level of total revenue. In other words, each point on the line represents sales revenue comprised of 37% from lemon cakes, 34% from carrot cakes and 29% from coffee cakes.

The line which connects points A, B, C and D is the line that represents the relationship between revenue and profit or loss on the assumption that we sell the cakes in the order of profitability (measured as the C/S ratio).

The Usefulness of this Multi-product Break-even Chart

The chart is useful because it gives an idea of the level of revenue at which we will make neither a profit nor a loss. This is particularly relevant in our case because these are new products in what is a new and specialised market for us and therefore we do not have experience at forecasting sales volumes. The sales team have given their best estimates for October, but there is no past experience to base this on, which means that its accuracy is questionable.

By knowing the break-even position, it helps to understand the margin of safety that we have from the forecast figures. The margin of safety is the amount by which revenue can fall from the expected revenue before a loss is made, usually measured as a percent. The expected level of revenue is B$1,356,000 and the line ABCD gives us a higher margin of safety (because the breakeven level of revenue is lower) compared to the straight line. The difference in these two measures is that the line ABCD assumes that we sell the most profitable products first and not a weighted average of what we expect to sell overall.

This information is useful because it might help management to decide if it is worthwhile focusing on carrot cake sales above the other two cakes so that fixed costs of production can be covered more quickly. However, we will need to be guided by what the customer wants (see point below).

However, there are some factors which limit the usefulness of this break-even analysis that you need to be aware of.

- It is likely that customers will want a range of the three cakes in each order and so realistically we will not be able to sell the products in the order of their respective C/S ratios. Therefore plotting the line ABCD is potentially meaningless in our situation.

- The figures used are estimates only. Production has not started yet and therefore it could be that the estimates of variable costs per cake and the overall level of fixed costs are wrong.
- The analysis assumes that we can define costs as fixed or variable. In reality, all costs are variable in the long term and even in the short term many costs that we think of as variable are fixed (for example, labour costs).

Aggressive Approach to Working Capital Management and Its Implement in the GA Facility

An aim of an aggressive approach to working capital management is to reduce the investment in working capital to the minimum level possible or at least to a very low level.

The investment in working capital is made up of inventory, trade receivables and cash net of trade payables and any overdraft. Therefore to minimise this investment is to reduce inventory and receivables balances as much as possible and to maximise trade payables. By doing this, less cash is tied up in working capital, which means that there are cost savings in terms of interest where it is funded by overdraft or opportunity savings where the cash can be invested elsewhere in the business.

The latest financial statements show that our core business currently has an overdraft and the review of the statement of cash flows indicates that there is a largely down to movements in working capital. Indeed in 2015, inventory and receivables both increased (despite a drop in revenue) and payables decreased. These movements in the working balances are contrary to an aggressive policy for working capital management and would seem to suggest that it might be difficult to actually implement such as policy in the new facility. Therefore in order to implement this approach, we will need to change the way that working capital is managed.

In respect of inventory, clearly discussions have already been made about JIT and therefore that aspect of inventory management will not be discussed here. However, it is important that in order to implement an aggressive approach that inventory levels are well managed and kept to as low a level as possible through careful and frequent ordering and ensuring that inventory is dispatched as soon as cakes are ready.

There are a number of measures which would be implemented to manage the level of receivables down in the new facility. These include the follows.

- Giving new customers lower credit terms than we would normally give.
- Setting up a settlement discount to encourage early payment. Care would be needed here though that the cost of this discount was not greater than the savings made as a result of a lower level of working capital investment.
- Ensuring that the credit control function is appropriately staffed and trained to ensure that outstanding monies are received quickly.

In terms of payables, the intention would be to take advantage as much as possible of supplier terms and to negotiate extended terms wherever possible. Essentially trade payables are a free form of finance and therefore we should ensure that we take full advantage of this. However, care is needed that we do not threaten our relationships with suppliers by starting to pay outside of the agreed terms or indeed create an ethical issue by not paying on time.

Thanks!

Management Accountant Assistant
First Class Bakery

试卷三　参考答案

任务一

发件人：管理会计助理

收件人：财务经理 Tim Walker

主题：GA 产品的成本核算

作业成本动因

材料采购——耗用的材料数

生产 GA 系列产品需要向 10 个不同的供应商采购 27 种不同的原材料，有可能会产生相当大额的与材料采购相关的间接费用，这就有必要把它当作一个独立的作业成本中心。

不同的 GA 蛋糕需要不同数量的原料：柠檬蛋糕只需要 5 种原料，胡萝卜蛋糕需要 10 种，而咖啡蛋糕需要 12 种。采取每块蛋糕均摊采购成本或武断地按照直接人工工时等指标分摊的做法都是不合适的，因为每块蛋糕消耗的作业水平不同。更者，一种原料只能供一种 GA 蛋糕使用，一些供应商可以批量发货而另一些则做不到，这意味着，生产每种蛋糕所需原料对应的订单数是不同的，从而增加了在各种 GA 蛋糕之间合理分配采购成本的复杂性。

就此看来，耗用的材料数是较为合适的成本动因。

生产线调整准备——调整准备次数

每生产一种蛋糕就需要一段调整准备的时间来清洗大桶、浇注产线以及调整机器。很显然，调整准备的次数越多，成本也就越高。因此，作业（也就是调整准备）与其成本动因（也就是调整准备次数）之间存在明显的联系。

就我们的例子来看，尽管我们希望可以按大致相同的批量生产不同种类的产品，但实际生产中，我们只能按不同的批量进行三种 GA 蛋糕的生产。以一年为期来看，生产不同种类的蛋糕要求的调整准备次数是不同的。因此，在计算不同种类蛋糕的生产成本时体现这一差异是颇为妥当的。

就此看来，调整准备次数是合适的成本动因。

质量控制——质量检验次数

我们的产品是食品，质量检验非常重要，因为我们不希望卖出去的蛋糕口味不达标，更不希望出现产品变质。因此，质量检验会产生大额的间接费用。如果我们用同样的方法对不同种类的蛋糕进行质量检验，那么以产量为基础分摊该项成本就是合适的。但是，我们要求对胡萝卜蛋糕和咖啡蛋糕进行比柠檬蛋糕更多的质量检验，那么不加区分的做法就不合适了。

就此看来，质量检验次数是合适的成本动因。

采用作业成本法的潜在好处及可能面临的问题

潜在好处

由于抓住了作业与作业成本动因之间的联系，作业成本法可以帮助我们更好地理解成本是如何产生的，换句话说，也就是到底是什么导致了成本的产生。较好地理解成本是如何发生的可以使我们更好地进行成本控制。以生产线调整准备成本为例。将调整准备成本作为一个作业意味着，只要进行一次调整准备就会产生一定数额的成本，而该成本是已知的、可得的。这种理念意味着，越关注生产计划的安排就越有可能使调整准备成本最小化，进而使总成本降至最低。这对我们在未来生产新的 GA 蛋糕意义非凡，但同时生产计划也会变得更复杂。

由于单位产品的成本来源于其所消耗的作业，而不是根据一个随意性的基础进行分摊，因此，作业成本法可以提供更为准确的成本信息，这将使我们结合预期毛利制定的价格策略变得更为合理。这一点对诸如 GA 这样即将推向市场的新产品尤其重要。

对于产品数量众多的企业来说，作业成本法特别有用。如果 GA 系列继续扩大到甜点或其他产品，那么更好地理解成本动因就可以为定价决策提供更多的信息。

潜在缺点

最重要的一点是实施的成本高昂。建立作业成本中心并确定相应的成本动因需要花费大量的管理时间。此外，还要在技术上有所投入才有可能根据成本动因收集合适的数据。在这个过程中，信息的收集随着产品数量的增加会变得越来越复杂。假设 Patrick 建议要确认 20 个作业成本中心，精细到这种程度的话，在系统建立时就要投入大量的时间，在未来的运行过程中也需要大量的监督时间。

另外一点是，还会产生一些间接费用，除了与产量相关的，例如机器工时或直接人工工时这样的计量指标外，很难确定其他的成本动因。因此在成本计算过程中，还是会有一部分间接成本需要采用武断的方法分摊进产品成本中。

感谢！

至臻糕点公司
管理会计助理

任务二

发件人：管理会计助理
收件人：财务经理 Tim Walker
主题：GA 项目

适时制

采用适时制进行存货管理的目的是使库存水平尽可能降低，这既包括流入的商品也包括对外发出的商品。

对至臻糕点公司及新的 GA 生产线来说，该理念的意义仅仅在于根据公司订单安排生产计划，确保产品一生产出来就可以马上发送给客户。此外，也只有在生产需要的时候才会购入原料。

采用适时制会给我们带来许多潜在的好处，包括降低存货持有成本、减少由于过期导致的原材料和蛋糕损耗等。不过，这些好处不会一在存货管理中采用适时制就自动产生，它要满足一系列的要求才能实现，这里考虑的因素包括供应商和生产流程。

供应商

我们要对我们的供应商抱有充分的信心，既要求他们有能力在我们需要的时候及时提供原料，还要求他们保证原料的质量，这样生产流程才会顺畅。因为 GA 产线，我们将拥有一大批新的供应商，如果要实施适时制，那么至关重要的一点就是，在签约之前，我们要评估他们在我们需要的时候提供符合质量要求的原料的能力。

另外，还要要求供应商在供货时间上有一定弹性，然而只有那些离我们很近的供应商才能做到，这一点很重要。它不但有助于实现弹性供货，而且也将为我们的蛋糕打上“本地采购”的标签，这一点对我们的品牌推广和广告营销也会有一点帮助。

很显然，我们在现阶段是否有能力与供应商建立这样的关系还是未知数。我们需要的很多原料都很特殊，相应的供应商有限，选择的空间也就很有限。也就是说，我们按照需求提出发货要求的可能性很小，这可能会制约我们运用适时制的能力。

生产流程

我们还要对我们的生产流程有信心。在原料准备和搅拌阶段使用技能匹配的工人很重要，这样才能保证产品的高质量。如果采用了适时制，容错空间就很小了，生产要求完全做到“一次到位”。相比选择供应商，这一点不是难题，因为我们已经有了一大批经验丰富、技能熟练的工人可以调动过去。

我们要确保生产线是符合目标要求的，并且它一旦启动运行之后也会得到恰当的维护。生产线的任何中断最终都意味着无法及时满足客户订单，由此也就会损害客户关系。不过，需要再一次声明的是，生产流程的管理在我们的可控范围之内。

此外，我们还要求生产流程具有一定的弹性。员工要能适应快速的变化，生产线要能快速地从一种产品的生产转变到另一种产品的生产。我有信心，我们可以通过训练使员工工作富有弹性，不过相比之下，生产线的弹性多少是个问题。我们一个时间只能生产一种产品，而调整需要大量的整备时间。我们需要找到解决这一问题的方法。

财务报告

在 GA 系列蛋糕的开发支出会计处理中，需要讨论以下三个主要的问题。

- 支出属于研究项目还是开发项目？
- 如果属于开发项目，那么是否符合费用资本化的要求？
- 哪些支出可以资本化？

研究支出还是开发支出？

研究支出和开发支出的区别是很重要的，因为它关系到是要把支出资本化（开发支出）还是直接加入当期损益（研究支出）。

在我们的案例中，这些开支属于开发支出，因为项目的成果——无麸质蛋糕将在生产设备建设完毕后马上推向市场。这里有一项潜在的无形资产，也就是我们在开发过程中获得的 GA 蛋糕的配方，该配方预期将在未来产生经济利益。

是否符合支出资本化的要求？

只有当符合一系列条件时，开发支出才可以资本化为无形资产。实际上，只有当一项支出完全符合以下条件时才可以被资本化。

- 形成无形资产并符合使用要求在技术上是可行的。在本案中，我们开发的配方和烘焙流程属于无形资产，并且从项目一开始就符合这项条件，因为我们的团队具有足够的专业知识和经验开发出该配方。

- ■ 有完成该无形资产并使其可供使用的意愿。在项目开始的时候我们就有了这种意愿。
- ■ 企业具有使用该无形资产的能力。从项目的一开始，我们就符合这项要求，因为该开发工作是在企业内部完成的。
- ■ 无形资产预期可以为企业带来未来经济利益。整个项目的目的就是开发 GA 产品配方，由此才可以推出新的蛋糕产品系列。无麸质蛋糕刚在市场上出现，该技术应用的最终产品就是它本身，这是客户愿意购买的产品。因此，从项目一开始，这个标准就得到了满足。
- ■ 现有资源足以完成该无形资产。同样，从项目一开始，我们就有意愿要开发可以对外销售的产品，因此该条件已经满足。
- ■ 有关无形资产的支出可以被可靠地计量。考虑到成本的性质，并配有一个专业团队在开发配方与烘焙流程，这一条件也从一开始就得到了满足。

因此，看起来在项目的开发过程中，所有这些条件都可以得到满足。关键点是要明确，在哪一个时点上，所有条件都能得到满足，因为从那一天开始，有关的开发支出就将被资本化。

哪些支出可以资本化?

Tony Swift 提供的表格中有两个项目不属于开发支出，它们是以下两项。

- ■ 在新产品开发过程中，厨房的新设备耗费 B$ 50 000。这是企业经营的有形资产，它们还可以继续用在公司未来开发的项目上，因此不构成开发支出。这 B$ 50 000 的资产应计入公司财务状况表的不动产、厂房和设备（PPE）当中。
- ■ 和其他不动产、厂房和设备项目一样，这些资产需要在使用年限内计提折旧。计提的折旧费用将会减少资产在财务状况表中的账面价值。通常来说，折旧费用也会冲减利润，在本案中，有一部分的折旧费用也许可以看作是公司开发支出的一部分。
- ■ 表格中还包括了 B$ 30 000 的一般管理费。根据国际会计准则第 38 号的要求，这不能包括在开发支出当中，因为它是分摊的公司的一般管理费用，而不是为开发成果直接产生的成本。它应作为当期费用直接反映在损益表中。

总而言之，我们可以在达到上述所有标准的时候，将开发支出（剔除 B$ 50 000 的不动产、厂房和设备与分摊的一般管理费）资本化。无形资产与不动产、厂房和设备都需要在经济寿命期内进行摊销或计提折旧，该费用会冲减各年的利润。

感谢！

至臻糕点公司
管理会计助理

任务三

GA 产品组合营销报告

关于网上组合营销应考虑的因素

我们可以把组合营销策略看作是一套可控的变量，利用它们的水平来影响目标市场。我们可以在 7P 的指引下，围绕组合营销来制订我们的营销行动计划，这 7P 所指代的内容如下。

产品（Product）

我们的产品开发团队将很大一部分精力集中在营养价值更高的 GA 产品系列上。产品的初期测试得到了市场广泛的认同。测试结果显示，零售商和个体消费者均认为我们的产品包装有创意，优于我们的竞争对手。这个产品系列已经形成了高品质的市场认同。由于具有无麸质特性，我们的产品对那些小麦制品不耐受的消费者将特别有吸引力。

价格（Price）

有许多因素会影响我们的定价决策。当然，从长期来看，我们需要确保价格足以补偿全部成本并能够实现盈利。我们要留意，有很多竞争对手也已经开发出了和 GA 系列相类似的无麸质产品。GA 产品市场品牌化水平很高，与此同时初步测试结果非常有利，我们必须注意不要将价格定得过高，尤其要考虑到 GA 品牌在市场上是个新生事物。

我们还需要认识到，客户会影响我们对 GA 产品的定价。超市购买力很强，我们在产品定价过程中要充分考虑这点。至于线上的个体消费者，我们需要了解他们的观念到底是追求“物有所值”，还是愿意对优质产品支付溢价。

促销（Promotion）

为了向现有客户及新客户推销 GA 产品，营销部门如何选择促销工具的组合至关重要。或许，例如广告等非个人化的、针对整个市场的大众媒体会比较适合于我们当前的情况。我们还可以开展促销，例如提供第一次下单折扣或线上优惠券。我们还要思考如何把销售网站整合进相应的促销组合当中。

场所（Place）

场所谈的是在什么地方销售这些产品。我们已经有完善的分销渠道，从地理上看已经覆盖了主要的超市。如果这些超市接受 GA 产品，那将给业务带来很大的好处。这会使我们的产品可以在市场上得到展示，进而也会加快线上客户对产品的认知速度。

就线上销售来说，发货速度对潜在的消费者可能是特别重要的。基于这一点，我们要认真选择 GA 产品的仓储地点以保证快速发货，同时也要优化我们的流程以便及时处理订单。

人（People）

我们要确保我们有足够的训练有素的员工及后勤服务来做好线上的咨询和销售工作。一旦线上订单处理不及时或方式不当，消费者马上就会跑掉。

流程（Processes）

这里指的是支撑消费者与至臻糕点公司互动的流程。这是我们需要确保无误的，例如付款和发货流程要做到稳健、可靠。

实物展示（Physical Evidence）

线上销售要获得成功，网站设计特别重要。网站的设计要注意让使用者感到亲切。例如对线上销售来说，便捷的导航链接就特别重要。

任务四

发件人：管理会计助理
收件人：财务经理 Tim Walker
主题：新产品线

对多产品盈亏平衡分析图的解读

A 点

在 A 点，企业没有销售收入，也就是销量为 0。由于固定成本不受产量或作业量的影响，因此这部分成本会照样产生。这意味着，在收入为 0 的情况下会出现金额为固定成本的亏损。从表中我们可以看到，10 月的固定成本大约是 B$ 440 000。只有当这部分得到补偿后，企业才有利润。

D 点

另一端的 D 点表示，在该月各种蛋糕都如期实现了预计的销量、边际贡献和包括大约 B$ 440 000 的固定成本的总收入和利润。该图显示，预期的销售收入为B$ 1 340 000，相应的，企业将会实现 B$ 80 000 的利润。

B 点和 C 点

B 点和 C 点的销售量处在 0（A 点）和 D 点的预期总销售量之间。这些点的绘制基于我们是以按 C/S 比计量的盈利性为序进行销售这一假设。C/S 指标等于每块蛋糕的边际贡献与单位售价的比，它说明每产生 B$ 1 的销售收入可以补偿多少经营过程中产生的固定成本。

很显然，如果先销售 C/S 比最高的产品，然后按 C/S 比率高低依次销售，意味着这会比我们按既定的产品组合销售更快弥补完所有固定成本。从表格下方的信息我们可以看到，胡萝卜蛋糕的 C/S 比最高，其后是咖啡蛋糕和柠檬蛋糕。这意味我们应优先销售胡萝卜蛋糕，然后是咖啡蛋糕，最后才是柠檬蛋糕。

B 点说明的是我们卖出了所有的胡萝卜蛋糕，而其他蛋糕一块都没有卖出的情况。C 点说明的是所有的胡萝卜蛋糕和咖啡蛋糕都卖出后的情况。

E 点

E 点是各条线的盈亏平衡点。

由图可知，直线的盈亏平衡点对应的销售收入是 B$ 1 225 000，也就是在该点企业处于不赢不亏的状态。这说明销售收入可以从预期的 B$ 1 356 000 下降到这个水平，如果再往下降，那么对应的边际贡献就不足以弥补固定成本了。曲线 ABCD 对应的盈亏平衡点和直线不同，该点对应的销售收入大约为 B$ 1 050 000，这意味着销售收入下降到这个水平之前就还不会发生亏损。

两条曲线的区别

连接 A 点和 D 点的直线表示不同收入水平下的预期盈亏，它假设我们预期不论销售收入是多少，总是保持固定的产品比例组合。换句话说，也就是该直线上的每一个点对应的销售收入当中都有 37% 来自柠檬蛋糕，34% 来自胡萝卜蛋糕，29% 来自咖啡蛋糕。

连接 A 点、B 点、C 点和 D 点的曲线表示，根据 C/S 比计算的盈利率的高低依次销售产品的情况下的收入和利润情况。

多产品盈亏平衡分析图的应用

该图是很有用的，因为它能够让我们理解销售收入在什么水平上，企业将处于不赢不亏的状态。这对企业来说关系重大，因为我们的新产品面对的是一个新的专业化的市场，我们缺乏预测销售量的经验。对 10 月的销售量，我们的销售团队尽最大可能做了估计，但由于缺乏历史经验作为基础，预测的精确性很成问题。

而一旦知道了盈亏平衡点，它就会帮助我们理解预测数据的安全边际。安全边际指的就是收入可以下降而不引起亏损的空间，通常以百分比表示。预期销售收入为B$ 1 356 000，相比直线，曲线ABCD提供了更大的安全边际，因为它对应的盈亏平衡点较低。二者的区别在于，曲线ABCD是假设按照盈利能力的优先顺序，而不是以加权平均的方式实现销售的。

该信息是很有价值的，因为它可能会帮助管理层做出胡萝卜蛋糕优先销售的决策，这样固定成本就可以较快地得到补偿。当然，我们仍要以市场需求为导向，这一点可以参见后面的分析。

不过，我们还需要注意盈亏平衡分析存在下面这样一些局限性。

- 一般来说，消费者会按个人的喜好购买这三种蛋糕，因此比较实际的情况是我们并不可能按照C/S比率依次安排销售。因此在我们的案例中，曲线ABCD可能并没有多少实际意义。
- 使用的数据都只是估值。生产还没有开始，每块蛋糕的变动成本和总体的固定成本数据都有可能出错。
- 分析过程中，我们假设可以将成本区分为固定的和变动的。但现实生活中，从长期角度来看，所有成本都是可变的，更有甚者，一些从短期角度看我们认为是变动的成本实际上是固定的，例如人工成本。

运营资金管理的激进法及其在GA生产线上的实施

采用激进法管理运营资金的目标之一是减少在运营资金上的投资，也就是要达到最小化或至少要做到尽可能的少。

企业在运营资金上的投资包括存货与扣除应付款及任何透支后的应收款和现金净额。因此，该项投资最小化的意思是要尽可能地减少存货和应收款余额，并使得应付款净额尽可能大。如此一来，运营资金中积存的现金减少，这意味着减少了诸如因为透支而产生的利息以及可以用于投资其他项目的机会成本。

最近一期的财务报表显示，目前我们的核心业务出现了透支，分析现金流量表可以看到，运营资金的流动性大幅度下降。的确，在2015年，尽管收入下降但存货和应收款都出现了上升，与此同时应付款却减少了。余额的这些变化与运营资金的激进管理方法是相违背的，看起来我们要在新产线上实施这项政策存在一定的难度。因此，如果要实施该方法，我们就有必要改变现有的运营资金管理方式。

关于存货，董事们已经很深入地探讨过适时制，因此有关存货管理的部分在此就不赘述了。不过，为了实施激进法，通过仔细和频繁地订货以及一生产就发货等做法来管理存货，使其保持在尽可能低的水平上是很重要的。

有一系列措施可以帮助降低新产线的应收款水平，包括以下几项。

- 给予新客户短于目前政策的信用期。
- 设置现金折扣鼓励提前付款。不过这里要小心，产生的折扣成本不要超过降低运营资金水平所带来的节约额。
- 确保合理安排信用管理人员，并加强培训，确保尽快收到欠款。

关于应付款管理，要尽可能地利用供应商的信用政策，并通过谈判尽量延长信用期。应付款本质上是一种免费的融资，要确保我们充分利用了这一优势。不过也要小心，不要因为付款超过协议约定的期限而危害到我们与供应商的关系，或者因为付款不及时引发伦理问题。

感谢！

至臻糕点公司
管理会计助理

Variant 3　Marking Guidance

Section	Technical skills		Business skills		People skills		Leadership skills		Integration	Total
1	Justification of three cost drivers specific to a new production line Potential benefits and drawbacks of using ABC for a new production facility	12 13								25
2	Accounting for research expenditure and development expenditure	12	Requirements for the successful operation of JIT and barriers to its operation	13						25
3					The marketing mix in the context of online sales	14			3	17
4	Interpretation of a break-even chart Usefulness of a specific break-even chart Working capital management	11 5 11					Usefulness of a specific break-even chart	6		33
Total marks available for each competency		64		13		14		6	3	100

试卷三　评分指南

部分	技术技能		商业技能		人际技能		领导技能		综合能力	总计
1	适合新生产线的三个成本动因及其理由 在新生产线上采用作业成本法的潜在好处及弊端	12 13								25
2	研究支出与开发支出的会计处理	12	成功实施适时制的要求及其潜在障碍	13						25
3					在线上销售的背景下开展组合营销	14			3	17
4	解读盈亏平衡分析图 盈亏平衡分析图的用处 运营资金管理	11 5 11					盈亏平衡分析图的用处	6		33
各技能评分合计		64		13		14		6	3	100

厦门大学名师解惑

本套题目的案例主体是至臻糕点公司，试卷一共有四项任务，考查了 E1、P1、F1 三门课程的知识点，具体包括作业成本法、研究支出与开发支出的会计管理、适时制的实施、组合营销、盈亏平衡图、运营资金管理。其中 P1（49）的知识点分数比重最高，其次是 E1（25），最后则是 F1（27）。这和 OCS 的考纲要求基本一致。该试卷考核了考生的四项能力，其中技术技能的分值占 64%，商业技能的分值占 13%，人际技能的分值占 14%，领导技能的分值占 6%，与 CGMA 管理会计能力框架的技能要求一致。考生在备考时应根据考试重点有所侧重。另外的 3 分是考查综合能力的，可能是对不同模块或不同能力的整合。这些得分点嵌在任务里，完成任务时能满足要求，就能得分。

该试卷的每项任务涉及以下知识点：

<table>
<tr><th>任务</th><th>问题</th><th>科目</th><th>知识点</th></tr>
<tr><td>任务一</td><td>新生产线的三个成本动因及其理由
在新生产线上采用作业成本法的潜在好处及弊端</td><td>P1</td><td>成本动因（cost drivers）
作业成本法（ABC）</td></tr>
<tr><td rowspan="2">任务二</td><td>成功实施适时制的要求及其潜在障碍</td><td>E1</td><td>适时制（JIT）</td></tr>
<tr><td>研究支出与开发支出的会计处理</td><td>F1</td><td>研究开发会计处理（account for research and development expenditure）</td></tr>
<tr><td>任务三</td><td>在新产品线上销售的背景下讨论组合营销策略</td><td>E1</td><td>组合营销（marketing mix）</td></tr>
<tr><td rowspan="2">任务四</td><td>解读多品种盈亏平衡分析图及其用处</td><td>P1</td><td>多品种盈亏平衡分析图（multi-product break-even chart）</td></tr>
<tr><td>解释如何实施激进的运营资金管理方法</td><td>F1</td><td>运营资金管理（working capital management）</td></tr>
</table>

上述各项任务要求以邮件、报告或工作笔记等形式来呈现答案，对问题的描述非常明确，答题时既要注意内容的针对性，也要注意形式的规范性。

对应知识点深度剖析

阐述成本动因及其依据，实施作业成本法的好处和弊端

本任务的要求非常明确，不仅需要选择合适的成本动因，还必须解释选择依据。这些依据要立足于问题出现的新场景，结合新产品使用了多种原料（具体阐述）、采购成本差异很大的实际情况来阐述。同样，对于质量的检验、设备的调整也要基于作业对资料的消耗存在差异性这一点来阐述。

作业成本法的优缺点，可参见教材所列。考生要能适当举例，说明其对于案例公司的实用性，例如，多品种的复杂生产模式下的成本可以得到更好控制。而在阐述缺点时，也应结合信息需求量的增加带来时间和成本的投入增加这一点展开论述。

考生注意事项

1. 作业成本法和成本动因是P1中的重要知识点。在本案例的背景资料下，属于大概率出现的考点，应重点关注。考题可能是针对背景资料中的现状，也可能是出现的新情况（本套试卷为新情况）。

2. 选择成本动因，除了要考虑知识点中的依据外，更重要的是要结合案例情景，并陈述其现实意义，即展示将知识应用于现实的能力。

成功实施适时制的要求及其潜在障碍

本题要避免过多阐述什么是适时制，而要针对任务的要求来回答问题。阐述适时制的好处时要结合案例公司的背景，特别是其引入了GA新生产线这一事件。例如，对供应商需要提出哪些要求，对生产流程应该做出哪些改变等，这是得高分的保障。

研究支出与开发支出的会计处理

本题需要了解国际会计准则（第16号、第38号）的相关规定，以下是处理业务的主要依据。

（1）研究支出或开发支出的区分和判断是否符合标准？

（2）资本化的条件和判断是否符合标准？

（3）对于可以资本化的项目，判断时需要结合案例公司的实际情景做分析。同时要能判别表格中不构成开发支出的项目，说明其应归属的项目（不动产、厂房和设备）及会计处理方法。

在线上销售新产品的背景下的组合营销策略

本题主要考核考生对营销模型（7P）的熟悉程度及应用能力。另外，由于是线上销售，所以考生要能特别指出，如何针对该渠道突出相应的“P”的处理。例如，保证线上咨询人员的数量和服务质量，线上的实物展示办法，以及确保线上交易流程稳健和可靠等。

多品种盈亏平衡图分析

该题首先要求考生能读懂图，了解 A ~ E 之间各点的经济含义，当然需要结合案例公司的背景做出解释。其中 B 点和 C 点稍微难些，要能识别出假定只卖胡萝卜蛋糕，而其他蛋糕一块都没有卖出的情况下的利润和假定只卖了胡萝卜蛋糕和咖啡蛋糕的利润。要具体点出是卖了什么产品，而不是笼统地说卖出一种、卖出两种。E 点是盈亏平衡点，考生还需要解释盈亏平衡点的含义，即边际贡献刚好弥补固定成本的界线。考生要能识别出不同产品 C/S 比的高低差异，并说明图中两条利润线的含义。利用该图，对新产品销售未来可能的变化做出预测，并陈述把握盈亏平衡点和安全边际的好处，同时也要考虑其潜在的局限。

运营资金管理

考生需要阐述运营资金的构成。激进的运营资金政策将尽量减少存货和应收款，并增加应付款的占用。不要把这个政策和融资策略混淆（即用短期资金支持运营资本）。

考生注意事项

学生在阅读背景材料时，可以根据相关资料对可能的考核范围做一些猜测。比如，从资料上看，该企业生产的两大类产品在生产复杂性上存在着较大差异，材料详细介绍了用料流程等，可以预测题目可能和成本核算有关，特别是和作业成本法有关。不过，本套题的场景是现有产品线以外的新产品，尽管无法准确预测，但是资料上给了无麸质产品的市场动态，可能会有知识点的考核。对于旧生产流程的了解，可以帮助理解该新生产线，从而提出比较合适的成本动因并做解释。资料还介绍了企业的研究开发，所以，出现研究开发方面的题目也不意外。本套题没有出现人力资源管理方面的考点，不过替换为组合营销。这个说明，在 E 领域内，学生需要掌握相对广博的知识，要全面复习相关知识。运营资金管理、盈亏平衡分析，这些都是比较基础的技能，所以一般都容易复习到。

在考试的时候，要避免只是就教科书的知识点简单复述，而要结合案例公司的实际情况作答，例如结合蛋糕的工艺流程来阐述成本动因的选择。运营资金管理的政策，需要基于对公司当前财务状况的了解。当然，也可以略施技巧，例如反复强调至臻糕点公司应如何等。

Variant 4

This examination is structured as follows：

Section number	Number of tasks	Time for section(minutes)
1	1	30
2	1	30
3	1	60
4	1	60

The time available for each section is for reading,planning and writing your answer(s).

Section 1

You receive the following email from Tim Walker.

From: Tim Walker, Finance Manager
To: Management Accountant Assistant
Subject: Production and demand constraints

We have just started negotiations with Better Quality Foods for the supply of a significant volume of desserts. If we are successful, we will need to expand dessert production capacity.

Better Quality Foods has asked us to produce desserts in two speciality flavours: (1) organic chocolate and (2) coffee and walnut. The terms in the contract are that we use high quality ingredients including a particular type of unrefined sugar, which is often in short supply.

Both dessert flavours will be manufactured in batches of 500 units and as far as I can tell, towards this project, the constraints in the coming three-month period are as follows.

- The unrefined sugar is only available from one supplier within Beeland. For the three-month production period, this supplier will be able to supply us with a maximum of 18,000 kilograms of the unrefined sugar.
- The production planning and control department have advised that there is a maximum of 280 machine hours and 2,000 labour hours available during the three-month period for the production of these new flavours.
- Better Quality Foods has informed us that there is an unlimited demand for the organic chocolate flavoured dessert but the demand for the coffee and walnut flavoured dessert will not exceed 200 batches.

The following information relates to these constraints:

	Organic chocolate	Coffee and walnut
Unrefined sugar per batch of desserts (kilogram)	40	30
Labour time per batch of desserts (minute)	180	240
Machine time per batch of desserts (minute)	50	40

Our senior accountant has used linear programming to prepare a graphical solution relating to the product mix decision under the constraints facing our business on the basis that First Class Bakery would wish to maximise contribution.

I would like you to prepare a briefing note for senior manager.

- Interprets the linear programme graph prepared by the Senior Accountant.
- Explains the usefulness of this graph to us.

Tim Walker

Finance Manager

First Class Bakery

Linear programming graph：

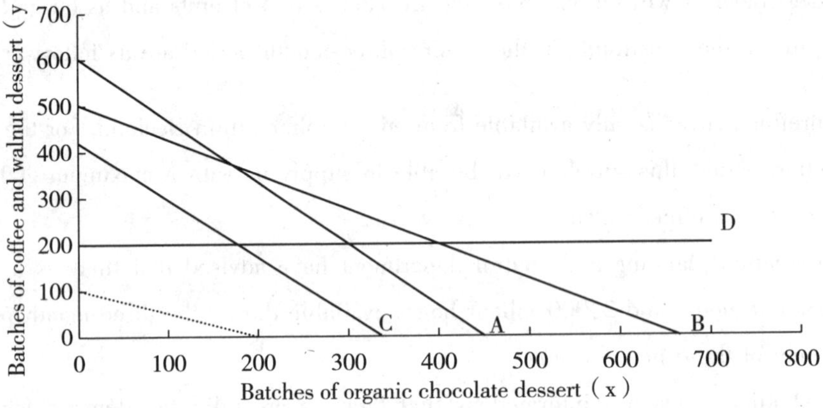

Line A：40x ＋ 30y ＝ 18,000 kilograms

Line B：180x ＋ 240y ＝ 120,000 minutes（2,000 hours）

Line C：50x ＋ 40y ＝ 16,800 minutes（280 hours）

Line D：y ＝ 200 batches

Notes：

In the graph, the dotted line represents the objective function based on anticipated contribution of B$ 500 for a batch of organic chocolate desserts and B$ 1,000 for a batch of coffee and walnut desserts.

Write your response to Tim Walker.

Section 2

A few weeks later, Tim Walker says to you:

The expansion of the desserts line has now been approved by Universal Foods. They are going to provide us with the funding and the plan is to start the construction of another production line within the month. In the meantime, the marketing and sales team have been at work building up our customer base for our own First Class Bakery label desserts and cakes. They've been focusing on other types of customers such as coffee shops, hotels and hospitals as well as our normal small independent food retailers. I am concerned about the potential impact of this change in customer base on our receivables balance and our ability to manage the receivables ledger.

Please send me an email with your thoughts on:

(1) The likely impact of these new customers on our finance function, recoverability risks and brand;

(2) Any measures that we should consider to mitigate any additional recoverability risks that might arise.

Write a response to Tim Walker.

Section 3

It is now two weeks later and you have just completed some work on setting new standards for ingredient usage and direct production labour hours. Rajiv had requested this to be done as the standards had not been updated for two years. You receive the following email from Tim Walker.

From: Tim Walker, Finance Manager
To: Management Accountant Assistant
Subject: Brand accounting and variance statement

Thank you for the work you did for me last week regarding the new standards for all of our products. As a result, I've rewritten the standard cost information. It was good to see that our efficiency in the usage of ingredients and labour is expected to be higher.

Rajiv has asked me to prepare a report to go to the next directors'meeting covering a couple of issues.

Firstly, many of the directors have been discussing the increasing value of our own brand due to the expansion in our desserts business and the acquisition of new customers for our own label cakes. They are keen that this increased value is reflected in our financial statements. Rajiv has already commented that this cannot happen because of IFRS. However, he would like to give the other directors a more detailed explanation of why this is the case.

Secondly, he asked me to prepare the variance statement for our most recent operating period using a planning and operational approach for the first time, given that we've just up-dated the standards. I've now prepared the variance statement; an extract showing only the planning variances is attached. I've not had time to prepare any commentary yet.

To help me prepare my report, please draft a section of the report.

- The reasons why IFRS prevent the inclusion of our brand value within our financial statements.
- The potential benefits and problems for us to split variances into planning and operational components.
- Possible reasons for each of the planning variances shown in the extract.

Many thanks.

Tim Walker
Finance Manager
First Class Bakery

Extract from variance statement — most recent operating period:

	B$ 000	**B$ 000**
Original budget contribution		1,350
Planning variances		
Ingredients price	(40) Adverse	
Ingredients usage	20 Favourable	

（续表）

	B$ 000	B$ 000
Labour rate	(10) Adverse	
Labour efficiency	20 Favourable	
Labour idle time	50 Favourable	
Selling price	—	
Revised budget contribution		1,390

Draft the sections of the report requested by Tim Walker.

Section 4

A week later, Tim Walker comes to your desk and hands you the following email that he has received from the new appointed quality manager, Ron Brookes.

To: Tim Walker, Finance Manager
From: Ron Brookes, Quality Manager
Subject: Quality within First Class Bakery

Despite the growing sales, it seems obvious to me that we have quality issues across our business. I am probably seeing things "with a fresh pair of eyes" having joined First Class Bakery very recently.

In my opinion, there has been some focus on product quality on the factory floor but it would appear that there has been very little focus on quality elsewhere within the business. I would suggest that we produce a cost of quality report in order to help improve our operating performance using appropriate classifications.

I also consider that operational improvements could be made via the application of quality initiatives such as TQM (total quality management). In this regard, the creation of quality circles could bring considerable benefits to our business. Of course, these initiatives would have implications for managing human resources.

Please can we discuss this at your earliest convenience?

Ron Brookes

Quality Manager

First Class Bakery

Tim Walker then says to you：

I had an interesting conversation with Ron as a result of this email. He has asked that we prepare a briefing report to go to senior management which covers each of the following.

- A brief explanation of each different classifications of quality cost. Please include an example relevant to our business for each of these classifications.
- How the use of a cost of quality report could benefit our business.
- The major considerations in the implementation of quality circles, in order to achieve operational improvements in our business.
- The implications for First Class Bakery of a TQM focus on human resource management.

Please prepare the first draft for me.

Write the draft report requested by Tim Walker.

试卷四

本次考试的结构如下：

序号	任务数	时间（分钟）
1	1	30
2	1	30
3	1	60
4	1	60

每个部分规定的时间可用于读题、组织和书写答案。

任务一

你收到了 Tim Walker 的邮件。

发件人：财务经理 Tim Walker

收件人：管理会计助理

主题：生产和需求限制

最后，我们启动了与 Better Quality Foods（优质食品公司）关于大规模供应甜点的谈判。如果谈判成功，我们将需要扩大甜点的生产规模。

Better Quality Foods 要求我们生产两种特殊口味的甜点：有机巧克力和咖啡加核桃。合同条款要求我们使用高质量的原料，包括一种特定类型的粗制糖，这种粗制糖经常供不应求。

这两种口味的甜点都要以 500 个为一批进行批量生产。据我所知，对于这个项目，未来三个月里还存在如下限制。

- 粗制糖只能从 Beeland 的一个供应商处获得。三个月的生产期里，该供应商最多能够提供 18 000 千克的粗制糖。
- 生产计划与控制部门建议，在新口味甜点三个月的生产期里，可用工时最多为 280 个机器工时和 2 000 个人工工时。
- Better Quality Foods 告知，有机巧克力口味甜点的需求量是无限的，但咖啡加核桃口味甜点的需求量不会超过 200 批。

相关限制可参考如下信息：

	有机巧克力	咖啡加核桃
每批甜点所需粗制糖（千克）	40	30
每批甜点所需人工工时（分）	180	240
每批甜点所需机器工时（分）	50	40

基于至臻糕点公司贡献最大化的目标，我们的高级会计师运用线性规划法，绘制了在各种限制条件下，最优产品组合决策的线性规划图。

你需要为高级经理准备一份简报。

■ 解释高级会计师绘制的线性规划图。

■ 解释该图表对我们的用处。

至臻糕点公司

财务经理

Tim Walker

线性规划图：

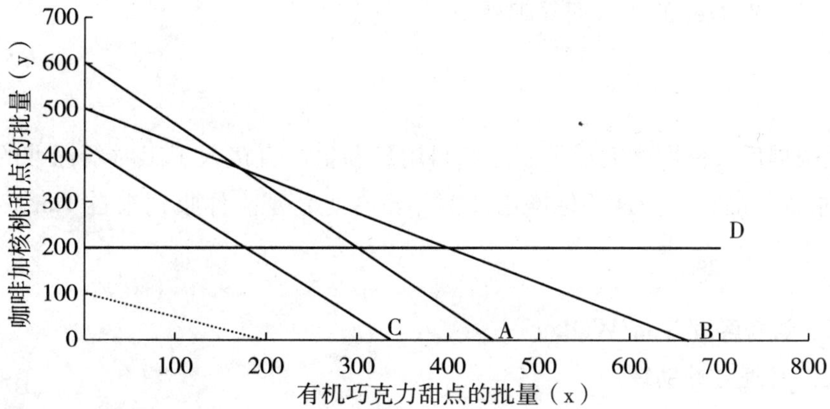

线 A：40x + 30y = 18 000 千克

线 B：180x + 240y = 120 000 分钟（2 000 小时）

线 C：50x + 40y = 16 800 分钟（280 小时）

线 D：y = 200 批

注：

图表中虚线代表目标函数，其假设每批有机巧克力口味甜点预计贡献 B$ 500，每批咖啡加核桃口味甜点预计贡献 B$ 1 000。

请根据 Tim Walker 的要求回复邮件。

任务二

几周后，Tim Walker 对你说：

甜点生产线的扩张现已得到通用食品公司的批准，他们将为我们提供资金，并计划在一个月内开始建造另一条生产线。与此同时，市场和销售团队一直在努力为至臻糕点公司自有品牌的甜点和蛋糕建立客户群。他们一直专注于其他类型的客户，如咖啡店、酒店、医院以及小型的独立食品零售商。我担心客户群的变化会对我们的应收账款余额和应收账款分类账管理能力带来潜在的影响。

请把你关于以下问题的想法发一封邮件给我。

（1）这些新客户对我们财务职能、坏账风险和品牌建设的潜在影响。

（2）我们可以采取哪些措施以降低新增坏账的风险？

请根据 Tim Walker 的要求回复邮件。

任务三

现在是两周后，你刚刚完成了制定原料用量和生产直接人工工时新标准的工作。这是 Rajiv 要求你做的，因为这些标准已经两年没有更新了。你收到来自 Tim Walker 的邮件，内容如下。

发件人：财务经理 Tim Walker
收件人：管理会计助理
主题：品牌核算和差异报告

谢谢你上周帮我制定了公司所有产品的新标准。基于你的工作，我更新了标准成本信息。很高兴看到我们的原料和劳动力使用效率将会得到提高。

Rajiv 要我准备一份报告以参加下一次董事会会议，内容应涉及以下几个问题。

第一，鉴于我们甜点业务的扩大以及自有品牌蛋糕新客户群体的增加，许多董事一直在讨论我们自有品牌的增值工作。他们非常希望品牌增值能够反映在财务报表中。Rajiv 已经说了，按照国际财务报告准则，这是行不通的。然而，他想给其他董事更详细地解释一下为什么会这样。

第二，鉴于我们刚刚更新了标准，他要我准备一份最近经营期间的差异报告，并且首次要求将差异分为计划性差异和经营性差异。我已经开始准备差异报告了，摘录只展示了计划性差异，但我还没来得及撰写评论。

请你帮我准备报告，并起草其中的部分内容，解释如下事项。

- 国际财务报告准则禁止在财务报告中确认品牌价值的原因。

■ 将差异分为计划性差异和经营性差异的潜在益处和问题。

■ 摘录中每项计划性差异产生的可能原因。

非常感谢。

至臻糕点公司

财务经理

Tim Walker

最近经营期间差异报告摘录：

	B$ 000	B$ 000
最初预算贡献		1 350
计划性差异		
原料价格	（40）不利	
原料用量	20 有利	
人工价格	（10）不利	
人工效率	20 有利	
人工闲置时间	50 有利	
销售价格	–	
修订后预算贡献		1 390

根据 Tim Walker 的要求草拟一份报告。

任务四

一周后，Tim Walker 来到你的桌前，并给你看他收到的来自新任质量经理 Ron Brookes（罗恩·布鲁克斯）的邮件，邮件内容如下。

收件人：财务经理 Tim Walker
发件人：质量经理 Ron Brookes
主题：至臻糕点公司的产品质量

虽然销售收入在增长，但我明显感觉到我们的业务存在一些质量问题。可能是我最近才刚加入至臻糕点公司，看待事情的角度比较新。

在我看来，工厂对产品质量一直有一定的重视度，但业务的其他方面对质量明显缺乏重视。我建议编制一份质量成本报告，用合适的分类帮助我们提高经营绩效。

另外，我认为可以通过开展诸如全面质量管理等质量管理行动来改善经营。在这方面，质量管理循环的建立可以给我们的业务带来可观的利益。当然，这些举措将对人力资源管理产生一些影响。

你最近什么时候方便，我们可以讨论下这个问题吗?

至臻糕点公司
质量经理
Ron Brookes

随后 Tim Walker 对你说:

基于这封邮件，我和 Ron 进行了一次有趣的谈话。他要求我们准备一份简报，并提交给高级管理层，其中包括如下内容。

- 简要解释每一种不同的质量成本分类，对于每个分类，举一个与我们业务有关的例子。
- 使用质量成本报告对公司业务的好处。
- 实施质量管理循环以改善经营需要考虑的主要因素。
- 开展全面质量管理对至臻糕点公司人力资源管理的影响。

请为我草拟一份报告。

请根据 Tim Walker 的要求草拟一份报告。

Variant 4 Suggested Answers

Section 1

Linear Programme Graph Report

Interpretation of the Linear Programme Graph

The lines on the graph represent potential constrained resource to our production of the new dessert flavours: line A relates to unrefined sugar, line B to labour hours, line C to machine hours and line D to demand for the coffee and walnut flavour. Each of the lines A, B and C represents the different combinations of production of x (organic chocolate) and y (coffee and walnut) that will utilise all of the resource and hence represents the maximum production under each resource. Line D is a demand constraint line.

In order to interpret the graph, we need to identify the "feasible region" of production. The feasible region is the area on the graph contained within all of the constraint lines (which are lines A, B, C and D). In situations where there are several constraints (as in this case), the feasible region will be the area below each of the lines that is common to all constraints. The reason why the feasible region is below the lines but not above the lines is because these lines represent why the maximum production or demand of x but y given the constraint in place, hence it is only possible to have production below the line but not above it.

In our graph, the feasible region (the area below each line which is common to all) is the area below both line C and line D, which means that line C (the machine hours constraint) and line D (the sales volume for coffee and walnut desserts constraint) are our binding constraints. The optimum solution for the production of organic chocolate and coffee and walnut desserts must therefore be in this feasible area, because it is only at production within this area that we will have enough machine hours and the production is less than demand for the coffee and walnut desserts.

Within this feasible region, the optimum solution will be where the combination of x (organic chocolate) and y (coffee and walnut) which gives us the greatest level of contribution. To find this point, we use the objective function line (which is the dotted line on the graph). This line is simply the line which represents the relationship between the contributions from each product.

The point at which contribution will be maximised will be the point on the graph where the objective function line (moving away from the origin of the graph) and the feasible area just touch.

The graph therefore shows that the point at which contribution can be maximised, within the constraints in place, is where lines C and D intersect. This corresponds to production of 200 batches of coffee and walnut and 180 batches of organic chocolate.

Usefulness of the Linear Programming Graph

The linear programming graph is a useful tool in situations where there are a number of potential resource constraints on production, as it does identify the optimum solution where contribution will be maximised within the boundaries of the constraints. In our case: production of 200 batches of coffee and walnut and 180 batches of organic chocolate. However, whilst this is the production plan that in theory maximises contribution, this ignores other factors such as customer requirements.

Also, a linear programming graph is only ever sensible for a very short term production decision or within a small range of production. This is because over time and volumes the nature of costs can change, linear programming works on the assumption of linearity, and therefore ignores changes over time and economies of scale.

Linear programming is however useful in terms of identifying opportunity costs, otherwise known as shadow prices for binding resources. A shadow price of a binding resource is the contribution increase that would arise from having one more unit of that resource. This would be potentially useful to calculate as it would show us the premium above the normal price what we would be prepared to pay for one more unit of that resource. However, this only applies for a small range because increasing the constrained resource will ultimately lead to that resource not being constrained.

Section 2

From: Management Accountant Assistant

To: Tim Walker, Finance Manager

Subject: The impact of the new customers

The Impact of the New Customers on the Finance Function, Recoverability Risks and Brand

The nature of the new customers that we will be taking on will have any number of impacts.

Firstly, there will be a significant increase in the volume of transactions that will need to be processed within the finance team. There are two aspects to this that will need to be addressed: ensuring that there is adequate employee resource to deal with the processing of orders and invoices as well as the ability of our systems to deal with the volume of data.

Secondly, there will be a potential detrimental impact on our cash flows. As we already know, our small independent retailers often pay late and it is likely that these new customers follow the same trend.

Thirdly, there will be an increase in the recoverability risk that the business faces. By their nature, small independent businesses are more likely to become insolvent or unilaterally cease to trade than larger corporations.

Lastly, and on a positive note, one key impact will be that our brand will benefit from an increased presence in the market. Although this benefit might be limited if hotels and coffee shops simply sell our cakes by the slice or serve our desserts, as the end consumer will be unaware of the fact that it is one of our products.

Measures to Mitigate any Additional Risk

There are a number of measures that we could adopt to manage the additional risks arising from selling to a greater number of small independent customers.

(1) Recruit appropriate qualified people for the finance department. It would be sensible to recruit an appropriate experienced and qualified credit controller to ensure that all new customers are assessed as to their credit worthiness and that the receivables are monitored and chased for payment as required in a timely manner. Currently the management accountant assistants cover this role between them.

(2) Ensure sound credit control procedures are in place. All potential customers should be assessed as to their creditworthiness prior to being accepted. This might involve purchasing credit agency reports or performing an internal assessment by looking at financial statements. In addition there should be procedures in

place for the regular monitoring of outstanding debts and for chasing up late payments through telephone calls and letters.

(3) Offer prompt payment discounts. We could look into offering prompt payment discounts to these customers as an incentive to pay earlier than they would usually do. This will clearly impact on our profit margin, but the benefits of receiving the cash earlier and the reduction in recoverability risk might be worth it.

(4) Finance through receivables factoring. Ultimately, to protect against the risk of irrecoverable debt, we could at a future date factor our receivables under a without recourse agreement. This would in effect mean that we would sell our outstanding debts to a finance company which would be responsible for recovering the monies and would take on the risk of recoverability. This would have the effect of immediately improving our cash flow, although it would be relatively expensive to implement.

Thanks!

Management Accountant Assistant
First Class Bakery

Section 3

Brand Accounting and Variance Report

Brand Accounting

Given the increasing presence of our First Class Bakery brand in the market, especially in respect of our desserts line, it is clear that our brand value is increasing. Whilst it is sensible to suggest that this might be included as an asset of the business, it fails to meet the criteria in IAS 38 Intangible Assets for recognition. This report will consider each recognition criterion in turn.

The Intangible Asset Gives Rise to Future Economic Benefit

The First Class Bakery brand, especially with its increasing prominence, will give us future economic benefits in terms of revenue and profit. A brand, by definition, engenders customer loyalty and hence continued sales. Therefore this criterion would appear to be met.

The Cost or Fair Value of the Intangible Asset Can Be Measured Reliably

To place a value on our brand is very subjective. Whilst there are various brand valuation methods and specialist consultants available to undertake such work, such a valuation is unlikely to meet the requirement of reliable measurement in the accounting standard. This is because of the large number of assumptions about the future which would be required. Therefore this criterion is not met.

The Intangible Asset Has Been Acquired or Is Capable of Separation from the Business

In order to capitalise the value of a brand, that brand needs to be either acquired from an external source (where there is therefore a reliable measurement base being the consideration paid) or be capable of separation from the rest of the business in the sense that it can be sold. In our case, clearly our brand value has been generated through internal means (through the work of our sales and marketing team) rather than as a result of an acquisition.

In addition, if we were to separate our brand with a view to selling it, we would be left with only the supermarket own label business as we would no longer have the right to use the First Class Bakery name. Indeed, if we sold our name, even the own label business could be in jeopardy because our customers are still reliant on the name as a measure of quality. Therefore again this criterion is not met.

Therefore we cannot capitalise the value of our brand in the statement of financial position.

The Potential Benefits and Problems of Splitting Variances

Potential Benefits

The analysis highlights those variances that are controllable (operational) and those that are non-controllable (planning).

There are several potential benefits from the calculation of planning variances within First Class Bakery. Firstly, it can help to generate more meaningful performance measurement in respect of our managers. Central to this is the concept of controllability and the premise that managers' performance should be assessed on how well they controlled those aspects that they can actually influence. In this way, reward schemes can be focused on what they actually achieve rather than things that they cannot control (or punish them).

Secondly, particularly in volatile and changing environments, standard costing and variance analysis are more useful using this approach. Operational variances should not only provide a fairer reflection of actual performance of operational managers but also provide up to date information about the current levels of efficiency.

Thirdly, operational variances are likely to make the standard costing system more acceptable to managers and to have a positive impact on their motivation as they know that they will not be held responsible for poor standard setting.

Lastly, the approach emphasises the importance of the planning function in the preparation of standards and helps in the identification of planning deficiencies. However, the planning and standard setting processes should improve; standards should be more accurate, relevant and appropriate.

Potential Problems

Potential problems include defining which aspects of performance are controllable and which are not from the perspective of our managers. It might will be the case that some aspects are not under the total control of our managers. This can lead to demotivation of managers as well as inaccurate performance measures.

It is difficult to decide in hindsight what the realistic standard should have been and invariably the determination of the ex-post standard involves an element of subjectivity.

It may be too easy to justify variances as being attributable to uncontrollable factors or bad planning.

There can be a conflict between planning and operational staff, which can give rise to a"blame culture". If we absolve operational managers from the responsibility for planning variances then do we place the responsibility upon planning staff? We wish to avoid the creation of such a culture, as the focus is trying to spread blame rather than achieving (and improving) our performance.

The approach is very time consuming because of the on-going need to establish up-to-date standards and calculate additional variances.

Possible Reasons for Each of the Planning Variances

The ingredients price planning variance is adverse overall. We know that the budget was set based on prices expected at the start of the year and therefore it is highly likely that some of the prices have changed. Overall the variance is adverse, which means that the effect of known price increases is greater than the effect of any known price decreases. It should be borne in mind that the ingredients price planning variance is outside the control of operational managers unless they could influence prices via negotiation.

The ingredients usage planning variance is favourable. This is because revised (ex-post) standards for usage are lower than the original (ex-ante) standards in respect of ingredients.

From the work I carried out last week, it was evident that we're now budgeting efficiencies in ingredient usage, perhaps as a result of less wastage or more accurate measuring and quality control of ingredients prior to mixing. This has created the favourable variance.

The labour rate planning variance is adverse. The labour cost standard is based on the weighted average of the rates for skilled and unskilled labour. Possibly we are planning to use more skilled labour than originally budgeted, which will push the weighted average wage rate up. Alternatively it could be that we have had to increase wage rates more than we had originally budgeted.

The labour efficiency planning variance is favourable. Like the ingredients usage planning variance, this is likely due to the increased efficiency as shown in the new standards. This could directly link into the rate variance above in that we are planning to use more skilled labour (which potentially will be more efficient).

The labour idle time planning variance is favourable. This could be attributable to the fact the revised standard reflects less idle time than was originally expected thereby giving rise to higher level of labour efficiency, perhaps as a result of better production scheduling. It might be the case that the originally planned idle time was too pessimistic (planned idle time cannot be favourable). If we had known what we know now, we would have planned more optimistically.

The selling price planning variance is zero. This indicates the selling price we expected at the start of the period is the same as what we have observed during the most recent operating period.

Section 4

Quality Report

Quality Related Costs

Prevention costs are costs incurred prior to or during production in order to prevent substandard or defective goods from being produced. Prevention costs within First Class Bakery include the costs of maintenance of equipment such as the weighing machines in the ingredients preparation area (this ensures that the correct quantities are mixed and therefore the consistency of the cakes are appropriate and to the correct quality).

Appraisal costs are costs incurred in order to ensure that outputs produced meet quality standards. An example within First Class Bakery is the cost of inspecting incoming ingredients to ensure that they are fit for purpose.

Internal failure costs are costs arising from inadequate quality which are identified before the delivery from us to our customers. An example within First Class Bakery is the costs of rework, such as redecoration of special occasion cakes.

External failure costs are costs arising from inadequate quality discovered after the delivery from us to our customers. An example within First Class Bakery is the cost incurred in dealing with customer complaints.

How the Use of a Cost of Quality Report Could Benefit Our Business

A cost of quality report would clearly segregate costs and identify them as non-value added, thereby providing a management focus on the reduction or elimination of those items.

A cost of quality report would provide a true indication of the current health of First Class Bakery because cost items would not be concealed within cost of sales, thereby hiding inefficiencies.

The segregation of costs under the headings of prevention, appraisal, internal failure and external failure magnifies the impact and increases management focus on such costs.

A cost of quality report provides a target, which not only can be shared by our entire organisation but also clearly measures the progress of a total quality programme in absolute terms. This will assist us in our achievement of "continuous improvement".

The cost of quality report encourages the use of more relevant measures of organisational performance and stimulates all employees to learn more about the operations in which they are involved.

The Major Considerations in the Implementation of Quality Circles in Order to Achieve Operational Improvements

Major considerations in the implementation of quality circles within First Class Bakery are as follows:

- Management should establish a quality circle comprising employees with a range of skills from all levels of the organisation to help ensure that work is defect free.

- They should meet voluntarily on a regular basis to discuss quality related issues and to develop solutions to problems within the business.

There are a number of ways in which management can encourage the development and use of a newly established quality circle.

- It is vital to ensure that there is high profile executive management commitment to support the initiative at all times. Successful employee-involvement programmes, such as Quality Circles, require genuine management involvement and full understanding throughout all levels of management concerning the multifaceted purposes served by the programme.
- Management must ensure that staff members have the training in problem solving and analysis which they need to identify problems and develop workable solutions.
- Management need to ensure that staff members who are involved in quality circles have sufficient spare time away from their normal day-to-day responsibilities to participate in meetings and activities.
- Management should review the information system in order to identify the information needs of quality circles, and to ensure that data required to assess performance and identify problems is available to them.
- Management need to demonstrate that they take the process seriously and take all necessary actions recommended by quality circles to resolve problems.
- Management need to develop an organisational culture that permits possible changes but tolerates the possibility of mistakes, and provide training for all staff to increase awareness of the importance and value of quality circles within the business.

The Implications of a TQM Focus on Human Resource Management

First Class Bakery will need a human resource strategy to support the introduction of TQM. Human resource practices should lead to a set of positive outcomes including high staff commitment to the TQM philosophy and highly flexible employees who are receptive to innovation and change.

A management audit could be undertaken with a view to assessing the current skills base and this would identify the"gap" between skills required and the current level of skills within First Class Bakery. Management could then put the plans to close the gap.

In recruiting new employees, it is vital to ensure that new recruits are"team players" as teamwork is a fundamental requirement of a successful TQM programme.

With regard to the induction of new employees then this would be an ideal opportunity to explain that TQM is central to the business strategy and part of the culture. This should facilitate the "buy-in" from new recruits.

Inevitably there will be a need for training of not only new staff but also existing staff. This will be important since existing staff will be affected in that aspects of their current roles will change. It would probably be best that a combination of formal and on-the-job training is used to meet the training needs identified by management.

Management should undertake a review of the human resource plan in order to measure the effective use of the human resources and their contribution towards the achievement of our business objectives.

试卷四　参考答案

任务一

线性规划图报告

线性规划图的解读

图中的直线代表生产新口味甜点的潜在资源限制。线 A 代表粗制糖限制，线 B 代表人工工时限制，线 C 代表机器工时限制，线 D 代表咖啡核桃甜点的需求限制。线 A、B、C 分别代表充分利用资源条件下产品 x（有机巧克力甜点）和 y（咖啡核桃甜点）的组合，因而也代表了每种资源约束条件下的最大产量。线 D 为需求限制线。

为了解释该图，我们需要找出生产的“可行解区域”。图中的可行解区域是包括所有限制线（线 A、B、C、D）之下的部分。当有若干个限制条件时（如本题所示），可行解区域即每条限制线之下的共同区域。可行解区域之所以位于限制线之下而非之上的原因在于，限制线代表了在既定限制条件下的最大产量，或 x 和 y 的最大需求量，因此，只能在限制线之下才可能进行生产，而非在其之上。

在本题图中，可行解区域是线 C 和线 D 之下的部分（每条限制线之下的共同区域），即线 C（工时限制）和线 D（咖啡核桃甜点需求限制）是强制性限制。有机巧克力甜点、咖啡核桃甜点的最优产量规划一定位于可行解区域内，因为仅位于此区域内时才有充足的工时进行生产，咖啡核桃甜点的产量才小于市场需求量。

在可行解区域内，最优产品规划是带来最高贡献的产品 x（有机巧克力甜点）和 y（咖啡核桃甜点）的组合。我们需要使用目标函数线（图中虚线）寻找最佳产品组合，这条线代表了每种产品贡献之间的关系。

图中贡献最大化点即为目标函数线（远离原点平行移动）和可行解区域相切的点。

因而，图中限制条件下贡献最大化的点为线 C 和线 D 的交点，即 200 批咖啡核桃甜点和 180 批有机巧克力甜点。

线性规划图的用途

线性规划图在一系列潜在的生产限制下是一种有用的方法，它可以找出在限制范围内最大化贡献的最优方案。在本案例中，即为 200 批咖啡核桃甜点和 180 批有机巧克力甜点。然而，这虽然是理论上能够最大化贡献的生产计划，但是它忽视了其他因素如消费者要求等。

除此之外，线性规划仅适用于超短期的生产决策或者小规模生产。原因在于随着时间的推移和产量的扩大，成本数额及性质会发生改变。线性规划基于线性假设，忽略了时间带来的改变和规模经济效应。

然而，线性规划在识别机会成本方面也大有用处，此时它也被叫作限制性资源的影子价格。限制性资源的影子价格是放宽一单位限制性资源限制带来的边际贡献。计算影子价格的潜在用途在于，影子价格代表了为多使用一单位限制性资源，可以支付的超过正常价格的溢价金额。但是这只在小范围的变化内适用，原因在于增加限制性资源的供应将最终导致其不再是限制性资源。

任务二

发件人：管理会计助理

收件人：财务经理 Tim Walker

主题：新客户影响

新客户对财务职能、坏账风险和品牌建设的影响

新客户的固有性质将对我们产生许多影响。

第一，财务部门需要处理的交易量大幅提升，这包括两点：一是确保有足够的员工来处理订单和发票，二是信息系统要有能力处理增加的数据量。

第二，对公司现金流可能产生潜在的不利影响。因为我们已知小型独立零售商经常延迟支付，而且这些新客户可能会跟风采用相同的做法。

第三，提高公司的坏账风险。小型独立公司从本质上看，破产和单方终止交易的可能性比大型公司更高。

最后，从积极的方面来看，一个关键的影响在于，由于市场存在感增加，我们的品牌将从中受益。但是如果酒店和咖啡店仅仅出售我们的小块蛋糕或甜点，最终消费者可能意识不到这是我们的产品，那么对品牌的宣传作用就可能较为有限。

减低新增坏账风险的措施

向更多小型独立客户销售带来了新增的坏账风险，对此，我们可以采用如下几种措施进行管理。

（1）为财务部门招聘合适的、有资格认证的人员。招聘一个有相关经验、有职业资格认证的财务信贷经理将是明智的选择，这能够确保所有新客户的信用得到评估，使应收账款处在监测之中并能及时催收。目前是由管理会计助理负责此类事务。

（2）确保拥有恰当的信用控制程序。在将其确定为新客户之前，需要考察所有潜在客户的信用。这可能需要购买信用机构的评价报告或查看财务报表进行内部评估。此外，需要定期检查其现有债务，并通过电话和信件催收延期支付的款项。

（3）提供即时支付折扣政策。我们可以向客户提供即时支付折扣（现金折扣），激励客户比往常更早支付货款。这显然会影响我们的毛利，但相对于提前收到货款的益处与坏账风险的降低来说，这是值得的。

（4）通过应收账款保理融资。最后，为了防范不可回收的坏账风险，我们可以在未来某一时间对应收账款进行保理，并选择不附追索权的形式。事实上这意味着我们将当前债务出售给债务公司，债务公司将负责收回现金并承担不可回收的风险。这可以产生即时改进现金流的效果，然而实施成本相对较高。

感谢！

至臻糕点公司

管理会计助理

任务三

品牌核算和差异报告

品牌核算

随着我们至臻糕点品牌，尤其是甜点在市场中知名度的提高，我们的品牌价值显著提升。虽然建议将品牌作为公司的一项资产纳入财务报表是合理的，但是这不符合国际会计准则第 38 号无形资产的确认标准。此报告将依次解读各项确认标准。

无形资产提升未来经济利益

随着至臻糕点品牌知名度的日益提高，以收入和利润为主要形式的经济利益将增加。从定义上看，品牌能够产生客户忠诚度并带来持续销售，因而，符合此标准的要求。

无形资产的成本或公允价值能够可靠计量

品牌估值是非常主观的行为，即使有各种各样的品牌估值方法和专业咨询师进行评估。此类评估不可能满足会计准则中可靠计量的要求。原因在于它需要对未来做大量的假设，因而，不满足此标准。

无形资产从外部购买或者能够从企业中分离出来

为了资本化品牌价值，品牌需要从公司外部购入（此时支付对价为可靠计量的基础），或者能够与公司其他资产分离开来，在此意义上，才可以将其对外销售。在本案例中，可以清楚地看到，我们的品牌价值产生于公司内部（通过市场营销团队的工作），而不是购买的结果。

除此之外，如果我们把品牌从企业经营中分离出来进行销售，我们将仅剩用超市品牌进行销售的业务，因为我们将不再拥有至臻糕点品牌的使用权。事实上，如果我们出售品牌，那么即使是我们的贴牌业务，也可能处于危险之中。因为我们的客户仍然信赖我们的品牌，并将此作为质量的衡量标准。因而，也不满足此标准。

综上，我们不能在资产负债表中资本化品牌价值。

将差异进行分拆的潜在益处和问题

潜在益处

分类分析将差异分成了经营性差异（可控差异）和计划性差异（不可控差异）。

对于至臻糕点公司来说，计算计划性差异有下列潜在益处。首先，有助于提供更有价值的经理人员业绩考评指标。这种指标的核心在于可控的理念，对管理者绩效的评估应基于管理者可施加影响的那部分的经营状况。因此，奖励制度（或受到惩罚）应集中于经理能实际掌控的部分，而非他们不可控的部分。

其次，当处于多变的环境中时，基于差异分类，标准成本法和差异分析将有更多用处。经营性差异不仅更公平地反映了经理人员的实际业绩，同时也提供了当前最新的效率信息。

再次，经营性差异分析使标准成本体系更易于被管理层接受，由于经理人知道他们不需要对不合适的标准负责，因而对激励有正向影响。

最后，此方法强调计划在编制标准中的重要性，并有助于识别计划的不足之处。但是，计划和标准设定的程序需要改进，同时标准应该更准确、更相关、更合适。

潜在问题

潜在的问题包括需要从管理层的角度界定哪些绩效是可控的，哪些是不可控的。而且可能有些部分对管理层来说是不完全可控的。这会导致对管理层的负向激励并产生不准确的绩效评价指标。

事后看来，确定真正的标准本应该是什么十分困难，事后标准的确定总带有一定的主观性。

可能因为太容易，反而无法将差异归因为不可控因素或计划失误。

这可能导致计划员工和运营员工之间的冲突，进而产生“怪罪文化”。如果我们认为运营经理不对计划差异负责，那么计划员工就应该对此负责吗？我们想避免此类文化的产生，因为它关注的焦点是互相责备而非实现（并改进）绩效。

由于需要持续更新标准以及计算额外差异，这种方法非常费时。

各计划差异可能的原因

原材料价格计划差异总体上为不利差异。我们知道，预算是基于年初预计价格设定的，因而很可能其中一些价格会发生变化。总体上为不利差意味着，已知价格上升的影响超过了已知价格下降的影响。应牢记于心的是，除非运营经理可以通过谈判影响价格，否则材料价格计划差异不在运营经理的控制范围之内。

原材料用量计划差异为有利差异，因为修改后的（事后）原材料用量标准比原始（事先）标准低。从上周我完成的工作中可以明显看出，我们正在把原料使用的效率编入预算，原因可能在于浪费减少、衡量更为准确以及原材料在混合之前的质量控制。这些导致了有利差异的产生。

劳动力价格计划差异为不利差异。劳动力成本标准的制定基于熟练工和非熟练工加权平均工资。有可能我们修改预算后，计划比原始预算使用了更多的熟练工，导致加权平均工资的上升，或者也可能是我们本应该提供比原始预算更高的工资。

劳动力效率计划差异为有利差异。与原材料用量计划差异类似，这可能是由于新标准中劳动力效率提高了。也许它与上述我们计划使用更多熟练工（意味着可能更有效率）带来的劳动力价格差异息息相关。

劳动力空闲时间计划差异为有利差异。这可以归因于修改后的标准比原始的空闲时间更少，进而提升了劳动力效率，这可能源于更科学的生产计划。也许是原始预算中对空闲时间的规划过于悲观（计划的空闲时间不可能为有利差异）。如果我们之前知道现在知道的情况，将进行更为乐观的预算。

销售价格计划差异为0，这意味着起初我们期望的销售价格与最近经营期间观测到的销售价格一致。

任务四

质量报告

质量相关成本

预防成本是在生产之前或生产过程中发生的，用于预防次品或残品而产生的成本。

在至臻糕点公司，预防成本包括机器设备的维护成本，如在原料准备环节的称重机（用以确保各种原材料以正确的数量混合，继而保证蛋糕的生产保持一致，并符合正确的质量要求）。

鉴定成本是确保生产的产品符合质量标准而产生的成本。以至臻糕点公司为例，检测购入的原材料以确保其符合要求而花费的成本即为鉴定成本。

内部失败成本是指在运送给客户之前发现质量不合格的产品而产生的成本，以至臻糕点公司为例，内部失败成本即再加工成本，如特殊场合蛋糕的再装饰成本。

外部失败成本是指在运送给客户之后发现质量不合格的产品带来的成本，以至臻糕点公司为例，外部失败成本即处理客户投诉产生的成本。

使用质量成本报告对公司的益处

质量成本报告可以清晰地识别、分离不再增加价值的成本，由此将管理重心引向减少或者消除此类项目。

质量成本报告可以真实体现至臻糕点公司当前运营的健康状况，因为此类项目不能被隐藏于销售成本，所以也无法隐藏效率低下问题。

将成本分为预防成本、鉴定成本、内部失败成本和外部失败成本，突出了各类成本的影响，提高了管理层对上述成本的关注。

质量成本报告不仅提供了一个全组织共同的目标，同时它可以用绝对量的形式清晰地衡量全面质量项目的进程。这有助于我们实现“持续改进”。

质量成本报告鼓励公司采用与组织绩效更相关的措施，刺激全员学习更多与之有关的企业运营知识。

实施质量管理循环以改进运营需要考虑的主要问题

至臻糕点公司实施质量管理循环需要考虑的主要问题如下。

- 管理层需要建立一个拥有多项技能、来自公司各个层级的员工组成的质量管理循环团队以保证此项工作无缺陷。
- 他们需要定时、自愿组织在一起讨论质量相关问题，并提出在企业内部解决问题的办法。

管理层可以使用多种方法开发和使用新成立的质量管理循环。

- 确保有一个有威望的高层管理者在任何时候均支持原创是非常关键的。想让成功的员工参与项目如质量管理循环，需要公司管理层真正参与、各级管理层全面理解项目目标的多样性。

- 管理层必须确保全体员工接受分析问题、解决问题的相关培训，使他们能够识别问题并提出可行的解决方法。
- 管理层需要确保参与到质量管理循环的员工在日常工作之余，有足够的空闲时间参与品控会议与活动。
- 管理层需要评估信息系统，识别质量管理循环的信息需求，并确保质量管理循环可以获得绩效评价、问题识别所需的信息。
- 管理层需要证明他们认真地遵循了上述程序，并采取了质量管理循环推荐的所有必要行动以解决问题。
- 管理层需要培养一种允许改变、包容错误的组织文化，并为全体员工提供培训，以提升其对质量管理循环在企业中的重要性和价值的认知。

全面质量管理对至臻糕点公司人力资源管理的影响

至臻糕点公司需要人力资源战略支撑全面质量管理的引入。人力资源实践应该产生一系列正面效果，包括员工对全面质量管理理念的高度认可，培养愿意接受创新和改变的高灵活性员工。

可以通过管理层审计评价当前的员工技能基础，并识别至臻糕点公司所需技能水平与当前技能水平之间的差距，就此，管理层可以提出弥补差距的计划。

在招募新员工时，至关重要的是确保新员工是“富有团队精神的人”，因为团队合作是成功的全面质量管理的基本要求。

新员工招聘是一个解释全面质量管理是公司战略的核心和文化组成部分的绝佳机会。这有助于新员工接受全面质量管理的理念。

不仅新员工必然需要培训，现有员工也需要培训。这非常重要，因为当现有员工当前的工作角色需要改变时，他们将受到影响。最好的方法可能是，将正式培训和在岗培训结合起来，以此满足管理层制定的培训要求。

管理层需要进行人力资源规划评价，以衡量人力资源使用的有效性及其对实现公司目标的贡献。

Variant 4　Marking Guidance

Section	Technical skills		Business skills		People skills		Leadership skills		Integration	Total
1	Usefulness of linear programming	9			Linear programming	2	Linear programming	6		17
2	Impact of new customers on finance function, recoverability risks and brand Measures to mitigate recoverability risk	9 8								17
3	Accounting for brands Benefits and problems of splitting variances into planning and operational variances Reasons for planning variances	11 11 11								33
4	Cost of quality	4	Cost of quality Benefits of a cost of quality approach Quality circles	4 7 4	Quality circles TQM	4 7			3	33
Total marks available for each competency		63		15		13		6	3	100

试卷四　评分指南

部分	技术技能		商业技能		人际技能		领导技能		综合能力	总计
1	线性规划的用途	9			线性规划	2	线性规划	6		17
2	新客户对财务职能、坏账风险和品牌建设的影响 降低新增坏账风险的措施	9 8								17
3	品牌会计核算 将差异分为计划性差异与经营性差异的好处与存在的问题 计划性差异可能的原因	11 11 11								33
4	质量成本	4	质量成本 质量成本方法的好处 质量管理循环	4 7 4	质量管理循环 全面质量管理	4 7			3	33
各技能评分合计		63		15		13		6	3	100

中南财经政法大学名师解惑

本套试卷模拟企业经营实际，在背景案例的基础上，根据生产经营中出现的新机遇与新问题，要求学生站在管理会计助理的视角，综合运用管理会计（P1）、组织管理（E1）和财务报告与税收（F1）三个模块的知识与理论，分析、解决会计助理日常工作遇到的各种问题，符合管理会计职业能力的框架要求。

考查的知识点涵盖线性规划图的解读与运用（P1）；开拓新客户对财务职能、坏账风险与品牌建设的影响，降低坏账风险的措施（F1）；品牌会计核算，国际会计准则第38号无形资产确认标准（F1）；将差异分为计划性差异与经营性差异的益处与潜在问题，产生每项计划差异的可能原因（P1）；质量成本的分类，质量成本报告（P1）；全面质量管理等（E1）。但管理会计（P1）、组织管理（E1）和财务报告与税收（F1）的考试并非相互独立，而是在企业运营的背景下，三者通过财务报告和绩效管理，最终提升企业绩效。因而如同企业经营实际，三部分内容相互作用，相辅相成，共同为提升企业价值服务。

需要注意的是，在运营级案例考试中，P1的知识点分数比重最高，其次是E1，最后则是F1。这和OCS的考纲要求基本一致。该试卷考核了考生的四项能力，其中技术技能的分值占63%，商业技能的分值占15%，人际技能的分值占13%，领导技能的分值占6%，与CGMA管理会计能力框架的技能要求一致。考生在备考时应根据考试重点有所侧重。另外的3分是考查综合能力的，可能是对不同模块或不同能力的整合。这些得分点嵌在任务里，完成任务时能满足要求，就能得分。

该试卷每项任务覆盖以下知识点内容：

任务	问题	科目	知识点
任务一	线性规划图的解读与用途	P1	线性规划图（linear programming graph）
任务二	分析新客户对财务职能、坏账风险和品牌建设的影响	E1	财务职能对经营和战略的影响（impact of new customers on the finance function）
	降低坏账风险的措施	F1	坏账风险（recoverability risk）
任务三	内部形成的品牌资本化的问题	F1	无形资产资本化（capitalization of intangible assets）
	将差异分为计划性差异与经营性差异的好处与存在的问题 出现计划性差异的原因	P1	计划性差异和经营性差异（planning variances and operational variances）

（续表）

任务	问题	科目	知识点
任务四	质量成本分类和质量成本计算的好处	P1	质量成本会计（quality costing）
	实施质量管理对人力资源管理的影响	E1	全面质量管理（TQM）

上述各项任务要求以邮件、报告或工作笔记等形式来呈现答案，对问题的描述非常明确，答题时既要注意内容的针对性，也要注意形式的规范性。

对应知识点深度剖析

线性规划图的解读和用途

该知识点为P1的内容，考生不需要列规划方程，也不需要用数学方法求解，但是要能看懂图、应用图。图上各个线条的含义要能理解。这个要结合任务所给的限制信息来阐述。另外，各条限制线所组合成的可行解区域要能够找出来。最后，找到等利润线，并根据等利润线与可行解区域的对应关系识别出最优解。

至于线性规划图的用途这类问题，要注意，解释模型的用途时，尽量从正反两个方面去阐述。其用处是什么（解决限制条件下最优产品组合问题）？为什么有用？存在什么缺陷？这样才能对方法做出全面评价。

解释新客户对财务职能、坏账风险和品牌建设的影响

只要深度了解背景材料，并结合考试时出现的信息就能很好地回答这个问题。注意回答问题的结构，建议设小标题，以确保对三个方面（财务职能、坏账风险和品牌建设）的影响能都阐述到。不要只是阐述理论，要结合案例背景来回答。既然新客户是小客户，那么就套用小客户常见的特点来阐述可能影响。

降低坏账风险的措施

这个问题，借助F1的相关知识点就能回答。尽量将措施完整回答，并对其可能的成本效益也做一定的分析。

内部形成的品牌资本化的问题

要完成这个任务，考生必须掌握国际会计准则第38号的认定标准，并将公司的实际情况与标准逐一对照分析，说明是否符合标准，以及不能在报表中确认品牌价值的原因。

将差异分为计划性差异与经营性差异的好处与存在的问题，计划性差异分析

考生要能解释区分计划性差异和经营性差异的原因，不要遗漏。差异结果的分析，首先要看懂差异的方向，是有利的还是不利的。要能解释出背后的可能原因，而不是简单说，因为标准价格调高了，所以出现了不利的计划性差异。这只是表象，原料短缺导致原料成本的增加才是真正原因。

质量成本分类和质量成本计算的好处

这个基本上是对照大纲陈述知识点，是一个比较容易作答的任务，但记住要结合公司的实际业务来举例说明可能的成本类型，同时要解释为什么这类业务的成本可以归属于某一类质量成本，例如鉴定成本。而质量成本计算的好处，则尽量列举完整。

质量管理对人力资源管理的影响

要注意审题，任务要求阐述的是全面质量管理对于人力资源管理的影响，因此需要阐述人力资源管理如何采取一系列措施来促进全面质量管理的实施。可以从人力资源的招募、培训、评价等方面来阐述。

考生注意事项

对管理会计（P1）的考查，不需要计算，如计划性差异与经营性差异的计算，而是要在已知差异计算结果的基础上，考查差异分类的好处与潜在问题、差异产生的原因等，这提示考生在学习时要更为注重理解各种管理会计方法的产生背景、适用性、优缺点等，做到知其然，知其所以然。在准备运营级案例考试时，要熟悉背景材料，揣摩背景材料中暗含的出题点，对应到教材知识点。考试作答时特别需要注意的是，一定要结合案例材料作答，切勿空谈知识点与理论。

Variant 5

This examination is structured as follows：

Section number	Number of tasks	Time for section(minutes)
1	1	45
2	1	45
3	1	45
4	1	45

The time available for each section is for reading,planning and writing your answer(s).

Section 1

You have just received the following email from Rajiv Patel.

From：*Rajiv Patel*, *Finance Director*

To：*Management Accountant Assistant*

Subject：*Environmental costing*

Yesterday I received an email from David Spencer, finance director of our parent Universal Foods.

He has asked the finance director of each subsidiary in the group to produce a report on environmental management and the environmental costs associated with its own business. Each report will ultimately be made available to all managers in that business but will also be sent to head office and collated into the group report.

Whilst we've obviously been aware of the environment and have a number of environmental policies (such as planting trees on new sites and selling food waste to local pig farms), we have never really thought about environmental costs. Currently any costs that we incur linked to environmental are not reported separately.

Please prepare the first draft of the following report sections requested by David in respect of First Class Bakery.

- The reasons why management awareness of the environmental impact of the business is important.
- How environmental costs can be categorised as environmental quality costs (prevention, appraisal, internal failure and external failure) with an explanation of what each type of cost means?
- Two examples of each category of environmental quality cost relevant to the business.

Thank you.

Rajiv Patel

Finance Director

First Class Bakery

Write the draft report sections requested by Rajiv Patel.

Section 2

Two weeks later, Tim Walker places a copy of the following internet press article on your desk with a note saying that a management meeting has been called to discuss the implications of this for the business.

The Emissions Legislation Issue

April 2016 **James Tyler**

The Government yesterday announced that new rules in respect of minimum vehicle emissions are to be fast tracked. By 1 January 2017, all vehicles within Beeland will need to comply with the new rules, or face a significant fine.

This is expected to hit hauliers the hardest. Most cars will already meet the minimum requirements thanks to legislation introduced two years ago. However, only a small proportion of trucks currently on our roads would meet the requirements, although most can be converted to ensure compliance.

Alan Jenkins from BeeHaulage, the largest road hauling business in Beeland, has said: "This new legislation has not really surprised us, we knew that the government was keen to champion the environment. It is going to cost us though to make the changes required to our fleet. We expect to have to replace some of our older trucks as it is unlikely that older engines can be converted successfully".

The next day, Tim Walker sends you the following email.

From: Tim Walker, Finance Manager

To: Management Accountant Assistant

Subject: The impact of the new emissions legislation

It was an interesting meeting yesterday. There is a difference of opinion within the management team about how we should deal with the new emissions legislation. We seem to have two options:

(1) Option 1 — spend B$ 125,000 on updating the vehicles' existing engines and exhaust systems so that our vehicles can comply with the legislation.

I know Frank Mitchell is keen on this option. The only concern he has is whether the expenditure of B$ 125,000 can be included as part of non-current assets or whether it will all affect profit straight away. We will need to look at the conditions for the capitalisation of subsequent expenditure in IAS 16 PPE to address his concern. As you know, currently we depreciate each vehicle as a single asset over a period of 10 years.

(2) Option 2 — sell our existing fleet of delivery vehicles and outsource the entire outbound logistics function.

Marilyn Groves, the operations manager, has been suggesting for a while that consideration should be given to outsourcing the outbound logistics function. Indeed she once said: "After all we are a bakery not a haulage business!" She suggested that we approach BeeHaulage which is the major provider of outsourced delivery services within Beeland.

I need to take a report to our next meeting on this whole issue. Please therefore draft the following sections for me.

- How the expenditure of B$ 125,000 will impact our financial statements, should we choose to keep the fleet, with reference to the subsequent expenditure rules in IAS 16 PPE?
- The potential benefits from outsourcing our entire outbound logistics function.
- The potential drawbacks from outsourcing our entire outbound logistics function.

Many thanks.

Tim Walker

Finance Manager

First Class Bakery

Write the report sections requested by Tim Walker.

Section 3

A few months later, Rajiv Patel catches you at lunch and says:

As you know, the board of directors recently announced our decision to outsource the outbound logistics function. This appears to have led to a decline in employee motivation.

We are now considering the introduction of a new reward scheme in order to maintain and improve employee motivation. The directors are keen to understand how we might achieve this.

On another matter, given that we decided to sell our delivery fleet, the directors wish to understand how this will affect our financial statements for the year ended 31 December 2016. I expect that we will start with our new outsource partner late in December and therefore are likely to sell our fleet of vehicles in January or February of 2017. There is already a buyer interested in the fleet and we are currently negotiating a price.

Please prepare sections of a report that I can take to the other directors which explain:

- the purposes of, and the factors to consider when establishing the new reward scheme;
- the implications for our financial statements for the year ended 31 December 2016 of the intention to sell the delivery fleet.

Write the report sections requested by Rajiv Patel.

Section 4

Two weeks later, you receive the following email from Tim Walker.

From: Tim Walker, Finance Manager

To: Management Accountant Assistant

Subject: New cake opportunity

Last week, I had a conversation with Anna Spring, the sales manager. She has been working with the product development team to secure customers for a new organic cherry slab cake that they have developed. The new cake will be called "Ultimate Cherry" and will be marketed as a healthier alternative to our normal cakes as a result of using unrefined sugars and organic cherries. Because this is an area of the market in which we have very limited experience, Anna has suggested that we do an initial pilot production run of the cake to see how it sells before we make firm commitments to suppliers.

The organic cherries will be supplied by a new supplier, TOCC, who has offered us a choice of contracts for the initial pilot production run. Each contract is for different purchase quantities at different cost points. We need to evaluate which of these contracts to undertake.

I've prepared both a pay-off table and a minimax regret table in respect of this decision regarding the pilot production run, which are included in the attached schedule. I've been asked by the directors to prepare a report on this decision.

I would be very grateful if you could send me an email containing the following.

- An interpretation of the information included in the payoff table (there is no need to recalculate any of the data).
- An explanation of the Maximax, Maximin and Minimax regret decision-making criteria including commentary on the risk attitudes of managers who employ such methods and the identification of which contract would be selected under each of these three decision criteria.
- An explanation of expected values and the potential benefits and problems of their use in the decision regarding the purchase of organic cherries.

Many thanks.

Tim Walker

Finance Manager

First Class Bakery

Schedule

Relevant information: all organic cherries will be purchased from a single supplier, TOCC. TOCC has offered a choice of four different contracts A, B, C and D for the supply of cherries in the pilot production run period.

	Contract A	Contract B	Contract C	Contract D
Number of cakes that can be manufactured from the cherries supplied	160,000	240,000	360,000	480,000
Cost of cherries per cake	B$ 1.30	B$ 1.00	B$ 0.80	B$ 0.70

- Demand in the above table relates to possible demand from food retailer customers for the organic cherry cakes made in the pilot production run.
- Any cakes made in the pilot production run period that are not sold to food retailer customers will be sold as animal feed.
- For the purposes of this analysis, we have assumed all cherries purchased under the contract will be used in the production of organic cherry cakes, in the anticipation that all cakes made will be sold to our food retailer customers. Each organic cherry cake has a five week shelf life.

	Contract A	Contract B	Contract C	Contract D
Demand (units)	Contribution (B$ 000)	Contribution (B$ 000)	Contribution (B$ 000)	Contribution (B$ 000)
480,000	152	300	522	744
240,000	152	300	126	(48)
160,000	152	36	(138)	(312)

Write your response to Tim Walker's email.

试卷五

本次考试的结构如下：

序号	任务数	时间（分钟）
1	1	45
2	1	45
3	1	45
4	1	45

每个部分规定的时间可用于读题、组织和书写答案。

任务一

刚刚，你收到来自 Rajiv Patel 的邮件。

发件人：财务总监 Rajiv Patel

收件人：管理会计助理

主题：环境成本

昨天，我收到了一封来自母公司通用食品公司财务总监 David Spencer 的电子邮件。他要求集团内部的每一个子公司的财务总监制作一份关于自身业务的环境管理和环境成本的报告。每一份报告最终都将提交给公司所有经理查阅，同时被寄往总部，整合进集团报告中。虽然我们已经有相当高的环境意识并配有许多环境政策（比如在新基地种树、将食品废料卖给当地的养猪场），但我们从没真正地考虑过环境成本。目前，任何与环境有关的成本我们都没有进行分开报告。

请按照 David 的要求，准备一份关于至臻糕点公司以下内容的报告初稿。

- 为什么使管理层了解环境对经营的影响非常重要？
- 如何将环境成本，即环境质量成本分类（预防成本，鉴定成本，环境内部失败成本和环境外部失败成本）？解释各种成本类型的含义。
- 列举两个与业务有关的各类环境质量成本的例子。

谢谢！

至臻糕点公司

财务总监

Rajiv Patel

请根据 Rajiv Patel 的要求草拟部分报告。

任务二

两周后，Tim Walker 将一篇网上的文章放在了你的桌子上并附上了便笺，通知你一个意在讨论文章内容对公司业务的影响的管理层会议已经宣布召开。

排放立法的相关问题

2016年4月　　James Tyler（詹姆斯·泰勒）

政府部门昨天宣布，有关汽车最小尾气排放量的最新规定将快速立法。到2017年1月1日，所有Beeland境内的汽车都需要遵守新规定，否则将面临巨额罚款。

这项举措预计将对承运者带来严重打击。归功于两年前提出的规定，大部分小轿车已经达到了最小的排放要求。然而，目前公路上只有少部分的货车能够达到这个要求，尽管其中大部分可以通过改装确保符合标准。

来自BeeHaulage的Alan Jenkins（阿兰·詹金斯）拥有Beeland最大的公路运输业务，他说："这项新的立法没有真的吓到我们，我们早已知道政府对环境保护的渴望。但是，此项立法将使我们花费成本来完成对车队必要的改造。预计我们需要替换一些旧货车，因为老旧的发动机似乎无法成功改装。"

第二天，Tim Walker 向你发了如下一封电子邮件。

发件人：财务经理 Tim Walker
收件人：管理会计助理
主题：新排放立法的影响

昨天的会议很有趣。管理层对于我们应该怎样应对新的排放立法有不同的意见。我们似乎有两个选择：

（1）选项1——花费B$ 125 000，更新汽车现有的发动机和排放系统，使它们符合立法标准。

我知道Frank Mitchell强烈建议选择此项。他唯一担心的是花费的B$ 125 000是否可以被归为非流动资产的一部分，还是这笔花费将全额直接影响利润。我们需要查看国际会计准则第16号固定资产中有关后续支出的资本化条件以解决他的问题。如你所知，目前我们将每辆车视为单独资产，折旧时间为10年。

（2）选项2——卖掉我们现有的运输车队并将整个配送物流部门外包。

运营总监Marilyn Groves一直建议我们应该考虑外包配送物流部门。实际上她曾经说过："我们毕竟是一个糕点公司而不是一个运输公司！"她建议我们向Beeland主要的运输外包服务提供商BeeHaulage寻求合作。我需要在我们下次的会议上提交一份有关以上所有内容的报告，请你为我草拟以下部分。

- 假如我们选择保留现有车队，根据国际会计准则第16号固定资产后续支出的相关规定，这B$ 125 000的支出将如何影响我们的财务报表？
- 整体外包配送物流部门的潜在好处。
- 整体外包配送物流部门的潜在缺陷。

十分感谢！

至臻糕点公司
财务经理
Tim Walker

请根据Tim Walker的要求草拟部分报告。

任务三

几个月后，Rajiv Patel在午饭时遇到你并对你说：

正如你所知，董事会最近宣布了我们将外包配送物流部门的决定。这似乎导致了员工士气的下降。

我们现在正在考虑引进一个新的薪酬激励体系来保持并改善员工的积极性。董事们强烈地想要了解我们该如何实现这一目标。另外，鉴于我们已经决定出售我们的运输车队，董事们希望获悉这将如何影响公司2016年的年度财务报表。我希望我们能在12月下旬和新的外包合伙人展开合作，因此我们的汽车车队很有可能在2017年的1月或者2月出售。目前已经有一个对车队感兴趣的购买者，我们正在与之谈判价格。请你准备一份报告以便我能提交给其他董事，这部分报告需要解释以下内容。

- 设立新的薪酬激励体系的目的以及需要考虑的要素。
- 出售运输车队对公司2016年财务报表将产生什么影响？

请根据Rajiv Patel的要求撰写部分报告。

任务四

两周后，你收到了来自Tim Walker的电子邮件，内容如下。

发件人：财务经理Tim Walker
收件人：管理会计助理
主题：新蛋糕的机会

上周我和销售经理Anna Spring面谈了一次。她已经和产品研发团队一起，为他们开发的一种新的有机樱桃切片蛋糕寻求客户。这个新品种的蛋糕将被命名为“终极樱桃”，并且因其使用的是粗制糖和有机樱桃，它将作为我们常规蛋糕的一种更健康的替代选择进行市场推广。由于我们在这个市场的经验非常有限，Anna建议我们在与供应商签订合约前，对这种蛋糕做一个初步试点生产，以观察其销售情况。有机樱桃将由一个新的供应商TOCC供货，它为我们提供了一些可供选择的初步试点生产的合同。每一份合同都依据不同的购买数量并以不同的成本计算。我们需要通过评估来确定签订哪份合同。为了这个初步试点生产的决定，我已经准备了与之相关的一份支付矩阵分析以及一个最小最大后悔表加在附表中。董事们要求我准备一份相关报告。如果可以，请发给我一封包含以下内容的邮件，我将不胜感激。

- 解释支付矩阵所包含的信息（没有必要重新计算其中的任何数据）。
- 解释最大最大决策法、最大最小收益法以及最小最大后悔值法决策标准，并对采用这些方法的经理的风险态度进行评论。此外，分别判断在这三个不同的决策标准下，哪一份合同将被采纳。

■ 解释期望值，并说明其运用在购买有机樱桃的决策中的潜在优势和弊端。

十分感谢！

至臻糕点公司

财务经理

Tim Walker

附表

相关信息：所有有机樱桃将从唯一的供应商 TOCC 处购买。TOCC 为在试点生产时期的樱桃供应提供了四种不同的合同 A，B，C 和 D。

	合同A	合同B	合同C	合同D
供应的樱桃可以生产出的蛋糕数	160 000	240 000	360 000	480 000
每个蛋糕耗费樱桃的成本	B$ 1.30	B$ 1.00	B$ 0.80	B$ 0.70

■ 上表中的需求量与试点生产中食品零售商对有机樱桃蛋糕的可能需求量有关。

■ 任何在试点生产期间生产的未向食品零售商售出的蛋糕将被作为动物饲料售出。

■ 为了便于分析，我们假设所有根据合同购买的樱桃将被用来生产有机樱桃蛋糕，并预期所有的蛋糕将被出售给我们的食品零售商客户。有机樱桃蛋糕的保质期是 5 周。

	合同A	合同B	合同C	合同D
需求量（单元）	毛利 （B$ 000）	毛利 （B$ 000）	毛利 （B$ 000）	毛利 （B$ 000）
480 000	152	300	522	744
240 000	152	300	126	(48)
160 000	152	36	(138)	(312)

请回复 Tim Walker 的邮件。

Variant 5 Suggested Answers

Section 1

Environmental Quality Costing Report

The Reasons why Management Awareness of the Environmental Impact of First Class Bakery Is Important

Just like Universal Foods, the vast majority of organisations are now recognising that awareness of the environmental impact and management of environmental costs are important for long-term survival.

The need to demonstrate effective environmental management has become a necessity in order to maintain a good public image. Organisations which are perceived by the public as lacking concern for the environment, can considerably weaken their position in their market place. The example of The Foods R Us Manufacturing Group which was subject to a heavy fine for failing to comply with environmental legislation and received a significant amount of adverse publicity is highly relevant in this respect. If we are to continue to develop our own brand presence, it is vital that we are perceived to be environmentally aware in order to maintain a good public image.

In the food and beverage industry, there are a significant number of regulations regarding treatment of waste. It is important that management are aware of situations where First Class Bakery might be in breach or close to breaching regulation so that corrective measures can be taken to avoid penalty.

There has been a significant increase in customers' needs and concerns relating to the environment health as evidenced by our most recent customer survey. This applies equally to our actual customers (who are mostly food retailers) but also to their customers who are the ultimate consumers. Very often customers are willing to pay more for products of organisations who promote their concern for the protection and maintenance of the environment, which means the potential to increase margins. Alternatively if our customers (especially our larger food retailer customers) switches to more environmentally aware manufacturers, a loss in revenue and profit will happen.

First Class Bakery needs to be able to manage the risk and potential impact of an environmental disaster as this also could damage our reputation. We should ensure that environmental considerations are part of capital investment decisions and that we are aware of how we might cause damage to the environment so that we can put measures in place to manage or mitigate it.

First Class Bakery can achieve significant cost savings through improved use of scarce resources such as fuel and water, leading to increased profits.

Classification of Environmental Quality Costs (Environmental Costs)

Environmental Prevention Costs

Environmental prevention costs are those costs associated with preventing adverse environmental impacts. Examples relevant to First Class Bakery are as follows.

- The costs incurred (largely management time) in the creation and maintenance of our environmental policy aimed at reducing the likelihood of adverse environmental impacts occurring.
- The costs incurred in the evaluation of potential suppliers in order to establish the extent of their "environmental concern".

Environmental Appraisal Costs

Environmental appraisal costs are the costs of those activities undertaken in order to determine whether products, services and activities are in compliance with environmental policies and standards. Examples relevant to First Class Bakery are as follows.

- Monitoring, testing and inspection costs incurred in order to ensure adherence to standards and internal policies.
- The costs incurred in monitoring supplier performance in relation to their environmental impact.

Environmental Internal Failure Costs

These are costs that are incurred after hazardous materials, waste or other contaminants have been produced. The costs are incurred in order to comply with both externally and internally imposed standards in order to eliminate the environmental impact. These costs are borne exclusively by the business. Examples relevant to First Class Bakery are as follows.

- The costs of recycling and disposing of waste. Packaging from raw materials is usually recycled by the supplier and most of our production waste is sent to local farms as pig feed. However, a small about of waste does exist for which we pay a charge to dispose of it. This charge is an internal failure cost.
- Any offset costs, for example, the trees are planted to offset the damage caused by the construction of additional buildings.

Environmental External Failure Costs

These are incurred when there are failures of internal control and hazardous materials, waste or contaminants have been introduced into the environment.

Examples relevant to First Class Bakery are as follows.

- Carbon emissions from our ageing vehicle fleet which affect our reputation with the ultimate consumers.
- Potential lost goodwill as a result of us being deselected by customers causing a reduction in turnover and profit.

Section 2

The Impact on the Financial Statements of the Additional Expenditure of B$125,000on the Delivery Fleet

The additional expenditure of B$125,000 constitutes subsequent expenditure on the fleet and therefore we need to look at the rules in IAS 16 PPE to see how this should be treated.

IAS 16 states that subsequent expenditure on an asset (in this case is our delivery vehicles) can only be capitalised if any of the following conditions are met.

- The expenditure improves the economic benefit associated with the asset. This is not the case here because the expenditure does not increase the life of the delivery vehicles or the capacity of the delivery vehicles in any way. It simply allows the vehicles to meet government new legislation and will stop First Class Bakery being fined for non-compliance.
- The expenditure replaces a component of the asset where the carrying amount of

the component replaced has been separately recognised. Again this does not apply here. The B$ 125,000 will be spent on changing parts of the engine and exhaust system; the whole engine will not be replaced.

- The expenditure relates to a major inspection for faults and the cost of the previous inspection was capitalised. Again this does not apply because the expenditure of B$ 125,000 is not an inspection cost.

To conclude, this additional expenditure does not meet any of the conditions in IAS 16 for the subsequent expenditure to be capitalised. As a result, this cost would need to be written off to profit or loss when incurred.

The Potential Benefits of Outsourcing Our Entire Outbound Logistics Function

Purchasing Benefits from Economies of Scale

BeeHaulage purchase thousands of vehicles each year and should be able to get substantial discounts from manufacturers. This means that their cost of operation is likely to be lower than ours and some of this benefit may be passed on to us.

Predictable Costs

Currently, the cost of running the delivery fleet is variable and a little unpredictable, especially in relation to fuel prices. Unpredictability is further compounded by the fact that our vehicles are ageing and are becoming less reliable, requiring increasing levels of maintenance. If we were to outsource then delivery costs would be detailed in a service level agreement (SLA) and this means that we would be able to budget delivery costs with far greater accuracy.

Reduced Overhead Costs — Garage and Purchasing

The overhead costs associated with the garage and maintenance employees will be saved as a result of outsourcing. There may also be an opportunity for realising income from the sale of the garage site. It is located in a residential area with no room for expansion and severe parking congestion. It may be possible to sell the garage for residential development for a significant amount. Alternatively we could use the premises in order to expand our manufacturing capacity and avoid any associated acquisition costs of such land.

Concentration on Core Business

The management of delivery function is not a core strategic requirement for First Class

Bakery. It must consume some elements of senior management time. Outsourcing frees up that time so it can be used to focus on issues directly relevant to the customers and the business of the bakery itself, especially plans for product development and profit growth.

The Potential Drawbacks from Outsourcing Our Outbound Logistics Function

Depression of Morale

As a result of outsourcing, we will need to make drivers and garage staff redundant. This will obviously have a cost implication in the short term, but might also damage the morale of our remaining workforce and the erosion of our organisational culture which has been a significant factor in our success in recent years.

Loss of Control

Outsourcing means that we will no longer have direct control over the delivery function. The responsibility for delivery will rest with BeeHaulage and we will potentially have little input into decisions regarding delivery time-slots. We also lose the interface with our customers.

Finality of Decision

Once the service has been outsourced, it may be difficult in operational terms to take back in-house at a later date due to a loss of in-house expertise. If BeeHaulage doesn't perform as they should, alternative hauliers would be available, but there would be a significant amount of time and resource needed to set this up.

Transaction Costs

These would arise as a consequence of the effort put into the specification of the service level required, coordinating delivery and monitoring of the quality levels provided by BeeHaulage.

Risk of Loss of Confidential Information

There is the risk that confidential information about First Class Bakery ends up in the "wrong hands". For example, sales information is obtained by a competitor.

Section 3

The Reward Scheme

The purpose of the reward scheme is to improve performance by linking performance to rewards in a clearly defined manner. Performance incentives may result in our staff focusing their efforts and attention on improving their own performance which, in turn, should lead to improved organisational performance. While the recent employee survey indicates that employee motivation and satisfaction appear to be high, it might well be the case that these levels increase upon the introduction of a well-constructed reward scheme.

In a commercial organisation such as ours, the long-term goal is maximising shareholder wealth and this means making long-term profits. It follows that the reward must, in the long-term, generate more benefit than it costs. The aims of a reward system should consider motivation of all staff. In particular the scheme should encourage desirable behaviour and recognise that different employees will be motivated by different factors.

Any reward scheme implemented within First Class Bakery should meet the following conditions.

- Be transparent. It must be clear and widely publicised. The criteria for rewards and the scale of rewards for different levels of performance must be clearly stated.
- Be attractive so that the appropriate calibre of employee is initially recruited and subsequently retained. A reward scheme can be made attractive in a variety of ways: financial reward in the form of bonuses or pay rises, non-financial reward in the form of for example health benefits, or job promotion.
- Provide a fair and consistent basis for motivating and rewarding individuals and should be perceived as equitable by all employees. It is therefore important that any reward scheme implemented is not seen to reward managers more favourably than other employees.
- Reward good performance, for example by promotion through developed career pathways. In this respect, we should acknowledge that non-cash rewards might sometimes be intangible in nature but nevertheless effective. For example, certain members of our staff would value recognition for good work, even if this does not involve a payment being made to them. The ability to earn 'credits' towards future promotion would also be a potentially powerful incentive.
- Give recognition to factors other than job performance, such as the level of responsibility or additional tasks of the jobholder.

- Assist management in the control of employee costs as a consequence of a more stable work force due to lower levels of staff turnover.
- Assist the organisation to achieve its goals as a result of improved employee commitment and motivation.
- Be flexible in order to deal with abnormal events that were not anticipated by the original scheme specification. Again, this must be transparent and must not permit any management patronage.
- Ensure that rewards comply with legal regulations, for example, the employment laws which include minimum pay and equal pay legislation to ensure that no groups are prejudiced against.

Implications for the Financial Statements

It is expected that we will sell our delivery fleet early in 2017 and so at the year end of 31 December 2016 we will still own the fleet.

Currently the fleet is included within non-current assets at cost less accumulated depreciation. This is the correct treatment on the basis that the business uses the delivery fleet to generate economic benefit. However, on 31 December 2016 we will no longer be using the fleet as we will be using our outsource partner for all deliveries. Therefore it is not appropriate to include the fleet as part of our PPE on that day, as these assets will not be used to generate future economic benefit for the business.

IFRS 5 Non-current Assets Held for Sale and Discontinued Operations, specifically deals with this situation, where an asset is no longer used by the business.

IFRS 5 states that where an assets carrying amount will be recovered principally from a sale transaction rather than its continuing use, then it should be shown separately on the face of the statement of financial position. This is clearly the case here as we expect to sell the fleet early in 2017.

Further there are a number of conditions that all need to be met in order to apply IFRS 5 in this situation, all of which we are likely to meet by the year-end. At the year-end, the delivery vehicles will be available for immediate sale in their present condition, the sale will be highly probable (there is already a buying in the pipe-line); a reasonable price will have been set (this has already been discussed with the buyer); the sale will be completed within 12 months from the date of classification (the sale will occur in January or February, clearly within 12 months).

At the year-end therefore we should show the delivery fleet as non-current assets held for sale. This will need to be disclosed separately on the face of the statement of financial position. We will need to effect this reclassification at the date that the decision was made to sell the fleet. Therefore we will need to depreciate the fleet up until the date of that decision to determine its carrying value on that date.

What we will then need to do is to carrying out an impairment test. If the carrying value of the fleet (after the depreciation charge) is higher than its fair value less costs to sell (which is the selling price that we will have agreed by then less any legal or other costs of selling), then we will need to record an impairment loss. This impairment loss will reduce profit.

To conclude, at 31 December 2016, the delivery fleet should be categorised as non-current assets held for sale and shown on the statement of financial position separately at a value which is the lower of carrying value and the net proceeds that we will expect to generate from the sale. No depreciation will be charged from the date that the asset was reclassified.

Section 4

From: Management Accountant Assistant
To: Tim Walker, Finance Manager
Subject: New cake opportunity

Interpretation of the Pay-off Table

The pay-off table shows a measure of the value or "pay-off" of each possible outcome in terms of the decision facing the directors.

A pay-off table can be a useful way to represent and analyse a scenario where there is a range of possible outcomes and a variety of possible responses. A pay-off table illustrates all possible gains/losses and as such is often used in decision-making under conditions of uncertainty.

In our case, there are four possible purchase levels for cherries from TOCC and there are three possible levels of demand from the customers. The pay-off table shows the level of contribution that would be earned by First Class Bakery as a result of entering each of the alternative contracts depending on the level of demand from customers.

The level of contribution would vary according to the contract size chosen. The price of organic cherries reduces as the contract size increases and therefore the contribution per cake would increase.

In situations where the contract size is greater than the level of customer demand then surplus cakes will be sold to local farmers.

The value of the table is very much dependent on the accuracy of the market research that has been undertaken.

Explanation of Maximax, Maximin and Minimax Regret

Maximax Approach

The Maximax rule to decision making involves selecting the decision option that would maximise the maximum pay-off potentially achievable. It is based on the assumption that the best pay-off will occur. This approach to decision making would be appropriate for a decision maker who has an optimistic approach to decision making and is prepared to select the decision option that would yield the best results if the most beneficial decision outcome were to occur. Under the Maximax decision criterion, contract D would be selected since it might result in the highest possible contribution of B$744,000.

Maximin Approach

The Maximin approach to decision-making involves choosing the decision option that would maximise the minimum "pay-off" achievable. The Maximin criterion is the opposite of the Maximax rule. The assumption underlying the Maximin criterion is that the worst possible outcome will always occur and therefore the decision maker should select the largest payoff under this assumption. This approach is appropriate for a decision maker who wishes to achieve the best outcome when the worst happen.

Applying a Maximin approach to this decision would result in the selection of contract A under which 160, 000 cakes worth of organic cherries would be supplied. Only contracts A and B if selected, would always result in a positive contribution when demand is based on the worst possibility.

Minimax Regret

The Minimax regret decision criterion is the one that would minimise the maximum regret on the part of the decision-maker. This decision strategy is useful when probabilities for decision outcomes are not available and/or where the decision maker wishes to avoid making a bad decision. "Regret" in this context could be regarded as the opportunity loss incurred as a result of making a less than optimal decision.

Applying a minimax regret approach, the smallest of the maximum regret will be under contract C at B$ 290,000. Therefore in order to minimise the maximum regret, contract C, would be chosen under which 360,000 cakes worth of organic cherries would be supplied.

Explanation of the Use of Expected Values in Managerial Decision-making

Expected Values

The expected value is calculated by weighting each of the contribution levels by its associated probability. The sum of these weighted amounts is called the expected value of the probability distribution. In other words, the expected value is the weighted arithmetic mean of the possible outcomes.

Potential Benefits

- Expected values are associated with risk neutrality and consider the probability of each possible outcome.
- The decision information is reduced and it's represented by a single number that facilitates decision making.
- The calculations are relatively straightforward.

Potential Problems

- The probabilities used are usually very subjective because two individuals will not necessarily assign the same probabilities to a particular outcome.
- The expected value is merely a weighted average and therefore has little relevance for a one-off decision.
- The expected value does not necessarily correspond to any of the actual possible outcomes as in this decision.

Thanks!

Management Accountant Assistant

First Class Bakery

试卷五　参考答案

任务一

环境质量成本报告

为什么提高至臻糕点公司管理层的环境意识非常重要

如通用食品公司一样，目前绝大多数企业都认为管理层的环境意识和环境成本管理对企业的长期发展非常重要。为了维护良好的社会形象，企业必须证明其有效的环境管理能力。被社会公众认定为没有环境意识的企业将会逐渐丧失市场地位。曾经因违反环境法规遭受大额罚款和大量负面报道的 R Us 食品制造集团就是很好的例证。如果我们想继续发展至臻糕点这个品牌，那么向社会公众证明我们具有环境意识，并树立良好的社会形象就至关重要。

有许多关于食品和饮品行业废料处理的法律法规。因此，至臻糕点公司管理层要对企业违反了或者将要违反这些法规的情况保持警觉，并采取合理的措施避免罚款。

最近的客户调查显示，客户对环境健康的需求与关心大幅增加，这一现象适用于我们的现有客户（大都是食品零售商）以及他们的客户，也就是最终消费者。客户愿意为那些保护环境的企业产品支付更高的价格，因此这些企业有增加毛利的潜力。如果我们的客户（尤其是大型食品零售客户）转到环境意识更强的制造商那里，我们的收入和利润就会降低。

至臻糕点公司要能够管理环境灾难的风险和潜在影响，因为它会破坏公司的声誉。我们要保证在做出资本投资决策时考虑到其对环境的影响，也要意识到我们哪些行为可能会破坏环境，并采取措施去管理或降低这个风险。

至臻糕点公司可以通过提高对燃料、水等稀缺资源的有效利用节约成本，从而增加利润。

环境质量成本（环境成本）分类

环境预防成本

环境预防成本指与防止产生负面环境影响相关的成本。至臻糕点公司中发生的环境预防成本主要有以下两种。

- 建立和维护降低发生负面环境影响可能性的政策所产生的成本（大多数为管理时

间）。

- 为评估潜在供应商“关心环境”的程度而产生的成本。

环境鉴定成本

环境鉴定成本指确定企业的产品、服务、相关活动是否遵守环境政策法规所引发的成本。至臻糕点公司中产生的环境鉴定成本主要有以下两种。

- 保证遵守环境政策法规和公司内部政策引发的监督、检查、测试成本。
- 监督供应商的环境影响所产生的成本。

环境内部失败成本

环境内部失败成本指危害物、废料或其他污染物产生后引发的成本。主要是为了降低对环境的影响，遵守企业内外政策法规而产生的成本，这些成本只能由企业来承担。至臻糕点公司产生的环境内部失败成本主要有以下两种。

- 回收利用和处置废料的成本。供应商会回收原料的包装，而大部分生产废料将送往当地农场用作猪饲料，但是，确实有少量废料需要我们出资处理，这项花费就是内部失败成本。
- 一些抵销费用。例如：种树以降低施工建设引起的环境破坏。

环境外部失败成本

环境外部失败成本指当内部控制失效，危害物、废料以及其他污染物影响外部环境时产生的成本。至臻糕点公司发生的外部失败成本有以下两种。

- 陈旧运输车队的高碳排放会影响公司在最终消费者中的声誉。
- 客户拒绝公司产品引起的潜在商誉下降，并由此导致的产品周转和利润下降。

任务二

支付 B$ 125 000 改造运输车队对财务报表的影响

用于改造运输车队的 B$ 125 000 被视为后续支出，因此，我们需要查阅国际会计准则第 16 号固定资产，确定此项后续支出的账务处理。

国际会计准则第 16 号规定，资产（本例中是运输车辆）的后续支出满足以下三个条件中的任何一个即可资本化。

- 支出提高了资产相关的经济利益。本例并不适用这一条件，因为支出并没有延长车辆的使用寿命或者提高其运输能力，仅仅是使车辆满足政府最新的政策法规，防止至臻糕点公司因违反规定受到罚款。
- 支出用于更换资产的组成部分，且被替换部分的账面价值已被单独确认。本例同样不适用这一条件。B$ 125 000 的支出只用作更换引擎和排气系统的一部分，并没有更换整个引擎。
- 支出用于故障的重大检查，并且以前的检查成本已被资本化。本例也不适用这一条件，支出的 B$ 125 000 并不是检查成本。

总之，此项支出并不满足任何国际会计准则第 16 号中后续支出的资本化条件。因此，此项支出应于发生时计入损益。

整体外包配送物流部门的潜在好处

源自规模经济的购置利益

BeeHaulage 每年购置数千辆车，因此能从制造商处获得巨大购买折扣。这意味着它的经营成本比我们低，我们因此可以获得一部分经济利益。

成本可预见

目前，车队的经营成本多变，不可预测，燃油价格尤为如此。并且，我们的车辆陈旧，可靠性下降，需要进行更多的维修，这一事实更加剧了成本的不可预测性。如果我们外包出去，运输费用将会在服务协议中详细写明，这也就意味着我们能更准确地预算运输成本。

降低间接费用——车库和购置

外包会降低与车库和维修人员相关的间接费用，还可能会增加来自车库出售的收益。这个车库位于居民区，交通拥堵严重，没有扩建的空间，可被出售用于居民住宅开发，从而获得巨额收益。我们也可以把这块土地用于生产扩建，避免产生新购置土地的成本。

集中于核心业务

运输部门的管理并不是至臻糕点公司的核心战略需求，它肯定会消耗高层管理者一部分时间。外包会消除这部分时间消耗，从而集中精力于与客户和面包直接相关的问题上，尤其是制订关于产品开发和利润增长的计划。

整体外包配送物流部门的潜在缺陷

降低员工士气

外包会导致我们的司机和车库员工被解雇。短期内显然会发生解雇成本，还可能会影响到在职员工的士气，瓦解企业的组织文化，而组织文化是近几年企业成功的关键因素之一。

失去控制

外包意味着我们失去了对运输部门的直接控制，运输工作完全依赖 BeeHaulage。很少参与运输时间安排的决策会使我们失去与客户的接触和交流。

决策的终局性

一旦将物流配送部门外包出去，就会由于失去内行专长人员，很难再将其作为一个内部部门来运营。如果 BeeHaulage 做得不够好，我们就需要花费很多时间和资源去寻找新的服务商。

交易成本

外包需要我们花费很多精力去规定服务水准、协调运输服务，以及监督 BeeHaulage 的服务质量，这就产生了交易成本。

商业机密泄露的风险

至臻糕点公司的商业机密可能会落入他人之手，比如销售信息被竞争对手获取。

任务三

薪酬激励体系

薪酬激励体系的目的在于通过一种清晰定义的方式将员工薪酬与业绩挂钩，从而促使员工提高业绩。在薪酬激励下，员工会集中精力努力提高个人业绩，进而提高公司业绩。最近的员工调查显示，员工的积极性和满意度都很高，这可能是因为我们新引进的薪酬激励体系架构合理的缘故。

在我们这样的商业化组织里，长期目标就是实现股东财富最大化，也就是要实现长期盈利。长远来看，薪酬体系所带来的经济利益要大于它的成本。设计薪酬体系时要考虑到所有员工的积极性，意识到不同的员工被不同的因素激励，尤其要鼓励出企业想看到的员工行为。

至臻糕点公司的薪酬激励体系应该做到以下几点。

- 透明度高，必须标准清晰并公开宣传。要详细说明不同业绩水平的薪酬等级和标准。
- 有足够的吸引力，能够招募到高素质员工并留住这些人才。有多种方式使得薪酬体系富有吸引力，例如津贴或加薪形式的物质性报酬，还有健康福利、职务晋升等非物质性报酬。

- 公平并一贯地激励和奖励每一位员工，让所有员工感到人人平等。因此，薪酬激励体系不能看起来对管理者有偏向，这一点很重要。
- 奖励好的业绩，例如提供成熟的职业晋升通道。我们要认识到，虽然非现金奖励是无形的，但往往很有效。例如，很多员工很重视领导对自己工作的认可，即使并未获得物质奖励。为未来的晋升赚取"荣誉"是强有力的激励。
- 重视除工作业绩外的其他因素。例如：责任心，员工的加班意识。
- 帮助管理层减少员工流失，稳定员工队伍，从而降低员工成本。
- 提高员工认可度，有效激励员工，帮助企业实现组织目标。
- 灵活应对企业计划外的特殊事项。这也要透明，不允许偏袒管理层。
- 保证薪酬制度符合法律法规。例如：遵从劳动法规定的最低工资制和同工同酬制，保证所有群体得到公平对待。

对财务报表的影响

我们计划于2017年年初出售车队，因此在2016年12月31日之前我们仍拥有车队的所有权。

目前这个车队在报表中列示为非流动资产，列示金额是成本扣除累计折旧。基于公司将持续使用此车队并获取经济利益，该处理是正确的。但是在2016年12月31日，公司已经决定由外包服务商提供运输服务，不再使用自己的车队。因此，仍将其作为固定资产列示是不合适的，因为车队已经不能给公司带来经济利益收入。

国际财务报告准则第5号持有待售的非流动资产和终止经营专门处理企业不再使用某项资产这种情形。

国际财务报告准则第5号规定，如果资产的账面价值主要通过出售而不是持续使用获得，则该项资产应该单独列示在资产负债表中。我们预计2017年年初出售车队就符合这种情形。

应用国际财务报告准则第5号的条件在2016年年底都能得到满足。在2016年年底，车队达到了可供出售的状态，出售交易很可能会发生（已经有买卖正在进行）；已经设定了合理价格（已经和买方协商一致）；自划分之日起12个月内完成出售交易（将于2017年1月或2月出售，肯定在12个月内）。

因此，在2016年年底，我们应该将车队列示为持有待售非流动资产，并在资产负债表中单独记录。只有到正式决定出售车队时才能重分类，因此对车队的折旧需要做到这个决策出台时为止，以确定车队的账面金额。

接下来我们要做的是减值测试。如果车队的账面价值（扣除折旧后）高于公允价值减去处置费用（也就是未来销售价格减去法律费用或其他销售费用），我们就需要确认减值失败，减值失败会降低利润。

总之，在2016年年底，我们需要在资产负债表上将车队单独列示为持有待售非流动资产，列示金额为账面价值和预计出售净收入中的较低者。自重分类日起停止计提折旧。

任务四

发件人：管理会计助理

收件人：财务经理 Tim Walker

主题：新蛋糕的机会

支付矩阵解读

支付矩阵是描述管理者面临决策选择时每一种可能结果的支付值。

支付矩阵可以有效分析有一系列可能结果和反应的情形，可以阐述不确定情况下决策选择的各种可能收益和失败。

在这个案例中，至臻糕点公司从TOCC购置樱桃生产蛋糕的数量有四种可能情况，客户需要蛋糕的需求量有三种情况。支付矩阵展示了樱桃蛋糕生产量和客户需求量组合下的至臻糕点公司可得收益。

贡献水平随购置数量变化而变化。随着购置数量增加，有机樱桃的价格会下降，每个蛋糕的贡献就会增加。

如果生产量大于客户需求量，多余的蛋糕就出售给当地的农民。

这个支付矩阵的价值很大程度上取决于市场调研的准确性。

最大最大决策法、最大最小收益法、最小最大后悔值法解读

最大最大决策法

最大最大决策法原则指找出每种选择下的最大可能支付，然后从中选择最大值，这一方法假设最大支付一定会发生。这一原则适用于乐观的决策者，他们选择在最有利的情况下能带来最好结果的方案。在最大最大值决策法标准下，选择合同D能带来最大B$ 744 000的潜在贡献。

最大最小收益法

决策中最大最小收益法找出每种选择下的最小可能支付，从中选择最大值，即选择

最小值中最大的方案。与最大最大决策法相反，它假设最坏的结果会发生，因此选择该种情形下的最大支付。这种方法适用于在最坏情形下得到最大收益的决策者。

在最大最小收益法下，我们会选择合同 A，供应 160 000 个有机樱桃蛋糕。在 160 000的最小需求下，只有选择合同 A 和 B 才能得到正贡献。

最小最大后悔值法

最小最大后悔值法选择最大后悔值中的最小值。这种方法适用于无法预计决策结果的发生概率，且/或决策者想避免做出坏决策的情况。这里的“后悔值”代表没做出最好决策的机会成本。

在最小最大后悔值法下，合同 C 的最大后悔值中的最小是 B$ 290 000。因此，为了最小化最大后悔值，应选择合同 C，供应 360 000 个有机樱桃蛋糕。

管理层决策中期望值的使用解读

期望值

期望值是贡献值和发生概率的加权平均数。这些加权数的总和就是概率分布下的期望值。换句话说，期望值就是各种可能结果的算术加权平均数。

潜在好处

- 期望值和风险中立相联系，它考虑了各种可能结果发生的概率。
- 决策信息简化并由一个数字代表，有利于决策制定。
- 计算相对简单。

潜在弊端

- 结果发生概率的确定非常主观。不同的人对同一结果发生的概率有不同的判断。
- 期望值仅仅是加权平均数，在一次性决策中参考意义不大。
- 期望值并非和实际可能发生的各种决策结果相一致。

感谢！

至臻糕点公司
管理会计助理

Variant 5　Marking Guidance

Section	Technical skills		Business skills		People skills		Leadership skills		Integration	Total
1	Environmental cost reporting	22							3	25
2	Accounting for subsequent expenditure on PPE	9	Benefits and drawbacks of outsourcing outbound logistics	16						25
3	Impact on the financial statements of selling the delivery fleet	13			The purposes and factors to consider when implementing a reward scheme	12				25
4	Interpretation of a pay-off table and the decision criteria Explanation of expected value and its benefits and problems	19					Application of maximax, maximin and minimax regret decision criteria	6		25
Total marks available for each competency		63		16		12		6	3	100

试卷五　评分指南

部分	技术技能		商业技能		人际技能		领导技能		综合能力	总计
1	环境成本报告	22							3	25
2	固定资产后续支出的会计处理	9	外包配送物流部门的好处与问题	16						25
3	出售车队对财务报表的影响	13			实施薪酬激励体系的目的与需要考虑的因素	12				25
4	解释支付矩阵和决策标准 解释期望值并说明其好处与存在问题	19					最大最大决策法、最大最小收益法和最小最大后悔值法的决策规则应用	6		25
各技能评分合计		63		16		12		6	3	100

中南财经政法大学名师解惑

本套题目的案例主体是至臻糕点公司，共四个任务，涉及 E1，P1 和 F1 的知识点。分别是：企业环境意识的重要性，企业流程外包的优缺点和薪酬体系的设计（E1）；环境成本的分类，管理层决策时期望值的运用，支付矩阵的含义以及最大最大决策法、最大最小收益法、最小最大后悔值法的运用（P1）；国际会计准则第 16 号固定资产后续支出资本化的条件，国际财务报告准则第 5 号中重分类为持有待售资产的条件和重分类后的账务处理及其在报表中的记录（F1）。

其中 P1（47）的知识点分数比重最高，其次是 E1（28），最后则是 F1（22）。这和 OCS 的考纲要求基本一致。该试卷考核了考生的四项能力，其中技术技能的分值占 63%，商业技能的分值占 16%，人际技能的分值占 12%，领导技能的分值占 6%，与 CGMA 管理会计能力框架的技能要求一致。考生在备考时应根据考试重点有所侧重。另外的 3 分是考查综合能力的，可能是对不同模块或不同能力的整合。这些得分点嵌在任务里，完成任务时能满足要求，就能得分。

该试卷的每项任务涉及以下知识点：

任务	问题	科目	知识点
任务一	认识环境对经营的影响 环境成本分类及举例	P1	环境对经营的影响（environmental impact of the business） 环境成本（environmental cost）
任务二	对车队后续支出的处理方式如何影响财务报表 运输服务外包的好处和问题	F1 E1	固定资产的后续支出（subsequent expenditure on fixed assets） 外包（outsourcing）
任务三	制定新的薪酬激励体系的考虑因素 出售运输车队对财务报表的影响	E1 F1	薪酬激励体系（reward scheme ） 出售资产对财务报表的影响（impact on the financial statements of selling fixed assets）.
任务四	解释支付矩阵 解释不确定性决策标准，评论风险态度及可能采纳的合同 解释期望值并说明其好处与存在问题	P1	支付矩阵（payoff matrix） 最大最大决策法（maximax），最大最小收益法（maximin）和最小最大后悔值法（minimax regret decision criteria） 期望值（expected value）

上述各项任务要求以邮件、报告或工作笔记等形式来呈现答案，对问题的描述非常明确，答题时既要注意内容的针对性，也要注意形式的规范性。

对应知识点深度剖析

环境意识——认识环境对经营的影响的重要性

在背景资料中有相关的环境问题的信息，例如食品加工过程中的环境污染问题和政府的立法等。要结合社会环境意识加强的背景，从正反两面论述，即重视环境问题的好处和不重视的可能后果。在回答时，要把背景信息融入答案中，提出具体方案，如有效利用能源和水资源等，减少生产对环境的影响。

环境成本分类及举例

环境质量成本的分类参照质量成本的分类法。考生要解释每一类别的含义，并结合公司背景举出适当的例子。例子需要突出的是环境质量成本，而不仅仅是质量成本。

对车队的后续支出方式对财务报表的影响

本题考查考生对国际会计准则第16号的理解程度和应用能力。要完整地阐述资产后续支出资本化的三个条件，并逐条对照判断本例中运输车辆的支出是否符合条件，解释判断依据。例如，支出是否带来经济利益？为什么需要增加支出？如果是为了达到立法要求，那么对于资产寿命和运输能力的改善就没有影响，所以没有带来经济利益，就不符合资本化条件的第一条。考生应逐条对照后依次做出判断。本例中三个条件都不满足，所以不能资本化。

运输服务外包的好处和问题

外包业务的好处和问题在大纲和教材中均有详细介绍。考生需要结合运输车队外包，对比自营对于公司的好处和不足来阐述。

考生注意事项

要熟读预览材料和题目，善于从中搜集有价值的信息，便于答题时为己所用。答题时要将课本上的知识点与案例分析结合起来，切记不能抛开案例罗列知识点，分析要条理清晰，有理有据。例如，题目中要求分析整体外包配送物流部门的优缺点，我们要首先回顾教材中关于企业流程外包的优点和缺点，列出答题的提纲，然后结合预览材料和题干中的信息，将知识点和案例资料结合起来作答。备考过程中，考生在充分掌握教材知识点的基础上应多做练习题，并通过题目提高知识点的运用能力，也可通过关注财经新闻报道提高实战能力。

制定新的薪酬激励体系的考虑因素

首先要阐述薪酬激励体系的作用，再进一步阐述需要考虑的因素，避免漏答。分析考虑因素时切记要结合案例，不要泛泛而谈。

出售运输车队对财务报表的影响

本题涉及国际财务报告准则第 5 号持有待售非流动资产的相关知识。答题时不仅要描述准则的规定，同时要结合案例来分析。例如，“出售业务将在 12 个月内完成”这条标准，就需要提到案例中业务的预计完成时间是在 1 月或 2 月，符合标准。

解释支付矩阵

这是一个容易漏答的问题。至少要提到，有 4 个采购价格各不相同的合同可供考虑，而需求存在 3 种可能，从而使决策存在不确定性。而每个单元格的数值，代表的是在各种可能的需求条件下 4 个采购合同各自的贡献值。另外还可以提到，市场需求是管理者无法控制的，需要决定的是采用哪个合同。提到“采购价格将影响贡献值”等都可以得到一些分数。

解释不确定性决策标准，评论风险态度及可能选择的合同

回答这个问题必须描述出最大最大决策法、最大最小收益法和最小最大后悔值法的决策标准，以及不同标准所对应的风险态度。同时结合案例，分析按各个标准判断时的决策结果分别是什么。

解释期望值，分析其好处与问题

此题需要解释期望值的含义，同时说明其好处和问题。特别注意要完整回答，不要漏答。好处是考虑了概率，但实际结果不一定与期望值一致。

考生注意事项

当考题涉及 F1 的某经济业务的会计处理问题时，答题思路基本类似：

（1）确定经济业务适用的准则条款；（2）完整准确地描述准则的规定标准；（3）结合案例对照分析是否符合标准；（4）最终得出结论。

案例二

CASE 2

桑切斯·纳瓦娜公司

SANCHEZ NAVARRA

Background Materials

Introduction

Sanchez Navarra is a company which manufactures and sells a range of luxury bath and body products. It is located in Keyland, a major developed economy which has the K$ as its currency.

All manufacturing is undertaken at the company's only production facility in the capital city of Keyland. The site where the production facility is located also includes a large warehouse for the storage of inventory and various offices where the directors and management are based. Currently there are three products: body wash, body lotion and hand & foot cream. Each of these products is manufactured in each of Sanchez Navarra's 10 unique fragrances.

Sanchez Navarra's products are seen by consumers as high quality and luxurious meaning that they are sold at a premium price compared to other bath and body products available in the market. They are currently sold in Keyland through a network of concession stands within major department store chains, on-line through the company website and in five Sanchez Navarra stores located throughout the country. Sanchez Navarra's products are not currently sold outside of Keyland.

The company was founded 16 years ago by Freda Jones and Nisha Shah, two friends from University with a passion for luxury bath and body products. With the help of bank loans and venture capital equity finance, Freda and Nisha have been able to grow the business. For the year ended 31 December 2015 its revenue was over K$31 million.

At the start of 2016, the venture capital investors sold their 30% of the equity holding in Sanchez Navarra to the TRU Group, a large multi-national group. At the same time Freda and Nisha each sold 15% of the equity stake in the business to the TRU Group. As a result, TRU Group now owns 60% of the equity of Sanchez Navarra, with the remaining 40% owned equally between Freda and Nisha.

Freda and Nisha both believe that becoming a subsidiary of TRU Group will lead to expansion on an international stage, given that TRU Group has subsidiaries which operate in over 50 countries.

You work in the finance department of Sanchez Navarra as a finance officer.

News Article about the Acquisition of Sanchez Navarra by the TRU Group

TRU Group Acquire a Controlling Stake in Keyland's Favourite Luxury Bath Products Business

15 January 2016　　James Retallack

It was announced yesterday that multi-national consumer products business TRU Group has acquired a controlling stake in one of Keyland's luxury bath and body products companies, Sanchez Navarra.

TRU Group has over 80 subsidiaries throughout the world. Over half of the subsidiaries are engaged in the beauty and hair care industry and the manufacture of luxury consumables. Sanchez Navarra is its first acquisition in Keyland. There are rumours that other beauty and hair care product manufacturers in Keyland are being targeted.

Nisha Shah, one of the original founders of Sanchez Navarra, said: "This acquisition makes perfect sense to Freda Jones, my co-founder, and me. We need to expand overseas and to develop new product ranges, which will be a whole lot easier with the backing, contacts and experience of TRU Group. Freda and I still have an equity stake in the business and we are going to be left to continue to run the business with TRU Group support, the best of both worlds!"

Three Extracts from Sanchez Navarra's Website

Extract 1 Welcome Message from the Sanchez Navarra Founders Hello from Nisha and Freda

Welcome to Sanchez Navarra. We met over 20 years ago at University, when Nisha was studying chemistry and Freda was studying business. Despite our different academic passions we were kindred spirits. Neither of us were ever really satisfied with the bath and body products we tried and often talked about developing our own. In our final year at university, we decided that may combine our chemistry and business skills and we should set up our own business, which is why Sanchez Navarra was born 16 years ago.

Freda Jones Nisha Shah

Our goals have been simple.

- To develop a body wash which foamed really well, did what it needed to in terms of cleansing, but which also smelled amazing: a smell that should stay on the body as long as possible.
- To develop a body lotion with great absorption properties and which not only hydrated the skin but also left it feeling silky smooth and loved.
- To use natural products as much as possible and to ensure that the fragrances we used were sourced sustainably.

The result of all of our work is the Sanchez Navarra range that you see today. We have body wash, body lotion and hand & foot cream in each of our 10 unique fragrances: emerald, ruby, sapphire, topaz, diamond, amber, jade, garnet, amethyst and opal. We here at Sanchez Navarra truly love all of our products and we're confident that you will too!

Nisha Shah　　　　　　Freda Jones
Managing Director　　　Finance Director

Extract 2　The Story so Far

Sanchez Navarra: The story so far...

2000	Sanchez Navarra is born. We start developing our luxurious body wash and body lotion base and the quest for unusual fragrances using combinations of natural spices, peppers, flowers and plants starts in earnest
2002	We secure our first contract with the major department store chain,Hawkins. We start with 15 concession stands in Hawkins' stores across Keyland selling body wash and body lotion in four fragrances: emerald, ruby, sapphire and topaz
2005	We secure a second contract with the major department store chain,Gamells.We also extend the number of concessions stands with Hawkins and launch our new fragrances: diamond and amber
2008	We open our first Sanchez Navarra store in the capital of Keyland to celebrate the launch of our next two fragrances: jade and garnet. We refresh our packaging design and improve the bases for both body wash and body lotion
2011	With the help of venture capital funding, we launch our own website based online-sales service direct to customers. We also significantly expand our production facility and launch our very rich and subsequently award winning hand & foot cream
2012	Our final two fragrances are launched: amethyst and opal. We open another four of our own stores in the major cities of Keyland
2014	We win the right to use the prestigious "Made in Keyland" label on all of our products. Only 20% of our competitors have the right to use this label
2016	As a result of our venture capital partners wishing to realise their investment, 60% of the business is acquired by the TRU Group, giving us access to new markets and product opportunities

Extract 3　Meet the Directors

Nisha Shah, Managing Director 	Nisha co-founded Sanchez Navarra soon after completing her university degree in chemistry. She has a keen interest in maintaining and enhancing the luxurious qualities of the products and heads up a small but dedicated product development team. Nisha spends a lot of time travelling the world looking for new but sustainable natural ingredients, either for use in the base product or for a new fragrance.
Freda Jones, Finance Director 	Freda co-founded Sanchez Navarra soon after completing her university degree in business. She has a keen interest in all aspects of business and finance and has completed qualifications in HR management. She also has a passion for fragrance and is always involved in the development of new fragrances. Although not a qualified accountant, Freda heads up the finance team. She is the liaison with the bank and was until recently the liaison with our venture capital providers.

Tomaz Green, Operations Director 	Tomaz has a post-graduate degree in chemistry and before joining Sanchez Navarra seven years ago worked for a major manufacturer of bath and body products. Tomaz has a keen interest in product and production quality and is a qualified quality standards inspector. Tomaz is responsible for the operation of the production facility.
Richard Procter, Sales & Marketing Director 	Richard is an experienced marketer and joined Sanchez Navarra very recently having worked for a major retailer before. Richard has been instrumental in Sanchez Navarra being awarded the right to use the "Made in Keyland" label. He is passionate about extending sales beyond Keyland. Richard is responsible for the sales and marketing functions of the business. He heads up the sales force.

Extracts from Sanchez Navarra's Production Employee Handbook

Products

We manufacture three products: body wash, body lotion and hand & foot cream. Each of our products is manufactured in each of our 10 unique fragrances.

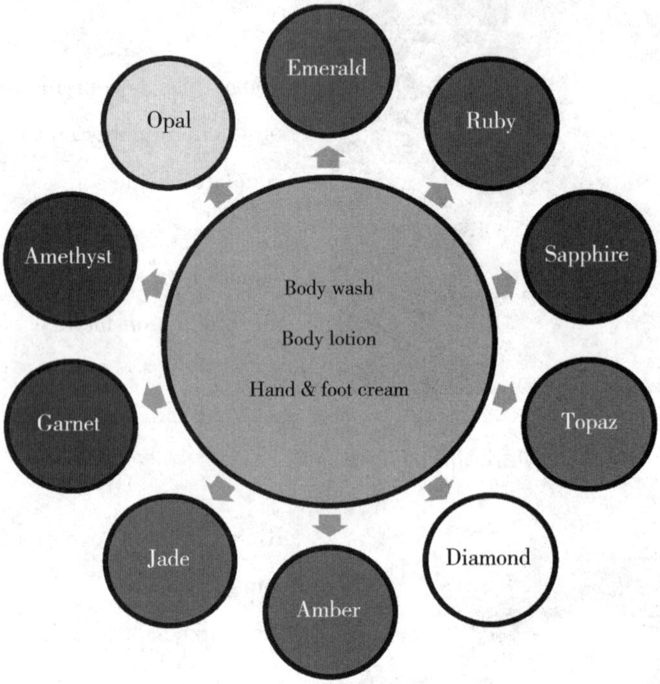

We aim to use at least 70% natural materials in our base products and to limit the use of synthetic compounds. Each fragrance is developed to utilise natural spices, peppers, salts, flowers and plant derived essential oils. We formulate our fragrances to have a long lasting effect on the body after use.

The Production Process

The production process for all of our products is essentially same: water based and oil based raw materials are initially mixed in a large mixing tank, which are then fed into a larger mixing tank where an emulsion is formed. After quality checking the contents of the larger mixing tank are fed into the mechanised bottling line. Please see diagram overleaf for an overview of this process.

Each of our products (body wash, body lotion and hand & foot cream) uses a different combination of raw materials which effectively create the base un-fragranced product. As we use different raw materials, the timings of each stage in the process and the temperature the product is heated to differs depending on whether it is body wash, body lotion or hand & foot cream.

The ingredients which create each of our unique fragrances are added to the process at different stages, depending on what the ingredient is. Therefore, only one fragrance at a time can be produced.

There are two production lines on site. One is exclusively used for the production of body wash, the other for the production of both body lotion and hand & foot cream. Once a production run is completed, a team of quality controllers check the quality of the end products. Once these checks are completed, the product is accepted and is bottled. The bottling line is mechanised and bottles are either 250 mL or 100 mL. The same shape plastic bottle is used for each product and each has a pump top added automatically by the bottling line.

At the end of the bottling line, the 250 mL finished products are packaged into cardboard boxes, with 200 bottles in each. These are then stored in the warehouse: some in the dedicated on-line sales area and the rest in another area ready to despatch to stores and concession stands.

The 100 mL bottles are packaged into cardboard boxes and moved to a separate area in the warehouse. There a small team of people assemble the gift sets. Either five or ten bottles of different products and fragrances are placed into gift bags, which are then put into a plastic bag to protect the gift bag and boxed up ready for despatch.

Overview diagram of the production process：

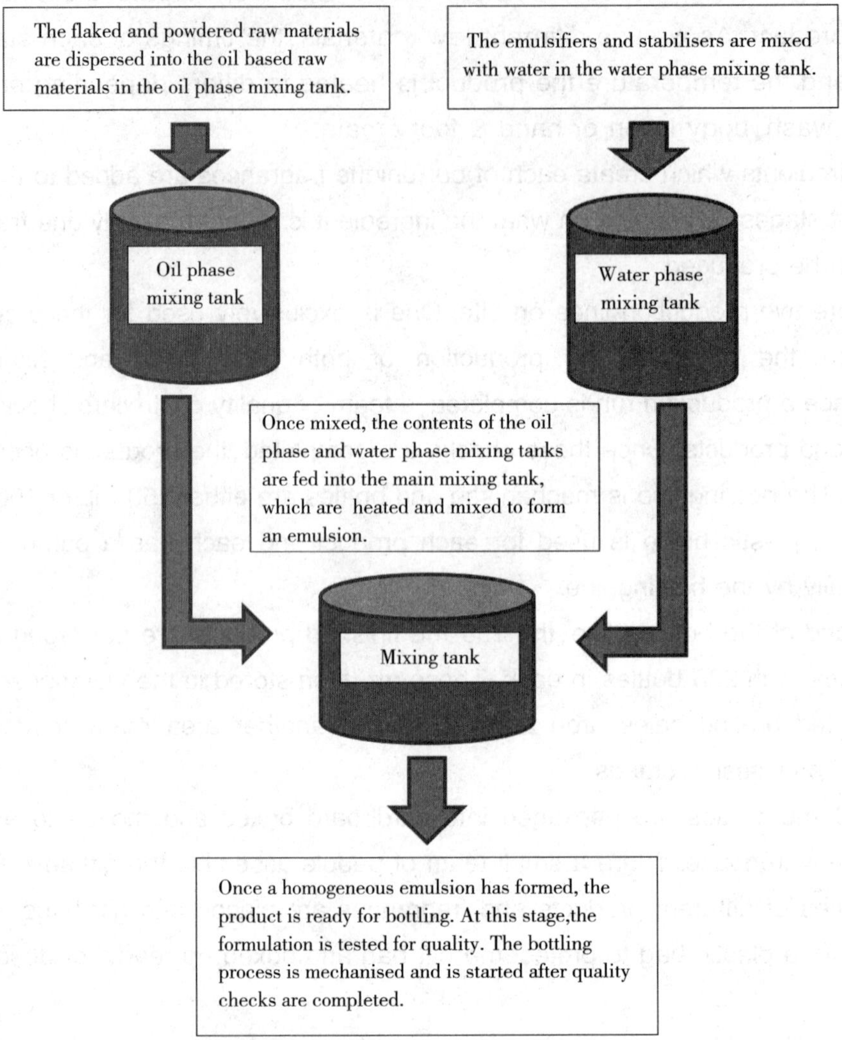

Key Raw Materials

Raw material	Explanation
Water	Water is a key element of all of our products. We have our own water purification system, which draws water from the main water supply and feeds it into water phase mixing tank
Surfactants	Surfactant is an ingredient which lowers the surface tension between two different compounds (which could be two different liquids or a liquid and a solid). Surfactants give cleansing and emulsifying properties to our products We use a number of different surfactants most of which are derived from vegetable fatty acids. Most of the surfactants we use are derived from coconut or soy bean oil
Emollients	Emollient is an ingredient with moisturising and conditioning properties. We aim to use natural emollients as many as possible and therefore use vegetable glycerine, aloe vera and jojoba based emollients in our products
Preservatives	Preservatives are necessary to ensure that the quality of our products is maintained after sale to the end consumer
Vitamins	We add Vitamin E to our hand & foot cream for its nourishing properties
Essential oils	A range of essential oils are used for their cleansing, nourishing and fragrance properties. Our essential oils are from all over the world
Other fragrance ingredients	To create our 10 unique fragrances we use a range of other ingredients including spices, peppers and flower and plant extracts

Employees

Organisation chart—key employees:

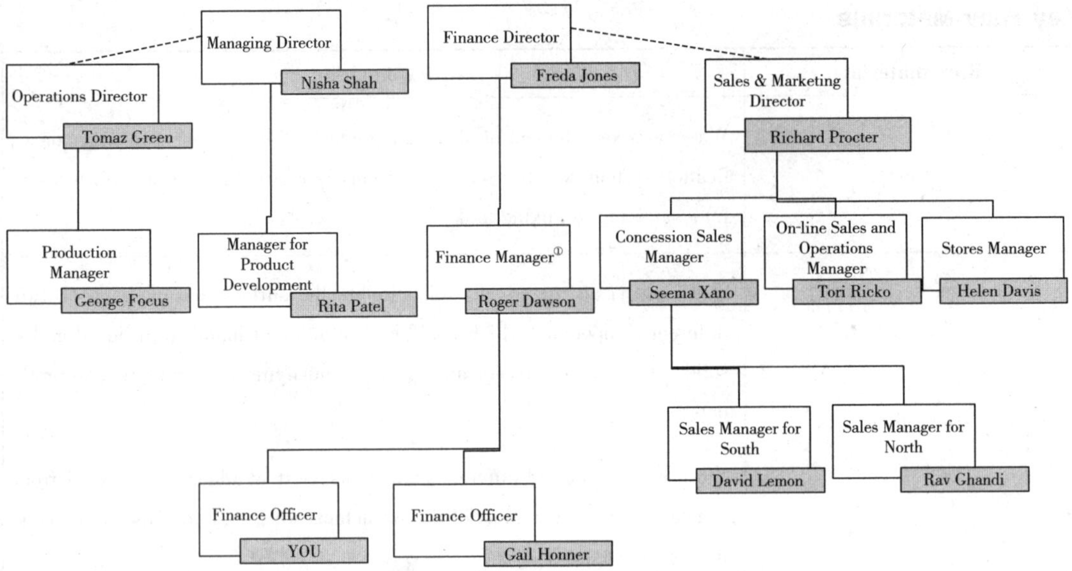

①The finance manager is a qualified accountant who has worked at Sanchez Navarra for over 10 years.

Break-down of Employee Numbers

	Number
Production	72
Selling and distribution	214
Administration	11
	297

Sales Channels and Pricing Strategy

Sales Channels

Sanchez Navarra currently sells its products in Keyland only.

Concession Stands in Department Stores

Sanchez Navarra has arrangements to run concession stands in two of Keyland's major department store chains. There are currently 120 concessions stands operating in a number of towns and cities across Keyland. Sales at concession stands account for approximately 70% by value of all of Sanchez Navarra's sales.

A concession effectively means that Sanchez Navarra rents a space in the department store to sell its products. The sales people on the concession stands are Sanchez Navarra employees and any specialised shelving or display equipment is supplied by Sanchez Navarra(the department store provides basic shelving and storage facilities for inventory).

When a sale is made to a consumer, it is initially recorded as a department store sale and the monies are paid over to the department store. In the month following the sale at the concession stand, the department store pays over the monies collected from customers(net of the rent due) to Sanchez Navarra.

On-line Sales through the Sanchez Navarra Website

Approximately 25% by value of all of Sanchez Navarra's sales are now made directly to the consumer through the company website. The website has been praised for being easy to use and in customer satisfaction surveys the company always scores highly in terms of promptness of delivery and quality of product.

There is a dedicated team of sales people who manage on-line sales ard are based in an office next to the warehouse. When a order is received, a picking list is created and sent to the warehouse. Within the warehouse there are two employees who deal exclusively with this list, picking and packaging the goods ordered ready for despatch. courier service is used for despatching on-line orders and this is organised by the on-line sales team.

Sales through Sanchez Navarra Stores

Sanchez Navarra operates five of its own retail stores. These are located in major cities within Keyland. Three of the stores are owned by the company and two are rented. The three stores that are owned are in prime real estate areas and since purchased their value has increased significantly. The directors decided to buy these stores rather than rent them as a form of investing surplus cash that was in the business. Approximately 5% by value of Sanchez Navarra's sales are through their own retail stores.

Pricing Strategy

The three products, body wash, body lotion and hand & foot cream, have recommended retail prices of K$ 12. 50, K$ 15. 00 and K$ 15. 00 respectively. This recommended retail price is the same irrespective of the fragrance. Each of the sales managers(see organisation chart) has the authority to reduce this recommended retail price at the point of sale in their region by up to 30%. This can be applied across all fragrances and all products or can be used on individual fragrances and products.

Extracts from the Financial Statements for the Year to 31 December 2015

Statement of Profit or Loss

	2015 (K$000)	2014 (K$000)
Revenue	31,300	29,690
Cost of sales	(10,642)	(9,800)
Gross profit	20,658	19,890
Distribution and selling costs	(15,153)	(14,245)
Administrative expenses	(3,300)	(3,250)
Finance costs	(15)	(15)
Profit before tax	2,190	2,380
Tax	(504)	(540)
Profit for the year	1,686	1,840

Statement of Financial Position

	2015 (K$000)	2015 (K$000)	2014 (K$000)	2014 (K$000)
Assets				
Non-current assets				
PPE		3,240		3,100
Current assets				
Inventories	6,030		5,500	
Trade and other receivables	1,950		1,880	
Cash and cash equivalents	517		345	
		8,497		7,725
Total assets		11,737		10,825
Equity and liabilities				
Ordinary share capital issued		5		5
Retained earnings		8,996		8,510
Revaluation reserve		772		320

（续表）

	2015 (K$000)	2015 (K$000)	2014 (K$000)	2014 (K$000)
Total equity		9,773		8,835
Non-current liabilities				
Bank loan		250		250
Current liabilities				
Trade and other payables	1,210		1,200	
Tax payable	504		540	
		1,714		1,740
Total equity and liabilities		11,737		10,825

Statement of Cash Flows

	(K$000)	(K$000)
Cash flows from operating activities		
Profit before tax	2,190	
Adjustments		
Depreciation	368	
Finance costs	15	
		2,573
Movements in working capital		
Increase in inventories	(530)	
Increase in trade and other receivables	(70)	
Increase in trade payables	10	
		(590)
Cash generated from operations		1,983
Tax paid	(540)	
Finance costs paid	(15)	
		(555)
Net cash from operating activities		1,428
Cash flows from investing activities		
Purchase of property, plant and equipment	(56)	
Net cash from investing activities		(56)

（续表）

	(K$000)	(K$000)
Cash flows from financing activities		
Dividend paid	(1,200)	
Net cash from financing activities		(1,200)
Net increase in cash and cash equivalents		172
Cash and cash equivalents at the beginning of the year		345
Cash and cash equivalents at the end of the year		517

Notes on preparation of financial statements:

(1) Cost of sales includes only the costs of producing the products. All distribution and selling costs are included below gross profit.

(2) Property is revalued every three years by a professional valuer.

Budget Information

Budgeted Sales for the Year Ended 31 December 2016

Standard sized 250 mL bottles:

	Body wash	Body lotion	Hand & foot cream	Total
Sales quantity	1,300,000	710,000	290,000	2,300,000
Sales price(K$)	12.50	15.00	15.00	
Sales(K$)	16,250,000	10,650,000	4,350,000	31,250,000

Gift sets(containing either 5 or 10,100mL bottles):

	Gift set1 500 mL	Gift set2 1,000 mL	Total
Sales quantity	50,000	35,000	85,000
Sales price(K$)	40.00	75.00	
Sales(K$)	2,000,000	2,625,000	4,625,000

The budgeted sales figures above are based on the full recommended retail price of each product.

Costings

Sanchez Navarra uses a standard costing approach for monitoring performance. For each fragrance of each product a standard cost card record is maintained, which is updated annually.

Standard cost card for a 250 mL bottle of product for the cheapest fragrance to produce, Opal is as follows:

Standard production costs for a 250 mL bottle of Opal	Body wash (K$)	Body lotion (K$)	Hand & foot cream (K$)
Raw materials (excluding fragrance ingredients)	0.58	1.20	1.40
Fragrance ingredients	0.18	0.18	0.18
Bottle and packaging	0.52	0.52	0.52
Production labour	0.46	0.62	0.95
Variable production overhead	0.35	0.47	0.72
Fixed production overhead	0.31	0.41	0.63
Total production cost	2.40	3.40	4.40

Standard cost card for a 250 mL bottle of product for the most expensive fragrance to produce, Diamond is as follows:

Standard production costs for a 250 mL bottle of Diamond	Body wash (K$)	Body lotion (K$)	Hand & foot cream (K$)
Raw materials (excluding fragrance ingredients)	0.58	1.20	1.40
Fragrance ingredients	1.95	1.95	1.95
Bottle and packaging	0.52	0.52	0.52
Production labour	0.76	0.91	1.24
Variable production overhead	0.58	0.70	0.95
Fixed production overhead	0.51	0.62	0.84
Total production cost	4.90	5.90	6.90

The differences in standard production cost between fragrances arise from：

(1) the fragrance ingredient costs；

(2) the time required to manufacture a product of the fragrance (usually the more expensive fragrance ingredients the longer it takes to dissolve). This results in different standard production labour costs. In addition because variable production overheads and fixed production overheads are based on direct labour hours, this also changes.

Each month, two types of variance report are produced by the finance team.

(1) A detailed sales variance report for each of the sales managers.

(2) A reconciliation between the actual cost of production and the standard cost of the actual level of production. This is prepared for the production manager.

The sales managers and the production manager are responsible for preparing a commentary about their variances, which is discussed at the monthly directors' meeting.

Schedule of Standard Gross Profit per Product for 250mL Bottles

Body wash	Selling price① (K$)	Production cost (K$)	Gross profit (K$)
Emerald	12. 50	3. 75	8. 75
Ruby	12. 50	4. 20	8. 30
Sapphire	12. 50	4. 75	7. 75
Topaz	12. 50	2. 60	9. 90
Diamond	12. 50	4. 90	7. 60
Amber	12. 50	4. 35	8. 15
Jade	12. 50	3. 60	8. 90
Garnet	12. 50	4. 10	8. 40
Amethyst	12. 50	3. 80	8. 70
Opal	12. 50	2. 40	10. 10

Body lotion	Selling price[①] (K$)	Production cost (K$)	Gross profit (K$)
Emerald	15.00	4.75	10.25
Ruby	15.00	5.20	9.80
Sapphire	15.00	5.75	9.25
Topaz	15.00	3.60	11.40
Diamond	15.00	5.90	9.10
Amber	15.00	5.35	9.65
Jade	15.00	4.60	10.40
Garnet	15.00	5.10	9.90
Amethyst	15.00	4.80	10.20
Opal	15.00	3.40	11.60

Hand & foot cream	Selling price[①] (K$)	Production cost (K$)	Gross profit (K$)
Emerald	15.00	5.75	9.25
Ruby	15.00	6.20	8.80
Sapphire	15.00	6.75	8.25
Topaz	15.00	4.60	10.40
Diamond	15.00	6.90	8.10
Amber	15.00	6.35	8.65
Jade	15.00	5.60	9.40
Garnet	15.00	6.10	8.90
Amethyst	15.00	5.80	9.20
Opal	15.00	4.40	10.60

① Standard selling price is the full recommended retail price. The standard production cost includes absorbed fixed production overhead.

Industry Information

The bath and body products industry in Keyland generated revenue of K$ 12,000 million in 2015, which is growing at around 2% a year.

It is dominated by three large manufacturers who account for around 92% of all sales by volume and 75% of all sales by value. These large manufacturers focus on bath and body products for everyday use with an average price per product of K$ 3.00.

The remaining 8% by volume of the market is made up of around 100 manufacturers who differentiate themselves on the basis of luxuriousness, natural ingredient quality, organic properties or a combination of these. Sanchez Navarra is one of these manufacturers. The average retail price for these products is K$ 12. 00, which is why this part of the market accounts for 25% of the market's revenue by value. This part of the market is growing at around 5% a year by value.

Tax Regime in Keyland

Corporate Profits

- The corporate tax to be applied to taxable profits is 25%.
- Unless otherwise stated below, accounting rules on recognition and measurement are followed for tax purposes.
- The following expenses are not allowable for tax purposes:
  —accounting depreciation;
  —amortisation;
  —entertaining expenditure;
  —donations to political parties;
  —taxes paid to other public bodies.
- Tax depreciation allowances are available on items of plant and machinery (including vehicles used for business purposes) at a rate of 25% per year on a reducing balance basis.
- Tax losses can be carried forward indefinitely to offset against future taxable profits from the same business.
- A company is deemed to be resident in Keyland if it has its principal place of management there. A resident company will pay Keyland corporate tax on all of its profit irrespective of which country in which the profit is earned. Sanchez Navarra is resident in Keyland.
- Where a resident company in Keyland owns a subsidiary company which is resident in another country, any dividends paid by that subsidiary to the parent company will be treated as income of the parent company and will be taxed at the corporate tax rate.
- Double taxation treaties exist with a number of other countries. All of these treaties give relief for double taxation in respect of any withholding and underlying tax suffered on dividends received. Relief is available using the tax credit method.

背景材料

介绍

桑切斯·纳瓦娜公司是一家生产和销售高档沐浴和护肤产品系列的公司，位于 Keyland（基兰德）境内。该国是一个主要的发达经济体，以 K\$ [①]为货币。

该公司的所有生产工作只在位于 Keyland 首都的唯一生产工场进行，同一地点还设有一个用于存储货物的大型仓库以及董事会和管理机构。目前，该公司主要生产 3 类产品：沐浴露、润肤乳、手足霜。每类产品具有 10 种香型，均为桑切斯·纳瓦娜公司所特有。

桑切斯·纳瓦娜公司的产品被消费者视为高质和高档产品，这意味着与市场上其他沐浴和护肤产品相比，该公司可以以更高的价格出售产品。目前，这些产品在 Keyland 境内销售，销售渠道主要是连锁百货公司的特许柜台、公司网站的在线销售以及散布在 Keyland 境内的 5 家专卖店。当前，桑切斯·纳瓦娜公司的产品还未在 Keyland 境外销售。

该公司是由 Freda Jones（弗蕾达·琼斯）和 Nisha Shah（妮莎·沙）在 16 年前创立的，她们二人在大学时期就开始热衷于高档的沐浴和护肤产品。在银行贷款和风险资本股权融资的帮助下，Freda Jones 和 Nisha Shah 得以开创她们的事业。截至 2015 年 12 月 31 日，公司的收入超过了 K\$ 3 100 万。

2016 年初，风险资本投资者将持有的桑切斯·纳瓦娜公司 30% 的股权出售给了一个大型跨国集团——TRU 集团。与此同时，Freda 和 Nisha 分别将持有的 15% 股权出售给了该集团。至此，TRU 集团已拥有桑切斯·纳瓦娜公司 60% 的股权，剩下 40% 的股权则由 Freda 和 Nisha 各持一半。

Freda 和 Nisha 都认为让桑切斯·纳瓦娜公司成为 TRU 集团的子公司将有利于她们

① 此处及下文出现的“K\$”，均指 Keyland 当地货币，该货币为虚拟货币。

开拓国际市场，因为TRU集团旗下的子公司遍布全球50多个国家。

你在桑切斯·纳瓦娜公司的财务部工作，是一名财务主管。

TRU集团收购桑切斯·纳瓦娜公司的新闻报道

TRU集团收购了Keyland最受欢迎的高档沐浴产品企业并获控股权

2016年1月15日　　James Retallack（詹姆斯·雷特兰克）

昨天，消费品跨国企业TRU集团宣布其收购了Keyland高档沐浴及护肤产品公司之一的桑切斯·纳瓦娜公司并获得控股权。

TRU集团拥有80多家子公司，遍布世界各地。超过一半的子公司从事美容和护发产业，以及高档消费品的生产。桑切斯·纳瓦娜公司是TRU集团在Keyland境内收购的第一家公司。有传言称，Keyland境内的其他美容美发产品制造企业也将成为其收购对象。

Nisha Shah是桑切斯·纳瓦娜公司的创始人之一，她谈道："这次收购对我和公司联合创始人Freda Jones而言意义非凡。我们需要拓展海外市场和开发新的产品系列，而在TRU集团的支持下，借助该集团的业务网络和经验，我们将更容易实现这一目标。我和Freda仍然持有公司的股权，将留下来继续经营企业，同时还能得到TRU集团的支持，这真是两全其美！"

桑切斯 · 纳瓦娜公司网站的 3 份摘录

摘录 1　桑切斯 · 纳瓦娜公司创始人的欢迎辞：来自 Nisha 和 Freda 的问候

欢迎来到桑切斯 · 纳瓦娜公司。20 多年前，我们——Nisha 和 Freda 在大学相遇，当时 Nisha 在学习化学专业，而 Freda 在学习商务知识。尽管我们热衷于不同的学科，但我们志趣相投。我们都不曾真正满意过我们使用的沐浴和护肤产品，我们经常谈论怎样开发自己的产品。在大学最后一年，我们认为可以将我们二人所学的化学知识和商业技能结合起来，从而创建属于自己的事业，这就是我们 16 年前创建桑切斯 · 纳瓦娜公司的初衷所在。

我们的目标很简单。

- 开发一种沐浴露，其泡沫丰富、清洁力强、味道迷人，且香味可以尽可能长时间地留在身体上。
- 开发一种吸收性良好的身体乳，其不仅可以让皮肤更加水润光泽，还能让皮肤如丝般光滑，备受呵护。
- 尽可能地使用天然材料，并确保我们所使用的香料可持续采购。

我们所有努力的成果就是你们今天所看到的桑切斯 · 纳瓦娜公司的系列产品。我们开发了沐浴露、润肤乳、手足霜，它们都具有我们公司特有的 10 种香型：祖母绿、红宝石、蓝宝石、黄玉、钻石、琥珀、翡翠、石榴石、紫水晶和蛋白石。我们真切喜爱桑切斯·纳瓦娜公司的所有产品，我们确信你们亦会如此！

Nisha Shah　　　　Freda Jones

总经理　　　　财务总监

摘录2　我们的发展故事

桑切斯·纳瓦娜公司：我们的发展故事……

2000年　桑切斯·纳瓦娜公司诞生。我们开始开发高档沐浴露和润肤乳的基础产品，通过混合天然香料、胡椒、鲜花和植物，努力追求不同寻常的香气

2002年　我们与大型的连锁百货公司Hawkins（霍金斯）签订了第一份合约。我们在 Hawkins遍布Keyland的门店中设立了15个特许销售柜台，出售4种香型的沐浴露和润肤乳：祖母绿、红宝石、蓝宝石和黄玉

2005年　我们与大型公司 Gamells（盖梅尔）签订了第二份合约。此外，我们还增加了Hawkins门店的特许销售柜台，推出了新的香型：钻石和琥珀

2008年　我们在Keyland首都开设了第一家桑切斯·纳瓦娜公司专卖店，以此来庆祝我们另外2种香型的推出：翡翠和石榴石。我们还重新设计了产品包装，改良了沐浴露和润肤乳的基础产品

2011年　在风险资本投资的帮助下，我们推出了基于自有网站的网上销售服务，直接面向客户销售产品。此外，我们还大幅扩建了生产设施，并推出了我们的王牌手足霜——富含滋润物质，曾获大奖

2012年　我们最后两款香型推出：紫水晶和蛋白石。此外，我们在Keyland的主要城市开设了另外4家专卖店

2014年　我们获得了可为我们的所有产品贴上颇具盛名的“Keyland生产”标签的权利。在我们的竞争对手中，只有20%有权使用这一标签

2016年　由于我们的风险资本合作伙伴希望变现他们的投资，TRU集团收购了我们公司 60%的股权。这项收购给予了我们进入新市场和开发新产品的机会

摘录3　高管一览

总经理 Nisha Shah

在完成大学的化学专业学习不久之后，Nisha 就与 Freda 共同创立了桑切斯·纳瓦娜公司。

她对保持和提升产品的奢华品质有着浓厚的兴趣，带领着一支规模不大但全员投入的产品开发团队。

Nisha 花了很多时间奔波于世界各地，寻找新的、可持续获取的天然成分，以用于生产基础产品或开发新香型。

财务总监 Freda Jones

在完成大学的商务专业学习不久之后，Freda 与 Nisha 共同创立了桑切斯·纳瓦娜公司。

她对商业和金融的各个方面都有着浓厚的兴趣，在人力资源管理方面也取得了相应资格。她还喜爱各种香味，经常参与新香型的开发工作。

Freda 虽然不是一个专业的会计师，但由她领导财务团队。她不仅负责与银行的沟通联络工作，还担当着风险资本投资人的联络人，直至最近风险资本退出。

运营总监 Tomaz Green（托马斯·格林）

Tomaz 拥有化学专业的硕士学位，7 年前加入了桑切斯·纳瓦娜公司。在此之前，他曾为一家主要生产沐浴及护肤产品的企业工作。

Tomaz 对产品和产品品质有着浓厚的兴趣，他是一名合格的质量标准检查员。

Tomaz 主要负责生产设施的运行。

市场营销总监 Richard Procter（理查德·普罗克特）

Richard 是一位经验丰富的营销人员，最近才加入桑切斯·纳瓦娜公司。在此之前，他为一家大型零售企业工作。

在桑切斯·纳瓦娜公司获得殊荣使用“Keyland 生产”标签的过程中，Richard 发挥了巨大的作用。他极有工作激情，试图将产品销售扩展到 Keyland 境外。

Richard 主要负责公司销售和市场营销部门的工作，管理销售队伍。

桑切斯 · 纳瓦娜公司生产员工手册的摘录

产品

我们生产 3 种产品：沐浴露、润肤乳和手足霜，每种产品都具备 10 种特有香型。

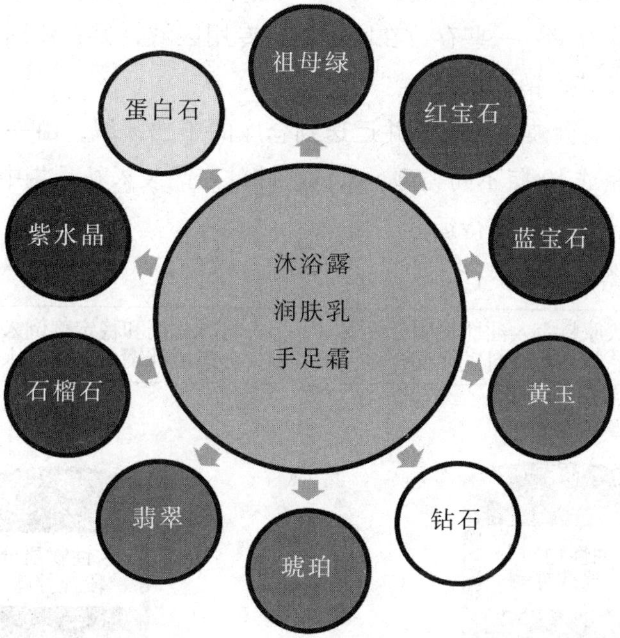

我们的目标是使基础产品中使用的原料至少有 70% 是天然材料，并限制合成化合物的使用。每一种香型都能使用天然香料、胡椒、盐、鲜花和植物所提取的精油进行开发，而香型配方则能够实现使用之后长时间散发香气的效果。

生产流程

我们所有产品的生产流程基本相同：首先，将水性和油性原料在大型搅拌罐中进行混合，然后倒入更大的搅拌罐并形成乳化液。经过质量检查之后，将搅拌罐内的物质倒入机械化灌装设施。生产流程概述请参阅生产流程概览图。

我们每个产品（沐浴露、润肤乳、手足霜）都使用不同的原料组合，能生产出不带香气的基础产品。由于产品所使用的原料的不同，生产流程每个阶段的加工时间以及各个产品的加热温度就因具体的产品类型——沐浴露、润肤乳、手足霜而不同。

形成我们产品独特香味的各种成分，将根据其性质，在生产流程的不同阶段添加到产品中。因此，我们一次只能生产一种香型的产品。

我们拥有两条生产线，一条专门用于生产沐浴露，另一条用于生产润肤乳和手足霜。一旦完成一轮生产，质检人员会查看最终产品的质量。检查合格之后，再接着完成产品的装瓶工作。瓶装线实现了机械化操作，瓶装规格是250毫升或100毫升。每种产品使用相同形状的塑料瓶，瓶装线会自动为瓶子加装按压式瓶盖。

在瓶装线的最后阶段，将250毫升的成品装入纸箱，每箱200瓶。随后，封装完毕的纸箱会被送到仓库存储：一些存放在网上销售专用区域，另一些则存放在其他区域并准备发送到专卖店和特许销售柜台。

100毫升的成品也会被装入纸箱并运送到仓库的单独区域，由一小组员工将其包装成礼品套装。将5瓶或10瓶不同类型、不同香味的产品装入礼品袋中，再在礼品袋外套上塑料袋进行保护，最后装箱待运。

生产流程概览图如下所示：

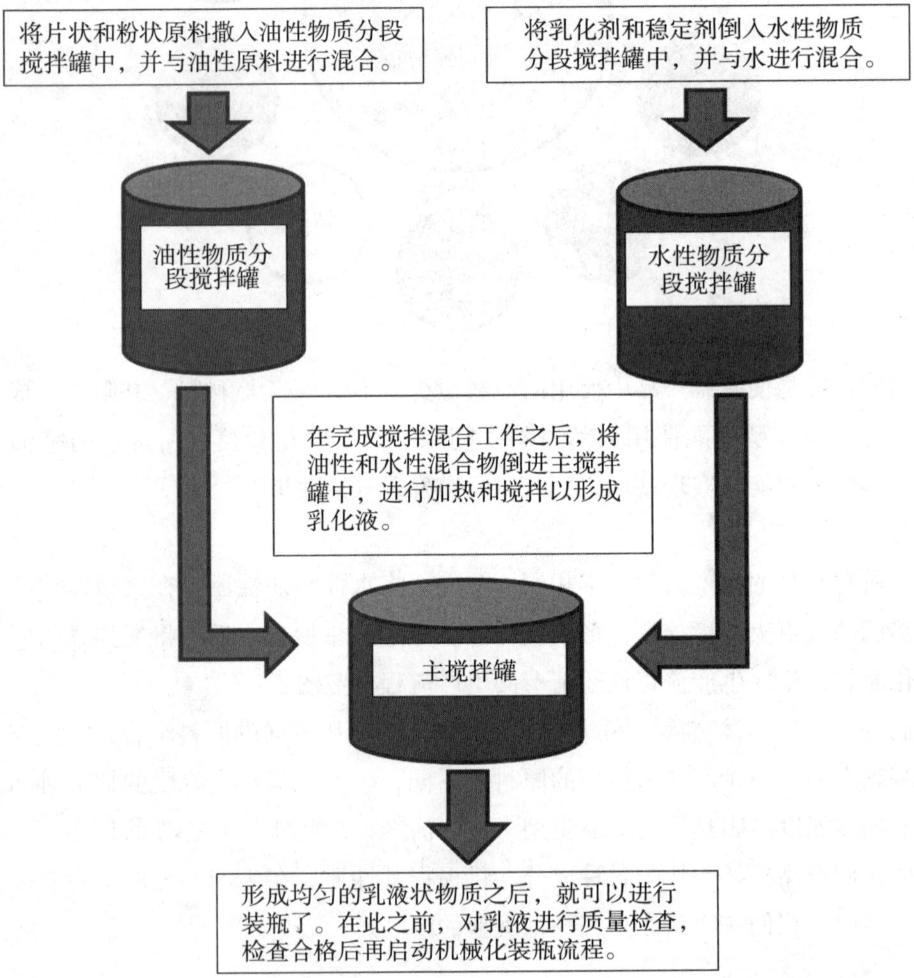

主要原料

原料	说明
水	水是我们所有产品的关键成分之一。我们拥有自己的水净化系统，它将水从主管中抽取出来并注入水性物质分段搅拌罐中
表面活性剂	表面活性剂是一种可以降低两种不同化合物（可能是两种不同的液体，或是一种液体和一种固体）表面张力的成分。表面活性剂能为我们的产品提供清洁和乳化性能 我们使用了许多不同的表面活性剂，其中大部分提取自植物脂肪酸。我们现在所使用的大多数表面活性剂都提取自椰子油或豆油
润肤剂	润肤剂是一种具有保湿和调理功能的成分 我们的目标是尽可能多地使用天然润肤剂，因此，我们产品采用的润肤成分是蔬菜甘油、芦荟和荷荷巴油
防腐剂	防腐剂是必不可少的，它可以确保我们的产品在销售给最终用户之后，质量仍是合格的
维生素	我们在手足霜中添加了维生素 E 以获得滋养性能
精油	我们在产品中使用一些精油以获得清洁、滋养性能并形成香味，而这些精油来自世界各地
其他香味成分	我们使用一些其他香味成分以形成我们产品独有的 10 种香型，其中包括香料、胡椒、鲜花和植物提取物

员工

组织结构图——主要员工：

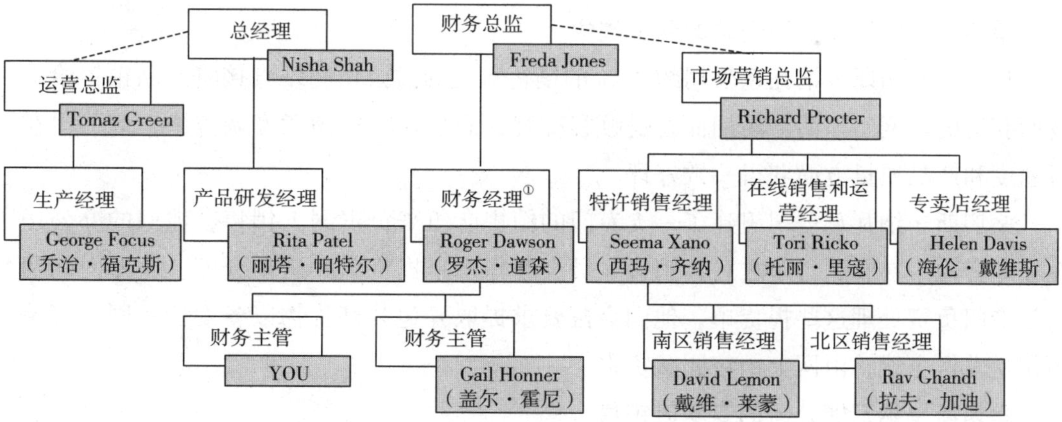

①财务经理是一名合格的会计师，他在桑切斯·纳瓦娜公司工作超过了 10 年。

员工细分

	人数
生产部门	72
销售与配送部门	214
管理部门	11
	297

销售渠道和定价策略

销售渠道

目前，桑切斯·纳瓦娜公司只在 Keyland 境内销售产品。

百货公司的特许柜台销售

桑切斯·纳瓦娜公司与 Keyland 境内的两家主要连锁百货公司签订了特许柜台销售合约。目前，公司在 Keyland 境内的许多城镇里共设立了 120 个特许销售柜台。特许柜台销售额约占桑切斯·纳瓦娜公司所有销售额的 70% 。

特许柜台销售是指桑切斯·纳瓦娜公司在百货公司租赁一个场地以摆放柜台出售产品。特许柜台的销售人员是桑切斯·纳瓦娜公司的员工，任何专用货架或陈列设施均由桑切斯·纳瓦娜公司提供（百货公司提供基本货架和货物的存放场所）。

向消费者售出产品后，交易首先会被记录为百货公司的销售，钱款也会支付给百货公司。在特许销售柜台完成销售交易的一个月后，百货公司会将客户支付的所有销售款项（扣除应付租金之后）转给桑切斯·纳瓦娜公司。

桑切斯·纳瓦娜公司网站的网上销售

目前，桑切斯·纳瓦娜公司约 25% 的销售额是通过公司网站直接将产品销售给消费者而获得的。网站因简洁易用而备受顾客称赞，而且在客户满意度调查中，该公司在交货速度和产品质量方面获得一致好评。

桑切斯·纳瓦娜公司组建了一支专门的销售队伍来负责网上销售，他们的办公场所在仓库旁边。在收到订单之后，销售人员会制作一个提货单并送到仓库。仓库内的两名员工专门负责处理这些提货单，他们会按要求提取并包装好货物以备发货。网上订单采用快递发送方式，由网上销售团队负责。

桑切斯·纳瓦娜公司的专卖店销售

桑切斯·纳瓦娜公司自己经营着 5 家零售专卖店，它们位于 Keyland 境内的主要城市。其中 3 家专卖店属于公司直接所有，另外 2 家专卖店则是租赁的。该公司自有的 3 家专卖店位于房地产黄金区域，自购买以来，其价格已经显著上涨。当初，公司高管决定购买这些专卖店而不是租赁，是想以此作为公司盈余资金的一种投资形式。桑切斯·纳瓦娜公司约 5% 的销售额是通过专卖店实现的。

定价策略

3 种产品——沐浴露、润肤乳和手足霜的建议零售价分别为 K$ 12. 50、K$ 15 和 K$ 15。不论具体香型为何，产品的建议零售价都是相同的。每个销售经理（参见组织结构图）都有权降低其负责区域销售点的建议零售价，最高幅度可达 30% 。这一策略可适用于所有香型和所有产品或个别香型和个别产品。

截至 2015 年 12 月 31 日的年度财务报表摘要

利润表

	2015 年 （K$ 000）	2014 年 （K$ 000）
收入	31 300	29 690
销售成本	（10 642）	（9 800）
毛利润	**20 658**	**19 890**
配送和销售费用	（15 153）	（14 245）
管理费用	（3 300）	（3 250）
财务费用	（15）	（15）
税前利润	**2 190**	**2 380**
税费	（504）	（540）
本年利润	**1 686**	**1 840**

资产负债表

	2015 年 （K$ 000）	2015 年 （K$ 000）	2014 年 （K$ 000）	2014 年 （K$ 000）
资产				
非流动资产				
不动产、厂房及设备		3 240		3 100
流动资产				
存货	6 030		5 500	

（续表）

	2015 年 (K$ 000)	2015 年 (K$ 000)	2014 年 (K$ 000)	2014 年 (K$ 000)
应收账款	1 950		1 880	
现金及现金等价物	517		345	
		8 497		7 725
总资产		11 737		10 825
所有者权益和负债				
发行的普通股本		5		5
留存收益		8 996		8 510
重估准备		772		320
所有者权益总额		9 773		8 835
非流动负债				
银行贷款		250		250
流动负债				
应收账款	1 210		1 200	
应交税费	504		540	
		1 714		1 740
所有者权益和负债总额		11 737		10 825

现金流量表

	(K$ 000)	(K$ 000)
经营活动现金流		
税前利润	2 190	
调整事项		
折旧费用	368	
财务费用	15	
		2 573
营运资金变动		
存货的增加	(530)	
应收账款的增加	(70)	
应付账款的增加	10	
		(590)
经营活动产生的现金流		1 983

（续表）

	(K$000)	(K$000)
已交税费	(540)	
	(15)	
已付财务费用		(555)
		1 428
经营活动产生的净现金流		
投资活动现金流		
购置不动产、厂房和设备	(56)	
投资活动产生的净现金流		(56)
筹资活动现金流		
已付股利	(1 200)	
		(1 200)
筹资活动产生的净现金流		
现金及现金等价物的净增加		172
期初现金及现金等价物		345
期末现金及现金等价物		517

财务报表编写附注：

（1）销售成本仅包括产品的生产成本；所有配送及销售费用均纳入毛利润的计算。

（2）每3年由专业评估师对公司财产进行重新估值。

预算信息

截至2016年12月31日的销售预算

250毫升标准规格：

	沐浴露	润肤乳	手足霜	总计
销售数量（个）	1 300 000	710 000	290 000	2 300 000
销售价格（K$）	12.50	15.00	15.00	
销售额（K$）	16 250 000	10 650 000	4 350 000	31 250 000

礼品套装（含5瓶或10瓶100毫升产品）：

	礼品套装 1 500 毫升	礼品套装 2 1 000 毫升	总计
销售数量（个）	50 000	35 000	85 000
销售价格（K$）	40.00	75.00	
销售额（K$）	2 000 000	2 625 000	4 625 000

上述销售预算数据是根据每个产品的建议零售价的全价计算得出的。

成本核算

桑切斯·纳瓦娜公司使用标准成本法来考查业绩。每种产品的每一香型都建有一个标准成本卡，每年更新一次。

最便宜香型——蛋白石香型 250 毫升产品的标准成本卡如下：

蛋白石香型 250 毫升产品的标准成本卡	沐浴露（K$）	润肤乳（K$）	手足霜（K$）
原材料（不包括香味成分）	0.58	1.20	1.40
香味成分	0.18	0.18	0.18
瓶子和包装材料	0.52	0.52	0.52
生产人工	0.46	0.62	0.95
变动生产费用	0.35	0.47	0.72
固定生产费用	0.31	0.41	0.63
生产总成本	2.40	3.40	4.40

最昂贵香型——钻石香型 250 毫升产品的标准成本卡如下：

钻石香型 250 毫升产品的标准成本	沐浴露（K$）	润肤乳（K$）	手足霜（K$）
原材料（不包括香味成分）	0.58	1.20	1.40
香味成分	1.95	1.95	1.95
瓶子和包装材料	0.52	0.52	0.52
生产人工	0.76	0.91	1.24
变动生产费用	0.58	0.70	0.95
固定生产费用	0.51	0.62	0.84
生产总成本	4.90	5.90	6.90

各香型产品的标准生产成本差异源于以下两个方面。

（1）香味成分的成本。

（2）生产各种香型所需的时间（通常是越昂贵的香料成分需要越长的时间进行分解）。这导致所消耗的标准生产人工成本不同。此外，变动生产费用和固定生产费用是基于直接人工时间的，因此也会有所不同。

每个月，财务团队都会编写两种不同类型的差异报告。

（1）编写详细的销售差异报告并提供给每个销售经理。

（2）编写实际生产成本与实际生产水平标准成本之间的对照报告并提供给生产经理。

销售经理和生产经理负责编写差异分析报告并在每月的董事会上进行讨论。

250 毫升标准瓶装产品的毛利表

沐浴露	售价① （K$）	生产成本（K$）	毛利（K$）
祖母绿	12.50	3.75	8.75
红宝石	12.50	4.20	8.30
蓝宝石	12.50	4.75	7.75
黄　玉	12.50	2.60	9.90
钻　石	12.50	4.90	7.60
琥　珀	12.50	4.35	8.15
翡　翠	12.50	3.60	8.90
石榴石	12.50	4.10	8.40
紫水晶	12.50	3.80	8.70
蛋白石	12.50	2.40	10.10

润肤乳	售价① （K$）	生产成本（K$）	毛利（K$）
祖母绿	15.00	4.75	10.25
红宝石	15.00	5.20	9.80
蓝宝石	15.00	5.75	9.25
黄　玉	15.00	3.60	11.40
钻　石	15.00	5.90	9.10
琥　珀	15.00	5.35	9.65
翡　翠	15.00	4.60	10.40
石榴石	15.00	5.10	9.90
紫水晶	15.00	4.80	10.20
蛋白石	15.00	3.40	11.60

手足霜	售价[①]（K$）	生产成本（K$）	毛利（K$）
祖母绿	15.00	5.75	9.25
红宝石	15.00	6.20	8.80
蓝宝石	15.00	6.75	8.25
黄　玉	15.00	4.60	10.40
钻　石	15.00	6.90	8.10
琥　珀	15.00	6.35	8.65
翡　翠	15.00	5.60	9.40
石榴石	15.00	6.10	8.90
紫水晶	15.00	5.80	9.20
蛋白石	15.00	4.40	10.60

①标准销售价格是指建议零售价格的全价。标准生产成本包括所吸收的固定生产费用。

行业信息

2015 年，Keyland 国内的沐浴及护肤产品行业的收入为 K$ 120 亿，每年约增长 2% 。

这一行业主要被三大生产厂商占据，它们的销售约占行业全部销售量的 92% 以及销售额的 75% 。这些大型生产厂商专注于生产和销售日常的沐浴和护肤用品，每件产品的平均售价为 K$ 3。

余下 8% 的销售量则由 100 家左右的厂商共同分享，它们在产品奢华性、天然成分的质量、产品有机性或组合方面追求差异化。桑切斯 · 纳瓦娜公司就是此类厂商之一。这些产品的平均零售价为 K$ 12，这就是为什么这部分市场能占据行业全部销售额的 25% 。就销售额而言，这部分市场正以每年 5% 左右的速度增长。

Keyland 的税制体系

企业利润

- 企业所得税为应税利润的 25% 。
- 除非另有说明，否则应该从税务的角度出发来执行下列的确认和计量会计规定。
- 以下费用不得税前扣除：

——会计折旧；

——摊销费用；

——文娱开支；

——政党捐款；

——支付给其他公共机构的税费。

- 厂房和机器设备（包括商用车辆）的折旧可以抵税，每年的抵扣率为25%，以其递减余额为基础。
- 可抵税损失可以进行结转，用于抵减同一企业未来的应税利润。
- 判断一个公司是否属于Keyland民营企业的主要依据是这个公司主要管理活动的所在地。Keyland民营企业应就其所有利润向Keyland纳税，而不论其具体利润来自哪个国家。桑切斯·纳瓦娜就属于Keyland的民营企业。
- 如果Keyland民营企业拥有一家子公司，其是另一个国家的民营企业，那么，子公司向总公司发放的任何股利都将被视为总公司的收入，并按企业税率向Keyland缴税。
- Keyland与其他一些国家签订了双重征税协定。所有此类协定围绕的企业所收到的股利涉及的代扣代缴税和股息税，免除双重征税。企业使用税收抵免法可享受这一优惠。

Variant 1

This examination is structured as follows：

Section number	Number of tasks	Time for section(minutes)
1	2	45
2	1	45
3	1	45
4	1	45

The time available for each section is for reading,planning and writing your answer(s).

Please note section 1 consists of two tasks and leave enough time to complete both parts.

Section 1

You arrive at office in the morning and receive the following email from Roger Dawson, finance manager.

From: Roger Dawson, Finance Manager

To: Management Accountant Assistant

Subject: Marginal costing and justification on marketing spend

The directors had a conference call yesterday with Mr C Tan, who is the TRU Group international operations director. They discussed a number of matters and the directors have now asked me to do a couple of things for them.

Firstly, Mr C Tan talked with them about changing from standard absorption costing to standard marginal costing. Apparently, many of the TRU Group subsidiaries use marginal costing and Mr C Tan would like us to as well. The directors have requested a briefing paper on this.

I have prepared a schedule using absorption costing which shows our budgeted gross profit for body wash for the next three months on the basis of what we have scheduled to produce in each month. We need to undertake some maintenance to the body wash production line in June, which means that production will be lower than normal in that month.

I would like you to prepare a briefing paper which explains the impact of marginal costing on our profit and inventory valuation and the benefits and drawbacks to our business if we used it. Please use the schedule that I have prepared to illustrate your explanation. There is no need to perform any calculations at this stage.

Secondly, in the conference call, Mr C Tan raised concerns about the amount that we spend on marketing our products, which in 2015 was 35% of the total spend on selling and distribution. He has therefore asked for a justification of the amount we spend on marketing in relation to the maintenance of our brand. Please prepare the first draft of a briefing paper for Mr C Tan on this matter.

Many thanks!

Roger Dawson

Finance Manager

Sanchez Navarra

Budgeted gross profit for body wash for the next three months based on forecast production levels:

	May(K$000)		June(K$000)		July(K$000)	
Sales		1,375		1,375		1,375
Opening inventory	2,275		2,415		2,240	
Production costs	525		210		385	
Closing inventory	(2,415)		(2,240)		(2,240)	
(Over)/under Absorption of fixed production overhead	(16)		21		0	
		(369)		(406)		(385)
Gross Profit		1,006		969		990

Notes:

(1) Inventory and production costs are valued at a full cost of production of K$3.50 per unit, which represents the weighted average across all body wash fragrances.

(2) Fixed production overheads are absorbed on the basis of 110,000 units of production for each of the months May, June and July. On this basis fixed production Overheads are K$0.41 per unit.

(3) Sales are based on budgeted sales of 110,000 units for each of the months May, June and July, at the recommended retail price of K$12.50 per unit.

Write the briefing paper for the directors on marginal costing.

Write the briefing paper for Mr C Tan on justification of the marketing spend.

Section 2

Three days later, Roger Dawson is on annual leave. Freda Jones, finance director sends you the following email.

From: Freda Jones, Finance Director

To: Management Accountant Assistant

Subject: Financial statement queries and group structure

Mr C Tan has sent a copy of the TRU Group financial control manual to me. This is an internal manual and he is keen that the relevant IFRS are dealt with correctly across the group.

I recently sent him the most recent Sanchez Navarra financial statements for the year ended 31 December 2015. He has come back to me with a couple of queries on them.

- He has asked for an explanation of why there is a revaluation reserve shown in the statement of financial position.
- He also asked why there is such a high receivables balance given that we sell directly to consumers through our concession stands, retail stores and on-line. He would also like to know the reasons why our cash balance at 31 December 2015 was not higher, given the company's profitability.

We are the most recent of a number of acquisitions made by TRU Group which include hygiene and hair care product manufacturers in several locations around the world. As a result, the directors of TRU Group are considering changing the organisational structure from the current geographical divisional structure to either a product based divisional structure or a matrix structure.

Also, in the "open forum" style of management operated by TRU Group, Mr C Tan has asked for our opinion on how both a product based divisional structure and a matrix structure would suit the group's current position and how we would see ourselves fitting in and benefiting from each structure.

Please send me an email with suitable responses that I can send to Mr C Tan in respect of;

- his queries on our financial statements for the year ended 31 December 2015;
- his queries on group structure.

Many thanks!

Freda Jones
Finance Director
Sanchez Navarra

Write the email requested by Freda Jones.

Section 3

It is two months later and Roger Dawson sends you the following email.

From: Roger Dawson, Finance Manager
To: Management Accountant Assistant
Subject: Retail stores

I've just come out of a meeting with the directors about how we might reorganize our sales channels. Richard Procter, sales & marketing director, believes that we should close our own five retail stores and invest instead in the on-line sales business.

He believes that the sales performance of the retail stores is not hitting budget and that the on-line environment is the future. In order for the directors to make a decision about this, I have been asked to prepare a briefing paper on how the retail stores have been performing against the sales budget for the first six months of 2016.

Gail Honner, your fellow finance officer, has produced a schedule of the summarized variances, which is attached. I think that the briefing paper needs to include an explanation of the figures in this schedule, together with any additional factors that the directors should consider when forming a judgment on the performance of the retail stores.

Richard Procter also thinks that we should retrain some staffs of the retail stores to work in the on-line sales office dealing with customers. As a result, the directors have also asked that our briefing paper includes an explanation of the steps that will need to be taken in order for the re-training programme to be effective.

Please prepare the draft of this briefing paper for me.

Many thanks!

Roger Dawson
Finance Manager
Sanchez Navarra

Summary of budgeted sales revenue and sales variances for retail stores for the six months to 30 June 2016:

	Body wash (K$000)	Body lotion (K$000)	Hand & foot cream(K$000)	Gift sets (K$000)	Total (K$000)
Budgeted sales revenue	400	270	105	300	1075
Actual sales revenue	341	300	88	312	1041
sales price variance	47A	75A	32A	0	154A
sales volume contribution variance	9A	76F	10F	5F	82F

A = Adverse, F = Favorable.

Notes:

(1) Budgeted sales are the budgeted volumes multiplied by the recommended retail price for each product.

(2) The budgeted volumes included above for the retail stores are exactly half of the budgeted volumes for the year. The total budgeted volume for the year was equal to the actual volumes sold in the previous year.

(3) The sales price and volume variances for each product are the totals of the individual variances for each fragrance.

(4) The average discount from the recommended retail price given by the retail sales manager, Helen Davis, was 12% for body wash, 20% for body lotion, 27% for hand & foot cream and nil for gift sets.

(5) The sales volume variances are calculated as the difference in volume multiplied by the average standard contribution per unit.

Write the draft of briefing paper requested by Roger Dawson.

Section 4

It is three months later and the directors decided to close the retail stores and to expand the on-line sales operation. There has been considerable unbudgeted expenditure as a result of this, which has resulted in a significant reduction in our cash balance.

You receive the following email from Roger Dawson.

From: Roger Dawson, Finance Manager

To: Management Accountant Assistant

Subject: Budgeting and financial statements

I've just had a conference call with Freda Jones, finance director, and Mr C Tan from TRU Group. Mr C Tan expressed his concern about a lack of accuracy and rigor in the budgeting process and has suggested that we could overcome this with the use of rolling budgets and ZBB.

Freda has asked me to prepare a briefing paper for her regarding the potential introduction of a rolling budget for our cash budget and ZBB for our on-line sales operation budget. I think that the briefing paper should include explanation of each approach together with its benefits to us.

On a slightly separate matter, Freda has also asked me for an explanation of the impact of closing the stores on the financial statements, with regard to the three properties that we own. She is particularly interested whether we should be classifying this as a discontinued activity in accordance with IFRS 5.

Please prepare the first draft of a briefing paper that I can send to Freda regarding both of her requests.

Thank you!

Roger Dawson
Finance Manager
Sanchez Navarra

Write the draft of briefing paper requested by Freda Jones.

试卷一

本次考试的结构如下：

序号	任务数	时间（分钟）
1	2	45
2	1	45
3	1	45
4	1	45

每个部分规定的时间可用于读题、组织和书写答案。

请注意任务一包括两项子任务，需留足时间。

任务一

早上你到办公室时，收到了来自财务经理 Roger Dawson 的邮件。

发件人：财务经理 Roger Dawson

收件人：管理会计助理

主题：营销支出的边际成本和合理性

董事会昨日与 TRU 集团国际业务总监谭先生进行了电话会议。他们讨论了一些问题，现在董事会要求我们做一些事情。

首先，谭先生和他们讨论了将全部成本法改为边际成本法。显然，TRU 集团的许多子公司都在使用边际成本法，谭先生希望我们也这样做。董事会要求我们提供一份关于这方面的简报。

我已经准备了一份使用全部成本法的时间表，它展示了未来 3 个月内根据每月计划生产沐浴露的预算毛利。沐浴露生产线将在 6 月进行一次维修，这意味着该月的产量将会比正常水平低。

我希望你准备一份简报，解释使用边际成本法核算对利润和存货估价的影响，以及对业务产生的影响。请使用我准备的时间表阐明解释，在这个阶段不需要计算。

其次，在电话会议中，谭先生对我们在产品营销方面的支出表示担忧。2015 年，市场营销部的支出约占销售和分销支出总和的 35%，因此，他要求我们对维护品牌而花费在营销上的支出做出解释。请就此事为谭先生准备一份简报文件的初稿。

十分感谢！

桑切斯·纳瓦娜公司
财务经理
Roger Dawson

根据预测的生产水平，预计未来 3 个月沐浴露的毛利润如下表所示：

	5 月（K$000）		6 月（K$000）		7 月（K$000）	
销售额		1 375		1 375		1 375
期初存货	2 275		2 415		2 240	
生产成本	525		210		385	
期末存货	（2 415）		（2 240）		（2 240）	
对固定生产费用的过度分摊（分摊不足）	（16）		21		0	
		（369）		（406）		（385）
毛利润		1 006		969		990

注释：

（1）库存产品和生产成本的价值均根据全部成本法计量，单位成本为 K$ 3.5，这代表所有香型沐浴露的加权平均成本。

（2）5、6、7 月份的固定生产成本以每月 110 000 单位为基础进行计算，每单位为 K$ 0.41。

（3）销售额以预计的 5、6、7 月份每月 110 000 单位为基础，每单位的建议零售价为 K$ 12.5。

请为董事会写一份关于边际成本核算的简报。

请向谭先生解释营销支出。

任务二

三天后，Roger Dawson 在休年假，财务总监 Freda Jones 给你发了一封邮件，内容如下。

发件人：财务总监 Freda Jones

收件人：管理会计助理

主题：财务报表问题和组织结构

谭先生发给我一份 TRU 集团的财务管理手册的副本。这是一份内部手册，谭先生希望整个集团能正确对待相关的国际财务报告准则。

近日，我给他寄了截至 2015 年 12 月 31 日的桑切斯·纳瓦娜公司的最新财务报表，他反馈给我一些问题。

■ 他要求解释重估财务状况表中的储备金额。

- 考虑到我们直接通过特许柜台、零售商和网店向客户出售商品，谭先生询问为什么应收账款的余额这么高；考虑到公司的盈利能力，他也想了解为什么我们2015年12月31日的现金结余没有增加。

我们公司是TRU集团最新收购的子公司，TRU集团包括世界各地的卫生和护发产品制造商。因此，TRU集团的董事正在考虑将集团的组织结构由当前的地理分工结构变为基于产品的部门结构或者矩阵结构。

另外，在TRU集团组织的管理模式“开放论坛”中，谭先生要求我们就产品分部结构、矩阵结构如何适应集团目前的状况以及我们如何将自己融入和从每个结构中获益提出意见。

请回复给我一封邮件，其中包括对下列问题的适当答复，让我可以发送给谭先生。

- 他对截至2015年12月31日的年度财务报表的质疑。
- 他对组织结构的疑问。

十分感谢！

桑切斯·纳瓦娜公司

财务总监

Freda Jones

请根据要求写下邮件。

任务三

两个月后，Roger Dawson发给你一封邮件。

发件人：财务经理Roger Dawson

收件人：管理会计助理

主题：零售店

我刚刚出席了董事会会议，讨论如何重组我们的销售渠道。销售与市场总监Richard Procter认为，我们应该关闭自己的5家零售店，投资在线销售业务。

他认为，零售商的销售业绩并没有达到预期，而且在线销售是未来的发展趋势。为了帮助董事会做出决定，我被要求准备一份关于零售店在2016年前6个月的销售预算执行情况的简报。

你的同事财务主任Gail Honner已经制作了一个差异汇总表（后附）。我认为，我们需要对这份简报中的数字做出解释，以及找出一些董事会对零售店业绩做出判断时应考虑的其他因素。

Richard Procter也认为，我们应该重新培训零售店的一些职工，让他们和线上销售的顾客打交道。因此，董事会还要求，我们对简报中采取的步骤进行解释，以使得再培训计划有效。

请帮我准备简报文件的初稿。

十分感谢！

桑切斯·纳瓦娜公司

财务经理

Roger Dawson

2016年1~6月零售店的预算销售收入和实际销售收入差异摘要

	沐浴露（K$000）	润肤乳（K$000）	手足霜（K$000）	礼品套装（K$000）	总计（K$000）
预算销售收入	400	270	105	300	1075
实际销售收入	341	300	88	312	1041
销售价格差异	47A	75A	32A	0	154A
销售量差异	9A	76F	10F	5F	82F

A=不利的，F=有利的。

注释：

（1）预算销售收入是预算销售量乘以每个产品的建议零售价格。

（2）上述零售店的预算销售量刚好是今年预算数量的1/2，全年的预算总量等于上一年的实际销售量。

（3）每种产品的销售价格和数量差异是每种香味的个体差异的总和。

（4）零售经理Helen Davis建议的零售价格的平均折扣是沐浴露的12%、润肤乳的20%、手足霜的27%，礼品套装为0。

（5）销售量差异的计算方法是数量的差异乘以平均的标准单位边际贡献。

请写下Roger Dawson要求的简报初稿。

任务四

三个月后，董事会决定关闭零售店，扩大在线销售业务。因此，相当大的一笔支出未列入预算，导致现金余额大幅度下降。

你收到了 Roger Dawson 的邮件，内容如下。

发件人：财务经理 Roger Dawson
收件人：管理会计助理
主题：预算和财务报表

我刚刚和财务总监 Freda Jones、TRU 集团的谭先生进行了电话会议。谭先生对预算编制过程缺乏准确性和严谨性表示担忧，并且建议我们通过使用滚动预算和零基预算来克服这一问题。

Freda 请我为她准备一份简报，介绍关于现金预算的滚动预算和在线销售运营预算的零基预算。我认为，这个简报应当包括每种方法的介绍以及其对我们的益处。

另外，Freda 还要求我解释关闭商店对我们拥有的 3 处房产的财务报表的影响。她还对我们是否应该根据国际财务报告准则第 5 号将其分类为终止经营活动这个问题特别感兴趣。

请准备一份简报的初稿，让我可以回复 Freda 上述的两个问题。

谢谢！

桑切斯·纳瓦娜公司
财务经理
Roger Dawson

请写下 Freda Jones 要求的简报草案。

Variant 1 Suggested Answers

Section 1

Briefing Paper to the Directors on Marginal Costing

Impact of Marginal Costing on Profit and Inventory Valuation

The main impact under marginal costing is that we would no longer absorb fixed production overheads into the cost of each product, instead these fixed production overheads would be treated as period costs.

Opening and closing inventory will no longer be valued at the fully absorbed cost, but will instead be valued at variable costs only (in our case raw materials, fragrance ingredients, bottling and packaging, direct labour and variable overheads). This means that the inventory value will always be lower under marginal costing. It also means that where inventory levels change in a period under marginal costing our profit would be different to that under absorption costing.

Focusing on the schedule we can see that inventory volumes are expected to increase in May. Production volumes must be greater than volumes sold because, firstly, there is over-absorbed fixed production overhead (meaning that more than 110,000 units of body wash were produced) and secondly, the value of closing inventory is higher than the value of opening inventory (both of which are valued at the same standard full cost per unit).

In June the opposite is true, inventory volumes are expected to fall, resulting in under-absorbed overheads and a reduction in closing inventory value. This fall in inventory is consistent with the maintenance time required on the production line for body wash.

In July we are forecasting to produce the same volume as we sell as evidenced by the inventory level staying the same and there being no over or under absorption.

All of these inventory movements mean that the gross profit under absorption costing is different each month, despite the fact that the sales value is the same and our production costs per unit are the same. The reason for these differences is that when inventory increases, a greater amount of fixed production overhead is carried into the next period, hence increasing profit.

If we were to use marginal costing, there would be three important differences in the schedule. Firstly, there would be no over or under absorption of overheads adjustment required. Secondly, the fixed production overheads would be as a single period cost and not reflected in the value of inventory. Lastly, the profit would be the same for each month.

It should be noted that in the long run these differences between marginal and absorption costing cancel each other out.

Benefits and Drawbacks to the Finance Team of Using Marginal Costing

Benefits

The main benefit to the business will be a considerable saving in time when preparing management reports. There will be no need to prepare calculations of absorption rates, nor will there need to be calculations of over and under absorption of production overhead in the monthly management accounts.

The information provided in the reports is more useful for decision making because the cost per product will be on a contribution basis rather than a full cost basis. Arbitrary absorption of overheads is avoided.

The fact that other TRU Group subsidiaries use marginal costing means that if we adopt it, it will make it easier at group level to compare results across subsidiaries. This is clearly a benefit to TRU Group, but it is also potentially beneficial to us in terms of group co-operation and support.

By using marginal cost as discussed above, all fixed costs are treated as period costs and inventory is valued at the variable cost of production only. This means that there is no incentive to over-produce to boost closing inventory and therefore to increase profit for a period in the management reports.

Drawbacks

Under marginal costing inventory is valued at variable costs of production only. This valuation basis is not consistent with that required by IFRS for the valuation of inventory in the financial statements. Therefore we will need to perform additional calculations at the year-end when preparing the financial statements to ensure that a share of fixed production overheads is included.

Briefing Paper for Mr C Tan

Marketing Spend in Relation to Branding

In 2015,35% of our total spend on sales and marketing did indeed relate to marketing spent to protect and boost our brand image. Whilst this is a significant portion of the costs in 2015,the benefits of this expenditure are long term and will help to boost profits in the future.

Branding in our business is all important. The business will survive or decline with the popularity of the brand and how it is perceived. We sell quality body care products that customers feel them are valued for their effectiveness and range of fragrances. Our brand makes a statement about our products and is a key asset of the business(although under IFRS we are not allowed to recognise this in our financial statements). Customers choose our products over our competitors because they like our brand. Properly managed, our brand will enable us to achieve premium prices.

Much of the marketing spend is linked to maintaining our brand image, emphasising our consistency of quality, associated with our distinctive brand name and our range of product features, which make it well known and popular. Not only are our products high quality, but our marketing campaigns need to be as well: our customers expect it.

As such our marketing spend has the objective of putting our brand at the forefront of our consumers' minds and therefore influencing their choice. Whilst this requires us to commit considerable resources, a strong brand can improve profitability by achieving high sales, through name awareness, and the perception of quality and strong association.

Maintaining the brand is essential to achieving higher prices, improving profitability, connecting with our customers and achieving brand loyalty encouraging repeat sales and influencing buying habits.

Whilst marketing spend on branding is difficult to accurately cost to products, we feel it is an essential element of our marketing mix.

Section 2

From：Management Accountant Assistant

To：Freda Shah，Finance Director

Subject：Mr C Tan's queries

Queries from the Financial Statements

Revaluation Reserve

The reason why we have a revaluation reserve is because we have a policy of revaluing our property assets. IAS 16 allows a choice between the cost model and the revaluation model for a class of assets（PPE）.

We have chosen to revalue our property assets because our properties are worth considerably more than their original purchase cost. Actually，We own three stores in prime retail locations where property prices have increased significantly. The benefit of revaluation is that these assets are reflected in the statement of financial position at a more realistic value than their cost.

The increase in value is not recognised as profit however. Instead it accumulates the revaluation reserve that Mr C Tan has commented upon. When an asset is revalued upwards，the value of the asset will be increased to the revalued amount and this increase，along with the accumulated depreciation at the date of revaluation，will be credited to the revaluation reserve. Depreciation is then calculated on the revalued amount.

The TRU Group must have not chosen to revalue any assets，even though International Financial Reporting Standards would allow to do this.

Receivables and Cash Position at 31 December 2015

Mr C Tan is correct in that we sell directly to the end consumer，however this does not necessarily mean that we receive the cash from the sale straight away. 70% of our sales arise through our concession stands in department stores，where we do not receive the cash until the month after the sale. Therefore，at the year-end our concession stand partners owe us money in respect of sales that were made in December.

In respect of the cash position there have been a number of drains on the cash balance at 31 December 2015，which are summarised in the statement of cash flows for the year.

Firstly, a dividend of K$ 1,200,000 was paid in the year. At the time these financial statements were prepared, Sanchez Navarra would have been partly owned by the venture capital investors who likely required the dividend to be paid as a part of their return on investment. Clearly as shareholders, Freda and Nisha will also have benefited from this payment. This dividend was a significant proportion of the cash generated from operations in the year.

Secondly, inventories increased by K$ 530,000 at the end of the year compared to the previous year. This results in a net cash outflow for the business. This may be a necessity in running the business and ensuring adequate inventory levels, but it is not in line with the increase in sales revenues.

Thirdly, the tax payment was another major cash outflow, presumably in line with our audited statements and agreed by the relevant authorities.

Discussion Regarding Proposed Structure

Proposed-product Based Divisional

In a product based divisional structure, the business will be split and therefore managed on the basis of product groups. TRU Group owns a range of subsidiaries which operate in different product markets including hair-care, hygiene, bath products and beauty products. each product group could have its own division.

Given the increasing global nature of trade, this form of divisionalisation is likely to be more beneficial to TRU Group than a geographical basis because of the specialist knowledge of the global product markets that would develop. It would allow for better sharing of ideas between subsidiaries operating in the same or similar product markets, which ultimately could boost trade and innovation across the group.

In respect of Sanchez Navarra, such a structure would suit us as we would potentially be better able to collaborate with other body product businesses and possibly share research and development facilities. We might also be able to benefit from trade links that other subsidiaries have in different markets. However, this will all depend on how close a competitor our fellow subsidiaries are.

Proposed-matrix Structure

In a matrix structure, there would be two dimensions of organisational split: across products and also across geographical regions. From a practical point of view this would mean that each subsidiary in the group would need to report to the regional manager for each region in which they operate and sell as well as to the manager for the product group(which would be bath products for Sanchez Navarra).

Such a structure would allow the TRU Group to liaise across divisions but there will be duplication of some functions such as finance and personnel, our decisions may not always fall in line with their thinking and there may be a lack of goal congruence between investment decisions and prioritisation of resources. Provided we continue to perform well this isn't likely to be a problem, but increasingly formalised controls in changed circumstances may stifle the business.

In respect of Sanchez Navarra, this is probably over complex for our purposes. Matrix structures are best suited to the effective coordination of complex situations and the manufacturing of sophisticated products such as motor cars. Our business is much simpler with the production of a number of similar products using similar techniques. It is likely that a matrix structure would cause conflict of command, many time consuming meetings and consequently higher costs, all issues that we should try to avoid.

Thanks!

Management Accountant Assistant

Sanchez Navarra

Section 3

Briefing Paper to the Directors

Sales Variances of Retail Stores

Analysis of Schedule

The schedule of variances shows that the actual revenue generated by the retail stores is lower than the budget, although not by much.

Looking at each product individually:

(1) Body wash was discounted on average by 12% which has resulted in an adverse price variance. For body wash there is also an adverse volume variance indicating that the volumes sold were less than budget. This could be the result of seasonality factors or could be because our body wash products were perhaps not dis-

counted enough.

(2) Body lotion was discounted by 20% on average across the fragrances. Unlike body wash this has resulted in a favourable volume variance. Indeed the favourable volume variance indicates that the additional sales will have generated additional contribution of K$ 76,000, which is greater than the adverse price variance of K$ 75,000. It would appear that the policy to discount by 20% has actually resulted in an increase in contribution and therefore profit. Perhaps this is an optimum level of discount.

(3) Hand & foot cream has been discounted, even more heavily than body lotion. Whilst this has increased the volumes sold (as evidenced by a favourable volume variance), it has not increased overall profit because the price variance is larger than the volume variance.

(4) There was no discounting of gift sets (hence the nil price variance), however we still managed to sell more than we had budgeted to.

Overall, the fact that the adverse sales price variance is greater than the favourable volume variance, does not automatically mean that the retail stores are not performing. Indeed body lotion, hand & foot cream and gift sets sales were higher than budget in terms of volumes sold.

Additional Factors to Be Considered

The first factor to be consider is whether the budget is realistic in the first place, there are three main concerns:

(1) The budgeted volumes are based on last year's actual sales: is this a realistic basis? The directors need to consider the wider environment in terms of the market for our products. Has the market grown or declined? What has our competition been doing? What is the economy like?

(2) Additionally the schedule has been prepared on the basis of a half of the budget for the year. It is possible that there are seasonal variations in volumes sold and that we are not really comparing like with like.

(3) Budgeted sales are based on the full recommended retail price and ignore the discounts that Helen Davis (retail stores manager) has the authority to give in order to promote products.

Secondly, the schedule only considers the sales position. The directors also need to consider how well the retail stores manage costs: after all performance is not just about revenue.

Thirdly, it would be useful to compare the performance of the retail stores with our own concession stands. Ultimately the selling environment is similar and we would expect a similar performance. If the concession stands are doing much better than the retail stores, then this is a more useful indicator.

Retraining Programme

As a result of closing our own stores, we will be increasing our on-line business and hence are considering retraining some of the staff we currently employ in the stores to work in the on-line business. In order for this retraining to be successful and effective we will need to undertake the following steps:

(1) Evaluate what the training need is and whether retraining is the best approach. We will need to establish how the role in the on-line environment differs from that in the retail role. In the on-line environment there will be less direct contact with customers, instead the employee will focus on monitoring, packaging and sending out orders and dealing with queries from customers over the telephone. On the one hand, It might be that our retail employees are not comfortable with this switch away from direct customer contact and might prefer to transfer to the concession stands or to another organisation. On the other hand, some employees might relish the prospect. Therefore the first step is to establish whether there is an appetite amongst the store employees to retrain. If there isn't then any efforts to retrain are likely to end in failure.

(2) Determine what training is required. What skills and competencies do the on-line sales employees require that are different to the retail sales employees? Clearly computer skills are important, as are organisational skills. Telephone skills are also important. The retraining programme needs to be designed to take all of these into account.

(3) Define the training objectives and plan the retraining programme. From step two we will know what skills and competencies we need to train our employees on, so the next step is to set the outcomes that we expect from the training programme

together with how it will be implemented. We will need to consider whether we need to bring in external experts or whether we have the facilities and capability to carry out the training ourselves. Given that we already have a strong on-line sales team, then it is very likely that we can do this in house as we already have considerable experience in this area.

(4) Implement the training and evaluate how successful it has been. Within the implementation phase of the training we will need to check that the employees have taken on board all of the training and that they are capable of doing the job required. For example, we could check their telephone skills by using mock customer complaints. Evaluating the training is important because it will help to inform future training programmes that we might need to undertake.

Section 4

Briefing Paper

Rolling Budget

Rolling budget is a budget that is continually updated for the latest plans as time moves on. When an accounting period ends then another new accounting period is added in (whether this is a month or on another basis).

For the cash budget I would suggest that we set out budget period for three months. Within the budget period we would then break it down further to weekly or possibly monthly periods. Each time a week or a month passes it would be removed from the budget and the next period added. That way the cash budget will always extend ahead for the whole budget period of three months

By continually up-dating the cash budget and keeping the overall budget period relatively short at three months, we will have a much better idea of what our cash position is likely to be and hence can plan accordingly. If a deficit is forecast then we can make arrangements to organise overdraft facilities or loan facilities.

It will allow us to plan and will focus on areas of the business where perhaps performance isn't as it should be. For example, the rolling cash budget could indicate that we are not receiving cash from our concession partners as quickly as we should and therefore we could take corrective action to rectify this.

Rolling cash budget would have been particularly useful in respect of our recent experience. As a result of closing the retail stores and investing in expanding the on-line sales operation we have incurred significant expenditure which was not budgeted. rolling cash budget, especially prepared for a short time period would have allowed us to more accurately predict the movement in cash and to arrange for funding if needed.

ZBB

ZBB involves essentially starting a budget from a zero position. Each budget holder has to justify their budget and will start by defining the objectives that they wish to achieve. Mutually exclusive decision packages are then developed which are different ways of achieving these objectives. These decision packages are then ranked alongside other decision packages and the budget set on the basis of the best way to achieve all the objectives.

In respect of the on-line sales department, the objective is going to be to deliver the correct goods to the customer in a timely manner. A key factor in meeting this objective will be the number of staff dealing with on-line orders and the mode of delivery to customers. Different decision packages could be created with different levels of staff and different delivery options: each would meet the objective but to different degrees. Management would then decide based on decision packages elsewhere in the business what the budget for the on-line sales department should be.

A benefit of using ZBB is that because each budget has to be justified and decision packages compared it means that resources are more effectively allocated and inefficiencies removed. In addition, the budget will be more forward looking.

Impact of Store Closures on the Financial Statements

Discontinued Operation

A discontinued operation is a component of an entity that either has been disposed of, or is classified as held for sale, and:

- represents either a separate major line of business or a geographical area of operations;
- is a part of a single co-ordinated plan to dispose of a separate major line of business or geographical area of operations;

- is a subsidiary acquired exclusively with a view to resale and the disposal involves loss of control.

Given those criteria we could not classify the store closures as a "discontinued operation", since the closure of these stores is a small percentage of our business at only 5% of total revenue and cannot be deemed major. We also do not have any further stores to close. The closures are not a part of a plan to dispose a separate major line of business or geographical area of operations.

Owned Properties

How we treat the owned properties once we have closed the stores depends on what we intend to do with them.

If we sell the properties before the year end we will need to record a profit or loss on the sale in the statement of profit or loss. This will be calculated as the difference between the carrying value of the properties and the sale proceeds. We will also need to transfer the revaluation reserve to retained earnings.

If we intend to sell the properties within 12 months of the year end date, we will classify these properties as assets held for sale. In order to do this there must be a committed plan to sell, the assets must be available for immediate sale, an active programme to locate a buyer is initiated and the sale is highly probable. Given those criteria, any non-current assets from the closed stores would be classified as "held for sale" and would be held at the lower of the carrying amount and the fair value less costs of disposal.

A third possibility is that we hold onto the properties (because they are in prime retail areas) and rent them to a third party. If we do this then the properties become investment properties and we would classify them separately on the face of the statement of financial position. We will be able to choose between the cost model and the fair value model. If we opt for the fair value model, this means that at each year end the investment properties would be revalued to their fair value. Any gain or loss would be taken to the statement of profit or loss. No depreciation would be charged.

试卷一　参考答案

任务一

给董事会的关于边际成本的简报

边际成本法对利润和存货估值的影响

边际成本法的主要影响是：我们不再将固定生产费用纳入每种产品的成本中，而是将这些固定生产费用视为期间成本。

期初和期末存货将不再以全部已负担成本计价，而是只以变动成本计价（在我们的案例中，变动成本包括原材料、香料成分、包装瓶、包装袋、直接人工和变动费用）。这意味着，在边际成本法下，存货的价值将会更低，也意味一段时期内，在边际成本法和在全部成本法下，存货水平的变动对利润的影响各不相同。

在时间表中，我们可以看到，5 月份的预计库存量将会上升。产量必然大于销量的原因是：首先，有过多的固定生产费用被分摊（生产了 110 000 多单位的沐浴露）；其次，期末存货价值高于期初存货（二者都以同一标准的每单位全部成本计量）。

6 月份正好相反，预计库存量将下降，导致分摊的固定生产费用不足，期末存货价值降低。这一库存的下降与沐浴露生产线的维护时间一致。

我们预测，7 月份将产销平衡，库存水平保持不变，没有固定生产费用的过剩或不足。

这些存货变动意味着，在全部成本法下，各个月份的毛利润是不同的，尽管事实上，销售价格和产品的单位生产成本是不变的。造成这些差异的原因是，当库存增加时，更多的固定生产费用将计入下一期，从而增加利润。

如果我们使用边际成本法，将会在表中发现 3 处显著的不同：第一，不需要对固定生产费用进行过剩或不足的调整；第二，固定生产费用将被列为期间成本，不在存货价值中体现；最后，每个月的利润都将一样。

应指出的是，边际成本法和全部成本法的差异可以在长期经营下抵消。

对财务团队而言，使用边际成本法的优点和缺点

优点

使用边际成本法最主要的好处是在准备管理报告时可以节约相当多的时间，既不需要计算固定生产费用分摊率，也不需要在每月的管理账户中计算固定生产费用的过剩或不足。

报告中提供的信息对决策更有用，因为每单位产品的成本将会基于边际贡献计算而不是基于全部成本，可以避免主观任意地分摊固定费用。

TRU 集团的其他子公司使用边际成本法核算的情况表明，如果我们公司采用边际成本法，将会使集团层面更容易比较子公司之间的业绩。这对 TRU 集团来说，显然是有好处的，但在集团合作和支持方面对我们也有潜在的好处。

通过使用如上所述的边际成本法，所有的固定成本都将被视为期间成本，从而使存货只以变动生产成本计价。这意味着，在管理报告中不存在过度生产以增加库存并因此在一段时间内增加利润的可能性。

缺点

在边际成本法下，存货只以可变成本计价，这种计价基准与国际财务报告准则对财务报表中存货估值要求的基准不一致。因此，在年底编制财务报表时，我们需要进行额外的计算，以确保其包括固定生产费用的一部分。

给谭先生的简报

与品牌有关的营销支出

2015 年，市场营销部总支出的 35% 确实与保护和提升我们的品牌形象的营销活动相关。尽管这部分支出占 2015 年成本的很大一部分，但是这笔支出对企业有长期的好处，并且有助于提高企业未来的利润。

品牌对于我们的公司十分重要。随着品牌的普及和大众熟知度的提升，公司将会生存或衰落。我们销售优质的身体护理产品，产品的效果和香味的多样吸引了客户。我们的品牌就为我们的产品做出了声明，并且品牌是公司的重要资产（尽管根据国际财务报告准则，我们不应该在财务报表中确认这一点）。客户在众多竞争者中选择我们的产品，是因为他们喜欢我们的品牌。妥善管理品牌，将会使我们实现巨大的盈利。

营销支出的大部分与维护品牌形象有关，强调品质的一致性，让其与我们独特的品牌名称和产品功能范围相关联，这使得我们的品牌广受欢迎。我们不仅需要使产品质量好，也需要让营销活动精彩，这是顾客的期望。

因此，我们营销支出的目标是让我们的品牌在客户心中位于首位，从而影响他们的选择。虽然这需要我们投入大量的资源，但是一个强大的品牌能够通过达到高销售量、品牌知名度、质量观念和强有力的联想来提高盈利能力。

维护品牌形象对获得更高的产品价格、提高盈利能力、联系客户和实现品牌忠诚度从而鼓励重复销售和影响购买习惯至关重要。

虽然在品牌上的营销支出难以准确地计入产品成本，但我们认为这是我们营销组合的重要部分。

任务二

发件人：管理会计助理

收件人：财务总监 Freda Shah

主题：谭先生的疑问

财务报表问题

储备金的重估

由于有一个重新评估我们资产的政策，所以我们重估了储备金。国际会计准则第16号允许对不动产、厂房和设备这一类资产在成本模型和重估模型之间做出选择。

我们选择重新评估我们的不动产，是因为我们的不动产的价值远高于它们的原始购买成本。事实上，我们主要零售地点的3家店铺的物业价格大幅上涨。重估的好处是，这些资产在财务状况表中会反映出比成本更加真实的价值。

然而增加的价值不会被视为利润，相反，它增加了谭先生提到过的重估准备金。但当资产价值重估上调时，增加的资产价值将会计入重估值，这部分增加值和重估日期的累计折旧将被计入重估储备金，然后根据重估金额计算折旧。

TRU集团必须选择不重估任何资产，即使国际财务报告准则允许这样做。

2015年12月31日的应收款项和现金状况

谭先生是正确的，我们确实直接将产品出售给最终消费者，然而这并不意味着我们能立即从销售中收回现金。我们销售额的70%是通过在百货公司中的特许经营柜台获得，这部分收入直到销售后一个月才能收到。因此，在年底时，我们的特许经营柜台的合作伙伴尚未向我们支付12月份的销售收入。

在现金状况方面，2015年12月31日的现金余额是有一些下降，这些变化汇总在今年的现金流量表中。

首先，本年度支付了K$ 1 200 000的股息。在准备这些财务报表时，桑切斯·纳瓦娜公司部分由风险资本投资者拥有，这些投资者更可能要求支付股息，作为他们投资回报的一部分。显然，作为股东，Freda和Nisha同样从这笔款项中受益。股息支出占本年度经营活动产生的现金的很大一部分。

其次，年末库存比上一年增加了K$ 530 000，这导致公司净现金流出。这可能是运营业务和确保足够库存水平的必要条件，但并不与销售收入的增长相一致。

最后，税收是另一个主要的现金支出，这大概与我们的审计报告一致，并且得到了相关部门的认证。

关于所提议的结构的讨论

基于产品部门的建议

在基于产品的部门结构中，业务将在产品组的基础上进行分割和管理。TRU 集团拥有大量子公司，其分布在不同的产品市场，包括护发产品、清洁产品、沐浴产品和美容产品。每种产品都有自己的部门。

考虑到贸易全球性的增强，这种产品部门分工化比以地理为基础的分工更加有利，因为全球产品市场的专业知识在不断增多。产品部门分工化有助于在相同或相似的产品市场运营的子公司之间分享观点，最终可以促进整个集团的贸易和创新发展。

在桑切斯·纳瓦娜公司，这样的结构会适合我们，因为我们可以更好地与其他护肤类产品业务部门合作，并且可能共享研发设施。我们或许还能够从与其他不同市场的子公司的贸易联系中受益。然而，这都取决于我们的子公司与竞争对手的接近程度。

基于矩阵结构的建议

在矩阵结构中，组织分裂将存在于两个方面：跨产品和跨地域。从实际角度来看，这意味着集团中的每一个子公司都需要同时向每一个区域的区域经理和产品组的经理报告运营成果和销售业绩（对桑切斯·纳瓦娜公司而言，报告的产品组就是沐浴产品组）。

这样的结构使得 TRU 集团可以跨部门联系，但是会存在一些职能重叠，例如财务和人事，我们的决定并不会总和他们的想法相一致，在投资决策和资源排序中可能会缺乏目标一致性。如果我们继续表现良好，这可能不是一个问题，但在不断变化的环境中，日益形式化的控制可能会扼杀企业。

对桑切斯·纳瓦娜公司而言，这可能太过复杂了。矩阵结构最适用于复杂情况下的有效协作以及精密产品的制造，比如汽车。我们的业务要简单得多，只是使用类似的生产技术生产类似的产品。矩阵结构很可能会引起命令的冲突，导致会议耗时从而带来更高的成本，所以我们应该尽量避免这些问题。

非常感谢！

桑切斯·纳瓦娜公司

管理会计助理

任务三

给董事会的简报

零售店的销售差异

时间表分析

差异表显示，零售店的实际收入低于预算，但是相差不大。

分别查看每一种商品：

（1）沐浴露的平均折扣是12%，这导致了价格上的不利差异。对于沐浴露来说，还存在数量上的不利差异，这表明销售量低于预算。这可能是季节因素的影响结果，或者是因为我们的沐浴露产品的折扣不够。

（2）润肤乳的整个芳香系列产品的平均折扣是20%。与沐浴露不同，打折为润肤乳带来了有利的数量差异。事实上，这种有利的数量差异表明增加的销售额会产生K$ 76 000的额外贡献，这大大高于价格产生的不利差异 K$ 75 000。这样看来折扣20%的政策实际上会使额外贡献增加，从而增加利润。也许这是一个最佳的折扣水平。

（3）手足霜的折扣比润肤乳的折扣更大。虽然这增加了销售量（可以从有利差异中看出），但是由于价格上的不利差异大于数量上的有利差异，总体利润并没有增加。

（4）礼品套装没有折扣（因此价格差异为零），然而我们依然成功卖出了多于预算的数量。

总体来看，不利的销售价格差异大于有利的销售量差异的这一事实并不能代表零售店业绩不佳。事实上，润肤乳、手足霜和礼品套装的销售量是高于预算销售量的。

需要考虑的其他因素

首先，需要考虑的第一个因素是预算是否切合实际，主要有3个问题。

（1）预算销售量是根据去年的实际销售量计算的：这是一个现实的基础么？董事会需要考虑我们产品市场的大环境，市场是增长还是下降？我们的竞争对手在做什么？经济环境如何？

（2）另外，这个时间表是根据全年预算的1/2编制的，销售量可能存在季节性的变化，但是我们进行比较的时候并没有考虑这个因素。

（3）预算的销售额是根据原本的建议零售价格计算的，忽略了零售店经理 Helen Davis 有权为促销产品提供折扣这一因素。

其次，时间表只考虑了销售情况，董事会还需要考虑零售店成本管理的情况，毕竟收入不是业绩的唯一体现。

最后，将零售店的业绩与我们的特许经营柜台进行比较是有用的。它们的最终销售环境相似，所以我们期待它们有相似的业绩表现。如果特许经营柜台比零售店表现好，那么这是一个比较有用的衡量指标。

再培训项目

由于关闭了自己的店铺，我们将增加在线业务，因此我们考虑重新培训目前店铺里雇佣的员工以使他们能够从事在线业务。为了使这次再培训取得成功并行之有效，我们将采取以下步骤。

（1）考虑培训需要什么，以及再培训是否是最佳方法。我们需要确定在线销售环境和零售店销售环境中员工角色的不同。在在线销售环境中，员工和顾客直接接触的机会较少，员工将会关注监控、包装、订单发出和电话处理客户的质询。一方面，我们零售店的员工或许并不愿意从事线上工作，可能更愿意调动到特许经营柜台或者另外一个组织。另一方面，有一些员工或许会更看好在线业务的前景。因此，第一步要确定零售店员工对再培训项目是否有兴趣，如果没有，为再培训计划做出的任何努力都可能会以失败告终。

（2）确定需要什么培训。要求在线销售人员具备的能力和技能与零售店的有什么不同？显然，电脑技能是十分重要的，组织技能也很重要，电话通信技能同样很重要。设计再培训计划时需要将这部分内容纳入考虑范围。

（3）确定培训目标，并制订再培训计划。从第二步中，我们将了解到培训员工所需的技能和能力，所以，下一步是确定我们需要从培训计划中得到的期望成果，以及如何实施这个计划。我们需要考虑我们是否需要引进外部专家，或是我们自己是否有能力和设施完成培训计划。鉴于我们已经有一个强大的在线销售团队，而且在这个领域已经有相当多的经验，因而我们很可能能够内部完成这件事。

（4）实施培训计划并评估其成功程度。在培训计划的实施阶段，我们需要检查员工是否接受了所有的培训，以及他们是否有能力胜任这份工作。例如，我们可以通过模拟客户投诉来检查他们的电话沟通技能。评估培训十分重要，因为这将能为我们未来可能开展的培训计划提供信息。

任务四

简报

滚动预算

滚动预算是指随着时间推移不断更新的最新预算计划。当一个会计期结束时，再增加另一个新的会计期（无论是一个月，还是另一个时期基础）。

对于现金预算，我建议我们设定3个月的预算期。在预算期内，我们可将其进一步分解为每周，或者每月。每当一周或者一个月过去，就将其从预算中删除，将后续的期间加入。这样，在3个月的整个预算期内，现金预算总会延续向前。

通过不断更新现金预算，使总预算周期维持在一个相对短的时间内——3个月内，我们将能更好地了解我们的现金状况，并可以据此做出相应的计划。如果预算出现赤字，我们可以安排透支额或者贷款工具。

这将使我们能够进行计划，并且关注那些绩效不佳的业务领域。例如，滚动现金预算可能表明我们没有按计划收到特许经营伙伴的现金款项，因此，我们要采取措施纠正这一点。

滚动现金预算对于我们最近的情况特别有用。由于关闭了零售店并且投资扩大了在线销售业务，我们已经产生了大量未经预算的支出。滚动现金预算，特别是准备一个短期的滚动预算，将能使我们更准确地预测现金流动，并在需要时安排资金。

零基预算

零基预算是指从零开始的预算，每一个预算编写者需证明预算的合理性，并确定他们想要实现的目标，然后提出通过不同途径实现目标的相互排斥的方案，将这些决策方案与其他决策方案以及基于实现所有目标的最佳途径而制定的预算一起排列。

在线销售部门的目标是及时向客户提供正确的货物。实现这一目标的关键因素是处理在线订单员工的数量和配送给顾客的方式。不同的员工水平和不同的配送方式可以创建出不同的决策：每一个决策都可以实现目标，但是实现程度不同。管理层会根据企业其他部门的决策方案来决定在线销售部门的预算应该是多少。

使用零基预算的好处在于，每一个预算都被合理化，并且各个决策之间进行了比较，这意味着资源被更有效地分配并且避免了低效。此外，预算将会更有前瞻性。

关闭店铺对财务报表的影响

终止经营

终止经营是指已被处置或分类为持有待售的实体的组成部分，以及其他部分。

- 代表一个独立的主要业务线或者一个地理区域的业务。
- 是处理一个独立的主要业务线的协调计划的一部分，或者是地理区域业务的一部分。
- 是专为转售而收购的附属公司，其处置失去了控制。

鉴于这些标准，我们不能将店铺关闭归类为“终止经营”，因为关闭的这些店铺只是我们业务的一小部分，仅占总收入的5%，不能视为主要业务。我们也没有更多的店铺关闭，并且，关闭店铺也不是处理单独业务或者地理区域的计划的一部分。

自有资产

关闭店铺之后，我们如何处理这些资产取决于我们打算用它们做什么：

如果我们在年底之前出售了这些资产，我们就需要在损益表中记录销售的盈亏，这将被计算为资产账面价值和销售收入之间的差额。我们还需要将重估储备金转为留存收益。

如果我们打算在年后12个月内出售这些资产，那么我们将把它们归类为持有待售的资产。为了做到这一点，必须有一个明确的出售计划，资产必须可以立即出售，可以发起一个积极的出售方案找到买家，并且交易很可能成功。鉴于这些标准，店铺关闭的所有非流动资产都应该归类为“持有待售”资产，并将以账面价值和处置的公允价值减去处置成本中的较低者计量。

第三种可能是，我们继续持有这些资产（因为它们位于黄金零售区）并将它们出租给第三方。如果我们这样做，那么这些资产将会成为投资资产，我们将根据财务报表对它们分别分类。我们可以在成本模型和公允价值模型之间选择计量方式。如果我们选择公允价值模型，这意味着在每年年底投资性资产将被重新估算公允价值，受益和损失都将计入损益表，同时不计提折旧。

Variant 1　Marking Guidance

Section	Technical skills		Business skills		People skills		Leadership skills		Integration	Total
1	Impact of marginal costing on profit and inventory valuation（P1）	13	Justification of marketing spend（E1）	3			Justification of marketing spend（E1）	6	3	25
2	Revaluation reserve and cash position（F1）	13	The wider organisational structure（E1）	12						25
3	Sales price, mix and quantity variances（P1）	13			Effective retraining programme（E1）	12				25
4	Rolling budgets and zero-based budgets（P1） Financial reporting implications of closing stores（F1）	12 13								25
Total marks available for each competency		64		15		12		6	3	100

试卷一 评分指南

部分	技术技能		商业技能		人际技能		领导技能		综合	总计
1	边际成本法对利润和存货估价的影响（P1）	13	营销支出的合理性（E1）	3			营销支出的合理性（E1）	6	3	25
2	储备资金和现金状况的重估（F1）	13	更广泛的组织结构（E1）	12						25
3	销售价格和数量的组合方差（P1）	13			有效的再培训计划	12				25
4	滚动预算和零基预算（P1） 关闭店铺对财务报告的影响（F1）	12 13								25
各种能力分数总计		64		15		12		6	3	100

中央财经大学名师解惑

试卷一共有四项任务，考查了 P1、F1、E1 三门课程的知识点，具体包括边际成本法、财务报表与组织结构、预算执行差异计算与分析、滚动预算、零基预算、终止经营的会计处理方法等。该试卷考核了考生的四项能力，其中技术技能的分值占 64%，商业技能的分值占 15%，人际技能的分值占 12%，领导技能的分值占 6%，与 CGMA 管理会计能力框架的技能要求一致。

该试卷的每项任务涉及以下知识点：

任务	问题	科目	知识点
任务一	边际成本核算方法对利润和存货估价的影响，及对企业的利弊	（P1）	边际成本法（marginal cost method）
	解释为维护品牌而花费的营销支出	（E1）	营销支出（marketing expenditure）
任务二	对财务报表项目储备金额、应收账款、现金结余进行解释	（F1）	财务报表（financial statements）
	考虑产品结构与矩阵结构的利弊	（E1）	组织结构（organization structure）
任务三	预算执行情况及差异分析	（P1）	预算分析（budget analysis）
	培训零售店职工		员工培训（staff training）
任务四	介绍现金预算的滚动预算	（P1）	滚动预算（rolling budget）
	介绍在线销售运营预算的零基预算	（P1）	零基预算（ZBB）
	关闭店铺后对自有资产的处理方式及影响	（F1）	终止经营（terminate the business）

上述各项任务要求以邮件、报告或工作笔记等形式来呈现答案，对问题的描述非常明确，答题时既要注意内容的针对性，也要注意形式的规范性。

其他答题注意事项包括：（1）仔细读题，一般每项任务都会涉及 2～3 个大的知识点，一定不能漏答；（2）答题要有条理，从是什么到为什么，从分析原因到提出解决办法，将每个知识点都解释清楚；（3）分层级列出各级小标题，让考官容易了解你的思路。

同时，答题时，要避免只是对教科书中的知识点进行简单复述，应结合案例公司的实际情况。注意回答时的措辞、格式、论述的结构、论点的鲜明性和整体性等。

对应知识点的深度剖析

边际成本法

在考虑边际成本法的影响时，首先要考虑边际成本法与全部成本法的差异，即固定生产费用不纳入每种产品的成本中，而是计入期间成本，期初期末存货只以变动成本计价。

考生需要准确理解边际成本法与全部成本法的核算差异，在全部成本法下，产量提高会使得产品分摊到的固定费用下降，毛利率上升，反之亦然。而边际成本法只计算生产成本，使得当售价与单位生产成本不变时，毛利率不变。

分析边际成本法的利弊时，考生应综合考虑管理层决策有用性与报表披露原则来进行衡量，结合内外部的使用途径进行综合分析。

营销支出

品牌对企业的业务开展十分重要，企业应维护自身品牌，以求在众多竞争者中获得优势。考生应恰当阐述品牌对企业的重要性，并结合题目中的具体信息进行说明。

财务报表

财务报表综合反映了企业的财务状况和经营成果，能对企业会计政策的运用做出即刻的体现。考生需了解应用不同会计准则对企业财务报表的影响，掌握不同企业运营模式所对应的财务报表数据的可能呈现形态，同时熟悉财务报告的勾稽关系。

组织结构

组织结构设计是企业管理的基本前提。考生在考虑组织结构时，首先，应了解企业自身的生产运营模式；其次，应明确每种组织结构形态的优势与劣势；最后，应从企业的现实状况出发，考虑企业应用不同组织结构的利弊。

结合题中所给信息，综合考虑 TRU 集团已有的子公司的产品市场分布情况、产品的专业性和分工化，以及报告的繁简程度，同时考虑组织结构对未来长期发展的影响，进行合理阐述。

考生注意事项

组织结构设计：

第一步：了解企业自身的生产运营模式；

第二步：明确基于产品的部门结构与矩阵部门结构相比各自的优势与劣势；

第三步：从企业的现实状况出发，考虑企业应用不同组织结构的利弊。

预算执行差异计算与分析

考生在对预算执行情况进行分析时，应同时考虑数量差异与价格差异，准确指出造成预算差异的有利因素和不利因素。

在进行业绩评价时，考生应主要考虑预算编制的现实性：（1）基期的销售状况是否合适；（2）销量是否受季节变化影响；（3）销售价格变化是否会影响销售量。同时注意结合企业的实际情况，如本题中提到的成本管理水平，运营模式等。

员工再培训

考生在设计再培训项目时，常规思路如下：（1）评估再培训是否为最佳方法及其针对对象；（2）确定需要什么类型的培训；（3）确定培训目标；（4）实施培训并评估其成功程度。考生需要理解表述出整个设计员工再培训方案的过程，同时，要基于题中所给信息进行回答，而不是只宽泛地描述。

滚动预算

滚动预算又称连续预算或永续预算，是根据上一期的预算完成情况，调整和具体编制下一期预算，并将编制预算的时期逐期连续滚动向前推移，使预算总是保持一定的时间幅度，从而保证预算的完整性、连续性，动态把握企业的未来，保证企业的经营管理工作稳定而有序地进行。滚动预算的核心在于：将原定的预算结果不断进行修改，这也是它优于普通年度预算之处，这种动态固定的特性使得预算的准确性逐步提高。

考生在解答此题时，可以先介绍滚动预算的特点，再根据滚动预算的实施步骤，结合题中提供的细节信息来回答。

零基预算

零基预算与传统的增量预算法不同，在编制成本费用预算时，不考虑以往的费用项目或数额，一切从零开始，根据预算期的实际需要和可能性，逐项审查预算期内各项费用的内容及其开支标准是否合理，在综合平衡的基础上编制费用预算。其优点是可以减少浪费，合理分配资金，提高预算管理水平。

考生在解答此题时，可以先介绍零基预算的特点，再根据零基预算的实施步骤，结合题目中提供的细节信息来回答。零基预算的关键步骤之一是对可选的决策方案进行成本效益分析，解答时需指出开展成本效益分析要取得哪些相关信息。

考生注意事项

零基预算的核心是在预算编制中引入一种质疑的态度，对现有的实践活动和费用开支提出疑问，诸如：这项活动是必需的吗？如果不进行这项活动，会带来什么后果？是否有其他可能的途径可以达到同样的目的？这项费用开支是否值得？通过回答这些问题使预算中的不合理因素被剔除，从而达到节约成本，提高资源利用效率的目的。

零基预算的三个核心步骤包括：(1) 根据组织目标，确认预算期内需要进行的业务项目及其费用开支，制订多个可能的备选方案（也称为决策方案）；(2) 对备选方案进行成本效益分析，评估项目费用开支的合理程度，确定先后顺序以及对组织业务活动的影响；(3) 按照预算期可动用的资金及其来源和项目的轻重缓急次序，分配资金，落实预算。考生可通过对核心步骤的阐述，结合企业现实情况，分析益处。

终止经营

国际会计准则第 5 号，将终止经营界定为被处置或归类为持有待售的实体的组成部分：代表一个独立的主要业务线或者地理区域的业务；是处理独立的主要业务线的协调计划的一部分，或者是地理区域业务的一部分；是专为转售而收购的附属公司，其处置涉及控制权。

要回答此题，考生需熟悉案例材料，对其有深入的理解和认识，同时注意与准则内容相契合。

Variant 2

This examination is structured as follows：

Section number	Number of tasks	Time for section(minutes)
1	1	50
2	1	45
3	1	45
4	1	40

The time available for each section is for reading,planning and writing your answer(s).

Section 1

You arrive at office in the morning and receive the following email from Roger Dawson, finance manager.

From: Roger Dawson, Finance Manager
To: Management Accountant Assistant
Subject: World class manufacturing and cost of quality

Yesterday the directors and the management team had a video conference call with some of the senior management teams at TRU Group, who expressed their desire that we move forward in the rapidly changing market.

TRU Group management has developed a considerable capacity for research and development over the years and is now planning to give us access to their research facilities and extensive product testing data. They are encouraging the development and production of new fragrances for the existing product range. This has become particularly urgent as a major competitor is rumored to be about to launch a similar range of products.

TRU Group operates world class manufacturing in many of its subsidiaries and is keen that we consider adopting it. Furthermore, it was suggested that we consider using a cost of quality report to enhance our commitment to quality throughout our business. Gail Honner, your fellow finance officer, has come up with a list of costs which she believes are quality related.

Freda Jones, finance director, has asked for a briefing paper which explains:

- How suitable the key principles of world class manufacturing are to our business and how we might implement them;
- How we should implement a cost of quality report and the benefits to us of doing so. Please include justification ion of how each cost identified in Gail's schedule should be classified within a cost of quality report.

Please prepare the briefing paper for Freda.

Many thanks!

Roger Dawson
Finance Manager
Sanchez Navarra

Gail Honner's list of potential quality costs.

- A training course for new employees on the proper use of machinery and equipment.
- The costs of staff downtime as a result of production machinery having to be repaired.
- The costs of renting testing equipment used to test the quality of raw materials.
- Maintenance of the production line.
- Costs of dealing with customer complaints.

Write the briefing paper for Freda Jones requested by Roger Dawson.

Section 2

The next day, you receive the following email from Freda Jones.

From: Freda Jones, Finance Director
To: Management Accountant Assistant
Subject: Inventory

Thank you for your input into the briefing paper yesterday. Roger told me that you had prepared the initial draft. I'd like your thoughts on a few other matters arising from the video conference call with TRU Group management.

Comments were made on the conference call about our inventory level. The TRU Group management pointed out that, at the end of June, our finished goods inventory for body wash represents 220 inventory days and has been increasing. They consider this is excessive and not compatible with their management philosophy of World Class Manufacturing.

As a result I asked Gail Honner, your fellow finance officer, to produce an aged inventory report, by fragrance for body wash, which is attached. Please prepare a briefing paper on the implications to our business of this aged inventory report and a brief outline of what we could do to reduce our body wash finished goods inventory level.

TRU Group management also raised concerns about how we prepare our budgets. I had explained to them that we prepare the budget annually using the budget for the year before as a starting point. They are concerned that this approach to budget preparation has resulted in inappropriate budgets in certain areas. In particular they commented about the number of recent machinery breakdowns resulting from insufficient maintenance of the machinery, which has been blamed on the budgeting process. Expenditure on machinery maintenance was limited to the initial budget allowance, but clearly this was not enough to keep the machines working properly. As a result we have had to spend more money fixing the machinery than we would have done had we spent a little more on maintenance. All of this has resulted in significant machinery repair cost overspends.

TRU Group management have therefore suggested that we use ZBB when setting next year's budget. Within the same briefing paper please include an explanation of how we could implement ZBB for our machinery maintenance cost budget and the benefits to us of doing so.

Many thanks!

Freda Jones
Finance Director
Sanchez Navarra

Schedule of finished goods inventory days by fragrance for body wash based on the inventory level at 30 June 2016 and cost of sales for the year to 30 June 2016:

Body wash	**Inventory days**
Emerald	355
Ruby	200
Sapphire	195
Topaz	12
Diamond	445
Amber	225

（续表）

Body wash	Inventory days
Jade	225
Garnet	155
Amethyst	20
opal	55
Average	220

Write the briefing paper requested by Freda Jones.

Section 3

A few months later there is much excitement in the company as a new fragrance, Tanzanite, is about to be launched. Roger Dawson, finance manager, is on annual leave and Freda Jones comes to your desk and says:

Our new fragrance, Tanzanite, is almost ready for launch. Having had access to TRU Group's facilities to develop the new fragrance, it is important to create a good impression with them and this fragrance is a success. As such we will need to ensure that we undertake an effective marketing campaign for this launch.

I'm having a meeting tomorrow with Richard Procter, sales & marketing director, about this launch and the associated marketing campaign. Richard is suggesting that we should undertake a large-scale mass media campaign. I'm not so sure that we need to do this. Before Roger left on his annual leave he prepared a schedule of the expected impact of three different levels of campaign expenditure on the sales of Tanzanite in the first six months, under three different market conditions.

I still have the schedule but have lost Roger's explanation of what it means and the different ways I could interpret it. I know his explanation of the schedule said something about extending the analysis if we could determine the probabilities, but I can't remember exactly what it said and have to rush straight into a meeting for the rest of today.

So that I'm prepared for my meeting with Richard tomorrow, please send me an email which firstly discusses the factors that we need to consider in order to run an effective marketing campaign; secondly explains and interprets the pay off and regret tables in Roger's schedule and what he meant by extending the analysis.

Pay off table of expected profit(net of campaign expenditure) from Tanzanite for the first six months:

	Campaign		
Market conditions	**A(K$000)**	**B(K$000)**	**C(K$000)**
Poor	150	140	100
Fair	200	210	150
Good	220	240	250

Regret table:

	Campaign		
Market conditions	**A(K$000)**	**B(K$000)**	**C(K$000)**
Poor	0	10	50
Fair	10	0	60
Good	30	10	0

Write the email requested by Freda Jones.

Section 4

It is now 3 January 2017 and you receive the following email from Roger Dawson.

From: Roger Dawson, Finance Manager
To: Management Accountant Assistant
Subject: Supplier issue

I've just had a conversation with George Focus, production manager. He informed me that the last batch of surfactants that we received from our supplier has created a major problem for us. We used it in the final week's production of body wash for 2016. Initially it all seemed fine, but it now appears that the products(which thankfully are still sitting in our warehouse) have started to separate in the bottles.

On investigation it appears that the surfactant was of inferior quality. We hadn't tested it upon receipt because we have always trusted our supplier to deliver good quality materials.

The terms of trade with our supplier quite clearly state that a final inspection should be made by us on receipt of the goods, but because of an error in our procedures this didn't happen. George Focus has suggested that we falsify the paperwork and claim that the inspection was carried out on receipt of the goods and therefore the quality issue has arisen since this initial inspection. George thinks that we should raise a credit note to the supplier for the full value of the supplies plus our full manufacturing costs.

Our inventory records at 31 December 2016 show K$ 150,000 as the cost value of the finished good inventory affected. It looks like we can rework the affected finished body wash at an additional cost of K$ 120,000. Once reworked the retail value of this inventory would be K$ 400,000. If we decide to scrap the body wash it is going to cost us K$ 20,000.

In addition, our inventory records at 31 December 2016 show K$ 105,000 for the unused poor quality surfactant. We plan to return this to the supplier.

I don't have time to think about this too much at the moment, so I would like you to send me an email in which you:

- draft a response that I can send to George Focus regarding his suggestion;
- explain how the above will potentially affect the inventory value and profit that we will include in our financial statements for the year ended 31 December 2016.

Many thanks!

Roger Dawson

Finance Manager

Sanchez Navarra

Write the email requested by Roger Dawson.

试卷二

本次考试的结构如下：

序号	任务数	时间（分钟）
1	1	50
2	1	45
3	1	45
4	1	40

每个部分规定的时间可用于读题、组织和书写答案。

任务一

你早上到达工作岗位后，收到了财务经理 Roger Dawson 的电子邮件。

发件人：财务经理 Roger Dawson
收件人：管理会计助理
主题：世界级制造业（WCM）和质量成本

昨天，董事会和管理团队与 TRU 集团的一些高级管理团队进行了视频电话会议，他们希望我们能在快速变化的市场中前进。

TRU 集团管理公司多年，具有相当出色的研发能力，目前他们正在计划给我们提供他们的研究设施和广泛的产品测试数据。他们也鼓励我们在现有产品系列内开发和生产新的香型。由于有传言称我们的一个主要竞争对手正在开发类似的产品系列，因此这项工作就变得尤为迫切。

TRU 集团的许多子公司在经营世界级制造业，并且希望我们考虑采用它。此外，有人建议，我们可以考虑使用质量报告的成本来提高我们对业务质量的承诺。财务人员 Gail Honner 提出了她认为与质量相关的成本清单。

财务总监 Freda Jones 想要一份简报，其中要说明：

- 世界级制造业的关键原则如何适应我们的业务，以及我们要如何实施；
- 我们应该如何实施质量报告的成本以及我们这样做的好处。请将其包括在 Gail 计划中并确定每一项成本如何在质量报告的成本中进行分类的理由。

请为 Freda 准备简报。

非常感谢！

桑切斯·纳瓦娜公司
财务经理
Roger Dawson

Gail Honner 的潜在质量成本清单。

- 为新员工提供正确使用机器设备的培训课程。

- 由于必须修理生产机械而导致人员停工的成本。
- 用于测试原材料质量的设备的租用费用。
- 维护生产线。
- 处理客户投诉的费用。

请根据 Roger Dawson 的要求为 Freda Jones 撰写简报。

任务二

第二天，您收到了 Freda Jones 的电子邮件。

发件人：财务总监 Freda Jones

收件人：管理会计助理

主题：库存

谢谢你昨天在简报中提出的意见。Roger 告诉我是你准备了初稿。我希望你对 TRU 集团管理层在视频电话会议上提出的一些其他问题也发表一些想法。

关于我们的库存水平在电话会议上也有讨论。TRU 集团管理层指出，截至 6 月底，我们的沐浴成品库存已达 220 天，而且还在不断增加。他们认为这是过度的，不符合世界级制造业的管理理念。

因此，我要求你的同事 Gail Honner 撰写了一份沐浴用香薰的陈年库存报告，随信附上。请你撰写一份关于这个陈年库存报告对我们业务的影响的简报，并简要介绍如何降低沐浴成品的库存水平。

TRU 集团管理层也对我们如何准备预算表示了担忧。我向他们解释说，我们每年用前一年的预算作为起点来编制预算。他们担心这种预算编制方式会导致某些领域的预算不恰当，特别是他们查看了由于维护不足而造成的机器故障数量后，已经将之归咎于预算过程。机械维修支出仅限于初始预算津贴，但显然这不足以使机器维持正常工作。因此，我们不得不花更多的钱来修理机器，如果我们当初花稍微多点钱来维护，就不会像现在这样了。所有这些都导致了机器维修费用严重超支。

因此，TRU 集团管理层建议，在设定明年预算时，我们应该使用零基预算。在同一个简报中，请说明我们如何为机器维护成本预算实施零基预算，以及我们这样做的好处。

非常感谢！

桑切斯·纳瓦娜公司
财务总监
Freda Jones

基于2016年6月30日的库存水平和截至2016年6月30日的销售成本的沐浴用香薰成品库存日期表：

沐浴露	存货周转天数
祖母绿	355
红宝石	200
蓝宝石	195
黄玉	12
钻石	445
琥珀	225
翡翠	225
石榴石	155
紫水晶	20
蛋白石	55
平均	220

请撰写Freda Jones要求的简报。

任务三

几个月后，公司的新香型“坦桑”即将上市，让人兴奋不已。财务经理Roger Dawson正在休假，Freda Jones来到你的办公桌前说：

我们的新香型坦桑，几乎已经可以上市了。用TRU集团的设施来开发新的香型，很重要的一点是要给他们一个良好的印象，而且这种香味是成功的。因此，我们需要确保为这次推广进行有效的营销活动。

我明天将与销售和市场总监Richard Procter就这次发布会和相关的营销活动举行会

议。Richard 建议我们进行大规模的大众媒体宣传活动，但我不太确定我们是否需要这样做。在 Roger 休年假之前，他制定了 3 个不同市场条件下的 3 个不同水平的活动支出对前 6 个月坦桑销售预期影响的时间表。

我仍然保有时间表，但是失去了 Roger 对于它的意义和不同的解释方式的说明。我知道他对时间表的解释是说，如果我们能够确定概率，那么我们就可以扩展分析，但是我不能完全记住它的意思，而且不得不在今天剩下的时间里参加会议。

因为我准备明天和 Richard 会面，所以请给我发一封电子邮件。首先，讨论我们需要考虑的因素，以便进行有效的营销活动；其次，解释 Roger 计划中的薪酬和遗憾值表及扩展分析的意思。

前 6 个月坦桑的预期利润支付表（扣除活动支出）：

	活动		
市场条件	A（K$000）	B（K$000）	C（K$000）
差	150	140	100
中	200	210	150
好	220	240	250

遗憾值表：

	活动		
市场条件	A（K$000）	B（K$000）	C（K$000）
差	0	10	50
中	10	0	60
好	30	10	0

请根据 Freda Jones 的要求进行回邮。

任务四

现在是 2017 年 1 月 3 日，您收到以下来自 Roger Dawson 的电子邮件。

发件人：财务经理 Roger Dawson

收件人：管理会计助理

主题：供应商问题

我刚刚和生产经理George Focus进行了交谈。他告诉我，我们从供应商处收到的最后一批表面活性剂为我们带来了一个重大问题。我们在2016年的最后一周的沐浴露生产中使用了它。起初一切似乎都很好，但现在这些产品（幸好还在我们的仓库里）已经开始在瓶子里分离了。

调查结果表明，表面活性剂的质量不合格。我们没有在收到货品后进行测试，因为我们一直相信我们的供应商提供的是优质的材料。

与供应商的贸易条款清楚地表明，我们在收到货物后应该进行最后的检查，但由于我们的程序错误，这并没有被执行。George Focus建议我们伪造文件，并声称这是在收到货物后进行的检查，因此从最初的检查开始，质量问题就出现了。George认为，我们应该向供应商提供一个信用报告，以获得全部的耗材价值及我们的全部制造成本。

我们2016年12月31日的库存记录显示K$150 000作为成品库存影响的成本价值。看起来我们可以对受影响的成品沐浴露进行加工，额外费用为K$120 000。一旦重新加工，此库存的零售价值将为K$400 000。如果我们决定废弃沐浴露，那么将花费我们K$20 000。

此外，我们2016年12月31日的库存记录显示，未使用的不良品质表面活性剂为K$105 000。我们计划将其退还给供应商。

我目前没有时间考虑这个问题，所以我希望你给我发一封电子邮件，其中包括：

- 就George的建议，起草一份我可以寄给他的回函；
- 解释上述情况将如何影响我们在截至2016年12月31日的年度财务报表中所包含的库存价值和利润。

非常感谢！

桑切斯·纳瓦娜公司
财务经理
Roger Dawson

请根据Roger Dawson的要求进行回邮。

Variant 2　Suggested Answers

Section 1

Briefing Paper for Freda Jones

World Class Manufacturing

WCM (World Class Manufacturing) is increasingly relevant in environments which change quickly and are becoming more unpredictable. The ability of our rivals to create competing products and to react quickly to rapidly changing market conditions and changes in buyer needs, means that we need to be able to do the same.

Customer satisfaction is an overriding priority of WCM. Whilst cost effectiveness is still vitally important, time-to-market, response to customer demands and innovation of products are all increasingly relevant to success.

Ultimately, customer satisfaction is underpinned by quality: of the product, of the production process and the service provided by us. Therefore WCM is essentially about quality and the principles of TQM are seen as the route to achieving this. By pursuing a policy of continuous improvement with the ultimate goal of zero defects, excellence in manufacturing can be achieved.

In order to achieve this, we will need to invest in our manufacturing equipment and in technology such as computers for analysing and testing products. In our business, revising the mixes of different fragrances, analysing test results and the ability to process large quantities of information are essential to ensure that we stay ahead of our competitors.

We trade in a truly global environment and we are now facing potential competition from across the world. Our competitors may be closer to the sources of raw materials and operate in cheaper economic areas , which giving them competitive advantage. We need to ensure our supply chains are lean and efficient.

Employee participation and empowerment of employees is another crucial factor in WCM. A team approach to the business which is designed to encourage all employees to work cooperatively eradicating traditional job demarcation is to be encouraged. Setting up quality circles might help to achieve this.

In conclusion, in the long run adopting WCM approach is likely to be beneficial to the business, in terms of enhancing customer satisfaction through consistently high quality products and a modern manufacturing environment which is flexible and adaptable to the needs of customers.

Cost of Quality

Implementing a Cost of Quality Report

A cost of quality approach is essentially a way of reporting on and considering those costs which are incurred by the business, which arise either as a result of ensuring that the appropriate quality is achieved or because the quality standard has not been achieved. It involves the preparation of a cost of quality report where costs are broken down into the costs of conformance (those costs which are incurred in order to ensure that a certain quality standard is achieved) and costs of non-conformance (those costs which are incurred as a result of failure to meet the quality standard). Conformance costs can either be prevention or appraisal and non-conformance costs are internal or external failure costs.

Looking at each of Gail's suggested quality costs in turn.

- The cost of training courses for new staffs on the use of machinery is a prevention cost. This is because the training is undertaken to ensure that the machinery is used correctly and hence the quality of production is as it should be. It is a cost incurred to prevent quality issues from occurring.
- The cost of staff downtime as a result of production machinery having to be repaired is an internal failure cost. The fact that the production machinery has broken down and needs to be repaired means that there has been a failure in quality which has resulted in the downtime. The fact that the failure occurs before the product has reached the end customer means that it is an internal failure cost.
- The costs of renting testing equipment used to test raw materials, is an appraisal cost. Raw materials are tested as part of the appraisal process to ensure that they are of the correct quality prior to being used in production.
- Maintenance of the production line is a prevention cost because if the production line is working properly then this can prevent quality issues from arising as a result of mechanical issues.

- The costs of dealing with customer complaints are an external failure cost. The fact that a customer is complaining means that there has been a failure in quality(either as a result of a poor product or poor service). The fact that it is the customer complaining means that it is external to the business.

The Benefits of Adopting a Cost of Quality Report

Given that WCM is being considered and that this is underpinned by quality and TQM, adopting a cost of quality approach will enhance and support this, because it focuses management attention onto quality issues.

By identifying and quantifying quality related costs in a cost of quality report, we will have a better idea of what we do to mitigate the risk of quality failure(in terms of our conformance costs) and the impact of not actually meeting quality(in terms of our non-conformance costs).

For example, if non-conformance costs are high(perhaps because of a poor quality batch of production which has had a significant impact of customer goodwill and hence reduced sales) then we need to consider whether a greater proportion of our budget should be allocated to quality control in house. This would have the impact of increased conformance costs, but this mitigation might potentially save us more in terms of future lost goodwill arising from more batches of production reaching the end customer.

Section 2

Briefing Paper on Inventory and Budget Control

Inventory

Implications of Aged Inventory Report

The aged inventory report indicates that the inventory level varies enormously with the fragrance. Indeed it would appear that for Diamond there is enough inventory on hand to satisfy demand for well over a year, whilst there is Topaz and Amethyst to satisfy less than a month.

From the analysis it would appear that we are holding excessive inventory for some of our fragrances(Diamond and Emerald in particular) and possibly risk stock-outs for other fragrances(Topaz and Amethyst).

Holding Excessive Inventory Levels Has a Number of Negative Implications for Our Business

- It is tying up cash within our working capital cycle that could be better used elsewhere in the business.
- It is costing us money to store the inventory, which has the effect of reducing our profit.
- There is a risk that these fragrance products lose quality and, if these are then sold to consumers, it could damage our reputation for quality production.
- There is also the risk at very excessive levels of inventory that our products become obsolete and unsaleable. This would reduce profit as this inventory would need to be written off.

Holding a Low Level of Inventory also Has a Number of Implications

- On the positive side, a low level of inventory means that the costs of storage are low and that a lower investment in working capital is required.
- However, there is a potential risk of stock-out. We have to spread our finished good inventory across a number of concession stands as well as our own stores and on-line sales warehouse. Therefore if the overall level of inventory is very low then almost certainly there will be locations where certain fragrances are out of stock and hence there are lost sales.

What We Could Do to Reduce Finished Goods Inventory Levels

The different levels of finished inventory by fragrance is likely the result of our current production scheduling system which is based on a "push" system where product is produced whether there are orders for it or not. It has always been important to ensure that all of our concessions stands, own stores and the on-line warehouse have adequate inventory, but producing for inventory rather than orders has led to the position we are now in.

In outline we could do the following to reduce our excessive inventory holdings of finished goods.

- Ensure that there are adequate and detailed inventory control systems to manage inventory holding at each location. This together with detailed sales forecasts by location should be used to determine the level of production of each fragrance.

- Implement a JIT philosophy to inventory management. JIT can be regarded as a pull through system: a system that responds to customer demand whereby fragrances are manufactured as required and raw materials are obtained only as they are required. This contrasts with our current push system of regular production runs of fragrances in rotation, regardless of demand.
- We could look to promote the fragrances with the highest levels of inventory in order to convert as much as possible into cash. However, care is needed not to discount too heavily as this could have a negative impact on our reputation and brand.

ZBB

ZBB would be implemented in a number of stages. Firstly, the production process would be split into decision units or departments. For example, this could be raw materials receiving and checking, oil based mixing, water based mixing, emulsification, quality control, bottling, packaging, warehouse handling and of course machinery maintenance.

Secondly, for each decision unit develop decision packages. A decision package is essentially an analysis and costing of different ways in which the objectives of the decision unit can be achieved. Taking machinery maintenance as an example, the objectives must be to ensure that the machinery is maintained so that there are no breakdowns and therefore production can continue without unnecessary interruptions.

Decision packages can either be mutually exclusive or incremental. For machinery maintenance mutually exclusive decision packages might be firstly to employ our own staff to carry out maintenance and secondly to set up a contract with an external party for monthly maintenance. Both of these would potentially achieve the objective of the decision unit and each will have different costs associated with them. These mutually exclusive decision packages could be further broken down into incremental decision packages. For example, the decision package to employ our own staff for maintenance as discussed above, could be split into a base package and then one or more incremental packages. The base package here could be to employ one person to cover all of the production lines. This might not fully meet the objective of zero breakdowns, and the impact of this would need to be factored into the decision package. There could then be an incremental package whereby two people are employed, which should result in no break-downs.

Finally, once all the decision packages are identified, each decision package is to review and rank on a cost benefit basis. Budget resources should then be allocated on this basis.

The benefits of using ZBB are as follows.

- Because decision packages need to be identified and quantified it focuses attention on activities and the achievement of objectives (such as zero machinery breakdowns). Ultimately this focus re-enforces these objectives, meaning that there is a greater chance that they are achieved.
- Because in effect budget setting starts from a position of zero, the decision packages that are accepted into the budget will need to be fully justified. Hence the budget should reduce budget slack and potential inefficient use of resources. It will also, potentially, increase the motivation of staff.

Section 3

From: Management Accountant Assistant
To: Freda Jones, Finance Director
Subject: Marketing campaign

Effective Marketing Campaign

A proper marketing campaign will enable us to get close to our customers and fulfil their needs, if we don't consider our competitors will.

In our case we have a zero level distribution network, dealing either directly with customers personally, or directly through our on-line channel.

As such a direct marketing pull strategy will be most appropriate. A "pull" strategy involves advertising through various media to create consumer demand, in our case this will be based around our existing brand values but with the addition of the new fragrance. This is especially important with the launch of our new fragrance and positioning is all important to us, we need to formulate a definitive market strategy around which the fragrance will be marketed to the target audience.

Consideration of the marketing mix will be required. The marketing mix involves working out the tactical details of the positioning strategy and as such consideration of the 4 P's product, price, promotion and place. With regard to product we already have a well-defined quality product, which we sell at premium prices to reflect the fragrance quality. Our distribution and selling network is also well developed. The promotion, therefore, will be heavily dependent on emphasising the new addition to the existing brand.

Brand in our business is all important. The business will survive, or decline with the popularity of the brand and what it stands for. In our case quality body care products that customers feel are valued for their effectiveness and range of fragrances. Our brand makes a statement about our products and is a key asset of the business. Customers choose our products over our competitors because they like our brand.

It is important that this link is maintained with our advertising campaign and that the marketing spend on the new fragrance is linked to maintaining our brand image, emphasising our consistency of quality, associated with our distinctive brand name and our range of product features, which make it well known and popular.

As such our marketing spend has the objective of putting our brand at the forefront of our consumer's minds and therefore influencing their choice. It is important that we establish and maintain this link in the customer's mind. Whilst this will require us to commit considerable resources, a strong brand should enable the link with name awareness, and the perception of quality and strong association of the new fragrance, with our well-established and reliable brand.

Roger's Schedule

Roger has created a pay-off table which enables the evaluation of alternative courses of action (the three possible campaigns) under different market conditions.

There is clearly uncertainty about how the market will react to the campaign which Roger has assumed depends on whether the market conditions are poor, fair or good. The end result is that there are nine possible combinations of market condition and campaign.

Interpretation of Schedule

Without probabilities there are three different ways in which Roger's schedule can be interpreted and the choice of which depends on your attitude to decision making.

Firstly, using a maximax approach we would select the campaign which gives the best possible result of all nine possible outcomes. This is campaign C, which in good market conditions returns the highest profit at K$ 250,000. This is an optimist approach, assuming that the best outcome will occur whatever else happens.

Secondly, using a maximin approach, which is a pessimistic approach, we would select campaign A, as this gives the best of all the worst outcomes, in poor market conditions of K$ 150,000.

Thirdly, using a minimax regret approach, we would select campaign B, because this gives the lowest of the maximum regrets, where regret is measured as the impact of making an incorrect decision.

Impact of Probabilities

If we had the probabilities of the likelihood of each of the three market conditions occurring, we would be able to extend the analysis by calculating the expected value of each campaign.

For each campaign the expected value would be the sum of each possible outcome of that campaign multiplied by its probability of occurrence. The campaign with the highest expected value would then be selected on the basis that this would give the highest expected return.

The benefits of using this technique is that it takes account of risk by considering the probability of each possible outcome and it produces a single result which is straightforward and easy to understand, compared to the three possible results identified above.

With probabilities we could take the analysis even further by calculating the standard deviation of each campaign. This is a statistical measure which tell us how risky each campaign is as a result of how wide the range of possible outcomes are.

Thanks!

Management Accountant Assistant

Sanchez Navarra

Section 4

From: Management Accountant Assistant

To: Roger Dawson, Finance Manager

Subject: Supplier issue

Explanation for George

Dear George,

I understand we have a considerable amount of redundant inventory as a result of production problems caused by faulty raw materials and that this has most likely happened because of our failure to follow correct procedures. As such I will have to advise that your suggestion that we should falsify various paperwork, and recharge our supplier with not only the cost of the materials but also our conversion costs is not acceptable. To do this would be dishonest and unethical.

As you are no doubt aware, as a member of a professional body I am bound by an ethical code which gives guidance in such circumstances. In particular the code refers to integrity which involves being straight forward honest and truthful in all professional and business relationships. If we falsify the paperwork and recharge our supplier, this will certainly not be so.

In order to prevent this type of situation happening again we will need to ensure that our procedures are reviewed and that this type of situation will not reoccur. Since we have a long standing relationship with this supplier, perhaps the best course of action would be to explain exactly what has happened and the situation with our redundant inventory. It may well be that we can come to agreement with them and solve the problem in an amicable and mutually agreeable manner.

Ultimately it is important that we maintain the good relationship with this supplier, therefore we should act honestly and with integrity.

Inventory Value in the Financial Statements for the Year Ended 31 December 2016

Even though we have found out about the defective materials in January 2017, this is actually evidence of a condition that existed at the reporting period date and therefore this is an adjusting event.

As you know, inventory at the year-end will need to be measured at the lower of cost and net realisable value.

In respect of the K$ 105,000 of raw material surfactant, we plan to return this to our supplier. Even though we did not check the quality prior to using some of the surfactant, it is likely, given our good relationship with the supplier, that they will accept return of this poor quality raw material. If that is the case then at the year-end we should make an accrual for the return that we will be making. This means effectively that the inventory value for this will be nil and there will be a corresponding receivable for the balance owed from the supplier.

If the supplier does not accept return of the surfactant, we will need to write the value of the unused surfactant down to nil as there has been an impairment in its value. This will reduce profit for the year by K$ 105,000. Any costs incurred scrapping the raw materials would be a cost in 2017, as the decision to scrap will have been made in 2017.

In respect of the K$ 150,000 of finished goods inventory, we will need to look at its net realisable value. The net realisable value will depend on whether we decide to rework the products or to scrap them.

If we rework the products, the net realisable value will be calculated as the ultimate sales proceeds from the sale of the inventory (K$ 400,000) less the estimated costs to complete the products (K$ 120,000) ther less any costs of selling the products, such as our distribution and selling costs (which are unknown at this stage). If this value is lower than the cost of K$ 150,000, we will need to record the inventory at the lower value.

If we decide to scrap the inventory, the value of the inventory at the year-end must be nil as there has been an impairment in its value. This will reduce profit for the year. The scrapping costs of K$ 20,000 should not be recorded in the year to 31 December 2016 as the decision to scrap will have been taken in 2017, and therefore there is no commitment at the year end.

Thanks!

Management Accountant Assistant
Sanchez Navarra

试卷二 参考答案

任务一

给 Freda Jones 的简报

世界级制造业

世界级制造业在变化迅速、越来越难以预测的环境中变得日益重要。我们的对手能够创造竞争产品，并能对快速变化的市场环境和买家需求的变化做出快速反应，意味着我们需要具备同样的能力。

客户满意度是世界级制造业的首要任务。虽然成本效率仍然至关重要，但上市时间、对客户需求的响应和产品的创新都越来越与成功息息相关。

最终，客户满意度是由质量——产品、生产过程和我们提供的服务——来支撑的。因此世界级制造业本质上与质量相关，而全面质量管理的原则被视为实现这一目标的途径。通过追求零缺陷的最终目标的持续改进，可以实现制造的卓越。

为了实现这一目标，我们需要投资我们的制造设备，以及用于分析和测试产品的计算机技术等。在我们的业务中，调配不同香料的混合，分析测试结果和处理大量信息的能力是确保我们领先竞争对手的关键。

我们在一个真正的全球化环境中进行贸易，我们现在面临着来自世界各地的潜在竞争。我们的竞争对手可能更接近原材料的产地，在较廉价的经济领域开展业务，这些给他们带来了竞争优势。因此，我们需要确保我们的供应链是精简高效的。

员工参与和员工赋权是世界级制造业的另一个关键因素。鼓励所有员工共同努力去消除传统的工作界限，这是一种被鼓励的团队合作方式。建立高质量的圈子可能有助于实现这一目标。

总之，从长远来看，采用世界级制造业方法可能有利于企业，通过始终如一的高质量产品和一个灵活的、可适应客户需求的现代制造环境来提高客户满意度。

质量成本

实施质量成本报告

质量成本法实质上是报告和考虑业务所产生的成本的一种方式，这些成本可能是由于确保达到适当的质量或由于质量标准尚未达到而产生的。它涉及质量报告的准备，其成本分为符合成本（为确保达到一定的质量标准而产生的费用）和不符合成本（产生的费用不符合质量标准）。符合成本可以是预防或评估，而不符合成本是内部或外部的失败成本。

依次看看 Gail 建议的每一个质量成本。

- 新员工使用机器培训课程的费用是预防成本。这是因为进行培训是为了确保机械被正确使用，因此生产的质量是应有的。这是为防止质量问题发生而产生的费用。
- 由于生产机器需要修理而造成的人员停工费用是内部故障成本。生产机械已经崩溃并需要修理的事实意味着质量的下降导致了停工。在产品到达最终客户之前发生故障的事实意味着它是内部故障成本。
- 租赁用于检测原材料的检测设备的费用是评估成本。作为评估过程的一部分，对原材料进行检测，以确保它们在生产前具备合格的质量。
- 生产线的维护费用是预防成本。因为如果生产线正常工作，那么就可以防止由于机械问题而导致的质量问题。
- 处理客户投诉的费用是外部失败成本。客户抱怨的事实意味着产品品质不佳（由于产品不良或服务差）。事实上，客户的抱怨意味着它是企业外部的业务。

采用质量成本报告的好处

鉴于世界级制造业正在被考虑，而且这是由质量和全面质量管理支撑的，采取质量成本法将会加强和支持这一点，因为它将管理层的注意力集中在了质量问题上。

通过在质量成本报告中识别和量化质量相关成本，我们将更好地了解如何降低质量失败的风险（在我们的符合成本方面）及实际上不符合质量的影响（根据我们的不符合成本）。

例如，如果不符合成本很高（可能是由于生产质量较差，对客户的商誉有显著的影响，从而减少了销售），那么我们就需要考虑是否将更大比例的预算分配给内部的质量控制。这将会影响符合成本的增加，但是从未来更多批次的生产到达最终客户所产生的商誉损失来看，这种缓解可能会为我们节省更多。

任务二

有关库存和预算控制的简报

库存

陈年库存报告的影响

陈年库存报告显示，库存水平与香味大不相同。事实上，对于钻石香味来说，似乎有足够的库存可以满足一年多的需求，而黄玉和紫水晶香味的库存只能满足不足一个月的需求。

从分析可以看出，我们正在对我们的一些香味（特别是钻石和翡翠）持有过多的库存，并且可能存在其他香料味（黄玉和紫水晶）的缺货风险。

过多的库存水平对我们的业务有很多负面影响

- 在我们的营运资金周期内占用的现金，可以被更好地利用在其他业务领域。
- 存储存货会花费资金，将会减少我们的利润。
- 这些香味产品存在质量不合格的风险，如果这些产品出售给消费者，可能会损害我们的质量生产声誉。
- 存在过高的库存水平的风险，我们的产品变得过时和滞销。这将减少利润，因为这个库存需要注销。

存货水平低也有一些影响

- 从积极的角度而言，低库存意味着存储成本低，只需要较低的营运资金投入。
- 然而，存在潜在的缺货风险。我们必须将我们的成品库存分散到许多特许柜台以及我们自己的商店和在线销售仓库。因此，如果整体库存水平非常低，那么几乎肯定会有某些地方的某些香味缺货，进而导致销售损失。

我们可以做些什么来降低成品库存水平

香味成品库存的不同水平可能是我们目前的生产系统调度的结果，该系统基于产品生产的“推送”系统，无论是否有订单。一直很重要的是要确保我们所有的特许经营柜台，自有的商店和在线仓库都有足够的库存，但生产存货而不是订单已经导致了我们现在的处境。

总而言之，我们可以采取以下措施来减少我们过剩的成品库存。

- 确保有适当和详细的库存控制系统来管理每个地点的库存。这些可与地点的详细销售预测一起应用于确定每种香味的生产水平。
- 对库存管理实施适时制。适时制可以被视为一个拉动系统：一个响应客户需求的系统，其中根据需要制造香味，原材料也只能根据需要获得。这与我们目前的常规生产香味的推动系统形成了鲜明的对比，即不管需求如何。
- 我们可以对库存水平最高的香水进行促销，以尽可能地将其转换为现金。然而，我们不能有太大的折扣，因为这可能会对我们的声誉和品牌产生负面影响。

零基预算

零基预算将分若干阶段实施。首先，生产过程将被分成决策单元或部门。例如，可能会被分为原材料的接收和检查、油基混合、水基混合、乳化、质量控制、灌装、包装、仓库处理，当然还有机器维护。

其次，为每个决策单元制定决策包。决策包本质上是不同的分析和成本核算方法，可以实现决策单元的目标。以机器维护为例，其目标必须是确保机器得到维护，以免发生故障，从而不会出现不必要的中断情况，使生产能够继续。

决策包可以是互斥的或增量的。对于机器维护而言，互斥的决策包可能首先是聘请我们自己的员工进行维护，其次是与外部人员签订月度维修合同。这两者都可能实现决策单元的目标，并且每种方法都具有与之相关的不同成本。这些互斥的决策包可以进一步细分为增量决策包。例如，如上所述使用我们自己的员工进行维护的决策包可以分为一个基本包和一个或多个增量包。这里的基本包可能是雇用一个人来覆盖所有的生产线，这可能不能完全达到零故障的目标，因此需要将其影响考虑到决策包中。那么可能会有一种增量式的方案，同时雇佣两个人，这样就可以实现零故障的目标了。

最后，一旦确定了所有的决策包，就会以成本效益为基础对每一个决策包进行审查和排名。因此，应在此基础上分配预算资源。

使用零基预算的好处。

- 因为决策包需要被识别和量化，所以它把注意力集中在活动和目标的实现上（例如零机器故障）。最终，这种焦点重新强化了这些目标，这意味着有更大的可能性实现它们。
- 因为实际的预算设定从零开始，所以在预算中被接受的决策包需要完全合理。因此，预算应该减少预算松动和潜在的资源利用效率低下。这也可能会提高员工的积极性。

任务三

发件人：管理会计助理

收件人：财务总监 Freda Jones

主题：营销活动

有效的市场营销

适当的营销活动能够使我们靠近我们的客户并满足他们的需求，如果我们不考虑竞争对手的意愿。

在我们的案例中，我们有一个零级的分销网络，直接与客户打交道，或者直接通过我们的在线渠道。

因此，直接的营销策略是最合适的。“拉动式”战略包括通过各种媒体进行广告宣传以创造消费者需求，在我们的案例中，新香型的增加是基于我们现有的品牌价值。这对于我们的新香型的发布和定位尤为重要，我们需要制定一个明确的市场策略，将香水推向目标受众。

需要考虑营销组合。营销组合包括制定定位策略的战术细节，以及对 4 个 P，即产品、价格、促销和地点的考虑。就产品而言，我们已经有了一个明确的优质产品，以高价出售，来反映香味的质量。我们的销售网络也很发达。因此，促销活动将在很大程度上依赖于强调现有品牌的新增。

品牌在我们的业务中是很重要的。随着品牌和它所代表的意义的普及，企业将会生存，或者衰落。在我们的案例中，客户之所以认为我们的身体护理产品的质量好，是因为产品的效果和香味的多样。我们的品牌对我们的产品做出了声明，是我们公司的一项重要资产。顾客选择我们的产品而不是竞争对手的产品，是因为他们喜欢我们的品牌。

重要的是，要通过我们的广告活动来维持这一联系，并且要清楚新香型的营销支出与维护品牌形象有关。其强调了我们与品牌的一致性，并与我们独特的品牌名称以及我们的产品功能范围相关联，这样才能使它知名和受欢迎。

因此，我们的营销支出的目标是把我们的品牌置于消费者心中的首位，从而影响他们的选择。重要的是我们要在客户的头脑中建立并保持这种联系。这需要我们投入大量的资源，一个强大的品牌应该能将我们的品牌意识及对新香型的质量和强烈联想的感知，与我们信誉良好的品牌联系在一起。

Roger 的时间表

Roger 制作了一个收益表，它可以在不同的市场条件下评估不同的行动方案（3 种可能的活动）。

很明显，市场对这场活动的反应有着明显的不确定性，而 Roger 的假设取决于市场状况是好是坏。最终的结果是，市场状况和营销活动有九种可能的组合。

关于时间表的解释

若不考虑概率，那么有三种不同的方式可以解释 Roger 的时间表，而怎么选择取决于你对决策的态度。

第一，使用最大化方法，我们将在所有九种可能结果中选择能够获得最佳结果的营销活动。假设这是活动C，在良好的市场条件下，其回报最高的利润为K$ 250 000。这是一种乐观的态度，假设不管发生什么，都会出现最好的结果。

第二，使用最小化方法，这是一种悲观的做法，我们将选择活动A，因为在K$ 150 000的糟糕市场条件下，这是所有最坏结果中的最好选择。

第三，使用极小遗憾的方法，我们将选择活动B，因为这是所有最大遗憾中的最好选择，遗憾值由做出错误决定的影响来衡量。

概率的影响

如果我们有三种市场情况发生的可能性的概率，我们就可以通过计算每一种活动的预期价值来进行扩展分析。

对于每个活动，期望值都是该活动的每个可能结果乘以其发生概率的总和。然后，预期价值最高的活动将被选中，因为这样可以获得最高的预期回报。

使用这种方法的好处在于，它通过考虑每种可能结果的概率来考虑风险，并且与上面所确定的3个可能的结果相比较而言，它产生了一个简单而易于理解的结果。

知道了概率，我们就可以通过计算每一场活动的标准差来做进一步分析。这是一种统计方法，它告诉我们每个竞选活动的风险有多大，因为可能的结果范围很广。

非常感谢！

桑切斯·纳瓦娜公司
管理会计助理

任务四

发件人：管理会计助理
收件人：财务经理 Roger Dawson
主题：供应商问题

对 Geoger 的解释

亲爱的 Geoger：

据了解，由于原材料不良导致了生产问题，所以我们有大量的冗余库存，而这很可能是由于我们未能遵循正确的程序而造成的。因此，我不得不指出您建议我们应该伪造各种文件，并让我们的供应商补充材料的成本以及我们的转换成本，这是不能接受的。这样做太不诚实和不道德了。

正如你所知道的，作为一个专业团体的成员，我被在这种情况下给予指导的道德准则所约束。特别是在所有的职业和商业关系中，准则都是正直和诚实。如果我们伪造文件，给我们的供应商加价，这肯定不是正直和诚实的。

为了防止这种情况再次发生，我们需要确保我们的程序得到了审查，并确保这种情况不会再发生。我们与供应商有着长期的合作关系，也许最好的行动方案是明确地向他们解释发生了什么事情及我们库存冗余的情况。这样可能我们可以和他们达成一致，以一种友好和双方一致同意的方式解决问题。

最终，我们保持与供应商的良好关系是很重要的，因此我们应该诚实正直地行事。

截至 2016 年 12 月 31 日的年度财务报表的存货价值

尽管我们已经在 2017 年 1 月发现了材料有缺陷，但这实际上是报告期内存在这种情况的证明，因此这是一个调整事项。

如您所知，年底库存需要以较低的成本和可变现净值来衡量。

关于 K$ 105 000 的表面活性剂原料，我们计划将其退还给我们的供应商。尽管我们在使用这些表面活性剂之前没有进行检查，但考虑到我们与供应商的良好关系，他们可能会接受这种质量低劣的原材料的退货。如果是这样的话，那么年底时我们应该为我们将要得到的回报做一个预提。这意味着我们有效的存货价值为零，并且会有相应的应收账款来抵消供应商的欠款。

如果供应商不接受表面活性剂的退货，那么我们就需要将未使用的表面活性剂的价值降到零，因为其价值已经减损。这将使本年度的利润减少 K$ 105 000。废弃原材料所产生的任何费用都将是 2017 年的成本，因为废弃的决定将在 2017 年完成。

关于价值 K$ 150 000 的成品库存，我们需要看看它的可变现净值。其可变现净值将取决于我们是决定重新加工产品，还是废弃产品。

如果我们重新加工产品，则可变现净值将计算为销售库存的最终销售收入（K$ 400 000）减去加工产品的估计成本（K$ 120 000），再减去销售产品的成本，例如我们的分销和销售成本（在这个阶段是未知的）。如果这个价值低于 K$ 150 000 的成本，那么我们将需要以较低的价值记录库存。

如果我们决定废弃库存，则年末库存的价值必须为零，因为其价值已经减损。这将减少本年度的利润。截至2016年12月31日，K$20 000的报废成本不用被记录下来，因为在2017年，报废的决定才会被做出，因此在年底也不会有责任。

非常感谢！

桑切斯·纳瓦娜公司

管理会计助理

Variant 2　Marking Guidance

Section	Technical skills		Business skills		People skills		Leadership skills		Integration	Total
1	Cost of quality (P1)	14	Application of world class manufacturing to the business (E1)	14						28
2	Aged inventory report and inventory management (F1) ZBB(P1)	13 12								25
3	Pay-off table (P1)	13			Marketing campaign (E1)	12				25
4	Inventory value and event after the reporting issue (F1)	11			Ethical issue (E1)	2	Ethical issue (E1)	6	3	22
Total marks available for each competency		63		14		14		6	3	100

试卷二　评分指南

部分	技术技能		商业技能		人际技能		领导技能		综合	总计
1	质量成本（P1）	14	世界级制造业在商业中的应用（E1）	14					3	28
2	陈年库存报告和库存管理（F1） 零基预算（P1）	13 12								25
3	收益表（P1）	13			营销活动（E1）	12				25
4	报告问题后的库存价值和事项	11			道德问题（E1）	2	道德问题（E1）	6	3	22
各种能力分数总计		63		14		14		6	3	100

中央财经大学名师解惑

试卷一共有四项任务，考查了 E1、P1、F1 三门课程的知识点，具体包括质量成本、库存报告和库存管理、零基预算、营销活动及职业道德问题等。该试卷考核了考生的四项能力，其中专业技能的分值占 63%，商业技能的分值占 14%，人际技能的分值占 14%，领导技能的分值占 6%，与 CGMA 管理会计能力框架的技能要求一致。

该试卷的每项任务涉及以下知识点：

任务	问题	科目	知识点
任务一	如何实施质量成本报告以及其好处	（P1）	质量成本（quality cost）
	世界级制造业的关键原则的具体实施办法	（E1）	世界级制造业（world class manufacturing）
任务二	说明存货报告对业务的影响及如何进行存货管理	（F1）	存货管理（inventory management）
	如何实施零基预算及其好处	（P1）	零基预算（ZBB）
任务三	对收益表进行解释	（P1）	收益表（income statement）
	如何进行有效的营销活动	（E1）	营销活动（marketing activities）
任务四	解释财务报告中的库存价值和事项	（P1）	库存价值（inventory value）
	说明其中的道德问题	（E1）	道德问题（moral issue）

上述各项任务要求以邮件、报告或工作笔记等形式来呈现答案，对问题的描述非常明确，答题时既要注意内容的针对性，也要注意形式的规范性。

其他答题注意事项包括：（1）仔细读题，一般每项任务都会涉及 2～3 个大的知识点，一定不能漏答；（2）答题要有条理，从是什么到为什么，从分析原因到提出解决办法，将每个知识点都解释清楚；（3）分层级列出各级小标题，让考官容易了解你的思路。

同时，答题时，要避免只是对教科书中的知识点进行简单复述，应结合案例公司的实际情况。注意回答时的措辞、格式、论述的结构、论点的鲜明性和整体性等。

对应知识点的深度剖析

质量成本

质量成本包括符合成本和不符合成本。符合成本是实现特定质量要求的成本，又可分成评估成本和预防成本。不符合成本是未达到质量标准所产生的成本，又分成内部失败成本和外部失败成本。

质量成本报告是指根据质量成本分析形成的报告，主要是为了制定质量的方针目标、评价质量体系的有效性和寻求质量改进的依据。它也是对质量成本管理活动或某一典型事件进行调查、分析和建议的总结性文件，并可常规性地放进月度的管理会计报告中。使用质量成本报告有助于公司加强质量管理，提高竞争力。

世界级制造业

为了达到世界级制造业的水平，企业必须广泛采用世界级制造业方法。通过广泛采用世界级制造业方法，可以不断改善企业的生产运营系统，提升企业的运作绩效，最终使企业成为“世界级制造”企业。世界级制造业的绩效评估体系包括：交货和用户服务绩效的度量、加工时间绩效的度量、制造系统柔性的度量、质量绩效的度量、财务绩效的度量、人才管理绩效的度量。企业实现世界级制造的步骤：（1）战略规划；（2）先进制造方式的选择与实施；（3）可行的绩效评估体系；（4）至臻至善，持续改进。

对于如何落实世界级制造业的关键原则这一问题，考生应明确其首要任务及最终目标，然后围绕如何实现该目标进行思考。

存货管理

存货作为一项重要的流动资产，直接关系到企业的资金占用水平及资产运作效率。因此，一个企业若要保持较高的盈利能力，就应当十分重视存货的管理。通过实施正确的存货管理方法，来降低企业的平均资金占用水平，提高存货的流转速度和总资产周转率，才能最终提高企业的经济效益。存货持有水平是存货管理的重要内容。

考生应恰当阐述存货持有水平高低对业务的影响以及如何加强存货的相关管理，并结合题目中的具体信息进行说明。

零基预算

零基预算与传统的增量预算法不同，在编制成本费用预算时，不考虑以往期间的费用项目或数额，一切从零开始，根据预算期的实际需要和可能性，逐项审查预算期内各项费用的内容及其开支标准是否合理，在综合平衡的基础上编制费用预算。其优点是可以减少浪费，合理分配资金，提高预算管理水平。

考生在解答此题时，可以先介绍零基预算的特点，再根据零基预算的实施步骤，结合题目中提供的细节信息来回答。零基预算的关键步骤之一是对可选的决策包进行成本效益分析，解答中需指出开展成本效益分析时还要取得哪些相关信息。

考生注意事项

零基预算的核心是在预算编制中引入一种质疑的态度，对现有的实践活动和费用开支提出疑问，诸如：这项活动是必需的吗？如果不进行这项活动，会带来什么后果？是否有其他可能的途径可以达到同样的目的？这项费用开支是否值得？通过回答这些问题使预算中的不合理因素被剔除，从而达到节约成本，提高资源利用效率的目的。

零基预算的三个核心步骤包括：(1) 根据组织目标，确认预算期内需要进行的业务项目及其费用开支，制定多个可能的备选方案（也称为决策包）；(2) 对备选方案进行成本效益分析，评估项目费用开支的合理程度，确定先后顺序以及对组织业务活动的影响；(3) 按照预算期可动用的资金及其来源和项目的轻重缓急次序，分配资金，落实预算。

收益表

收益表是公司的一种报表，报告某段时期（通常为一年）的销售收入或收益，所售商品的合理成本，还有剔除成本后所剩的利润（净收入）。对收益表进行分析是为了分析企业如何组织收入、控制成本费用支出、盈利，并评价企业的经营成果。同时还可以通过分析收支结构和业务结构，评价各部门的业绩成长对公司总体效益的贡献，以及不同分公司的经营成果对公司总体盈利水平的贡献。

考生需掌握如何利用收益表评估不同的行动方案。

营销活动

营销活动是企业在变化的市场环境中，为满足消费者需求和实现企业目标，综合运用各种市场营销手段，把商品和服务整体地销售给消费者的一系列市场经营活动。营销活动不仅能够增加品牌的影响力，提升消费者的忠诚度，同时也能吸引更多的媒体关注。完整的市场营销活动应当从市场分析开始，然后制定营销战略，确定营销计划和营销组合，接着实施计划，最后是衡量与评估成果。

实施有效的营销活动，考生必须结合案例中企业的具体情况，按照市场营销的基本思路进行思考。

库存价值

对企业存货价值（即成本）进行计量可以帮助企业的仓库管理人员对库存商品进行详尽、全面的控制和管理，同时由此提供的各种库存报表和库存分析可以为企业的决策提供依据，实现降低库存、减少资金占用的目标，保证企业的经营活动顺利进行。而存货的计价方法包括：先进先出法、后进后出法、加权平均法和个别计价法。资产负债表规定，存货应当通过比较成本与可变现净值来进行计量。存货成本高于可变现净值的，应当按计提存货跌价准备，计入当期损益。其中，可变现净值是指在日常活动中存货的估计售价减去至完工时估计将要发生的成本、估计的销售费用以及相关税费后的金额。

考生应熟练掌握存货价值的估值方法，以及可能涉及的存货计价方法以及存货计量等会计问题。

道德问题

职业道德是指从业人员在职业活动中应该遵循的行为准则，涵盖了从业人员与服务对象、职业与职工、职业与职业之间的关系。职业道德要求我们必须办实事，求实效，坚决反对和制止在工作上弄虚作假，如果为了满足自己的私利或迎合某些人的私欲而弄虚作假、虚报浮夸，就会背离实事求是这一最基本的职业道德原则。

考生应当学会从职业道德角度出发，围绕案例对企业经营管理中发生的行为进行评述。

Variant 3

This examination is structured as follows：

Section number	Number of tasks	Time for section(minutes)
1	1	55
2	1	45
3	1	40
4	1	40

The time available for each section is for reading,planning and writing your answer(s).

Section 1

You arrive at work in the morning and receive the following email from Roger Dawson, finance manager.

From: Roger Dawson, Finance Manager
To: Management Accountant Assistant
Subject: Supplier price increase

We recently received information that our suppliers of coconut and soy bean oil have formed a trade association to protect their collective trading positions. This is going to result in an increase in the price that we pay for these raw materials. These raw materials are used in body wash and body lotion, but not hand & foot cream.

Yesterday, Tomaz Green, operations director, asked for a schedule giving an indication of what our profitability would be based on the original budget and the revised budget (which takes into account the increased costs). Gail Honner, your fellow finance officer, prepared a schedule of workings and sent it to Tomaz.

Tomaz has come back to me with some queries and requests. Here is what he said in this email:

I'm having difficulty understanding Gail's schedule of workings. Please send me an explanation of what I should interpret from this schedule in respect of the original and revised budgets. Please tell me how useful Gail's schedule is as a means of assessing the profitability of individual product groups.

If this type of cost increase were to happen again, I don't think that we would want to pass this increased cost onto our customers. Therefore please send me your suggestions as to what steps we could take to improve our trading position.

Our current purchasing policy is to use a number of different suppliers and bargain for the best price, so it is disappointing to find that we are now facing price increases. In the light of this, I think we need to review our purchasing policy so we don't get any more surprises. I'd like to know your view on our current policy and how we might change it to our advantage.

I need to send Tomaz a briefing paper addressing his four queries. As Gail is not here today, please prepare the first draft of this for me.

Many thanks!

Roger Dawson
Finance Manager
Sanchez Navarra

Accessory

Based on original budget for the year to 31 December 2016:

	Body wash (K$000)	Body lotion (K$000)	Hand & foot cream (K$000)	Gift sets (K$000)	Total (K$000)
Revenue(note 1)	14,300	9,500	3,800	4,300	32,000
Variable cost(note 2)	(4,300)	(2,800)	(1,400)	(1,090)	(9,590)
Contribution	10,000	6,800	2,400	3,210	22,410
Specific fixed costs(note 3)	(630)	(670)	(380)	(240)	(1,920)
Contribution less specific fixed costs	9,370	6,130	2,020	2,970	20,490
Other fixed costs(note 4)					(17,800)
Total budgeted profit					2,690
C/S ratio(%)	69.9	70.8	63.2	74.7	70.0

Notes:

(1) Revenue for each products stated after adjusting for the expected level of discount on the recommended retail price for that product.

(2) Variable cost includes the variable costs of production only.

(3) Specific fixed costs are the fixed production costs plus marketing costs from product targeted campaigns. The fixed production costs associated with the body wash production line have been wholly allocated to body wash. The fixed production costs associated with the other production line have been split between body lotion and hand & foot cream on the basis of numbers of units sold. The fixed production costs associated with assembly of gift sets is wholly allocated to gift sets.

(4) Total(specific and other) fixed costs are K$ 19,720,000. Other fixed costs include administrative costs, and those sales and distribution costs which have not been specifically allocated.

Revised budget：

Following the price increase total contribution would reduce by K$ 906,000. The revised C/S ratio would be：

	Body wash	Body lotion	Hand & foot cream	Gift sets	Total
Revised C/S ratio(%)	65.9	68.6	63.2	71.9	67.2

Break-even and margin of safety calculations for all products：

Measure	Original budget	Revised budget
Break-even revenue(K$)	28,171,429	29,345,238
Margin of safety(%)	12.0	8.3

Write the draft of briefing paper requested by Roger Dawson.

Section 2

A few days later Roger Dawson sends you the following email.

From：Roger Dawson, Finance Manager
To：Management Accountant Assistant
Subject：Marketing issues

I had a meeting yesterday with the directors. We discussed the briefing paper that we'd prepared for Tomaz and one of the conclusions was that we need to undertake an additional marketing campaign across our range of products to boost sales and better cover the fixed costs.

There was some disagreement on what form this marketing campaign should take and how much should be spent on it. Three options are being considered：spending K$ 150,000, spending K$ 100,000 or spending K$ 75,000. Richard Procter, sales & marketing director, talked about using a combination of different promotions, although he didn't discuss which form these promotions should take or how effective they might be. He did, however, rule out a mass media advertising campaign. He recommended that K$ 150,000 should be spent on the campaign.

After the meeting Richard sent those of us who attended the meeting a schedule which he said this is his argument for the largest of the three potential marketing campaign budgets. Nisha Shah and Freda Jones have asked me to prepare a report for them before they meet with Richard again, so that they fully understand the reasoning behind his recommendation. They are also keen to hear about any ideas we have regarding what form our promotions should take. They would like the report to include:

- an explanation and evaluation of the approach Richard has used to reach his conclusion and any alternative conclusions that could be reached by using the statistical information provided;
- suggestions of three different forms of promotion that we could use in this campaign and the associated benefits and drawbacks of each one.

Please prepare a report for Nisha and Freda on the above.

Many thanks!

Roger Dawson

Finance Manager

Sanchez Navarra

Schedule of the Impact of Different Marketing Spends

If we spend K$ 150,000 on the campaign:

Probability	Impact on profit	Expected value
0.4	(30)	(12)
0.4	190	76
0.2	300	60
	124	
Standard Deviation = K$ 132,000, Coefficient of variation = 1.06		

If we spend K$ 100,000 on the campaign:

Probability	Impact on profit	Expected value
0.1	10	1
0.6	100	60
0.3	160	48
	109	
Standard Deviation = K$ 42,532, Coefficient of variation = 0.39		

If we spend K$ 75,000 on the campaign:

Probability	Impact on profit	Expected value
0.4	10	4
0.5	90	45
0.1	150	15
	64	
Standard Deviation = K$ 47,371, Coefficient of variation = 0.74		

Notes:

(1) The impact on profits measured as the possible additional contribution generated by each campaign less the costs of the campaign.

(2) Each level of spend relates to a different form of campaign. As a result the probabilities associated with each possible outcome differ between campaigns.

Conclusion：

My recommendation is to spend K$ 150,000 on the campaign on the basis of expected value.

Write the report requested by Roger Dawson.

Section 3

The following day, Roger Dawson says to you：

Tomaz Green is looking into changing a number of the suppliers of raw materials. He has just handed me a schedule of information that he has accumulated about six potential suppliers of emollients. They all offer the same quality of emollient and are all offering to supply us at very similar prices. Tomaz is unsure of which one or two of these suppliers is used and has asked me to look at his schedule to see what I think about their suitability as suppliers. Please you look at the schedule and send me your assessment based on the information provided, together with any further information that we will need to consider before making a decision.

On a related matter, as a result of the recent increase in the coco nut and soy bean raw material costs brought about by suppliers forming a trade association, our standards for raw materials prices are out of date. Changing suppliers is only going to compo und this issue which is potentially going to make our variance reports less meaningful. I've been thinking about splitting our variances into planning and operational variances to deal with this, although I'm concerned about engaging our managers in this.

I will need to justify this change to the directors and therefore would like you to send me an explanation of the approach(using the raw materials cost variances to illustrate), its benefits and also its drawbacks to the business, which I can use them as justification. Please send me this in the same email as your assessment of Tomaz's schedule.

Schedule of information relating to six potential suppliers of emollients：

Each potential supplier would be able to supply us in full the amount that we would require.

Potential supplier	Location	Annual revenue 2015 (K$ million)	Operating cash inflow or outflow in 2015	Ownership	Credit terms offered (days)
Supplier 1	Keyland	16	inflow	subsidiary of a large international group	30
Supplier 2	Keyland	166	outflow	quoted on the Keyland market	40
Supplier 3	Meyland	27	inflow	privately owned business	45
Supplier 4	Keyland	14	outflow	privately owned business	60
Supplier 5	Keyland	13	outflow	subsidiary of a large international group	20
Supplier 6	Seyland	250	inflow	quoted on the Seyland stock market	30

Meyland uses the M$ as its currency and Seyland is the S$. For supplier 3 and 6 the annual revenue figures in the above table have been translated into K$ at the average rate of exchange for 2015 for the purposes of this analysis.

Write the email requested by Roger Dawson.

Section 4

Two months later you receive the following email from Roger Dawson.

From: Roger Dawson, Finance Manager
To: Management Accountant Assistant
Subject: Working capital position and supplier issue

I need to prepare a report for the next directors'meeting and I would like you to draft a couple of sections for me.

Firstly, the directors would like an analysis of our working capital position at the end of June 2016 compared both with our position at the end of June 2015 and with one of our major competitors which has a year-end of April. This competitor operates concessions in large department stores and has a number of corporate contracts to supply hotels with its products.

I've pulled together the following information in respect of this:

	Based on our 30 June 2016 balances	Based on our 30 June 2015 balances	Based on our competitor's balances at 30 April 2016
Inventory days	240 days	207 days	180 days
Receivable days	45 days	23 days	47 days
Payable days	35 days	42 days	65 days
Working capital cycle	250 days	188 days	162 days

Secondly, it has come to Tomaz Green's, operations director, attention that one of our new suppliers has been using child labour to harvest its crops. Apparently employment laws

in their country state that children can work if they are given adequate breaks and work no more than 30 hours a week. Tomaz is concerned because in Keyland children are not allowed to work more than five hours a week and then only in a service industry. In their meeting the directors have asked for an idea of the factors that they need to consider in respect of this potential issue.

Please prepare the two sections for the report that I am preparing for the directors.

Many thanks!

Roger Dawson

Finance Manager

Sanchez Navarra

Write the report requested by Roger Dawson.

试卷三

本次考试的结构如下：

序号	任务数	时间（分钟）
1	1	55
2	1	45
3	1	40
4	1	40

每个部分规定的时间可用于读题、组织和书写答案。

任务一

您早上工作时，收到了财务经理 Roger Dawson 的以下电子邮件。

发件人：财务经理 Roger Dawson

收件人：管理会计助理

主题：供应商涨价

最近，我们收到相关信息，我们的椰子和大豆油供应商组建了一个贸易协会来保护他们的交易地位。这将导致我们为这些原材料支付的价格上涨。这些原料用于沐浴露和身体乳，但不用于手足霜。

昨天，运营总监 Tomaz Green 要求我们给他提供一个明细表，在其中要说明基于原始预算和修订预算（考虑到成本增加）的我们的盈利能力。财务总监 Gail Honner 准备了一份工作明细表，并将其发送给了 Tomaz。

Tomaz 已经回复了我，并提出了一些疑问。这是他的电子邮件的具体内容：

我很难理解 Gail 提供的工作明细表。请给我一个能让我从这个明细表中理解原始和修订的预算的说明。请告诉我，Gail 的明细表是如何有效地评估个别产品组的盈利能力的。

如果这种成本增加再次发生，我不认为我们应该把增加的成本转嫁到我们的客户身上。因此，请您给我一些建议，我们可以采取什么措施来改善交易状况。

我们目前的采购政策是使用不同的供应商，并进行讨价还价，所以我们现在面临的价格上涨是令人失望的。鉴于此，我认为我们需要重新审视我们的采购政策，这样我们就不会再受到更多惊吓了。我想知道您对现行政策的看法，以及我们如何将它改变为我们的优势。

我需要给 Tomaz 发送一份关于他这四个疑问的简报，因为 Gail 今天不在这里，请你为我准备这份简报的初稿。

非常感谢！

桑切斯 · 纳瓦娜公司

财务经理

Roger Dawson

附件

基于2016年12月31日的原始预算：

	沐浴露（K$000）	润肤乳（K$000）	手足霜（K$000）	礼品套装（K$000）	总计（K$000）
收入（附注1）	14 300	9 500	3 800	4 300	32 000
变动成本（附注2）	(4 300)	(2 800)	(1 400)	(1 090)	(9 590)
贡献	10 000	6 800	2 400	3 210	22 410
特定固定成本（附注3）	(630)	(670)	(380)	(240)	(1 920)
贡献减去特定固定成本	9 370	6 130	2 020	2 970	20 490
其他固定成本（附注4）					(17 800)
总预算利润					2 690
C/S 比率（%）	69.9	70.8	63.2	74.7	70.0

附注：

（1）根据该产品的建议零售价调整预期折扣水平后每种产品的收入。

（2）可变成本仅包括生产的可变成本。

（3）特定固定成本是固定生产成本加上产品定位活动的营销成本。与沐浴露生产线相关的固定生产成本已全部分配给沐浴露；与其他生产线相关的固定生产成本在销售单位数量的基础上，在润肤乳与手足霜之间分摊；与礼品套装生产线相关的固定生产成本全部分配给礼品套装。

（4）总固定成本（特定和其他）为K$ 19 720 000。其他固定成本包括行政费用，以及尚未明确分配的销售和分配成本。

修订预算：

在价格上涨之后，总贡献将会减少K$ 906 000。经修订的C/S比率是：

	沐浴露	润肤乳	手足霜	礼品套装	总计
修订的C/S比率（%）	65.9	68.6	63.2	71.9	67.2

所有产品的盈亏平衡和安全边际计算：

度量变量	原始预算	修订预算
盈亏平衡收入（K$）	28 171 429	29 345 238
安全边际（%）	12.0	8.3

请撰写Roger Dawson要求的简报初稿。

任务二

几天后，Roger Dawson 向您发送了以下电子邮件。

发件人：财务经理 Roger Dawson
收件人：管理会计助理
主题：营销问题

昨天我和董事们开了个会。我们讨论了我们为 Tomaz 准备的简报，其中一个结论是，我们需要对我们的产品进行额外的营销活动，以增加销售额并更好地分摊固定成本。

但是我们对于这场营销活动应该采取什么样的形式，以及应该花多少钱，有一些分歧。目前，我们正在考虑 3 个选择：花费 K$ 150 000，花费 K$ 100 000 或花费 K$ 75 000。销售与市场总监 Richard Procter 谈到使用不同促销活动的组合，尽管他并没有讨论这些促销活动应该采取哪种形式和它们的效果。不过，他否定了采用大众媒体进行宣传的方案，并且建议在活动中花费 K$ 150 000。

会后，Richard 给我们这些参加会议的人发了一份计划表，他说这是他支付 3 种营销活动预算中最多的那个的理由。Nisha Shah 和 Freda Jones 已经要求我为他们准备一份报告，需要在他们再次与 Richard 会面之前准备好，以便他们充分了解 Richard 建议的背后的原因。他们也很乐意听到我们有关促销活动应该采取什么形式的任何想法。他们希望报告包括以下两个方面。

- 对 Richard 所用的可以得出这个结论的方法的解释和评价，以及利用所提供的统计资料所能得出的任何其他结论。
- 关于我们可以在这次活动中使用的三种不同形式的促销活动的建议以及每种促销活动的优点和缺点。

请根据上述要求为 Nisha 和 Freda 准备一份报告。

非常感谢！

桑切斯·纳瓦娜公司
财务经理
Roger Dawson

不同营销支出影响下的明细表

如果我们在活动上花费 K$ 150 000：

概率	对利润的影响	期望值
0.4	(30)	(12)
0.4	190	76
0.2	300	60
	124	
标准差 = K$ 132 000，变异系数 = 1.06		

如果我们在活动上花费 K$ 100 000：

概率	对利润的影响	期望值
0.1	10	1
0.6	100	60
0.3	160	48
	109	
标准差 = K$ 42 532，变异系数 = 0.39		

如果我们在活动上花费 K$ 75 000：

概率	对利润的影响	期望值
0.4	10	4
0.5	90	45
0.1	150	15
	64	
标准差 = K$ 47 371，变异系数 = 0.74		

附注：

（1）对利润的影响由每个活动可能产生的额外贡献减去活动的成本来衡量。

（2）每种支出水平都涉及不同形式的活动。因此，每个可能结果的概率在不同的营销活动中是不同的。

结论：

基于期望值，我的建议是在营销活动上花费 K$ 150 000。

请根据 Roger Dawson 的要求撰写报告。

任务三

第二天，Roger Dawson 对你说：

Tomaz Green 正在调查一些原材料供应商的变化，他刚刚递交了一份他调查到的 6 个潜在润肤剂供应商的信息明细表。这些供应商都提供了同样质量的润肤剂，并且都给我们提供了非常相似的价格，Tomaz 不确定我们应该使用这些供应商中的哪一个或哪两个，并要求我查看他的明细表，以便知道我对他们是否适合作为我们的供应商的看法。请你看一下明细表，并根据提供的信息将你的评估结果及在你做出决定之前我们需要考虑的任何进一步信息发送给我。

与此相关的是，由于最近供应商组成了贸易协会使得椰子油和大豆原材料的成本上涨，所以我们之前制定的原材料价格标准已经过时了。不断变化的供应商只会使这个问题复杂化，也可能会使我们的差异报告变得更没有意义。尽管我很担心让我们的经理参与进来，但我一直在考虑将我们的差异分解为规划和运营差异来处理这个问题。

我需要向董事们证明这一变化的合理性，因此，希望你可以向我发送这个方法的说明（使用原材料成本差异来说明）、对业务的好处和缺点，我可以以此作为理由。请将包括你对 Tomaz 明细表评估结果和这些内容的邮件发送给我。

有关 6 个潜在润肤剂供应商的信息一览表：

每个潜在的供应商都能够为我们提供足够的数量。

潜在供应商	位置	2015 年年收入（百万 K$）	2015 年经营现金流入或流出	所有权	信用期（天）
供应商 1	Keyland	16	流入	一个大型国际集团的子公司	30
供应商 2	Keyland	166	流出	在 Keyland 股市上市	40
供应商 3	Meyland	27	流入	私营企业	45
供应商 4	Keyland	14	流出	私营企业	60
供应商 5	Keyland	13	流出	一个大型国际集团的子公司	20
供应商 6	Seyland	250	流入	在 Seyland 股市上市	30

Meyland 用 M$ 作为货币，Seyland 用 S$ 作为货币。对于供应商 3 和供应商 6，为了达到分析的目的，上表中的年度收入数据以 2015 年的平均汇率折算为 K$ 。

请根据 Roger Dawson 的要求撰写电子邮件。

任务四

两个月后，您收到了 Roger Dawson 的电子邮件。

发件人：管理会计助理

收件人：财务经理 Roger Dawson

主题：流动资金状况和供应商问题

我需要为下一次的董事会议编写一份报告，我希望你能帮我起草几个章节。

首先，董事们希望在 2016 年 6 月底对我们的营运资金状况进行分析，并与我们在 2015 年 6 月底的状况和我们以 4 月份为会计年度末的主要竞争对手之一进行比较。这个竞争对手在大型百货公司有特许经营权，并与多家公司签订合同，为酒店供应产品。

我已经将相关信息汇集在一起，如下：

	基于我们 2016 年 6 月 30 日的余额	**基于我们 2015 年 6 月 30 日的余额**	**基于我们的竞争对手在 2016 年 4 月 30 日的余额**
存货周转天数（天）	240	207	180
应收账款周转数（天）	45	23	47
应付账款周转天数（天）	35	42	65
流动资金周转天数（天）	250	188	162

其次，运营总监 Tomaz Green 注意到，我们的新供应商之一一直在使用童工来收割作物。显然，他们国家的就业法规定，如果孩子们能得到足够的休息时间，并且每周的工作时间不超过 30 个小时，那么他们是可以工作的。Tomaz 对此感到担心，因为在 Keyland，孩子们每周不允许工作超过 5 个小时，而且只能在服务行业工作。在会议上，董事们已经要求了解这些潜在问题需要考虑的因素。

请帮我准备我正在为董事们准备的报告的这两部分内容。

非常感谢！

桑切斯·纳瓦娜公司

财务经理

Roger Dawson

请根据 Roger Dawson 的要求撰写报告。

Variant 3 Suggested Answers

Section 1

Briefing Paper to Tomaz Green, Operations Director

Interpretation of Gail's Schedule

Because we are selling a number of different products, Gail has prepared her schedule on the basis of each product group as far as possible. However, because we cannot allocate many of our fixed costs to individual product groups she has considered overall profitability, and break-even, on the basis of the total weighted average position. To do this she has assumed that we sell our products in a constant mix (the budgeted mix).

The C/S ratio is a measure of profitability based only on variable costs. It is the contribution earned from a product group divided by the revenue from that product group expressed as a percent: it is a contribution margin. Based on the original budget the C/S ratio shows that when we consider only the variable costs of production, gift sets have the highest contribution margin at 74.7% and hand & foot cream the lowest at 63.2%.

The price increase for coconut and soy bean oil has a direct impact on the C/S margin because as a variable cost it will directly affect contribution. As a result of the price increase the schedule shows that the contribution margin falls for body wash, body lotion and gift sets (which include both body lotion and body wash), whilst stays the same for hand & foot cream. This is because the price increase for coconut and soy bean oil will only affect body wash and body lotion: the raw material is not used in the production of hand & foot cream.

The break-even position is shown in terms of overall revenue. This is calculated as the total of the fixed costs (both specific and other) divided by the weighted average contribution margin for all of our products. Based on the original budget this means that revenue of K$28,171,429 would be just enough to cover the fixed costs and the variable costs at that level of sales. After adjusting for the price increase the break-even revenue rises to K$29,435,238 which is a significant increase. It must be noted that this is based on the assumption that we sell our products in the standard mix.

Lastly the margin of safety has been calculated. Based on the original supplier prices, this shows that our budgeted revenue (after adjusting for the discounts given by the sales managers) of K$ 32,000,000 could fall by 12%, assuming the same sales volume mix and we would still make a profit. This drops to 8.3% after the raw material price increase is included.

Product Range Profitability

As explained above the C/S ratio is indeed a measure of profitability, although only in respect of how much revenue a product group generates compared to its variable costs. As we can see from the schedule the C/S ratios indicate that all of our product groups generate relatively high levels of contribution, although this is adversely affected by the raw material price increase.

However, this is not the complete picture. To have a full understanding of a product group's profitability we need to include fixed costs, as ultimately these are deducted in arriving at profit.

Gail has made some attempt to allocate fixed costs to product groups by including those fixed costs that can be specifically related to each product group in her schedule. But the basis on which these have been allocated needs to be considered. For all product groups the allocation of specific marketing campaign costs is appropriate. However, the allocation of the fixed production costs is perhaps too simplistic for a complete picture of profitability.

We have two production lines: one exclusively for body wash and the other for body lotion and hand & foot cream. Each will have separate fixed costs of operation and Gail has allocated all of the body wash line costs to that product group and has split the second line costs to body wash and hand & foot cream on the basis of volumes sold. There are potentially two issues with this allocation: firstly, a portion of the costs for each line also relate to gift sets and secondly, hand & foot cream takes longer to produce than body lotion (as evidenced from our standard cost cards) and therefore there is an argument that hand & foot cream should be allocated a greater share of the production line fixed costs.

In addition Gail's schedule shows that there is a significant amount of fixed cost which cannot be specifically assigned to product groups. In our business a lot of this costs relate to general marketing campaigns and the cost of running our concession stands, stores and on-line sales operations. It is very difficult to pin these down to specific product groups because, they are incurred in order for the business to operate as a whole. Indeed it is possible that some of our distribution costs are variable in nature rather than fixed, although in the short term the value of this is likely to be small.

Therefore, whilst Gail's schedule is a useful guide to the profitability of product groups, it is not the complete picture.

Further Cost Increases and Improving our Trading Position

We can look at various areas to improve our trading position.

(1) Increasing sales revenue by controlling discounts and considering our pricing policy generally, increasing prices where possible.

(2) Improving the sales mix by targeting promotions of higher margin fragrances.

(3) Considering changing our sales channel mix: more online sales will be more cost effective, although a public presence will be required.

(4) Improving our manufacturing processes possibly to create efficiencies which reduce for example energy consumption and therefore production costs.

(5) Improving our purchasing function to ensure we are purchasing at the best rates possible.

(6) Producing more meaningful management information to help improve our cost controls. Breaking down our selling distribution and administration costs into meaningful reports with budgets for different categories. Introducing a system of rolling budgets to ensure changes such as prices can be incorporated easily and quickly and comparisons made.

Purchasing Policy

We have always operated an opportunistic supply chain policy, and our supply arrangements can be typically defined as competitive. We have always sought out the lowest prices and often switched suppliers in order to obtain the lowest prices.

Given that we are a premium supplier of quality products and with the supply issues we are now facing, it is time to change our attitude towards our suppliers to a more collaborative approach. We need to get closer to our suppliers. We need premium ingredients to manufacture our products and, given the market scenario, price issues should not have come as a great surprise.

A more collaborative arrangement may be typified by a sole sourcing agreement with one supplier. Giving more commitment to a particular supplier may be advantageous in the long run. With more knowledge of our products, our supplier may be able to source better quality raw materials for us. We may be able to improve our mixes, improving quality and reducing the quantity of mixes required, consequently leading to cost savings.

We also need to take care of our image and brand: producing a premium product, we should be using premium ingredients. This should enable us to be more price flexible in the market. Maintaining our brand value is key, any indication that we are using the cheapest materials available may cause considerable damage.

There may also be opportunities for price negotiations related to volume commitments. We may ultimately be better off with a more collaborative approach to purchasing.

Section 2

The Report to Nisha Shah and Freda Jones on Marketing Campaign

Richard Procter's Schedule

Basis of Richard's Conclusion

Richard has concluded that the marketing campaign with the largest budget of K$ 150,000 should be undertaken. His conclusion is based on the fact that this campaign would give the highest expected value of K$ 124,000 compared to K$ 109,000 and K$ 64,000 for the other campaigns.

The expected value for each campaign is calculated as the sum of each of the possible outcomes multiplied by its probability of occurrence. In other words the expected value represents the average of all of the possible outcomes weighted by the probability that it will happen. It does not in itself represent what will actually happen, but is simply an average.

Richard has concluded that because the K$ 150,000 campaign has the highest expected value, this is the campaign that will potentially have the greatest positive impact on profit.

However, this conclusion is flawed because using expected value in this way ignores the range of possible outcomes in the decision due to the fact that expected value is simply an average.

Using Standard Deviation and Coefficient of Variation

Establishing the standard deviation gives us a statistical measure of risk for each of the campaigns. The standard deviation is a measure of how much the possible outcomes vary compared to the average(expected value)and is therefore a measure of how risky or how variable the possible returns are.

Richard has already provided this information in his schedule and it shows that the K$ 100,000 campaign has the lowest standard deviation. Therefore if we were to take a risk adverse approach we might choose the K$ 100,000 option because although its expected value is lower than the K$ 150,000 campaign,the possible profits are subject to less variation. Indeed choosing this campaign would,based on the figures provided, guarantee a positive return compared to the K$ 150,000 campaign where there is a 40% chance of making a loss.

In order to assess each of these campaigns against each other,we should look at the coefficient of variation which is the standard deviation divided by the expected value. In effect this takes into account both the expected value and the risk as measured by standard deviation,and an optimal decision would be to choose that option with the lowest coefficient of variation. The schedule shows that the K$ 100,000 campaign is the best option with the lowest coefficient of 0. 39.

Three Possible Promotions

Free Gift Offer

We could offer a free gift of,saying,a wash bag with each purchase of saying three full sized and full priced bottles of the fragrances being targeted. This could be rolled out nationally to all concession stands as well as our own stores and on-line sales.

In this way we will target our existing customer base to perhaps try a fragrance they haven't tried before(although this could be at the expense of other fragrances). Promotional displays on concession stands might also entice passing customers of the department store to try our products for the first time.

The promotion itself would be relatively easy to set up,especially as we already have contacts for the supply of wash bags. However,the main drawback of this approach will be the cost of both the gift bags and the promotional displays for each of our numerous concession stands. In addition this approach will only reach those people who are already customers or those that happen to use the store. It might not bring in a lot of new customers, which ultimately is what we need to do.

Using Social Media

We could create a buzz on social media about the fragrances that we're targeting. We could create an advert featuring these fragrances with a competition attached, which can only be entered by liking the advert. The competition prize could be a year's supply of products or even a holiday linked to the origins of the fragrance. This is an example of viral marketing.

The main benefit of this approach is that the scope of social media is vast. Our products could reach a much wider audience and attract new customers. Consumers are less likely to feel that they have been bombarded with an advert a result of the competition element.

The downsides are that the advert itself will need to be engaging within a very short period of time and the prizes attractive (and therefore potentially expensive).

Targeted Email Promotion

We could set up a targeted campaign by sending emails to potential consumers with a discount code of saying 10% off one bottle, 20% off two bottles, or such like.

Clearly we already have email addresses of each of our on-line customers, but in order to reach a wider audience we will need extend this base. We could look to acquire a list of email addresses for likely customers from an independent third party data provider. This would of course be costly, however, would potentially give us access to a wide base. Alternatively we could liaise with our department store partners and seek to acquire their consumer lists.

This type of approach clearly has its benefits as it directly connects with the consumer and creates a relationship, assuming that the consumer wants to engage. However, many people get frustrated by spam email and may consider this approach as an intrusion. It could therefore put some people off our brand.

Section 3

From: Management Accountant Assistant

To: Roger Dawson, Finance Manager

Subject: Financial factors and variance reporting

Assessment of Potential Suppliers

When assessing the suitability of a supplier it is important to consider its financial stability and ability to operate as a going concern. It is important once selected that we have continuity of supply and therefore we should ensure the business looks like it will be able to continue to operate into the future by having sufficient cash flows. The fact that a business is generating operating cash outflows could indicate cash flow problems: this is the position of supplier 2, 4 and 5. However, we will need to consider whether this is just a one off in 2015 or a part of a trend. In addition the ownership of the supplier is also important here. Supplier 1 and supplier 5 are owned by large international groups and therefore are likely to be supported by them financially. Supplier 4 is privately owned and, given its relatively small size (only K$ 14,000,000 of revenue a year), there is considerable uncertainty surrounding this suppliers ability to continue to trade compared to the other.

Another factor to consider here is using suppliers based in another country. Supplier 3 is based in Meyland and supplier 6 in Seyland. We will need to consider whether there will be any increase in currency risk and how easy it will be to pay the supplier in their own currency if they should wish that. Currency movements are going to add variability to our costings and we will need to take this into our review of budget performance. It would be useful to know how stable the currencies are in Meyland and Seyland before disregarding these suppliers on the basis of currency risk.

The other piece of information on the schedule relates to the credit terms the suppliers are offering us. Our payables balance is an important part of how we fund our operating cash flows: effectively it is a free form of finance and ideally we would want suppliers that offered us the longest credit term. The schedule shows that supplier 4 is offering the longest terms at 60 days, but as mentioned above this is the supplier that based on this information has the biggest chance of ceasing to operate, therefore, it is unlikely that this is the best option overall.

Other aspects of the financial terms to consider are whether there are prompt payment discounts available if we choose to pay earlier than the standard terms, or indeed whether there are bulk discounts available for larger orders. This is information that we don't currently have. Both of these have a potential cost saving benefit to our business, although we would need to weigh this up against the associated costs (earlier use of cash or higher inventory holding costs) to evaluate whether this was ultimately worthwhile.

Variance Reporting

A planning variance is based on the difference between the original standard (also known as ex-ante) and the revised standard (also known as ex-post), whilst an operational variance is based on the difference between the revised standard and the actual result. A key factor of splitting variances in this way is that managers should only be held accountable for those variances that they can control (typically operational variances).

Take for example the raw material cost variances. For each material the price variance arising from changing supplier could potentially be identified as a planning variance, whilst any further changes would be attributable to operational issues. These price changes could also have a knock-on impact on the usage as well, so we could find that there is also a usage planning variance, possibly as a result of having to use slightly more of a slightly different compound to what we've been used to.

The benefits of using this approach are as follows.

- A better analysis of what elements of our variances are controllable and due to operational issues and which are not controllable by the production team such as the price increases arising from suppliers coming together in a trade association.
- A variance report motivates managers better as they know that they will only be held accountable for operational variances. Therefore it is likely that our managers will be more engaged and not less engaged as a result of splitting the variances in this way.
- A better basis for preparing the standards in following years because we will have a better understanding through the planning variances of what changes regularly.

The drawbacks of using this approach are as follows.

- Variance reports will be more time consuming to prepare which puts pressure on us in the finance team, as we have to do this preparation.
- It is sometimes difficult to justify what is a planning variance and what is an operational variance. Using the raw material pricing issue, clearly the unforeseen change as a result

of the trade association is not controllable and therefore should be included as a planning variance. However, any further changes that arise as a result of changing suppliers could arguably be operational variances, because the decision to change supplier will be made by the production team, whose performance is being measured with these variances.

Section 4

Sections of the Report

Analysis of Working Capital Position

2016 Compared to 2015

Our working capital cycle has increased by 62 days at the end of June 2016 compared to 2015, which will have had a detrimental effect on our cash flows.

Inventory days have increased significantly. This could indicate that the marketing efforts we undertook earlier in the year have not generated the additional sales that were anticipated. We might have produced too much inventory, and we now need to be careful that some of this inventory does not become past its best date and obsolete. Proper inventory rotation in the warehouse is very important.

Receivable days have also increased significantly. The balance at the end of June should represent solely the amounts receivable from our department store concession partners in respect of sales made in department stores in June. In 2015 receivable days of 23 days was in line with this (given that 70% of our sales comes from concessions). The fact that it is now 45 days is cause for concern. Potentially one or more of our department store partners is withholding payment and we need to ascertain why.

Payables days have decreased. This is likely due to changing some of our suppliers who perhaps have offered a shorter credit period. Alternatively it could be that we have been able to claim a prompt payment discount by paying earlier.

Compared to Our Competitor

In respect of comparing our position against our competitor's there are two notes of caution.

(1) The competitor's year end is April and therefore it is entirely possible that seasonal factors will affect the comparison.

(2) The competitor operates slightly differently in that they have corporate customers as well as concessions. This will have an impact on receivable days.

Overall the competitor has a lower operating cycle which will be beneficial for their cash flow. Inventory days are lower than ours: it's possible that because of their corporate customers the competitor does not need to hold as much inventory, and possibly production is carried out to specific orders.

Receivable days are in line with our position at the end of June 2016, although given that they have corporate clients we would actually expect it to be higher than our position. Again this highlights that we have a potential issue with our receivables balances at the end of June 2016.

Payable days are higher than ours. This could be the result of extended payment terms that our competitor has negotiated with its suppliers. Alternatively it could be that our competitor deliberately pays later and does not treat its suppliers ethically.

Children Labour Issue

The Factors to Consider

Essentially this is a corporate social responsibility issue. As a corporate organisation we have a responsibility to act in a legal and ethical manner.

Legal responsibilities are about making sure that we, either directly or indirectly through our customers and suppliers, carry out all activities within the laws by which we or our partners are bound. In this situation, there is a potential that no laws have been broken. It is entirely possible that the supplier applies the Seyland law accurately, so we would need to investigate this through looking at press reports or legal case records for any indications that this is not the case.

Ethical responsibility goes beyond this and is about us operating in a way which is fair and just to all, even if the law does not compel us to operate in that way. Here the fact that in Keyland the practice of employing children would not be allowed for such work is a factor to be considered. There is a potential ethical responsibility on us as an organisation that we are not associated with child labour.

We need to consider the impact on our customers if they were to know the position. We pride ourselves on our Made in Keyland badge and our customers see our product as a premium product. Therefore, it is highly likely that if it were known that child labour was used in the harvest of some of our raw materials then our customers would view this as unethical and it would have a very detrimental effect on sales and our brand image.

One last factor to consider is the position of TRU Group. As a large multi-national group, TRU Group must have corporate social responsibility policies which we will need to adhere to. It is entirely possible that the policies include clauses about child labour. We should seek advice on this from the management of TRU Group.

试卷三　参考答案

任务一

给运营总监 Tomaz Green 的简报

对 Gail 明细表的解释

因为我们正在销售很多不同的产品，所以 Gail 已经尽可能地在每个产品组的基础上准备了明细表。然而，由于我们无法将多项固定成本分摊给个别产品组，所以她基于总加权平均原则考虑了整体的盈利能力和盈亏平衡。为了做到这一点，她假设我们以不断的组合（预算组合）销售我们的产品。

C/S 比率仅是基于可变成本的盈利能力的度量，用产品组所得的毛利润除以该产品组的收入的百分比表示：它是一个毛利润率。根据原始预算中的 C/S 比率显示，仅考虑生产可变成本时，礼品套餐的最高毛利润率达 74.7%，手足霜的最低毛利润率为 63.2%。

椰子油和大豆油的价格上涨对 C/S 的利润率有直接的影响，因为可变成本会直接影响毛利润。由于价格上涨，明细表表明，沐浴露，润肤乳和礼品套装（包括润肤乳和沐浴露）的边际毛利润将会下降，而手足霜则保持不变。这是因为椰子油和大豆油的价格上涨只会影响沐浴露和润肤乳：这两种原料不用于生产手足霜。

盈亏平衡情况以总体收入呈现，由固定成本（特定和其他）的总和除以我们所有产品的加权平均边际毛利润得出。根据原始预算，这意味着 K$ 28 171 429 的收入足以支付该销售水平的固定成本和可变成本。价格上涨后经过调整，盈亏平衡收入上升至 K$ 29 435 238，显著增长。必须注意的是，这是基于我们以标准组合销售我们产品的假设。

最后计算了安全边际。若根据原始的供应商价格，我们的预算收入（调整了销售经理的折扣后）K$ 32 000 000 可能会下降 12%，假设销售量相同，我们仍然可以获利。如果将原材料价格上涨计算在内，这一数字将降至 8.3%。

产品系列的盈利能力

如上所述，C/S 比率确实是衡量盈利能力的一个标准，尽管它只代表产品组获得的收入与可变成本之间的差值。从明细表可以看出，C/S 比率表明，我们所有的产品组都会产生较高的毛利润，尽管这受到了原材料价格上涨的不利影响。

但是，这并不完整。要充分了解产品组的盈利能力，我们需要纳入固定成本，最终将这些成本扣除得出利润水平。

Gail 已经尝试将固定成本分摊给产品组，通过在明细表中包含与每个产品组具体相关的固定成本。但是，需要考虑这种分摊的依据。对于所有产品组来说，具体营销活动成本的分摊是适当的。然而，固定生产成本的分摊对于完整盈利能力来说可能过于简单。

我们有两条生产线：一条专门用于生产沐浴露，另一条用于生产润肤乳和手足霜。每条生产线都有独立的固定运营成本，而 Gail 将所有沐浴露生产线的成本分摊给了该产品组，并将第二条线的成本以销售量为基础分摊给了沐浴露和手足霜。这一分摊方式可能存在两个问题：首先，每一条生产线的部分费用与礼品套装相关；其次，手足霜比沐浴露需要更长的生产时间（我们的标准成本卡可以证明），因此有一个观点认为，手足霜应该被分摊更多的生产固定成本。

此外，Gail 的明细表显示有大量固定成本不能特定地分摊给产品组。在我们的业务中，很多这样的成本涉及一般营销活动和我们的特许摊位的运行，商店和在线销售业务，将它们归结到特定的产品组是非常困难的，因为它们是为了使业务整体运行而产生的。事实上，我们的一些分销成本有可能本质上是变化的，而不是固定的，尽管在短期内这种成本的价值可能很小。

因此，虽然 Gail 的明细表对于产品组的盈利能力是一个有用的指南，但它并不完整。

进一步增加成本并改善我们的交易状况

我们可以看看如何从各个方面来改善我们的交易状况。

（1）通过控制折扣和综合考虑我们的定价政策来增加销售收入，尽可能提高价格。

（2）通过促销高利润香水来改善销售组合。

（3）考虑改变我们的销售渠道组合：更多的在线销售将更具成本效益，尽管公众参与成为必要的因素。

（4）在可能的情况下改进我们的生产流程，以提高效率，例如降低能源消耗，从而节约生产成本。

（5）改善采购功能，确保我们能以最优惠的价格进行采购。

（6）提供更有价值的管理信息，以帮助改进成本控制。将销售分销和管理成本分解为具有不同类别预算的有意义的报告，再引入一个滚动预算系统，以确保价格等变化能够容易、快速地并入并进行比较。

采购政策

我们一直实行机会主义的供应链政策，我们的供应安排通常可以被定义为具有竞争力。我们一直寻求最低的价格，并经常更换供应商以获得最低的价格。

鉴于我们是高质量产品的优质供应商，以及我们现在所面临的供应问题，现在是时候改变我们对供应商的态度，采取更合作的方式。我们需要和供应商的关系更为密切。我们需要优质的材料来制造我们的产品，并且根据市场情况来看，价格问题不应该让我们感到过于惊讶。

一个更有合作精神的方案可能是与供应商签订特许采购协议。从长远来看，给予特定供应商更多的承诺可能是有利的。随着对我们产品的了解更多，我们的供应商可能会为我们提供更好的原材料，我们就有可能能够改善我们的配方，提高质量并减少所需的混合物的数量，从而节省成本。

我们还需要注意我们的形象和品牌：生产优质的产品，我们应该使用优质的成分。这也许能使我们在市场上的价格更具弹性。保持我们的品牌价值是关键，任何表明我们使用最便宜材料的迹象都可能会造成相当大的损失。

也可能存在与数量承诺相关的价格谈判的机会。或许我们最终可能会采用更合作的方式来采购。

任务二

给 Nisha Shah 和 Freda Jones 的关于营销活动的报告

Richard Procter 的明细表

Richard 的结论基础

Richard 认为应该进行最大预算 K$ 150 000 的营销活动。他的结论是基于这样一个事实：这次活动将给出最高的 K$ 124 000 的预期价值，而其他活动的预期价值则为 K$ 109 000 和 K$ 64 000。

每个活动的期望值计算为每个可能结果乘以其发生概率的总和。换句话说，期望值代表所有可能结果的平均值加权的概率。它本身并不代表实际发生的事情，只是一个平均值。

Richard 的结论是，由于 K$ 150 000 的活动具有最高的期望值，这一活动就可能对利润产生最大的积极影响。

然而，这个结论是有缺陷的，因为以这种方式使用期望值忽略了决策中可能出现的结果的范围，因为期望值只是一个平均值。

使用标准差和变异系数

建立标准差给我们提供了每个活动的风险统计量度。标准差是衡量可能结果与平均值（期望值）的差异程度的指标，因此它是衡量可能回报的风险程度或变化程度的指标。

Richard 已经在他的明细表中提供了这些信息，并且显示了 K$ 100 000 的活动具有最低的标准差。因此，如果我们要规避风险，我们就可能会选择 K$ 100 000 的预算，因为尽管它是期望值低于 K$ 150 000 的活动，但相应的利润会有更少的变化性。的确，根据所提供的数据，选择这一活动将保证有一个正值的回报，相比之下，K$ 150 000 的活动有 40% 的可能性会造成损失。

为了通过相互比较来评估这些活动，我们应该将目光转向变异系数，也就是标准差除以期望值的值。实际上，这同时考虑到了期望值和标准差测量到的风险，最佳决策是选择具有最低变异系数的选项。明细表显示，具有最低变异系数 0. 39 的 K$ 100 000 的活动是最佳选择。

三种可能的促销方式

免费礼品

我们可以提供一个免费的礼物，比如给每一次达到设定购买目标的客户一个洗漱包，这个设定目标可以是购买 3 瓶全尺寸和全价格的香味产品。这个方法可以推广到全国所有特许销售柜台，以及我们自己的零售店和在线销售。

通过这种方式，针对我们现有的客户群，他们或许会尝试以前没有尝试过的香型（尽管这可能是以牺牲其他香型为代价）。特许销售柜台的促销展示也可能吸引路过的百货公司的客户首次尝试我们的产品。

促销活动本身比较容易建立，特别是因为我们已经有了提供洗漱包的供应商。不过，这种方法的主要缺点是礼品袋和我们众多特许经营柜台的促销展示需要费用。此外，这种方法只能接触到那些已经是客户或那些碰巧使用商店的人，它可能不会带来很多新客户，而这是我们最终需要做到的。

使用社交媒体

我们可以在社交媒体上制造关于我们目标香型的相关舆论。我们可以创建一个以这些香型为特色的广告，并附带一个比赛，并规定促销活动只能通过观看广告来参加。比赛奖品可能是一年的产品供应，甚至是与香料起源相关的一次度假。这是病毒式营销的一个例子。

这种做法的主要好处是社会媒体的范围很广，我们的产品可以被更多消费者了解，从而吸引新客户。消费者不太可能觉得他们在被广告轰炸，也是竞争元素存在的结果。

缺点是广告本身需要在非常短的时间内发挥作用，并且奖品要有吸引力（因此可能是昂贵的）。

目标性电子邮件推广

我们可以通过向潜在消费者发送电子邮件来设置有针对性的活动，包含折扣代码，比如 1 瓶 10% 的折扣，2 瓶 20% 的折扣等等。

显然，我们已经有了每个在线客户的电子邮件地址，但为了吸引更多的客户，我们需要扩大这个基础。我们可以从独立的第三方数据提供商那里获取可能的客户的电子邮件地址列表。这当然是昂贵的，但是，这可能会使我们得到一个广泛的客户基础。或者，我们可以与我们的百货公司的合作伙伴联络，寻求获取他们的消费者名单。

这种方式显然有其好处，因为它直接与消费者联系，并建立了一种关系——假设消费者想要参与。但是，很多人对垃圾邮件感到厌烦，可能会觉得这种做法是一种侵扰。因此，这种方法也可能让一些人远离我们的品牌。

任务三

发件人：管理会计助理

收件人：财务经理 Roger Dawson

主题：财务因素和差异报告

对潜在供应商的评估

在评估供应商的适用性时，重要的是要考虑其作为一个经营主体的经济稳定性和经营能力。更重要的是，一旦选定了供应商，我们就要求其能保证供应的连续性，因此我们应该确保这家企业看起来能够通过充足的现金流继续经营到未来。企业产生经营性现金流出的事实可能表明现金流存在问题：这是供应商 2、4、5 的状况。但是，我们需要考虑这是否仅仅是2015 年的一次性下降或部分趋势。此外，供应商的所有权在哪里也很重要。供应商 1 和供应商 5 由大型国际集团拥有，因此我们有可能得到他们的财务支持。供应商 4 是私有的，规模相对较小（每年只有 K$ 14 000 000 的收入），与其他供应商相比，其继续贸易的能力有很大的不确定性。

另一个要考虑的因素是使用位于另一个国家的供应商。供应商 3 的总部设在 Meyland，供应商 6 的总部设在 Seyland。我们需要考虑货币风险是否会有所增加，以及如果他们愿意的话，以他们自己的货币交易的容易程度是多少。汇率变动将增加我们的成本变动，我们需要将其纳入我们对预算绩效的审查中。在根据货币风险不考虑这些供应商之前，最好先了解 Meyland 和 Seyland 的货币稳定程度。

附表中的另一条信息涉及供应商向我们提供的信用期。我们的应付账款余额是我们组建经营性现金流的重要组成部分：实际上它是一种自由的融资形式，理想情况下，我们想要可以为我们提供的是最长信贷期限的供应商。明细表显示，供应商 4 提供的最长期限是 60 天，但是如上所述，这是基于这些因素最有可能停止运营的供应商，因此，它并不是最佳选择。

要考虑的财务条款的其他方面是，如果我们选择早于标准条款付款，是否有即时支付折扣可用，或是否确实有大批量折扣可用于较大的订单，这是我们目前没有的信息。这两者都对我们的业务有潜在的成本节约的好处，尽管我们需要将其与相关成本（早期使用现金或更高的库存持有成本）进行比较来评估这最终是否是值得的。

差异报告

计划差异基于原始标准（也称为事先）与修订标准（也称为事后）之间的差异，而运作差异基于修订标准与实际结果之间的差异。以这种方式分割差异的一个关键因素是，管理人员只应该对他们可以控制的差异（通常是运营差异）负责。

以原材料成本差异为例。对于每一种材料，由于更换供应商而引起的价格差异可能被认定为计划差异，而任何进一步的变化都可能归因于运作问题。这些价格变化也可能会对使用造成冲击，所以我们可以发现，使用计划方面也有差异，这可能是由于我们不得不使用稍微更多的和我们原先使用的略微不同的化合物的结果。

使用这种方法的好处如下。

- 能更好地分析造成我们差异的哪些因素是可控的，只是由于操作问题，哪些因素是不受生产团队控制的，例如由于供应商聚集在同一个行业协会而引起的价格上涨。
- 差异报告能更好地激励管理者，因为他们知道他们只对运作差异负责。因此，由于以这种方式分割差异，我们的管理人员很可能会更投入，而不是更少地参与。
- 在接下来的几年中我们会有更好的准备标准的基础，因为我们会对规律变化的计划差异有更好的理解。

使用这种方法的缺点如下。

- 准备差异报告将会花费大量时间，因为我们必须做这个准备工作，这对我们的财务团队造成了压力。
- 有时难以证明什么是计划差异，什么是运作差异。以原材料定价问题为例，显然由于贸易协会引起的不可预见的变化是不可控制的，因此这应该被当作计划差异。然而，由于变更供应商而产生的任何进一步变化都可以说是运作差异，因为改变供应商的决定是由生产团队做出的，生产团队的绩效将用这些差异来进行衡量。

任务四

部分报告

流动资金状况分析

2016 年与 2015 年相比

2016 年 6 月底，我们的流动资金周期比 2015 年增加了 62 天，这会对我们的现金流产生不利影响。

库存周转天数明显增加。这可能表明我们今年早些时候进行的营销工作没有产生预期的额外销售额。我们可能生产了太多存货，我们现在需要注意的是这些库存中是否有一些错过了最佳日期或者已经过期。适当的库存轮换非常重要。

应收账款周转天数也大幅增加。6 月底的余额仅为本公司百货商店特许经营合伙人 6 月份在百货商店销售的应收款项。2015 年应收账款周转天数为 23 天符合这一条件（因为 70% 的销售来自特许经营），现在 45 天的事实令人担忧。我们的一个或多个百货商店合作伙伴可能会拒绝付款，我们需要查明原因。

应付账款周转天数减少。这可能是因为我们更换上了一批提供较短信用期的供应商。或者，可能我们可以通过提前支付来取得立即支付折扣。

与我们的竞争对手相比

在比较我们与竞争对手的情况时，有两个注意事项。

（1）竞争对手的年终是 4 月份，因此季节性因素完全有可能影响比较结果。

（2）竞争对手的经营方式与我们略有不同，他们既有企业客户，也有特许权。这将对应收账款周转天数产生影响。

总体而言，竞争对手的经营周期较短，对现金流有利。他们的库存周转天数低于我们：这可能是因为他们有企业客户，不需要持有尽可能多的库存，其生产可能是按特定的订单进行的。

其应收账款周转天数与我们 2016 年 6 月底的状况一致，尽管他们有企业客户，但实际上我们预期他们的应收账款周转天数会多于我们的天数。这再次强调，我们 2016 年 6

月的应收账款余额有潜在的问题。

其应付账款周转天数也高于我们的。这可能是我们的竞争对手与其供应商谈判的延长付款期限的结果。或者是我们的竞争对手故意延期付款，不道德地对待他的供应商。

童工问题

需考虑的因素

本质上，这是一个企业社会责任问题。作为一个企业组织，我们有责任以合法和道德的方式行事。

法律责任是确保我们通过我们的客户和供应商直接或间接地在我们或我们的合作伙伴受法律约束的范围内进行所有活动。在这种情况下，不存在任何违反法律规定的可能。供应商完全有可能完全遵守了 Seyland 的法律，所以我们需要通过查看新闻报道或法律案件记录来进行调查，以证明情况并非如此。

道德责任超越了这一点，它要求我们以一种对所有人都公平公正的方式运作，即使法律不强制我们这样做。事实上，在 Keyland，这样的工作雇用童工是不被允许的，这是一个我们要考虑的因素。我们作为一个与童工无关的组织有潜在的道德责任。

我们需要考虑如果客户知道了这个情况，会产生什么影响。我们以“Keyland 制造”徽章为荣，我们的顾客将我们的产品视为优质产品。因此，如果知道我们在收获一些原材料时使用童工，那么我们的客户会认为这是不道德的，这样就会对我们的产品销售和品牌形象产生非常不利的影响。

最后一个要考虑的因素是 TRU 集团的情况。作为一个大型跨国集团，TRU 集团有需要我们遵守的企业社会责任政策。这些政策完全有可能包括关于童工的条款，所以我们应该向 TRU 集团的管理层征求意见。

Variant 3　Marking Guidance

Section	Technical skills		Business skills		People skills		Leadership skills		Integration	Total
1	Break-even and assessment of profitability（P1）	15	Purchasing policy（E1）	7			Trading position（P1）	6	3	31
2	Decision making with risk and uncertainty（P1）	13			Promotional tools（E1）	12				25
3	Financial factors to consider in respect of selecting new suppliers（F1） Variance reporting（P1）	11 11								22
4	Analysis of working capital position（F1）	11	CSR issue（E1）	9	CSR issue（E1）	2				22
Total marks available for each competency		61		16		14		6	3	100

试卷三　评分指南

部分	技术技能		商业技能		人际技能		领导技能		综合	总计
1	盈亏平衡与盈利能力评估（P1）	15	采购政策（E1）	7			交易状况（P1）	6	3	31
2	具有风险和不确定性的决策（P1）	13			促销手段（E1）	12				25
3	考虑选择新供应商的相关财务因素（F1） 差异报告（P1）	11 11								22
4	流动资金状况分析（F1）	11	企业社会责任问题（E1）	9	企业社会责任问题（E1）	2				22
各种能力分数总计		61		16		14		6	3	100

西安交通大学名师解惑

试卷一共有四项任务，考查了 P1、F1、E1 三门课程的知识点，具体包括盈亏平衡与盈利能力评估、采购政策、交易状况、具有风险和不确定性的决策、促销手段、选择新供应商的财务因素、流动资金状况分析、企业社会责任问题等。该试卷考核了考生的四项能力，其中技术技能的分值占 61%，商业技能的分值占 16%，人际技能的分值占 14%，领导技能的分值占 6%，综合能力占 3%，与 CGMA 管理会计能力框架的技能要求一致。

该试卷的每项任务涉及以下知识点：

任务	问题	科目	知识点
任务一	采购政策的制定	E1	采购政策（purchasing policy）
	对交易状况的分析和改善交易状况的方法	P1	交易状况（trading position）
	基于 C/S 比率分析盈利能力	P1	盈亏平衡与盈利能力评估（break-ever and assessment of profitability）
任务二	制定促销策略	E1	促销手段（promotion approaches）
	通过分析标准差和变异系数来进行具有风险和不确定性的决策	P1	风险决策（decision making with risk）
任务三	选择新供应商时应该考虑的财务因素	E1	财务因素（financial factors）
	差异报告的定义和优缺点	P1	差异报告（variance report）
任务四	流动资金状况的横向和纵向分析	F1	流动资金（working capital）
	童工带来的企业社会责任问题	E1	企业社会责任（corporate social responsibility）

上述各项任务以要求撰写邮件、报告或工作笔记等形式来呈现答案，对问题的描述非常明确，答题时既要注意内容的针对性，也要注意形式的规范性。

其他答题注意事项包括：（1）仔细读题，一般每项任务都会涉及 2～3 个大的知识点，一定不能漏答；（2）答题要有条理，从是什么到为什么，从分析原因到提出解决办法，将每个知识点都解释清楚；（3）分层级列出各级小标题，让考官容易了解你的思路。

同时，答题时，要避免只是对教科书的知识点进行简单复述，应结合案例公司的实际情况；注意回答时的措辞、格式，注意论述的结构，论点的鲜明和整体性等。

对应知识点深度剖析

采购政策

采购过程中所遇到的情况千差万别，采购人员应根据具体情况采用不同的采购策略来降低采购成本，在产品开发、质量、价格、物流4个方面形成最佳采购供应链。根据题中给出的背景和信息，考生在制定策略时，应该注意高质量和低成本的结合。

交易状况

考生应当分析整个背景，从成本、定价、销售等多方面入手，全面梳理问题，分析问题，提出改善交易状况的具体建议。这是训练学生综合运用知识的能力的任务。

盈亏平衡与盈利能力评估

盈亏平衡点又称零利润点、保本点、盈亏临界点、损益分歧点、收益转折点。其通常是指全部销售收入等于全部成本时（销售收入线与总成本线的交点）的产量。以盈亏平衡点为界限，当销售收入高于盈亏平衡点时企业盈利，反之，企业就亏损。盈亏平衡点可以用销售量来表示，即盈亏平衡点的销售量；也可以用销售额来表示，即盈亏平衡点的销售额。本题用盈亏平衡点和C/S比率来分析产品组的盈利能力，考生应用所学公式进行基本运算。

促销手段

促销手段是指企业利用各种有效的方法和手段，使消费者了解和注意到企业的产品，激发消费者的购买欲望，并促使其实现最终的购买行为。给出自己的促销建议是一个较为综合的考查，考生可在上述回答的基础上考虑风险和不确定性因素，提出建议。考生需有发散性思维。

风险决策

风险决策是在多种不定因素的作用下，对两个或两个以上的活动方案进行选择，由于有不定因素存在，活动方案的实施结果的损益值是不能预先被确定的。风险已经被量化，考生只需套用公式算出标准差和变异系数即可得出答案。

财务因素

分析财务因素是会计的重要技能。从基本要素出发，量化考虑。考生要根据已知条件对供应商做多方面的财务分析，从每个财务角度出发，逐条分析即可。

差异报告

考查差异报告的定义及优缺点。考生应注意熟记这些书本上的基础知识点。在本题中，要根据具体题目说明如何进行差异分析。

流动资金

本题要计算和分析报表中的流动资金状况，就需计算出流动资金的周期、库存的周转天数、应收账款的周转天数、应付账款的周转天数，并与过去的年度进行纵向比较，再与竞争者进行横向比较，分析可能的原因。只要考生平时有足够的积累和全面的知识体系，这道题就很容易得分。

企业社会责任

企业社会责任是指企业在创造利润、对股东和员工承担法律责任的同时，还要对消费者、社区和环境承担责任。企业社会责任要求企业必须改变把利润作为唯一目标的传统理念，强调企业要在生产过程中关注人的价值，强调其对环境、消费者、社会的贡献。本题要求结合社会问题分析对企业造成的影响，考生只需用具体情境结合知识点分析即可。

从总体来看考查重点在专业技能上，其所占比例远高于其他技能。因此对基础专业技能的掌握程度十分重要，做好了基于课本知识点的专业性分析，就成功了一大半。

可以看出，涵盖采购、生产、销售以及现金流等流程的知识模块都是主要考点，其中的组成部分，比如供应商选择、原材料议价、生产成本分摊、存货控制、促销方式和工具、现金流控制和资金链、应收应付账款等都是常见考点，考生需要理解记忆，多做多练，才能做好分析。

决策的风险和不确定性是很重要的考点，涉及期望值、标准差、变异系数等概念和工具，考生需熟练掌握，做好基础分析。

但是给出促销建议则需要发散思维。企业社会责任作为近年来的考核热点，考生需要运用所学知识点进行深入分析，并有自己的见解。同时，差异报告这种特定概念会考到基本概念，如定义、优缺点等，考生需掌握相关知识点。

Variant 4

This examination is structured as follows：

Section number	Number of tasks	Time for section(minutes)
1	1	60
2	1	60
3	1	35
4	1	25

The time available for each section is for reading,planning and writing your answer(s).

Section 1

Freda Jones, finance director, calls a short meeting for the entire finance team, where she says:

Thanks for being here. I just wanted to get you all up to speed with a few things.

Richard Procter, sales and marketing director, is negotiating with a number of potential new customers (including a major hotel chain) for new corporate business. Richard firmly believes that this is a section of the market in which we can expand our sales and is keen to ensure that we have the production capacity to be able to deal with this.

If all of our production plant were operating optimally, this wouldn't be a problem, certainly in the short term. However George Focus, production manager, has informed me of some mechanical issues with the production line that we currently use for body lotion and hand & foot cream, which have led to a number of batches to be thrown away due to poor product quality. As a result of having to re-work production we have had to buy in additional raw materials quickly at higher than normal prices. We have also had to pay overtime, the cost of which is included in the production labour cost.

George says that the body wash production line is not affected by these mechanical issues. On that line a new materials measurement and inputting process has been developed.

It would appear that maintenance of the production line has not been carried out as it should have for the last year. In any event, the production line is old, so I will be asking at the next directors' meeting for approval of the capital expenditure needed to set up a new production facility sooner than we had originally planned.

After a week, Roger Dawson sends you the following email.

From: Roger Dawson, Finance Manager
To: Management Accountant Assistant
Subject: Production cost variances and quality

I have just been on the telephone to the finance manager at TRU Group who has asked me to send him a summary of our recent months'production materials and labour cost variances. They would like an explanation of reasons for the variances. Gail Honner, finance officer, your fellow has prepared the summary of the data as follows:

Production	Body wash	Body lotion	Hand & foot cream
Budgeted production (bottles of 250mL)	108,000	60,000	25,000
Actual production (bottles of 250mL)①	110,000	48,000	17,000
Standard production cost for actual (K$)	396,000	210,000	95,200
Overall variances for actual production	(K$)	(K$)	(K$)
Materials price	0	4,100 A	3,500 A
Materials usage	500 F	29,500 A	22,200 A
Labour rate	0	350 A	500 A
Labour efficiency	2,000 F	9,900 A	9,850 A

Note: A = adverse, F = favourable.

The TRU Group finance manager also asked why we didn't use a cost of quality report to complement our variance reports as part of our assessment of production performance. He would like us to consider it, as we would find it useful.

In addition, Freda Jones and Tomaz Green, together with people from TRU Group have been discussing using the principles of TQM throughout our production process. Freda has asked for an explanation of how introducing quality circles within the business might help us to meet TQM principles.

Please send me an email which includes:

(1) an explanation of the above variance summary that I could forward onto the TRU Group finance manager;

(2) four examples, specific to our business, of the costs that we might include in a cost of quality report, including justification of which quality cost category they relate to;

(3) an explanation of how a cost of quality report would benefit our business, using the recent

① Actual production refers to the amount of good output and excludes the batches that were thrown away as a result of quality issues.

mechanical issue to illustrate;

(4) an explanation of how introducing quality circles within the business might help us meet TQM principles.

Many thanks!

Roger Dawson
Finance Manager
Sanchez Navarra

Write the email requested by Roger Dawson.

Section 2

A few weeks later, Roger Dawson is absent from work and Jack Forbes, an assistant in the sales & marketing department, sends you the following email.

From: Jack Forbes, Sales & Marketing Assistant
To: Management Accountant Assistant
Subject: One-off contract and new corporate customers

We have been offered a one-off contract to supply 10,000 gift sets to one of Keyland's major fashion businesses which will be exhibiting at Keyland Fashion Week. The business is going to be giving away "Made in Keyland" gift bags to its important customers at the Keyland Fashion Week and would like to include one of our gift sets in each bag. They are prepared to pay K$ 30.00 for each 500 mL gift set, giving us total revenue of K$ 300,000.

Richard Procter, sales & marketing director, has asked me to look into whether this contract is worthwhile. He told me that there is shortage of capacity given the mechanical issues with our production line for body lotion and hand & foot cream. Tomaz Green, operations director, has looked into this and estimates that if we spend K$ 225,000 on a temporary fix for the system, we would be able to produce enough to meet normal demand as well as this contract. If there is no fix we will only be able to meet our normal demand. He anticipates that the fix will last for three months, by which time the new production facility will be ready.

Based on our standard gross profit per gift set of K$ 27.85 (see attached schedule) it would appear that the additional gross profit that we would make on this contract of K$ 278,500 (10,000 × K$ 27.85) would more than cover the temporary fix cost of K$ 225,000. Hence I think that we should go ahead with the contract and fixing the production system. I'm not sure though that my logic is right. I do know that we will be using some old gift set bags that we have in inventory, which we no longer use in gift sets. I also know that in the short term we would keep all of the production workers employed regardless of whether we took on the contract. If we took on the contract we would need to work some overtime in order to fulfil the order as well as our normal production.

Firstly I am interested to hear your view on whether my logic is correct and if not correct how it needs to be amended. Don't need you to do any calculations, just need to understand the principles. Secondly, I would also like your assessment of any other factors that we should consider before accepting this contract.

As well as this contract Richard is negotiating with a number of new corporate customers to supply our products to them on a regular basis. This includes two major hotel chains and 10 smaller independent hotels. These negotiations are still in the early stages, but already one question that some of the potential customers have asked is the credit terms that they can expect to receive from us. Richard is keen to understand how credit terms are decided in the first place and on suitable ways to reduce the risk that customers fail to pay us. Therefore as a third matter, please can you send me some notes with which I can explain to Richard.

I'd really appreciate it if you could send me an email addressing each of these three things.

Many thanks!

Jack Forbes

Sales & Marketing Assistant

Sanchez Navarra

Breakdown of the standard gross profit per unit for 500 mL gift sets:

	(K$)
Revenue	40.00
Material cost of body wash and body lotion bottles	(6.40)
Material cost of gift bag	(2.50)
Production labour cost	(1.25)
Variable production overhead	(1.25)
Fixed production overhead	(0.75)
Gross profit	27.85

Write the email requested by Jack Forbes.

Section 3

A month later you receive the following email from Roger Dawson.

From: Roger Dawson, Finance Manager

To: Management Accountant Assistant

Subject: New production facility

We've just signed all the paperwork to buy the piece of land next door to our existing production site. This is where the new production facility is going to be built. The plan is that construction will be completed by the end of October and that the facility will be tested throughout November to then be commissioned and ready to operate from 1 December 2016.

Yesterday I compiled the final budget for the whole build project and circulated it to the directors. Freda and Nisha have both asked how these various costs will be reflected in our financial statements at the year end. They are keen to capitalize as much as possible.

Due to the on-going expansion we need to recruit a new finance officer to help support the business. Freda has already been working on a job analysis for the role and is keen to also get a person specification. She has asked for our recommendations on what would need to be included in the person specification for the new finance officer.

Because I'm pushed for time it would really help me out if you send me an email with your explanation of:

- how the costs in the attached budget schedule should be dealt with in the financial statements for the year ended 31 December 2016;
- what should be included in the person specification for the new finance officer that needs to be recruited.

Many thanks!

Roger Dawson

Finance Manager

Sanchez Navarra

Schedule of the construction budget for the new production facility:

	(K$ 000)
Purchase price of land, Including legal fees	500
Site preparation costs	120
Building contractor costs	250
Total interest to be paid on a 5 year loan taken out to fund the construction	300
Purchase price of plant and equipment cost	1,200
Import duties paid in respect of the plant and equipment	120
Costs of testing the plant	150
Costs of training staff to use the plant	80
Share of general overheads	290
Total budgeted cost of construction	3,010

Write the email requested by Roger Dawson.

Section 4

It is now 2 January 20 17 and Roger Dawson, finance manager is on annual leave. The new production facility has been fully operational since 1 December 20 16. Tomaz Green, operations director, sends the following email to Freda Jones, finance director, which she forwards to you.

From: Tomaz Green, Operations Director

To: Freda Jones, Finance Director

Subject: Potential product recall

It would appear that we have a contamination issue in the new facility. I've recently been notified by Keyland's National Water Authority that they released potentially harmful chemicals into the main water supply in December 2016. As we purify our water before using it in production, this should have been filtered out, but it would appear that the water purification system in the new facility was not working correctly (I have now arranged for this to be fixed).

This means that all of our production from the new facility is contaminated and will need to be thrown away. We have finished goods inventory in the new facility warehouse with a cost value of K$ 290,000.

Luckily we had only despatched contaminated products with an invoiced value of K$ 15,000 to concessions and stores, none of which has been sold to consumers. We have however, despatched K$ 30,000 of products directly to consumers through on-line sales. I understand that because of the way we manufacture, the effects on a consumer of using our products contaminated by this water is minimal.

We'll obviously do a product recall, but I'm concerned how our customers will react.

Many thanks!

Tomaz Green

Operations Director

Sanchez Navarra

Later that day, Freda Jones says to you:

I'm concerned about the impact of this product recall on both our financial statements and our customer relationships. Given that we've only just found out about this I think that we should deal with it in the 2017 financial statements rather than the 2016 financial statements, although I would like your view on this and what the impact of any adjustments required will be.

Like Tomaz, I'm also worried about how our customers will react. We need to protect our brand at all costs. Please let me know how you think we should communicate the product recall to have the minimum adverse effect on our brand.

Please email me on both of these points.

Write the email to Freda Jones.

试卷四

本次考试的结构如下：

序号	任务数	时间（分钟）
1	1	60
2	1	60
3	1	35
4	1	25

每个部分规定的时间可用于读题、组织和书写答案。

任务一

财务总监 Freda Jones 为整个财务团队召开了一个简短会议，会上她说：

感谢大家能来开会，我只是想让大家了解一些新情况。

销售和市场总监 Richard Procter 正在与一些潜在的新客户（包括一家主要的连锁酒店）进行新业务的谈判。Richard 坚信这是我们能够扩大销售市场的机会，并且热切希望我们有生产能力来应对这一问题。

如果在短期内我们所有的生产设备都在最佳运作状态，这个提议将不存在任何问题。然而，生产经理 George Focus 告诉我，我们目前用于生产润肤乳和手足霜的生产线存在一些机械问题，导致很多批产品由于质量差而被淘汰。由于必须重新生产这些产品，我们不得不以高于正常价格的价格迅速购买额外的原材料。我们还必须支付加班费，其包括在生产劳动力成本中。

George 说，沐浴露生产线不受这些机械问题的影响，已经在该生产线上开发了一种新的材料测量和输入工艺。

看来，这条生产线的维护工作没有像去年那样坚持进行。无论如何，生产线还是旧的，所以我会在下一次董事会议上就比原计划提前设立新生产设施所需的资本支出征求同意。

一周后，Roger Dawson 向您发送了电子邮件。

发件人：财务经理 Roger Dawson
收件人：管理会计助理
主题：生产成本差异和质量

我刚刚打电话给 TRU 集团的财务经理，对方要求我向他发送一份我们最近几个月的生产资料和人工成本差异的汇总信息。他们想要我们对差异原因的解释。您的同事 Gail Honner 已经准备好了数据汇总，如下：

产品	沐浴露	润肤乳	手足霜
预算产量（250 毫升/瓶）	108 000	60 000	25 000
实际产量（250 毫升/瓶）①	110 000	48 000	17 000

① 实际产量是指产出的良好产品数量，不包括由于质量问题而丢弃的批次。

（续表）

产品	沐浴露	润肤乳	手足霜
实际生产成本标准	K$ 396 000	K$ 210 000	K$ 95 200
实际生产的总体差异	K$	K$	K$
材料价格	0	4 100 A	3 500 A
材料用途	500 F	29 500 A	22 200 A
劳动率	0	350 A	500 A
劳动效率	2 000 F	9 900 A	9 850 A

注：A = 不利的，F = 有利的。

TRU 集团的财务经理还问我们为什么没有使用质量成本报告来补充我们的差异报告，并将其作为我们对生产绩效评估的一部分。他希望我们考虑一下，因为我们会发现它很有用。

此外，Freda Jones 和 Tomaz Green 以及 TRU 集团的人员一直讨论在我们的整个生产过程中使用全面质量管理的原则。Freda 要求我们解释如何在业务中引入质量圈来帮助我们满足全面质量管理原则。

请给我发送一封电子邮件，内容包括：

（1）我可以转发给 TRU 集团财务经理的针对上述差异汇总的解释；

（2）有关我们成本业务的 4 个例子，可能包括在质量成本报告中，以及与其相关的质量成本类别的理由；

（3）使用最近发生的机械问题来说明质量成本报告如何有利于我们的业务；

（4）关于在业务中引入质量圈会怎样帮助我们满足全面质量管理原则的解释。

非常感谢！

桑切斯 · 纳瓦娜公司

财务经理

Roger Dawson

请根据 Roger Dawson 的要求撰写邮件。

任务二

几周后，Roger Dawson 缺席工作，销售和市场部的助理 Jack Forbes 向您发送了电子邮件。

发件人：销售与营销助理 Jack Forbes

收件人：管理会计助理

主题：一次性合同和新的企业客户

我们已经获得了一份一次性的合同，向 Keyland 的一个主要时尚企业提供 10 000 套礼品套装，这些套装将在 Keyland 时装周上展出。该企业将在 Keyland 时装周上向重要客户赠送"Keyland 制作"的礼品袋，并希望每个袋子中都包含一个礼品套装。他们准备为每件 500 毫升礼品套装支付 K$ 30.00，总收入为 K$ 300 000。

销售与市场总监 Richard Procter 已经要求我研究这个合同对我们是否有利。他告诉我，我们的润肤乳和手足霜生产线上存在的机械问题导致了产能不足。运营总监 Tomaz Green 已经调查了这一点，并估计如果我们能花费 K$ 225 000 来暂时解决这个问题，那么我们就可以生产出足够的产品来满足正常的合同需求。如果这个问题，我们就只能满足我们的正常需求。他预计该修复将持续 3 个月，届时新的生产设备将会准备就绪。

根据我们每套礼品的标准毛利 K$ 27. 85（见附表）来看，我们在本合同项下获得的额外毛利 K$ 278 500（10 000 × K$ 27. 85）将超过临时固定成本 K$ 225 000。因此，我认为我们应该继续签订合同并完善生产系统。我不太确定我的判断是否是正确的。我知道我们会使用一些我们库存的不再用于礼品套装的旧礼品袋。我也知道，在短期内，我们将保留所有的生产工人，无论我们是否接受合同。如果我们签了合同，我们就需要加班加点，以便履行订单和正常生产。

首先，我想听听你对我的判断是否正确的看法，如果我的判断不正确的话，需要如何修改，这不需要你做任何计算，只需要了解原则就可以了。其次，我也希望你对签订本合同之前我们应该考虑的任何其他因素进行评估。

除了这份合同之外，Richard 还在与一些新的企业客户进行谈判，以定期向他们提供我们的产品，这包括两家大型连锁酒店和 10 家较小的独立酒店。这些谈判仍处于早期阶段，但是一些潜在客户已经提出了一个问题，即他们期望从我们这里获得的信用条件。Richard 渴望了解如何在一开始就确定信贷条件，并找到合适的方式来减少客户拒绝支付的风险。因此，第三件事就是请你给我发一些关于上述问题的笔记，以便我向 Richard 介绍。

我将会很感激，如果你可以给我发送一封解决这三件事情的电子邮件。

非常感谢！

桑切斯·纳瓦娜公司
销售和营销助理
Jack Forbes

每件 500 毫升礼品套装的标准毛利明细：

	（K$）
收入	40.00
沐浴露和润肤乳的包装瓶的材料成本	(6.40)
礼品袋的材料成本	(2.50)
生产劳动力成本	(1.25)
变动生产费用	(1.25)
固定生产费用	(0.75)
毛利润	27.85

请根据 Jack Forbes 的要求撰写邮件。

任务三

一个月后，您收到来自 Roger Dawson 的电子邮件。

发件人：财务经理 Roger Dawson
收件人：管理会计助理
主题：新生产设施

我们刚刚已经签署了所有的文件，购买了我们现有生产基地附近的一块土地。在这里，我们将要兴建新生产设施，我们计划在 10 月底之前完成建设施工，在 11 月份进行全面测试，随后于 2016 年 12 月 1 日起投入运行。

昨天我编制了整个建设项目的最终预算，并将其分发给了董事们。Freda 和 Nisha 都问到这些不同的成本将如何在年末的财务报表中反映出来。他们渴望尽可能多地积累资本。

由于业务的持续扩张，我们需要招聘一名新的财务人员来协助完成业务。Freda 已经在为该职位做职业需求分析，并且渴望得到一份岗位说明书。她已经要求我们提出关于新财务干事的岗位说明中需要包括什么的建议。

因为我的时间紧迫，如果你能给我发送一封电子邮件解释一下，真的会帮到我。

■ 截至 2016 年 12 月 31 日的年度财务报表应如何处理附加预算表中的费用。
■ 招聘新财务干事的岗位说明书应包括哪些内容。

非常感谢！

桑切斯·纳瓦娜公司
财务经理
Roger Dawson

新生产设施建设预算表：

	（K$）
土地购买价格，包括法律费用	500
预备场地费用	120
建筑承包商费用	250
5 年期贷款的利息总额	300
工厂和设备的采购价格	1 200
关于工厂和设备的进口关税	120
测试工厂的成本	150
培训员工使用新设施的成本	80
一般管理费用的份额	290
建设的总预算成本	3 010

请根据 Roger Dawson 的要求撰写电子邮件。

任务四

现在是 2017 年 1 月 2 日，财务经理 Roger Dawson 正在休年假。新的生产设施自 12 月 1 日起已经全面投入运行。运营总监 Tomaz Green 向财务总监 Freda Jones 发送了以下电子邮件，她又转发给了你。

发件人：运营总监 Tomaz Green
收件人：财务总监 Freda Jones
主题：潜在的产品召回

我们的新工厂似乎存在污染问题。我最近被 Keyland 国家水务局通知，他们在 2016 年 12 月将潜在的有害化学物质排放到了主要供水系统中。由于我们在生产之前对水进行了净化，所以应该已经将其过滤掉了，但似乎新工厂的净水系统没有正常工作（我现在已经安排了进行修复工作）。

这意味着我们所有新工厂生产的产品都受到了污染，需要被丢弃。我们已经在新工厂的仓库中完成了货物库存，其成本价值为 K$ 290 000。

幸运的是，我们只向特许经营商和专卖店发送了发票价值 K$ 15 000 的污染产品，并且没有一个产品被卖给消费者。但是，我们通过在线销售直接向消费者发送了价值 K$ 30 000 的产品。据了解，由于我们生产的方式，使用我们这种被水污染的产品对消费者影响很小。

很明显，我们会进行产品召回，但我担心客户的反应。

非常感谢！

桑切斯·纳瓦娜公司
运营总监
Tomaz Green

那天晚些时候，Freda Jones 对你说：

我担心这次产品召回对我们的财务报表和我们的客户关系产生的影响。鉴于我们刚刚发现了这一点，我认为我们应该在 2017 年的财务报表中处理这个问题，而不是在 2016 年的财务报表中，尽管我需要知道你对这一点的看法以及所需调整的影响是什么。

像 Tomaz 一样，我也担心客户的反应如何。我们需要不惜一切代价保护我们的品牌。请让我知道你认为我们应该如何进行产品召回以对我们的品牌产生最小的不利影响。

请就这两个问题给我发一封电子邮件。

请写下给 Freda Jones 的电子邮件。

Variant 4 Suggested Answers

Section 1

From: Management Accountant Assistant

To: Roger Dawson, Finance Manager

Subject: RE: Production cost variances and quality

Production Cost Variances

The production cost variances shown in the schedule show that our performance in the most recent month was significantly affected by the mechanical issues on the body lotion and hand & foot cream production line.

Body Wash

There have been no reported mechanical issues on the body wash production line and hence the variances for the month are low compared to body lotion and hand & foot cream. Indeed overall we were able to produce more than budgeted and have a favourable labour efficiency variance. It would appear that the changes made to the process of measuring and loading the raw materials into the production process have been beneficial, hence we have had to use less labour time.

There has also been a saving in the usage of materials as evidenced by the favourable usage variance, probably as a result in the changes to the measuring and inputting process. It should be noted that the saving in labour cost is greater than the raw material cost saving and indicates that the main benefit of the changes has been the time saving.

Body Lotion and Hand & Foot Cream

We produced significantly less good output than we had budgeted to produce for both body lotion and hand & foot cream. This is because of mechanical issues with the production line resulting in low quality product which had to be thrown away and started again.

In respect of the significant adverse variances for materials usage can be explained by this. We have had to use significantly more materials to produce our 17,000 bottles of hand & foot cream and 48,000 bottles of body lotion than we should have based on our standards. We have in effect wasted raw materials.

In addition as a result of having to order raw materials to be delivered quickly, we have had to pay a premium, resulting in adverse raw material price variances for both body lotion and hand & foot cream.

The mechanical issues have also resulted in adverse labour efficiency variances. A greater number of labour hours have had to be used in production than having been for this level of good output. Overtime has been worked by production staff, as evidenced by the adverse labour rate variance.

Four Examples of Costs of Quality Linked to Our Production Line

Cost of Maintaining the Production Lines

The costs that we incur maintaining our production lines would be classified as a prevention cost within a cost of quality report. Maintenance of the lines ensures that the production that is achieved on the line is of the correct standard. If the lines were not maintained the production could be defective and sub-standard, which would be detrimental to the business. Thus, maintenance of the machinery is a prevention cost.

Costs of Quality Control Staff

The costs that we incur in respect of employing quality control staff within the production process are appraisal costs within a cost of quality report. There are two main areas where we employ quality control staff: in the raw materials receiving area and at the end of the production line prior to bottling. At each point the raw materials or finished products are checked for their quality, hence why this is categorised as an appraisal cost.

Cost Incurred Scrapping Poor Quality Production

The costs incurred scrapping poor quality production (such as the raw materials wasted, labour wasted and charges for disposal of waste) are internal failure costs in a cost of quality report. Such costs are incurred after the quality issues has arisen and are therefore seen as failure costs. The fact that the issue has been identified prior to despatching to customers means that this is an internal failure cost.

The Potential Loss of Customer Goodwill

If we had a situation where poor quality products were sold to customers we could potentially lose some of our customer goodwill which will impact on future sales. In this instance this lost future revenue would be an external failure cost: failure is because the poor quality has caused the issue and external is because it has arisen after the goods have been despatched. This is very hard to quantify.

How a Cost of Quality Report Might Benefit Our Business

A cost of quality report would show the total cost to Sanchez Navarra of ensuring the quality of production (in the form of conformance costs) and also any costs associated with production not being at the correct quality level (which are non-conformance costs). It would be useful to look at this alongside our traditional variance reports that we produce every month as there are important links between the two.

Using the example of the mechanical issues with the body lotion and hand & foot cream production plant, additional employee time was used to re-make batches of production that had to be scrapped and there would have also been additional quality checks as a result of the known problem.

This additional time is the adverse labour efficiency variance, which looking at the variances in isolation would be viewed as negative (because it is adverse). However, if we were to think about this from a quality perspective the time taken re-doing batches was necessary, so that the quality of the products reaching the end consumer was not impaired. A cost of quality report would highlight this alongside the adverse variance.

A cost of quality report can also be used as a check with regard to which quality costs we would have expected to see. One of the prevention costs that I identified above is the cost of maintaining the production line. If we had produced a cost of quality report in previous periods, it would have been easier to identify where expenditure was lower than it should have been. We might have identified that lack of maintenance and hence been able to act before the mechanical issues actually arose.

Introducing Quality Circles to Achieve TQM Principles

A quality circle is a team of people from all levels and departments of the business who meet regularly to discuss issues relating to the quality of the product. In our case the circle should include representatives from production as well as sales people, managers as well as production operatives. We could also potentially include an employee that works either in one of our stores or on a concession stand who has first-hand experience of the customer perception of quality. The team should also include someone from the product development team.

At meetings, the team should discuss collaboratively ideas for improving the product and the production process. Suggestions, no matter how small, should be taken on board by management and acted upon, or at least considered. For example, an idea might be to change the way that some of the fragrance materials are stored to increase their intensity or to improve their longevity. Another idea might be to change the order of mixing so that the mix was able to emulsify more easily.

Acting on such suggestions would help to achieve a number of the TQM principles.

- Prevention of poor quality production through using fragrance materials which were keeping their best.
- Elimination of waste through the efficient use of resources such as the mixing machine.
- Continuous improvement through listening to those involved in the process first hand.

In addition, quality circles also include all levels of staff working collaboratively encourage participation, teamwork and empowerment which are also key principles of TQM. By involving all departments it can aid quality throughout the business. For example, the current quality issues resulting from the mechanical problems have resulted in batches of production being thrown away. If there were a quality circle meeting to discuss this issue, it might well be that the sales people could give guidance on which fragrances to focus on in production, given possible constraints.

Many thanks!

Management accountant assistant

Sanchez Navarra

Section 2

From: Management Accountant Assistant

To: Jack Forbes, Sales and Marketing Assistant

Subject: One-off contract and new corporate customers

Basis of Decision

A decision such as this which is for a one-off contract should be decided using the principles of relevant costs and revenue.

A relevant cost or revenue is one which is a future cash-flow and is incremental to the decision, or in other words is only incurred or earned as a result of the decision. You are correct with part of your analysis in that the cost of the temporary fix of K$ 225 000 is a relevant cost because it only arises as a result of the decision. However, we need to compare this to the net of the relevant revenue and costs that arise from the contract itself.

In terms of relevant revenue, this will be the K$ 300,000 that the fashion label will pay us (and not based on the K$ 40 per gift set that is the standard revenue). This means that as long as the total relevant costs (which includes the temporary fix costs of K$ 225,000) are less than this, we should accept the contract.

In terms of relevant costs there are a number of considerations.

- The material cost of the body wash and body lotion will be relevant to the decision. We are asked to use bottles of body wash and body lotion that we use in our normal sets, thus any inventory we use will need to be replaced. This is a cost of K$ 6. 40 a gift set.
- The cost of the gift bag is possibly not a relevant cost. This is because we have bags in inventory which we do not currently use for our normal gift bags. If there are no plans to use these bags in the future then the relevant cost is zero.
- The bulk of the labour cost is likely to be not relevant. This is because in the short term we will still employ all of the workers regardless of this contract. However, any additional overtime worked as a result of the contract would be a relevant cost and should be included.
- In respect of variable overhead we expect these to vary with production and therefore these will be relevant to the decision.
- Fixed overheads by nature do not change with the level of activity and therefore will not be relevant.
- We will need to check whether there are any additional costs arising as a result of taking on this contract.

Other Factors to Consider in Respect of the One-off Contract

There are a number of factors that need to be considered in respect of the contract before a decision is made.

Brand Awareness

Even if, from a relevant costing perspective, this contract does not appear to be worthwhile, but the exposure of our brand will have could more than make up for any shortfall. Keyland Fashion Week is likely to be attended by people from all over the world and exposure of our brand in this way could help with expansion into other countries.

Availability of Cash

If we undertake the contract then we will need to spend K$ 225,000 up front in order to temporarily fix the production plant. In addition we will need to buy additional inventory of raw materials. We will not receive payment from the fashion label until possibly a month or so after delivery. The question therefore is whether we have sufficient cash to fund this.

Accuracy of the Information Supplied

If we accept the contract, we will be committed to fulfil it. This will not be an issue as long as the repairs do fix the plant as Tomaz Green believes. There is a risk that the repairs do not work as planned and therefore we are unable to produce enough to satisfy both the contract and our normal sales. as a result We could potentially lose sales and customer goodwill.

Attitude of Employees

Overtime is likely to be required in order to produce enough for both the contract and normal sales. We need to be sure that there is enough capacity in the workforce to be able to meet this requirement and that production employees are happy to do the overtime. There could be morale and motivation issues if too much is expected. We might need to provide incentives to ensure that this is not the case, which will potentially be an additional relevant cost.

Credit Terms and Encouraging Payment

Credit Terms

There are two inter-linked aspects that you will need to consider in respect of establishing appropriate credit limits for the new corporate customers.

(1) The amount of credit that is given (the maximum amount a customer can owe at

any one time).

(2) The time limit for payment(how long a customer has to pay from the date of the invoice).

You mention that there are two major hotel chains and a number of smaller independent hotels that you are already negotiating with. These customers will vary in respect of the size of their order and in their ability to pay us. Each customer will need to be assessed separately.

The key factor to assess is the potential creditworthiness of the customer, in other words its ability to pay for goods that it has received. The large hotel chains due to their size are likely to have better creditworthiness than the independent hotels, therefore they could probably be granted a higher amount of credit and time limit for payment.

However, this would need to be confirmed by carrying out a check on creditworthiness for each potential customer. This involves looking at financial statements for signs that liquidity is an issue, obtaining credit reports and /or reviewing any press reports about them.

We will also need to establish what the industry norm is for the time allowed to repay. We would not want to be too different from the industry norm, otherwise it could act as a disincentive for them to purchase from us.

Ways to Reduce the Risk That the Customers Do not Pay for Goods Received

Firstly, we need to ensure that we follow sound credit control procedures at all times. This means that customers are only allowed to order goods to the value of their credit limit less the amount that they owe us. That is, credit limits are strictly adhered to, and reviewed and changed if necessary to limit our exposure to irrecoverable debts.

Secondly, we could offer prompt payment discounts. This involves allowing say a 1% discount on the invoice value if the customer pays within 7 days from the date of invoice. Ultimately if the customer takes this up this will affect our profit, but we will have received the money early and will have reduced the risk that they don't pay.

Thirdly, we could take out credit insurance on our customer balances. This would involve paying a premium, but if a customer did not pay because it had ceased trading for example, the insurer would usually honour up to 75% of the balance owing.

Fourthly, we could factor our debts without recourse. This would involve effectively selling our receivable balances to a factoring company, who would then manage our receivables ledger and be responsible for any debts not received. This would however be potentially very costly.

Many thanks!

Management accountant assistant
Sanchez Navarra

Section 3

From: Management Accountant Assistant
To: Roger Dawson, Finance Manager
Subject: New production facility

Accounting Treatment of Construction Costs

IAS 16: PPE, states that expenditure associated with an item of property, plant and equipment can be capitalised if it is either part of the purchase price (including import duties) or directly attributable to getting the asset ready for its intended use.

From the budget the purchase prices of the land and the plant and equipment clearly fall into this first category. The building contractor costs and the import duty also fit this category.

The costs that can be said to be directly attributable costs including the site preparation costs and the costs of testing the plant. Both of these are necessary in order to first build the facility and secondly to ensure that the plant and equipment is operating as it should.

The interest costs are dealt with in IAS 23: Borrowing Costs. IAS 23 says that where an asset is constructed like this, any borrowing costs incurred up until the point the construction is complete and the asset is ready for its intended use should be capitalised. Therefore we will be able to capitalise the interest incurred up until 1 December 2016, which is the date that the facility will be ready for use. We also need to check when the borrowings were taken out. We should only capitalise interest incurred after construction commenced, which might be later than when the borrowing was actually taken out.

The costs of training staff and the general overheads are likely not to be directly attributable costs and hence need to be expensed as incurred. In respect of the overhead this is an apportionment rather than directly incurred and hence in accordance with IAS 16 cannot be capitalised.

In respect of the training costs, the answer is less clear cut. It will be hard to argue that training costs are incurred in order to get the asset ready for its intended use. The production facility is likely to be ready for its intended use, even if staff need to be trained to use it. Even if we could argue that training costs are directly attributable to getting the production facility ready for use, the fact that it is the staff that are being trained, who are free to leave the business at any time, means that these costs do not meet the definition of an asset in terms of being able to control the economic benefits expected to arise. It is likely that our auditors will expect the training costs to be expensed as incurred.

Person Specification

The person specification need to include those personal characteristics, qualifications, skills and qualities that we are looking for in respect of the new finance officer that we need to recruit.

There are a number of models which can be used to help in establishing what to include in the person specification. Using Fraser's Five Point Plan the Finance Officer candidates will need to demonstrate.

(1) Flexibility and adjustment in terms of how well they take instruction, work with or without supervision and deal with potentially stressful situations. As a finance office they need to be able to work on their own as well as under the guidance of the finance manager, Roger Dawson and other members of the management team, including the directors. There are times of the year when there are peaks of work, such as budget setting time and month end, when the finance officer will need to manage time and workload.

(2) Their impact on other people. It's important that there is an ethos of teamwork within the business. A finance officer will ultimately become involved in many aspects of the business and need to get along with all types and grades of employ-

ee. Thus, they will also need good communication skills.

(3) The required qualifications. It is important that the finance officer has the appropriate business and accountancy qualifications as well as the appropriate experience in the field. Additional qualifications that might be useful given the nature of our business would include Health and Safety and First Aid.

(4) Motivation in terms of achievement and progression plans. Clearly we want to employ motivated people but we must recognise that motivation takes many forms and also that not all jobs can offer promotion.

(5) Innate abilities in terms of aptitude and general intelligence. We need to ensure that we employee people who will be able to understand the role that will be required of them and be willing to learn and pick up new skills as required.

Many thanks!

Management accountant assistant
Sanchez Navarra

Section 4

From: Management Accountant Assistant
To: Freda Jones, Finance Director
Subject: Product recall

Impact of Product Recall on the Financial Statements

We will need to adjust for this product recall in the financial statements for the year ended 31 December 2016, because the notification of the contamination gives us the evidence of a condition existing at the reporting period date. It is an adjusting event in accordance with IAS 10: Events After the Reporting Period.

The contaminated water was used in production in December, and given that the new facility only started production in December all of the inventory will be affected. Therefore at 31 December 2016, the contamination issue exists and the notification in January is simply evidence of it.

In terms of the impact on the financial statements we will need to write off all of the contaminated inventory. This will be a cost in the statement of profit or loss. In addition we need to create a payable for any amounts that we will need to repay to on-line customers that have purchased this inventory.

Communication and Marketing of the Product Recall

It is important that we act in an ethical and socially responsible manner and communicate as clearly as possible with our on-line customers. We need to explain the nature of the problem and clearly communicate that the potential effects on the consumer of using our products is minimal.

Given that they are on-line customers, it should be relatively easy to communicate with them because we will have their email addresses and postal addresses.

We need to send an email or a letter in the post to each of the on-line customers in order to clearly explain the issue. Given that it arose initially from a contamination of the main water supply, it is likely that consumers will already be aware of the issues, albeit they might not expect that their Sanchez Navarra products have been affected.

We need to ask the customers to return the products (using a free post service) and offer them some sort of recompense. We could offer to refund the money or provide a replacement. Alternatively, we could refund the money automatically and just send a replacement as a goodwill gesture. We could also offer a short term discount on future orders.

In terms of protecting our brand we also need to communicate to the market as a whole, perhaps through a press release.

Many thanks!

Management accountant assistant
Sanchez Navarra

试卷四　参考答案

任务一

发件人：管理会计助理

收件人：财务经理 Roger Dawson

主题：生产成本差异和质量

生产成本差异

汇总表中显示的生产成本差异表明，我们最近一个月的生产业绩深受润肤乳和手足霜生产线的机械问题的影响。

沐浴露

目前还没有关于沐浴露生产线的机械故障报告，因此与身体乳和手足霜相比，本月的差异较小。总的来说，我们的生产能力超过预算，并且有一个有利的生产效率差异。看来，将原材料的测量和装载环节并到生产过程的变化是有益的，因此我们必须减少劳动时间。

使用方面的有利差异也可以节省材料的使用，可能是由于测量和输入过程发生了变化。但需要注意的是，劳动力成本的节省要大于原材料的成本节约，这表明改变的主要好处是节省了时间。

润肤乳和手足霜

我们生产的产品明显少于我们预计生产的润肤乳和手足霜。这是因为生产线的机械问题导致产品质量不佳，不得不被丢弃并重新生产。

对于材料使用方面的显著的不利差异可以由此解释。根据标准，我们不得不使用更多的材料来生产我们的 17 000 瓶手足霜和 48 000 瓶润肤乳，我们实际上浪费了原材料。

此外，由于必须快速订购原材料，我们不得不支付额外费用，导致了润肤乳和手足霜的原材料价格差异不利。

机械问题也导致了不利的劳动效率差异。生产中必须使用的劳动时间要比这种水平的良好产出所需要的劳动时间要多。生产人员一直在加班，这可以从不利的劳动比率差异中看出。

质量成本应用到我们生产线的 4 个实例

维护生产线的成本

我们维护生产线所产生的成本将在质量报告成本中被分类为预防成本。维护生产线是为了确保在生产线上实现的生产是正确的标准。如果不维护生产线，生产可能会有缺陷，不符合标准，这对业务是不利的。因此，机器的维护成本是预防成本。

雇用质量控制人员的成本

我们在生产过程中雇用质量控制人员所产生的成本是质量报告成本中的评估成本。我们采用质量控制人员的主要领域有两个：原料接收区域和装瓶前的生产线末端区域。在每一点，他们都要检查原材料或成品的质量，因此将其归类为评估成本。

劣质产品的成本

劣质产品的生产成本（如原料浪费，劳动力浪费和废弃物处理的费用）是质量报告成本的内部失败成本。这些费用是在质量问题出现之后产生的，因此被视为失败成本。这个问题在发送给客户之前就已经确定了，这意味着这是一个内部失败成本。

客户信任的潜在损失

如果我们遇到将质量差的产品出售给客户的情况，我们可能会损失一些客户的信任，也可能会对未来的销售产生影响。在这种情况下，这种损失的未来收入将会是一个外部失败成本：失败是因为是质量差导致了这个问题；外部是因为它是在货物发货后出现的。这很难量化。

质量报告成本如何有益于我们的业务

质量成本报告将显示桑切斯·纳瓦娜公司确保生产质量（以符合成本的形式）的总成本，并且与生产相关的任何不在合格的质量水平下的成本（这是不符合成本）。与我们每个月生产的传统方差报告一起研究是很有用的，因为这两者之间有重要的联系。

以润肤乳和手足霜生产工厂的机械问题为例，使用额外的劳动时间来重新生产必须报废的批次产品，并且还会因为已知的问题进行额外的质量检查。

这个额外的时间是不利的劳动效率差异，将孤立的差异视为消极的（因为它是不利的）。但是，如果我们从质量的角度考虑这一点，重新生产所花费的时间是必要的，这样到达最终消费者手里的产品质量才没有缺陷。质量成本报告将突出显示这种不利的差异。

质量成本报告也可用作检查我们预期的质量成本。以上我提到的预防成本之一是维护生产线的成本。如果我们在前一时期已经产生了质量成本报告，那么更容易确定哪里的支出低于原本的水平。我们可能已经发现机械缺乏维护，因此在机械问题真正出现之前就能够采取行动。

引入质量圈来实现全面质量管理原则

质量圈是由来自企业各级和各部门的人员组成的团队，他们定期开会讨论与产品质量有关的问题。在我们的案例中，这个圈子应该包括生产和销售人员的代表，管理人员和生产人员。它也可以包括在我们的一家专卖店或特许经营柜台工作的员工，他们具有客户对质量认知的第一手经验。这个团队还应包括产品开发团队的人员。

在会议上，团队应共同讨论改进产品和生产过程的想法。无论多么微小的建议，都应由管理层采纳并采取行动，或至少进行考虑。例如，一个想法可能是改变一些香料的存储方式以增加其香味或延长其保质期。另一个想法可能是改变混合的顺序，使得混合物能够更容易乳化。

根据这些建议采取行动，将有助于实现一些全面质量管理原则。

- 通过使用香味处于最佳时期的香料，防止劣质产品。
- 通过有效利用混合机等资源，消除浪费。
- 通过直接聆听过程中涉及的内容，持续改进。

此外，质量圈还包括各级共同工作的员工，鼓励参与，团队合作和授权，这也是全面质量管理的关键原则。通过所有部门的参与，它可以帮助提升整个业务的质量。例如，目前由机械问题导致的质量问题使得批量产品被放弃。如果有一个质量圈会议来讨论这个问题，可能销售人员就会在考虑到可能的限制因素的情况下，提供关于在生产中应该关注哪些香味的指导。

非常感谢！

桑切斯·纳瓦娜公司

管理会计助理

任务二

发件人：管理会计助理

收件人：销售和营销助理 Jack Forbes

主题：一次性合同和新的公司客户

决策基础

这样的一项关于一次性合同的决策应该根据相关成本和收入的原则来决定。

相关的成本或收入是指未来的现金流，对决策而言是增量的，换句话说，只是由于决策而产生或获得的。您的部分分析结果是正确的，因为临时固定费用 K$ 225 000 是相关费用，因为它只是决策的结果。但是，我们需要将其与合同本身产生的相关收入和成本的净额进行比较。

在相关收入方面，这是时尚品牌将支付给我们的 K$ 300 000（而不是基于每个礼品套装 K$ 40 的标准收入）。这意味着只要相关费用总额（其中临时固定费用为 K$ 225 000）低于此，我们就应该接受合同。

在有关成本方面，这儿有一些考虑。

- 沐浴露和润肤乳的材料成本与决策有关。我们被要求使用我们在正常套装中使用的瓶装沐浴露和润肤乳，因此我们使用的所有库存都需要被替换。这是一件 K$ 6.40 的礼品套装。
- 礼品袋的成本可能不是相关费用。这是因为我们目前没有使用我们正常礼品袋的库存袋。如果将来没有计划使用这些袋子，则相关费用为零。
- 大部分劳动力成本可能不是相关费用。这是因为在短期内，我们仍然会雇佣所有的工人，而不考虑这份合同。但是，由于合同而产生的加班的任何额外费用都是相关费用，应包括在内。
- 关于可变开销，我们预计这些将随生产而变化，因此这些与决策相关。
- 固定费用本身并不随着活动水平而变化，因此不相关。
- 我们需要检查是否因接受这份合同而产生了额外费用。

关于一次性合同的其他考虑因素

在做出决策之前，有一些与合同相关的因素需要被考虑。

品牌意识

即使从相关的成本核算角度来看，这份合同似乎不划算，但我们的品牌的曝光足以弥补任何损失。Keyland 时装周可能有来自世界各地的人参加，以这种方式曝光我们的品牌可以帮助我们扩展到其他国家。

现金可用性

如果我们签订合同，那么我们需要预先花费 K$ 225 000 来临时修理生产车间。另外，我们还需要购买额外的原材料库存。我们大概在交货后一个月左右才能从时尚标签收到付款。因此，问题是我们是否有足够的现金来支持这一计划。

所提供信息的准确性

如果我们签订这份合同，我们将承诺履行合同。只要工厂如 Tomaz Green 所认为的那样修复，这就不是问题。但我们依然承担着维修工作没有按计划完成的风险，这样我们就不能生产出足够满足合同以及正常销售所需要的产品。我们可能会因此失去销售渠道和客户的信任。

员工态度

可能需要加班，以便为合同和正常销售生产出足够的产品。我们需要确保在劳动力方面有足够的能力来满足这一要求，并且生产员工乐意加班。如果预期过高，可能会产生士气和激励问题。我们可能需要提供奖励，以确保这种情况不会发生，这可能是额外的相关成本。

信用条款和鼓励付款

信用条款

在为新的公司客户建立适当的信用额度时，您需要考虑两个相互关联的方面。

（1）给定的信用额（客户在任何时间都可以承受的最大金额）。

（2）付款期限（客户从发票开出之日起可以支付的最晚时间）。

你提到有两家主要的连锁酒店和一些你正在与之谈判的较小的独立酒店。这些客户的订单规模和支付能力会有所不同。因此，每个客户都需要分开评估。

评估的关键因素是客户的潜在信誉，换句话说，就是它能够支付已收到的商品的能力。规模大的连锁酒店可能比独立酒店具有更好的信誉，因此可能会获得更高的信用额度和更长的付款期限。

然而，这需要通过对每个潜在客户进行信誉检查来确认。这涉及查看财务报表中是否有迹象表明流动性存在问题，获得信用报告和/或审查关于它们的任何新闻报道。

我们还需要确定允许偿还时间的行业规范。我们不希望与行业规范有太大的不同，否则可能会阻碍他们向我们购买。

降低客户不付款的风险的方法

首先，我们要确保我们始终遵循良好的信用管理程序。这意味着客户只被允许按其信用额度的价值订购货物，而不被允许按欠我们的金额订购，也就是说，我们要严格遵守信贷限额并在必要时进行审查和更改，以限制我们对不可收回的债务的敞口。

其次，我们可以提供及时的支付折扣。如果客户在发票开出之日起 7 天内支付，则允许发票价值有 1% 的折扣。最终，如果客户接受这一点，这将会影响我们的利润，但是我们会尽快收到这笔钱，并且降低他们不支付的风险。

再者，我们可以对客户的余额进行信用保险。这将涉及支付保险费，但如果客户例如因为停止交易而没有付款，则保险公司通常会给我们兑换余额的 75%。

最后，我们可以无追索权地把我们的债务考虑在内。这将涉及有效地将应收账款余额出售给一家保理公司，该公司随后将管理我们的应收账款分类账，并对未收到的任何债务负责。然而，这可能是非常昂贵的。

非常感谢！

桑切斯·纳瓦娜公司
管理会计助理

任务三

发件人：管理会计助理
收件人：财务经理 Roger Dawson
主题：新的生产设施

建筑成本的会计处理

国际会计准则第16号不动产、厂房和设备指出，与不动产、厂房和设备相关的支出，如果是采购价格（包括进口关税）的一部分，或直接归属于达到资产预计可使用状态前所发生的必要、合理的支出，则可以资本化使用。

从预算来看，土地、厂房和设备的采购价格明显属于第一类。建筑承包商的费用和进口关税也符合这一类别。

可以说直接归因成本包括现场准备成本和测试工厂的成本。这两者都是必要的，以便首先建造设施，然后确保工厂和设备正常运行。

利息费用在国际会计准则第23号借款费用中有所说明。国际会计准则第23号规定，如果资产如本例所示的方式构建，那么直到建设完成并且资产准备好用于其预期用途之前发生的任何借贷成本都应该资本化。因此，我们能够将所产生的利息资本化到2016年12月1日，即设施准备使用的日期。我们还需要检查借款何时被取出。我们应该仅资本化施工开始后产生的利息，这可能晚于实际开始借款的时间。

培训人员的费用和一般管理费用可能不是直接归因成本，因此需要支付费用。关于一般管理费用，这是一种分摊而不是直接发生的，因此根据国际会计准则第16号不能资本化。

在培训费用方面，答案不太明确。很难认为培训费用是为了使资产准备好用于其预期用途而产生的。即使员工需要接受培训，但生产设备也可能已经准备就绪。即使我们认为培训成本可直接归因于准备使用的生产设备，但正在接受培训的员工随时可以自由离职的事实意味着这些成本不符合资产在能够控制预期经济利益方面的定义。我们的审计人员很可能会期望培训费用按发生费用被支出。

岗位说明

该岗位说明需要包括我们正在招聘的新财务人员的个人特征、资格、技能和素质。

有许多模型可用于帮助确定岗位说明中应包含的内容。根据 Fraser 五点计划，财务人员候选人将需要证明以下几点。

（1）在接受命令、在没有监督的情况下工作及处理潜在的压力情况方面，懂得灵活变通。作为一个财务部门，他们需要能够在财务经理 Roger Dawson 和其他管理团队成员（包括董事）的指导下独立开展工作。一年中有几个工作高峰期，比如预算设定时间和月末，财务总监需要管理时间和工作量。

（2）他们对别人的影响。企业内部的团队合作精神很重要。财务人员最终将参与到业务的许多方面，并需要与所有类型和等级的员工相处，因此他们也需要良好的沟通能力。

（3）从业资格。财务人员必须具备适当的业务和会计资格以及相关经验。鉴于我们业务的性质，可能要求的附加条件包括健康与安全和急救。

（4）在成就和进步计划方面的动机。显然，我们想要雇佣有进取心的人，但我们必须认识到，激励有很多形式，也不是所有的工作都能提供晋升机会。

（5）天赋才能和一般智力。我们需要确保我们的员工能够了解他们所担当的角色，并愿意根据需要学习和发展新技能。

非常感谢！

桑切斯 · 纳瓦娜公司

管理会计助理

任务四

发件人：管理会计助理

收件人：财务总监 Freda Jones

主题：产品召回

产品召回对财务报表的影响

在截至 2016 年 12 月 31 日的年度财务报表中，我们需要对此次产品召回事项进行调整，因为污染通知已经向我们证明了报告期内此情况的存在。根据国际会计准则第10号报导期间后事项，这是一个调整事项。

受污染的水在去年12月被用于生产，鉴于新工厂在12月才开始生产，所有库存都会受到影响。因此，在2016年12月31日，污染问题就已经存在，1月的通知仅仅是证明了这一事实。

就对财务报表的影响而言，我们需要注销所有受污染的库存，这将是损益表中的成本。此外，我们需要为我们需要偿还给已购买此库存的在线客户的任何款项创建一个应付款项。

产品召回的沟通和营销

重要的是，我们必须以一种道德和富有社会责任的方式行事，并尽可能清晰地与我们的在线客户沟通。我们需要解释问题的性质，并明确地说明使用我们的产品对消费者的潜在影响是最小的。

鉴于他们是在线客户，因为我们有他们的电子邮件地址和邮政地址，所以与他们沟通应该相对容易。

我们需要向每位在线客户发送一封电子邮件或一封信，清楚地解释这个问题。鉴于这个问题最初来自主要供水的污染，消费者很可能已经意识到这些问题，尽管他们可能没有预料到他们的桑切斯·纳瓦娜公司的产品受到了影响。

我们需要让客户退回产品（使用免费的邮政服务），并向他们提供某种补偿。我们可以提供退款或提供更换。或者，我们可以开启自动退款通道，只需发送一个替换作为一个善意的姿态。我们也可以为未来的订单提供短期折扣。

在保护品牌方面，我们也需要通过新闻报道与整个市场进行沟通。

非常感谢！

桑切斯·纳瓦娜公司

管理会计助理

Variant 4　Marking Guidance

Section	Technical skills		Business skills		People skills		Leadership skills		Integration	Total
1	Explanation of variances (P1) Cost of quality reporting (P1) Costs in a cost of quality report (P1)	8 4 8	Quality circles (E1) Cost of quality reporting (P1)	5 4	Quality circles (E1)	4				33
2	Relevant costing (P1) Qualitative factors in the decision (P1) Credit terms for new customers (F1)	11 8 5					Credit terms for new customers (F1)	6	3	33
3	Capitalisation of new production facility (F1)	10			Person specification (E1)	10				20
4	Accounting for product recall (F1)	7	Impact on the brand (E1)	7						14
Total marks available for each competency		61		16		14		6	3	100

试卷四　评分指南

部分	技术技能		商业技能		人际技能		领导技能		综合	总计
1	对差异的解释（P1） 质量成本报告（P1） 质量报告成本（P1）	8 4 8	质量圈（E1） 质量成本报告（P1）	5 4	质量圈（E1）	4				33
2	相关成本的计算（P1） 决策的定性因素（P1） 对新客户的信用条款（F1）	11 8 5					对新客户的信用条款（F1）	6	3	33
3	新生产设施的资本化（F1）	10			职位要求（E1）	10				20
4	产品召回的会计记录（F1）	7	对品牌的影响（E1）	7						14
各种能力分数总计		61		16		14		6	3	100

西安交通大学名师解惑

试卷一共有四项任务，考查了 P1、F1、E1 三门课程的知识点，具体包括生产成本差异、质量成本、质量成本报告、质量环、外部质量损失成本、决策中的定性因素、新生产设施的资本化、对新客户的信用条款等。该试卷考核了考生的四项能力，其中技术技能的分值占 61%，商业技能的分值占 16%，人际技能的分值占 14%，领导技能的分值占 6%，与 CGMA 管理会计能力框架的技能要求一致。

该试卷的每项任务涉及以下知识点：

任务	问题	科目	知识点
任务一	对生产成本差异的解释	P1	差异分析（variance analysis）
	质量成本给公司带来的影响	P1	质量成本（cost of quality）
任务二	利用成本收益分析原则进行决策	P1	成本收益分析（cost-benefit analysis）
	提供给新客户的信用条件	F1	对新客户的信用条款（credit given to new customers）
任务三	如何处理附加预算表中的费用	F1	新资产设施的资本化（capitalisation）
	招聘新财务干事的岗位说明书所包含的内容	E1	职位要求（job requirements）
任务四	产品召回对财务报表的影响	F1	对产品召回的会计记录（accounting treatments of product recall）
	对品牌产生最小不利影响的沟通召回方式	E1	产品召回对品牌的影响（effects on brand）

上述各项任务要求以邮件、报告或工作笔记等形式来呈现答案，对问题的描述非常明确，答题时既要注意内容的针对性，也要注意形式的规范性。

同时，答题时，要避免只是对教科书的知识点进行简单复述，应结合案例公司的实际情况；注意回答时的措辞、格式，注意论述的结构，注意论点的鲜明性和整体性等。

对应知识点的深度剖析

差异分析

通过对预算成本与实际成本之间差额的分析来确定差异形成的原因和责任，考生要重点关注润肤乳和手足霜的生产中由生产线的机械问题带来的原材料浪费和快速采购成本的增加。

质量成本给公司带来的影响

关于质量成本给公司带来的影响，4 个成本的确定相对较容易，但对质量圈及质量圈会议概念及其用处、优点的把握易成为考生的丢分点。

利用成本收益分析原则进行决策

判定 Richard 的思考逻辑是否正确的标准，从公司层面来说，大体上应采用成本收益分析原则，即运用所给出的数据分析成本和收入。除此之外，正如分析企业运营状况一样，还应考虑除利润外的财务因素（如流动性）以及非财务因素（如企业文化、员工态度）。

提供给新客户的信用条件

考生应综合考虑给定的信用额及付款期限两个方面来决定合适的信用额度，之后还需要结合实际情况提出可能采用的评估客户信用风险的方法。

新生产设施的资本化

本题目涉及较多的会计专业知识，如会计费用的确认及计量。在处理附加预算表中的费用时，应充分联想并引用国际会计准则中的相关规定（第 16 号不动产、厂房和设备；第 23 号借款费用）。

职位要求

招聘说明书的内容相对较开放，有多种模型可供选择和运用，如答案给出的 Fraser 五点计划。

对产品召回的会计记录

本题涉及期后事项的确认及处理。我们可以从 1 月的通知中合理推断出在 2016 年 12 月 31 日时污染问题已经明显存在，因此其应当被视作调整事项在上一年度的财务报表中反映，不论我们的客户会怎样解读所披露的信息。

产品召回对品牌的影响

为了尽量减少消费者的负面情绪，我们可以在附注中明确说明我们产品的潜在影响很小，这样在遵从职业道德规范的同时又能保护品牌的措施是值得采用的。

Variant 5

This examination is structured as follows：

Section number	Number of tasks	Time for section(minutes)
1	1	45
2	2	45
3	1	45
4	1	45

The time available for each section is for reading,planning and writing your answer(s).

Please note section 2 consists of two tasks. Please leave enough time to complete both parts.

Section 1

Roger Dawson, finance manager is on annual leave. You receive the following email from Freda Jones, finance director.

From: Freda Jones, Finance Director
To: Management Accountant Assistant
Subject: Expansion of sales into Feyland

I've just had a very interesting conversation with Richard Procter, sales & marketing director, about expansion into Feyland. Feyland is a country with a similar economic profile to Keyland and has the F$ as its currency. Richard has been working closely with the Sales & Marketing team at TRU Group to make contact and to start negotiations with potential department store partners in Feyland. The most promising lead at the moment is Stars, a major national department store chain in Feyland.

Stars has agreed to rent us space for concession stands in its ten largest stores, which are all in major cities. The arrangement with Stars will be the same as our Keyland department store partners here, in that sales receipts net of rents will be collected and paid over to us after a month. We will need to provide our own sales employees for each concession stand. We will also need to set up an office and warehouse in Feyland (probably on a single site), which the whole Feyland operation will be managed and inventory stored and distributed to the concession stands.

Richard is confident that our products will sell well in Feyland, especially with our "Made in Keyland" badge. Apparently Feyland consumers are really keen on any products from Keyland because they have a reputation for being high quality goods. Richard believes that once we've established ourselves at Stars we can launch our website there and extend our on-line sales.

We now need to discuss, as a management team, some of the operational issues associated with setting up in Feyland and so I am preparing a report on the matter.

Please you send me an email with your assessment of the following.

- Why it is important that we establish what our level of demand might be in Feyland and how we might do this using survey and statistical approaches.
- The financial reporting and tax implications of operating in Feyland if we set up a subsidiary

which is incorporated there. I know that Feyland uses IFRS. The tax rules in Feyland are exactly the same as Keyland except that the corporate tax rate is 30% and no withholding tax is applied to dividends paid. A double taxation treaty exists between the two countries.

Thank you!

Freda Jones
Finance Manager
Sanchez Navarra

Write the email requested by Freda Jones.

Section 2

A week later, Roger Dawson is still on annual leave and Freda Jones, finance director sends you the following email.

From: Freda Jones, Finance Director
To: Management Accountant Assistant
Subject: Feyland budget

Thank you for the email that you sent me last week. At the directors' meeting we decided to go ahead the arrangement with Stars, although we decided not to set up as a subsidiary initially. We will be launching a marketing campaign in Feyland to promote our brand, which is organised and paid for from Keyland.

At our meeting Richard Procter, sales & marketing director, was talking about our marketing strategy for Feyland. He kept mentioning guerrilla, viral and experiential marketing. This is all very new to Nisha and me as we've always been quite traditional in our marketing approach. So that we can talk knowledgeably about this with Richard we would be very grateful if you could send us a briefing note on what guerrilla, viral and experiential marketing are all about, with examples of how we might implement them in Feyland.

We will be setting up an office and warehouse in Feyland on a single site. The whole Feyland operation will be run from this office as a profit center separated from the rest of the business in

Keyland. We will employ a manager with overall responsibility for the profit Centre, its staffing and its budget. Our products will be shipped from Keyland to the Feyland warehouse and will be charged to the profit center at standard cost of production plus freight costs. Each of the ten Stars concessions stands will be serviced from this warehouse. The Feyland manager will have the same authority with respect to the recommended retail price of goods sold to customers as our sales managers in Keyland.

We need to start putting the budget together for the Feyland profit centre. In particular I am unsure of how we should set the volumes for the sales budget, if it is set at a high level, will this be motivational for the manager? Please send me, in an email, an explanation of the different elements that should be included in this budget, the degree of control that the Feyland manager will have for each of these elements and whether in your view setting a high sales volume target would be motivational for the manager.

Many thanks!

Freda Jones

Finance Manager

Sanchez Navarra

Write the briefing note about marketing.

Section 3

Six month later, the ten concession stands in Stars stores are operating. Jacob Perez is the Feyland manager. You receive the following email from Roger Dawson, finance manager.

From: Roger Dawson, Finance Manager

To: Management Accountant Assistant

Subject: Variance report and investment of surplus cash

The directors have asked for a briefing paper for their meeting later today on a couple of matters.

Firstly, the directors have received the latest sales variance report for body wash from Jacob

Perez(the manager of the Feyland business). The directors would like to know what the report is telling them in terms of how the Feyland profit centre is performing in sales of body wash, especially as there are some adverse variances.

To help you with this know that Jacob has the same authority to reduce the standard selling price for each product as do our Keyland sales managers. Our products are transferred to the Feyland profit centre at our budgeted standard cost of production plus freight charges adjusted at a fixed exchange rate. This transfer value has not changed in the period and the exchange rate has been stable and is expected to remain at the same level in the foreseeable future.

Secondly, despite the adverse variances, the Feyland business has really helped to boost the overall cash position of the business. At the moment there is around F$1,000,000 in our business bank accounts. The directors have already decided that in four months'time F$950,000 will be needed to expand the production facility. However, in the short term they are keen that any currently surplus money should earn some form of return (at the moment no interest is earned on either of the business bank accounts). They have therefore asked that the briefing paper includes explanations of the factors that they need to consider when choosing how to invest this money and suggestions of suitable investments.

Please prepare the first draft of this briefing paper for me.

Many thanks!

Roger Dawson
Finance Manager
Sanchez Navarra

Extract of Sales Variance Report for Feyland Profit Centre

Sales of body wash for the month:

Fragrance	Standard gross profit per unit(F$)	Price variance (F$)	Sales mix variance (F$)	Sales quantity variance(F$)
Emerald	9.50	1,950A	1,330 F	380A
Ruby	8.96	300A	5,018A	358A
Sapphire	8.30	—	1,328A	332A
Topaz	10.88	6,000A	9,140 F	435A
Diamond	8.12	—	2,111A	325A
Total		8,250A	2,013 F	1,830A

A = Adverse, F = Favourable.

Notes:

(1) Total budgeted gross profit is F$ 54,912 for the month.

(2) The standard gross profit per unit is the standard retail selling price less the standard cost of buying in the product from the production facility. This has been used to calculate the volume variances.

(3) The standard selling retail price per unit is F$ 15, irrespective of the fragrance.

(4) The budget was based on selling 6,000 units in total(1,200 for each fragrance). Actual sales were 5 800 units in total (which would equate to 1,160 units of each fragrance at the budgeted mix).

Write the draft of briefing paper requested by Roger Dawson.

Section 4

A few weeks later Roger Dawson phones you and says:

The directors are now thinking about launching the on-line sales service in Feyland. They are not sure whether we should operate this within the Feyland profit centre or outsource the whole on-line sales function(which will include dealing with orders, distribution and customer care. There are two potential outsource partners: a TRU Group subsidiary based in Feyland which sells luxury bedding through its own on-line sales function and a third-party distribution and customer care specialist, also based in Feyland, which manages on-line sales for a number of clients.

Richard Procter, sales & marketing director, has prepared a schedule concerning the impact on profit for the first year of operation of each of these three options (in-house, outsource to TRU

Group subsidiary or outsource to a third-party). He is now away at a conference but I do remember him saying that there were different ways to interpret the tables shown in his schedule. The other directors would like to know what the schedules are showing as well as what the various interpretations are. The directors would also like to know the benefits of carrying out the on-line sales function in house compared to outsourcing to either the TRU Group subsidiary or the third party specialist .

Please come and pick up Richard's schedule and then prepare the first draft of a briefing paper to the directors addressing these matters.

After the phone call, you collect Richard's schedule from Roger.

Schedule Prepared by Richard Procter, Sales & Marketing Director

Impact of on-line sales on profit for the first year of operation:

Possible volume of sales in units	Possible increase in profit from on-line sales		
	In-house (F$ 000)	TRU subsidiary (F$ 000)	Third party (F$ 000)
180,000	1,400	1,650	1,590
310,000	2,600	2,750	2,800
430,000	3,800	3,500	3,990

Regret table:

Possible volume of sales in units	Regret		
	In-house (F$ 000)	TRU subsidiary (F$ 000)	Third party (F$ 000)
180,000	250	0	60
310,000	200	50	0
430,000	190	490	0

Notes on preparation of schedule:

(1) There are three possible volumes of sales: 180,000 units, 310,000 units and 430,000 units. The level of sales depends on the market conditions.

(2) The in-house profits are based on the contribution per unit and fixed costs keep constant at all levels of sales.

(3) Both the TRU Group subsidiary and the third-party are offering us a set charge per unit despatched. This charge per unit dispatched varies with volumes sold.

- For the TRU Group subsidiary the charge per unit will be higher at higher volumes. This is because they will need to expand operations if they need to dispatch more than 320,000 units of our product in the year.
- For the third party, the charge per unit decreases at higher volumes as a result of economies of scale.

Write the draft of a briefing paper requested by Roger Dawson.

试卷五

本次考试的结构如下：

序号	任务数	时间（分钟）
1	1	45
2	2	45
3	1	45
4	1	45

每个部分规定的时间可用于读题、组织和书写答案。

请注意任务二包括两项子任务，需留足时间。

任务一

财务经理 Roger Dawson 在休年假。你收到了来自财务总监 Freda Jones 的以下邮件。

发件人：财务总监 Freda Jones
收件人：管理会计助理
主题：扩张销售市场至 Feyland

我刚刚与销售和市场总监 Richard Procter 进行了一次非常有趣的谈话，内容是关于将销售市场扩张到 Feyland。Feyland 是一个与 Keyland 有着相似经济状况的国家，以 F$ 为货币。Richard 一直与 TRU 集团的销售和营销团队紧密合作，以便与 Feyland 的潜在百货商店合作伙伴建立联系，开展谈判。目前最有前景的领军者是 Feyland 一家大型的全国百货连锁店 Stars。

Stars 已经同意将其十个最大商店的摊位租给我们来进行特许经营，这些商店都分布在一些主要城市。Stars 的安排与我们这边的合作伙伴 Keyland 百货商店一样，将在收到扣除租金的销售收入的一个月后集中支付给我们。我们需要为每个特许柜台配备我们自己的销售人员。我们还需要在 Feyland（可能在一个地点）设立一个办公处和仓库，来管理 Feyland 的整个运营、存货存储以及存货向特许经营场所的分发。

Richard 相信我们的产品在 Feyland 会很畅销，尤其是有了我们的“Keyland 制造”的品牌。显然，Feyland 的消费者对 Keyland 的任何产品都很热衷，因为 Keyland 的产品以高品质而闻名。Richard 认为，一旦我们在 Stars 站稳脚跟，我们就可以在那里推出我们的网站并扩大在线销售。

我们作为管理团队，现在需要讨论与在 Feyland 发展业务相关的一些运营问题，所以我正在编写一份有关这个问题的报告。

请你发给我一封对下述问题的分析邮件。

- 为什么我们需要确定我们的产品在 Feyland 的需求水平，以及我们可以通过怎样的调查和统计方法来确定需求水平。
- 若我们成立一家在那里注册的子公司，那么会对在 Feyland 经营的财务报告和税收带来什么影响。我知道 Feyland 使用国际财务报告准则。除了公司税率为 30%，分红不征收预扣税款之外，Feyland 的税收规定与 Keyland 完全相同。两国之间存在着双重征税条约。

谢谢！

桑切斯·纳瓦娜公司
财务总监
Freda Jones

请根据 Freda Jones 的要求回复邮件。

任务二

一周后，Roger Dawson 还在休年假，财务总监 Freda Jones 给你发了一封邮件。

发件人：财务总监 Freda Jones
收件人：管理会计助理
主题：Feyland 的预算

感谢您上周发送给我的电子邮件。在董事会会议上，我们决定继续与 Stars 合作，尽管我们最初决定不设立子公司。我们将在 Feyland 开展营销活动来推广我们的品牌，该活动将由 Keyland 的公司组织和支付费用。

在我们的会议上，销售和市场经理 Richard Procter 谈到了我们在 Felyand 的营销策略。他不断提到游击营销、病毒营销和体验营销。Nisha 和我对此感到非常新鲜，因为我们在营销方法上一直比较传统，因此，我们想和 Richard 针对这个谈一谈。如果你能给我们发送一份有关游击营销，病毒营销和体验营销的简要说明，以及举一些我们如何在 Feyland 实施这些策略的例子，我们将非常感谢。

我们将在 Feyland 的同一个地点开设一个办事处和仓库。整个在 Feyland 的运营将作为一个利润中心由这个办事处运作，并与其他在 Keyland 的业务分开。我们将聘请一名经理，全面负责利润中心、人员配置和预算。我们的产品将从 Keyland 运送到 Feyland 的仓库，并将以标准生产成本加上运费向利润中心收取费用。这个仓库将为 Stars 的十个特许经营柜台提供服务。Feyland 的经理与我们在 Keyland 的销售经理，在对销售给客户的商品的建议零售价格上具有同等的权力。

我们需要开始为 Feyland 的利润中心制定预算。我尤其不确定如何设定销售预算的数额，如果设定在高水平，这对于经理来说会有激励作用吗？请以邮件的形式，发给我一份对于这个预算中所应包含的不同要素的说明，Feyland 的经理对每一个要素的控制程度，以及在你看来设定高销量目标对经理是否有激励作用。

非常感谢！

桑切斯·纳瓦娜公司
财务总监
Freda Jones

请根据 Freda Jones 的要求撰写简报。

任务三

6 个月后，Stars 百货连锁商店的十大特许经营柜台正在运作。Jacob Perez 是 Feyland 的经理。你收到了财务经理 Roger Dawson 的以下电子邮件。

发件人：财务经理 Roger Dawson
收件人：管理会计助理
主题：差异报表及盈余现金的投资

董事们要求我为今天晚些时候的会议准备一份简报，介绍几件事情。

首先，董事们收到了 Jacob Perez（Feyland 的业务经理）最新的沐浴露销售差异报告。董事们想知道，报告关于 Feyland 利润中心在销售沐浴露的表现如何是怎样介绍的，特别是当那边有一些不利的变化时。

为了帮助你了解，就要知道 Jacob 与 Keyland 的销售经理在降低每个产品的标准销售价格上拥有同等的权利。我们的产品按照我们预算的标准生产成本加上以固定汇率调整的运费转入 Feyland 利润中心。在此期间，转移价值未发生变化，汇率稳定，预计在可预见的将来仍保持同一水平。

其次，尽管有不利的变化，但 Feyland 的业务确实对提升企业整体的现金状况有所帮助。目前，我们的商业银行账户中大约有 F$1 000 000。董事会已经决定，在四个月的时间里，需要 F$950 000 来扩大生产设施。不过，短期来看，他们渴望目前任何盈余的资金都能赚取某种形式的回报（目前，任何一家商业银行的账户都不会产生利息），因此，他们要求简报包含对他们在选择如何投资这些钱时需要考虑的因素的解释，以及合适的投资建议。

请准备一份简报的初稿给我。

非常感谢！

桑切斯·纳瓦娜公司

财务经理

Roger Dawson

Feyland 利润中心的销售差异报告的摘录

本月沐浴露的销售情况：

香型	每单位标准毛利（F$）	价格差异（F$）	销售组合差异（F$）	销售数量差异（F$）
祖母绿	9.50	1 950A	1 330F	380A
红宝石	8.96	300A	5 018A	358A
蓝宝石	8.30	—	1 328A	332A
黄玉	10.88	6 000A	9 140 F	435A
钻石	8.12	—	2 111A	325A
合计		8 250A	2 013 F	1 830A

A = 不利，F = 有利。

注：

（1）本月总预算毛利为 F$ 54 912。

（2）每单位的标准毛利是标准零售价格减去从生产设备购买产品的标准成本。这已被用于计算产量差异。

（3）单位标准零售价为 F$ 15，无论何种香型。

（4）预算建立在总销量为 6 000 个单位的基础上（每种香型销量为 1 200）。实际总销量为 5 800 个单位（相当于按预算组合，每种香水销售 1 160 个单位）。

请根据 Roger Dawson 的要求撰写简报初稿。

任务四

几星期后 Roger Dawson 给你打电话说：

董事们正在考虑在Feyland推出线上销售服务。他们不确定我们是应该在Feyland利润中心之内运作这个业务，还是外包整个在线销售职能（包括处理订单，分销和客户关怀）。我们现在有两个潜在的外包合作伙伴，一个是位于Feyland的TRU集团的子公司，它通过自己的线上销售功能销售豪华床上用品；另一家是一个同样位于Feyland的第三方分销和客户服务专家，它为很多客户管理线上销售。

销售和市场总监Richard Procter，已经准备了一个计划表，其内容有关三个选择（内部运作，外包给TRU集团的子公司或外包给第三方）对第一年经营利润所产生的影响。他现在不在会议上，但我记得他说过，有不同的方式来解释他的计划表中列出的表格。其他董事想知道这些表格展现了什么，以及对它们都有哪些不同的解读。董事们也想知道，相比外包给TRU集团的子公司或第三方专家，内部实施在线销售职能的好处。

请来拿Richard的计划表，然后为处理这些事宜的董事们准备一份简报的初稿。

在通话结束后，您从Roger那里拿到了Richard的计划表。

销售与市场总监Richard Procter制定的计划表

在线销售对第一年营业利润的影响：

预期销售数量	通过在线销售预期增加的利润		
	内部（F$000）	TRU子公司（F$000）	第三方（F$000）
180 000	1 400	1 650	1 590
310 000	2 600	2 750	2 800
430 000	3 800	3 500	3 990

遗憾值表：

预期销售数量	遗憾值		
	内部（F$000）	TRU子公司（F$000）	第三方（F$000）
180，000	250	0	60
310，000	200	50	0
430，000	190	490	0

准备计划表的备注：

（1）有三种可能存在的销量：180 000单位，310 000单位和430 000单位。销售水平与市场状况有关。

（2）内部利润基于每个单位的贡献而定，固定成本在各个销售水平都是不变的。

（3）TRU 集团的子公司和第三方都向我们提供了每单位货物的固定费用。这笔每单位货物的费用因销售量而异。

- 对于 TRU 集团的子公司而言，单位费用将以较高的数量增加。这是因为如果他们需要在今年发货超过 320 000 台的产品，就需要扩大运营。
- 对于第三方来说，由于经济规模的原因，单位费用将以较大的数量减少。

请写下 Roger Dawson 所要求的简报初稿。

Variant 5 Suggested Answers

Section 1

From: Management Accountant Assistant

To: Freda Jones, Finance Director

Subject: Expansion of sales into Feyland

Why IT's Important That We Establish Our Level of Demand in Feyland

It is important that we estimate our level of demand as accurately as possible so that we are able to plan.

Firstly, we need to plan the additional production that will be required. We need to ensure that we have enough of each fragrance and given that we can only make one fragrance at a time, it is important that production is carefully planned. Otherwise, we risk stock-outs of popular fragrances or incur additional costs for holding excess inventory of a certain fragrance.

Secondly, we need to be able to plan shipping the products to Feyland and need to have an idea of quantity to be able to secure the best deal with the freight company.

Thirdly, we will need to prepare budgets and set targets for the sales people. If we set an unrealistic budget because we have not tried to forecast demand sensibly, it could result in de-motivation of the sales people and hence have an adverse effect on sales overall.

How We Can Establish What Our Level of Demand Might Be in Feyland

There are a number of tools available to us to help us determine what the demand for our products might be in Feyland, which can broadly be categorised into two: survey and statistical based methods.

Survey Based

We could undertake market research in Feyland to canvas the opinions of the end consumers on our products.

Given that Feyland is a completely new market and we do not have any knowledge of it, the best option is likely to be to engage a marketing consultant from Feyland. The consultant could conduct surveys and report back to us on the scope of the market for our products. The cost of using a consultant is likely to be outweighed by the benefits of expert knowledge: the end result is likely to be more useful and accurate than if we did it by ourselves.

Any survey undertaken would need to be targeted to our likely end consumers. Possibly we could arrange with Stars and the expert consultant to have promotional stands in stores with samples of all of the products that we wish to sell.

From the survey information, the expert consultant would be able to use their knowledge of the market and the economy of Feyland to predict sales levels.

Statistically Based

On the assumption that the economy and market in Feyland is similar to Keyland, we could use historical data on sales from our own market.

We could start with data from ten concession stands based in large city based department stores and create a time series for each product and each fragrance we could identify the trend and any seasonal variations (such as Christmas or holiday time) which would need to be factored into any production planning. We could make adjustments for any known differences in the markets between Keyland and Feyland.

Alternatively, because using Keyland information relies on the two economies having similar features (such as demographics and disposable incomes), and this might not be the case, we could see if statistical information based on the Feyland market was available, from external marketing organisations in the country.

In reality, the best result is likely to be a combination of both the survey and statistical approach.

Financial Reporting and Tax Implications of Setting Up in Feyland as a Subsidiary

Financial Reporting Implications

If we set up the Feyland operation as a subsidiary this will mean that it will be a separate entity from Sanchez Navarra, albeit a part of the Sanchez Navarra.

From a financial reporting point of view, this means that we will need to prepare a separate set of financial statements for the subsidiary. Feyland uses IFRS and therefore the basis for the preparation of the subsidiary's financial statements will be the same as we use.

In addition we will possibly need to prepare group financial statements. This means that as well as the two sets of financial statements for Sanchez Navarra and the subsidiary, we will need to prepare a third set of financial statements which combines them. This involves adding the income, expenses, asset and liabilities of each entity together and eliminating inter-company balances and transactions (of which there will be many).

We could however claim exemption from preparing group financial statements because we are a partly owned subsidiary of a larger group. However, in order to use the exemption we will need to check that:

- the TRU Group will prepare its own group financial statements;
- both Nisha and Freda, as the non-controlling shareholders in Sanchez Navarra, do not object.

Tax Implications

From a tax perspective each company is seen as a separate entity and is taxed on that basis. Therefore, setting up a subsidiary in Feyland means that it will be subject to Feyland corporate tax at a rate of 30%. It will need to pay corporate tax based on its profits to the Feyland tax authority.

Any dividends paid to us by the Feyland subsidiary, will therefore have been subject to underlying tax, because they will have been paid out of taxed profits. These dividends received by us will also be taxable income in Keyland and subject to tax at our corporate rate of 25%. Therefore, potentially this income will be taxed twice.

However, a double tax treaty exists between Feyland and Keyland which means that relief is available to prevent such double taxation. Under the tax credit method, we will be able to offset the amount of underlying tax on the dividend that was paid in Feyland against our equivalent tax liability in Keyland. However such relief can only be claimed to the extent of our liability in Keyland and no refund can be claimed. Given that the Keyland tax rate is lower than the Feyland tax rate this means that we will not be able to claim relief for all of the underlying tax.

Many thanks!

Management accountant assistant

Sanchez Navarra

Section 2

Briefing Note on Digital Marketing

Guerrilla Marketing

Guerrilla marketing is a about creating a buzz around a product as a result of surprising potential consumers. It is a non-conventional form of marketing and is about organising a creative stunt to draw attention to a product rather than a drawn out campaign. It is usually a relatively cheap form of marketing which can have a massive impact.

We could for example engage a well-known celebrity in Feyland and project his image with our product onto the front of the 10 Stars department stores in which we will be selling our products. Or we could project a giant picture of a bottle of body wash onto the buildings coloured with the Keyland flag to identify it as a "Made in Keyland" product.

Viral Marketing

Viral marketing is about using the social media networks that already exist to spread awareness of the brand. The idea is that we create an advert or a video within these networks which is then spread throughout the network by people sharing the message.

We could for example, create a short promotion video about Sanchez Navarra products(possibly using a well-known celebrity in Feyland) and link this to a competition to win a range of the products. By sharing or liking the advert, the potential consumer would be entering the competition and also more importantly for us spreading brand awareness through their friendship group and beyond. This would potentially reach a wider audience than a television advert alone.

Experiential Marketing

Experiential marketing is about creating an emotional link between a potential consumer and the brand through having experience of the brand.

This could be achieved by setting up a roadshow which travels around Feyland allowing potential consumers to experience our products. This would be particularly good for the body lotion and hand & foot cream as potential consumers could easily access this. Indeed we could extend this and possibly create a "Body Beautiful" campaign where we look for real consumers to feature in a television campaign.

The Email to Freda Jones

From: Management Accountant Assistant
To: Freda Jones, Finance Director
Subject: Feyland budget

As a profit centre the Feyland budget will need to include all of the revenue and costs associated with the sales operation there.

Budgeted Revenue

Revenue will be driven by two factors: volumes budgeted to be sold and the price charged to the consumer.

The Feyland manager will have the same authority to discount the recommended retail price of our products as our Keyland sales managers and this means that he or she could discount any of our products by up to 30%. The question is whether we budget on the basis of the full recommended retail price (which is what we do for the Keyland business) or whether we take account of an average level of discount when setting the budget.

The volumes of products sold at the 10 Star's concession stands will partly be under the control of the Feyland manager. Ultimately the volume of sales will be the result of the Feyland manager's decisions on pricing and staffing levels at each stand. It will also depend on how well sales staff are trained to sell the products, which again will be within the manager's control. However, the volumes sold in Feyland will also be influenced by the marketing campaign there, which is being controlled in Keyland and over which the Feyland manager will have no input.

Budgeted Costs

There are a number of costs that need to be included in the budget. These costs and the ability of the Feyland manager to control them are discussed below.

(1) The costs of buying in the products from the Keyland production facility. This is going to be based on the standard cost of production plus freight costs and is therefore fixed and controlled in Keyland. The Feyland manager will not be able to control these costs and therefore should not be held responsible for any changes to this cost that we in Keyland impose.

(2) The costs of employing sales staff at each of the concession stands. The Feyland

manager will need to decide how to staff each of the stands. There will need to be cover on all stands at all times that the stores are open, however there is flexibility in how this is done. There could be a mixture of full-time and part-time staff, with possible overtime if required. The manager could decide to employ more staffs in order to push promotions at busy times. Therefore the manager should be held responsible for these costs, although the effect of any changes in saying national wage rates, or employee taxes should be identified separately, as these are not under the control of the Feyland manager.

(3) The costs of running the distribution of products to stores. There will be a central distribution warehouse, but the manager is responsible for how often deliveries are made to concessions stands and how this is done. This will clearly be a cost that they will be responsible for.

Budgeted Sales Volumes

When setting budgets it is important that the targets set are seen by the budget holder as achievable, otherwise it could have a demotivating effect. If we set a high and unrealistic budget for sales volumes, then it is likely that the Feyland manager would feel that this was unattainable and hence they would not even attempt to reach it. If the target was achievable then the likelihood is that they would work harder to achieve it.

In respect of the Feyland operation it is important that we have a good forecast for the level of sales that we could expect so that we are able to set a motivational but achievable budget.

Section 3

Briefing Paper

Sales Variance Report from Feyland Business

Sales Price Variances

The price variance indicates that the prices of Emerald, Ruby and Topaz have been reduced by Jacob Perez, presumably as a means to boost sales of these fragrances. The prices of Sapphire and Diamond have not been changed.

It would appear that Topaz has seen the largest price reduction, followed by Emerald. Ruby has seen only a small decrease.

Jacob's policy would seem to be to discount those fragrances with the highest standard gross margin. Topaz has the highest margin and has been discounted the most.

Despite the price variance being adverse, this is not necessarily negative for the business as a whole. The authority to reduce prices is given to the sales managers so that they have the flexibility to promote the fragrances and hence in theory increase the volumes sold. Therefore we should not look at the sales price variances in isolation. We need to consider the whole picture.

Sales Mix Variances

The sales mix variances show the impact on gross profit of selling the fragrances in a different proportion to the original budget. We originally budgeted to sell 1,200 of each fragrance, a total of 6,000 units. If we flex the budget for actual total sales of 5 800 then should have sold 1,160 units of each fragrance.

The sales mix variances show that we have sold more than 1,160 units of Emerald and Topaz, which is to be expected given that these were two of the fragrances discounted. It is perhaps surprising that we didn't also sell more Ruby. Indeed, Ruby has the largest adverse mix variance, which might indicate that it isn't the right fragrance for the Feyland market.

Sales Quantity Variances

The sales quantity variances show the impact on gross profit of the overall volume of sales being less than budgeted. It is calculated for each fragrance as 1,200 less 1,160 multiplied by the gross profit per unit. Each fragrance shows an adverse variance because overall we sold less than the budget. This variance represents the difference between the budgeted sales in the budgeted mix and the actual sales in the budgeted mix.

Overall

Overall the report shows that the impact of the price reductions is not met by the increase in volumes sold on a total level. This could be because the volumes were incorrectly forecast in the first place, or that the discount was not enough to encourage greater sales or was ineffective at generating additional sales. Alternatively, it could be that the wrong products were discounted or that some fragrances (such as Ruby) are just not suited to the Feyland market.

Looking at individual fragrances it would appear that only Topaz has exceeded the budget. The adverse price variance of F$ 6,000 is less than off-set by the F$ 9,100 favourable mix variance, despite the F$ 440 adverse quantity variance. Therefore, Jacob's decision to heavily discount this fragrance is justified. Possibly this approach should be taken on other fragrances.

We will need to obtain clarification of the above, together with any additional explanations from Jacob Perez. We will then consider whether we will need to revise production schedules and inventory levels to fit with a revised budget.

Investment of Surplus Cash

Factors to Consider When Investing Surplus Cash

Firstly there is a need to determine exactly how much cash is effectively surplus to short term requirements. This can be achieved by preparing a detailed cash forecast which takes into account all receipts and payments. This needs to include all potential payments, including any interest, loan repayments or payments required to our parent company.

Once this is established then you will need to decide whether you require a buffer of cash available for any unforeseen circumstances that might arise. I suggest that a buffer is retained.

Once the amount of cash that is truly surplus is determined the other factors that need to be considered can be broadly categorised into three considerations: profitability, liquidity and safety.

Profitability relates to the return to be gained from the investment. You have already stated that this is a concern as the bank account is currently not giving any return. Clearly there is a need to earn as high a return as practicable, however high return usually correlates with high risk in an investment. Thus, it is important that any considerations regarding return are balanced with considerations about the risk of the investment. The risk of the investment is linked to its liquidity and especially its safety.

Liquidity relates to how easily the investment can be converted into cash. Usually the easier it is to convert, the lower the level of return. From the Sanchez Navarra perspective, as long as we are confident that this is surplus cash then we could invest the funds for the full four months, which is when we'll need the funds for investment in the new production facility.

Safety relates to how safe the investment is. Usually the safer the investment, the lower its return. Clearly there is a need to protect the capital value of our investment as we are need the funds in four months' time for the new production facility.

Suggestions of Suitable Investments

Interest Bank Deposit Account

The surplus funds could be invested in an interest bearing bank deposit account for a period of four months. This is likely to be a safe investment(even if the bank were to find themselves in difficulty they would likely be government backed in some form with deposits protected, although we would need to check this). The return is likely to be low on this investment.

Money Market Deposits

With the help of our bank, the funds could be placed on money market deposit. This is likely to give a higher rate of return than a normal deposit account. This is only available for very large sums of money and therefore we will need to check with our bank whether this is feasible. If it is then it would probably give a higher return than a normal deposit.

Marketable Securities

We could invest in short term bonds or gilts on the money market. These types of investment are riskier than deposits, especially if the bonds are corporate, however they usually offer the opportunity of a greater return. One way to reduce the risk would be to invest in government bonds such as Treasury Bills. Because these are government backed the risk is negligible, although as a result the return will be lower.

Section 4

Briefing Paper

The Sales & Marketing Director's Schedule

The schedule shows the expected additional profit from on-line sales, at three different levels of demand, for each of the options being considered: operate the on-line sales function in-house, outsource to a TRU Group subsidiary or outsource to an expert third party.

Presumably, three different sales volumes have been considered because there is uncertainty over how much we will be able to sell as this is still a relatively new market for us. Richard believes that sales could be low at 180,000 units, intermediate at 310,000 units or high at 430,000 units.

The difficulty with this decision is that in each of the options being considered the costs incurred vary in different ways. It is not simply the case that one of the options is the cheapest and therefore generates the greatest profit, which depends on what the volume of sales ends up being.

There are a number of ways that we can use this table to make a decision, depending on the attitude of the directors.

Maximax Approach

A maximax approach is seen as an optimist approach. Using this approach we would select the option which gave the maximum return (in this case profit) assuming that the best was to happen.

In this table, this would be to use the third party, because in the best situation (sales of 430,000 units), this would give the highest profit.

Maximin Approach

A maximin approach is seen as a pessimist approach. Using this approach we would select the option which gave the maximum profit assuming that the worst was to happen.

In this table, this would be use the TRU Group subsidiary, because in the worst situation (sales of 180,000 units), this would give the highest profit.

Minimax Regret Approach

We could also use a minimax regret approach, which is where we would select the option which minimises our maximum regret. This would be appropriate if the directors were most concerned about making the wrong decision. Using this criteria we choose the alternative which gives the lowest of the maximum regrets that could arise after the decision has been taken and the actual demand has become known. In effect, regret is the effect of getting the decision wrong in the first place and we seek to minimise this possible regret.

Based on the regret table, the optimum decision would be to use the third party, as the maximum regret here would only be F$60,000 (compared to F$490,000 for the TRU Group subsidiary and F$250,000 for in-house).

Conclusion

Ultimately the approach that you take will depend on your attitude towards making an incorrect decision or whether you wish to take a pessimistic of optimist view.

The above analysis indicates that either of the outsourcing options would be an optimal decision depending on criteria used. It also clearly indicates that the in-house option is not an optimal decision under any of the criteria.

However, the decision cannot be made just on the basis of this table, other non-financial factors need to be considered.

Benefits of In-house Compared to Outsourcing

The main benefit of the on-line sales function being in-house is that we would have control over it. This means that we would be able to ensure that orders were fulfilled accurately, that products were packaged appropriately and delivered in a timely manner. If we use either of the outsource options we will lose this control. The TRU subsidiary is not familiar with our products (selling luxury bedding) and therefore there is a risk that less care is taken in packaging products for despatch. We do not know what type of products the third party despatches, however, given that they are experts, perhaps the risk will be reduced.

One way to mitigate against this loss of control over the operation is to have a detailed SLA (Service Level Agreement) in place, which specifies packaging and maximum delivery times and penalties for non-compliance. However, there is a cost attached to setting this up in the first place and then monitoring and managing it. If the operation is in-house then clearly there is no need for a SLA.

Another benefit of retaining the on-line sales function in-house it what we would have direct access to the customers. We would be able to create a database of emails and contacts, which we could use in marketing and promotional activities.

We would also be able to access information about customer buying patterns and trends more easily than if we out-sourced. Such information would help in preparing budgets and scheduling production.

Linked to this by involving an outsource partner the risk of our confidential sales data getting into competitors hands is increased. This risk is particularly relevant for the third party outsource partner, which presumably has a number of contracts with different businesses. It is perhaps less of an issue for the TRU subsidiary as we are all part of the same group and it does not undertake the function for any outside parties.

试卷五 参考答案

任务一

发件人：管理会计助理

收件人：财务总监 Freda Jones

主题：扩张销售市场至 Feyland

为什么确定我们在 Feyland 的需求水平如此重要

它重要在我们要尽可能准确地估计需求水平，以便能够实施计划。

首先，我们需要规划额外的生产需求。我们需要确保每一种香型都足够，并且考虑到我们每次只能生产一种香型，所以仔细计划生产是很重要的。否则，我们将有流行香型库存不足的风险，或者会因持有某些香型的过剩库存而产生额外费用。

其次，我们需要计划怎样将产品运送到 Feyland，并且需要对数量有大体估计才能确保与货运公司达成最佳协议。

最后，我们需要制定预算，为销售人员设定目标。如果我们制定了不切实际的预算，那么可能因为我们没有试图对需求进行理智的预测，导致销售人员的积极性减弱，从而对整体销售产生不利影响。

如何确立我们在 Feyland 可能的需求水平

有很多工具可用于帮助我们确定我们的产品在 Feyland 的可能需求水平，这些工具大致分为两种：基于调查和基于统计的方法。

基于调查

我们可以在 Feyland 进行市场调研来了解最终消费者对我们产品的看法。

鉴于 Feyland 是一个全新的市场，而我们对此并不了解，最好的选择可能是聘请来自 Feyland 的营销顾问。顾问可以进行调查并向我们报告我们产品的市场范围。使用顾问的成本可能会被专业知识带来的好处超过：最终结果可能比我们自己做的更有用和准确。

进行的任何调查都需要针对我们可能的最终消费者。也许我们可以与 Stars 和专家顾问一起在商店中推广我们希望销售的所有产品的样品。

通过调查信息，专家顾问将能利用他们对 Feyland 市场和经济的了解来预测销售水平。

基于统计

假设 Feyland 的经济和市场状况与 Keyland 相似，我们就可以使用我们自己市场的销售历史数据。

我们可以先从位于大型城市的百货商店的 10 个特许摊位开始统计，并为我们可以识别趋势及季节变化（如圣诞节或假期）的每个产品和每种香型创建一个时间序列，这种季节差异需要被纳入所有的生产计划。我们可以调整 Keyland 和 Feyland 市场之间的任何已知的差异。

另外，因为使用 Keyland 信息依赖于具有相似特征的两个经济体（例如人口和可支配收入），但这实际上并不一定。我们可以通过来自这个国家的外部营销组织看到，基于 Feyland 市场的统计信息是否可用。

实际上，最好的方法可能是调查和统计方法的结合。

在 Feyland 设立子公司对税收和财务报告的影响

对财务报告的影响

如果我们在 Feyland 以子公司的形式运营业务，这意味着尽管它是桑切斯·纳瓦娜公司的一部分，但它将是与桑切斯·纳瓦娜公司分离的一个独立实体。

从财务报告的角度来看，这意味着我们需要为子公司编制一套单独的财务报表。Feyland 使用国际财务报告准则，因此编制子公司财务报表的依据将与我们所用的相同。

另外，我们可能需要编写集团财务报表。这意味着，除了桑切斯·纳瓦娜公司和子公司的 2 套财务报表，我们还需要编制第三套合并财务报表。这涉及将每个实体的收入、费用、资产和负债加在一起，并消除公司内部的余额和交易（会有很多）。

不过，我们可以要求免除编制集团财务报表，因为我们是一个较大集团的全资子公司的一部分。但是，为了获得豁免，我们需要核对：

- TRU 集团将编制自己的集团财务报表；
- 作为桑切斯·纳瓦娜公司非控股股东的 Nisha 和 Freda 不反对。

对税收的影响

从税收的角度来看，每个公司都被视为一个独立的实体，并在此基础上纳税。因此，在 Feyland 设立子公司意味着其将以 30% 的税率缴纳企业税。子公司需要根据利润向 Feyland 税务机关缴纳企业税。

因此，Feyland 的子公司向我们支付的任何股息都将因从税后利润中支付而被征税。

我们收到的这些股息也将作为在 Keyland 的应税收入，并以 25% 的企业税率纳税。因此，这笔收入可能会被征税两次。

然而，Feyland 与 Keyland 之间存在双重征税协定，这意味着可以通过减免来防止这种双重征税。根据税收抵免方式，我们可以把在 Feyland 支付的股息的应交税款与在 Keyland 的等值应交税款相抵消。但是，这种减免只能在我们在 Keyland 的责任范围内提出，并且不能要求退款。鉴于 Keyland 的税率低于 Feyland 的税率，所以我们将无法申请对所有相关税收进行减免。

非常感谢！

桑切斯·纳瓦娜公司

管理会计助理

任务二

关于数字营销的简要说明

游击营销

游击营销是指通过使潜在消费者惊讶来制造一种产品的轰动效应。这是一种非传统的营销形式，是组织一种创造性的噱头来引起人们对产品的关注，而不是一场冗长的活动。它通常是一种可以产生巨大影响，但相对便宜的营销形式。

例如，我们可以雇佣一个 Feyland 的名人，将他的形象与我们的产品一起投射到我们销售产品的 10 个 Stars 百货商店的前面。或者我们可以将一瓶沐浴露的巨幅照片投射到用 Keyland 旗帜着色的建筑物上，以将其标识为“Keyland 制造”的产品。

病毒营销

病毒营销是利用已经存在的社交媒体网络来传播品牌意识。我们的想法是在这些网络中创建一个广告或视频，然后通过人们共享消息在整个网络中传播。

例如，我们可以创建一个关于桑切斯·纳瓦娜公司产品的简短宣传视频（可能借助 Feyland 的名人），并将其链接到一个可以赢得一系列产品的竞赛。通过分享或点赞广告，潜在的消费者将会进入竞赛。更重要的是，我们将通过他们的友谊团队及其他达到品牌知名度传播的目的，这可能比仅靠电视广告吸引的受众更广泛。

体验营销

体验营销是指通过体验品牌来建立潜在消费者与品牌之间的情感联系。

这可以通过设置在Feyland的巡回路演来实现，路演允许潜在消费者体验我们的产品。这对于润肤乳和手足霜来说特别有益，因为潜在的消费者可以很容易地接触到它们。事实上，我们可以将这一范围扩展，开展一个“美体”活动，寻找真正的消费者来参加电视竞选。

给财务总监 Freda Jones 的邮件

发件人：管理会计助理

收件人：财务总监 Freda Jones

主题：Feyland 的预算

作为一个利润中心，Feyland的预算需要包括与当地销售业务有关的所有收入和成本。

收入预算

收入将由两个因素驱动：预算销售量和实际售价。

Feyland的经理与我们的Keyland的销售经理，对我们产品的建议零售价打折，享有相同的权力，这意味着他或她可以将我们的任何产品打折30%。问题是我们是否按照完整的建议零售价格（这是我们为Keyland的业务做的）进行了预算，还是在制定预算时考虑了平均折扣水平。

10个Stars特许经营点出售的产品数量部分将由Feyland的经理控制。最终，销售量将是Feyland的经理对每个经营点的定价和人员配置水平的决定的结果。这还取决于销售人员在销售产品方面的培训情况，这也在经理的控制之内。然而，Feyland的销售数量也将受到当地市场营销活动的影响，该活动在Keyland受到控制，但Feyland的经理对这个活动没有投入。

成本预算

预算中需要包括一些费用，这些费用和Feyland的经理控制这些成本的能力讨论如下。

（1）从Keyland生产工厂购买产品的成本。这将以标准生产成本加运费为基础，因此在Keyland是固定和被控制的。Feyland的经理将无法控制这些费用，因此不应对我们在Keyland所造成的任何费用变动负责。

（2）给每个特许经营场所聘用销售人员的费用。Feyland的经理将需要决定如何对每个地点进行人员安排。当商店营业时所有营销点都需时时刻刻有人，但达成这一要求的方式具有灵活性，可能会有全职和兼职人员的搭配，如有需要也可能加班。经理可以决定雇佣更多的员工，以便在繁忙时间推动促销活动。因此，经理应对这些费用负责，尽管一些变化（如国家工资水平或员工税）的影响应单独确定，因为这些变动不受 Feyland 的经理的控制。

（3）将产品配送到商店的费用。将有一个中央配送仓库，但经理需负责多久向特许摊位送货一次以及如何完成这项工作。这显然是他们需负责的费用。

销售量预算

在制定预算时，重要的是要让预算执行者看到所设定的目标是可实现的，否则可能会产生消极效果。如果我们为销售量设定了一个高而不切实际的预算，那么 Feyland 的经理很可能觉得这是无法实现的，因此甚至不会尝试去达成它。如果预算目标是可以实现的，那么他们可能会更努力地去实现目标。

在 Feyland 的业务运作方面，对预期的销售水平有一个良好的预测很重要，以便我们能够制定一个激励人心的但可实现的预算。

任务三

简报

Feyland 业务的销售差异报告

销售价格差异

价格差异表明，祖母绿，红宝石和黄玉的价格已经被 Jacob Perez 降低，这大概是促进这些香型销售的一种手段。蓝宝石和钻石的价格没有改变。

黄玉已经得到最大幅度的降价，其次是祖母绿，红宝石只有小幅度降价。

Jacob 的策略似乎是对高毛利率的香型进行折扣销售。黄玉具有最高的利润，被打折最多。

尽管价格差异是不利的，但这并不一定对整个企业都是不利的。将降低价格的权力给予销售经理，是让他们灵活地推广香型，从而在理论上增加销量，所以我们不应该孤立看待销售价格的差异，我们需要考虑整体情况。

销售组合差异

销售组合差异显示了以与原始预算不同的比例销售香型对毛利的影响。我们最初预算是每一种香型出售 1 200 个单位，总共 6 000 个单位的香型产品。如果我们假定实际的销售总量为 5 800 个单位的香型产品，那么每种香型应该卖出 1 160 个单位。

销售组合差异显示，我们已经出售了超过1 160单位的祖母绿和黄玉，这是可以预料的，因为这两款是有折扣的。也许令人惊讶的是，我们还没有销售出更多的红宝石。事实上，红宝石有最大的不利组合差异，这也许表明它不是适合Feyland市场的香型。

销售数量差异

销售数量差异显示销售总额对毛利的影响小于预算。每种香型的价格计算方式为1 200减1 160乘以每单位的毛利润。每种香型销量都呈现出负变动，因为我们的销售总额低于预算，这种差异代表预算组合中的预算销售额与预算组合中的实际销售额之间的差额。

总体

总体而言，报告显示，降幅的影响并不能由总销售量增加而抵消。这可能是因为销量最初被错误地预测，或者折扣不足以刺激更大的销售额或无法产生额外的销量。或者，可能是错误的产品被折扣销售或一些香型（如红宝石）不适合Feyland市场。

但看每一种香型，只有黄玉已经超出了预算水平。尽管有F$ 440的不利差异，但是F$ 6 000的不利差异低于F$ 9 100的有利组合差异。因此，Jacob决定对这种香型大打折扣是有道理的。这种方法也许可以应用于其他香型。

我们将需要获取对上述内容的阐明，以及Jacob Perez的任何其他解释。然后我们将需要考虑是否修改生产计划表和库存水平以与修订的预算相符。

盈余现金的投资

投资盈余现金时需考虑的因素

首先，需要准确确定有多少现金是对短期需求的有效盈余。这可以通过进行详细的现金预测来实现，其中要考虑到所有的收支。其包括所有潜在的付款，即我们母公司所需的任何利息，贷款还款或付款。

一旦确定了这一点，那么您将需要决定是否设立现金缓冲区，以备可能出现的任何不可预见的情况。我建议保留缓冲区。

一旦真正实现盈余的现金数额被确定，其他需要考虑的因素可以大致分为3类：盈利能力，流动性和安全性。

盈利能力与投资收益相关。因为银行账户目前没有任何回报，您已对此表示担忧。显然，您希望获得尽可能高的回报，但高回报通常与投资的高风险相关。因此，关于回报的任何考虑都与投资风险的考虑相关。投资的风险与流动性特别是其安全性有关。

流动性涉及如何将投资轻易地转换为现金，通常转换越简单，回报水平越低。从桑切斯·纳瓦娜公司的角度来看，只要我们确信这是盈余现金，那么我们就可以在4个月的时间里进行投资，这是我们需要投资新生产设施的资金。

安全性与投资的安全有关，通常投资越安全，回报越低。显然，投资的资本价值需要被保护，因为我们要在4个月的时间内筹集资金用于新的生产设施。

合适的投资建议

利息银行存款账户

盈余资金可以投资一个有息银行存款账户，为期4个月。这可能是一个安全的投资（即使这家银行发现自己陷入困境，他们可能会得到政府以某种形式支持的存款保护，尽管我们需要验证这一点），但回报可能会很低。

货币市场存款

在我们银行的帮助下，这些资金可以放在货币市场上，可能会获得比普通的存款账户更高的回报率。但这只适用于非常大的金额，因此我们需要向银行查询这是否可行，如果可行的话，它可能会得到高于普通存款的回报。

有价证券

我们可以在货币市场上投资短期债券或金边债券。这些类型的投资比存款风险更大，尤其是公司债券，但是他们通常会提供更多回报。降低风险的一种方式是投资国库券等国债。这些都是政府支持的，因此风险可以忽略不计，但是回报率将会降低。

任务四

简报

销售和市场经理的计划表

该计划表显示了3种不同需求水平下在线销售的预期额外利润。每个水平都考虑了3种情况：在内部运行在线销售功能，外包给TRU集团子公司或外包给专业第三方。

三种不同的销售量都被考虑在内，大概是因为我们不确定能够销售多少，毕竟这个市场对我们来说仍然是一个相对较新的市场。Richard认为，销售量的最低值为180 000个单位，中值为310 000个单位，最高值为430 000个单位。

这个决策的难点在于，在所考虑的每种情况中，所花费的成本在不同方面有所不同。它并不是选择最便宜的就会产生最大的利润这么简单，销售量的多少也会对其有影响。

根据董事的态度，我们可以通过多种方式来使用这个表格以做出决定。

最大的最大值法

最大的最大值法被视为一种乐观主义的方法。使用这种方法，我们将在最好情况发生的假设下，选择可以获得最大回报（在这种情况下是利润）的选项。

在这个表格中，这将是选择第三方，因为在最好的情况下（销售430 000个单位），它将给予我们最高的利润。

最大的最小值法

最大的最小值法被视为一种悲观的做法。使用这种方法，我们将在最坏情况发生的假设下，选择可以获得最大利润的选择。

在这个表格中，这将是选择TRU集团的子公司，因为在最糟糕的情况下（销售180 000个单位），这样会获得最高的利润。

最小的最大后悔值法

我们也可以使用最小的最大后悔值法，选择能最大限度减少我们最大后悔值的选项。如果董事们很担心会做出错误决定，这种方法是适当的。我们用这个标准选择，在决策施行且实际需求水平被知晓后，可以产生最小的最大后悔值。实际上后悔值是指，在首先做出错误决定后，我们力求尽量减少这种可能后悔值。

基于后悔值表，最佳选择是使用第三方，因为这里最大的后悔值只有F$ 60 000（TRU集团子公司F$ 490 000，内部F$ 250 000）。

结论

最终，你所采取的方法取决于你对做出错误决定的态度，或是你希望采取乐观态度或是悲观态度。

上述分析表明，选择两种外包之一将是最佳决策，这取决于所使用的标准。这也清楚地表明，内部选择不是任何标准下的最佳决策。

但是，不能仅仅在这个表的基础上做出决定，还需要考虑其他非经济因素。

相较外包，内部运作的好处

在线销售功能在内部运作的主要优点是我们可以控制它，这意味着我们能够确保订单能够准确地实现，产品被妥善包装并及时交付。如果我们使用任何一种外包选择，我们将失去这种控制力。TRU集团的子公司不熟悉我们的产品（销售高档床上用品），因此存在不仔细包装便发出产品的风险。我们不知道第三方开发的是哪种类型的产品，但是鉴于他们是专家，也许风险会被降低。

减轻对操作失去控制权的一种方法是制定详细的SLA（服务水平协议），规定包装和最大交货时间以及不符合规定的处罚。然而，要想做到这一点，首先需要一定成本，其次需要监控和管理它。如果操作是内部的，那么显然不需要SLA。

保留在线销售功能的另一个好处是我们可以直接访问客户。我们将能够创建一个电子邮件和联系人数据库，在营销和促销活动中使用。

相较外包，内部运作也可以让我们更容易地访问有关客户购买模式和趋势的信息，这些信息将有助于编制预算和安排生产。

与外包合作伙伴相关联的是，我们的机密销售数据流入竞争对手手中的风险增加了。这种风险与第三方外包合作伙伴尤其相关，他们可能同时与许多不同的企业签订了合同。或许这对于TRU集团的子公司来说并不是一个问题，因为我们都是同一个组织的一部分，不对任何外部团体负责。

Variant 5 Marking Guidance

Section	Technical skills		Business skills		People skills		Leadership skills		Integration	Total
1	Forecasting demand（P1） Financial reporting and tax implications of setting up a subsidiary（F1）	12 13								25
2	Budget（P1）	13			Guerrilla，viral and experiential marketing（E1）	12				25
3	Sales variances（P1） Investment of surplus cash（F1）	7 6	Sales variances（P1）	3			Investment of surplus cash（F1）	6	3	25
4	Pay-off table（P1）	12	Relative benefits of outsourcing（E1）	13						25
Total marks available for each competency		63		16		12		6	3	100

试卷五　评分指南

部分	技术技能		商业技能		人际技能		领导技能		综合	总计
1	需求预测（P1） 设立子公司对财务报告和税收的影响（F1）	12 13								25
2	预算（P1）	13			游击营销，病毒营销和经验营销（E1）	12				25
3	销售差异（P1） 盈余现金的投资（F1）	7 6	销售差异（P1）	3			盈余现金的投资（F1）	6	3	25
4	支付表（P1）	12	外包策略的益处（E1）	13						25
各种能力分数总计		63		16		12		6	3	100

西安交通大学名师解惑

试卷一共有四项任务，考查了P1、F1、E1三门课程的知识点，具体包括需求预测、设立子公司的税收影响、营销策略、预算、销售差异等。该试卷考核了考生的五项能力，其中技术技能的分值占63%，商业技能的分值占16%，人际技能的分值占12%，领导技能的分值占6%，综合能力的分值占3%，与CGMA管理会计能力框架的技能要求一致。

该试卷的每项任务涉及以下知识点：

任务	问题	科目	知识点
任务一	确定需求水平的重要性以及调查、统计方法	P1	需求预测（forecasting demand）
	成立子公司对公司的财务报告和税收带来什么影响	F1	设立子公司对财务报告和税收的影响（financial reporting and tax implications of setting up a subsidiary）
任务二	有关游击营销，病毒营销和体验营销的简要说明以及实施案例	E1	游击营销、病毒营销和经验营销（guerrilla，viral and experiential marketing）
	预算中应包含的不同要素及公司经理对应的控制程度，高销量目标对经理是否有激励作用	P1	预算（budget）
任务三	报告对利润中心的销售表现是怎样介绍的，特别是当发生一些不利的变化时	P1	销售差异（sales variances）
	投资盈余现金需要考虑的因素，以及合适的投资建议	F1	盈余现金的投资（investment of surplus cash）
任务四	支付表展现了什么，以及对其不同的解读	P1	支付表（pay-off table）
	相比外包，自己实施在线销售职能的好处	E1	外包策略的益处（relative benefits of outsourcing）

上述各项任务要求以邮件或简报的形式来呈现答案，对问题的描述非常明确，答题时既要注意内容的针对性，也要注意形式的规范性。

对应知识点的深度剖析

需求预测

需求预测是指估计未来一定时间内整个产品或特定产品的需求量和需求金额。

为什么要进行需求预测？即其必要性、好处和重要性。需求预测的整体目的在于通过提出切合实际的预算目标，从而制订购需求计划，指导原材料或商品订货。之后，考生应结合预测过程中每个环节对应的作用来做进一步的细分回答。

预测方法可大致分为基于调查和基于统计两类。基于调查的方法需要考虑到 Feyland 是一个全新市场，可能需要当地专家顾问的帮助；基于统计的方法则需要通过材料中提供的相应数据和地区特征来写，考核考生的逻辑和综合思维能力。

设立子公司对财务报告和税收的影响

对于财务报告，考生应该联想到会计准则对子公司报表和合并报表的编制要求，豁免合并报表的条件要求，并结合材料所给的约束条件进行作答。

考生注意事项

游击营销：与传统营销的区别主要集中在媒介选择和品牌公关活动上。在媒介选择上，游击营销选择媒介的主要标准是费用和与目标消费者的互动，这使得它们基本上不考虑大众媒体，而是倾向于自己创造独特的传播路径。而在公关活动上，相对于传统营销倾向于利用大型的、有声势的活动吸引公众的视线，如赞助大型社会公益活动的正面进攻方式，游击营销对冠名权、赞助等形式则“敬而远之”，偏重于创意活动。

病毒营销：又称病毒性营销、基因营销或核爆式营销，是利用公众的积极性和人际网络，让营销信息像病毒一样传播和扩散。病毒营销是一种常见的网络营销方法，常用于进行网站推广、品牌推广等。由于这种传播是用户之间自发进行的，因此是几乎不需要费用的网络营销手段。

体验营销：体验营销是通过看（see）、听（hear）、用（use）、参与（participate）的手段，充分刺激和调动消费者的感官（sense）、情感（feel）、思考（think）、行动（act）、关联（relate）等感性因素和理性因素。其认为消费者消费时是兼具理性与感性的，消费者在消费前、消费时、消费后的体验，才是研究消费者行为与企业品牌经营的关键。

而对税收的影响则考查了考生对于母子公司税收政策的熟悉程度。可从税率、应纳税所得额（考虑到子公司的股息和红利）以及双重征税协定的角度进行作答。

游击营销，病毒营销和经验营销

营销本身是一个需要发散性思维和个人见解的活动，也是对考生交际能力的考查，但本题中的考查主要针对基础知识点的具体运用：写出游击营销、病毒营销和经验营销的基本定义，以及将其套用到本题中，如何结合材料所给的地区名人等条件。可以看出营销也成了近年的考查热点，考生应多加关注，牢记相关知识点。

预算

本部分对于预算（P1）的考查也较为贴近课本。Feyland 作为一个利润中心，收入、成本是关键预算要素。其中收入等于销售量乘以单价，费用又细分为可控费用和不可控费用。可控成本显然是需要经理控制的对象，这就确认了本题的讨论思路。考生需注意结合题干信息来回答分析如何设定预算额及其作用。

销售差异

销售差异分析是衡量实际销售额和计划销售额的差异及原因，即围绕销售这一环节进行差异分析，将销售中的要素分点考虑，如数量、价格等。而销售量差异可进一步细分为两种差异：销售组合差异和销售数量差异。要注意，各因素的变动不是孤立的，它们之间可能会相互影响，例如：销售价格差异显示由计划价格或标准价格收取不同销售价格所产生的总收入差异。本题中，产品降价导致负的价格差异。但注意，低价理论上将带来销售量的正向提高，因此要整体分析各因素变化带来的影响。

盈余现金的投资

投资盈余现金前，首先要考虑短期内对于现金的需求有多少，以防投资后发生短期资金流动困难，影响公司的正常运营及投资机会。在确立了真正实现盈余的现金数额后，可以通过了解公司对于投资回报、流动性和安全性的需求进行进一步的分析决策。

支付表

支付表显示了 3 种不同条件下的预期额外利润，我们可以很容易联想到 P1 中利用支付表做决策的相关内容。在作答支付表展现了什么时，考生不仅需要根据理解介绍支付表的直观内容，也应解释支付表这样设置的原因和决策目的。要求解读支付表，主要是要考查在做决策时使用到的 3 种方法：最大的最大值法、最大的最小值法以及最小的最大后悔值法。使用不同的方法得出的决策可能不同。

考生注意事项

最大的最大值法：是一种乐观主义的方法。指在最好情况发生的假设下，选择能够获得最大回报（在这种情况下是利润）的选项。

最大的最小值法：也叫悲观法、保守法、瓦尔德决策准则、小中取大法，是一种悲观的做法。指在最坏情况发生的假设下，选择能够获得最大利润的选项。

最小的最大后悔值法：也叫最小遗憾值法。是一种根据机会成本进行决策的方法，它根据各方案的机会损失大小来判断方案的优劣。即首先计算各方案在各自然状态下的后悔值，并找出各方案的最大后悔值，然后进行比较，再选择最大后悔值最小的方案作为最终方案的一种决策方法。

外包策略的益处

外包是一个战略管理模型，是指企业从战略的角度出发，将一些非核心的或者成本处于劣势的业务，转移到企业之外，使企业将有限的资源使用在那些期望取得长期成功，能够创造出独特价值，或者能使企业成为行业领先者的核心业务领域。战略外包被认为是一种企业有效降低产品成本，引进和利用外部资源，帮助企业提高核心竞争力的有效手段。

但与此同时，外包策略也有一系列缺点。例如：当外包服务不再受公司的控制时，就失去了灵活性，企业难以根据环境的改变做出迅速的反映；外包带来的成本；供应商质量和服务的隐患；商业秘密的外部化等。这都是考生可以参考的作答点，此题要结合产品及子公司和第三方的特性作答。

这套试题的重点在于对专业能力的考查，要求在基础上发散思维和进行具体分析，强调要结合知识点和题干作答，提醒大家注意较为具体的知识点的记忆。

案例三

CASE 3

智选酒店

WISE CHOICE HOTELS

Background Materials

Introduction

Wise Choice Hotels is a family run business which currently operates four hotels in Macland, a country with a mature economy and a warm climate. Macland has the M$ as its currency.

Wise Choice Hotels was started in 2005 after brother and sister, John Hayes and Molly Patel, inherited a significant sum of money after their elderly parents died. On receipt of their inheritance John and Molly purchased their first hotel. This is known within the business as Hotel 1 and is situated in Southcastle, a large city in the south of Macland.

In 2008 and 2012 respectively Hotels 2 and 3 were purchased. At the start of 2015 Hotel 4 was purchased. Each hotel is situated in either Southcastle or Fordtown a large town 40 kilometres from Southcastle.

All four hotels were purchased as going concerns. Hotels 1, 2 and 3 were in need of refurbishment and so immediately after purchase, each bedroom and communal area was refitted and the building redecorated throughout. In respect of Hotel 4, other than redecoration and changing a few of the bedrooms which had been damaged by a flood, little has been done.

The hotels each have bar and restaurant facilities, but there are currently no spa or gym facilities in any of them. Each hotel has its own identity and is managed independently by a dedicated hotel manager responsible for the day-to-day running. Each hotel has its own bank account and the manager is responsible for maintaining the basic accounting records.

Wise Choice Hotels is incorporated and its equity shares are owned equally by John Hayes, managing director, and Molly Patel, operations director. The finance director is Molly's husband, Rav Patel. John's wife, Pam Hayes, works part-time in the business as the marketing director.

The directors are based in a suite of offices in Hotel 1, but frequently visit all four hotels to deal with different issues. You are one of two finance officers based in the suite of offices that work directly for Rav Patel, the finance director.

Profile of the Four Hotels

Hotel 1:
Acquired by Wise Choice Hotels in 2005
Location: Southcastle, business district
Hotel manager: Tara Gomez
Number of rooms: 80
Average budgeted room rate for 2016: M$ 105
Budgeted occupancy rate for 2016: 90%

Hotel 2:
Acquired by Wise Choice Hotels in 2008
Location: central Fordtown
Hotel manager: Pierre Vert
Number of rooms: 90
Average budgeted room rate for 2016: M$ 100
Budgeted occupancy rate for 2016: 80%

Hotel 3:
Acquired by Wise Choice Hotels in 2012
Location: Southcastle, shopping and theatre district
Hotel manager: Patrick Jenkins
Number of rooms: 95
Average budgeted room rate for 2016: M$ 100
Budgeted occupancy rate for 2016: 80%

Hotel 4:
Acquired by Wise Choice Hotels in 2015
Location: Southcastle, financial district
Hotel manager: Seema Kahn
Number of rooms: 105
Average budgeted room rate for 2016: M$ 110
Budgeted occupancy rate for 2016: 80%

Article in the Local Business Press on the Acquisition of Hotel 4

Southcastle Gazette

7 January 2015　No. 7823　　M$ 1.20

Wise Choice Hotels Extend Hotel Portfolio in Southcastle

Lorna Gomez, Business Correspondent

After months of being on the market, the old Forbes Hotel in the financial district of Southcastle has been sold to Wise Choice Hotels.

Wise Choice Hotels already own two other hotels in other areas of Southcastle and one hotel in neighbouring Fordtown.

Forbes Hotel has long been the resting place of weary business and leisure travellers and has been under threat of closure due to the death early last year of its previous owner, Callum Stinger.

John Hayes, managing director of Wise Choice Hotels said: "We had been considering a number of different investment opportunities in Southcastle and the Forbes Hotel was the best option for us. It allows us to expand our hotel portfolio into a different district of Southcastle. We're not planning to make any significant changes to the hotel, certainly for a year or so and we will keep all the existing staff."

This comes as a relief to the staff at the hotel who had been threatened with losing their jobs had a buyer not been found.

Overall Organisational Structure

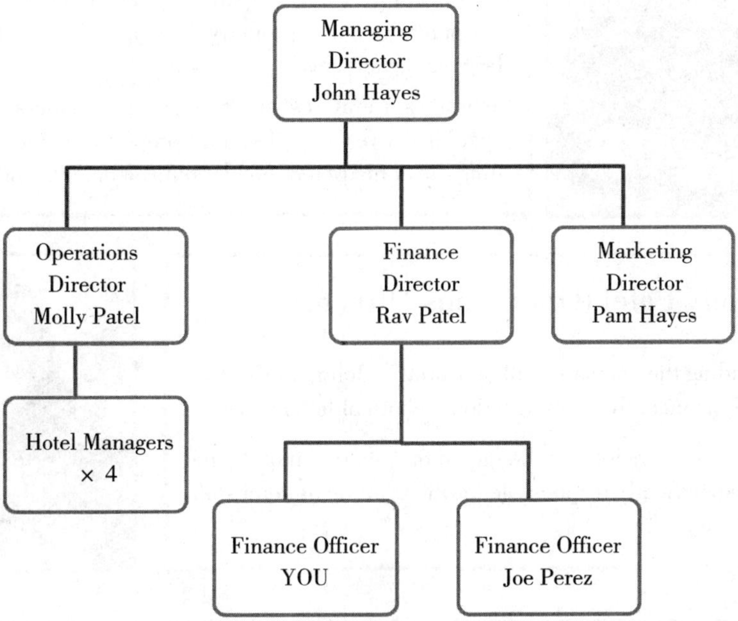

Each hotel manager reports directly to the operations director on a day-to-day basis, but also report to the other three directors where appropriate.

There are also two secretarial and administrative assistants who work part time for the directors.

Organisation Structure at Each Hotel

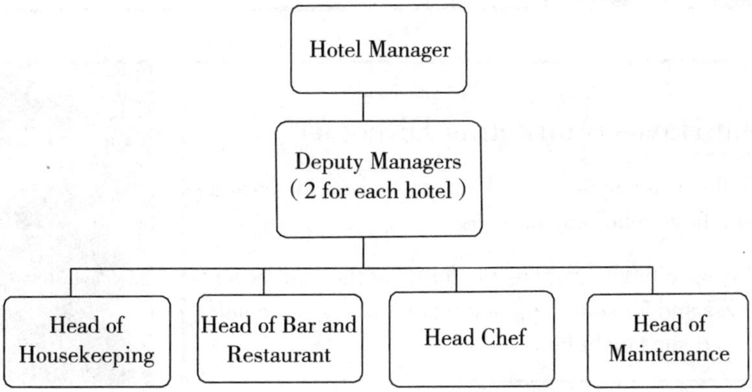

John Hayes (Managing Director)

- Before founding the company in 2005, John Hayes worked for many years as a property developer, involved in both large-and small-scale projects.
- As well as overall responsibility for the business, John Hayes is specifically responsible for all property related matters, including the aquisition of hotels, refurbishments and maintenance.

Molly Patel (Operations Director)

- Before founding the company with her brother John, Molly Patel was a hotel manager for an international chain of hotels.
- Molly Patel is responsible for the day-to-day operation of the hotels and is specifically responsible for the training of hotel staff and quality control.

Rav Patel (Finance Director)

- Before joining the company in 2005, Rav Patel was a bank manager. He is not a qualified accountant, although has a good grasp of accounting from his banking experience.
- Rav Patel is specifically responsible for the financial records, payroll and HR. An external firm of accountants is used to prepare statutory financial statements and to deal with all the tax affairs of the business.

Pam Hayes (Marketing Director)

- Before joing the company in 2007, Pam Hayes was a marketing manager for a large retail business.
- Pam Hayes is specifically responsible for all of the marketing of the business and for setting up and maintaining each hotel's website (a skill she taught herself).

Key Responsibilities of Managers

Position	Key responsibilities
Hotel Manager	The hotel manager is responsible for: ■ Recruiting, interviewing and appointing, along with two of the directors, deputy hotel managers and heads of department ■ Dealing with staff disciplinary issues, including termination of employment for junior staff. If there is a disciplinary issue with a deputy hotel manager or a head of department, the directors will also be involved ■ Maintaining a personnel file for each member of staff ■ Creating the staff roster (with information from the deputy managers and their direct reports) and collating the hours worked on a weekly basis for all weekly paid staff ■ Liaising with corporate customers, including setting credit terms ■ Ensuring that the booking system is operating appropriately and notifying the marketing director of any changes to be made to the hotel's website ■ Authorising expenditure on property maintenance (including the building and fixtures and fittings) up to the value of M$ 1,000. Any expenditure above this amount must be authorised by both the finance director and the managing director
Deputy Managers	The deputy managers are responsible for: ■ Guest bookings, reception services and dealing with guest complaints, in the first instance ■ Deputising for the hotel manager when he, or she, is not on the hotel premises. It is expected that either the hotel manager or one of the deputy managers will be on site in the hotel at all times. In rare circumstances such as illness, one of the directors will take this role ■ Recruiting and the day-to-day management of reception staff
Head of Housekeeping	The head of housekeeping is responsible for: ■ Ensuring that the rooms are cleaned and replenished to the correct standard on time ■ Recruiting and managing the team of housekeeping staff on a day-to-day basis ■ Ensuring that laundry is sent to the external laundry service provider in a timely manner ■ Ordering cleaning products and complimentary items when required. Any changes to the cleaning products used or complimentary items are agreed with the hotel manager

（续表）

Position	Key responsibilities
Head of Bar and Restaurant	The head of bar and restaurant is responsible for: ■ Selecting the beverages for the bar and for ensuring that there is an appropriate level of inventory in the bar ■ The quality of service given to guests in the bar and restaurant ■ Deciding on staffing levels on a day-to-day basis and the recruitment of bar and waiting staff ■ Dealing with guest complaints in the first instance. They have the authority to issue refunds or vouchers if required ■ Setting the prices to guests for beverages and food (together with the head chef and the hotel manager)
Head Chef	The head chef is responsible for: ■ Designing and selecting the meals to be included on the menu ■ Sourcing and ordering ingredients ■ Ensuring that the quality of the food leaving the kitchen is appropriate ■ Recruiting kitchen staff and the day-to-day staffing levels ■ Setting the prices to guests for beverages and food (together with the head of bar and restaurant and the hotel manager)
Head of Maintenance	The head of maintenance is responsible for: ■ Ensuring the upkeep of the hotel's structure and decoration, both internally and externally, and liaising with the managing director where external contractors are required ■ Ensuring that all minor repairs are carried out in a timely manner ■ Recruiting and managing maintenance staff on a day-to-day basis.

Further Information About How the Hotels Operate

Each hotel is run as an independent unit, with its own bank account, booking and accounting systems.

Customers

Each of the hotels caters to both business and leisure guests. Based on the actual guests in 2015, the proportions of each at each hotel are shown below:

Hotel	Proportion of business to leisure guests shown as a ratio	Percentage of business guests linked to corporate customers(%)
Hotel 1	70 : 30	75
Hotel 2	50 : 50	60
Hotel 3	20 : 80	80
Hotel 4	60 : 40	60

All leisure guests pay when they check out of their room. Business guests either do the same or are linked to one of the hotel's corporate customers, who use the hotel as accommodation for their employees travelling on business.

Corporate customers pay according to agreed credit terms set with the hotel manager. On average, for the business as a whole, this is 30 days after the corporate guest has checked out. All corporate customers are based in Macland.

If a room has been booked and the booking is cancelled not less than 24 hours before the check in time, there is no charge for the cancellation. If the guest cancels within the 24 hour period, or does not turn up, an invoice is sent for the price of the room, either directly to them, or to the corporate customer. Typically, 75% of these invoices get paid.

Websites and Bookings System

Each hotel has its own website which is linked to its independent bookings system, a simple software package. Each time a booking is made through the website the system up-dates room availability. This software is not linked in any way across the hotels.

At least 70% of leisure guests book directly through the website, with the rest booking over the phone. To ensure room availability, the person taking the phone booking updates the system whilst on the call. If, when trying to make a booking for a Southcastle hotel the required room is not available on the date specified the potential guest is re-directed to a nearby Wise Choice Hotel.

Corporate customers usually request bookings via email, these are processed on the system as soon as possible. If a room is not available for the dates requested, the corporate customer is contacted and redirected to the next closest Wise Choice Hotel.

Accounting System

Each hotel uses the same standard accounting package. It is a finance officer's responsibility to process all transactions, make payments to suppliers and reconcile the bank account.

Astandard payroll package is also used at each hotel. The processing of payroll and payments to staff are carried out by a finance officer, after the approval of the payroll by the finance director.

At the end of the month, the finance officer generates monthly accounts from the system and uses these to prepare performance reports for each hotel. These performance reports include a comparison of actual performance against the original budget and key statistics, such as receivable and payable days and cash generation.

There is no central accounting system: each hotel operates its own system and bank account.

An external firm of accountants is used to prepare the end-of-year financial statements at and deal with all of the company's tax affairs (excluding payments for payroll taxes which are actioned by a finance officer and approved by the finance director).

Finance Officer Role

- Visiting each hotel on a rotational basis and:
  - processing all purchase and sales transactions.
  - generating payments to suppliers.
  - ensuring that corporate customer accounts are paid in a timely manner and chasing for payment if required.
  - processing the payroll and making payments to hotel staff.
  - reconciling the hotel's bank account each month.
  - preparing performance reports for each hotel on a monthly basis.
  - transferring cash balances from the hotel's own bank account into the central business bank account.
- Reconciling the central business bank account each month.
- Preparing analysis of financial information for the business as required by the directors.
- Assisting in the preparation of budget information in respect of each hotel. This will be prepared once a year (usually in November) for the forthcoming calendar year.

- Preparing reports and explanations for the directors as required on matters affecting the business.

Extracts From Wise Choice Hotels Financial Statements for the Year Ended 31 December 2015

Wise Choice Hotels

Statement of profit or loss for the year ended 31 December:

	2015 (M$ 000)	2014 (M$ 000)
Revenue	11,138	7,925
Operating costs	(8,984)	(6,023)
Profit before tax	2,154	1,902
Tax	(643)	(571)
Profit for the year	1,511	1,331

Wise Choice Hotels

Statement of financial position at 31 December:

	2015 (M$ 000)	2015 (M$ 000)	2014 (M$ 000)	2014 (M$ 000)
Assets				
Non-current assets				
Intangible assets(note 2)	733		423	
PPE(note 1)	5,844		3,829	
		6,577		4,252
Current assets				
Inventory	362		260	
Trade and other receivables	378		224	
Cash and cash equivalents	4,344		4,961	
		5,084		5,445
Total assets		11,661		9,697
Equity and Liabilities				

（续表）

	2015 (M$ 000)	2015 (M$ 000)	2014 (M$ 000)	2014 (M$ 000)
Ordinary share capital issued		1,500		1,500
Retained earnings		8,625		7,114
Total equity		10,125		8,614
Current liabilities				
Trade and other payables	893		512	
Tax payable	643		571	
		1,536		1,083
Total equity and liabilities Wise		11,661		9,697

Choice Hotels

Statement of cash flows for the year ended 31 December 2015

	(M$ 000)	(M$ 000)
Cash flows from operating activities		
Profit before tax		2,154
Adjustments		
Depreciation	305	
Amortisation	90	
		395
Movements in working capital		
Increase in inventories	(102)	
Increase in trade and other receivables	(154)	
Increase in trade payables	381	
		125
Cash generated from operations		2,674
Tax paid		(571)
Net cash from operating activities		2,103
Cash flows from investing activities		
Purchase of PPE	(2,320)	

（续表）

	(M$ 000)	(M$ 000)
Purchase of intangible assets	(400)	
Net cash from investing activities		(2,720)
Net increase in cash and cash equivalents		(617)
Cash and cash equivalents at the beginning of the year		4,961
Cash and cash equivalents at the end of the year		4,344

Notes:

(1) Wise Choice Hotels has a policy of depreciating items of PPE for a full year in the year of purchase and not depreciating in the year of disposal.

(2) Intangible assets comprise the purchased goodwill from the acquisition of hotels. Each of Hotels 1,2,3 and 4 was acquired as a going concern, with Wise Choice Hotels purchasing the assets and liabilities of the business, rather than the equity shares of the company which owned the hotel business. Goodwill arose because the price paid for the hotel business for each of Hotels 1,2,3 and 4 was greater than the net of the assets and liabilities acquired. The purchased goodwill has been capitalised as an intangible asset and is amortised annually.

Wise Choice Hotels Summary Budget Information

Budgets are prepared by Rav Patel, finance director, annually on an incremental basis. This requires the assistance of the finance officers, the other directors and the four hotel managers.

Total budgeted profit:

	Budget for the year ended 31 December 2016 (M$ 000)	Budget for the year ended 31 December 2015 (M$ 000)
Revenue from hotels	13,582	12,391
Variable hotel operating costs	(4,414)	(4,089)
Contribution from hotels	9,168	8,302
Fixed hotel operating costs	(4,358)	(4,248)
Operating profit from hotels (note 1)	4,810	4,054
Central costs:		
Depreciation and amortisation (note 2)	(413)	(413)
Marketing	(650)	(650)

（续表）

	Budget for the year ended 31 December 2016 (M$ 000)	Budget for the year ended 31 December 2015 (M$ 000)
Directors' salaries	(320)	(300)
Central administrative costs	(575)	(560)
Budgeted profit	2,852	2,131

Notes:

(1) The budgeted operating profit from hotels is derived from the detailed budget for each hotel. Each hotel's budget includes analysis of revenues and operating costs in regard to two distinct operating areas; room and bar & restaurant.

(2) Depreciation and amortisation are treated as central costs and are not attributed to hotel operating profit for the purposes of budgeting.

Total budgeted hotel revenue for the years ended 31 December 2016 and 2015:

Hotel	Budget for the year ended 31 December 2016*			Budget for the year ended 31 December 2015		
	Room revenue (M$ 000)	Bar & restaurant revenue (M$ 000)	Total (M$ 000)	Room revenue (M$ 000)	Bar & restaurant revenue (M$ 000)	Total (M$ 000)
Hotel 1	2,759	552	3,311	2,628	526	3,154
Hotel 2	2,628	497	3,125	2,497	473	2,970
Hotel 3	2,774	416	3,190	2,635	305	2,940
Hotel 4	3,373	583	3,956	2,951	376	3,327
Total	11,534	2,048	13,582	10,711	1,680	12,391

* The major changes budgeted in respect of revenue generation in 2016 compared to 2015 are:

- To increase the occupancy of Hotel 4 from 70% to 80%, by not increasing room rates.
- To increase guest usage and spend per head in the bars and restaurants for Hotels 3 and 4.

Room Revenue Income Stream

Total budgeted room revenue for the year ended 31 December 2016:

Hotel	Number of rooms	Budgeted average occupancy (%)	Budgeted occupied rooms in the year	Budgeted average room rate* (M$)	Budgeted room revenue (M$ 000)
Hotel 1	80	90	26,280	105.00	2,759
Hotel 2	90	80	26,280	100.00	2,628

（续表）

Hotel	Number of rooms	Budgeted average occupancy(%)	Budgeted occupied rooms in the year	Budgeted average room rate* (M$)	Budgeted room revenue(M$ 000)
Hotel 3	95	80	27,740	100.00	2,774
Hotel 4	105	80	30,660	110.00	3,373
Total					11,534

* The average room rate is for the room for the night plus breakfast in the morning. In all of the Wise Choice Hotels there is only one grade of room available, however the price charged for each room varies depending on when the booking is made. This budgeted room rate is based therefore an average of the room rates.

Total budgeted hotel operating costs related to room revenue for the year ended 31 December 2016:

Hotel	Variable costs related to room revenue(M$ 000)	Fixed costs related to room revenue(M$ 000)	Total hotel operating costs related to room revenue(M$ 000)
Hotel 1	850	813	1,663
Hotel 2	860	840	1,700
Hotel 3	894	831	1,725
Hotel 4	1,002	962	1,964
Total	3,606	3,446	7,052

Notes:

(1) Variable costs vary with the level of occupancy in respect of room revenue. The budgeted variable costs in the above table are based on the budgeted occupancy rates.

(2) The variable costs associated with room revenue includes the costs of food and beverages for breakfast provision, housekeeping costs (the costs of complimentary items and cleaning products used), the costs of laundering towels and bedding, as well as 85% of total hotel energy costs and the variable element of staff costs associated with housekeeping, reception and maintenance.

(3) The fixed costs related to room revenue includes the fixed element of staff costs in respect of housekeeping, reception and maintenance and 85% of the total hotel property related costs.

Bar and Restaurant Income Stream

Total budgeted bar and restaurant revenue for the year ended 31 December 2016:

Hotel	Budgeted occupied rooms per year	Budgeted proportion of guests using facilities (%)	Budgeted number of guests using facilities in the year	Budgeted bar and restaurant revenue for each guest using facilities(M$)	Budgeted bar and restaurant revenue (M$ 000)
Hotel 1	26,280	60	15,768	35.00	552
Hotel 2	26,280	60	15,768	31.50	497
Hotel 3	27,740	50	13,870	30.00	416
Hotel 4	30,660	50	15,330	38.00	583
Total					2,048

Total budgeted hotel operating costs related to bar and restaurant revenue for the year ended 31 December 2016：

Hotel	Variable costs related to bar and restaurant revenue(M$ 000)	Fixed costs related to bar and restaurant revenue (M$ 000)	Total hotel operating costs related to bar and restaurant revenue(M$ 000)
Hotel 1	206	210	416
Hotel 2	201	246	447
Hotel 3	175	213	388
Hotel 4	226	243	469
Total	808	912	1,720

Notes：

(1) Variable costs vary with the level of guest usage in respect of bar and restaurant revenue. The budgeted variable costs in the above table are based on the budgeted guest usage rates.

(2) The variable costs related to bar and restaurant revenue includes the costs of food and beverage purchases associated with this revenue, 15% of total hotel energy costs and the variable element of bar and restaurant staff costs.

(3) The fixed costs related to bar and restaurant revenue includes the fixed element of bar and restaurant staff cost and 15% of total hotel property related costs.

Additional notes on budgeted costs：

(1) All hotels send laundry to an external laundry service which is situated 30 kilometres from Hotel 1. This is the large laundry facility which has contracts with a number of hotels in the area.

(2) Housekeeping costs are the costs of cleaning and restocking the bedrooms with

complimentary items such as tea, coffee, cookies, shampoo and body wash. The budgeted cost of replenishing complimentary items is based on the average level of replacements per room occupied.

(3) The budgeted breakfast cost has been calculated at M$5 per room per night occupied. This is an average cost adjusted for the average number of guests that occupy a room.

(4) 20% of staff costs are variable in nature and 80% fixed for all hotels.

(5) Property cost includes property insurance and general repairs and maintenance. It also includes M$250 per room per year for the replacement of bedding and towels. For both 2015 and 2016 no significant refurbishment expenditure was budgeted.

Budgeted Contribution for the Year Ended 31 December 2016

From room revenue:

Hotel	Budgeted total contribution (M$ 000)	Budgeted occupied rooms per year	Budgeted room contribution per room occupied (M$)
Hotel 1	1,909	26,280	72.64
Hotel 2	1,768	26,280	67.28
Hotel 3	1,880	27,740	67.77
Hotel 4	2,371	30,660	77.33
Total	7,928		

From bar and restaurant revenue:

Hotel	Budgeted total contribution (M$ 000)	Budgeted number of guests using the facilities in the year	Budgeted bar and restaurant contribution per guest using the facilities (M$)
Hotel 1	346	15,768	21.94
Hotel 2	296	15,768	18.77
Hotel 3	241	13,870	17.38
Hotel 4	357	15,330	23.29
Total	1,240		

Employees

Number of Employees

	Directors	Managers/Heads	Other	Total
Hotel 1	—	7	22	29
Hotel 2	—	7	25	32
Hotel 3	—	7	22	29
Hotel 4	—	7	29	36
Head office	4	—	4	8
Total	4	28	102	134

Employment Policy

The directors of Wise Choice Hotels pride themselves on their employment policy. Each member of staff is contracted to work a minimum of 30 hours a week. This is unusual in Macland's hotel industry, where it is common for employees to be employed on zero-hour contracts (where there is no guarantee of any work for employees).

Each week, the hotel manager is responsible for preparing the staff roster and ensuring that these minimum hours are allocated to each employee. Usually, employees work at least 38 hours a week. If occupancy is higher than average, this can increase to 45 hours a week. If occupancy is lower than average, this can decrease to 30 hours a week. In rare cases where there is not enough normal hotel work to fill the 30 hours, employees are utilised in deep cleaning or tidying areas of the hotel.

Employees are paid for the hours that they work each week, based on an hourly rate. This rate is above the national minimum wage for Macland (which again is unusual for the hotel industry). An overtime premium is paid when an employee works more than 42 hours in a week.

All employees are entitled to free meals at the hotel whilst at work. If an employee works beyond ten o'clock in the evening the business pays for a taxi for them to get home. If rooms are unoccupied and it is difficult for an employee to get home, they are allowed to stay at the hotel free of charge.

Environmental Concerns

Each hotel bedroom has a notice which offers guests the chance to not have their towels washed on a daily basis, in a bid to save water and energy. Recently, all light bulbs in all hotels were replaced with energy saving bulbs.

All food and beverage waste is sent to a composting facility and each hotel is encouraged to recycle as much beverage and food packaging as possible. There is a fee for transporting both food waste and recycling to the relevant facilities. Towels and bedding that are no longer fit for purpose are also recycled in this way.

The Wider Community

Wise Choice Hotels makes regular donations to local charities and sponsors a children's football team in Fordtown.

Examples of Guest Reviews Which Were Posted on the Respective Hotel's Website

Hotel 1: Average Score is 8. 8 Out of 10

Rating: 9/10

What a charming little find. This is the first time I've stayed at Hotel 1 and it won't be the last. Breakfast was excellent, as was dinner the night before. Great location for the business district and the staff on the reception desk could not have been more helpful.

Rating: 8/10

This is the third time that my employer has booked me a room at Hotel 1 and as usual it was a great stay. It was convenient for work, lovely food and friendly and helpful staff. The only slight comment I would make is that the décor is looking a little bit tired, although the facilities were all that I needed.

Hotel 2: Average Score 9. 1 Out of 10

Rating: 10/10

This hotel is excellent value for money. Breakfast was stunning: lots of choice and really well cooked. I will definitely be back. I loved the fact that the hotel not only offers the chance to save energy and water by not having towels washed, but actually acts on it. I've stayed in hotels offering the same, but even though I selected not to have my towels washed they were changed anyway.

Rating: 8/10

I stayed for the weekend as I had a family party to attend. Very convenient for the centre of town and the hotel itself was great. Noise was a bit of an issue though, in the early hours of Saturday and Sunday morning. I was in a room at the front: I would ask for a room at the back of the hotel in future.

Hotel 3: Average Score 8. 1 Out of 10

Rating: 8/10

This is a good hotel if you want a central base for shopping in Southcastle. The exterior of the hotel does not look too appealing, but inside the rooms are lovely and well appointed. I did have to send my breakfast back as it had arrived cold; although this was rectified very quickly.

Rating: 5/10

The hotel itself was good; but dinner in the restaurant was poor. We waited over an hour to receive our meals after ordering and then the food was bland and uninteresting.

Response from Patrick Jenkins, hotel manager:

Sorry to hear about your experience in our restaurant, we hope that it will not deter you from coming to stay with us again; especially as we have just launched a new menu.

Hotel 4: Average Score 6. 9 Out of 10

Rating: 6/10

The hotel itself is a beautiful building and the rooms have everything needed for a comfortable stay. I did have an issue that my bathroom was not as clean as I would have expected and my bed linen had stains on it. After complaining a member of housekeeping was sent to rectify the situation; although not for over an hour. I would have expected it to be a little better.

Breakfast was as I would expect, although the dining room is looking a little tired and in need of modernisation.

Rating: 4/10

I was not impressed by my stay at Hotel 4. The furniture in my bedroom was old-fashioned and the bathroom needs a complete overhaul in my view. Breakfast was fine and staff helpful enough, but the hotel just lacks any real character.

Response from Seema Kahn, hotel manager:

Sorry to hear that you were not impressed with your stay in our hotel. We will be embarking on a complete refurbishment programme within the next two years and hope that you will come and see us after this has been completed.

Industry Information

Types of Guest

There are a wide range of hotels available in Macland that cater for a wide range of budgets. Guests that stay in the hotels can be categorised into two types: business or leisure.

Typically guests that travel for business purposes require hotels in the main towns and cities of Macland. The length of stay booked by this type of guest is on average two nights.

Those guests traveling for leisure do so for a number of reasons. If they require a relaxing vacation then they are more likely to book a hotel in a coastal resort (of which there are many in Macland because of its warm climate) or in the country. Typically hotels that cater to this type of guest will have swimming and gym facilities: many also have golf courses. The length of stay booked by this type of guest is usually either 7 or 14 nights.

Alternatively, many guests travel for leisure to visit towns and cities, to see the sights and take advantage of theatres and shopping. The length of stay booked for this type of guest is, on average, three nights.

The Leisure Travel Market

There are a number of leisure travel companies in Macland who act as agents between the leisure hotels and guests, typically for vacation trips for a week or more. In 2005 there were 95 such companies, in 2015 this had fallen to 30. The reason for this decline was guests' increasing confidence in sourcing hotels themselves, through the hotels' own website. The 30 companies that survive do so because they have specialised, or differentiated their service, in some way. The leisure travel company market in Macland is now thought to be in a steady state.

There is an organisation in Macland called the MLTA (Macland Leisure Travel Authority), which was set up to protect the rights of leisure travellers. Each of the remaining 30 leisure travel companies is a member of MLTA, as are all of the major hotel chains. By booking a hotel room through a member of MLTA a guest is able to claim back any deposit, or advance booking monies, that have been paid.

Similarly, a smaller hotel can claim protection against any debts owing from trading with a leisure travel company.

Most small independent hotel chains, including Wise Choice Hotels, are not members of MLTA and do not trade with leisure travel companies.

The Hotel Market

There are eight major hotel chains with hotels located all around the country, accounting for 75% of all hotels in Macland. The other 25% of hotels are either wholly independent or are part of a small group. Many of these independent and small hotel groups are family owned businesses, like Wise Choice Hotels. Within the Southcastle and Fordtown area, Wise Choice Hotels represents 10% of the market in terms revenue generation.

Tax Regime in Macland

Corporate Profits

- The corporate tax to be applied to taxable profits is 30%.
- Unless otherwise stated below, accounting rules on recognition and measurement are followed for tax purposes.
- The following expenses are not allowable for tax purposes:

  accounting depreciation;

  amortisation;

  impairment charges;

  entertaining expenditure;

  donations to political parties;

  taxes paid to other public bodies.
- Tax depreciation allowances are available on items of plant and equipment (including vehicles used for business purposes) at a rate of 25% per year on a reducing balance basis.
- Where a company is in receipt of a government grant, the tax treatment will depend on the nature of the grant. For tax purposes, capital grant money received in the year is netted off the capital value of the asset to which it relates prior to tax depreciation allowances being calculated. Any capital grant income released to profit or loss in the year is not taxable. Revenue grants released to profit or loss in the year are treated as income for tax purposes.

- Tax losses can be carried forward indefinitely to offset against future taxable profits from the same business.
- A company is deemed to be resident in Macland if it has its principal place of management there. A resident company will pay Macland corporate tax on all of its profit irrespective of the country in which the profit is earned. Wise Choice Hotels is resident in Macland.
- Where a company resident in Macland owns a subsidiary company which is resident in another country, any dividends paid by that subsidiary to the parent company will be treated as income of the parent company and will be taxed at the corporate tax rate.
- Double taxation treaties exist with a number of other countries. All of these treaties give relief for double taxation in respect of any withholding and underlying tax suffered on dividends received. Relief is available using the tax credit method.

背景材料

介绍

智选酒店(Wise Choice Hotels)是一家家族经营企业,目前在Macland(麦克兰德)境内经营四家酒店。Macland这个国家属于成熟经济体,拥有宜人的气候,该国的货币为M$[①]。

智选酒店创建于2005年,John Hayes(约翰·海斯)和Molly Patel(莫莉·帕特尔)兄妹在其父母过世后继承了大笔遗产,随后就购买了他们的第一家酒店。这家酒店在企业内被称为一号酒店,位于Macland南部大城市Southcastle(南堡)。

而后,兄妹二人分别于2008年和2012年购买了二号酒店和三号酒店,并在2015年年初购买了四号酒店。这些酒店位于Southcastle或40公里外的大城镇Fordtown(福特镇)。

所购买的四家酒店都是为了开展持续经营。一号、二号、三号酒店需要翻新,这项工作在购买之后立即展开。每间卧室和公共区域都进行了改装,整座建筑都进行了重新装修。而四号酒店,除了重新装修和改造一些被洪水毁坏的卧室外,并未进行更多的翻修。

每家酒店都有酒吧和餐厅设施,但目前均没有水疗和健身设施。每家酒店都有各自的身份,并由一名专职酒店经理独立负责其日常运行。各家酒店都开设了自己的银行账户,由经理负责维护基本的会计记录。

智选酒店是一个有限责任公司,其股份由总经理John Hayes和运营总监Molly Patel平均持有。财务总监是Molly Patel的丈夫Rav Patel(拉夫·帕特尔),John Hayes的妻子Pam Hayes(帕姆·海斯)则担任企业的兼职市场营销总监。

董事的办公场所位于一号酒店内,但董事们会经常视察所有四家酒店以便处理不同问题。你是两名财务人员之一,在一号酒店内办公,直接听命于财务总监Rav Patel。

① 此处及以下所称“M$”,均指Macland当地货币,该货币为虚拟货币。

四家酒店简介

一号酒店：

2005年被智选酒店收购
位置: Southcastle商业区
酒店经理：Tara Gomez（塔拉·戈麦斯）
房间数量:80
2016年预算的平均房价：M$105
2016年预算的入住率：90%

二号酒店：

2008年被智选酒店收购
位置：Fordtown中心城区
酒店经理：Pierre Vert（皮埃尔·维特)
客房数量：90
2016年预算的平均房价：M$100
2016年预算的入住率：80%

三号酒店：

2012年被智选酒店收购
位置：Southcastle购物和剧院区
酒店经理：Patrick Jenkins（帕特里克·詹金斯）
客房数量：95
2016年预算的平均房价：M$100
2016年的预算入住率：80%

四号酒店：

2015年被智选酒店收购
位置：Southcastle金融区
酒店经理：Seema Kahn（西玛·卡恩）
客房数量：105
2016年预算的平均房价：M$110
2016年预算的入住率：80%

当地商业媒体对四号酒店收购事项的报道

Southcastle 公报

2015 年 1 月 7 日　7823 号　　　M$ 1.20

智选酒店扩展其位于 Southcastle 的酒店投资组合

Lorna Gomez(洛娜 · 戈麦斯),商业记者

在挂牌转让几个月之后,位于 Southcastle 金融区、业已陈旧的福布斯酒店终于卖给了智选酒店。

智选酒店在 Southcastle 其他区域已经拥有两家酒店,在邻近的 Fordtown 拥有一家酒店。

长期以来,福布斯酒店一直是疲劳的商务客人和休闲旅客的休憩之所,自去年年初酒店前任老板 Callum Stinger(卡勒姆 · 斯廷杰)去世之后,该酒店一直面临着关门的威胁。

智选酒店总经理 John Hayes 谈道:"我们对 Southcastle 范围内一系列不同的投资机会进行了考虑,而福布斯酒店是我们最好的选择。通过这一交易,我们可以扩展自己的酒店投资组合,覆盖 Southcastle 不同地区。我们不打算对该酒店做任何重大改造,在一年左右的时间内,这一点是确定的;同时,我们将保留所有在职员工。"

如果福布斯酒店未找到接手的买家,那么酒店员工将面临失业,这一交易让员工们都松了一口气。

总体组织结构

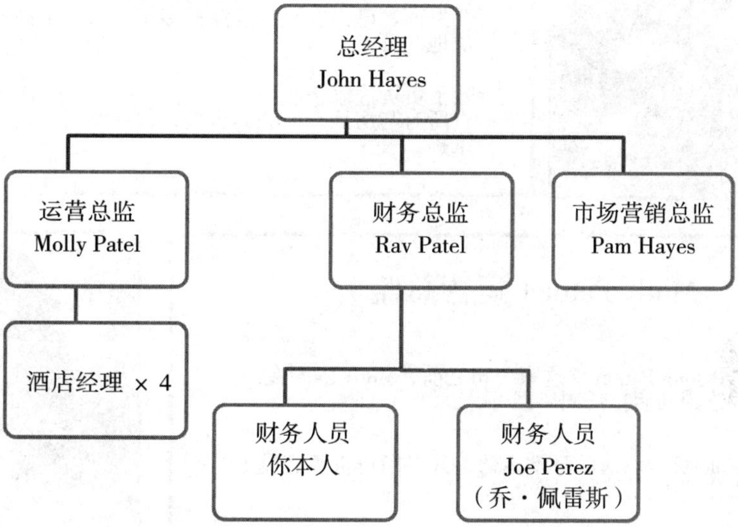

酒店经理直接向营运总监汇报每日工作，如果需要的话，也向其他三位总监汇报工作。此外，还有两名兼职秘书兼行政助理，他们服务于总监。

各家酒店的组织结构

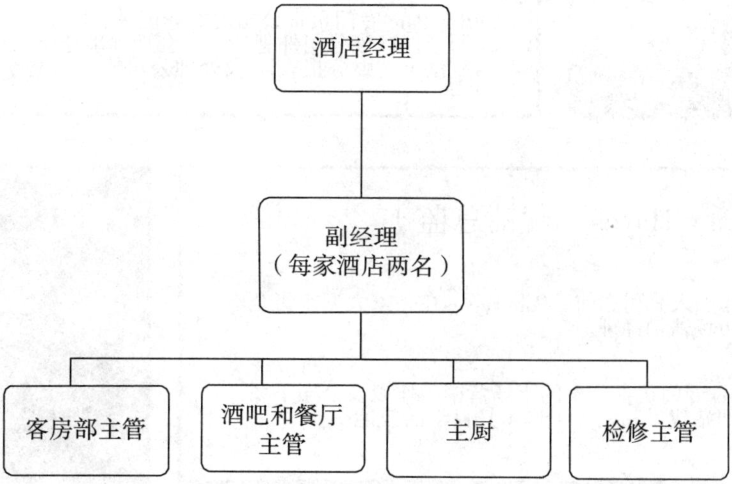

John Hayes（总经理）

- 在2005年成立这家公司之前，John Hayes作为一名房地产开发商，已经在该行业深耕多年，参与了许多大大小小的房地产开发项目。
- 除了负责这家企业的整体工作以外，John Hayes还专门负责所有与房地产有关的事项，包括酒店的收购、翻新以及维护。

Molly Patel（运营总监）

- 在与哥哥John Pate成立这家公司之前，Molly Patel在一家国际性连锁酒店担任酒店经理。
- Molly Patel负责酒店的日常运营，并专门负责酒店员工的培训工作 和质量控制工作。

Rav Patel（财务总监）

- 在2005年加入这家公司之前，Rav Patel是一名银行经理。虽然通过其银行工作经验，他能很好地了解会计，但他并不是一名合格的会计师。
- Rav Patel专门负责公司的财务记录、职工薪酬和人力资源工作。该公司外聘了一家会计师事务所，负责为公司制法定的财务报表以 及处理公司的一切税务相关事务。

Pam Hayes（营销总监）

- 在2007年加入公司之前，Pam Hayes在一家大型零售企业担任市场营销经理。
- Pam Hayes专门负责公司的市场营销工作以及公司下属酒店的网站建设和维护工作（其自学的技能）。

管理人员的主要职责

职位	主要职责
酒店经理	酒店经理负责： ■ 与其他两名董事一起，招聘、面试和任命酒店副经理和部门负责人 ■ 处理员工纪律问题，包括终止雇用初级员工。如果纪律问题涉及酒店副经理或部门负责人，其他董事也将参与进来 ■ 保管员工的人事档案 ■ 创建员工花名册（利用副经理提供的信息及他们的直接报告），为所有领取周薪的员工整理每周工作时间 ■ 联系企业客户，包括设定信用期限 ■ 确保预订系统运行正常，告知市场营销总监酒店网站所需进行的任何更改 ■ 在 M$ 1 000 的范围内，可授权物业维护支出（包括建筑、设施和配件）。超过这个金额的任何支出都必须经财务总监和总经理共同批准
副经理	副经理职责： ■ 客人预订、接待服务并在第一时间处理客人投诉 ■ 酒店经理不在酒店时，代行其职责。要确保在任何时候，酒店经理和副经理需有一人在酒店当班。在极为少见的情况下，如因生病不能保证当班，则由董事之一承担这一职责 ■ 招聘接待人员并负责其日常管理
客房部主管	客房部主管负责： ■ 确保客房按照正确的标准得到及时清扫，物品得以及时补充 ■ 招募客房保洁人员并负责其日常管理 ■ 确保及时将清洗物品送到外部洗衣房 ■ 按需订购清洁用品和免费物品。若有任何变动，需征得酒店经理的同意
酒吧和餐厅主管	酒吧和餐厅主管负责： ■ 挑选酒吧酒水，并确保酒水适当的库存水平 ■ 向客人提供高质量的酒吧服务和餐厅服务 ■ 决定每日的人员配置水平以及招聘吧台和服务人员 ■ 第一时间处理客人投诉。如果需要的话，有权退款给客人或赠送代金券 ■（与主厨和酒店经理一起）确定客人的酒水和食品价格

（续表）

职位	主要职责
主厨	主厨负责： ■ 设计和选定菜单餐食 ■ 采买和订购原料 ■ 确保厨房的出品食物具有适当的品质 ■ 招聘厨房员工，并负责人员的日常配置水平 ■（与酒吧和餐厅主管以及酒店经理一起）确定客人的酒水和食品价格
检修主管	检修主管负责： ■ 确保维护酒店的内外部结构和装饰，如果需要外部承包商，则需请示总经理 ■ 确保所有小规模修复工作得到及时开展 ■ 招聘维护人员，并负责其日常管理工作

关于酒店运营的进一步信息

每家酒店作为一个独立单位运行，拥有自己的银行账户、预订系统和会计核算系统。

客户

每家酒店都面向商务和休闲客人。根据2015年的实际客人数据，每家酒店的各类客人比例如下所示：

酒店	商务客人与休闲客人的比例	企业客户中商务客人的占比(%)
一号酒店	70 : 30	75
二号酒店	50 : 50	60
三号酒店	20 : 80	80
四号酒店	60 : 40	60

所有休闲客人需在办理退房手续时付款。商务客人可在办理退房手续时付款，也可以记到酒店企业客户的账下。这些企业客户将酒店指定为出差员工的住宿酒店。

企业客户可根据与酒店经理达成的信用期限进行付款。就公司整体而言，平均的信用期限为企业客户办理退房手续后的30天。所有企业客户都位于Macland境内。

如果客人已经预订客房，但在距离入住时间不少于24小时的情况下取消预订，酒店则不收取任何费用。如果客人在 24 小时内取消预订或未现身办理入住,酒店就会按照房价直接将发票寄送给这些客户或是企业客户。通常,75% 的发票得到实际支付。

网站和预订系统

每家酒店都拥有自己的网站,与其独立的预订系统连接,即一个简单的软件包。每完成一次网站预订,预订系统就会更新可用客房信息。这个软件不以任何方式与其他酒店连接。

至少 70% 的休闲客人直接通过网站预订客房,剩余的休闲客人则通过电话预订。为了确保客房的可用性,接听订房电话的人员需在接听的同时更新预订系统。如果客人试图预订位于 Southcastle 的酒店,但在指定日期没有所需的客房,那么酒店会给潜在客人推荐附近的其他智选酒店。

企业客户通常通过电子邮件预订客房。酒店应尽快在系统中处理这些预订要求。如果在指定日期没有可用客房,酒店需联系企业客户,向他们推荐最近的其他智选酒店。

会计核算系统

每家酒店都使用相同的标准会计核算包。财务人员的职责是处理所有交易,向供应商支付款项以及进行银行对账。

此外,每家酒店还使用标准的工资包。财务人员负责员工工资的处理和支付,在支付工资之前需由财务总监进行审批。

月底,财务人员通过系统生成月度账目,并基于此编写每家酒店的业绩报告。这些业绩报告内容包括实际业绩与初始预算、关键数据之间的比对,如应收账款和应付账款的天数以及现金生成情况。

公司没有中央会计核算系统:每家酒店负责自己的系统和银行账户。

公司外聘会计师事务所来编写年终财务报表,处理公司的所有税务事项(但不包括工资税的支付,这项工作需要经财务总监批准,并由财务人员操办)。

财务人员的职责

- 轮流视察每家酒店并:

  处理所有采购和销售交易。

  向供应商付款。

  确保企业客户及时付款,如有需要,催讨账款。

  处理和支付酒店员工的工资。

  处理酒店每个月的银行对账工作。

编写各家酒店的月度业绩报告。

将各家酒店银行账户的现金余额转到中央商业银行账户。

- 处理中央商业银行账户每月的对账工作。
- 按照董事的要求，编写公司的财务信息分析报告。
- 协助每家酒店进行预算信息的编制工作。预算编制针对即将到来的自然年度，每年一次，通常在11月进行。
- 根据董事的要求，就影响公司的事项编写报告并进行解释。

智选酒店截至2015年12月31日的年度财务报表摘要

智选酒店

截至2015年12月31日的年度利润表：

	2015年（M$ 000）	2014年（M$ 000）
收入	11 138	7 925
运营成本	（8 984）	（6 023）
税前利润	2 154	1 902
税费	（643）	（571）
本年利润	1 511	1 331

智选酒店

截至2015年12月31日的资产负债表：

	2015年（M$ 000）	2015年（M$ 000）	2014年（M$ 000）	2014年（M$ 000）
资产				
非流动性资产				
无形资产（注2）	733		423	
不动产、厂房和设备（注1）	5 844		3 829	
		6 577		4 252
流动资产				

（续表）

	2015 年 (M$ 000)	2015 年 (M$ 000)	2014 年 (M$ 000)	2014 年 (M$ 000)
存货	362		260	
应收账款	378		224	
现金及现金等价物	4 344		4 961	
		5 084		5 445
总资产		11 661		9 697
所有者权益及负债				
发行的普通股本		1 500		1 500
留存收益		8 625		7 114
所有者权益总额		10 125		8 614
流动负债				
应付账款	893		512	
应交税费	643		571	
		1 536		1 083
所有者权益及负债总额		11 661		9 697

智选酒店

截至 2015 年 12 月 31 日的现金流量表：

	(M$ 000)	(M$ 000)
经营活动现金流		
税前利润		2 154
调整项		
折旧	305	
摊销	90	
		395
营运资金的变动		
存货增加	(102)	
应收账款的增加	(154)	
应付账款的增加	381	
		125

（续表）

	（M$ 000）	（M$ 000）
经营活动产生的现金流		2 674
已付税款		（571）
经营活动的净现金流		2 103
投资活动现金流		
购置不动产、厂房和设备	（2 320）	
购置无形资产	（400）	
投资活动的净现金流		（2 720）
现金及现金等价物的净增加		（617）
期初现金及现金等价物		4 961
期末现金及现金等价物		4 344

注：

（1）智选酒店对不动产、厂房和设备的折旧政策是：在购置当年按全年折旧，而在处置当年不再折旧。

（2）无形资产包括通过收购酒店所购买的商誉。一号、二号、三号、四号酒店都出于持续经营的目的而进行收购，智选酒店购买的是这些酒店的资产和负债，而不是这些酒店业务所属公司的股权。商誉的形成是因为一号、二号、三号、四号酒店的酒店业务收购价格要高于所收购资产和负债的净值。所购买的商誉作为无形资产已经进行资本化，按年度予以摊销。

酒店的预算信息

预算由财务总监 Rav Patel 编制，采取年度递增方式。这项工作要求财务人员、其他董事和四名酒店经理提供协助。

预算总利润：

	截至 2016 年 12 月 31 日的年度预算（M$ 000）	**截至 2015 年 12 月 31 日的年度预算（M$ 000）**
酒店收入	13 582	12 391
酒店的变动运营成本	（4 414）	（4 089）
酒店的收入贡献	9 168	8 302
酒店的固定运营成本	（4 358）	（4 248）
酒店的营业利润（注 1）	4 810	4 054

（续表）

	截至2016年12月31日的年度预算（M$ 000）	截至2015年12月31日的年度预算（M$ 000）
总公司成本：		
折旧与摊销（注2）	（413）	（413）
市场营销	（650）	（650）
董事薪资	（320）	（300）
总公司行政费用	（575）	（560）
预算利润	2 852	2 131

注：

（1）根据每家酒店的详细预算来推算出酒店的预算营业利润。每家酒店的预算包括针对客房、酒吧和餐厅这两个不同经营领域的收入和运营成本分析。

（2）折旧及摊销被视为总公司成本，在编制预算过程中，未将其纳入酒店预算营业利润的考量。

截至2016年12月31日及2015年12月31日的酒店年度预算总收入：

酒店	截至2016年12月31日的预算*			截至2015年12月31日的预算		
	客房收入（M$ 000）	酒吧和餐厅收入（M$ 000）	总计（M$ 000）	客房收入（M$ 000）	酒吧和餐厅收入（M$ 000）	总计（M$ 000）
一号酒店	2 759	552	3 311	2 628	526	3 154
二号酒店	2 628	497	3 125	2 497	473	2 970
三号酒店	2 774	416	3 190	2 635	305	2 940
四号酒店	3 373	583	3 956	2 951	376	3 327
总计	11 534	2 048	13 582	10 711	1 680	12 391

* 与2015年相比，2016年收入创造方面的重大预算变化表现在：

■ 将四号酒店的入住率从70%提高到80%，但不提高房价。

■ 提高三号酒店和四号酒店的酒吧和餐厅的客人光顾率和人均消费水平。

客房收入流

截至2016年12月31日的客房预算总收入：

酒店	客房数量	预算平均入住率（%）	预计的年度客房使用量	预算平均房价*（M$）	预算客房收入（M$000）
一号酒店	80	90	26 280	105.00	2 759
二号酒店	90	80	26 280	100.00	2 628
三号酒店	95	80	27 740	100.00	2 774
四号酒店	105	8	30 660	110.00	3 373
合计					11 534

* 平均房价包含客房过夜价格和早餐。所有智选酒店的可用客房只有一种规格，但是客房价格会有所不同，这取决于订房时间。因此，该预算房价是基于平均房价。

截至2016年12月31日与酒店客房收入相关的预算总运营成本：

酒店	客房收入中的变动成本（M$000）	客房收入中的固定成本（M$000）	房屋收入涉及的总运营成本（M$000）
一号酒店	850	813	1 663
二号酒店	860	840	1 700
三号酒店	894	831	1 725
四号酒店	1 002	962	1 964
合计	3 606	3 446	7 052

注：

（1）在客房收入方面，可变成本随客房入住情况的不同而不同。上表中的预算可变成本是基于预算入住率。

（2）与客房收入相关的可变成本包括早餐所提供食物和饮料的成本、客房清扫成本（包括免费物品和所用的清洁用品）、毛巾和床上用品的清洗成本、酒店能源总成本的85%，以及与客房、接待和维护员工相关的变动成本。

（3）与客房收入相关的固定成本包括与客房、接待和维护员工相关的固定成本，以及酒店物业相关总成本的85%。

酒吧和餐厅的收入流

截至2016年12月31日的酒吧和餐厅预算总收入：

酒店	预计的客房年度使用量	预计客人使用服务的比例（%）	预计使用服务的年度客人数	使用服务的客人预计带来的人均酒吧和餐厅收入（M$）	酒吧和餐厅预算收入（M$000）
一号酒店	26 280	60	15 768	35.00	552
二号酒店	26 280	60	15 768	31.50	497

（续表）

酒店	预计的客房年度使用量	预计客人使用服务的比例（%）	预计使用服务的年度客人数	使用服务的客人预计带来的人均酒吧和餐厅收入（M$）	酒吧和餐厅预算收入（M$000）
三号酒店	27 740	50	13 870	30.00	416
四号酒店	30 660	50	15 330	38.00	583
合计					2 048

截至2016年12月31日与酒吧和餐厅收入相关的酒店预算总运营成本：

酒店	酒吧和餐厅收入中的变动成本（M$000）	酒吧和餐厅收入中的固定成本（M$000）	酒吧和餐厅收入涉及的总运营成本（M$000）
一号酒店	206	210	416
二号酒店	201	246	447
三号酒店	175	213	388
四号酒店	226	243	469
合计	808	912	1 720

注：

（1）在酒吧和餐厅收入方面，可变成本随客人服务使用情况的不同而不同。上表中的预算可变成本是基于预算的客人使用率。

（2）与酒吧和餐厅收入相关的可变成本包括食品和酒水的采购成本、酒店能源总成本的15%，以及与酒吧和餐厅员工相关的变动成本。

（3）与酒吧和餐厅收入相关的固定成本包括与酒吧和餐厅员工相关的固定成本，以及酒店物业相关总成本的15%。

预算成本的补充附注：

（1）所有酒店将需要清洗的物品送到距离一号酒店30公里处的外部洗衣房。这是一家大型的清洗服务提供商，它与该地区的多家酒店签订了服务合同。

（2）客房清扫成本包括客房打扫成本、补充免费物品的成本，如茶、咖啡、饼干、洗发水和沐浴露。免费物品的预算补充成本是基于每间入住客房免费物品的平均更换水平。

（3）早餐的预算成本为每间入住客房每天M$5。这一平均成本会根据每间入住客房的平均客人数量进行调整。

（4）对于所有酒店而言，员工成本的 20% 属于变动成本，员工成本的 80% 属于固定成本。

（5）物业成本包括财产保险和一般维护费用。此外，它还包括每间客房每年更换床上用品和毛巾的费用 M$ 250。2015 年和 2016 年均不涉及重大的翻新费用预算。

截至 2016 年 12 月 31 日的预算年度收入贡献

客房收入：

酒店	预算的收入贡献总额（M$ 000）	预计的客房年度使用量	每间入住客房的预算收入贡献（M$）
一号酒店	1 909	26 280	72. 64
二号酒店	1 768	26 280	67. 28
三号酒店	1 880	27 740	67. 77
四号酒店	2 371	30 660	77. 33
合计	7 928		

酒吧和餐厅收入：

酒店	预算的收入贡献总额（M$ 000）	预计使用服务的年度客人数	使用服务的客人预计带来的人均酒吧和餐厅收入贡献（M$）
一号酒店	346	15 768	21. 94
二号酒店	296	15 768	18. 77
三号酒店	241	13 870	17. 38
四号酒店	357	15 330	23. 29
合计	1 240		

员工

员工人数

	董事	酒店经理/部门主管	其他	总计
一号酒店	—	7	22	29
二号酒店	—	7	25	32

（续表）

	董事	酒店经理/部门主管	其他	总计
三号酒店	—	7	22	29
四号酒店	—	7	29	36
总公司	4	—	4	8
合计	4	28	102	134

用工政策

智选酒店的用工政策让董事们引以为豪。每名员工的合同保证其每周至少工作 30 小时。这一规定在 Macland 酒店行业并不常见，行业的通常做法是签署零小时的雇佣合同（员工得不到任何的工作保证）。

每个星期，酒店经理负责准备员工花名册，确保每名员工分配到最低的工作时长。通常，员工每周至少工作 38 小时。如果入住率高出平均水平，则可能增加到每周 45 小时。如果入住率低于平均水平，则可能减少至每周 30 小时。在极少数情况下，酒店的正常工作量无法满足员工每周至少 30 小时的工作时长，那么酒店会安排员工深入清洁或整理酒店区域。

员工按照每周的工作时长以及小时工资率获得报酬，所采用的小时工资率高于 Macland 的全国最低工资水平（同样，这在酒店行业也是不常见的）。如果员工每周的工作时间超过了 42 小时，酒店则会支付加班津贴。

上班期间，所有员工均能享受酒店提供的免费工作餐。如果员工的下班时间超过晚上 10 点，那么酒店会支付打车回家的费用。如果酒店还有空余客房且下班回家路程对于员工来说非常困难，那么酒店会允许员工免费使用客房。

关注环境

酒店会在每间客房放置一个提示，客人有机会选择是否每天更换毛巾，此举是为了节约水和能源。最近，酒店的所有灯泡都换成了节能灯。

所有食品和酒水类废物会送到垃圾堆肥场，公司鼓励每家酒店尽可能多地回收饮料和食品包装。将食品类废物和回收的包装送到相关设施会产生一定的费用。淘汰下来的毛巾和床上用品也会以这种方式加以回收处理。

更广泛的社区

智选酒店会定期给当地的慈善机构捐款，同时还赞助了 Fordtown 的儿童足球队。

各家酒店网站上的客户评价

一号酒店：平均得分为8.8分，满分为10分

评价：9/10

多么令人欣慰的小小发现。这是我第一次入住一号酒店，但绝不会是最后一次。早餐非常丰盛，前一日的晚餐也很棒。该酒店位于商业区，地理位置优越，前台员工也非常热心。

评价：8/10

这已经是我的老板第三次为我预定一号酒店的客房了，与往常一样，这家酒店的入住体验非常棒。工作便利，食物美味，员工友善且乐于助人。唯一不足的是，虽然酒店设施能满足我的所有需要，但装饰看上去有点陈旧。

二号酒店：平均得分为9.1分，满分为10分

评价：10/10

这家酒店很好，物有所值。早餐绝对大赞：种类丰富、烹饪精心。我肯定会再次入住这家酒店。让我非常认同的一点是，这家酒店不但让客人有机会选择是否更换毛巾以节约能源和水，并且切实践行。虽然我入住的其他酒店也提供类似选择，但即使我选择不更换毛巾，它们依然会更换掉。

评价：8/10

我因参加周末的家庭聚会而入住了该酒店。酒店位于中心城区，位置非常便利，并且酒店本身也很棒。但在周六和周日的清晨，噪音是个问题。我这次入住的客房临街，我想下次我会要求安排背街的客房。

三号酒店：平均得分为8.1分，满分为10分

评价：8/10

如果你想在Southcastle市中心购物，那么这家酒店是一个很好的选择。酒店的外观虽不太吸引人，但客房内部舒适，布局和安排都很好。但是在早上用餐时，我不得不要求重上早餐，因为食物已经凉了，好在这个问题很快得到了解决。

评价：5/10

酒店本身很好，但餐厅的晚餐服务很糟糕。我们订餐后等待了一个多小时才上菜，而且食物平淡无味，让人提不起胃口。

酒店经理Patrick Jenkins的回复：

对于您这次用餐体验，我深表歉意。我们希望这不会影响到您再次选择我们的酒店，特别需要说明的是，我们刚刚推出了新菜单。

四号酒店：平均得分为 6.9 分，满分为 10 分

评价：6/10

酒店建筑本身就很漂亮，并且客房物品一应俱全，令人舒畅。但我碰到的问题是，浴室不像我预期的那样干净，床单上也有污渍。在我投诉之后，酒店重新打扫了房间，所用时间不超过一小时。我希望酒店在这方面能有所改进。

早餐符合我的预期，但餐厅看起来有点陈旧，需要进行现代化改造。

评价：4/10

四号酒店未能给我留下深刻印象。客房家具非常老式，浴室在我看来需要彻底翻新。早餐很好，员工服务周到，但酒店缺乏真正特色。

酒店经理 Seema Kahn 的回复：

对于我们酒店的入住体验未能给您留下深刻印象，对此我们深表遗憾。未来两年，我们将着手酒店的彻底翻新工作，我们希望完工之后您能再次光顾。

行业信息

客人类型

Macland 境内拥有各类酒店，可以广泛满足不同的预算要求。住店客人可以分为两类：商务客人或休闲客人。

商务客人通常需要位于 Macland 主要城镇的酒店。这类客人的平均停留时间为两晚。

休闲客人选择酒店出于不同考虑。如果他们希望度过一个轻松愉快的假期，那么他们更有可能会选择位于海滨度假胜地（由于 Macland 气候宜人，有很多此类酒店）或位于乡间的酒店。能够满足客人此类需要的酒店通常都配备游泳和健身设施，此外，很多酒店还拥有高尔夫球场。这类客人的停留时间通常为 7 晚或者 14 晚。

另外，许多客人的旅游目的是游览城镇、欣赏风景、借机观剧和购物。这类客人的停留时间平均为 3 晚。

旅游休闲市场

Macland 境内有许多旅游休闲公司，它们充当中介，为休闲酒店和客人牵线搭桥。度假时间通常为一个星期或以上。2005 年，有 95 家公司从事此类业务，而 2015 年，这一数字已降至 30 家，出现这种情况的原因是客人日益相信自己能通过酒店网站搜寻酒店。剩下的 30 家公司之所以能够得以幸存是因为它们在某种程度上实现了业务的专业化或差异化。当前，Macland 境内的旅游休闲市场处于一个稳定状态。

Macland 境内有一个名为 MLTA（Macland 休闲旅游管理局）的组织，其旨在保护休闲旅客的权益。幸存下来的 30 家旅游休闲公司以及所有的主要连锁酒店都是 MLTA 的会员。如果通过 MLTA 会员预订酒店客房，客人能够收回已支付的任何押金或预订款项。

与此相似，小规模酒店也可要求获得保护，向旅游休闲公司追讨拖欠的业务款项。大多数独立的小规模连锁酒店，包括智选酒店，并不是 MLTA 的会员，与旅游休闲公司没有任何业务往来。

酒店市场

Macland 境内有 8 家大型的连锁酒店，旗下酒店遍布全国各地，它们占了 Macland 酒店数量的 75%，另外 25% 的酒店是完全独立的酒店或小型集团的旗下酒店。许多像智选酒店这样独立的小规模酒店集团都是家族企业。在 Southcastle 和 Fordtown 地区，智选酒店的业务收入占市场份额的 10%。

Macland 的税收体系

企业利润

- 企业所得税为应税利润的 30%。
- 除非另有规定，否则应该从税务的角度出发来执行下列的确认和计量会计规定。
- 以下费用不得税前扣除：

  会计折旧；

  摊销费用；

  减值支出；

  文娱开支；

  政党捐赠；

  支付给其他公共机构的税费。
- 厂房和机器设备（包括商用车辆）的折旧可以抵税，每年的抵扣率为 25%，以其递减余额为基础。
- 如果公司获得了政府补贴，具体的税务处理要视补贴的性质而定。站在税务的角度，企业收到的资本补贴可在收到拨款的当年，在计算折旧抵税之前，用于抵减相关资产的资本价值。当年盈利或损失所涉及的任何资本补贴收入无须纳税。站在税务的角度，当年盈利或损失所涉及的收入补贴应视为应税收入。
- 可抵税损失可以进行结转，用于抵减同一企业未来的应税利润。

- 判断一个公司是否属于 Macland 居民企业的主要依据是这个公司主要管理活动的所在地。Macland 居民企业应就其所有利润向 Macland 纳税，而不论其具体利润来自哪个国家。智选酒店属于 Macland 居民企业。
- 如果 Macland 居民企业拥有一家子公司，其属于另一个国家的居民企业，那么子公司向总公司发放的任何股利将视为总公司的收入，并按企业税率向 Macland 缴税。
- Macland 与其他一些国家签订了双重征税协定。所有此类协定围绕企业所收到的股利涉及的代扣代缴税和股息税，免除双重征税。企业使用税收抵免法可享受这一优惠。

Variant 1

This examination is structured as follows：

Section number	Number of tasks	Time for section(minutes)
1	1	45
2	1	45
3	1	45
4	1	45

The time available for each section is for reading,planning and writing your answer(s).

Section 1

The directors of Wise Choice Hotels are currently in the later stages of negotiations with Westport Hotels to acquire a chain of three hotels, which are all located in Westport, a city 50 kilometres west of Southcastle.

They are negotiating to buy 100% of the equity of Westport Hotels.

You arrive at work to find the following email from John Hayes, managing director:

From: John Hayes, Managing Director
To: Management Accountant Assistant
Subject: Audit report and relevant costing

Whilst Rav Patel is away for a few days, I need your help on a couple of things.

Firstly, the advisors we are using for the acquisition recently sent me Westport Hotels' financial statements for the last three years. I've had a look at them and there is something that has slightly alarmed me. In the financial statements for the year ended 31 December 2014 the audit report is modified, but the report for the year ended 31 December 2015 is not.

Secondly, I visited one of the Westport Hotels yesterday to have a look around. Whilst I was there I overheard a conversation between staff on the reception desk about the hotel's pricing policy. Apparently, they have a policy that, in order to stop a late arriving potential guest moving to another hotel, the price charged for a room can be lowered to the point at which the relevant costs are covered. I must admit I'm a little confused about what relevant costs means in the context of a one-night stay at Hotel 4 and whether we should consider adopting this Westport Hotels' policy in our own hotels.

Please send me an email that explains:

- The seriousness of this modified audit report of Westport Hotels and the grounds for this modification as I don't understand the accounting terminology. Please also explain whether this modified audit report means that we should not acquire the company.
- What the relevant costs of a one-night stay in Hotel 4 are likely to be and the suitability of adopting this Westport Hotels' policy in our own hotels. There is no need to quantify what the relevant costs are at this stage.

Many thanks!

John Hayes

Managing Director

Wise Choice Hotels

Extracts from the Modified Audit Report for Westport Hotels for the Year Ended 31 December 2014

Basis for Qualified Opinion

The company has changed its accounting policy in respect of property balances from the cost model to the revaluation model. At 31 December 2014 the properties were valued at M$ 3,200,000, which generated a revaluation surplus of M$ 500,000. The company has treated this as a realised gain and has additionally not charged any depreciation on the property assets for the year. Both of these constitute departures from International Financial Reporting Standards. If management had treated the revaluation surplus and depreciation charge in accordance with International Financial Reporting Standards, profit for the year would have decreased by M$ 628,000 and shareholder's equity by M$ 128,000.

Audit Opinion

In our opinion, except for the possible effects of the matters described in the Basis for Qualified Opinion paragraph, the financial statements present fairly, in all material respects, the financial position of Westport Hotels at 31 December 2014 and of its financial performance and cash flows for the year then ended in accordance with International Financial Reporting Standards.

Write the email requested by John Hayes.

Section 2

It is now three months later. The three Westport Hotels were acquired five weeks ago. They all have the same management staff and operate in the same way as they did before the acquisition. The finance manager of Westport Hotels, Anna Copeland, has been retained and is responsible for the day-to-day financial affairs of the Westport hotels.

The directors of Wise Choice Hotels have appointed Stephen Nichols as overall manager for all of the Westport hotels. He has responsibility for the operation of the three hotels and reports directly to Wise Choice Hotels' directors.

You receive the following email from Rav Patel, finance director:

Director: From: Rav Patel, Finance Director

To: Management Accountant Assistant

Subject: Induction programme and cost of quality

I've just had a meeting with Stephen Nichols. Although he is obviously new to both our businesses, he does have a lot of experience in the hotel industry. He made a couple of observations about the Westport hotels.

His first observation was on the high level of staff turnover at the hotels. A large proportion of staff that left had completed less than one year's service. Stephen believes that part of the problem is that there is no formal induction programme in place in any of the hotels. On their first day new staff are given a quick tour of the hotel and are told what their role is by a more senior member of staff. Apparently, sometimes even this does not happen and some staff report that they have just been left to get on with it. I mentioned this to Molly Patel, operations director, and we agreed that this should be a priority for the directors to consider.

His second observation was about the restaurants at the Westport hotels. In his experience he knows that service quality is a critical success factor in the restaurant operation. He referred to the complaints register for the hotels which showed a number of complaints about the quality of both the food and the service. He mentioned that his previous employer used a cost-of-quality reporting approach to monitor hotel operations. He thinks that we could adopt this, not only for the Westport hotels but across all our hotels, especially for the restaurant operations.

Please prepare a first draft of the following sections for a report that I am preparing:

- What should be included in a formal induction programme for new hotel staff, together with the benefits (other than a reduction in staff turnover) that might be gained by us from doing so?
- The benefits to be gained from the adoption of a cost-of-quality reporting approach to the monitoring of operations within Wise Choice Hotels. Please include actions that could be taken within our restaurant operations to achieve these benefits.

Rav Patel

Finance Director

Wise Choice Hotels

Write the draft report sections required by Rav Patel.

Section 3

A week later, Rav Patel is absent from work and you receive the following email from John Hayes, managing director:

From: John Hayes, Managing Director

To: Management Accountant Assistant

Subject: Variance report and consolidated financial statements

I've just received, from finance manager Anna Copeland, our first variance report for the Westport Hotel hotels, and I'm having difficulty understanding some of it. I've attached her October summary variance report for Hotel A and I have a few queries, as it is presented differently to our existing variance reports:

- What does the "Flexed Budget" column represent? I've never seen this in any of our reports.
- Comparing the "Actual" and "Budget" columns there is an adverse variance of M$ 13,838. Comparing the "Actual" and "Flexed budget" columns there is an adverse variance of M$ 26,925. Why is the latter variance worse?
- Our actual room revenue is lower than our original budget by M$ 10,050. I see from note 3 of Anna's schedule that, as a result of competition from the Eagle Hotel Group, the Westport hotels have reduced prices in a bid to price match. Is the adverse variance of M$ 10,050 entirely due to the bid to price match?
- I see that the number of complaints has doubled. How might these complaints relate to the figures contained in the variance report?

In addition, our year-end is rapidly approaching and I am interested to know how our acquisition of 100% of the equity share capital of Westport Hotels will impact on the financial statements of

Wise Choice Hotels. I believe that we will need to prepare consolidated, as well as individual, financial statements. I know that it will be different to when we've purchased hotels in the past, as we acquired the company, rather than just the business assets and liabilities. However, I would like to know how it will be different.

Please send me an email which:

- Addresses each of my four queries.
- Explains how the acquisition of the Westport Hotels company on 1 October 2016 will impact our individual and consolidated financial statements for the year ended 31 December 2016, and how this is different from any of our previous hotel acquisitions.

Thank you!

John Hayes

Managing Director

Wise Choice Hotels

Summary variance report from Anna Copeland, finance manager, Westport Hotels for Hotel A for the month of October 2016

	Budget (M$)	Actual (M$)	Variance against budget (M$)	Flexed budget (M$)	Variance against flexed budget (M$)
Room revenue	220,000	209,950	(10,050)	236,500	(26,550)
Food and beverage revenue	44,000	41,662	(2,338)	47,300	(5,638)
Total revenue	264,000	251,612	(12,388)	283,800	(32,188)
Total variable costs	89,500	94,200	(4,700)	96,213	2,013
Total fixed costs	89,750	86,500	3,250	89,750	3,250
Operating profit	84,750	70,912	(13,838)	97,837	(26,925)

Notes:

- The budget for Westport Hotel A was based on budgeted room occupancy of 80%.
- All figures in the budget column are exactly 1/12th of the budget for the year.
- Due to strong competition from The Eagle Hotel Group in Westport we tried to "price match" the room rate offered by them and also attempted to exercise better cost control during the month. Wherever possible staffing schedules were reorganised in order to use staff with less than twelve months service as they are paid at a lower rate than staff that have completed one year of service.
- The actual occupancy level in October 2016 was 86%.

Our records show that in October 2016 the number of complaints from guests more than doubled compared with the previous month.

Write the email requested by John Hayes.

Section 4

A month later Rav Patel asks you to come to his office and says the following to you:

We've just had a directors' meeting where we discussed the performance of Westport Hotels B and C. There are significant adverse variances against budget for both the hotels and we've identified three main reasons for this: firstly, an unrealistic budget set by the previous owners of the company; secondly, excessive spending in certain areas, despite measures to reduce costs; thirdly, a huge variation in the rates at which rooms were charged to guests.

There are four different grades of room at each of the Westport hotels and it seems to me that there is no consistency regarding the pricing of these rooms. So that I can report back to the other directors please prepare a briefing paper which explains the factors that will influence price setting with regard to the rooms on offer at the Westport hotels under each of the headings cost, competition, customers and corporate objectives.

We've always used incremental budgeting for our Wise Choice hotels but in terms of the budget for the Westport hotels I think that we need to start from scratch; indeed I think we need to consider using ZBB. I think that this will help to curb excessive spending, motivate staff and provide other benefits from encouraging their involvement in the budgeting process. In the same briefing paper please explain whether ZBB is appropriate for our business including commentary on the advantages that might be gained as a result of encouraging the participation of our staff in our budgeting process. Thank you.

Write the briefing paper requested by Rav Patel.

试卷一

本次考试的结构如下：

序号	任务数	时间（分钟）
1	1	45
2	1	45
3	1	45
4	1	45

每个部分规定的时间可用于读题、组织和书写答案。

任务一

智选酒店的主管和韦斯特波特酒店（Westport Hotels）的合作谈判已经进入后期。智选酒店想要和三家酒店连锁经营，这三家酒店都位于韦斯特波特，一个位于 Southcastle 西边 50 公里的城市。

双方在协商由智选酒店购买韦斯特波特酒店 100% 的股份。

你收到了以下来自总经理 John Hayes 的邮件：

发件人：总经理 John Hayes

收件人：管理会计助理

主题：关于审计报告和相关成本的计算

财务总监 Rav Patel 离开了数天，我需要请你来帮忙做以下几件事。

第一，我们的顾问最近发给我一份韦斯特波特酒店过去三年的财务报表，里面有一些地方引起了我的注意。在该财务报表中，对于 2014 年 12 月 31 日的审计报告我有保留意见，对于 2015 年 12 月 31 日的审计报告我没有意见。

第二，我昨天参观了韦斯特波特酒店其中的一家酒店。我在参观时无意间听到了前台员工关于这家酒店定价政策的对话。他们的政策是，为了防止晚到的潜在客户移步去其他酒店，房间的价格可以降到房间的相关成本价。我对在四号酒店住一晚的相关成本是多少以及我们是否应该在我们的酒店也借鉴该政策有些疑惑。

请就以下内容发邮件给我：

- 韦斯特波特酒店保留意见的审计报告的严重性和出具保留意见的原因。因为我不熟悉会计的专业术语，请解释这份修改过的审计报告是否意味着我们不应该继续这次合作。
- 在四号酒店住一晚的相关成本是多少，以及在我们自己酒店也借鉴该政策的可行性。现阶段不需要考虑相关成本。

非常感谢！

智选酒店

总经理

John Hayes

韦斯特波特酒店年度截止日为2014年12月31日的保留意见的审计报告的摘录

出具保留意见的依据

该公司将房产的资产计量方面的会计处理方法从成本模型转换成了公允价值计量模型。2014年12月31日，资产估值为M$ 3 200 000，重新估值后增长了M$ 500 000。公司将此计入了已确定收益，并且未对当年的不动产计提折旧。这两项都违反了国际会计准则。如果管理人员将重估价利润和折旧按照国际会计准则计量，年利润将减少M$ 628 000，股东权益将减少M$ 128 000。

审计师的意见

我们认为，除了上述保留意见提到的可能影响外，上述财务报表在所有重大方面均按照国际会计准则的规定编制，公允地反映了韦斯特波特酒店在2014年12月31日的财务状况以及2014年度的经营成果和现金流。

给总经理John Hayes回复邮件。

任务二

现在是3个月之后了，韦斯特波特酒店的那三家酒店在5周前已被收购。这三家酒店皆由被收购前的员工按照未被收购时的管理模式继续经营。韦斯特波特酒店的财务经理Anna Copeland（安娜·科普兰）继续留任并负责韦斯特波特酒店每日的财务。

智选酒店的主管已任命Stephen Nichols（斯蒂芬·尼克尔斯）作为韦斯特波特酒店的总负责，Stephen将负责这三家酒店的运营，并直接向智选酒店的主管汇报。

你收到了以下来自财务总监Rav Patel的邮件：

发件人：财务总监Rav Patel

收件人：管理会计助理

主题：入职培训方案和质量成本

我刚刚会见了Stephen Nichols。虽然他和我们都是第一次进行商业合作，但他显然在酒店行业有着丰富经验。他对韦斯特波特酒店的运营提出了以下几点考察意见。

第一，关于公司高级员工的流失问题。他发现留下的大部分员工服务经验不满一年。Stephen Nichols相信一部分原因在于这三家酒店都没有员工的入职引导。通常新员工在入职的第一天，往往会在经验丰富的老员工带领下去参观酒店并被告知自己的工作内容。显然，这些入职引导在我们酒店已经很少做了，新员工们反映他们往往被直接安排开始工作。我把这件事向运营总监 Molly Patel 反映了，我们决定把这件事当作首先需要解决的事情。

第二，关于韦斯特波特酒店的餐厅。根据他以往的经验，服务质量是餐厅运营成功的重要因素。他检查了酒店的意见登记簿，发现不少客人对酒店食物和服务有抱怨。他提到他以前的上司会使用质量成本报告来监管酒店的运营。他认为，我们不仅仅要在收购的这三家韦斯特波特酒店的酒店借用这种管理方法，而且要在我们旗下所有的酒店借用这种管理方法，尤其是在餐厅的运营管理上借用这种方法。

请帮我起草含以下内容的报告：

- 新员工入职引导应包含哪些项目以及这些项目将给我们带来的益处（除了减少员工流失）是什么？
- 在智选酒店采用质量成本报告来监管运营的益处。请列举能改善餐厅运营的举措。

智选酒店
财务总监
Rav Pate

根据财务总监 Rav Patel 的要求回复邮件。

任务三

一周后，Rav Patel 缺席工作，你收到了来自总经理 John Hayes 的邮件：

发件人：总经理 John Hayes
收件人：管理会计助理
主题：差异报告和合并财务报表

我刚收到财务经理 Anna Copeland 发来的我们的首个韦斯特波特酒店的差异报告，里面有些地方我不太理解。我附上了她做的 2016 年酒店 A 10 月份的差异汇总报告，这份报告和我们现在使用的报告不同，因此我有一些疑问。

- “弹性预算”① 列代表什么意思？我之前从未在我们的报告中见过。

① 有很多书翻译成“变动限额预算”。

- “实际”和“预算”有M$ 13 838的不利偏差，“实际”和“弹性预算”有M$ 26 925的偏差，为何后者的差异更糟？
- 我们实际的房间收入比预算低了M$ 10 050。我看到Anna在注释3中说，这是因为与老鹰酒店集团的竞争，韦斯特波特酒店在价格战中降低了价格。M$ 10 050的差异是否是价格战的后果？
- 我看到顾客的投诉数量翻倍了，这和差异报告中的数据有什么关联？

另外，年终就要到了。我想知道我们对韦斯特波特酒店100%的股权收购将会对智选酒店的财务报表产生怎样的影响。我想我们需要制作财务报表和合并财务报表。我知道这和我们之前的收购不同，因为我们收购了整个公司，不只是营业资产和债务，我想知道具体会有什么不同。

请发给我邮件。

- 解释我的四个问题。
- 解释2016年10月对韦斯特波特酒店公司的收购将会怎样影响我们2016年12月31日的独立财务报表和合并财务报表。这和我们之前的收购有什么不同？

非常感谢！

智选酒店

总经理

John Hayes

2016年10月酒店A差异汇总报告

	预算（M$）	实际（M$）	预算差额（M$）	弹性预算（M$）	弹性预算差额（M$）
客户收入	220 000	209 950	（10 050）	236 500	（26 550）
食物和饮料收入	44 000	41 662	（2 338）	47 300	（5 638）
总收入	264 000	251 612	（12 388）	283 800	（32 188）
变动成本总额	89 500	94 200	（4 700）	96 213	2 013

（续表）

	预算（M$）	实际（M$）	预算差额（M$）	弹性预算（M$）	弹性预算差额（M$）
固定成本总额	89 750	86 500	3 250	89 750	3 250
营业利润	84 750	70 912	（13 838）	97 837	（26 925）

说明：

- 韦斯特波特酒店 A 的预算基于房间 80% 的入住率。
- 预算图表中的所有数据都正好是全年预算的 1/12。
- 为了应对位于韦斯特波特的老鹰酒店集团的竞争，我们试图在房租上和他们打价格战，同时在本月尝试更合理的成本控制。我们重新编制员工的工作时间表，尽量使他们的工作时间少于 12 个月，这样可以付给他们低于全年的工资。
- 2016 年 10 月的实际入住率是 86% 。

我们的记录显示 2016 年 10 月收到的客户投诉超过先前月份的两倍还多。

请根据总经理 John Hayes 的要求回复邮件。

任务四

一个月后，Rav Patel 叫你到他的办公室并对你说：

我们刚刚召开了董事会，讨论韦斯特波特酒店 B 和 C 的经营状况，实际花费和预算有很大不同。我们找到了三个主要原因：第一，公司以前设定的预算不切实际；第二，尽管有些措施降低成本，但在某些领域过度支出；第三，客房收费差异很大。

每家韦斯特波特酒店都有四个不同等级的房间。在我看来，这些房间的价格没有一致性。为了便于我向其他董事汇报，请准备一份简报，介绍韦斯特波特酒店在不同房型的成本、竞争、客户和公司政策方面影响价格的因素。

我们一直为我们智选酒店使用增量预算，但在韦斯特波特酒店的预算问题上，我想我们需要从头开始。我认为，我们应该考虑零基预算，这有助于遏制过度开支，激励员工，并鼓励他们参与预算编制过程。请在同一个简报中，请说明零基预算是否适合我们的业务，以及可能获得哪些支持，最终能否鼓励员工参与我们预算过程。谢谢。

根据财务总监 Rav Patel 的要求写一份简报。

Variant 1　Suggested Answers

Section 1

From: Management Accountant Assistant

To: John Hayes, Managing Director

Subject: Audit report and relevant costing

Audit Report

The Seriousness of Westport Hotel's Modified Audit Report

The modified audit report of Westport Hotels means that the auditors, when undertaking their work, found that there was a material misstatement in the financial statements and have therefore issued a qualified opinion.

This means that the auditors disagree about the accounting treatment of one or more aspects of the financial statements which has a material impact on those statements in terms of profit and shareholders' equity. Therefore they have concluded that "except for" this material misstatement the financial statements of Westport Hotels are fairly stated.

Any modified audit report is potentially serious and in this case shows that Westport Hotels did not apply International Financial Reporting Standards appropriately in respect of its property balances.

However, a qualified, "except for" opinion is not the most serious type of audit modification in this type of situation. Had the auditors been of the opinion that the impact of this misstatement was pervasive, so that a user of the financial statements would not have been able to understand or rely on the financial statements, they would have given an adverse opinion. An adverse opinion would mean that in the auditor's opinion the financial statements would not have been fairly stated.

Why the Audit Report for the Year Ended 31 December 2014 Was Modified

The reason why the auditors modified their audit report is highlighted in the "Basis for Qualified Opinion" paragraph.

It appears that Westport Hotels changed their accounting policy in the year in respect of property balances. This in itself is allowed under IAS 16 PPE, however it appears that the gain that arose on the revaluation was not treated correctly.

When an asset is revalued for the first time, any upward valuation surplus (which is the situation here) should be recorded in a revaluation reserve in the statement of financial position. It should not be treated as a realised gain (which means that it has been recorded in profit or loss). It should however be shown as part of other comprehensive income in the statement of other comprehensive income.

In addition, in accordance with IAS 16, all assets, excluding land, should be depreciated annually. The fact that an asset has been revalued does not change this accounting rule. Therefore the directors of Westport Hotels were incorrect in not recording any depreciation on the properties. The depreciation charge of M$128,000 would have reduced profit for the year as well as shareholders' equity.

Impact on Our Decision to Acquire Westport Hotels

It is interesting to note that the audit report for the year ended 31 December 2015 was unmodified. This means that the auditors' opinion would have been that the financial statements for that year were fairly stated and materially in agreement with all International Financial Reporting Standards.

Therefore it seems likely that the directors changed the accounting treatment to be in line with the standards. It would be interesting to understand why the directors of Westport Hotels didn't adjust the financial statements in 2014, but the modified audit report should not preclude us from acquiring the business.

Relevant Costs

The Relevant Costs in Respect of a One-night Stay at Hotel 4

"Relevant costs" are future cash flows arising as a direct consequence of the decision under consideration. In this situation relevant cost are those costs that change as a result of one of our rooms being occupied as opposed to remaining unoccupied for a night.

Examples of relevant costs for a one night stay are as follows:

- The electricity costs that will be incurred to power the hotel room for the night. This will include power for lighting and electrical equipment such as the kettle and the television.

- The energy costs incurred to provide hot water for the guest, although it is possible that there might be enough hot water anyway and therefore there will be no incremental cost here.
- The costs of laundering the bedding and towels once the guest has checked out.
- The costs of any complimentary toiletries and refreshments that the guest uses. This is likely to vary by guest as not all guests use all of the complimentary items, and therefore this could be hard to quantify.
- The cost of providing breakfast to the guest in the morning (assuming that the guest has breakfast).
- Any additional costs incurred in respect of cleaning the room such as any additional time paid to housekeeping staff and any cleaning products used.

Suitability of Adopting This Policy

There is a risk that if guests are aware of the policy that they seek to wait until the last minute to book accommodation so that they can pay a lower price per room. However, this risk is probably minimal as the vast majority of guests wish to have the assurance that their accommodation has been booked with "certainty" and therefore will not want to leave it to the last minute as there might actually not be any room available.

The policy itself is likely to only apply to potential guests who for whatever reason find themselves searching for accommodation at the last minute. This will especially be the case if, say, the policy only applies after a cut-off point of time in the evening (e. g. 9pm).

Ultimately, as long as the price covers the relevant costs then it is worthwhile us accepting these types of guest on the assumption that they are only prepared to pay a lower price (it could actually be that we could charge a higher price anyway, especially if our competing hotels are full). The goodwill that this creates for a weary traveller could help secure future bookings and enhance guest loyalty. Another benefit may be the extra revenue created by the guest using the restaurant and bar facilities, or other facilities not included in the price of the room.

Thanks.

Management Accountant Assistant
Wise Choice Hotel

Section 2

Induction Programme

The Components of a Formal Induction Programme for Hotel Staff

A formal induction programme for hotel staff should include the following:

- A welcome and introduction to immediate colleagues, other colleagues and their line manager. This could be given by Molly Patel our operations director.
- An explanation of the nature of the job. This would be made easier if there is a clear job description for every type of job outlining responsibilities, time scales, priorities, measurements or KPIs, and how their role fits in with the bigger picture.
- An explanation of safety rules and procedures. It is important to communicate and clarify basic standards of dress, staff behaviour, time keeping, break allowance, staff meals, security, food safety and health and safety.
- An explanation of the terms and conditions of employment. We could issue a booklet giving full details of essential matters such as details of the minimum 30 hour contracts, authorisation of absence and overtime, holidays, probation period, disciplinary and grievance procedures and Internet and email policy.
- An explanation of the culture and values of the hotel. The orientation to the wider mission of the hotel group should be clearly explained. This is particularly important in service businesses such as ours because of the importance of staff attitude and motivation in the provision of high quality service. We should specify our standards for welcoming and greeting guests, including the booking procedures if this is part of their role. Even those staff who are not guest-facing need to know the protocol for greeting guests or dealing with their questions.
- Explanation of any systems of continuing training, coaching and mentoring within our business. This is a vital component of "expectations management" as we ex-

pect many of our employees to undertake significant amounts of training. Rules relating to attendance and gaining qualifications from colleges that specialise in Hotel and Catering Management must be clearly explained.

Benefits of an Induction Programme for Our Hotel Staff

The induction process would familiarise our new recruits with the staff and business processes of the hotel that they are working in. It will enable them to become productive quickly.

Induction training also helps to provide new staff with a professional impression of our business and its aims and objectives, which will motivate our new recruits to work towards these aims and exceed them.

An induction programme can assist the Hotel Manager in question to deliver a consistent message to all new recruits. It also helps to make the new recruits feel part of the hotel and a valued member of staff.

Given that we are a service business, guest satisfaction is of paramount importance. Having staff that are motivated and prepared and ready to deliver this quality service will enhance the guest's experience.

Cost of Quality

The benefits to be gained from the adoption of a "cost of quality" approach to the monitoring of operations within Wise Choice Hotels can be viewed as resulting from investing in the costs of conformance which are prevention costs and appraisal costs so that the costs of failure (both internal and external) do not happen.

Firstly, benefits can result from incurring prevention costs which seek to identify potential problems before they occur. Staff who are directly involved in the provision of the customer experience in food service should be encouraged to identify problems before they happen.

The head of bar and restaurant and head chef could use simulations and role plays to help staff take a more proactive approach to identify all types of food service failures along with effective recovery strategies.

We should form a quality planning team to establish action plans to ensure that failures do not arise. Extensive training of all staff should be undertaken to enhance the entire guest experience within Wise Choice Hotels.

Secondly, there are the benefits that can be obtained as a result of incurring appraisal costs. Appraisal activities should be undertaken to ensure that food and services meet the specific quality levels that will satisfy the guests' requirements.

There are also the benefits from identifying serving failures that will enable our restaurants to assess overall food and service quality. The restaurant staff should be encouraged to use self-inspection to ensure that the meals are prepared to meet the precise order specification of our guests.

Staff could also use "successive inspection" in which the next person in the service delivery chain verifies the quality and accuracy of the previous employee's work to ensure customer satisfaction. Staff should undertake inspection of all foodstuffs to uncover potential defects and fix them before they become food and service failures.

Empowering all employees within the restaurant will assist in the reduction of failure costs. Training kitchen employees to use the equipment properly will reduce wastage before the meal is delivered to the customers.

We should aim to empower all customer-facing serving staff to fulfil their responsibilities, as it is likely that they will try to meet or exceed them. The benefits to the restaurant are that service quality will be improved, as well as increased productivity which may lead to fewer waiting staff being required. The level of customer satisfaction should increase as a consequence of serving staff being more alert in identifying potential failure points before they occur.

Once external service failure occurs, the employee basic recovery goal is to act immediately on the customers' complaints. Our restaurants should pursue the goal of immediate service recovery and if achieved will reduce the overall expense of retaining the customers. Also, it is more likely that our restaurants will have repeat businesses from customers and, the customers will be more inclined to recommend our restaurants to their friends giving us the benefit of free advertising and promotion.

Section 3

From: Management Accountant Assistant

To: John Hayes, Managing Director

Subject: Variance report and acquisition of Westport Hotels

Variance Report Queries

Query 1

The budget column is based on an occupancy level of 80%. The column headed "Flexed budget" shows the budget for the actual level of occupancy during October, which must have been higher than 80% given that the flexed room revenue is higher than the budget column. Indeed we know that is was 86%. Flexing the budget allows us to look at the consequences if the planned level had been actual occupancy rather the budgeted occupancy. This enables a much more meaningful comparison to be made between our actual and budgeted revenues and costs as we are now comparing like with like. It gives us a fairer reflection of performance during the month.

Query 2

Comparing the actual and budget columns is slightly misleading because as explained above we were not comparing like with like. At occupancy of 86% we would expect our room revenue and bar and restaurant revenue to be higher than the original budget, although we would also expect our variable costs to be higher (though not our fixed costs). The impact of this increased occupancy is therefore reflected in the flexed budget and an increase in the expected operating profit. The actuals have fallen short of this increased expected flexed profit by M$26,925. Indeed even against the original budget there is a shortfall, although as already mentioned this is comparing expected profit at an 80% occupancy with actual profit at occupancy at 86%. The reason that the variance is worse is a function of the movement in occupancy.

However, it is not all bad news. Looking at the detailed variances against the flexed budget we can see that for both variable costs and fixed costs there are favourable variances, indicating that there has indeed been better cost control.

Query 3

The room revenue variance against the flexed budget is M$26,550 adverse. The adverse room revenue variance is likely the result of attempting to price match the room rate offered by The Eagle Group. Given that we sold a higher number of rooms than we had budgeted to sell and still fell M$26,550 short of flexed budget for room revenue then it is fair to say that the attempt to price-match The Eagle Group has severely impacted our performance during October. Whether the shortfall in room revenue is entirely due to our attempt to match the Eagle Group cannot be confirmed without further investigation. A further issue may be the basis on which the original budget has been split exactly into 1/12th of the budget for the year. It could be that October is a slack month and that lower room rates apply than for the rest of the year.

Query 4

You are correct in that the number of complaints is not measured in terms of M$. The nature of complaints from guests will vary but they invariably relate to "service". The favourable cost variances are partly attributable to the fact that, wherever possible we have reorganised our staffing schedules. It is possible that the use of less experienced staff has precipitated an increase in the number of complaints from guests. The effect of this is also then seen in the adverse variance for food and beverage revenue. It would appear that guests have spent less that we budgeted in the bar and restaurant, perhaps as a result of poor service, although this will have resulted in fewer food and beverage variable costs potentially.

Accounting for the Acquisition of Westport Hotels

Difference in Business Acquisition

When we have acquired hotels in the past we have always acquired the assets and liabilities of that hotel business: we did not buy the equity shares of the company in which that hotel was included. As a result we included these assets and liabilities in our statement of financial position and recorded any difference between the carrying value of these assets and liabilities at the date of purchase and the price we paid for them as goodwill.

This time we have brought the equity shares of the company, which means that we have brought an investment in another company, rather than just its assets and liabilities. This means that we are now a group with a 100% owned subsidiary and have to prepare consolidated financial statements.

Wise Choice Hotel's Individual Financial Statements

Our investment in Westport Hotels will impact our individual financial statements for the year ended 31 December 2016 as follows:

- In the statement of financial position there will be a line called "Investments" within non-current assets. This will initially be recognised at the price that we paid for the equity shares in Westport Hotels.
- The only other affect will be in the statement of profit or loss if the subsidiary pays us a dividend, in which case it would be recorded as other income.

Wise Choice Hotel's Consolidated Financial Statements

Our investment in Westport Hotels will impact our consolidated financial statements for the year ended 31 December 2016 as follows:

- In the statement of financial position we will add together the assets and liabilities of both companies and record these for the group.
- In the statement of profit or loss we will include all of Wise Choice Hotel's income and expenses and 3/12ths of Westport Hotel's income and expenses. We pro-rata the subsidiary's results because it has only been part of the group since 1 October 2016.
- In the statement of financial position we will include a figure for goodwill within non-current assets. This will be calculated as the difference between the price we paid for the equity shares and the fair value of the net assets that we have acquired.
- If there is any form of inter-company trade or maybe loans or management charges given by Wise Choice Hotels to Westport Hotels, these will need to eliminated on consolidation.

Thanks.

Management Accountant Assistant

Wise Choice Hotel

Section 4

Influences on Price Setting

The pricing of the rooms may be determined by reference to the following factors.

Cost

We must understand our own cost structure in order to ensure that all costs are covered in order to make a profit. However, cost alone cannot be the foundation of our pricing structure. We need to charge a price that covers the costs of providing our hotel services. Costs take two forms, fixed and variable costs. Fixed costs are costs that remain the same irrespective of level of occupancy within our hotels, such as insurance, property costs, and a significant portion of staff costs. Variable costs are costs that change with the level of occupancy, such as laundry costs. It is vital that we have a precise understanding of the nature of our cost base as a starting point in determining our pricing policy.

Competition

There is more to look at than simply what rate our competitors are charging. We should give consideration to the outside influences that would affect our market conditions, such as booking lead-time and nearby attractions. Our competitors might well have multiple room-rates and so it is important that we look at the various rate structures, such as refundable vs. non-refundable and rates for the different room types and different amenities. Basically, we have to be certain that we are comparing like with like when adjusting room-rates based on competitors' strategies. We also need to consider the impact on the average daily rate as a consequence of changing the mix of bookings.

Some value items to explore when comparing with our competitors are: early check-in or late check-out, free Wi-Fi, gym, guestroom amenities and refundable vs. non-refundable rooms.

We need to give consideration as to how we would respond if competitors change their prices. Would we be willing to offer prices that are above a competitor on one day and significantly below on another day?

Customers

We should aim to develop a brand with elements that meet the needs of a variety of customer segments. Wherever possible, we should aim to deliver a significantly different value proposition to our customers and not simply look to improve marginally on what currently is on offer. We can influence our customers' perception of value by modifying the room-rate. Also we need to ensure that we do not charge too low a price in certain markets as customers might doubt the quality of our product. In this regard it is vital that our prices match the "value to the customer" of our product.

Corporate Objectives

Good pricing strategies not only drive revenue in the short term, but also ensure that brand value is maintained and/or enhanced in the long term thereby assisting in building sustainable revenue streams. Our pricing strategy view should be aligned with and support our overall brand strategy. We must be clear as to how we want to be positioned in the market place, how our brand drives "value" for our customers which makes pricing a key component of our brand strategy.

ZBB

Whether is ZBB Appropriate

Given that this is the first time that we will be involved in budget setting for the Westport hotels it is the ideal opportunity to take a different approach to what we've always done at Wise Choice. ZBB will allow us to look at the operations of the hotel in detail to determine the best way to achieve our hotel service objectives. It is a method that could be rolled out to our other hotels as well.

We are seeking to reduce costs and thereby increase profits and ZBB is particularly useful when making decisions regarding reorganisation aimed at improving efficiency and reducing costs as it enables the identification and removal of non-value-added operations.

The use of ZBB is appropriate for our hotel business because variable costs comprise a large proportion of our cost base. Alternative levels of provision for each activity we undertake such as cleaning and maintenance are possible and costs and benefits attaching to each level are separately identifiable.

ZBB would focus the attention of our Hotel Managers and staff on the need to avoid unnecessary expenditure. It would also ensure that changes in our business environment are responded to and questions our current cost base.

It should be noted however that ZBB is potentially costly in terms of using management time; although this can be mitigated by have an staged implementation, hotel by hotel or even one area of operation (such as bar and restaurant) at a time.

Before making a commitment to ZBB, other forms of budgeting such as ABB should be given consideration. ABB has many of the same advantages as ZBB and could be linked into a change to the costing system as well, which ultimately could benefit the business.

Advantages of Increased Participation in Budget Setting

Motivation levels may be improved as managers would set targets that were consistent with their future objectives and those of the business as opposed to targets forced onto them by the directors. The additional work required in ZBB ensures that employees benefit by re-thinking an activity from its starting point and creating efficiencies and costs savings as a result. The fact that staff are involved means as well that the budget is likely to be more realistic and focused on the objectives of that operation.

As ZBB aims to eliminate slack, staff raise the expectations of their own achievement and enhance their motivation via increased job satisfaction.

The advantages of encouraging employee participation in budgeting lies in the fact that employees who are familiar with specific operations will provide information for the budget and knowledge spread among several tiers of management could be collated.

试卷一　参考答案

任务一

发件人：管理会计助理

收件人：总经理 John Hayes

主题：关于审计报告和相关成本的计算

审计报告

韦斯特波特酒店集团非标准审计报告的严重性

韦斯特波特酒店集团的非标准审计报告意味着审计师在开展工作时发现该集团的财务报表中存在实质性错报，因此签发了保留意见。

这意味着审计师对财务报表中一个或多个方面的会计处理表示不赞同，而这些方面在利润和股东权益领域对这些报表产生了实质性影响。因此，他们的结论是“除了”这项实质性错报之外，韦斯特波特酒店集团的财务报表为公允表述。

任何非标准审计报告都可能十分严重，这个案例表明韦斯特波特酒店集团在房产结余方面并未适当运用国际财务报告准则。

但是，在此类情况下，包含“除了”的保留意见并不是最严重的审计修改类型。如果审计师认为此项错报的影响是普遍的，那么财务报表的使用者就无法理解或依赖这些财务报表，他们就会给出否定意见。否定意见意味着在审计师看来，这些财务报表并非公允表述。

为什么截至 2014 年 12 月 31 日的年度审计报告为保留意见

审计师之所以修改其审计报告，其原因在“保留意见的基础”段落中加以强调。

韦斯特波特酒店集团在该年度中针对房产结余调整了会计政策。这一举措本身在国际会计准则第 16 号不动产、厂房和设备中是允许的，但似乎重新估值所产生的收益并未得到正确处理。

如果一项资产首次被重新估值，估值上调盈余（本案例中的情况）应在资产负债表内记录在重估值准备金中，它不应该作为已实现收益处理（意味着已经记录在损益中）。但是，它应该在其他综合损益表中显示为其他综合收入的一部分。

此外，根据国际会计准则第 16 号，除土地外，所有资产应每年折旧。资产已被重新估值的这一事实并不会影响这项会计规则。因此，韦斯特波特酒店集团的董事并未记录房产的折旧，这是不正确的。M$ 128 000 的折旧费用原本应该减少当年的利润和股东权益。

对我方收购韦斯特波特酒店集团的决策所产生的影响

值得指出的是，截至 2015 年 12 月 31 日的年度审计报告未经修改。这意味着审计师认为该年度的财务报表为公允表述，并且与所有国际财务报告准则基本一致。

因此，董事很可能为了符合国际财务报告准则而变更会计处理。需要了解的是为什么韦斯特波特酒店集团的董事没有在2014 年调整财务报表，但非标准审计报告不应阻止我们收购该企业。

相关成本

在四号酒店入住一晚的相关成本

"相关成本"是因为所考虑决策的直接后果而产生的未来现金。在这个案例中，相关成本是因为我们的一间客房有人入住而不是当晚无人入住而改变的成本。

入住一晚的相关成本示例包括以下内容。

- 当晚为酒店客房供电将产生的电费成本。这将包括照明以及电水壶和电视机等电气设备所使用的电力。
- 为客人提供热水而产生的能源成本。尽管可能始终存在充足的热水，因此将不存在增量成本。
- 客人退房后洗涤床上用品和毛巾的成本。
- 客人使用的免费洗漱用品和点心的成本。这项成本很可能会随着客人的变化而变化，因为并非所有客人都会使用所有免费商品，因此可能难以量化。
- 早晨为客人供应早餐的成本（假设客人享用早餐）。
- 清洁客房所产生的额外成本，比如为客房清洁人员支付的额外工作时间的费用以及所使用的清洁产品的费用。

采用这项政策的适宜性

风险在于，客人如果知道这项政策，会设法等到最后一分钟再预订酒店，以便能够支付更低的客房单价。但是，这项风险可能极低，因为绝大多数客人都希望其酒店被"确定"预订了，因此不希望等到最后一分钟再预订，因为可能到时已经没有空房。

这项政策本身很可能仅适用于无论出于何种原因都会在最后一分钟搜索酒店的

潜在客人。如果这项政策仅适用于夜晚的某个截止时间点（如晚上 9 点），将尤其符合。

最终，只要价格能够抵销相关成本，我们就值得接受此类客人，因为假设他们只准备支付较低的价格（可能实际上可以收取较高的价格，尤其是在竞争酒店均已客满的情况下）。这给疲惫的旅行者带来的善意有助于吸引他们在未来预订，并提高客人忠诚度。另一个好处是客人使用餐厅和酒吧设施或其他不包含在房间价格中的设施所创造的额外收入。

感谢！

智选酒店
管理会计助理

任务二

入职培训项目

为酒店员工提供正式入职培训项目的组成部分

针对酒店员工的正式入职培训项目应包括以下内容。

- 同组同事、其他同事及其基层经理的欢迎和介绍。我们的运营总监 Molly Patel 可提供此类欢迎和介绍。
- 解释工作性质。如果每种职位类型都存在明确的职位描述、概括职责、工作时间、首要任务、绩效衡量或关键绩效指标（KPI）及其角色如何融入企业的整体概况，将会令此类解释更加简便。
- 说明安全规则和程序。应传达并阐明有关着装、员工行为、考勤、休息、工作餐、安保、食品安全与健康，以及安全等方面的基本标准。
- 解释雇佣条款与条件。我们可分发一份小册子，其中详细介绍各种重要事项，比如最低 30 小时合同、缺勤和加班授权、休假、试用期、纪律和申诉程序，以及互联网和电子邮件政策的详细信息。
- 解释酒店的文化和价值观。应明确表明酒店集团更广泛的使命，这一点在我们这样的服务企业中尤为重要。因为在提供优质服务时，员工态度和激励至关重要。我们应详细规定欢迎和问候客人的流程，如果职责中包括预订流程，则预订流程也应该包含在内。不与客人直接接触的员工也需要了解问候客人或应对客人提问的规程。

- 介绍企业内部的持续培训、辅导和指导制度。这是“期望值管理”的关键要素之一，因为我们期望许多员工接受大量培训。与出勤以及酒店和餐饮管理专业学院获取资质等方面有关的规则必须明确解释。

入职培训项目为酒店员工带来的好处

入职培训流程将让新员工熟悉所在酒店的老员工和业务流程。这将让他们迅速变得富有成效。

入职培训还有助于新员工对我们的企业及其目标留下专业印象，这将激励我们的新员工朝着这些目标努力，并超越这些目标。

入职培训项目可协助相应的酒店经理向所有新员工传达一致的信息，还可以让新员工对酒店建立归属感，感受到自身是深受重视的员工团队的一分子。

我们是一家服务企业，因此客人满意度极为重要。让员工充满动力，时刻准备为客人提供优质的服务能够提升客人的体验。

质量成本

对智选酒店内的运营监督采用“质量成本”模式所带来的效益可以视为源于对符合性成本的投资，即预防成本和评估成本，从而避免（内部和外部的）损失成本。

第一，效益来自产生预防成本，在潜在问题发生之前加以辨别。应鼓励直接参与提供餐饮服务客户体验的员工在问题发生之前及早辨别。

酒吧和餐厅主管以及主厨可运用模拟和角色扮演等方式，协助员工以更加积极主动的方式发现各类餐饮失误问题，同时配合有效的补救策略。

我们应成立质量规划团队，制订行动计划，确保不会发生失误。应对所有员工组织培训，提高智选酒店内部的整体客人体验。

第二，产生评估成本也可能会实现效益。应开展评估活动，确保食品和服务符合相应的质量水平，能够满足客人的要求。

辨别服务失误也能带来效益，从而让我们的餐厅能够评估食品和服务的总体质量。应鼓励酒店员工通过自我检验来确保餐食的烹制准确，从而符合客人的要求。

员工也可采用“连续检查”流程，让服务交付链中的下一位员工验证上一位员工的工作质量和准确性，从而确保客户满意度。员工应该对所有食品进行检验，以便发现潜在缺陷，并且在缺陷成为食品和服务失误之前加以解决。

为餐厅内的所有员工赋能，将有助于减少损失成本。培训厨房员工正确使用设备，在把餐食送往客户前减少浪费。

我们应该对与消费者直接接触的所有服务人员加以赋能，鼓励他们履行职责，因为他们往往会试图实现或超越自身的职责。这样做对餐厅的好处是服务质量将得到改善，同时提高生产效率，或许可以减少所需的服务人员数量。随着服务人员能够在失误发生之前更加敏锐地辨别潜在失误点，客户满意度也将相应提高。

一旦发生外部服务失误，员工的基本补救措施是对顾客投诉立即采取行动。我们的餐厅应追求立即服务补救的目标，如果能够实现这个目标，将降低保留客户的总体费用。这样，我们的餐厅也就更有可能迎接回头客，客户也将更加倾向于将我们的餐厅推荐给他们的朋友，为我们带来免费宣传和推广的效益。

任务三

发件人：管理会计助理

收件人：总经理 John Hayes

主题：差异报告和合并财务报表

有关差异报告的询问

询问 1

预算列基于 80% 的入住率。名为“弹性预算”的一列显示了 10 月实际入住率水平的预算，由于弹性客房收入高于预算列，因此肯定高于 80% 。事实上，入住率为 86% 。弹性预算让我们能够了解计划水平如果达到实际入住率，而不是预算入住率，将会产生怎样的结果。这样能够在实际收入、预算收入及成本之间进行更有意义的比较，因为这是在进行同类对比。因此，这将更加公允地反映当月的业绩。

询问 2

在实际和预算列之间进行比较，这种做法略微具有误导性，因为正如上文所解释的，这样做并不是同类对比。当入住率为 86% 时，预期客房收入以及酒吧和餐厅收入都将高于原始预算，尽管预期变动成本也将更高（而固定成本不变）。因此，入住率提高的影响反映在弹性预算中，同时还有预期经营利润的上升。而实际数据比上升后的预期弹性利润低 M$ 26 925。事实上，即使对比原始预算也存在差额，尽管如上所述，这意味着对 80% 入住率下的预期利润和 86% 入住率下的实际利润进行比较。差异较大的原因在于入住率的变动。

但是，这种做法并非一无是处。如果分析相对弹性预算的详细差异，可以发现变动成本和固定成本都存在有利的差异，这表明确实有更加有效的成本控制。

询问3

相对弹性预算的客房收入差异为 – M$ 26 550。客房收入的负差异很可能是因为试图将价格匹配老鹰集团所提供的客房价格。由于我们的客房销售数量高于销售预算，而相对客房收入的弹性预算仍存在 M$ 26 550 的缺口，因此可以认为，与老鹰集团进行价格匹配的尝试对企业的 10 月业绩造成了严重影响。客房收入的不足是否完全源于我们试图与老鹰集团进行价格匹配，在没有进行进一步调查之前很难确定。另一个问题可能是原始预算精确划分为当年预算的 1/12。有可能 10 月属于淡季，酒店所采用的客房价格低于全年的其他月份。

询问4

你说的没错，投诉数量并非以 M$ 为单位加以衡量。客人投诉的原因各不相同，但总是与“服务”有关。正的成本差异部分可归因于我们已尽可能重新调整了人员配备日程。有可能采用经验较不丰富的员工，导致客人投诉数量增加。此后，企业影响也导致餐饮收入的负差异。似乎客人在酒吧和餐厅的消费金额低于我们的预算，或许是由于服务质量低下，虽然后者也有可能会降低餐饮变动成本。

收购韦斯特波特酒店集团的会计核算

企业收购差异

以往在收购酒店时，我们始终收购酒店企业的资产和负债：我们并没有收购酒店所属企业的股票。因此，我们将这些资产和负债纳入财务状况表内，并记录收购之日这些资产和负债的账面价值，以及我们作为商誉为这些资产和负债所支付价格之间的差异。

这一次，我们收购了这家公司的股票，这意味着我们收购了对另一家企业的投资，而不仅仅是资产和负债。这表明我们目前是拥有 100% 独资子公司的企业集团，必须编制合并财务报表。

智选酒店的独立财务报表

我们对韦斯特波特酒店集团的投资将对自身截至 2016 年 12 月 31 日的年度独立财务报表产生以下影响。

- 在资产负债表的非流动资产中，将有“投资”一行。期初将确认我们为韦斯特波特酒店集团的股票而支付的价格。

■ 如果子公司向我们支付股息，那么唯一的其他影响将存在于损益表中，这应该被记录为其他收入。

智选酒店的合并财务报表

我们对韦斯特波特酒店集团的投资将对我们截至2016年12月31日的年度合并财务报表产生以下影响。

■ 在资产负债表中，我们将累加两家企业的资产和负债，并记录为集团资产和负债。
■ 在损益表中，我们将包含智选酒店的所有收入和费用以及韦斯特波特酒店集团3/12的收入和费用。我们按比例计算子公司的结果，因为该公司从2016年10月1日起加入集团。
■ 在资产负债表中，我们将在非流动资产中包含商誉数据。商誉将计算为我们为股票支付的价格和我们所收购的净资产公允价值之间的差异。
■ 如果存在任何企业间交易或是智选酒店向韦斯特波特酒店集团提供的贷款或管理费，则需要在合并中扣除。

感谢！

智选酒店

管理会计助理

任务四

对定价的影响

可通过考虑以下因素来确定客房定价。

成本

我们必须了解自身的成本结构，以便确保抵销所有成本，产生利润。但是，成本单独无法作为定价结构的基础。我们需要收取的价格应抵销提供酒店服务的成本。成本采用两种形式，即固定成本和变动成本。无论酒店内的入住率如何，固定成本都保持不变，如保险、物业费和大部分员工成本。变动成本会随着入住率水平的变化而变化，如洗衣成本。我们应确切了解成本基础的性质，方可确定定价政策。

竞争

我们不应只聚焦于竞争对手收取的价格。还应考虑影响市场状况的外部因素，如提前确定时间和附近景点。我们的竞争对手可能采用多重客房价格，因此我们必须分析不同的价格结构，如可退款还是不可退款，以及不同客房类型和不同设施的价格，等等。基本上，在根据竞争对手的策略调整客房价格时，我们必须确定进行同类比较。我们还需要考虑变更预订组合将会对平均每日价格产生的影响。

在与竞争对手进行比较时，值得探索的部分价值因素包括：提前入住或延迟退房，免费 Wi-Fi，健身房，客房设施，以及可退款和不可退款的客房。

需要考虑的是，如果竞争对手调整价格，我们将如何做出反应。我们是否愿意在某一天提供高于竞争者的价格，而在另一天提供远低于竞争者的价格？

消费者

我们应致力于开发品牌，其中蕴含的要素能够满足不同消费者细分市场的需求。如果可能，我们应尽量努力为消费者提供与众不同的价值主张，而不仅仅是对目前提供的价值加以略微改进。我们可以通过调整客房价格，影响消费者的价值感知。此外，我们也需要确保不会在特定市场中收取过低的价格，因为消费者可能会因此质疑我们的产品质量。在这个方面，我们的价格必须匹配产品“对于消费者的价值”。

企业目标

完善的定价策略不仅能够在短期内提高营业收入，还可以确保在长期范围内保持和/或加强品牌价值，从而协助建立可持续的收入流。我们的定价策略观点应符合并支持企业的总体品牌战略。我们必须明确自身希望在市场中处于何种定位，我们的品牌如何为消费者推动“价值”，从而使定价成为品牌战略中的关键要素。

零基预算

零基预算方式是否适当

由于这是我们首次参与韦斯特波特酒店集团的预算编制，因此这是相对智选酒店传统实践采用不同模式的理想机会。零基预算能够让我们详细分析酒店运营，从而确定实现酒店服务目标的最佳途径。这种方法也可在集团旗下的其他酒店中加以开展。

我们旨在降低成本，提高利润。而在降低成本和提高效率的重组决策中，零基预算尤为有效，因为它有助于辨别和排除非增值运营。

我们的酒店业务适合采用零基预算，因为变动成本在我们的成本基础上占据较大部分，如清洁和维护等。我们开展的每项活动都可以存在不同的供应水平，与每种水平相对应的效益可分别辨别。

零基预算将让酒店经理和员工的注意力集中在避免不必要的开支上，还可以确保商业环境的变化得到及时响应，并对当前成本基础提出问题。

但是也应指出，零基预算将占用管理层时间，因此可能造成较高的成本。然而分阶段实施可减轻这个问题，如逐家酒店实施，或每次只针对一个运营领域（如酒吧和餐厅）实施。

在实施零基预算之前，作业预算等其他预算编制形式也应予以考虑。作业预算具备与零基预算相同的许多优点，并且也可关联成本核算系统的变化，最终将对企业带来效益。

在预算编制中提高参与度的优势

可能会提高激励水平，因为管理者所制定的预算将与自身和企业的未来目标保持一致，而不是由企业董事强加给他们的指标。零基预算所需的额外工作确保员工从零开始重新思考某项作业，因而创造效率和成本节约，产生效益。员工参与也意味着预算很可能更具现实意义，聚焦于具体运营的目标。

由于零基预算旨在消除松懈，员工将提高对自身成就的期望值，并通过职业满意度的提升产生激励。

鼓励员工参与预算编制的优势在于，熟悉具体运营的员工将为预算提供信息，可以在多个管理级别中传播知识。

Variant 1 Marking Guidance

Section	Technical skills		Business skills		People skills		Leadership skills		Integration	Total
1	Relevant costing principles Audit reports and accounting issue	12 10	Audit reports and accounting issue	3						25
2	Cost of quality	9			Induction programme	13			3	25
3	Variance reporting and budgeting Accounting for an acquisition	6 13					Variance reporting and budgeting	6		25
4	Zero-based budgeting	12	Pricing policy	13						25
Total marks available for each competency		62		16		13		6	3	100

试卷一　评分指南

部分	技术技能		商业技能		人际技能		领导技能		综合	总计
1	相关成本计算原则 审计报告和会计问题	12 10	审计报告和会计问题	3						25
2	质量成本	9			入职计划	13			3	25
3	差异报告分析和编制预算 收购的会计核算	6 13					差异报告分析和编制预算	6		25
4	零基预算	12	定价政策	13						25
各种能力分数总计		62		16		13		6	3	100

上海立信会计金融学院名师解惑

试卷一共有四项任务，考察了 P1、F1、E1 三门课程的知识点，具体包括短期决策分析、营运资金管理、本量利分析、现金管理、质量成本和供应商关系管理等。该试卷考核了考生的四项能力，其中技术技能的分值占 62%，商业技能的分值占 16%，人际技能的分值占 13%，领导技能的分值占 6%，与 CGMA 管理会计能力框架的技能要求一致。

该试卷的每项任务涉及以下知识点：

任务	问题	科目	知识点
任务一	审计报告中出具保留意见的原因	F1	国际会计准则第 16 号不动产、厂房和设备（IAS 16 PPE）
	在四号酒店一晚的相关成本	P1	相关成本（relevant cost）
任务二	新员工入职引导应包含哪些项目，以及项目给酒店带来的益处	E1	设计和实施新员工入职引导项目（the design and implementation of induction programmes）
	智选酒店采用质量成本报告来监管运营的益处	P1	质量成本报告（cost of quality reporting）
任务三	弹性预算的定义和偏差分析，以及差异报告分析	P1	弹性预算（flexible budget）
	收购对酒店的独立财务报表和合并财务报表的影响	F1	编制合并财务报表（consolidated statement of financial position and consolidated statement of comprehensive income）
任务四	影响不同房型价格的因素	P1	定价决策影响因素（issues arise in pricing decision）
	零基预算对于酒店的适合性	P1	增量预算（incremental budgeting）和零基预算（ZBB）

上述各项任务要求以邮件、报告或工作笔记等形式来呈现答案，对问题的描述非常明确，答题时既要注意内容的针对性，也要注意形式的规范性。

对应知识点深度剖析

国际会计准则第16号不动产、厂房和设备

国际会计准则16号不动产、厂房和设备中允许企业使用成本模型或重新估值模型对不动产、厂房和设备等资产进行计量。当不动产、厂房和设备被初始确认为一项资产以后，使用成本模型时，它们应按其成本减去累计折旧和累计减值后的金额入账；使用重新估值模型时，资产的账面金额等于公允价值减去累计折旧和累计减值后的金额。

此外，根据国际会计准则第16号，除土地外，所有资产应每年折旧。资产已重新估值的这一事实并不会影响这项会计规则。因此，韦斯特波特酒店的董事并未记录房产的折旧，这是不正确的。

考生注意事项

（1）重新估值模型下估值上调的处理方式：

估值上调时，盈余应在资产负债表内增加重新估值准备金，而不应作为已实现收益来处理。同时，应在其他综合损益表中显示为其他综合收入的一部分。

（2）重新估值模型下估值下调的处理方式：

估值下调时，如果降低额未超过同一资产所保持的重新估值准备金，该降低额应直接从重新估值准备金中扣除。如果超出了重新估值准备金的总额，超出的部分应做估值损失处理，记入当期的利润表。

（3）重新估值后资产的折旧：

这种变化应作为会计估计的变化予以核算，并且对当期和以后期间的折旧费加以调整。

相关成本

“相关成本”指的是受企业经营决策的直接影响，而产生的未来现金。一般而言，相关成本是预计的未来成本。决策是面向未来的，与之相关的成本也只能是未来要发生的成本。决策不能改变已经发生的历史成本，因而过去发生的历史成本与现在要做的决策毫无关系。在这个案例中，相关成本是因为我们的一间客房有人入住而额外增加的成本。

新员工入职引导项目

入职培训项目的目的是为了有效地让新员工融入企业中，为员工和公司带来最大的利益。一般而言，新员工入职引导项目包括以下一些项目：

（1）同组同事、其他同事及其基层经理的欢迎和介绍。

（2）明确各个职位说明安全规则和程序的职责、性质和考核标准等信息。

（3）说明安全规则和工作流程。

（4）解释雇佣条款与条件。

（5）解释酒店的文化和价值观。

（6）介绍企业内部的持续培训、辅导和指导制度，让员工明确今后的职业发展路径。

考生注意事项

入职培训项的益处：

（1）熟悉所在酒店的老员工和业务流程，让他们迅速提高工作效率。

（2）有助于新员工了解企业及其目标和目的，激励新员工朝着这些目标努力。

（3）协助管理者向新员工传达连贯一致的信息，增强员工的责任心。

（4）培养新员工对公司的归属感，降低员工的流失率。

采用“质量成本”模式所带来的效益

对智选酒店内的运营监督采用“质量成本”模式所带来的效益可以视为源于对符合成本的投资，即提高预防成本和鉴定成本的投入，这样就可以降低（内部和外部的）损失成本。

增加预防成本，在潜在问题发生之前加以预防。应鼓励为消费者直接提供服务的员工在问题发生之前及早发现问题。酒吧和餐厅主管以及主厨可运用模拟和角色扮演等方式，协助员工以更加积极主动的方式发现各类餐饮失误问题。

弹性预算

使用实际发生的成本和预算直接进行比较，这种做法具有误导性，因为这样做并不是同类对比。一般而言，更高的产出必然会带来更高的成本。弹性预算相对于固定预算来说，它是指以预算期间可能发生的多种业务量水平为基础，分别确定与之相应的费用数额而编制的能适应多种业务量水平的费用预算。

案例中使用弹性预算可以让我们了解如果达到实际入住率，将会产生怎样的结果。这样能够在实际和预算收入及成本之间进行更有意义的比较，也将更加公允地反映当月的业绩。

考生注意事项

准备弹性成本预算时，各项成本必须基于实际的业务量进行计算。

合并财务报表

当母公司获得对子公司的控制权时，就必须要编制合并财务报表。控制权指的是投资企业有控制被投资企业的财务和经营政策的权力。一般而言，投资方直接拥有被投资单位50%以上的表决权视为拥有对被投资单位的控制权。

考生应该注意的是母公司和子公司的交易，在母公司的独立报表和合并报表中处理的方式是截然不同的。比如子公司向母公司支付股息，在母公司的独立利润表中应记录为“其他收入”，但是在合并报表中必须要剔除这部分收入。同样，如果存在任何集团内的交易或贷款及管理费等，都需要在合并报表中扣除。

考生注意事项

合并报表编制的关键点：

（1）编制合并报表时应该遵循统一的会计政策。

（2）合并资产负债表中累加两家企业的资产和负债，并记录为集团资产和负债。

（3）合并资产负债表中非流动资产部分应该包含商誉。商誉计算为母公司支付的价格和所收购的净资产公允价值之间的差异。

（4）母公司对子公司的“投资”与子公司的净资产（权益）在合并报表中相互抵销。

（5）集团股本和股本溢价只包含母公司的股本和股本溢价。

（6）子公司的净资产在并购发生时应该进行公允价值的调整。

（7）集团内部交易产生的利润（亏损）在合并报表时应该剔除。

（8）任何集团内的交易或贷款及管理费等，都需要在合并报表中扣除。

定价决策影响因素

企业制定价格时需要考虑的一个重要因素是成本，我们必须了解自身的成本结构，以便确保收回所有成本并产生利润。但是，仅仅考虑成本无法作为定价的全部依据。我们还需要考虑成本的不同类型，即固定成本和变动成本，以便制定更灵活的定价策略。

另外一个需要考虑的因素是竞争，但是我们不应只聚焦于竞争对手的价格。还应考虑影响市场状况的外部因素，如提前确定时间和附近景点。在应对竞争对手的价格调整时还需要考虑：提前入住或延迟退房，免费 Wi-Fi，健身房，客房设施，以及可退款和不可退款的客房，等等。

同时，我们在制定价格时还应该考虑品牌的开发问题，尽量能够满足不同消费者细分市场的需求，为消费者提供与众不同的价值主张。最后，我们的定价策略应符合并支持企业的总体品牌战略。明确自身在市场中的定位，思考我们的品牌如何为消费者推动“价值”。

增量预算和零基预算

我们在案例中发现，韦斯特波特酒店和智选酒店一样都在使用增量预算，这种方法以过往期间的预算或实际业绩为基础来编制，并在此基础上增加额外的收支以及诸如通货膨胀等外部因素的调整。

与增量预算不同，零基预算在准备过程中不依赖往年的财务数据，它抛开了已有的假设，从零开始准备将来的预算。目前，韦斯特波特酒店连锁酒店 B 和 C 在成本控制上都出现了不利差异。使用零基预算能够从细节上摸清目前运营中存在的问题，从根本上找到解决方案，帮助企业在竞争中占据优势。

考生注意事项

增量预算的优点：

（1）预算编制工作量较少且比较稳定，不同期间的预算变化较小。

（2）可以避免生产经营业务和日常管理工作产生剧烈的波动。

（3）系统相对容易操作和理解，协调预算容易实现，它比较适合内外部环境比较稳定的企业或部门。

增量预算的缺点：

（1）首先它假设经营活动以及工作方式都以相同的方式继续下去。

（2）难以找到已有工作流程中的无效或者较少增加价值的活动。

（3）缺乏对目前业绩表现的挑战，无法给员工带来降低成本的动力。

（4）同时它还间接地鼓励基层管理者将预算全部用光，以便明年可以保持相同的预算。

零基预算的适应性和优点：

（1）适合像韦斯特波特酒店这样处于并购或重组中的企业，它更容易帮助企业找到并削除流程中未增加价值的部分。

考生注意事项

（2）重新审视目前费用支出的必要性，并关注外部环境的变化对已有费用支出情况可能带来的影响。

（3）促使员工重新思考其工作的有效性，找到节约成本的新方法。

零基预算的缺点：

（1）在准备过程中，更加费时费力。在实际操作中，我们可以选择逐步进行的方法。

（2）熟悉工作流程和企业运营现状的员工参与度决定了此方法是否能够成功。

Variant 2

This examination is structured as follows：

Section number	Number of tasks	Time for section(minutes)
1	1	45
2	1	45
3	2	45
4	1	45

The time available for each section is for reading,planning and writing your answer(s).

Please note section 3 consists of two tasks and answer screens. Please leave enough time to complete both parts.

Section 1

The directors recently discussed the need for the business to improve the performance of all four hotels. It was decided that, in order to facilitate this, investment in a new, integrated, IT system should be considered. In addition, the directors decided to focus on ways of improving the profit generated from each guest.

You arrive at work to find the following email from Rav Patel, finance director:

From: Rav Patel, Finance Director

To: Management Accountant Assistant

Subject: Guest profitability and a new, integrated, IT system

In light of our recent directors' meeting, I commissioned a study of guest profitability from a consultant. The consultant looked at three guests who stayed at Hotel 2 for different lengths of time. He calculated the actual average daily profit generated by each guest. He used ABC principles to determine the operating costs applicable to each guest and has suggested that we consider using it as our costing system.

I've already discussed the concept of ABC with the rest of the directors, but I now need to talk them through the consultant's findings, as well as extending the discussion about whether implementing ABC, as our costing system, would be beneficial to our business. I would appreciate your help with this.

Also, I have started to look into the benefits of investing in a new, integrated, IT system. I am compiling a report on all the various benefits and would like you to prepare a section for me on how such an investment would facilitate improvements in both the supplier and customer sides of our supply chain.

Please can you send me an email in which you:

- explain, for each activity identified in the consultant's activity table, how it will have affected the average daily profit of each guest (no need for any calculations though), together with an explanation of the advantages to us of using ABC in our hotels;
- include the draft report section I've asked for on investing in a new IT system.

Many thanks.

Rav Patel

Finance Director

Wise Choice Hotels

Report From the Consultant

Guest room revenue profitability(ignoring bar and restaurant revenue)：

	Guest A(M$)	Guest B(M$)	Guest C(M$)
Actual average profit per night using ABC	43. 60	37. 40	34. 12

- Guest A stayed 14 nights, guest B six nights and guest C one night.
- Each guest paid a room revenue rate of M$ 100 per night.
- Actual average profit was calculated as the total profit for the period of the stay divided by the number of nights of the stay. The total profit was calculated as room revenue for the stay less operating costs incurred, calculated on the basis of the activities consumed.
- Prior to the ABC approach, the budgeted profit per night is M$ 35. 31. This budgeted profit is based on bedding and towels being replaced every day on the assumption that the guest is only staying one night.

Examples of some of the activities used to calculate costs：

Example activity	Cost driver	Guest A 14 night stay	Guest B 6 night stay	Guest C 1 night stay
Check in	Number of check ins	1	1	1
Towel change	Number of towel changes	6	6	1
Complimentary item replenishment	Number of items replaced	7	20	4

Write your email to Rav Patel.

Section 2

The next day, Rav Patel calls you into this office and says：

Thank you for your email yesterday. Molly Patel, operations director, and I have been discussing the results of the consultant's work on profitability. We feel that we need a better idea of what the potential revenues for our hotels could be and want to prepare a more accurate forecast. Our budgets so far for each hotel have been based on a certain level of occupancy. I am interested to hear your view on the factors that we should consider when preparing a sales forecast for our hotels.

In terms of profitability, another problem that we discussed was the high levels of inventory in our bars and the amount of out-of-date beverages we seem to be throwing away. The Head of Bar and Restaurant at Hotel 4 tells me that he always orders beverages in bulk, to take advantage of discounts and to reduce delivery charges (the main suppliers charge a fixed rate per delivery, irrespective of its size). However, I'm convinced that this is not the correct policy, due to the amount that we have to throw away. I have read somewhere that it is possible to calculate optimum order sizes for inventory using an EOQ (economic order quantity) model, where the total costs of holding inventory and ordering inventory are minimised. I would like to know the nature of the costs associated with bar inventory and whether it would be appropriate for us to use EOQ to establish how much to order each time.

Please send me an email on both matters. Thank you.

Write the email requested by Rav Patel.

Section 3

A week later you arrive at work to find the following email from Rav Patel, finance director:

From: Rav Patel, Finance Director

To: Management Accountant Assistant

Subject: Restaurant quality and accounting for IT costs

I have just been talking to Molly Patel, operations director, about our aim to improve profitability in our bars and restaurants. Part of the issue, is that many of our guests don't use our restaurant to eat in the evening, or only use it once during their stay. It would appear from guest feedback that, perhaps, we have some quality issues in both the food and the service, particularly in Hotels 3 and 4.

Molly has prepared a list of what she believes are some of the quality related costs incurred in our restaurants. I have recently read about cost of quality reporting and I am interested in us looking into this. I would like you to have a look at the list and send me an email justifying how we could include each cost in a cost of quality report. There is no need to define each type of quality cost, as I already know this from my reading.

On a separate matter, we have engaged IT Solutions to help us regarding our new IT system. They have sent us a proposal for a complete up-grade of both our hardware and software, the costs of which are as follows:

	Cost
New computer terminals and printers (hardware), expected to last four years before they need to be replaced	M$ 84,000
Server equipment (from a supplier in Tacland, who we will need to pay in T $'s in December 2016)	T$ 58,000
Software licenses (for a three year period)	M$ 42,000
A fee to IT solutions for sourcing, installing and training of staff on the new system	M$ 45,000

I need to prepare a briefing paper for the other directors on how we will need to account for all of these costs in our financial statements for the year ended 31 December 2016 and in future years. Please prepare the first draft of this for me.

Thank you.

Rav Patel

Finance Director

Wise Choice Hotels

List of Quality Costs for the Restaurants

Costs incurred when:

- designing the meals on the restaurant menus;
- replacing meals that have been returned by guests;
- maintenance of the kitchen ovens.

- repairing kitchen equipment;
- inspecting products from suppliers;
- giving complimentary meal vouchers in respect of customer complaints.

Write the email requested by Rav Pate.

Write the briefing paper for the directors on how to account for the IT system costs.

Section 4

A few weeks later, Rav Patel, finance director sends you the following email:

From: Rav Patel, Finance Director

To: Management Accountant Assistant

Subject: Marketing campaign and investment in new IT systems

Pam Hayes, marketing director, and I have been looking at marketing campaigns to attract new customers to our hotels and their restaurants. We have come up with two mutually-exclusive campaigns: campaign A, costing M$40,000 and campaign B, costing M$70,000. Based on our experience from past campaigns, we have established the additional profit that could be generated under the following three conditions, the campaign is: not successful, reasonably successful, or very successful.

A consultancy firm, called Expert Consultants, has said that for a fee of M$25,000 it will manage our chosen campaign to improve the chance of its success. I had sent the consultants our original estimates of additional profit under each possible outcome and they sent me back a report which shows the position if we do it ourselves and the position if we engage them to manage the chosen campaign. They recommend we engage them to manage the M$70,000 campaign.

I need to prepare a briefing paper on this, for the other directors, which I would like you to draft for me. Please include an explanation of how to interpret the information contained in Expert Consultants' report, in terms of making a decision purely based on the expected value of the additional profit. Also show how we should interpret the coefficient of variation information and any other factors about basing our decision on expected value that we should consider before making a decision.

On another matter we have now agreed to accept the IT Solutions proposal for the new, integrated, IT system. Other than Pam Hayes, who knows a bit about website design, we really don't have anyone in the business with any great IT knowledge. We are going to be reliant on IT Solutions, who have told me that there are a number of alternative approaches to system changeover. I know that the other directors are interested to know what they are.

In the same briefing paper please explain the alternative system changeover methods that might be used, including commentary on the potential benefits and potential problems of each approach for our business.

Thank you!

Rav Patel
Finance Director
Wise Choice Hotels

Report from Expert Consultants

Expected value of additional profit (net of campaign costs) without Expert Consultants assistance:

	Campaign A			Campaign B		
	Probability	Additional profit/(loss) (M$ 000)	Expected value (M$ 000)	Probability	Additional profit (M$ 000)	Expected value (M$ 000)
Not successful	40%	(10)	(4)	60%	(30)	(18)
Reasonably successful	30%	20	6	20%	60	12
Very successful	30%	50	15	20%	90	18
	Expected profit		17	Expected profit		12
Coefficient of variation of campaign A		1.67	Coefficient of variation of campaign B			4.36

Expected value of additional profit (net of campaign costs but before the fee to Expert Consultants) with Expert Consultants assistance:

	Campaign A			Campaign B		
	Probability	Additional profit/(loss) (M$ 000)	Expected value (M$ 000)	Probability	Additional profit (M$ 000)	Expected value (M$ 000)
Not successful	10%	0	0	30%	(10)	(3)
Reasonably successful	40%	40	16	40%	80	32
Very successful	50%	70	35	30%	100	30
	Expected profit before fee		51	Expected profit before fee		59
	Fee		(25)	Fee		(25)
	Expected profit		26	Expected profit		34
Coefficient of variation of campaign A before fee		0.43	Coefficient of variation of campaign B before fee		0.78	

Value of Expert Consultants assistance:

The value of having Expert Consultants assistance is therefore M$ 17,000 (M$ 34,000 – M$ 17,000).

Write the briefing paper for the directors on Expert Consultants summary report and IT systems changeover.

试卷二

本次考试的结构如下：

序号	任务数	时间（分钟）
1	1	45
2	1	45
3	2	45
4	1	45

每个部分规定的时间可用于读题、组织和书写答案。

请注意任务三包括两项子任务，需留足时间。

任务一

各位经理最近在讨论如何提高 4 家酒店的业绩。他们最终决定，为了达成该目标，他们应考虑投资新的一体化 IT（信息技术）系统。另外，他们决定将重点放在如何从每位顾客中获取更多的利润。

你到达办公室后发现了来自财务经理 Rav Patel 的邮件：

发件人：财务总监 Rav Patel

收件人：管理会计助理

主题：顾客的盈利性和新一体化 IT 系统

根据我们最近的董事会会议决议，我委托了一位顾问调查顾客的可赢利空间。该顾问调查了 3 位住在二号酒店的顾客，他们居住的时间长短不一。他计算了每位顾客产生的实际平均日利润，并利用作业成本法来确定每位顾客的经营成本，并建议我们考虑使用它作为我们的成本核算方法。

我已经与其他董事讨论了作业成本法的概念，但我现在需要通过顾问的一些发现来讨论这些问题，并进一步讨论是否将作业成本法作为我们的成本核算方法，这将有益于我们的业务发展。我非常感谢你的帮助。

另外，我也开始调查投资新的一体化 IT 系统的好处并正在编写一份报告，希望你为我准备一个章节，说明这种投资将如何促进我们供应链的供应商和客户方双方的改进。

请发一封邮件给我，并包含以下内容：

- 解释顾问的活动表中的每个活动是如何影响每位顾客的平均日利润（不需要有计算），以及解释在我们的酒店中采用作业成本法的优势。
- 包括我所要求的投资新 IT 系统的草案报告部分。

非常感谢！

智选酒店

财务总监

Rav Patel

咨询报告

客房的盈利能力（不包括酒吧和餐馆的收入）：

	顾客 A（M$）	顾客 B（M$）	顾客 C（M$）
作业成本法下每晚的实际平均利润	43.60	37.40	34.12

- 顾客 A 住了 14 晚，顾客 B 住了 6 晚，顾客 C 住了 1 晚。
- 每个顾客每晚支付的房费都是 M$ 100/间。
- 实际平均利润计算为逗留期间的总利润除以住宿天数。总利润的预算是基于总利润计算为房间收入减去运营费用。
- 使用作业成本法之前，预算中每间房每晚的成本是 M$ 64.69，每晚房费是 M$ 100，净利润是 M$ 35.31。这个预算收入情况假设每个房客只住 1 晚，每天都需更换床具和毛巾。

运营费用：

活动项目	花费项目	顾客 A	顾客 B	顾客 C
		住 14 晚	住 6 晚	住 1 晚
登记	登记次数	1	1	1
更换毛巾	换毛巾数量	6	6	1
赠品的更新更换	赠品更新的数量	7	20	4

请根据财务总监 Rav Patel 的要求回复邮件。

任务二

第二天，Rav Patel 打电话到你的办公室并说：

感谢你昨日的来信。根据我同运营总监 Molly Patel 就顾问提出的盈利事项进行的讨论，我们一致认为还有收益更高的酒店运营方案。我们希望在接下来看到更精准的预测报告。鉴于公司对每家酒店的预算有限，我希望在接下来的报告里能看到你关于影响酒店销售额的几个要点的预测和分析。

我们还谈到了影响盈利的另一个方面，即存在酒吧库存过剩和大量过期、面临处理的饮料的问题。四号酒店的酒吧和餐厅主管告诉我，为了争取折扣和降低运费（其中的主要供应商按次收取运费而不论体积），他总是整件进货。基于目前需要扔掉的饮料数量，我并不赞同这种做法。我了解到如果运用经济订货批量（EOQ）的办法，我们可以计算出使库存利用最大化的订量。这样还能把维持库存和订货的成本降至最低。我想了解维持酒吧库存的成本，经济订货批量是否适合我们公司，以及如何据此决定每次订量。

请发邮件告诉我你关于这两个问题的想法。谢谢。

请根据财务总监 Rav Patel 的要求回复邮件。

任务三

一周后，你回到办公室，发现一封来自财务总监 Rav Patel 的信：

发件人：财务总监 Rav Patel
收件人：管理会计助理
主题：餐厅质量和 IT 支出账目

目前，我和运营总监 Molly Patel 谈到的关于如何提高酒吧和餐厅的盈利性。我认为，一部分问题在于许多客人并不选择在餐厅吃晚餐，或是在下榻期间只在餐厅吃过一次饭。根据顾客的反映，我认为这也许是因为我们的菜品及服务质量欠佳。这个问题在三号和四号酒店尤为突出。

Molly 已经列出了她认为对餐厅影响最大的几项质量成本，而我最近也读到了关于质量成本的报告。我认为，多了解这方面信息对我们是有帮助的。因此，我希望你能在看完该列表后发邮件告诉我如何将各项成本融合进质量成本报告里。我已事先有所了解，故无须再详细阐释各项质量成本。

此外，我们已正式请 IT 技术部帮助解决新 IT 系统的问题。以下是他们提交的关于升级整套硬件和软件的成本方案：

	支出
新电脑终端机及打印机（硬件），预计使用期限为 4 年	M$ 84 000
服务器设备（由来 Tacland 的供应商供货，我们需在 2016 年 12 月以 T $ 支付）	T $ 58 000
软件许可证（3 年）	M$ 42 000
支付 IT 部门对于新系统提供的技术支持、安装配件、员工培训的费用	M$ 45 000

我需要准备一份对上述各项开支做出详细说明的简报，以便分发给其他主管和完成截至 2016 年 12 月 31 日和今后的财务报表。请将初稿整理好后发送给我。

谢谢。

智选酒店
财务总监
Rav Patel

餐厅的质量成本表

- 设计主菜单中出现的菜品。
- 更换被顾客退回的菜品。
- 厨房烤箱维护。
- 厨房设备维修。
- 供货商对产品进行检查。
- 提供顾客投诉的免费餐券。

请根据财务总监 Rav Patel 的要求回复邮件。

请写一份简报给各位总裁，讲述如何对新 IT 系统成本进行会计计量。

任务四

几周后财务总监 Rav Patel 给你发了如下邮件：

发件人：财务总监 Rav Patel
收件人：管理会计助理
主题：市场营销活动和对新 IT 系统投资

我和市场营销总监 Pam Hayes 考虑开展一系列市场营销活动，以便吸引新的顾客光临酒店和餐厅。目前，我们有两个独立方案：方案 A 花费 M$4 000，方案 B 花费 M$7 000。根据以往的经验，我们计算出在 3 种情况中的额外盈利方案，3 种预想情况为：活动不成功、活动比较成功和活动非常成功。

一家收费 M$25 000 且名为“专家顾问”的咨询公司表示可以帮助我们提高活动成功率。在看过我们最初的基于 3 种情况设定预计的额外盈利之后，该公司列出了每种情况下我们自己负责和交由他们负责的盈利对比报告。并且，他们的建议是采用花费 M$7 000的方案。

我需要你起草一份简报便于我之后提交给其他主管。由于制定决策是基于预计获利情况，因此在该报告中，请阐明对该咨询公司各项说明的分析。此外，请说明可能影响最终决策的各变异系数或其他因素。

此外，我们已通过IT技术部关于更新整合系统的报告。由于Pam Hayes之外，我们公司没有可用的精通IT的人才，IT技术部将由他们全权负责。他们告诉我接下来将有一系列的系统转换升级。我相信其他主管也会表示对此有兴趣。

请在简报中一并陈列可能运用的系统转换法法，并附上你对这些系统将对公司产生的好与不好的影响的观点。

谢谢!

智选酒店
财务总监
Rav Patel

专家顾问公司的报告

没有专家顾问公司协助的额外收入的预期值（活动的净成本）：

	方案A			方案B		
	概率	额外的收入（损失）（M$ 000）	期望价值（M$ 000）	概率	额外的收入（损失）（M$ 000）	期望价值（M$ 000）
不成功	40%	(10)	(4)	60%	(30)	(18)
比较成功	30%	20	6	20%	60	12
非常成功	30%	50	15	20%	90	18
预期利润			17	预期利润		12
方案A的变异系数			1.67	方案B的变异系数		4.36

专家顾问公司协助下的额外收入的预期值（付费前的活动净成本）：

	方案A			方案B		
	概率	额外收入（损失）（M$ 000）	预期价值（M$ 000）	概率	额外收入（M$ 000）	预期价值（M$ 000）
不成功	10%	0	0	30%	(10)	(3)
比较成功	40%	40	16	40%	80	32

（续表）

	方案 A			方案 B		
	概率	额外收入（损失）(M$ 000)	预期价值 (M$ 000)	概率	额外收入 (M$ 000)	预期价值 (M$ 000)
非常成功	50%	70	35	30%	100	30
收费前的预期利润			51	收费前的预期利润		59
咨询费用			(25)	咨询费用		(25)
预期利润			26	预期利润		34
方案 A 付费前的变异系数			0.43	方案 B 付费前的变异系数		0.78

专家顾问公司协助价值：

专家顾问公司协助的价值是 M$ 17 000（M$ 34 000 – M$ 17 000）

请完成关于专家顾问公司的总结报告和 IT 系统更新的简报。

Variant 2　Suggested Answers

Section 1

From: Management Accountant Assistant

To: Rav Patel, Finance Director

Subject: RE: Guest profitability and a new, integrated, IT system

Guest Profitability

Comparison of Guest Profitability and Implications

The different levels of profitability per night are because each guest has generated different costs over the course of their stay as a result of the number of hotel activities that they have triggered.

Looking at the specific hotel activities listed in the report:

Each guest required one check in. For the guest staying for one night the cost generated will be fully reflected in the profit per night figure. For guest B who stayed six nights only 1/6th of this cost will be reflected in the profit per night figure. For guest A staying 14 nights only 1/14th of the cost affects the profit per night figure. Hence this will have contributed to guest A having the highest profit per night and guest C the lowest.

It is hotel policy that towels are changed when requested by guests (rather than automatically changed daily). It would appear from the data that guests A and B each had six changes of towels which meant that there were six laundry services incurred, effectively the same cost for both guests. However because guest A stayed for 14 nights this cost will be spread over these 14 nights rather than the six nights for guest B. This will have increased the profitability of guest A compared to guest B.

We will obviously only need to replenish complimentary items in the room where the guest uses the item in the first place. From the data we can see that guest B used up 20 items, compared to guest A that stayed for longer and only used seven items. Each time an item is replenished it costs our hotel money, therefore the greater the number of items replenished the higher our cost and therefore the lower the profit per night of the guest.

Would ABC Be Beneficial to Our Business

A key benefit of an ABC system is that it provides more meaningful cost information because it recognises that costs are driven not necessarily by the number of nights that a guest stays but by the decisions that a guest makes(for example the number of complimentary items they use). By using the guest data to establish the costs that are generated it might be possible to alter pricing policy so that for example a guest staying more than three or four nights would obtain a discount on the room rate(on the basis that they generate less costs). This in turn could attract more, long-term guests as they might feel that they were getting a good bargain.

Analysing cost information with regard to activities generating the cost might also allow us to be able to better control our costs. By understanding how many times an activity is undertaken, it might be that we can identify ways in which the number of activities can be reduced(for example, by understanding the cost of a check in or check out we might be able to change procedures to reduce this cost).

However, there are also potential issues if we were to implement ABC as a costing system, not least the time involved and the potential cost of setting it up and then monitoring activity usage. It is possible that the benefits of ABC will not outweigh these costs.

In addition, there is going to be no set pattern to how guests use each activity. From the consultant's report we can see that a guest staying for 14 days only used seven complimentary items, yet a guest staying for half that time used 20. Each guest is an individual and will make their own decisions regarding usage of items and towel renewal, which makes it very difficult to establish a standard level of activity for a particular type of guest.

New it Systems

Supply Side Benefits

One of the key elements in our supply chain is the local food producers and suppliers. Information technology will enable us to capture data on guests with regard to their opinions on our catering facilities, which in turn will enable us to focus attention on areas that we might need to improve. If, for example, guests complain about the quality of the ingredients used in our food then we could if we wish make changes within our upstream supply chain and raise the level of "customer value" within our business and in so doing improve our competitive position.

Information Technology will facilitate e-procurement, which is the key activity of upstream supply chain management, within our business. E-procurement comprises three stages, these being e-sourcing, e-purchasing and e-payment. We can benefit under each of these stages of e-procurement as follows:

- E-sourcing: We could issue electronic invitations to tender and requests for quotations from our food suppliers which will reduce our purchasing costs.
- E-purchasing: We could create recurring requisitions and shopping lists for regularly purchased items. These standard lists will form the basis of regular orders which can be amended for each specific order that we place with our chosen suppliers. This will reduce the time taken to create purchase orders and result in a further reduction of our purchasing costs.
- E-payment: We would have the capability to receive invoices and make payments to our suppliers electronically. This would make payment processes more efficient not only for us but also our suppliers, and would result in a reduction of costs for both parties.

Customer Side Benefits

Information Technology enables the gathering of information. So for example, customer relationship management software can be used to determine the needs of guests, booking patterns, and individual preferences. By the same token we can communicate with guests in order to try and trigger repeat bookings.

The new IT system might enable us to cope with any excess demand at any of our hotels. For example, if one of our hotels is at full capacity on any given date the system might be able to offer alternative accommodation within one or more of our other hotels on that date thereby reducing "lost bookings".

Thanks.

Management Accountant Assistant

Wise Choice Hotel

Section 2

From: Management Accountant Assistant

To: Rav Patel, Finance Director

Subject: Forecasting and inventory management

Forecasting

Factors that should be considered the preparation of a sales forecast for our hotels include the following.

Seasonality

Information will be available in respect of previous years and can be used to give us a much better understanding of the sales revenue patterns that might be generated in future periods. Past sales information can be analysed in order to identify any seasonal variations.

Reservation Mix

The mix of reservations between first time guests and repeat guests will also assist us in our prediction of potential revenue patterns within our hotels. In this respect it useful to look at the extent to which we were successful in converting the enquiries received from both existing and new guest enquiries into hotel bookings during previous periods.

Special Events

It is probable that revenues will increase when there are special events held close to a hotel's location. Hotel 3 is based in a theatre district and if a particularly popular play is scheduled then it will impact on the demand for the rooms within our hotels.

Competition

It is important to retain the history of our closest competitor's room availability and rates per room charged at different times throughout the previous budget period. This information is an important part of the understanding of future demand patterns within our hotels. It would be useful to give consideration to changes in their selling price strategies at different times throughout the previous budget period and to assess the impact on the demand for rooms within our hotels. It would be helpful to compare their selling prices during the forecast period with the prices they charged during the corresponding period of the previous budget year.

Advertising

We should give detailed consideration to the level and timing of anticipated advertising expenditure during the forthcoming budget year as this can impact upon the demand for rooms within our hotels. In this regard it would be useful to look at previous advertising campaigns we have undertaken in order to assess the degree of correlation between advertising expenditure and demand for rooms within our hotels.

Economic Environment

We should consider the forecast economic conditions within Macland which could impact the demand for our rooms. For example a recession within Macland would be likely to cause a downturn in the demand for hotel rooms from leisure guests who might wish to conserve their disposable income. Similarly, a recession could result in reduced demand from business guests. Conversely a "boom" economy leads to increased consumer spending and may result in an increase in demand for our hotel rooms.

Beverage Inventory Managment

The Nature of the Costs Associated With our Bar Inventory

Ordering costs will include the fixed delivery fee that we pay each time the supplier delivers an order to us as well as the cost of the time taken to administer the order by hotel staff.

Holding costs will include the costs of storing the beverages in terms of the energy consumed to hold them in a temperature controlled environment and a share of the insurance cost. It will also include the cost of any beverage inventory that we throw away as a result of going beyond its best before date and the cost of the working capital funds that are tied up in the value of inventory.

There are also other costs associated with our bar inventory such as lost sales where a particular beverage is not available and lost discounts if we do not purchase in bulk.

Appropriateness of EOQ

The EOQ model in principle is useful because it can determine an order quantity that minimises the total of holding and ordering costs. Discounts can also be factored into the calculations to see if it is worth taking them.

The problem for us though is that it would be very difficult to apply the model as we hold many different lines of inventory, each with different levels of demand. In addition the EOQ model assumes that demand for the product over the period is constant, which is an unrealistic assumption. Demand at our bars is dependent upon a number of factors such as the number of guests at the hotel (the occupancy), whether there is a function on and whether there are special events happening outside the hotel which take our guests away. Therefore demand is not constant.

The EOQ also ignores shortage costs, which are potentially quite significant for our business. If we consistently have beverages which are not available, this means lost sales as well as creating a bad guest impression.

Whist EOQ does consider the ordering and holding costs of inventory, it assumes the holding costs can be established per unit of inventory. Thus it assumes that holding costs are essentially variable in nature. In our situation this is not necessarily the case. Irrespective of the level of inventory on hand we are likely to incur the same amount of energy costs as we have to ensure that the shortage area is at the appropriate temperature anyway. Similarly, our insurance costs are fixed. Therefore it is unrealistic to establish a holding cost per unit.

To conclude, in practical terms EOQ is not likely to be very helpful in respect of managing inventory levels in the bars. The nature of demand means that the head of bar and restaurant is the still the best person to procure inventory (in terms of quantity and frequency) as they will be able to best anticipate peaks in demand from the expected occupancy levels and known function. However, perhaps more guidance needs to be given regarding accepting discounts and a new delivery charge negotiated with our suppliers so that smaller orders are not penalised.

Thanks.

Management Accountant Assistant
Wise Choice Hotel

Section 3

From: Management Accountant Assistant

To: Rav Patel, Finance Director

Subject: Restaurant quality

Quality Costs

Designing the Meals to Be Included on the Restaurant Menus

This is a prevention cost as it represents the cost of an action taken to reduce defects and failures of quality. It is possible to reduce perishable food purchasing costs through better menu design. Many restaurants offer standard meals with set vegetables that some customers may not always want.

Re-making Meals that Have Been Returned by Guests

This is an external failure cost as it represents a cost arising from inadequate quality discovered after the transfer of ownership to the restaurant customer. The meal that has to be re-made means that the original meal has to be scrapped and extra ingredients, energy and staff time used to re-make it. The returned meal represents evidence of customer dissatisfaction that can also result in lost customer goodwill.

Maintenance of the Kitchen Ovens

This is a prevention cost as it represents a cost incurred prior to or during production in order to prevent sub-standard meals from being produced. Prevention costs are discretionary costs which would be incurred with the intention of eliminating the costs of internal and external failure within our restaurants.

Repairing Kitchen Equipment That Has Broken Down

This is an internal failure costs as it represents a cost arising from inadequate quality which is identified before any meals have been transferred to the customer. Internal failure costs are costs of non-conformance which can only be reduced by increasing the costs of conformance.

Inspecting of Incoming Products from Suppliers

This is an appraisal cost as it represents costs incurred in order to ensure that the ingredients used in the meals that will be produced meet the required quality standards. Appraisal costs are discretionary costs which would be incurred with the intention of eliminating the costs of internal and external failure within our restaurants.

Giving Complimentary Meal Vouchers in Respect of Customer Complaints

This is an external failure cost as it represents a cost arising from inadequate quality discovered after the transfer of ownership of the meal to the customer. A complimentary meal voucher given to a guest represents acknowledgement of poor service (either in terms of the meal or service). This will entitle the guest to effectively a free meal; it is the cost of creating and serving this free meal which is the external failure cost.

Thanks.

Management Accountant Assistant
Wise Choice Hotel

Briefing Paper on Accounting for IT System Costs

Computer Terminals and Printers (Hardware)

The computer terminals and printers are tangible assets that will be capitalised as part of PPE in accordance with IAS 16 PPE. We can classify them as PPE because they will be used to generate economic benefit for our business for a period of more than 12 months and the cost can be reliably measured because it is the purchase cost.

We will need to depreciate these assets over a period of four years (which is their useful economic life), with a full year's charge in the year of acquisition.

Server Equipment

The server equipment is also a tangible asset which is to be classified as PPE in the same way as the hardware. It will need to be depreciated over its useful economic life which is still to be established.

The one complication with the server is that we will need to pay for it in T$ as it will be coming from Tacland. The asset will be capitalised at its cost of T$58,000 converted into M$ on the date of the purchase. If the payment for the purchase is delayed then an exchange difference might arise on the settlement of the transactions which will affect profit. The recorded cost of the asset, in the statement of financial position, will not change though.

Software Licences

Because the software licences are for a period of three years we will be able to capitalise the cost as an intangible asset in accordance with IAS 38 intangible assets. The licences give us the contractual right to use the software and to generate economic benefit. It is a purchased intangible asset which means that it can be capitalised.

The asset will need to be amortised over the three year life of the licence.

Fee to IT Solutions

The fee to IT solutions needs to be split into two. The element that relates to training staff cannot be capitalised as it does not meet the definition of an asset. Whilst the fact that the staff are trained to use the system potentially generates economic benefit to the business, the staff are free to take this knowledge with them and hence we cannot control it. Therefore training costs need to be written off to profit or loss.

The element that relates to sourcing and installing the hardware and software can be capitalised as part of the cost of the hardware (PPE) and software (intangible) accordingly.

Section 4

Campaign Decision

Decision on the Basis of Expected Value

There are two decisions facing Wise Choice Hotels, these are; whether to spend M$ 40,000 or M$ 70,000 on the campaign and whether to engage Expert Consultants to manage the campaign.

If we do not engage Expert Consultants then the best decision using only expected values would be to choose campaign A. This is because it has the highest expected value of the two campaigns at M$ 17,000 (compared to M$ 12,000 for B).

If we engage Expert Consultants then the best decision using only expected values would be to choose campaign B. This is because we would gain M$ 34,000 after allowing for the consultants' costs of M$ 25,000, compared with only M$ 26,000 from campaign A.

Considering the two decisions together, on the basis of expected values alone, we should select campaign B and engage Expert Consultants as the expected value of M$ 34,000 is greater than the M$ 17,000 from campaign A if the consultants are not engaged. This difference of M$ 17,000 represents the additional expected value to be created by engaging Expert Consultants to manage campaign B.

Coefficient of Variation

The coefficient of variation describes the amount of variability relative to the mean. It can be calculated by dividing the standard deviation by the expected value. Campaign B has a higher coefficient of variation which means that it has a greater spread of possible outcomes from a loss of M$ 10,000 to a profit of M$ 100,000. This means that campaign B is riskier than campaign A. The report from the Expert consultants shows that the coefficient of variation improves for both projects when their services are used and this claim needs to be substantiated.

Factors to Consider for this Decision

An expected value is an average of the possible outcomes weighted by the probabilities of those outcomes occurring. It represents an average of the possibilities over a long period of time: it does not represent one of the possible outcomes. As a result, using the expected value rule to make a decision is only really appropriate over the long run where either the decision in question is repeated or the probabilities used can be based on long-run experience.

A number of estimates are used here including the possible profits and losses and the probabilities. Given that Expert Consultants have a vested interest in selling their services to us, it is possible that the improvement in probability and expected profit that they predict is over-stated. Indeed it would seem that under campaign B they expect to reduce the probability of a loss to 30% from 60% and to also improve the end result under not successful conditions by M$ 20,000. This seems very optimistic; especially when we consider the improvement in the coefficient of variation (essentially the risk of the project) that they are predicting. It would be useful to undertake sensitivity analysis on the estimated probabilities as well as the revenue and costs associated with each decision option to understand how much each of these variables would need to change in order for the decision to change.

This decision basis is a risk neutral basis: it ignores the range of the possible outcomes. The downside risk of campaign B is bigger than that of campaign A and expected values alone do not identify this. If we do not use the consultants there is a 60% chance of making a loss of M$30,000 with campaign B compared to a 40% chance of a loss of only M$10,000 with campaign A. With the consultant the relationship between campaign's A and B is the same in that the chance of a loss for B(30% chance of a total loss of M$35,000) is greater than that for campaign A(a 10% chance of a total loss of M$25,000).

If the directors were risk adverse then campaign A is likely to be preferred as the coefficient of variation of campaign A is much lower than the coefficient of variation of campaign B.

System Changeover Methods

There are a number of approaches to system changeover that we could use, each of which varies in terms of time the potential benefits and problems to our business.

Four such approaches to system changeover and the associated benefits and problems are as follows:

Direct Changeover

This is a "Big Bang" approach to systems changeover where our existing systems would be completely replaced by the new system in one move at a designated point in time. The benefit to us of this method is that it is quick and low cost, as it would require minimal resources. This might appear to be an attractive option as there are currently no IT support staff. However, there are potential problems with this approach that are particularly important when dealing with real-time systems such as those in our hotels. The most likely time for a system to fail is during the early days and weeks of its implementation. If our new system does fail, then we have no system to fall back on. We rely on our system for real-time advice to guests, booking and billing. Can we afford to take the risk of the direct changeover method, even if the software and hardware are well proven elsewhere?

Parallel Running

This would involve running the existing system and the new system in parallel for a period of time. They both process current data that enables the output information of both systems to be compared and hence verifies the results produced by the new system prior to "going live" with it. This reduces many risks because, if anything goes wrong with the new system, it can be corrected and the old system can continue to run to deliver our real-time services to guests. This is a high cost low risk approach to systems changeover. This method might cause much "organisational pain" as it is time consuming due to the additional workload and at present we have limited IT resources. We would need to engage staff with the appropriate skills and more money to pay them.

Pilot Operation

Pilot operation would involve selecting one of our hotels to operate the new system in parallel with our existing system. When the hotel operating the system is satisfied with the new system it would cease to use the existing system. The new system would then be piloted in another hotel. Pilot operation provides a greater degree of safety than a direct changeover and is less resource consumptive and lower cost and easier to control than parallel running. However this changeover method is not as safe as complete parallel running and can take a long time to achieve a total changeover.

Phased (or Modular) Changeover

Phased (or modular) changeover would involve selecting one sub-system such as the room reservations system for a direct changeover. When this sub-system is running satisfactorily, another sub-system is switched until eventually the whole of the existing system has been replaced by the new system. A phased series of direct changeovers is lower risk than a single direct changeover as any problems and disruption should be isolated in an area of operations. This could work well within Wise Choice Hotels. For example, we could set up the customer records sub-system first, and then move on to booking and billing. We would not need to implement inventory control and purchasing until later since there is little or no link between this and the customer-related sub-systems.

This changeover method can take a long time to achieve a total changeover.

试卷二　参考答案

任务一

发件人：管理会计助理

收件人：财务总监 Rav Patel

主题：回复：顾客的盈利性和新一体化 IT 系统

顾客盈利能力

顾客盈利能力比较及其意义

每晚不同的盈利能力水平是因为每位顾客在入住期间导致不同数量的酒店作业，在此过程中产生不同的成本。

分析报告中列出的具体酒店作业如下：

每位顾客需要一次入住手续。对于入住 1 晚的顾客 C 而言，其所产生的成本完全反映在每晚利润的数据中。对于入住 6 晚的顾客 B 来说，此项成本只有 1/6 反映在每晚利润的数据中。对于入住 14 晚的顾客 A 来说，此项成本只有 1/14 反映在每晚利润数据中。因此，这将导致顾客 A 的每晚利润最高，顾客 C 的每晚利润最低。

酒店的政策是在顾客提出要求时更换毛巾（而不是自动每日更换）。数据似乎表明顾客 A 和顾客 B 分别更换了 6 次毛巾，这意味着产生了 6 次洗衣服务，即两位顾客的成本相同。但是，由于顾客 A 入住了 14 晚，这项成本将分摊到 14 晚，而不是顾客 B 的 6 晚。相对于顾客 B 而言，这将提高顾客 A 的盈利能力。

显然，只有当顾客使用客房内的免费用品时，才需要加以补充。从数据中可见，顾客 B 使用了 20 件商品，而顾客 A 虽然入住时间较长，但只使用了 7 件商品。每次补充商品时，都会对酒店造成成本，因此补充的商品数量越多，我们的成本就越高，顾客产生的每晚利润也就越低。

作业成本法是否对我们的企业有益

作业成本法的关键优势之一是提供更有意义的成本信息，因为它认识到成本不一定只在于顾客入住的天数，也在于顾客做出的决策（如顾客使用的免费用品数量）。通过运用顾客数据来确定产生的成本，或许可以调整定价政策，比如入住超过 3 晚或超过 4

晚的顾客可享受客房价格折扣（原因是他们将产生较低的成本）。因而，这又会吸引更多的长期客户，因为他们会觉得物超所值。

根据产生成本的作业分析成本信息，也可以让我们能够更好地控制成本。通过了解某项作业实施的次数，我们可以确定如何减少此项作业的数量（例如，通过了解入住或退房手续的成本，我们可以调整程序，降低这项成本）。

但是，如果我们要实施作业成本法，将有潜在问题，尤其是建立作业成本法和监督作业使用情况所涉及的时间和潜在成本。作业成本法产生的效益可能无法抵销这些成本。

此外，顾客如何使用每项作业并不存在固定模式。顾问公司的报告显示，一位顾客入住了 14 晚，只使用了 7 件免费商品；而另一位顾客只入住了一半的时间，却使用了 20 件免费商品。每位顾客都各不相同，他们会独立做出有关免费商品使用和毛巾更换的决策，因此很难为特定类型的顾客建立标准的作业水平。

新 IT 系统

供应侧效益

我们供应链中的关键要素之一是本地食品生产商和供应商。信息技术将让我们能够针对顾客对于餐饮设施的观点捕捉数据，因此能够让我们将注意力集中在可能需要改进的领域。例如，如果顾客投诉餐饮所用食材的质量欠佳，那么我们可以在上游供应链中进行调整，提高企业内的“消费者价值”水平，并因而提高自身的竞争地位。

信息技术将促进电子采购，而这是我们企业内部上游供应链管理的关键作业。电子采购包括 3 个阶段：电子寻购、电子购买和电子支付。电子采购的每个阶段都将给我们带来以下效益。

- 电子寻购：我们可以发出电子招标邀请函，向食品供应商征求报价，从而降低采购成本。
- 电子购买：我们可以针对定期采购的商品创建循环请购和采购清单。这些标准清单将构成定期订购的基础，可以对我们与所选择的供应商签订的具体订单进行修改。这将缩短创建采购单所需的时间，可进一步降低采购成本。
- 电子支付：我们将能够通过电子方式收到发票，向供应商付款。这将使我们自身乃至供应商的支付流程更加高效，从而为双方降低成本。

客户侧效益

信息技术使信息的收集成为可能。例如，客户关系管理软件可用于确定顾客的需求、预订模式和具体偏好。根据同样的系统，我们可以与顾客进行沟通，以便尝试并触发重复预订。

新 IT 系统或许能够让我们应对酒店中的超额需求。例如，如果一家酒店在某个特定日期客满，那么系统当日就能在集团旗下的一家或多家其他酒店中提供备选客房，从而减少“预订流失”。

谢谢。

智选酒店

管理会计助理

任务二

发件人：管理会计助理

收件人：财务总监 Rav Patel

主题：预测和存货管理

预测

在为酒店编制销售预测时，应考虑以下因素。

季节性

上一年的信息可供使用，便于让我们更加准确地了解未来可能产生的销售收入模式。可以分析以往的销售信息，确定季节性变化。

预订组合

新顾客和老顾客之间的预订组合也将有助于我们预测酒店内的潜在收入模式。在这个方面，可以分析以往我们将收到的新老顾客咨询成功地转化为酒店预订的情况。

特殊活动

如果在酒店所在地附近举办特殊活动，那么收入很可能会增加。三号酒店位于剧院区，如果特别热门的剧目被安排上演，那么这将提高酒店内的客房需求。

竞争

必须保存与我们最为接近的竞争对手在上一个预算期内不同时期的客房可用性和所

收取的客房单价的历史记录。此类信息是了解酒店未来需求模式的重要因素。应考虑竞争对手在上一个预算期内不同时期的销售价格策略调整，评估对我们酒店客房需求的影响，这将是有益的。这将有助于比较竞争对手在预测期内的销售价格与他们在上一个预算年度中相应时期所收取的价格。

广告宣传

我们应详细考虑未来预算年度中预期广告开支的水平和时机，因为这可能会影响顾客对我们酒店客房的需求。在这个方面，应分析之前开展的广告宣传活动，从而评估广告开支和酒店客房需求之间的关联程度。

经济环境

我们应考虑 Macland 地区的预测经济状况，这可能会对我们酒店客房需求产生影响。例如，Macland 的经济衰退将很有可能导致休闲顾客对酒店客房的需求下降，后者可能希望保留可支配收入。同样，经济衰退也可能会造成商务顾客的需求下降。相反，经济繁荣会提高消费者开支，可能会提升顾客对我们酒店客房的需求。

饮料库存管理

与酒吧库存相关的成本性质

订购成本包括供应商每次送货时我们需支付的固定送货费，以及酒店员工用于管理订单而花费的时间成本。

持有成本包括储存饮料的成本，比如将饮料储存在温控环境中所消耗的能源以及一定比例的保险成本。其中还包括因为超过保质期而丢弃的饮料储存成本以及饮料库存所占用的流动资金成本。

酒吧库存还存在其他相关成本，比如某种饮料缺货造成的销售额流失以及并非大批量采购所导致的折扣损失等。

经济订货批量模式的适宜性

原则上，经济订货批量模式十分有效，因为它能够确定令持有和订购总成本最小化的订购数量。也可将折扣纳入计算中，确定是否值得考虑。

然而，我们所面临的问题是极其难以应用这个模式，因为我们持有大量不同类型的库存，每种库存的需求水平各不相同。此外，经济订货批量模式假设产品在一个时期内的需求保持恒定，但这个假设缺乏现实意义。酒吧的需求取决于一系列因素，比如酒店顾客数量（入住率），是否有大型集会，以及酒店外是否有吸引顾客外出的特殊活动，等等。因此，需求并非固定不变。

经济订货批量还忽略了短缺成本，而这项成本对我们的企业非常重要。如果某些饮料一直缺货，那么这意味着销售额会下降，并且会给顾客留下不好的印象。

虽然经济订货批量模式的确考虑了库存的订购和持有成本，但它假设每单位库存都可以确定持有成本。因此，它假设持有成本本质上是可变的。而对我们的企业而言，情况不一定是这样。无论目前的库存水平如何，我们都往往会产生同样的能源成本，因为我们必须始终确保短缺区域达到适宜的温度。同样，我们的保险成本也是固定的。因此，确定单位持有成本缺乏现实意义。

总之，就实践意义而言，经济订货批量模式对于管理酒吧库存水平并非十分有效。需求性质意味着酒吧和餐厅主管仍然是负责采购库存（包括数量和频率）的最佳人选，因为他们能够最准确地根据预期入住率水平和已知函数预测需求峰值。但是，或许需要就接受折扣以及与供应商谈判新送货费等问题为他们提供指导，以免小批量订购处于不利境地。

谢谢。

智选酒店

管理会计助理

任务三

发件人：管理会计助理

收件人：财务总监 Rav Patel

主题：餐厅质量

质量成本

设计餐厅菜单上的餐食

这是预防成本，因为它代表为了减少质量缺陷和失误而采取行动的成本。更加完善的菜单设计，可以降低易腐食品的采购成本。许多餐厅提供包含固定蔬菜的标准套餐，但一些消费者可能并不一定希望享用此类蔬菜。

重新制作顾客退货的餐食

这是外部损失成本，因为它代表了在所有权移交用餐的顾客后发现质量不足所产生的成本。需要重新制作的餐食意味着原先的餐食必须丢弃，重新制作将消耗额外的食材、能源和员工时间。被退货的餐食也是消费者不满的证据，也可能会使消费者对餐厅失去好感。

厨房烤箱维护

这是预防成本，因为它代表着在生产之前或期间为了预防生产出不达标准的餐食而产生的成本。预防成本是为了消除餐厅内部和外部损失成本而产生的酌量性成本。

维修出现故障的厨房设备

这是内部损失成本，因为它代表了在餐食送往消费者之前发现的质量不足所产生的成本。内部损失成本是不符合成本，只能通过提高符合性成本加以降低。

检验供应商的送货

这是鉴定成本，因为它代表着为了确保餐食中所使用的食材符合所需质量标准而产生的成本。评估成本属于酌量性成本，其目的是为了消除餐厅内的外部和内部损失成本。

针对消费者投诉赠送免费餐券

这是外部损失成本，因为它代表着在餐食的所有权转移到消费者之后发现质量不足所造成的成本。向顾客赠送的免费餐券代表承认质量低劣（餐食或服务）。餐券将让顾客能够享用一顿免费餐食，将产生制作并供应免费餐食的成本，即外部损失成本。

谢谢。

智选酒店

管理会计助理

IT 系统成本会计核算简报

计算机终端与打印机（硬件）

计算机终端和打印机是有形资产，根据国际会计准则第 16 号不动产、厂房和设备，可作为不动产、厂房和设备的一部分进行资本化。我们可以将这些设备归类为 PPE，因为它们将用于为我们的企业创造超过 12 个月的经济效益，而且其成本能够可靠地计量，即采购成本。

我们将需要在 4 年（其经济使用寿命）内对这些资产进行折旧，采购当年计为全年费用。

服务器设备

服务器设备也是有形资产，将与硬件一样被归类为 PPE。服务器设备需要在其经济使用寿命中折旧，但具体使用寿命待定。

服务器的复杂问题之一在于我们需要为其支付 T$ ，因为它来自 Tacland。我们将在采购之日把 T$ 58 000 的成本转换为 M$，对这项资产进行资本化。如果采购付款被延迟，那么交易结算可能会产生汇率差额，这将对利润产生影响。但在资产负债表中，所记录的资产成本将不变。

软件许可

由于软件许可有效期为 3 年，我们可以根据国际会计准则第 38 条无形资产，将这项成本作为无形资产进行资本化。软件许可通过合同方式让我们有权使用软件并产生经济效益，它属于已采购的无形资产，意味着可以资本化。

这项资产将需要在许可的 3 年有效期内摊销。

为 IT 解决方案支付的费用

为 IT 解决方案支付的费用需要分为两个部分。与培训员工有关的部分无法资本化，因为它不符合对于资产的定义。尽管培训员工使用这个系统可能会为企业产生经济效益，但这项技能由员工自由持有，我们无法加以控制。因此，培训成本需要冲销为损益。

与采购和安装软硬件有关的部分可分别作为硬件（不动产、厂房和设备）和软件（无形资产）成本实现资本化。

任务四

宣传活动设计

有关期望值基础的决策

智选酒店面临着两项决策，即对这项宣传活动应花费 M$ 40 000 还是 M$ 70 000，以及是否应聘请专家顾问公司来管理这项宣传活动。

如果不聘请专家顾问公司，仅仅取决于期望值的最佳决策为选择宣传活动方案 A。这是因为它具备两项方案中最高的期望值，即 M$ 17 000（而方案 B 的期望值为 M$ 12 000）。

如果聘请专家顾问公司，仅仅取决于期望值的最佳决策为选择宣传活动方案 B。这是因为在扣除 M$ 25 000 的顾问成本后，收益为 M$ 34 000，而方案 A 的收益仅为 M$ 26 000。

仅仅根据期望值同时考虑这两个决策，我们应选择宣传活动方案 B，并聘请专家顾问公司，因为其期望值为 M$ 34 000，高于不聘请顾问公司时方案 A 所产生的 M$ 17 000。M$ 17 000 的差额代表聘请专家顾问公司管理宣传活动 B 所创造的附加期望值。

变异系数

变异系数描述相对均值的可变性程度。将标准差除以平均值，可计算变异系数。宣传活动方案 B 的变异系数较高，意味着可能的结果分布范围较大，从 M$ 10 000 的亏损到 M$ 10 000 的利润。这表示宣传活动方案 B 的风险高于方案 A。专家顾问公司的报告显示，采取其服务时，两个项目方案的变动系数均有所改善，但这一诉求有待证实。

此项决策需要考虑的因素

期望值是可能结果通过其发生概率加权而产生的平均值，它代表了在长期范围内的可能性平均值，它不代表某个可能结果。因此，只有在长期范围内，当所述决策重复发生或所用概率可能以长期经验为基础时，才适合使用期望值规则来进行决策。

这里使用了一系列估计值，包括可能的损益和概率。由于专家顾问公司向我们销售其服务存在既得利益，有可能会高估所预测的概率和预期利润改进。事实上，似乎在宣传活动方案 B 项下，他们预期亏损概率将从 60% 下降至 30%，在非成功条件下，最终成果也将提高 M$ 20 000。这种观点似乎极为乐观，尤其考虑到他们所预测的变动系数（项目风险）改善。应对所估计的概率以及每个决策选项的收入和成本开展敏感性分析，以便了解每项变量需要实现何种程度的变化方可调整决策。

这项决策基于风险中性基础，它忽略了可能的结果范围。宣传活动方案 B 的下行风险高于方案 A，而仅仅期望值无法揭示这一点。如果我们不聘请顾问公司，宣传活动方案 B 产生 M$ 30 000 亏损的概率为 60%，而方案 A 产生仅 M$ 10 000 亏损的概率为 40%。在聘请顾问公司的情况下，宣传活动方案 A 和 B 之间的关系相同，即方案 B 的亏损概率（总亏损达到 M$ 35 000 的概率为 30%）高于方案 A（总亏损达到 M$ 25 000 的概率为 10%）。

如果企业董事希望规避风险，那么宣传活动方案 A 可能是首选，因为方案 A 的变异系数远远低于方案 B 的变异系数。

系统转换方式

多种系统转换方式可供我们使用，每种方式在时间以及对企业带来的潜在效益和问题方面各不相同。

4 种系统转换方式及其相应的效益和问题如下。

直接转换

这是“大爆炸式”的系统转换方式，是指在指定的时间点用新系统一次性完全取代现有系统。这种方式为我们带来的效益是快速、低成本，因为它需要的资源最少。这个选项看似颇具吸引力，因为企业目前并没有 IT 支持人员。但是，这种方式存在潜在问题，在处理像我们酒店这样的实时系统时尤为重要。系统最有可能出现故障的时间是实施后的最初几天和最初几周。如果新系统真的出现故障，那么我们将没有系统可用。我们依赖于自身的系统来为顾客提供实时建议、订购和出账。虽然其软件和硬件在其他企业中经过了充分验证，但是我们能否承担起直接转换方式的风险还值得考虑。

平行运行

这涉及将现有系统和新系统同时运行一段时间。两个系统都将处理当前数据，以便对两个系统的输出信息进行比较，从而验证新系统产生的结果，之后再正式上线。这样能够减少大量风险，因为如果新系统出现问题，可及时加以纠正，而老系统则可以继续运行，为顾客提供实时服务。这是高成本、低风险的系统转换方式。这种方式可能会引起大量“组织努力”，因为它非常耗费时间，需要增加额外的工作量，而且我们目前的IT资源有限。我们需要聘用具备适当技能的员工，并向他们支付更高的薪资。

试运行

试运行即选择一家酒店，将新系统与现有系统同时运行。如果采用试运行的酒店对新系统感到满意，可停止使用现有系统。然后，继续在另一家酒店对新系统进行试运行。与直接转换相比，试运行可提供更高的安全性，而与平行运行相比，它使用的资源较少，成本较低，也更容易控制。但是，这种转换方式并不像完全平行运行那么安全，而且完全转换可能需要较长的时间。

阶段性（或模块化）转换

阶段性（或模块化）转换是指选择一个子系统（如客房预订系统）进行直接转换。如果这个子系统的运行令人满意，那么可着手进行下一个子系统的转换，直到现有系统最终完全被新系统取代。阶段性直接转换系列的风险低于一次性直接转换，因为任何问题和中断都将局限于某一个运营领域。这种方式可能十分适合智选酒店。例如，我们可以首先设置客户记录子系统，然后转换预订和出账子系统。我们暂时无须实施库存控制和采购子系统，因为这个子系统与客户相关的子系统之间没有或几乎没有关联。采用这种转换方式，实现完全转换可能需要较长的时间。

Variant 2 Marking Guidance

Section	Technical skills		Business skills		People skills		Leadership skills		Integration	Total
1	Activity based costing and profitability	13	Impact of new IT systems on the supply chain	12						25
2	Forecasting revenue Inventory management	10 8	Inventory management (appropriateness)	4					3	25
3	Cost of quality Accounting for investment in new IT systems	12 13								25
4	Short-term decision making under risk	6			IT system changeover methods	13	Short-term decision making under risk	6		25
Total marks available for competency		62		16		13		6	3	100

试卷二　评分指南

部分	技术技能		商业技能		人际技能		领导技能		综合	总计
1	作业成本法和赢利能力	13	新 IT 系统对供应链的影响	12						25
2	预期收入 存货管理	10 8	存货管理（适合）	4					3	25
3	质量成本 对投资新 IT 系统的财务计算	12 13						6		25
4	风险下进行短期决策	6			IT 系统转变方法	13	风险下进行短期决策	6		25
各种能力的分数总计		62		16		13		6	3	100

上海立信会计金融学院名师解惑

试卷一共有四项任务，考察了 P1、F1、E1 三门课程的知识点，具体包括短期决策分析、营运资金管理、本量利分析、现金管理、质量成本和供应商关系管理等。该试卷考核了考生的四项能力，其中技术技能的分值占 62%，商业技能的分值占 16%，人际技能的分值占 13%，领导技能的分值占 6%，与 CGMA 管理会计能力框架的技能要求一致。

该试卷的每项任务涉及以下知识点：

任务	问题	科目	知识点
任务一	活动表中的每个活动是如何影响利润的？解释在酒店采用作业成本法的优势	P1	作业成本法的优缺点（advantages and disadvantages of ABC）以及作业成本法下成本的计算
	投资 IT 系统如何促进供应链中供应商和客户双方的改进？	P1	信息系统在企业的运用（value of information systems in organisations）和供应链（supply chain）
任务二	计算出经济订货批量，分析经济订货批量是否适合我们公司以及如何据此决定每次订量	P1	经济订货批量（EOQ）
任务三	如何将各项成本融合进质量成本报告？	E1	质量成本报告（cost of quality report）
	如何对新 IT 系统进行会计计量？	F1	国际会计准则第 38 号无形资产（IAS 38 intangible assets）
任务四	起草一份简报，使用期望值来进行决策，同时考虑不同项目的风险	P1	期望值（expected value）和变异系数（coefficient of variation）
	在简报中陈列可能运用的系统转换方式，并不同方式对公司产生的影响	P1	系统转换方式（system changeover methods）

上述各项任务要求以邮件、报告或工作笔记等形式来呈现答案，对问题的描述非常明确，答题时既要注意内容的针对性，也要注意形式的规范性。

对应知识点深度剖析

作业成本法

成本作业法的核心在于，主张将活动量作为分配间接成本的基础。成本作业法认为，每一个企业都是在设计、生产、销售、发送和辅助其产品的过程中进行各种活动的集合体。各种耗费资源的活动“驱动”了成本的发生，每种产品的成本取决于其对不同活动的需要量。

成本作业法分为两步：

第一步，识别不同活动的成本，并把它们分配到成本库中。成本库可以根据企业实际经营所发生的各种活动灵活加以确定。它们可能包括设置调试机器、订货、材料处理、储存、发运、生产过程监管等。每个成本库都会有对应的驱动因素，对成本驱动因素的分析有助于确定把制造费用分配到各个产品或产品系列上的适当比率。

第二步，根据耗用的成本驱动因素量把成本库中的制造费用分摊到各个产品中。

考生注意事项

成本作业法对企业的正面作用：

（1）提供更有意义的成本信息。因为它认识到成本不一定只和生产的数量或销售量有关，从而进行更合理的产品定价。

（2）能够更好地控制成本。通过了解某项作业实施的次数，可以确定如何减少此项作业的数量。

运用成本作业法的挑战：

（1）很难准确地为每项间接费用找到合适的驱动因素。

（2）建立作业成本法并监督作业使用情况所涉及的成本有可能超过带来的效益。

（3）顾客如何使用每项作业不存在固定模式，难以为不同顾客建立标准作业量。

信息系统

信息系统在企业中有两个重要的职能：第一个主要职能是为了辅助运营，主要是处理和记录交易信息；第二个主要职能是为了帮助管理者做好商业决策，包括更合理地进行计划预算，以及更准确地进行运营绩效评估和管理控制。对信息系统进行成本效益分析时，我们应该考虑以下一些因素。

考生注意事项

信息系统的起始成本：

（1）信息系统的设计发展费用以及相关硬件、软件设施的采购费用。

（2）调试和安装成本。

（3）培训费用。

信息系统的运营费用：

（1）人员费用。

（2）材料耗用、零部件更换、系统升级等费用。

（3）技术支持、咨询等支出。

信息系统可能的效益：

（1）信息使用效率的提升。

（2）更准确及时的信息。

（3）获取信息的便捷性提升。

（4）更便捷的信息共享。

（5）更高效的沟通效率。

（6）更高效全面的决策以及更完善的客户服务体验。

供应链

供应链是指商品到达消费者手中之前各相关者的连接或业务的衔接，围绕核心企业，通过对信息流、物流、资金流的控制，从采购原材料开始，制成中间产品以及最终产品，最后通过销售网络把产品送到消费者的手中，将供应商、制造商、分销商（零售商、批发商等）和最终用户连成一个整体的功能网链结构。案例要求考生分析如何使用IT系统来提升价值链中供应侧及客户侧的效益。对于服务业企业而言，信息技术能让我们针对顾客对于餐饮设施的要求收集数据，让企业将注意力集中在可能需要改进的领域。例如，如果顾客投诉餐饮食材质量，那么我们可以在上游供应链中，进行供应商或者供应方式的调整，以满足客户的食材需求，进而提高自身的竞争力。另外，还可以通过投资改善电子采购的三个阶段（电子寻购、电子购买和电子支付）来提升采购效率和质量。

此外，信息系统还可供收集信息。通过客户关系管理软件来确定顾客的需求、预订模式和具体偏好。使用这个系统还能够提升我们与客户的沟通效率。因为客户的订购记录、地址等信息已经记录在系统中，客户在进行重复预订时，可以避免重复输入采购信息，从而提升我们的服务速度。

经济订货批量

库存管理中需要考虑的成本包括三类，分别是订购成本、持有成本和其他成本。其中，订购成本包括供应商送货时企业需支付的固定送货费，以及企业员工用于管理订单而花费的时间成本。持有成本包括储存成本，以及因为管理不善而丢弃的库存材料和库存所占用的流动资金成本。其他相关成本包括缺货造成的销售额流失以及错失的批量折扣等。

理论上，经济订货批量能够确定最优的订购数量，使持有和订购总成本最小化。另外，它还可将批量折扣纳入计算，确定是否值得大批量采购。但是在实践中使用经济订货批量模式管理案例中的酒吧库存，有很大的局限性。因为我们持有大量不同类型的库存，每种库存的需求水平各不相同。此外，经济订货批量模式假设产品在一个时期内的需求保持恒定，但这个假设缺乏现实意义。经济订货批量还忽略了短缺成本，而这项成本对我们的企业可能相当重要。如果某些饮料一直缺货，将导致销售额流失，并破坏酒店的声誉。

最后，经济订货批量模式假设持有成本为变动成本。而对案例中的酒店而言，情况不一定是这样。因为无论库存水平如何，能耗成本、安保成本及保险成本都是相对固定的。

质量成本报告

案例中智选酒店的财务总监 Rav Patel 在电子邮件中提到了质量成本这个概念。在回答案例的这个问题之前，我们有必要重温一下质量成本的概念和分类。

质量成本是指企业为确保或提高产品质量而发生的费用支出，以及由于未能达到质量标准而造成的损失，即质量成本不仅包括为提高质量而实际支出的费用，而且还包括产品低下导致的返修、处理客户投诉以及客户流失等造成的损失。

按照列支范围可大致将质量成本划分为三类：

一是预防成本，是指为了保证和提高产品质量，采取预防性措施而发生的费用，一般包括提高质量发生的设计和服务费、质量信息收集整理费、员工质量培训费、故障安全装置费等。

二是鉴定成本，是指为了检验和鉴定产品质量而发生的费用，一般包括对原材料、半成品、工序或产品的质量检验费、化验费等；前两种成本发生的目的都是为了让产品合规，它们也被称为符合成本。

三是损失成本，指因不满足规定的要求而造成损失的费用不符合成本。损失成本又可细分为内部损失成本和外部损失成本。内部损失成本是指产品出厂前发生的废次品造成的损失费用，如废次品造成的损失返修、停工损失、减产损失、产品等级下降损失等。外部损失成本是指在产品销售后用户使用过程中发生的损失，如返修费用、折价损失、索赔费用、公司声誉损失等。这些概念是在准备案例时同学们必须掌握的内容。但是，一定要注意案例中财务总监 Rav Patel 明确说明他已经了解了这些概念，不需要再对这些概念进行复述。

考生注意事项

质量成本的分类：

（1）如果费用发生在准备阶段，生产还未正式开始，一般而言可以归类为预防成本。

（2）如果已经进入了产品的正式生产阶段但产品还未出厂，发生的费用与原材料或产品的质量检测相关，则应归类为鉴定成本。

（3）如果发生的费用与生产过程中的设备损坏停工、废次品返修、解决产能低下问题等相关，则应该归类为内部损失成本。

（4）如果是在产品已经出厂之后发生的任何与质量相关的费用，则一定属于外部损失成本。

国际会计准则第 38 号无形资产

根据国际会计准则第 38 号无形资产，定义无形资产为用于商品或劳务的生产或供应、出租给其他单位或管理目的而持有的、没有实物形态的、可辨认非货币资产。当且仅当满足以下条件时，无形资产应予以确认：（1）归属于该资产的未来经济利益很可能流入企业；（2）该资产的成本可以可靠地计量。尽管案例中培训员工可能会为企业产生经济效益，但此项技能由员工自由持有，我们无法加以控制。因此，培训成本应当确认为当期费用。此外，内部产生的商标、商誉、刊头、报刊名、客户名单和本质上类似的项目都不应确认为无形资产，

在运营案例阶段，同学们最常见的与内部产生的无形资产关联的两类支出分别为研发费用和开发费用。一般而言，研发费用应在其发生时确认为费用。开发费用如果满足以下条件便可以确认为无形资产：（1）使用或销售，完成该无形资产在技术上可行；（2）有意完成该无形资产并使用或销售它；（3）有能力使用或销售该无形资产；（4）该无形资产可以产生可能未来经济利益；（5）为完成该无形资产开发，并使用或销售该无形资产，有足够的技术、财务资源和其他资源的支持；（6）对归类于该无形资产

开发阶段的支出，可以可靠地计量

无形资产的应折旧金额应在其使用年限内系统地摊销，摊销应自无形资产可利用之日起开始进行。具有无限使用年限的无形资产不进行摊销，但需要每年进行减值测试。

考生注意事项

汇率变化对资产成本的影响：

如果企业的资产在海外进行采购，因为支付的并非本国货币，需要在采购当日转换成本国货币进行会计计量。但如果汇率发生变化，付款时可能会产生汇率差额，对利润产生影响。但在资产负债表中，所记录的资产成本保持不变。

期望值

在使用预期值进行投资决策时，我们会选择有较高期望值的选项。但是，我们需要注意的是期望值是各个可能的结果与其发生概率加权而产生的平均值。它代表了在长期范围内的可能性平均值，而非某个可能的实际结果。因此，只有在长期范围内需要重复相同决策或所用概率以长期经验为基础时，才适合使用期望值进行决策。所以，对于一次性的决策问题来说，这个方法没有太多实际意义。

此外，期望值基于风险中性基础，而忽略了可能的结果范围。例如，在此案例中使用顾问公司后项目 B 的期望值为 M$ 34 000，高于项目 A 的 M$ 17 000，但是却忽略了 B 的亏损率为 30%，大大高于 A 的 10%。

变异系数

当需要比较两组数据的离散程度大小时，如果两组数据的度量单位或平均数不同，那么直接使用标准差来进行比较就不合适。而变异系数可以做到这一点，它是原始数据标准差与原始数据平均数的比。一般来说，变异系数越高的项目其离散程度的测度值越大，风险也就越大。

考生注意事项

变异系数的计算：

变异系数的计算公式 =（标准偏差 / 平均值）×100%

$CV = \sigma / \mu$

系统转换方式

一共有 4 种系统转换方式可以供企业选择，分别为直接转换、平行运行、试运行和阶段性（或模块化）转换。

直接转换为激进的转换方式，是指在指定的时间点用新系统一次性完全取代现有系统。这种方式为我们带来的效益是快速、低成本，因为它需要的资源最少。但同时是风险较大的一个选项，因为如果系统转换失败将没有可以使用的系统来支持当前的运营。所以，只有对新系统充满绝对的信心（已经在其他企业或部门验证过），或者转换的系统并非企业的核心系统时才能采取这个方法。

平行运行为风险相对较低的转换方式。它要求现有系统和新系统同时运行一段时间，并进行比较。对新系统验证之后，再正式上线。这是高成本、低风险的系统转换方式，因为它非常耗费时间，而且需要增加额外的工作量。这种方法适用于特别重要的系统，或者从未在其他地方验证过的新系统。

试运行即选择一家酒店，将新系统与现有系统同时运行。试运行后，如果对新系统感到满意，那么再停止使用现有系统并选择另一家酒店对新系统进行试运行。其成本和安全性介于直接转换和平行运行之间，完全转换可能需要较长的时间。

阶段性（或模块化）转换是指选择一个子系统（如客房预订系统）进行直接转换。如果这个子系统的运行令人满意，那么可着手进行下一个子系统的转换，直到现有系统最终完全被新系统取代。这种方式也许比较适合酒店行业，因为诸如客户系统与库存系统、采购系统没有太大关联性，但不一定适合像生产系统与制造系统有极大关联性的行业。

不同的方法有不同的优缺点，案例中的酒店需要根据新系统的可靠性、充足的IT资源、转换的紧迫性、不同行业的特点等因素进行综合考虑来决定最优化方式。

Variant 3

This examination is structured as follows：

Section number	Number of tasks	Time for section(minutes)
1	1	45
2	1	45
3	1	45
4	1	45

The time available for each section is for reading,planning and writing your answer(s).

Section 1

Five months ago the directors at Wise Choice Hotels agreed to build a new hotel in a coastal resort close to Southcastle. The hotel, to be known as Hotel 5, is currently under construction. Once completed it will have a golf course, spa facilities, an outdoor pool and separate bar and restaurant facilities. The new hotel will be very close to a beach and to a small local airfield, which amongst other events hosts the three day Southcastle Air Show every year. Some of Hotel 5's rooms will have sea views.

You arrive at work to find the following email from Rav Patel, finance director:

From: Rav Patel, Finance Director
To: Management Accountant Assistant
Subject: ABC and increasing revenue

I have a meeting tomorrow with the other directors to discuss a few matters relating to Hotel 5. I would like you to prepare a briefing paper on a couple of issues for me.

Firstly, I've been thinking about how we should prepare our budget for the new hotel. It strikes me that Hotel 5 is very different to our other four hotels. For a start there will be different grades of room and a wider variety of revenue generating opportunities.

I recently attended a business breakfast where the presentation was about using ABC in a service organisation. I've got a basic understanding of the principles of ABC and think that we should consider implementing it, initially for Hotel 5. I would like your briefing paper to include an explanation of the relevance and potential benefits of using ABC for Hotel 5 and the potential problems that might result from its implementation. There is no need, at this stage, to include any examples of potential cost drivers.

Secondly, at tomorrow's meeting, we are going to discuss the different ways we can generate revenue at Hotel 5, so that we can consider our marketing approach. I would like your briefing paper to explain:

- four ways in which we could price our rooms at different times of the year, for different types of guests, in order to maximise total room revenue at Hotel 5;
- four ways in which we could generate revenues (excluding room, bar and restaurant revenues from our guests) in Hotel 5 by using its facilities.

Thank you.

Rav Patel

Finance Director

Wise Choice Hotels

Write the briefing paper requested by Rav Patel.

Section 2

One week later Hotel 5 is still being constructed. You receive the following email from Rav Patel, finance director:

From: Rav Patel, Finance Director

To: Management Accountant Assistant

Subject: Capitalisation of costs for Hotel 5 and ABC

The other directors and I had a meeting to discuss Hotel 5. Construction of the hotel and its swimming pool will be completed shortly and we plan to be open for business in early October. The golf course will be completed by spring 2017.

John Hayes, managing director, has prepared a schedule of the costs (excluding the golf course) that he believes might be capitalised as PPE in respect of Hotel 5. He has asked for a justification of whether each entry on his schedule can be capitalised in our statement of financial position, or not.

At the meeting we decided to go ahead with implementing an ABC system for Hotel 5. We are thinking of creating different package deals for Hotel 5's vacation guests. We are currently thinking of six packages, all with different lengths of stay and different levels of access to spa and golf facilities. In order to price these we will need the costings to be as accurate as possible.

We are going to start by analysing the daily housekeeping service, which includes bed making, a light clean, towel swapping, if requested, and restocking of complimentary refreshments and toiletries (although most guests who stay for more than a few days tend to use their own toiletries). Unless there is a new guest coming into the room, bedding is changed twice a week and bedrooms are set up once a week. A bedroom set up means the room is thoroughly cleaned, complimentary fresh fruit, water and complimentary items are placed in the room.

Please send me an email which includes:

- A draft response to John Hayes' query about PPE.
- An explanation of three activities and associated cost drivers for the housekeeping operation. Please include an explanation of the nature of the costs that would be included in the associated cost pools as well as justification of why it is appropriate for the activity to be separately identified.

Thank you!

Rav Patel

Finance Director

Wise Choice Hotels

Schedule of Hotel 5 Construction Costs Prepared by John Hayes

	(M$ 000)
Land purchase	1,200
Legal fees associated with land purchase and planning applications	140
Architect's fees	160
Construction costs of the hotel and swimming pool paid to an external building contractor	2,800
Purchase of furniture, kitchen, spa and swimming pool equipment	1,100
Interest on a loan taken out to fund the purchase of furniture (the loan is for 5 years at a cost of M$ 20,000 a year, giving a total cost of M$ 100,000)	100
Operating loss expected in the first two weeks of operation	240
Cost of external consultancy to train new staff	25
Suggested total costs to be capitalised as PPE	5,765

Write the email to Rav Patel.

Section 3

A few months later you arrive at work to find the following email from Rav Patel, finance director:

From: Rav Patel, Finance Director
To: Management Accountant Assistant
Subject: Sales variances and potential leisure travel company customers

I have just been looking at the first operating statement for Hotel 5. I like how you have analysed the room occupancy figures using variances (and I've checked that all the numbers are right!). I showed your analysis to John, but he didn't understand it and has asked for an explanation of, and possible reasons for, each variance.

As Hotel 5's guests mainly stay for vacations, I've been looking into linking in with leisure travel companies. The idea would be that Hotel 5 would be included in the leisure travel companies' hotel portfolios, their customers could then book and pay for a stay at Hotel 5 through them. After the guests' stay, at a point in time to be agreed with the hotel manager, the leisure travel companies will pay us. We would pay a commission to the leisure travel companies. I think that this would be a good way to attract guests from other countries.

To start with, we will approach leisure travel companies in Bacland and Tacland, our two closest neighbours. First we need to assess their creditworthiness before accepting them as customers and agreeing credit terms (which would be on similar terms to our corporate customers). Please send me an explanation of the factors that we will need to consider and the actions that we should take in this assessment of creditworthiness.

I just need one email from you which includes:

- an explanation of what each variance means and possible reasons for each variance;
- my request in respect of potential new leisure travel company customers.

Thank you!

Rav Patel
Finance Director
Wise Choice Hotels

Room related sales variances for Hotel 5 for the quarter ended 31 December 2016：

Sales variance	Sea-facing room(M$)	Non-sea-facing room(M$)
Price	44,160 Favourable	27,600 Adverse
Mix *	13,904 Favourable	11,850 Adverse
Quantity *	10 384 Favourable	11,850 Favourable

* Mix and quantity variances are measured using the standard contribution per type of room, per night occupied, of M$ 88 for sea-facing rooms and M$ 75 for non-sea-facing rooms. The mix variance is calculated using the individual units method. For the purposes of calculation the number of rooms occupied in the mix and quantity variances has been rounded to the nearest whole number.

This is the information used to correctly calculate the variances：

- Hotel 5 has 50 sea-facing rooms and 75 non-sea-facing rooms.
- Average budgeted room rates are：

  Sea-facing rooms-M$ 143 a night.

  Non-sea-facing rooms-M$ 130 a night.
- The budgeted occupancy rate for the quarter ended 31 December 2016 was 90% for sea-facing rooms, and 80% for non-sea-facing rooms.
- The actual room rate charged is on a sliding scale for each type of room. Typically, (but not always) the smaller the time gap between the booking and the occupancy, the lower the price.

Actual occupancy during the quarter was 96% for sea-facing rooms and 80% for non-sea-facing rooms.

Write the email requested by Rav Patel.

Section 4

A week later you receive the following email from Rav Patel, finance director：

From：Rav Patel, Finance Director

To：Management Accountant Assistant

Subject：Workplace flexibility and a celebrity golf tournament

I was reading an article in a management journal about workplace flexibility and it got me thinking as to whether, or not, it was something that we should look into as we recruit the staff for Hotel 5. If it works there we could possibly roll it out to all of our hotels.

On another matter, we have decided to hold a pro-celebrity golf tournament. Invitations will be sent out to golf professionals and celebrities from the entertainment industry in Macland. It is intended that the admission fees will be paid to charity, but our intention is that Wise Choice Hotels will benefit from sales of food and beverages on the golf course, as well as from increased occupancy and use of hotel facilities, such as our restaurant and spa.

We are considering three alternative dates on which to hold the tournament: 1 April, 1 June or 1 August. We do not yet know which golf professionals and celebrities will be available on the different dates, which, along with the weather on the day, will have an impact on attendance figures.

Recently, we engaged Prospero Consultants to undertake research on the levels of attendance we could expect from holding the tournament on the three alternative dates. We provided Prospero Consultants with cost and budget data to help them to estimate the expected profit that would be earned.

They have looked at the three different decision options and have now sent us a schedule of their results with the comment: "that the choice of date on which to hold the celebrity golf tournament depends on the directors' attitudes to risk." I know that the directors need an explanation of the schedule and also the comment made by Prospero Consultants.

Please prepare a briefing note which can be circulated ahead of our next directors' meeting which explains:

- How we could achieve numerical, financial and task flexibility for the workforce at Hotel 5 and the potential benefits, and possible disadvantages to us, of doing this.
- The meaning of the data contained in the schedule from Prospero Consultants and how different "attitudes to risk" affect our decision on which date to hold the pro-celebrity golf tournament.

Rav Patel

Finance Director

Wise Choice Hotels

Schedule from Prospero Consulting

1 April:

Predicted additional profit(M$)	Probability of occurrence	Expected value(M$)
170,000	0.4	68,000
180,000	0.3	54,000
190,000	0.3	57,000
		179,000
Standard deviation = M$ 8,306		
Coefficient of variation = 4.64%		

1 June:

Predicted additional profit(M$)	Probability of occurrence	Expected value(M$)
140,000	0.5	70,000
180,000	0.4	72,000
250,000	0.1	25,000
		167,000
Standard deviation = M$ 33,481		
Coefficient of variation = 20.05%		

1 August:

Predicted additional profit(M$)	Probability of occurrence	Expected value(M$)
120,000	0.1	12,000
200,000	0.5	100,000
215,000	0.4	86,000
		198,000
Standard deviation = M$ 26,944		
Coefficient of variation = 13.61%		

Write the briefing note for the directors.

试卷三

本次考试的结构如下：

序号	任务数	时间（分钟）
1	1	45
2	1	45
3	1	45
4	1	45

每个部分规定的时间可用于读题、组织和书写答案。

任务一

5个月前，智选酒店的管理层同意在Southcastle附近的海滨度假胜地建造一座新酒店，即五号酒店，该酒店目前正在建设中。建成后的五号酒店将拥有高尔夫球场、SPA（水疗）会所、户外游泳池以及独立的酒吧和餐厅。五号酒店靠近海滩，毗邻本地机场，这个机场每年都会举办三次Southcastle航空展。五号酒店的一些客房是海景房。

你来到办公室后，收到一封来自财务总监Rav Patel的邮件：

发件人：财务总监 Rav Patel

收件人：管理会计助理

主题：作业成本法和收入增加

我明天要和其他管理者讨论一些与五号酒店有关的问题。请为我准备一份简报，包括以下内容。

第一，我一直在考虑如何做好五号酒店的预算问题。我认为，五号酒店和其他4家酒店不同。五号酒店客房档次较高，有更多的创收机会。

最近，我在一次商务早餐上，听说服务业也可以采用作业成本法。我了解了作业成本法的原则，我认为我们从五号酒店开始试点引进。请你准备一份简报解释五号酒店采用作业成本法的相关问题和潜在收益，以及可能会带来的潜在问题。无须对成本驱动进行举例。

第二，我们将在明天的会议上讨论五号酒店的创收模式，因此需要考虑营销手段。希望你在简报中解释以下问题：

- 为了使五号酒店的客房收入最大化，请列举我们可以针对不同类型的客人、在不同的时间、提供4种不同的价格。
- 为充分利用五号酒店的设施，请列举4种创收模式（不包括客房收入、酒吧和餐厅的收入）。

谢谢。

智选酒店

财务总监

Rav Patel

请根据 Rav Patel 的要求做出简要回答。

任务二

一周后，五号酒店仍在建造中。你收到来自财务总监 Rav Patel 的邮件：

发件人：财务总监 Rav Patel
收件人：管理会计助理
主题：五号酒店的成本资本化和作业成本法

昨天，我与管理层讨论了五号酒店的问题。该酒店主体及其游泳池即将完工，计划于 10 月初开业。高尔夫球场计划于 2017 年春季竣工。

总经理 John Hayes 已经编制了一份关于五号酒店需要资本化处理的成本项目表（不包括高尔夫球场），他要求我们在资产负债表中说明每个项目是否可以成本资本化。

我们已经决定在五号酒店采用作业成本法。五号酒店为前来度假的客人提供不同的消费套餐。目前，酒店有 6 个套餐，不同的套餐有不同的住宿时间、不同级别的 SPA 和高尔夫设施。我们需要精确核算成本以便为这 6 个套餐进行定价。

以客房服务成本分析为例，包括床上用品、客房保洁、毛巾更换，以及补充免费的茶点和洗漱用品（大多住几天以上的客人都会自备洗漱用品）等成本。如果客人长住，每周需要更换两次床上用品，进行一次客房保洁。客房保洁包括彻底打扫客房，摆放新鲜的水果、水和免费的物品等。

请在给我的回复中包括以下内容：

- 简要回答 John Hayes 关于固定资产问题的提问。
- 解释客房服务的 3 项活动及相关成本动因，包括成本池中每项成本的属性以及单独确认各项作业的理由。

谢谢！

智选酒店
财务总监
Rav Patel

John Hayes 编制的五号酒店建造成本项目表

	（M$ 000）
购买土地	1 200
土地购买和规划申请的法律费用	140
建筑设计费	160
支付给外部建筑承包商的有关酒店和游泳池的建筑成本	2 800
购买家具、厨房、SPA 和游泳池设备	1 100
为购买家具而支付的贷款利息（贷款期限为 5 年，年利息为 M$ 20 000，总成本为 M$ 100 000）。	100
试运营两周的预计投入	240
培训新员工的外部咨询成本	25
资本化处理为固定资产的总成本	5 765

请按 Rav Patel 的要求写一封邮件。

任务三

几个月后，你来到办公室后收到一封来自财务总监 Rav Patel 的邮件：

发件人：财务总监 Rav Patel
收件人：管理会计助理
主题：销售差异和潜在的商务休闲客户

我刚刚看了五号酒店的第一份经营情况报告。我觉得你采用差异分析法来分析销售差异的做法不错（我检查了你所用的数据也都是正确的）。我将你的分析结果向 John 进行了传达，但他不是很理解，希望你对每个差异进行解释并分析原因。

五号酒店主要提供度假服务，为此我已经多次接洽几家休闲旅游公司。他们同意将五号酒店纳入他们的商务休闲酒店范围，这样客户可以通过休闲旅游公司来预订我们的五号酒店。客人消费结束后，休闲旅游公司再与我们的酒店经理约定打款时间。我们向休闲旅游公司支付佣金。我认为，此举有利于吸引外国客人。

为此，我们要开始与 Bacland（巴克兰德）和 Tacland（塔克兰德）的休闲旅游公司接洽。在决定将它们列作合作对象和拟定信用条款（信用条款的拟定要参考我们现有的信用政策）前，先评估它们的信用级别。请列出我们在信用评估中需要考虑的因素，并解释我们需要采取的行动。

请在你的回复中包括以下内容：

- 每项差异的解释及可能的原因分析。
- 对休闲旅游公司客户的要求。

谢谢！

智选酒店

财务总监

Rav Patel

截至 2016 年 12 月 31 日五号酒店房费销售差异的季度数据：

销售差异	海景房（M$）	非海景房（M$）
价格差异	44 160 有利差异	27 600 不利差异
组合差异*	13 904 有利差异	11 850 不利差异
数量差异*	10 384 有利差异	11 850 有利差异

* 组合差异和数量差异按单间客房标准边际贡献、每晚入住率、海景房价格为 M$ 88、非海景房价格为 M$ 75 来计算，组合差异采用单位法来计算。为了计算方便，组合差异和数量差异计算中的入住客房数量四舍五入到整数。

下列信息用于正确计算差异：

- 五号酒店有 50 间海景房和 75 间非海景房。
- 平均预算房费分别为：
  海景房每晚 M$ 143。
  非海景房每晚 M$ 130。
- 截至 2016 年 12 月 31 日，本季度的海景房预算入住率为 90%，非海景房为 80%。
- 实际房费是浮动的。通常情况下（但并非总是），预订与入住之间的时间间隔越小，价格就越低。
- 本季度海景房实际入住率为 96%，非海景房实际入住率为 80%。

请按 Rav Patel 要求写一封邮件。

任务四

一周后，你收到一封来自财务总监 Rav Patel 的邮件：

发件人：财务总监 Rav Patel
收件人：管理会计助理
主题：工作灵活性和名人高尔夫球赛

我在一本管理杂志上读到一篇关于工作灵活性的文章，这让我开始思考，当我们为五号酒店招聘员工时，这是否是我们应该研究的问题。如果工作灵活性在五号酒店试行有效，我们就可以把这个方法推广到所有的酒店中。

此外，我们还打算举办一场名人高尔夫球赛，并向 Macland 的高尔夫专业人士和娱乐圈名人发出邀请函。门票收入将捐赠给慈善机构，智选酒店也会因此增加食物和饮料销售，增加餐厅和 SPA 的营业收入。

高尔夫球赛有 3 个备选日期：4 月 1 日、6 月 1 日、8 月 1 日。我们尚不知道受邀人士在什么时间方便，也无法预知比赛当天的天气会对出席人数产生何种影响。

最近，我们委托普罗斯佩罗顾问咨询公司就上述 3 个日期的参赛人数进行了调研，我们向该公司提供了成本和预算数据，要求他们为我们估计预期利润。

普罗斯佩罗顾问咨询公司交来了一份研究结果，并附加以下评论："名人高尔夫球赛日期选择取决于管理者的风险态度。"管理层需要这份研究结果的解释及上述评论的解释。

请在下次董事会之前准备一份简报，解释以下问题。

- 我们如何实现五号酒店数据、财务和工作的灵活性，以及工作灵活性有哪些潜在的优劣点？
- 普罗斯佩罗顾问咨询公司研究结果中数据的含义，以及不同的"风险态度"对决定名人高尔夫球赛日期有何影响。

智选酒店
财务总监
Rav Patel

普罗斯佩罗顾问咨询公司的研究结果

4 月 1 日：

预计附加利润（M$）	发生的概率	期望值（M$）
170 000	0.4	68 000
180 000	0.3	54 000
190 000	0.3	57 000
		179 000
标准差 = M$ 8 306		
离散系数 = 4.64%		

6 月 1 日：

预计附加利润（M$）	发生的概率	期望值（M$）
140 000	0.5	70 000
180 000	0.4	72 000
250 000	0.1	25 000
		167 000
标准差 = M$ 33 481		
离散系数 = 20.05%		

8 月 1 日：

预计附加利润（M$）	发生的概率	期望值（M$）
120 000	0.1	12 000
200 000	0.5	100 000
215 000	0.4	86 000
		198 000
标准差 = M$ 26 944		
离散系数 = 13.61%		

请为管理者做出简要注释。

Variant 3 Suggested Answers

Section 1

ABC at Hotel 5

The Relevance and Benefits of Using ABC

As with many service organisations we have a high proportion of fixed costs; our 2016 budget indicates that these total almost the same as our variable costs, some M$4.4 million. Whereas variable costs can easily be linked proportionally to activity, we should also recognise that fixed costs are also caused by something. If we can understand what causes the various fixed costs to arise, then we can plan more effectively and also take action to reduce these costs.

What is needed is an analysis of our various fixed costs in order to determine the respective driver that causes each cost to arise. Some of these costs will be genuinely fixed in nature, for example our local tax may well be a fixed amount that we can do nothing about. On the other hand, it may be possible to establish the drivers for other costs in staffing and property. For example, we budget M$250 per room per year for the replacement of towels and bedding. This presupposes that all towels and bedding wear out at the same rate. A more accurate driver might be the number of times that items are washed, which in turn depends on both room occupancy and the extent to which guests are content to use the same towels for more than one day. Some fixed property costs might also be driven by occupancy; a rarely used room will not need redecorating as frequently as a well-used one.

In Hotel 5 there will be a greater number of services available to guests compared to our existing hotels and hence these services will be tailored to the guest specifications. ABC could be used in conjunction with customer profitability analysis to give a more accurate view of the profitability earned from servicing particular customers.

We operate in a very competitive market and we need to be able to assess the profitability of the products on offer to our guests, which ABC would allow us to do. Using ABC as the basis of budgeting and longer term forward planning of our overhead costs would provide more realistic budgets of them which should improve our system of performance management. By controlling the incidence of the cost driver the level of the associated cost could be controlled. ABC can provide a fairer allocation of costs and which would enable better decision making within our business.

The Potential Problems That Might Result from the Implementation of ABC

Setting up an ABC system can be expensive and time consuming. As the hotel activities are analysed, they must be broken down into each activity's individual components. The entire process can use up valuable resources as data is collected, measured and entered into the new system. An ABC system might also prove to be expensive to run and manage once implemented.

We potentially lack the resources to implement an ABC system and would probably have to hire an outside consulting firm to assist with the set-up of such a system and provide training in its operation. This would be costly.

Even in an ABC system some overhead costs are difficult to assign to activities and customers and therefore such costs still have to be arbitrarily applied. For example, we would probably still need to apportion our costs in respect of property insurance and building depreciation at the cost pooling stage.

A major issue in the implementation of an ABC system lies in the correct identification of appropriate cost drivers of the activities undertaken within our business. The selection of inappropriate cost drivers could seriously undermine the value gained from such an investment as our management would be receiving and making decisions on the basis of inaccurate information produced by the system.

Four Ways We Could Price Our Rooms in Order to Maximise the Generation of Room Revenues

We could charge higher prices per room at times of events such as the Southcastle Air Show. This is a form of price discrimination, in that we set the price in line with peaks in demand. This would give a higher level of sales revenue if demand for hotel accommodation exceeds the available supply at the time of the show.

We could charge higher prices per room during the high season when people tend to take their vacations and have a willingness to pay a higher rate for a room because potentially the weather is better. In this respect the location of our new hotel being not only on the coast but also offering sea-views will add to this willingness to pay more for our rooms and this might well result in a higher level of sales revenue. Again this is a form of price discrimination.

We could offer inclusive "hotel and golf packages" . Golf is a very popular sport and such an offer might appeal to a very wide audience. We could potentially charge a premium for the room associated with the package. The costs of the golf course are likely to be predominantly fixed in nature and so any premium in room rate for such packages would not only boost our sales revenue but also our profit.

We could reduce our prices per room for senior citizens during the low season in an attempt to increase our occupancy rate. Senior citizens have more available time for leisure activities than the working population. Perhaps a package that includes the provision of free transport to and from their homes could be offered to them in order to increase the perceived value of a stay at our hotel. Again, as long as the selling price of our rooms exceeds the variable cost of the room plus transport then such a package would not only boost our sales revenue but also our profit.

Four Ways We Could Generate Other Revenues at Hotel 5

- The golf course could be made available to the public. This would boost the sales revenue and profit of our hotel. Care would have to be taken when scheduling bookings for the golf course to ensure that hotel guests are given first priority.
- The restaurant could be opened to the public for meals, which would again boost our sales revenues and profit.
- We could promote our hotel as a wedding venue. This would create an additional income stream. This might not only increase the volume of our business but enable us to charge premium prices leading to a boost in both sales revenue and profit.
- We could launch spa day packages to draw people in that are not guests of the hotel. The package could include lunch in the restaurant, full use of the swimming pool and a certain number of spa treatments. The price charged for such a package is likely to cover any additional variable costs incurred by a considerable margin.

Section 2

From: Management Accountant Assistant

To: Rav Patel, Finance Director

Subject: Capitalization of costs for Hotel 5 and ABC

Capital Expenditure

In order to capitalise the expenditure incurred in respect of Hotel 5 as part of PPE an asset must have been created. There are two criteria that must be met in order to recognise an asset. Firstly, it is probable that the expenditure will result in future economic benefits to our business; secondly, the expenditure can be reliably measured. Both of these are met: the hotel once constructed will generate future economic benefits in the form of profit and because the expenditure is cash related it can be reliably measured.

Further, to be classified as PPE, IAS 16 PPE states that the asset is held for the supply of goods and services and will be held for more than one accounting period. Clearly, our hotel and associated facilities will be used to supply services for our guests and we intend to hold the hotel for more than a year: therefore the hotel and facilities are PPE.

The next consideration is which of the costs in John's schedule can be included as part of a PPE asset. The general rule is that purchase costs and those costs directly attributable to bringing the asset to its working condition for its intended use can be included.

There are a number of purchase costs identified in John's schedule: land, furniture and equipment. These can be capitalised, although it should be noted that they will be capitalised as individual assets for the purposes of calculating depreciation. The construction costs of the hotel and swimming pool are also in effect purchase costs. This amount of M$2. 8 million will need to be broken down into the hotel building itself and the swimming pool, as each will have a different useful economic life.

Costs that are directly attributable will include legal and professional fees, hence the legal fees and architect fees can be included in the cost of the hotel.

The costs that cannot be capitalised are:

- The interest on the five year loan for the purchase of the furniture. It is possible to capitalise interest where a loan has been taken out to fund the construction of a qualifying asset: an asset which has taken a substantial time to get ready for its intended use. However our loan is for furniture. Had the loan been associated with the construction of the hotel then a portion of the interest could be capitalised.

- The operating loss for the first two weeks is not a cost directly attributable to getting the hotel ready for its intended use. The hotel is ready for its intended use the minute that the first guest arrives.
- The cost of an external consultant to train the staff. Whilst it could be argued that the training of staff is required in order for the asset(the hotel)to be ready for its intended use, expenditure on training of staff cannot be capitalised because the staff themselves are free to leave and take their training with them.

ABC—Housekeeping Operation

Restocking of Complimentary Refreshments and Toiletries

An activity within the housekeeping operation is the restocking of the complimentary refreshments and toiletries. The cost pool for this activity will include the costs of the complimentary items plus a share of the labour cost associated with housekeeping staff. A suitable cost driver here is the number of complimentary items restocked when a room is serviced.

This is an appropriate activity because guests who stay for a week or more, typically bring and use their own toiletries, whilst those staying for only a few days use the complimentary ones. Thus the usage of this activity is potentially different depending on the length of guest stay and therefore the type of guest package.

Bed Changing

Another activity within the housekeeping operation is bed changing. The cost pool for this activity will include the cost of laundering a set of bedding plus the labour cost associated with the physical activity of changing the bed. A suitable cost driver here will be the number of bed changes.

This is an appropriate activity because different guest packages will have a different number of bed changes. Guests who stay for a week or more only have bedding changed twice a week(therefore every 3 or 4 days). If a guest stays only one night then obviously the bed will need to be changed ready for the next guest.

Bedroom Set Up

Another activity within the housekeeping operation is bedroom set up. The cost pool for this activity will include the costs of the complimentary fruit and water and the labour cost associated with the extra time taken to thoroughly clean and set the room up. A suitable cost driver here would be the number of bedroom set ups.

This is an appropriate activity because each package may have a different number of set ups. A guest staying for more than one week will have this done twice, whilst a guest staying for a week or less will have this done once, whether it be a one night stay or a seven night stay.

Thanks!

Management Accountant Assistant
Wise Choice Hotel

Section 3

From: Management Accountant Assistant
To: Rav Patel, Finance Director
Subject: Sales variances and potential leisure travel company customers

Explanation of the Sales Variances for Hotel 5

Room Price Variances

The room price variance is favourable for sea-facing rooms but adverse for non-sea-facing rooms. This is because the average room rate charged for sea-facing rooms was higher than the budgeted room rate, whilst that for non-sea-facing rooms was lower. The overall price variance will be favourable meaning that the effect of the higher prices charged for the sea facing rooms is outweighing the effect of the adverse price variance for non-sea-facing rooms.

It is possible that the sea-facing rooms were booked earlier than the non-sea-facing rooms because they would have been booked when room rates were higher on the sliding scale. The opposite is true for the non-sea-facing rooms: although it possible that this was due to guests waiting for a good deal.

Room Revenue Mix Variances

Our hotel has in effect two products on offer namely sea-facing and non-sea facing rooms. The room mix variances have arisen during the period because we have sold our two products in different proportions from those contained in our budget for the quarter ended 31 December 2016.

The room mix variance is calculated by reference to the budgeted contribution per room, which is higher for sea-facing rooms. The mix variance is favourable for sea-facing rooms and adverse for non-sea-facing rooms because the effect on contribution of sea-facing rooms is greater than for non-sea-facing rooms. The mix variance overall is favourable which means the impact of the change in the mix of rooms sold is an increase in contribution: in terms of the total number of rooms occupied in the period, a greater proportion of these were sea-facing rooms.

It is possible that the actual mix of rooms sold is different to budget, because more people than we thought were prepared to pay a premium for a sea-view. It is likely that those people who definitely wanted a sea-view booked early (hence the higher room rate), but those who were not bothered waited.

Room Revenue Quantity Variances

The room quantity variance is calculated by comparing our actual level of rooms occupied in budgeted proportions with our original budget and is measured on the basis of contribution per room type. The room quantity variances are favourable for both sea-facing and non-sea-facing rooms due to the fact that our overall level of room sales exceeded our budgeted level of sales during the period. What is important here is the overall position rather than the individual variances and therefore these individual variances should be shown as one figure.

Looking at non-sea-facing rooms specifically we can see that the mix and quantity variances exactly match each other giving a nil volume variance for this type of room: which is as we would expect given that the budgeted and actual occupancy levels are the same at 80%.

It is possible that we underestimated our budget. Alternatively it could be that guests are curious and hence were keen to come and use our facilities in the first few months. It will be interesting to see if this trend continues.

Potential Leisure Travel Company Customers

Factors to consider assessing creditworthiness:

The main issue to consider before we actually link with a new customer is the ability of the customer to pay us. We need to be reasonably confident that the customer is not going to go out of business, or that they will struggle to pay us in a timely manner.

This is particularly important for leisure travel companies. More and more guests now book directly with hotels (even those in other countries), through hotel websites. As a result, certainly in Macland, many leisure travel companies have ceased trading in the last 10 years.

Having said that, many of the leisure travel companies that remain in Macland have evolved in some way to offer additional services to their customers: they have had to in order to survive. As a result they are successful and thriving businesses.

We will need to assess whether the story in Macland is the same in Bacland and Tacland. If the markets and guest behaviours in Bacland and Tacland are 10 years behind us, then this increases the risk that our customer ceases to trade. However, it could be that the same evolution has already happened in these countries and therefore this somewhat limits this risk.

We should also consider whether Bacland and Tacland have a similar organisation to MLTA. If they do then this might offer us some form of protection against a customer ceasing to trade owing us money. We will need to check whether our potential customers are members of such an organisation though before accepting them.

We can get a good idea about whether a business is creditworthy by analysing their financial statements (assuming that we can get hold of them from Bacland and Tacland). In particular we should look at the cash and working capital position. We could calculate current ratios and look at the statement of cash flows. We could look at payable days to assess how quickly they pay hoteliers.

Another factor that we should consider is the age of the business. If the business is new then, especially in the current market, there is a greater risk of default. However as per my comment above given the changes in the market the age of the business might not be that reliable a factor to consider.

We should also consider if there are any references available from banks, other hotel customers, credit reference agencies, alongside any reports in the press or on-line about the business and their trading history.

Thanks!

Management Accountant Assistant

Wise Choice Hotel

Section 4

Workforce Flexibility

Within Hotel 5 we could seek to achieve three types of flexibility. These are as follows：

Numerical Flexibility

This could be achieved through the use of temporary workers who might be contractors or agency staff. This would enable us to be better positioned to cope with fluctuations in demand on our services. We ought to give consideration to the use of contractors for some of our ancillary services such as maintenance, catering, security and the swimming pool service.

Financial Flexibility

This is achieved through variable systems of reward such as performance related pay, bonus schemes and profit sharing. We should recognise that achieving a good performance/rewards linkage will help to realise a number of performance improvements within the hotel.

Task Flexibility

This is also referred to as functional flexibility and involves having employees who are able to undertake a wide range of tasks. If we could introduce task flexibility within Hotel 5, employees might be able to undertake a wider range of tasks at the same level (horizontally) or undertake tasks previously carried out by employees at higher or lower levels (vertically). The achievement of task flexibility would enable us to react to changes in service requirements and levels in demand: for example, in the provision of our catering services.

Potential benefits of flexibility are as follows：

- a reduction in our labour costs as a result of operating at lower staffing levels which would be more noticeable in the low season when our occupancy level is lower and yet we still have the burden of our fixed costs；
- better utilisation of equipment (such as catering equipment or the pool equipment) as a consequence of the increased multi-tasking capabilities of employees；
- increased employee motivation and productivity as a consequence of the investment in training, given in order to give employees the capabilities to multi-task; higher motivation might in turn lead to reductions in levels of absenteeism and staff turnover at

Hotel 5——this is important as we operate in an industry in which levels of absenteeism and staff turnover are relatively high;

- the achievement of flexibility would represent a shift away from the "fixed workforce" with its fixed cost burden to our business.

Potential disadvantages of flexibility are as follows:

- There could be a dilution of our organisational culture, as employees would see less of each other.
- This in turn might give rise to problems with continuity and team working at Hotel 5.
- Flexibility would be at a cost to the business via the investment in training to achieve multi-skilling.

Prospero Consultant's Schedule

The data in the table:

The table prepared by Prospero Consultants shows the expected value of each of the possible tournament dates: 1 April, 1 June and 1 August.

The data in the table indicates that there are three possible outcomes for each tournament date. The possible outcomes for each tournament date are shown in the first column indicating predicted additional profit. These are all different and represent the net effect of additional revenues less additional costs.

The probabilities are the likelihood of each outcome arising based on Prospero's estimates. The expected value is the sum of each outcome multiplied by its associated probability. Thus the expected value is the weighted average of all outcomes where the weighting is by probability.

In general a higher expected value is more attractive than a lower one, but please see my comments on attitudes to risk below.

In the case of the attached schedule August has the highest expected value and June the lowest.

The expected value alone gives no indication of the range of possible outcomes. The expected value is not the most likely result, it might not even be one of the possible outcomes of the three decision options. The expected value is the long-run average outcome if the same event was to be repeated over and over again.

Care should be exercised when using expected values in a "one-off" decision as it is simply a weighted average.

It should also be borne in mind that the probabilities used in the calculations of the expected value of each of the decision options might be subjective in nature, although the fact that Prospero Consultants are experts at what they do does limit this subjectivity.

Risk Attitudes

It is highly probable that all decision makers will not have the same attitude to risk. In this regard a director within Wise Choice Hotels may be a "Risk Seeker", "Risk Neutral" or "Risk Averse".

- A "Risk Seeker" is a decision-maker who is interested in the best outcomes no matter how small the likelihood that they will occur. June has the highest standard deviation and also the highest coefficient of variation. This indicates high upside potential as evidenced by the possible outcome of M$250,000. For this reason this type of decision maker would be attracted to June.
- A "Risk Neutral" decision maker will select the strategy that maximises the expected value or benefit. In the case of Wise Choice Hotels a risk neutral decision would select August which has the highest expected value of the three dates under consideration. This type of decision maker would ignore both the standard deviation and coefficient of variation.
- A "Risk Averse" decision maker tries to avoid risk. April has the lowest standard deviation and also the lowest coefficient of variation. This indicates that April is most likely to result in an outcome which is closer to the expected value and therefore has a low downside risk. For these reasons this type of decision maker would be attracted to April.

The final decision regarding the choice of date on which to hold the celebrity golf tournament would be influenced by the "collective" risk attitude of you, the directors.

试卷三　参考答案

任务一

五号酒店作业成本法

采用作业成本法的相关性和好处

作为一家门店众多的服务企业，五号酒店的固定成本较高。在2016年的预算中，固定成本与变动成本几乎持平，大约为M$ 440万。变动成本一般与经营业务量相关，而固定成本也有相应的成本动因。如果能找出固定成本的产生原因，就可以更好地计划固定成本，并有效降低固定成本。

我们需要分析不同的固定成本项目并确定每项成本的动因。有些固定成本金额恒定不变，如地方税，我们无法施加影响；也有些固定成本源于人工和财产等成本动因，如预算每间客房每年更换毛巾和床上用品的成本为M$ 250，这是假定所有的毛巾和床上用品都会以同样的速度受到磨损。事实上，客房的入住率和客人使用毛巾的频率才是这些物品清洗次数及磨损速度的真正动因。一些固定的物业成本可能也取决于入住率的高低，比如闲置较多的客房无须像高频使用客房那样经常翻修。

五号酒店为客人提供定制服务，入住率会高于其他酒店。作业成本法有利于结合客户获利能力分析，从而能更精确地衡量不同客户的盈利能力。

酒店业竞争十分激烈，采用作业成本法有助于我们准确评估不同服务的盈利能力。基于作业成本法的预算和长期管理费用计划，有助于改善我们的业绩管理。通过控制成本动因，相关成本的实际水平能得到有效控制。作业成本法有利于公平分摊成本，改善业务决策。

采用作业成本法的潜在问题

搭建一个作业成本法系统比较费时费力。在分析酒店作业时，需要将所有的作业分解为不同的组件。收集、测量相关数据并将其输入作业成本法系统会耗用企业宝贵的资源。此外，作业成本法的运行和管理成本也会非常昂贵。

如果我们自己缺乏实施作业成本法的资源，那么我们就需要花重金聘请外部咨询机构协助我们建立核算系统并培训相关员工。

在作业成本法系统中，有些管理成本很难分配给具体的业务和客户，只能按主观进行分配。例如，财产保险成本及折旧成本的分摊。

实施作业成本法还要正确识别作业的成本动因。如果成本动因选择不当，就会错误低估投资回报，致使管理者根据系统产生的错误信息来做相应决策。

实现客房收入最大化的房费定价方法

我们可以在 Southcastle 航空展期间提高房费。在需求高峰时段涨价虽是一种价格歧视行为，但在航空展期间，酒店住宿供不应求，涨价有利于增加酒店的销售收入。

在旺季，由于气候宜人，很多人前来度假并愿意支付更高的房费，这也可以给我们带来更高的收入。五号酒店毗邻海岸线，能提供高品质的海景房。提高房费可以增加我们的销售收入。当然这也是一种价格歧视。

我们还可以开发“酒店 + 高尔夫”打包服务，对打高尔夫球的客人收取额外费用。高尔夫是一项非常流行的运动，“酒店 + 高尔夫”打包服务可以吸引更多的客人。高尔夫球场主要是固定成本，与酒店业务打包，不仅有利于增加销售收入，还能增加利润。

为了提高入住率，我们还可以在淡季为老年客人提供低价房。相对而言，老年人有更多的休闲时间，向他们提供免费接送服务可以增加他们在酒店的消费。只要收取的房费收入超过客房的变动成本加往返交通费，这样的打包服务就有利于提高我们的销售收入和利润。

五号酒店增加收入的其他 4 种方式

- 向公众开放高尔夫球场将有利于提高酒店的销售收入和利润。但必须注意，在安排高尔夫球场预订时，要优先考虑酒店入住客人的需求。
- 向公众开放餐厅也有利于提高销售收入和利润。
- 将酒店作为婚礼场地有利于创造额外的收入，不仅可以增加业务品类，还可以通过收费提高销售收入和利润。
- 向非酒店客人提供 SPA 套餐，包括餐厅的午餐、游泳池及 SPA 服务。这个打包服务的价格应该能弥补所有的额外变动成本。

任务二

发件人：管理会计助理

收件人：财务总监 Rav Patel

主题：五号酒店的成本资本化和作业成本法

资本支出

五号酒店的开支可以列为固定资产（不动产、厂房和设备）。将支出进行资本化处理有两个标准：第一，可以带来未来经济效益；第二，可以准确度量。五号酒店的支出也要满足两个标准：第一，酒店建成后会产生未来经济效益及利润；第二，所有支出都与现金有关，可以准确度量。

此外，国际会计准则第 16 号关于固定资产的准则规定，固定资产是用于提供商品和服务并且持有期超过一个会计期间的资产。显然，五号酒店的投资将用于为客人提供服务，我们打算持有 1 年以上，因此酒店和设施可以列为固定资产。

在 John 的开支项目表中，需要确定哪些支出可以列为固定资产。一般来说，购买资产并将其准备到可使用状态所发生的成本都应计入固定资产。

John 的开支项目表中包括：土地、家具和设备的购买成本。这些成本都可以单独进行资本化处理并计提折旧。酒店和游泳池的建造成本也是实际购买成本。总额为 M$ 280 万的资金需要分解为不同的经济寿命的酒店大楼和游泳池，分别入账。

法律费用和专业建筑设计费用属于直接成本，直接计入酒店大楼成本。

不能进行资本化处理的成本有以下 3 种。

- 购买家具的 5 年期贷款利息。如果贷款用于符合固定资产要求的资产的建造，其利息可以资本化处理。所谓符合固定资产要求，指的是花费较长时间准备达到其预计用途的资产。但我们的贷款只用于购买家具，而不用于酒店建设，因此不可以进行资本化处理。
- 前两周试运营的投入并不是为酒店达到预计用途而发生的成本，酒店在第一个客人到达之前已经完工。
- 培训员工的外部咨询成本。对员工进行培训是为了使酒店达到可使用标准，但员工未来可能会离职，他们也有权决定是否参加培训，所以员工培训费不能资本化处理。

作业成本法——客房服务

茶点和洗漱用品的补充

客房服务中有一项作业是补充茶点和洗漱用品。该作业的成本池包括补充用品的成本及相关客房服务人员的人工成本。对该成本项目进行分配的动因是客房服务时补充用品的数量。

有些长期入住的客人一般会自备洗漱用品，而一般短期入住的客人才会使用酒店的洗漱用品。所以，客房服务作业还受客人住店时间和客人类型的影响。

整理床铺

客房服务的另一项作业是整理床铺。该作业的成本池包括床上用品的清洗成本和整理床铺的人工成本。该成本项目进行分配的动因是整理床铺的次数。

不同的客人需要不同的整理床铺次数，长期入住的客人一般每周需要整理两次床铺（即每3到4天一次）。如果客人只住1个晚上，那么第二天就需要为下一位客人整理床铺。

客房保洁

客房服务还有一项作业是整理卧室。该作业的成本池包括水果和饮用水的成本及整理卧室所需要的人工成本。该成本项目进行分配的动因是整理卧室的次数。

不同的客人需要不同的整理卧室次数，入住一周以上的客人一般每周需要整理两次卧室，入住一周以内（不管是住1个晚上还是7个晚上）的客人可能只需一周整理一次卧室。

感谢！

智选酒店

管理会计助理

任务三

发件人：管理会计助理

收件人：财务总监 Rav Patel

主题：销售差异和潜在的休闲旅游公司客户

五号酒店销售差异解释

客房价格差异

海景房价格存在有利差异，而非海景房价格存在不利差异。这是因为海景房平均房价高于预算房价，而非海景房平均房价低于预算房价。全部客房价格差异是有利差异，即海景房有利差异超过了非海景房的不利差异。

一般预订海景房的时间比预订非海景房的时间要早，顾客在预订海景房后，可能平均房费会有所下降，而非海景房刚好相反。当然也可能是客人在预订时希望等到更优惠的价格而推迟预订时间。

房费收入组合差异

五号酒店有海景房和非海景房两种产品。由于在2016年最后一个季度按不同的价格和不同的比例销售了这两种产品，从而导致了房费收入的组合差异。

房费收入的组合差异是根据每个客房的预算贡献来计算的，其中海景房的预算贡献更高。海景房的组合差异是有利差异，而非海景房的组合差异是不利差异，这是因为海景房的贡献高于非海景房。总的组合差异是有利差异，说明所提供客房组合的贡献额是增加的，即海景房所占比例更大。

房费收入的实际组合可能不同于预算组合，因为很多客人愿意为海景房支付更高溢价。可能那些只想住海景房的人会提前预订，而不想住海景房的客人不会提前太早预订。

房费收入数量差异

房费收入的数量差异是按预算入住率计算的实际客房数与最初预算数的差额，乘以每种房型的贡献计算出的。海景房和非海景房的数量差异都是有利差异，因为我们预算期间的实际客房收入超过预算水平。注意这里说的房费收入的数量差异是不同房型的整体差异，而不是每间客房的收入差异。也就是说，将所有客房的收入和数量差异合并为同一个数字。

非海景房的组合差异和数量差异刚好抵销，因此当非海景房预算入住率和实际入住率都为80%时，组合差异和数量差异之和为零。

出现这样的结果可能是因为我们预算偏保守，也可能是因为客人只是在开业的头几个月比较感兴趣。我们希望试营业结束后，我们的设施仍然可以吸引客人。

潜在的休闲旅游公司客户

信用评估的影响因素主要有如下几个方面。

在与新客户合作之前，我们要着重考查客户的支付能力，我们要避免与濒临破产的企业合作，或者说要保证能及时收回合同款项。

这一点对于选择合作的休闲旅游公司来说尤为重要。现在越来越多的客人通过酒店网站直接预订酒店（甚至国外酒店）房间。在Macland，很多休闲旅游公司近10年都几乎没有什么业务。

许多Macland的休闲旅游公司为了生存，开发了针对客户的新服务。所以，现存的休闲旅游公司都是成功的企业。

我们需要评估Bacland和Tacland的情况是否与Macland相同。如果Bacland和Tacland的旅游业只是我们10年前的水平，那么未来合作终止的风险就比较高。如果这些地方与Macland情况相同，风险就会大大降低。

我们还要调查Bacland和Tacland是否也有类似于MLTA的机构。如果有，这些机构也可以在一定程度上保护我们的权益，防止休闲旅游公司截留资金。在签约之前，我们需要调查该公司是否归属于此类机构。

如果可以从Bacland和Tacland获得公司的财务报表，那么我们就可以分析它们的财务报表，评估其商业信誉。我们要特别关注它们的现金和营运资金状况，计算流动比率，研究其现金流量表。计算其应付账款周转天数，评估他们的付款速度。

我们还要考虑这些公司的经营年限。如果对方是一家新公司，那么在当前市场环境下，违约风险就会更大。但是根据上文分析，在市场变化的环境下，无须太在意企业的经营年限。

我们还要参考银行、其他酒店客户和信用评级机构的资料，并且关注该业务的交易新闻或网上报道。

感谢！

智选酒店

管理会计助理

任务四

工作灵活性

五号酒店可以实现如下3类灵活性。

用工量灵活性

根据不同时期的用工量雇用临时员工，包括寻找承包商或通过劳务机构聘请临时人员。一些辅助性的服务，如维修、餐饮、安保和游泳池服务等可以外包给承包商。

财务灵活性

通过绩效奖励机制实现财务灵活性，如绩效工资、奖金计划和分红制。良好的绩效奖励机制有助于改进酒店的各方面业绩。

工作任务灵活性

工作任务灵活性也称为功能灵活性，包括雇用全能型的员工。如果五号酒店实现了工作任务灵活性，员工可以在同一水平（横向）从事多项任务，或者在不同水平（纵向）从事多项任务。实现任务灵活性有助于我们灵活应对餐饮服务要求和需求层级的变化。

工作灵活性的潜在好处如下：

- 在淡季，固定成本不变，但入住率下降，减少员工数量有利于降低劳动力成本；
- 员工具备多项业务的能力可以提高设备（如餐饮设备或游泳池设备）使用效率；
- 培训全能型员工有利于提高员工的积极性和生产力，酒店业的员工缺勤率和流动率相对较高，更高的奖励措施有助于降低员工的缺勤率和流动率；
- 实现工作灵活性意味着将“固定劳动力”的固定成本转移到具体业务上。

工作灵活性的潜在缺点如下：

- 员工之间交流减少，从而导致企业文化淡漠；
- 这反过来又会影响五号酒店工作的持续性和团队合作；
- 培训全能型员工以实现工作灵活性的成本较高。

普罗斯佩罗顾问咨询公司的研究结果

表中数据说明如下文。

普罗斯佩罗顾问咨询公司编制的表格分析了3个比赛日期（4月1日、6月1日和8月1日）的预期值。

3个比赛日期有3个不同的结果。第一列是每个比赛日期的可能结果，即预计的附加利润，等于附加收入减去附加成本的净额。3个不同的比赛日期下附加利润各不相同。第二列是3种情况发生的概率，第三列是根据每个结果乘以相应概率得出的期望值。所以，总的期望值是所有结果的加权平均值，权数是概率大小。

一般来说，期望值越高越具有吸引力，但请参阅下面关于风险态度的评述。

在附表中，8月比赛的期望值最高，6月最低。

但所计算的期望值不能界定可能出现结果的变化范围，也不能指出哪个是最可能出现的结果。也就是说，最可能出现的结果并不是这三个期望值中的任何一个。如果无限重复计算，得出的期望值就等于长期平均值。

在“一次性”决策中使用期望值时，要注意它只是一个加权平均值。

此外，在计算每个决策期望值时所使用的概率都是主观的，当然普罗斯佩罗顾问咨询公司的咨询师都是领域内的专家，这在一定程度上降低了预测的主观性。

风险态度

一般来说，不同决策者的风险态度是不一样的。智选酒店的管理者可能是“风险偏好者”、“风险中性者” 或“风险厌恶者”。

- “风险偏好者” 是指那些不顾概率高低而追求最好结果的人。风险偏好者会选择6月比赛，但6月比赛的标准差和离散系数较高，这表明 M$25 万预计利润的实现可能性较低。
- “风险中性者” 是指那些选择预期值或预期利润最高的人。风险中性者会选择8月比赛，因为8月比赛的预期值最高。风险中性者不关心标准差和离散系数高低。
- “风险厌恶者” 尽量规避风险。风险厌恶者会选择4月比赛。4月比赛的标准差和离散系数最低，说明4月比赛最有可能产生一个与期望值相接近的结果，所以风险最低。

所以，名人高尔夫球赛的日期最终取决于管理者整体对风险的态度。

Variant 3　Marking Guidance

Section	Technical skills		Business skills		People skills		Leadership skills		Integration	Total
1	ABC	10	Pricing policy	12					3	25
2	Treatment of construction costs ABC	13 12								25
3	Sales variances Assessing creditworthiness of new customers	12 9	Assessing creditworthiness of new customers	4						25
4	Dealing with risk in short-term decision making	6			Workforce flexibility	13	Dealing with risk in short-term decision making	6		25
Total marks available for competency		62		16		13		6	3	100

试卷三　评分指南

部分	技术技能		商业技能		人际技能		领导技能		综合	总计
1	作业成本法	10	定价策略	12					3	25
2	建筑成本的处理 作业成本法	13 12								25
3	销售差异 新客户信用度评估	12 9	新客户信用度评估	4						25
4	短期决策方面的风险管控	6			工作灵活性	13	短期决策方面的风险管控	6		25
各种能力分数总计		62		16		13		6	3	100

湖北经济学院名师解惑

试卷一共有四项任务，考察了 P1、F1、E1 三门课程的知识点，具体包括作业成本法、收入预算差异分析、建筑成本的会计处理、销售差异分析、新客户信用度分析与长期决策、工作灵活性的短期决策风险等。该试卷考核了考生的四项能力，其中技术技能的分值占 62%，商业技能的分值占 16%，人际技能的分值占 13%，领导技能的分值占 6%，与 CGMA 管理会计能力框架的技能要求一致。

该试卷的每项任务涉及以下知识点：

任务	问题	科目	知识点
任务一	采用作业成本法的相关问题	P1	作业成本法的优缺点（advantages and disadvantages of ABC）
	营销手段和创收方法	E1	定价策略和营销（pricing policy and promotion）
任务二	固定资产成本资本化的项目	F1	国际会计准则第 16 号不动产、厂房和设备（IAS 16 PPE）
	作业成本法中的作业、成本动因及理由	P1	成本动因（identifying cost drivers）
任务三	销售差异的分析	P1	差异分析法（variance analysis）
	新客户信用度分析要点	F1	信用度评估（assessing credit worthiness）
任务四	工作灵活性的方式及优缺点	E1	工作灵活性（workforce flexibility）
	短期决策风险中的数据分析及风险态度的影响	P1	决策中的不确定性和风险（uncertainty and risk in decision making）

上述各项任务要求以邮件或简报等形式来呈现答案，对问题的描述非常明确，答题时既要注意内容的针对性，也要注意形式的规范性。

对应知识点深度剖析

作业成本法的优缺点

相比于传统成本法而言，作业成本法的系统设置费钱费力，因此只有在合适的条件下才能推广作业成本法。优点：（1）更精确；（2）更易于理解成本；（3）成本分配更合理；（4）更好的成本控制；（5）应用于更复杂的情况；（6）应用于生产过程之外；（7）可用于服务业。缺点：（1）相关性不足；（2）成本分配存在主观性；（3）需要找到合适的成本动因和作业；（4）比较复杂；（5）操作费钱费力。

考生需要理解、应用并且表达出作业成本法的使用条件和优缺点。

结合题中所给信息，案例公司固定成本较高，作业成本法有利于结合客户获利能力分析，从而能更精确地衡量不同客户的盈利能力。酒店业竞争比较激烈，采用作业成本法有助于准确评估不同服务类别的盈利能力。基于作业成本法的预算和长期管理费用计划，有助于改善业绩管理，通过控制成本动因有效控制相关成本的水平。作业成本法有利于公平分摊成本，改善业务决策。

在讨论作业成本法时，考生结合题中内容，考虑该方法对长期发展产生的影响。整体回答需基于本案例企业的具体特征，而不是宽泛讨论。

考生注意事项

作业成本法的优缺点：

优点：（1）更精确；（2）更易于理解成本；（3）成本分配更合理；（4）更好的成本控制；（5）应用于更复杂的情况；（6）应用于生产过程之外；（7）可用于服务业。

缺点：（1）相关性不足；（2）成本分配存在主观性；（3）需要找到合适的成本动因和作业；（4）比较复杂；（5）操作费钱费力。

定价策略

定价策略是市场营销组合中一个十分关键的组成部分。价格通常是影响交易成败的重要因素，同时又是市场营销组合中最难以确定的因素。企业定价的目标是促进销售，获取利润。这要求企业既要考虑成本的补偿，又要考虑消费者对价格的接受能力，从而使定价策略具有买卖双方双向决策的特征。此外，价格还是市场营销组合中最灵活的因素，它可以对市场做出灵敏的反映。

本例中，案例企业可以通过营销组合进行定价来提高收入，考生需要对酒店行业提出相关的具体策略，包括在合适的时候提高房费，推出打包服务或在淡季为老年客人提供低价房等。此外，还要求考生举出 4 种增加收入的措施。这里是考营销组合的知识点，一般的营销手段包括广告、促销、公众关系、个人销售和直接邮件等。结合本题内容，可以考虑一些更为具体的可行方式，如提供婚礼场地等。

固定资产成本资本化的会计处理

资本化是指符合条件的相关费用支出不计入当期损益，而是计入相关资产成本，作为资产负债表的资产类项目管理。简单地说，资本化就是公司将支出归类为资产的方式。

固定资产是用于提供商品和服务并且持有期超过一个会计期间的资产。五号酒店会产生未来经济效益及利润；所有支出都与现金有关，可以准确度量。五号酒店的投资是为客人提供服务并持有 1 年以上，因此酒店和设施可以列为固定资产。其中土地、家具和设备的购买成本都可以单独进行资本化处理并计提折旧。酒店和游泳池的建造成本也是实际购买成本。法律费用和专业建筑设计费用属于直接成本，可直接计入酒店大楼成本。但购买家具的 5 年期贷款利息、前两周试运营投入和培训员工的外部咨询成本等不能资本化处理。

考生注意事项

国际会计准则第 16 号关于固定资产资本化处理的标准有两条：

（1）可以带来未来经济效益；

（2）可以准确度量。

成本动因分析

成本动因是导致对于资源消耗变化、影响质量和周期时间的任何事件与情形。一个作业可能具有多个动因。成本动因并不需要数量化，但是它对于作业动因和资源动因的选择具有重要影响。

考生在运用作业成本法时，需要找到每个作业的成本动因，找到的成本动因必须与成本具有相关性，且易于计量。

考生需要针对酒店的业务来确定客房服务的各项成本和成本动因：补充茶点和洗漱用品成本项目进行分配的动因是客房服务时补充用品的数量，整理床铺成本项目进行分配的动因是整理床铺的次数，客房保洁成本项目进行分配的动因是整理卧室的次数。

销售差异分析

销售差异分析是衡量实际销售额和计划销售额的差异及原因。

销售差异包括实际销售价格与标准价格之间的销售价格差异，以及预计销售数量与实际销售数量之间的销售数量差异。销售价格差异是实际销售价格与标准价格之间的差异导致的收入变化，销售数量差异是实际销售量与预计销售量不同而对销售收入的影响。

考生注意事项

成本动因有以下三类。

（1）执行动因。若某项作业被重复执行，每次作业消耗的资源费用差别很少，这时作业的执行次数即可作为成本动因。

（2）数量动因。当某项作业多次执行时，资源费用的消耗表现出明显的变异，若资源费用的消耗跟作业时间或其他数量量度之间存在近似的正比例关系，这时称成本动因为数量动因。

（3）强度动因。有些产品、劳务或顾客需要一些具有特殊性的作业，在作业执行过程中资源的耗费并不具备执行动因或数量动因的条件，这时需要对作业进行个别追踪记录，直接把作业成本归属为成本计算对象。这种成本动因被称为强度动因，由于直接归属作业成本，所以不需要计算成本动因率。

考生需要注意，本例中酒店的销售价格差异是两种房型的房费导致的差异，海景房价格是有利差异，非海景房价格是不利差异，而两种房型的全部客房价格差异是有利差异。原因是部分海景房预订后可能房费会有所下降，而非海景房刚好相反。收入组合差异是由海景房和非海景房两种产品按不同的价格和不同的比例销售导致的。海景房的组合差异是有利差异，而非海景房的组合差异是不利差异，总的组合差异是有利差异。

房费收入数量差异是按预算入住率计算的实际客房数与最初预算水平的差异，乘以每种房型的贡献计算出的。海景房和非海景房的数量差异都是有利差异。

考生注意事项

销售差异分析的目的包括如下4点。

（1）明确实际销售完成情况与预算目标的不同。

（2）分析企业内外部因素各自对预算差异的影响。

（3）提供激励销售预算有关人员的数据依据。

（4）确定成本和利润预算差异分析的基础。

新客户信用度分析

客户信用度分析是指为有效控制客户信用风险，实现资金的安全性、流动性和收益性，从客户经营能力、盈利能力、偿债能力、发展能力以及客户素质和信用状况等方面对客户进行综合评价和信用等级的确定。企业不仅需要对所有的新客户进行信用度分析，还要定期对老客户进行信用度分析。一般而言，影响信用度的因素有很多，包括外部因素（本例中的国家和地方旅游业发展水平、行政主管机构）和内部因素（公司财务报表、经营年限及公司在其他地方的资料记录，如银行、往来单位、信用评级机构等）。此外，还有交易新闻或网上报道。

考生注意事项

客户信用管理的影响因素从以下几个方面展开分析：

（1）行业信息；

（2）区域信息；

（3）财务信息；

（4）客户信用记录信息；

（5）客户基本面信息。

工作灵活性

工作灵活性包括很多方面，如工作任务（或功能）灵活性、用工量灵活性、财务灵活性和工作安排灵活性等。案例中五号酒店可以根据不同时期的用工量雇用临时员工实现用工量灵活性，通过绩效奖励机制实现财务灵活性，雇用全能型的员工实现工作任务灵活性。实现任务灵活性有助于灵活应对餐饮服务要求和需求层级的变化。工作灵活性有利于降低劳动力成本，提高设备（如餐饮设备或游泳池设备）使用效率，提高员工的积极性和生产力，降低员工的缺勤率和流动率，但同时也会造成员工之间的交流减少，从而导致企业文化淡漠，影响五号酒店工作的持续性和团队合作，而且整个项目实施下来成本较高。

考生需要对工作灵活性从正反两个方面进行分析，并且结合案例特定的情况和要素展开讨论。

决策中的不确定性和风险

期望值是将不同的可能结果乘以其发生概率而得出来的。从长期来说，期望值就是长期平均值。期望值并不一定是最终出现的结果，只是在“一次性”决策中使用的一个加权平均值。我们计算期望值时所使用的概率都是主观的。

决策者的风险态度有 3 种：“风险偏好者”、“风险中性者” 和 “风险厌恶者”。“风险偏好者”是指那些不顾概率高低而追求最好结果的人，“风险中性者”是指那些选择预期值或预期利润最高的人，“风险厌恶者”尽量规避风险。管理者整体对风险的不同态度导致最终决策结果也不同。

考生注意事项

期望值 = EV = $\sum px$

其中，x 为未来的可能结果，p 为可能结果发生的概率。

Variant 4

This examination is structured as follows:

Section number	Number of tasks	Time for section (minutes)
1	1	45
2	1	45
3	1	45
4	2	45

The time available for each section is for reading, planning and writing your answer(s).

Please note Section 4 consists of two tasks and answer screens. Please leave enough time to complete both parts.

Section 1

You arrive at work to find, left on your desk, the following extract of a directors' meeting that was held a week ago.

Minutes of Directors' Meeting

August 2016 Hotel performance

Concern was expressed about the large adverse variances across all hotels in the first half of 2016. Profitability in every hotel is down, which can be attributed to two main issues:

- a decline in occupancy levels, compared to budget, especially in Hotels 3 and 4;
- escalating costs in certain areas, including house-keeping, restaurant and bar and staffing.

There has been a noticeable decline in guest feedback scores and quite a lot of adverse comments relating to the state of the décor and the age of some of the bedroom facilities. There are also increasing comments about our restaurants in Hotels 3 and 4, especially about menu choice and the lack of healthy options.

As directors, we have decided to tackle this in four ways:

- a large scale programme of refurbishment across all hotels, starting with Hotel 4—we still have significant funds in the bank and have the capacity to borrow if needed;
- a refocusing of the restaurants in Hotels 3 and 4;
- looking to achieve cost savings where we can;
- looking at ways to reward staff better and improve their motivation.

After you have read the extract of the minutes from the directors meeting, Rav Patel, finance director, sends you the following email:

From: Rav Patel, Finance Director

To: Management Accountant Assistant

Subject: Responsibility accounting and reward scheme

I hope you've had a chance to read the extract of the directors' meeting minutes that I left on your desk; we have a few challenges ahead! I need you to look at a couple of things for me.

Firstly, I was talking to an accountant friend of mine yesterday, about our escalating costs and falling revenues and how we could get better control of both. He thinks we should make each hotel's heads accountable for their own cost centres. He mentioned having some as profit centres. At the moment, the only person that is really accountable to us for hotel performance is the Hotel Manager.

I've been thinking about it ever since, especially in relation to the Head Chef and Head of Bar and Restaurant, as I suspect that there is a lot of overlap between the two. Please send me an email explaining how they influence costs and revenues within their respective areas of operation, and suggesting how we could split these operations into cost and/or profit centres.

Secondly, we need to design, and implement, a new reward scheme for staff. I am convinced that this is essential in order to improve our performance. Such a scheme would need to build in the potential to recognise, and reward, individual members of staff. I'm not interested in setting up a straight forward bonus scheme, as I would like the new scheme to focus on non-financial rewards.

I'll need to brief the other directors on this. Please send me an explanation of why it is important for us to reward our staff beyond just basic wages and financial bonuses. Please also explain how we could use this to recognise good individual staff performance, as well as improving hotel performance.

Please send both explanations in the same email.

Thank you!

Rav Patel

Finance Director

Wise Choice Hotels

Write the email requested by Rav Patel.

Section 2

Two months later Rav Patel, finance director and Molly Patel, marketing director are on annual leave. You receive the following email from John Hayes, managing director:

From: John Hayes, Managing Director

To: Management Accountant Assistant

Subject: Hotel 3 operating statement and marketing mix

Before Molly went on annual leave, she said that we should consider revising our marketing mix. She also said that we currently focus on the elements of the traditional marketing mix and we ought to place a greater focus on the three service extension PS. She did not explain any further than that. I'm intrigued now by what she means.

Please send me an explanation of the three service extension PS in our marketing mix, with examples of each element relevant to us.

Also, thank you for sending me the operating statement for Hotel 3 for the month of September. I notice that you have identified some variances as planning and some as operational, but I'm not sure why. Surely a variance is a variance and all that is important is whether it is favourable, or adverse, isn't it?

Please send me an explanation of what planning and operational variances mean with reference to the information contained in the attached operating statement for Hotel 3. Please include an explanation of how each of the actions identified on the schedule affect the operating statement.

Please include both your explanation on the marketing mix and planning and operational variances in a single email.

Thank you!

John Hayes

Managing Director

Wise Choice Hotels

Summary operating statement for Hotel 3 for the month of September:

	(M$ 000)
Original budgeted profit	90
Variable cost planning variance	3
Fixed cost planning variance	(5)

（续表）

	(M$ 000)
Revised budgeted profit	88
Room revenue and bar and restaurant revenue price variance	(2)
Occupancy variance(based on contribution)	10
Variable costs variance	9
Fixed costs variance	(4)
Actual profit	101

Actions taken solely by the directors in respect of Hotel 3:

- Negotiating a reduction in laundry costs with our laundry services provider.
- Changing the property insurance provider to reduce the premium paid.
- Deciding that a new head chef should be recruited at a higher salary than the existing one.

Changes to costs as a result of the actions taken by the directors have been incorporated into a revised budget.

Actions taken solely by Patrick Jenkins, hotel manager:

- Engaging a nutritionist for advice in respect of changing the menu, at a one-off cost of M$5,000.
- Reducing the number of complimentary toiletries available in each bedroom.
- Reducing the prices charged in the restaurant for meals, with the agreement of the new head chef and the head of bar and restaurant.

Write the email requested by John Hayes.

Section 3

A week later, Rav Patel calls you into his office and says:

The more I think about how we prepare budgets and monitor hotel performance, the more I think that we need to take a fresh approach. I recently read that ZBB is a good approach, because it eliminates budget slack and therefore helps a business control costs. I'm happy that I know the benefits of such an approach, but I'm interested in your views on how we might implement it. Please explain, in an email, how ZBB can be implemented in our business using the costs associated with housekeeping to illustrate (include the costs of replenishment of complimentary items such as toiletries, the annual cost of replacing bedding and towels and the cost of laundry).

As well as that, I would like your help regarding information that John Hayes has asked me for. He has been identifying those assets that will no longer be required, as a result of a major refurbishment of Hotel 4, and has placed them into three categories: assets to be sold in December 2016, assets to be sold in January 2017 and assets that will be stored and used on a temporary basis, if there are breakages. He has prepared a summary schedule of this, together with a few notes. He would like to know how these three asset categories will impact on the financial statements for the year ended 31 December 2016. In the same email as your explanation about zero-based budgeting please prepare a response that I can send to John. Thank you.

Schedule of replaced assets at hotel 4:

Category	Net book value (M$ 000)	Expected sale proceeds (M$ 000)
Assets to be sold in December 2016	125	135
Assets to be sold in January 2017	80	40
Assets to be retained	50	N/A (as not expected to be sold)

Notes:

(1) The assets identified above are all items of plant and equipment. The net book value stated above is as at 1 January 2016.

(2) The refurbishment of Hotel 4 will be completed before the end of December.

(3) There are no costs associated with selling any of the assets in either December or January.

Write the email requested by Rav Patel.

Section 4

A month later you receive the following email from Rav Patel, finance director:

From: Rav Patel, Finance Director

To: Management Accountant Assistant

Subject: Health club at Hotel 4

I have just had a conversation with John Hayes, managing director, about the improvements in hotel performance, especially at Hotel 4. Guest feedback comments and scores have seen a marked improvement, with many guests saying that they cannot wait to come back.

John is of the view that we should reflect this increasing guest goodwill in our financial statements. He commented that we already have goodwill recorded in our statement of financial position, within intangible assets, so we should increase this value. I told him that I didn't think that was possible, as the goodwill in our financial statements was a different form of goodwill. I said that I'd get back to him on the matter.

Please draft a briefing paper that I can send to John which includes an explanation of:

- How the goodwill we have recorded in our financial statements arose.
- The reasons why IFRS do not allow goodwill arising from the satisfaction and loyalty of our guests to be recorded in the individual financial statements of a company.

On another matter, at our directors' meeting last week, we discussed establishing a health club at Hotel 4. It would provide gym facilities, fitness classes, sports massage, health treatments such as reflexology, together with well-being and health advice for customers.

We engaged Better Consultants to help us formulate a decision about our customer fee strategy. We plan initially to have a fixed price for a trial period of three months. Customers will be charged a daily fee. The day will include full access to the gym, a session of sports massage, two fitness classes, one health treatment and lunch in the hotel restaurant.

Better Consultants have sent us a schedule showing a pay-off table and a regret table, in respect of our pricing decision and have said that we can use a maximax, maximin or minimax regret approach to this decision.

Please prepare a first draft of a briefing paper which I can circulate to the other directors, that:

- Interprets the information in the pay-off table.
- Explains the three approaches to the decision that Better Consultants have suggested. Please include the appropriate decision under each approach.

Rav Patel

Finance Director

Wise Choice Hotels

Pay-off table of expected contribution for the three month trial period:

Variable costs per customer per day (M$)	Daily fee (M$)		
	100	115	135
60	136,160	156,860	165,600
40	204,240	213,900	209,760
30	238,280	242,420	231,840

Regret table for the expected contribution for the three month trial period:

Variable costs per customer per day (M$)	Daily fee (M$)		
	100	115	135
60	29,440	8,740	0
40	9,660	0	4,140
30	4,140	0	10,580

Notes:

(1) There are 92 days in the period.

(2) There are three levels of daily fee being considered. The three daily fee levels are M$ 100, M$ 115 or M$ 135.

(3) The maximum number of customers is 40 in any one day. Demand is dependent upon the daily fee.

(4) There are three possible levels of variable costs that will arise depending on the degree to which customers use the facilities and the lunch option chosen.

Write the draft briefing paper requested by Rav Patel about accounting for goodwill.

Write the draft briefing paper requested by Rav Patel about the Hotel 4 health club pricing strategy.

试卷四

本次考试的结构如下：

序号	任务数	时间（分钟）
1	1	45
2	1	45
3	1	45
4	2	45

每个部分规定的时间可用于读题、组织和书写答案。

请注意任务四包括两项子任务，需要留足时间。

任务一

你来到办公室后在办公桌上发现一份一周前的董事会会议记录。

董事会会议记录

2016 年 8 月酒店业绩

2016 年上半年，我们旗下所有酒店都存在相当大的不利差异，大家对此表示担忧。每个酒店的盈利能力都在下降，主要表现为以下两个方面：

- 酒店入住率低于预算水平，尤其是三号酒店和四号酒店；
- 客房管理、餐馆、酒吧和人工等成本不断上升。

客户打分明显下降，有很多客户抱怨客房装饰和设施不够健全。三号酒店和四号酒店餐厅的负面评论也越来越多，主要集中在菜品选择和忽视健康问题方面。

管理层决定采用以下 4 种方法来解决问题：

- 从四号酒店开始对所有酒店进行大规模翻新——我们存在银行的资金充足，必要时还有一定的借款能力；
- 集中整改三号酒店和四号酒店的餐厅；
- 尽可能节约成本；
- 奖励员工，提高他们的积极性。

在你读完董事会会议记录后，财务总监 Rav Patel 给你发来以下邮件：

发件人：财务总监 Rav Patel
收件人：管理会计助理
主题：责任会计和员工奖励计划

我希望你能仔细阅读我放在你办公桌上的董事会会议记录，思考一下我们当下存在的一些问题。

第一，我昨天和一位会计朋友聊天时谈到如何应付成本上升和收入下降的问题。他建议，任命每个酒店的负责人为成本中心负责人。他也提议将部分成本中心确定为利润中心。目前，对酒店业绩负责的是酒店经理。

他的话引起了我的思考，特别是酒店负责人与主厨和酒吧负责人的关系非常复杂。

请给我回复一封电子邮件，解释他们在各自业务范围内如何影响成本和收入，并就如何将这些业务分成成本中心和/或利润中心提出建议。

第二，我们需要重新设计一套员工奖励机制并在日常工作中实施，这是提高业绩的必要条件。新的奖励机制应该能有效识别并奖励优秀员工。我不主张直接发奖金，我希望新的奖励机制能专注非财务奖励。

我需要向其他高管做一个简要介绍。请解释我们在基本工资和奖金之外还要给员工提供奖励机制的理由。同时，请解释我们如何使用这一奖励机制来识别优秀员工的表现以及改善酒店的业绩。

请用同一邮件回复上述两个问题。

谢谢。

智选酒店
财务总监
Rav Patel

请根据 Rav Patel 的要求回复邮件。

任务二

两个月后，财务总监 Rav Patel 和营销经理 Molly Patel 在休年假，你收到一封来自总经理 John Hayes 的邮件：

发件人：总经理 John Hayes
收件人：管理会计助理
主题：3 号酒店经营差异和营销组合

在 Molly 休年假之前，她就提出了营销组合修改方案。她强调，我们目前比较关注一些传统营销组合的要素，今后的工作重点是要扩展三项服务，但她没有对此进行深入解释。我对她的提议很感兴趣。

请解释在我们的营销组合中如何扩展三项服务，并各举一个与我们业务相关的例子。

同时，感谢你 9 月给我发来的关于三号酒店的营业情况简报。我看到你将某些差异列为计划差异，将某些差异列为实际差异，但我不明白这样分类的原因。对于差异，我们更应该关注这是有利差异还是不利差异。请在邮件中解释三号酒店经营情况简报中的计划差异和实际差异，并请解释每项差异对经营情况的影响。

请在邮件中对营销组合方案进行解释，并解释经营情况简报中的计划差异和实际差异。

谢谢。

智选酒店

总经理

John Hayes

三号酒店9月份经营情况说明摘要：

	(M$ 000)
原始预算利润	90
变动成本计划差异	3
固定成本计划差异	(5)
修订后预算利润	88
客房收入及酒吧和餐厅收入价格差异	(2)
入住率差异（基于贡献）	10
变动成本差异	9
固定成本差异	(4)
实际利润	101

三号酒店的具体做法包括：

- 与洗衣房协商降低洗衣成本；
- 变更财产保险公司降低保险费；
- 以高于现在的薪水聘请一位新主厨。

上述措施导致的成本变化已被纳入修订后的预算。

酒店经理 Patrick Jenkins（帕特里克·詹金斯）提出以下方案：

- 支出 M$5 000 用于营养专家咨询费，更换菜单；

- 减少客房洗漱用品的数量；
- 征得新主厨及酒店和餐厅老板同意后，降低餐厅消费价格。

请根据 John Hayes 的要求写一封邮件。

任务三

一周后，Rav Patel 把你叫进他的办公室，说：

我认为，我们需要变更预算方法和业绩监督方法。我最近了解到，零基预算有助于消除预算松弛和控制企业成本。零基预算非常有效，我想知道你对我们实施零基预算有什么看法。请在邮件中解释我们如何实施零基预算，并用与客房管理相关的费用进行解释（包括洗漱用品等补充用品成本，以及每年床上用品的更换费用和洗衣费等）。

此外，我希望你帮我收集 John Hayes 需要的资料。他提到四号酒店的翻新导致有些资产需要处置。这类资产主要有 3 种：2016 年 12 月出售的资产、2017 年 1 月出售的资产和因破损暂不出售的资产。他已经列好了一份简报，并做了相应注释。他想知道上述 3 种资产对 2016 年的财务报表存在何种影响。

请为我准备一份回复给 John 的邮件，对零基预算进行解释。谢谢。

四号酒店处置资产表：

项目	账面净值（M$ 000）	预期销售收入（M$ 000）
2016 年 12 月出售的资产	125	135
2017 年 1 月出售的资产	80	40
因破损暂不出售的资产	50	N/A（因为不处置）

注：

（1）上述所有资产均为固定资产，其账面净值的取值时间为 2016 年 1 月 1 日。

（2）四号酒店翻新工作将在 12 月底之前完成。

（3）12 月或 1 月处置的所有资产不考虑其他相关成本。

请根据 Rav Patel 的要求写一封邮件。

任务四

1 个月后，你收到了下面这封来自财务总监 Rav Patel 的邮件。

发件人：财务总监 Rav Patel

收件人：管理会计助理

主题：四号酒店健康俱乐部

我刚刚和总经理 John Hayes 讨论了如何提高酒店业绩，尤其是四号酒店的情况。四号酒店的客人反馈意见和评分有了明显提高，许多客人表示愿意再来消费。

John 认为，我们应该在财务报表中反映这种来自客人的美誉度。他认为，我们在财务报表中有“商誉”这个项目，我们应该将客人的美誉度当作商誉计入无形资产。我认为这种做法有点不妥，因为财务报表中的“商誉”与来自客人的美誉度有区别。我会就这事与他再沟通。

请你帮我草拟一份寄给 John 的简报，解释下列问题：

- 财务报表中的商誉是如何产生的；
- 《国际财务报告准则》不认可将客人的满意度和忠诚度记入商誉的原因是什么。

此外，在上周的董事会上，我们讨论在四号酒店建立一个健康俱乐部。它将为客人提供健身设施、健身课程、运动按摩、康复治疗（如反射疗法），以及有关健康方面的咨询服务。

我们聘请更好顾问（Better Consultants）咨询公司帮助我们制定客户收费政策。我们将在 3 个月的试营业期间内按天固定收费，客人支付一天的费用可使用健身房，进行一次运动按摩，参加两个健身班，体验一次健康治疗和享受一顿酒店午餐。

更好顾问咨询公司给我们提供了定价决策，并编制了一张收费表和一张后悔值表，同时建议我们可以使用大中取大法、小中取大法或大中取小法来做出决定。

请准备一份简报的初稿，以便我发给其他的管理人员，内容包括：

- 解释付费信息；
- 解释更好顾问咨询公司提出的 3 种收费方法，并对每一种方法做出相应的评价。

智选酒店

财务总监

Rav Patel

3 个月试营业期的盈利：

每人每天变动成本（M$）	每天收费（M$）		
	100	115	135
60	136 160	156 860	165 600
40	204 240	213 900	209 760
30	238 280	242 420	231 840

3 个月试营业期的预期贡献的后悔值：

每人每天变动成本（M$）	每天收费（M$）		
	100	115	135
60	29 440	8 740	0
40	9 660	0	4 140
30	4 140	0	10 580

注：

（1）试营业期为 92 天。

（2）每天收费有 3 个标准，分别为 M$ 100、M$ 115 或 M$ 135。

（3）每天客户最多 40 人，客户量取决于每天收费高低。

（4）变动成本有 3 种可能，取决于客户使用多少设备和是否享用午餐。

请根据 Rav Patel 的要求写一份解释“商誉”的简报。

请根据 Rav Patel 的要求写一份关于四号酒店健康俱乐部定价决策的简报。

Variant 4 Suggested Answers

Section 1

From: Management Accountant Assistant

To: Rav Patel, Finance Director

Subject: RE: Responsibility accounting and reward scheme

Restaurant And Kitchen Responsibility Accounting

In order for a manager to be held accountable for either cost or revenue generation that manager must in a position to influence or control that cost or revenue.

Responsibility for Costs

The head chef at Hotel 4 is responsible for the operation of the kitchen. This includes development of menus, selection of ingredients used and the number of staff that he has working in the kitchen. Each of these has an inter-related cost implication.

The menu will determine which ingredients need to be purchased and the head chef has a choice whether to source the best quality ingredients or to have lower quality and hence reduce costs. The head chef can also choose to have inexperienced staff or experienced kitchen staff with a different cost implication. As a result the head chef has control over the majority of costs generated by the operation of the kitchen and hence it is appropriate that they are held accountable for this.

The head of bar and restaurant at Hotel 4 is responsible for the operation of the bar and restaurant. This includes determining the number of waiting staff and bar staff on a particular day as well as selecting the range of beverages to stock in the bar. It is appropriate for the Head of Bar and Restaurant to be responsible for these staffing and purchase costs as they influence them.

Responsibility for Revenues

Responsibility for costs is fairly clear cut. However responsibility for the bar and restaurant revenue is not so clear cut. At the moment prices for food and beverages sold are agreed jointly between the head chef, bar and restaurant manager and hotel manager.

The revenue generated by the bar and restaurant is for beverages and meals sold to guests. There is a question mark over who has the greatest influence in respect of this revenue being generated.

The head chef clearly influences this revenue in terms of how attractive the menus are and the quality of the meals that leave the kitchen. If a guest is staying more than one night, they are unlikely to return to the restaurant if there are issues with menu choice or quality. Similarly if the menu is unattractive or offers little choice then a guest staying for a single night is unlikely to use the restaurant. The head of bar and restaurant also has influence over the revenue generation in terms of the quality of service provided by the waiting staff and the range ofbeverages on offer in the bar.

I would suggest that we need to split the bar and restaurant revenue into two：that for the sale of beverages in the bar and revenue from meals sold. The Head of bar and restaurant should be held responsible for the bar revenue（in a "bar" profit centre）and the head chef held responsible for the revenue from meals（in a "kitchen" profit centre）. On balance the head chef has more influence on the meals revenue generation than the other manager, who ultimately is reliant on the kitchen doing a good job by producing quality meals in a timely manner to provide a good waiting service.

Reward Scheme

Our employees are our biggest asset and maximising their performance and ensuring employees are able to develop the skills and knowledge to deliver a high level of customer service is essential for our business. We are in a very competitive market place and we are under pressure to attract guests that want to return. Ensuring staff members are satisfied and motivated in their roles will assist in the achievement of this goal.

It is important that we take the necessary steps to ensure that every individual staff member feels that they are appreciated and that they play a valuable role within Wise Choice Hotels. Staff who are not fully engaged and do not feel valued may disassociate themselves with the structure of our chosen working practices.

To achieve success, reward schemes must be tailored to our employees and suited to their aspirations. To achieve this, our Hotel Managers need to know what drives their people, as different things will motivate different people. Flexible, widely encompassing schemes that engage at different performance levels and in different ways, are essential to success. Communication via team talks is a great way to engage staff and gives management an opportunity to motivate and resolve any issues.

The hotel managers need to be motivated themselves, and so we must drive motivation from the top down. Being a preferred employer and offering pensions, employee benefit programmes and additional benefits can give rise to higher levels of motivation and improved performance.

When designing a reward scheme it is important to incorporate scope for "personal recognition". It is important to drive interest and engagement. Posters displayed at each hotel showing who has been nominated and who has won awards are excellent techniques to maintain employee interest and act as an aspirational driver.

The value of personalised rewards is also important and helps deliver employee engagement. Nominations, for example, for "employee of the month" awards deliver a personalised and tailored message which helps each staff member feel appreciated.

Other techniques which work particularly well within the hotel industry are points-based websites, such as Rewardbanking. com, which allows organisations to run incentive and motivation programmes. Such programmes work well when set up for each hotel in a chain and each recipient within the workplace. Points deposited into reward banking enable recipients to claim the rewards they have earned and use as they choose, and again, this is an excellent motivator for staff.

Providing individual hotel managers with discretionary pots to award employees for more ad-hoc efforts, such as customer feedback or serving according to the company's code of practice also helps to maintain the focus of each member of staff on their own performance. Although of course we would need to be sure that this is used in an equitable way across all hotel staff.

Thanks!

Management Accountant Assistant
Wise Choice Hotel

Section 2

From：*Management Accountant Assistant*

To：*John Hayes*，*Managing Director*

Subject：*RE*：*Hotel* 3 *operating statement and marketing mix*

People

Service businesses such as ours invariably have a high person-to-person contact. Therefore it is vital that we focus on the need to instil values of quality and reliability and generate a service ethic in our staff who are the interface between our customers and our business. In order to achieve this focus on the achievement of excellence and a strong customer orientation we need to invest in our staff via high quality training. In particular customer-facing staff must be selected，trained and motivated with a major focus on customer care and public relations.

The physical presence and appearance of people performing services such as our reception and restaurant staff is a vital aspect of customer satisfaction. Such staff are performing a service and also liaising with our customers to promote the services that we offer，gather information and respond to customer needs.

We need to ensure that that our staff have the range of skills and knowledge to support the services that we offer and that there are staff uniforms available to give a professional image at each hotel. For example our reception staff should wear suits or corporate uniform and be trained in upselling，encouraging our guests to use the restaurant.

Processes

These are the systems through which our services are delivered and used to support our customers' interaction with us. We must recognise that efficient processes can create a marketing advantage for Wise Choice Hotels. If our check-in and check-out process is made as efficient as possible then guests' first and last impressions of Wise Choice Hotels will be favourable and create "customer value" which can lead to further bookings and higher revenues. Other processes such as our on-line bookings process should be streamlined and create a favourable impression to our potential guests. Customers need to be completely satisfied by such important processes（for example, the security attached to the making of on-line payments).

We should undertake periodic reviews of our processes for their level of efficiency paying particular attention to issues such as queuing and waiting times and the accessibility of facilities, premises, personnel and the services that we have on offer.

Physical Evidence

Physical evidence relates to how our products and services are perceived in the market place. The physical evidence of our service provision can be incorporated into the design and specification of our service environment by designing our hotel premises to reflect the quality and types of service that we offer. In this regard we should give consideration to environmental factors such as fixture and fittings, decor, colour schemes, noise levels, background music, fragrances and general ambience. Thus physical evidence embraces the comfort and facilities that we have on offer.

A critical component of the provision of physical evidence is our website which must be well designed in order to facilitate easy navigation by both existing and potential visitors to our hotels. We should recognise that our website will frequently give potential customers their first impressions of our business.

Variances

As a result of the actions taken by the directors in respect of Hotel 3, a revised budget has been prepared. The operating statement now reconciles between the original budget and the revised budget and also the revised budget and the actual performance.

The variances which reconcile between the original and revised budgeted profit are the planning variances. Planning variances are not related to operating performance and are not controllable by operational management. They are the result of the directors' decisions and therefore it would be unfair to hold the Hotel Manager responsible for the effect of these decisions.

The operating statement shows that the overall effect of these planning variances is a reduction in our revised budgeted profit from M$ 90,000 to M$ 88,000. Looking at each of the directors' actions identified underneath the operating statement:

- Action one will have reduced our budgeted laundry costs. Laundry costs are a variable cost and therefore will have contributed favourably towards the variable cost planning variance.

- Action two will have reduced our budgeted property costs. Property costs are fixed and therefore this will have contributed favourably to the fixed cost planning variance.
- Action three will have increased staff costs and because the Head Chef will be on a permanent contract it is likely that this will be part of fixed costs. This will therefore have created an adverse fixed cost planning variance. The net impact of action two and action three by the directors has made to reduce the revised budgeted profit by M$5,000.

The variances which reconcile between the revised budget and actual performance are the operational variances. These are a better measure of the performance of the hotel because they will have arisen as a result of the actions taken by the Hotel Manager and how he and his team have managed the hotel. The Hotel Manager will be responsible for these.

It should be noted that the operational variances are favourable overall(as shown by the fact that the actual profit is higher than the revised budget). This is due to two main effects though: increased occupancy shown by the favourable occupancy variance and an overall decrease in costs.

In respect of each of the actions of the Hotel Manager:

- Action one will have increased the costs associated with the restaurant. This will be an increase in fixed cost and will have contributed to the adverse fixed cost variance.
- Action two will reduce housekeeping costs and hence has contributed to the favourable variable costs variance.
- Action three will have reduced the revenue from the restaurant and will have contributed to the adverse price variance.

Thanks!

Management Accountant Assistant
Wise Choice Hotel

Section 3

From：Management Accountant Assistant

To：Rav Patel，Finance Director

Subject：RE：ZBB and disposal of assets

ZBB

The implementation of a ZBB system will require Hotel Managers and Heads of Department to engage in several major planning，analytical and decision-making processes.

The manager responsible for each operation within Wise Choice Hotels（such as the Head of Housekeeping for example）would be responsible for developing a description of each programme of activities to be operated in the next budget year. It may be necessary for them to involve other staff members in their department to collect the required information. In the context of ZBB such programmes are referred to as decision packages，and each decision package usually will have three or more alternative ways of achieving the decision package's objectives.

Briefly，each decision package alternative must contain as a minimum，goals and/or objectives，activities，resources and their associated costs. Each decision package should contain a description of how it will contribute to the attainment of the objectives of Wise Choice Hotels.

Each manager will then be required to review each decision package and its alternatives in order to be able to assess and justify its operation and in doing so，several questions must be answered. In particular，each manager will need to answer the following questions：

- Does this decision package support and contribute to the goals of our business？
- What would be the impact on our business if the decision package were to be eliminated？
- Can this decision package's objectives be accomplished more effectively and/or efficiently？

A ranking process，based upon cost/benefit analysis is used to establish a prioritised ranking of decision packages. Ranking is a way of evaluating all decision packages in relation to each other. The ranking process could prove to be problematic insofar as it will require our managers to make value judgements and thus subjectivity is an inherent factor in the application of ZBB. Although difficult, the ranking of decision packages is fundamental to the process of ZBB.

Here at Wise Choice Hotels, within housekeeping we have various costs such as staff, laundry, toiletries bedding and towels. The amount that we spend on these items is partly dependent on the volume of business that we do, but also partly discretionary. Using toiletries as an example, the volume of business will be one key factor in determining the total number of times that we change the toiletries and therefore the amount of inventory that we consume in doing this. Beyond this, though, we have discretionary expenditure. Should we supply premium branded, middle of the range or low-cost toiletries? In order to answer this question we would set up a number of decision packages; each with a different quality of toiletries in its specification. Each of these packages would be relatively easy to cost, but we would also need to evaluate the benefits of each. This would be more difficult because the benefits would be intangible. The managers could then consider each package in the light of our corporate objectives and financial constraints and select the package that is most appropriate for us.

Further examples of decision packages within housekeeping would relate to the quality of bed linen and the quality level of towels supplied in each guest room. Where these items are subject to annual contract then we have the flexibility to upgrade or downgrade accordingly.

Disposal of Assets

Assets to be Sold in December 2016

When we sell the assets in December 2016 we will need to derecognise the assets as part of PPE and recognise a profit on disposal in the statement of profit or loss. Because we will have disposed of these assets during the financial year we will not record any depreciation on these assets for the year in line with our depreciation policy.

Asset to be Sold in January 2017

At the year end of 31 December 2016 we will still own these assets, however we will no longer be using them for business purposes because the refurbishment will be complete by then. However, at the year-end there will be plan to sell these assets and it would appear that a sales value has already been established. Also the assets will be sold within 12 months. Therefore these assets would need to be recognised separately in the statement of financial position as "assets held for sale".

The value that these assets should be recognised at is the lower of their carrying value on the date they become held for sale and the net proceeds of sale (M$ 40,000). In order to determine the carrying value we will need to depreciate these assets up until the date that they become held for sale. It is likely though that the carrying value will be significantly lower than the net proceeds of sale and therefore a loss equal to the difference will need to be recorded in the statement of profit or loss.

Assets to be Retained

The assets to be retained should be retained within PPE at the year end. We will still need to depreciate these assets even though we will potentially only use them in temporary situations. However, we will also need to undertake an impairment review to make sure that there has been no impairment in their value. This involves comparing the assets carrying value with the higher of their value in use (the benefit that we still expect to get out of them) and their estimated net realisable value. Given the nature of these assets, it is highly likely that there will be an impairment loss which will be recorded in the statement of profit or loss for the year to 31 December 2016.

Thanks!

Management Accountant Assistant
Wise Choice Hotel

Section 4

Briefing Paper on Accounting for Goodwill

Goodwill in Our Financial Statements

The goodwill in our statement of financial position arose when we acquired each of our hotels. So far, we have always purchased hotels as going concerns, which means that the consideration that we paid for each hotel would have included the value of the tangible assets PPE and any current assets and liabilities (such as inventory, hotel receivables and payables). The consideration paid would also have included an amount to reflect the experience of the staff at the hotel, the strength of customer loyalty and the strength of the business as a going concern. This means that each time we acquired a hotel we would have paid more than the value of its PPE and net current assets. This additional element of consideration is known as purchased goodwill and can be capitalised because it arose only as a result of a business combination. This is the goodwill that is recorded in our statement of financial position and it is recorded as an intangible asset because it relates to the factors identified above in respect of customer loyalty and staff experience.

Once purchased goodwill has been recorded international financial reporting standards state that it cannot be revalued upwards because there is no active market in which to determine a reliable value. However, it should be subject to annual impairment reviews with any impairment losses taken to profit or loss.

Reasons Why Goodwill Arising from Guest Satisfaction and Loyalty is Not Recognised

There are two main reasons why international financial reporting standards do not allow goodwill that arises from guest satisfaction and loyalty (which is a form of internally generated goodwill) to be recognised.

Firstly, it is not possible to reliably measure its value. Whist there are specialist companies that do value goodwill and other intangible assets such as brands, significant assumptions have to be made which compromise reliability. There is no market place for goodwill and hence the concept of market value cannot apply. If organisations were to place their own values on their internally generated goodwill, there would be scope for them to inflate the value of their businesses resulting in an unfair or even fraudulent view of the business to the reader of the financial statements.

Secondly, internally generated goodwill cannot be separated from the rest of the business and sold in its own right. If we think about Hotel 4, the increase in customer satisfaction and therefore goodwill is part of Hotel 4. We could not sell the goodwill without selling the whole hotel.

Briefing Paper on Health Club Pricing

The pay-off table shows a measure of the value or "pay-off" of each possible outcome facing the directors. In our case there are three possible levels of customer daily fee under consideration. We have control over this decision. There is uncertainty though over how much each customer would use the facilities and hence the amount of variable cost that would be incurred.

The pay-off table shows the level of contribution that would be earned by us as a result of setting the daily fee at M$ 100,M$ 115 or M$ 135. At each price point it has been estimated that there will be a certain number of customers each day(the higher the daily fee the fewer the customers).

The payoff table looks at each possibility. At a daily fee of M$ 100,we expect there to be a certain number of customers a day. If these customers used the services fully then variable costs would be M$ 60 for the day and hence contribution M$ 136,160. Alternatively it's possible that customers use the facilities up to a point of generating M$ 30 of variable cost and therefore contribution is higher at M$ 238,280.

At each of the three different levels of daily fee,there are three possible levels of variable cost per customer and so there are nine possible levels of contribution for the three months.

It should be noted that the value of the table is very much dependent on the accuracy of the market research that has been undertaken and the assumptions that underpin it in terms of numbers of customers per day.

Decision Criteria

The maximax decision rule involves choosing the fee that offers the best possible result,in this case choosing the fee which maximises contribution. The decision maker is an optimist and would therefore choose the daily fee of M$ 115 as this could result in a contribution of M$ 242,420(but only if all customers used the facilities at the lower end of usage).

The maximin decision rule involves choosing the fee that offers the best of the worst outcomes,in this instance choosing the fee which maximises the minimum contribution for each price point. The decision maker is a pessimist and would therefore choose the daily fee of M$ 135 which has the best of the lowest possible contributions at M$ 165,600.

The minimax regret decision rule involves choosing the fee that minimises the maximum regret from making the wrong decision,in this instance choosing the fee which minimises the maximum opportunity cost from making the wrong decision. From the regret table we can see that the minimax regret decision strategy would be to choose a daily fee of M$ 115 as the most the regret can be here is M$ 8,740.

试卷四　参考答案

任务一

发件人：管理会计助理

收件人：财务总监 Rav Patel

主题：责任会计和员工奖励计划

餐厅和厨房责任会计

为了使经理对成本或收入负责，必须赋予他们影响甚至控制成本或收入的权利。

成本责任

四号酒店的主厨负责该酒店厨房的运营，包括开发菜单及确定食材品质和厨房工人数量等。每项工作都会影响成本。

开发菜单需要确定购买哪些食材，主厨要决定采用食材的品质高低，以及决定聘用熟练员工还是非熟练员工，这些都会影响成本。可见，主厨控制了厨房运营过程中的大部分成本，因此他们也必须为成本负责。

四号酒店的酒吧和餐厅主管负责酒吧和餐厅的运营，包括确定某一天等候的员工数量和酒吧工作人员的数量，以及酒吧库存的饮料种类等。酒吧和餐厅主管应该为这些人工成本和采购成本负责。

收入责任

酒吧和餐厅的成本责任较容易界定，但收入责任的界定就有一定难度。目前，食品和饮料的售价由主厨、酒吧和餐厅经理以及酒店经理共同商定。

酒吧和餐厅的收入源于向客人销售饮料和菜品，但很难确定到底哪一项对收入的影响最大。

主厨对收入的影响取决于他所开发的菜单是否有吸引力，以及从厨房端出的菜品品质如何。如果一些长住客人对菜单和菜品质量不满意，那么他们就不会再次光顾餐厅。如果菜单缺乏吸引力或可选择的菜品不多，那么短住客人也不会使用餐厅。酒吧和餐厅主管对收入的影响也体现在所雇用的服务员的服务质量和所销售的饮料种类上。

我建议将酒吧和餐厅的收入分成两部分：饮料销售收入和菜品销售收入。酒吧和餐厅主管对酒吧收入（“酒吧”利润中心）负责，主厨对菜品收入（“厨房”利润中心）负责。总的来说，主厨对菜品收入的影响大于其他经理，因为菜品收入主要依赖于厨房是否能及时提供优质的菜品和良好的服务。

奖励计划

员工是我们最大的资产。最大限度地调动员工积极性，充分开发员工的技能和扩展他们的知识，提高服务水平，这对我们来说至关重要。在竞争激烈的市场，我们要努力吸引回头客，而员工对其工作角色的满意度和积极性有助于实现这一目标。

我们需要制定相应的制度，确保每个员工都能在智选酒店发挥其自身的价值。员工如果参与感不强、不受重视，则无法用心做好自己的工作。

为了取得成效，员工奖励计划要为员工量身打造，满足员工的诉求。为此，酒店经理需要明白如何有针对性地奖励员工。有效的奖励计划应该做到灵活度高、涵盖面广，且针对不同的业绩采用不同的奖励方式。有效的团队沟通有利于吸引员工的兴趣，为管理者提供奖励的机会，并有效解决所有问题。

因为酒店经理也需要得到奖励，所以奖励机制应该是自上而下的。成为首选雇主，为员工提供养老金、福利计划和额外福利，有助于激励员工，最终促使他们提升业绩。

在设计奖励计划时，要强调“个人认同感”，激发员工的工作热情和参与度。例如，在每个酒店张贴海报，展示优秀员工的提名者和获奖者的风采，能有效激发员工的工作热情，发挥奖励效应。

设计个性化奖励方案也有助于提高员工参与度。例如，为提名的“本月之星”设计个性化和量身定制的展示信息，从而鼓励每位员工有机会获得赏识。

另外，在酒店业还可以采用积分银行（Rewardbanking. com）的方式设计奖励计划，员工完成酒店的相关工作可以赚取相应的积分。员工可以根据他们所积攒的积分选择相应的奖励方案，这也是奖励员工努力工作的动力。

酒店经理也可以根据顾客的反馈情况或员工对公司业务规范的遵守情况，评估每位员工的业绩。做到奖勤罚懒。当然，我们需要确保公平对待所有酒店员工。

感谢！

智选酒店

管理会计助理

任务二

发件人：管理会计助理

收件人：总经理 John Hayes

主题：三号酒店经营差异和营销组合

人员

像我们这样的服务业总是强调人际关系。因此，我们需要强调人品的重要性，并着重培养外联员工的服务道德意识。为此，我们应该以客户为导向，通过高质量的培训来提高员工素质。特别是选择、培训并奖励外联员工，做好客户关怀和公共关系。

形象服务（如前台和餐厅工作人员的服务）是影响客户满意度的关键因素。这些形象服务通过与客户联系提高服务水平，收集客户需求信息并满足客户需求。

在所有的酒店，我们要确保员工拥有相应的技能和知识，以支持我们提供的服务，要求员工穿着统一的制服，树立专业形象。例如，前台工作人员必须穿西服或工作制服，并接受促销训练，鼓励入住客人使用餐厅。

业务流程

我们设计了方便客户使用的系统，支持客户与我们互动。有效的业务流程会为智选酒店带来市场优势。如果能加速客人的入住和退房程序，就会提高他们对智选酒店的首次消费体验和最终印象，创造“客户价值”，从而给未来带来更多订单和更高收入。此外，我们要进一步精简在线预订程序（如提高在线支付的安全性），创造良好形象以吸引潜在客户。这些重要的业务流程需要得到客户的高度满意。

我们要定期对工作程序和工作效率进行检查，注意客户排队等候时间，还要注意我们提供的设施、客房、工作人员及其服务对顾客的方便性。

市场口碑

市场口碑是指市场对我们的产品和服务的看法。有关我们酒店服务的市场口碑，与我们在酒店提供的服务质量和服务类别息息相关，我们将重点改进酒店环境设计和服务规范。为此，我们需要关注一些环境细节，如固定装置、配件、装饰、配色方案、噪声水平、背景音乐、香水和一般氛围等。能否获得市场口碑取决于我们是否能为顾客提供舒适和便利的服务。

现在，提高市场口碑还有一点是精细设计我们的网站，方便原有和潜在的客人能顺利通过导航找到我们的酒店。网站是潜在客户对我们酒店的第一印象。

差异分析

管理层对三号酒店的整改方案已经开始实施，修订了原有预算，并根据原有预算、修订预算和实际业绩对经营报表进行了调整。

原有预算和修订预算利润差是计划差异。计划差异与经营业绩无关，经营管理无法影响计划差异的大小。计划差异源于管理层的决策，因此不应该由酒店经理负责。

经营报表显示，计划差异为预算利润从 M$ 90 000 降至 M$ 88 000。以下是酒店经理在经营报表上提出的方案。

- 方案一，降低洗衣成本预算。洗衣成本是变动成本，降低洗衣成本预算有利于实现变动成本的有利差异。
- 方案二，降低财产保险预算。财产保险是固定成本，降低财产保险预算有利于实现固定成本的有利差异。
- 方案三，增加员工成本，因为主厨一般会与酒店签订长期合同，这是一项固定成本，因此增加员工成本会导致固定成本的不利差异。同时采取方案二和方案三会使预算利润降低 M$ 5 000。

修订预算和实际业绩之间的差异是运营差异。由于酒店经理及其团队的努力改善了酒店实际业绩，这个有利差异应归功于酒店经理。

应该指出的是，利润差异是有利差异（实际利润高于修订的预算利润），说明入住率有所增加，成本有所下降。

酒店经理 Patrick Jenkins 提出的上述 3 个方案的实际效果也完全不同。

- 方案一会增加餐厅相关成本，也会增加固定成本，从而导致固定成本不利差异。
- 方案二会降低客房服务成本，从而导致变动成本有利差异。
- 方案三降低餐厅收入，从而导致价格不利差异。

感谢！

智选酒店

管理会计助理

任务三

发件人：管理会计助理

收件人：财务总监 Rav Patel

主题：零基预算和处置资产

零基预算

执行零基预算要求酒店经理和部门负责人参与重大规划、分析和决策过程。

智选酒店的各部门经理（如客房服务经理）负责本部门下一个预算年度的预算，他们需要与部门员工一起收集预算所需的信息。在零基预算的情况下，每个方案是一个决策包，实现每个决策包的目标至少有 3 个路径。

每个决策包必须包括预计目标、具体活动、所需资源及相关成本，还要解释这些决策包如何有助于智选酒店总目标的实现。

每位部门经理需要审查每个决策包及其实现方案，以及评估方案的可实施性，并回答以下问题：

- 该决策包是否有利于实现我们的业务目标？
- 不采纳该决策包会对我们的业务产生什么影响？
- 是否可以更有效地完成该决策包的目标？

我们需要采用成本效益分析法对决策包进行优先排序。排序是对所有的相关决策包进行评估。排序过程中需要部门经理进行主观的价值判断，这可能会导致排序结果出现偏颇，也就是说零基预算具有一定的主观性。即便如此，零基预算仍然需要对决策包进行排序。

在智选酒店，客房服务成本有员工成本、洗衣成本、洗漱用品和毛巾成本等。这些成本项目的高低部分取决于业务量大小。以洗漱用品为例，业务量大小决定洗漱用品的补充次数，并因此决定洗漱用品库存量的高低。此外，还有一些自主性开支。关于洗漱用品的档次的选择问题可以制定系列决策包，每个决策包包括高、中、低不同档次的洗漱用品。每个决策包的成本容易估计，但评估其收益比较困难，因为有些收益是无形的。部门经理需要结合企业目标和财务限制来考量每个决策包，并选择最适合的方案。

再如，客房服务的决策包括床单和毛巾的质量高低。如果这些物品不受年度合同的约束，我们可以灵活地调整这些物品的档次。

资产处置

2016 年 12 月出售的资产

在 2016 年 12 月出售资产时，需要将这些固定资产从账上注销并在损益表中确认为损益。由于这些资产在该财年内会被处置，所以无须提取折旧。

2017 年 1 月出售的资产

虽然这些资产在 2016 年 12 月 31 日仍然存在，但因为即将被处置，所以不再用于商业目的。这些资产已经确定了销售价值并将在短期内出售，所以在财务状况表上单独列为“待售资产”。

这些资产的计量应遵循账面净值与预计销售收入（M$ 40 000）孰低原则。账面价值指的是截止到出售日之前的折余价值，如果账面净值低于预计销售收入，则两者差额将计入损益表。

因破损暂不出售的资产

因破损暂不出售的资产在年末留在固定资产账上。如果还会暂时使用这些资产，则需要对其提取折旧。此外，还需要对这些资产进行减值评估，确定其价值是否减少。对这些资产进行减值评估包括将资产账面净值、使用价值（预期可获得收益）和可变现净值进行对比。鉴于这些资产的性质，预计减值损失计入 2016 年年度损益表中。

感谢！

智选酒店

管理会计助理

任务四

商誉会计简报

财务报表中的商誉

我们在并购酒店时会产生商誉。一般在并购业务中，会将并购标的视为持续经营主体，并购酒店的报价除了购买其现有的有形资产（固定资产）、流动资产和负债（如库存、应收账款和应付账款）外，还包括所并购酒店的员工经验、客户忠诚度和持续经营业务优势等。也就是说，所支付的并购款一般会高于其固定资产和净流动资产的价值，多出来的部分就是对商誉的购买。商誉可以资本化处理，因为它源于企业合并行为。商誉之所以在财务状况表中列入“无形资产”科目，是因为商誉与客户忠诚度和员工经验等无形因素有关。

根据国际财务报告准则，由于没有确定商誉价值的活跃市场，一旦所购入的商誉被确认入账，企业便不能对其进行重新估值。但企业需要每年对商誉进行摊销，并计入当年损益。

由客人满意度和忠诚度带来的商誉不能确认为无形资产

国际财务报告准则规定，由客户满意度和忠诚度（企业内部产生的商誉）带来的商誉不能确认为无形资产，原因有两个。

第一，价值无法计量。有些专家认为，基于假设前提下将商誉和其他无形资产（如品牌）确认入账，违背了可靠性原则。商誉没有可交易市场，无法适用市场价值概念。如果企业将内部产生的商誉进行估值，就会夸大其业务价值，从而误导或欺骗财务报表的使用者。

第二，内部产生的商誉无法与其他业务分离出来并单独出售。比如四号酒店客户满意度是该酒店商誉的一部分，但我们无法单独将四号酒店的商誉对外出售。

健康俱乐部定价简报

3 个月试营业期的盈利表显示了管理者面临的每种可能的盈利水平。本例中，每天 3 种收费决策是公司可控的因素，但每个客户使用多少设施并因此产生多少变动成本是不可控的。

盈利表列出了每人每天收费为 M$ 100、M$ 115 或 M$ 135 三种价格下的盈利情况。价格不同，每天的客户量也不同（价格越高，客户越少）。

从盈利表来看，如果每天收费 M$ 100，每天客户量会达到一定规模。如果这些客户使用所提供的全部服务，则变动成本为 M$ 60，此时盈利总额为 M$ 136 160；如果客户只使用部分设施，则变动成本为 M$ 30，盈利总额可增至 M$ 238 280。

在 3 种不同的收费水平下，每种收费水平又有 3 种可能的变动成本，因此在试运营的 3 个月内有 9 个可能的盈利水平。

值得注意的是，该盈利表的准确性有赖于市场调研的准确性以及每天客户数量假设的准确性。

决策标准

盈利额大中取大法是指选择能导致最好结果的收费水平，即选择贡献额最大的收费水平。这种方法也叫乐观法。如果每天收费 M$ 115，则客人使用设施最少，可产生 M$ 242 420的最高盈利额。

盈利额小中取大法是指从最坏结果中选择最大贡献额的收费水平，即选择在每个收费水平下 3 个最小贡献额中的最大值。这种方法也叫悲观法。如果每天收费 M$ 135，则产生 M$ 165 600 的最低盈利额。

后悔值大中取小法是指从每种收费水平的最大后悔值中选择最小值对应的收费水平，即选择错误决策导致的最大机会成本中的最小值。从后悔值表中可以看出，按后悔值大中取小法，如果每天收费 M$ 115，则最大后悔值中最小的为 M$ 8 740。

Variant 4　Marking Guidance

Section	Technical skills		Business skills		People skills		Leadership skills		Integration	Total
1	Responsibility accounting	11	Reward scheme	4	Reward scheme	7			3	25
2	Planning and operational variances	13	Marketing mix	12						25
3	ZBB Disposal of property, plant and equipment	12 13								25
4	Accounting for purchased goodwill Short-term decision making with uncertainty	7 6			Short-term decision making with risk	6	Accounting for internally generated goodwill	6		25
Total marks available for competency		62		16		13		6	3	100

试卷四　评分指南

项目	技术技能		商业技能		人际技能		领导技能		综合	总计
1	责任会计	11	奖励计划	4	奖励计划	7			3	25
2	规划运营差异	13	营销组合	12						25
3	零基预算 固定资产处置	12 13								25
4	购买商誉的会计处理 不确定性短期决策	7 6			短期风险决策	6	内部产生商誉的会计处理	6		25
各种能力分数总计		62		16		13		6	3	100

湖北经济学院名师解惑

试卷一共有四项任务，考察了P1、F1、E1三门课程的知识点，具体包括责任会计、奖励计划、营销组合、差异分析、零基预算和不定性短期决策等。该试卷考核了考生的四项能力，其中技术技能的分值占62%，商业技能的分值占16%，人际技能的分值占13%，领导技能的分值占6%，与CGMA管理会计能力框架的技能要求一致。

该试卷的每项任务涉及以下知识点：

任务	问题	科目	知识点
任务一	运用责任会计区分责任中心（成本中心和/或利润中心）	P1	责任会计与成本控制（responsibility accounting and controllability of costs）
	非财务员工奖励计划的理由及优点	E1	员工奖励（reward systems）
任务二	营销组合及具体方案	E1	营销组合（mixed marketing）
	预算差异中计划差异和实际差异的分析	P1	差异分析法（variance analysis）
任务三	零基预算的介绍	P1	零基预算（ZBB）
	固定资产的处置及其对财务报表的影响	F1	非流动资产（non-current assets）的核算
任务四	商誉的产生及核算范围	F1	无形资产（intangible assets）的核算
	不确定性短期决策下的后悔值分析法	P1	大中取大、大中取小和小中取大后悔值法（maxima，maximin and minmax regret）

上述各项任务要求以邮件或简报等形式来呈现答案，对问题的描述非常明确，答题时既要注意内容的针对性，也要注意形式的规范性。

对应知识点深度剖析

运用责任会计区分成本中心和/或利润中心

责任会计是指为了适应企业内部经济责任制的要求，对企业内部各责任中心的经济业务进行规范与控制，以实现业绩考核与评价的一种内部会计控制制度。企业组织结构与其责任会计系统有着密切的关系，责任会计系统应反映并支撑企业组织结构。

考生需要根据对成本或收入的影响成立成本中心和责任中心。本例中，主厨决定着所采用食材的品质的高低和被聘用员工的熟练程度等厨房运营过程中的大部分成本，因此他们也必须为成本负责。酒吧和餐厅主管负责酒吧和餐厅的运营方面的人工成本与采购成本。

考生需结合本例背景材料，将酒吧和餐厅的收入分成两部分：饮料销售收入和菜品销售收入。酒吧和餐厅主管对酒吧收入（“酒吧”利润中心）负责，主厨对菜品收入（“厨房”利润中心）负责。

考生注意事项

责任会计的职责包括如下3个基本原则。

（1）责任原则。要确定责任单位，明确责任指标，使企业内部的各个单位都有定量的经济责任指标（资金、成本费用、利润），企业的总指标都能分解落实到责任单位。

（2）定价结算原则。按照一定价格分成不同的责任单位进行核算，包括各单位之间往来结算和各责任单位的责任指标完成情况的核算。

（3）利益原则。对各责任单位指标完成情况要进行考核，在考核的基础上进行奖惩。

上述3个基本原则事实上就是事先确定目标、事中核算监督和事后考核奖惩3个环节。

员工奖励

员工是企业最重要的资产。企业需要制定相应的制度，让每个员工都能发挥其自身的价值。有效的奖励计划应该做到灵活度高、涵盖面广，且针对不同的业绩采用不同的奖励方式。员工奖励计划要为员工量身打造，满足员工的诉求。

奖励机制是自上而下的，要强调“个人认同感”，激发员工的工作热情和参与度。设计个性化奖励方案有助于提高员工参与度，还可以采用积分银行的方式设计奖励计划。

制订员工奖励计划是实际商业环境中经常遇到的决策问题，该问题考查考生综合解决问题的能力。我们一般在提出具体奖励计划时都需要考虑企业发展、财务状况、营运能力、经营规模和员工组成等要素，再基于每个点，结合公司现状进行拓展叙述。

营销组合

营销组合是企业的综合营销方案，即企业针对目标市场的需要对自己可控制的各种营销因素的优化组合和综合运用，使之协调配合，扬长避短，发挥优势，以便更好地实现营销目标。

企业在规划营销组合时，考虑 4 个 P，即产品（product）、地点（place）、营销（promotion）和价格（price）；而服务业还要注意其他的 3 个 P，即人（people）、过程（process）和形象服务（physical evidence）。结合本例，在设计营销组合时需要强调人品的重要性，着重培养外联员工的服务道德意识，以客户为导向，通过高质量的培训来提高员工素质。形象服务（如前台和餐厅工作人员的服务）是影响客户满意度的关键因素。要求前台工作人员必须穿西服或工作制服，并接受促销训练，鼓励入住客人使用餐厅。设计出方便客户使用的系统，支持与客户互动。定期对工作程序和工作效率进行检查。

服务业要十分注重市场口碑，即市场对企业服务的看法。市场口碑与服务质量和服务类别息息相关，能否获得市场口碑取决于我们是否能为顾客提供舒适和便利的服务，所以还需要关注一些环境细节。

最后，考生还要注意结合酒店业现在的通行做法提及酒店的网站，网站是给潜在客户的第一印象。

考生注意事项

营销组合具有以下特性：

（1）可控性；

（2）动态性；

（3）复合性；

（4）整体性。

因此，考生在提出相应的方案时，需要确定所提出的方案是否符合上述特征，避免所提的方案缺乏操作性。

预算差异中的计划差异与实际差异分析

预算差异分析是通过比较实际执行结果与预算目标，确定差异额及差异原因。如实际成果与预算标准的差异太大，企业管理者应审慎调查并判定其发生原因，以便采取适当的矫正措施。差异分析一般分两种差异：计划差异和运营差异。原有预算和修订预算利润之间的差异是计划差异，修订预算和实际业绩之间的差异是运营差异。计划差异源于管理层的决策，与经营业绩无关，不应该由酒店经理负责。而酒店经理及其团队的努力改善了酒店实际业绩，运营差异的有利差异应归功于酒店经理。

考生注意事项

计划差异＝修订预算业绩－原有预算业绩

运营差异＝实际业绩－修订预算业绩

零基预算的介绍

零基预算是指在编制成本费用预算时，不考虑以往会计期间所发生的费用项目或费用数额，而是以所有的预算支出为零作为出发点，一切从实际需要与可能出发，逐项审议预算期内各项费用的内容及其开支标准是否合理，在综合平衡的基础上编制费用预算的一种方法。执行零基预算要求酒店经理和部门负责人参与重大规划、分析和决策过程。

考生注意事项

零基预算的优点：

（1）有利于提高“投入—产出”意识；

（2）有利于合理分配资金；

（3）有利于发挥基层单位参与预算编制的创造性；

（4）有利于提高预算管理水平。

零基预算的缺点：

（1）编制工作量大，费用相对较高；

（2）分层、排序和资金分配时，可能有主观影响，容易引起部门之间的矛盾；

（3）过分强调项目，可能是有关人员只注重短期利益，忽视本单位作为一个整体的长远利益。

固定资产处置

在提交报表之前出售固定资产，企业需要将这些资产从账上注销并在损益表中确认为损益。这些资产无须提取折旧。

那些即将被处置且不再用于商业目的的资产，已经确定了销售价值并且将在短期内出售，所以在资产负债表上应被单独列为“待售资产”。其计量应遵循账面净值与预计销售收入孰低原则。账面价值是指截止到出售日之前的折余价值，如果账面净值低于预计销售收入，则两者差额将计入损益表。

因破损暂不出售的资产在年末留在固定资产账上。如果还要暂时使用这些资产，则需要对其提取折旧。此外，还需要对这些资产进行减值评估，确定其价值是否减少。对这些资产进行的减值评估，包括将资产账面净值、使用价值（预期可获得收益）和可变现净值进行对比。

考生需要仔细分析不同日期的固定资产的会计处理，具体情况具体分析。

商誉的核算

国际会计准则第 38 号对“无形资产”的定义为：“无形资产是指为用于商品或劳务的生产或供应、出租给其他单位，或管理目的而持有的、没有实物形态的、可辨认非货币资产。”

商誉通常是指企业在同等条件下，能获得高于正常投资报酬率所形成的价值。这是由于企业所处的地理位置具有优势，或者是由于经营效率高、历史悠久、人员素质高而使其与同行企业相比可以获得超额利润。商誉能在未来期间为企业经营带来超额利润，是企业预期的获利能力超过可辨认资产正常获利能力（如社会平均投资回报率）的资本化价值。商誉是企业整体价值的组成部分。在企业合并时，它是购买企业投资成本超过被合并企业净资产公允价值的差额。

本例中，并购的报价包括商誉，它在资产负债表中被列入“无形资产”科目。但国际财务报告准则规定，由客户满意度和忠诚度（企业内部产生的商誉）带来的商誉能确认为无形资产，因为价值无法计量，并且内部产生的商誉无法与其他业务分离出来，因而也无法单独出售。

考生不仅需要了解国际会计准则关于无形资产的界定，还需要分析案例中的具体业务，判断客户满意度和忠诚度是否属于无形资产。这个结论可以用于其他的相似情况。

不确定型短期决策

后悔值法为不确定型决策的决策方法之一。假设已选定某个方案，但实际情况证明，如选定另一个方案将产出更高的利润，决策后将因实际得到的利润小于可能获得的利润而后悔，各种可能状态在所有方案中的最高期望利润，减去该方案在某种可能状态下的估计利润，即为最大潜在后悔值。

考生注意事项

在不确定性下的决策有如下3种方法。

(1) 盈利额大中取大法，是指选择能导致最好结果的收费水平，即选择贡献额最大的收费水平。这种方法也叫乐观法。

(2) 盈利额小中取大法，是指从最坏结果中选择最大贡献额的收费水平，即选择在每一个收费水平下3个较小贡献额中的最大值。这种方法也叫悲观法。

(3) 后悔值大中取小法，是指从每种收费水平的较大后悔值中选择最小值对应的收费水平，即选择错误决策导致的最大机会成本中的最小值。

Variant 5

This examination is structured as follows:

Section number	Number of tasks	Time for section(minutes)
1	1	45
2	2	45
3	1	45
4	1	45

The time available for each section is for reading,planning and writing your answer(s).

Please note Section 2 consists of two tasks. Please leave enough time to complete both parts.

Section 1

It is the middle of August and Rav Patel, finance director, sends you the following email:

From: Rav Patel, Finance Director

To: Management Accountant Assistant

Subject: Six-month hotel performance statements

Molly Patel (Operations Director) will be conducting her six monthly appraisal with each of the hotel managers over the next two weeks. Molly has asked for a summary of performance for each hotel for the first six months of the year.

Yesterday, Joe Perez, your fellow Management Accountant Assistant, prepared a schedule for Hotel 1, which includes two statements for the six months to 30 June 2016; a reconciliation of the budgeted to actual profit; a reconciliation of operating profit to operating cash flow for both actual and budgeted performance.

In March a new eco-neutral hotel called Envirohotel opened one street away from Hotel 1. It has a fantastic restaurant with a world-class chef. As a result of the increased competition, Hotel 1's manager, Tara Gomez, has changed the complimentary toiletry products to a luxury brand, we publicise this on our website. A major redecoration project started in April, a year ahead of schedule, after approval from managing director John Hayes.

In preparation for her appraisal session with Tara Gomez, Molly has requested an explanation of what Joe's operating statement shows about the performance of the hotel, with possible reasons for the variances. Molly would also like an analysis of the actual operating cash flow generated against budget in the six months and any implications arising from the analysis in respect of working capital management.

Joe Perez is ill today, so I would like you to prepare a first draft of a briefing paper for Molly on both of these matters.

Many thanks!

Rav Patel

Finance Director

Wise Choice Hotels

Schedule of Operating Statement and Operating Cash Flow Reconciliation of Hotel 1

Operating statement for the six months to 30 June 2016:

	Room revenue income stream (M$ 000)	**Bar and restaurant income stream (M$ 000)**
Budgeted operating profit	548	68
Occupancy volume contribution variance	(85)	
Bar and restaurant volume contribution variance		(42)
Room revenue rate variance	60	
Bar and restaurant revenue rate variance		(18)
Variable costs variance	(8)	—
Fixed costs variance	(13)	—
Actual operating profit	502	8

- Budgeted operating profit included above is 50% of the budgeted operating profit for the year for each of the room revenue and bar and restaurant income streams.
- The actual level of occupancy in the hotel for the six months was 82%.
- The proportion of guests using the bar and restaurant facilities was 50%.
- Budgeted contribution per room occupied has been used to calculate the occupancy volume contribution variance. Budgeted bar and restaurant contribution per guest has been used to calculate the bar and restaurant volume contribution variance.

Operating cash flow reconciliation for the six months to 30 June 2016:

	Actual (M$ 000)	**Budget (M$ 000)**
Hotel 1 operating profit	510	616
Movement in inventory	(34)	10
Movement in receivables	(112)	45
Movement in payables	(80)	(15)
Hotel 1 operating cash flow	284	656

- In the six months to 30 June 2016, 65% of guests were business travellers of which 75%

were paid for by corporate account.

- The balances at 31 December 2015 were M$ 92,000 for inventory, M$ 115,000 for receivables and M$ 206,000 for payables.

Depreciation is not charged to individual hotels and hence is not included in the above reconciliation.

Write the briefing paper to Molly Patel, as requested by Rav Patel.

Section 2

One week later Rav Patel calls you into his office and says:

John Hayes, managing director, recently attended a business owners' breakfast at the new Envirohotel. At the breakfast, the owner of Envirohotel, Paul Kano, gave a short presentation about how the ethos and strategies of his hotel are embedded in corporate social responsibility (CSR) principles, with a particular focus on the hotel's impact on the environment. John was very impressed with the presentation and with Envirohotel itself.

John is keen that we, as a business, look into this further, because he feels that Wise Choice Hotels is now at a competitive disadvantage. Hotel 1, in particular, has seen a declining occupancy rate, with guests seemingly switching to Envirohotel. He thinks that in order to stop this trend and to grow the business, we need to be much more aware of our corporate responsibilities. He is also keen that we all have a better understanding of how our business affects the environment, so that, perhaps, we can make changes to counteract any harmful impact.

He has asked for a briefing paper to be circulated to all directors and hotel managers, to include explanations of:

- the economic, legal, ethical and philanthropic corporate social responsibilities that our business faces and any measures already in place that meet these responsibilities;
- how we could categorise our environmental costs, in an environmental cost of quality report, and an example of each category of environmental cost which is relevant to our business. Please include justification of the categorisation for each of your examples.

Please prepare the first draft of this briefing paper for me.

Write the draft briefing paper requested by Rav Patel.

Section 3

The next week Rav Patel, finance director, sends you the following email:

From: Rav Patel, Finance Director
To: Management Accountant Assistant
Subject: Environmental project

John Hayes, managing director, is keen on making some significant changes to our hotels so that we can start to lessen the impact that they have on the environment. He has already made enquiries into the most technologically advanced solar panels as a means to generate some of our own electricity. These solar panels have a useful economic life of 10 years.

The Macland government is currently offering two incentives to encourage businesses to invest in these technologically advanced solar panels. John would like to know how these incentives will impact our financial statements and tax charge for the year to 31 December 2016. The incentives are as follows:

- a government grant of 10% of the cost of the solar panels. This grant would be given at the point when the solar panels start to produce energy. Once granted the monies will not need to be repaid as long as the solar panels continue to be used by the business for a period of three years.
- 100% first year tax allowances in respect of the purchase cost of these solar panels.

John was impressed with the section, in the briefing paper we sent him last week, about the contents of an environmental cost of quality report, as he hadn't heard of this before. He is keen to understand though how such a report will help us to improve our environmental and financial performance.

Please draft a response to John that explains:

- How the receipt of the government grant will impact the financial statements and tax charge of the business for the year to 31 December 2016 on the assumption that the grant is received at the end of December 2016.
- How tax allowances usually affect our tax charge and how the 100% first year allowances

will affect our tax charge for the year to 31 December 2016 on the assumption that the solar panels are purchased during 2016.

- How an environmental cost of quality report will help us to improve our environmental and financial performance.

Many thanks!

Rav Patel

Finance Director

Wise Choice Hotels

Write your response to Rav Patel.

Section 4

Two weeks later, Rav Patel, finance director is on holiday with his wife, Molly Patel (operations director). In their absence, John Hayes, managing director, sends you the following email:

From: John Hayes, Managing Director
To: Management Accountant Assistant
Subject: Laundry services

I've been thinking about the environmental impact of our hotels. It seems to me that laundry is one of our major environmental issues. At the moment, we use the same external contractor for all of our hotels laundry. We have no control over the contractor's environmental policies. In addition, laundry is a significant expense. I've often wondered whether it would be better to set up a facility and do the laundry in-house.

I would like to discuss this with the rest of the directors, when Rav and Molly are back from their holiday. I have already done some preliminary work on this, in terms of how we might set up a laundry facility and the costs involved. There is an ideal, ex-laundry, building close to Hotel 1. I know that it has been unused and empty for a number of years and, therefore, could be rented on an annual basis for M$ 70,000 a year.

I propose that we initially rent machinery for a one-year trial period. There are two options that

I think we need to consider; whether to set up enough washing machines, driers and ironing presses to cover just our requirements, or, whether we double the capacity and sell the laundry services to external parties. I was discussing this with my son (who is at university studying accountancy) at the weekend and he drew up a decision tree for me, which I have attached. He didn't quite have time to finish it, before he went back to university, but he has included some notes.

I would be very grateful if you could prepare a briefing paper, which I can use as the basis of my discussions with the other directors, that explains:

- the potential benefits and drawbacks to us of setting up our own facility for laundry, rather than continuing to contract out laundry services;
- how we can arrive at a decision, using the decision tree, by explaining what points C, D and E on it mean and any potential problems of basing our decision solely on this decision tree. There is no need to provide any further calculations.

Many thanks.

John Hayes
Managing Director
Wise Choice Hotels

Decision Tree of the Net Costs Associated with Laundry Provision

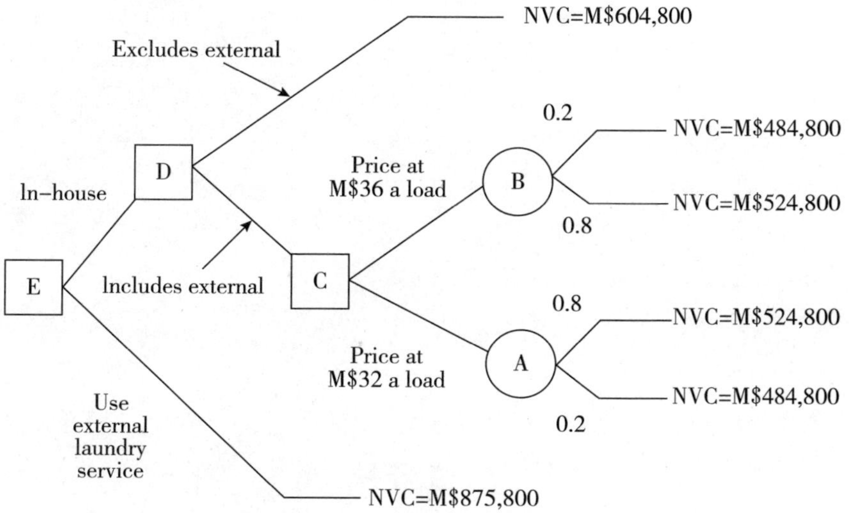

Notes:

(1) NVC stands for net variable costs. This represents the variable costs incurred less any revenue we would earn if we offered the laundry service externally.

(2) If no laundry facility is set up the contracted cost of laundry for the year is M$ 875,000.

(3) If the laundry facility is set up just for Wise Choice Hotels laundry, fixed costs are estimated at M$ 250,000 for the year.

(4) If the laundry facility is doubled in capacity so that laundry services can be sold externally, the fixed costs are estimated at M$ 350,000 for the year.

(5) If the capacity is doubled, there are two possible prices that could be charged: M$ 36 a load or M$ 32 a load. The price per load will determine the level of external customer demand. For each price per load there are two possible outcomes. The probability attached to each outcome is shown on the decision tree.

(6) Expected values are M$ 532,800 at point A and M$ 516,800 at point B.

Write the briefing paper requested by Rav Patel.

试卷五

本次考试的结构如下：

序号	任务数	时间（分钟）
1	1	45
2	2	45
3	1	45
4	1	45

每个部分规定的时间可用于读题、组织和书写答案。

请注意任务二包括两项子任务，需留足时间。

任务一

8 月中旬，财务总监 Rav Patel 给你发了以下电子邮件：

发件人：财务总监 Rav Patel
收件人：管理会计助理
主题：酒店半年业绩报告

运营总监 Molly Patel 将在接下来的两周内对每一位酒店经理进行为期 6 个月的评估。Molly 需要一份今年上半年每家酒店业绩的简报。

昨天，你的同事，另一位管理会计助理 Joe Perez 编制了一号酒店 2016 年上半年的两份资料：一份是预算利润与实际利润的调节表；另一份是根据经营利润计算的经营现金流的预算和实际调节表。

今年 3 月 1 日，酒店附近新开了一家环保酒店（Envirohotel）。该酒店拥有高规格的餐厅，聘请了世界顶级的主厨。为了适应不断加剧的市场竞争，一号酒店的经理 Tara Gomez 决定提升客户洗漱用品的品质，我们也在网站上发布了这一消息。在征得总经理 John Hayes 的同意后，今年 4 月启动了重大装修工程，这一工程比原计划提前了 1 年。

Molly 正在准备与 Tara Gomez 的评估会议材料，解释 Joe 提供的资料中关于酒店业绩的说明，并解释预算数与实际数差额产生的原因。Molly 还需要公司半年内实际经营现金流与预算水平差异的分析，以及营运资金管理对该差异的影响。

Joe Perez 今天身体有恙，烦劳你准备一份解释上述两件事情的初稿。

谢谢！

智选酒店
财务总监
Rav Patel

一号酒店的经营情况及经营现金流预算数和实际数

2016 年上半年的经营情况：

	客房收入（M$ 000）	酒吧和餐厅收入（M$ 000）
预算经营利润	548	68
入住量贡献差异	(85)	
酒吧和餐厅贡献差异		(42)
客房收入价格差异	60	
酒吧和餐厅价格差异		(18)
变动成本差异	(8)	—
固定成本差异	(13)	—
实际经营利润	502	8

- 上表中半年客房收入及酒吧和餐厅收入的预算经营利润是全年预算的一半。
- 上半年酒店的实际入住率为 82%。
- 使用酒吧和餐厅的房客占 50%。
- 计算每间客房入住量贡献差异时使用单间客房的预计入住量。计算酒吧和餐厅贡献差异时使用每位客人的酒吧和餐厅预计贡献。

2016 年上半年经营现金流预算数和实际数：

	实际数（M$ 000）	预算数（M$ 000）
一号酒店经营利润	510	616
存货变化	(34)	10
应收账款变化	(112)	45
应付账款变化	(80)	(15)
1 号酒店经营现金流	284	656

- 截至 2016 年 6 月 30 日，65% 的客人是商务客人，其中有 75% 是通过对公账户支付。
- 2015 年 12 月 31 日的存货余额为 M$92 000、应收账款为 M$115 000、应付账款为 M$206 000。
- 单个酒店不提取折旧，因此上述调节表不包括折旧金额。

请根据 Rav Patel 的要求向 Molly Patel 做一份简报。

任务二

Rav Patel 把你叫到办公室并对你说：

前不久，总经理 John Hayes 参加了一次新开业的环保酒店的业主早餐。当时，环保酒店老板 Paul Kano（保罗·卡诺）做了一个简短的演讲，谈及企业社会责任的精神和战略，尤其要关注酒店业对环境的影响。此次演讲和环保酒店给 John 留下了深刻印象。

John 认为，智选酒店现在处于竞争劣势，需要深入研究并寻找出路。特别是一号酒店的入住率下降，部分客人流向环保酒店。他认为，为了防止情况进一步恶化并大力开展业务，我们也需要关注企业社会责任。同时，他希望我们大家都能意识到酒店业务对环境的破坏，并尽可能消除负面影响。

他需要向管理层和酒店经理准备一份简报，并解释以下问题：

- 我们所面临的有关经济、法律、道德和慈善事业的企业社会责任，以及为此所做的努力；
- 我们如何在质量环境成本报告中对环境成本进行分类，请对每一类环境成本举一个例子，并说明理由。

请为我准备这份简报的初稿。

请根据 Rav Patel 的要求写一份简报。

任务三

发件人：财务总监 Rav Patel

收件人：管理会计助理

主题：环境计划

总经理 John Hayes 迫切希望在环境保护方面有所作为。他打算引进最新的太阳能电池板技术以实现部分电能的自给自足。这种太阳能电池板可以使用 10 年。

Macland 政府有两项鼓励企业投资太阳能电池板的奖励措施。John 想了解这些奖励措施对 2016 年 12 月 31 日的财务报表和税收的影响。政府奖励措施的要点包括如下两条。

- 政府承担太阳能电池板 10% 的成本。只要太阳能电池板开始发电，就可以获得这笔政府补助。连续 3 年使用太阳能电池板，这笔政府补助就无须偿还。
- 太阳能电池板的全部采购成本在采购当年可以全额抵税。

John 对此很感兴趣，在上周我们发给他的简报中提到的关于质量环境成本报告的内容，他以前没有听说过。他很想知道如何通过这份报告帮助我们改善环境和提高业绩。

请向 John 解释以下问题。

- 如果政府补助在2016年年底前可以到位，那么该笔资助款对2016年的财务报表和税收有什么影响。
- 如果2016年内购买太阳能电池板，那么税收补贴和第一年全额抵扣对2016年的税收有什么影响。
- 质量环境成本报告将如何改善环境和提高财务业绩。

谢谢！

智选酒店
财务总监
Rav Patel

请写上你对Rav Patel的回复。

任务四

两周后，财务经理Rav Patel和他的妻子Molly Patel（运营总监）一起去度假了。由于他们两位的缺席，总经理John Hayes直接给你发了以下邮件：

发件人：总经理John Hayes
收件人：管理会计助理
主题：洗衣服务

我很关心我们酒店的环境问题。我认为，洗衣排放是我们的主要环境问题之一。目前，我们的洗衣服务全部外包，我们无法控制外部承包商的环境政策。此外，外包洗衣服务成本较高，我在考虑是否需要自建洗衣房。

Rav和Molly度假回来后，我打算和其他高管一起讨论这个问题。我已经就自建洗衣房方案和相关成本做了一个初步预算。在一号酒店附近有一个比较不错的洗衣房，已闲置多年，可对外出租，估计每年租金M$ 70 000。

我提议我们可以先行试用租赁上述洗衣房，在此期间，我们考虑以下两种方案：一是购置满足我们要求的洗衣机、烘干机和熨烫机；二是将洗衣产能扩大一倍并向外承接洗衣服务。我和读会计专业的儿子讨论过这个问题，他为我画了一个决策树（见后文）。他的学业紧张没时间跟我仔细解释，但是已经在重要的地方做了一些标记。

希望你能为我准备一份简报以便我和其他高管讨论，简报包括以下内容。

- 自建洗衣房而不外包洗衣业务的潜在利弊。
- 如何根据决策树来做出决策，解释决策点C、D和E的含义，并指出仅仅依靠决策树进行决策的潜在问题。此问题无须更多计算。

谢谢。

智选酒店
总经理
John Hayes

与洗衣有关的决策树

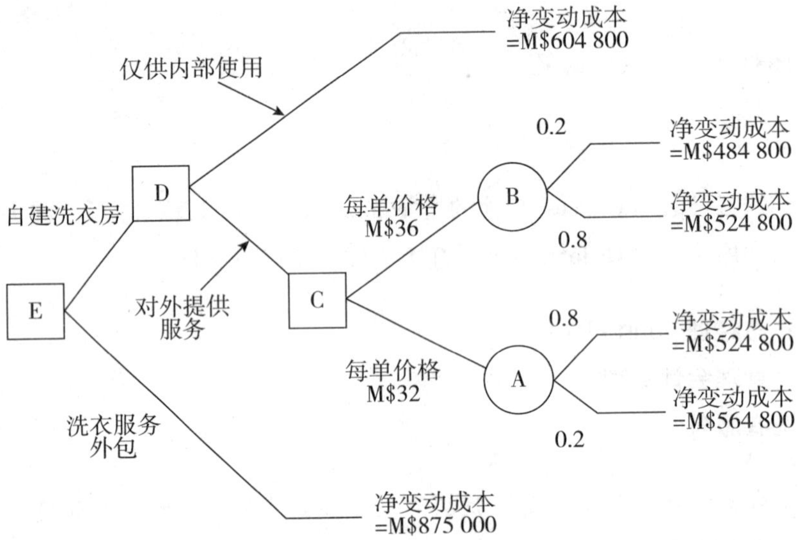

注：

（1）净变动成本是向外提供洗衣服务收入减去相关变动成本的差额。

（2）如果不自建洗衣房，那么每年的洗衣费用是 M$ 875 000。

（3）如果自建洗衣房仅供内部使用，那么每年固定成本为 M$ 250 000。

（4）如果洗衣房产能增加一倍，那么可向外提供洗衣服务，预计每年固定成本为 M$ 350 000。

（5）如果产能增加一倍，那么可以向外承接洗衣服务，有两种收费选择：每单 M$ 36 或 M$ 32。对外服务订单量取决于每单收费价格。每种收费标准都有两个可能的结果。每个结果发生的概率都显示在决策树上。

（6）在决策点 A 的预期值为 M$ 532 800，而在决策点 B 的预期值为 M$ 516 800。

请针对 John Hayes 的要求回复一份简报。

Variant 5 Suggested Answers

Section 1

Operating Statement

The operating statement shows that actual operating profit was significantly lower than budgeted from both the room revenue and bar and restaurant income streams.

Room Revenue

In respect of the room revenue income stream the largest factor to affect operating profit is the occupancy of the hotel, as shown by an occupancy volume contribution variance of M$ 85,000 adverse. Actual occupancy was 82% compared to the budget of 90%. It's likely that this is a result of the new eco-neutral hotel opening nearby which has possible taken some of our potential guests. Alternatively, because this statement is for the first six months of the year only it's possible that this rate of 82% is representative of this time of the year and there will be a seasonal improvement in the rate for the second half.

Despite the reduction in the room occupancy level, the average revenue achieved per room has increased. This is evidenced by the favourable room revenue rate variance of M$ 60,000. On average the rooms occupied have been sold at above the budgeted average rate. This could be because of the time of the year in that we would expect a higher rate in the first six months.

The variable cost variance is adverse and means that more was spent per room than budgeted on breakfast service, laundry, house-keeping, or possibly there has been a greater proportion of variable staffing used. One aspect of this will be the up-grade in the toiletries provided free in the bedrooms which will have increased the house-keeping costs per room occupied. Possibly there have also been price increases that weren't budgeted; this needs to be investigated further.

Fixed costs are also higher than budget. Fixed costs are not affected by occupancy so the adverse variance of M$ 13,000 is the result of an increase in expenditure. The redecoration of the hotel is likely to be the reason for this. The project has been brought forward by a year and therefore will not have been included in the original budget.

Bar and Restaurant

The adverse volume contribution variance measures the effect on contribution of less guests using the bar and restaurant facilities. We budgeted for 60% of guests to use them and the actual proportion of guests using them was 50%. In addition our occupancy was only 82% compared to the budget of 90%

Bar and restaurant revenue is also lower than budgeted for the actual level of usage, as shown by the adverse rate variance. This means that the average revenue earned per guest is lower than that budgeted. Perhaps the new eco-neutral hotel restaurant is attracting our guests, the result being that they are spending less on food and beverages in our bar and restaurant.

The costs incurred by the bar and restaurant facility are in line with the budget as there are no cost variances here.

Analysis of Cash Generation and Implications for Working Capital Mangement

Analysis of Cash Generation

Overall we were budgeting that the movement in working capital would have a net positive effect on cash flow. However the opposite has happened and the movement in working capital has reduced cash flow and therefore Hotel 1's cash balance over the six month period.

Inventory Movement

We were budgeting for a small reduction in the inventory level to boost cash flow but there has actually been an increase in inventory of M$34,000 during the period. This is a significant increase on the balance at the end of the year.

It's possible that the reduction in occupancy level and the reduction in guest spending in the bar and restaurant has led to an increase in food, beverage and housekeeping inventory. Possibly order sizes have not been reduced to compensate of the reduction in use. Switching to the new luxury toiletries might also be a factor; bulk orders may have been required.

The implication of this increase is that an assessment of the age of the inventory needs to be made. The higher the level, the greater the risk of obsolescence; especially for food and beverage items.

Receivables Movement

We were budgeting for a reduction in the receivables balance but there has actually been an increase of M$112,000 which has the effect of reducing operating cash flow. This increase is surprising given that the proportion of business travellers to leisure travellers has fallen from the 70% budgeted to 65% and that the level of occupancy generally is down.

There has been no change in the proportion of business travellers that are linked to corporate accounts. Therefore the increase must be the result of either an increase in the credit terms given to Hotel 1's corporate customers or less efficient collection of money from corporate customers.

The implication of this is that an aged receivables report needs to be reviewed, to see if there is a general increase across all customers (in which case credit control procedures need to be tightened up) or one particular customer is not paying promptly (in which case that customer needs to be targeted).

Payables Movement

We were budgeting for a small reduction in the payables balance but there has actually been a relatively large reduction. This has had a negative impact on cash flow because cash is leaving the business more quickly than we had anticipated.

It's possible that the new supplier of toiletries has low credit terms or that other suppliers have changed their terms of trade. Alternatively it could just be the payments are being made too early and we are not taking full advantage of the credit terms given to us.

Trade payables are a form of free finance for the business and therefore we need to ensure that we utilise credit terms offered; although we do need to be careful that we don't over-extend these terms else we risk losing our suppliers' goodwill.

Section 2

Corporate Social Responsibility

Economic Responsibilities

Any business has an economic responsibility to its shareholders in terms of being able to generate a good return on investment. In the case of Wise Choice Hotels, you as directors are also shareholders and therefore this objective is at the fore-front of all the decisions that you make regarding the business.

However, economic responsibility goes beyond just the shareholders. It extends to employees and ensuring that they receive fair conditions of employment and remuneration. We already meet this as we have a staff welfare policy which offers free meals and accommodation. Our wages are also above the national minimum wage.

Economic responsibility also extends to our guests, in that they receive a good service for a fair price. Evidence in respect of our occupancy rates and guest feedback ratings suggest that we meet this responsibility.

Legal Responsibilities

There is an obligation for our business to follow the laws and regulations of Macland. Often laws are in place to protect interested parties such as employees and customers. We adhere to laws especially in relation to employees; indeed we go above and beyond what is required of us legally. We pay above the national minimum wage and we have contracts of employment which guarantee a minimum of 30 hours a week, even though many other hotel businesses use zero hours contracts.

Ethical Responsibilities

There is also an ethical responsibility for a business to act in a manner which is fair and just even where there is no legal responsibility. One major area here is in respect of the impact that our business has on the environment: it could be said that we have an ethical responsibility to minimise the impact of the business on the environment.

As a hotel business there are many ways that we impact the environment (see the second part of this briefing paper). We do have an environmental policy whereby we offer guests the opportunity not to have towels changed every day and we have introduced energy saving lightbulbs throughout every hotel. However, there is possibly more that could be done.

Philanthropic Responsibilities

The final level of responsibility is that of corporate philanthropy; giving something back to the community in which our business is embedded. We already do this in two ways; our donations to charity and sponsorship of a local children's football team. Such actions are often seen as desirable but not required.

Environmental Cost of Quality Report

Within an environmental cost of quality report there are four categories of environmental cost: prevention, appraisal, internal failure and external failure.

Environmental Prevention Costs

These are the costs that we incur to prevent an environmental impact from happening. The cost of replacing normal lightbulbs with energy saving light-bulbs is one example of an environmental prevention cost that we have incurred. It is a prevention cost because by using these bulbs we reduce the amount of energy that we use and therefore our carbon footprint on the environment.

Environmental Appraisal Costs

These are the costs incurred in order to assess whether we are complying with environmental standards and policies, whether these be internally or externally set.

The cost of the time that management will need to take developing environmental performance measures upon which the hotels can be appraised will be an appraisal cost. In addition the cost of the time taken to monitor the environmental impact of our suppliers such as our laundry service would be an appraisal cost.

Environmental Internal Failure Costs

These are the costs that are incurred in order to mitigate any environmental impacts that the business has created. These are costs that are borne by the business.

With regard to Wise Choice Hotels, one example is the cost that we incur scrapping our food waste. Our policy is to pay for food waste to be sent to a composting facility. This is an internal failure cost because if we had better control of food orders and the use of food in the kitchens there would be no food waste; hence no cost.

Environmental External Failure Costs

These are the costs that the environment suffers as a result of the actions of our business in generating harmful emissions.

As a hotel business we use a significant amount of energy in terms of lighting, heating and providing hot water for guests. Our laundry service provider will also use a lot of energy and although we do not directly create the carbon emissions, we are responsible for them. These emissions affect the environment at large and are external to our business. They area failure cost because there are ways in which we could have prevented at least some of the effect (such as solar panels and reducing the kilometres travelled to the laundry, assuming there was a laundry service closer).

Section 3

From: Management Accountant Assistant

To: Rav Patel, Finance Director

Subject：RE：Environmental project

Investment Incentives

Government Grant

The government grant is a capital grant because it is to be used to fund the capital purchase of the solar panels.

In accordance with IAS 20 Government Grants there are two options available to account for a capital grant in the financial statements.

The first option is to net the value of the grant off the cost of the solar panels and capitalise this net cost as PPE. This net cost would then be depreciated over the useful economic life of the solar panels，which is 10 years.

The second option is to capitalise the full cost of the solar panels as PPE and to create a deferred revenue account（which is a liability）for the value of the grant. This deferred revenue account would then be released to profit each year over the life of the solar panels.

Whichever option is taken，the impact on profit for the year will be exactly the same. One tenth of the value of the grant will be released to profit each year，which will have the impact of increasing profit. All that changes is the presentation in the statement of financial position.

The government grant will be taxed on the basis of it being a capital grant. As per Macland's tax rules this means that the total of the grant will be deducted from the cost of the solar panels and this net amount will be subject to writing-down allowances. In the tax computation the amount of grant income released to profit or loss（as well as the depreciation of the solar panels）will be shown as an adjustment to arrive at taxable profit.

First Year Tax Allowances

A tax allowance is a relief that a business can claim against its taxable profit in a year. The relief is set down in tax legislation and in Macland this relief is usually given at a rate of 25% a year on a reducing balance basis for purchases of plant and equipment.

This means that when we purchase a new piece of equipment，such as a new oven in the kitchen，we will be able to claim 25% of the value of the purchase as a deduction from our taxable profit before the calculation of the tax charge. In the following year，we can then claim 25% of the tax carrying value of the oven(which will be its cost less tax allowance claimed in the first year). Each year the tax allowance will get smaller for an individual asset(and hence the tax saved will get smaller) because the carrying value of the asset is reduced each year.

A first year tax allowance of 100% means that we will be able to claim 100% of the cost of the solar panels(net of the associated grant) as a reduction in taxable profit for the year. This means that we will be able to claim all of the available relief in respect of our asset purchase in one year, rather than have it spread over a number of years.

The impact of this for us is that a tax charge for 2016 and therefore the amount of tax that we will pay in 2017 will be reduced. However in future years, we will lose the benefit of any capital allowances on the solar panels.

How an Environmental Cost of Quality Report Can Help Us to Improve Our Environmental and Financial Performance

There are many ways in which our business affects the environment, especially in relation to our usage of energy and water, which ultimately generates carbon emissions which affect the world at large. As a business, we do have measures in place to try and mitigate some of this, such as the energy saving light bulbs and our towel washing policy. An environmental cost of quality report makes both our impact on the environment and what we do to mitigate this visible.

By identifying both internal and external failure costs, management can see the impact that our business has as a result of creating carbon emissions or waste. These are our costs of non-conformance and mean that we have failed to stop our business negatively affecting the environment.

It is important that management understand the nature and level of these costs to both our business directly(internal failure costs) and to the wider environment(external failure costs) so that we as a business can do something about them.

If we know the level of carbon emissions that are generated by, say, an old oven or an inefficient hot water system then we can look to replace them with new more efficient equipment. This will potentially have two impacts: firstly carbon emissions are reduced and hence our negative impact on the environment is lessened and secondly we end up using less energy and hence reduce the amount of money that we spend on electricity. In both ways we improve performance: firstly in terms of impact on the environment and secondly in terms of an increase in profit.

Understanding what our environmental prevention and appraisal costs are is equally important in respect of performance. High prevention and appraisal costs indicate that as a business we are doing things to mitigate our environmental impact, such as the energy efficient light bulbs and investment in solar panels. Whilst this is an immediate cost to our business (and therefore a drain on profit) the impact on our performance in the long-term is more intangible.

By knowing exactly what we are doing and being able to quantify the costs it means that we are able to promote ourselves on a more environmental basis which in our current market is likely to generate greater customer loyalty and goodwill. Ultimately this has a long-term benefit on our performance.

Thanks!

Management Accountant Assistant
Wise Choice Hotel

Section 4

Potential Benefits and Drawback to Setting up In-house Laundry Facility

Potential Benefits

One benefit of setting up our own laundry facility is that we will not be reliant on a third party for the quality of the laundry service. Whilst this can be safeguarded to some extent by a service level agreement (in which we can stipulate what we consider acceptable levels of service in terms of cleanliness and delivery and the penalties if these levels are breached), this agreement will need to be monitored and acted on, which utilises management time.

Another benefit of setting up our own laundry facility is that it will give us a potentially good source of revenue in the future. The laundry service that we use is 30 kilometres away and there is no alternative closer. In the long-term, there could be a lucrative market locally that we could service.

Another benefit of setting up our own facility is that outsourcing is potentially going to be more expensive than doing it ourselves. The external laundry service provider will include a profit margin on the price that they charge us and therefore setting up our own facility will eliminate this.

Potential Drawbacks

The main drawback of setting up our own facility rather than outsourcing a service such as laundry is that the external provider of the service is likely to be an expert in its field. Our current provider of laundry services has a large facility and we are just one of many contracts. They have expertise in laundry services(which we would need to develop if we set up our facility) which means that they are able to deal with issues such as stubborn stains. They also have staff that have already been trained which means that the quality of the service is likely to be higher than we can achieve(certainly in the short-term).

Further, by continuing to outsource we can safeguard the level of service quality by having a service level agreement.

Another of the drawbacks of setting up our own facility is that we increase the uncertainty over our future cash flow. Whist we might be able to fix the cost of the rent of the premises and the equipment for the year, the prices of the variable costs are likely to be subject to change. By outsourcing we will be able to fix a price within the service level agreement.

Another drawback is that we will have to focus energy and resources into an area of business which is not core to the hotel operation. Setting up a facility could be time consuming in terms of recruiting and training appropriate staff and could end up being a distraction for management.

Using a Decision Tree

Within the decision tree each branch represents one of the possible actions that we could take: use an external laundry service provider, set up in-house with enough capacity for just our own laundry, set up in-house with enough capacity for provided a laundry service to external parties at either a cost of M$ 36 or M$ 32 a load.

Point C

Point C is a decision point in respect of the branch that relates to setting up in-house and selling the laundry service externally. The decision to be evaluated here is whether to charge M$ 36 or M$ 32 a load. At this point we can if we charge M$ 36 the expected value of this decision is a net cost of M$ 516,800, at a price of M$ 32 it is a net cost of M$ 532,800.

We should select the lower cost, therefore at point C the decision would be to charge M$ 36 a load.

Point D

Point D is another decision point. Here the decision is whether to set up the facility purely for Wise Choice Hotels laundry or whether to double the capacity and charge M$ 36 a load to external parties (which is the best decision at point C).

We know from the decision tree that the net variable cost of setting up for just our own laundry is M$ 604,800 and that the fixed costs of this are M$ 250,000.

We also know that if we were to set up to provide external laundry services then the expected value of the variable costs is M$ 516,800 (at a price of M$ 36). The fixed costs however are M$ 350,000.

To evaluate this decision we need to compare the total expected costs (variable and fixed) for each option. Even without performing any calculations we can see that the difference between the variable costs is less than M$ 100,000, with the own laundry only option having the higher cost. The difference in the fixed costs is exactly M$ 100,000, therefore the best option would be to set up just for our own laundry.

Point E

Point E is the final decision point. Here the decision is whether to continue outsourcing the laundry service at a cost of M$ 875,000 or to do it in-house (for our needs only). The cost of in-house is M$ 604,800 plus M$ 250,000.

The decision will be based on which option has the lower of these two totals.

Potential Problems

Firstly, many of the decisions above are quite close on financial grounds; a small error in our estimates or changes in the assumptions used could easily change some of these decisions. In particular, in respect of the probabilities, it will be important to understand what these are based on (especially given that we have not undertaken anything like this before and they have not been derived from an expert in this field). We also are unlikely at this stage to have a good idea of what the demand for our external laundry service would be, especially as we will be new to the market and will not have the experience or expertise of existing laundry operations.

Secondly, the decision tree approach, with its reliance on expected values, is really more appropriate for long-run repeated decisions. This is a major one-off decision where expected values are less appropriate. It might be that the best case outcome for setting up a double capacity in-house laundry would actually result in lower total costs than the decision that we are proposing.

Thirdly, the decision tree uses expected values which assume that the decision maker is risk neutral. This means that the decision maker is concerned with the most likely outcome, rather than potentially the best return (a risk taking decision maker) or on the action which stops the worst possible outcome from happening (a risk adverse decision maker). You will need to consider the decision given by the decision tree in light of the directors' attitudes to decision making.

Lastly, the decision tree analysis ignores non-financial factors such as the impact on our reputation as a hotel business of undertaking external laundry and the fact that it will utilise management time which could instead be spent focusing on the core hotel operation.

试卷五　参考答案

任务一

经营情况

经营情况表明，公司客房以及酒吧和餐饮方面的实际营业利润明显低于预算水平。

客房收入

影响客房经营利润变化的最大因素是酒店入住率，如客人贡献差异为M$85 000。客房的预计入住率为90%，实际为82%。产生这种差异的部分原因是附近新开了一家环保酒店，使得我们流失了一部分潜在客人。还有，经营情况显示上半年的客房入住率为82%，下半年可能会出现季节性的改善。

尽管客房入住率有所降低，但每间客房的平均收入却有所增加。房价收入存在M$60 000的有利差异。客房平均售价高于预算，原因可能是因为上半年我们预计房费偏低。

变动成本存在不利差异，原因可能是客房早餐、洗衣和保管费用开支高于预算，或者是因为变动人工成本占比较大。超出预算方面可能是卧室提供的免费洗漱用品品质升级或价格上涨所致，具体原因需要进一步调查。

固定成本也超过预算水平。固定成本不受入住率影响，所以M$13 000的不利差异是由于固定支出增加所致，如酒店的装修项目提前一年开工，因此未被列入原来的预算。

酒吧和餐厅

在酒吧和餐厅消费的客人数量低于预算水平，从而产生了不利数量差异。我们预算有60%的客人会在酒吧和餐厅消费，而实际数只有50%。此外，预算入住率为90%，而实际仅为82%。

酒吧和餐厅的收入也低于预算，由此产生了一个不利价格差异，这意味着客人在酒吧和餐厅的人均消费低于预算。原因可能是新开的环保酒店吸引了我们的部分客人，导致酒吧与餐厅的食物和饮料消费收入降低。

酒吧和餐厅设施的费用与预算相符，没有成本差异。

营运资金变化对现金流差异的影响

现金流分析

我们预计营运资金的变化会对现金流产生积极影响。现实却刚好相反，营运资金的变化导致现金流的减少，因此也降低了一号酒店上半年的现金余额。

库存变化

我们预算的库存水平会略有下降，导致现金流会有所增加，但实际情况是库存量增加 M$ 34 000。这是年末数据中的一个重要增加项。

酒店和餐厅的入住率下降减少了客人消费，就会导致食品、饮料和家具库存的增加。而酒店对这些物品的订单规模并没有因此减少，加上酒店提高了客房洗漱用品的档次，公司还需要增加高品质洗漱用品的订单量。

库存量增加，我们需要对库存时间长短进行追踪。一般来说，库存时间越长，过时或者说过期的风险越大，尤其是食品和饮料等库存。

应收账款变化

我们预计应收账款余额会有所减少，但实际上增加了 M$ 112 000，应收账款的增加导致经营性现金流入量的减少。这个差异有点意外，因为预计商务旅客占休闲旅客的比例是 70%，而实际上只有 65%，而且入住率也有所下降。

来自企业客户的商务旅客比例没有变化，因此应收账款的增加可能是由于一号酒店放宽了公司客户的信用条件或公司收账不力所致。

基于此，我们需要对应收账款的账龄进行分析，以确定所有客户的应收账款是否都有所增加（这种情况下需要收紧信用政策），或者其中某些客户未及时付款（这种情况下需要对此类客户进行重点追踪和催收）。

应付账款变化

我们原本预计应付账款余额会有所减少，而实际上是大幅增加。这说明现金流出量比预计额大，因此会减少经营现金净流量。

原因有可能是新的洗漱用品供应商提供的信用政策比较严格，或者是有些供应商提高了信用条件。当然也可能是因为我们付款太积极而放弃享用供应商为我们提供的信用条件。

应付账款是企业能够享受的一种无息贷款，我们应该尽量利用这些信贷条件。当然应付账款的使用也要十分谨慎，避免延期付款而导致供应商失去对我们的信任。

任务二

企业社会责任

经济责任

每个企业都必须为股东创造投资回报。作为智选酒店的管理者和股东，你在做任何投资决策时都要以投资回报为前提。

然而，企业所肩负的经济责任不仅要为股东创造投资回报，还要充分考虑员工的利益，为员工提供就业机会和劳动报酬。这一点我们公司做得不错，我们为员工提供免费的膳食和住宿，员工的工资也高于全国最低工资。

履行经济责任还包括以合理的价格为客户提供优质服务。我们在这一点上的成绩体现为较高的入住率和较好的客户反馈。

法律责任

法律一般是保护员工和客户等利益相关者的权益。我们严格遵循 Macland 法律，保护员工和客户的权益。事实上，我们所做的事情大大超出了法律的要求，比如，我们的员工工资水平高于国家最低工资要求，我们与小时工签订雇佣合同确保他们每周工作 30 小时以上，而很多同行并没有为员工提供最低工作时间保障合同。

道德责任

企业道德是指即使没有法律要求，企业也应该坚持公平合理的态度，如环境保护。我们恪守企业道德，尽量降低对环境的影响。

酒店业务对环境的影响方式较多（见本简报的第二部分）。我们鼓励客人尽量不要每天更换毛巾，并使用节能灯泡。当然在环境保护方面我们还有很长的路要走。

慈善责任

企业的终极责任是慈善事业，回馈我们业务所涉及的社区。我们自愿向慈善机构捐款，并赞助当地的儿童足球队。

质量环境成本报告

在环境成本质量报告中，环境成本分为 4 类：预防成本、鉴定成本、内部损失成本和外部损失成本。

环境预防成本

我们为环境保护已经花费了很多成本，如用节能灯泡代替普通灯泡。这是一种环境预防成本，因为使用节能灯泡可以减少能量耗费并降低碳排放。

环境鉴定成本

环境鉴定成本是指为评估我们是否遵守环境标准和政策而发生的内部成本和外部成本。

管理层为开发酒店环境绩效指标而花费的时间成本也是一项鉴定成本。同样，为监控供应商（如洗衣房）的环境影响所花费的时间也是一项鉴定成本。

环境内部损失成本

环境内部损失成本是指由企业承担的、为减轻业务造成的环境影响而产生的成本。

以智选酒店为例，减少食品浪费也会产生相关成本。我们的政策是将食物垃圾交给肥料制造厂。这就是一个内部损失成本的例子，因为如果我们控制好食品订单，并在厨房里合理规划食材，就会减少食物垃圾，降低相应处理成本。

环境外部损失成本

环境外部损失成本是指酒店业务引起的有害排放物对环境破坏而产生的成本。

我们的酒店业务在照明、供暖和热水方面耗用了大量能源，洗衣服务供应商也是能源消耗大户，尽管这些能耗不是我们直接产生的碳排放，但我们也必须对此负一定的责任。这些排放会影响到我们的业务范围之外的整个环境。采用一些有效方法来减少碳排放，如采用太阳能电池板、就近选择洗衣服务商等，这些都是环境外部损失成本。

任务三

发件人：管理会计助理

收件人：财务总监 Rav Patel

主题：环境计划

投资奖励

政府补助

政府补助金是一项资本补助，用于购买太阳能电池板。

根据国际会计准则第 20 号，财务报表中的政府补助金核算有两种方式。

第一种是将太阳能电池板的价值列为“固定资产”，将太阳能电池板的成本在其有效经济寿命（10 年）内计提折旧。

第二种是将太阳能电池板的全部成本进行资本化处理，记入“固定资产”并按其价值创建“递延收入”科目（这是一个负债类科目）。随后，在太阳能电池板的有效经济寿命期内将递延收入逐年转化为利润。

上述两种核算方法对每年的利润影响是一样的，都是每年将补助总额的1/10转化为利润，从而增加当年的利润水平。所有这些都需要在资产负债表中进行说明。

作为资本补助，政府补助金必须纳税。根据Macland的税法规定，政府补助金总额将从太阳能电池板的成本中扣除，所得余额作为计提折旧的基础。在税收计算中，政府补助金对收入（和太阳能电池板的折旧）的影响被列为调整项以计算应税利润。

第一年免税额

税收减免是根据税法规定，企业一年内可以用于抵扣其应税利润的一种抵扣项。Macland税法规定该抵扣项采用余额递减法计算，按厂房和设备逐年余额的25%计算抵扣额。

也就是说，假如我们购买一个新的设备（如烤箱），当年可以按购买价的25%记为应税利润的抵扣项。第二年再按账面余额（即原价减去第一年的抵扣额）的25%计算抵扣额。由于资产的账面价值逐年减少，每年抵扣额也逐年减少（因此免税额也逐年减少）。

如果第一年将全部采购价格用于税收减免，即将全部太阳能电池板成本（扣除相关政府补助）用于税收抵减，则我们能够在一年内将资产总额用于抵税，而无须在数年内分摊。

也就是说，2016年的抵税额会减少2017年所支付的税款。然而，在未来的几年中，我们将无法享受购置太阳能电池板的所有好处。

环境成本质量报告如何帮助我们改善环境和提高业绩

酒店业务对环境的影响较大，特别是能源和水资源的消耗，最终影响全世界的碳排放。我们已经为降低碳排放采取了一些措施，如鼓励客人不要每天更换毛巾以及采用节能灯泡等。环境成本质量报告不仅披露了我们对环境的影响，还披露了我们为降低环境污染而采取的措施。

通过界定内部和外部损失成本，管理层可以意识到由于碳排放或浪费而造成的影响。这些都是我们破坏环境的代价，说明我们未能有效预防酒店业务对环境的不利影响。

管理层需要了解此类成本的属性和大小（内部损失成本）以及对外部环境的影响（外部损失成本），以采取相应的措施。

如果我们计算出旧烤箱或低效热水系统碳排放较高，那么可以考虑更新设备。更新设备会产生两个影响：一是减少碳排放，缓解对环境的负面影响；二是最终会降低能源耗费，从而减少耗电量。这两个影响都有利于我们提高绩效：前者可以改善环境，后者有利于提高利润。

在考虑企业绩效方面，环境预防成本和鉴定成本的考量同样重要。环境预防成本和鉴定成本较高，说明企业正在努力降低对环境的破坏，如采用节能灯泡和太阳能电池板等。这些虽然会在短期内产生直接成本（因此降低利润），但从长期来看会提高企业业绩。

通过了解环境保护投入并量化其成本，我们能够在更健康的基础上发展业务，从而在目前的市场中提高客户忠诚度和企业商誉。这些将促进我们的业绩取得长足的发展。

感谢！

智选酒店

管理会计助理

任务四

自建洗衣房的潜在优缺点

潜在优点

自建洗衣房可以摆脱对第三方洗衣服务商的依赖。虽然第三方的洗衣服务质量可以通过服务协议来保障（例如，可以在服务协议中规定我们认可的清洁程度和运送服务，以及违反协议的处罚），但是对协议的执行情况进行监督也需要占用管理时间。

自建洗衣房也可以创收。目前，最近的第三方洗衣服务商距离酒店 30 公里。从长远来说，我们需要一个当地的洗衣服务商。

自建洗衣房还可以降低洗衣服务外包成本。如果自建洗衣房，可以挤掉第三方洗衣服务商赚取的利润，降低成本。

潜在缺点

自建服务（如洗衣服务）的主要缺点是没有意识到外部服务商可能是洗衣领域的行家。目前，我们的洗衣服务提供商都是规模很大的商家，为很多大客户提供洗衣服务。他们拥有专业的洗衣服务，能高效处理顽固污渍等问题。他们拥有大量的熟练员工，从短期来看，他们能够提供服务的质量高于我们可以实现的水平，如果我们自建洗衣房，还需要投入大量的开发成本。而且，如果继续选择外包服务，我们可以通过服务水平协议来确保洗衣服务质量。

自建洗衣房的第二个缺点是增加未来现金流的不确定性。虽然洗衣房的房屋和设备租金等固定成本是既定的，但变动成本难以预计，而外包服务可以在合同条款中锁定价格。

自建洗衣服务的第三个缺点是将精力和资源用于酒店非核心业务。自建洗衣设施需要招聘和培训员工，耗时较长，并打乱管理重心。

决策树

在决策树中，每个分支代表一个可能的方案：一是使用第三方洗衣服务；二是自建仅供内部使用的洗衣房；三是自建可供外部使用的洗衣房，并按每单收取 M$ 36 或 M$ 32洗衣费。

C 点

C 点是关于自建洗衣房并向外出售洗衣服务的决策点。对外收费标准为每单 M$ 36 或 M$ 32。如果每单收费为 M$ 36，那么该决策的净支出额为 M$ 516 800；如果每单收费 M$ 32，那么该决策的净支出额为 M$ 532 800。

根据成本最低原则，在 C 点的决策是选择每单收费 M$ 36。

D 点

另一个决策点 D 点决定是否自建仅供内部使用的洗衣房，还是扩大两倍产能，向外部提供洗衣服务并收取每单 M$ 36（C 点的最佳决策）。

从决策树中可知，自建洗衣房的变动成本为 M$ 604 800，固定成本为 M$ 250 000。

如果提供外部洗衣服务，那么预计变动成本为 M$ 516 800（价格为 M$ 36），固定成本为 M$ 350 000。

在决策时，需要对比每个决策的预期总成本（包括变动成本和固定成本）。可以看出，自建洗衣房仅供内部使用和向外提供洗衣服务两个决策的变动成本差额不大（不到 M$ 100 000），其中仅供内部使用决策的变动成本较高；两个决策的固定成本差额正好为 M$ 100 000。因此，最优决策是自建仅供内部使用的洗衣房。

E 点

E 点是最终决策点。在此决定是继续以 M$ 875 000 的成本外包洗衣服务，还是自建仅供内部使用的洗衣房。后者的总成本为 M$ 604 800 的变动成本加上 M$ 250 000 的固定成本，即总成本为 M$ 854 800。E 点的决策是选择总成本较低的选项，即自建仅供内部使用的洗衣房。

潜在问题

首先，上述许多决策都是以财务数据为基础，一个小小的估计误差或所使用的假设发生变化就会影响最终决策，而且概率的估计缺乏客观基础（尤其是第一次做出某种决策并无法从该领域的专家那里获得相关消息时）。目前，我们面临不断变化的市场环境，也缺乏洗衣行业经验或专业知识，我们很难了解洗衣服务市场的真实情况。

其次，决策树方法依赖于预期价值，更适用于长期重复的决策。而本案例中关于是否自建洗衣房决策是一次性决策，不适合采用期望值做决策。可能自建两倍产能的洗衣房的实际成本低于上述预期成本。

再次，决策树中使用的预期值是基于决策者是风险中性型的假设。也就是说，决策者只关心最可能的结果，而不追求可能出现的最佳结果（决策者是风险偏好型），或阻止最坏结果（决策者是风险厌恶型）。你需要根据管理者对决策的态度，来考虑决策树的结果。

最后，决策树分析没有考虑非财务因素，如对外承接洗衣业务对酒店声誉的影响，自建洗衣房对管理精力的影响，以及可能忽视酒店核心业务的影响等。

Variant 5　Marking Guidance

Section	Technical skills		Business skills		People skills		Leadership skills		Integration	Total
1	Operating statements Operating cash flows and working capital management	10 8	Operating cash flows and working capital management	4					3	25
2	Environmental cost of quality reporting	12			Corporate Social Responsibility	13				25
3	Accounting for government grants and 100% tax allowances Environmental costing	16 9								25
4	Short-term decision making using a decision tree	7	Outsourcing	12			Short-term decision making using a decision tree	6		25
Total marks available for competency		62		16		13		6	3	100

试卷五 评分指南

部分	技术技能		商业技能		人际技能		领导技能		综合	总计
1	经营报告 经营现金流和营运资金管理	10 8	经营现金流和营运资金管理	4					3	25
2	质量环境成本报告	12			企业社会责任	13				25
3	政府补助金和全额抵税 环境成本	16 9								25
4	基于决策树的短期决策	7	外包	12			基于决策树的短期决策	6		25
各种能力分数总计		62		16		13		6	3	100

湖北经济学院名师解惑

试卷一共有四项任务，考察了 P1、F1、E1 三门课程的知识点，具体包括经营报告、企业社会责任、质量环境成本报告、政府补助、环境成本和决策树等。该试卷考核了考生的四项能力，其中技术技能的分值占62%，商业技能的分值占16%，人际技能的分值占13%，领导技能的分值占6%，与 CGMA 管理会计能力框架的技能要求一致。

该试卷的每项任务涉及以下知识点：

任务	问题	科目	知识点
任务一	预算差异分析	P1	差异分析法（variance analysis）
	经营现金流的差异分析及营运资金管理对差异的影响	F1	营运资金管理（working capital management）
任务二	酒店业的企业社会责任及具体做法	E1	企业社会责任（corporate social responsibility）
	质量环境成本报告中环境成本的分类及解释	P1	环境管理会计（environmental management accounting）
任务三	政府补助对税收和报表的影响	F1	政府补助（government grant）
	质量环境成本报告对环境与财务业绩的影响	P1	环境管理会计（environmental management accounting）
任务四	自建或外包决策的利弊分析	E1	外包（outsourcing）
	决策树中各决策点的分析及决策树法的局限性	P2	短期投资（short-term investment）

上述各项任务要求以邮件或工作简报等形式来呈现答案，对问题的描述非常明确，答题时既要注意内容的针对性，也要注意形式的规范性。

对应知识点深度剖析

预算差异分析

预算差异分析就是通过比较实际执行结果与预算目标，确定差异额及其差异原因。如果实际成果与预算标准的差异过大，公司管理层应审慎调查，并判定其发生原因，以便采取适当的矫正措施。

本例中，影响客房经营利润变化的最大因素是酒店入住率，部分原因是附近新开了一家环保酒店。房价收入存在有利差异，可能是因为上半年案例企业预计房费偏低。

变动成本不利差异的原因可能是客房早餐、洗衣和保管费用开支高于预算，或者是因为变动人工成本占比较大。固定成本超过预算水平是由于固定支出增加所致。

在酒吧和餐厅消费的客人数量低于预算水平，同时也存在不利价格差异。这些差异都可能有多种原因，考生要学会分析，结合案例陈述自己的理解和看法。

考生注意事项

差异分析法的步骤：

（1）确定分析对象及分解标准；

（2）收集信息；

（3）差异计算与分解；

（4）判断差异重要程度；

（5）对重要差异进行解释；

（6）差异原因报告与确认。

经营现金流的差异及营运资金管理的影响

营运资金的变化导致现金流的减少，因此也降低了一号酒店上半年的现金余额。

结合题目中的信息，考生需要按营运资金的类别进行分析。

由于酒店和餐厅的入住率下降减少了客人消费，导致库存的增加。一般来说，库存时间越长，过时或者说过期的风险越大，尤其是食品和饮料等库存。

应收账款的增加导致经营性现金流入量的减少，这可能是由于放宽了公司客户的信用条件或公司收账不力所致。为此，建议考生进行应收账款的账龄分析，以确定是否所有客户的应收账款都有所增加（这种情况下需要收紧信用政策），或者其中某些客户未及时付款（这种情况下需要对此类客户进行重点追踪催收）。

应付账款余额大幅增加，这说明现金流出量比预计额大。原因可能是供应商的信用政策比较严格，或者是有些供应商提高了信用条件，也可能是我们放弃使用供应商的信用条件。当然应收账款的使用也要十分谨慎，避免延期付款而导致供应商对我们失去信任。

考生注意事项

营运资金公式：

营运资金＝流动资产＝流动负债

＝（总资产－非流动资产）－（总资产－所有者权益－长期负债）

＝（所有者权益＋长期负债）－非流动资产＝长期资本－长期资产

企业社会责任

企业社会责任是指企业在创造利润、对股东承担法律责任的同时，还要承担对员工、消费者、社区和环境的责任，企业的社会责任要求企业必须超越把利润作为唯一目标的传统理念，强调要在生产过程中对人的价值的关注，强调对环境、消费者和社会的贡献。

考生注意，本题中要求从经济责任、法律责任、道德责任和慈善责任等方面展开企业社会责任的分析，分析企业如何为股东、员工、客户、环境和社区等利益相关者实现权益最大化。考生需要注意，在环保意识越来越强的今天，酒店业务对环境的影响是该行业被舆论指责的重点，需要着重分析。

考生注意事项

企业社会责任一般从以下几个方面展开：

（1）办好企业，把企业做强、做大、做久；

（2）企业一切经营管理行为应符合道德规范；

（3）社区福利投资；

（4）社会慈善事业；

（5）自觉保护自然环境。

质量环境成本报告

环境成本是指某一项商业生产活动造成环境污染而使环境功能水平下降的代价，从资源开采、生产、运输、使用、回收到处理，解决环境污染和生态破坏所需的全部费用。环境成本分为4类：预防成本、鉴定成本、内部损失成本和外部损失成本。

环境预防成本是指为环境保护花费的成本；环境鉴定成本是指为评估是否遵守环境标准和政策而发生的内部与外部成本；环境内部损失成本是指由企业承担的、为减轻业务造成的环境影响而产生的成本；环境外部损失成本是指酒店业务产生的有害排放物破坏环境而产生的成本。

考生在解题时需要注意的是，题目要求对每一个成本项目进行举例说明，这些具体的例子要结合酒店业的特征，包括具体业务，如洗衣业务对环境的影响等，理解环境成本项目的真实意义。

政府补助

政府补助是指企业从政府无偿取得货币性资产或非货币性资产，但不包括政府作为企业所有者投入的资本。主要的政府补助包括财政贴息、研究开发补贴和政策性补贴。国际会计准则第20号规定，财务报表中对政府补助金核算有两种方式：第一种是将全部补助列为"固定资产"，在其有效经济寿命内计提折旧；第二种是对政府补助进行资本化处理，记入"固定资产"，并按其价值创建"递延收入"科目（这是一个负债类科目）。随后，在太阳能电池板的有效经济寿命期内将递延收入逐年转化为利润。

上述两种核算方法对每年的利润影响是一样的，都是每年将补助总额的一部分转化为利润，从而增加当年利润水平。所有这些都需要在财务状况表中进行说明。

在税收计算中，政府补助金对收入（和太阳能电池板的折旧）的影响被列为调整项，以便计算应税利润。

考生注意事项

余额递减法折旧：

折旧额 =（固定资产原值 − 上年累积折旧额）× 折旧率

环境成本质量报告对环境和业绩的影响

考生需要了解环境成本的属性和大小（内部损失成本）以及对外部环境的影响（外部损失成本），以采取相应措施。有的环境成本既可以改善环境，又有利于提高利润。

有的环境预防成本和鉴定成本在短期内会产生直接成本（因此降低利润），但从长期来看，会提高企业业绩。

对环境成本进行有效控制有利于提高客户忠诚度和企业商誉，从而促进业绩的长足发展。

自建或外包洗衣房决策的利弊分析

自建洗衣房是企业的一项投资决策，是以洗衣房为对象的长期投资行为。外包是指企业动态地配置自身及其他企业的功能和服务，并利用企业外部的资源为企业内部的生产和经营服务。

自建洗衣房的优点在于可以摆脱对第三方洗衣服务商的依赖，可以创收，还可以降低服务外包成本。

自建洗衣房的缺点则包括没有意识到外部服务商可能是洗衣领域的行家，需要投入大量的开发成本，增加未来现金流的不确定性，同时将精力和资源用于酒店非核心业务。

考生需要注意的是，自建洗衣房的优点和缺点即外包洗衣服务的缺点和优点，所以在答题过程中可以从自建和外包两个方面进行思考，确保考虑周全。

决策树中各决策点的分析及决策树法的局限性

决策树是在已知各种情况发生概率的基础上，通过构建决策树来评价项目风险，判断其可行性的决策分析方法，是直观运用概率分析的一种图解法。在决策树中，每个分支代表一个可能的方案。

本例中，有 3 种可能的方案：使用第三方洗衣服务，自建仅供内部使用的洗衣房，自建可供外部使用收费的洗衣房。其中 3 个决策点分别计算了 3 种方案下的总变动成本。考生需要对这 3 个决策点的计算过程进行分析，并解释其中的含义。

但基于决策树的短期决策存在一些潜在问题：首先，以财务数据为基础，概率的估计缺乏客观基础；其次，依赖于预期价值，更适用于长期重复的决策；再次，预期值的计算是基于决策者是风险中性型的假设；最后，没有考虑非财务因素。

考生需要注意，决策树的更详细的学习是在 P2 课程阶段，但本题已经给出决策树，考生要学会解读决策树中每一个数字表达的意思，总结这些数字在决策中的作用和局限性。这需要考生更灵活地运用短期投资决策内容，并结合题目展开分析。

CGMA

全球特许管理会计师考试 综合案例与解析 [运营级]

CGMA CASE STUDY
EXAMINATION AND ANALYSIS
(Operational Level)

下

国际注册专业会计师公会◎编著

中信出版集团 · 北京

目 录（下册）

案例四

CASE 4

摩利兹能源公司

MARICI POWER

Background Materials

Job Description

You are one of three assistant management accountants for Marici Power. Your main role is to assist with the production of the annual budget, produce the monthly management accounts and provide information to management as required.

Company Background

Marici Power is located in Freeland, a country in western Europe. Freeland's currency is the F$.

The company offers solar power solutions to customers in Freeland and the rest of Europe. It provides a wide portfolio of products that enable private and commercial users to generate electricity cleanly, efficiently and profitably from the power of the sun. Its products include solar panels as well as complete solar power systems which incorporate Marici Power panels and system components such as inverters, frames and roof-mounted racks. In the home market, it supplies both commercial customers and installers who deal directly with the public. The supply to the rest of Europe is through distributors and represents 15% of the company's turnover.

All manufacturing of solar panels and solar cells, which are the key component for the solar panels, is undertaken at Marici Power's only production facility which is located in the capital city of Freeland. At the same location, there is a large warehouse for the storage of inventory and office accommodation where the directors and management are based.

Over the past 20 years Marici Power has invested heavily, and has designed and developed increasingly more sophisticated and efficient solar panels. It has developed a strong brand and has established a reputation for producing high quality panels with high conversion efficiency. As a result, it is now the largest manufacturer of solar panels in Freeland.

Marici Power's origins is the research and development division of a large oil company, Saltenergy, also based in Freeland. Saltenergy recently decided to divest what they considered to be peripheral businesses and concentrate on their "core" business of energy from fossil fuels. As a result, in February 2016, Marici Power was sold to Wala Solar, a major global supplier of solar products with manufacturing plants throughout Europe and America. Marici Power now operates as a strategic business unit in the Wala Solar and benefits from the renewable energy market knowledge available within the group.

What Are Solar Panels

Solar panels are active solar devices that use PV (photovoltaic) technology to convert sunlight into electricity. They come in a variety of rectangular shapes and are usually installed in combination to produce electricity.

Solar panels are fully equipped for generating electricity (direct current) from sunlight. Direct current power can be used at the generation location itself, either immediately or stored in a battery for later use. Inverters convert this direct current to alternating current to allow the system to be connected to the public grid and give owners the flexibility to use both solar energy and electricity from the public grid. Any excess power generated from the solar system that is not required by the owners can be sold to the power company, as shown in the figure.

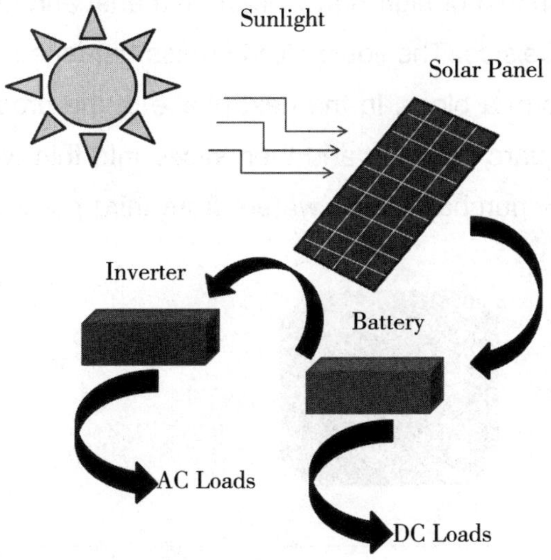

Web Page from www. maricipower. com

HOW ARE SOLAR PANELS MADE?

Silicon

Silicon is the starting point of our solar production cycle. It is extracted from quartzite rock or sand, which is primarily made up of silicon dioxide. As the second most common element in the earth's crust, there is a virtually endless supply of silicon. Polysilicon is a high purity form of silicon.

Solar Wafers

The next step is the production of solar wafers. These are the main component for solar cells.

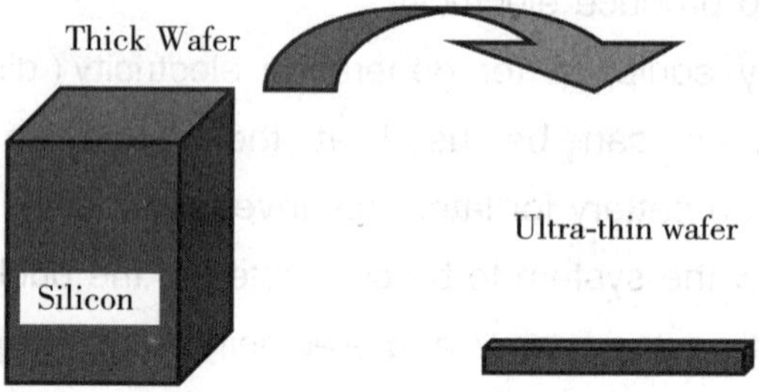

To produce the polysilicon wafers used in most solar panels, the high-purity silicon is cast into a coated mould of high-purity quartz material and melted at temperatures over 1,400 degrees Celsius. The liquid silicon mass hardens and thousands of small crystals combine to form a block. In the next phase of the production process, these blocks are cut into square columns and then sliced into thin wafers.

At Marici Power, we purchase solar wafers from third party suppliers who use the highest purity silicon.

Solar Cells

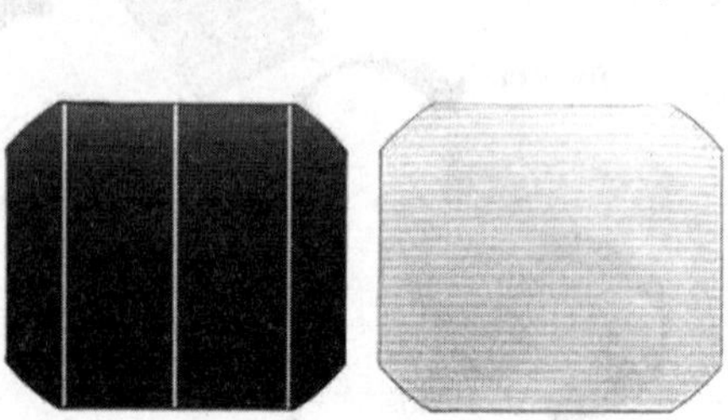

The next part of the production process involves the production of solar cells from the wafers. These are the key components of the solar panels. These cells house all of the technical characteristics required to generate electricity from sunlight. Light radiation releases positive and negative charge carriers, resulting in flows of electrical current(direct current).

At Marici Power, we manufacture solar cells using one of the most advanced solar cell production facilities in the world. Through a series of chemical and heat treatments, we convert the wafers into productive cells i. e. cells that are capable of producing electricity.

Solar Panels

In the panel production process, solar cells are combined to form larger units—panels. Panels are enclosed in frames and weather-proofed. Solar panels are finished, which are fully equipped for generating electricity(direct current) from sunlight.

In the finishing phase, the solar panels are carefully cleaned and inspected. The panels are then loaded on pallets for delivery to homes and businesses.

Future Strategy

(Extract from Marici Power 2015 Annual Report and Accounts)

Branding

At Marici Power, we will continue to sell our solar panels under our established brand names: Solar Bright, Solar Glow, Solar Eclipse and Solar Halo.

Quality

We will continue to develop our brand and our reputation as a producer of high quality panels with high conversion efficiency. We will strive to maintain our position as the largest solar panel manufacturer in Freeland.

Customer Focus

Customer needs drive the entire business and all processes within Marici Power. Product differentiation and comprehensive customer service will create added value for the customer.

Innovation

Solar power systems, in which panels are combined with other components to form a complete solution, will continue to be strategically important to us. We will continue working to improve the electricity generation capacity of our panels. In 2017, we will offer the customers an enhanced panel design with reduced weight and a better self-cleaning effect. These panels will be available in various sizes and types.

Sales Growth

We plan to continue to utilise the opportunities as the largest manufacturer in Freeland, to increase shipments and gain market share. One of our ongoing goals is to grow our complete solar power solutions business since greater differentiation from the competition is possible in this sector.

Cost Efficiency

We expect to achieve economies of scale in production in 2017, due to volume growth, enabling the reduction of manufacturing cost per unit. We also plan to make cost reductions in all organizational units and at all stages of the supply chain with the aim of optimising cash flow and profit.

Introduction to the Solar PV Energy Industry

Renewable energy technologies are clean sources of energy that have a much lower environmental impact than conventional energy technologies. Renewable energy will not run out whilst other sources of energy are finite and will someday be depleted. Solar energy is one of the main forms of renewable energy. Solar energy provides more than 1% of the world's electricity demand or the equivalent of 33 large coal fired power plants.

The solar energy industry is divided, based on the technology involved, into two segments:CST(concentrated solar thermal) and photovoltaic.

PV technology is where absorbed light is directly converted into electricity(photo-effect). CST technology is where direct light is focused into one point in order to heat a liquid. The heat is subsequently used to drive a generator as in a conventional power station.

In absolute terms, electricity generation from photovoltaic is still a relatively small market. The worldwide installed capacity at the end of 2015 was 178 gigawatts(GW), of which 40 GW was installed in 2015, as shown in the figure.

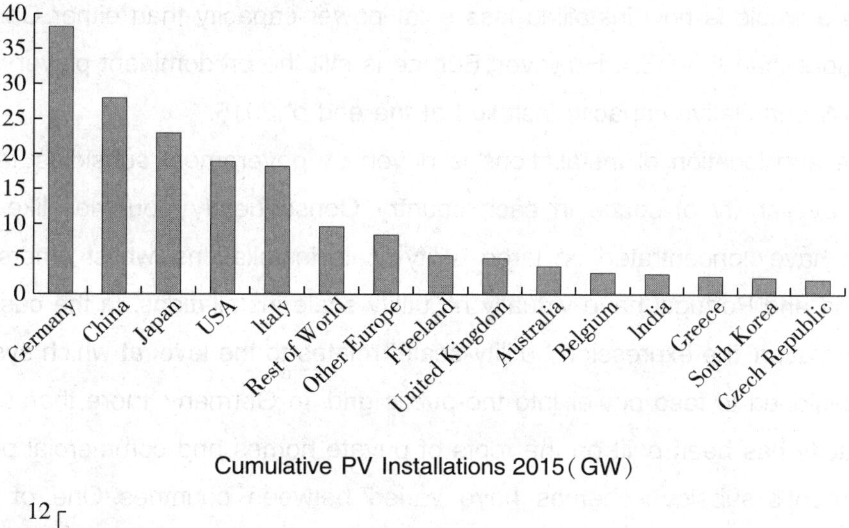

Cumulative PV Installations 2015(GW)

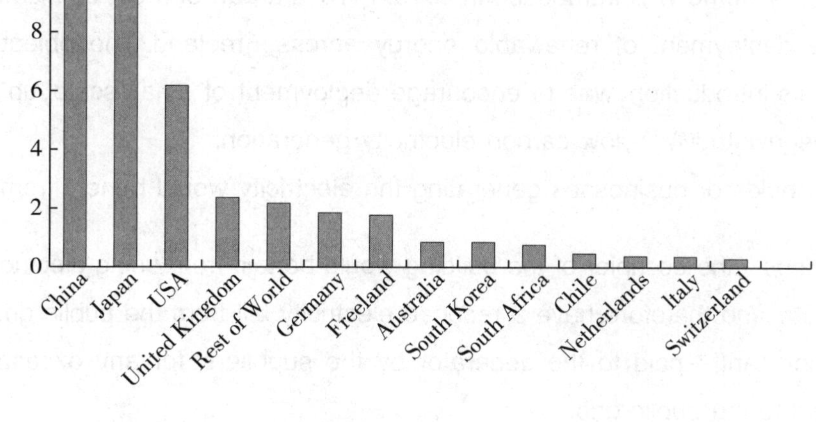

PV Installations 2015(GW)

The global market for PV installations used to be dominated by Europe. In 2009, Germany held 50% of the market share, however by 2015 the market had shifted to Asia (with over 50% of new installations), America and Africa.

The solar panel market reached an annual capacity installed of 40 GW for the first time in 2015. This level of installations has been achieved due to both the growth of the Asian and American markets and, to some extent, the emergence of new markets.

After years of rapid development, the rate of market growth in Europe slowed down in 2014 and this trend continued in 2015. With around 7 GW of capacity installed in 2015, Europe as a whole is now installing less solar power capacity than either China or Japan, but more than the USA. However, Europe is still the predominant player with more than 88 GW cumulative capacity installed at the end of 2015.

The size and location of installations is driven by government subsidies, tariff structures and availability of space in each country. Consequently, countries like Romania and Spain have concentrated on large utility-scale installations, whilst others such as Netherlands and Portugal have virtually no utility-scale installations. In the case of solar power generation, the expression "utility-scale" relates to the level at which systems are typically designed to feed power into the public grid. In Germany, more than 60% of all solar capacity has been built on the roofs of private homes and commercial premises.

Government's subsidy schemes have varied between countries. One of the most popular schemes in Europe is the FITs (Feed-in Tariff scheme). The Freeland government's scheme was introduced in 2010. FITs is a part of a set of initiatives to encourage the deployment of renewable energy across Freeland. The objective of the scheme, on its introduction, was to encourage deployment of small scale, up to and including 5 megawatt (MW), low-carbon electricity generation.

The households or businesses generating the electricity would benefit from it.

- Bill savings—the occupier of the building would benefit from using electricity generated onsite, and therefore have a reduced electricity bill from the public grid supplier.
- An export tariff—paid to the generator by the suppliers, for any excess electricity exported to the public grid.
- A generation tariff—paid to the generator by the supplier, designed to incentivize the

deployment of the low-carbon technology as opposed to fossil fuel alternatives.

The subsidies paid through FITs are funded by additional charges, levied by the government, on the energy bills of all consumers. In order to limit the impact of the charges on consumer bills, the total amount of subsidies available is capped by the government.

Other government initiatives to encourage the further development of solar power include a range of tax incentives. The Freeland government has set a reduced value added tax(VAT) rate of 5% on solar panel and other solar components.

Industry History

In less than a decade, the solar energy industry has transformed from a cottage industry to a $100 billion business with global reach. Among the factors contributing to its growth were government subsidies, significant capacity additions from existing and new entrants and continual innovation.

Between 2007 and 2011, the solar energy industry grew at approximately 70% per year driven by government subsidies that made the installation and use of solar power units economically attractive for many consumers. As demand rose, new entrants flocked to the industry, and the pace of innovation accelerated. This rapid growth meant that production was hard pressed to keep up with demand. As a result, those companies that were able to increase capacity could gain market share.

Manufacturing capacity increased dramatically, particularly after large-scale, low-cost Chinese manufacturers entered the market. Between 2009 and 2011, Chinese solar panel production quadrupled to more than the entire global demand. Chinese-made panels were selling for as much as 45% cheaper than those made in Europe and the USA. The price drop fuelled demand but put pressure on margins. As a result of this excess supply, prices of solar cells began to tumble as companies fought to reduce inventories and many smaller producers simply suspended manufacturing operations.

The main reason of solar cell prices dropped so much in 2011, was the price of the key raw material, polysilicon, which makes up a very significant part of the total cost, dropped significantly.

In 2007—2008, there was a worldwide shortage of capacity for the manufacture of polysilicon, the raw material used to produce the solar wafers which are incorporated into solar cells. This shortage led to an increase in the price of polysilicon to around \$400 per kg. Suppliers, attracted by the high prices, added significant additional capacity. Consequently, there was a huge polysilicon manufacturing over capacity which eventually resulted in falling prices. At the beginning of 2011, prices for polysilicon had fallen to around \$80 per kg but by the end prices were around \$20 to \$25 per kg.

As a result of the falling prices of solar panels, due mainly to cheap imports from China and over-capacity in the market, almost all of the companies in the solar industry were unprofitable from 2011 to 2014.

In 2012, the USA government imposed tariffs on the import of Chinese solar cells and panels on the basis that the manufacturers benefited from unfair subsidies from their government.

In 2013, the European Commission decided to impose punitive import duties on solar panels from China in a move to guard against what was seen as "dumping" of cheap goods in Europe. After negotiations between the governments of the EU and China, a minimum price undertaking was agreed for imports of solar panel and components.

Major Market Trends

While 2015 undoubtedly remained a challenging time for the solar industry, it did mark a turning point in the industry's development. Sales volume grew significantly, mainly due to government policy in China. Solar power is now broadly recognized as a cost competitive, reliable and sustainable energy source.

The growth experienced in the industry improved the utilisation rates of manufacturing capacities and reduced the pressure on prices, leading to a continued recovery of the industry around the world. In 2015, manufacturers of solar cells and panels were able to significantly improve their financial results with many reporting profits for the first time in a number of years.

This return to profitability for manufacturers and their strengthening financial position has resulted in new investment in the industry. Several manufacturers have announced that they have placed orders for innovative equipment to upgrade their current production lines or to put new ones in place. At the same time, new solar panel factories are opening within, or close to, emerging markets although some continue to close in Europe.

In Europe, the minimum price undertaking, agreed with the Chinese government, maintained the prices of solar products from Chinese producers at higher than market levels. Other Asian manufacturers however continued to sell to the market at cheaper prices.

Future Outlook

A large part of solar power development until the end of 2015 has been driven by the regulatory framework adopted by national governments, including tax incentives, subsidies and other ad hoc support schemes. In the short term, market growth is strongly dependent on continued government support. However, its sustained development will ultimately depend on its ability to compete with conventional sources of electricity.

Demand will still be highly concentrated in a handful of countries, presenting significant risk to those companies who do not have a strong market presence in these countries. The rapid price declines seen by the industry has opened up solar to an enormous number of countries around the world but the global solar market will remain driven by those countries using supporting regulatory frameworks, e. g. in Asia and America.

The decision of some European countries to reduce or end FITs is concerning and could have a major impact on the extent of future installations. Companies will need to convince customers that the reduced costs of their electricity bills, without other additional incentives, is sufficient to justify the investment.

Historically, solar panel development has been driven by distributed installations where electricity is produced at, or near, the point where it is used. In 2014, utility-scale solar power grew to the extent of becoming the largest segment, in terms of GW, installed globally. In 2015, both types of installations were balanced, with around 20 GW each. The respective development of each segment will depend on the regulatory framework adopted by the national governments but looking at current trends the global development of utility-scale solar power seems to be favoured, driven by its increasing cost-competitiveness.

Web Page from www. maricipower. com

Extract from the Glossary of Terms Used in the Solar PV Industry

G：	
Grid-connected	A grid-connected solar power system generates its own electricity and feeds its excess power into the public grid for later use. Grid-connected solar electric systems are eligible for many incentives and rebates
I：	
Inverter	The inverter electronically converts direct current(DC)power into alternating current (AC)power and is required for grid-connected solar power systems
P：	
PV technology	Photo = light; volt = electrical potential(literally: electricity from light). Einstein won a Nobel Prize for discovering that when light shines on certain materials(like silicon),an electrical current is generated
Polysilicon	Polysilicon is a high-purity form of silicon. Due to its semiconductor-like properties, polysilicon is used in most solar energy applications
Public grid	The public grid is an interconnected network of generating stations that produce electrical power,high-voltage transmission lines that carry power from distant sources to demand centres,and distribution lines that connect individual customers
PV array	A PV array is the complete power-generating unit,consisting of any number of solar (or PV)panels
S：	
Semiconductor	A material that conducts current,but only partly. The conductivity is somewhere between that of an insulator,which has almost no conductivity,and a conductor,which has almost full conductivity
Silicon	The basic material used to make solar cells. It is the second most abundant element in the earth's crust,after oxygen

（续表）

Solar cell(or PV cell)	Semiconductor device that converts sunlight into direct current electricity
Solar panel(or PV panel)	Solar panels consist of solar cells sealed in an environmentally protective laminate and are the fundamental building block of solar(or PV) systems
Standalone system (or off-grid system)	Energy generated by these systems is stored in batteries and then subsequently used. Also known as "off-grid," these systems are not connected to the public grid

Extract from Marici Power Organisation Chart

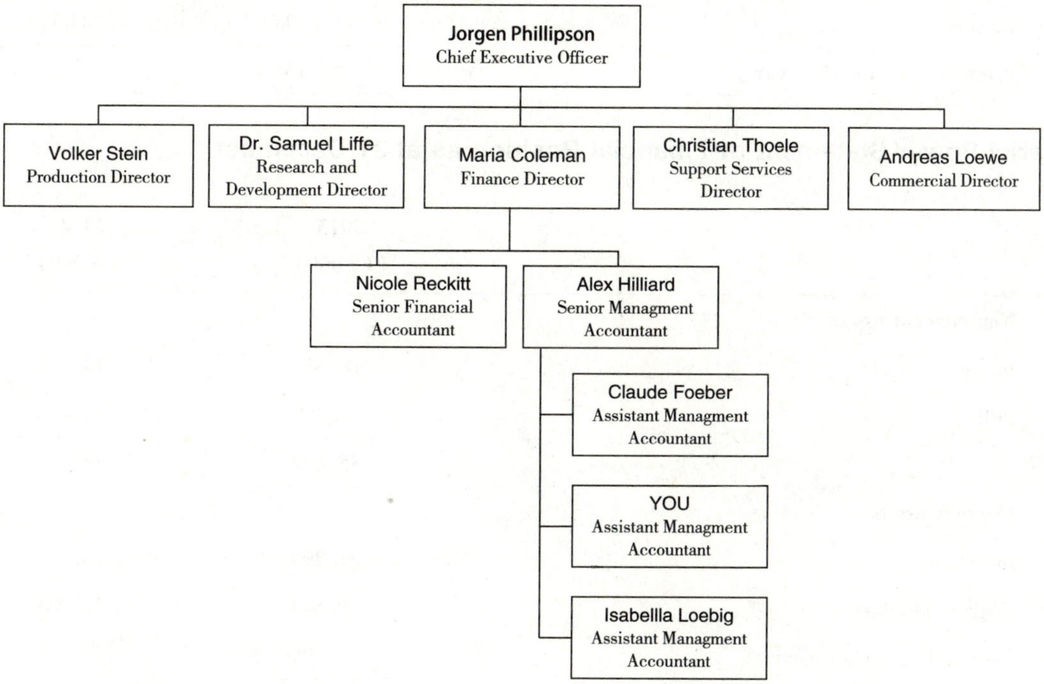

Extracts from Marici Power 2015 Financial Statements

Marici Power Statement of Profit or Loss for the Year Ended 31 December

	2015 (F$000)	2014 (F$000)
Revenue	69, 993	60, 895
Cost of materials	(37, 705)	(33, 258)
Personnel expenses	(14, 111)	(12, 692)
Amortisation and depreciation	(2, 412)	(2, 263)
Other operating expenses	(13, 530)	(12, 872)
Operating profit	2, 235	(190)
Finance costs	(1, 978)	(2, 156)
Profit before tax	257	(2 346)
Taxation	(106)	(65)
Profit /(loss) for the year	151	(2 411)

Marici Power Statement of Financial Position as at 31 December

	2015 (F$000)	2014 (F$000)
Non-current assets		
Intangible assets	18, 430	17, 800
PPE	17, 409	17, 474
	35, 839	35, 274
Current assets		
Inventories	21, 299	20, 767
Trade receivables	10, 604	10, 788
Cash and cash equivalents	206	75
	32, 109	31, 630
Total assets	67, 948	66, 904
Equity and liabilities		

（续表）

	2015 (F$000)	2014 (F$000)
Share capital	1, 490	1, 490
Retained earnings	34, 946	34, 795
Total equity	36, 436	36, 285
Non-current liabilities		
Long-term borrowings	21, 322	22, 664
Current liabilities		
Trade payables	8, 396	6, 729
Short-term borrowings	1, 688	1, 161
Current tax liabilities	106	65
	10, 190	7, 955
Total equity and liabilities	67, 948	66, 904

Marici Power Statement of Cash Flows for the Year Ended 31 December 2015

	2015 (F$000)	2014 (F$000)
Cash flows from operating activities		
Profit/(loss) before tax	257	(2, 346)
Depreciation and amortisation	2, 412	2, 263
Net finance costs	1, 978	2, 156
(Increase)/decrease in inventory	(532)	(425)
(Increase)/decrease in trade and other receivables	184	224
Increase/(decrease) in trade and other payables	1, 667	567
Cash generated from operations	5, 966	2, 439
Interest paid	(1, 978)	(2, 156)
Tax paid	(65)	(125)
Net cash generated from operating activities	3, 923	158
Cash flows from investing activities		

（续表）

	2015 (F$ 000)	2014 (F$ 000)
Purchase of property, plant and equipment	(2, 347)	(1, 594)
Increase in intangibles	(630)	(245)
Net cash used in investing activities	(2, 977)	(1, 839)
Cash flows from financing activities		
Increase in short-term borrowings	527	1, 200
Repayment of long-term borrowings	(1, 342)	(605)
Net cash from/(used in) financing activities	(815)	595
Net increase/(decrease) in cash and cash equivalents	131	(1, 086)
Cash and cash equivalents at beginning of the year	75	1, 161
Cash and cash equivalents at the end of the year	206	75

Tax Regime in Freeland

Corporate Profits

(1) The corporate tax rate applicable to taxable profits is 20%.

(2) Unless otherwise stated below, accounting rules on recognition and measurement are followed for tax purposes.

(3) The following expenses are not allowable for tax purposes:

- accounting depreciation;
- amortisation;
- entertaining expenditure;
- donations to political parties;
- taxes paid to other public bodies.

(4) Tax depreciation allowances are available on items of plant and machinery (including vehicles used for business purposes) at a rate of 25% per year on a reducing balance basis.

(5) Tax losses can be carried forward to offset against future taxable profits from the

same business.

Marici Power Management Accounting Information

- The company produces an annual budget with all managers participating in its production.
- The company operates a standard absorption costing system and produces a monthly variance analysis report reconciling actual profit to budgeted profit.
- KPIs are reported on a monthly basis.
- A detailed daily sales report is available to managers to enable close monitoring of sales units and selling prices.

Budget Information 2017

Solar panel sales budget 2017					
	Solar Bright	**Solar Glow**	**Solar Halo**	**Solar Eclipse**	**Total**
Selling price per unit(F$)	275	300	350	450	
Number of units	55,000	58,000	62,000	60,000	235,000
Sales mix(units)(%)	23.4	24.7	26.4	25.5	
Total sales(F$ 000)	15,125	17,400	21,700	27,000	81,225
Sales mix(sales value)(%)	18.6	21.4	26.7	33.3	

Budgeted standard gross profit per unit				
	Solar Bright **F$**	Solar Glow F$	**Solar Halo** **F$**	**Solar Eclipse** **F$**
Selling price	275	300	350	450
Material cost	140	150	190	245
Labour cost	40	45	50	65
Variable production overheads	2.2	2.5	2.8	3
Fixed production overheads	22	25	28	30
Standard gross profit	70.8	77.5	79.2	107

News Article

Solar Power News

16 September 2016 No. 78 F$4.70

Government Cuts to Solar Panel Subsidies – a "Hammer Blow" to the Industry

Damien Valence, Business Correspondent

The Freeland government has decided to cut subsidies to householders installing rooftop solar panels by 60%, despite admitting that the move could result in the loss of up to 18,000 jobs.

A second subsidy scheme for large commercial projects has also been cut. The solar industry and environmentalist groups have described the moves as "reckless and short-sighted".

The government argues it needs to protect wider energy bills from the rising impact of renewable energy subsidies.

The new figures from James Claville, the energy secretary, are less than the original government proposal to slash subsidies by a whopping 87%, which was met by a storm of criticism.

"My priority is to keep energy bills for householders and businesses as low as possible whilst ensuring there is a sensible level of support for low carbon technologies. We have to get the balance right and I believe that subsidies should be temporary, not part of a permanent business model. The reduced cost of solar technologies should be followed by a reduction in consumer-funded support."

The shadow energy secretary, Lisanne Furwell, said the cuts were misguided.

"These short-sighted cuts will place great pressure on our solar industry and lead to thousands of job losses. At a time when energy bills are a concern for everyone, it makes no sense to limit one of the cheapest forms of clean energy."

News Article

Solar Technology

15 September 2016 No. 23　　F$5.25

Keeping the Sun Shining – the Future Is Bright

Johan Steiff, Business Correspondent

Energy from renewable sources is a really "hot" topic but whilst capacity is increasing and prices are going down, there remains one major constraint to solar power developing into a major, cost-competitive alternative to fossil fuels — storage.

For renewable sources of electricity to be viable they must be able to provide a continuous supply of energy and meet peaks and troughs in demand. Unfortunately, we cannot guarantee that the sun will always be shining. Then there is the matter of night-time.

In order for there to be electricity during the night, solar energy must be captured and stored during the day while the sun is out. But as people are using electricity during the day, solar panels need to capture as much sun as possible, enough to fulfil daytime electricity dem ands and enough to fill up batteries for the night.

The problem is that cheap battery packs have longevity or reliability issues. While quality battery packs are prohibitively expensive to produce.

The renewable energy industry is working on this problem but has so far been unable to bring the expensive technology down to a realistic cost. However, developments in the electric vehicle industry have meant that lithiumion storage — the most promising technology for solar — is becoming a more viable proposition.

背景材料

工作说明

你是摩利兹能源公司的3名管理会计助理之一，主要职责是协助编制年度预算，生成月度管理账目并按要求向管理层提供信息。

公司简介

摩利兹能源公司位于西欧国家Freeland，该国货币为F$①。

摩利兹能源公司向Freeland及欧洲其他地区的客户提供太阳能发电产品。它提供的丰富的产品组合，能够满足家用及商业用户的要求，以环保、高效、有益的方式来利用太阳能发电。摩利兹能源公司所提供的产品包括太阳能电池板和完整的太阳能发电系统，该系统整合了摩利兹能源公司的电池板和逆变器、支架和屋顶安装机架等组件。在国内市场上，摩利兹能源公司的主要客户为商业用户及直接面向公众的安装商。欧洲其他地区则是通过经销商来供货，这些地区的销售收入占该公司营业额的15%。

摩利兹能源公司唯一的生产厂房位于Freeland的首都，用于制造所有的太阳能电池板及太阳能电池的关键组件。在同一地点，摩利兹能源公司还拥有一个大型存储仓库和董事及管理层的办公场所。

过去20年，摩利兹能源公司进行了大量投资，设计并开发了日益成熟和高效的太阳能电池板，凭借高质量的电池板和出色的能源转换效率，打造了过硬的品牌并赢得了良好的声誉。如今，该公司已经发展成为Freeland最大的太阳能电池板制造商。

摩利兹能源公司是在Freeland大型石油公司Saltenergy（索尔特能源）的研发部门的基础上发展而来的。近年来，Saltenergy决定剥离非核心业务，着重发展核心业务——化石燃料能源。因此，Saltenergy于2016年2月将摩利兹能源公司卖给了Wala Solar集团

① 此处及以下所称“F$”，均指Freeland当地货币，该货币为虚拟货币。

（瓦拉太阳能集团）。Wala Solar 集团是一家大型的全球性太阳能产品供应商，其生产工厂遍布欧洲和美国。如今，作为 Wala Solar 集团的战略业务单位，摩利兹能源公司可以充分利用该集团可再生能源市场的相关资源。

什么是太阳能电池板

太阳能电池板是活跃的太阳能设备，它采用光伏技术将太阳能转化为电能，呈方形，通常组合起来安装以生成电力。

太阳能电池板完全具备从太阳光取能发电（直流电）的能力。直流电可供发电站本身使用，直接使用或储存在电池内以后使用都可以。逆变器能将直流电转换为交流电，从而可将太阳能发电系统接入公共电网，让用户自由选择使用太阳能电力或公共电网供电。用户还可将太阳能系统产生的多余的电量出售给电力公司，如下图所示。

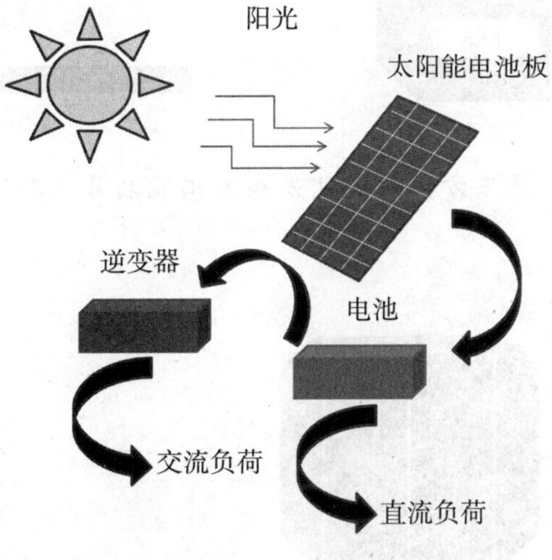

摘自 www. maricipower. com 的网页

> **如何制造太阳能电池板？**
>
> **硅**
>
> 硅是我们太阳能电池板生产周期的起点，它提取自石英岩或石英砂，主要由二氧化硅构成。硅作为地壳中的第二常见元素，我们几乎取之不尽。多晶硅是硅的高纯度形式。

太阳能晶片

制造太阳能电池板的第二个步骤是生产太阳能晶片，它们是太阳能电池的主要组成部分。

大部分太阳能电池板需要使用多晶硅晶片，为了生产这些晶片，需将高纯度的硅注入高纯度石英材料涂层的模具中，并在1 400摄氏度以上的高温下进行融化。液体硅质量变硬，数以千计的小晶体结合成块状。在生产过程的下一个阶段，这些晶块将被切割成方块，随后再被切割成薄晶片。

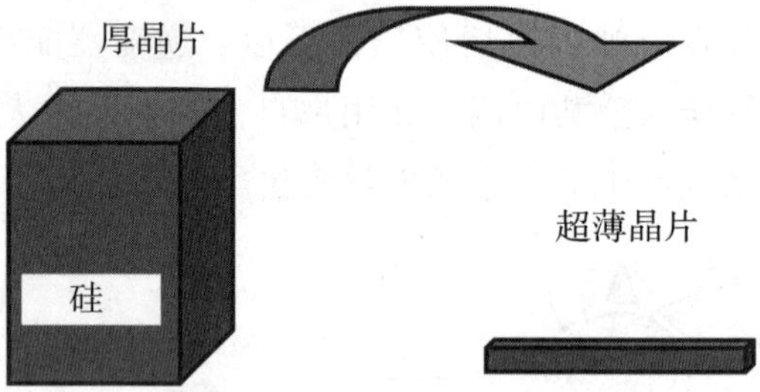

摩利兹能源公司从第三方供应商处采购太阳能晶片，而供应商使用最高纯度的硅来生产太阳能晶片。

太阳能电池

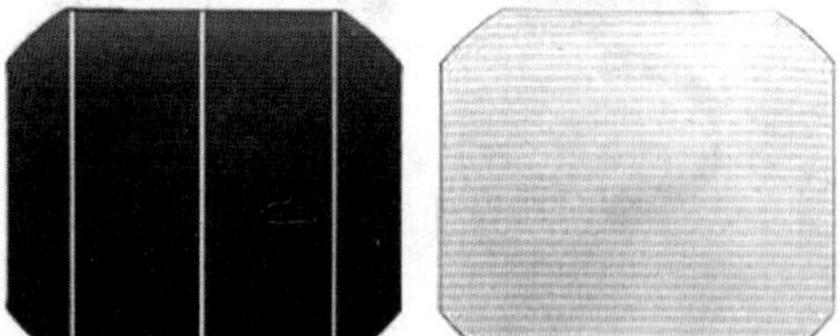

生产过程的下一阶段是利用晶片生产太阳能电池，晶片是太阳能电池板的重要元件。太阳能电池具备太阳能发电所需的全部技术特性，光辐射释放出正负电荷载体，从而形成电流（直流电）。

摩利兹能源公司使用世界上最先进的太阳能电池生产设施制造太阳能电池。经过一系列的化学和热处理之后，晶片转换为具有生产能力的电池，即能够发电的电池。

太阳能电池板

在电池板的生产过程中，需将太阳能电池组合成更大的单元——电池板。电池板被封闭在框架之中，具备较强的气候抵御能力。完工后的太阳能电池板已完全具备利用太阳光取能发电的能力（直流电）。

在生产过程的最后包装阶段，对太阳能电池板进行出厂前的仔细清理和检查，随后装运并发送给家用和商业客户。

未来战略

（摘自摩利兹能源公司 2015 年的年度报告和财务报表）

品牌化

摩利兹能源公司将继续以现有品牌名称销售太阳能电池板，即 Solar Bright（明亮太阳能）、Solar Glow（辉光太阳能）、Solar Eclipse（日蚀太阳能）和 Solar Halo（光环太阳能）。

质量

作为高质量及高转换效率的太阳能电池板的生产商，我们将继续发展品牌，建立声誉。此外，我们将努力巩固自己作为 Freeland 最大的太阳能电池板生产商的地位。

客户为先

客户需求是摩利兹能源公司所有业务和生产流程的推动因素。产品差异化和全方位的客户服务将为客户带来附加值。

创新

太阳能系统是由太阳能电池板与其他元件共同组成的一个完整的发电系统。对于我们而言，太阳能系统仍然是我们的战略重点，我们将继续努力提高太阳能产品的发电能力。我们计划在 2017 年进一步改进电池板的设计，减轻重量，实现更好的自洁效果，为客户提供不同规格和类型的太阳能电池板。

销售增长

作为 Freeland 最大的太阳能产品制造商，我们将继续抓住机遇，增加出货量，扩大市场份额。发展完整的太阳能发电系统业务是我们一直以来的目标之一，因为就这一市场而言，通过竞争实现更大的差异化是有可能的。

成本效益

我们希望在2017年通过生产量的增长实现规模经济，降低产品的单位生产成本。除此之外，我们还计划削减所有组织部门和供应链条各个部分的成本，以期优化公司的现金流和利润水平。

太阳能光伏发电产业介绍

可再生能源技术是清洁能源的来源，与传统的能源技术相比，它对环境的影响要小得多。可再生能源并不会被消耗殆尽，而其他形式的能源则是有限的，终有一天会枯竭。太阳能是可再生能源的一种主要形式，它能满足全世界电力需求的1%以上，发电量等同于33个大型煤电厂。

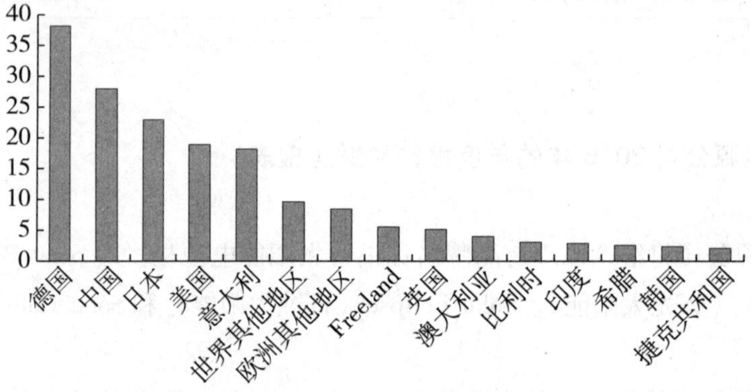

2015年光伏发电的累计装机容量（GW）

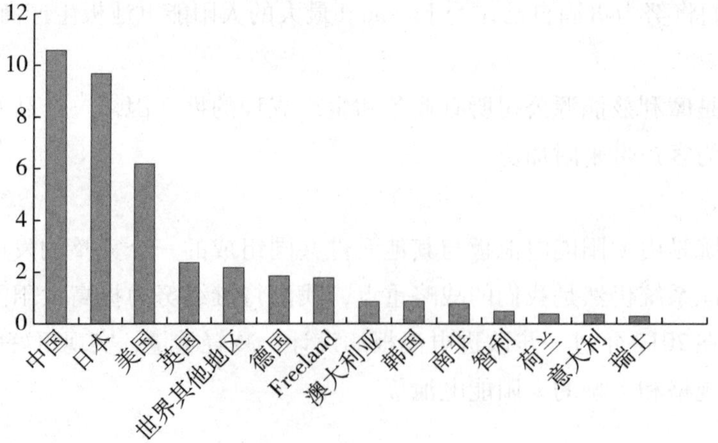

2015年光伏装置量（GW）

按照所使用的技术，太阳能产业主要分为两部分：集中式太阳能光热发电（CST）和光伏发电（PV）。

光伏发电技术的原理是将所吸取的光直接转换为电能（光效应）；集中式太阳能光热发电技术的原理则是将直射阳光聚焦到一点并加热某种液体，所产生的热能随后被用于驱动发电机，就像在传统的发电站一样。

从绝对值来看，光伏发电的市场份额仍相对较小。截至2015年年末，全球光伏发电的装机容量为178GW，其中40GW是在2015年完成安装的。

过去，光伏设备装机的全球市场一直由欧洲主导。2009年，德国占据了市场份额的50%。然而2015年，市场重心转移到了亚洲（占新装机量的50%以上）、美洲和非洲。

2015年，太阳能电池板市场的年装机容量首次达到40GW，这得益于亚洲和美洲市场的增长，在某种程度上也得益于新兴市场的出现。

经历数年的快速发展之后，欧洲市场的增长速度在2014年开始放缓，且2015年进一步萎缩。2015年，整个欧洲市场的装机容量约为7GW，低于中国或日本的太阳能发电设备装机容量，但仍超过美国。然而，截至2015年年末，欧洲仍然是主要的市场参与者，累积装机容量超过88GW。

各国的政府补贴政策、关税结构和可使用空间决定了太阳能发电设备的安装规模和地理位置。在罗马尼亚和西班牙等国，太阳能发电设备主要采取的是“公用工程规模”的大规模安装方式，而在荷兰和葡萄牙等国，基本上没有“公用工程规模”的安装。就太阳能发电而言，“公用工程规模”通常是指设计的系统的发电能力达到了向公共电网输送电力的水平。在德国，超过60%的太阳能发电设备安装在私人住宅和商用场所的屋顶。

各国政府的补贴计划各不相同。欧洲最受欢迎的政府补贴计划之一是“上网电价补贴”（FITs）。Freeland政府在2010年推出了补贴计划，“上网电价补贴”就是其中之一，政府希望借此鼓励业界在Freeland布局可再生能源。其推出这个计划的初衷是鼓励太阳能产业在Freeland境内布局最高发电量能达到5MW（含5MW）的小规模低碳发电设备。

利用太阳能发电的家庭或企业能获得以下益处。

- 节省开支——建筑物用户可使用楼宇太阳能发电设备所产生的电能，从而降低公共电网的用电成本。

- 出口补贴——发电者将多余电量输入公共电网，从而获得供电企业提供的出口补贴。
- 发电补贴——为鼓励部署和使用低碳技术而非化石燃料，供电企业给发电者提供的补贴。

“上网电价补贴”计划的资金源于政府针对所有用电用户所征收的附加费用。为了限制用电附加费用对消费者的影响，政府为补贴总额设定了上限。

为进一步鼓励太阳能的开发，政府制订的其他计划包括一系列的税收减免优惠。Freeland 政府针对太阳能电池板及其他太阳能元件，将增值税税率降低了 5% 。

产业历史

在不到 10 年的时间内，太阳能产业已从家庭作坊式作业发展成为市场规模超 1 000 亿美元的全球性产业。推动其发展的因素包括政府补贴、现有市场参与者及新进入者的重大扩容贡献，以及持续不断的创新。

2007—2011 年，政府补贴让许多用户看到了经济效益，吸引他们开始安装和使用太阳能设备，这让太阳能行业实现了 70% 左右的年度增长。随着需求量的增加，新的参与者不断涌入这一行业，创新步伐加快。太阳能行业的快速增长意味着产能难以满足需求，因此，能够提升产能的公司将获得更多的市场份额。

太阳能产业的产能出现剧增，特别是在大规模、低成本生产的中国制造商进入市场之后。2009—2011 年，中国的太阳能电池板产量是全球需求量的 4 倍多，且售价比欧洲和美国同类产品的售价便宜 45% 。尽管价格下降刺激了需求，但也压缩了企业的利润空间。由于供过于求，太阳能电池的价格开始大跌，许多公司力求降低库存，而许多小规模的制造商甚至直接停产。

2011 年，太阳能电池价格大幅下跌的主要原因是太阳能电池的重要原材料——多晶硅的价格出现了大幅的下降，而多晶硅在产品总成本中占了很大比例。

多晶硅是生产太阳能晶片的原材料，而太阳能晶片则用于组装太阳能电池。2007—2008 年，全球多硅晶的产量低于需求量，这一短缺导致多晶硅的售价上涨至每千克 400 美元左右。受到高价格的驱动，多晶硅供应商纷纷大幅度提升产能，造成了多晶硅产能的极大过剩，最终导致了价格的下滑。2011 年年初，多硅晶的价格下滑至每千克 80 美元左右，而 2011 年年底，则进一步下降为每千克 20 ~ 25 美元。

2011—2014 年，由于中国的低价出口和市场产能过剩，太阳能电池板的价格出现下滑，导致在太阳能行业内，几乎所有的公司都无法实现盈利。

2012年，美国政府以中国制造商获得了中国政府不公平的补贴为由，对中国太阳能电池和太阳能电池板征收进口关税。

2013年，欧盟委员会认为中国太阳能企业以低价向欧洲倾销产品，因此决定对从中国进口的太阳能电池板征收惩罚性的进口关税。欧盟与中国政府经过协商之后，双方确定了进口太阳能电池板和元件的最低售价。

主要市场趋势

2015年对于太阳能产业而言无疑是充满挑战的一年，行业发展出现了转折点，这主要是因为中国政府的利好政策极大地提振了太阳能设备的销售。现在，太阳能作为具有成本竞争力、可靠和可持续获取的能源已经获得了广泛认可。

太阳能产业的增长改善了产能利用率并缓解了价格压力，从而推动了全球太阳能产业的持续复苏。2015年，太阳能电池和太阳能电池板制造商的财务状况得到了显著改善，其中不少制造商实现了多年以来的首次盈利。

制造商重新获利，财务状况也得以改善，这引发了新一轮的行业投资。多家制造商宣布他们计划购入创新设备以升级现有生产线或增加生产线。与此同时，新建的太阳能电池板工厂大多位于或靠近新兴市场，而欧洲境内的几家制造商则陆续倒闭。

在欧洲，欧盟与中国政府商定的最低售价让中国厂商的太阳能产品售价高于市场水平。然而，其他亚洲制造厂商仍能以较低的价格在欧洲销售太阳能产品。

展望未来

截至2015年年末，太阳能产业的发展在很大程度上得益于各国政府所采用的监管框架，其中包括税收优惠、补贴和其他专项支持计划。从短期来看，市场增长将主要依赖于政府的持续支持。然而，太阳能行业的持续发展终究需要依靠自身与传统电力能源的竞争能力。

太阳能发电产品的需求仍高度集中在少数几个国家，这对于在这些国家缺乏市场覆盖的公司而言，是一个重大风险。该行业所经历的产品价格快速下滑为其打开了许多国家的太阳能市场，但全球太阳能市场的发展仍由那些采用支持性监管框架的国家所驱动，如亚洲和美洲的国家。

一些欧洲国家决定减少或终止“上网电价补贴”，这令人感到担忧，它可能会对未来太阳能设备的装机量产生重大的影响。企业需要让消费者相信，即便在没有其他额外补贴的情况下，用电成本的减少也足以证明太阳能的投资价值。

从历史上看，太阳能电池板的发展是由分布式安装推动的，即发电位置与用电位置相同或接近。2014 年，就装机容量而言，“公用工程规模”的太阳能装机方式在全球范围内已经占据最大市场份额。2015 年，太阳能设备的两类装机容量大致相同，均为 20GW 左右。两类装机方式的发展将取决于各国政府所采用的监管框架，但从现有发展趋势来看，“公用工程规模”的太阳能装机方式凭借其日益显现的成本竞争优势，在全球范围内似乎更胜一筹。

摘自 www. maricipower. com 的网页

太阳能光伏发电行业的术语表摘录

G：	
光伏并网	联网的太阳能发电系统能够自行发电并将多余的电量输入公共电网供后续使用。联网的太阳能发电系统可获得多项奖励和部分退款
I：	
逆变器	逆变器能将直流电转换为交流电，联网的太阳能发电系统需安装这个部件
P：	
光伏技术	光 = 光线；伏 = 电量潜能（其字面意思就是通过光线产生的电能）。爱因斯坦（Einstein）发现将光照射到某些材料（例如硅）上能产生电流，并因此获得了诺贝尔奖
多晶硅	多晶硅是硅的高纯度形态。由于具有类似半导体的性质，多晶硅常用于大部分太阳能发电设备
公共电网	公共电网是一个相互连接的发电站网络，由以下三个部分组成：提供电力的发电站、将电力从发电站远距离输送到变电站的高压输电线、连接单个用户的配电线路
光伏阵列	光伏阵列是一个完整的发电单元，可由任何数量的太阳能（光伏）电池板组成

（续表）

S：	
半导体	半导体是指仅能部分导电的材料。半导体的导电性介于基本不具导电性的绝缘体与几乎完全导电的导体之间
硅	硅是用于生产太阳能电池的基本材料。除了氧之外，硅是地壳中含量最丰富的元素
太阳能电池（或光伏电池）	将阳光转化为直流电的半导体设备
太阳能电池板（或光伏面板）	太阳能电池板包括密封在保护层内的太阳能电池，它是太阳能（或光伏）系统的基本组成部分
独立系统（或离网系统）	这些系统所生成的电力储存在电池内以供后续使用。独立系统也被称为“离网系统”，它并不接入公共电网

摩利兹能源公司的组织结构摘要

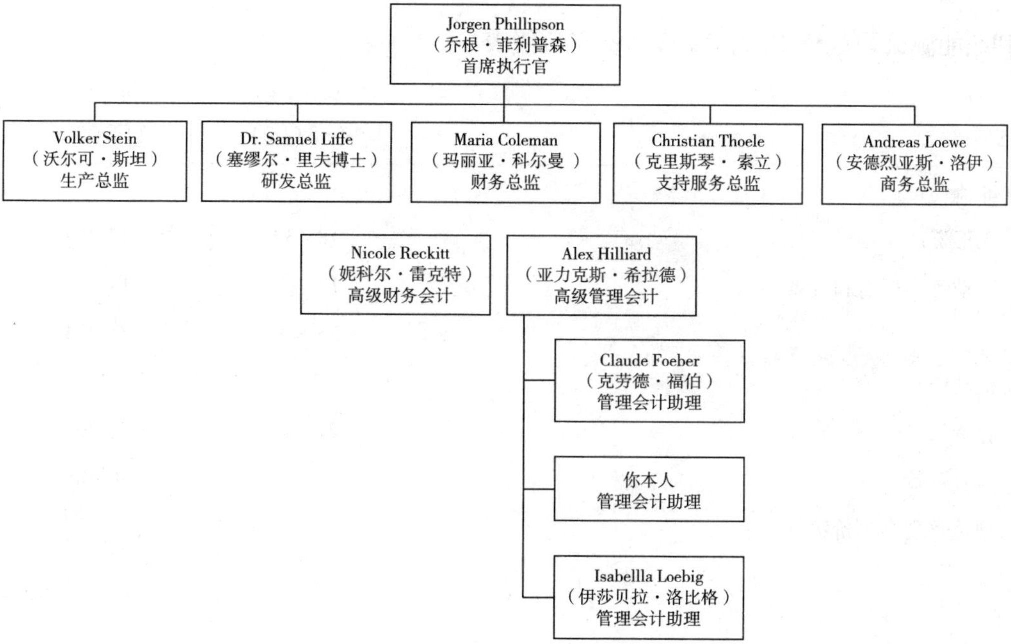

摩利兹能源公司2015年财务报表摘要

摩利兹能源公司截至12月31日的年度利润表

	2015年 (F$000①)	2014年 (F$000)
收入	69 993	60 895
原材料成本	(37 705)	(33 258)
人员费用	(14 111)	(12 692)
摊销和折旧	(2 412)	(2 263)
其他运营费用	(13 530)	(12 872)
经营利润	2 235	(190)
财务费用	(1 978)	(2 156)
税前利润	257	(2 346)
税费	(106)	(65)
本年利润/（亏损）	151	(2 411)

摩利兹能源公司截至12月31日的资产负债表

	2015年 (F$000)	2014年 (F$000)
非流动资产		
无形资产	18 430	17 800
不动产、厂房和设备	17 409	17 474
	35 839	35 274
流动资产		
存货	21 299	20 767
应收账款	10 604	10 788
现金及现金等价物	206	75
	32 109	31 630

① F$000，即1000F$。

（续表）

	2015 年 (F$ 000)	2014 年 (F$ 000)
总资产	67 948	66 904
所有者权益和负债		
股本	1 490	1 490
留存收益	34 946	34 795
所有者权益总额	36 436	36 285
非流动负债		
长期借款	21 322	22 664
流动负债	8 396	6 729
应付账款	1 688	1 161
短期借款	106	65
当期所得税负债	10 190	7 955
所有者权益和负债总额	67 948	66 904

摩利兹能源公司截至 2015 年 12 月 31 日的年度现金流量表

	2015 年 (F$ 000)	2014 年 (F$ 000)
经营性现金流		
税前利润（亏损）	257	(2 346)
折旧和摊销	2 412	2 263
财务费用净额	1 978	2 156
存货（增加）/减少	(532)	(425)
应收账款的（增加）/减少	184	224
应付账款的增加/（减少）	1 667	567
经营活动产生的现金流	5 966	2 439
已付利息	(1 978)	(2 156)
已付税费	(65)	(125)

（续表）

	2015 年 （F$ 000）	2014 年 （F$ 000）
经营活动产生的净现金流	3 923	158
投资活动现金流		
购买不动产、厂房和设备	（2 347）	（1 594）
无形资产的增加	（630）	（245）
投资活动所使用的现金净额	（2 977）	（1 839）
筹资活动现金流		
短期借款的增加	527	1 200
偿还的长期借款	（1 342）	（605）
筹资活动获得/（使用）的净现金额	（815）	595
现金及现金等价物的净增加/（净减少）	131	（1 086）
期初现金及现金等价物	75	1 161
期末现金及现金等价物	206	75

Freeland 的税收体系

企业利润

（1）企业税率为应税利润的 20%。

（2）除非另有规定，否则应该从税务的角度出发来执行下列的确认和计量会计规定。

（3）以下费用不得税前扣除。

- 会计折旧。
- 摊销费用。
- 文娱开支。
- 政党捐款。
- 支付给其他公共机构的税费。

（4）厂房和机器设备（包括商用车辆）的折旧可以抵税，每年的抵扣率为 25%，以其递减余额为基础。

（5）可抵税损失可以进行结转，用于抵减同一企业未来的应税利润。

摩利兹能源公司的管理会计信息

- 该公司所有管理人员共同参与年度预算的编制。
- 该公司采用标准吸收成本核算系统，每月编制实际利润与预算利润之间的差异分析报告。
- 该公司每月考核 KPIs（关键绩效指标）。
- 该公司向管理人员提供详细的每日销售报告，以便其密切监控销售数量和销售价格。

2017 年预算信息

2017 年太阳能电池板的销售预算					
	Solar Bright	Solar Glow	Solar Halo	Solar Eclipse	合计
单位售价（F$）	275	300	350	450	
售出数量	55 000	58 000	62 000	60 000	235 000
销售占比（数量）（%）	23. 4	24. 7	26. 4	25. 5	
销售总额（F$ 000）	15 125	17 400	21 700	27 000	81 225
销售占比（销售金额）（%）	18. 6	21. 4	26. 7	33. 3	

单位产品的预算标准毛利				
	Solar Bright (F$)	Solar Glow (F$)	Solar Halo (F$)	Solar Eclipse (F$)
销售价格	275	300	350	450
材料成本	140	150	190	245
人员成本	40	45	50	65
变动生产费用	2. 2	2. 5	2. 8	3
固定生产费用	22	25	28	30
标准毛利润	70. 8	77. 5	79. 2	107

新闻报道

太阳能行业资讯

2016年9月16日　78号　F$4.70

政府削减太阳能电池板补贴——太阳能行业发展受阻

Damien Valence（达米安·瓦伦斯），商业记者

Freeland政府决定削减家庭安装屋顶太阳能电池板的补贴，幅度高达60%，尽管该国政府承认此举可能会导致18 000个工作岗位的丧失。

此外，政府还削减了针对大型商业项目的另一项补贴计划。太阳能行业及环保机构批评政府此举“鲁莽和短视”。

而政府表示，由于新能源补贴支出日益增加，政府需要考虑并保证更广泛的能源发展需要。

政府最初提出的补贴削减比例高达87%，消息一出立刻遭到了强烈反对。而根据能源部部长James Claville（詹姆斯·克拉维乐）提供的最新数据，实际削减比例要低于这一数字。

“我们的工作重点是确保将家庭和企业的用电成本维持在尽可能低的水平，与此同时，确保为低碳技术提供合理的支持。我们必须在两者之间寻求适当的平衡，而且我认为补贴应该只是暂时性的，不能作为长期的商业模式。随着太阳能技术相关成本的降低，我们理应降低由消费者负担的资金支持力度。”

能源部影子部长Lisanne Furwell（利萨安娜·弗维尔）表示，削减补贴可能产生错误的指导作用。

“政府削减补贴的举动显得目光短浅，这将给我们的太阳能行业带来巨大的压力，导致数以万计的工作岗位消失。在人们普遍关心能源开支的时代，太阳能作为最便宜的清洁能源之一，限制其发展是毫无道理的。”

新闻报道

太阳能技术

2016 年 9 月 15 23 号　　F$5.25

让阳光一直灿烂——太阳能的光明前景

Johan Steiff（约翰·斯特弗），商业记者

可再生能源已经成为真正的热点话题，产能不断扩大，价格一路走低，但太阳能想要发展成为主要的、具成本竞争力的、可替代化石燃料的能源，面临的最大挑战是储能问题。

可再生能源发电想要实现广泛应用，必须能够持续供电，并能够根据用电高峰和用电低谷进行调节。然而不幸的是，我们不能保证太阳一直高挂天空，毕竟还有夜晚的存在。

为了保证夜间的用电需求，太阳能发电设备必须在白天获取和储存足够多的太阳能。但由于人们在白天也有用电需求，因此太阳能电池板需要尽可能多地吸收阳光，在满足白天用电需求的同时，还能存储到电池中以满足夜晚的用电需求。

但问题是价格便宜的电池组存在使用寿命和可靠性问题，而高品质的电池组价格太过高昂，妨碍了它的生产。

可再生能源行业正致力于解决这一问题，但迄今为止，未能将这一昂贵技术的成本降至切实可行的水平。然而，电动汽车行业的发展意味着锂离子储能或许能成为太阳能领域最具前景的储能技术，且更切实可行。

Variant 1

This examination is structured as follows：

Section number	Number of tasks	Time for section(minutes)
1	1	50
2	1	30
3	1	45
4	1	55

The time available for each section is for reading,planning and writing your answer(s).

Section 1

The following article was published in *Solar Industry News* recently.

Solar Industry News

7th November 2016 No. 775 F$5.80

Price of Solar Wafers Set to Skyrocket as Demand Outstrips Supply

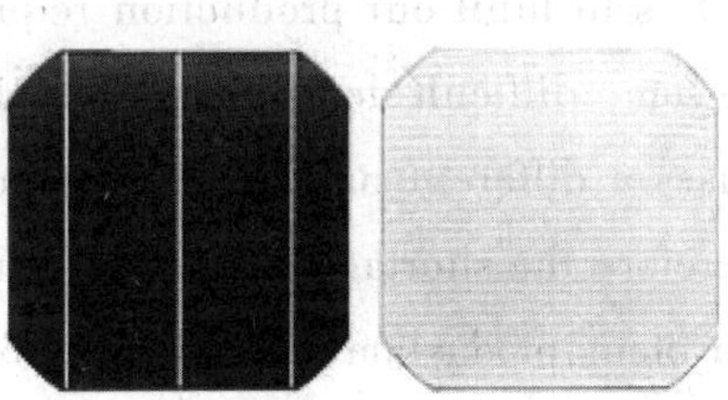

Joseph Versace, Business Correspondent

Industry observers are predicting a solar wafer supply shortage throughout the entire supply chain as they forecast another record year for solar panel installations in 2017. This comes despite recent announcements of large capacity expansions from leading solar panel manufacturers.

The solar industry's capacity expansions plans are unlikely to keep pace with the forecast for demand growth in 2017. Most solar wafer suppliers have limited product availability, until the second half of 2017.

Compared to the overall solar panel industry, capacity expansions in the solar wafer sector are far more capital intensive, while margins for wafer manufacturers are currently much smaller than for most panel manufacturers. This is one of the reasons wafer capacity expansion plans have been much more conservative than new panel capacity announcements. A, second reason is that many large manufacturers have increased their in-house panel capacity, while keeping a significantly lower wafer capacity. Instead, they are opting to purchase wafers from third-party companies, to reduce their capital expenditures and allow greater flexibility in their manufacturing capacity.

As a result of strong market demand and insufficient supply, the average selling prices of solar wafers has slowly started to rise since June.

You receive the following email from Maria Coleman, finance director.

From: Maria Coleman, Finance Director
To: Management Accountant Assistant
Subject: Supply shortage of solar wafers

I have circulated a copy of an article from the *Solar Industry News* to all staffs. The board is concerned about the implication of the shortage of solar wafers for our current production schedule. They also want to ensure continuity of supply for the future.

We have been advised by our major suppliers that they will not be able to supply sufficient wafers to fulfil our production requirements for the next quarter. Therefore, we need to make some difficult decisions about what we are going to produce. Each solar panel produced uses a different number of solar cells, but each cell uses the same number of wafers, therefore the shortage of wafers restricts our production of both solar cells and panels.

Volker Stein, production director, has provided some data for each of our main product lines (see attached). He has suggested that we use the available wafers to produce the products that make the highest gross profit per panel. Andreas Loewe, commercial director, however is keen that we should produce as much as possible of "Solar Halo" as he believes that this is going to be a market leader in the future.

I am also going to be meeting next week with Harold Foyle, the purchasing manager, to discuss the factors we would need to consider when selecting a new supplier.

Please produce a report for me to use in my discussions with Volker, Andreas and Harold. You should include the following areas in the report.

- How we should determine which products to supply if we are trying to maximise our short-term profits and what other factors would need to be considered.
- The factors we would need to consider when selecting another supplier.

Regards.

Maria Coleman
Finance Director
Marici Power

Data on solar panel models：

	Solar panel models			
	Solar Bright	Solar Glow	Solar Halo	Solar Eclipse
Contribution per panel(F$)	89.8	99.5	104.2	134
Gross profit per panel(F$)	70.8	77.5	79.1	107
No. of cells per panel	55	50	65	75

Write the report for Maria Coleman, finance director.

Section 2

Two weeks later, you meet Nicole Reckitt, senior financial accountant in the lunch queue at the staff canteen. After the usual pleasantries, she says：

You may have heard that we have now agreed a contract for future supplies of wafers with Solar Systems who are based in Germany. The only problem is that they have offered us only 30 days' credit compared to our existing supplier who gives us 60 days. I suppose we could just pay late but the Finance Director is against that idea as it could jeopardise future supplies. She is also concerned about the effect of the price rise for wafers on our profit and cash flow.

She would like me to look in particular at our working capital cycle. Firstly, she wants me to suggest ways in which we could reduce the length of our working capital cycle and secondly, to consider the impact of a shorter working capital cycle on our ability to operate efficiently and on our relationship with customers and suppliers.

At the moment, I have got one member of staff off sick and another off on holiday. I have discussed this with Alex, senior management accountant, and he has suggested that I ask you to do it for me. Would you mind? It would be a great help if you could do it.

You reply that you would be happy to do it and tell her you will send her an email.

Write the email to Nicole Reckitt.

Section 3

A few days later, you receive the following email from Alex Hilliard, senior management accountant.

From: Alex Hilliard, Senior Management Accountant
To: Management Accountant Assistant
Subject: Budget revisions

As you know, we completed the annual budget for 2017 a few weeks ago. We would not normally make any changes after the budget has been finalized but we are faced with a lot of uncertainty in the industry around demand, selling prices and raw material costs. We now believe that the assumptions we made in the budget are overly optimistic. The board had an emergency meeting yesterday and they want to see some revised budget figures as soon as possible.

I have put together some revised figures but they have also asked us to provide some indication of the sensitivity of these figures. I have attached an extract from the revised budget.

Please prepare a report for me that includes the following:

- how we could apply CVP (cost-volume-profit) analysis and sensitivity analysis to these figures;
- the potential benefits and limitations of this analysis.

Our revised cash budget is showing cash deficits in January and February 2017 which we will not be able to meet by our existing short-term borrowing arrangement. You looked at how to reduce the working capital cycle and I have incorporated your suggestions into my calculations, but unfortunately we are still showing a deficit.

Please also review the cash budget and let me know what steps we could take to improve our net cash flow in order to avoid the deficits arising.

Thanks!

Alex Hilliard

Senior Management Accountant

Marici Power

Extract from Revised Budget

Revised sale budget：

	Solar Bright	Solar Glow	Solar Halo	Solar Eclipse
Sales mix based on sales revenue(%)	15	25	32	28
Selling price(F$)	265	290	340	440
Contribution per panel(F$)	79.5	92.8	95.2	127.6

The revised budget for fixed costs is F$ 18,000,000.

Revised cash budget：

Revised cash budget for the period January 2017 to March 2017			
	January	February	March
Receipts：	(F$ 000)	(F$ 000)	(F$ 000)
From sales	6,400	6,500	6,700
Sales of non-current assets			1,000
Total receipts	6,400	6,500	7,700
Payments：			
Payments to suppliers	3,700	3,900	4,100
Personnel expenses	1,200	1,200	1,200
Marketing expenses	250	400	180
Selling and distribution expenses	300	320	350
Administration expenses	345	315	325
Research and development expenditure	100	150	80
Payment of dividends		700	
Purchase of machinery	2,000		
Total payments	7,895	6,985	6,235
Opening cash balance	1,200	(295)	(780)
Net cash flow for the period	(1,495)	(485)	1,465
Closing cash balance	(295)	(780)	685

Write the report for Alex Hilliard, senior management accountant.

Section 4

Marici Power

Extract from the Minutes of a Meeting of the Board of Directors

The board of directors noted the report from the production director regarding the quality issues with the wafers being supplied by Solar Systems. It was also noted that the quality issues had resulte in both production delays and customer returns of faulty products.

The board expressed concern regarding the lack of detailed financial information on the potential impact of this on company profits. They were also surprised that this problem had been ongoing for the past two months and was only now being brought to the board's attention.

The board directed that immediate steps be taken to ensure that suppliers meet the company's normal high quality standard. They also required the finance director to provide a report with suggestions for potential improvements to the monthly management accounting information to ensure that, in the future, attention would be directed to this type of issue at an earlier stage.

You receive the following email from Alex Hilliard, senior management accountant.

From: Alex Hilliard, Senior Management Accountant

To: Management Accountant Assistant

Subject: Supplier quality issues

The finance director has asked me to represent her in the working group that is looking at the quality issues that have arisen with the new wafer supplier. Please draft some working notes for me to take into the first meeting of the group.

You should include the following areas in your notes.

- How can we manage supplier relationships to ensure that the problems experienced with our new supplier do not arise again, either with this, or our other suppliers?
- How would the use of quality cost reporting have helped to avoid this issue arising and what future benefits would it give us?
- It would also be helpful if you could give some examples of quality costs that relate to our business, which we could include in future monthly management accounts. Please use the four standard quality cost categories and include two well explained examples of quality costs for each category.

Many thanks!

Alex Hilliard
Senior Management Accountant
Marici Power

Write the working notes for Alex Hilliard, senior management accountant.

试卷一

本次考试的结构如下：

序号	任务数	时间（分钟）
1	1	50
2	1	30
3	1	45
4	1	55

每个部分规定的时间可用于读题、组织和书写答案。

任务一

下面这篇文章发表在近期的《太阳能行业资讯》中。

太阳能行业资讯

2016年11月7日 775号　　F$5.80

太阳能晶片供不应求，价格将飙升

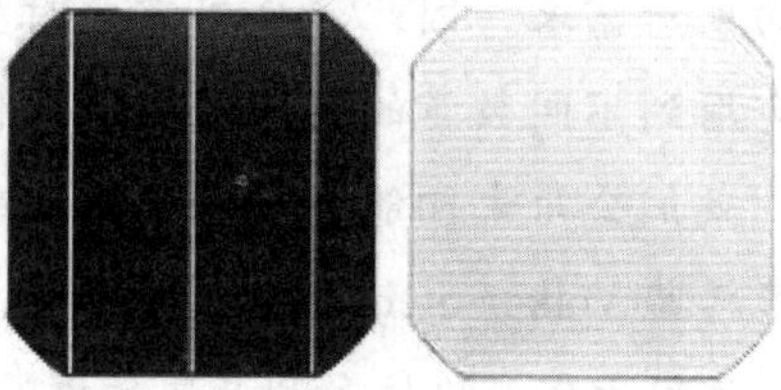

商业记者Joseph Versace（约瑟夫·弗塞斯）

据业内观察人士预计，2017年太阳能电池板安装量将再创历史新高，整个供应链将出现晶片供应短缺问题。尽管最近主要的太阳能电池板制造商宣布了大规模扩张以提升产能的消息，这种情况依然会出现。

2017年太阳能产业的扩张计划不大可能跟得上预计的需求增长，直到2017年下半年，大多数太阳能晶片供应商的供应能力仍将是有限的。

与整个太阳能电池板工业相比，太阳能晶片产能扩张的资本密集程度更高，而且目前晶片制造商的利润率低于大多数电池板制造商。这是造成晶片产能扩张计划比新的电池板产能增加更为保守的原因之一。还有一个原因是许多大型制造商提高了内部电池板的产能，而保持了明显较低的晶片产能。相反，他们选择从第三方公司购买晶片，以减少资本性支出，并在制造能力上获得更大的灵活性。

由于市场需求旺盛和供应不足，自6月以来，太阳能晶片的平均售价已经开始缓慢上升。

你收到了来自财务总监 Maria Coleman 的邮件。

发件人：财务总监 Maria Coleman
收件人：管理会计助理
主题：太阳能晶片供应短缺

我已经把一篇从《太阳能行业资讯》上摘录的文章传给了全体员工。董事会担心太阳能晶片的短缺会对我们公司目前的生产进度产生影响，同时也希望能够确保未来供应的连续性。

公司已经收到来自主要供应商的通知，他们将不能提供足够的晶片来满足公司下一个季度的生产需求。因此，公司需要对生产什么产品做出一些艰难的决定。每种太阳能电池板会用到不同数量的太阳能电池，但每个电池使用的晶片数量相同，所以晶片的短缺会限制我们公司太阳能电池和电池板的生产数量。

生产总监 Volker Stein 提供了每一个主要产品线的部分数据（见附件）。他建议公司把现有的晶片用于生产单位毛利最高的电池板产品。然而，商务总监 Andreas Loewe 却认为公司应该尽可能多地生产"Solar Halo"，因为他相信该产品将会是未来的市场领导者。

我还将在下周与采购经理 Harold Foyle（哈罗德·福耶尔）会面，讨论挑选新供应商时需要考虑的因素。

请你为我提供一份报告，供我在与 Volker，Andreas 和 Harold 的讨论中使用。报告应该包括以下内容：

- 如果公司希望使短期利润最大化，该如何确定生产哪种产品，以及有什么其他需要考虑的因素；
- 在选择另一个供应商时，公司需要考虑哪些因素。

诚挚的问候。

摩利兹能源公司
财务总监
Maria Coleman

太阳能电池板的数据：

	太阳能电池板类型			
	Solar Bright	Solar Glow	Solar Halo	Solar Eclipse
单位边际贡献（F$）	89.5	99.5	104.2	134
单位毛利（F$）	70.8	77.5	79.2	107
每块电池板需用的电池个数	55	50	65	75

请为财务总监 Maria Coleman 写一份报告。

任务二

两周后，你在员工食堂的午餐队伍里遇见了高级财务会计师 Nicole Reckitt。在简单的寒暄后，她说道：

你可能听说了，公司已经和德国的太阳能系统公司（Solar Systems）签订了一份未来的晶片供应合同。唯一的问题是他们只给我们 30 天的信用期，而现在的供应商给的是 60 天。我想我们可以晚一点付款，但财务总监表示反对，因为这可能危及未来的供应，而且她还担心晶片价格上涨会对公司的利润和现金流产生影响。

她希望我特别关注一下公司的营运资金周期。首先，她想要我提出一些能够缩短营运资金周期的建议；其次，还要考虑较短的营运资金周期对公司有效运作的能力，以及客户和供应商关系的影响。

目前我手下的一个员工生病了，还有一个在休假。我和高级管理会计师 Alex 讨论过这个问题，他建议我找你帮忙做这件事。你愿意吗？如果你能做的话，那可是帮了大忙了。

你回答说你很乐意效劳，并告诉她你会给她发电子邮件。

请给高级财务会计师 Nicole Reckitt 写一封电子邮件。

任务三

几天后，你收到了来自高级管理会计师 Alex Hilliard 的邮件。

发件人：高级管理会计师 Alex Hilliard

收件人：管理会计助理

主题：预算修正

正如你所知道的那样，几周前公司完成了2017年的年度预算编制。通常情况下预算编制完成后，不会再做出任何改变。但鉴于公司目前在产品需求、售价和原材料成本等方面面临着诸多行业内的不确定性因素，我们认为之前预算编制中做出的一些假设过于乐观了。董事会昨天召开了一次紧急会议，希望能够尽快修正预算数据。

我已经整理了一些修正后的数据，但董事会要求我们提供对这些数据的敏感性分析。邮件后附上了修正后的预算的摘录。

请帮我准备一份报告，报告中要包括以下内容。

- 我们如何运用本量利分析法和敏感性分析法对这些数据进行分析。
- 这些分析的潜在好处和局限性。

修正后的现金预算表明，2017年1月和2月出现了现金赤字，这是我们现有的短期借款安排无法解决的。你已经研究了如何缩短营运资金周期，我把你提出的建议加入到了我的计算中，但不幸的是，仍然显示赤字。

请你也复核一下现金预算，让我知道公司可以采取什么措施来提升净现金流，以避免赤字的出现。

十分感谢！

摩利兹能源公司
高级管理会计师
Alex Hilliard

修正后的预算表摘录

修正后的销售预算表：

	Solar Bright	Solar Glow	Solar Halo	Solar Eclipse
销售收入占比（%）	15	25	32	28
单位售价（F$）	265	290	340	440
单位边际贡献（F$）	79.5	92.8	95.2	127.6

修正后的固定成本预算是F$ 18 000 000。

修正后的现金预算表：

2017 年 1 ~ 3 月修正后的现金预算表			
	1 月	2 月	3 月
现金流入：	（F$ 000）	（F$ 000）	（F$ 000）
销售收入	6 400	6 500	6 700
处置非流动资产而收到的现金净额			1 000
现金流入合计	6 400	6 500	7 700
现金流出：			
原材料支出	3 700	3 900	4 100
人员费用	1 200	1 200	1 200
营销费用	250	400	180
销售及配送费用	300	320	350
管理费用	345	315	325
研发费用	100	150	80
分配股利		700	
设备费用	2 000		
现金流出合计	7 895	6 985	6 235
期初现金及现金等价物余额	1 200	（295）	（780）
现金及现金等价物本期净流量	（1 495）	（485）	1 485
期末现金及现金等价物余额	（295）	（780）	685

请为高级管理会计师 Alex Hilliard 写一份报告。

任务四

> **摩利兹能源公司**
>
> **董事会会议记录摘要**
>
> 董事会注意到，生产总监报告了太阳能系统公司提供的晶片存在质量问题，而且这一问题已经导致了生产延误，以及客户将不合格产品退回等情况。
>
> 尚无详细的财务信息表明晶片质量问题对公司利润的潜在影响，董事会对此表示担心。更令他们惊讶的是，这一问题已经持续了两个多月，却直到现在才引起董事会的注意。
>
> 董事会要求立即采取措施，以确保供应商们能够达到公司要求的高质量标准。他们还要求财务总监提交一份报告，对每月的管理会计报告提出可能的改进建议，以确保今后这类问题在早期阶段就能引起关注。

你收到了一封来自高级管理会计师 Alex Hilliard 的邮件。

发件人：高级管理会计师 Alex Hilliard
收件人：管理会计助理
主题：供应商质量问题

财务总监让我代表她参加一个研究新晶片供应商带来的质量问题的工作小组。请你为我准备一份工作笔记，以便我带去参加第一次小组会议。

笔记中应该包括以下内容。

- 我们如何管理与供应商的关系，以确保今后不再出现类似问题？包括这个新供应商和其他供应商。
- 如何使用质量成本报告来帮助公司避免这类问题的发生，并且它未来会给我们带来什么样的好处？
- 如果你能列举出一些和公司业务相关的质量成本的例子，并能够放进每月的管理会计报告中，那么将会有很大的帮助。请根据 4 个标准的质量成本类别，并针对每类质量成本给出两个详细阐述的例子。

十分感谢！

摩利兹能源公司
高级管理会计师
Alex Hilliard

请为高级管理会计师 Alex Hilliard 撰写一份工作笔记。

Variant 1　Suggested Answers

Section 1

Solar Wafer Shortage and Selection of New Suppliers

Production Scheduling Based on Profit Maximization

We have a shortage of solar wafers which is limiting our production of solar cells. As the same number of solar wafers is used to produce each solar cell, we would want to make the best use of the solar cells as possible. Each of our products uses a different quantity of solar cells therefore we should maximise the contribution per solar cell and not the gross profit per unit as suggested by Volker. Our total fixed costs will not be affected in the short-term by the mix of products produced and therefore for short-term decisions such as these it is appropriate to focus on contribution per solar cell.

We can calculate the contribution per cell by dividing the contribution per panel by the number of solar cells used in each panel. We would then need to rank the products on the basis of the contribution per solar cell. The product with the highest contribution per solar cell would rank 1st and the product with the second highest contribution would rank 2nd and so on. We would then determine the production schedule based on this ranking.

This would give us a production schedule based on short-term profit maximisation. However, the fact that there is a shortage of solar wafers means that we will leave the production requirement, and consequently demand, for at least one of our products unfulfilled. This may have implications for the longer term, which we would need to consider.

(1) Andreas has suggested that "Solar Halo" is going to be a market leader in the future. What effect would restricting the supply of "Solar Halo" in the short term have in the longer term sales of the product? If we do not supply the full requirement of "Solar Halo", it may give an opportunity for one of our competitors to take up some of our planned market share and affect our long term returns.

(2) What effect would offering a reduced supply of one of our products have on customers who want to purchase the full range of our products? If we do not supply them with at least some of the four products, would they seek an alternative sup-

plier for meeting all their requirements? By failing to supply our customer requirements there may be a loss of customer goodwill. An alternative approach may be to prioritise our most important customers and then use the remaining resources based on the ranking given for short-term profit maximization.

In conclusion therefore, rather than pursuing a short-term profit maximization objective, we may be better to take a longer term view of the decision.

Factors to Be Considered When Selecting a Supplier

An important consideration for the choice of future supplier is price, however we should not make a decision on which supplier to be used based solely on price. The need for a new supplier arose as a result of a market shortage of wafers and we need to ensure continuity of future supplies. We therefore should consider a number of qualitative factors in relation to the supplier.

(1) Will the supplier be prepared to enter into a long-term contract to ensure continuity of supply? How long regularly will the agreed price be revised?

(2) What credit terms will the supplier be prepared to offer?

(3) What production capacity does the supplier have available and what are its plans for further expansion of capacity? We want to ensure continuity of supply as our business grows.

(4) Does the supplier meet the quality standards we would expect from one of our suppliers? Our quality standards are of vital importance to us and it is therefore important that our suppliers are able to maintain these high standards.

(5) Where is the supplier located? A supplier that is located in Freeland or in a nearby country may be able to fulfil our orders more quickly. Supplies from an overseas supplier are subject to risk of delay due to weather or other external factors.

(6) How reliable is the supplier? Would the supplier be able to produce the quantities required at the right time? Delays in supply would result in us being unable to meet our customers' requirements and potentially a loss in customer goodwill and future business.

(7) Is the supplier financially secure? If the supplier failed we would be unable to meet customer's demand until we could source a new supplier. We would need to review the potential suppliers' financial performance and track record in terms of reliability. We should also consider how well the supplier is managed.

(8) What is the culture of the supplier? Does the supplier have the same ethos as us with regard to environmental issues and sustainability? We should also consider the supplier's reputation in terms of corporate and social responsibility.

Section 2

From: Management Accountant Assistant
To: Nicole Reckitt, Senior Financial Accountant
Subject: reducing the working capital cycle

Working Capital Cycle

The working capital cycle represents inventory days plus receivable days less payable days. The longer the working capital cycle, the longer capital is tied up and not earning a return.

However businesses need sufficient working capital to survive and therefore working capital needs to be managed to balance these two requirements.

Reducing the Working Capital Cycle

There are a number of steps that could be taken to reduce the working capital cycle as follows.

Inventory

Our current inventory levels are high at F$ 21 million. What is the breakdown of this between raw material, work in progress and finished goods?

We could reduce our raw material inventory holdings by reviewing slow moving stock, re-order levels and re-order quantities. In the longer term, we might also consider the use of JIT purchasing. Better supplier relationships may also help to ensure the correct inventory is received at the right time and reduce the lead time between order and receipt of goods.

It must however be borne in mind that reducing inventory levels could result in the loss of discounts for bulk purchases and we may also incur additional costs as a result of price rises. There is also the danger of stock-outs which may result in production delays and failure to meet our customers' orders on time.

We could review our production techniques and efficiency levels with a view to reducing work in progress.

Our main production is of four standardised products. Do we need to hold such large inventories of these products? We could reduce our finished good inventory by reorganizing our production scheduling and distribution methods. In the longer term, we could also consider the introduction of JIT production. We must however ensure that any changes do not affect our ability to satisfy customer's demand and result in a reduction in sales.

Accounts Payable

We could obtain more finance from suppliers by delaying payments. This is considered by some people to be unethical and could result in the withdrawal of credit and/or future supplies. The finance director is concerned to jeopardise supplier relations, we should therefore do this through negotiation with the supplier. We may however lose potential early settlement discounts or incur additional charges as a result of this policy.

Accounts Receivable

Are our customers paying according to agreed credit terms or is there evidence of late payment? We could reduce the credit given to customers although this may result in a loss of sales. We could however ensure that we invoice customers and follow up outstanding amounts more quickly, without damaging customer relations. We could also offer early payment discounts to customers although we would need to evaluate whether the reduced cash payment would be outweighed by the benefit of receiving cash quicker.

Another alternative would be to factor our debts or use invoice discounting. This would generate immediate cash flow however there would also be interest costs and fees involved. We would need to decide if these costs are justified compared to the benefits offered. We would also need to carefully consider whether factoring is appropriate since it may cause our customers to question our financial stability.

Thanks!

Management Accountant assistant
Marici Power

Section 3

The Report of CVP Analysis and Sensitivity Analysis

CVP/Sensitivity Analysis

Using the figures that you have calculated for our range of solar panels, we can calculate the break-even point and the margin of safety, if we assume that the sales mix is constant.

To do this we need firstly to calculate the contribution to sales ratio for each of the products by dividing the contribution per unit by the selling price. We can then calculate the weighted average contribution to sales ratio by weighting the contribution to sales ratio by the percentage sales revenue mix. We can then divide the fixed costs by the weighted average contribution to sales ratio which will give us the break-even sales volume in F$.

If we compare this figure to our budgeted sales we can calculate the margin of safety. This tells us by how much sales can fall before we make a loss. We can also express the margin of safety as a percentage by dividing the budgeted sales minus the breakeven sales by the budgeted sales.

We can also calculate the sales revenue required to make a required profit target by adding the required profit target to the fixed costs and dividing by the weighted average contribution to sales ratio.

We can also apply sensitivity analysis by changing the variables in the CVP model. We could change each of the variables, selling price per unit, variable cost per unit, sales mix ratios to assess the impact on profit and breakeven point.

Benefits/Limitations of the Analysis

The major benefit of CVP analysis is that it indicates the lowest amount of activity necessary before we make losses. It promotes decision making as it explains the relationship between cost, volume and profit. It can be extended using "what-if" or sensitivity analysis to explain how changes in the relationship between fixed and variable costs or in revenues will affect profit levels and break-even.

However, the analysis is fairly limited as we have assumed a constant sales mix which may not actually occur. It is also based on our assumptions about the behaviour of revenue, costs and volume. Other factors, beside volume will affect profits, including changes in selling price, unit costs of inputs and efficiency. We have assumed that all costs can be divided into fixed and variable elements and that fixed costs remain constant over the relevant range of the CVP analysis. We have also assumed that variable costs are directly proportional to volume over the relevant range.

Cash Flow Deficit

There are a number of steps that we could take to avoid the short-term cash deficit arising.

(1) Approaching the bank to arrange additional short-term borrowings. This may be relatively straight forward as we have a good track record with the bank and they already hold security for the existing overdraft.

(2) If we currently hold any short-term investments we could sell these, although we would need to consider any penalties that may be imposed as a result of early withdrawal or sale.

(3) The main reason for the deficit is the purchase of the new machinery in January. Are we already committed to this purchase or can it be delayed until a later date? We need to be careful however that a deferral does not compromise our other plans. It may be possible to arrange a loan or lease finance for the purchase.

(4) Is it necessary to make the dividend payment in February? Delaying the payment of the dividend until March would deal with the majority of the deficit in February leaving only the January deficit, which is significantly lower, to be dealt with.

(5) Postponing non-essential capital or revenue expenditure such as the additional advertising spend in February. We should be careful however as whilst advertising expenditure tends to be classified as discretionary expenditure, a reduction or delay in the expenditure may result in reduced turnover at a later date. The same point could also be made about the R&D expenditure.

(6) Is it possible to bring forward the planned disposal of non – current assets? If the asset is not required we could sell the asset sooner or perhaps arrange with the purchaser to pay a deposit.

Section 4

Supplier Quality Issues Notes

Managing Supplier Relationships

We could in future use a relationship approach to managing our suppliers. Relationships could be formed to ensure our suppliers are performing well, in particular to ensure the quality of supply.

If we actively manage our relationship with suppliers we may be able to positively influence the price paid and negotiate discounts for swift payment, loyalty or bulk orders. However rather than emphasize price, we should build relationships with suppliers in order to jointly manage the entire supply chain better so that mutual benefits can accrue. Strong relationships are also needed with our suppliers, in order to ensure a continuity of supply and goodwill. We should attempt to actively manage the relationship with our suppliers because we may need the supplier's cooperation when there are "rush" orders or changes in purchasing requirements at short notice.

Relationships such as this are built on trust between the two parties but this is normally supported by a formal contractual agreement. A service level agreement would include details of expectations from each of the parties. In particular, we would want it to cover areas such as expected quality standard and delivery lead times. We would also need to give commitments to the suppliers in respect of minimum annual volumes and payment terms.

Finally, we would need to specify the penalties that would be imposed for default by either party. Drawing up the agreement would involve input from our department and both Volker's and Samuel's departments. With such an agreement, both parties can plan for the long-term with confidence in future business and the way that business will be conducted.

In the longer term, we could introduce a TQM approach and work with our suppliers to ensure that they do the same. This is especially important if we want to operate just in time approaches. TQM would give us a competitive edge in our dealings with suppliers and the drive towards continuous improvement would give us a more motivated and committed staffs which can only lead to an improvement in supplier relations.

Other initiatives that could be considered include inspection of goods delivered and regular feedback to suppliers, selection of suppliers with a similar ethos to ours, involvement of suppliers in new product design and arranging regular visits to suppliers.

Actively managing our relationship with suppliers may allow us to gain a relative competitive advantage over rival firms which do not currently practice relational procurement and operations.

Quality Cost Reporting and Benefits

Quality cost reporting would provide an important addition to our current management accounting information.

A cost of quality report would have directed our attention to the rise in quality costs as a result of the failure with the quality standards from the new supplier. The proposed quality report below shows the type of costs that we would include. Conformance costs are concerned with the costs of achieving quality standards, whilst non-conformance costs are concerned with the consequences of failing to achieve these standards. Conformance costs are further divided into prevention costs (costs incurred to ensure that things do not go wrong) and appraisal costs (costs incurred to check for quality problems before they lead to failures). Non-conformance costs are also further divided into internal failure costs (where there has been a quality failure that has been detected and dealt with before the product has been delivered to the customers) and external failure costs (where the failure occurs after the goods have been delivered to the customers). The quality problems with Solar Systems would have arisen in the form of non-conformance costs as there was a quality failure. Quality cost reporting would have enabled us to take remedial action at an earlier stage.

The quality failure may have been avoided had we spent more on both prevention costs, for example, the initial evaluating of Solar System as a supplier and /or appraisal costs, for example the inspection of the solar wafers when they were received in the warehouse. The conformance costs of quality whilst reducing profits can potentially avoid significant non-conformance costs at a later date.

If we use cost of quality reporting in the future, it will enable us to identify potential areas for improvement which will lead to effective quality programmes and eventually improve overall organizational performance. This is particular important for our organisation as our high quality standards are respected in the industry.

Cost of quality reporting will help to reduce operational costs thus enhancing our competitiveness through higher quality and lower costs.

The use of cost of quality data will also be helpful in the future evaluation of capital investment alternatives. It helps justify and steer investments in prevention activities, which lower quality costs. It also helps justify and steer other quality improvement efforts and investments. As it is the accounting department that is preparing the information, the quality data is likely to be more readily accepted.

The cost of quality system will also enable us to develop more advanced performance measures in the areas of customer satisfaction, production and design.

Examples of Quality Costs

I have given some examples below of quality costs that would be relevant to our business:

Cost of conformance	Appraisal costs	Costs of inspection of solar wafers when received into the warehouse—these costs would be expected to be higher for goods received from new suppliers and gradually reduce as confidence in quality standards are attained
		Costs of inspection of solar panels, to ensure the panels meet the required quality standards, before delivery to customers
	Prevention costs	Evaluation costs of a new supplier to ensure quality standards prior to supplier selection—this is an important stage in ensuring acceptable quality standards from a new supplier
		Costs of staff training in quality control procedures and processes to ensure our high quality standards are maintained
Cost of non-conformance	Internal failure costs	The costs of faulty panels which have failed to meet our quality control standard, cannot be reworked including both labour and material costs
		The labour costs and costs of replacement parts involved in reworking faulty panels that have failed to meet our quality control standard
	External failure costs	The costs of processing customer complaints from customers who have received faulty panels
		The labour, material and delivery costs of replacing panels which have proved to be faulty either before or after installation but after delivery to customers

试卷一　参考答案

任务一

太阳能晶片供应短缺和挑选新供应商

基于利润最大化的生产计划

太阳能晶片的短缺限制了公司太阳能电池的生产。由于生产每个太阳能电池所用的晶片数量相同，我们需要尽可能充分地利用太阳能电池。因为每种电池板产品都使用不同数量的太阳能电池，所以我们应该使太阳能电池的单位边际贡献最大化，而不是像Volker建议的那样，使太阳能电池板的单位毛利最大化。短期内总固定成本不会因产品生产组合的不同受到影响，因此像这种短期决策，重点关注太阳能电池的单位边际贡献是恰当的。

太阳能电池的单位边际贡献可以用太阳能电池板单位边际贡献除以每个电池板使用的电池数量来计算。然后，根据电池单位边际贡献的大小对电池板产品进行排序。电池单位边际贡献最高的产品排在第一位，第二高的产品排在第二位，依次类推。最后，我们将根据这个排序来确定电池板的生产计划。

这将为公司确定一个能够使短期利润最大化的生产计划。然而，太阳能晶片短缺的事实意味着公司将背离生产要求，继而至少有一种产品不能完全满足市场需求。我们需要考虑这种状况可能带来的长期影响。

（1）Andreas 认为“Solar Halo”未来将成为市场的领导者。在短期内限制“光环太阳能”的供应会对长期销售产生什么影响？如果公司不能满足“Solar Halo”的全部市场需求，可能会给某个竞争对手一个机会，侵占一些我们计划中的市场份额，这将影响到公司的长期回报。

（2）减少一种产品的供应将会对想要购买全部产品的客户产生什么影响？如果公司不能做到至少部分供应4种产品，客户是否会为了满足需求转而寻找替代供应商？如果不能满足客户需求，可能会损害公司在客户中的信誉。另一种可选择的方法是优先保障供应公司最重要的客户，然后再根据短期利润最大化的排序来使用剩余资源。

总而言之，我们不能仅仅追求短期利润最大化的目标，而应更长远地看待这一决策。

选择供应商需考虑的因素

选择未来供应商需要考虑的一个重要因素是价格，但是不应仅仅根据价格就决定使用哪个供应商。晶片市场供应短缺产生了对新供应商的新需求，我们还需要确保未来供应的连续性。因此，我们应考虑诸多与供应商有关的定性因素。

（1）供应商是否准备签订长期合同以确保供应的连续性？约定价格多久调整一次？

（2）供应商准备提供什么样的信用条件？

（3）供应商生产能力如何，以及进一步扩大产能的计划是什么？公司希望随着业务的增长，能够确保供应的连续性。

（4）供应商是否符合公司期望的质量标准？公司的质量标准对公司至关重要，因此供应商能够达到这些高标准是很重要的。

（5）供应商位于哪里？位于 Freeland 或附近国家的供应商可能能够更快地完成我们的订单。海外供应商存在由于天气或其他外界因素而延误的风险。

（6）供应商的可靠性如何？能否在需要的时间生产出所需的数量？供应延迟将会导致公司无法满足客户的需求，可能会有损于公司的信誉和未来业务。

（7）供应商的财务安全吗？如果供应商遭遇财务危机无法正常生产，将导致公司无法满足客户的需求，除非能够找到新的供应商。我们需要查看潜在供应商的财务绩效和追踪记录是否可靠。此外，还应该考虑供应商的管理情况是否良好。

（8）供应商的企业文化是什么？在环境问题和可持续发展方面，供应商是否与我们公司具有相同的企业精神？我们还应该考虑供应商在企业和社会责任方面的声誉。

任务二

发件人：管理会计助理

收件人：高级财务会计师 Nicole Reckitt

主题：缩短营运资金周期

营运资金周期

营运资金周期等于存货周转天数加上应收账款周转天数减去应付账款周转天数。营运资金周期越长，资金被占用的时间就越长，并且这期间不能获得收益。然而，企业需要充足的营运资金才能维持生存，因此需要管理营运资金来平衡这两方面的要求。

缩短营运资金周期

公司可以采取以下的方法来缩短营运资金周期。

存货

公司目前的库存水平高达 F$2 100 万，细分为原材料、在产品和产成品库存，其分别是多少呢？

我们可以通过检查滞留库存、再订货水平和再订货数量来减少原材料库存。从长远来看，也可以考虑使用适时制采购。良好的供应商关系也有助于确保在适当的时间收到正确数量的存货，并缩短订货和交货之间的交付周期。

然而必须记住，降低库存水平有可能导致失去批量采购可获得的折扣，也可能因价格上升而带来额外的成本。此外还存在缺货风险，可能会导致生产延误和不能按时向客户交货。

公司还可以审查生产技术和效率水平，以减少在产品。

公司主要生产 4 种标准化产品，有必要持有大量的产品库存吗？公司可以通过重新规划生产安排和配送方法来减少产成品库存。从长远来看，也可以考虑引入适时制生产，但是必须确保任何改变都不会影响到公司满足客户需求的能力和导致销售额降低。

应付账款

公司可以通过延迟付款来获得更多供应商的资金。有些人认为这是不道德的，并且可能导致信用期被取消或未来的供应中断。财务总监考虑到不能危害公司和供应商的关系，所以应该通过与供应商的协商来达到这一目的。然而，公司会因为这项政策而丧失提早结算可能获得的现金折扣，或者产生额外的费用。

应收账款

我们的客户是否都按照商定的信用条件付款，有证据表明存在延迟付款吗？公司可以缩短给予客户的信用期，尽管这可能会导致销售额的损失。公司还可以更快地向客户开具发票并跟踪未付款项，而不损害客户关系。公司也可以为客户提供提早支付的现金折扣，尽管这需要评估客户少付的现金是否超过了公司更快收到现金带来的利益。

另一个选择是保理我们的债权或使用发票贴现。这将产生即时的现金流，但也会带来利息费用和其他费用。公司需要确定与所获得的利益相比，这些成本是否合理，还需要仔细考虑保理是否合适，因为这可能会导致我们的客户质疑公司的财务稳定性。

十分感谢！

摩利兹能源公司

管理会计助理

任务三

本量利分析及现金赤字问题的报告

本量利（CVP）分析/敏感性分析

如果假定销售组合不变，利用您计算的太阳能电池板系列的数据，我们就可以计算盈亏平衡点和安全边际。

为此，首先需要用单位产品边际贡献除以销售价格来计算每种产品的边际贡献率。然后，用销售收入占比为权数来计算加权平均的边际贡献率。接下来将固定成本除以加权平均边际贡献率得到以F$为单位的盈亏平衡点的销售额。

如果我们将这个数字与预算销售额进行比较，就可以计算出安全边际。这个指标告诉我们，销售额下降多少将会导致亏损。我们也可以通过百分比的方式来表示安全边际，安全边际率等于预算销售额减去盈亏平衡点的销售额再除以预算销售额。

如果将要求获得的目标利润加上固定成本，再除以加权平均边际贡献率，就能计算出要实现目标利润所需的销售额。

通过更改本量利分析模型中的变量，还可以进行敏感性分析。我们更改每个变量，如单位销售价格，单位变动成本，销售组合比率，以评估其对利润和盈亏平衡点的影响。

本量利分析和敏感性分析的优点/局限性

本量利分析的主要优点在于它指出了为避免亏损所需的最低业务量。它解释了成本、业务量和利润之间的关系，有助于决策。若使用“如果怎么样，将会怎么样”或敏感性分析的方法扩展这个模型，就可以解释固定成本和变动成本之间的变化或收入的变化，将如何影响到利润水平和盈亏平衡点。

然而，本量利分析的作用是相当有限的，因为它基于一个可能不会实际发生的恒定的销售组合比例假设，同时也基于对收入、成本和业务量性态的假设。除了业务量影响利润，其他因素包括销售价格、投入的单位成本和效率的变动也会影响利润。在本量利分析中，我们假定所有成本都可以分为固定的部分和变动的部分，并且假定固定成本在相关范围内保持不变，变动成本在相关范围内与业务量成正比。

现金赤字

我们可以采取一些措施来避免出现短期现金赤字。

（1）与银行协商安排额外的短期借款。这可能是相对直接的，因为公司在银行有良好的记录，银行已经拥有现有透支额的担保。

（2）如果公司目前持有任何短期投资，可以出售这些资产，尽管需要考虑提前撤出或出售可能遭受的任何处罚。

（3）造成赤字的主要原因是1月要购置新机械。公司是否一定要购置，或者可以推迟到以后？我们需要小心的是推迟购置是否会损害公司的其他计划。还有一种可能是为该项购置安排贷款或采用融资租赁的方式。

（4）是否有必要在2月支付股利？将股利延期到3月支付就能解决2月的大部分赤字，只剩下1月的赤字，这样需要解决的赤字明显降低很多。

（5）推迟非必要的资本性或收益性支出，如2月额外的广告支出。但是我们也要小心，广告支出往往被归类为酌量性费用，减少或延迟该项支出有可能导致以后的销售下降。对研发支出的考虑也是同样的。

（6）是否有可能提前实施非流动资产的处置计划？如果该项资产是不需要的，就可以尽快出售，或者可能要求购买方先支付定金。

任务四

供应商质量问题的工作笔记

管理供应商关系

我们以后可以采用一种关系方法来管理我们的供应商。关系的建立是为了确保我们的供应商表现良好，特别是确保供应的质量。

如果我们能积极地管理好与供应商的关系，就能够对所支付的价格产生有利影响，也有助于获得快速付款的折扣及忠诚度或批量订单的折扣。然而我们与供应商建立良好关系的目的是为了更好地共同管理整个供应链，从而实现互惠互利，而不应只强调价格。与供应商建立牢固的关系，也是为了确保供应和信誉的连续性。我们应该尝试积极管理与供应商的关系，因为在短时间内有“紧急”订单或采购需求变化时，都需要供应商的配合。

这样的关系建立在双方相互信任的基础上，但通常还需要一份正式的合同协议来保障。服务水平协议包含双方期望的细节，特别是我们希望它能够涵盖预期的质量标准和交货时间等方面。我们还需要就最低年度采购数量和付款条件对供应商做出承诺。最后，还需要规定双方违约的处罚。制定这项协议将涉及我们部门以及 Volker 和 Samuel 的部门。有了这样一个协议，双方才能有信心对未来业务和企业的发展方式进行长期规划。

从长远来看，我们公司可以引入全面质量管理方法，并与供应商合作，确保他们也采用同样的方法。如果公司想要采用适时制生产方式，这一点尤其重要。与供应商的交易中，全面质量管理方法将赋予我们竞争优势，持续改进的动力能使我们更好地激励和约束员工，而这只会带来与供应商关系的改善。

其他可以考虑的措施包括检验到货质量，向供应商定期反馈情况，选择与我们公司具有相似企业精神的供应商，让供应商参与新产品设计，定期访问供应商等。

在与那些当前还没有实行关系采购和经营的对手公司的竞争中，积极管理与供应商的关系可以让我们获得相对的竞争优势。

质量成本报告及其好处

质量成本报告将为公司目前的管理会计信息提供重要的补充。

质量成本报告将引导公司关注那些因新供应商达不到质量标准而导致的质量成本上升。下面给出的质量成本报告显示了应包括的成本类型。符合成本指为实现质量标准而耗费的成本，而不符合成本则与未能达到质量标准而引起的后果有关。符合成本进一步分为预防成本（确保事情不会出错的成本）和评估成本（在导致故障之前检查质量问题所产生的成本）。不符合成本也被进一步分为内部失败成本（在产品交付给客户之前发现和处理的质量问题）和外部失败成本（货物交付给客户后出现问题）。太阳能系统公司的质量问题会造成不符合成本，因为存在质量问题。质量成本报告将使我们能够在早期阶段采取补救行动。

如果公司花费更多的预防成本（例如对太阳能系统公司作为供应商进行初步评估）和/或评估成本（例如在太阳能晶片入库的时候进行检验），质量故障就有可能避免。符合成本的增加会降低利润，但这可能会在以后避免重大的不符合成本的产生。

今后如果我们使用质量成本报告，就能使我们确定潜在的改进领域，进而实施有效的质量改进计划，并最终提高公司的整体绩效。这对我们公司尤为重要，因为公司一向以高质量标准在行业中备受尊重。

质量成本报告将有助于降低运营成本，从而通过更高的质量和更低的成本提高我们的竞争力。

未来对质量成本数据的应用也将有助于投资项目选择的评估。它有助于评判和引导对预防活动的投资，从而降低质量成本，它也有助于评判和指导其他质量改进工作和投资。由会计部门来准备质量成本数据，这些数据可能会更容易被接受。

质量成本体系还将使公司能够在客户满意度、生产和设计方面发展更为先进的绩效指标。

一些关于质量成本的例子

以下给出了一些与我们公司业务相关的质量成本的例子：

<table>
<tr><td rowspan="2">符合成本</td><td>评估成本</td><td>太阳能晶片入库时的检验成本——对于来自新供应商的货物，这些成本预计会更高，而随着对货物达到质量标准的信心增加而逐渐减少
太阳能电池板的检测成本，确保在交付给客户之前，电池板达到了所要求的质量标准</td></tr>
<tr><td>预防成本</td><td>在选择供应商之前，为确保质量标准而对新供应商进行评估的成本——这是确保新供应商能够达到可接受的质量标准的重要步骤
对员工进行质量控制程序和流程培训的成本，以确保能够维持公司的高质量标准</td></tr>
<tr><td rowspan="2">不符合成本</td><td>内部失败成本</td><td>不符合质量控制标准且不能返工的、有缺陷的电池板的成本，包括人工和材料成本
不符合质量控制标准的、有缺陷的电池板返工所耗费的更换零部件成本和人工成本</td></tr>
<tr><td>外部失败成本</td><td>处理买到有缺陷的电池板的客户投诉的成本
交付给客户后，在安装之前或之后，更换被证明是有缺陷的电池板的人工、材料和运输成本</td></tr>
</table>

Variant 1　Marking Guidance

Section	Technical skills		Business skills		People skills		Leadership skills		Integration	Total
1	Short term decision making where there is a constraint to production	7	Other factors to consider in respect of a production decision Factors to consider when selecting suppliers	6 4	Factors to consider when selecting suppliers	6	Factors to consider when selecting suppliers	3		26
2	Reducing working capital cycle and its impact	18								18
3	CVP analysis The benefits and limitations of CVP analysis Improving a cash deficit	10 9 7								26
4	Benefits of quality cost reporting Examples of quality costs	3 9	Management of supplier relationships Benefits of quality cost reporting	3 3	Management of supplier relationships Benefits of quality cost reporting	4 3	Management of supplier relationships	2	3	30
Total marks available for each compertency		63		16		13		5	3	100

试卷一　评分指南

部分	技术技能		商业技能		人际技能		领导技能		综合	总计
1	当生产受到约束时的短期决策	7	生产决策需要考虑的其他因素 选择供应商需要考虑的因素	6 4	选择供应商需要考虑的因素	6	选择供应商需要考虑的因素	3		26
2	缩短营运资金周期及其影响	18								18
3	本量利分析 本量利分析的优点和局限性 改善现金赤字	10 9 7								26
4	质量成本报告的好处 质量成本举例	3 9	供应商关系管理 质量成本报告的好处	3 3	供应商关系管理 质量成本报告的好处	4 3	供应商关系管理	2	3	30
各种能力分数总计		63		16		13		5	3	100

江西财经大学名师解惑

试卷一共有四项任务，考查了 P1、F1、E1 三门课程的知识点，具体包括短期决策分析、营运资金管理、本量利分析、现金管理、质量成本和供应商关系管理等。该试卷考核了考生的四项能力，其中技术技能的分值占63%，商业技能的分值占16%，人际技能的分值占13%，领导技能的分值占5%，与 CGMA 管理会计能力框架的技能要求一致。

该试卷的每项任务涉及以下知识点：

任务	问题	科目	知识点
任务一	当生产受到约束时的短期决策及需要考虑的其他因素	P1	限制因素分析（limiting factors analysis）
	选择供应商需要考虑的因素	P1	短期决策（short-term decision making）
任务二	缩短营运资金周期及其影响	F1	营运资金周期（working capital cycle）
任务三	本量利分析和敏感性分析的运用及其优点和局限性	P1	本量利分析和敏感性分析（CVP analysis and sensitivity analysis）
	改善现金赤字	F1	现金管理（cash management）
任务四	质量成本报告的好处和质量成本举例	E1	质量成本（quality cost）
	供应商关系管理	E1	供应商关系管理（management of supplier relationship）

上述各项任务要求以邮件、报告或工作笔记等形式来呈现答案，对问题的描述非常明确，答题时既要注意内容的针对性，也要注意形式的规范性。

其他答题注意事项包括：（1）仔细读题，一般每项任务都会涉及2～3个大的知识点，一定不能漏答；（2）答题要有条理，从是什么到为什么，从分析原因到提出解决办法，将每个知识点都解释清楚；（3）分层级列出各级小标题，让考官容易了解你的思路。

对应知识点的深度剖析

限制因素分析

在公司存在限制因素时，应如何最大化短期利润。常规思路是：（1）判断限制性因素；（2）计算每种产品单位限制因素边际贡献；（3）根据单位限制因素边际贡献对产品排序；（4）决定生产计划。

考生需要理解、应用并且表达出整个限制因素分析的过程。

结合题中所给信息，每个太阳能电池板都使用不同数量的太阳能电池，但每个电池使用的晶片数量相同。所以我们应该最大化每个太阳能电池的边际贡献，而不是生产总监 Volker 建议的每个电池板的毛利。然后根据单位太阳能电池的边际贡献大小来排序，再做出生产决策。

在公司存在限制因素时，结合题中商务总监 Andreas 的建议，考虑其对长期发展产生的影响。整体回答需基于对限制因素的假设上，而不是宽泛讨论。

考生注意事项

限制因素分析计算

第一步：判断限制因素（limiting factor/bottle neck），基于是否可以满足销售需求。

第二步：计算每种产品的单位限制因素边际贡献（contribution per bottle neck）。

第三步：按每种产品的单位限制因素边际贡献排序，确定不同产品的生产顺序。

第四步：确定最优生产计划，按不同产品的生产顺序，依次满足其销售需求，直至用尽限制因素。

短期决策

为了保障未来晶片供应的持续性，选择供应商需要考虑哪些因素呢？这是实际商业环境中经常遇到的决策问题，考核了考生综合解决问题的能力。一般在选择供应商时，都需要考虑其质量、财务状况、生产能力、经营规模、价格等要素，再基于每个点结合公司现状进行拓展叙述。

营运资金周期

营运资金周期 = 存货周转天数 + 应收账款周转天数 - 应付账款周转天数。

营运资金周期越长，资金被占用的时间就越长，对公司的发展显然是不利的。缩短该周期需降低存货周转天数（即降低存货水平），降低应收账款周转天数（即尽快收回客户的应收账款），增加应付账款周转天数（即递延应付账款支付）。

考生需会计算各项周转天数，并且理解其背后的意义。

考生注意事项

存货周转天数 =365 天/存货周转次数 =365 天/销售成本 × 平均存货金额。

存货周转天数这个数值越低越好，越低说明公司存货周转速度越快，反映了良好的销售状况。

应收账款周转天数 =365 天/应收账款周转次数 =365 天/销售收入 × 平均应收账款。

应收账款周转天数越少，说明应收账款变现的速度越快，资金被客户占用的时间越短，管理工作的效率越高。

应付账款周转天数 =365 天/应付账款周转次数 =365 天/销售收入 × 平均应付账款。

通常应付账款周转天数越长越好，说明公司可以更多地占用供应商货款来补充营运资金，而无需向银行短期借款。

本量利分析和敏感性分析

本量利分析法包含计算盈亏平衡点、安全边际、实现目标利润所需要的销售额、边际贡献率等。敏感性分析是分析更改某个变量时，对利润和盈亏平衡点的影响。

本量利分析和敏感性分析的优点在于提供决策建议，但是局限性也是明显的，因其整个模型建立在很多个假设基础上，而这些假设基础在现实商业环境中很难百分之百实现。

考生需会计算和陈述这两种分析方式。

考生注意事项

本量利分析法：

盈亏平衡点销售量（实物单位）=固定成本/单位边际贡献；

盈亏平衡点销售额（金额单位）=固定成本/边际贡献率；

安全边际量（额）=现有或预计销售量（额）－盈亏临界点销售量（额）；

实现目标利润所需要的销售量 =（固定成本 + 目标利润）/单位边际贡献；

实现目标利润所需要的销售额 =（固定成本 + 目标利润）/边际贡献率。

敏感性分析是研究制约利润的有关因素在特定条件下发生变化时，对利润所产生的影响程度的一种分析方法。单因素敏感性分析，指每次只变动一个因素而其他因素保持不变时所做的分析。如果某个因素的小幅度变化能够导致利润的较大变化，则称此因素为敏感性因素，反之则称其为非敏感性因素。

现金管理

避免现金赤字，即增加现金流入，降低现金流出。在本案例的现金预算中，有明显的月度特殊事项（处置非流动资产、增加营销费用、购置固定资产、支付股利），并且对于整体月度现金流产生了较大的影响。在现金流不够充沛时，是否建议公司实施这些事项需谨慎考虑。同时也可以提出其他可以解决现金赤字的方式。

质量成本

质量成本包括符合成本和不符合成本。符合成本是实现特定质量要求的成本，又分成评估成本和预防成本。不符合成本是未达到质量标准所产生的成本，又分成内部失败成本和外部失败成本。

质量成本报告是指根据质量成本分析形成的报告，主要是为了制定质量方针目标、评价质量体系的有效性和寻求质量改进的依据。它也是对质量成本管理活动或某一典型事件进行调查、分析和建议的总结性文件，并可常规性地放进月度的管理会计报告中。在本案例中该公司面临明显的质量问题，使用质量成本报告可以有助于公司加强质量管理，提高竞争力。

供应商关系管理

供应商关系管理要基于质量、价格、交货时间、数量、付款和违约等要素综合考虑，并达成以相互信任为基础的服务水平协议。从战略层面，全面质量管理法、适时制生产都是建立在供应商关系管理基础上的整合性管理方式。

考生需要对供应商关系管理给出具体建议，并且结合案例中的特定情况和要素。

Variant 2

This examination is structured as follows：

Section number	Number of tasks	Time for section(minutes)
1	1	55
2	1	50
3	1	35
4	1	40

The time available for each section is for reading,planning and writing your answer(s).

Section 1

As you log in to your computer this morning a message pops up on the company intranet. It is to all staff from Martin Lerwick, chief executive officer of Wala Solar.

> **Wala Solar and Marici Power – Creating"TrueValue"Together**
>
> When Marici Power joined the Wala Solar group a few months ago, I outlined my vision for the group. Part of that vision was to create a group that provide "TrueValue" for our customers.
>
> After consultation with various stakeholders, the group directors have decided to develop a corporate branding strategy under the umbrella of"TrueValue"."TrueValue" reflects the Wala Solar group's ethos and beliefs and will enable us to further differentiate ourselves from the competition. Every employee will be involved in delivering the"TrueValue" message to our customers.
>
> Our intention has always been to share the knowledge and expertise of both companies and so far that process has been progressing well. It is now time to move to phase 2 of the integration. Over the next 12 months further policies and procedures will be integrated across the group. Working parties, with contributors from all areas, will be set up to develop our plans and implement the changes. I appreciate that any change can be just as difficult as it can be exciting and would urge you to get involved in the working parties wherever you can, so that you can be apart of the change.
>
> Together we can create"TrueValue" for our customers!
>
> Regards.
>
> Martin Lerwick
> CEO
> Wala Solar Group

You receive the following email from, Maria Coleman, finance director.

From: Maria Coleman, Finance Director

To: Management Accountant Assistant

Subject: Corporate branding strategy

As you were aware from Martin Lerwick's communication, we are developing a corporate branding strategy so that we have one combined, cohesive strategy for our brands. This is obviously very important for the future success of the group and I would like to better understand how effective brand management, under the umbrella of TrueValue, will benefit us in both financial and non-financial terms.

One of the initiatives to achieve the strategy will be to utilise digital marketing to deliver the TrueValue message to our distributors and installers. I would therefore like to consider how Marici Power could use digital marketing and the potential benefits of its use.

On another matter, Nicole Reckitt has gone on honeymoon for four weeks and the management accounting team are helping to cover her responsibilities while she is away. Wala Solar's finance director has asked for our help in accounting for the separately identifiable Marici Power brands that were purchased as a part of the acquisition. In particular, they are trying to establish the useful life of the brands as required by IAS 38 Intangible Assets. I know that you are interested in this area so I would appreciate your assistance.

Please draft a report covering the following areas.

- The financial and non-financial benefits to our company of effective brand management.
- The ways in which we could use digital marketing to deliver the TrueValue message to our distributors and installers and the other potential benefits of its use.
- How the useful life of the Marici brands would be established, in accordance with IAS 38 Intangible Assets.

Regards.

Maria Coleman
Finance Director
Marici Power

Write the report for Maria Coleman, finance director.

Section 2

A few days later, you receive the following email from Alex Hilliard, senior management accountant.

From: Alex Hilliard, Senior Management Accountant
To: Management Accountant Assistant
Subject: Budgeting

As a part of the ongoing integration of policies and procedures throughout the Wala Solar group, a working party has been reviewing the budgeting approaches at both Marici Power and Wala Solar. At Marici Power, we have always used an incremental budgeting approach but Wala Solar uses a ZBB approach for discretionary costs.

I have been asked to give a presentation at the next meeting of the working party on the potential use of ZBB in Marici Power. I thought it would be interesting to use the finance department as an example of where ZBB could be applied. I have had a number of discussions with Maria about our department's specific objectives and how we could potentially achieve these objectives. I have provided more details in the attachment to this email.

Another a part of the working group's remit is to look at how effectively we use budgets for performance evaluation, with a view to incorporating best practice across the Wala Solar group.

In the past, the budget for our sales team has been set at the start of each year and this has provided the basis for performance evaluation throughout the year. However, with the current changes to our branding strategy and the uncertainty surrounding the introduction of new products, we can see a potential conflict between the targets we have set in the budget and their use for performance evaluation.

Please provide briefing notes for me covering the following areas.

(1) How the details of the activities given in the attachment would be used to set the finance department's budget if a ZBB approach was taken. Please also include details of the other information that would be needed to enable the budget to be produced and subsequently evaluated by the budget committee.

(2) How the different purposes of budgeting, particularly in our uncertain environment, conflict with using the budget for performance evaluation and how this conflict could be minimised.

Many thanks!

Alex Hilliard
Senior Management Accountant
Marici Power

Accessory

Finance Department—Possible Activities

The finance department has three possible activities. Activity 1 would be considered the base package. Activity 2 and 3 are additional incremental options that could be added to the base package. Activities 2 and 3 are not dependent on each other.

- Activity 1 (Annual cost F$460,000) includes the implementation of statutory accounting requirements, providing all financial accounting services, producing annual budget information and basic management accounting information.
- Activity 2 (Annual cost F$160,000) would provide for an internal audit function that will improve the quality of control operations and reduce external audit fees.
- Activity 3 (Annual cost F$200,000) would provide for additional management accounting staffs to improve the current management accounting information and to assist in the implementation of a TQM programme.

Write the briefing notes for Alex Hilliard, senior management accountant.

Section 3

You receive the following email from Maria Coleman, finance director.

From: Maria Coleman, Finance Director
To: Management Accountant Assistant
Subject: Maintenance costs and employee engagement

As you know, Alex has been representing this department on the working party that has been reviewing our budgeting systems. The working party has been considering whether an ABB approach could be used to budget our indirect labour costs. Alex has gone on annual leave and I will be attending the next meeting of the working party.

The 2017 budget for the maintenance department includes funding for two additional members of staff to cope with the planned growth in production. The budget was prepared using an incremental budgeting approach. Alex was planning to use the maintenance department as an example of how we could apply ABB. Before he went on leave he prepared a schedule(attached) of the different activities carried out by maintenance staffs and the cost drivers for these activities. We were keen to see whether the two additional staff would be justified using an ABB approach.

On a separate issue, I am concerned that the extent of the changes over the last few months may have adversely affected staff's motivation and morale. I have discussed this with the Human Resources Manager, who reports to Christian Thoele. We are keen to develop an incentive scheme to encourage employee engagement with the new group. In my experience an incentive scheme linked to an individual's annual appraisal is the most effective. However, in light of the recent changes to our organisation and the need for integration, I would also like to consider an incentive scheme based on the achievement of the overall Wala Solar group's objectives.

Please draft a report for me covering the following areas.

- How we could use the activity information to produce the labour cost budget for the maintenance department, including details of the other information that we would need to make sure that the budget is as realistic as possible.
- The factors we would need to take into account when decide whether Marici Power should use an individual or a group based incentive scheme, including details of the type of and the reasons for the scheme you would recommend.

Regards.

Maria Coleman

Finance Director

Marici Power

Activities and Cost Drivers

Activity	Description of activity	Cost driver
Machine service	Servicing the machinery to keep it in good working order including lubrication, checking for wear and tear on moving parts and stripping down parts of the machong for full cleaning	Carrying out a service
Repairs	If a machine is not operating at full efficiency, or breaks down, the maintenance staff will repair the machine. Each problem with a machine is classed as a "fault"—a broken down machine may have more than one fault	Rectifying a fault
Ordering of parts	When repairs are required and new parts are needed, maintenance staff raise a purchase requisition. The purchasing department will then order the parts from external suppliers	Raising a purchase requisition
Cleaning	The machinery is cleaned down by maintenance staff at the end of each production run to keep the machines free from dust and dirt	Cleaning a machine

Write the report for Maria Coleman, finance director.

Section 4

A week later you receive the following email from Alex Hilliard, senior management accountant.

From: Alex Hilliard, Senior Management Accountant
To: Management Accountant Assistant
Subject: Impact of proposed policy changes

As you are well aware, there have been a number of changes to our policies and procedures over the past few months as a result of the integration of Marici Power into the Wala Solar group. There are a couple of proposed changes that will affect our cost accounting and performance management systems so that I need to look at in more detail.

The group's finance director has requested that we change our depreciation policy to bring it in line with the group policy. In the past, we have depreciated our production machinery using straight line depreciation over periods of up to 10 years but the rest of the Wala Solar group uses a maximum useful life of 8 years.

As Nicole is still on honeymoon, Maria has asked me to explain the financial reporting requirements when an accounting policy changes and the potential impact of the change on our reported profit from operations for 2016.

The Board of Directors is also considering the introduction of a JIT purchasing and production system in order to improve our inventory management. Whilst I understand the principles of JIT, I would like to consider in more detail how we could measure the effectiveness of the JIT systems.

I would be grateful if you could assist, by sending me a report covering the following areas.

- The financial reporting requirements when an accounting policy changes and the impact of the change on our reported profit from operations for 2016.
- Four suggested performance measures that Marici Power could use to measure the effectiveness of JIT purchasing and production, explaining why these performance measures would be appropriate.

Many thanks!

Alex Hilliard
Senior Management Accountant
Marici Power

Write the report for Alex Hilliard, senior management accountant.

试卷二

本次考试的结构如下：

序号	任务数	时间（分钟）
1	1	55
2	1	50
3	1	35
4	1	40

每个部分规定的时间可用于读题、组织和书写答案。

任务一

当你早上登录电脑时，一条信息突然在公司内网上弹出，这条信息是由瓦拉太阳能（Wala Solar）集团的总裁 Martin Lerwick（马丁·勒威克）发给全体员工的。

瓦拉太阳能集团和摩利兹能源公司共同创造“TrueValue（真实价值）”

当几个月前摩利兹能源公司加入瓦拉太阳能集团的时候，我就勾画好集团愿景的轮廓了，其中包括建立一个能够为我们的客户提供“TrueValue”的集团。
在咨询了不同的利益相关方之后，集团董事们决定在“TrueValue”商标下发展公司品牌战略。“TrueValue”反映了瓦拉太阳能集团的精神和信仰，使我们能够进一步与竞争对手区分开来。每位员工都将参与向我们的客户传递“TrueValue”信息这一行动。

一直以来我们的目标都是在这两家公司之间分享知识和专业技能，到目前为止，这个过程进展良好，现在是时候进行第二阶段的整合了。未来的12个月里，更多的政策和程序会在整个集团里被整合起来。来自各个领域的成员将会组成工作小组，去发展我们的计划以及进行改变。我明白任何改变都既是困难的也是令人兴奋的，无论你身在何方，改变都会推动你加入工作小组，因此你可以成为改变的一分子。

让我们一起来为我们的顾客创造“TrueValue”吧！

致好！

瓦拉太阳能集团
总裁
Martin Lerwick

你收到了来自财务总监 Maria Colemen 的邮件。

发件人：财务总监 Maria Coleman
收件人：管理会计助理
主题：企业品牌战略

正如你从 Martin Lerwick 先生的来函中了解到的，我们正在制定一个公司品牌战略，以便使我们的各种品牌有一个紧密结合的战略。显然这对于集团未来的成功非常重要，我想更好地了解在 TrueValue 商标之下，有效的品牌管理在财务和非财务两方面怎样使我们获益。

实现该战略的举措之一将是利用数字营销向我们的分销商和安装商传递 TrueValue 商标的信息。因此，我想了解摩利兹能源公司如何使用数字营销以及这么做的潜在好处。

还有一件事，Nicole Reckitt 已经去度蜜月了（4 周），在她离开的这段时间里，管理会计团队正在替她分担职责。瓦拉太阳能集团的财务总监要我们帮忙说明可单独辨认的摩利兹能源公司品牌的情况，这些是作为收购的一部分被买入的，特别是他们想要根据国际会计准则第 38 号无形资产准则的要求，确定这些品牌的预计使用寿命。我知道你对这方面感兴趣，所以我很感谢你的帮助。

请起草一份包括以下几方面内容的报告。

- 进行有效的品牌管理在财务方面与非财务方面给公司带来的收益。
- 如何利用数字营销向我们的分销商和安装商传递 TrueValue 理念，以及数字营销带来的其他潜在好处。
- 根据国际会计准则第 38 号无形资产准则，摩利兹品牌的预计使用寿命将如何确定。

致好！

摩利兹能源公司
财务总监
Maria Coleman

请为财务总监 Maria Coleman 写一份报告。

任务二

几天后，你收到了以下来自高级管理会计师 Alex Hilliard 的电子邮件。

发件人：高级管理会计师 Alex Hilliard
收件人：管理会计师助理
主题：预算

作为整个瓦拉太阳能集团持续进行的政策和程序整合的一部分，工作小组一直在审查摩利兹能源公司和瓦拉太阳能集团的预算方法。在摩利兹能源公司，我们一直使用增量预算法，但瓦拉太阳能集团对于酌量性成本使用零基预算。

我需要在下一次的工作小组会议上介绍零基预算法在摩利兹能源公司的可能用途。我想以财务部门作为零基预算应用的例子应该会很有趣。我已经和 Maria 多次讨论过财务部门的具体目标，以及如何才能实现这些目标。我会在这封邮件的附件中提供更多的详细信息。

工作小组的另一项职责是审查我们如何有效地利用预算进行绩效评价，以期在瓦拉太阳能集团中整合最佳实践。

过去，销售团队的预算在每年年初就已经被制定好，这为全年的绩效评价提供了基础。然而，随着目前公司品牌战略的变化以及引进的新产品的不确定性，我们可以看出预算中设定的目标与其应用于绩效评价之间存在潜在冲突。

请为我提供一份简要说明，包括以下几个方面：

(1) 如果采用零基预算方法，附件中给出的活动细节将如何用于制定财务部门的预算，还请列出预算委员会编制预算并进行后续评估所需的其他资料的细节；

(2) 预算编制的不同目的，特别是在不确定的环境下，会怎样与利用预算进行绩效评价相冲突，以及如何使这种冲突最小化。

十分感谢！

摩利兹能源公司
高级管理会计师
Alex Hilliard

附件

财务部——可能的活动

财务部有三项可能的活动。活动 1 被视为基本包，活动 2 和活动 3 是可以添加到基本包的额外增量选项。活动 2 和活动 3 相互独立。

- 活动 1（年度费用 F$ 460 000）包括执行法定会计要求，提供所有财务会计服务，编制年度预算资料和基本管理会计资料。
- 活动 2（年度费用 F$ 160 000）提供内部审计职能，以改善控制业务的质量并减少外部审计费用。
- 活动 3（年度费用 F$ 200 000）提供额外的管理会计人员以完善目前的管理会计信息，并协助实施全面质量管理方案。

请为高级管理会计师 Alex Hilliard 写一份简要说明。

任务三

你收到了来自财务总监 Maria Coleman 的邮件。

发件人：财务总监 Maria Coleman
收件人：管理会计师助理
主题：维修费用和员工投入度

如你所知，Alex 已经代表本部门加入工作小组并审查了我们的预算制度。工作小组一直在考虑是否可以使用一种基于作业的预算方法来编制我们的间接人工成本预算。Alex 已经在休年假了，而我将参加下一次的工作小组会议。

维修部门的 2017 年预算包括增加两名员工所需的资金，以应对计划中的生产增长。这个预算是采用增量预算法编制的。Alex 打算用维修部门作为如何应用作业基础预算法的示例。他在休假之前，准备了维修人员进行的不同作业的清单（附件）及这些作业的成本动因。我们热切地希望通过使用作业基础预算法来判断增加两名员工是否合理。

此外，我担心过去几个月的变化可能对员工的积极性和士气产生了不利影响。我已经跟人力资源经理讨论过这个问题，他是 Christian Thoele 的下属。我们想要制订一项奖励计划来鼓励员工投入新团队的工作。根据我的经验，与个人年度考核挂钩的奖励计划是最有效的。然而，鉴于近期我们公司的变化和整合的需要，我也在考虑一个基于实现瓦拉太阳能集团总体目标的奖励计划。

请帮我起草一份报告，包括以下内容：

- 我们如何使用作业信息来制定维修部门的人力成本预算，包括确保预算尽可能现实可行的其他细节信息；
- 当决定摩利兹能源公司是否应该建立一项基于个人或团体的奖励计划时，我们需要考虑哪些因素，包括具体的奖励计划类型及你推荐这一计划的理由。

致好！

摩利兹能源公司

财务总监

Maria Coleman

作业项目及成本动因：

作业名称	作业描述	成本动因
机器维护	维护机器以使之保持良好的运转状态，包括润滑，检查运动部件的磨损和拆下机器部件进行全面清洁	维护次数
维修	如果机器没有全面运行或出现故障，维修人员就要维修机器。机器的每个问题都被归类为一个“故障点”——一台出故障的机器可能有不止一个故障点	维修故障点的个数
订购零部件	当需要维修和新的零部件时，维修人员会提出采购申请。采购部门将从外部供应商处订购零件	提出采购申请的次数
清洁	每个生产批次结束时，维修人员都要清理机器，以使机器免受灰尘和污垢的影响	清洁机器的次数

请为财务总监 Maria Coleman 撰写报告。

任务四

一周后，你收到了来自高级管理会计师 Alex Hilliard 的电子邮件。

发件人：高级管理会计师 Alex Hilliard

收件人：管理会计师助理

主题：所提议的政策变化的影响

你很清楚由于摩利兹能源公司加入了瓦拉太阳能集团，过去几个月来，我们的政策和程序发生了许多变化。有几项计划中的调整将影响到我们的成本会计和绩效管理系统，我需要更仔细地审视一下。

集团财务总监要求我们改变折旧政策，使其与集团保持一致。过去我们对生产机器在不超过 10 年的期限内用直线法计提折旧，但瓦拉太阳能集团的其他分部使用最多不超过 8 年的折旧年限。

由于 Nicole 还在度蜜月，Maria 要求我来解释会计政策发生变化时的财务报告要求，并且说明这一变化对我们 2016 年营业利润报告的潜在影响。

董事会正在考虑引入适时制采购和生产系统，以改善我们的存货管理。虽然我明白适时制的一般原则，但我想更详细地了解如何衡量适时制系统的有效性。

如果你能协助我，并给我提供一个涉及以下内容的报告，我将不胜感激。

- 会计政策变更时的财务报告要求，以及变更对我们 2016 年营业利润报告的影响。
- 提出 4 个摩利兹能源公司可以用来衡量适时制采购和生产系统有效性的绩效指标，并解释为什么这些绩效指标是适当的。

十分感谢！

摩利兹能源公司
高级管理会计师
Alex Hilliard

请为高级管理会计师 Alex Hilliard 撰写报告。

Variant 2　Suggested Answers

Section 1

Corporate Branding Strategy Report

Effective Brand Managment

Financial and Non-financial Benefits

An effective brand management strategy, which will involve bringing the Marici Power brands under the umbrella of the Wala Group marketing plan and TrueValue, seeks to establish long-term benefits by creating a recognizable and attractive set of brands in the eyes of the customer base. Ultimately, the benefit is improved profitability through the brand.

Non-financial Benefits

- A stronger way to connect with our installers and distributors, by talking to them about what TrueValue means for them and all of the Wala Group brands. The brand should dovetail with our wider marketing efforts. By using the TrueValue brand, the advertising and launch of new products could be carried out from a very strong platform.
- This can help develop further trust and confidence in the brands and the group, which should generate customer loyalty. Although our product may be a long-term one-off purchase for the end customer, there may be some repeat business for example through the ongoing servicing of the product. We would certainly hope to achieve loyalty and repeat purchases from our installers and distributors (so they choose our brands over our competitors and therefore repeat sales are increased).
- It also offers differentiation from the competition, to distinguish our organisation and brands from our competitors, so acts as a source of competitive advantage. This should lead customers to prefer our products and, possibly, to pay premium prices for them. Unless our installers and distributors are tied to exclusive contracts, then this differentiation could be a key to us achieving preferred supplier status with them.

- It enables us to connect with our customers at a deeper level, to talk about areas such as quality and service, rather than focussing on price.

Financial Benefits

- A recognized brand may enable us to charge higher prices giving an immediate boost to revenues and profits. Our installers and distributors may be willing to pay these higher prices if, in turn, the end users are also prepared to pay high prices for the brand.
- An increase in customer loyalty should lead to increased sales which should then lead to greater profitability.
- The brand is a valuable asset. If this appears on the statement of financial position, then this represents a visible aspect of the company's wealth. Even if it does not, then it is still valuable because future business and profits will flow from it.

Ways to Incorporate Digital Marketing

For Marici Power the customers are distributors and installers, so our customer model is B2B (business to business). Therefore the majority of our digital marketing will be to these customers rather than to the end customer. Our installers and distributors represent a relatively small, and known, number of customers. This helps us in targeting our digital marketing efforts rather than engaging in speculative mass marketing to a much wider audience.

Digital marketing is the promotion of brands using electronic media, such as email, the internet, mobile phones or social media. Compared to non-digital methods, digital marketing has the benefit of being able to monitor and evaluate the marketing in a timely and cost-effective way (for instance by monitoring what is being viewed on an internet page).

The type of information that we may wish to disseminate would include corporate developments, specific product developments, special offers, competitive performance, and independent reviews.

Internet—our website should promote the TrueValue message so that any visitors to the website will receive a consistent message. It also allows us to deliver a good quality, up-to-date message. Our other marketing can direct customers to our website, with specific parts of the website dedicated to different types of customers. The company website needs to be up-to-date, well designed and easy to navigate. Since this will be accessed by a range of different interested parties, then they all need to be directed quickly and easily to those pages that are of particular interest to them. For example, perhaps the installers would be more concerned with practical technical issues to a degree that distributors would not.

Email—email can provide sophisticated segmentation opportunities so that messages and promotions can be sent via email to specific segments of our market, so helping to develop a more intimate customer relationship where possible. For instance, if a distributor specializes in only one of our products, then we can focus our messages on that alone. It is important here to distinguish our emails from the frequent junk mail that the installers and distributors will undoubtedly receive. Emails should be sufficiently significant and interesting to encourage the distributors and installers to want to read them.

Social media marketing—social media sites such as Facebook and Twitter have a large number of users, and whilst firms use these sites for marketing purposes and market research this is mainly used for B2C (business to consumer) models. However it is useful to monitor brand name mentions on these sites to capture any reviews of our products or our competitor products. Consumers are using social media more recently for raising the profile of customer complaints, and the message can reach a large number of people very quickly, so knowing about this and conducting an appropriate response is very important.

Useful Life of a Purchased Brand Name

A purchased brand name is classed as an intangible asset under IAS 38 Intangible Assets, which is defined as an identifiable non-monetary asset without physical substance.

The entity must assess the useful life of an intangible asset as either finite or indefinite. An intangible asset with a finite useful life should be amortised over its expected useful life, whereas an intangible asset with an indefinite useful life should not be amortised (but should be tested for impairment at least annually). It is very unusual for an intangible asset to be deemed to have an infinite life.

There are four main issues that should be considered in determining useful life: expected usage, possible obsolescence, industry stability and market demand. There are some interrelationships between these issues and they can be considered in the Marici Power/Wala Solar situation as follows.

We operate in an industry that has a degree of stability, but that has (and continues to) experienced some dramatic changes. There has been considerable growth in the industry as solar power has become more widely accessible and acceptable. This has inevitably increased competition as new entrants have sought to exploit the profit opportunities of an expanding market. The early demand for the products was impacted by the generous government incentive packages. However, changes to government policy have sometimes adversely affected demand which has undermined the industry stability. The extent to which the industry can sustain itself with little or no government incentives will be a factor in determining the useful life of the brand.

The possible obsolescence of the products and brands is the next issue. How long do we expect solar power to be required? There is optimism here that this will be a very long time indeed. As an ultra-long-term renewable energy source, we can reasonably expect solar power to be used long after fossil based energy sources have ceased to be significant.

However, obsolescence can also arise due to technological changes. How soon might we expect our current technology to be superseded by new technology (perhaps one that is significantly cheaper or more efficient)?

We should also consider the demand for the product represented by the brand. There may be an assumption that the output from the products (which is electricity) will continue indefinitely. However, will electricity continue to be required in the same volumes as it is today?

Section 2

ZBB

Setting the Budget

Using ZBB, every activity has to be justified (in comparison to incremental budgeting where the figures from last year are used as a base). ZBB is applicable for discretionary costs, where any expenditure or the amount of the expenditure is at the discretion of management. In the case of the finance department there is clearly discretion over how much we spend and the finance director has determined the activities that are the object of incremental decision packages. In this case, it is the addition of an internal audit function and the expansion of the management accounting function.

The finance director will have scrutinised each activity by asking whether the activity should be undertaken at all, how much of the activity should be done and to what standard. These would be in addition to the base package (which would be a minimum spend). The base package would be considered essential. We need to determine what the base package can achieve and how the benefits can be measured and evaluated.

The next step is to prepare a number of alternatives decision packages (so in this case it would either be whether to create an internal audit function and/or expand the management accounting function). The finance director will have considered how each activity should be done and how much each alternative would cost. ZBB encourages creative thinking concerning different ways of achieving objectives. We would need further information about the internal audit function to evaluate the benefits and likewise with the option of expanding the management accounting function; what would be the expected benefits in terms of control, risk management and improved decision making?

The evaluated packages should then be presented to the budget committee for a final decision about how we will actually operate the Finance Department next year. In making this decision, the budget committee will take a wider view over the whole organisation. This will include resource constraints (not the least of which will be cash) and the conflicting calls upon these constrained resources. The budget committee would review each of the decision packages and decide the resources that should be allocated to the Finance Department depending on the combination of activities that are approved.

ZBB can result in significant cost savings, as all activities and costs are budgeted from scratch, but can also mean an increased budget for a function or activity based on the evaluation, or the same budget as before.

Conflicting Purposes of Budgeting

When developing the budget for the forthcoming year the plans for that year are taken into account and their likely effect on revenue and costs is estimated. However there are a number of areas that could cause conflict when the budget is used for performance evaluation.

For example, one purpose is for the accurate planning of resources. If the budget for the sales team reflects what we genuinely believe we will sell, then we can gear our production to this volume. We can plan for raw material purchases, labour requirements, overtime, machine usage and so on with confidence. However, the motivational aspect of budgeting suggests that sales targets should be such that we encourage the highest possible efforts from the sales team. It is argued that targets should be higher than those that are actually achievable but only marginally so. In this way, sales staffs are motivated to achieve a target that they think is possible, but that is not so difficult that it becomes demotivating.

Clearly if we set motivating budget targets that are not quite achievable then there are concerns about planning on this basis. We would probably plan for too many raw material purchases, too much production and too much inventory. A further concern is that, if we set a challenging but not quite achievable target, we might penalise the sales team for falling short of it. This would be unfair and demotivating if the actual performance was as good as could reasonably be expected and was an improvement in the previous year. It might therefore be appropriate to use different budgets for different purposes: a motivating target for the sales team, but a realistic target for resource planning.

Circumstances during the budget period may have changed from what was anticipated, as inevitably there is always an element of uncertainty in the budget. This can be particularly evident where there is a chance of significant changes during the year. The market environment in which Marici Power operates is changing rapidly. There is uncertainty surrounding raw material prices and the potential effect of the cut to government subsidies on sales demand. The integration of Marici Power also raises question about the future including the changes to the branding strategy and the potential release of new products which may not be included in the budget.

For performance evaluation other factors may affect the usefulness of the budget. For example, if the production department do not meet their budgeted production this could detrimentally affect the sales team's performance or delay the release of a new product. If performance evaluation is linked with the rewards system, sales team may try to set easy sales targets, in the knowledge that these would be exceeded, in order to increase their rewards.

To minimise these conflicts a rolling budget (also known as a continuous budget) could be used, so that rather than using a static annual budget for the target for the year, projections are produced each month to reflect any changes in the underlying assumptions of the budget. As actual sales figures become available for each month these are updated in the rolling budget in place of the forecast figures, and a further month is added to the rolling budget.

Section 3

Maintenance Costs and Employee Engagement

Labour Cost Budget for Maintenance Department

The first step in introducing ABB is to identify cost pools or activities and to establish a cost driver for each activity. The schedule provided by Alex shows four cost pools and their cost drivers. We can build up the budget by each activity in turn.

For each of the activities we need to estimate the time taken to carry out the activity. This could be done by asking the maintenance function staffs to provide estimates, or by conducting a work study over a short period of time. The cost of idle time also need to be included in the budget. There will be periods when not all of the maintenance teams are fully occupied. We also have to take into account lunch breaks and rest breaks. We also need to recognise that experienced members of the maintenance function are likely to take less time on an activity than a new member of staff. This will be particularly relevant as additional members of staff are expected to be required. The new staffs will need training and go through a learning curve for the different activities that are undertaken.

For each activity, we then need to estimate the number of cost drivers that we expect to be performed within the budget period. For example, for repairs we would estimate the total number of faults that we expect to arise and then multiply this by the time required to carry out the repair to give the total hours needed. The estimate for the number of cost drivers could be based on information from previous year, if available, adjusted for changes in the expected activity level.

We need to establish the costs per hour for each activity. For example, do repair staffs get paid more than cleaning staffs? Each of the total times can be multiplied by the labour costs per hour to give the cost of each activity. We would also need to add any employer related costs to the total cost for all activities.

The breakdown of activities and the cost drivers for each activity should be analysed in more detail to check that the activities chosen are appropriate and that the cost drivers are a good reflection of the cause of the cost arising.

If the activities do not arise smoothly throughout the budget period, then the costs may need to be budgeted by month. We should also be aware of any anticipated pay rises that might arise during the budget period and factor these into the budget.

Incentive Schemes/Employee Engagement

A good incentive scheme links reward to improved performance, and helps to give a clear direction to employees of where their efforts are needed most. Clear communication of objectives and a financial reward based on these objectives can increase employee commitment, motivation and engagement. We need to consider whether the group or the individual scheme will be more effective for Marici in enhancing morale and motivation. We also need to consider which will be deemed fairer by our staffs. The incentive scheme is a morale and motivation factor in itself.

An incentive scheme based on individual performance is motivational to the employees as they can see their own efforts and achievements being recognized and rewarded directly. However, this may encourage selfish thinking which we would not wish to encourage. There can be difficulties in determining an individual's performance level where outputs cannot objectively be determined by individuals. This leads to performance assessment being subjective, and can lead to a notion of bias.

A group incentive scheme, or as you suggest an incentive scheme based on the organisation's overall performance, is based on the performance of the identified group (for instance the maintenance team achieving or exceeding their targets). Collective team work might be a worthy outcome of a group scheme, but we need to be careful that high performing employees are not penalised by their rewards being dragged down by an average that includes the efforts of less able/hard working colleagues. A scheme based on the organisation's overall performance (usually measured by meeting or exceeding a target profit) encourages employees to work together across different departments and parts of the organisation (for instance with Wala Solar head office) as they are all working towards the same goal. This type of scheme can prove very popular when times are good, but can be the cause of resentment when the business is not doing as well. Employees may perceive that they have contributed well and achieved their objectives but it is another part of the organisation or external forces, which have meant that the overall incentive has not been achieved.

My recommendation would be to consider a combination of the two schemes—an element of incentive for an individual's performance against carefully prepared and agreed objectives, and a further, larger element based on the overall performance of the Wala Solar group to encourage employees' interest and engagement with the new group.

Section 4

Impact of Proposed Policy Changes

Changes in Accounting Policy and Our Changes in Estimated Useful Economic Life

A change in accounting policy can be made where there is a change in an accounting standard or where it can be justified on the grounds of improving the reliability of the information in the financial statements. Where the change in accounting policy has a material effect on either current, prior or future periods, certain disclosures are required, namely the reasons for the change, the nature of the change, the fact that comparative information has been adjusted and the amount of adjustments for current periods and comparative periods.

IAS 8 requires retrospective application of a change in accounting policy, which means that the change of policy needs to be applied to transactions, events and conditions in all comparative information. So all comparative information should be restated as if the new policy had always been in place, with amounts relating to earlier periods reflected in an adjustment to opening reserves of the earliest period presented.

In this instance this is not actually a change in accounting policy. It is instead a change in accounting estimate, in that the useful life of the assets will be amended so that we are in line with the treatment adopted by group. Such a change will be carried out prospectively and impact the profit for this year and future years. We will need to calculate the depreciation on our assets for 2016 as carrying value divided by the remaining useful economic life based on an overall life of 8 years. For many assets, it is likely that the remaining life is reduced which will lead to an increase in the depreciation charge and a reduction in profit for 2016.

JIT—Performance Measures

Number of Quality Failures or Number of Machine Breakdowns

JIT production provides no buffer inventory to cover for quality problems. Accordingly, the reporting of quality issues becomes of vital performance. Quality is essential for JIT to work—with materials arriving just in time to produce the finished product, good quality control prevents any delays or stoppages in the production pipeline that would prevent JIT from working.

Number of Incorrect Deliveries Received or Number of Late Deliveries

Vendor rating is needed to determine if suppliers are performing to the required standard. As suppliers are delivering in smaller batches and more frequently, we will need an efficient system to record the deliveries, preferably with an automated checking of them against purchase orders. The number of incorrect or late deliveries received from individual suppliers would be measures, which could be used in rating suppliers.

Average Delivery Time or Throughput Time

JIT relies on speed in terms of delivery of materials and in production of the products. The lead time between ordering the material and the material being delivered is therefore of vital importance. Throughput in production must be fast so that customer orders can be met by production. Without fast throughput it will be necessary to hold some inventory to meet customer orders.

Material Handling Time or Set-up Time

The JIT philosophy is based on continuous improvement and the elimination of waste. Waste is defined as any activity that does not add value. This would include unnecessary movement of material or people including moving material from one production area to another. Set-up time is also non-productive. The aim is to achieve quick set-up times and low cost set-ups.

试卷二　参考答案

任务一

企业品牌战略报告

有效的品牌管理

财务与非财务收益

一个有效的品牌管理战略，涉及把摩利兹能源公司的品牌纳入瓦拉太阳能集团的营销计划和“TrueValue”商标下，力求通过创建在顾客眼中可识别的、有吸引力的一系列品牌来获得长期利益。最终通过品牌提升盈利能力。

非财务收益

- 一种更强大的连接安装商和分销商的方式，告诉他们TrueValue对他们和瓦拉集团的全部品牌意味着什么。品牌应该与公司更宽泛的营销手段相吻合。通过使用TrueValue商标，公司的广告和新产品的上市可以在一个非常强大的平台上进行。
- 有助于进一步建立顾客对品牌和集团的信任和信心，从而产生顾客忠诚度。虽然对最终消费者来说，我们的产品可能是长期的一次性购买，但还是有一些重复业务，例如持续的产品服务。我们当然希望获得安装商和分销商的忠诚度和重复购买（他们选择了我们的品牌而不是竞争者的，因此增加了重复销售）。
- 它也提供了与竞争产品之间的差异性，使我们的公司和品牌与竞争者区分开来，因而成为一个竞争优势的来源。这会使顾客偏爱我们的产品，并可能为之支付更高的价格。除非我们的安装商和分销商被排他性的合同条款限制，这种差异性是使我们成为他们优先选择的供应商的关键。
- 它使我们与顾客的联系更深，使顾客关注质量和服务等各个方面，而不是仅仅关注价格。

财务收益

- 一个被认可的品牌可以让我们收取更高的价格，从而快速提高收入和利润。要是最终消费者也准备为这个品牌支付更高的价格，那么我们的安装商和分销商就会愿意支付更高的价格。

- 顾客忠诚度的提高会带来销量的提高，从而产生更高的利润。
- 品牌是一笔有价值的资产。如果它出现在资产负债表上，就代表着企业财富中可视化的一面。即使不在报表上，它也依然是有价值的，是未来业务和利润的来源。

引入数字营销的方法

对摩利兹能源公司来说，顾客是分销商和安装商，所以我们的顾客模式是 B2B（企业对企业）。因此我们数字营销的主体是针对这些顾客而不是最终消费者。安装商和分销商是一个数量相对小的且已知的顾客群体，这有助于我们有针对性地确定数字营销方式，而不是面向更广阔对象的投机性大众营销。

数字营销是指利用电子媒体比如邮件、网络、手机或社交媒体对品牌进行推广。相较于非数字营销，数字营销的好处是能够及时地以低成本的方式去管理和评估营销过程（例如监控网页上正在被查看的内容）。

我们希望传播的消息包括公司发展，特定产品的发展，特别优惠，竞争绩效和独立检查。

网络——我们的网站应该推送 TrueValue 的消息，使任何一个浏览网页的人都能收到一致的消息。这使我们能推送优质的最新消息。其他的营销手段可以引导顾客访问我们的网站，其针对不同类型的顾客有不同的内容。公司的网站需要及时更新，要精心设计，易于操作。众多不同的利益相关方都会访问网站，他们都需要被简单快速地引导到他们特别感兴趣的页面。举例来说，安装商会在一定程度上更加关心实际的技术问题，但分销商不会。

电子邮件——电子邮件可以提供复杂的细分机会，以便相关信息和促销活动可以通过邮件发送到特定的细分市场，因而有助于在可能的情况下建立更密切的客户关系。例如，如果一个分销商只专注于我们的某一种产品，那么我们就可以把信息都集中在这一产品上。重要的是要将我们的电子邮件与安装商和分销商无疑经常会收到的垃圾邮件区分开来。电子邮件应该足够重要和有趣，使分销商和安装商想要打开阅读。

社交媒体营销——像脸书和推特这样的社交媒体网站拥有大量用户，公司可利用这些网站开展营销和市场调研，这种方式主要用于 B2C（商对客）模式。然而，监控这些网站上提及的品牌名称的情况，以获取对我们或竞争对手产品的任何评价是非常有用的。最近消费者越来越多地使用社交媒体来吸引大家对顾客投诉的注意，而且信息可以很快地传播给许许多多的人，所以了解这一点并给予适当的反应是非常重要的。

购入的品牌名称的预计使用寿命

按照国际会计准则第 38 号无形资产准则，购入的品牌名称应被列为无形资产，无形资产的定义是无实物形态的、可辨认的非货币性资产。

公司必须评估无形资产的预计使用寿命是有限期的还是无限期的。预计使用寿命有限的无形资产应在其预期的使用寿命内摊销，而预计使用寿命无限期的无形资产不应摊销（但至少每年进行一次减值测试）。无形资产被认定为使用寿命无限期的情况非常少见。

确定无形资产的预计使用寿命时，需要考虑四个主要因素：预期使用情况，可能的陈旧过时，行业稳定性和市场需求。这四个方面相互关联，摩利兹能源公司或瓦拉太阳能集团可做如下考虑：

我们在一个具有一定稳定性的行业中经营，但已经（并将继续）经历了一些戏剧性的变化。随着太阳能的广泛普及，该行业已经取得了巨大的发展。在一个扩张的市场上，新进入者试图攫取利润机会，这不可避免地加剧了竞争。早期的产品需求受到政府慷慨的一系列激励措施的影响。然而，政府政策的改变有时会对需求造成不利影响，从而破坏了行业稳定。该行业在没有或很少得到政府激励的情况下能够维持自身发展的程度，将是决定该品牌预计使用寿命的因素之一。

接下来要考虑产品和品牌可能过时。我们预期一下人们对太阳能的需求将持续多长时间？乐观地说，这将是一个很长的时间。太阳能作为一种超长期的可再生能源，我们可以合理地预测，在化石能源不再重要之后，太阳能将被长期使用。然而，技术的变化，也可能导致品牌过时。我们目前的技术预期会在什么时候被新技术（也许是非常便宜或更加高效的）所取代？

我们还应该考虑品牌所代表的产品需求。我们假定产品（即电力）的输出将无限期地持续下去，但对电力的需求会一直维持在现在的水平上吗？

任务二

零基预算

预算编制

采用零基预算，每项活动都需要被判定是否合理（与以去年的数据作为基础的增量预算法不同）。零基预算法适用于酌量性成本，即任何依据管理决策而定的费用项目或支出金额。在财务部门的案例中，需要清楚地决定我们花费多少，财务总监已经确定了作为增量决策对象的活动类型。在这个案例中，是指增加内部审计职能和扩大管理会计职能。

财务总监将仔细审查每项活动，询问这项活动到底是否真的需要进行，活动量是多少，要达到什么标准。这些会被加入基本包（最低支出）中。基本包是必需的，我们要确定基本包可以实现什么，以及如何衡量和评估其收益。

下一步是准备一些可选的决策方案包（在这个案例里，它要么是增加内部审计职能，要么是扩大管理会计职能）。财务总监将考虑每项活动应如何进行及每项备选方案的费用是多少。零基预算鼓励通过不同途径去实现目标的创造性思维。我们需要有关内部审计职能的进一步信息去评估其收益，对扩大管理会计职能的选项亦如此，还有在控制、风险管理和改进决策方面，预期收益是什么？

然后，评估后的方案包将被提交给预算委员会，以决定明年财务部将如何运作。要做出这项决定，预算委员会将对整个组织进行一个广泛地考量，包括资源约束（不仅仅是现金）和这些约束性资源的需求冲突。预算委员会将审查每个决策方案包，并根据批准的活动组合确定分配给财务部的资源量。

零基预算能带来显著的成本节约，因为所有的活动和成本的预算都是从零开始，但也可能基于评估为一项功能或活动增加预算，或者得到与之前同样的预算。

预算目标的冲突

在为来年制定预算时，要考虑到这一年的计划，并估计它们对收入和成本的可能影响。然而，当预算用于绩效评价时，可能会在许多领域引起冲突。

例如，预算的目标之一是为了精确地规划资源。如果销售团队的预算反映了我们真正相信会实现的销售量，我们就可以根据这个量做好生产准备。我们就可以有信心地计划原材料采购、人力需求、加班安排、机器使用等等。然而，预算的激励性意味着销售目标应该能够鼓励销售团队尽最大努力去实现。有人认为，预算目标应该比实际能够实现的目标要高，但仅仅是略高一些。这样的话，销售人员就会被激励去实现他们认为可能实现的目标，但不能因难度太大而带来消极影响。

显然，如果我们设定的激励性预算目标不太可能实现，那么以此为基础的计划就值得担忧了。我们很可能计划了过多的原材料采购、过多的生产和过多的库存。更令人忧虑的是，如果设定一个具有挑战性但不可能实现的目标，我们可能就会惩罚没有达到目标的销售团队。而实际绩效达到了合理预期并且比上一年有所进步的话，这将是不公平的，而且会挫伤团队的积极性。因此，为不同的目的设定不同的预算可能是比较合适的：为销售团队设定激励性的目标，但为资源计划设定切实可行的目标。

预算期间的情况可能与之前预期的相比有所不同，因为预算中不可避免地存在着不确定性因素。在年度内有可能发生重大变化的情况下，这一点表现得尤其明显。摩利兹能源公司经营所处的市场环境正在飞速变化。原材料价格和政府补贴的削减对需求的潜在影响存在不确定性。摩利兹能源的整合也对企业未来带来了挑战，包括品牌战略变化和没有包括在预算内的可能发行的新产品。

对绩效评价来说，其他因素也可能影响预算的有用性。例如，如果生产部门不能达到预算产量，必然会对销售团队的绩效产生不利影响或推迟新产品的发布。如果绩效评价与薪酬体系挂钩，销售团队可能会为了增加奖金，试图设定容易达到的销售目标，他们知道这些目标会被超过。

为了尽量减少这些冲突，可以使用滚动预算（也称为连续预算），而不是使用一个基于年度目标的静态年度预算，这样就可以每月做出预测，以反映预算所依据的假设的变化。当每个月的实际销售数据出来，就更新滚动预算，用实际数据替代预测数据，并再增加一个月的预算。

任务三

维修费用和员工投入度

维修部门的人工成本预算

引入作业基础预算法的第一步是确定成本库或者划分作业，以及为每一项作业确定成本动因。Alex 提供的清单列出了 4 个成本库和相应的成本动因，我们可以依次通过每个活动来增加预算。

对于每项作业，我们都需要估计作业耗费的时间，可以通过询问维修人员去估计，或者通过一个短期的工作研究来完成。闲置时间的成本也需要被包括在预算中。如果并不是全部的维修团队都在满负荷工作，闲置时间就总是存在的。我们也要把午饭时间和休息时间考虑进去，还需要认识到有经验的维修人员很可能会比新手花费更少的时间就可以完成一项作业。当需要增加额外的员工时，这一点尤其要考虑。新员工需要培训，从事不同作业时都将经历一个学习曲线。

接下来我们需要估计每项作业将在预算期间内耗费的成本动因数量。以修理来说，我们将估计可能发生的故障总数量，然后用这个数量乘以需要的修理时间来得到总工时。对于成本动因数量的估计可以基于前一年的信息，如果有的话，还需要根据预期作业水平的变化加以调整。

我们需要为每项作业确定单位时间成本。例如，从事修理的员工是否比从事清洁的员工报酬更高？每项作业的总工时乘以单位人工成本就可得到每项作业的成本。我们也需要把雇主的相关成本加到全部作业的总成本中。

作业的分类和每项作业的成本动因应该要详细分析，以确定所划分的作业是适当的，以及成本动因能够较好地反映成本发生的原因。

如果作业在整个预算期间并不是均匀发生的，就可能需要按月预算成本。我们还应该认识到预算期间可能出现的加薪，并将这些因素纳入预算。

奖励计划/员工投入度

一个好的奖励计划是将奖励与绩效提升联系起来，其有助于向员工提供他们最需要努力的明确的方向。明确的目标和基于目标的财务奖励能够增加员工的努力程度、积极性和投入度。我们要考虑的是团体或个人的奖励计划对于摩利兹能源公司来说，哪个在提高士气和积极性方面更有效。我们还要考虑哪个奖励计划在员工看来更公平。奖励计划本身就是一种士气和激励因素。

基于个人绩效的奖励计划对于员工来说是很有激励作用的，因为他们可以看到自己的努力和成就被认可并直接获得回报。然而，这有可能会助长我们并愿不鼓励的自私想法。当生产量不能由个人来客观地决定时，评估个人的绩效水平就很困难。这使得绩效评价变得主观，并可能导致偏见。

一个团体奖励计划，或者如您建议的基于企业整体绩效的奖励计划，是基于特定团队的工作表现的（例如维修团队达到或超过他们的目标）。集体工作在团体奖励计划下可能获得有价值的成果，但我们需要注意的是绩效好的员工不会被抑制，他们获得的奖励不会被包含没有能力或不够努力工作的同事的平均水平所拖累。一个基于企业整体绩效（通常由达到或者超过目标利润来衡量）的奖励计划会鼓励员工跨部门和企业不同分部（例如和瓦拉太阳能集团总部）一起工作，因为他们是为了同一个目标而工作。这种奖励计划制在经营状况好的时候很受欢迎，但经营状况不好时也可能引起怨恨。员工可能认为他们做得很好，也实现了他们的目标，但绩效不好是由企业的其他部门或外部压力导致的，这意味着整体激励并未实现。

我的建议是可以考虑把两种计划结合起来——奖励计划的一部分与个人绩效相关，基于精心确定的、一致同意的目标，另外更大的部分与瓦拉太阳能集团的整体绩效相关，激发员工对于新集团的兴趣和投入度。

任务四

所提议的政策变化带来的影响

会计政策的变化和预计使用寿命的变化

在会计准则发生变化，或者会计政策调整可以提升财务报表信息的可靠性的情况下，会计政策就可以改变。会计政策的变化对当期、前期或未来期间产生重大影响时，会被要求进行一定的披露，即变化的原因、性质，比较信息的调整情况，以及当期和比较期的调整金额。

国际会计准则第 38 号准则要求会计政策的变化要具有可追溯性，这意味着政策的变化需要应用于所有交易、事项和状况的比较信息中。所以，所有比较信息需要像新政策一直存在一样被重述，包括反映在最早时期的期初盈余调整中的前期调整金额。

在这个例子中并不是真正的会计政策变更。这是会计估计变更，资产的预计使用寿命需要被修正，以便和集团采用的处理方法保持一致。这个改变是具前瞻性的，并将会影响当年或未来年度的利润。我们将需要以 8 年的总预计使用寿命为基础，用账面价值除以剩余的预计使用寿命来计算 2016 年度的资产折旧额。对于很多资产来说，剩余使用寿命减少将导致 2016 年的折旧费用上升而利润下降。

适时制——绩效考核

质量缺陷的数量和机器故障次数

适时制生产没有缓冲库存来应对质量缺陷问题。因此，质量报告变得至关重要。质量对适时制的有效运行必不可少——随着材料准时到达用以生产成品，良好的质量控制可以预防任何会阻碍适时制运行的生产流水线延误或停顿。

交货错误的数量或迟交的数量

对供应商进行评级是需要确定其是否执行了要求的标准。由于供应商将以更小的批次、更频繁地送货，所以我们需要一个有效的系统来记录交货，最好是能够自动地与采购订单进行核对。要计算供应商交货错误的数量或迟交的数量，用作供应商评级的依据。

平均交货时间或产出时间

适时制依赖于原材料的交货速度和产品的生产速度，因此原材料订购和交付之间的交货时间是至关重要的。产出速度要快，以便生产能够满足客户的订单需求。如果没有快速的产出，就必须保留一些库存量以满足客户的订单。

材料搬运时间和生产准备时间

适时制的理念是以不断改进和消除浪费为基础的。浪费被定义为任何不增加价值的活动，包括不必要的材料或人员的移动，即将材料从一个生产区域转移到另一个生产区域。生产准备时间也是非生产性的。我们的目标是实现快速生产准备和低成本。

Variant 2　Marking Guidance

Section	Technical skills		Business skills		People skills		Leadership skills		Integration	Total
1	Useful economic life of intangible assets	10	Benefits of effective brand management Digital marketing and its potential benefits	7 10	Benefits of effective brand management	3				30
2	Zero-based budgeting Conflicts in respect of the purposes of budgeting	13 4			Conflicts in respect of the purposes of budgeting	4	Conflicts in respect of the purposes of budgeting	3	3	27
3	Activity based budgeting	10			Incentive schemes	7	Incentive schemes	3		20
4	Changes in accounting policies and estimates Just-in-time effectiveness	11 12								23
Total marks available for each competency		60		17		14		6	3	100

试卷二　评分指南

部分	技术技能		商业技能		人际技能		领导技能		综合	总计
1	无形资产的经济使用寿命	10	有效的品牌管理的好处 数字营销及其潜在的好处	7 10	有效的品牌管理的好处	3				30
2	零基预算 预算目标的冲突	13 4			预算目标的冲突	4	预算目标的冲突	3	3	27
3	作业基础预算	10			奖励计划		奖励计划	3		20
4	会计政策和会计估计变更 适时制的有效性	11 12								23
各种能力分数总计		60		17		14		6	3	100

江西财经大学名师解惑

试卷一共有四项任务，考查了 P1、F1、E1 三门课程的知识点，具体包括品牌管理、数字营销、无形资产的经济使用寿命、零基预算、预算目标、作业基础预算、绩效奖励计划、会计政策和会计估计变更和适时制等。该试卷考核了考生的四项能力，其中技术技能的分值占 60%，商业技能的分值占 17%，人际技能的分值占 14%，领导技能的分值占 6%，与 CGMA 管理会计能力框架的技能要求一致。

该试卷的每项任务涉及以下知识点：

任务	问题	科目	知识点
任务一	有效的品牌管理带来的好处	E1	品牌管理（brand management）
	数字营销的方式及潜在的好处	E1	数字营销（digital marketing）
	根据国际会计准则第 38 号确定品牌的预计使用寿命	F1	无形资产的预计使用寿命（useful life of intangible assets）
任务二	零基预算编制方法	P1	零基预算（ZBB）
	不同预算目标的冲突	P1	预算目标冲突（conflicting purposes of budgeting）
任务三	作业基础的人工成本预算	P1	作业预算（ABB）
	建立绩效奖励计划应考虑的因素	E1	绩效奖励计划（incentive scheme）
任务四	会计政策变更的报告要求	F1	会计政策与会计估计变更（changes in accounting policies and estimates）
	衡量适时制系统的有效性	P1	适时制（JIT）

上述各项任务要求以报告或简要说明的方式来呈现答案，对问题的描述非常明确，答题时既要注意内容的针对性，也要注意形式的规范性。

其他答题注意事项包括：（1）仔细读题，一般每项任务都会涉及 2～3 个大的知识点，一定不能漏答；（2）答题要有条理，从是什么到为什么，从分析原因到提出解决办法，将每个知识点都解释清楚；（3）分层级列出各级小标题，让考官容易了解你的思路。

对应知识点的深度剖析

品牌管理

有效的品牌管理可以给企业带来财务和非财务收益。财务收益主要围绕增加销量和利润来阐述。这一点很容易理解，当消费者缺乏直接判断不同商品质量和性能差异的能力，却又需要购买的时候，品牌知名度常常是决定购买的重要因素。非财务收益可以从增强与利益相关者（如供应商、竞争者和顾客）之间的关系和提升产品竞争力两个方面来讨论。考生在解答时应结合案例中提供的具体信息，如问题中提到的分销商和安装商，避免泛泛而谈。

数字营销

数字营销是指使用电子传播渠道来推广产品和服务的活动。在当今这个网络时代，数字营销显然是企业不能忽视的重要营销手段。这个问题结合时代热点，考查了考生的商业能力，要求考生基于对现实经济生活的观察、了解和认识，来分析在该案例背景下有哪些适合的数字营销方式。在解答问题时，考生首先需要解释什么是数字营销，再结合案例提出各种可能的数字营销方式并说明其优点，言之有理即可。

无形资产的预计使用寿命

购入的品牌符合国际会计准则第 38 号无形资产准则对无形资产的定义，应被确认为无形资产。在确定品牌的预计使用寿命时，需要考虑四个主要因素：预期使用情况，可能的陈旧过时，行业稳定性和市场需求。此问题的解答要求考生熟悉案例预览材料，对案例的行业背景有深入的理解和认识，阐述时要明确提出每个方面需要具体考虑的因素，还要注意四个方面的相互关联。

考生注意事项

在国际会计准则第 38 号无形资产准则中，无形资产被定义为“无实物形态的、可辨认的非货币性资产”，以便与商誉清楚地区分开来。无形资产可用于生产产品或提供劳务，出租或管理目的。常见的无形资产类型包括专利、商标、品牌名称、著作权等。在无形资产的后续会计处理中，企业首先需要评估无形资产的预计使用寿命是有限的，还是无限的。使用寿命有限的无形资产需要将成本在其使用寿命的最佳估计期限内进行系统摊销，使用寿命无限的无形资产不用摊销，但每年至少进行一次减值测试。估计无形资产的预计使用寿命需要考虑很多因素，包括资产的预期使用情况、产品生命周期、可能的陈旧过时、行业稳定性、市场需求变化、竞争者或潜在竞争者的预期行动等。

零基预算

零基预算与传统的增量预算法不同，在编制成本费用预算时，其不考虑以往期间的费用项目或数额，一切从零出发，根据预算期的实际需要和可能性，逐项审查预算期内各项费用的内容及其开支标准是否合理，在综合平衡的基础上编制费用预算。其优点是有助于减少浪费，合理分配资金，提高预算管理水平。考生在解答此题时，可以先介绍零基预算的特点，再根据零基预算的实施步骤，结合附件中提供的细节信息来回答。零基预算的关键步骤之一是对可选的决策包进行成本效益分析，解答中需指出开展成本效益分析时还要取得哪些相关信息。

考生注意事项

零基预算的核心是在预算编制中引入一种质疑的态度，对现有的实践活动和费用开支提出疑问，诸如：这项活动是必需的吗？如果不进行这项活动，会带来什么后果？是否有其他可能的途径可以达到同样目的？这项费用开支是否值得？通过回答这些问题使预算中的不合理因素被剔除，从而达到节约成本，提高资源利用效率的目的。

零基预算的三个核心步骤包括：（1）根据组织目标，确认预算期内需要进行的业务项目及其费用开支，制订多个可能的备选方案（也称为决策包）；（2）对备选方案进行成本效益分析，评估项目费用开支的合理程度，确定先后顺序以及对组织业务活动的影响；（3）按照预算期可动用的资金及其来源，依据项目的轻重缓急次序，分配资金，落实预算。

预算目标冲突

该问题中的预算目标冲突是指当预算用于绩效评价时，可能引起的冲突。设定激励性的预算目标本意是鼓励员工努力提升绩效，但如果难度过大，反而会带来消极的影响。预算期间的不确定因素，也可能使之前的预算目标变得不可行。不同部门间的预算目标的实现也会相互影响。当绩效评估与报酬挂钩，容易导致预算编制中的预算松弛行为。减少这些冲突的可行方法之一是使用滚动预算法，持续更新预算，以反映预算所依据的假设发生的变化。考生解答此问时要注意问题中提及的两个关键词——“不确定”和“绩效评价”，把握好问题设定的语境。

作业基础预算

作业基础预算是以作业成本计算为基础的预算编制方法。作业成本法的基本原理是“作业消耗资源，产品消耗作业”。考生需要熟悉这一原理，按照作业基础预算的实施步骤，结合案例来阐述。作业基础预算的主要步骤包括：（1）划分作业，确定成本动因；（2）预计每单位产品或劳务消耗的作业量；（3）根据每单位产品或劳务消耗的作业量和预计产出量估计预算期需要的总作业量；（4）确定每单位作业消耗的资源量；（5）用每单位作业消耗的资源量乘以第3步中预测出来的作业需求量，预测出可以满足作业消耗需求的资源量。因为本案例讨论的是维修部门的人工成本预算，所以每项作业需要估计单位人工工时。估计单位人工工时需要考虑到闲置时间、人工效率差异、学习曲线等因素。

绩效奖励计划

绩效奖励计划是指员工的薪酬随着个人、团队或组织绩效的某些衡量指标所发生的变化而变化的一种薪酬设计。本案例主要讨论采用个人绩效奖励计划还是团体绩效奖励计划。显然两种方式各有利弊，考生需要了解两种绩效奖励计划的优缺点和适用性。将两种奖励计划结合起来应用，是现实中企业的常见选择。

考生注意事项

个人奖励计划的优点是可以加强薪酬和绩效之间的联系，使公司更公平地分配薪酬，但是也可能导致员工过分依赖设定的绩效目标，并可能带来不良的工作行为。个人奖励计划适合于可以通过客观的方法来考核的员工绩效，员工有足够的能力控制工作结果，并且奖励计划不会导致员工间的不良竞争的情形。

团体奖励计划有利于鼓励员工间的相互协作，避免不良竞争，但也使员工无法看到自己的绩效与奖励之间的直接联系，较个人奖励计划缺少提高绩效的动力，并可能导致“搭便车”等消极行为。这种奖励计划适合于产出是团队合作的结果，个人对产出的贡献难以衡量的情形。

会计政策与会计估计变更

考生需要熟知国际会计准则第8号准则的相关内容，能够区分会计政策变更和会计估计变更，以及两者不同的财务报告要求。本案例中固定资产折旧年限的调整，属于会计估计变更，而不是会计政策变更。会计估计变更采用未来适用法，仅对当年和未来年度的利润产生影响。

考生注意事项

会计政策变更与会计估计变更的区别在于该事项是否涉及会计确认、计量基础选择或列报项目的变更。当至少涉及其中一项划分基础变更的，该事项是会计政策变更；不涉及上述划分基础变更时，该事项可以判断为会计估计变更。

根据国际会计准则第8号准则的规定，会计政策变更采用追溯调整法，调整资产负债表年初留存收益，以及利润表上年数栏有关项目。会计估计变更采用未来适用法，不必调整变更当年年初的留存收益，只在变更当年采用新的会计政策。会计政策的变化对当期、前期或未来期间产生重大影响时，要求披露变化的原因、性质，比较信息的调整情况，以及当期和比较期的调整金额。

适时制

适时制采购和生产系统采用需求拉动式的生产组织方式，要求企业必须根据客户订货或市场要求的数量、品种、质量标准和交货时间组织生产，安排采购，从而减少甚至消除存货，导致了存货管理和质量控制方面的重大变革。适时制强调质量和及时，考生可以从这两个方面来考虑衡量适时制有效性的绩效指标。

Variant 3

This examination is structured as follows：

Section number	Number of tasks	Time for section(minutes)
1	1	45
2	1	45
3	1	35
4	1	55

The time available for each section is for reading,planning and writing your answer(s).

Section 1

The following extract is from the customer review pages of www. maricipower. com.

> Poor delivery service from Marici—delivery was two days late and when it did arrive it was two panels short.
>
> *Joyce Johnson, Freeland*
> *23th November 2016*
>
> I had organised for the installers to arrive on Wednesday morning but by Wednesday lunchtime the panels had not arrived. I phoned Marici but they didn't seem to have any idea what was happening. I eventually got the panels three days later and I am now waiting for the installers to arrange a new date for the installation.
>
> *Harper Jones, Freeland*
> *18th November 2016*
>
> Don't use Marici solar panels!! Their delivery service is awful!!!!
>
> *Marta Wabera, Freeland*
> *10th November 2016*
>
> The quality of the panels is excellent and my installers were brilliant. Just a shame the delivery service from Marici is so unreliable. I received the panels late and was sent twice the quantity that had been ordered.
>
> *Jodie Venchetska, Freeland*
> *3rd November 2016*

You receive the following email from Maria Coleman, finance director.

From: Maria Coleman, Finance Director
To: Management Accountant Assistant
Subject: Issues with delivery to customers

You should have seen the recent customer reviews on our website and we have also received a number of complaints from our recommended installers. The board is concerned about the implication of these delivery problems to our reputation. They have asked that an immediate investigation be carried out to identify why the problems have arisen and what steps we can take to ensure they don't occur again in the future.

We have carried out some initial investigations and it would appear that there are a number of problems, from receiving customers' orders through to delivery to the customer. I have had discussions with Christian Thoele, the support services director, and we have agreed that we should use BPR (business process re-engineering) to improve the efficiency and effectiveness of our business processes. I realise however that this is likely to be very unsettling for staffs and the last thing we want to see is a fall in staff morale.

I would be grateful if you would prepare some notes that I can use for a presentation to staffs. Please include an explanation of what business process re-engineering involves and the benefits of using it in this situation. I would like to consider introducing a quality report as a part of our monthly management accounts. In view of the current situation I would like it, at this stage, to focus on external failures. The directors have expressed their concern that we had not identified this issue earlier. I have had a look at the historical monthly management accounts and it is clear that we should have picked up this issue. As a result, I would like to issue guidelines to the finance department staffs regarding the investigation of variances.

I would appreciate it if you could also include the following in your notes.

- An explanation of three external failure quality costs that we would expect to arise as a result of the poor delivery service and three non-financial indicators that would have enabled early identification of the quality failure.
- An explanation of how to determine which variances should be investigated, using the external failure quality costs identified to illustrate your explanation.

Regards.

Maria Coleman
Finance Director
Marici Power

Write the report for Maria Coleman, finance director.

Section 2

A few days later, you receive the following email from Maria Coleman, finance director.

From: Maria Coleman, Finance Director

To: Management Accountant Assistant

Subject: Issues with delivery to customers

As you know, there has been a lot of discussions in recent board meetings about the problems we have been experiencing with our delivery to customers.

Christian Thoele, the support services director, has been looking at the possibility of outsourcing the distribution operation. He has had some initial discussions with a logistics company and has asked the finance department to carry out an appraisal of this option. I have asked Alex to do some work on this, but I would also like you to help with some of the aspects.

The price offered by the logistics company is F$ 75 per delivery based on a standard mix of volume, weight and distance. Christian is keen to go ahead as it is lower than our current cost per delivery, based on the standard mix(see attached).

One of the advantages of outsourcing our distribution service is that it will change some of our fixed costs into variable costs and reduce our operational gearing. I would like you to review the figures in more detail and in particular look at the implications in terms of our cost structure. I would also like to consider the other potential benefits and limitations of outsourcing.

I would be grateful if you could draft a report that I can send to Christian. I would like it to cover the following areas.

- A review of the figures shown in the attached schedule including your views on the impact that outsourcing would have on our cost structure and operational gearing.
- The potential benefits and limitations of outsourcing for Marici Power!

Regards.

Maria Coleman

Finance Director

Marici Power

Accessory

Delivery costs：

Monthly cost of the current delivery operation	
	（F$）
Fuel costs	17,000
Tyres	3,000
Maintenance	4,400
Repairs	5,600
Depreciation	12,000
Taxes and permits	600
Insurance	6,000
Drivers' salaries	30,000
Administration costs	6,000
Total cost	84,600

Cost per delivery	
Total cost（F$）	84,600
Number of deliveries per month	1,000
Cost per delivery（F$）	84.60

Draft the report for Maria Coleman, finance director.

Section 3

Two weeks later, you receive the following email from Alex Hilliard, senior management accountant.

From：Alex Hilliard, Senior Management Accountant
To：Management Accountant Assistant
Subject：Outsourcing of distribution operation

The board has considered the financial and other implications of outsourcing and has decided to go ahead and outsource the distribution operation from 1st January next year.

It means that there will potentially be a need for redundancies of the delivery truck drivers and the administration staffs working in distribution. The board are keen to try to avoid compulsory redundancies and that we do everything possible to support any staffs who are being made redundant.

We also need to dispose of the delivery trucks we own, as they will no longer be required. We have asked the outsourcing companies whether they would be interested in purchasing them but they have informed us that they already have enough vehicles.

The board has asked for a report on the impact of the outsourcing decision on the financial accounts. I am putting together some figures on the potential redundancy payments, but would appreciate your help with some of the other costs that may be involved. I don't need detailed figures at this stage just some indication of the types of costs involved.

Please produce a report covering the following areas.

- Whether the delivery vehicles should be treated as "assets held for sale" in the financial statements, under IFRS 5 Assets Held for Sale and Discontinued Operations, if they are not sold to a third party before the 2016 financial year end. How should "assets held for sale" be shown in the financial statements?
- How we could avoid or limit any compulsory redundancies and the potential costs, other than redundancy payments, involved in the redundancy process.

Regards.

Alex Hilliard

Senior Management Accountant

Marici Power

Write the report for Alex Hilliard, senior management accountant.

Section 4

A few days later, you receive the following email from Alex Hilliard, senior management accountant.

From: Alex Hilliard, Senior Management Accountant

To: Management Accountant Assistant

Subject: Variance report

We have been reviewing the performance of our range of solar panels for last month and are concerned at the overall sales performance. We seem to be making significantly less profit than we had anticipated in the budget on our Solar Eclipse model.

I think that the poor performance is mainly due to a couple of issues. Firstly, the problems we have had with our delivery service which appears to have impacted on our sales in November. Secondly, there has been some debate about the budget that we set for Solar Eclipse in the first place. It seems that we failed to acknowledge in the budget that our main competitor was due to release a new model in November which is very similar to our Solar Eclipse.

I have produced a sales variance analysis which the finance director is going to discuss at the board next week. I dont have time to write the narrative to accompany the figures and would be grateful if you could complete the report for me. Please include the following areas.

- An explanation of the variances and what they tell us about our customers' preferences and market conditions.
- Whether you think it might be beneficial, in future, to split the variances into their planning and operational elements.

As a result of the reduced sales and pressure on margins, the cash budget is showing a cash deficit for the next two months which we will not be able to cover with our existing overdraft arrangements. We are already managing our inventory as efficiently as possible and there is no scope for improving our cash flow through better inventory management.

Please also include in your report a consideration of different forms of short-term finance that we could use to cover the deficit.

Many thanks!

Alex Hilliard

Senior Management Accountant

Marici Power

Sales Variance Analysis

Sales variance analysis November 2016

Sales price variance

	Actual sales quantity(units)	Standard selling price(F$)	Actual selling price(F$)	Variance (F$)	Total variance (F$)
Solar Bright	4,000	250	260	10F	40,000F
Solar Glow	4,400	280	270	10A	44,000A
Solar Halo	4,600	330	304	26A	119,600A
Solar Eclipse	4,400	430	392	38A	167,200A
	17,400				290,800A

Sales mix variance

	Actual sales quantity (units)	Actual sales @ budgeted mix(units)	Variance (units)	Standard contribution (F$)	Total variance (F$)
Solar Bright	4,000	3,828	172A	90	15,480F
Solar Glow	4,400	4,350	50F	100	5,000F
Solar Halo	4,600	4,698	98A	105	10,290A
Solar Eclipse	4,400	4,524	124A	135	16,740A
	17,400	17,400			6,550A

Sales quantity variance

	Budget sales quantity (units)	Actual sales @ budgeted mix(units)	Variance (units)	Standard contribution (F$)	Total variance (F$)
Solar Bright	4,070	3,828	242A	90	21,780A
Solar Glow	4,625	4,350	275A	100	27,500A
Solar Halo	4,995	4,698	297A	105	31,185A
Solar Eclipse	4,810	4,524	286A	135	38,610A
	18,500	17,400			119,075A

Write the report for Alex Hilliard, senior management accountant.

试卷三

本次考试的结构如下：

序号	任务数	时间（分钟）
1	1	45
2	1	45
3	1	35
4	1	55

每个部分规定的时间可用于读题、组织和书写答案。

任务一

以下是摘录自 www. maricipower. com 的客户评论页。

★☆☆☆☆

Marici 的送货服务差——送货时间晚了两天，等终于送到时还少了两块电池板。

Joyce Johnson，Freeland

2016 年 11 月 23 日

★☆☆☆☆

我已经约了安装人员星期三的上午来，但直到星期三的午餐时间，电池板还没送到。我打了一个电话给摩利兹能源公司，但他们似乎并不知道发生了什么事。三天后我终于拿到了电池板，现在正在等待安装人员重新安排安装时间。

Harper Jones，Freeland

2016 年 11 月 18 日

★☆☆☆☆

不要使用摩利兹能源公司太阳能电池板!! 他们的送货服务很糟糕!!!!

Marta Wabera，Freeland

2016 年 11 月 10 日

★★☆☆☆

电池板的质量非常好，安装人员也很棒。只可惜摩利兹能源公司的送货服务是如此的不可靠。不仅我收到的时间迟了，而且错发了订单的两倍数量。

Jodie Venchetska，Freeland

2016 年 11 月 3 日

你收到了来自财务总监 Maria Coleman 的电子邮件。

发件人：财务总监 Maria Coleman

收件人：管理会计助理

主题：交货问题

你想必已经看到了公司网站上最近的客户评论，我们也收到了很多来自我们推荐给客户的安装人员的投诉。董事会很关注这些给客户交货方面的问题对公司声誉的影响。他们要求立即进行调查，以找到问题产生的原因，以及我们可以采取什么措施，确保今后不会再发生类似情况。

我们已经进行了一些初步的调查，似乎从接收客户订单到货物交付给客户的过程中的确存在一些问题。我与支持服务总监 Christian Thoele 讨论过了，我们一致认为公司应该通过企业流程重组（BPR）来提高业务流程的效率和效益。然而，我想这可能会令员工感到非常不安，最终导致员工士气的下降。

如果你能帮我准备一些说明让我展示给员工，我将不胜感激。请在说明中解释企业流程重组涉及什么及当前情况下这么做的好处。我还考虑引入质量成本报告作为我们每月管理会计报告的一部分。鉴于目前的情况，我想现阶段的重点是关注外部故障。董事们对于我们没有更早地发现这个问题表示担忧。我翻阅了过去的月度管理会计报告，很明显我们应该正视这个问题。因此，我想向财务部工作人员发布一份有关差异调查的工作指南。

如果你还可以在说明中包含以下内容，我将不胜感激。

- 解释三种由于送货服务不到位而导致的外部损失成本，以及三个有助于早日发现质量故障的非财务指标。
- 说明如何确定哪些差异需要进行调查，应用识别出来的外部损失成本来解释你的说明。

致好！

摩利兹能源公司
财务总监
Maria Colem

请为财务总监 Maria Coleman 撰写一份报告。

任务二

几天后，你收到了来自财务总监 Maria Coleman 的电子邮件。

发件人：财务总监 Maria Coleman
收件人：管理会计助理
主题：交货问题

正如你所知，最近的董事会会议多次讨论了我们在给客户交货中遇到的问题。

支持服务总监 Christian Thoele 一直在考虑将配送服务外包的可能性。他与物流公司进行了初步的讨论，并要求财务部门对这一计划进行评估。我已经要求 Alex 在这方面做一些工作，但我希望你也能帮一点忙。

物流公司提供的价格是每次配送 F$ 75，基于一个根据体积、重量和距离的标准组合。Christian 很有兴趣推进，因为这个价格低于公司目前基于标准组合（见附件）的每次配送成本。

外包配送服务的优点之一是可以将一些固定成本转化为变动成本，并降低我们的经营杠杆。我希望你更详细地审查一下这些数据，特别是其对于我们成本结构的影响。我还需要考虑外包的其他潜在好处和局限性。

如果你可以为我起草一份发给 Christian 的报告，我将不胜感激。我希望它涵盖以下几个方面。

- 对附表数据的审查说明，包括你对外包如何影响公司成本结构和经营杠杆的看法。
- 外包配送服务对摩利兹能源公司的潜在好处和局限性。

致好！

摩利兹能源公司
财务总监
Maria Coleman

附件

配送成本：

当前每月配送成本总额	
	F$
燃油费用	17 000
轮胎	3 000
保养	4 400
修理	5 600
折旧	12 000

（续表）

当前每月配送成本总额	
	F$
税收及许可证	600
保险	6 000
司机工资	30 000
管理费用	6 000
总成本	84 600

每次配送成本	
总成本（F$）	84 600
每月的配送次数	1 000
每次配送成本（F$）	84.60

请为财务总监 Maria Coleman 起草一份报告。

任务三

两周后，你收到了来自高级管理会计师 Alex Hilliard 的电子邮件。

发件人：高级管理会计师 Alex Hilliard
收件人：管理会计助理
主题：配送业务外包

董事会考虑了外包的财务和其他方面的影响，并决定从明年1月1日起将配送业务外包。

这意味着有可能需要对卡车司机和配送部门的行政管理人员进行裁员。董事会非常希望能够避免强制性的裁员，我们将竭尽全力支持那些被裁员的员工。

我们还需要处理公司拥有的、不再需要的运输卡车。我们问过外包公司是否有兴趣购买，但对方说他们已经有足够的车辆了。

董事会要求提供一份有关外包产生的财务影响的报告。我正在汇总一些可能的裁员补偿款数据，但是希望你可以帮助提供其他可能涉及的成本。目前阶段我还不需要详细的数据，只要列出一些涉及的成本类型即可。

请写一份包括以下内容的报告。

- 根据国际财务报告准则第 5 号“持有待售的非流动资产和终止经营”，如果在 2016 财政年度结束前，运输车辆还没有出售给第三方，是否应被视为财务报表中的“持有待售的非流动资产”。“持有待售的非流动资产”在财务报表中应该如何列示？
- 在裁员的过程中，除了裁员补偿款以外，我们如何避免或减少任何强制性裁员和潜在成本。

致好！

摩利兹能源公司
高级管理会计师
Alex Hilliard

请撰写一份提供给高级管理会计师 Alex Hilliard 的报告。

任务四

几天后，你收到了来自高级管理会计师 Alex Hilliard 的电子邮件。

发件人：高级管理会计师 Alex Hilliard
收件人：管理会计师助理
主题：差异报告

我们一直在审查上个月不同类型的太阳能电池板的业绩，并关注了整体销售业绩。Solar Eclipse 产品的利润似乎明显低于预算。

我认为该产品表现不佳有几个主要原因。首先，我们在送货服务方面出现的问题似乎影响到了 11 月的销售。其次，对于我们最初确定的 Solar Eclipse 预算，本来就存在一些争议。我们的主要竞争对手预计会在 11 月份发布一款与 Solar Eclipse 非常相似的产品，但似乎我们没能在预算中反映出来。

我已经做了一份销售差异分析，财务总监下周将在董事会讨论。我没有时间写下对这些数据的解释，如果你能帮我完成报告，我将不胜感激。报告请包括以下几个方面。

- 对差异的解释以及我们可以从中得知的客户偏好和市场情况。

■ 你是否认为今后将差异分解为计划差异和运营差异两个部分会有好处。

由于销售量下降和利润率的压力，现金预算显示在未来两个月会出现赤字，我们将无法用现有的透支协议来弥补。我们已经尽可能有效地管理库存了，所以无法通过更好的存货管理来改善现金流。

请在报告中加入以下内容：

■ 对于我们可以用来弥补赤字的不同形式的短期融资的考虑。

十分感谢！

摩利兹能源公司

高级管理会计师

Alex Hilliard

销售差异分析

2016 年 11 月销售差异分析					
销售价格差异					
	实际销售数量（件）	标准销售价格（F$）	实际销售价格（F$）	差异（F$）	总差异（F$）
Solar Bright	4 000	250	260	10F	40 000F
Solar Glow	4 400	280	270	10A	44 000A
Solar Halo	4 600	330	304	26A	119 600A
Solar Eclipse	4 400	430	392	38A	167 200A
	17 400				290 800A
销售组合差异					
	实际销售数量（件）	实际销售量@预计组合（件）	差异（件）	标准边际贡献（F$）	总差异（F$）
Solar Bright	4 000	3 328	172F	90	15 480F
Solar Glow	4 400	4 350	50F	100	5 000F

（续表）

2016 年 11 月销售差异分析					
销售组合差异					
	预计销售数量（件）	实际销售量@预计组合（件）	差异（件）	标准边际贡献（F$）	总差异（F$）
Solar Halo	4 600	4 698	98A	105	10 290A
Solar Eclipse	4 400	4 524	124A	135	16 740A
	17 400	17 400			6 550A
销售数量差异					
Solar Bright	4 070	3 328	242A	90	21 780A
Solar Glow	4 625	4 350	275A	100	27 500A
Solar Halo	4 995	4 698	297A	105	31 185A
Solar Eclipse	4 810	4 524	286A	135	38 610A
	18 500	17 400			119 075A

请为高级管理会计师 Alex Hilliard 撰写一份报告。

Variant 3 Suggested Answers

Section 1

Customer Delivery Issues

BPR

BPR involves the fundamental rethinking and redesign of existing business processes to achieve improvements in performance as measured in terms of cost, quality, service and speed. The main objective of BPR is to enable us to meet the needs of our customers which we are failing to do at the moment.

BPR will challenge our managers and staff to totally rethink the way they do things in order to improve organizational effectiveness. It may involve setting targets for improvements in performance not previously contemplated.

The first stage of BPR will be to identify and review our existing processes. In this case we would need to review all the process from the point where we receive customers' orders to the point where we deliver the goods to the customers. We can then establish whether the process is necessary, adding value or supporting another value adding process. Those processes which are not adding value or which are not essential to supporting another value-adding process can be eliminated. The remaining processes can be redesigned so that they work in the most efficient way possible. The re-engineered processes can then be implemented resulting in our company working in the most efficient manner possible.

BPR often includes the creative use of IT wherever this can enhance business processes. In this case we will need to look at how our IT systems operate and the linkages between different parts of the system. We might consider the use of an enterprise resource planning (ERP) system to help solve some of the problems that we are currently experiencing.

We will need to handle the review carefully as the introduction of new processes may involve new working patterns and potentially redundancies and loss of staff goodwill. It is important therefore as you have suggested that we explain clearly to staffs what the process involves and its potential benefits. It is essential that we deal effectively with the current issues to secure the long-term future of the business and employees.

The benefits to the company may be significant in terms of reducing organizational complexity by concentrating on core processes and eliminating unnecessary or uneconomic activities. It may also provide us with a cost advantage over our competitors. It should certainly result in an improvement in our customer service.

The use of BPR is a radical solution however, and requires careful consideration as this involves a fundamental review and possibly a costly reorganization of the way in which we conduct our operations.

Quality Reporting

External Failure Quality Costs

The current issues in respect of customer deliveries will have resulted in significant external failure costs. The following financial indicators would have been useful in helping us identify the issues.

Excess delivery costs arising from the need to make good short deliveries and to return the excess of over deliveries.

Cost of processing complaints from customers in respect of delayed deliveries and under or over deliveries.

Inspection costs of returned goods to establish whether the panels can be returned to stock, need to be reworked/repaired or will require disposal.

Non-Financial Indicators

Non-financial indicators will be important to help us identify quality issues and to measure our progress in rectifying the quality issues.

Number of customer complaints—a rise in customer complaints would have provided an indicator that there was a quality issue which we could then have investigated further to establish the specific reasons.

Number of incorrect deliveries—if our systems had been operating effectively there should be no incorrect deliveries. This would be a clear indicator that we have an issue with our deliveries and trigger action to rectify the problems.

Average score on customer reviews—our website enables customers to rate the quality of our products and services. This feedback should be monitored regularly and will provide early indicator of any issues. We can clearly see from the information given that customer rating are very low.

Investigation of Variances

We could potentially adopt a policy where we investigate every reported variance, but this would be expensive and time consuming and would lead to the investigation of variances that would not result in improvements of operations even if the cause of the variance was determined. The objective of the policy should be to investigate those variances that yield benefits in excess of the cost of the investigation.

We would need to consider the following factors before deciding whether to investigate a variance.

(1) The size of the variance—costs tend to fluctuate around a norm and therefore variances may be expected on most costs. We will need to decide how large a variance must be before it is considered "abnormal" and worthy of investigation. The size could be determined in terms of an absolute amount or a predetermined percentage of the standard cost. It may be appropriate to set different percentages for different cost items. For example, we may want to set a fairly low level for goods returned inwards since the effect of a variance relates not only to the costs of the goods returned which are quantifiable but also to the damage to our reputation which is not quantifiable. The problems with deliveries to our customers should have been apparent from both an adverse variance on goods returned inwards and delivery costs which we have failed to recognise.

(2) The likelihood of the variance being controllable—managers may know from experience that certain variances may not be controllable even if a lengthy investigation is undertaken to determine their cause. Managers may argue that a material price variance is less easily controlled than a material usage variance as it is determined by external factors. On the other hand a material price variance may be due to the efficiency of the purchasing department and this would only be apparent after further investigation. We would need to consider each of the reported variances and determined which ones, if any, would be considered uncontrollable.

(3) The standard set—a variance may arise when changes in the price of inputs occur resulting in standard prices being outdated. Any investigation of variances would indicate a general change in market price rather than efficiency or inefficiency in acquiring the resources. Any investigation of these variances would indi-

cate a need to revise the standards. Ideally, standards should be reviewed frequently and updated to avoid variances being reported due to out of date standards.

Section 2

Delivery Outsourcing Report—Cost Analysis, Advantages/Disadvantages

Analysis of Delivery Costs

We can influence to a certain extent the level of fixed and variable costs in our cost structure. Companies with lower variable costs and higher fixed costs have a higher contribution margin and higher operational gearing. Operational gearing measures the sensitivity of profits to changes in sales. Higher degrees of operational gearing can provide significantly greater profits when sales are increasing but higher percentage decreases will also occur when sales are declining. High operational gearing results in a higher risk since the company has a high level of fixed costs which must be paid even if volumes and hence contribution, are low. We currently have high variable costs and therefore relatively low operational gearing. If we were to outsource our distribution service it would reduce further our operational gearing but will have a fairly minor impact.

Our current distribution service uses a mixture of both fixed and variable costs. Fuel costs, tyres, maintenance and repairs would be considered variable costs since these are all likely to vary with the number of miles travelled. Taxes and permits, insurance and drivers' salaries are all likely to be considered stepped fixed costs since these would take a stepped increase if our activity level increases significantly and result in the need for additional vehicles.

Administration costs would be considered fixed costs although these are likely also to take a stepped increase outside a large relevant range.

As the activity level increases, for example the number of deliveries or the number of miles travelled, the total variable costs will increase in direct proportion and the fixed costs will remain the same up to a certain level of activity. As the volume of activity rises, the cost per delivery will fall as the fixed costs per delivery fall.

If we decide to outsource the distribution service the price per delivery from the outsourcing company would be a variable cost. The logistics company is offering to provide the service at a cost of F$75 per delivery which is below our current cost per delivery.

We could also calculate an indifference point, that is, the number of deliveries where we would be neither better nor worse off using the logistic company's service. If our number of deliveries is not expected to rise above the indifference point, then we would be better off, in the short-term, using the outsourcing company. However this is not a short-term decision since it would commit the company for the medium to longer term. We should also bear in mind that there may be other costs involved with outsourcing, for example, administration costs in managing the relationship with the company.

Benefits of Outsourcing

If we believe that delivery to customers is not one of our core activities then outsourcing our delivery service will enable us to focus on our core activities, of manufacturing and selling solar panels, as these are the things we best understand. The delivery service might more effectively be provided by a third party on our behalf. Outsourcing would enable us to focus on our core business and by so doing become more specialised and proficient in that business without the distractions of carrying out other functions in which we have limited expertise.

Outsourcing organisations are often able to provide services at a lower cost than if we were to carry out the activities in-house. The cost of services charged by an external provider may often be lower because of the particular expertise and economies of scale that the provider enjoys.

Outsourcing may result in improvements in the quality of the distribution service because the external supplier can provide specialist expertise, knowledge, equipment and best practice not possessed by ourselves.

Disadvantages of Outsourcing

If the distribution service is considered to represent (or contribute to) a core competence for us, for example, customer service, then outsourcing would be inadvisable as the basis of our competitive advantage could be threatened unnecessarily. Quality and customer service is an important aspect of our business and if we do decide to outsource we need to ensure that the quality standards provided by the delivery company meet the standards we would expect and also our customers' expectations.

There may be resistance from staff groups and unions representing in-house workers whose jobs may be threatened. This may harm industrial relations and possibly lead to disruption in performance. Under these conditions, the initiative may be counter-productive. Outsourcing and a threat of job losses could affect staff relations and lead to a lack of motivation within the workforce.

The move to outsourcing may detract from our positive organizational culture by eroding shared values and goodwill.

Additional costs will be incurred associated with determining service specifications and ultimately monitoring performance.

Once the distribution service has been contracted out, it may be very difficult to take it back in-house at a later date, if things do not work out.

Section 3

Delivery Outsourcing Report—Impact on Financial Statements, Redundancies

Treatment of the Delivery Vehicles in the Financial Statements

Non-current assets will be classified as "assets held for sale" if their carrying amount is recovered principally through a sales transaction rather than through continuing use.

In general, the following conditions must be met for an asset (or "disposal group") to be classified as held for sale.

- Management is committed to a plan to sell.
- The asset is available for immediate sale.
- An active programme to locate a buyer is initiated.
- The sale is highly probable, within 12 months of classification as held for sale (subject to limited exceptions).
- The asset is being actively marketed for sale at a sales price reasonable in relation to its fair value.
- Actions required to complete the plan indicate that it is unlikely that plan will be significantly changed or withdrawn.

The outsourcing of the delivery service has been decided and the vehicles are available for sale. We are actively seeking a buyer for the vehicles at a reasonable price and given the nature of the assets it is highly probable that a buyer will be found within 12 months. The delivery vehicles would therefore be classified as "held for sale". These would be shown in the statement of financial position, under non-current assets, at the lower of the carrying amount and the fair value less costs of disposal.

Managing Redundancies

The directors are keen to avoid compulsory redundancies if possible and there are a number of methods we can use to avoid or at least limit the number of compulsory redundancies.

Some staffs affected may wish to volunteer for redundancy particularly if we offer redundancy payments above the statutory minimum. For the remaining staffs, we would need to assess whether it is possible for any of them to be offered a different position within the organisation. We should delay any further external recruitment until we have assessed whether the staffs affected by redundancy could fill any of the current vacancies. This may involve fairly minimal retraining costs to enable the administration staffs to move to other administration roles with the company, but for the delivery vehicle drivers there may be significant retraining costs required to make up for any skill deficiencies.

We may also be able to create other job opportunities by encouraging staffs over normal retirement age inducements to retire. We should also give consideration to adopting more flexible working practices such as offers of job-sharing between two or more people, and/or a shorter working week for certain groups.

There will also be costs associated with managing the redundancy process.

We will need to consider and discuss possible alternative actions with the relevant trade unions and/or staff representatives and be clear as to how we intend to conduct the process and the timescales involved. The process will need to be sensitively handled and management should seek to cushion negative impacts upon any individuals affected. We will need to ensure that there is effective communication and transparency of processes. This will involve administration costs mainly in respect of HR employee's time but also in producing literature to keep employees and interested parties informed.

There will also be costs involved in providing support for staffs affected by the redundancies.

We should consider appropriate and varied forms of support for individuals affected by job reductions. This might involve organizing counselling and peer support groups, in order to support for those retiring early and if, as a last resort, there is a need for compulsory redundancies, we must follow any established and agreed processes. For those workers made redundant we should do all we can to assist displaced individuals to find new works by offering a range of opportunities such as retraining, career coaching, sessions in CV writing and financial advice, outplacement consultants and job fairs, in order to get redundant workers back into work as soon as possible.

We need to recognise that it is important, as suggested by the directors, that redundancies should be avoided wherever possible. Staff redundancies will have an impact on both the company's reputation and the motivation and performance of our existing employees.

Section 4

Variances and Short-term Finance

Sales Variances

It is clear from the variance report that we are not performing as well as budget. For the month of November we are showing a total adverse variance.

The price variance has accounted for F$ 290,800 of the total variance. Each of our models has an adverse price variance which probably reflects the need to cut prices in response to the bad publicity about the delivery issues. It may also reflect the level of competition in the market. The highest variance however is in the Solar Eclipse model where we have probably had to make significant price reductions to achieve sales.

The sales mix and quantity variance give us an interesting insight into what is happening in the market. In total, the sales volume variance was adverse. Sales volumes are 1,100 units less than budget, despite the reductions in sales prices. By breaking this down further into the sales mix and sales quantity variance, we can see that we are F$ 6,550 worse off because the sales mix is different to what we estimated in the budget. There has been a switch from the "Solar Eclipse" model and "Solar Halo" brands to the "Solar Bright" and "Solar Glow" brands. The "Solar Bright" brand produces the lowest contribution and, if this trend continues, it will impact significantly on the company's profits. The variance reflects the competition in the market from the new competitor product but possibly also a movement towards lower cost solar panels. The sales quantity variance of F$ 119,075 is even more significant and tells us that our customers are not only switching towards our lower priced brands but are also buying less from us. This again is an indication of the competition in the market and possibly the effect on our reputation from the recent bad publicity.

We also need to look at the impact of the lower solar panel sales on our other products i. e. kits, inverters etc.

Planning and Operational Variances

Standards are normally based on the anticipated environment. It could be argued that if the environment is significantly different from the expected environment, actual performance should be compared with a standard that takes account of these changed conditions. This would provide a more meaningful measure of managerial performance.

The planning variances may not be controllable but does provide some useful information to managers on the accuracy of their planning and could help to improve the accuracy of future plans. It appears that our planning was inaccurate as the potential effect on prices of the market competition has not been incorporated in the budget.

Operational variances are considered to be controllable and hence they provide a better measure of the operating efficiency. If we are trying to assess the performance of the sales manager, it would be better to separate out the planning variances from the operational variances. It is important though to identify who has responsibility for the reduced sales. It would be unfair to evaluate the sales manager on the adverse sales variances if the main reason for the variances was the issues with the delivery to customers.

Sources of Short-term Finance

The main sources of short-term finance are as follows.

Trade Payables

Trade credit is a source of short-term finance. We could delay payment to our suppliers which would help to alleviate our cash flow difficulties but we would lose any early settlement discounts. Delaying payment without prior agreement from our suppliers is also unethical and suppliers may stop further supplies or take legal action against us. Both of these would be harmful to our reputation and credit rating. It is important therefore that we ensure agreement with our suppliers before taking this course of action.

Trade Receivables

We could use our trade receivables as a source of short-term finance by factoring the debts or using invoice discounting. There would be interest costs and fees involved with either of these options and we would need to evaluate whether this was worthwhile. Invoice discounting has the advantage that it is a confidential service whereas with factoring the customers are aware that the debt is being factored and this may raise a question mark over our financial stability.

Bank Borrowings

Bank overdraft: we could try to increase our bank overdraft facility. This has the advantage that it is flexible and that we only pay interest on the amount used which means it is a relatively cheap source of finance. The interest rate is variable which means we are exposed to any changes in bank base rate and makes it more difficult for us to budget for the interest costs. We should however be able to increase our overdraft but would need to check our current security arrangements with the bank. They will probably require us to provide up to date cash and profit forecasts to support our application for an increase in the facility.

Bank loan: alternatively, we could agree a short-term loan with the bank to cover the period of the additional cash deficit over and above our overdraft limit. Interest however will be payable on the whole sum of the loan for the specified period of the loan. This is therefore liable to be more expensive than an increase in the overdraft. We may also have to provide further security for the loan.

试卷三　参考答案

任务一

交货问题

企业流程重组

企业流程重组是对现有业务流程进行根本性的反思和重新设计，以实现成本、质量、服务和速度方面的业绩提升。企业流程重组的主要目标是使我们能够满足当前未能满足的客户需求。

企业流程重组将给我们的管理人员和员工带来挑战，让他们彻底地重新思考做事的方式，以提高组织的效益。它包括设定以前没有仔细考虑过的业绩改进目标。

企业流程重组的第一阶段是识别和审查我们现有的流程。在这种情况下，我们需要审查所有的流程，从收到客户订单到把货物送到客户手中。然后，确定这些流程是否必要，是否增加价值或支持另一个增值流程。那些不增加价值的，或对支持另一个增值流程不是必需的流程部分可以取消。其余的流程可以重新设计，以便用可能最有效的方式工作。经过重组的流程可以使我们公司以可能最有效的方式运转。

企业流程重组通常包括创造性地使用信息技术，无论在什么地方，都能加快业务流程。在这种情况下，我们需要研究我们的信息技术系统是如何运作的，以及系统不同部分之间的联系。我们可以考虑使用企业资源规划（ERP）系统来帮助我们解决目前遇到的一些问题。

我们要认真对待这项审查，因为引进新的流程可能会带来新的工作模式、可能的裁员及公司在员工眼中的声誉损失。因此正如你所建议的那样，重要的是向员工解释清楚流程重组所涉及的内容及潜在的好处。有效地处理当前的问题，以确保企业和员工的长久未来，是十分必要的。

通过集中精力于核心流程和消除不必要的或不经济的活动，来降低组织的复杂性，对公司来说意义重大。它还可以为我们提供超越竞争对手的成本优势，所以肯定也会改善我们的客户服务。

然而，实施企业流程重组是一个根本性的解决方案，需要仔细考虑，这涉及一个基础性的审查，也可能要对我们的经营方式进行一个成本高昂的重组。

质量成本报告

外部失败成本

目前，有关给客户交货的问题将导致大量的外部失败成本。下列财务指标将有助于我们查明问题。

由于需要快速送货和退还超出的货物而导致的超额配送成本。

在延迟交货和交货过多或不足的情况下处理客户投诉的成本。

退回货物的检验费用，用以确定电池板是可以直接退回到仓库，还是需要进行返工/修理或处理。

非财务指标

非财务指标对于帮助我们找出质量问题，以及衡量整改质量问题取得的进展是很重要的。

客户投诉数量——客户投诉数量的上升表明质量存在问题，我们可以进一步调查以确定具体原因。

错误配送的次数——如果我们的系统已经有效运行，就不应该存在错误的配送。这个指标能清楚地表明我们在交货中遇到的问题，并触发纠正问题的行动。

客户平均评分——我们的网站能够让客户评价产品和服务质量。这些反馈意见应被定期监测，其提供了问题发生的早期指示。从之前给出的信息中我们可以清楚地看到，客户评分很低。

差异调查

我们可以采取调查每项报告差异的策略，但这将是昂贵和耗时的，并且可能会导致无效的差异调查，即使确定了差异产生的原因也并不能改善经营。该项政策的目标应该是调查那些产生的利益超过调查成本的差异。

在决定是否调查一项差异之前，我们需要考虑一些因素。

（1）差异的大小——成本往往在正常范围内波动，因此大多数的成本差异是可以预期的。我们需要确定差异多大时才会被认为是“异常”并值得去调查的。差异的大小可以根据绝对量或标准成本的预计百分比来确定。恰当的方式可以是为不同的成本项目设置不同的百分比。例如，我们可能想要为货物退回产生的成本差异设定一个相当低的百分比，因为它不仅与可量化的退货成本有关，而且涉及不可量化的声誉损害。从因退货和未能估算到的配送成本导致的不利差异，可以明显看出我们给客户交货存在问题。

（2）差异的可控性——管理人员可以从经验中得知，即使进行漫长的调查去确定差异产生的原因，某些差异可能仍无法控制。管理人员可能认为材料价格差异不如材料用量差异易于控制，因为它是由外部因素决定的。另一方面，材料价格差异也可能是由于采购部门的效率造成的，这只有在进一步调查后才会知道。我们需要考虑每项报告的差异，并确定哪些（如果有的话）将被视为不可控差异。

（3）标准设立——当购入价格变化导致标准价格过时的时候，差异就出现了。差异调查表明这是由市场价格的正常波动造成的，而不是因为获取资源的效率高低。对这些差异的调查也表明标准需要被修订。在理想情况下，应经常审查和更新标准，以避免报告的差异是因为过时的标准而产生的。

任务二

配送外包报告——成本分析，优点/缺点

配送成本分析

我们可以在一定程度上影响成本结构中固定和变动成本的水平。变动成本较低而固定成本较高的公司具有更高的边际贡献率和经营杠杆。经营杠杆衡量利润对销售变化的敏感性。当销售额增长时，更高的经营杠杆率会带来更显著的利润增加，但销售额下降时，利润也会下降更大的百分比。高经营杠杆会导致更高的风险，因为公司具有高水平的固定成本，即使销售数量和边际贡献都很低也必须支付。我们公司目前变动成本较高，因此经营杠杆相对较低。如果我们外包配送服务，将进一步降低公司的经营杠杆，但只会造成相当小的影响。

公司目前的配送服务成本是固定和变动成本的混合。燃油、轮胎、维护和维修成本被视为变动成本，因为这些成本都可能随着运输里程数而变化。税金、许可证费用、保险费用和司机薪酬被归为阶梯式固定成本，因为如果我们的业务量水平显著增加，并且需要增加额外的车辆，这些费用就会呈阶梯上升。管理费用算作固定成本，虽然这些成本也可能在超过较大的相关范围时发生阶梯式增长。

随着业务水平的提高，例如配送次数或运输里程数，变动成本的总额将成正比例增加，固定成本则在一定的业务量水平上保持不变。随着业务量的增加，每次配送成本将随着每次配送分摊的固定成本下降而下降。

如果我们决定外包配送服务，外包公司的每次配送价格将是变动成本。有一家物流公司可以按每次 F$ 75 的价格提供这项服务，这低于我们目前的单位配送成本。

我们还可以计算一个成本无差别点，即我们使用物流公司服务时不会更好也不会更糟的配送次数。如果我们的配送次数预计不会高于成本无差别点，那么在短期内，还是使用外包公司更好。然而，这不是一个短期决策，因为它将给公司带来中期到长期的制约。我们还应该记住，外包可能还会产生其他成本，例如管理与外包公司关系的成本。

外包的优点

如果我们认为向客户交付不是我们的核心活动之一，那么外包配送服务将使我们能够专注于核心活动，即制造和销售太阳能电池板，因为这些是我们最了解的。由第三方代表我方提供的配送服务有可能会更高效。外包将使我们能够专注于核心业务，并通过这样做我们可以对这些业务变得更加专业和精通，而不会因履行其他职能而分心，对那些职能我们只有有限的专业知识。

外包组织通常能够以比我们在内部开展活动更低的成本提供服务。由于服务提供者所享有的特定专业知识和规模经济，外部服务提供者收取的服务费用往往较低。

外包可能带来配送服务质量的提高，因为外部供应商可以提供我们不具备的专业技能、知识、设备和最佳实践。

外包的缺点

如果配送服务被认为代表着（或有助于）我们的核心竞争力，例如客户服务，那么外包将是不合适的，因为我们的竞争优势的基础可能会受到不必要的威胁。质量和客户服务是公司经营的重要方面，如果我们决定外包，就需要确保运输公司提供的质量标准既符合我们期望的标准，也能满足我们客户的期望。

外包可能会遭到来自员工团体和代表内部工人的工会的抵制，因为这威胁到了他们的工作。这也可能会损害劳资关系，并可能导致业绩受损。在这种情况下，这一举措可能会产生反效果。外包和失业的威胁可能会影响员工关系，并导致员工缺乏动力。

外包可能会对我们的共同价值观和声誉产生侵蚀，从而损害我们积极的组织文化。

确定服务规格和最终监控其表现的相关额外成本将产生。

一旦配送服务已经被外包出去，如果问题仍没有解决，以后可能就很难再将其重新置于内部。

任务三

配送外包报告——对于财务报告和裁员的影响

财务报表对运输车辆冗余的处理

如果非流动资产的账面价值将主要通过销售交易而不是持续使用得以收回，该资产就将被归类为“持有待售的非流动资产”。

一般来说，资产（或“处置组”）必须符合以下条件才能被归类为持有待售资产。

- 管理层已着手制订出售计划。
- 该资产可立即出售。
- 积极寻找买方的行动已经展开。
- 在被划分为持有以备出售的12个月内，出售是很可能发生的（除有限的例外情况）。
- 资产正在以符合其公允价值的合理价格积极地出售。
- 完成此出售计划所需的行动表明不可能对出售计划做出重大修改或予以撤销。

外包配送服务已经被确定了，车辆也可以出售了。我们正在以合理的价格积极寻求车辆的买方，鉴于资产的性质，很有可能在12个月内找到买家。因此，运输车辆可以被归类为“持有待售的非流动资产”。这些资产将列示在资产负债表中的非流动资产下，以账面价值和公允价值减去处置成本两者中的较低者列报。

管理裁员

如果可能的话，董事们非常希望避免强制性的裁员，我们可以使用一些方法来避免或至少限制强制性裁员的数量。

一些受到影响的员工可能希望自愿离职，特别是如果我们能提供超过法定最低限度的裁员补偿的话。对于其余的工作人员，我们需要评估他们是否有可能在组织内担任另一个职位。我们应该推迟任何进一步的外部招聘，直到我们评估完受到裁员影响的员工是否可以填补目前的空缺。使管理人员能够担任公司的其他管理角色，这可能只涉及相当少的再培训费用，但对于运输车辆的司机来说，就可能需要大量的再培训费用来弥补他们的技能缺陷。

我们也可以通过鼓励已超过正常退休年龄的员工退休，以此来创造其他工作机会。我们还应该考虑采取更灵活的工作方式，例如在两个人或更多的人之间实施轮班制，或者让某些群体缩短工作时间。

管理裁员的过程也将产生相关的成本。

我们需要与有关工会和（或）员工代表一起考虑和讨论可能的替代方案，明确我们打算如何实施这一过程并制定时间表。这个过程需要谨慎处理，管理层应该设法减轻对受影响的个人的负面影响。我们也需要确保有效的沟通和过程的透明度。这将产生管理成本，主要是耗用了人力资源部门职员的时间，也涉及制作宣传资料，用以向员工和相关方通报情况。

为受到裁员影响的员工提供支持也要付出成本。

我们应该考虑为因裁员而受影响的员工提供适当的和多种形式的支持。这可能包括组织咨询和同伴互助团体，以此去帮助那些提早退休的人。最后如果需要强制性裁员，我们就必须按照既定的和协商好的程序进行。对于那些被解雇的员工，我们应该竭尽所能地去帮助他们找到新的工作，通过提供一系列的机会，例如再培训、职业指导、简历写作、财务咨询、职业顾问和招聘会等，来让被解雇的人员尽快回到工作岗位。

我们需要认识到，正如董事们所建议的那样，尽可能避免裁员是很重要的。裁员将对公司的声誉和现有员工的积极性和表现产生影响。

任务四

差异和短期融资

销售差异

从差异报告中可以清楚地看出，我们的业绩没有达到预算目标。11 月份呈现出总的不利差异。

在总差异中，价格差异达到了 F$ 290 800。每种类型的产品都出现了不利的价格差异，这可能反映了我们需要降价以应对配送问题带来的负面影响，也可能反映了市场竞争的水平。然而，差异最大的是日蚀太阳能这种类型，我们可能不得不大幅降价以促进销售。

销售组合和数量差异给我们提供了一个了解市场上正在发生的情况的有趣的视角。总体而言，销售量差异是不利的。尽管销售价格有所下降，总销售量仍比预算低了1 100 个单位。通过将差异进一步细分为销售组合差异和销售数量差异，我们可以看到，由于销售组合与预算中估计的不同，收益下降了 F$ 6 550。对“Solar Eclipse”和“Solar Halo”的需求已经转向了“Solar Bright”和“Solar Glow”。“Solar Bright”的单位边际贡献是最低的，如果这种趋势持续下去，将会对公司的利润产生重大影响。这种差异反映了来自市场上新对手产品的竞争，但也可能反映了一种转向成本较低的太阳能电池板的趋势。销售数量差异为 F$ 119 075，更为显著地表明，我们的客户不仅转向了我们的低价位品牌，而且减少了购买数量。这再次表明了市场竞争的态势，也可能是近期的负面消息对我们的声誉造成了影响。

我们还需要研究一下太阳能电池板销售下降对我们的其他产品，如配套元件、逆变器等的影响。

计划差异与运营差异

标准制定通常基于预期的环境。可以这样认为，如果实际环境与预期环境有显著差异，则应将实际绩效与考虑到这些变化情况后的标准进行比较。这将为绩效管理提供一个更有意义的衡量指标。

计划差异可能是不可控的，但是它确实为管理人员的计划准确性提供了一些有用的信息，有助于提高未来计划的准确性。看来我们之前的计划并不准确，因为市场竞争对价格的潜在影响未被纳入预算。

运营差异被认为是可控的，因此可以用来更好地衡量经营效率。如果我们试图评估销售经理的绩效，最好将计划差异与运营差异分开，这对于确定谁应该对销售量减少负责是很重要的。如果造成差异的主要原因是货物配送上出现的问题，那么用不利的销售差异来评估销售经理就是不公平的。

短期融资的来源

主要的短期融资来源有以下几个方面。

应付账款

贸易信贷是短期融资的来源之一。我们可以延迟付款给供应商，这将有助于减轻我们的现金流困境，但我们将失去早期结算可获得的折扣。未经供应商事先同意的延迟付款也是不道德的，供应商可能会停止进一步供应或对我们采取法律行动，这两者都将对公司的声誉和信用评级造成损害。因此，重要的是在采取此行动之前，我们必须确保与供应商达成一致。

应收账款

我们可以利用应收账款，通过债务保理或发票贴现的方式作为短期融资的来源。这些方法将带来利息费用和其他相关费用，我们需要评估这么做是否值得。发票贴现的优点在于它是一种保密服务，然而在保理业务下，客户如果意识到债务被保理了，可能会对我们的财务稳定性产生疑问。

银行借款

银行透支：我们可以尝试增加银行透支额度。它的优点是灵活，而且我们只需对使用的金额支付利息，这意味着它是相对便宜的资金来源。利率是可变的，这意味着银行基准利率的任何变化都会对我们造成影响，使我们更难以预算利息费用。然而，我们应该能够增加透支额度，但需要检查我们目前与银行的保证金安排。银行可能会要求我们提供最新的现金和利润预测，以支持我们增加透支额度的申请。

银行贷款：或者，我们可以与银行达成短期贷款协议，以弥补超出透支限额的额外现金赤字。基于贷款总额的利息将在贷款期限内被支付。因此，这可能会比增加透支额的成本更高。我们还得为这笔贷款提供进一步的担保。

Variant 3 Marking Guidance

Section	Technical skills		Business skills		People skills		Leadership skills		Integration	Total
1	External failure costs and non-financial indicators Investigation of variances	9 8	Business process re-engineering	3	Business process re-engineering	4	Business process re-engineering	1		25
2	Impact of outsourcing on operational gearing and cost structure	9	Impact of outsourcing on operational gearing and cost structure Benefits and limitations of outsourcing	3 6	Benefits and limitations of outsourcing	2	Impact of outsourcing on operational gearing and cost structure Benefits and limitations of outsourcing	1 1	3	25
3	Assets held for sale	10	Limiting redundancy and associated costs	4	Limiting redundancy and associated costs	4	Limiting redundancy and associated costs	2		20
4	Sales variances Planning and operational variances Financing a cash deficit	10 7 10			Planning and operational variances	3				30
Total marks available for each competency		63		16		13		5	3	100

试卷三 评分指南

部分	技术技能		商业技能		人际技能		领导技能		综合	总计
1	外部失败成本和非财务指标 差异调查	9 8	企业流程重组	3	企业流程再造	4	企业流程重组	1		25
2	外包对经营杠杆和成本结构的影响	9	外包对经营杠杆和成本结构的影响 外包的优点和局限性	3 6	外包的优点和局限性	2	外包对经营杠杆和成本结构的影响 外包的优点和局限性	1 1	3	25
3	持有待售的资产	10	限制裁员和相关成本	4	限制裁员和相关成本	4	限制裁员和相关成本	2		20
4	销售差异 计划差异和运营差异 弥补现金赤字	10 7 10			计划和运营差异	3				30
各种能力分数总计		63		16		13		5	3	100

江西财经大学名师解惑

试卷一共有四项任务，考查了P1、F1、E1三门课程的知识点，具体包括企业流程再造、外部质量失败成本、外包、持有待售的非流动资产、限制裁员、销售差异、计划差异和运营差异、短期融资等。该试卷考核了考生的四项能力，其中技术技能的分值占63%，商业技能的分值占16%，人际技能的分值占13%，领导技能的分值占5%，与CGMA管理会计能力框架的技能要求一致。

该试卷的每项任务涉及以下知识点：

任务	问题	科目	知识点
任务一	解释企业流程重组并说明其优点	E1	企业流程重组（business process re-engineering）
	说明3种外部质量失败成本和3个识别质量失败的非财务性指标	P1/ E1	外部质量失败成本（external failure quality cost）
	确定需要调查的差异	P1	差异调查（investigation of variances）
任务二	外包对成本结构和经营杠杆的影响	P1/E1	外包（outsourcing）
	外包的优点和局限性	P1/E1	外包（outsourcing）
任务三	根据国际财务报告准则第5号，持有待售的非流动资产应如何报告	F1	持有待售的非流动资产（non-current assets held for sale）
	限制裁员和相关成本	E1	裁员（redundancy）
任务四	解释销售差异并分析客户偏好和市场状况	P1	销售差异（sales variance）
	区分计划差异和运营差异	P1	计划差异和运营差异（planning variance and operational variance）
	用于弥补现金赤字的短期融资	F1	短期融资（short-term finance）

上述各项任务要求以报告的方式来呈现答案，考生所要回答的问题一般都非常明确，不需要自己再去归纳问题。这套试题考查的3门课程所涉及的知识点比重相当，很多解答要点都可以从考试教材上直接找到，所以考生要做到对教材内容非常熟悉。特别是F1中的知识点，如被判定为持有待售的非流动资产必须符合的条件，是国际财务报告准则第5号里明确规定的，一定要熟记。这套试题在考查P1的知识点时，差异分析

是重点。平时的课程学习中，考生对这个知识点关注的重点是怎样计算差异，但在案例分析考试中，答题时以解释原理及应用为主，并不涉及具体的差异计算。解答一定要结合案例的具体情况，特别是涉及 E1 的知识点时尤其如此。

对应知识点的深度剖析

企业流程重组

企业流程重组强调以业务流程为改造对象和中心，以关心客户的需求和满意度为目标，对现有的业务流程进行根本的再思考和彻底的再设计，以实现成本、质量、服务和速度方面的业绩提升。考生需要能够解释企业流程重组的流程，分析企业流程重组对员工和企业的影响，描述企业流程重组带来的好处及可能的不利影响。虽然问题中没有明确要求列出企业流程重组的不利影响，但从回答问题的完整性角度考虑，也要提及一下。

外部失败成本

标准的质量成本四分法将质量成本划分为预防成本、鉴定成本、外部失败成本和内部失败成本四个类别。外部失败成本是指产品交付给客户之后，发现质量问题而由企业支付的一切费用的总和。考生容易想到的、常见的外部失败成本项目有赔偿、退货、产品折价和保修等等，但在本案例中，外部失败成本主要指由配送服务不佳带来的，而非产品本身的质量问题。考生在解答时要思考配送服务不佳可能会带来哪些成本增加，回答要有针对性。在提出三项可能的外部质量失败成本之后，识别质量缺陷的非财务指标就相应地针对造成这三项质量成本的原因来设计。

差异调查

对一项差异是否要深入调查，主要依据成本效益原则来判断，只有当调查差异带来的利益超过成本时，才值得这么做。在决定是否调查一项差异之前，需要考虑的因素包括差异的大小、变动趋势、可控性、调查成本、所用标准的类型和差异间的相互影响等等。注意问题中特别指出的，考生可以结合外部质量损失成本来解释，所以要避免每个要点只有一句概念性的陈述，要结合案例进行拓展说明。

外包

当公司的成本结构中固定成本所占比例较高时，会有较高的经营杠杆，反之，则经营杠杆较低。该案例中如果外包配送服务，将降低公司的固定成本，增加变动成本，导致经营杠杆下降。由于案例中的公司的变动成本所占比例本来就较高，所以外包对公司经营杠杆的影响并不大。考生需要理解成本结构和经营杠杆的关系，并能够具体分析配送服务的成本构成以及外包带来的成本变化。由于案例中并未明确提供配送次数的数据，所以在比较自营和外包两个备选方案的成本时，成本无差别点分析可以帮助企业在短期内做出更好的选择。考生不应忽视的是，外包并非是一个简单的短期决策，公司也要考虑到外包带来的中长期影响。外包优缺点的阐述要结合案例情境来适度展开。

考生注意事项

经营杠杆，又称营业杠杆或营运杠杆，反映销售和EBIT（息税前利润）的杠杆关系，指在企业生产经营中由于存在固定成本而使利润变动率大于产销量变动率的规律。在一定产销量范围内，产销量的增加一般不会影响固定成本总额，但会使单位产品的固定成本降低，从而提高单位产品利润，并使利润增长率大于产销量增长率；反之，产销量减少，会使单位产品的固定成本增加，从而降低单位产品利润，并使利润下降率大于产销量的下降率。经营杠杆的大小一般用经营杠杆系数表示，即EBIT变动率与销售量变动率之间的比率。

经营杠杆系数＝EBIT变动率/产销量变动率

＝（经营收入－变动成本）/（经营收入－变动成本－固定成本）

经营杠杆系数越大，经营杠杆的作用和经营风险越大；反之，则相反。

持有待售的非流动资产

按照国际财务报告准则第5号“持有待售的非流动资产及终止经营”中的规定，符合条件而被分类为持有待售的资产，金额以账面价值和公允价值减去销售成本孰低者计量，并停止对该类资产计提折旧，这类资产需要在财务状况表中单独披露。该资产必须在其当前状况下仅根据销售此类资产的通常和惯用条款即可立即出售，而且其出售必须是很可能的。这个认定条件可进一步划分为管理层已着手制订出售计划，该资产可立即出售，积极寻找买方的行动已经展开，资产正在以符合其公允价值的合理价格积极地出售等6个要点。考生需要熟知国际财务报告准则第5号的相关规定，对照案例中描述的情形，就能判定运输车辆可以被归类为“持有待售的非流动资产”。

裁员

裁员的初衷主要是节约开支，降低成本，但企业做出这一决策时需要充分考虑由此带来的负面影响，例如对企业声誉的损害和留任员工士气的影响等。企业通常会采取措施以尽量避免强制裁员，或努力把裁员的负面影响降到最低。裁员过程中以及之后也会发生相关成本，如管理裁员过程的成本，为被裁掉的员工提供再培训和职业指导发生的成本等。考生需要对这些问题有较为全面的思考和认识。

销售差异

本案例中不仅提供了销售价格差异，还将总销售量差异细分为销售组合差异和数量差异，考生需要清楚这三项差异的内涵和每项差异产生的可能原因，结合案例情境来进行综合分析。很明显，考生需要知道当各种产品的实际销售量比例和预期的不同时，反映出市场发生了怎样的变化。

考生注意事项

销售价格差异是由于产品实际销售价格不同于标准（预算）销售价格所导致的，当产品实际的销售价格低于预算价格时，会产生不利的销售价格差异，反之产生有利的价格差异。

当企业销售不止一种产品时，总销售量差异可以进一步细分为销售组合差异和销售数量差异。销售组合差异是由于产品实际销售比例不同于标准（预算）销售比例造成的。销售数量差异是由于实际销售数量不同于预算销售数量造成的。销售差异既可以表示为利润的差异额，也可以表示为边际贡献的差异额。当产品实际销售数量组合中，单位利润或单位边际贡献高的产品所占比例高于预期，而单位利润或单位边际贡献低的产品所占比例低于预期时，将产生有利的销售组合差异，反之产生不利差异。当实际总销售量高于预算总销售量时，将产生有利的销售数量差异，反之产生不利差异。

计划差异和运营差异

当把差异作为绩效评价的依据时，区分计划差异和运营差异就变得必要，这样才有利于为绩效管理提供更有意义的衡量指标。计划差异通常是由于实际环境与预期环境的不同造成的，可能是不可控的，但可以为管理人员提高未来计划的准确性提供有用信息。运营差异通常被认为是可控的，可以用于更为公平地评价经营效率。再次强调，考生在阐述这两类差异的不同时，不要忘记结合案例材料。

考生注意事项

在绩效评价中，当出现管理者不可控的因素造成原始预算或标准不可行或不适合时，就需要对原始预算或标准进行调整。调整后的预算或标准和原始预算或标准之间的差异，被称为计划差异。实际结果和调整后的预算或标准之间的差异，被称为运营差异。

短期融资

常见的短期融资来源包括应付账款、应收账款、银行透支和短期贷款等。考生在解答这一问题时，应具体解释每种融资方式是如何获得资金的，分析其相关成本，列出其优缺点，注意回答的完整性。

Variant 4

This examination is structured as follows：

Section number	Number of tasks	Time for section(minutes)
1	1	50
2	1	45
3	1	45
4	1	40

The time available for each section is for reading,planning and writing your answer(s).

Section 1

The following article was published in the *Daily Independent*.

Daily Independent

7th November 2016 No. 823 F$2.80

Double Blow for the Solar Panel Industry as VAT Rate Is Set to Increase

Maisie Wells, Business Correspondent

The Treasury Department has outlined proposals to replace the current reduced rate of 5% VAT on solar panels with the standard rate of 20%.

The Treasury Department has said that the impact of the rate increase on households is negligible but the Solar Panel Trade Association (SPTA) has said that the move is likely to add around F$900 to the price of a typical 4Kw installation which is currently selling for about F$6,400.

John Jones, head of SPTA said that:

"Urgent action is required from both the Freeland government and the European Commission. The industry has already been affected by the reduction in government subsidies and will not survive this double blow."

Renewable energy campaigners branded the proposals as "ridiculous" and completely at odds with the government's rhetoric on tackling climate change. George Perman of "Go for Green" said that: "This makes the proposed cuts in subsidies for solar panels even more misguided — these changes will push up the cost of renewables which means the government will surely need to revise its proposals to cut support for these technologies".

You receive the following email from Maria Coleman, finance director.

From: Maria Coleman, Finance Director

To: Management Accountant Assistant

Subject: VAT increase

You should have seen the press report about the proposed increase in value added tax on solar panels. I have just come out of an urgent board meeting and the directors have requested an analysis of the potential impact of the change on future profits.

I have had discussions with the commercial director, Andreas Loewe, about the possible impact of the VAT increase on our sales demand and selling price. We have also considered the effect that the current wage dispute is likely to have on our labour costs. Andreas has arrived at some probabilities for the expected sales demand and contribution per unit for our Solar Eclipse panel. The details are shown in the table below. The probabilities he has given for each of the variables are independent. Using this information, I have produced the probability distribution that is attached to this email.

The probabilities of the expected sales demand and contribution per unit for Solar Eclipse panel:

Demand (units)	Probability (%)	Contribution per unit (F$)	Probability (%)
60,000	25	135	15
55,000	45	125	45
50,000	30	115	40

I would be grateful if you could produce a report that I can discuss with Andreas, covering the following areas.

- An explanation of the figures shown in the probability distribution and how we could use these in the assessment of risk.
- The limitations of using expected value for risk assessment and the potential benefits from the additional information provided by a probability distribution.

It was apparent during the meeting that some of the directors did not understand how the VAT system operates. They seemed to think that our reported sales revenue was going to go up by the increase in the VAT rate. I tried to explain how the system works but I am not sure that they understood.

Please also explain in your report: How the change in the VAT rate would impact on our sales revenue and how VAT is reported in the financial accounts. Please include details of how the VAT system works and how it is accounted for through the supply chain.

Regards.

Maria Coleman
Finance Director
Marici Power

Probability distribution:

Demand(units)	Contribution per unit(F$)	Total contribution (F$)	Joint probability	Expected value (F$)
60, 000	135	8, 100, 000	0. 0375	303, 750
	125	7, 500, 000	0. 1125	843, 750
	115	6, 900, 000	0. 1000	690, 000
55, 000	135	7, 425, 000	0. 0675	501, 188
	125	6, 875, 000	0. 2025	1, 392, 187
	115	6, 325, 000	0. 1800	1, 138, 500
50, 000	135	6, 750, 000	0. 0450	303, 750
	125	6, 250, 000	0. 1350	843, 750
	115	5, 750, 000	0. 1200	690, 000
				6, 706, 875

Write the report for Marian Coleman, finance director.

Section 2

A few days later, you receive the following email from Maria Coleman, finance director.

From: Maria Coleman, Finance Director
To: Management Accountant Assistant
Subject: Initiatives to improve sales and profits

The board has reviewed the revised budgets and as a result we have been considering various initiatives to improve sales and profit.

One of the areas that we discussed was the possible implementation of an ABC system. The current absorption costing system uses a machine hour absorption rate. I am not sure whether an ABC system would result in a significant difference in our product costs.

Andreas Loewe, the commercial director also suggested that we should use business to customer marketing. Our marketing effort at the moment is mainly on B2B marketing but Andreas seems to think that we could increase our sales if we marketed directly to the end customer. Our marketing budget is currently fully committed and he is looking for an increase in the budget in order to include B2C. I would like to be sure that this approach is going to give a return on the additional spend.

I need you to produce a report that I can present at next week's board meeting. Please include the following in your report.

■ A discussion on whether an ABC system would result in an improved method for calculating product costs compared to our current absorption costing system and what other benefits we might get from using an ABC system.

■ The differences between B2B and B2C marketing and the potential benefits to us of increasing the marketing budget to enable a B2C marketing effort.

Regards.

Maria Coleman
Finance Director
Marici Power

Write the report for Maria Coleman, finance director.

Section 3

A few days later, you receive the following email from Alex Hilliard, senior management accountant.

From: Alex Hilliard, Senior Management Accountant
To: Management Accountant Assistant
Subject: Lean Manufacturing

The board of directors are considering the introduction of a system of lean manufacturing in the company. I have been asked to produce a report on the potential costs and benefits of introducing such a system and would like some help from you in understanding what would be involved in implementing lean manufacturing. I understand that it would include the introduction of just-in-time purchasing and production.

I would be grateful if you could produce a report for me to include the following areas.

- The main features of lean manufacturing and how it defines waste, explaining how its introduction would help to eliminate, or reduce, waste at various stages in our manufacturing process.
- An explanation of JIT purchasing and production, and the implications of its use on our relationship with our suppliers.

Volker Stein, the production director, has estimated that implementing "lean" would require an investment of F$ 500,000 in new machinery, which will have a resale value of F$ 100,000 at the end of five years. Our normal accounting policy is to depreciate the machinery on a straight line basis over its useful life but I also need to consider the tax implications of the investment.

Please also include the following in your report: An explanation of how the investment would be treated in our tax computations and the adjustments to accounting profit that are required to arrive at a taxable profit, with an explanation of the effect on both our accounts and tax computation if the disposal proceeds from the machinery are different from our estimate.

Thanks!

Alex Hilliard
Senior Management Accountant
Marici Power

Write the report for Alex Hilliard, senior management accountant.

Section 4

The following month, you receive an email from Andreas Loewe, commercial director.

From: Andreas Loewe, Commercial Director
To: Management Accountant Assistant
Subject: Special order from a new buyer

As you are aware, our sales demand has been lower than expected and we therefore have spare production capacity that we are unlikely to fill with orders from our regular customers.

I have been in negotiations with a potential new customer who has offered to place a substantial order, but the price they want to pay is around 30% below our normal selling price. The panels they are requesting have a slightly higher specification than our standard panels. I am keen to go ahead with the order despite the low price, as this is a major customer who may give us significant future business. I have had a discussion with Maria Coleman, the Finance Director, and she has suggested that I ask you to review the figures before we make a final decision. I have attached my calculations to this email and would be grateful if you could have a look at them.

She has asked that you do a relevant cost analysis but I am not entirely sure what she means. I would be grateful if you could explain what is meant by relevant costs and why each of the cost items included in the attached calculations is relevant or irrelevant. Please also suggest how we should decide whether or not to accept the order and what other non-financial factors we should consider before making a final decision.

I look forward to receiving your email in the near future.

Regards.

Andreas Loewe
Commercial Director
Marici Power

Sales order calculations：

	Notes	(F$ 000)
Material		
Solar wafers in inventory at original cost	1	200
Metal for panels (original purchase price)	2	30
Inverters (all to be purchased for this order)		18
Labour		
Skilled labour	3	54
Non-skilled labour	4	30
Supervisory staff	5	10
Manufacturing overheads (based on a machine hour absorption rate)	6	60
Selling and administration overheads (based on a percentage of sales revenue)	7	12
Total cost		414
Price offered by buyer		360
Net loss		(54)

Notes:

(1) Solar wafers are in continual use in the business. Due to a shortage in supply the price of the wafers in inventory has risen significantly and the items in inventory would now cost F$220,000 to replace.

(2) The metal for the panels is different from our standard specification. It was ordered some weeks ago for another special order and is no longer required. It now has a resale value of F$ 21,000.

(3) The skilled labour will be transferred to this order from working on other orders. They would be replaced by different workers, for the period of this order, at a cost of F$ 37,000.

(4) The non-skilled labour will be specifically employed for the order.

(5) The supervisory staff will be retained, whether or not the order is accepted, at their present salary levels.

(6) Manufacturing overheads have been charged using a machine hour absorption rate. Only F$15,000 of the total cost would be avoided if the order does not go ahead.

(7) All selling and administration overheads will be incurred whether the order goes ahead or not.

Write the email to Andreas Loewe, commercial director.

试卷四

本次考试的结构如下：

序号	任务数	时间（分钟）
1	1	50
2	1	45
3	1	45
4	1	40

每个部分规定的时间可用于读题、组织和书写答案。

任务一

下面的文章是发表在《独立日报》（*Daily Independent*）上的一篇报道。

独立日报

2016年11月7日 823号 F$2.80

因增值税提高，太阳能电池板行业即将遭受双重打击

商业记者**Maisie Wells**

财政部已经提出议案，要将太阳能电池板的增值税率从现行的减按5%调整为20%的标准税率。

财政部表示，税率的上升对家庭住户的影响是微乎其微的，然而SPTA（太阳能电池交易协会）指出，这项税率的上涨将会使一个典型的4千瓦太阳能电池板基于现售价F$6 400再上涨大约F$900。

SPTA的会长John Jones（约翰·琼斯）表示，Freeland政府与欧盟委员会都必须采取紧急措施。这个行业已经受到了政府补贴下调的影响，无法再承受税率上涨这样的双重打击。

可再生能源支持者认为这项提议是“可笑的”，并且完全与政府要处理气候变化的那些说辞相背离。“走向绿色（Go for Green）”的George Perman说“这使得之前提议缩减对太阳能电池补贴的议案更加令人不解，这些举动都会使可再生能源的成本上涨，这意味着政府必须修改这些削减技术支持的提议。”

你收到了一封来自财务总监 Maria Coleman 的邮件。

发件人：财务总监 Maria Coleman
收件人：管理会计师助理
主题：增值税上涨

你一定已经看见了关于提议太阳能电池板的增值税上涨的新闻报道。我刚刚参加完一场紧急的董事会议，董事们要求我就增值税上涨对未来利润的潜在影响做出分析。

我刚刚与商务总监 Andreas Loewe 就增值税的上涨对于销售需求与售价的影响进行了分析讨论。我们也考虑到了目前的工资纠纷可能对我们的人工成本所造成的影响。Andreas 针对“Solar Eclipse”这种电池板的预期销售需求量和单位贡献给出了相应的发生概率，具体数据如下表所示。他给予的每个变量的概率都是相互独立的，根据这些信息，我已经做出了概率分布并附在了此邮件里。

Solar Eclipse 的预期销售需求量和单位贡献的发生概率：

需求量（个）	概率（%）	单位贡献（F$）	概率（%）
60 000	25	135	15
55 000	45	125	45
50 000	30	115	40

我要跟 Andreas 进行讨论，请准备一份报告供我在讨论时使用，非常感谢。报告内容应包括以下两点。

- 对概率分布表中的数据进行解释，以及我们怎么利用这些数据来评估风险。
- 使用期望值进行风险评估的局限性，以及概率分布表所提供的附加信息的潜在优点。

很明显，在会议期间，一些董事并不了解增值税税制是如何运作的。他们似乎认为随着增值税税率的上升，我们的销售收入也会随之上升。我试图去解释这个税制是如何运作的，但我不确定董事们是否能够理解。

所以请你在报告中解释：增值税税率的变化会如何影响我们的销售收入，以及增值税在我们的财务账目中是如何体现的。你的解释应包含增值税税制在整个供应链中如何运作以及相应的账务处理的细节。

致以问候！

摩利兹能源公司
财务总监
Maria Coleman

概率分布：

需求量（个）	单位贡献（F$）	总贡献（F$）	联合概率	期望值（F$）
60 000	135	8 100 000	0.0375	303 750
	125	7 500 000	0.1125	843 750
	115	6 900 000	0.1000	690 000
55 000	135	7 425 000	0.0675	501 188
	125	6 875 000	0.2025	1 392 187
	115	6 325 000	0.1800	1 138 500
50 000	135	6 750 000	0.0450	303 750
	125	6 250 000	0.1350	843 750
	115	5 750 000	0.1200	690 000
				6 706 875

请写出给财务总监 Maria Coleman 的报告。

任务二

几天后，你收到了财务总监 Maria Coleman 的邮件。

发件人：财务总监 Maria Coleman
收件人：管理会计师助理
主题：提高销量和利润的措施

董事会已经审查了修改后的预算，因此我们一直在考虑各种措施来提高销量和利润。

我们讨论的其中一个方面是关于作业成本法系统的可能实施。现行的全部成本法（AC）系统是以机器工时作为依据来计算分摊率的。我不确定采用作业成本法系统是否会导致我们的产品成本产生显著差异。

另外，商务总监 Andreas Loewe 建议我们使用 B2C 的营销模式。我们目前的营销重点都放在 B2B 上，但 Andreas 似乎认为如果我们能直接面向最终顾客进行营销会增加我们的销售额。我们的营销预算现在已经全部被投入了，他正打算增加预算以纳入 B2C 营销模式。我想要确认的是在 B2C 营销模式上的额外支出是否会带来回报。

我需要你写一份报告，我会在下周的董事会上提交这份报告。该报告应该包括以下内容。

- 请讨论与现行的全部成本法系统相比，在计算产品成本时作业成本法系统是否带来了方法上的改进。除此之外，使用作业成本法系统我们还能获得什么好处。
- B2B 与 B2C 营销的不同之处是什么？我们增加营销预算来实行 B2C 会带来什么潜在好处。

致以问候！

摩利兹能源公司
财务总监
Maria Coleman

请写出给财务总监 Maria Coleman 的报告。

任务三

几天后，你收到了高级管理会计师 Alex Hilliard 的邮件。

发件人：高级管理会计师 Alex Hilliard
收件人：管理会计师助理
主题：精益生产

董事会正在考虑在公司引入精益生产系统。关于引进这样一个系统可能带来的成本与收益，他们需要我就此给出一份报告，我希望你能帮助我了解实施精益生产所涉及的内容。我知道的是在精益生产系统中应该引入适时制采购与生产。

请你为我撰写一份相关报告，非常感谢。报告内容应该包括以下两个方面。

- 精益生产的主要特点以及它如何界定浪费，并解释引入精益生产将如何帮助我们消除或减少在各个生产环节中的浪费。

■ 解释适时制采购与生产，以及它们如何影响我们与供应商的关系。

生产总监 Volker Stein 觉得要实施“精益”将需要投资 F$ 500 000 用于购买新机器，该机器在 5 年后能够有 F$ 100 000 的变卖价值。通常我们使用的会计折旧政策是在机器的有效使用年限内按直线法计提折旧，但我也需要考虑投资的税收影响。

所以报告还应解释如何进行该项投资的税金计算，以及如何将会计利润调整为应税利润。同时，解释若该机器的处置收入与之前估计的不一致，将会对我们的账目与税金计算产生什么影响。

谢谢！

摩利兹能源公司
高级管理会计师
Alex Hilliard

请写出给高级管理会计师 Alex Hilliard 的报告。

任务四

一个月后，你收到了商务总监 Andreas Loewe 的邮件。

发件人：商务总监 Andreas Loewe
收件人：管理会计师助理
主题：来自新买家的特殊订单

如你所知，我们的销售需求低于预期，因此我们有了更多的富余产能，使得我们不再局限于只满足常规客户的订单需求。

我一直在与一位潜在的新客户进行谈判，他愿意为我们提供一个数额巨大的订单，但他愿意支付的价格比我们平常的售价低了 30% 左右。他需要的电池板也比我们平常的标准电池板的规格略高一些。这是一个重要的客户，因为在未来他将会给我们带来大宗业务，所以尽管价格很低，我还是很想签下这份订单。我已经和财务总监 Maria Coleman 进行了交流，她建议在做出最终决定之前，让你再审核一下这些数据。我已经把我的计算附在了邮件后面，希望你看一下，非常感谢。

她要求你做一个相关成本分析，但我并没有完全明白她的意思是什么。如果你能解释一下什么是相关成本，并解释在附表里的各项成本为什么是相关的或不相关的，我将十分感谢。另外，请对我们如何决定是否接受这个订单提出建议，以及在做出最终决定前我们还需考虑哪些非财务性因素。

希望能很快收到你的回复。

致以问候。

摩利兹能源公司

商务总监

Andreas Loewe

销售订单的计算：

	附注	(F$000)
原材料		
以原始成本计量的太阳能晶片库存	(1)	200
用于电池的金属（以原始购买价格计量）	(2)	30
逆变器（为了这次订单所购）		18
人工		
熟练工	(3)	54
非熟练工	(4)	30
监管人员	(5)	10
制造费用（按机器工时分摊）	(6)	60
销售与管理费用（基于收入的百分比）	(7)	12
总成本		414
买家愿意支付的价格		360
净亏损		(54)

附注：

(1) 太阳能晶片在企业中是被持续使用的。由于供给的短缺，库存的太阳能晶片的价格大幅上涨。这些存货的重置价格为 F$ 220 000。

(2) 用于电池板的金属的规格与我们的标准规格不一致，这种金属是几周前我们为了另一个特殊订单而采购的，目前别无他用。这些金属现在的变卖价格为 F$ 21 000。

（3）熟练工将被从其他订单的作业中，调来为这项订单工作。在这个订单作业期间，他们原本的工作将会被其他的工人替代，这将花费 F$ 37 000。

（4）非熟练工是为这一订单而特别雇佣的。

（5）无论是否接受这个订单，监管人员的工资水平都和现有水平一样。

（6）制造费用是通过机器工时分摊的。若不接受这个订单，总成本中将只有 F$ 15 000 是可以避免发生的。

（7）无论是否接受这个订单，销售与管理费用都会发生。

请写一封给商务总监 Andreas Loewe 的邮件。

Variant 4　Suggested Answers

Section 1

Report

Probability Distribution and vat Increase

Probability Distribution

The probability distribution shows the nine possible outcomes, that is, three different levels of demand combined with three different contribution levels. The total contribution for each of the nine possible outcomes is calculated by multiplying the demand by the contribution per unit. The probability of each outcome is the joint probabilities of the variables. This is calculated by multiplying the probability of the sales demand with the probability of the contribution per unit. We can then multiply the contribution for each outcome by the joint probability for each outcome. The total of this represents the expected value of the total contribution.

The same figure for expected value can be calculated from Andreas's table. Expected value of demand can be calculated by multiplying each level of demand by the associated probability and then totaling the subsequent figures. The expected value of the unit contribution can be calculated using the same approach. The expected value of demand can then be multiplied by the expected value of the unit contribution to give the expected value of the total contribution.

The probability distribution is useful as it allows us to carry out further analysis. We can establish the probability of the total contribution being above or below a particular level. Alternatively, we could determine the most likely outcome, that is, the contribution with the highest joint probability. If we know the fixed costs for the product we could also calculate the probability of making a profit or loss.

It may also be appropriate to extend the analysis to compare the new data with the situation before the VAT increase.

Benefits and Limitations of the Analysis in Measuring Risk

The figures produced by Andreas could have been used to calculate the expected value of the total contribution. However this is limited as this is a one-off situation and the expected value is the weighted average outcome if the decision is repeated several times. The resultant expected value may not, and in this case does not, correspond to any of the actual possible outcomes. The expected value also gives no indication of the dispersion of possible outcomes around the expected value, that is, the risk.

Calculating the standard deviation of the data will give us a clearer indication of the risk. The standard deviation is the square root of the sum of the squared deviations of each outcome from the expected value taking account of the associated probabilities. The higher the standard deviation, the more widely dispersed is the distribution and therefore the greater the inherent risk. The standard deviation can be considered in respect of how comfortable the directors are with the situation in light of their attitude to risk.

Measures such as expected value and standard deviation are used to summarise the characteristics of a probability distribution but they are limited in representing the probability distribution. The presentation of the entire probability distribution can provide useful information to management as the distribution indicates the probability for each of the possible outcomes.

The analysis however is very dependent on the accuracy of the probabilities which are subjective and based on Andreas's knowledge of the market.

Operation of a VAT System

VAT is a system of indirect taxation on the sale of goods and services to final consumers (individuals). The tax is collected in stages through what is called "the chain of supply", and sales of goods and services in the VAT system are referred to as "supplies".

How It Works

VAT registered businesses charge VAT on their sales (output tax) and recover VAT on their purchases and expenses (input tax) and pay the difference to the tax authorities. They submit returns to their tax authorities on a regular basis where they declare the value of their output tax and input tax in that period which is accompanied by the relevant payment.

Our company purchases goods and services from a range of suppliers each of whom is registered for VAT and charges VAT on their supplies. We then use the purchases to make a number of solar panels that we sell to one of our installers for a price including VAT.

Our VAT return will show a VAT payable figure of the total of output tax which we have charged to our installers less the total VAT reclaimable figure of the input tax which we have paid to our suppliers.

In the next stage, the installers sell all of the solar panels to retail customers. They will charge VAT on the sales. The installers VAT return will show a VAT payable figure of the total of output tax which they have charged to their customers less the total VAT reclaimable figure of the input tax which they have paid to us for the panels.

Each business involved in the manufacturing and retailing of the goods—from the businesses who supply goods and services to the manufacturer—to the manufacturer right through to the retailer—creates a "chain of supply" and some of the VAT is collected in stages from the businesses rather than it all being collected from the retailer at the point of final sale.

As demonstrated above, it is the consumer who finally bears the VAT as they are not VAT registered and cannot reclaim the VAT charged. The intermediary parties in the supply chain effectively pay no VAT since, whilst they pay over to the government everything that they collect, they also reclaim everything that they pay. They are therefore tax collectors for the government.

In our accounts, the reported sales revenue is ex-VAT and therefore will not be directly affected by the increase in the VAT. However, if the full impact of the VAT increase is passed on to the final consumer we may see a reduction in demand with a consequent pressure on prices.

Section 2

Report

ABC and Marketing

ABC

An ABC system will be appropriate for use in any organisation with the following features.

- When consumption of overheads is not primarily driven by volume.
- When overhead costs are high relative to direct costs.
- Where there is diversity in the product range resulting in varied overhead resource

input.

In our business our production overhead costs are relative low compared to our direct costs. The range of products which we sell is fairly homogenous and does not vary significantly in terms of resource consumption. We would not therefore expect to see significantly different gross profits for each of the products compared to that shown under the current absorption costing system.

However we may be able to benefit from utilising aspects of an activity based system. The identification of our activities and the cost drivers for those activities would provide information to management to enable them to take actions to improve the overall profitability of the company. Cost driver analysis will provide information to management about how costs can be controlled and managed. An activity based system gives more detailed information about how costs are incurred and the potential for cost reduction by reducing activity levels. We would also be able to identify value added and non-value added activities and performance management could be improved by measuring efficiency through cost driver rates. Using ABC to allocate our non-production overhead costs to products may also result in a better indication of total product cost and would be useful for assessing product profitability and for setting prices.

B2B vs B2C Marketing

B2B marketing is concerned with targeting goods or services at businesses that will use the products to produce the goods or services that they sell. B2C marketing is concerned with marketing the goods or services to individuals who purchase them for their own or family use.

At present, we sell our products directly to commercial customers and private customers through our distribution network of installers. For this reason we have concentrated on B2B marketing.

In B2B marketing, demand for the product is derived from consumer demand, that is, the demand from our customers is derived from the demand from the individual households wanting to install solar panels. We have few customers and therefore it is important to understand their individual requirements. Our customers also have significantly higher purchasing power than individual consumers. The financial value of our customers' purchase orders is large and the frequency low therefore it is important to maintain close contact with them. Our customer relationships are extremely valuable and need to be managed. Our brand identity has been created based on the personal relationship we have with our customers. The B2B marketing effort is therefore fairly complex as we are entering into agreements for the supply of our products for a period of years and negotiation of the supply contract can be quite lengthy.

B2C marketing, in contrast, is concerned with a large number of consumers who individually have low purchasing power and where the success of the marketing often depends on the ability to invoke an emotional response rather than demonstrate value. We would be required to target the customers using different techniques across multiple channels based on which demographics are most likely to access them. We already use a form of B2C marketing through our website which is available to be accessed by the general public.

B2C marketing may prove to be effective and would provide support to our distribution network in their marketing effort. As mentioned earlier, demand for our products is derived from consumer demand and therefore targeting the consumer directly may be an effective way to increase our sales. It would also enable us to deliver our brand message directly to the consumer.

Section 3

Report

Lean Manufacturing, JIT and the Impact of Machinery Purchases

Lean Manufacturing

There are several key principles involved with lean manufacturing.

(1) Elimination of waste.

One of the most critical features of lean manufacturing is the elimination of waste. Waste takes various forms and can occur at every stage of the production process. For example, holding unnecessary inventory wastes space and incurs costs including insurance, pilferage and obsolescence. Waste also arises when there are production delays as employees are likely to be paid even when they are waiting for materials or when production has been halted due to machine breakdowns. Waste arises when there are quality failures and products have to be reworked or scrapped. The layout of the production facility can also result in waste where time is spent moving raw materials, work in progress and finished goods from one location to another.

The idea of waste elimination is to review all areas in the organisation, determine where the work is non-value added and reduce or eliminate it.

(2) Improved production scheduling.

Production is initiated by customer demand rather than the ability and capacity to produce and production is demand-pull not supply-push. This will ensure that the company is not over producing and holding excess inventory.

(3) Established quality standard.

Quality is built into the manufacturing process, the design of the parts and into the packaging. Throughout all areas of the product, from design to shipping, quality is a major consideration.

In lean manufacturing the focus must be on doing it right the first time. This will reduce quality failures and the costs associated with these failures.

(4) Continuous improvement.

Continuous improvement or Kaizen is one of the most critical principles of lean manufacturing. Continuous improvement promotes constant, necessary change toward the achievement of a desired state. The process is continual as there is always room for improvement. Continuous improvement should be a mind-set throughout the whole organisation.

JIT Production and Purchasing

JIT purchasing is a method of purchasing that involves ordering materials only when production of a customer's order is about to commence. When the goods are received, they go straight into production.

JIT production is about producing what is required, when it is required and in the quantity required. Production is driven by demand for the finished products (a pull system), whereby each component on a production line is produced only when it is needed for the next stage. This means that components are not used in products that are not required and no time is wasted making unsaleable products.

The use of a JIT system is likely to result in a reduction in the number of suppliers. It will be preferable for us to work with suppliers who are in close proximity therefore reducing delivery times and costs. For the system to be effective we must avoid any disruptions to the process. We need to "get it right, first time". In order to do this, we need to build strong relationships with our suppliers to ensure high quality and reliability. If we work closely with our suppliers we will be able to improve the quality of supplies. This will minimise production delays as there are less inspection, fewer returns and less reworking of products. We will also be able to rely on frequent and on-time deliveries, which allows us to maintain low inventories.

Accounting Depreciation Versus Tax Depreciation

Accounting depreciation is not an allowable expense for tax purposes. It is replaced by tax depreciation. In Freeland tax depreciation allowances are available on items of plant and machinery (including vehicles used for business purposes) at a rate of 25% per year on a reducing balance basis.

In our tax computations for each year, we would add back the accounting depreciation to the accounting profit and deduct the tax depreciation to arrive at the taxable profit. The accounting profit and taxable profit will be different since our accounting depreciation is calculated by taking the initial cost of the asset less its residual value and charging this over the useful life of the assets whilst the tax depreciation charge is based on a rate of 25% of the reducing balance.

If the proceeds from the sale of the machinery are higher (lower) than the net book value or carrying amount we would show an accounting profit (loss) on disposal. An accounting profit or loss would be treated as disallowable for tax purposes. A profit will be deducted from the accounting profit and a loss will be added to the accounting profit. This would then be replaced by a balancing charge or allowance for tax purposes. A balancing charge will be added back to the accounting profit and a balancing allowance will be deducted from the accounting profit when computing the taxable profit.

The tax balancing allowance or charge in Year 5 would be the amount that allows the total tax depreciation claimed over the period, to equal the initial cost of the asset less the disposal proceeds.

Section 4

From：Management Accountant Assistant
To：Andreas Loewe，Commercial Director
Subject：Re：Special order from new buyer

Special Order From a New Buyer

Relevant Cost Analysis

Relevant costs and revenues are the costs and revenues appropriate to a specific decision，and they are represented by future cash flows whose magnitude will vary depending upon the outcome of the management decision made. Relevant costs and revenues are therefore future，incremental cash flows that arise as a result of the decision.

In this case，the decision is whether to accept a special order at below our normal selling price and as such，we need to consider the incremental costs，that is，the additional costs that will be incurred as a direct consequence of accepting the order. The incremental costs could be the variable costs of the contract and any additional specific fixed costs incurred.

General fixed overheads which will be incurred whether the contract is accepted or not are unavoidable costs and，as such，are irrelevant costs.

With reference to the schedule and notes that you have provided.

(1) The relevant cost of the solar wafer is F$ 220, 000 as the wafers are in continual use and will be replaced. The future cash flow is therefore the replacement cost.

(2) The metal for the panels has already been ordered and is a committed cost. If not used in this contract however it could be sold for F$ 21, 000. The relevant cost is therefore the opportunity cost of F$ 21, 000.

(3) The inverter need to be purchased for the contract therefore the relevant cost is the purchase cost of F$ 18, 000.

(4) The incremental cost is the cost of hiring the less skilled workers.

(5) The cost of hiring the non-skilled labour is directly related to the contract and a relevant cost.

(6) Since the supervisory staffs will be retained whether or not the contract is accepted，the cost is unavoidable and therefore irrelevant.

(7) Only the avoidable manufacturing costs are relevant.

(8) The selling and administration overheads are unavoidable and therefore irrelevant.

We can calculate the total cost of the contract on a relevant cost basis and compare this to the price. If the order makes a profit on a relevant cost basis it should be accepted and if not, it should be rejected.

This type of analysis assumes that the decision will be made on the basis of short term cash flows however there are wider issues that we should consider before making a final decision.

Is this really a one-off order or will it have an impact on future orders? It is suggested that the customer will provide future business if we accept this order. If this future business is expected to be profitable then there may be a case for accepting this order even if it makes a small loss. However, we need to consider what the effect of accepting this order at a low price will be on future orders. Have we set a precedent with this order which means that the customer would be reluctant to accept a price increase on future orders?

We would also need to consider the potential effect of accepting this order on our existing customers. We rely on our existing customers for the majority of our business and it is important that we keep them happy and maintain their future business. If our existing customers find out that we have given a highly discounted price to this new customer they may react badly. They may ask for a similar price to be given to them on future orders and if this is not forthcoming, they may take their business to a competitor.

Is this a long-term decision rather than a short-term decision? Is there an over-capacity issue and should we consider getting rid of the excess capacity?

Thanks!

Management Accountant Assistant

Marici Power

试卷四　参考答案

任务一

报告

概率分布和增值税增加

概率分布

概率分布表显示出了9种可能的结果，即3种不同级别的需求水平与3种不同的贡献情况组合而成。这九种组合中每一种组合的总贡献都是用销售需求量乘以单位贡献而得到的。每个结果的概率是两种变量的联合概率，这是用每种销售需求对应的概率乘以每种单位贡献对应的概率来计算的。然后，我们将每一个组合的贡献乘以它的联合概率，并将这些结果汇总相加，就得到了总贡献的期望值。

同样的期望值也可以从Andreas提供的表中计算得出。首先计算销售需求量的期望值，用每一级别的需求量乘以对应的概率，最后再将这些数字相加。单位贡献的期望值也可以用同样的方法来计算。最后，销售需求量的期望值乘以单位贡献的期望值即可得到总贡献的期望值。

概率分布是十分有用的，它使得我们可以做更多深入的分析。我们可以知道总贡献低于或高于某一特定水平时的概率。或者，我们可以确定最可能出现的结果，即最高联合概率下的贡献。如果我们知道产品的固定成本，我们也可以计算出盈利或亏损的概率。

我们也可以拓展这种分析，将新数据与增值税增加之前的相应数据进行比较。

风险评估分析的好处与局限性

Andreas提供的数据可以用来计算总贡献的期望值。但是，因为这是一个一次性事件，而期望值是一个加权平均数，需要类似的决策重复多次，所以这是有局限的，这样算出来的期望值和实际结果可能会不一致（本案例也是如此）。期望值并不能显示出各个可能结果与期望值的离散程度，这就是风险。

计算这些数据的标准差将使我们能更清楚地分析出风险。在考虑联合概率的情况下，期望值的方差的平方根即为标准差。标准差越大，分布越分散，固有风险越大。根据董事们对风险的态度，标准差还可以用来考量董事们对现状的适应程度。

像标准差与期望值这样的测量方式是用来总结概率分布的特点的，但是它们在表述概率分布时还存在着不足。因为分布代表了每种可能结果的概率，所以只有对整个概率分布进行表述才能为管理者提供有用的信息。

这项分析还十分依赖于概率的精确性，但这些概率是主观的，是基于 Andreas 对市场的认知。

增值税税制的实施

增值税是一项间接税，根据商品的销售与劳务的提供向最终消费者征税。增值税在所谓的“供应链”里被环环征收，增值税系统中商品的销售与劳务的提供被认为是“供应品”。

增值税是如何运作的

增值税注册企业对其销售征收税款（销项税），而在其发生费用与进行采购时抵扣一部分增值税（进项税），将销项与进项的差额上缴给税务机关。他们需要定期向税务机关提交所得税申请表以说明与本期相关的支付的进项增值税额与销项增值税额。

我们公司从已注册增值税的各供应商处采购商品和接受服务，并对他们所供给的商品和服务收取增值税。我们使用所采购的材料制造太阳能电池板，然后将这些太阳能电池板以包含增值税的价格卖给我们的客户。

我们的增值税申报单上会显示出我们应纳的增值税额，即我们向客户收取的销项增值税额减去向供应商缴纳的可抵扣进项增值税额。

在下一环节，客户（安装商）把所有太阳能电池板卖给零售客户，在销售中同样也收取增值税。他们的增值税申报单也将显示出他们的应纳税款，即向顾客征收的销项税减去之前买电池板时向我们缴纳的可抵扣的进项增值税。

所有涉及在制造与零售商品过程中的企业，从供应物品与劳务的供应商到制造商再到零售商，形成了一条供应链，其中的一些增值税在经营过程中被企业按环节征收，而不是将零售商作为最后环节来征收全部税额。

如上所述，因为消费者不是增值税注册者，他们并不能收取可抵扣进项增值税，所以增值税最终是由消费者承担的。因为供应链中间的企业向政府缴纳销项税的同时也向顾客收回了进项税，所以这些企业实际上并没有交纳增值税。因此这些企业实际上是政府税收的征收者。

在我们的账目中，销售收入是不含增值税的，所以增值税的增加并不会直接影响销售收入。但是，如果增值税增加所带来的影响被完全传递给了最终消费者，那么在价格上涨的压力下我们将会看到需求的下降。

任务二

报告

作业成本法与营销

作业成本法

作业成本法适用于任何具有以下特点的企业。

（1）间接成本的发生不是由产量所决定。

（2）相对于直接成本，间接成本的比重较高。

（3）产品的多样化导致了所消耗的资源的多样化。

在我们的经营过程中，生产间接成本相对于直接成本来说是较低的。我们销售的产品种类是比较一致的，消耗的资源也没有很大的差异。所以我们在从现行的全部成本法变为作业成本法后，每种产品的利润也不会出现较大的变化。

但是我们仍会从作业成本法的使用中获益。对各项活动进行识别划分并找出它们的成本动因，这可以为公司管理提供有效信息，促使管理者采取行动以提高公司整体的盈利性。成本动因分析可以就如何控制和管理成本为管理者提供管理信息。作业成本法系统能为我们提供一些更详细的信息，包括成本是如何发生，以及通过降低作业水平来降低成本的可能性。我们还将可以识别增值活动与非增值活动，并且通过成本动因率来评价效率，以提升绩效管理水平。作业成本法可以将非生产间接费用分配给各种产品，这就可以更好地反映产品的总成本，并有助于衡量产品的盈利性与制定价格。

B2B 与 B2C 营销

B2B 营销是将产品或服务的市场定位于企业，这些企业再对购买来的产品和服务进行加工以生产或提供他们所销售的商品和服务。B2C 营销是向个人消费者推销商品或服务，这些消费者购买商品或服务主要是供自己或家庭使用。

目前，我们通过安装商的分销网络将产品直接卖给商业客户和私人客户。由于这个原因，我们的营销策略集中在 B2B 营销上。

在 B2B 营销中，对产品的需求来自消费者需求，即我们客户的需求来自想要安装太阳能电池板的单个家庭的需求。我们的客户数量很少，因此了解他们各自的需求是很重要的。我们的客户的购买力也明显高于个人消费者，采购订单都是大订单，且订购频率较低，因此与他们保持密切的联系是很重要的。我们与客户之间的关系非常有价值，需要好好管理，因为我们的品牌形象就是建立在我们与客户的个人关系之上的。因此 B2B

营销工作相当复杂，因为我们签订的是长期的产品供应协议，且供应合同的谈判过程也可能很冗长。

相比之下，B2C 营销则关注的是大量的个人消费者，他们的购买力较低，这种市场营销的成功往往依赖于激发起这些消费者的情绪反应的能力而非展示价值。我们需要通过各种渠道（人口统计特征与客户相近），利用各种技术来定位客户。我们已经在我们的网站上采用了 B2C 营销策略，任何人都可以进入浏览我们的网站。

B2C 营销可能是有效的，可以为我们的分销网络的营销努力提供支持。如前所述，对我们产品的需求来自于消费者的需求，因此直接瞄准消费者可能是增加销售的有效途径。这还将使我们能够直接向消费者传递我们的品牌信息。

任务三

报告

精益生产、适时制和购买新机器的影响

精益生产

精益生产涉及许多重要原则。

（1）消除浪费。

精益生产最重要的一个特点就是消除浪费。浪费有很多种形式，并且在生产过程的每一个环节都有可能发生，比如，持有不必要的存货会浪费空间并且会产生成本，包括保险费用，偷窃或存货过期造成的损失。同样，在原料还未送到或机器出现故障停运而造成生产拖延时，也会发生浪费，因为这种时候仍要给工人支付工资。当出现质量问题时，产品必须被返工或者丢弃，这时也会产生浪费。生产设施的布局也有可能造成浪费，因为时间都被花费在搬运原材料、在产品与成品上了。

消除浪费旨在审查企业的所有领域，确定非增值的工作，进而减少或者消除它。

（2）改进生产安排。

生产是由客户的需求决定的，而不是生产的产能与能力，再者生产应是需求拉动而不是供给推动。这样就会保证公司不会过度生产并持有过量存货。

（3）建立质量标准。

质量理念需要贯穿于生产制造、设计及包装等各个环节中。在产品的各个方面，从设计到运送，质量都是需要考虑的主要因素。

在精益生产中，重点是第一次就把事情做好。这就可以降低质量失败的可能性，并减少与质量失败相关的成本。

（4）持续改进。

持续改进或改善是精益生产最重要的原则之一。持续改进就是不停地向着理想的状态进行必要的、持续的改变。因为总有改进的空间，所以这个过程是持续的。持续改进应该成为整个组织的思维模式。

适时制生产与采购

适时制采购是一种只有当客户订单即将开始生产时才进行原材料采购的方法。原材料一旦到货就立刻投入生产。

适时制生产是指在指定时间，生产指定数量的指定产品。生产是由对成品的需求驱动的（拉动系统），生产线上的每一个部件都只有在被下一环节需要时才会被生产。这意味着生产中用不到的部件将不会被生产，我们也不会浪费时间去生产无法销售的产品。

采用适时制系统很有可能会导致供应商数量的减少。与距离较近的供应商进行合作可以减少运送时间与成本，这对我们来说是更好的选择。为了使这一系统有效，我们必须避免生产出现中断。我们需要“第一次就把事情做好”，为了做到这一点，我们需要与供应商建立牢固的关系来保证高质量与可靠性。如果我们与供应商保持紧密的联系，供应商供应的商品的质量就会得到提高。这有利于将生产延迟的可能性降到最低，因为这可能会减少产品检查、产品退回和产品返工的次数。我们也同样可以依靠频繁的、按时的运送来保持较低的存货水平。

会计折旧与税收折旧

会计折旧是不可抵税的，需要用税收折旧代替。在 Freeland，厂房和机器设备可以享受税收折旧减免（包括商用汽车），均按 25% 的折旧率以余额递减法计提折旧。

在每年的税务计算中，我们需在会计利润上加回会计折旧，再减去税收折旧来得到应纳税利润。会计折旧是用资产的原始成本减去它的残值并把差值分摊到该资产的使用年限上，而税收折旧是按 25% 的折旧率以余额递减法计提折旧，所以会计利润与应纳税利润是不同的。

如果最终出售机器所取得的收入高于（或低于）它的账面净值或账面价值，我们将得到会计上的处置利得（或损失）。无论是会计上的利得还是损失都是不可抵税的，利得将从会计利润中扣除，亏损将加回到会计利润中。这些都将出于税收原因而被余额计税和余额抵税所取代。在计算应税利润时，如果是余额计税则要计入应纳税所得额；如果是余额抵税，则可以抵减应纳税所得额。

在第 5 年，无论是余额计税还是余额抵税，总的税收折旧等于资产的初始成本减去处置收益。

任务四

发件人：管理会计师助理

收件人：商务总监 Andreas Loewe

主题：新买家的特殊订单

新买家的特殊订单

相关成本分析

相关成本与相关收入是与特定决策相适应的成本与收入。它们由未来的现金流表示，其现金流取决于管理决策的结果。因此，相关成本和相关收入是由于某项特定决策而产生的未来的、增量的现金流。

因此，在这种情况下，是否接受一个低于我们正常销售价格的特殊的订单，我们需要考虑增加的成本，也就是说，接受订单的直接后果是产生额外成本。增加的成本可以是这个合同的变动成本，也可以是额外发生的特定的固定成本。而不管是否接受订单，一般的固定成本都会发生，它们是不可避免的成本，因此这些成本是不相关的成本。

根据您所提供的明细表和注释，我做了一些分析。

（1）太阳能晶片的相关成本是 F$ 220 000，因为晶片是连续使用并需要更替的，所以未来的现金流就是重置成本。

（2）太阳能电池板中所使用的金属已经被订购，属于已承付成本。然而如果这些金属没有用于本合同，它们可以以 F$ 21 000 的价格出售。因此，相关成本即为 F$ 21 000 的机会成本。

（3）为了这项合同，需要购买逆变器，所以相关成本即为购买的价格 F$ 18 000。

（4）雇佣非熟练工人的成本是一种增量成本。

（5）雇佣非熟练工人的成本与合同直接相关，因此是相关成本。

（6）无论合同是否签订，监管人员都会被保留，这项成本是不可避免的，因此是无关成本。

（7）只有可以避免的制造成本是相关的。

（8）销售费用和管理费用是不可避免的，所以是不相关的。

我们可以基于相关成本计算出合同的总成本，并将其与订单的价格进行比较。在此基础上，如果这项订单可以获得利润，我们就应该接受这项订单，如果不能获得利润，则不应该接受。

在这种类型的分析中，它假定决策是基于短期现金流的，但是在我们做出最终决策前还有很多问题要考虑。

这真的是一项一次性的订单吗？或者它会对未来的订单产生影响吗？如果我们接受这个订单，这个客户就会为我们带来未来的业务。如果预期未来的业务是可以带来利润的，那么即使有一些损失，这项订单也是可以接受的。但是，我们需要考虑以低价接受这个订单会对我们未来的订单产生什么影响。这个订单是否会成为一个先例，使我们的客户不愿意接受未来订单的价格上涨？

我们也需要考虑接受这个订单对我们现有客户的潜在影响。我们的大部分业务都依赖于现有的客户，使他们保持满意并继续合作对我们来说是很重要的。如果他们发现我们给新客户提供了一个非常高的折扣，他们也许会有激烈的反应。他们也会要求我们在将来的业务中提供同样的价格，如果我们不同意，他们也许就会将业务提供给我们的竞争对手。

如果这是一个长期决策而不是短期决策呢？是否会有产能过剩的问题，我们是否应该考虑解决产能过剩的问题？

谢谢！

摩利兹能源公司
管理会计师助理

Variant 4　Marking Guidance

Section	Technical skills		Business skills		People skills		Leadership skills		Integration	Total
1	Probability distribution Limitations of expected values Operation of VAT system	9 8 8	Operation of VAT system	3						28
2	Activity based costing	13	B2B versus B2C marketing	5	B2B versus B2C marketing	4	B2B versus B2C marketing	1	3	26
3	Lean manufacturing Tax depreciation allowances	3 9	Lean manufacturing JIT production and purchasing	2 3	Lean manufacturing JIT production and purchasing	2 4	Lean manufacturing JIT production and purchasing	1 1		25
4	Short term decision regarding a one-off order using relevant costing principles	12	Short term decision regarding a one-off order using relevant costing principles	4	Short term decision regarding a one-off order using relevant costing principles	3	Short term decision regarding a one-off order using relevant costing principles	2		21
Total marks available for each competency		62		17		13		5	3	100

试卷四　评分指南

部分	技术技能		商业技能		人际技能		领导技能		综合	总计
1	概率分布 期望值的局限性 增值税税制的实施	9 8 8	增值税税制的实施	3						28
2	作业成本法	13	B2B 与 B2C 营销	5	B2B 与 B2C 营销	4	B2B 与 B2C 营销	1	3	26
3	精益生产 税收折旧减免	3 9	精益生产 适时制生产与采购	2 3	精益生产 适时制生产与采购	2 4	精益生产 适时制生产与采购	1 1		25
4	使用相关成本法处理一次性订单，做出短期决策	12	使用相关成本法处理一次性订单，做出短期决策	4	使用相关成本法处理一次性订单，做出短期决策	3	使用相关成本法处理一次性订单，做出短期决策	2		21
各种能力分数总计		62		17		13		5	3	100

天津财经大学名师解惑

试卷一共有四项任务，考查了 P1、F1、E1 三门课程的知识点，具体包括短期决策分析、营运资金管理、本量利分析、现金管理、质量成本和供应商关系管理等。该试卷考核了考生的四项能力，其中技术技能的分值占62%，商业技能的分值占17%，人际技能的分值占13%，领导技能的分值占5%，与 CGMA 管理会计能力框架的技能要求一致。

该试卷的每项任务涉及以下知识点：

任务	问题	科目	知识点
任务一	概率分布及期望值的局限性	P1	概率分布（probability distribution）与期望值（expected value）
	增值税税制的实施	F1	增值税（VAT）
任务二	作业成本法	P1	作业成本法（ABC）
	B2B 及 B2C 营销	E1	B2B 与 B2C
任务三	精益生产及适时制采购与生产	E1，P1	精益生产（lean production）与适时制（JIT）
	税收折旧减免	F1	税收折旧（tax depreciation）
任务四	使用相关成本法处理一次性订单，做出短期决策	P1	相关成本法（relevant cost）和短期决策（short-term decision）

上述各项任务要求以邮件、报告或工作笔记等形式来呈现答案，对问题的描述非常明确，答题时既要注意内容的针对性，也要注意形式的规范性。

对应知识点的深度剖析

概率分布

（1）通过概率分布表我们可以计算出期望值。期望值是指在一个离散性随机变量试验中每次可能结果的概率乘以其结果的总和。在该题中可通过两种方法进行计算，一是求出联合概率，二是使用 Andreas 的图表。

（2）使用期望值来评估风险的好处与局限性。

好处：可以根据期望值计算出标准差，能够更准确地反映风险。

局限性：依赖于概率的精确性，而概率的估计是基于人的主观判断；期望值是一个需要多次决策才能得出的加权平均数，不适用于一次性的决策；期望值不能显示出各个可能结果与期望值的离散程度。

考生注意事项

期望值（EV）=每种可能的产出×对应概率，然后求和。

联合概率=两变量各自概率的乘积。

标准差=期望值的方差的平方根。

增值税

增值税是以商品（含应税劳务）在流转过程中产生的增值额作为计税依据而征收的一种流转税。从计税原理上说，增值税是对商品生产、流通、劳务服务中多个环节的新增价值或商品的附加值征收的一种流转税。实行价外税，也就是由消费者负担，有增值才征税，没增值不征税。

增值税注册企业对其销售征收税款（销项税），而在其发生费用与进行采购时抵扣一部分增值税（进项税），将销项与进项的差额上缴给税务机关。他们定期向税务机关提交所得税申请表以说明与本期相关的、支付的进项增值税额与销项增值税额。

作业成本法

作业成本法把直接成本和间接成本（包括期间费用）作为产品（服务）消耗作业的成本同等地对待，拓宽了成本的计算范围，使计算出来的产品（服务）成本更为准确真实。

作业成本法的分析过程

（1）定义业务和成本核算对象（通常是产品，有时也可能是顾客、产品市场等）。这一过程很耗时间。如果两种产品满足的是顾客的同一种需求，那么在定义业务时，选择顾客要比选择单个产品更为恰当。

（2）确定每种业务的成本动因，即成本的决定因素，如订单的数量。

（3）将成本分配给每个成本核算对象，对各对象的成本和价格进行比较，从而确定其盈利能力的高低。

作业成本法适用于任何具有以下特点的企业。

（1）间接成本的发生不是由产量所决定的。

（2）相对于直接成本，间接成本的比重较高。

（3）产品的多样化导致了消耗的资源的多样化。

作业成本法的优缺点

优点：能更准确地计算产品和产品线的成本；有利于改进成本控制；为战略管理提供信息支持（经营管理）。

缺点：开发和维护费用较高；确定成本动因比较困难；不符合对外财务报告的需求。

B2B 和 B2C 营销

B2B 是指企业与企业之间通过专用网络，进行数据信息的交换、传递，开展交易活动的商业模式。它将企业内部网和企业的产品及服务，通过 B2B 网站或移动客户端与客户紧密结合起来，通过网络的快速反应，为客户提供更好的服务，从而促进企业的业务发展。

B2C 的中文简称为“商对客”。“商对客”是电子商务的一种模式，也就是通常所说的直接面向消费者销售产品和服务商业零售模式。

考生注意事项

两者的区别主要表现在概念及交易模式方面。

概念区别

B2B 是企业与企业之间通过互联网进行产品、服务及信息的交换。

B2C 是电子商务按交易对象分类中的一种，即表示商业机构对消费者的电子商务。这种形式的电子商务一般以网络零售业为主，主要借助于因特网开展在线销售活动。例如经营各种书籍、鲜花、计算机、通信用品等商品。

交易模式区别

B2B 使企业之间的交易减少了许多事务性的工作流程和管理费用，降低了企业经营成本。网络的便利及延伸性使企业扩大了活动范围，企业跨地区跨国界发展更方便，成本更低廉。

B2C 是企业到客户，是指利用因特网进行全部的贸易活动，即在网上将信息流、资金流、商流和部分的物流完整地实现连接。在今天，B2C 电子商务以完备的双向信息沟通、灵活的交易手段、快捷的物流配送、低成本高效益的运作方式等在各行各业展现了强大的生命力。

适时制和精益生产

精益生产是通过进行系统结构、人员组织、运行方式和市场供求等方面的变革，使生产系统能更快适应用户需求的不断变化，并能使生产过程中一切无用的、多余的东西被精简，最终达到包括市场供销在内的生产的各方面的最好结果的一种生产管理方式。与传统的大生产方式不同，其特色是“多品种、小批量”。

明确精益生产的原则：消除浪费、改进生产安排（需求拉动生产）、建立质量标准、持续改进。考生需要了解和掌握以上几条生产原则，同时应结合本题的案例进行分析。

适时制的基本思想是“只在需要的时候，按需要的量，生产所需的产品”，也就是追求一种无库存，或库存达到最小的生产系统。适时制的基本思想是生产的计划和控制及库存的管理。

适时制以准时生产为出发点，首先暴露出生产过量和其他方面的浪费，然后对设备、人员等进行淘汰、调整，达到降低成本、简化计划和提高控制的目的。适时制模式分为适时制生产和适时制采购两种。适时制采购是指只有当客户订单即将开始生产时才进行原材料的采购，原材料一旦到货就立刻投入生产；而适时制生产是指在指定时间，生产指定数量的指定产品。

适时制模式对供应商具有很大的依赖性，因此需要企业和供应商保持良好的关系以确保供应的质量和数量和适时制模式的正常运行。

该考点考查适时制和精益生产的知识点，学生需要熟悉实施适时制和精益生产的背景条件，掌握适时制和精益生产的联系和区别。适时制与精益生产不仅在E1中占很大篇幅，在P1中也有很多阐述，为考试中经常出现的考点，需要考生们重点关注。

考生注意事项

（1）适时制（包括生产与采购）与精益生产的定义。

（2）适时制的基本原则与特点：

品质——寻找、纠正和解决问题；

柔性——小批量、一个流；

投放市场时间——把开发时间减至最小；

产品多元化——缩短产品周期、减小规模效益影响；

效率——提高生产率、减少浪费；

适应性——标准尺寸总成、协调合作；

学习——不断改善。

（3）一定要结合案例本身，针对公司存在的问题指出适时制存在的意义与重要性，以及在财务与非财务方面能带来哪些影响。

相关成本和决策

相关成本是指对企业经营管理有影响或在经营管理决策分析时必须加以考虑的各种形式的成本。相关成本主要包括机会成本、付现成本等。而非相关成本是指过去已经发生的，与某一特定决策方案没有直接联系的成本，指不适用于决策分析的成本。不可避免成本、沉没成本等均属于非相关成本。

相关成本三要素：（1）现金形式（影响现金流）；（2）反映先前成本的变化；（3）影响未来现金流。考生可根据此三项来判定某项成本是否为相关成本。

该考点考核学生对相关成本的掌握程度，学生需要掌握判定相关成本的方法，区分相关成本和非相关成本，并运用相关成本做出决策。

在考题中，通常会给出一系列数据让考生判断其是否为某一决策的相关成本并依据自己的判断来进一步说明是否应该实施此项决策。这种题型一般比较灵活，书本上的最基本的判断准则是必须掌握的根本（futher，relevant，cash），考生需要在每个情景中仔细判断，并解释是或不是相关成本的理由。此题一般任务量较大，需要考生们在平时多练习，以形成快速判断的能力。

在判断是否实施决策时，要比较该决策能带来的收益与相关成本，无关的收益与成本不能被考虑在内，所以在第一环节中一定要准确判断其是否为相关成本。

但除此之外，在考虑是否接受该决策时还需要我们有更多的考量，比如首先在这种类型的分析中，它假定决策是基于短期现金流的，未顾虑到长期影响，并且我们也没有考虑到其对现有客户的影响。所以我们仍要继续分析，从非财务与长远角度来继续阐述潜在的影响，给予一个更为全面及深层次的理解。这需要考生们有更多的交际能力与领导力。

应税利润和税收抵扣

会计折旧、税收抵扣、应税利润与营业利润。

会计折旧是用资产的原始成本减去它的残值并把差值分摊到该资产的使用年限上。

税收折旧是按 25% 的折旧率以余额递减法计提折旧。

应税利润 = 会计利润 + 会计折旧 – 税收折旧。

营业利润 = 营业收入 – 营业成本 – 营业税金及附加 – 销售费用 – 管理费用 – 财务费用 – 资产减值损失 + 公允价值变动收益（ – 公允价值变动损失） + 投资收益（ – 投资损失）。

该考点考核学生对税收的掌握情况，学生需要掌握利润调整的方法，并熟悉应税利润和营业利润的区别。

考生注意事项

会计折旧是不可抵税的，需要用税收折旧代替。

由于在计算税收时使用的基础为应税利润，所以我们首先要对会计利润进行调整，加回会计折旧，而减去税收折旧。

如果最终出售机器所取得的收入高于（或低于）它的账面净值或账面价值，我们将会得到会计上的处置利得（或损失）。无论是会计上的利得还是损失都不可抵税。利得将从会计利润中扣除，亏损将加回到会计利润中。这些都将出于税收原因而被余额计税和余额抵税所取代。在计算应税利润时，如果是余额计税则要计入应纳税所得额；如果是余额抵税，则可以抵减应纳税所得额。

Variant 5

This examination is structured as follows：

Section number	Number of tasks	Time for section(minutes)
1	1	35
2	1	45
3	2	45
4	1	55

The time available for each section is for reading,planning and writing your answer(s).

Please note section 3 consists of two tasks. Please leave enough time to complete.

Section 1

The following article was published in *Home Energy Solutions*.

Home Energy Solutions

7th November 2016 No. 23 F$2.40

Marici Power Announces Next-generation Solar Power Storage System

Benjamin Novak, Business Correspondent

Marici Power says it expects to launch its revolutionary home battery storage system at the end of February 2017 with the first residential installations set to take place in March 2017. This will be Marici's first entry into residential energy storage.

The battery storage unit can be combined with Marici's solar panels to provide a fully integrated system. The company said it was already seeing "substantial interest" in the home battery units.

Lighter, more modular and easier to install than the current market offerings, the new storage unit maintains industry-leading standards for performance, reliability and safety and is suitable both for installation into existing home solar systems and for packaging together with new solar panels. All of these features give solar providers the flexibility and choice they need to integrate storage into their customer offers.

"Marici Power is always seeking ways to deliver the best energy solutions for our customers," said Mark Rawson, Marici's R&D manager. "We strive to satisfy our customers' increasing desire for energy savings. This new system provides even more options and choice."

You receive the following email from Maria Coleman, finance director.

From: Maria Coleman, Finance Director

To: Management Accountant Assistant

Subject: Launch of the new energy storage system

You will have seen yesterday's press report about our new solar energy storage system. It's great news and should make a major impact in the market.

One of our main priorities is to decide on an appropriate selling price for the new product. commercial director Andreas Lowe has carried out a review of the market and believes that we should set the selling price at either F$ 6, 000, F$ 6, 250 or F$ 6, 500. He has had various discussions with our installers to establish the possible customer reaction to the new product and thinks it could be strong, moderate or weak. I have attached a table showing the estimated contribution for each of the nine possible outcomes.

Andreas wants to go ahead with a selling price of F$ 6, 000 as it offers the maximum possible outcome but I dont believe that the maximax decision criterion is the right approach to take in this case. I would like to look at other approaches that we could take to making the decision.

I would be grateful if you could prepare a report that I can discuss with Andreas covering the following areas.

(1) An explanation of the other decision criteria that we could apply, given the uncertainty about the market reaction, and the price that would be selected under each criterion.

(2) What further data we would require if we wanted to base our decision on expected value and what are the limitations of that approach.

Regards.

Maria Coleman

Finance Director

Marici Power

Estimated contribution for the 6 month period to March 2017—August 2017：

	Selling price(F$)		
	6,000	6,250	6,500
Customer reaction			
Strong	4,500,000	4,000,000	4,250,000
Moderate	3,500,000	3,400,000	3,600,000
Weak	2,750,000	3,000,000	2,500,000

Write the report for Maria Coleman, finance director.

Section 2

A few days later, you receive the following email from Alex Hilliard, senior management accountant.

From：Alex Hilliard, Senior Management Accountant
To：Management Accountant Assistant
Subject：New product budgets

We have decided that the selling price for the new product will be F$ 6,250. I have now prepared a profit and cash budget for the first six months period for the new energy storage units (see profit and cash budget) assuming a moderate level of customer reaction.

We have also decided to use a system of flexible budgeting and responsibility accounting which are new concepts for some of the directors. Maria Coleman, the finance director, is going to present the figures at the board meeting next week. She has asked that we provide a narrative to explain how the budget figures will be used as a control mechanism to monitor our actual performance against budget and for the performance evaluation of our managers. She would also like an explanation why the net cash movement in the period is lower than the projected profit.

I am going on holiday tomorrow and won't have time to do this before I go, so I would appreciate it if you could do it instead.

I suggest that you include the following information.

(1) An explanation of both, how a budget acts as a control mechanism, and the concept of re-

sponsibility accounting.

(2) Why it would be appropriate for us to use a flexible budgeting system.

(3) An explanation of why there is a difference between the profit and the net cash movement for the period.

Many thanks!

Alex Hilliard

Senior Management Accountant

Marici Power

Profit and cash budget:

New energy storage system Budgeted profit and loss for the period March 2017—August 2017	
	(F$ 000)
Sales revenue	6, 250
Material costs	1, 875
Labour costs	625
Variable manufacturing overheads	150
Non-manufacturing variable overheads	200
Contribution	3, 400
Fixed manufacturing overheads	800
Non-manufacturing fixed overheads	200
Amortisation of research and development costs	800
Net profit	1, 600

New energy storage system Cash budget for the period March 2017—August 2017	
Receipts	(F$ 000)
Sales receipts	4, 200
Payments	

（续表）

New energy storage system Cash budget for the period March 2017—August 2017	
	(F$ 000)
Payments to suppliers	2, 125
Manufacturing wages and salaries	625
Non-manufacturing wages and salaries	150
Research and development costs	200
Total payments	3, 100
Opening cash balance	0
Net cash flow for the period	1, 100
Closing cash balance	1, 100

Write the report for Maria Coleman, finance director.

Section 3

The following week, you receive an email from Maria Coleman, finance director.

From: Maria Coleman, Finance Director

To: Management Accountant Assistant

Subject: Ethics investigation / R&D expenditure

I have just come out of a meeting with Dr. Liffe, the research & development director, and Martin Lerwick, the group CEO.

Martin Lerwick has just informed me that there has been an investigation into unusual trading in the shares of our parent company. It would appear that the details of the new product were leaked before the official announcement. It is clear that the leak has come from within this company either from someone in the research & development department or the finance department.

This is a very serious issue and I am planning to call a meeting of all finance department staff for tomorrow morning. As members of CIMA we are all bound by the CIMA Code of Ethics.

I would be grateful if you could prepare some notes for me on how the CIMA Code of Ethics would apply in this situation and why such a failure in business ethics could be detrimental to our company.

On a completely different issue, Dr. Liffe mentioned that he was looking at the budget for the new product (see profit and cash budget) and was slightly confused as to how we have treated the research and development expenditure. He said that he knows that we have incurred significantly more expenditure developing the new product than is shown in the budgeted profit figures.

Please send him an email explaining the accounting requirements under IAS 38 Intangible Assets and how we have treated the expenditure on the new product.

Regards!

Maria Coleman

Finance Director

Marici Power

Profit and cash budget:

New energy storage system Budgeted profit and loss for the period March 2017—August 2017	
	(F$ 000)
Sales revenue	6,250
Material costs	1,875
Labour costs	625
Variable manufacturing overheads	150
Non-manufacturing variable overheads	200
Contribution	3,400
Fixed manufacturing overheads	800
Non-manufacturing fixed overheads	200
Amortisation of research and development costs	800
Net profit	1,600

New energy storage system Cash budget for the period March 2017—August 2017	
Receipts	(F$ 000)
Sales receipts	4, 200
Payments	
Payments to suppliers	2, 125
Manufacturing wages and salaries	625
Non-manufacturing wages and salaries	150
Research and development costs	200
Total payments	3, 100
Opening cash balance	0
Net cash flow for the period	1, 100
Closing cash balance	1, 100

Write the notes for Maria Coleman, finance director and wirte the email for Dr. Liffe, the research & development director.

Section 4

A few days later, you receive the following email from Alex Hilliard, senior management accountant.

From: Alex Hilliard, Senior Management Accountant
To: Management Accountant Assistant
Subject: Certified partnership scheme

You may probably have heard by now that the directors are considering the introduction of a Certified Partnership Scheme. Under such a scheme, we would certify that our installers are fully trained and accredited specialists in assessing, installing and maintaining our new innovative energy systems. Certification means each partner has made a commitment to ensure they deliver the highest standards of service.

The new scheme is very important for the long term survival of our business and it is imperative that we know that the installers who are working with our products are applying high quality standards.

There has been a lot of debate about whether the certified partnership scheme is worthwhile. A few of our colleagues have said that if we go ahead with this scheme we need to make sure that the partners not only provide high quality standards but are also seen to have the same ethos as us in terms of environmental management and sustainability. Maria Coleman, the Finance Director, is suggesting that we should require all certified partners to report on a selection of quality and environmental measures on a quarterly basis.

A project group has been formed with representation from various departments in the company and I would like you to represent the Finance Department. I am really keen that we should be seen to be making a significant contribution to this type of project so it is important that you have well prepared for the first meeting.

I suggest that you prepare some working notes covering the following areas.

- What the potential benefits to our company and our certified partners of operating a certified partnership scheme are.
- Your recommendation, including justification, for measures that we could use to monitor the performance of our certified partners in relation to the quality of their work and environmental practices, providing three quality and three environmental measures covering different areas of the installers' operations.

Best of luck!

Alex Hilliard
Senior Management Accountant
Marici Power

Write the working notes for Alex Hilliard, senior management accountant.

试卷五

本次考试的结构如下：

序号	任务数	时间（分钟）
1	1	35
2	1	45
3	2	45
4	1	55

每个部分规定的时间可用于读题、组织和书写答案。

请注意任务三包含两项子任务，需留足时间。

任务一

下面这篇文章发表在《家庭能源解决方案》上。

家庭能源解决方案

2016 年 11 月 7 日 23 号　　F$2.40

摩利兹能源公司

宣布了下一代太阳能储存系统

摩利兹能源公司声称，将于2017年2月底发布具有创新性的家用电池存储系统，并计划在2017年3月进行首次住宅安装。这将是摩利兹能源公司首次进入住宅能源存储领域。

电池存储单元能够跟摩利兹能源公司的太阳能电池板相结合来提供一个综合系统。公司声称已经看见了家用电池类产品的巨大利益。

与当前市场上的产品相比，新一代电池存储系统更轻、更模块化、更易安装，并在性能、可靠性、安全性方面保持着行业领先的标准。此外，它不仅可以在当前已有的太阳能系统中使用，也可以和新的太阳能电池板配合使用。所有的这些特征给予了太阳能产品供应商灵活性，他们向顾客提供产品时在整合存储系统方面有了更多的选择。

"摩利兹能源公司一直致力于为客户提供最优的能源解决方案。"摩利兹能源公司研发部经理 Mark Rawson说道，"我们尽全力满足客户在节约能源方面不断上升的需求，这个新系统为我们提供了更多的可能和选择。"

你收到了一封来自财务总监 Maria Coleman 的邮件。

发件人：财务总监 Maria Coleman
收件人：管理会计师助理
主题：新能源存储系统的发布

你一定看过了昨天关于我们新型太阳能存储系统的报道了。这是一个好消息，应该会对市场产生较大的影响。

我们需要优先考虑的主要事情之一是给新产品确定一个合适的销售价格。商务总监Andreas Lowe已经对市场进行了调查并且认为我们应该把售价定在F$6 000，F$6 250或者F$6 500。他已经和我们的安装人员进行了多次讨论，以此来了解客户对新产品可能做出的反应，并认为这些反应可能是强烈的、温和的或是微弱的。附表中是我对这九种可能的后果带来的贡献进行的估计。

Andreas认为应该定价为F$6 000，因为它有可能带来最大收益，但是我并不认为在现阶段采用“Maximax”这种方法进行判断是正确的选择。我想寻找一些适合我们做出决策的其他方法。

我要跟Andreas进行讨论，请准备一份报告供我在讨论时使用，非常感谢。报告内容应包括：

（1）考虑到市场反应的不确定性，以及在每种标准下可能采用的销售价格说明我们可以使用的其他决策方法；

（2）如果我们想根据期望值来做出决策，我们还需要哪些额外的数据？这种方法的局限性是什么？

致以问候。

摩利兹能源公司

财务总监

Maria Coleman

2017年3月到8月的估计贡献：

	售价（F$）		
	6 000	6 250	6 500
客户反应			
强烈	4 500 000	4 00 000	4 250 000
温和	3 500 000	3 400 000	3 600 000
微弱	2 750 000	3 000 000	2 500 000

请根据财务总监Maria Coleman的要求写一份报告。

任务二

几天后，你收到了来自高级管理会计师 Alex Hilliard 的一封邮件。

发件人：高级管理会计师 Alex Hilliard
收件人：管理会计师助理
主题：新产品预算

我们已经决定将新产品的销售价格定为 F$6 250。假设客户的反应是温和的，我准备了一份关于新能源存储单元在前 6 个月内的利润预算和现金预算（见利润和现金预算表）。

我们已经决定了使用弹性预算系统和责任会计制度，这对很多董事来说是新的概念。财务总监 Maria Coleman 即将在下周的董事会上展示这些数据。她要求我们提供一份文字材料来解释一下，预算数据作为一种控制机制，将被如何运用于对实际绩效和预算的监控及对经理们的绩效评估。她也希望我们对在此期间的净现金流比预期的利润低这一现象做出合理解释。

我明天即将休假，没有时间完成这些工作，所以如果你可以替我完成它们，我将非常感谢。

我建议在你文字材料中包含以下内容。

（1）解释预算是如何作为控制机制运行的，解释责任会计的概念。

（2）解释为什么使用弹性预算系统对我们来说是合适的。

（3）解释期间内利润和净现金流存在差异的原因。

非常感谢！

摩利兹能源公司
高级管理会计师
Alex Hilliard

利润和现金预算表：

新能源存储系统 2017 年 3～8 月利润预算表	
	（F$ 000）
销售收入	6 250
材料成本	1 875
人工成本	625
变动制造费用	150
非制造变动费用	200
贡献	3 400
固定制造费用	800
非制造固定费用	200
研发成本的摊销费	800
净利润	1 600
新能源存储系统 2017 年 3～8 月现金预算表	
收入	（F$ 000）
销售收入	4 200
支出	
给供应商的付款	2 125
生产部门的工资和薪酬	625
非生产部门的工资和薪酬	150
研发成本	200
总支出	3 100
期初现金余额	0
本期净现金流	1 100
期末现金余额	1 100

请写出给财务总监 Maria Coleman 的报告。

任务三

一个星期后，你收到了一封来自财务总监 Maria Coleman 的邮件。

发件人：财务总监 Maria Coleman

收件人：管理会计师助理

主题：道德调查/研发支出

我刚刚和研发总监 Dr. Liffe、集团首席执行官 Martin Lerwick 进行了会谈。

Martin Lerwick 刚才通知我，我们母公司的股票因为存在非正当交易而正在接受调查。新产品的细节在官方发布之前似乎被泄露了。很明显，泄密者肯定是公司内部的人，要么来自研发部门，要么来自财务部门。

这是一个十分严重的问题，我打算明天早上召集全体财务部门的人员开会。作为 CIMA 的会员，我们都应该遵守 CIMA 的道德规范。

我希望你可以为我准备一些资料，说明一下 CIMA 道德规范在这种情况下是如何应用的，以及为什么在商业道德上的失败会对公司造成损害。非常感谢！

此外，Dr. Liffe 提到他在查看新产品的预算表（见利润和现金预算表）时对于我们如何处理研发费用感到困惑。他认为我们用于开发新产品的费用远多于利润预算表中披露的数字。

请给他发一封邮件，解释国际会计准则第 38 号无形资产的核算要求，以及对新产品的研发费用的处理方法

致以问候。

摩利兹能源公司

财务总监

Maria Coleman

利润和现金预算表：

新能源存储系统 2017 年 3 ~ 8 月利润预算表	
	（F$ 000）
销售收入	6 250
材料成本	1 875

（续表）

新能源存储系统 2017 年 3 ~ 8 月利润预算表	
	（F$ 000）
人工成本	625
变动制造费用	150
非制造变动费用	200
贡献	3 400
固定制造费用	800
非制造固定费用	200
研发成本的摊销费	800
净利润	1 600
收入	
销售收入	4 200
支出	
给供应商的付款	2 125
生产部门的工资和薪酬	625
非生产部门的工资和薪酬	150
研发成本	200
总支出	3 100
期初现金余额	0
本期净现金流	1 100
期末现金余额	1 100

请根据要求给财务总监 Maria Coleman 和研发总监 Dr. Liffe 准备资料及回复邮件。

任务四

几天后，你收到了一封来自高级管理会计师 Alex Hilliard 的邮件。

发件人：高级管理会计师 Alex Hilliard

收件人：管理会计师助理

主题：认证合作伙伴计划

你可能已经听说了董事们正在考虑引入认证合作伙伴计划。在此计划下，我们需要证明在评估、安装和维护我们新的创新能源系统方面，我们的安装人员都是经过全面培训的、可信任的专家。认证就意味着每一个和我们合作的伙伴都做出了承诺以确保他们能够提供最高标准的服务。

这个新的计划对我们公司的长期发展至关重要，同时，我们也有必要了解安装我们的产品的安装人员是否提供了高质量标准的服务。

大家对"认证合作伙伴计划是否有价值"这一议题存在很多争论。一些同事认为，如果实施这个计划，我们就需要确保合作伙伴不仅能够提供高质量的服务，而且还要与我们在环境管理和可持续发展方面有相同的理念。财务总监 Maria Coleman 建议我们应该要求所有被认证的合作伙伴以一个季度为期间，报告他们采用的质量和环境措施。

公司不同部门将分别派出代表，组成一个项目组，我希望你能代表财务部加入该项目组。我非常希望财务部能够在这个项目中做出巨大的贡献，所以你为第一次会议做好充分的准备是至关重要的。

我建议你准备的工作资料中应包含以下方面。

- 实施认证合作伙伴计划对我们公司和被认证的合作伙伴有哪些潜在的好处。
- 我们可以采用哪些方法来监督被认证的合作伙伴在工作质量和环境实践中的表现，给出你的建议（在质量和环境方面各列举三种方法，涵盖安装人员不同的工作领域），并做出合理的解释。

好运！

摩利兹能源公司

高级管理会计师

Alex Hilliard

请给高级管理会计师 Alex Hilliard 准备工作资料。

Variant 5 Suggested Answers

Section 1

Report

Price of the New Energy Storage System

Other Decision Criterion

Maximin Criterion

Under the maximin criteria we would select the alternative that maximises the minimum pay-off achievable under each alternative. This is where a pessimistic approach is taken.

The minimum pay-offs are as follows.

- If we choose a selling price of F$ 6, 000, F$ 2, 750, 000.
- If we choose a selling price of F$ 6, 250, F$ 3, 000, 000.
- If we choose a selling price of F$ 6, 500, F$ 2, 500, 000.

We would therefore choose a selling price of F$ 6, 250 as this gives us the maximum contribution if the worst outcome were to happen.

Minimax Regret Criterion

Under this criterion the alternative that minimises the maximum regret under each alternative is selected. This is generally used where we want to avoid making a bad decision. "Regret" refers to the opportunity loss through having made the wrong decision. This is also where a pessimistic approach is taken to the decision.

We can produce a regret matrix which shows the regret depending on the customer reaction to the product and which selling price we choose. For example, if the customer reaction is strong we would have no regret if we had chosen a selling price of F$ 6, 000. The regret for each of the other two selling prices would be the difference between a contribution of F$ 4, 500, 000 and the contribution for each selling price.

Having calculated the regret for each different customer reaction, we can then establish the maximum regret for each selling price. We then choose the selling price with the minimum of the maximum regrets.

Expected Value

If we wish to base the decision on expected value we would need to first of all determine the probabilities for each of the customer reactions. Andreas should be able to use his experience of the market to arrive at the probabilities. The probabilities will however be subjective since they are based purely on Andreas' judgement.

Expected value is calculated by weighting each of the possible outcomes by their associated probability. The expected value is therefore the weighted average of the possible outcomes based on estimates of their probability.

Expected value has a number of limitations.

- The probabilities used are usually very subjective. As discussed above they rely on Andreas' judgement of the market.
- The expected value is merely a weighted average if the decision is repeated several times. In business there are few decisions that would be repeated many times. In this case, the launch of the new solar energy storage system and the price to charge is a major one-off decision so reliance solely on expected value would be unwise.
- The expected value gives no indication of the dispersion of possible outcomes around the expected value, that is, the risk. For example, a price of F$6,250 has a relatively small range of possible outcomes whereas a price of F$6,000 has a much wider dispersion. Expected value takes a risk-neutral approach to decision making.
- The expected value may not correspond to any of the actual possible outcomes as it is an average.

Section 2

Report

Budgeting

Budgetary Control / Responsibility Accounting

Budgetary control is about comparing actual performance against budgeted performance and taking corrective action where necessary.

It focuses on the costs for a department, business unit or in this case, a product. The responsibility for the costs will be allocated to an individual manager. If there are any differences between actual and budgeted performance we would expect the manager responsible to act either to correct the budget or bring the cost under control.

For the system of responsibility accounting to be effective, the managers' performance will have to be evaluated only on the costs that they can control. Using our standard costing system we are able to split variances from budget into those that relate to efficiency and those that relate to price. For example, we can split the total material cost variance into a material usage variance and a material price variance. The production manager would be responsible for the material usage variance whilst the purchasing manager would be responsible for the material price variance.

Flexible Budget

A fixed budget, which is what we have used in the past, remains unchanged regardless of the actual level of activity. A flexible budget shows the same information but for a number of different levels of activity. Flexible budget can be used for both planning and control purposes.

In drawing up the budgets we have assumed that the customers' reaction will be moderate but we could have produced budgets for both strong and weak customer reaction.

In this situation with the launch of a new product, there is the considerable uncertainty and it is likely the actual activity level will differ from the budgeted level. If our costs were mainly fixed, a change in level of activity would not cause many problems for cost comparison with a fixed budget. However, a significant proportion of our costs are of a variable nature and therefore it is difficult to control expenditure satisfactorily using a fixed budget.

A flexible budget will help us to make more valid comparisons. It would be unfair to evaluate managers' performance against a fixed budget since we would expect changes in activity levels to result in a change in variable costs. A flexible budget is designed to show the allowed expenditure for the actual numbers of units produced and sold. Comparing a flexible budget with the actual expenditure will enable us to distinguish genuine efficiencies and inefficiencies.

The use of flexible budget therefore is linked with the concept of responsibility accounting.

Differences Between Profit and Cash

The profit budget for the new product has been produced on an accruals basis, that is, a sale is recognized when the goods have been delivered to the customer and costs are recognized when the expense has been incurred. The cash budget, in contrast, is a forecast of payments and receipts. We will begin to make sales of our new product in March 2017 but as we extend credit to our customers, we will not receive payment until April 2017 at the earliest. This is why our sales receipts are F$ 4, 200, 000 compared to sales revenue of F$ 6, 250, 000.

Similarly, we have purchased materials to produce the products but as we get credit from our supplier we will not pay for them immediately. However purchases need to happen before production which is why payments to suppliers are in line with material and other costs.

Some profit or loss items are derived from accounting conventions and are not cash flows, for example, the depreciation of non-current assets. The depreciation of machinery used to produce our new product is included in fixed manufacturing overheads but the depreciation is not included in the cash budget. Instead the cash budget would show the payment of the purchase price of the machinery which we will incur prior to the budget period shown.

The research and development cost shown in the profit budget is the amortisation cost of the development expenditure that we had previously capitalized. Whereas, the amount shown in the cash budget is the cash payments we expect to make for further development of the product over the six months period.

Section 3

CIMA Code of Ethics

CIMA members and registered students throughout the world have a duty to observe the highest standards of conduct and integrity, and to uphold the good standing and reputation of the profession. They must also refrain from any conduct which might discredit the profession.

The code incorporates five fundamental principles. I have assessed each of these based on the alleged offence：

Integrity means conducting oneself in an honest and truthful manner in all business dealings. To take advantage of insider knowledge is a breach of this since it is an attempt to obtain personal financial reward in a dishonest way.

Objectivity means not allowing conflict of interest to override professional judgement. There is conflict of interest in that the apparent personal and third party gain conflicts with the responsibility to Marici.

Professional competence includes conducting oneself according to the relevant professional standards. Professional standards include not using inside information for personal gain.

Professional behaviour means obeying laws and regulations. In most countries，insider dealing is a criminal offence hence there is a clear breach in this case.

Confidentiality requires that CIMA members respect the confidential nature of information acquired through professional relationships such as past or current employment. CIMA members should not disclose such information unless they have specific permission or a legal or professional duty to do so. They should also never use confidential information for their own or another person's gain.

Business ethics are important for any organisation and our stakeholders expect us to operate to certain ethical standards. A failure such as this would be detrimental to our reputation with stakeholder groups. An ethical framework is a part of good corporate governance and suggests a well-run business. Any ethical failure calls into question our corporate governance policy and procedures. Investors may be concerned by this failure and about our approach es to risk management. Our employees may be demotivated if they believe that they operate in an environment of poor ethical corporate behaviour.

IAS 38

Accounting Treatment of R&D（Research and Development）Costs

The accounting for R&D is dealt with under IAS 38 Intangible Assets.

Definitions of Research and Development

Research is investigation undertaken to gain new scientific or technical knowledge and understanding.

Development is the application of research findings or other knowledge to plan or design for the production of new or substantially improved processes, products or services before the start of commercial production.

Research expenditure must be written off as an expense to the statement of profit or loss. Development expenditure, which is what we are concerned with, can be capitalized provided it meets all of the criteria explained below.

From: Management Accountant Assistant
To: Dr Liffe, Research and Development Director
Subject: Research and development expenditure

Capitalisation of Development Expenditure

Under IAS 38, an intangible asset arising from development must be capitalized if an entity can demonstrate a number of criteria. In respect of this development project all of the following criteria would have been assessed, and at the point that they were all met, further expenditure on the project would have been capitalized.

(1) The technical feasibility of completing the intangible asset so that it will be available for use or sale. At the point where the knowledge gained from the development project indicated that the new energy storage system was feasible, this criterion would have been met.

(2) Intention to complete and use or sell the intangible asset. At the point that management had decided to complete the project and to start selling the new system, this criterion would have been met.

(3) Ability to use or sell the intangible asset. We already have an existing market for our current products and the new product is an extension of this.

(4) Existence of a market or, if to be used internally, the usefulness of the intangible asset. At the point that we had established that there was a market for the new product, this criterion would have been met.

(5) Availability of adequate technical, financial, and other resources to complete the

intangible asset. At the point that our budgets showed that we had adequate resources to complete the project, this criterion would have been met.

(6) The cost of the intangible asset can be measured reliably. The costs relating to the new product have been separately recorded.

If any of the recognition criteria are not met then the expenditure must be charged to the statement of profit or loss as incurred. If the recognition criteria have been met, capitalisation must take place, but only those costs incurred from the point that all criteria are met can be capitalized.

Once we recognized that the project met the criteria above, the development expenditure was capitalized and is shown in our statement of financial position.

Treatment of Capitalized Development Expenditure

If development costs have been capitalized, the asset should be amortised over its finite life. Amortisation should begin when the asset is available for use.

The development expenditure that we previously capitalised will be amortised over the life of the product. The amount that you have seen in the budgeted profit figures is the amortisation charge for the six months period.

Thanks!

Management Accountant Assistant

Marici Power

Section 4

Certified Partnership Scheme

Potential Benefits

There are a number of benefits that we could get from operating a certified partnership scheme. The scheme would involve us actively managing the relationship between our company and our installers, which has a number of advantages.

It is preferable to work with our installers to add value to the supply chain so that the overall benefits that accrue can be shared amongst all the parties involved. Rather than emphasize price, we should build relationships with the installers in order to jointly manage the entire supply chain better.

Our dependency on these installers is high as there are only a few installers in the industry for this new product. Actively managing our relationship with installers may allow us to gain a relative competitive advantage over rival firms which do not currently operate such a scheme.

Our brand identity is dependent on the perceived quality of our product and this could be compromised should our installers not apply the standard of service we would expect. A certified partnership scheme would enable us to work together with the installers to ensure that the quality standard of the installation meets the same high standard of our product.

Using a certified partnership scheme would enable us to build long term, loyal relationships with the installers. Frequently changing installers would cause increased administrative effort and a lack of coherence in our external dealings.

Relationships based purely on price may destabilise our installers financially making them more vulnerable to going out of business, so potentially jeopardising future business. A certified partnership scheme would help to avoid this happening.

Environmental and Quality KPIs

The following environmental measures would be appropriate.

(1) Packaging material: tonnes sent to landfill or tonnes recycled.

Our products are delivered to the installers using wooden frames to secure the panel and covered in cardboard and water-proofing material. It would be appropriate to measure what volume in tonnes or as a percentage of the total is sent to landfill and what volume is recycled.

(2) Distribution vehicles: fuel usage or miles travelled or CO_2 emissions.

Our installers use transport to take the workers and the products to their customers. The amount of fuel used and the emissions from the vehicles would be an important measure. Alternatively the amount of miles travelled would give us an indirect measure of these.

(3) Energy and water usage: total water usage (in m^3) or fossil fuel energy usage (KW · h).

The use of energy and water at the installer's offices would also be appropriate. We would expect our installers to be using solar power but they may also have a need to use fossil fuels. When fitting the solar panels they will use water to clean the panels and the customer's buildings after installation.

The following quality measures would be appropriate：

（1）Prevention costs：training costs（F$）or average training expenditure per employee.

Prevention costs is concerned with ensuring that no quality failures arise. A measure for this could be the expenditure on training and development to ensure that installers are working at the highest possible standards in terms of service，safety and reliability.

（2）Internal failure costs：cost of rework or number of rework incidents.

Internal failure costs are concerned with the consequences of failure before the product or service has not been handed over to the customer. Damage caused to the panel during the installations which would involve the installer in either replacing or repaired the damaged panel would be an appropriate measure of this.

（3）External failure costs：cost of dealing with customer complaints or number of customer complaints.

External failure costs are concerned with the consequences of failure after the product or service has been handed over to the customer. This could be measured as the cost of dealing with customer complaints as a result of the solar system not operating correctly or the breakdown of the system. The number of customer complaints would also be an appropriate measure.

试卷五　参考答案

任务一

报告

新能源存储系统的定价

其他决策标准

Maximin 法

在这种方法下，我们将每种方案中的最小贡献值进行比较，选择其中的最大值。这个方法被认为是较为悲观的方法。

最小贡献值如下所示。

- 如果选择售价为 F$6 000，则贡献为 F$2 750 000。
- 如果选择售价为 F$6 250，则贡献为 F$3 000 000。
- 如果选择售价为 F$6 500，则贡献为 F$2 500 000。

因此我们应当选择将售价定为 F$6 250。因为如果最坏的情况出现，在此价格下，我们能够获得最大的贡献值。

Minimax regret 法

在这个方法下，我们将选择所有方案中最大后悔值中最小的数值。当我们想避免做出错误决策时，通常使用这个方法。“后悔值”是指做出的一个错误决定可能会带来的机会损失。这种方法也被认为是较为悲观的方法。

我们可以制作一个后悔矩阵，体现客户对产品的不同反应和我们选择的不同售价下各自的后悔值大小。例如，我们选择了 F$6 000 的售价，如果客户反应是强烈的，那么就不存在后悔值。如果选择了其他两种售价，那么就会产生后悔值，每一个后悔值是 F$4 500 000的贡献值和每种售价的贡献值之差。

在计算出不同客户反应下的后悔值之后，我们可以得到每种售价下的最大后悔值，从中再选择出最小的后悔值，其对应的价格就是我们最终选择的价格。

期望值

如果我们想要基于期望值来定价，那么我们首先需要确定每种客户反应的概率。Andreas 应该可以根据他的市场经验获得这些概率。然而，这些概率是主观的，因为它完全取决于 Andreas 的个人判断。

每种可能的结果按其相关概率加权，就可以计算出期望值。因此，期望值是基于概率估计的所有可能结果的加权平均数。

期望值法有以下几个局限性。

- 概率通常是非常主观的。如上所述，概率完全取决于 Andreas 对市场的个人判断。
- 期望值是一个加权平均数，需要类似的决策重复多次。在商业活动中，极少有重复多次的决策。在这个案例中，新能源存储系统的实施及其定价都是一次性的决策，因此，仅仅依赖期望值来做决策是不明智的。
- 期望值法没有考虑到每种结果与期望值的离散程度，也就是所谓的风险。比如，定价为 F$6 250 时离散程度较小，而定价为 F$6 000 时离散程度较大。期望值法是风险中立的决策方法。
- 期望值只是一个平均数，并不代表某一实际的可能结果。

任务二

报告

预算

预算控制/责任会计

预算控制就是将实际绩效和预算绩效进行比较，并在必要时采取纠正措施。

预算控制主要关注部门、业务单元或者某个产品的成本。各种成本的责任会分派到每个管理者身上。如果实际绩效和预算绩效存在差异，我们希望管理者能够对此负责，修改预算或者控制成本。

为了使责任会计制度实施起来更有效，管理者的绩效必须根据在他们控制范围内的成本状况来进行评估。在标准成本法系统中，我们能够将预算差异分解为与效率相关的差异和与价格相关的差异。例如，我们能够将材料总成本差异分为材料的使用差异和材料的价格差异，生产经理对材料的使用差异负责，而采购经理则对材料的价格差异负责。

弹性预算

固定预算是我们过去使用的一种预算方法，不论实际的活动水平如何，此种预算都不会发生变化。同样的信息，弹性预算是基于不同的活动水平来反映的。弹性预算可以用于计划和控制。

在制定预算的过程中，我们假设客户的反应是温和的，但是我们也应该针对顾客的强烈反应和微弱反应做出预算。

当发布一个新产品时，存在着很多不确定因素，实际的活动水平和预算的活动水平可能存在差异。如果我们的成本大多都是固定的，那么在固定预算模式下活动水平的变化可能并不会引发很多问题。但是，我们成本中大部分都是变动成本，所以很难通过固定预算来有效控制成本费用。

弹性预算将会帮助我们进行更多有效的比较。既然我们预计活动水平的变化会导致变动成本的变化，那么用固定预算来评价管理者的绩效就是不公平的。弹性预算反映了在实际产量和销量下允许产生的费用支出。将弹性预算数和实际支出数进行比较，有助于我们区分有效与无效行为。

因此，弹性预算的使用和责任会计这一概念是相关的。

利润和现金的差异

新产品的利润预算是在权责发生制的基础上编制的，也就是说，产品运送到客户手中后确认为销售收入，费用发生后确认为成本。相反，现金预算是对现金收支的预测。我们会在 2017 年 3 月开始销售我们的新产品，但是由于我们允许客户赊购，所以我们最早也要等到 2017 年 4 月才能收到货款。这就是为什么我们确认的销售收入是F$ 6 250 000而销售现金流入只有 F$ 4 200 000。

同样地，我们采购了一批原材料来生产产品，但是，我们是从供应商处赊购的，所以我们不需要立刻付款。但是购买先于生产，这就解释了为什么支付给供应商的费用与原材料和其他成本相一致。

一些损益类项目来自会计准则，它们并不是现金流，例如，非流动资产的折旧。生产新产品的机器的折旧费是算在固定制造费用里的，但是折旧并不包含在现金预算中。相反，现金预算能反映机器采购款的支付行为，而这个采购行为发生在预算期之前。

可以将之前已经资本化的开发支出进行摊销，以研发费用列示在利润预算中。然而，现金预算中显示的支出数额是未来六个月内我们为进一步开发产品而准备的。

任务三

CIMA 道德准则

全球 CIMA 的会员和注册学员都有义务遵守关于行为和诚信的最高标准，并维持良好的信誉和职业声望。他们还必须避免任何可能败坏这一职业的行为。

这个准则包括 5 个基本原则。根据这五个基本原则，我对被指称的过错做出以下评价：

正直，意味着在所有商业往来中以诚实和真实的态度行事。利用内部消息是对这一原则的违背，因为这是一种企图以不诚实的方式获得个人利益的行为。

客观，意味着不允许利益冲突凌驾于职业判断之上。个人利益、第三方利益与摩利兹能源公司的责任之间存在明显的冲突。

职业能力，是指应按照相关专业标准进行自我管理，专业标准包括不使用内部信息谋取私利。

专业行为，意味着遵守法律法规。在大多数国家，内幕交易都是一种刑事犯罪，因此在这个案例中明显之间存在违法行为。

保密原则，要求 CIMA 会员尊重通过职业关系获得的信息的机密性，比如过去或现在的雇佣关系。CIMA 会员不应该泄漏这样的信息，除非他们得到特殊的批准或有法律义务和职业职责的要求。他们也绝不应该用保密的信息谋取私利或为他人牟利。

商业道德对任何组织都十分重要，我们的利益相关者也希望我们按照一定的道德标准行事。一次道德上的失败可能会对我们公司在利益相关者群体中的声誉产生损害。道德框架是好的公司治理的一部分，并意味着企业运营良好。任何道德失败都会使我们公司的治理政策和程序被质疑。投资者可能会关注这一失败及对我们管理风险的方法感到担忧。如果员工觉得他们在一个道德不良的环境里工作，他们的工作态度就可能变得消极。

国际会计准则第 38 号

研发成本的会计处理

研发成本的核算是根据国际会计准则第 38 号无形资产进行处理的。

研发的定义

研究是指为了获得科学上或技术上的新知识和新理解而进行的调查活动。

开发是指在商业生产开始之前，利用研究阶段的发现或其他知识，对产品生产、提供服务、改善流程等方面进行计划和设计。

研究支出在损益表中作为一项费用，抵减当期利润。我们所关注的开发支出若符合以下标准就可以被资本化。

发件人：管理会计师助理

收件人：研发总监 Dr. Liffe

主题：研发支出

开发支出资本化

国际会计准则第 38 号规定，如果一个企业能满足一些标准，那么其开发中产生的无形资产就必须被资本化。关于这个开发项目，以下所有的标准都需要被评估，当所有的标准都达标后，后续的项目支出就应该被资本化。

（1）完成该无形资产，使其达到可使用或销售状态，具有技术上的可行性。如果从开发的项目中所获得的信息表明新型能源存储系统是可行的，那么这个标准就已经达到了。

（2）有完成、使用或销售无形资产的意图。当管理层决定完成该项目并开始出售新系统时，这个标准就达到了。

（3）有使用或者销售无形资产的能力。我们已经有一个销售当前产品的现存市场，而新产品是当前产品的扩展。

（4）能够证明无形资产自身存在市场或者无形资产将在内部使用，应当证明其有用性。当我们确保新产品有市场时，我们就满足了该标准。

（5）有足够可用的技术资源、财务资源和其他资源来完成该无形资产。我们的预算显示我们有足够的资源来完成这个项目，所以这个标准也达到了。

（6）无形资产的成本能够被可靠地计量。和新产品相关的成本已经被分别记录。

如果没能达到其中任何一条标准，支出就必须按照实际发生额记录在利润表中。如果所有的标准都已经达到了，那么支出就一定要被资本化，但是只有那些所有标准都满足之后所发生的成本才可以被资本化。

一旦我们确认该项目满足了上述所有标准，开发支出就要被资本化，并且列示在资产负债表中。

资本化的开发支出的处理

如果开发成本已经被资本化，资产应该在使用年限内进行摊销。摊销应该从资产达到可用状态时开始。

上述资本化的开发支出将在该产品使用年限内进行摊销。你在预算利润表中看到的数据是 6 个月的摊销额。

非常感谢！

摩利兹能源公司
管理会计师助理

任务四

认证合作伙伴计划

潜在好处

开展认证合作伙伴计划有许多好处。这一计划将促使我们积极管理公司与安装商之间的关系，而这会使我们收获良多。

与安装商一起工作会实现供应链的价值增值，这是一个更好的选择，所有的参与方都可以从中分享利益。我们应该与安装商建立良好的关系来联合管理供应链，而不是仅仅强调价格。

在本行业内这种新产品的安装商很少，所以我们对安装商有着很高的依赖性。积极管理与安装商的关系可以让我们获得一定的竞争优势，尤其是和那些还没有实施这一计划的竞争对手相比。

我们的品牌识别依赖于客户对我们的产品质量的认知，如果我们的安装人员不能提供我们所期望的服务标准，那么品牌识别度就可能会受到损害。认证合作伙伴计划可以促使我们与安装商合作，以确保安装的质量标准与我们产品的高标准相一致。

实施认证合作伙伴计划能够使我们与安装商建立一个长远的、忠诚的合作关系。频繁更换安装商将增加我们的管理工作，也会使对外事务缺乏连贯性。

单纯以价格为基础的关系可能会使得安装商在经济上不稳定，使其更容易破产，这也会危及未来的业务。而认证合作伙伴计划将会避免这一情况的发生。

环境和质量的关键绩效评估指标

下列环境指标是适当的。

（1）包装材料：成吨填埋或回收。

我们的产品是用木制的框架来固定面板，并且用木纸板和防水材料覆盖包装，以保证电池板安全地被送到安装商处。我们可以按照吨数或者总量的百分比来计量被送到废弃物填埋场的包装材料，如果是回收的方式可以使用回收的数量来计量。

（2）运输车辆：燃料使用量、行驶里程或二氧化碳排放量。

安装商使用交通工具将工人和产品运送至客户处。燃料的使用量和交通工具的排放量可能是一个重要的测量指标。或者，行驶里程数也可以作为一种间接的测量方式。

（3）能源和水的使用量：总用水量（立方米）或者化石燃料能源使用量（千瓦·时）。

安装商办公室所使用的能源和水也是合适的测量指标。我们希望我们的安装商使用太阳能，但是，他们可能也需要使用化石能源。当安装完成后，安装商会用水清理电池板和客户的建筑物。

下列质量指标是适当的。

（1）预防成本：培训成本或者每个员工的平均培训费用。

预防成本是用来确保不产生质量问题的。这一指标可以是员工培训和发展的支出，以确保安装人员在服务、安全性和稳定性方面按照最高标准来工作。

（2）内部失败成本：返工成本或返工次数。

内部失败成本是指产品或服务未被移交给客户之前由于质量问题而引发的成本。安装过程中电池板可能会受到损坏，安装商需要替换或维修受到损坏的电池板，由此产生的成本可以作为一个合适的指标。

（3）外部失败成本：处理客户投诉的成本或者客户投诉的数量。

外部失败成本是指产品或者服务移交给客户之后由于质量问题而引发的成本。太阳能系统的非正常运行或者系统的崩溃会引起客户投诉，处理这些投诉的成本可以用来衡量外部失败成本。另外，客户的投诉量也是一个合适的指标。

Variant 5 Marking Guidance

Section	Technical skills		Business skills		People skills		Leadership skills		Integration	Total
1	Decision making under uncertainty Expected values in decision making	8 9					Decision making under uncertainty Expected values in decision making	2 1		20
2	Responsibility accounting and budgets for control Flexible budgeting Comparison of cash flow and profit statements	4 4 8	Flexible budgeting	2	Responsibility accounting and budgets for control Flexible budgeting	4 2			24	
3	Ethical issue IAS 38：Research and Development	2 12	Ethical issue	4	Ethical issue	4		3	25	
4	Quality and environmental performance measures	16	Benefits of a certified partnership scheme	10	Benefits of a certified partnership scheme	2	Benefits of a certified partnership scheme	3		31
Total marks available for each competency		63		16		12		6	3	100

试卷五　评分指南

部分	技术技能		商业技能		人际技能		领导技能		综合	总计
1	存在不确定性时的决策 期望值在决策中的应用	8 9					存在不确定性时的决策 期望值在决策中的应用	2 1		20
2	责任会计和预算控制 弹性预算 现金流量表和利润表的比较	4 4 8	弹性预算	2	责任会计和预算控制 弹性预算	4 2				24
3	道德问题 国际会计准则第38号：研发	2 12	道德问题	4	道德问题	4			3	25
4	质量和环境的绩效评估方法	16	认证合作伙伴计划的优点	10	认证合作伙伴计划的优点	2	认证合作伙伴计划的优点	3		31
各种能力分数总计		63		16		12		6	3	100

天津财经大学名师解惑

试卷一共有四项任务，考查了 P1、F1、E1 三门课程的知识点，具体包括风险决策应用、责任会计、预算控制、CIMA 道德准则、研发成本的会计处理（国际会计准则第 38 号：无形资产）、认证合作伙伴计划、环境和质量的关键绩效评估指标等。该试卷考核了考生的四项能力，其中技术技能的分值占 63%，商业技能的分值占 16%，人际技能的分值占 12%，领导技能的分值占 6%，与 CGMA 管理会计能力框架的技能要求一致。

该试卷的每项任务涉及以下知识点：

任务	问题	科目	知识点
任务一	存在不确定性时的决策标准及其相对应的销售价格	P1	风险管理（risk management） Maximin 法、Maximax 法、Minimax regret 法、期望值法
	期望值法的应用及其局限性	P1	期望值（expected value）
任务二	预算控制机制的运行及责任会计	P1	预算控制（budgeting control） 责任会计（responsible accounting）
	弹性预算的适用性	P1	弹性预算（flexible budgeting）
	利润和现金流的差异分析	F1	利润预算（income budgeting） 现金流预算（cash flow budgeting）
任务三	CIMA 道德准则	P1、E1	正直（integrity） 客观（objectivity） 职业能力（professional competence） 专业行为（professional behaviour） 保密（confidentiality）
	研发成本的会计处理（国际会计准则第 38 号：无形资产）	F1	研究与开发（research and development） 开发支出资本化（capitalization of development expenditure）
任务四	认证合作伙伴计划的潜在好处	E1	供应链价值增值（supply chain value added） 竞争优势（competitive advantages） 品牌识别（brand identity） 供应商关系（relationships） 未来业务（future business）

（续表）

任务	问题	科目	知识点
任务四	环境和质量的关键绩效评估指标	P1	预防成本（prevention cost） 评估成本（appraisal cost） 内部失败成本（internal failure cost） 外部失败成本（external failure cost）

上述各项任务要求以邮件、报告或工作笔记等形式来呈现答案，对问题的描述非常明确，答题时既要注意内容的针对性，也要注意形式的规范性。

对应知识点的深度剖析

风险决策

由于市场存在不确定性，企业采取不同的销售价格可能会引起不同的消费者反应，从而造成不同的贡献值。常规思路是：（1）选择不同的风险决策方法；（2）根据估计贡献表格，分析在不同的风险决策方案下，最合适的销售价格。

管理者的风险态度会造成不同的风险决策方法，从而使销售价格不同。具体的风险管理方法有：Maximin 法、Maximax 法、Minimax regret 法、期望值法。

考生需要理解、应用并且表达出整个风险决策分析的过程。

Maximax 法：将每种方案中的最大贡献值进行比较，选择其中的最大值。

Maximin 法：将每种方案中的最小贡献值进行比较，选择其中的最大值。

考生注意事项

风险决策分析计算

第一步：选择不同的风险决策方法（Maximin 法，Maximax 法，Minimax regret 法）。

第二步：计算不同的销售价格下，各个市场客户做出反应后的贡献值。

第三步：根据不同风险决策方法的选择标准，对不同销售价格的贡献值进行排序选择。

第四步：确定最优生产计划，按不同产品的生产顺序，依次满足其销售需求，直至用尽限制因素。

Minimax regret 法：选择所有方案中最大后悔值中最小的数值。当我们想避免做出不利的决策时，通常使用这个方法。“后悔值”是指做出的一个错误决定可能会带来的机会损失。

期望值法

期望值法，首先要分析和估计项目风险概率和项目风险可能带来的损失（或收益）大小，然后将二者相乘求出项目风险的损失（或收益）期望值，并使用项目损失期望值（或收益）去度量项目风险，从而选择损失期望值（收益期望值）最小（最大）的方案。

如果我们想要基于期望值来定价，常规思路是：（1）首先确定每种客户反应的概率；（2）根据不同销售价格下每种可能的结果乘以它们对应的概率得到最终的期望值。

期望值 = 每种可能的结果 × 对应概率。

期望值的局限性

（1）概率通常非常主观。（2）需要决策重复多次，而新能源存储系统的实施及其定价都是一次性的决策，不具有适用性。（3）期望值法没有考虑每种产出与期望值的离散程度，也就是所谓的风险。（4）期望值法只是一个加权平均数，并不代表某一实际的可能结果。

考生注意事项

期望值 = 每种可能的结果 × 对应概率，然后求和。

本考点考查考生期望值的知识点，要求考生掌握期望值的概念，计算和结合案例理解并讨论其局限性。

预算控制和责任会计

预算控制就是将实际绩效和预算绩效进行比较，并在必要时采取纠正措施。责任会计旨在实现不同的管理者对其控制范围内的所有负责，管理者的绩效是根据在他们控制范围内的成本状况来进行评估，以便更好地进行预算控制。

本考点不仅考查考生对预算控制机制的运行模式和实质的理解，而且要求考生掌握责任会计的内容。

弹性预算

弹性预算是基于不同的活动水平来反映预算状况的。弹性预算可以用于计划和控制。本案例中的企业成本大部分是变动成本，弹性预算更有利于进行预算与实际的比较，进而提高生产效率和减少非效率行为。

考生需要对题中提到的固定预算和弹性预算进行比较，结合案例实际生产产品时的不确定因素（如生产成本变动性、生产模式等）分析两种预算方法的适用性，提出最合适的建议和结论。

考生注意事项

弹性预算与固定预算（结合案例中生产新产品时的不确定因素分析两种预算的适用性）。

责任会计与预算控制是相关的，需结合分析。

利润预算和现金流预算

利润预算是在权责发生制的基础上编制的，即商品送达客户手中时确认收入，费用发生时确认成本；现金预算是对现金收支的预测，即赊销赊购、折旧费用等现金流不计入现金预算。由于两种预算的计量标准不同，造成了利润和现金流的预算的差异。

差异主要源于：

（1）赊销赊购等没有实质性现金流入或流出的活动行为；

（2）一些损益类项目是来自会计准则，它们并不是现金流，如：固定资产折旧费用；

（3）非预算期的现金提前支付行为；

（4）摊销期间前资本化的开发支出，以研发费用列示在利润预算中，现金预算中显示的支出数额是未来六个月内我们为进一步开发产品而发生的。

考生需要全面分析利润预算和现金流预算存在差异的主要原因，并结合案例中的实际情况进行举例分析。

CIMA 道德准则

这一准则包括 5 个基本原则。

（1）正直：意味着在所有商业往来中以诚实和值得信赖的态度行事。你不应该与任何你认为含有实质性虚假或误导性陈述的信息联系在一起。

（2）客观：意味着不允许冲突、偏见、利益或他人的影响凌驾于职业判断之上。

（3）职业能力：是指为人处事应遵循有关专业标准，其中包括不使用内部信息谋取私利。

（4）专业行为：意味着遵守法律和规定。避免做出损害职业声誉的行为。

（5）保密原则：要求尊重通过职业关系获得的保密信息，比如过去或现在的雇佣关系。在未得到特殊批准时，不得泄露职业的相关信息。

考生注意事项

在回答此题时，不能仅仅罗列知识点和解释每一个原则的含义，要结合具体案例，在每一个准则后加入对具体情况的分析。

研发成本的会计处理（国际会计准则第38号无形资产）

研究与开发的定义：研究是指为了获得科学上或技术上的新知识和新理解而进行的调查活动。开发是指在商业生产开始之前，利用研究阶段的发现或者其他知识，对产品生产、提供服务、改善流程等方面进行计划和设计。

研究与开发的会计处理：研究支出在损益表中作为一项费用，抵减当期利润。

开发支出只有符合以下标准才可以被资本化，并列示在资产负债表中。

（1）完成该无形资产，使其达到可使用或销售状态，具有技术上的可行性。比如，企业已经完成了全部计划、设计和测试活动。

（2）有完成、使用或销售无形资产的意图。

（3）有使用或者销售无形资产的能力。

（4）能够证明无形资产自身存在市场或者无形资产将在内部使用的，应当证明其有用性。无形资产是否能够为企业带来经济利益，应当对运用该无形资产生产产品的市场情况进行可靠预计，以证明所生产的产品存在市场并能够带来经济利益，或能够证明市场上存在对该无形资产的需求。

（5）有足够的、可用的技术资源、财务资源和其他资源来完成该无形资产。企业应能够证明可以取得无形资产开发所需的技术、财务和其他资源，以及提供获得这些资源的相关计划。

（6）无形资产的成本能够被可靠计量。比如，直接发生的研发人员工资、材料费，以及相关设备折旧费等。同时从事多项研究开发活动的，所发生的支出应当按照合理的标准在各项研究开发活动之间进行分配，无法合理分配的，则需计入当期损益。

认证合作伙伴计划

主要考虑的是与供应商之间的关系的改善，涉及以下几个方面。

（1）供应链的价值增值。供应链增值体现在多个方面，比如降低成本、增加利润、提升产品质量或服务水平、提高供应链运作效率、加快供应链对市场的反应速度、降低供应链风险、减少库存、使信息更及时准确等。

（2）改善与供应商的关系来获得竞争优势。当行业中的供应商数量较少时，企业对供应商就会存在极高的依赖性，与供应商建立良好的合作关系，会在采购环节获得极大的竞争优势。

（3）品牌认知度。品牌与产品质量紧密相关，在选择合作伙伴时，要确保其服务质量。

（4）合作伙伴的忠诚度。长远、稳定的合作关系能使双方获利，频繁更换合作伙伴会增加工作量。

（5）考虑长远利益。与合作伙伴之间的关系不能仅仅建立在价格上，这有可能会导致合作的失败，损害长远利益。

环境和质量的关键绩效评估指标

质量的关键评估指标有 4 个。

（1）预防成本：用来确保不产生质量问题。如员工的培训和发展支出。

（2）评估成本：为判定产品或劳务是否符合客户或制造要求而发生的成本。如检验和测试成本。

（3）内部失败成本：是指产品或服务未移交给客户之前由于质量问题而引发的成本。如废品损失、返工损失、停工损失、产量损失等。

（4）外部失败成本：是指产品或服务移交给客户之后由于质量问题而引发的成本。如索赔费用、退货损失、保修费用、诉讼费用、产品降价损失等。

预防成本与评估成本被统称为符合成本，内部失败成本和外部失败成本被统称为不符合成本。符合成本一般都发生在生产之前，而且这一类成本若发生，往往会使不符合成本下降。

考生注意事项

预防成本与评估成本被统称为符合成本，内部失败成本和外部失败成本被统称为不符合成本。符合成本一般都发生在生产之前，而且这一类成本若发生，往往会使不符合成本下降。

案例五

CASE 5

梅维斯·文德柏公司

MAVIS VENDERBY

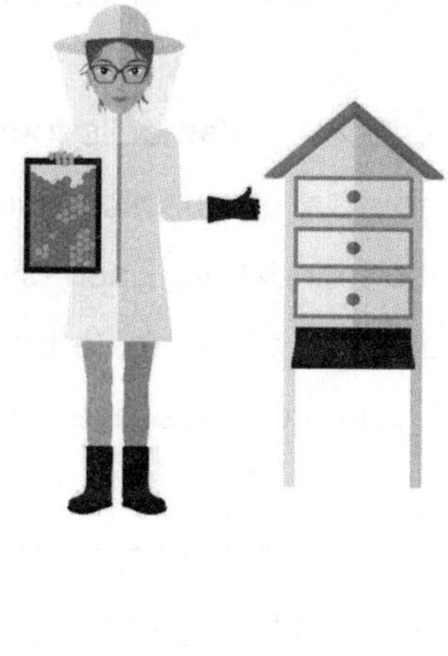

Background Materials

Introduction

Mavis Venderby is a business that manufactures and retails wooden beehives. The business was established 70 years ago by Mavis Venderby and her husband Benjamin. It is based in Tucland, which has the T$ as its currency. Tucland has a temperate climate and is situated in the Northern hemisphere.

Mavis Venderby is owned equally by Thomas Venderby, managing director, and Jacinta Cory, sales and marketing director, who are the great grandchildren of Mavis and Benjamin.

Two types of beehive are manufactured and sold by Mavis Venderby: box hive and slatted hive. Each type of hive has the same component parts and functionality but has a different shape. Each type of hive is manufactured in two different types of wood: cedar and pine. All hives are sold flat packed, meaning that customers have to assemble them for themselves.

As well as wooden hives, Mavis Venderby also sells foundation and frames. Foundation is a base on which bees will form a comb into which honey will be placed. The frame is a wooden support around the foundation. Each hive, when constructed, will hold up to 20 framed foundations. Frames used to be made by Mavis Venderby, but are now bought in and sold on because it is more cost effective. Foundation is still manufactured by Mavis Venderby.

Foundation and frames are sold and packaged separately from the wooden beehives.

Mavis Venderby sells all of its products directly to the public. It has its own store located at the factory site. The majority of sales are made direct to customers through the Mavis Venderby website or over the telephone.

The business has four directors: Thomas Venderby as managing director, Jacinta Cory as sales and marketing director, Joseph Perez as production director and Pene Lopez as finance director. It employs a range of skilled and unskilled people.

Mavis Venderby recently moved from a small industrial unit to new premises. The new premises used to be farm estate offices with associated barns and outbuildings. There is now plenty of scope for expansion.

Honey Bees: the Perfect Team!

Written by: Pete Sampson

Have you ever wondered where the honey that you spread on your toast in the morning comes from? Obviously from honey bees, but did you know how much team work is involved? The creation of honey really is a wonder of nature.

Honey bees live in colonies, either in the wild, wherever they can find a hollow space, or within man-made hives. At the peak of the honey season, a single colony contains around 60,000 bees: one female queen, around 1,000 male drones and the rest are female workers. Each type of bee has a very specific role within the colony.

The queen is central to any bee colony and has the sole responsibility of laying eggs. She will destroy any potential queen rivals before they hatch and when another queen arrives from another colony, she will battle to the death to retain supremacy.

Throughout her lifetime, the queen secretes a pheromone which ensures that no other female in the colony can produce young. A male drone's sole purpose is to mate with her so that she continually lays eggs.

Worker bees, as their name suggests, do everything else. They collect nectar from flowers and take this to the hive where it is secreted into combs (which are essentially storage compartments). The flapping of the worker bee's wings dehydrates the nectar to form honey within the comb. Once full each part of the comb, it will be sealed with a wax cap produced by the bees. As well as producing the honey, worker bees also take responsibility of all other aspects of the colony including looking after the young and defending it from attack.

The working of a bee colony is finely tuned. Without the queen and drones there can be no young and therefore no new worker bees and without the worker bees there can be no honey, which is the colony's source of food (until we come along and steal it from them). Team work at its natural best!

Mavis Venderby Products

Product Listing

Product	Picture of Products in Use	Information
Box hive Cedar: Retail price T$ 375 Pine: Retail price T$ 290		All hives are supplied flat-packed and have the same component parts From the bottom upwards, these components are: (1) hive stand; (2) hive floor; (3) brood box; (4) queen excluder; (5) super box; (6) crown board; (7) roof. Each component is explained in our guide to the beehive (shown on the next page)
Slatted hive Cedar: Retail price T$ 460 Pine: Retail price T$ 380		
Foundation Retail price T$ 20		Foundation is manufactured on site at Mavis Venderby. It is sold in one size equivalent to brood box size This is further explained in our guide to the beehive (shown on the next page)
Frames Retail prices: Brood T$ 2. 60 Super T$ 1. 80		Frames are available in brood box and super box sizes This is further explained in our guide to the beehive (shown on the next page)

Mavis Venderby: Guide to the Beehive

Component	Explanation
Hive stand	The hive stand is a simple base on which the hive sits. It is designed so that the hive is held off the ground to reduce the amount of pests invading it
Hive floor	The hive floor includes a bottom board(which acts as the actual floor) and a landing area for the bees which protrudes slightly from the rest of the hive. It also includes a slatted rack above the bottom board, the purpose of which is to provide ventilation to the hive
Brood box	The brood box is the largest of the hive boxes. The brood box will hold the brood frames with foundation(see below), which is where the queen lays her eggs and where the young are looked after by the worker bees. Essentially this is the living quarters for the bee colony
Foundation	Foundation is made from beeswax which is strengthened with wire. This is the base onto which bees build their own wax to form combs into which eggs are laid(in the brood box) and honey is stored(in the super box)
Frame	The frame is a wooden rectangular holder for a foundation
Queen excluder	The queen excluder is a rack made from wood and wire mesh with holes large enough for the worker bees to crawl through but too small for the queen. This ensures that the queen cannot access the super box
Super box	The super box is a smaller version of the brood box. This box will hold the frames where the bees store honey. It is this honey which is extracted as a human food product
Crown board	The crown board acts as a lid to the top hive box. It has a hole in the middle for ventilation
Roof	The roof of the hive sits above the crown board and is reinforced with galvanised steel to add protection against the weather

Mavis Venderby manufactures all of the above components, except for frames which are bought in from a supplier and then sold onto customers.

Sales Pattern

The peak months for sales of hives, foundation and frames are the months of March through to July. During this five month period 70% of all sales by value are made. This period corresponds with the peak honey production time in Tucland, which is late spring through to summer. Sales are usually at their highest in March and April as the season starts.

Production Processes

Production is scheduled to be reasonably even throughout the year. Therefore because sales are seasonal, inventory levels vary throughout the year.

Beehives

The production process for beehives has three stages as follows:

DRYING

- All wood is dried on site prior to being used in production. A combination of air drying in a large drying shed and kiln drying is used for both types of wood. Due to differences in properties, cedar is usually dried for approximately six months and pine for approximately four months. The actual time needed is dependent upon climatic conditions
- Each type of wood is purchased in 3 metre planks and stacked upon receipt. Initially the wood is left to air dry and the individual planks of wood within each stack are rotated on a regular basis. Half way through drying time, the planks are placed in a drying kiln for up to two days. The length of time in the kiln is dependent upon the general climatic conditions. After this, the planks are stacked again and air dried until ready for use

CUTTING

- Once the wood has dried, the next stage is cutting all of the component parts of each hive. Programmable machinery is used for this. Box and slatted hives require different cutting programmes and therefore setting-up time is required
- Once cut, some components (such as the stand and roof) are assembled by hand and all components are sanded and quality checked. At this point, any knots in the pine are sealed with a painted on sealant
- Typically cedar is easier to work with than pine as there are fewer imperfections in the wood. As a result, wastage of pine is higher than cedar in the cutting process

PACKING

- After qualitiy checks have been performed, all of the components for a single hive are shrink wrapped for protection and are then placed into the finished goods storage area
- Once an order has been received, the appropriate number and type of hives are collected from this area and are then re-packaged with polystyrene protection into cardboard boxes ready for shipment. At this point, the necessary screws, nails, glue, instructions and other fittings are included in the cardboard box
- All orders are shipped to customers via a courier service

Foundation

Foundation is made in the following way：

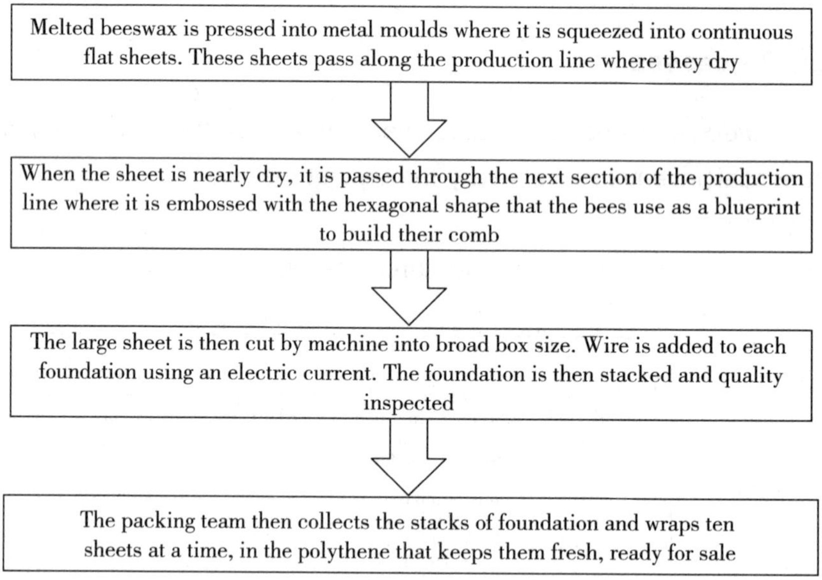

Customers and Suppliers

Customers

Mavis Venderby's customers are a mixture of hobby beekeepers (who usually have less than 10 beehives) and commercial beekeepers (with anything up to 500 beehives, occasionally more). In the year to 29 February 2016, 50% of sales by value were made to hobby beekeepers and 50% by value to commercial beekeepers. This compares to a 40% (hobby)/60% (commercial) split in the year to 28 February 2010. Mavis Venderby's customers are very loyal, with many of them having been customers for many years.

There are three sales channels: the on-site store, through the website and over the phone. For the year ended 29 February 2016, 20% of sales by value were made through the store, 35% over the telephone and 45% through the website. The proportion of store sales is relatively high because beekeepers (especially hobbyists) are prepared to travel many kilometres not only to buy their hives but also to discuss beekeeping issues with the sales staff (who are all very knowledgeable on the subject).

Commercial beekeepers are allowed standard credit terms of 30 days. Hobby beekeepers make payment at the point of ordering.

Customers have a choice of either cedar or pine when buying a beehive. Cedar naturally repels moths and is not as prone to rotting and warping as is pine. Cedar is also a good insulator. Therefore, a cedar hive tends to be longer lasting than a pine hive and has superior properties. However, it costs more to manufacture (due principally to the higher cost of the wood) and hence is more expensive to buy. Each customer has their own preference for either cedar or pine.

Hives are sold flat packed. This means that customers have to construct the hive for themselves. Once constructed, most customers paint or treat their beehive to protect the wood.

Suppliers

Mavis Venderby sources wood from two suppliers. These suppliers have not changed in 20 years and both offer exceptionally long credit terms, as a result of the close working relationship. Mavis Venderby takes advantage of significant bulk purchasing discounts offered by these suppliers.

The suppliers of the other materials offer terms in line with the accepted industry norms, which are 30 days. Mavis Venderby keeps basic data relating to their lead times and reject rates for all suppliers.

Key People in Mavis Venderby

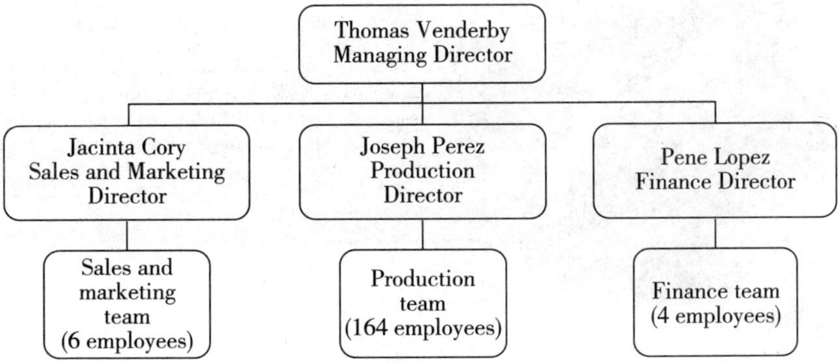

Thomas Venderby—Managing Director

Thomas is 40 and recently took over as managing director from his father. He has always worked in the family business and was previously the production director, with a keen interest in product quality. Thomas now has specific responsibility for Human Resources (although he is not qualified in HR) but is involved across the business. He is keen to expand the customer and product base and to maintain the quality of production, whilst also enhancing service and brand strength

Pene Lopez—Finance Director

Pene is 32 and a qualified accountant. She has been finance director for two years and was previously a finance manager in a clothing manufacturing business. She has ultimate responsibility for all financial and accounting matters and manages the finance team

The Finance Team

Cormac Jones Senior Finance Officer	■Cormac is a newly qualified accountant who has been with the business for two months. He is responsible fo rpreparing the monthly management reports, collating budget information and for wrting the first draft of the financial statements at the year end
You Finance Officer	■You have worked at Mavis Venderby for three years and started as a finance assistant. You are studying for your professional exams and assist both Pene Lopez and Cormac Jones with a wide range of tasks. You also assist other directors and managers when asked
Susie Ronaldo Finance Assistant	■Susie has worked as a finance assistant at Mavis Venderby for 10 years. She is responsible for processing the weekly payroll and for dealing with petty cash. She also assists the finance officers when required
Duncan Scoby Finance Assistant	■Duncan is relatively new to the business. He is responsible for the processing and coding of invoices and payments for both purchases and sales. He is also responsible for reconciling the bank account each month

Jacinta Cory—Sales and Marketing Director

Jacinta is 38 and has been the sales and marketing director for eight years. like her brother Thomas, she has always worked in the family business. Jacinta is a keen bee-keeper herself and has made strong links with a number of regional and the national beekeeping associations. She is specifically responsible for marketing, maintenance of the website and the sales and marketing team management

The Sales and Marketing Team

The sales and marketing team consist of a professional manager and five assistants. The sales and marketing manager is Toby Venger, who is an expert beekeeper and very knowledgeable about all aspects of beekeeping, such as queen rearing, bee diseases and hive products. He has been with Mavis Venderby for 15 years and is responsible for managing his team of five assistants and works closely with Jacinta Cory regarding targeting new customers and maintaining relationships with existing customers.

Toby and his team of assistants (who like Toby are all very knowledgeable about beekeeping) operate the on-site retail store and deal with orders from the website and on the telephone.

Toby maintains 10 beehives near the Mavis Venderby site and is always looking for ways in which beehive construction can be improved. Currently he is working on developing a special pheromone to put on foundation to deter pests and to encourage quicker honey production.

Joseph Perez—Production Director

Joseph is 58 and has worked at Mavis Venderby for 40 years. He started as a trainee in the production department and worked his way up through the business to production manager (a position he held for 20 years). He became production director when Thomas Venderby became managing director. Joseph has responsibility for production. He is a skilled wood craftsman and along with Thomas is keen to expand the range of wood products that Mavis Venderby make. He is currently developing animal houses

The Production Team

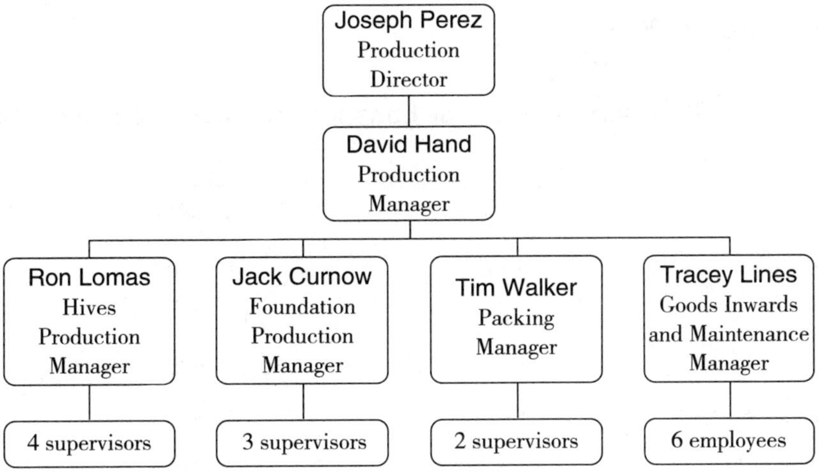

In total there are 165 production employees, broken down as follows:

	Number	Number
Indirect		
Production Director	1	
Managers	5	
Supervisors	9	
Goods inwards and maintenance employees	6	
Total indirect		21
Total direct		144
Total production employees		165

Notes:

(1) Goods inwards and maintenance is a support function to the production activities. The six employees cover the maintenance of machinery and property as well as the purchasing of raw materials.

(2) The direct employees are assigned to specific production areas and many are multi-skilled.

(3) Mavis Venderby has a rolling programme of employing around eight new trainees a year. Trainees are paid a flat rate of T$ 9 an hour until they pass their six month probationary period. After this probationary period, if positions are available these trainees will be taken on as full time employees.

Latest Director Approved and Audited Financial Statements for the Year Ended 29 February 2016

Mavis Venderby's Statement of Profit or Loss for the Year Ended 29 February 2016

	2016 (T$ 000)	2015 (T$ 000)
Revenue	17,860	17,909
Cost of sales	(13,324)	(13,199)
Gross profit	4,536	4,710
Other operating costs	(2,441)	(2,036)
Profit on disposal of PPE	864	—
Profit before tax	2,959	2,674
Finance cost	(48)	—
Profit before tax	2,911	2,674
Tax	(710)	(696)
Profit for the year	2,201	1,978

Mavis Venderby's Statement of Financial Position for the Year Ended 29 February 2016

	2016 (T$ 000)	2016 (T$ 000)	2015 (T$ 000)	2015 (T$ 000)
Assets				
Non-current assets				
PPE		8,872		5,760
Current assets				
Inventory	4,351		3,510	
Trade and other receivables	587		473	
Cash and cash equivalents	412		903	
		5,350		4,886
Total assets		14,222		10,646

（续表）

	2016 (T$ 000)	2016 (T$ 000)	2015 (T$ 000)	2015 (T$ 000)
Equity and liabilities				
Ordinary share capital issued		50		50
Retained earnings		11,293		9,092
Total equity		11,343		9,142
Non-current liabilities				
Bank loan		1,250		—
Current liabilities				
Bank loan	250		—	
Trade and other payables	674		814	
Tax payable	705		690	
		1,629		1,504
Total equity and liabilities		14,222		10,646

Mavis Venderby's Statement of Cash Flows for the Year Ended 29 February 2016

	T$ 000	T$ 000
Cash flows from operating activities		
Profit before tax		2,911
Adjustments		
Depreciation	752	
Profit on sale of PPE	(864)	
Finance costs	48	
		(64)
Movements in working capital		
Increase in inventories	(841)	
Increase in trade and other receivables	(114)	
Decrease in trade and other payables	(140)	
		(1,095)
Cash generated from operations		1,752
Tax paid		(695)
Finance costs paid		(48)

（续表）

	T$ 000	T$ 000
Net cash from operating activities		1,009
Cash flows from investing activities		
Purchase of PPE	(8,350)	
Sale of PPE	5,350	
Net cash from investing activities		(3,000)
Cash flows from financing activities		
Proceeds from borrowing	1,500	
Net cash from financing activities		1,500
Net decrease in cash and cash equivalents		(491)
Cash and cash equivalents at the beginning of the year		903
Cash and cash equivalents at the end of the year		412

The financial statements for the year ended 29 February 2016 are the latest set of financial statements to have been approved by the directors. The auditors gave an unmodified opinion of these statements.

Budget Information for the Year Ended 28 February 2018

Sales and Production Budget for the Year Ended 28 February 2018

	Box cedar	Box pine	Slatted cedar	Slatted pine	Frame	Foundation
Sales quantity(units)	10,000	7,000	9,000	6,000	198,000	396,000

Budgeted Profit or Loss for the Year Ended 28 February 2018

	Box cedar (T$ 000)	Box pine (T$ 000)	Slatted cedar (T$ 000)	Slatted pine (T$ 000)	Frame (T$ 000)	Foundation (T$ 000)	Total (T$ 000)	Total (T$ 000)
Sales	3,750	2,030	4,140	2,280	436	6,336		18,972
Less：materials cost								
Wood	518	183	616	210			1,527	
Galvanised steel	47	33	42	28			150	

（续表）

	Box cedar (T$ 000)	Box pine (T$ 000)	Slatted cedar (T$ 000)	Slatted pine (T$ 000)	Frame (T$ 000)	Foundation (T$ 000)	Total (T$ 000)	Total (T$ 000)
Steel mesh	4	3	4	3			14	
Ply wood	6	4	5	4			19	
Wax						1,996	1,996	
Frame					390		390	
Wire						95	95	
								(4,191)
Less: direct labour cost								
Drying	280	122	334	141			877	
Cutting	510	387	551	398			1,846	
Foundation						1,236	1,236	
Packing	65	46	70	47		51	279	
								(4,238)
Less: production overhead								
Drying	466	164	555	189			1,374	
Cutting	599	381	604	370			1,954	
Foundation						1,307	1,307	
Packing	294	206	317	212	36	194	1,259	
								(5,894)
Gross profit								4,649
Less: non-production overhead								
Employees							564	
Delivery							683	
Administration and selling							1,236	(2,483)
Operating profit								2,166

Budgeted Gross Profit per Hive-box Hive

Box hive in cedar	Quantity used	Cost per metre, hour or absorption basis used(T$)	T$	T$
Materials(measured in metres)				
Cedar	2.80	18.50	51.80	
Galvanised steel	0.42	11.20	4.70	
Steel mesh	0.40	1.10	0.44	
Ply wood	0.25	2.30	0.58	
Total material cost				57.52
Labour(measured in hours)				
Drying	2.00	14.00	28.00	
Cutting	3.00	17.00	51.00	
Packing	0.50	13.00	6.50	
Total direct labour cost				85.50
Production overhead				
Drying(on basis of wood value)	51.80	0.90	46.62	
Cutting(on basis of machine hour)	0.825	72.60	59.90	
Packing(on basis of direct labour hour)	0.50	58.76	29.38	
Total production overhead cost				135.90
Total production cost				278.92
Selling price				375.00
Budgeted gross profit per hive sold				96.08

Box hive in pine	Quantity used	Cost per metre, hour or absorption basis unit(T$)	T$	T$
Materials(measured in metres)				
Pine	2.90	9.00	26.10	
Galvanised steel	0.42	11.20	4.70	
Steel mesh	0.40	1.10	0.44	
Ply wood	0.25	2.30	0.58	
Total material cost				31.82
Labour(measured in hours)				
Drying	1.25	14.00	17.50	

（续表）

Box hive in pine	Quantity used	Cost per metre, hour or absorption basis unit(T$)	T$	T$
Cutting	3.25	17.00	55.25	
Packing	0.50	13.00	6.50	
Total direct labour cost				79.25
Production overhead				
Drying(on basis of wood value)	26.10	0.90	23.49	
Cutting(on basis of machine hour)	0.75	72.60	54.45	
Packing(on basis of direct labour hour)	0.50	58.76	29.38	
Total production overhead cost				107.32
Total production cost				218.39
Selling price				290.00
Budgeted gross profit per hive sold				71.61

Budgeted Gross Profit per Hive-slatted Hive

Slatted hive in cedar	Quantity used	Cost per metre, hour or absorption basis unit(T$)	T$	T$
Materials(measured in metres)				
Cedar	3.70	18.50	68.45	
Galvanised steel	0.42	11.20	4.70	
Steel mesh	0.40	1.10	0.44	
Ply wood	0.26	2.30	0.60	
Total material cost				74.19
Labour(measured in hours)				
Drying	2.65	14.00	37.10	
Cutting	3.60	17.00	61.20	
Packing	0.60	13.00	7.80	
Total direct labour cost				106.10
Production overhead				
Drying(on basis of wood value)	68.45	0.90	61.61	
Cutting(on basis of machine hour)	0.925	72.60	67.16	
Packing(on basis of direct labour hour)	0.60	58.76	35.26	
Total production overhead cost				164.03

（续表）

Slatted hive in cedar	Quantity used	Cost per metre, hour or absorption basis unit(T$)	T$	T$
Total production cost				344. 32
Selling price				460. 00
Budgeted gross profit per hive				115. 68

Slatted hive in pine	Quantity used	Cost per metre, hour or absorption basis unit(T$)	T$	T$
Materials(measured in metres)				
Cedar	3. 90	9. 00	35. 10	
Galvanised steel	0. 42	11. 20	4. 70	
Steel mesh	0. 40	1. 10	0. 44	
Ply wood	0. 26	2. 30	0. 60	
Total material cost				40. 84
Labour(measured in hours)				
Drying	1. 68	14. 00	23. 54	
Cutting	3. 90	17. 00	66. 30	
Packing	0. 60	13. 00	7. 80	
Total direct labour cost				97. 64
Production overhead				
Drying(on basis of wood value)	35. 10	0. 90	31. 59	
Cutting(on basis of machine hour)	0. 85	72. 60	61. 71	
Packing(on basis of direct labour hour)	0. 60	58. 76	35. 26	
Total production overhead cost				128. 56
Total production cost				267. 04
Selling price				380. 00
Budgeted gross profit per hive				112. 96

Budgeted Gross Profit for Foundation

Foundation is made in one set size, equivalent to the size of the brood box frame. Each brood box foundation can be cut in half by customers to fit into a super box frame.

	T$
Wax	5.04
Wire	0.24
Foundation direct labour	3.12
Packing labour	0.13
Production overhead	3.30
Packing overhead	0.49
Total cost per unit	12.32
Selling price	16.00
Gross profit	3.68

Notes on Budget Preparation

(1) The budget for the year ended 28 February 2018 has just been completed, ready for the start of the new financial year. It was based on the budget for the year ended 28 February 2017 with changes made to sales and production volumes, selling prices and expected changes to costs per unit of raw material, labour rates and overhead costs. No changes were made to the standards for direct labour or machine hours.

(2) Selling prices are based on full budgeted production cost plus a margin.

(3) Mavis Venderby uses standard costing and absorbs production overhead into unit costs.

(4) The standard quantities for wood are gross of a normal wastage of 10% due to off-cuts in the cutting process.

(5) The expected quality reject rates are 4% for all cedar hives produced and 7.5% for all pine hives produced. The expected losses are built into the standard cost of goods production and all rejects are detected at the end of the production process.

(6) The standard rates for various types of labour are an average for the year based

on the pay rates for different skill levels and the budgeted mix of skilled, unskilled and trainee workers. Pay rises happen in September every year. Overtime premium which is scheduled and production worker bonus are included within production overhead.

(7) The standard hours for cutting include time taken for reworking items which initially fail quality checks.

(8) Production overheads are ALL treated as fixed costs and include depreciation, energy, property related costs, the cost of indirect production employees, maintenance, consumables and packaging materials. Costs are first specifically allocated to one of five cost centres: drying, cutting, foundation, packing and goods inwards and maintenance. Other costs are then apportioned to the relevant cost centre on an appropriate basis (for example, floor space and number of employees). The goods inwards and maintenance costs are then re-apportioned on the basis of number of purchase orders.

(9) A production overhead absorption rate is calculated for each production cost centre. For drying the rate is per T$1 of wood value, for cutting the rate is per machine hour, for packing the rate is per packing direct labour hour and for foundation the rate is per foundation direct labour hour.

(10) The budgeted cost per hive is all of the packaging costs associated with the hive, including the cost of shrink wrap and the cost of the final packaging to the customer. These costs are treated as overheads. At the year-end, adjustments are required to these unit costs to value in progress and finished goods at an appropriate cost amount for the financial statements.

Article on the Rise of Beekeeping

Tucland Daily Bugle

16 January 2017 | No. 7823 T$1.20

The Rise of Beekeeping in Tucland

Jackson Percy, Business correspondent

It seems that there has been somewhat of a revival in beekeeping in recent times in Tucland,fuelled by two factors:its increased popularity as a hobby and the increase in Tucland' s appetite for home grown honey.

Five years ago,we imported more than 70 of the honey that we consumed as a country.Now this is down to around 50 and potentially could fall further.

It would seem we as consumers are getting more particular about what we eat and are demanding to know more about the provenance of our food.Honey produced in Tucland is known for its sweetness and purity,qualities which consumers are now prepared to pay a premium for.Tucland also seems immune to many of the diseases attacking bee colonies in other countries. Experts put this down to our climate and the resilience of our bees.

The demand for Tucland honey is at an all time high and according to industry experts, the growth in demand shows no signs of slowly down any time soon,despite the recent economic downturn.

To meet this increased demand, the number of commercial honey farms in Tucland has increased by 200 from five years ago,with an average of one new farm being established every week.Each farm can have anything up to 500 hives,so not only is this improving our trade deficit but it is also helping to support other niche businesses such as beehive manufacturers and beekeeping equipment retailers.

The increase in commercial honey producers is not the whole story.Beekeeping as a hobby is also flourishing.It is estimated that there are now approximately 200, 000 hobby beekeepers in Tucland (equating to 1 of the population).Whilst much of the honey produced is consumed by themselves,these hobby beekeepers are driving the growth in demand for all forms of beekeeping equipment and add on services.

According to the Tucland Beekeepers Association (one of many national and regional beekeeping associations and groups),hobby beekeepers are more likely to buy gadgets and to have the latest equipment.They are also more inclined to try new things and are always seeking advice on the best way to keep and treat their bees.The provision of beekeeping courses has more than tripled in this country in the last 10 years.These hobby beekeepers have money to spend on their hobby.This can only be good news for niche businesses such as Mavis Venderby and Griggs Hives.

Extract from a Thread on the Popular Honeypot Beekeepers' Forum

Posted by：Freda Banko on 19 January 2017

I am having a real dilemma at the moment, regarding which is the best hive to use in Tucland. I've been reading a lot about it over the last couple of weeks and to be honest have got to the point where I am going round in circles.

The problem is that in my mind based on everything I've read, polystyrene hives seem to make a lot of sense. Firstly and most importantly, they have better waterproof and insulating properties. I live in the countryside, so our temperatures in the middle of winter (or any time really) tend to be a couple of degrees lower than they are in town. They are lighter and so easier for a small woman like me to lift. Also they are cheaper and as they don't rot, maintenance will be easier too.

Polystyrene hives are used in Tucland. I saw an article the other day about how a bee-keeper up north has moved over to all polystyrene recently, about 500 hives. Now you don't make that kind of decision and financial investment lightly.

On the other hand, everyone I speak to about it just says that they will stick with wooden hives but none of them really seem to have much justification for it, other than to say that it has worked for the past 100 years. The only possible valid reasons anyone has given is the possibility of condensation dripping on the bees in the middle of winter as that would definitely kill them off, and the fact that the hives cannot be scorched with a blow torch to kill off all the mites and diseases.

I am obviously going to stick with the box hives as everyone else around here uses them, so it makes borrowing kit much easier. I am not sure how interchangeable the polystyrene and wooden hives are though.

So maybe I am going to come to a decision that I will buy polystyrene, unless anyone who has used them can give me a good reason not to! Next decision is who to buy from... Any recommendations folks?

Mavis Venderby's Position in the Beekeeping Equipment Supply Market

(All percentages used below relate to data for the year ended 31 December 2016)

Mavis Venderby is the largest Tucland based manufacturer of wooden beehives. It sells all of its beehives within Tucland, which represents 20% by volume of all the wooden beehives purchased in Tucland. Mavis Venderby has an excellent reputation with beekeepers for quality beehives.

Its closest competitor in Tucland, in terms of volume, is a business called Griggs Hives. Griggs Hives has a similar reputation for quality to Mavis Venderby and sells wooden beehives in cedar only. Griggs Hives sells 6% of all wooden beehives purchased in Tucland. In addition, Griggs Hives rears and sells queen bees and has an excellent reputation for this. Griggs Hives also sells beekeeping equipment such as smokers, bee suits, beehive spares as well as foundation and frames.

Of all the wooden beehives purchased in Tucland, 70% are manufactured there (the rest are imported). There are ten Tucland based manufacturers in total, each of which sells directly to beekeepers. Wooden beehives account for 65% of the Tucland beehive market by volume. The other 35% relates to polystyrene beehives (which are growing in popularity).

All polystyrene beehives are currently manufactured outside of Tucland and are imported into the country. Of the ten wooden beehive manufacturers, six also import and sell polystyrene beehives as well as other beekeeping equipment. Some also sell live bees.

Currently Mavis Venderby does not sell polystyrene beehives, beekeeping equipment or live bees.

Tax Regime of Tucland

Corporate Profits

- The corporate tax to be applied to taxable profits is 25%.
- Unless otherwise stated below, accounting rules on recognition and measurement are followed for tax purposes.
- The following expenses are not allowable for tax purposes:
  —accounting depreciation;
  —amortisation;
  —impairment charges;
  —entertaining expenditure;
  —donations to political parties;
  —taxes paid to other public bodies.

- Tax depreciation allowances are available on items of plant and equipment (including vehicles used for business purposes) at a rate of 25% per year on a reducing balance basis.
- Where a company is in receipt of a government grant, the tax treatment will depend on the nature of the grant. For tax purposes, capital grant money received in the year is netted off the capital value of the asset to which it relates prior to tax depreciation allowances being calculated. Any capital grant income released to profit or loss in the year is not taxable. Revenue grants released to profit or loss in the year are treated as income for tax purposes.
- Tax losses can be carried forward indefinitely to offset against future taxable profits from the same business.
- A company is deemed to be resident in Tucland if it has its principal place of management there. A resident company will pay Tucland corporate tax on all of its profit irrespective of the country in which the profit is earned.
- Where a company resident in Tucland owns a subsidiary company which is resident in another country, any dividends paid by that subsidiary to the parent company will be treated as income of the parent company and will be taxed at the corporate tax rate.
- Double taxation treaties exist with a number of other countries. All of these treaties give relief for double taxation in respect of any withholding and underlying tax suffered on dividends received. Relief is available using the tax credit method.

背景材料

简介

梅维斯·文德柏（Mavis Venderby）公司是一家木制蜂箱的生产零售企业，由梅维斯·文德柏和她的丈夫 Benjamin（本杰明）在 70 年前创立。公司位于 Tucland（塔克兰德），该国的货币为 T$ ①。Tucland 位于北半球，气候宜人。

该公司的总经理 Thomas Venderby（托马斯·文德柏）和销售与市场营销总监 Jacinta Cory（杰辛塔·科里）各持有梅维斯·文德柏公司一半的所有权，他们是 Mavis 和 Benjamin 的曾孙。

梅维斯·文德柏公司制造和销售两种类型的蜂箱：盒式蜂箱和板式蜂箱。这两类蜂箱具有相同的组件和功能，只是形状不同而已。每类蜂箱都由两种不同类型的木材制成：雪松和松木。所有蜂箱都采用扁平包装进行销售，这意味着客户必须自行组装。

除了木制蜂箱外，梅维斯·文德柏公司还销售底基和框架。蜜蜂可以利用底基来构造单个蜂房，存放蜂蜜。框架是底基四周的木制支架，每个蜂箱最多可容纳 20 个框架式底基。梅维斯·文德柏公司以前自行制造框架，但现在采用从供应商处购进后再出售的方式，因为后者更具成本效益，而底基则仍由梅维斯·文德柏公司自行制造。底基和框架与木质蜂箱独立包装，分开销售。

梅维斯·文德柏公司面向公众直接销售所有产品，并在工厂所在地设立了销售门店。梅维斯·文德柏公司大部分销售是通过网站或电话完成的。

公司设有 4 名董事：总经理 Thomas Venderby、销售和市场营销总监 Jacinta Cory、生产总监 Joseph Perez（约瑟夫·佩雷斯）、财务总监 Pene Lopez（佩妮·洛佩斯）。雇员分为熟练员工和非熟练员工。

---

① 此处及以下所称“T$”，均指 Tucland 当地货币，该货币为虚拟货币。

最近，梅维斯·文德柏公司从原来的小型厂房搬迁到了新厂房。新厂房曾经是农场办公室，配建了谷仓和附属建筑物，有很大的扩建空间。

蜜蜂：完美的团队！

作者：皮特·桑普森（Pete Sampson）

每个早晨，在将蜂蜜涂抹到吐司面包上时，你有没有想过，蜂蜜是怎么来的？答案显而易见，当然是来自蜜蜂，但你知道采蜜这一过程涉及多少团队合作吗？蜂蜜的生产真的是大自然的一个奇迹。

不论野生还是家养，不论是野外找到的空洞还是人造蜂箱，蜜蜂都是以群居方式生活的。在产蜜季节的高峰期，每个蜂群约有6 000只蜜蜂：1只蜂王，约1 000只雄蜂，其余则为雌性的工蜂。在蜂群中，每类蜜蜂的角色分工都非常明确。

蜂王是蜂群的核心，她唯一的职责就是产卵。在任何一个潜在的竞争对手孵化之前，蜂王就会破坏其蜂卵；如果面对来自另一个蜂群的蜂王，她会与之战斗直至死亡，以确保自己在蜂群中至高无上的地位。

在蜂王整个生命历程中，她会分泌一种信息素，以确保蜂群中的其他雌蜂无法生育后代。雄蜂的唯一职责就是与蜂王交配，以便蜂王能够不断地产卵。

工蜂，正如其名，它们需要负责余下的所有工作：从花朵中收集花蜜，带回蜂巢，并存放到蜂房（基本上用作储藏室）中。工蜂要不断扇动翅膀以帮助花蜜脱水，最终在蜂房内形成蜂蜜。一旦蜂房装满蜂蜜，工蜂就会分泌蜂蜡将蜂房密封。除了生产蜂蜜外，工蜂还要负责蜂群的方方面面，其中包括照顾幼蜂、对抗外来攻击、保护蜂巢。

蜂群的分工协作是经过精心设计的。没有蜂王和雄蜂，就没有下一代，就不会有新的工蜂；没有工蜂，就没有蜂蜜，蜂群就没有食物来源（直到我们从蜜蜂那里偷走蜂蜜）。这是最杰出的团队协作！

梅维斯·文德柏公司的产品

产品清单

产品	所使用的产品图片	信息
盒式蜂箱 雪松： 零售价 T$ 375 松木： 零售价 T$ 290		所有蜂箱都采用扁平包装，具有相同的构造组件 从下到上，这些组件包括： (1) 蜂巢底座； (2) 蜂巢底板； (3) 育蜂箱； (4) 蜂王隔离网； (5) 超级箱； (6) 顶板； (7) 屋顶。 我们在蜂巢组件指南中对其做了进一步说明（如下页所示）
板条蜂箱 雪松： 零售价 T$ 460 松木： 零售价 T$ 380		
底基 零售价 T$ 20		梅维斯·文德柏公司自行制造底基，只有一个尺寸，与育蜂箱的尺寸匹配 我们在蜂巢组件指南中对其做了进一步说明（如下页所示）
框架 零售价： 育蜂箱框架 T$ 2.60 超级箱框架 T$ 1.80		框架有两个尺寸，分别对应育蜂箱和超级箱 我们在蜂巢组件指南中对其做了进一步说明（如下页所示）

梅维斯·文德柏公司：蜂巢组件指南

组件	说明
蜂巢底座	蜂巢底座为蜂巢提供了一个简单基座，其设计宗旨是抬高蜂巢，以远离地面，减少害虫的入侵数量
蜂巢底板	蜂巢底板包括一个底层木板（作为实际的楼板）和蜜蜂的着陆区域，它比蜂巢的其余部分略微突出。此外，它还包括底板上方的板条架，其目的是为蜂巢提供通风
育蜂箱	育蜂箱是最大的蜂巢箱，它由具有蜂房底基的育蜂架组成（见下文）。此处是蜂王产卵以及工蜂照顾幼蜂的场所。就本质而言，育蜂箱是蜂群的生活区
底基	底基是由蜂蜡制成的，并用线材进行加固。蜜蜂可以在此基础上用自己的蜂蜡再建造蜂房，用于存放蜂卵（育蜂箱）和储存蜂蜜（超级箱）
框架	框架是一个木制的矩形支架，用来框住底基
蜂王隔离网	蜂王隔离网是一个用木材和金属网格制成的支架，其中留有孔眼，孔径足以让工蜂通过，但对蜂王来说却太小。这样可以确保蜂王无法接近超级箱
超级箱	超级箱是育蜂箱的缩小版本，其中的支架用于存储蜂蜜。养蜂人正是从此处提取蜂蜜以供人类的饮食
顶板	顶板是蜂箱顶部的盖板，中间留有一个通风孔
屋顶	蜂箱的屋顶位于顶板上方，采用镀锌钢筋加固，以抵御天气的影响

除了框架是从供应商处购买再卖给客户外，其他组件均由梅维斯·文德柏公司自行制造。

销售模式

蜂箱、底基和框架的销售高峰期是 3 ~7 月，这 5 个月能完成全年销售额的 70% 。这段时间对应着 Tucland 晚春和整个夏季的蜂蜜生产高峰。蜂箱销售的最高峰通常在 3 月和 4 月，也就是产蜜季节之初。

生产流程

全年的生产计划要保持合理平均。由于销售存在季节性，因此库存水平在全年有所不同。

蜂箱

蜂箱的生产过程分为三个阶段：

烘干

- 在生产之前，对所有木材进行现场烘干。两种类型的木材都采用大型烘干棚空气干燥结合窑炉烘干的方式。由于材质不同，雪松的干燥期大约为6个月，松木约为4个月。实际干燥时间取决于气候条件
- 每类木材按3米长的板材规格进行采购，到货之后先进行堆放。最初，木材采用空气干燥方式，对每个堆垛中的木板定期翻转。在干燥期过半的时候，将木材移至窑炉进行长达两天的烘干。窑炉烘干时间的长短取决于气候条件。之后，将木板重新堆放并进行空气干燥，直至符合使用条件

切割

- 一旦木材干燥完毕，下一个步骤就是使用可编程机器，按照蜂箱的各个组件切割木材。盒式蜂箱和板式蜂箱需要采用不同的切割程序，因此，需要花费一些时间对机器进行设置
- 切割工作完成之后，某些组件（如底座和屋顶）需要手工组装，且所有组件都要进行打磨和质量检查。在这一环节，松木上的任何树节都需要涂上密封胶加以密封
- 通常，雪松比松木更易处理，因为木材本身的缺陷较少。因此，在切割过程中，松木的浪费高于雪松

包装

- 在完成质量检查之后，单个蜂箱的所有组件都将被热缩塑料包装以保护木材，然后送至成品存放区域
- 接到订单后，从成品存放区域提取正确数量和类型的蜂箱，用聚苯乙烯保护膜再次包装并放入纸箱以备运输。在这一环节，产品组装所需的螺丝、钉子、胶水、说明书和其他配件都会一并放入纸箱
- 通过快递将产品发送给客户

底基

底基按以下方式制造：

将熔化的蜂蜡注入金属模具中，将其挤压成完整的平板，然后再传送到生产线上进行干燥

当平板接近干燥时，将其传送至生产线的下一个阶段，压制成六边形的形状，蜜蜂可以以此为基础建造蜂房

随后，按照箱体的尺寸用机器对大片的平板进行切割，利用电流为每个底基焊上金属网线，然后采用堆垛方式存放并进行质量检查

包装团队在收到底基之后，以10片为单位，用聚乙烯进行包装以保持新鲜，至此，底基已做好出售准备

客户和供应商

客户

梅维斯·文德柏公司的客户包括养蜂爱好者（拥有的蜂箱通常少于10个）和商业养蜂人（拥有的蜂箱可高达500个，有时甚至更多）。截至2016年2月29日之前，养蜂爱好者和商业养蜂人分别贡献了该公司营业额的50%；而在2010年2月28日之前，养蜂爱好者和商业养蜂人的营业额贡献率分别为40%和60%。梅维斯·文德柏公司的客户非常忠诚，许多客户已与公司保持了多年的业务关系。

公司拥有三个销售渠道：门店销售、网站销售和电话销售。截至2016年2月29日，门店、电话、网站这三种销售方式分别贡献了20%、35%和45%的销售额。选择门店销售方式的人数占比相对较高，养蜂人（特别是养蜂爱好者）愿意跋涉数十公里[①]，因为他们不仅是为了购买蜂箱，同时还为了与公司的销售人员探讨养蜂问题（销售人员对于这些问题非常在行）。

公司给予商业养蜂人的标准信用期限为30天，而养蜂爱好者需要在下订单时即时付款。

在购买蜂箱时，客户可以选择雪松或松木。雪松天然就能抵御蛾子，且相比于松木，它没那么容易腐烂和卷曲。此外，雪松也是一种很好的绝缘体。因此，雪松制成的蜂箱比松木制成的蜂箱更经久耐用，具有更好的品质。然而，由于雪松蜂箱的制造成本

① 1公里=1千米。——编者注

更高（主要是因为木材的成本较高），因此购买价格也更高。选择雪松还是松木，每个客户都有各自的偏好。

蜂箱采用扁平的方式包装和出售。这意味着客户必须自行组装蜂箱。在完成组装之后，绝大多数客户会在蜂箱外层涂漆或进行处理以保护木材。

供应商

梅维斯·文德柏公司从两家供应商处采购木材。这种供应关系已经维持了 20 年，鉴于这种紧密的合作关系，两家供应商都为该公司提供了非常长的信用期限。梅维斯·文德柏公司利用批量采购优势，从这些供应商那里获得了采购折扣。

其他材料供应商提供的信用期限符合行业常规，一般为 30 天。梅维斯·文德柏公司针对所有供应商，保留了它们的备货期以及拒收率等方面的基本数据。

梅维斯·文德柏公司的关键人员

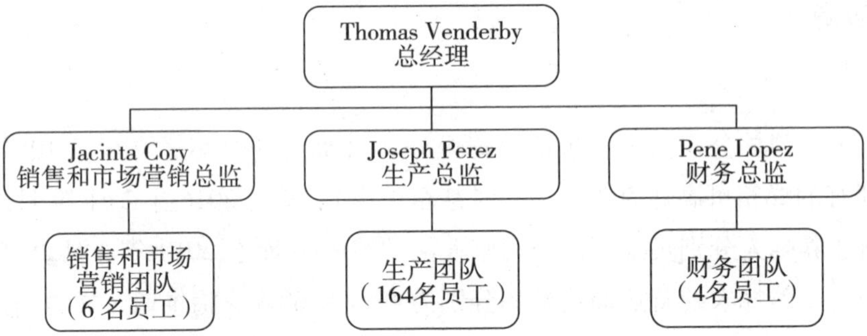

Thomas Venderby——总经理

Thomas，40岁，最近刚从父亲手中接任总经理一职。他一直在家族企业中工作，之前担任过生产总监，尤其关注产品质量。如今，Thomas具体负责人力资源事务（尽管他不具备人力资源相关经验），同时还要把握企业全局。他热衷于拓展客户基础和丰富产品种类，在保持生产质量的同时，还注重提升服务和品牌实力

Pene Lopez——财务总监

Pene，32岁，是一名合格的会计师。她担任财务总监一职已有两年时间，在此之前，她曾担任服装制造企业的财务经理。她对公司内所有财务和会计事务负有最终责任，并负责管理财务团队

财务团队

（Cormac Jones） 戈迈克·琼斯 高级财务主管	■ Cormac不久前获得会计师资格认证，刚入职两个月。他负责编制月度管理报告、整理预算信息，以及年度财务报表的初稿
你本人 财务主管	■ 你在Mavis Venderby公司工作了3年，最初职务是财务助理。你正在备考专业考试，负责协助Pene Lopez和Cormac Jones处理一系列复杂事务。个别情况下，你还需要为其他董事和经理提供协助
Susie Ronaldo （苏茜·罗纳尔多） 财务助理	■ Susie在mavs Venderby公司担任财务助理长达10年。她负责处理每周的工资以及小额现金收付事宜。有时她还需要为财务主管提供协助
Duncan Scoby （邓肯·斯科比） 财务助理	■ Duncan刚进入企业不久，还是一名新手。他负责发票的处理和编码以及采购和销售的付款工作。此外，他还负责每个月的银行对账事宜

Jacinta Cory——销售和市场营销总监

Jacinta，38岁，担任销售和市场营销总监一职已长达8年。与哥哥Thomas一样，她一直在家族企业中工作。Jacinta自己就喜欢养蜂，并与许多地区和国家的养蜂协会建立了紧密的联系。她具体负责市场营销、网站维护以及销售和市场营销团队的管理工作

销售和市场营销团队

销售和市场营销团队由一名专职经理以及5名助理组成。销售和市场营销经理是Toby Venger（托比·文格尔），他是一名养蜂专家，对养蜂工作的方方面面都非常了解，比如蜂王的养育、蜜蜂相关疾病以及蜂巢产品。他已经在Mavis Venderby公司工作了15年，负责管理5人助理团队，与Jacinta Cory密切配合开展工作，开拓新客户并维护现有的客户关系。

Toby和他的助理团队（与Toby一样，助理们也非常精通养蜂事宜）负责经营零售门店，处理网站和电话订单。

Toby在梅维斯·文德柏公司厂房附近养了10箱蜜蜂，他一直致力于改良蜂箱的建造方法。目前，他正在研发一种特殊的信息素，将其喷涂在底基上，一方面可以抵御害虫，另一方面也可以促使蜜蜂更快产蜜。

Joseph Perez——生产总监

Joseph，58岁，在梅维斯·文德柏公司已工作40年。刚入职时，他在生产部门做实习生，而后一路晋升，直至成为生产经理（他担任这一职务长达20年时间）。在Thonas Uenderby公司担任总经理之后，他升任生产总监。Joseph负责管理生产事务，他是一名技艺娴熟的木匠。目前，Thomas热衷于扩大公司的木制产品系列，而Joseph正着手开发动物屋

生产团队

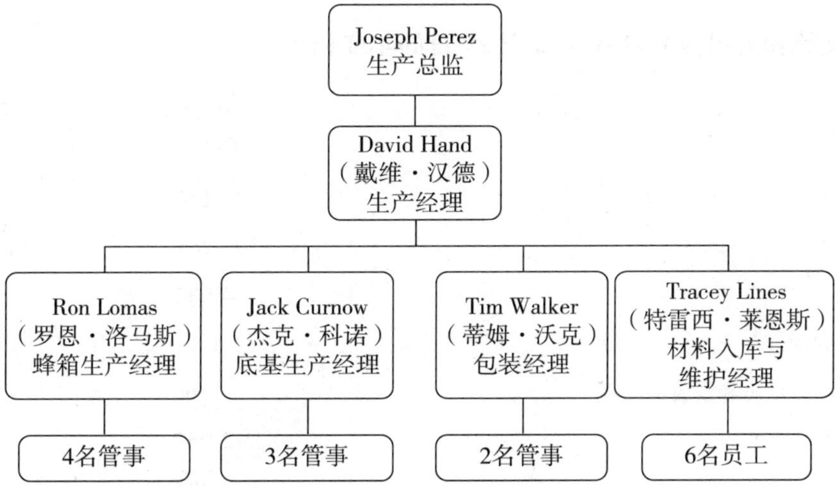

该公司共有165名生产员工，细分如下：

	人数	人数
间接生产人员		
生产总监	1	
经理	5	
管事	9	
材料入库与维护人员	6	
间接生产人员总数		21
直接生产人员总数		144
生产人员总数		165

注：

（1）材料入库与维护工作是生产活动的辅助工作。6名员工负责机器和厂房的维护以及原材料的采购工作。

（2）直接生产人员被分配到特定的生产区域，许多人同时承担几项工作。

（3）梅维斯·文德柏公司制订了一个人员滚动计划，每年雇用8名左右的实习生。支付给实习生的固定工资为每小时T$9，直至他们通过为期6个月的试用期。试用期之后，如果有适合岗位，这些实习生将成为全职员工。

经董事批准审计的截至2016年2月29日的最新年度财务报表

梅维斯·文德柏公司截至2016年2月29日的年度利润表

	2016年 (T$ 000)	2015年 (T$ 000)
收入	17 860	17 909
销售成本	(13 324)	(13 199)
毛利	4 536	4 710
其他营运成本	(2 441)	(2 036)
处置不动产、厂房和设备的收益	864	—
息税前利润	2 959	2 674
财务费用	(48)	—
税前利润	2 911	2 674
税费	(710)	(696)
本年利润	2 201	1 978

梅维斯·文德柏公司截至2016年2月29日的资产负债表

	2016年 (T$ 000)	2016年 (T$ 000)	2015年 (T$ 000)	2015年 (T$ 000)
资产				
非流动资产				
不动产、厂房和设备		8 872		5 760
流动资产				
存货	4 351		3 510	
应收账款和其他应收款	587		473	
现金及现金等价物	412		903	
		5 350		4 886
资产合计		14 222		10 646
所有者权益和负债				
已发行普通股股本		50		50
留存收益		11 293		9 092

（续表）

	2016 年（T$ 000）	2016 年（T$ 000）	2015 年（T$ 000）	2015 年（T$ 000）
所有者权益合计		11 343		9 142
非流动负债				
银行贷款		1 250		—
流动负债				
银行贷款	250		—	
应付账款和其他应付款	674		814	
应付税费	705		690	
		1 629		1 504
所有者权益和负债合计		14 222		10 646

梅维斯·文德柏公司截至 2016 年 2 月 29 日的年度现金流量表

	T$ 000	T$ 000
经营活动产生的现金流		
税前利润		2 911
调整		
折旧	752	
出售不动产、厂房和设备的收益	（864）	
财务费用	48	
		（64）
运营资本的变动	（841）	
库存的增加	（114）	
应收账款和其他应收款的增加	（140）	
应付账款和其他应付款的减少		（1 095）
		1 752
经营活动产生的现金		（695）
已付税费		
已付财务费用		（48）
经营活动产生的现金流净额		1 009
投资活动产生的现金流	（8 350）	
购买不动产、厂房和设备	5 350	

（续表）

	T$ 000	T$ 000
出售不动产、厂房和设备		（3 000）
投资活动产生的现金流净额		
筹资活动产生的现金流	1 500	
借款收益		1 500
筹资活动产生的现金流净额		（491）
现金及现金等价物的净减少额		903
年初现金及现金等价物		412
年末现金及现金等价物		

截至2016年2月29日的年度财务报表，是经董事会批准的最新财务报表，且审计人员给出了无保留的审计意见。

截至2018年2月28日的年度预算信息

截至2018年2月28日的年度销售和生产预算

	雪松蜂箱	松木蜂箱	雪松板材	松木板材	框架	底基
销售数量（单位）	10 000	7 000	9 000	6 000	198 000	396 000

截至2018年2月28日的年度预算损益

	雪松蜂箱（T$ 000）	松木蜂箱（T$ 000）	雪松板材（T$ 000）	松木板材（T$ 000）	框架（T$ 000）	底基（T$ 000）	总计（T$ 000）	总计（T$ 000）
销售额	3 750	2 030	4 140	2 280	436	6 336		18 972
减去：材料成本								
木材	518	183	616	210			1 527	
镀锌钢							150	
金属网格	47	33	42	28			14	
胶合板	4	3	4	3			19	
蜂蜡	6	4	5	4	1 996	1 996		

（续表）

	雪松蜂箱 (T$ 000)	松木蜂箱 (T$ 000)	雪松板材 (T$ 000)	松木板材 (T$ 000)	框架 (T$ 000)	底基 (T$ 000)	总计 (T$ 000)	总计 (T$ 000)
框架					390		390	
线材						95	95	
								(4 191)
减去：直接人工成本								
烘干	280	122	334	141			877	
切割	510	387	551	398			1 846	
底基						1 236	1 236	
包装	65	46	70	47		51	279	
								(4 238)
减去：生产费用								
烘干	466	164	555	189			1 374	
切割	599	381	604	370			1 954	
底基						1 307	1 307	
包装	294	206	317	212	36	194	1 259	
								(5 894)
毛利								4 649
减去：非生产费用								
雇员							564	
运输							683	
管理和销售							1236	(2 483)
营业利润								2 166

每个蜂箱的预算毛利——盒式蜂箱

雪松盒式蜂箱	使用量	每米、每小时或所使用吸收基数的成本（T$）	T$	T$
材料（以米计）				
雪松	2.80	18.50	51.80	
镀锌钢	0.42	11.20	4.70	
金属网格	0.40	1.10	0.44	
胶合板	0.25	2.30	0.58	
材料总成本				57.52
人工（以小时计）				
烘干	2.00	14.00	28.00	
切割	3.00	17.00	51.00	
包装	0.50	13.00	6.50	
直接人工成本合计				85.50
生产费用				
烘干（以木材价值为基数）	51.80	0.90	46.62	
切割（以机器小时为基数）	0.825	72.60	59.90	
包装（以直接劳动时间为基数）	0.50	58.76	29.38	
生产间接成本合计				135.90
生产总成本				278.92
售价				375.00
每售出一个蜂箱的预算毛利				96.08

松木盒式蜂箱	使用量	每米、每小时或所使用吸收基数的成本（T$）	T$	T$
材料（以米计）				
松木	2.90	9.00	26.10	
镀锌钢	0.42	11.20	4.70	
金属网格	0.40	1.10	0.44	
胶合板	0.25	2.30	0.58	
材料总成本				31.82
人工（以小时计）				
烘干	1.25	14.00	17.50	

（续表）

松木盒式蜂箱	使用量	每米、每小时或所使用吸收基数的成本（T$）	T$	T$
切割	3.25	17.00	55.25	
包装	0.50	13.00	6.50	
直接人工成本合计				79.25
生产费用				
烘干（以木材价值为基数）	26.10	0.90	23.49	
切割（以机器小时为基数）	0.75	72.60	54.45	
包装（以直接劳动时间为基数）	0.50	58.76	29.38	
生产间接成本合计				107.32
生产总成本				218.39
售价				290.00
每售出一个蜂箱的预算毛利				71.61

每个蜂箱的预算毛利——板式蜂箱

雪松板式蜂箱	使用量	每米、每小时或所使用吸收基数的成本（T$）	T$	T$
材料（以米计）				
雪松	3.70	18.50	68.45	
镀锌钢	0.42	11.20	4.70	
金属网格	0.40	1.10	0.44	
胶合板	0.26	2.30	0.60	
材料总成本				74.19
人工（以小时计）				
烘干	2.65	14.00	37.10	
切割	3.60	17.00	61.20	
包装	0.60	13.00	7.80	
直接人工成本合计				106.10
生产费用				
烘干（以木材价值为基数）	68.45	0.90	61.61	
切割（以机器小时为基数）	0.925	72.60	67.16	
包装（以直接劳动时间为基数）	0.60	58.76	35.26	
生产间接成本合计				164.03

（续表）

雪松板式蜂箱	使用量	每米、每小时或所使用吸收基数的成本（T$）	T$	T$
生产总成本				344.32
售价				460.00
每售出一个蜂箱的预算毛利				115.68

松木板式蜂箱	使用量	每米、每小时或所使用吸收基数的成本（T$）	T$	T$
材料（以米计）				
松木	3.90	9.00	35.10	
镀锌钢	0.42	11.20	4.70	
金属网格	0.40	1.10	0.44	
胶合板	0.26	2.30	0.60	
材料总成本				40.84
人工（以小时计）				
烘干	1.68	14.00	23.54	
切割	3.90	17.00	66.30	
包装	0.60	13.00	7.80	
直接人工成本合计				97.64
生产费用				
烘干（以木材价值为基数）	35.10	0.90	31.59	
切割（以机器小时为基数）	0.85	72.60	61.71	
包装（以直接劳动时间为基数）	0.60	58.76	35.26	
生产间接成本合计				128.56
生产总成本				267.04
售价				380.00
每售出一个蜂箱的预算毛利				112.96

底基的预算毛利

底基按统一尺寸制作，其规格与育蜂箱框架差不多。客户可将每个育蜂箱的底基再切割成两半，即与超级箱框架大小相当。

	T$
蜂蜡	5.04
线材	0.24
底基直接人工	3.12
包装人工	0.13
生产费用	3.30
包装费用	0.49
每单位总成本	12.32
售价	16.00
毛利	3.68

预算编制说明

（1）截至2018年2月28日的年度预算刚刚完成，这说明我们已为新财年的开始做好了准备。它以截至2017年2月28日的年度预算为基础，对销售量、生产量、销售价格做了调整；对原材料的单位成本、人工成本、间接成本做了预期调整；未对直接人工标准和机器小时标准进行任何调整。

（2）销售价格是全面预算的生产成本加上一定利润得出的。

（3）梅维斯·文德柏公司采用标准成本核算法，将生产费用吸收到单位成本之中。

（4）由于切割过程中的错误操作，木材的标准数量要包含10%的正常损耗。

（5）该公司生产的雪松蜂箱因质量问题而导致的拒收率预计为4%，松木蜂箱拒收率预计为7.5%。预期损失已经纳入正常生产的标准成本，但在生产过程结束之际，所有瑕疵品都要挑拣出来。

（6）各类人工的标准工资以不同技术水平的工资率以及熟练工人、非熟练工人与实习生的工资混合预算为基础，计算当年的平均工资而得出的。每年9月进行调薪。计划中的加班工资以及生产工人奖金都包含在生产费用之中。

（7）切割工作的标准时间包括对未通过质量检查的项目重新加工所耗费的时间。

（8）生产费用**全部**视为固定成本，包括折旧、能源费用、物业相关成本、间接生产员工的成本、维护费用、耗材和包装材料的成本。公司首先将成本专门分配给五个成本中心之一：烘干、切割、底基、包装、材料入库与维护；而后，采用适当的基数（例如，占地面积和雇员人数），将其他成本分配给相关成本中心。材料入库与维护成本将根据采购订单的数量重新分摊。

（9）公司为每个生产成本中心计算生产费用吸收率。对于烘干流程而言，效率为每T$ 1 木材价值；对于切割流程而言，效率为每一机器小时；对于包装流程而言，效率为每一直接劳动小时；对于底基流程而言，效率为每个底基的直接劳动小时。

（10）每个蜂箱的预算成本是指与蜂箱包装相关的所有成本，包括收缩膜包装材料的成本以及向客户发货的最终包装成本。这些成本被视为间接费用。在年底，公司需要对这些单位成本进行调整，以便按照恰当的成本金额对在产品和产成品进行估值，以供财务报表之用。

报道文章：养蜂业的兴起

Tucland 号角日报

2017年1月16日 | 第7823期　　T$1.20

养蜂业在 Tucland的兴起

商业记者 Jackson Percy（杰克逊 · 柏西）

近来，Tucland的养蜂业似乎有所复苏，这主要得益于两个因素的推动：作为一项业余爱好，养蜂业人气渐增；Tucland国民对家酿蜂蜜的喜爱有所增加。

5年前，Tucland作为蜂蜜消费国，70%以上的蜂蜜都从国外进口。现在这一比例降至50%左右，且有望进一步下降。

作为消费者，我们似乎越来越关注我们食用的东西，要求更多地了解食物的来源。Tucland生产的蜂蜜因其甜度和纯度而声名远扬，现在，消费者愿意以更高的价格购买高品质的产品。此外，Tucland的蜂群似乎对其他国家蜜蜂所遭受的诸多疾病具有免疫能力，专家把这归功于我们的气候以及我国蜜蜂的恢复能力。

市场对Tucland蜂蜜的需求处于历史最高点，根据行业专家的估计，尽管近来经济出现下滑，但人们对蜂蜜需求的增长并没有放缓的迹象。

为了满足增长的需求，Tucland的商业养蜂 农场相比5年之前数量已经增长了200%，即平均下来，每周都有一家新农场建成。每个农场拥有的蜂箱数量可高达500个，这不仅可以帮助Tucland改善贸易逆差，而且还能为其他小众企业提供助力，如蜂箱制造商和养蜂设备零售商。

除了职业蜂蜜生产商的增加，养蜂作为一项爱好也得到了蓬勃发展。据统计，Tucland现有约20万名养蜂爱好者（相当于人口总数的1%）。虽然养蜂爱好者生产的大部分蜂蜜都用于自己消费，但他们推动了各类养蜂设备以及附加服务的需求增长。

根据Tucland养蜂人协会（为数众多的国家及地区性养蜂协会和团体之一）的统计，养蜂爱好者更希望购买小配件和最新的设备。此外，他们也更倾向于尝试新鲜事物，在如何以最好的方式养育和治疗蜜蜂方面，他们一直在寻求建议和意见。在过去10年间，Tucland的养蜂课程已经增加了3倍多。这些养蜂爱好者拥有足够的金钱，能够支撑自己这一爱好。这对于梅维斯 · 文德柏公司和格里格斯 · 海夫斯（Griggs Hives）公司等小众企业而言是好消息。

“蜜罐养蜂人论坛”热门讨论摘要

发布者：Freda Banko（弗雷达·班科），2017 年 1 月 19 日

最近，我面临着一个真正的困境，我不知道在 Tucland 境内哪类蜂箱最好用。在过去的几周，我阅读了很多相关资料，但坦白地说，还是在原地打转而已。

根据我所阅读的资料，聚苯乙烯蜂箱似乎很具吸引力。首先，也是最为重要的一点，它们具有更好的防水和绝缘性能。我住在农村地区，当地隆冬时节（事实上，任何季节）的温度要比城镇的温度低几度。对于我这样的小个子女人来说，聚苯乙烯蜂箱质量更轻，搬起来更容易。此外，它们的价格还更低，由于不会腐烂，维护工作也更加容易。

聚苯乙烯蜂箱已在 Tucland 得到采用。我几天前曾看过一篇文章，讲北方地区的某个养蜂人最近将蜂箱全部更换为聚苯乙烯蜂箱，约有 500 个。现如今，没有人会草率地做出这样的决定，进行这样的财务投资。

但在另一方面，我与许多养蜂人就聚苯乙烯蜂箱进行了交流，所有人都表示要坚持使用木质蜂箱，虽然他们之中似乎没有人能给出足够充分的理由，只是表示过去一百年以来大家一直都在使用木质蜂箱。他们所给出的或许有效的理由：在隆冬时节，聚苯乙烯蜂箱上可能形成冷凝水并滴落到蜜蜂身上，这无疑将杀死蜜蜂；而且，此类蜂箱不能采用喷灯来炙烤和消灭所有害虫和疾病。

显而易见，我仍然会像周围的养蜂人一样坚持使用盒式蜂箱，这样，借用工具什么的也更为方便。但我并不清楚聚苯乙烯蜂箱与木质蜂箱之间的互换性如何。

因此，或许我会决定购买聚苯乙烯蜂箱，除非有人在使用这类蜂箱之后给出具有说服力的理由来建议我不要这么做！下一个决定是从谁那里购买蜂箱，你们有何建议？

梅维斯·文德柏公司在养蜂设备供应市场上的地位

（以下所有使用的百分比均是截至 2016 年 12 月 31 日的数据）

梅维斯·文德柏公司是 Tucland 最大的木制蜂箱生产商，所有销售都在 Tucland 境内完成，占 Tucland 木制蜂箱采购量的 20%。梅维斯·文德柏公司生产高质量的蜂箱，在养蜂人中拥有良好的口碑。

就销售数量而言，梅维斯·文德柏公司在 Tucland 的最大竞争对手是格里格斯·海夫斯公司。在质量方面，格里格斯·海夫斯公司与梅维斯·文德柏公司不相上下，它只

销售雪松木制蜂箱，其销售量占 Tucland 木制蜂箱销售量的 6%。此外，格里格斯 · 海夫斯公司还培育和出售蜂王，并因此而声名大噪。与此同时，格里格斯 · 海夫斯公司还销售养蜂配套设施，如烟熏器、防护装备、蜂箱配件以及底基和框架。

在 Tucland 境内销售的木制蜂箱中，70% 属于本地制造，其余则是进口。该国共有 10 家蜂箱生产商，它们都面向养蜂人直接销售产品。就数量而言，木质蜂箱占了 Tucland 蜂箱市场 65% 的份额，其余 35% 则是聚苯乙烯蜂箱（正在日益普及之中）。

目前，所有的聚苯乙烯蜂箱都在 Tucland 境外生产，然后进口到该国。在这 10 家木制蜂箱生产商中，有 6 家进口和销售聚苯乙烯蜂箱以及其他养蜂设备。此外，还有厂商从事活蜂销售业务。

目前，梅维斯 · 文德柏公司并不销售聚苯乙烯蜂箱、养蜂设备或活蜂。

Tucland 的税收体制

企业利润

- 企业所得税为应税利润的 25%。
- 除非另有说明，否则在税务方面，应遵守下列关于确认和计量的会计准则。
- 以下费用不得税前扣除：
  ——会计折旧；
  ——摊销费用；
  ——减值支出；
  ——文娱开支；
  ——政党捐款；
  ——缴纳给其他公共机构的税款。
- 厂房和机器设备（包括商用车辆）的折旧费用可以抵税，抵扣基础为递减余额，年抵扣率为 25%。
- 如果公司获得了政府补贴，具体的税务处理要视补贴的性质而定。站在税务的角度，企业收到的资本补贴可在收到拨款的当年，在计算折旧费用抵税之前，用于抵减相关资产的资本价值。当年盈利或损失所涉及的任何资本补贴收入则无须纳税。站在税务的角度，当年盈利或损失所涉及的收入补贴应视为应税收入。
- 可抵税损失可以无期限结转，以抵减同一企业未来的应税利润。
- 判断一个企业是否属于 Tucland 居民企业的依据是 Tucland 是否是该企业主要管理

活动的所在地。居民企业应就其所有利润向 Tucland 纳税，不论其具体利润来自哪个国家。

- 如果 Tucland 居民企业拥有一家子公司，且这家子公司属于另一个国家的居民企业，那么，该子公司向总公司派发的任何股利将视为总公司的收入，并按企业税率向 Tucland 缴税。
- Tucland 与某些国家签订了双重征税协定。此类协定规定企业股利涉及的代扣代缴税和股息税可免于双重征税。企业使用税收抵免法可享有这一税收优惠。

Variant 1

This examination is structured as follows：

Section number	Number of tasks	Time for section(minutes)
1	1	45
2	1	45
3	1	45
4	1	45

The time available for each section is for reading,planning and writing your answer(s).

Section 1

You arrive at work to find the following email from Pene Lopez, finance director.

From: Pene Lopez, Finance Director
To: Management Accountant Assistant
Subject: Polystyrene box hives

The directors made the decision last week to begin retailing polystyrene box hives (poly box hives). At this early stage, we do not want to commit to manufacturing the poly box hives in-house, but would rather work with a specialist manufacturer to design and produce a quality product that we can then sell as a Mavis Venderby hive. This is a major departure from our core business and there are a number of concerns, not least the negative effect that the decision will have on our wooden box hive business.

Thomas recently attended a training course where he learnt about the Five Spokes of Cousin's Strategic Supply Wheel (which he told me were: competences and skills, performance measures, cost benefit, relationships and organisational structure). He thinks that it would be a good idea to use this in our search for the right supplier to ensure that we consider all aspects of the poly box hive supply chain and how can we prepare our business smoothly.

However, Jacinta is convinced that selling poly box hives will adversely affect sales of our wooden box hives and I am sure that she is right. We need an accurate sales forecast for our wooden box hives as changes in demand will have an effect on production and purchasing. I have done the preliminary work regarding this using regression analysis to establish a trend line and have identified seasonal variations relevant to our business. I have attached a schedule of my preliminary work to this email.

I would like you to draft two sections for a report that I will present later this week to the other directors, which includs:

- Details what we should be considering using Cousin's Strategic Supply Wheel in respect of the selection and retention of a specialist poly box hive manufacturer.
- Explains, in non-technical terms, the trend line and seasonal variations that I have produced in my attached notes. Please also include explanation of any limitations of using

simple linear regression when forecasting.

Many thanks!

Pene Lopez

Finance Director

Mavis Venderby

The Schedule of the Preliminary Work on Forecasting

The Trend

The actual sales trend data is from a business called Petroc Hives which operates in a country called North Republic. They started selling poly box hives 15 years ago and I have retrospectively used regression analysis to determine the trend line for their wooden box hive sales. Petroc Hives is a similar size to Mavis Venderby and this data represents the first two years sales of wooden box hives after the launch of their poly box hives.

The trend line is:

$Y = 17{,}000 - 700Q$

Y = the total number of wooden box hives sold

Q = the number of quarters (where Q = l represents the first quarter following the launch; Q = 2 represents the second quarter following the launch, and so on.)

Seasonal Variation

The seasonal variation data that we have collected here at Mavis Venderby over the years, using a multiplicative (proportional) method, is as follows:

Period	Seasonal Variation
Q1 (March—May)	+60%
Q2 (June—August)	+40%
Q3 (September—November)	-60%
Q4 (December—February)	-40%

Write the report sections requested by Pene Lopez, finance director.

Section 2

Two weeks have passed and you arrive at work to find the following on your desk.

Extract from a Thread on the "Honeypot Beekeepers' Forum"

I am intending to expand my apiary this year and have decided to buy thirty poly box hives. After a lot of research, I have decided to go with the model sold by Aches Hives, even though I have slight reservations about their flimsy plastic crown board. The fact is that every model on the market has something that I don't like: one has pans that are not interchangeable with my wooden box hives, another has an integrated feeder that I don't want and a third has a roof that doesn't fit properly.

I heard at my local bee farmers meeting that Mavis Venderby are going to sell their own poly box hive soon. Obviously if I am spending this much money, I want to buy the best kit. Can anyone tell me when the Mavis Venderby poly box hive will be available?

Pene Lopez calls you into her office and says:

Now that it seems to be public knowledge that we are going to be selling our own-brand poly box hive. Thomas wants us to be focused on the design, development and launch of the new hive. He suggests us all to work as a team, cross-functionally as he calls it, to get the best results. He thinks that the two key factors for the success of the poly hive are the selection of the right supplier and appropriate marketing.

David Hand has compiled a list of six potential suppliers, all of which would meet our quality standards, have very similar prices and also have the capacity to supply enough hives (based on our forecast sales). I would like you to take a look at the schedule and email me your assessment of the suppliers, based on the information provided.

Linked to that, Jacinta wants us to produce a marketing mix, detailing our ideas of how the poly box hive marketing will differ from our traditional hives. Naturally we will have most to say about the price but it is possible that we might think of something that she hasn't considered with the other aspects of the marketing mix. Please include in your email your ideas for the marketing of the poly box hive under the four headings of the marketing mix.

Pene Lopez then hands you the schedule, compiled by David Hand.

Schedule of Information Relating to Six Potential Suppliers of Poly Box Hives

Potential supplier	Country supplier is based in	Time trading	Revenue for the year to 31 December 2016 (T$ million *)	Usual credit terms offered (day)
supplier A	Tucland	14 months	4	60
supplier B	North states	20 years	121	20
supplier C	North Republic	9 years	65	30
supplier D	Tucland	7 years	24	40
supplier E	Hutland	9 years	40	20
supplier F	Tucland	2 years	20	40

* North States has the NS $ as its currency, North Republic the NR $ and Hutland the H $. For suppliers B, C and E the revenue figures in the above table have been translated into T$ at the average rate of exchange for 2016.

Write the e-mail requested by Pene Lopez, finance director.

Section 3

A number of months have passed. You arrive at work and read the following email.

From: Pene Lopez, Finance Director

To: Management Accountant Assistant

Subject: Variance report for wooden box hives for June—August 2017

Thomas has read the variance report for wooden box hives for the quarter June—August 2017 and has made the comment that the purchasing and production teams have some explaining to do. We know that the phenomenal success of the poly box hives has made a nonsense of our original budget for wooden hives, as sales have fallen and we have had to reduce production volumes. I don't think Thomas knows that we are still using the original budget to calculate variances. I have been sent the following comments from the purchasing and production managers.

Tracey Lines

I worked flat out with the poly hive suppler during the design stage. However, since the launch the work has been a challenge; firstly fixing teething problems and then having to collaborate to increase the volume of every order. The wood supplier relationships were neglected as there were simply not enough hours in the day to do all the work. We reduced the quantity of wood purchased from June onwards as it is clear that we will be making less wooden box hives in the future. Luckily the world price of cedar has fallen by 30% since February.

Ron Lomas

I have lost 14 of my most able staff this year to a business making bespoke garden furniture! I have replaced some of them with trainees but they are not up to speed yet. I have restricted their work to pine box hive production where they can do least damage. The experienced staff are unhappy at the moment as it is obvious to everyone that the demand for wooden hives is falling. There has been no opportunity to work overtime this peak period and as the annual pay increase is not due until next month, they are missing the money.

I have attached a copy of the variances that I need to explain to Thomas. As Cormac is on leave please draft and email me the following:

- An explanation of the likely causes of the variances in light of the managers' comments above.
- The advantages and disadvantages to us of splitting variances into their planning and operational components, together with an explanation of the usefulness of this split to evaluate and control management performance.

There is no need to recalculate any of the variances.

Pene Lopez
Finance Director
Mavis Venderby

Variance Report for Wooden Box Hives for the Quarter June—August 2017

Production

	Cedar box hives	Pine box hives
Budgeted production (units)	3,000	2,500
Actual production (units)	2,500	1,400

Variances

Variance	Cedar box hives(T$)	Pine box hives(T$)	Notes
Material price—wood	2,190 FAV	1,500 ADV	All inventorics arc valued at standard cost. Cedar was purchased for T$ 18. 20 and pine for T$ 9. 30 per metre
Material usage—wood	5,550 ADV	8,460 ADV	
Labour rate—cutting	6,080 FAV	16,200 FAV	Average hourly rates paid were T$ 16. 70 for cedar hives and T$ 14. 00 for pine hives
Labour efficiency—cutting	1,700ADV	1,450 ADV	

Write the email requested by Pene Lopez, finance director.

Section 4

It is now September 2017 and you receive the following email.

From: Pene Lopez, Finance Director

To: Management Accountant Assistant

Subject: Break-even and financial statements

This morning, there was a senior management meeting where the latest management accounts and the draft financial statements for last year(the year ended 28 February 2017) were discussed.

At the meeting, the poly hive success was applauded, and I made the point that our wooden and poly hives affect our business profitability in different ways. Thomas asked for further information regarding this. I have prepared an analysis, using our budget for the year ended 28 February 2018, showing the effects of the poly hives on our business' breakeven in response to this, but have not done any more yet.

Since the meeting I have had two emails. Firstly, Jacinta told me that a customer went into liquidation this morning(she has just received confirmation). This customer bought 200 hives from us in January 2017 and the debt is pan of the receivables balance at year end. I was surprised that this customer hadn't already paid us. Secondly, Thomas has suggested that we change the way that we value inventory in the financial statements. He wants us to use LIFO, FIFO or weighted average instead of standard cost. He believes that, as there is inflation in the economy, this might save us having to pay so much corporate income tax.

I would like to circulate a briefing paper to all directors which addresses all of these issues. Please prepare a first draft to include an explanation of:

- Why the introduction of the poly hives has lowered our CIS ratio but caused our overall break-even point and margin of safety to increase? Please include comments on the implications for our business. There's no need to do any calculations.
- How the customer that has gone into liquidation will affect our financial statements for the year ended 28 February 2017? Are there any implications of this event for our receivables management?
- Should we change the inventory valuation method in our financial statements for the year ended 28 February 2017 as suggested by Thomas ? What is the potential impact if it is changed?

Pene Lopez

Finance Director

Mavis Venderby

Break-even analysis

	Original budget for year ended 28/2/2018 (no poly hives)	**Revised budget for year ended 28/2/2018 (with poly hives)**
Sales (number ot hives)	32,000	37,000
Sales (T$ 000)	12,200	13,580
Weighted average sales/contribution ratio	62%	57%
Break even sales	10,243	11,255
Margin of safety	16%	17%

Notes: There are no additional fixed costs incurred in the purchase and sale of poly hives.

Write the briefing paper requested by Pene Lopez, finance director.

试卷一

本次考试的结构如下：

序号	任务数	时间（分钟）
1	1	45
2	1	45
3	1	45
4	1	45

每个部分规定的时间可用于读题、组织和书写答案。

任务一

回到公司，你收到一封来自财务总监 Pene Lopez 的邮件。

发件人：财务总监 Pene Lopez
收件人：管理会计助理
主　题：聚苯乙烯盒式蜂箱

上星期，董事们正式决定开始销售聚苯乙烯盒式蜂箱。在起步阶段，我们不打算自主制造聚苯乙烯盒式蜂箱。我们准备与一家专业生产商合作，设计和生产高品质的产品，并把这些产品作为本公司的蜂箱出售。由于这种模式与我们的核心业务有很大分别，所以我们也特别关注此项业务，尤其是这一决定对我们木质盒式蜂箱所带来的负面影响。

最近，Thomas 出席了一个训练课程。在课程中，他学习了 Cousins（考辛斯）供应轮模型的五大辐条，分别为：能力与技能、业绩衡量、成本收益分析、关系和组织结构。他认为，这一模型能够帮助我们全面地考虑如何选择合适的聚苯乙烯盒式蜂箱供应商，以及如何有序开展准备工作。

然而，Jacinta 坚信推出聚苯乙烯盒式蜂箱不利于木质蜂箱的销售。这点我也十分赞同。由于需求的改变会影响我们的生产和采购，所以我们需要准确地预测一下木质盒式蜂箱未来的销量情况。在这方面我已经做了初步的工作。我运用回归分析法确定了趋势图，并区分了我们在不同季节中的不同数据。我把初步分析作为附件一并发给你。

希望你能够帮我撰写报告初稿，解释以下两件事，以便我能在本周后期提交给其他董事：

- 详细解释，如何运用 Cousins 的供应轮模型选择及保留聚苯乙烯盒式蜂箱的制造商。
- 运用浅显的语言解释一下附件中的趋势图和季节变化数据，并说明用简单线性回归法进行预测的局限性。

谢谢！

梅维斯·文德柏公司
财务总监
Pene Lopez

销量预测的初期工作

趋势

我制作的趋势图基于从彼得罗夫斯·海夫斯（Petroc Hives）公司得到的真实销售数据。Petroc Hives 公司位于 North Republic（北共和国），在 15 年前开始销售聚苯乙烯盒式蜂箱。我运用回归分析法确定了木质盒式蜂箱的销售趋势图。彼得罗夫斯·海夫斯公司和梅维斯·文德柏公司的规模差不多，且这些数据包括了他们在推出聚苯乙烯盒式蜂箱之后的头两年，木质盒式蜂箱的销量变化。

该趋势线为：

Y = 17 000 – 700Q

Y = 木质盒式蜂箱的总销量

Q = 季度数目（例如，在推出之后的第一个季度，Q = 1；在推出之后的第二个季度，Q = 2，以此类推。）

季节变化

以下的表格统计了梅维斯·文德柏公司多年来的数据资料，并运用乘法模型编制出季节变化数据。

季度	季节变化
Q1（3～5 月）	+60%
Q2（6～8 月）	+40%
Q3（9～11 月）	–60%
Q4（12～2 月）	–60%

请撰写财务总监 Pene Lopez 所要求的简报内容。

任务二

两星期后，你回到公司并发现在你桌上放着以下文件。

“蜜罐养蜂人论坛”讨论摘要

我准备在今年扩充我的蜂房，并决定购买 30 个聚苯乙烯盒式蜂箱。经过一番研究后，我决定从 Aches Hives（艾之思·海夫斯）公司购买蜂箱。虽然我对他们那薄薄的顶板略有意见，但事实上，对市场上的所有款式我都有不满之处。有的在组件上不能和我的木质蜂箱互相替换；有的则有我不想要的综合饲糖盒，或是屋顶并不合适。

我在养蜂场的聚会中得知，梅维斯·文德柏公司将会推出聚苯乙烯盒式蜂箱。既然我注定要为此花一笔钱，那么当然希望买到最好的。可否告诉我梅维斯·文德柏公司的聚苯乙烯盒式蜂箱何时推出呢?

Pene Lopez 召你到她的办公室，并说：

现在，大众似乎已经得知我们正准备推出自己品牌的聚苯乙烯盒式蜂箱。Thomas 希望我们在新蜂箱的设计、研发和发行上多投入精力。她建议我们组成多功能型的团队，以此取得最理想的效果。她认为，选取合适的供应商和适当的营销是两个成功的主要因素。

David Hand 已经编制了 6 家潜在供应商的资料。这些供应商都符合我们的质量标准，提供差不多的价格，而且有足够的供给能力以满足我们的生产（基于预算销售额），请你帮我研究一下附表中的资料，并回复邮件，就 6 家供应商做出分析。

同时，Jacinta 希望我们能设计一套营销组合方案，指出聚苯乙烯盒式蜂箱的市场营销与传统的蜂箱有何分别。当然我们会最重视价格策略，但可否就营销组合的其他角度也提出一些意见？请在回邮中分别以营销组合的四要素为题，提供你对聚苯乙烯盒式蜂箱的营销意见。

接着，Pene Lopez 把 David Hand 编制的附表交给你。

关于 6 家潜在供应商的资料

潜在供应商	供应商所在地	创立时间	截至 2016 年 12 月 31 日的年度收入（T$ 百万*）	授予该客户的一般信用期限（天）
供应商 A	Tucland	14 个月	4	60
供应商 B	North States（北州）	20 年	121	20
供应商 C	North Republic	9 年	65	30
供应商 D	Tucland	7 年	24	40
供应商 E	Hutland（赫之兰迪）	9 年	40	20
供应商 F	Tucland	2 年	20	40

* North States 的货币为 NS$，North Republic 的货币为 NR$，Hutland 的货币为 H$。附表中供应商 B、C 和 E 的收入已按照 2016 年的平均汇率换算至 T$。

请撰写财务总监 Pene Lopez 所要求的邮件内容。

任务三

几个月后，你收到以下的邮件。

发件人：财务总监 Pene Lopez

收件人：管理会计助理

主　题：2017 年 6~8 月木质盒式蜂箱的差异分析报告

Thomas 已经阅读了 2017 年 6 月至 8 月期间木质盒式蜂箱的差异作析报告，并希望采购团队与生产团队就差异做出解释。我们知道，聚苯乙烯盒式蜂箱的火爆使木质蜂箱的销量下降，我们也因此减少了它的生产量。这令我们原来的木质蜂箱预算变得不合理。我相信 Thomas 并不知道我们仍然使用原来的预算数据来计算差异。我收到了来自采购经理和生产经理的评论，内容如下。

Tracey Lines

在设计阶段，我已尽最大的努力和聚苯乙烯盒式蜂箱的供应商开展合作，但在推出该产品后，挑战仍源源不绝。首先，我们要解决修复初期的问题，其次就是要与他们商讨如何增加每一笔订单的订货数量。与此同时，由于没有充足的时间去处理所有事宜，我们忽略了与木材供应商的关系。因为我们预计木质盒式蜂箱将会减产，所以自 6 月开始，就减少了木材的订购数量。幸运的是，雪松木的国际价格自 2 月起下降了 30% 。

Ron Lomas

今年，我们有 14 位最能干的员工辞职了，改为从事定制花园家具的工作。我把他们的部分工作分配给学徒，但学徒们的工作速度较慢。由于松木盒式蜂箱在生产上的损坏率较低，所以我只分配学徒们去生产松木盒式蜂箱。另外，因为木质蜂箱的需求正在下降，较有经验的员工在生产高峰期内均失去了可以加班的机会，再加上本年度的加薪下个月才进行，所以现在很不满意。

附表是我将要向 Thomas 解释的差异分析。由于 Cormac 正在放假中，所以请你帮我准备以下两部分的内容：

- 一是就以上两位经理的评论，解释为何出现差异；
- 二是阐述把差异分拆为计划差异和运营差异的好处和坏处，并解释该分拆对管理绩效的评估和控制有何作用。

你并不需要再进行任何差异计算。

梅维斯·文德柏公司
财务总监
Pene Lopez

2017 年 6 ~8 月木质盒式蜂箱的差异分析

生产

	雪松盒式蜂箱	松木盒式蜂箱
预算生产量（单位）	3 000	2 500
实际生产量（单位）	2 500	1 400

差异

差异	雪松盒式蜂箱（T$）	松木盒式蜂箱（T$）	备注
直接材料价格——木材	2 190 有利差异	1 500 不利差异	所有存货均运用标准成本法来计价。雪松的成本价格为每米 T$ 18. 20，松木的成本价格则为每米 T$ 9. 30。
直接材料用量——木材	5 550 不利差异	8 460 不利差异	
直接人工价格——切割	6 080 有利差异	16 200 有利差异	雪松蜂箱的平均人工价格为每小时 T$ 16. 70，松木蜂箱的平均人工价格则为每小时 T$ 14. 00。
直接人工效率——切割	1 700 不利差异	14 450 不利差异	

请撰写财务总监 Pene Lopez 所要求的邮件内容。

任务四

现在是2017年9月。你收到一封来自Pene Lopez的邮件。

发件人：财务总监Pene Lopez
收件人：管理会计助理
主　题：盈亏平衡和财务报表

今早，管理阶层召开了会议。他们在会议中讨论了最新的管理报告以及截至2017年2月28日的年度财务报表初稿。

在会议中，我们都为聚苯乙烯盒式蜂箱的成功而感到高兴。与此同时，我指出木质蜂箱和聚苯乙烯盒式蜂箱对利润的影响是不同的。Thomas希望我就此提供有关的资料。我对截至2018年2月28日的年度预算进行了非常初步的分析，说明了聚苯乙烯盒式蜂箱对我们盈亏平衡的影响。

会议过后，我收到两封邮件。第一封是来自Jacinta的。她刚确认了有一位客户在今早已进入了清盘阶段。该客户在2017年1月购买了200个蜂箱，而未缴付的金额则包括在年底的应收账款内。奇怪的是，为何该客户仍未缴付全额？第二封则来自Thomas。他建议我们改变存货在财务报表中的计价方法，由标准成本法改为后进先出法、先进先出法或加权平均成本认列法。他认为，在通货膨胀的情况下，此改动能帮助我们缴纳较少的企业所得税。

我打算写一份简报来处理这些问题，并将其提交给所有董事。请替我准备简报的初稿，并解释以下问题。

- 为什么在推出聚苯乙烯盒式蜂箱后，我们的销售贡献率下降，而整体的盈亏平衡点和安全边际却上升？请分析此现象对我们的意义，你不需要做任何计算。
- 该客户进入清盘阶段后，对我们截至2017年2月28日的财务报表有什么影响？这事件对我们的应收账款管理有什么启示？
- 我们应否听从Thomas的建议，改变我们在截至2017年2月28日的财务报表中存货的计价方法？该计价方法改变后，又会有怎样的影响？

梅维斯·文德柏公司
财务总监
Pene Lopez

盈亏平衡分析

	截至 2018 年 2 月 28 日 原本的年度预算 （未推出聚苯乙烯蜂箱）	经修改后截至 2018 年 2 月 28 日的年度预算 （推出聚苯乙烯蜂箱）
蜂箱的销售数量（单位）	32 000	37 000
销售额（T$ 000）	12 200	13 580
加权平均销售贡献率（%）	62	57
盈亏平衡数	10 243	11 255
安全边际（%）	16	17

注：在购买及售卖聚苯乙烯蜂箱的过程中，公司并未产生额外的固定成本。

请撰写财务总监 Pene Lopez 所要求的简报内容。

Variant 1　Suggested Answers

Section 1

Strategic Supply Wheel and Forecasting Report

Cousin's Strategic Supply Wheel

Competences and Skills

We at Mavis Venderby are skillful at producing and retailing wooden hives. However, our knowledge of polystyrene hives is limited, therefore in our search for the right supplier, we need to recognise our need to fill our knowledge gap with external experts. The supplier chosen will need to have good communication skills as we will need to work collaboratively to produce the best design and manage future supply chain issues.

Performance Measures

These are the metrics by which we monitor the success of the supply strategy. At Mavis Venderby we already have in place a number of tactical measures, such as lead time and reject rate. As with all agency transactions, the need to build trust is paramount. We would need to find further appropriate quality control checks to ensure our brand and reputation are not tarnished by sub-standard poly hives.

Cost/Benefit

In choosing a new supplier, our primary concern must be quality and expertise. Therefore we need to focus on the benefits a specialist manufacturer will bring to our portfolio. The cost is a secondary concern, however, it must be calculated and a viability study performed to ensure the long-term success of our business.

Relationships

This symbiotic relationship between us and the manufacturer means in Cousin's term our relationship would need to be "collaborate" rather than "competitive". We would need to see our suppliers as partners, working together to achieve long-term success. We already have a great long-term working relationship with our wood suppliers, however this time, we would have to go even further and collaborate on the design and manufacture stages.

Organisational Structure

It is important that supply management can work cross functionally as a team. At Mavis Venderby, it is important that we do not be stuck in our functional silos to damage the success of our overall strategy. For example, consideration of suppliers from a financial perspective may prefer a particular supplier whereas Tracey may prefer a supplier that will despatch a special order quickly. The decision to choose a sole supplier of poly hives will require a project like approach.

Forecasting

The Trend Line

The regression line Y = 17,000 − 700Q, is the trend line for Petroc Hives. It is based on observations of past sales to model the relationship between Y, the total number of wooden hives sold and Q, the time period (which in this case is quarters).

17,000 represents the number of wooden box hives sold in the base year, that is, the year before Petroc Hives sold poly hives. This represents a size of demand close to our own at Mavis Venderby, which suggests that we can expect similar results.

−700Q means that for every three month period (quarter) that Petroc Hives traded, the demand for wooden hives fell, on average, by 700 hives.

Given the similarity of our businesses, we can use this relationship to forecast what will happen to our wooden hives sales once we start to sell poly hives.

Seasonal Variation

We are a seasonal business and make most of our sales in March to July. Therefore in addition to our trend line, which is at its most simple, just an average sales figure, we need to adjust for differences due to the time of year.

Q_1 is the first quarter of the financial year and sales are likely to be 60% above the average (trend). As Q_2, the second quarter of the financial year, is less busy sales, being only 40% above the average (trend).

For our business, the multiplicative method is more useful than the additive as our seasonal variation is proportionate to our total sales. So for example, if our annual sales are down due to, for example, poor weather, the proportion of seasonal variation is likely to remain constant.

Limitations

The simple regression assumes linearity, in that there is a linear relationship between time and the fall in volume sales of wooden box hives. Using this assumption, we will sell no wooden box hives at all after approximately six years of poly hive sales. While this is possible, it is unlikely.

Linear regression is based on past sales. The assumption is that the trend will continue in the future as it has in the past. This is not a safe assumption particularly as we are basing the trend on only two years' sales data.

We are also assuming that the buying pattern of beekeepers in the North Republic will be replicated by the beekeepers of Tucland and also that data which is 15 years old is still relevant. This may not be the case as perhaps the climate in the North Republic is colder than in Tucland or the technology that produces poly hives may have advanced and become more desirable.

Section 2

From: Management Accountant Assistant

To: Pene Lopez, Finance Director

Subject: Supplier selection and marketing mix

Assessment of The Six Potential Suppliers

Financial Stability

We have only two indicators of financial stability: the size of the revenue and the time that the supplier has been trading. The revenue of each of the suppliers can indicate an ability to survive in the short to medium term. The revenue of supplier A is the smallest of all the suppliers under consideration. The smaller the revenue, the greater proportion of their business will be taken up by our orders. On this basis, supplier A is by far the riskiest choice.

The most likely time for a business to cease trading is in the months following start-up. In this category, it is once again supplier A that would be the least stable as they have only been trading for a little over a year. supplier F has also only traded for a short period of time.

Location and Currency

From a financial perspective, it is easier to trade with suppliers A, D and F as they operate within Tucland, which means that we will receive and pay invoices in T$. suppliers B, C and E will invoice in their own currency and we will have to consider the currency risk of using them as suppliers. In addition, it will be less easy to pay suppliers in a foreign currency, which could lead to problems with payment and additional administration.

Different locations also have implications for lead times. The closer a supplier is to us, the easier it is to manage inventory and to limit the environmental damage caused by transporting goods. Furthermore, if we import abroad, we may have to pay import duties or higher delivery charges which would increase the cost of the goods.

Credit Terms

The schedule shows that supplier A is offering the best terms at 60 days, however, we should be wary of choosing supplier A for the reasons already listed. The second best are suppliers D and F and, although 40 days is much shorter than we currently receive from our wood supplier, they are the best available. supplier D would appear the best option of the two as they have slightly larger revenues and have been trading for longer. We should also consider though whether there are prompt payment discounts on offer; as this will reduce these standard terms potentially.

Similarly, there may be bulk discounts available for larger orders. Although larger orders will increase our inventory holding costs (such as the cost of financing inventory, insurance and store management) as a seasonal business, we might find that a bulk discount benefit could outweigh the cost. The availability of discounts needs further investigation.

The Marketing Mix

Product

Obviously our products are hives, but we need to consider the features of a poly hive that makes it more attractive to our customers. The extract from the Honeypot Beekeepers' Forum was probably written by a commercial beekeeper (given the volume of hives ordered) who can value a product where honey bees can enjoy an ideal environment for producing as high a honey yield as possible. The poly hive is made from a material that, due to its insulating properties, makes it easier for the bees to regulate the internal temperature, being less draughty and waterproof. In other words, better for honey yield than wooden hives. In addition, the poly hive will not rot, which will mean less time and expense spent on maintenance. This will mean a better financial yield.

It is also important that the poly hive is designed in order that the parts are interchangeable with the wooden hives that we sell. Few beekeepers (hobby or commercial) will want to replace their entire hive stock in one go.

Price

We have always priced our hives using a cost plus approach. However in the minds of our customers, the price of a poly hive will have a benchmark which is the price of a wooden hive. In effect it is likely that if the price of a poly hive rises then the customer will switch to a wooden hive and vice versa. To this extent, the price that we charge for a poly hive will be anchored with the price of a wooden hive. As our market is quite competitive, the prices that we charge are probably going to be influenced by what our competitors are charging. The going rate price will influence our price to some extent but if we can differentiate our poly hives, in terms of a superior design or brand we will be able to sell at a higher price.

We have been able to charge a premium price for our wooden hives because of our strong brand name. It is likely that we will be able to charge a premium price for our poly hive for the same reason. As usual, commercial beekeepers are likely to buy in bulk and suitable discount can be available to them for this.

Promotion

We will promote the poly hive in the same way that the wooden hives are promoted, via the national beekeeping magazines, through local beekeeping and bee farming associations as trade shows and of course through the website. The poly hive is a new product with different attributes to the wooden hives. In the early months of the lifecycle of the poly hive, customers are likely to need more help and guidance than they need for the established wooden versions. Our sales staff must be able to give this advice.

Place

Our poly hives will be sold via the website and also through our shop. In the shop, they will need to be displayed assembled at the side of our wooden hives. At our premises, we have a number of bee colonies. The presence of a poly hive and the resulting evidence of a bumper honey crop will aid promotion. We will also need to ensure that the poly hives have prominence on our website.

Many Thanks!

Management Accountant Assistant

Mavis Venderby

Section 3

From: Management Accountant Assistant

To: Pene Lopez, Finance Director

Subject: Cause of variance and planning variance and operational variance

Variances

Materials

The cedar price variance is marginally favourable, which means that we bought cedar at less per metre than the original standard set in February 2017. However, as the world price for cedar has fallen by almost a third since this standard was set, a much more favourable variance could be expected. In effect, the world cedar price drop masked an adverse variance. This operational variance may be a result of the lack of contact between Tracey and the suppliers during the time when she had to work almost exclusively with the poly hive suppliers, it is possible lower prices need negotiating.

This pine price variance is adverse as we paid more for a metre than standard. This is probably due to the loss of bulk purchase discounts as we will buy less wood if we are making less hives.

Usage is adverse for both the pine and the cedar hives, which means that we are using more wood for each hive built than standard. The pine usage can be explained by the fact that all of the new trainees have been working on the pine box production and they are more likely to make mistakes and errors. The adverse usage on the cedar hives is likely to be due to the poor staff motivation. The cutting staff may be worried about the possibility of losing their jobs as it is obvious that the demand for wooden hives is falling.

Labour

The pine rate variance is favourable as this is where we employed sixtrainees. All trainees are paid a basic T$9 per hour not the full T$17 per hour until they complete their six-month probationary period. The weighted average hourly will have reduced as the lower paid trainees have replaced the more expensive experienced staff on the pine box hives. The cedar rate variance is less favourable than the pine and is probably due to the fact that the annual pay rise has not yet been awarded.

The pine labour efficiency variance is due to the high proportion of trainee workers working on this product. As they are not yet fully trained, they take longer than standard to manufacture a hive and they are more likely to make sub-standard hives. The reason cedar box hive adverse efficiency variance is less clear, but possibly due to the motivational issues as discussed above.

Planning and Operational Variances

Advantages and Disadvantages

A planning variance is caused by differences between the revised standard cost of actual output and the original standard cost of actual output, whereas the operational variance is caused by differences between the actual costs and the revised standard cost of actual output.

Standards are usually based on the environment which is anticipated when they are set. We produced the current standard cost card during January and February this year, using the information available to us at that time. We could not have anticipated the world cedar price fall that has happened since. If we split our variances into planning and operational, this price fall would be categorised as a planning variance. Splitting the variances is useful when factors in the environment change unexpectedly.

The information used in setting the ex-post standards can be used in future budget periods, making them more accurate and therefore more useful for performance appraisal and control. For example, the material price variance was calculated on a standard price that assumed that the demand for wooden hives required more wood to be purchased than the previous year. In fact, the volume of wood purchased is likely to be lower than the previous year and so it is likely that bulk purchase discounts will be lost and the price of wood higher. Therefore the standard does not reflect true performance. When we set the standard for the next year, we will factor this into the standard rate we establish.

The division of variances into planning and operational elements can be subjective. The mix of trainees during this quarter could be argued to be a normal variation with our usual operations or an abnormal "blip" caused by the garden furniture manufacturer paying much higher wages. Managers will want to argue this point depending on their own perspective, and this can lead to conflicts within the business.

Finally the re-working of variances into their planning and operational elements is a time consuming process, which will rely on good analysis skills. However, we have limited resources within the finance function to deal with this.

Management Performance

Managers should only be held responsible for factors that are within their control. As our managers had no control over the reduced demand for wooden hives, it is unfair to appraise their performance on the fact that they have produced less hives. In this case, splitting the variances into the planning and operational elements would have been useful. On the contrary, it would be misleading not to split the variances, as detailed above.

When actual performance is compared with a standard that is up to date and takes account of any changed conditions, it provides a more meaningful measure of managerial performance. This can mean that a manager is not blamed or indeed praised for factors that they have not influenced. For example, Tracey should not be rewarded for a favourable cedar price variance. This means that these variances are more motivational as they are more equitable.

The use of planning variances will allow us to assess how effective our planning process has been. Where a revision of standards is required due to environmental changes that were not foreseeable at the time the budget was prepared, the planning variances are uncontrollable. However, standards that failed to anticipate known market trends when they were set will reflect faulty standard setting. As the standards were set not long before the start of the new financial year, perhaps the fall in world cedar price should have been anticipated.

Many Thanks!

Management Accountant Assistant
Mavis Venderby

Section 4

Breakeven and Financial Accounting Treatment-report

Breakeven Analysis

Breakeven Point

The breakeven point is higher when poly hives are included, meaning that we need a higher level of sales to cover our fixed costs in order to breakeven. The reason that the break-even point is higher is because the weighted average C/S ratio has fallen as a result of increasing the sales of poly hives.

The weighted average C/S ratio with the inclusion of the poly hives is lower because we will be making a higher contribution margin on those products that we make in-house than the poly hive which we buy in. It is reasonable to expect a lower contribution margin for the poly hives as all of the costs are variable costs whereas the wooden hives have a high proportion of fixed costs. We are adding less value to the poly hive than we do to the raw materials that we purchase.

It is also possible that our weighted average C/S ratio is lower with the inclusion of poly hives because we will make less wooden hives which means that we buy less materials and may lose any bulk purchase discount. This will increase our cost and reduce the contribution margin.

Margin of Safety

The margin of safety is higher with the inclusion of poly hives, meaning that the gap between our budgeted sales and breakeven sales is bigger than without poly hives. This is because of our overall sales increase. In effect we gain more customers (sales) overall if we sell poly hives.

Business Implications

Overall the increase of the breakeven point increases our business risk as we have to make more sales to cover our fixed costs. However, the risk is offset to some extent by the increased margin of safety, as this shows that we are achieving higher levels of sales.

The poly hive business is purely variable cost based and it could be useful for us to investigate other outsourcing opportunities. As there is no additional fixed cost incurred in the purchase and sales of poly hives, every additional poly hive that we sell will generate contribution and profit. However, in reality it is likely that the sales of poly hives will have some incremental fixed costs.

Customer in Liquidation

IAS 10: Events after the reporting date, states that where there is evidence that a condition existed at the reporting period date and the financial statements have not yet been approved by the director, those financial statements should be adjusted to reflect the change.

Although the customer was not declared insolvent until many months after the reporting period date of 28 February 2017, the debt owed relates to sales made in the year leading up to that date. Within our draft financial statements for the year ended 28 February 2017, there is a receivable balance for this customer(the conditions) and we now have evidence that this money is not going to be collected. In accordance with IAS 10, this is an adjusting event.

In terms of the impact on our financial statements, we will need to reduce the receivables balance by the amount that the customer owes and debit the irrecoverable debt expense in the statement of profit or loss(which will increase administrative expenses).

The implication of this for our receivables management is that we need to ensure that we review all receivables balances(both at 28 February 2017 and now) for any other amounts that might not be recovered. This debt has been outstanding for many months and it was a surprise that it had not been paid. Possibly as a result of all the changes to the business and the increased workload regarding credit customers, monitoring of receivables balances has been ignored. We need to ensure that an aged receivables report is prepared, reviewed and acted on regularly.

Changing Inventory Valuation Method

IAS 2: Inventories allows the weighted average and FIFO methods to value inventory but not LIFO.

IAS 8: Accounting Policies, Changes in Accounting Estimates and Errors, states that a change of this nature is a change in accounting policy, which if allowed would require a retrospective adjustment to the financial statements. This means that we would have to restate the inventory value using the weighted average or FIFO method for the comparatives in the financial statements as well as the opening position in retained earnings.

The impact of changing to the FIFO method of valuation on the financial statements would increase the recorded value of the inventory at the year end. The weighted average method of valuation is likely to give a similar recorded value to the standard cost. The impact on profit will depend upon the opening inventory position(as this will also change). In any event, any profit differences are only temporary as the closing inventory for this February 2017 will be the opening inventory for the year ended 28 February 2018. In the long term, there is no tax benefit.

Changes in accounting policy are only permitted if required by a standard or if it results in the financial statements providing more reliable and more relevant information. We will need to assess if this is the case. Currently we use standard costs to value inventory in our financial statements and in accordance with IAS 2, these will need to be adjusted by a share of the variances at the year end to give an approximation of cost. If either FIFO or weighted average give us a better approximation for cost then it is possible that the auditors will agree this change.

One final point is that it is not ethical to manipulate profits in order to pay less taxation. Even if there was a tax benefit (which in the long term there isn't), this could be seen as tax avoidance, which although not illegal, is viewed negatively.

试卷一　参考答案

任务一

供应轮模型及有关预测报告

Cousins 的供应轮模型

能力与技能

梅维斯·文德柏公司能熟练地制造并出售木质蜂箱，但由于我们对聚苯乙烯蜂箱的认识有限，所以在选择供应商时，我们必须考虑到该供应商能否帮助我们弥补知识差距。该供应商需要具备良好的沟通技巧，使双方能紧密合作以生产出最好的产品，并解决未来在供应链上的问题。

业绩衡量

这些指标是我们监察采购策略成功与否的标准。梅维斯·文德柏公司已有不少战术衡量指标，如前导时间和废品率等。与其他代理业务一样，诚信是最重要的，所以在选择供应商时，我们要确定有合适的质量控制检查，以确保我们的品牌和声誉不会因不合规格的聚苯乙烯蜂箱而受到损害。

成本收益分析

在选择新的供应商时，我们的首要条件是质量和技术过硬，因此我们要注意该专业生产商能为我们的产品组合带来的益处是什么。虽然成本是次要的考虑因素，但我们仍要计算该产品的成本，并进行可行性研究，确保这业务长期成功。

关系

根据 Cousins 的论述，在建立我们与生产商相辅相成的关系时，需要的是彼此合作而不是互相竞争。我们需要视供应商为合作伙伴以实现长期的成功。我们已与木材供应商建立了长期的合作关系，但在设计与生产阶段，与供应商的合作需要我们付出更多努力。

组织结构

使供应管理以一个跨职能团队开展工作是十分重要的。在梅维斯·文德柏公司，我们不能让工作卡在一个职能部门而影响了整体策略的成功。比如说，在选择供应商时，若从财政的角度出发，会选择某一特定供货商；但 Tracey 或许会选择一家能够快速发货的供应商。选择单一的聚苯乙烯蜂箱供应商时，我们应基于项目的方法做决定。

预测

趋势图

附表中的回归线 $Y = 17\ 000 - 700Q$ 是 Petroc Hives 的趋势图。该回归线根据以往的销售量分析，得出 Y（代表木质蜂箱的总销量）和 Q（代表季度的数目）之间的关系。

17 000 代表了在基年（即在 Petroc Hives 开始售卖聚苯乙烯蜂箱之前的那一年）卖出的木质盒式蜂箱的数目。这一数目与梅维斯·文德柏公司的需求相近，所以我们预计会得出差不多的结果。

$-700Q$ 是指 Petroc Hives 开始售卖聚苯乙烯蜂箱后每三个月（即每一季）木质蜂箱的销售量平均减少 700 个。

基于我们与 Petroc Hives 的业务相近，我们可以用这一关系去预测当我们开始售卖聚苯乙烯蜂箱后，木质蜂箱的销售量将会受到怎样的影响。

季节变化

我们开展的是季节性的业务，销售高峰期是 3 月 ~7 月。由于该趋势图是基于最简单的平均销量，我们需要根据时间对该图做出调整。

Q_1是年度首季，其销量比平均水平多 60% 。Q_2为年度中的第二季，销量较少，只比平均水平多 40% 。

对于我们的业务，由于季节变化与总销售量成比变化，乘法模型比加法模型更为有效。比如说，如果我们的年度销量因天气原因而下降，季节导致的变化则可保持相对不变。

用简单线性回归法进行预测的局限性

简单回归模型假设了线性的关系，即是说我们假设时间和木质盒式蜂箱的销量下降存在着线性关系。这一假设意味着在推出聚苯乙烯蜂箱 6 年后，我们将卖不出任何木质盒式蜂箱。虽然有可能出现此情况，但可能性不高。

线性回归法用以往的销售数据做分析，这假设了以往的趋势在未来也会继续。这样的假设并不太周全，更别说我们只用了两年的数据。

我们假设 North Republic 养蜂人的购买模式和 Tucland 的相似，我们还假设了 15 年前的数据仍然有效。这些假设未必成立，因为 North Republic 的天气可能比 Tucland 寒冷，又或者技术的进步能更有效地生产聚苯乙烯蜂箱。

任务二

发件人：管理会计助理

收件人：财务总监 Pene Lopez

主　题：潜在供应商的分析和营销组合

6 个潜在供应商的分析

财务稳定性

在财务稳定性方面，我们只有两项指标，分别是收入多少和该供应商的创立时间。供应商的收入能表示他们在短期至中期内能否继续生存。供应商 A 在所有备选供应商中收入最少。收入越少，我们的订单占他们业务的比重便越高。从这个角度考虑，供应商 A 是风险最高的选择。

一家公司最有可能在刚创立的头几个月倒闭。供应商 A 只创立了一年多，所以它是最不稳定的，供应商 F 的创立时间也颇短。

所在地和货币

从财务上的角度出发，由于供应商 A、D 和 F 的所在地都是 Tucland，我们能够以 T$ 缴付账单，所以与他们进行交易比较方便。由于供应商 B、C 和 E 将会以他们自己的货币作为账单单位，我们在选择他们时需要考虑货币风险。再者，以外币来编付账单会带来付款和额外的行政问题，所以一般来说会比较困难。

供应商的所在地也会对前导时间产生影响。供应商与我们越近，就越容易管理存货，也越能减少运货对环境的损害。另外，如果选择从外国引进货品，我们有可能需要缴付进口税或更多的运费，所以存货成本也可能相应地增加。

信用期限

根据附表中的资料，供应商 A 授予的 60 日信用期限是最好的。但基于上述原因，我们对选择供应商 A 需提高警觉。供应商 D 和 F 均授予 40 日的信用期限。虽然此信用期限较我们当下与木材供货商所定下的期限少很多，但这已是最好的条款。在这两家供应商中，由于 D 的收入稍高而且创立时间更长，所以供应商 D 似乎是最佳选择。当然，我们要考虑这些供应商是否会授予提前付款折扣，因为这些折扣会间接降低标准信用期限。

同样的，供应商可能会提供批量采购折扣。虽然是季节性的业务，较大的订单会增加我们的库存持有成本（如存货融资成本、保险和存货管理等），但批量采购折扣带来的利益会超过成本，所以我们应进一步研究一下这项折扣的实用性。

营销组合建议

产品

显然，我们的产品是蜂箱，但我们需要思考如何令聚苯乙烯蜂箱更具市场吸引力。那篇“蜜罐养蜂人论坛”摘要的发布者，从他的订货数量来看，估计是商业养蜂人。他们相当重视产品能否给蜜蜂提供一个最好的环境去生产更多蜜蜂。用来制造聚苯乙烯蜂箱的物料有更好的绝缘性能，蜜蜂更容易控制巢内的温度，加上聚苯乙烯蜂箱通风性更强而且防水，所以蜂蜜产量会更多。另外，聚苯乙烯蜂箱不会腐烂，维护工作也更加容易，所以从金钱上来说是更划算的。

需要注意的是，在设计聚苯乙烯蜂箱时，要考虑其蜂巢组件与木质蜂箱的互换性。相信很少养蜂人（不论是养蜂爱好者或是商业养蜂人）会一次性把他们的蜂箱全换掉。

价格

我们一向用成本加成定价法来决定蜂箱的价格。可是，客户会以木质蜂箱的价格为基准来衡量聚苯乙烯蜂箱的价格。这样一来，若聚苯乙烯蜂箱价格上涨，客户就会转买木质蜂箱，反之亦然。因此，聚苯乙烯蜂箱的可定价格与木质蜂箱的价格息息相关。再者，由于市场竞争激烈，竞争对手的定价也会影响我们在这方面的决定，所以不得不考虑采用随行就市法定价。但如果我们能在设计或品牌上和市场上的聚苯乙烯蜂箱区别开来，定价则可以高一点。

基于我们的品牌优势，我们可以给木质蜂箱定一个较高的价格。同理，聚苯乙烯蜂箱的定价也可以稍高一点儿。另外，商业养蜂人通常会批量采购，我们也可以如往常一样给予他们一个合理的折扣。

促销

木质蜂箱和聚苯乙烯蜂箱的促销手法一样，都是通过国家的养蜂杂志和本地的养蜂协会商展以及网站促销。聚苯乙烯蜂箱是新产品，它与木质蜂箱的特色不同，所以在售卖初期，客户可能需要更多的辅助和指导。我们的销售人员必须提供这方面的指引。

分销

我们的聚苯乙烯蜂箱将会通过网站和门店进行销售。在门店内，聚苯乙烯蜂箱会放置在木质蜂箱附近。在我们的工厂内有很多蜂群，如果我们放置一个装满蜜糖的聚苯乙烯蜂箱作为样品，会有利于产品的推广。同时，我们需要在自己的网站中重点突出聚苯乙烯蜂箱。

十分感谢！

梅维斯·文德柏公司

管理会计助理

任务三

发件人：管理会计助理

收件人：财务总监 Pene Lopez

主　题：差异原因及计划差异和运营差异

差异

材料

雪松的价格差异为轻微的有利差异，意思是相比起在 2017 年 2 月定下的标准价格，我们可以用更便宜的价格购入单位长度的雪松木材。可是，在定下标准价格后，雪松的国际价格下降了差不多三分之一。我们估计这会带来更大的有利差异。事实上，价格下降掩盖了不利差异。此项运营差异可能是因为 Tracey 差不多把所有时间都放在聚苯乙烯蜂箱的供应商上而忽略了木材供应商。如果我们想降低木材价格，采购部需要与供应商进一步洽谈。

松木的价格差异为不利差异。我们购买单位长度松木的价格比标准价格高。这是由于我们的木质蜂箱生产量下降，购入松木的数量有所减少，所以我们失去了批量采购的折扣优势。

雪松蜂箱和松木蜂箱的材料用量差异都是不利差异，这意味着我们制造蜂箱的实际木材用量比标准用量多。一方面，由于我们分配了学徒去生产松木盒式蜂箱，而他们的犯错率较高，所以松木的用量增多。另一方面，因为木质蜂箱需求正在下降，切割工人可能会担心失去工作，在缺乏激励的情况下，雪松木的用量也多了。

人工

松木蜂箱的人工价格差异为有利差异。我们分配学徒生产松木盒式蜂箱，在学徒试用期内，其固定工资为每小时 T$ 9。学徒取代了全职员工，而全职切割员工的工资为每小时 T$ 17，所以平均来说，每小时支付的工资减少了。雪松蜂箱的有利人工价格差异比松木蜂箱的少，这可能是因为本年度的加薪还没有进行。

松木蜂箱的人工效率差异是因为在这个项目上我们分配了学徒去完成。由于他们对生产过程还不熟练，犯错率更高，所以实际耗用的工时较标准工时长。至于雪松蜂箱的不利人工效率差异的原因则不太明显，可能与上述的激励因素有关。

把差异分拆为计划差异和运营差异两部分

好处和坏处

计划差异的产生源于修正后的实际产出标准成本与原本的实际产出标准成本之间的差额。运营差异则是源于实际成本与修正后的实际产出标准成本之间的差额。

标准通常基于可预计的情况而设定。我们在今年的 1 月和 2 月定下了标准，并利用当时的信息制定了标准成本卡。彼时，我们无法预测到雪松木的国际价格会下降。如果我们把差异分拆为计划差异和运营差异，那么这一价格下降将归纳为计划差异。当环境因素在不可预计的情况下发生改变，那么差异分拆是一个比较好的选择。

在编制预算时，我们可以利用制定事后标准的信息来使预算变得更准确，同时，使绩效评估和控制变得更为有效。比如说，直接材料价格差异是根据木质蜂箱较去年需求增长而购买更多木材计算得出的。但实际上，由于推出聚苯乙烯蜂箱，我们较去年木材采购量减少了，不能再享受批量采购的优惠，所以木材价格有所上升。因此，已定下的标准并不能反映真实的绩效。在制定下一年的标准时，我们应把这一因素考虑在内。

把差异分拆为计划差异和运营差异的过程是很主观的。在本季度把工作分配给学徒可以说是一项正常的变动，但同时也可以说是一项由于花园家具生产商提供更高薪水导致员工离职而发生的突发变动。经理们可能从他们自己的角度出发来发表意见，因而容易产生内部冲突。

最后，把差异分拆为计划差异和运营差异十分费时，而且需要良好的分析技巧。对此，我们的财务团队只具备有限的资源。

管理绩效

经理只需要为他们能够控制的因素负责。由于我们的经理并不能控制木质蜂箱需求的减少，所以如果以蜂箱生产量降低来评估绩效的话对他们是不公平的。在此情况下，把差异分拆为计划差异和运营差异有利于问题解决。反之，根据以上所述，不把差异分拆则会令人产生误解。

当把实际情况与最新的已考虑环境变动的标准做比较时，管理绩效便能更有效地做出评估。这能够确保经理们不会因为他们不能控制的因素而受到责备或表扬。比如，Tracey 不应因为雪松蜂箱的有利价格差异而得到奖赏。在此情况下，差异分析才会更具激励性和公平性。

使用计划差异能够帮助我们评估规划是否有效。如果我们在编制预算时不能预计环境的变动而需要对标准做出修改，那么该计划差异是不能控制的。但如果在制定标准时未能把已知的市场趋势考虑在内，该标准则是错误的。由于标准在新财年开始前不久才定下，雪松木的国际价格下降趋势可以说是可预计到的。

十分感谢！

梅维斯·文德柏公司
管理会计助理

任务四

盈亏平衡及财务会计事宜简报

盈亏平衡分析

盈亏平衡点

聚苯乙烯蜂箱的推出提高了我们的盈亏平衡点。这意味着我们需要增加销量来覆盖固定成本，保持盈亏平衡。盈亏平衡点的提升是因为聚苯乙烯蜂箱的收入上升导致了加权平均销售贡献率下降。

在推出聚苯乙烯蜂箱后，我们的加权平均销售贡献率下降了。因为相比于我们直接购入的聚苯乙烯蜂箱，自行制造的产品边际贡献较高。聚苯乙烯蜂箱的成本全部是变动成本，而木质蜂箱的成本大部分都是固定成本，所以我们可以合理地认为聚苯乙烯蜂箱的边际贡献较低。相比起我们购买材料再加工制造，购入成品的聚苯乙烯蜂箱的附加价值较低。

除了以上原因外，加权平均销售贡献率在推出聚苯乙烯蜂箱后有所下降可能是因为木质蜂箱生产量减少，所以购入的材料自然也少了。我们失去了批量采购的折扣优势而导致成本上升，边际贡献也因而下降。

安全边际

聚苯乙烯蜂箱的推出提升了我们的安全边际。这意味着相比还没推出聚苯乙烯蜂箱前，销售预算和盈亏平衡销量的差距加大了。这是由于推出聚苯乙烯蜂箱之后，我们的客户多了，整体的销售额也增加了。

对业务的影响

整体来说，盈亏平衡点的上升意味着我们需要增加销量来覆盖固定成本。这提高了我们的商业风险。但与此同时，销量提升也能使安全边际上升，所以这在某种程度上抵消了上述的商业风险。

聚苯乙烯蜂箱的业务完全是基于变动成本的，我们也可以考虑一下其他的外包机会。由于在采购和销售聚苯乙烯蜂箱的过程中并没有产生额外的固定成本，所以每卖出一个额外的聚苯乙烯蜂箱都会带来贡献和利润。可是事实上，销售聚苯乙烯蜂箱很可能会产生一些额外的固定成本。

客户进入清盘阶段

国际会计准则第 10 号：报导期间后事项指出于报导期间结束日至通过发布财务报表日间，若发生的事项在报导期结束日之情况提供了佐证，该公司需要调整认列于财务报表之金额，以反映报导期间后调整事项。

虽然该客户在报导期间之后几个月才进入清盘阶段，但未缴付的金额来自 2017 年 2 月 28 日前的销售。在截至 2017 年 2 月 28 日的年度财务报表初稿中，该客户的未缴付金额仍然包括在年底的应收账款内，然而现在有证据证明该笔款项并不能收回，根据国际会计准则第 10 号，此事项应当作报导期间后调整事项。

从财务报表的角度来说，我们需要把该笔未缴付金额从应收账款中扣除。同时，坏账费用会使损益表中的管理费用上升。

从应收账款管理的角度来说，这件事使我们明白，我们需要检阅一下所有于报导期末和现在的应收账款，并决定能否收回账款。若某债务已未付多时，而我们仍然对该客户未缴付金额感到意外，可能是由于业务上的改变和赊户带来的工作量导致我们疏忽了应收账款的监控。我们必须定期准备并检阅应收账款分析报表，并对此采取适当的措施。

存货计价方法的改变

国际会计准则第 2 号：存货允许采用先进先出或加权平均成本公式分配存货的成本。企业不可以使用以后进先出的成本分配方法。

国际会计准则第 8 号：会计政策、会计估计变动及错误，此改变属于会计政策变动，所以在许可的情况下，企业应在财务报表中采用追溯适用的方法。据此，我们需要采用加权平均法或先进先出法来调整存货成本的比较数字和留存收益的初始余额。

采用先进先出法分配存货成本会使我们在财务报表中已记录的年末存货上升。若采用加权平均法分配存货的成本的话，所得出的成本与采用标准成本法计算出来的结果应该差不多。这一改变对盈利的影响则取决于期初存货。由于在2017年2月的期末存货会成为2018年2月28日的期初存货，所以在任何情况下，在盈利上的变化都只是短暂的。长远来说，这一改变并不会带来税务优惠。

企业若要变动其会计政策，必须符合以下条件之一：（1）财务报导准则要求改变；（2）这一改变能使财务报表提供更为可靠且更加重要的信息。我们需要就以上条件做出评估。当下我们采用标准成本法来计量存货成本。根据《国际会计准则第2号》，我们需要把年末的差异调至存货成本，使其结果接近成本，若采用先进先出或加权平均法能够提供更接近成本的结果，核数师可能会认同这一改变。

最后，通过操纵利润来减少税额是不道德的。即使能带来税务优惠（虽然长远来说并没有任何利益），但这一举动可能被认定为避税。虽然避税并不违法，但却会带来负面影响。

Variant 1　Marking Guidance

Section number	Technical skills		Business skills		People skills		Leadership skills		Integration	Total
1	Forecasting using linear regression	12	Cousin's Strategic Supply Wheel	3	Cousin's Strategic Supply Wheel	10				25
2	Supplier selection based on financial information	7	The Marketing Mix in respect of a new product	12	Supplier selection based on financial information	3			3	25
3	Reasons for direct raw materials variances and direct labour variances Planning and operational variances and performance evaluation	12 7					Planning and operational variances and performance evaluation	6		25
4	Breakeven analysis in respect of a change in product mix Impact in the financial statements of the liquidation of a customer Changing the inventory valuation method in the financial statements	9 8 8								25
Total marks available for each competency		63		15		13		6	3	100

试卷一　评分指南

序号	技术技能		商业技能		人际技能		领导技能		综合	合计
1	线性回归预测分析	12	Cousins 供应轮模型	3	Cousins 供应轮模型	10				25
2	利用财务资讯选择供应商	7	新产品的营销组合	12	利用财务资讯选择供应商	3			3	25
3	直接材料差异和直接人工差异的原因 计划差异、运营差异和绩效评估	12 7					计划差异、运营差异和绩效评估	6		25
4	产品结构改变后的盈亏平衡分析 客户进入清盘阶段对财务报表的影响 改变财务报表的存货计价方法	9 8 8								25
各技能评分合计		63		15		13		6	3	100

香港中文大学名师解惑

本套题目的案例主体是一家生产销售木制蜂箱的企业，名为 Mavis Venderby。试卷一共有四项任务，考查了 P1、F1、E1 三门课程的知识点。其中，以 P1（46）的知识点分数比重最高。其次是 F1（26），最后则是 E1（25）。这和 OCS 的考纲要求基本一致。该试卷考核了考生的四项能力，其中技术技能的分值占 63%，商业技能的分值占 15%，人际技能的分值占 13%，领导技能的分值占 6%，与 CGMA 管理会计能力框架的技能要求一致。考生在备考时应根据考试重点有所侧重。

该试卷的每项任务涉及以下知识点：

任务	问题	科目	知识点
任务一	Cousins 供应轮模型	E1	营运管理（operational management）
	线性回归预测分析	P1	预测方法（forecasting techniques）
任务二	利用财务资讯选择供应商	F1	财务资讯的运用（use of financial information）
	新产品的营销组合	E1	营销组合分析（elements of the Marketing Mix）
任务三	直接材料差异和直接人工差异的原因	P1	差异分析（variance analysis）
	计划差异、运营差异和绩效评估	P1	
任务四	产品结构改变后的盈亏平衡分析	P1	盈亏平衡分析（breakeven analysis）
	客户进入清盘阶段对财务报表的影响	F1	
	改变财务报表的存货计价方法	F1	国际会计准则的应用（IAS 10；IAS 2；IAS 8）

上述各项任务要求以邮件、报告或工作笔记等形式来呈现答案，对问题的描述非常明确，答题时既要注意内容的针对性，也要注意形式的规范性。

考前准备

背景资料是提前下发的，考生在阅读时，可以根据相关资料对考核范围做一些猜测。宏观来看，梅维斯·文德柏公司是一家生产企业。考生可从 E1，P1 和 F1 的知识点中抽取与生产企业有关的课题重点复习，例如，成本计算方法（P1）、预算方法和差异分析（P1）、瓶颈处理方法（E1）和存货管理（F1）等。

此外，由于背景资料的后半部分（尤其是那篇论坛摘要）提到聚苯乙烯蜂箱和木质蜂箱的区别，而梅维斯·文德柏公司并未销售聚苯乙烯蜂箱，因此也可以合理推测将会有涉及新产品的问题。新产品的营销策略（E1）应该是考核的一个主要内容。而聚苯乙烯蜂箱是木质蜂箱的代替品，新产品会影响现有产品的销量，所以有可能对新产品如何影响企业产品结构的知识点做出考核。在成本会计的层面来看，这一调整可能会改变企业的盈亏平衡点，考生应就此进行准备。

另外，梅维斯·文德柏公司是一家生产销售企业，从最近两年的资产负债表来看，存货均占了流动资产的70%以上，且该比例有上升的趋势。这当然与存货管理有关，但从财务会计的层面来推测，很有可能会有涉及存货计价方法的会计问题。最后需要注意的是，本套题目颇为重视技术技能，学生应对成本会计（P1）和国际会计准则（F1）的专业知识做出充足的准备。

对应知识点深度剖析

营运管理

营运管理是E1的知识点，而供应商关系则是营运管理其中的一环。供应商的选择对新产品来说尤其重要。在决定供应商时，企业要就多方面进行考量。Cousins的供应轮模型除了为企业进行多方面考量提供了一个框架之外，也能够帮助企业衡量其采购成熟度。

考生注意事项

Cousins供应轮模型的五大辐条：

（1）能力与技能：能否与供应商共享知识，能否对内部员工进行培训。

（2）业绩衡量：成本与订单的精确度、开发的速度以及企业责任等。

（3）成本收益分析：根据定价或战略协作因素确定采购。

（4）关系：供应商数量的多与少。

（5）组织结构：初级职能能否支持生产，高级职能能否参与战略决策。

考生除了要仔细了解以上五大辐条外，还要能够应用并陈述每项辐条对梅维斯·文德柏公司在选择新产品供应商时的影响。

预测方法

预测方法是P1的知识点。考生应对时间序列、趋势分析、回归分析和季节变化等预测技巧有充分的了解。本项考试要求考生对趋势图和季节变化做出简单阐述，考生无需进行计算。

财务资讯的运用

题目提供了 6 家供应商的资料，其中包括所在地、创立时间、年度收入、授予客户的信用期限、货币等信息。考生要充分利用这些资料，整合、分析，并针对供应商的选择提出意见。

营销组合分析

营销组合是企业市场营销战略的一个重要组成部分，其目的是使企业能够从整体上满足消费者的需要。本套试题要求考生替梅维斯 · 文德柏公司的新产品设计一套营销组合。

考生注意事项

营销组合包括：

（1）产品（product）：注重产品的功能和独特的卖点。

（2）价格（price）：市场定位、竞争对手所定的价格等。

（3）促销（promotion）：刺激消费者的购买欲以促进销售。

（4）分销（place）：建立销售网络（例如：门店销售、网上销售等）。

差异分析

差异分析是经营会计中的一大课题。简单来说，差异是计算实际绩效与预算绩效的偏差，而差异分析则是进一步分析这些差异并确定其原因的过程。差异主要分为不利差异（unfavourable variance）和有利差异（favourable variance）两大类。本套试题要求考生进行差异分析，并在无需计算的情况下，解释差异的原因。

考生注意事项

总成本差异包括：

（1）直接材料差异：①直接材料价格差异；②直接材料耗用量差异。

（2）直接人工差异：①直接人工价格差异；②直接人工效率差异。

（3）变动制造费差异。

（4）固定制造费差异。

盈亏平衡分析

盈亏平衡分析应用边际成本法，目的在于研究产量变化对利润造成的影响。与此相关的是销售贡献率。销售贡献率有助于企业根据营收来计算对固定成本的贡献。此外，还有安全边际。安全边际是预算作业水平和盈亏平衡作业水平之间的差异。

虽然本次考试并不需要考生进行以上计算，但考生需要解释其背后的意义。

考生注意事项

（1）盈亏平衡数 = 固定成本/单位贡献

（2）销售贡献率 = 固定成本/盈亏平衡收入

（3）安全边际 =（预算产量 - 盈亏平衡数）/预算产量

国际会计准则的应用

财务会计准则是 F1 的考试重点，而且涉及内容广泛。考生应充分准备，否则在考试时无法把相关知识应用在案例中。以本次考试为例，考生要明确客户进入清盘阶段这一事宜属于报导期间后事项，并以国际会计准则第 10 号：报导期间后事项作为依据进行分析。

考生注意事项

国际会计准则第 10 号：报导期间后事项

（1）报导期间结束日至通过发布财务报表日之间所发生的事，可分为两种类型：①报导期间后调整事项（adjusting event）；②报导期间后非调整事项（non-adjusting event）。

（2）报导期间后调整事项：对报导期间结束日之前发生的情况提供佐证的事项。

（3）报导期间后非调整事项：对报导期间之后发生的情况提供佐证的事项。

回答此类问题的一个困难之处，是财务会计准则的关联性。考生应指出相关的准则并结合问题灵活应用。比如，本次考试要求考生分析梅维斯·文德柏公司是否应该改变存货的计价方法，其中涉及国际会计准则第 2 号中的存货和国际会计准则第 8 号中的会计政策、会计估计变动及错误。缺少以上任何一项都会影响答案的全面性。

考生注意事项

国际会计准则第 2 号：存货的计价方法

（1）先进先出法（FIFO）；

（2）加权平均法（weighted average）。

后进先出法（LIFO）是不允许的。

考生注意事项

国际会计准则第 8 号：会计政策、会计估计变动及错误。

（1）会计政策的变动：采用追溯适用的方法（retrospective adjustment）。

（2）会计估计的变动于下列期间推延认列为损益：①变动当期；②变动当期及未来期间（prospective change）。

（3）错误：采用追溯适用的方法（retrospective adjustment）。

答题技巧

在答题时，一方面要有选择性地回答问题，避免把所有背诵过的知识点全写下；另一方面，要避免只是就教科书的知识点简单复述，而要结合案例公司的实际情况加以阐述。比如，在提出 Cousins 供应轮模型的五大辐条后，学生应结合公司的实际情况进一步展开分析。这一点也适用于营销组合的四大范畴。

最后，注意答题的措辞、格式、论述的结构完整性和论点的鲜明和整体性等。例如，在回答优缺点时，应用鲜明的标题，分点分行明确列出，这是综合分的得分点。

Variant 2

This examination is structured as follows：

Section number	Number of tasks	Time for section(minutes)
1	1	45
2	1	45
3	1	45
4	1	45

The time available for each section is for reading,planning and writing your answer(s).

Section 1

Today is 8 March 2017. On the night of 28 February 2017, there was a major storm and the roof on one of the storage buildings collapsed, damaging all of the cedar hive finished goods inventory and a fork-lift truck.

You arrive at work to find the following email from Pene Lopez, finance director:

From: Pene Lopez, Finance Director
To: Management Accountant Assistant
Subject: Storm damage

David Hand, Production Manager, has just given me a list of the items damaged by the storm last week. David believes that about half of the cedar hives are a complete write off but that, with some work, the balance can be made serviceable and sold, although at about half the price of a perfect hive. A fork-lift truck has also been damaged but, although badly dented and scratched, is still as safe and functional to use as before the storm.

All of the damaged cedar hive finished goods inventory had been included in our inventory count on 28 February 2017. Thomas wants to know how both the damage to the inventory and the fork-lift truck will be reflected in our financial statements for the year ended 28 February 2017.

Given that we now do not have any finished goods inventory of cedar hives, we need to produce as many cedar hives as we can. We have orders for 450 cedar box hives from important customers that must be shipped next week.

Before the storm, the production departments were working close to full capacity and there are only so many cutting and packing hours available. In addition, cedar is a particular problem as it takes so long to dry and we only have 2,800 metres of dried cedar available for immediate production. As there are so many variables to consider, I have used a linear programming graph to estimate our optimal production plan for cedar hives given our current resource constraints for dried cedar, cutting hours and packing hours.

Thomas Venderby, managing director, wants to know if it is worth buying in ready dried cedar, which is in plentiful supply. In addition, there are two staff members in packing and one in cutting who are willing to give up a day's planned leave to help. If we accepted their offer, we would have to pay for an extra ten hours for each member of staff.

I have meetings all day so I would like you to draft a briefing note for Thomas to explain.

- How the damage to the finished goods inventory and the fork-lift truck will affect our financial statements for the year ended 28 February 2017? Please make reference to the appropriate financial reporting rules.
- How we have used the linear programming graph to estimate our optimal production plan? Please also explain whether we should consider buying additional dried cedar and take up the offer of the three members of staff. There is no need to do any calculations at this stage.

Pene Lopez
Finance Director
Mavis Venderby

The Linear Programming Graph

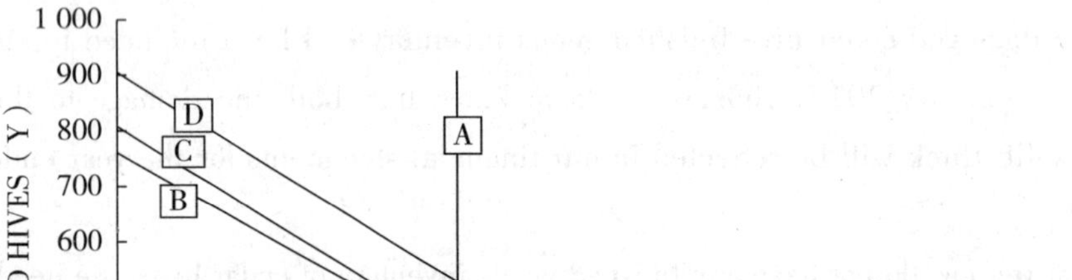

Notes：

X represents the number of cedar box hives produced and Y represents the number of cedar slatted hives produced.

Objective function is to maximise contribution（Z）

$Z = 231.98X + 279.71Y$

Subject to the constraints

Line A: $X \geq 450$

Line B (dried cedar): $2.8X + 3.7Y \leq 2,800$

Line C (cutting hours): $3X + 3.6Y \leq 2,900$

Line D (packing hours): $0.5X + 0.6Y \leq 540$

Optimal production plan

$X = 637, Y = 274$

Writing the briefing note required by Pene Lopez, finance director.

Section 2

Five weeks later, you receive the following email from Pene Lopez, finance director.

From: Pene Lopez, Finance Director
To: Management Accountant Assistant
Subject: Sales variance report and bonus scheme

After the damage to the cedar hives and resulting production issues in March, a number of issues have arisen.

The sales variances for the month are quite unlike anything we have seen before. I have decided to issue the other directors with a detailed report explaining the reasons for the sales variances; I would like your help with this.

In addition, there was a meeting earlier this week between a few representatives of the drying, cutting and packing departments and David Hand. The production workers believe that the bonus system that we have used for years is unfair. The workers were upset that they earned less bonus for March than they did earlier in the year when business was slower. David tells me that morale in the work shop is poor and that there is a high level of absenteeism this week. This contrasts quite sharply with the weeks after the storm when everyone pitched in; a few members of staff even cancelled annual leave to help out then.

As you know, we pay our drying, cutting and packing workers a bonus of T$ 1.00 for each cedar hive sold and T$ 0.20 for each pine hive sold. I have checked and it appears that the bonus for March was 24% lower than budgeted. I have read that a good bonus scheme should: (1) be motivational; (2) reward good performance; (3) be consistent and fair; (4) be in line with organisatlonal goals.

Please can you prepare draft sections for a report to the directors which explains:

- The sales variances (details of which are attached to this email) and the reasons for them. There is no need to explain how they are calculated.
- Whether our existing production worker bonus scheme achieves the four principles of a good bonus scheme, with suggestions of how it could be improved.

Many thanks!

Pene Lopez

Finance Director

Mavis Venderby

Sales Variances March 2017

Budgeted and Actual Sales Information

	Box cedar	Box pine	Slatted cedar	Slatted pine	Total
Budgeted sales units	2,000	1,400	1,800	1,200	6,400
Actual sales units	1,200	1,700	1,350	1,400	5,650
Standard selling price perunit(T$)	375. 00	290. 00	460. 00	380. 00	
Standard gross profit perunit(T$)	96. 08	71. 61	115. 68	112. 96	

Sales Variances

Variance type	Box cedar	Box pine	Slatted cedar	Slatted pine	Total
Sales price(T$)	0	25,500 A	0	28,000 A	53,500 A
Sales miX	1,881 F	12,898 A	3,891 A	4,617F	10,291 A
Sales quantity					74,554 A

Notes:

(1) In addition to the actual sales figures above 600 cedar hives that were damaged in the storm were sold for T$ 145,000. There was no bonus paid to the production workers for these sales.

(2) Pine hives were sold at a discounted price to those customers for whom we could not supply cedar hives due to the stock-outs.

(3) Sales quantity and mix variances are calculated on a weighted average basis at budgeted gross profit per hive.

(4) The standard weighted average profit per hive is T$ 99. 40.

Write the draft report sections requested by Pene Lopez, finance director.

Section 3

A few weeks later, Pene Lopez and Cormac Jones are both absent from work and you receive the following email from Jacinta Cory, sales and marketing director.

From: Jacinta Cory, Sales and Marketing Director

To: Management Accountant Assistant

Subject: Honey Show and hobby beekeepers

We have just been offered a one off contract to supply 300 slatted cedar hives to the organisers of the Tucland National Honey Show. I have costed the work, and we will make T$ 29,274 additional profit if we accept the contract (see attached).

As the hives will be sold to hobby beekeepers, the organisers want the hives to be ready-assembled and painted with preservative. They will pay T$ 500 per hive but we have to produce and ship the hives within the next three weeks. A courier service has quoted T$ 6,000 to pack them with protective padding and deliver them to the venue.

David tells me that we are still short of labour capacity following the storm damage, but I am sure that enough employees will work overtime to assemble and paint the hives. David thinks that each hive will take one hour to assemble and half an hour to paint. Ron knows of three students who are looking for temporary work would clean and set up a room, ready for the hive assembly work. This would take them a week and we will have to pay them T$ 9 per hour. Ron also thinks that they would be capable of painting the hives.

The preservative is an additional material and it's said that this would cost T$ 15 per hive (each hive needs half a litre). Tracey has enough preservative left over from we renovated the farm buildings last year. We wouldn't use it for anything else, which is lucky as the price has gone up by T$ 4 per litre since we bought it.

This order has made me wonder if we have overlooked the potential of the hobby beekeeper market segment. We believed that as hobby beekeepers usually buy only one hive at a time and have endless questions before they buy, they were less profitable than the commercial bee farmers who buy in bulk. We could be wrong and I think it's time to take a closer look at the Marketing Mix for this market. I would like to gather views across all of the business about it and I am asking a number of people for their thoughts.

Please email me:

- Your views on whether my costing is correct. I don't need you to do any calculations, I just need to understand the costing principles. Can you think of any other factors that I should consider before committing to the order?
- Your thoughts on how the Marketing Mix(4 Ps) of the hobby beekeepers is likely to be different to that of the commercial beekeepers.

Jacinta Cory
Sales and Marketing Director
Mavis Venderby

Costing for the Tucland National Honey Show Contract

Assembled Slatted Cedar Hives

Adjusted Standard Cost per Hive

	T$
Usual standard gross profit for a slatted cedar hive	155.68
Plus: additional revenue(T$ 500 – T$ 460)	40.00
Less: additional material – preservative	(15.00)
Less: additional labour cost① (1.5 hours × T$ 13.00)	(19.50)
Revised standard gross profit	121.18

Total contract profit

	Working	T$
Revised standard gross profit	T$ 121.18 × 300 hives	36,354
Less: room preparations	T$ 9.00 × 3 students × 40 hours	(1,080)
Less: courier		(6,000)
Total profit		29,274

Write the email requested by Jacinta Cory, sales and marketing director.

① The standard hourly rate for labour has been used.

Section 4

Four weeks later, Pene Lopez calls you into her office and says:

Following the incredible success of our "Just add bees" hives at the honey show last week, Jacinta has done further research into the buying behaviour of hobby beekeepers. She has concluded that hobby beekeepers buy a substantial amount of other beekeeping equipment at the same time that they buy a hive. She has investigated the products that some of our competitors sell and the gross margins are excellent.

As we have plenty of space to expand, we have decided to extend our sales range to include all the peripheral equipment that beekeepers need. I will give you a list of these items, together with my notes in a moment. The whole retail operation is going to be run by Toby Venger as a single and separate new department. New people will be recruited and all purchasing, storage, sales order processing, picking, packing, despatch and the factory shop will be managed by him. Toby will have full budget responsibility for the department.

This is a substantial investment and it is our job to detail the indirect costs involved in running this new department. In order to do this, I am considering using ABC principles and I am planning on buying software to help us analyse our costs. If this pilot works out, we may wish to "roll out" ABC across the rest of the business.

Please email me your suggestions together with your thoughts on whether or not you think that using ABC for this new department would be beneficial to our business.

In addition, it is obvious that the new department's inventory management is going to be more complex than for our existing operations and Toby will need some help and guidance. Please include in your email an explanation of the economic order quantity (EOQ) model of inventory management. Include an explanation of how appropriate the model is for building and maintaining a good working relationship with our new suppliers during this crucial start-up period."

Pene Lopez then hands you her notes and the list of new items that Mavis Venderby intends to sell.

Beekeeping Equipment to Sell

- Protective clothing: beekeeper suits in four different sizes.
- Hive equipment: smokers, fuel, hive tools, hive carriers, syrup, cleaning chemical and medi-

cines.

- Queen rearing: grafting kits, mating hives, pheromone sprays.
- Honey extraction: extracting machines, uncapping trays, buckets, filters, labels and jars.
- Candle making: moulds, wax, wax melters, dyes and wicks.
- Books, guides and other small sundry items.

Notes:

(1) Many of the above items are delicate, others are bulky and some, (the chemicals) can be dangerous.

(2) The value of the products ranges from a single T$ 1 to several T$ 1 000.

(3) The new suppliers will charge a standard delivery fee irrespective of order size.

Write the email requested by Pene Lopez, finance director.

试卷二

本次考试的结构如下：

序号	任务数	时间（分钟）
1	1	45
2	1	45
3	1	45
4	1	45

每个部分规定的时间可用于读题、组织和书写答案。

任务一

今天是2017年3月8日。2017年2月28日晚上下了一场暴雨，导致一座仓储大厦的屋顶倒塌，损毁了所有已经完工的雪松蜂箱存货和一辆叉车。

你到达办公室后发现一封来自财务总监Pene Lopez的邮件：

发件人：财务总监Pene Lopez

收件人：管理会计助理

主　题：风暴损毁

我刚从生产经理David Hand那里获得一份在上星期的暴风雨中损毁的物件清单。David认为大约一半的雪松蜂箱完工产品存货彻底报废，而剩余的一半若加以修补能以半价销售并重新使用。虽然叉车有很多凹痕和刮擦却无损功能，仍旧可以如常安全使用。

2017年2月28日存货盘点的余额里包括所有在暴风雨中损毁的雪松蜂箱完工产品。Thomas想知道存货和叉车的损毁对截至2017年2月28日的年度财务报表的影响。

假设我们目前没有任何雪松蜂箱完工产品存货，需要尽可能地生产雪松蜂箱。我们的重要客户预定了450个雪松盒式蜂箱，并要求下个星期必须发货。

暴风雨前，生产部门已经接近满负荷工作，仅剩余有限的切割和包装时间。此外，雪松的干燥期很长，目前我们只有2 800米已烘干的雪松能立即投入生产。由于需要考虑的因素很多，我已经利用线性规划图预估了在考虑已烘干的雪松、切割以及包装工时限制后的最优生产计划。

总经理Thomas Venderby想知道我们是否应该直接购入市场上供应充足的已烘干雪松。除此之外，两个包装工人和一个切割工人愿意取消休假计划继续工作，如果我们接受他们的好意，对每一个人我们将额外支付10个小时的工资。

由于我全天都有会议要参加，希望你能准备一份简报，向Thomas解释以下问题。

- 暴风雨对完工存货以及叉车造成的损毁将如何影响截至2017年2月28日的年度财务报表？请参考相应的财务报告准则。
- 我们是如何利用线性规划图预估最优生产计划的？此外，请论述我们是否需要额外购买已烘干的雪松以及是否需要接受上述三个员工的好意。目前不需要提供任何计算。

梅维斯·文德柏公司

财务总监

Pene Lopez

线性规划图

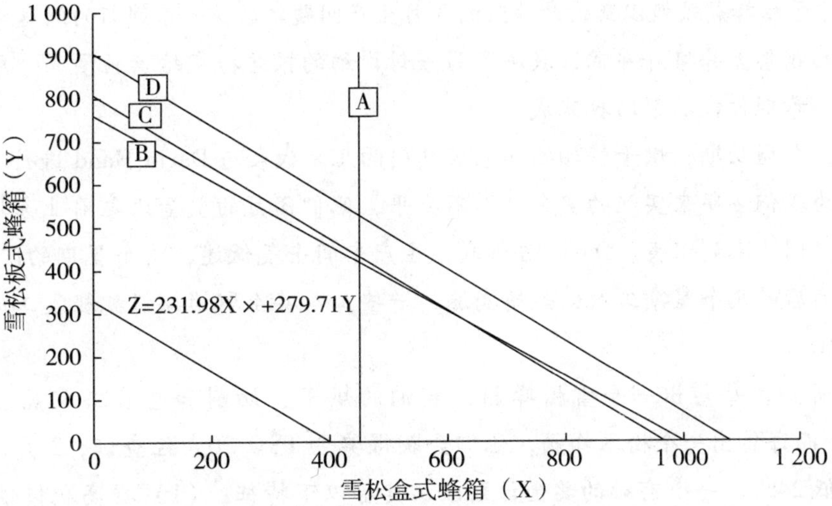

注：X 代表雪松盒式蜂箱的生产量，Y 代表雪松板式蜂箱的生产量。

目标函数是边际收益最大化

Z = 231. 98X + 279. 71Y

约束方程

直线 A：X ≥ 450

直线 B（已烘干的雪松）：2. 8X + 3. 7Y ≤ 2 800

直线 C（切割工时）：3X + 3. 6Y ≤ 2 900

直线 D（包装工时）：0. 5X + 0. 6Y ≤ 540

最优生产计划

X = 637，Y = 274

请依据财务总监 Pene Lopez 的要求，撰写简报。

任务二

5 个星期后，你从财务总监 Pene Lopez 那收到了以下邮件：

发件人：财务总监 Pene Lopez

收件人：管理会计助理

主　题：销售差异报告和奖金计划

经历了雪松蜂箱被毁以及由此导致的 3 月生产问题之后，一系列新的问题又出现了。

本月的销售差异格外异常，我决定写一封详细的报告提交给其他董事，解释销售差异的原因。希望你能够帮助我完成。

另外，本周初期，烘干、切割和包装部门的几个代表与 David Hand 进行了会晤。生产工人认为我们多年来实施的奖金计划不公平，他们 3 月的奖金比之前业务增长缓慢期的还要少，因此感到沮丧。David 告诉我，生产车间士气低迷，这个星期的旷工率很高。这与暴风雨后的几个星期工人们热情高涨，一些工人甚至取消休假积极复工的场面形成了鲜明对比。

如你所知，每售出一个雪松蜂箱，我们的烘干、切割和包装工人就会获得奖金 T$ 1.00，而每售出一个松木蜂箱，他们会获得奖金 T$ 0.20。经查证，3 月工人们的奖金比预算低 24% 。一个有效的奖金计划应该具备以下特征：（1）提高积极性；（2）奖励好业绩；（3）一致且公平；（4）与企业目标结合。

请你准备一份报告，向董事们解释：

- 销售差异（附件中是详细资料）以及它们的成因。你不需要解释它们是怎么被计算出来的。
- 目前我们的生产工人奖金计划是否具备以上 4 个特征，应当如何改进。

非常感谢！

梅维斯·文德柏公司

财务总监

Pene Lopez

2017 年 3 月的销售差异

销售预算和实际销售信息

	雪松盒式蜂箱	松木盒式蜂箱	雪松板式蜂箱	松木板式蜂箱	总计
预算销售量	2 000	1 400	1 800	1 200	6 400
实际销售量	1 200	1 700	1 350	1 400	5 650
标准售价（T$）	375.00	290.00	460.00	380.00	
标准单位毛利（T$）	96.08	71.61	115.68	112.96	

销售差异

差异种类	雪松盒式蜂箱	松木盒式蜂箱	雪松板式蜂箱	松木板式蜂箱	总计
销售价格（T$）	0	25 500A	0	28 000A	53 500A
销售组合	1 881F	12 898A	3 891A	4 617F	10 291A
销售数量					74 554A

注：

（1）除了以上的实际销售数据，600 个在暴风雨中被损坏的雪松蜂箱的销售收入是 T$ 145 000。与这项收入相关的奖金没有支付给生产工人。

（2）对于那些需要雪松蜂箱我们却没有库存的客户，我们以折扣价向他们出售松木蜂箱。

（3）销售数量和销售组合差异是用预算单位毛利的加权平均值算出来的。

（4）标准单位毛利的加权平均值是 T$ 99.40。

请依据财务总监 Pene Lopez 的要求，撰写报告。

任务三

几个星期后，Pene Lopez 和 Cormac Jones 没有上班。你从销售和市场营销总监 Jacinta Cory 那收到以下邮件。

发件人：销售和市场营销总监 Jacinta Cory

收件人：管理会计助理

主　题：蜂蜜展和养蜂爱好者

我们刚刚得到了一份合同，为 Tucland 全国蜂蜜展的组织者一次性提供 300 个雪松板式蜂箱。我已经计算了成本，如果我们接受这一合约，将获得利润T$ 29 274（参考附件）。

由于蜂箱将被售予养蜂爱好者，展会组织者要求蜂箱是组装好并涂上防腐剂的。他们愿意支付的价格是单价T$ 500，但是要求我们必须在未来三个星期内生产和发出蜂箱。一家快递公司愿意收取T$ 6 000的费用帮我们用保护垫包装蜂箱并送达指定地点。

David告诉我，风灾过后我们仍旧面临劳动力短缺的问题，但我确信我们有足够的员工可以加班组装蜂箱并涂抹涂料。David认为，一个蜂箱需要一个小时组装和半个小时涂抹涂料。Ron了解到有三个学生正在寻找临时工作，他们可以清洁和布置房间，以便组装蜂箱。这将花费一个星期的时间，而我们将支付他们每小时T$ 9的劳务费。同时，Ron也认为这些学生还能承担给蜂箱涂抹涂料的工作。

防腐剂是额外材料，据说每个蜂箱将会花费价值T$ 15的防腐剂（每个蜂箱使用半升）。Tracey那里有足够的防腐剂，是我们去年修复农场建筑时剩余的。我们将不会在任何其他地方使用这些防腐剂。幸运的是，自从我们购买以来，每升防腐剂的价格已经上升了T$ 4。

这个订单让我反思，我们是不是忽略了养蜂爱好者市场的潜力？过去我们认为，养蜂爱好者每次只购买一个蜂箱，而且在购买前有无数个疑问，所以相较于大量购买的商业养蜂人，他们带来的利润更低。我们的想法可能是错的，是时候重新审视我们的市场营销组合了。我希望收集关于这个行业的各种观点，而且我也正在向很多人询问他们的想法。

请写邮件告诉我：

- 我的成本计算在你看来是否是正确的？我不需要你做任何计算，只想知道相关的成本计算原则。你觉得还有什么因素是我在接受这个订单前需要考虑的？
- 关于养蜂爱好者和商业养蜂人的市场营销组合（4Ps），你有什么看法？

梅维斯·文德柏公司

销售和市场营销总监

Jacinta Cory

Tucland 全国蜂蜜展的订单成本——组装好的雪松板式蜂箱

调整后每一个蜂箱的标准成本

	T$
一个雪松板式蜂箱的正常标准毛利	115.68
加上：额外收入（T$ 500 – T$ 460）	40.00
减去：额外材料——防腐剂	(15.00)
减去：额外人工成本①（1.5 小时 × T$ 13.00）	(19.50)
调整后的标准毛利	121.18

合约总利润

		T$
调整后的标准毛利	T$ 121.18 × 300 个蜂箱	36 354
减去：房间准备	T$ 9.00 × 3 个学生 × 40 小时	(1 080)
减去：快递		(6 000)
总利润		29 274

请依据销售和市场营销总监 Jacinta Cory 的要求，撰写邮件。

任务四

4 个星期之后，Pene Lopez 请你到她的办公室，说道：

继上个星期蜂蜜展上“只加蜜蜂”蜂箱取得巨大成功之后，Jacinta 进一步研究了养蜂爱好者的购买行为。她得出的结论是，养蜂爱好者在购买蜂箱的同时会大量购买其他养蜂装备。经过对一些竞争对手的产品研究，她发现其中的利润非常可观。

由于我们有足够的空间扩张，我们决定扩大产品范围，加入所有养蜂爱好者需要的衍生装备。过一会儿，我给你一份产品清单，上面有我写的注释。整个零售经营将会成立一个唯一且独立的部门，由 Toby Venger 掌管。他将负责招聘新员工，所有的采购、仓储、订单处理、选择、包装、分派以及工厂门店的管理也都由他负责。Toby 将会对部门的预算承担全部责任。

① 一直使用的标准小时工资。

这是一笔大额投资，我们需要提供经营新部门间接成本的相关信息。为了达到目标，我正在考虑运用作业成本法原则并购买软件帮我们分析成本。如果试运行成功，我们希望把作业成本法推广到公司的其他业务上。

请发邮件告诉我你的建议，并说说你对在新部门运用ABC法是否有利于我们的经营的看法。

另外，很明显新部门的存货管理将比我们现有的更为复杂，Toby需要帮忙与指导。请你在邮件里解释一下，存货管理中的经济订货批量模型，以及这个模型在目前关键的起步时期，帮我们建立和维持与新供应商之间的良好合作关系的可行性。

然后，Pene Lopez 把带有她注释的梅维斯·文德柏公司即将销售的货品清单交给了你。

即将销售的养蜂装备

- 防护服：4种不同尺寸的养蜂人套装。
- 蜂箱装备：烟熏器、燃料、蜂箱工具、蜂箱支架、糖浆、化学清洁剂以及药物。
- 蜂王培育：嫁接工具包、交配蜂箱、信息素喷雾。
- 蜂蜜提取：提取机器、提升托盘、桶、过滤器、标签和罐子。
- 蜡烛制作：模具、蜡、熔蜡炉、染料和灯芯。
- 书、指南以及其他小杂物。

注：

（1）上述许多物品极易损坏，另一些物品比较笨重，还有一些（比如化学产品）属于危险品。

（2）产品价格从几个T$到几千T$不等。

（3）无论订单大小，新供应商将会收取标准的运货费用。

请依据财务总监 Pene Lopez 的要求，撰写邮件。

Variant 2　Suggested Answers

Section 1

Financial Reporting Issues—Brief Notes

Finished Goods Inventory—Cedar Hives

The fundamental principle of IAS 2: Inventory should be stated at the lower of cost and net realisable value (NRV). The storm has caused a physical deterioration in the cedar finished goods inventory and therefore it is likely that NRV is less than cost. Indeed, at least half of our cedar box and slatted hives are now worthless and therefore these should now be excluded from the valuation of the stock counted inventory. The effect of this is that our finished goods inventory value will be lower than would otherwise have been the case. This has the effect of increasing cost of sales for the year ended 28 February 2017 as closing inventory will be lower than it should be. In effect the inventory will be written off, which will reduce profit for the year, as this is wasted production.

For the rest of the inventory which can be salvaged we need to consider its NRV. Given that they are likely to be sold for half of our normal price, NRV will be lower than cost. NRV is the estimated sales price less estimated costs of completion less estimated costs necessary to make the sale. The estimated selling price is going to be much lower than our usual price: a good estimate would be the price any of our competitors charge for non-perfect products (assuming they do). Alternatively Jacinta, Joseph or Toby may already have a price in mind; ultimately it will depend just how damaged the hives are. The estimated costs of completion will be the costs of making the hives serviceable. The estimated costs necessary to make the sale will be the cost of the usual packaging, distribution costs and any other costs that might need to be incurred in order to sell the damaged hives.

The effect to our financial statements is the same as for the inventory that is worthless, although the effect will be smaller because we will be able to record the inventory at NRV.

Fork-lift Truck

The roof falling due to the storm is an impairment event and we need to determine the extent of any impairment loss specific to the fork-lift truck that has been damaged.

An impairment loss will arise if the carrying amount of the fork-lift truck exceeds its recoverable amount. Carrying amount is the amount at which the fork-lift truck is included within PPE, which will be its cost less accumulated depreciation to 28 February 2017. Recoverable amount is the higher of the fork-lift truck's fair value less cost to sell and its value in use. The fair value in the case of our fork-lift truck would be the amount that we could sell it for in its current condition while the value in use is the present value of the future cash flows, expected to be derived from using the fork-lift truck in the business.

As the fork lift truck is likely to generate the same future cash inflows as it did before the storm damage; hence its value in use is unchanged; it is likely that there is no requirement to impair the asset. Therefore the damage will have no effect on the financial statements for the year ended 28 February 2017. Any repair costs will be treated as expenses when incurred.

Linear Programming Solution

How the graph has been used to determine the optimal production plan

Each of the labelled lines on the graph represents a potential constraint to our production of cedar hives. These have been established in order that we can identify the feasible region of production.

The feasible region is the area on the graph where all of the constraints are met. The feasible region will be below the lines B, C, and D, because these lines represent the maximum production of cedar box hives and cedar slatted hives, given the amount of resources that each consume. The feasible region is to the right of line A because this represents the minimum amount of cedar box hives that must be produced as we have to ship the order of box hives to the special customers. The optimal solution is the point within the feasible region where we maximise the contribution that we can generate given the constraints.

The slope of the ISO contribution line is due to the different contributions earned from each of the different types of hive. We have determined the point that will maximise contribution by moving the ISO contribution line away from the origin until it touched the furthest edge of the feasible region. On our graph, this is where lines C and B intersect.

C(cutting hours) and B(dried cedar) are the binding resources as these are the constraints that prevent us from being able to make any more hives. Packing hours is a non-binding resource and this means that when we make as many hives as we are able, given the binding constraints, we have surplus packing hours.

Our optimum production plan is 637 box hives and 274 slatted hives given our existing level of resource constraint.

Buying Additional Production Resource

We would like to have enough resource to make as many hives as we have demand for, but we do not want the cost of the resource to exceed the benefit that it will generate as our objective is to maximise contribution.

The extra contribution that could be generated from an extra unit of a non-binding resource (the shadow price) is zero and so we should not pay for the two packing department staff to cancel their leave to work in the packing department. We can see from the graph that we have surplus packing labour and so more labour in this department will not generate any extra contribution. However, as many members of our workforce have been trained in different areas of the business, it may be possible to move some of the surplus packing labour to work in the cutting department, making cedar hives. If this is the case, then we should take up the offer from the two packing department employees.

At present, the binding resources (dried cedar and cutting labour) are preventing us from meeting demand for cedar hives and we are likely to have stock outs. Therefore we will want to accept the offer from the cutting department's staff and we will want to buy ready-dried cedar. We need to consider the shadow price of each resource in turn, in order to determine how much we should pay for them if we intend to maximise contribution. If we have more of these binding constraints' resource, then the constraint lines (lines B and C) on the linear programming graph will move further away from the origin. As we will only have ten hours of the cutting labour, this shift will be quite small and will become the only binding resource as the plentiful supply of ready-dried cedar will move line B to the right of cutting labour (line C). Once all of the cutting labour has been used, it is not worth buying any more dried cedar as it will not generate any additional contribution.

Section 2

Sales Variance and Bonus Scheme Report

Variance Report

Following the storm and consequential damage to the cedar box and slatted hives last month, Mavis Venderby was not able to meet the full demand for hives in one of our busiest months. This is reflected in the variance report.

Sales Price Variance

Both types of cedar hives were sold at the full list price, as evidenced by a nil price variance. This is to be expected as there was a shortage of hives and there would be no need to offer discounts as an incentive to buy.

On the other hand, the pine hives were sold at below list price. This can be explained by the discounts given to customers disappointed by the lack of cedar hives for sale.

Sales Quantity Variance

This is T$74,554 adverse as the total number of hives sold is less than the 6,400 budgeted. Therefore any additional pine hives sold has not compensated for the gross profit lost due to the reduced level of cedar hives sold.

Sales Mix Variance

This T$10,291 adverse variance means that when we compare the actual quantity of hives sold in the expected mix with the actual quantity of hives sold in the actual mix, it results in a lower gross profit overall. This indicates that we may have sold proportionately less of the higher margin hives and more of the lower margin hives.

This is confirmed by the individual mix variances as follows.

Box Cedar (T$1,881 F)

The actual quantity of cedar hives sold is less than the standard mix for actual sales. This can be explained by the reduced quantity of hives available for sale, due to the storm. This variance can be explained by the fact that we have sold less of hives that achieve below average profitability (T$96.08 against T$99.40).

Box Pine(T$12,898 A)

The actual quantity of pine hives sold is more than the standard mix for actual sales. This can be explained in part by the discounts offered. This variance can be explained by the fact that we have sold more of this relatively less profitable hives (T$71.61 against T$99.40).

Slatted Cedar(T$3,891 A)

The actual quantity of cedar hives sold is less than the standard mix for actual sales. This can be explained by the reduced quantity of hives available for sale, due to the storm. This variance can be explained by the fact that we have sold less of this relatively more profitable hive(T$115.68 against T$99.40).

Slatted Pine(T$4,617 F)

The actual quantity of pine hives sold is more than the standard mix for actual sales. This can be explained in part by the discounts offered. This variance can be explained by the fact that we have sold more of this relatively more profitable hives (T$112.96 against T$99.40).

It should be noted that the sales mix variances and sales quantity variances are subsets of the sales profit volume variance.

Incentive Systems

The purpose of any incentive system is to motivate staff to produce work that is congruent with the aims of the organisation. A good bonus scheme should satisfy the following points.

Motivational

A good bonus scheme should encourage workers to be effective and productive. Our bonus scheme fails to meet the criteria of a good financial incentive scheme because the staff are demotivated and unhappy. This has been demonstrated recently during the meetings with David Lines, an increase in absenteeism with the general poor atmosphere.

A Reward for Good Performance

What's more, a good bonus scheme should reward performance: last month the wood shop workers agreed to help the business by working overtime, in some cases giving up their leave-days in order to meet demand following the storm, only to find that this month they are no better off financially as their bonus is much less than usual. The extra effort and sacrifice was not rewarded by the scheme.

The hives that were damaged were produced by a good standard—this is the performance that should be rewarded. Our bonus scheme should be linked to the work that the workers have control over. We should link their reward to efficiency in their work (perhaps linking it to the standard costs) when the work is performed but not months later when other factors outside of their control devalue their work.

In addition, the fact that we pay T$1.00 for each cedar hive but only T$0.20 for a pine hive is inconsistent with the level of effort needed to make each type of hive and so does not reward good performance.

Consistent and Fair

A good bonus scheme should be consistent and fair. The production workers have no control over the sales which depend upon the marketing team doing their job, but more importantly on seasonal factors. In addition, the 600 damaged hives that were sold did not result in any bonus payment for the production workers. This is unfair as time to make them to a salable standard has been incurred twice by the production workers; once when the hives were originally made (see above) and again when salvaged and repaired after the storm but without reward.

It is more logical and fair to base the bonus on production rather than sales because this is what our production workers have control over. Our bonus scheme should also apply to all work that is undertaken, otherwise vital tasks could be neglected.

Goal Congruent

Finally, a good bonus scheme should comply with organisational goals. The scheme rewards the sales of the cedar hives more than the pine hives but not only is this outside of the control of the production workers (as above), but it does not focus on the goals of the organisation. The margin of the different types of hive does not merit the greater bonus for cedar hives.

Our business is renowned for the quality products and this is the key factor to our success. A bonus scheme that rewards quality production should be introduced. A bonus scheme based on quality measures (right first time, a reduction of wastage and rejects) would be more appropriate than volume sales.

Section 3

From: Management Accountant Assistant

To: Jacinta Cory, Sales and Marketing Director

Subject: Basis of the Decision and Marketing Mix

Basis of the Decision to Sell 300 Assembled Slatted Hives

A one-off decision like this one should be taken using the principles of relevant costs and relevant revenues. A relevant cost or revenue is cash based, in the future and incremental to the decision (in other words, a future cash flow that arises is only as a result of the decision).

The starting point for your schedule is the standard cost card for a flat pack slatted cedar hive, which is adjusted for the additional costs and revenue. This is an acceptable method so long as you also adjust any non-relevant costs included within the standard cost. In the case of this one-off contract, we can deduct the packing labour as this will not be incurred when we manufacture an assembled hive. In addition, the fixed production overhead is not relevant as it will remain constant in the short term regardless of whether we accept this contact or not and we should also deduct this.

In your schedule, you are correct to include the additional revenue earned from the contract as this is incremental. The incremental material cost however is not correct as we will be using preservative that has already been purchased and which will not be used for any other purpose. This is known as a sunk cost and will not be affected whether we undertake the contract or not. The relevant cost for preservatives therefore will be zero.

The incremental labour cost is correctly identified as 1.5 hours per hive in addition to the usual labour, but I think that the labour rate charge is incorrect for two reasons. Firstly, the standard labour rate per hour is based on the basic hourly rate. This contact will require all work to be paid at an overtime rate. Therefore it is likely to be higher than the standard rate. Also there is a possibility that for 0.5 hours per hive the rate can be set at T$9 per hour as the painting will be undertaken by the student labour.

The additional one-off costs of preparing the area (T$1,080) and additional courier packing charges (T$6,000) are also incremental costs and you have included them correctly to arrive at the profit figure.

Other Factors

The fixed overhead per flat packed hive is T$164.03, a significant amount and worth additional consideration. If we assume that our production overheads are all fixed (although in reality this is unlikely to be true), we could afford to sell the assembled hives at much lower prices and still generate profit. If further similar one-off opportunities arise, this should be borne in mind.

Before we commit to providing the assembled hives, we should be sure that the production workers will want to work overtime when it is necessary. We have no spare labour currently and recent issues with the bonus scheme may mean that our production workers are unwilling to extend their goodwill at the moment.

We need also consider that this is the first time for us to produce ready-assembled hives and we do not have any quality control systems in place to ensure that the work is done to the correct standard. Any lack of consistency or quality with these hives may tarnish our brand. Finally, we need to consider the effect that a failure to deliver these hives would have on our reputation.

The Marketing Mix

Product

What does our customer want from our products? Our hobby beekeeping customers want a hive that they can "just add bees" to, they want to buy a hive that is ready to use as soon as it is delivered. Hobby beekeepers hold less spare equipment than the commercial beekeepers and have limited time to pursue their hobby. Therefore, they don't want to spend time finding the correct tools to assemble hives. In addition, the hobby beekeepers are much more likely to be concerned about the aesthetics of a hive than commercial beekeepers.

If we extend our product range, this is likely to suit hobby beekeepers who would probably prefer a "one stop shop" for all of their beekeeping supplies, as this minimises shipping costs and research time, allowing plenty of time to enjoy their hobby.

Price

At Mavis Venderby, we have always tried to achieve a margin on cost and this will continue to be the case regardless of which market segment we are providing. However, it is likely that the hobby beekeepers are less price sensitive than the commercial beekeepers and are more likely to pay for items that are not necessary for the health of the bees and honey yield, but for the enjoyment of the beekeeping process. Hobby beekeepers will also expect and receive less bulk discount than the commercial beekeepers.

At Mavis Venderby, we will be able to charge a premium price for our products because of our strong brand name. Also, our product will extend beyond the simple physical items as hobby beekeepers will need the advice and expertise from our staff. This will enable us to charge higher prices than average. Commercial beekeepers do not often need this level of advice.

Promotion

Hobby beekeepers are likely to hear about Mavis Venderby through their local beekeeping association and the courses they run. Word of mouth and testimonials have always been a prominent part of our promotion. We will continue to advertise our hives via the National Beekeepers magazine, through local beekeeping associations, at honey shows and of course through the website.

As a seasonal business, we will focus the main promotional campaign at the end of the winter season. This coincides with the majority of beekeeper associations running beginners courses. It has been demonstrated that hobby beekeepers are far more likely to be brand-loyal so if the first hive they buy is a Mavis Venderby hive, so will all subsequent hives purchase.

Place

Our hives are sold via the website and also through our shop. It is important that our staff are able to offer advice and to demonstrate the functionality and quality of any other products that we may sell in the future. I expect that the hobby beekeepers who visit the shop will find that the environment is clean and the hives that we offer are displayed fully assembled. Similarly the website should detail the functionality and use of all our products.

Many thanks!

Management Accountant Assistant
Mavis Venderby

Section 4

From: Management Accountant Assistant

To: Pene Lopez, Finance Director

Subject: ABC and EOQ

Is ABC Beneficial?

ABC is most useful where the indirect cost is a high proportion of total cost. In our case, the current level of indirect costs in the manufacturing business is approximately 60% of total costs. With the new retail department, the indirect costs are unlikely to be this high, as the bought in cost of the products is likely to be more substantial. However, we will incur additional non-direct costs such as picking and packaging and ABC will help us to analyse and control these.

ABC also benefits businesses where there are a variety of different products with a high level of customisation. ABC would give us an accurate costing basis on which to control and perhaps reduce costs. The new department will be selling a very wide range of products that will require handling in different ways. The chemicals will require extra security, the fragile items need extra packaging. The different handling will mean that costs are incurred at different rates for different products, this can influence our decision to stock some lines. In addition, a better understanding of cost can help us to price our products more effectively.

ABC is not merely a more detailed and accurate overhead absorption costing system, it will ensure that we focus on key activities not only reducing cost but also increasing value to our customers. We have now identified two distinct customer segments: commercial beekeepers and hobby beekeepers. It is probable that, in a retail environment, these two segments will use different amounts of activities. For example, hobby beekeeper might place many small orders compared to the commercial beekeeper who may place only a very few large ones. The same amount of work will be involved in processing the sales order, but the revenue will be much less. ABC will help us to identify when to offer incentives to the hobby beekeepers in order to maximize profit.

On the downside, it could be argued that even if we determine that a line of a particular product is consuming more resource than the selling price, we will keep selling it anyway as the hobby beekeeper will want a one stop shop. These unprofitable products will serve as loss leaders.

As you have already stated, ABC is expensive to implement. Even if we buy the software, as suggested, it will involve a lot of time and effort to implement correctly. We will need to conduct the depth analysis of all of our operational activities before we are able to extract any real benefit from ABC. This will mean that we need cooperation and enthusiasm from the new department in all aspects. It is unlikely that Toby will want to take the time to help implement a whole new system on top of his other new responsibilities.

Finally, there is always likely to be some overhead that will be absorbed into the product using some arbitrary basis. If this is at a significant level, it can negate many of the advantages.

Inventory Management

The EOQ method of managing inventory aims to compute the optimal order size by minimising the total of holding costs and ordering costs. The holding cost of inventory is defined as the cost of holding one item in inventory for year. This cost includes the cost of insurance, risk of obsolescence, the opportunity cost of the space to store the goods, the administration and the cost of financing the investment in the inventory.

We have plenty of suitable space to store the new retail items. However, the holding costs are likely to be significant as: insurance will be based on a higher inventory value; breakages will occur as some of our products are delicate; our safety and security procedures will be more onerous due to the hazardous chemicals we will store. The most significant holding cost will probably be the effect on our working capital due to the outlay needed to stock the quantities and ranges of bought-in products.

The cost of ordering inventory include the purchasing costs including the administration costs of placing the orders, the cost of goods inwards checking (see above) and the cost of ensuring that we check and pay the invoices correctly. This is in addition to the supplier's own delivery charge which will remain at a fixed charge, irrespective of the number of items ordered.

How Appropriate is the Model to Build and Maintain a Good Working Relationship with Our New Suppliers?

One of the assumptions of the EOQ is that demand is constant. The model assumes that inventory will be purchased at a point in time and it will be used(sold)at a constant rate over time.

Our business is a seasonal business with the majority of our sales occurring in March through to June. It is unlikely therefore that we can build a relationship with our new suppliers based upon regular and evenly sized orders.

As our new department is essentially a start-up business, we cannot hope to know the annual demand with any degree of certainty for the products that we will be ordering from our new suppliers. It will therefore be difficult to formulate the EOQ. It is likely that in the early months of our new business, we will be far more likely to place frequent small orders and agree to additional delivery charges with our suppliers, than rely on the EOQ. In many ways, this abandoning of EOQ should enable us to get to know how reliable and consistent our suppliers are earlier.

The sheer diversity of our new product range will also make the EOQ difficult to use. It is probably better for us to focus on forming a relationship with our suppliers that allows for changes in order quantity and frequency, at least in the short term. We have also to remember that we hope to gain a significant share of this market in the long-term and our new suppliers are much more likely to focus on that than the short-term inconvenience of extra delivery costs.

Many Thanks!

Management Accountant Assistant
Mavis Venderby

试卷二　参考答案

任务一

财务报告问题的简报

完工产品存货——雪松蜂箱

国际会计准则第 2 号的基本原则：存货的计量应以成本和可变现净值的较低者为准。暴风雨对雪松蜂箱完工产品存货造成了损毁，因此存货的可变现净值可能低于成本。事实上，至少一半的雪松盒式蜂箱和板式蜂箱已经完全损毁，它们应该从期末存货中剔除出去，所以我们的完工产品存货价值将会比预期的低。注销已损毁的完工产品存货将会增加截至 2017 年 2 月 28 日的财政年度销售成本并减少期末存货价值。随着存货的注销，同年的利润也会一并减少。因为报废的存货等于是白白浪费了。

至于剩下的可以修补的完工产品存货，我们要考虑它们的可变现净值。假设我们能以正常价格的一半出售，可变现净值将会低于成本。可变现净值等于预计销售价格扣除预计的完工成本以及必要的销售成本。预计销售价格将会远低于我们的正常售价。我们可以参考竞争对手对残缺产品的定价（如果有的话），或者 Jacinta、Joseph 或 Toby 心中的预期。无论如何，预计销售价格最终取决于蜂箱的受损程度。预计完工成本代表受损蜂箱的修补成本。这包含了所有所需材料和人工成本。预计的必要销售成本代表正常的包装、分销成本以及其他在销售过程中可能产生的成本。

完工产品存货折价销售对财务报表的影响与完工产品存货报废的影响类似，但因为能实现可变现净值，所以程度比较轻。

叉车

仓储大厦屋顶坍塌会导致资产减值，因此我们需要评估叉车的受损程度以及任何相关的价值减损。

当叉车的账面价值高于可回收价值时，就会产生减值损失。在财务报表上，叉车属于物业、厂房和设备类别。账面价值等于成本减去截至 2017 年 2 月 28 日的累计折旧。可回收价值是叉车的公允价值扣除销售成本以及使用价值中的较高者。公允价值是叉车基于现状的销售价值，而使用价值是使用叉车产生的未来现金流的折现值。

由于暴风雨并没有改变使用叉车的未来现金流，叉车的使用价值与风暴雨前一致，所以我们有可能不需要计提资产减值。因此，暴风雨对叉车的损害没有影响截至2017 年

2 月 28 日的年度财务报表。如有任何减值成本，当年的费用将相应增加。

线性规划方案

利用线性规划图制订最优生产计划

图中每一条标注的直线代表生产雪松蜂箱的一个约束条件。通过这些直线我们可以找到满足所有约束条件的生产组合区域。

满足所有约束条件的生产组合区域在直线 B、C 和 D 的下面以及直线 A 的右边，因为直线 B、C 和 D 代表满足资源约束的雪松盒式蜂箱以及雪松板式蜂箱的最大产量，而直线 A 代表雪松盒式蜂箱的最小产量，同时也是重要客户预定的必须于下周发出的盒式蜂箱。最优生产计划是满足所有约束条件同时又带来最大边际收益的生产组合。

ISO 边际收益直线的斜率取决于不同雪松蜂箱产品的边际收益。我们通过将 ISO 边际收益直线朝远离原点的方向移动来确定最优生产计划。当 ISO 边际收益直线穿过满足所有约束条件的生产组合区域的最后一点时，这点就代表最优生产计划。如图所示，最优生产计划是直线 C 和直线 B 的交点。

直线 C（切割工时）和直线 B（已烘干雪松）是绑定资源，因为我们的产量受制于这些资源。包装工时为非绑定资源，这意味着由绑定资源决定的生产计划不会导致包装工时短缺，我们总有多余的包装工时。

基于现有资源限制，我们的最优生产计划是生产 637 个盒式蜂箱以及 274 个板式蜂箱。

购买额外的生产资源

我们希望有足够的资源，生产尽可能多的蜂箱，但是我们不希望获得资源的成本超过它所能产生的效益，因为我们的目标是边际收益最大化。

获取额外非绑定资源（影子价格）所产生的额外边际收益为零，所以我们不应该要求包装工人取消休假加入工作并支付他们额外的工资。我们有多余的包装工时，获取更多的包装工时并不能带来额外的边际收益。但是，由于许多员工曾经接受过多方面的训练，我们也许能让多余的包装工人负责切割和制造雪松蜂箱。如此，我们可以考虑让两位包装工人取消休假投入工作。

目前，绑定资源（已烘干雪松和切割工时）限制了我们的雪松蜂箱产量，这可能导致存货短缺。因此我们应该让切割工人取消休假继续工作，并且购买已烘干的雪松。我们需要考虑每一种资源的影子价格，决定我们为了实现边际收益最大化应该支付的资源成本。如果我们能获得更多的绑定资源，那么在线性规划图中，约束条件直线（直线 B 和直线 C）将会朝远离原点的方向移动。由于能额外获得的切割工时只有 10 个小时，十分有限，而市场上的已烘干雪松可以无限供应，切割工时将会成为唯一的绑定资源。由此，无限供应的已烘干雪松会导致约束条件直线 B 移到约束条件直线 C（切割工时）的右边。当切割工时全部用尽时，我们应停止购买已烘干的雪松，因为获得多余的已烘干雪松已经不能再产生额外的边际收益了。

任务二

销售差异及奖金计划报告

差异报告

继上个月的暴风雨及其导致的雪松盒式和板式蜂箱损毁之后，梅维斯·文德柏公司经历了最忙碌的一个月，但还不能完全满足客户对蜂箱的需求。这一点可以从差异报告反映出来。

销售价格差异

两种雪松蜂箱都是按定价销售，所以没有销售价格差异。可能是因为雪松蜂箱供应有限，我们没必要折价吸引客人购买。

另一方面，松木蜂箱的实际售价低于定价。这可能是因为我们希望通过折价销售松木蜂箱来平复想购买雪松蜂箱而没有存货的客人的不满。

销售数量差异

不利差异 T$ 74 554 意味着蜂箱的总销售数量小于预算销售数量 6 400，因此额外售出的松木蜂箱并不足够弥补雪松蜂箱销售数量下降造成的毛利损失。

销售组合差异

不利差异 T$ 10 219 意味着根据实际销售数量和预算销售组合算出来的毛利高于根据实际销售数量和实际销售组合算出来的毛利。这表明，相对来说，我们实际销售了更少的高利润蜂箱以及更多的低利润蜂箱。

每一种蜂箱的销售组合差异进一步说明了这一问题。

盒式雪松蜂箱（有利差异 T$1 881F)

雪松蜂箱的实际销量小于根据标准销售组合和实际销售数量计算出来的销量。这说明暴风雨导致了可销售蜂箱的数量减少。此项差异产生的原因是我们销售了更少的利润低于平均值的蜂箱（T$ 96. 08 相对 T$ 99. 40）。

盒式松木蜂箱（不利差异 T$12 898 A)

松木蜂箱的实际销量大于根据标准销售组合和实际销售数量计算出来的销量，其部分原因是折价销售。此项差异产生的原因是我们销售了更多利润相对较低的蜂箱

（T$ 71.61 相对 T$ 99.40）。

雪松板式蜂箱（不利差异 T$3 891 A）

雪松蜂箱的实际销量小于根据标准销售组合和实际销售数量计算出来的销量。这说明暴风雨导致了可销售蜂箱的数量减少。此项差异产生的原因是我们销售了更少的利润相对较高的蜂箱（T$ 115.68 相对 T$ 99.40）。

松木板式蜂箱（有利差异 T$4 617 F）

松木蜂箱的实际销量大于根据标准销售组合和实际销售数量计算出来的销量，其部分原因是折价销售。此项差异产生的原因是我们销售了更多利润相对较高的蜂箱（T$ 112.96 相对 T$ 99.40）。

需要注意的是，销售组合差异和销售数量差异都属于销量差异的一部分。

激励机制

任何激励机制的目的都是为了鼓励员工为实现企业目标而努力工作。有效的奖金计划应该满足如下几点。

提高积极性

一个好的奖金计划应该鼓励工人高效且多产。我们的奖金计划不是一个好的财务激励计划，因为我们的员工依然态度消极，情绪低落。正如在最近和 David Lines 的会晤中提到的，员工缺勤率增高且士气低迷。

奖励好的业绩

再者，一个好的奖金计划应该奖励好的业绩：上个月，生产车间的工人愿意加班来应对暴风雨后的市场需求，有些人甚至取消休假复工。然而，工人们最终发现当月的奖金不仅没有增加，相较于平常甚至更少。额外的付出和牺牲并没有被现有的奖金计划认可。

在风暴中损毁的蜂箱是根据高质量标准制造的，工人的业绩应该被认可并得到奖励。我们的奖金计划应该与工人可控范围内的业绩挂钩。换句话说，他们的奖金应该取决于工作的效率（可以与标准成本挂钩），而并非取决于几个月后受到非可控因素影响的业绩。

除此之外，每制作一个雪松蜂箱我们支付 T$ 1.00，而每制作一个松木蜂箱我们支付 T$ 0.20。这样的激励与工人在制造不同种类蜂箱过程中付出的努力并不匹配。换而言之，我们并没有做到奖励好的业绩。

一致且公平

好的奖金计划应该保持一致、公平。生产工人无法控制销售业绩的好坏，它取决于市场团队的努力，更受季节因素的影响。另外，生产工人没有从 600 个被损毁的蜂箱的销售中获得奖金。这是不公平的，因为工人们付出了双倍的时间和努力，才使这些蜂箱能够正常销售。一次是原先的正常生产（如上），而另一次是蜂箱损毁后的修复，然而他们都没有因此获得奖金。

更为合理公平的奖金基础应该是生产而非销售，因为生产工人并不能控制销售业绩。奖金计划还应该覆盖所有执行过的工作，否则关键性的任务可能被忽略。

目标一致

最后，好的奖金计划应该与企业目标一致。目前的奖金计划鼓励销售雪松蜂箱胜于松木蜂箱。这不仅超过了生产工人的可控范围（如上），还忽视了企业的目标。不同种类蜂箱的利润显示，我们并不值得为雪松蜂箱支付更高的奖金。

我们的公司因产品质量闻名，这也是我们成功的关键因素。我们应该实施一种基于高质量生产的奖金计划。这个计划的衡量标准应该基于质量（首次准确率、浪费率和退货率），而非销量。

任务三

发件人：管理会计助理

收件人：销售和市场营销总监 Jacinta Cory

主　题：决策依据以及市场营销组合

销售 300 个已组装的板式蜂箱的决策依据

类似这样的一次性决策应该考虑相关成本和相关收入原则。相关成本和相关收入以现金为形式，发生在将来并因决策而产生（换言之，它们是由于决策而产生的未来现金流）。

你的计划基于平包的雪松板式蜂箱的标准成本卡，并在此之上调整了额外的成本和收入。只要你同时调整了标准成本里的非相关成本，这一方法是可以接受的。对于这个一次性合约，我们可以扣减包装人工费，因为对于制造已组装好的蜂箱来说，这个成本不会产生。除此之外，固定制造间接费用是不相关的，因为不管我们是否接受合约，这个成本在短期内都是固定不变的，因此我们应该将它扣减掉。

在你的计划里，你正确地考虑了合约带来的额外收入，因为它们是额外增加的。然而，增加的材料成本是不正确的，因为我们将要使用的防腐剂早已购买且没有其他用途。这是一个沉没成本，无论我们是否接受合约都无法改变。因此，防腐剂的相关成本等于零。

除了正常的人工成本，每个蜂箱增加的 1.5 小时人工是正确的，但是我认为设定的工时工资是不对的。这有两个原因：一是标准工时工资基于基本工时工资，然而合约需要支付的是加班工资，所以其工时工资有可能高于标准工时工资；第二，涂抹涂料每半小时的工资可以设成每小时 T$ 9，因为这道程序将由学生劳工执行。

额外的一次性场地准备成本（T$ 1 080）和快递包装成本（T$ 6 000）也是增加成本，你已经在计算利润时予以正确处理。

其他因素

一个平包蜂箱的固定间接成本是 T$ 164.03，这是一个大数目，需要进一步考虑。如果我们假设所有的生产间接成本都是固定的（虽然现实中不太可能），那么我们能在保持盈利的同时以低得多的价格销售已组装的蜂箱。如果类似的一次性机会再次出现，我们要谨记于心。

在我们承诺提供已组装的蜂箱前，我们应该确定生产工人在必要时愿意加班。目前我们没有多余的劳动力，而且最近由奖金计划产生的问题也意味着，我们的生产工人就目前来说不会愿意展示更多好意。

此外，这是我们第一次生产已组装的蜂箱，我们并没有现成的质量控制体系保证完成的工作符合正确标准。缺乏一致性和质量低下将会损害我们的品牌。不能按时交货也会对我们的口碑产生影响。

营销组合

产品

我们的客户对产品的期望是什么？我们的养蜂爱好者客户希望购买一运到就可以立即使用的蜂箱，他们只要装进蜜蜂就可以。相较于商业养蜂人，养蜂爱好者需要更少的配件并且只有有限的时间发展兴趣爱好。因此，他们不愿意花时间寻找组装蜂箱时需要的正确工具。另外，相较于商业养蜂人，养蜂爱好者更加关心蜂箱的外观。

如果我们扩展产品范围，有可能会迎合养蜂爱好者的需求。他们可能更愿意在同一间店里购买所有的养蜂材料，减少运费和调查时间，从而有更多的时间享受他们的兴趣爱好。

价格

在梅维斯·文德柏公司，不管在哪一个细分市场，我们永远尽力赚取利润。然而与商业养蜂人相比，养蜂爱好者可能对价格不太敏感。他们更容易购买对蜜蜂健康和蜂蜜生产来说不必要的产品，但这些产品却能让他们更加享受养蜂的过程。养蜂爱好者获得的价格折扣预计也会比商业养蜂人少。

因为梅维斯·文德柏公司的品牌优势，我们能设定更高的产品价格。另外，我们的产品不仅仅是实物，养蜂爱好者还需要我们的职员提供建议和专业知识，这能让我们设定高于平均水平的价格。商业养蜂人则不常需要同等水平人士的建议。

宣传

养蜂爱好者也许能从他们当地的养蜂协会以及协会提供的课程上听说梅维斯 · 文德柏公司。口碑和推荐一直是我们宣传活动的重点。我们将继续通过国家养蜂杂志、当地养蜂协会、蜂蜜展以及网页为我们的蜂箱打广告。

作为季节性产业，我们的主要宣传活动集中在冬季末。这与大部分养蜂协会举办的入门课程时间一致。事实证明，养蜂爱好者对品牌的忠诚度更高，所以如果他们购买的第一个蜂箱是梅维斯 · 文德柏公司蜂箱，他们将会继续购买我们的蜂箱。

渠道

我们的产品通过网络和门店销售。对于将来我们可能销售的任何产品，我们的职员要能够提供建议并演示产品功能和质量，这一点是很重要的。我希望当养蜂爱好者参观门店时能发现，我们的环境清洁，展示的蜂箱组装完好。同样，网页应该有关于我们所有产品的功能和使用的细节说明。

十分感谢！

梅维斯 · 文德柏公司

管理会计助理

任务四

发件人：管理会计助理

收件人：财务总监 Pene Lopez

主　题：作业成本法及经济订货批量模型

作业成本法的益处

当间接成本在总成本中占比很大时，作业成本法最有用。在我们的案例中，制造业目前的间接成本大概是总成本的 60% 。随着新零售部门的成立，间接成本的比例不可能维持这么高，因为产品的购入成本可能会变得更多。然而，我们将产生额外的非直接成本，比如选择和包装，作业成本法将帮我们分析和控制这些成本。

当企业提供多种类别的、不同的、高度定制化的产品时，作业成本法也十分有益。

作业成本法为我们提供了控制，或者减少成本的成本基础。新部门将出售各种需要以不同方式处理的产品。化学产品需要额外安全措施，易碎产品需要额外包装。不同的处理方式意味着不同产品消耗的成本不同，这会影响我们对存货的决定。除此之外，更好地理解成本能帮我们更有效地定价。

作业成本法不仅仅是一种更详细、更精确的间接成本吸收法，它还让我们关注那些既能降低成本又能为客户创造价值的主要活动。我们现在已经确定了两个不同的客户群：商业养蜂人和养蜂爱好者。在零售环境下，这两种客户群可能对经营活动有不同的需求。比如说，相较于商业养蜂人数量少的大订单，养蜂爱好者可能有数量多的小订单。虽然订单的处理工作差不多，但是收入将会少很多。作业成本法将帮助我们确认何时向养蜂爱好者提供激励以实现利润最大化。

不利的方面是，即便我们发现某一产品消耗的资源高于售价，我们也将继续销售，因为养蜂爱好者想要的是一站式店铺。这些不盈利的产品将导致亏损。

如你所述，实施作业成本法十分昂贵。就算我们按建议买了软件，仍旧需要花费大量的时间和精力保证其正确实施。在我们从作业成本法中获得实际收益前，我们需要对我们的经营活动进行一次深入的分析。这意味着我们需要与新部门展开各方面的合作，并得到其热情的支持。Toby 不可能在他的新职责外，再花时间帮忙实施一个全新的系统。

最后，我们无法避免用一些主观的分配基础把某一些间接成本分配到产品上，如果程度较高，它将抵消许多有利方面的作用。

存货管理

存货管理中的经济订货批量模型旨在计算最优订货量，从而使持货和订货的总成本最小化。存货的持有成本是指持有单件货品一年时间所产生的成本，包括保险成本、过期风险、仓储空间的机会成本、以及对存货投资的管理和融资成本。

我们有大量合适的空间可以储存新的零售商品，然而持货成本可能很高，原因如下：保险费将基于更高的存货价值；一些易损坏的产品可能会报废；由于储存危险化学产品，我们的安全和保安程序将会更加繁重。最重要的持货成本可能是储存数量多、品种多的购入产品需要的支出对营运资金的影响。

订货成本包括：涵盖下单行政费的购买成本、来货检验以及确保单据正确的成本。不论订单大小，这些成本是供应商收取的固定运费之外的费用。

这个模型帮我们建立并维持与新供应商的良好工作关系的适当性？

经济订货批量模型的一个假设是需求固定。模型假设存货在一个固定的时间点被购买，并随着时间推移按照一个固定的使用率（销售率）慢慢消耗。

我们的业务具有季节性，大部分销售在3月~6月发生。因此，我们不可能通过定期等量的订单与新供应商建立关系。

由于我们的新部门才刚刚起步，我们不能完全准确地预计全年产品的需求量，也就是我们将重新供应商那购买的数量。因此，使用经济订货批量模型比较困难。在展开新业务的最初几个月，我们更可能经常发出小订单并支付供应商收取的额外运费，而较少地依赖经济订货批量模型。从另一个角度看，不依赖于经济订货批量模型也能让我们更早地了解供应商的可靠性和一致性。

新产品的多样性也会增加经济订货批量模型使用的困难。也许至少在短期内，我们更应该将重心放在与接受灵活订单的供应商建立关系上。我们也应该记得，从长远来看，我们希望在这个市场获得显著的市场份额，那么新供应商会更愿意关注这个目标而容忍额外运输成本造成的短期麻烦。

十分感谢！

梅维斯·文德柏公司

管理会计助理

Variant 2　Marking Guidance

Section number	Technical skills		Business skills		People skills		Leadership skills		Integration	Total
1	Impact of potential asset impairments on the financial statements Linear programming in the situation of limited resources	12 7			Linear programming in the situation of limited resources	6				25
2	Sales price, mix and quantity variances	12			Elements of a good bonus scheme	7	Elements of a good bonus scheme	6		25
3	Applying relevant cost principles to a one-off decision	13	The Marketing Mix for different types of customer	12						25
4	Benefits of using ABC The appropriateness of the EOQ model for inventory management	11 7	The appropriateness of the EOQ model for inventory management	4					3	25
Total marks available for each competency		62		16		13		6	3	100

试卷二　评分指南

序号	技术技能		商业技能		人际技能		领导技能		综合	合计
1	潜在资产减值对财务报表的影响 资源有限时的线性规划	12 7			资源有限时的线性规划	6				25
2	销售价格、销售组合和销售数量差异	12			有效的奖金计划的基本元素	7	有效的奖金计划的基本元素	6		25
3	利用相关成本原则进行一次性决策	13	营销组合	12						25
4	作业成本法的益处 经济订货批量模型	11 7	经济订货批量模型	4					3	25
各技能评分合计		62		16		13		6	3	100

香港中文大学名师解惑

本套题目的案例主体是一家生产销售木制蜂箱的企业，名为 Mavis Venderby。试卷一共有四项任务，具体包括资产减值对财国报务的影响，利用线性规划制订最优生产计划，销售价格、销售组合和销售数量差异，有效的奖金计划的基本元素，利用相关成本原则进行一次性决策，不同客户的营销组合，ABC 法的益处，以及 EOQ 模型。考查了 P1、F1、E1 三门课程的知识点。其中，以 P1（49）的知识点分数比重量高。其次是 E1（36），最后则是 F1（12）。这和 OCS 的考纲要求基本一致。该试卷考核了考生的四项能力，其中技术技能的分值占 62%，商业技能的分值占 16%，人际技能的分值占 13%，领导技能的分值占 6%，与 CGMA 管理会计能力框架的技能要求一致。考生在备考时应根据考试重点有所侧重。

该试卷的每项任务涉及以下知识点：

任务	问题	科目	知识点
任务一	解释资产减值对财务报表的影响	F1	国际会计准则第 2 号：存货（IAS 2 Inventories） 国际会计准则第 36 号：资产减值（IAS 36 Impairment of Assets）
	分析资源限制对生产计划的影响	P1	利用线性规划制订最优生产计划（linear programming）
任务二	解释销售差异的原因	P1	销售价格差异（sales price variance） 销售数量差异（sales quantity variance） 销售组合差异（sales mix variance）
	评价现有的奖金计划	E1	有效的奖金计划的 4 个组成元素（four principles of a good bonus scheme）
任务三	决定是否接受一次性订单	P1	相关成本及其他因素（relevant costs and other factors）
	分析商业养蜂人和养蜂爱好者的购买行为	E1	营销组合（marketing mix）
任务四	分析作业成本法是否有利于改善经营	P1	作业成本法
	解释经济订货批量及其在案例中的适用性	E1	经济订货批量

上述各项任务要求以邮件、报告或工作笔记等形式来呈现答案，对问题的描述非常明确，答题时既要注意内容的针对性，也要注意形式的规范性。

其他答题注意事项包括：（1）仔细读题，一般每项任务都会涉及2～3个大的知识点，一定不能漏答；（2）答题要有条理，从是什么到为什么，从分析原因到提出解决办法，将每个知识点都解释清楚；（3）分层级列出各级小标题，让考官容易了解你的思路。

回答时要避免只是对教科书的知识点进行简单复述，应结合案例公司的实际情况；注意回答时的措辞、格式；注意论述的结构，论点的鲜明整和体性等。

对应知识点深度剖析

国际会计准则第2号：存货

根据国际会计准则第2号的基本原则，存货应按成本与可变现净值中的较低者来加以计量。可变现净值是指在正常经营过程中，估计销售价格减去完工和销售估计所需费用后的净额。

本案例中，暴风雨已经对雪松蜂箱的完工产品存货造成了实际损毁，因此，存货的可变现净值可能低于成本。考生需要根据存货损毁的程度来决定减值的多少，并分析减值对财务报表的影响。

考生注意事项

第一步：判断完工产品存货的损毁程度。

第二步：完全损毁存货应从期末存货中剔除，而可修补存货则需要计算可变现净值。

第三步：分析存货减值对财务报表的影响，比如对资产和利润的影响。

国际会计准则第36号：资产减值

根据国际会计准则第36号，如果资产的账面价值超过通过使用或销售而回收的价值，该资产就是按超过其可回收价值计量的。如果是这样，则该资产应视为已经减值，企业应确认资产减值损失。

本案例中，仓储大厦屋顶坍塌导致资产减值，我们需要评估叉车的受损程度以及任何相关的价值减损。

考生注意事项

第一步：判断叉车的被损毁程度。

第二步：计算叉车的可回收价值。可回收价值是叉车的公允价值扣除销售成本以及使用价值中的较高者。公允价值是叉车基于现状的销售价值，而使用价值是使用叉车产生的未来现金流的折现值。

第三步：比较叉车的账面价值与可回收价值，确定其是否产生减值损失。

第四步：如有资产减值，分析资产减值对财务报表的影响，比如对资产和利润的影响。

利用线性规划制订最优生产计划

线性规划是研究在有限的资源条件下，如何进行资源优化配置并制订最优的生产计划。线性规划模型的建立需要两个条件：(1) 最优目标（也称目标函数），比如最大边际收益；(2) 约束条件，比如原材料、市场需求、人力时间和设备等。最优生产计划是在满足所有约束条件的同时又带来最大边际收益的生产组合。

考生要明白，获得更多的某项资源未必能增加最大边际收益，因为最终的生产计划受制于绑定资源。只有在增加绑定资源的情况下，才有可能增加边际收益。

考生注意事项：

第一步：根据案例背景以及提供的线性规划图找出所有表示约束条件的直线。

第二步：通过将 ISO 边际收益直线朝远离原点的方向移动来确定最优生产计划。当 ISO 边际收益直线穿过满足所有约束条件的生产组合区域的最后一点时，这点就代表最优生产计划。

第三步：判断哪些资源是绑定资源，哪些资源是非绑定资源。考生要明白，获取额外非绑定资源所产生的额外边际收益为零。

第四步：分析包装工人取消休假加入工作以及购买已烘干的雪松对边际收益的影响。

销售差异分析

销售差异分析旨在衡量实际销售额和计划销售额的差异，并分析差异形成的原因。销售差异可以细分为销售价格差异、销售数量差异和销售组合差异。考生不仅要知道怎么计算这些差异，还要了解有利差异以及不利差异背后的经济含义。考生要根据案例背景有针对性地进行分析，切忌简单罗列差异产生的可能原因。

考生注意事项

销售价格差异：当存在销售价格差异时，实际销售价格不同于预计（标准）销售价格。可能的原因包括市场供需变化、质量控制和市场竞争等。考生要根据案例背景有针对性地进行分析，列出最可能的原因。

销售数量差异：当存在销售数量差异时，实际总销售量不同于预计（标准）总销售量。可能的原因包括原材料限制、产能限制、市场营销手段、市场供需变化、质量控制、市场竞争等。考生要根据案例背景有针对性地进行分析，列出最可能的原因。

销售组合差异：当存在销售组合差异时，实际销售组合不同于预计（标准）销售组合。

可能的原因包括原材料限制、产能限制、市场营销手段、市场供需变化、质量控制、市场竞争等。考生要根据案例背景有针对性地进行分析，列出最可能的原因。

有效奖金计划的4个组成元素

任何奖励机制的目的都是鼓励员工为实现企业目标而努力工作。有效的奖金计划能提高员工的积极性，所以奖金计划应该跟绩效挂钩。由于绩效同时受到不可控因素的影响，所以制订奖金计划时还需要考虑员工承担的额外风险。考生需要根据案例提供的信息，从有效的奖金计划的4个组成元素方面评价案例中的奖金计划。

考生注意事项

有效的奖金计划包括以下4个元素：

（1）提高积极性；

（2）奖励好的业绩；

（3）一致且公平；

（4）与企业目标一致。

相关成本

相关成本和收入以现金为形式，发生在将来并因决策而产生（换言之，是由决策导致的未来现金流）。考生应根据案例提供的资料，分析销售300个已组装的板式蜂箱的相关成本。

考生注意事项

相关成本必须同时满足以下条件：

（1）以现金为形式；

（2）发生在将来；

（3）因决策而产生。

同时，考生还需了解影响决策的非财务因素。如本案例中，员工的加班意愿以及产品的质量控制都可能影响最终的决策。

营销组合

营销组合是企业市场营销战略的一个重要组成部分，其目的是使企业能够从整体上满足消费者的需要。考生需要比较养蜂爱好者和商业养蜂人的购买行为，提出关于营销组合的看法。

考生注意事项

营销组合的内容：

（1）产品（product）：注重产品的功能和独特的卖点。

（2）价格（price）：取决于市场定位、竞争对手所定的价格等。

（3）促销（promotion）：如何刺激消费者的购买欲来促进销售的增长。

（4）分销（place）：如何建立销售网络（例如：门店销售、网上销售等）。

作业成本法

作业成本法的核心思想是“成本对象消耗作业，作业消耗资源”。依据这个指导思想，企业以成本对象例如产品所需的作业为基础，把资源成本分摊到成本对象上。作业成本法提供了更合理的间接费用分摊方法，从而能获得更准确的产品成本信息。考生应该了解作业成本法的原理及其益处。

考生注意事项

作业成本法的益处：

（1）分析控制成本；

（2）有效地定价；

（3）关注创造价值的作业。

经济订货批量

当企业按照经济订货批量来订货，可实现持货和订货的成本之和最小化。存货的持有成本是指持有单件货品一年时间所产生的成本，包括保险成本、过期风险、仓储空间的机会成本，以及对存货投资的管理和融资成本。订货成本包括：涵盖下单行政费的购买成本、来货检验以及确保单据正确的成本。不论订单大小，这些成本是供应商收取的固定运费之外的费用。经济订货批量的一个假设是需求固定。模型假设，存货会在一个固定的时间点被购买，并随着时间推移按照一个固定的使用率/销售率慢慢消耗。考生需要根据案例提供的信息，判断经济订货批量在案例中的适用性。

考生注意事项

经济订货批量：

$$\mathrm{EOQ}=\sqrt{\frac{2DP}{C}}$$

其中，D 表示商品年需求量，P 表示单次订货成本，C 表示单位商品年持货成本。

Variant 3

This examination is structured as follows：

Section number	Number of tasks	Time for section(minutes)
1	1	45
2	1	45
3	1	45
4	1	45

The time available for each section is for reading,planning and writing your answer(s).

Section 1

Joseph Perez, Production Director, has been working on developing new products. As a result of that Mavis Venderby recently approached a medium-sized chain of pet shops called Upper-Class Pets (UCP) with prototype chicken houses and rabbit hutch, with a view to them adding these to their existing range of products. UCP have agreed to buy 100 units of the rabbit hutch and the medium and large size chicken houses on a trial basis every month. UCP have stated that if all goes well, it is likely that the order size will increase in the future. Joseph Perez and the rest of the production team have planned and executed the changes needed to incorporate the new products into the existing business. The extra 300 products each month can be easily managed within the existing production capacity. It is intended to start the production of the UCP's products next week and the first order is due in two weeks' time.

You arrive at work to find the following email.

From: Pene Lopez, Finance Director
To: Management Accountant Assistant
Subject: Mesh shortage and TQM

There was a senior management meeting this morning. It seems that no-one told Tracey Lines, goods inwards and maintenance manager, to order the specialist wire mesh that UCP insist that we use. With enough notice, this mesh is plentiful, but at the moment Tracey can only obtain 600 square metres in time for the first month's production. She is trying to persuade a supplier to sell us some mesh, but it is highly likely that we will only have 600 square metres to work with this month. We have taken the decision to manufacture a minimum of 50 units of each product, regardless of the effect on profit, so that we at least give the customer the full product range, if not the quantity ordered.

David Hand thinks that we need to introduce a TQM system to ensure that this problem will be not repeated in the future, but Joseph is reluctant to make any more changes at the moment. As a result of these discussions, I have been asked to write a report to circulate to senior management. I would like you to draft two sections for me.

Firstly, I need a section regarding our production decision. I've prepared a schedule (which is attached to this email) but please can you draft:

- An explanation of how the schedule has been used to determine the proposed production plan.
- An explanation of how much we should be prepared to pay for any additional mesh, including any non-financial issues that you think is relevant.

Secondly, I need a section on how TQM principles apply to our business, specifically: senior management support, prevention and participation. In particular, I would like the report to focus on how these principles solve the problems that we have experienced this week.

Pene Lopez
Finance Director
Mavis Venderby

Proposed Production Schedule

	Medium chicken house (per unit)	Large chicken house (per unit)	Rabbit hutch (per unit)
Revenue(T$)	360	410	285
Material cost(T$)	58	64	59
Labour cost(T$)	78	82	61
Contribution(T$)	224	264	165
Wire mesh required(square metres)	3. 0	4. 0	1. 5
Contribution per square metre of wire mesh(T$)	75	66	110
Proposed production plan(number of units)	83	50	100
wire mesh used(square metres)	249	200	150

Write the email requested by Pene Lopez, finance director.

Section 2

A few months have passed and UCP have now offered Mavis Venderby a long-term contract to supply 400 of each of the three products(rabbit hutch, medium chicken house and large chicken house) every month. This would necessitate the expansion of the production facilities; new staff would need to be recruited and an old grain store will be convened into a manufacturing facility for the UCP products.

You get to work and open the following email.

From: Pene Lopez, Finance Director

To: Management Accountant Assistant

Subject: ABC and HRM

I was at a meeting until late last night, discussing the UCP offer at which two issues were raised regarding the costing of the new products and production staffing implications. Before we agree to the contract, we will need to negotiate selling prices as UCP are asking for a significant discount. We have always priced our products using full cost plus a margin but I am not convinced that our costing information is accurate enough for this to be appropriate for the UCP products.

I want to use ABC to establish the full cost of all our wood products(hives, chicken houses and the rabbit hutch) before we negotiate a price with UCP.

We have a wide range of staff at Mavis Venderby from trainees to experienced craftsmen. Each year we've taken on new trainees and either employed them permanently as other people left or had to let them go when their trainee period ended. We've never really had a formal plan and now it is time that we should do. As we have no qualified Human Resource Manager(HRM) and the finance department compile the standard cost cards and pay the salaries, we have been asked to draft an HR plan.

As I have so much to do, before we meet with UCP, I need you to help me with a couple of things.

Firstly, using the attached schedule, identify and justify an appropriate cost driver for each of the following overheads:

- Machine set up cost
- Inspection cost

For each, explain how we would calculate the total budgeted cost driver activity and how this information can be used to help identify where we can reduce the cost of the UCP products. There is no need for any calculations at this stage.

Secondly, please draft an outline of the stages in developing a Human Resource plan and how this will apply to our business if we accept the UCP contract.

Pene Lopez
Finance Director
Mavis Venderby

Schedule of Budgeted Activities in the Cutting Department

	Box pine	Box cedar	Slatted pine	Slatted cedar	Rabbit hutch	Chicken large	Chicken medium
Budgeted production(units)	10,000	7,000	9,000	6,000	4,800	4,800	4,800
Number of units per batch	100	100	80	80	25	50	50
Number of batches per set – up	4	4	3	3	2	3	3
Number of inspections per batch	5	5	5	5	5	10	10
Time taken per inspection(minutes)	12	12	15	15	20	20	20

Notes:

(1) UCP insist that 20% of all of their products are quality inspected.

(2) All machine's set-ups take the same amount of time.

Write the email requested by Pene Lopez, finance director.

Section 3

Three more months have passed and the building work for the new production facility has been completed and experienced staff have been moved to this production area. New trainees have therefore been recruited and are now working on pine hive production in the cutting department. However, there are issues with the quality of the finished hives.

You receive the following email.

From: Pene Lopez Finance Director

To: Management Accountant Assistant

Subject: Hive cutting department variance report and working capital

Ron Lomas has just left my office. We discussed the variance report that you sent him for comment yesterday. Ron told me the following:

- October was the first full month that the trainees worked in the cutting department.
- Trainees were only allowed to work on the pine hives as errors on pine are less expensive than cedar.
- Ron put the more able trainees to work on the more complicated slatted hives.
- Trainees were not allowed to work overtime and were all paid by the standard rate of T$ 9 per hour.
- One of the machines on the cedar hives' line (I forget which one) developed a fault that took a few hours to rectify, this cost us 50 labour hours in total.

There is going to be a senior managers meeting about the performance of the business now that we've had the first full month of full-scale production for UCP. As well as the issues with hive production, there are also concerns about the length of our working capital cycle, which has increased considerably over the last few months. It has certainly been a challenge for Tracey to fit all the extra cedar in the drying space and for Duncan to keep control of UCP's receivables balance. UCP have been given 45 days' credit terms, but usually pay a few days after this time.

I've drafted parts of the report that I am going to present at the meeting, but I need your help with a couple of things:

Firstly, please draft a commentary that explains the labour variances (I have attached a copy of the variances that you need to comment on). Please prepare your commentary by product rather than variance type.

Secondly, explain why our working capital cycle has significantly increased over the last few months and the potential problems that this can cause. Also, please suggest ways by which we can reduce the risk of UCP not paying us in time.

Pene Lopez

Finance Director

Mavis Venderby

Hive Cutting Labour Variance Report for October 2017

Budgeted and Actual Production

	Box cedar	Box pine	Slatted cedar	Slatted pine
Budgeted units	1,000	700	900	600
Actual units	1,125	600	875	500
Percent of units produced rejected due to quality faults	2%	12%	6%	7.5%

Notes:

Budgeted and actual units are the gross units produced before hives were inspected and categorised into "first quality" and "rejects".

Variances

Variance type	Box cedar (T$)	Box pine (T$)	Slatted cedar (T$)	Slatted pine (T$)
Idle time			850A	
Labour efficiency	1,275F		748F	
Labour mix		1,829A		44A
Labour yield		4,971A		126A

Notes:

Because of the unusually high number of trainees employed during October, new operational standards were applied to the pine hives that allowed for a mix of the two grades of labour: skilled and trainee.

Write the email requested by Pene Lopez, finance director.

Section 4

Four days have passed since the variance report that you wrote was presented to the senior management. You arrive at work to find the following extract of the minutes of the meeting on your desk.

David Hand made the following points regarding the cutting machine breakdown in October:

(1) We lost 50 labour hours as the machine had to be stripped down and reset. The hive parts that were on the machine at the time had to be scrapped. We had to pay a fortune to get the pan we needed delivered to us by special courier. To ensure that we met our production targets, we had to pay overtime that we had not budgeted for.

(2) Following the receipt of a letter of complaint, was from the Middletown Beekeeping Association who bought two faulty hives from us, Jacinta spent two hours trying to put things right. She called them personally and apologised, arranged for replacements to be delivered to them by special courier. She also sent them a substantial number of frames and foundation for free. She said that they still seemed quite cross, even after all of that. These hives were from a batch produced on that machine the day it broke down.

(3) I want Tracey to introduce a maintenance program where all machines are serviced every month (during time that the production workers are not using them) and I also want to introduce a few more quality checks throughout the production process rather than just at the end.

Pene Lopez then calls you into her office and says the following to you:

Thomas wants us to produce a monthly report that puts a monetary value on the cost of quality. David used to produce one at his previous employment. He claims that it really does emphasise the importance of getting it (right first time).

Now that the building work in the old grain barn is complete and the UCP' production is running smoothly within it, Thomas wants a final total of the expenditure involved. He wants us to capitalise as much of the expenditure on the building work as we can. I have produced a schedule of the expenditure and will give it to you in a moment.

I have to be in meetings all day and as Cormac is on leave, I want you to prepare the draft of a briefing paper for Thomas in which you:

- Firstly, explain quality costs using the extracts from the minutes that I left on your desk and give examples of the different categories of quality costs. I know that you can't quantify any of these costs right now, but please explain how we could get the information that we need.
- Secondly, explain, with reference to relevant international financial reporting standard rules, what expenditure in my schedule can be capitalised and what cannot.

Thank you!

Schedule of Expenditure for the New Production Facility

Expenditure	Detail	T$
Architects fees/legal		3,500
Site preparation	Levelling the floor of the store and testing for ground contamination	4,200
Loan Interest	Loan from bank taken for four years to fund the new production facility. This represents the interest for the term of the loan	64,400
Building contractor's cost		420,000
Purchase price of new plant and equipment		96,000
Import duties paid in respect of the plant and equipment		8,500
Installation cost in respect of plant and equlp-ment	Work undertaken by our maintenance staff and selected production workers	6,100
Training costs	Costs required to train installation workers	1,700
Share of general overheads		4,000
Marketing to get new customers	Additional work undertaken to fill the new facility to capacity	3,000

Write the briefing paper requested by Pene Lopez, finance director.

试卷三

本次考试的结构如下：

序号	任务数	时间（分钟）
1	1	45
2	1	45
3	1	45
4	1	45

每个部分规定的时间可用于读题、组织和书写答案。

任务一

生产部经理 Joseph Perez 正在进行新产品的研发。最近，梅维斯·文德柏公司准备运营一条名为顶级宠物（Upper-Class Pets，简称 UCP）的中型宠物商店产业链，他决定将标准的鸡舍或兔笼加入已存在的商品范围。UCP 同意每个月试验性地购入 100 个兔笼和中大型鸡舍。UCP 已经开始运作，如果一切顺利的话，未来将会有更多订单。针对将新产品融入现有的业务所需要做出的改变，Joseph Perez 与其余的生产团队成员已经有所计划并逐一落实了。另外的 300 件产品可以在现有的生产能力下被轻松管理。UCP 产品的生产将于下个星期开始，第一份订单将于两周内产生。

工作时，你收到了下面这份邮件。

发件人：财务总监 Pene Lopez

收件人：管理会计助理

主　题：网格短缺以及全面质量管理

早上有一个高层管理者会议。看起来好像没有人告诉货物采购与维护经理 Tracecy Lines 去预订一些 UCP 建议我们使用的专用金属网格。如果足够上心，网格是够用的，但是当时 Tracey 只能获得600 平方米的网格来支持第一个月的生产。她尝试说服供应商卖给我们一些网格，但是很有可能我们只能得到600 平方米去完成这个月的生产工作。我们决定每个产品最少生产 50 件，不论其对利润的影响。即使不能完成所有订单，我们至少可以给顾客提供所有种类的产品。

David Hand 认为我们需要引进全面质量管理系统以确保未来这种问题不会再次发生，但是 Joseph 不愿意在此时做出更多改变。在这次谈话结束后，我被要求准备一份报告以供高管们传阅。我希望你可以完成其中的两部分。

首先，我需要一份关于我们生产决策的分析。我已经准备了一份计划表（在附件里），请你撰写初稿：

- 说明这份表格是如何决定被提议的生产计划的。
- 说明我们需要为增加的网格支付多少钱，包括一些你认为与其相关的非财务问题。

其次，我需要一份关于全面质量管理原则如何应用于我们企业的分析，特别是：高级管理层支持、风险防范与公众参与方面。请你准备一份报告，重点分析这些原则如何解决我们本周遇到的问题。

梅维斯·文德柏公司
财务总监
Pene Lopez

生产提议计划表

	中型鸡窝（每单位）	大型鸡窝（每单位）	兔窝（每单位）
收益（T$）	360	410	285
原材料成本（T$）	58	64	59
人工成本（T$）	78	82	61
贡献（T$）	224	264	165
金属织物需求量（平方米）	3.0	4.0	1.5
单位面积的金属织物贡献（T$）	75	66	110
建议生产计划（单位数量）	83	50	100
金属织物用量（立方米）	249	200	150

请根据财务总监的要求，回复邮件。

任务二

几个月过去了，UCP 公司已经与梅维斯·文德柏公司签订了长期合同，合同规定 UCP 每月为 Mavis Venderby 提供每种 400 个产品（兔子窝、中型鸡舍和大型鸡舍）。这些使生产部门不得不进行扩张，为了生产 UCP 的产品，生产部门将雇佣新员工，旧的储粮仓也需要改造成制造工厂。

你准备开始工作，打开了下面这封邮件。

收件人：财务总监 Pene Lopez

发件人：管理会计助理

主　题：作业成本法和人力资源管理（HRM）

直到昨晚，我一直在开会讨论 UCP 的供货出现的两个问题，即新产品的成本和生产雇员的影响。在我们同意这份合同之前，我们需要商议销售价格，因为 UCP 要求我们提供很大折扣。我们一直在用完全成本加成法定价，但我认为，我们的成本信息不够准确，无法合理地为 UCP 的产品定价。

在我们与 UCP 商议价格之前，我想用作业成本法来建立我们木制产品的成本模式（蜂巢、鸡舍、兔窝）。

在梅维斯·文德柏公司，从新员工到有经验的工匠，我们有大量的员工。每年我们都会聘请新的实习生，也会继续录用一些人，而另一些人会自行离开或者在实习期结束后不得不离开。我们从来没有正式的计划，而现在到了我们该做决定的时候了。因为我们缺少有资质的人力资源经理，由财务部门负责制定标准成本卡并支付工资。我们被要求拟定一个人力资源计划。

因为我有很多事要做，在与 UCP 见面前，我需要你帮我完成一些事。

首先，用后面附的表格，为以下各项间接费用确认一个合适的成本动因并予以评估：

- 机器启动成本；
- 检查费用。

对于上面的每项费用，解释如何计算总预算的成本驱动活动以及这些信息如何帮助我们识别哪些可以减少 UCP 产品的成本。在本阶段，你不需要进行任何计算。

其次，请拟定一份发展人力资源计划各阶段的大纲，并解释若我们接受 UCP 的合同，这些大纲将如何应用于我们的企业。

梅维斯·文德柏公司
财务总监
Pene Lopez

切割部门的活动预算表

	松木盒子	雪松盒子	板状松木	板状雪松	兔窝	大型鸡窝	中型鸡窝
产品预算（单位）	10 000	7 000	9 000	6 000	4800	4 800	4 800
每批的单位数量	100	100	80	80	25	50	50
每装配一批的数量	4	4	3	3	2	3	3
每批检查的数量	5	5	5	5	5	10	10
每次检查花费时间（分）	12	12	15	15	20	20	20

注：

（1）UCP 声称所有产品的 20% 要接受质量检查。

（2）所有机器装配一次所花费的时间相同。

请根据财务总监的要求，回复邮件。

任务三

又 3 个月过去了，新的生产设备的建设工作已经完成，有经验的员工也已经被转移到了这个生产区域。新的实习生也已招聘，现在在进行松木蜂箱的切割工作。然而，已经完成的松木蜂箱出现了质量问题。

你收到了如下邮件。

发件人：财务总监 Pene Lopez

收件人：管理会计助理

主　题：松木切割部门差异报告和营运资本

Ron Lomas 刚刚离开了我的办公室。我们讨论了昨天你给他发送的报告中对差异的评论。Ron 告诉我如下信息。

- 10 月是这些实习生在切割部门工作的第一个完整的月份。
- 实习生仅仅被安排在松木蜂箱部门，因为松木的犯错成本比雪松低。

■ Ron 让更有能力的实习生切割更复杂的板状蜂箱。

■ 实习生不允许加班，工资标准都是每个小时 T$ 9。

■ 雪松蜂箱生产线上的一个机器（我忘了是哪个了）出现了故障，我们花费了许多时间去修理它，这总共占用了我们 50 个工时。

在 UCP 产品大规模地生产了一整个月后，一个关于公司绩效的高管会议即将召开。在蜂箱生产上也有一些问题，我们的运营资本周期在最后几个月内飞速拉长，这一点令人担忧。Tracey 要为额外的雪松寻找一个干燥空间，Duncan 也需要对 UCP 的应收账款余额保持控制，这确实很有挑战。UCP 有 45 天的信用期间，但他们总会晚几天支付。

我已经起草了一份我要在会议中演示的报告，但还有一些事我需要你的帮助：

第一，请起草一份针对人工差异的说明（我已经附上了你可能会需要评论的差异的副本）。最好结合生产而不是差异种类。

第二，请解释我们的营运资本周期在过去的几个月中增长显著的原因及其可能造成的问题。关于如何降低 UCP 不及时支付款项的风险，也请给出你的建议。

梅维斯 · 文德柏公司

财务总监

Pene Lopez

2017 年 10 月松木切割部门人工差异报告

预算和实际生产

	雪松盒式蜂箱	松木盒式蜂箱	雪松板式蜂箱	松木板式蜂箱
预算单位	1 000	700	900	600
实际单位	1 125	600	875	500
每单位产品由于质量问题而报废的百分比	2%	12%	6%	7.5%

注：在蜂箱检查并被分为“一等品”和“废品”之前，预算和实际单位都是总共的单位产品。

差异

差异类型	雪松盒式蜂箱（T$）	松木盒式蜂箱（T$）	雪松板式蜂箱（T$）	松木板式蜂箱（T$）
闲置时间			850A	
人工效率	1 275F		748F	
人工组合		1 829A		44A
人工产量		4 971A		126A

注：

因为通常很多实习生都是在十月引进的，因此针对松木蜂箱出台了新的营运标准，它允许两个层级的员工组合工作：熟练工人和实习生。

请根据财务总监的要求，回复邮件。

任务四

从将你写的差异报告提交给高层管理者已经过了4天。你开始工作，并在桌子上发现了下面的会议记录摘要。

针对10月切割机器的损坏，David Hand提出如下几点：

（1）因为机器不得不拆卸后重新组装，我们损失了50个工时。而且机器上的蜂箱部件不得不成为废弃品。我们也必须花费一笔钱以购买我们需要特殊快递邮寄的部件。为了能达到我们的生产目标，我们要支付一部分未做预算的加班费。

（2）下面这封投诉信的收据来自Middletown Beekeeping Association，这个组织购买了我们公司两个有损的蜂箱，Jacinta花了两个小时试图解决好此事。她亲自打电话给他们道歉，计划用特殊的快递重新发新货给他们。她还免费给他们赠送了大量的蜂箱底基和框架。即便如此，她说这仍然没能使他们消气。这些蜂箱是用那天坏了的机器制造出来的一批货。

（3）我想让Tracey引进一项维修程序，每个月对所有机器进行维护（这期间生产工人不再使用机器），我也想在整个生产过程中引进更多的质量检查，而不是仅仅在完工后。

Pene Lopez 随后把你叫到办公室并说：

Thomas 希望我们完成一份在质量成本分析中加入货币价值的月度报告。David 在他先前的岗位上曾做过一份。他指出，做报告真正重要的是“一次就过”。

现在旧粮仓的建造完成了，UCP 在那经营得也很顺利，Thomas 想要一份最终总共的费用支出统计。他希望我们尽可能把所有建造工作的开支资本化。我准备了一份支出明细表，一会儿交给你。

我一整天都要开会，由于 Cormac 正在休假，希望你能为 Thomas 准备一份简报草稿。

- 首先，结合我放在你桌子上的会议记录摘要，解释一下质量成本，并举几个不同的质量成本分类的例子。我知道你现在不能确定任何成本数据，但请解释一下我们该如何得到需要的信息。
- 其次，参考相关的国际财务报告准则，解释在我们的明细表里，哪些支出可以被资本化而哪些不可以。

谢谢！

新生产设备的支出明细表

支出	细节	T$
建筑费/法律		3 500
场地准备	储藏地板校平和土地污染测试	4 200
贷款利息	从银行贷款，为期 4 年，为新生产设备提供资金	64 400
房屋建造成本		420 000
新厂房和设备的购买价格		96 000
厂房和设备进口时所付关税		8 500
厂房和设备的安装成本	维修的员工和挑选出的生产工人负责安装	6 100
培训费用	安装员工的培训费用	1 700
一般费用分担		4 000
获取新顾客的市场营销	为新设备投入所需额外工作	3 000

请根据财务总监的要求，回复邮件。

Variant 3　Suggested Answers

Section 1

From: Management Accountant Assistant

To: Pene Lopez, Finance Director

Subject: Mesh shortage and TQM

Explanation of the Schedule

The production schedule has been produced using a technique called limiting factor analysis.

The production schedule shows the contribution for each of the three new products that we have agreed to make for UCP. We use contribution but not profit per unit as fixed costs because they are assumed to be fixed in the short term. Therefore the contribution per unit is constant whereas the profit per unit will change at different volumes.

If there were no scarcity of mesh, the large chicken house would be considered to be the most profitable product and rabbit hutch the least profitable. However, as mesh is a scarce resource, we have to maximise the contribution that we can earn for each square metre of this resource in order to maximise profit. From the schedule, we can see that we earn T$110 a square metre for each rabbit hutch we make, T$75 for each medium chicken house and only T$66 for each large chicken house. This is the ranking that we prefer to make the products in, in order to maximise contribution and therefore profit.

If we had not made the decision to make at least 50 units of each product, we would have made more medium-sized chicken houses in preference to the large-sized chicken houses, as this would have generated more contribution.

The optimal production plan shows that the best mix of products that we can make, given the minimum production restriction, in this case is 83 of medium-sized chicken houses, 50 large-sized chicken houses and 100 rabbit hutch. At this point, we will have used up almost all of the available mesh.

How Much to Pay for any Additional Mesh

If Tracey is able to source extra mesh, we would use it to manufacture medium-sized chicken houses in the first instance, until we have made the maximum demand of 100 units. The most that we should pay for this extra mesh would be T$75, plus the standard price per square metre of mesh. T$75 is the contribution that we can earn for each extra square metre, known as the shadow price. Once we have made the maximum demand of medium chicken houses, we would then manufacture the large chicken houses. Each extra square metre of mesh we obtain would then generate T$66 contribution. Thus we would be willing to pay T$66 plus the standard price of mesh. Once we have secured enough mesh to produce 100 of each of the products, we will not buy any more mesh at a premium price.

As this is the first month that we are going to deliver products to UCP, it is important that we get it right. It could be more important to prove to our partner that we are professional and reliable rather than be profitable in the short term.

UCP have stated that they will increase the order size in the future and this could mean long-term benefits. This may not happen if we let them down on the very first order. Therefore, we could argue that almost any price is worth paying to ensure that we have enough wire mesh.

In addition, we should consider that our reputation will suffer if we let our customers down and this may affect our brand image and future hive sales.

TQM

Senior Management Support

Any TQM program that is not supported by the senior management is unlikely to succeed. Introducing a TQM system at Mavis Venderby will require a cultural change and this will be difficult to achieve without the passion and commitment of the top level managers. This week, we have seen the senior management involve themselves in a quality issue and it is likely that they will continue to do this as it is already part of our culture. As the production director, Joseph is a key senior manager, his 40 years of experience and extensive knowledge means that he is respected by all. It is a concern that he is reluctant to adopt TQM because without his support, any initiative is likely to fail.

Prevention

TQM requires that costs caused by mistakes which have to be rectified by consuming more resources, are eliminated. We will have to spend extra resource trying to source additional mesh. The senior management and purchasing manager have already spent considerable time and effort trying to minimise the damage caused by the forgotten wire mesh order. It is likely that there is more work to do before the problem is fully resolved. If this level of error is repeated frequently, it will reduce the long-term profit of the business.

Prevention of poor quality is often accompanied by the phrase "right first time", where the focus is placed on the design of processes and systems in order to ensure that mistakes are minimised.

Participation by All

In order to ensure an efficient process with a quality output, TQM discourages silo thinking. Each aspect of the supply chain (external and internal) contributes to the quality of the final product and its profitability.

Our employees will be expected to work cross-functionally, often in teams, to solve quality problems. To a small extent, this has been demonstrated with the mesh problem as production, purchasing and finance are working together to try and ensure that customers get their goods on time.

The customer is the entity that defines quality in any TQM system. UCP have specified the materials and approved the prototypes of the new products. This is the standard output that we now have to achieve in order to satisfy our customer. They have defined the quantity of products each month and the delivery time, which are parts of the standard that we should meet. We need to participate with our customer in order that we can achieve the quality standard that they require, otherwise we will reduce our ability to make profit.

The suppliers to the business will also have to be included in the participation process. The mesh that our customer specified as a key quality issue could not be supplied at very short notice this week. In future, we must ensure that we have sufficient resource to make the products needed.

Many thanks!

Management Accountants Assistant
Mavis Venderby

Section 2

From: Management Accountant Assistant
To: Pene Lopez, Finance Director
Subject: ABC and HRM

ABC

We have already determined cost pools for the machine set-up and the inspection activities within the cutting department. In order for us to absorb the overhead into products using ABC, we need to determine what causes the cost of each activity (the cost driver).

Machine Set-up Costs

The activity that will cause the total cost of machine set-ups to increase or reduce is the resetting of the machine. Therefore the cost driver is the number of machine set-ups.

To establish the total number of machine set-ups, we need to firstly calculate the number of batches required for each product type and secondly, the number of set-ups in total per product type.

In order to reduce the cost of the product that we sell to UCP, we need to try to reduce the amount of activity (machine set-ups) that each of the products uses. For example, with rabbit hutch we need to question why the batch size is so small? Is there a good reason that there are half the number of items in a batch of rabbit hutches compared to the other UCP products? If we could increase the batch size to be in line with the other UCP products (assuming that the number of batches per set-up stays the same as it is now), the number of machine set-ups would reduce, and therefore the set-up cost per rabbit hutch would also reduce.

Inspection Costs

Total inspection cost is driven by total inspection time. The factors that drive total inspection time are the number of inspections per batch and the actions taken during each inspection. These actions when multiplied by the total number of inspections needed will determine the total amount of time taken for the inspections. Therefore the cost driver is inspection time.

To establish the total inspection time, we need to firstly calculate the number of batches required for each product type and secondly, the total amount of inspection time needed for each product type.

In order to reduce the cost of the product that we sell to UCP, we need to establish why it is that the UCP products require a longer amount of time to inspect? UCP mandates that one in every five items are inspected and we will therefore not be able to reduce the number of inspections, but it could be that we are performing unnecessary checks during the inspection itself and that we could save time by eliminating these.

HR Plan

There are considered to be 5 main stages in developing an HR plan as follows.

Strategic Analysis

Planning for an increase or decrease in the staffing levels and the mix of skills required in the longer term depend upon the strategic goals and directions that our business takes. At present, we are extending our product range into new markets, albeit using existing resources and experience, this may mean that a long-term increase in the number of employees is needed. In addition to the wood working skills, other skills, such as negotiating prices with customers and suppliers, are increasing in importance.

Wider environmental factors should also be considered, for example, changes in legislation that restrict the length of time that employees are allowed to work each week. We are a seasonal business and we frequently rely on overtime working during the busy months.

Inventory of Existing Human Resources

This is an audit of the existing work force composition, the organisational structure details levels of authority and responsibility.

Included within this audit will be our policy with regards to flexible working, overtime, quiet periods and so on.

Identify the Gaps

Based on steps one and two, this is an evaluation of the differences between the current and future needs of our business with regards to the workforce. Its purpose is to identify potential skills shortages in specific areas—for example the negotiating skills needed in the purchasing department. This will identify the need for succession planning and management.

Develop the Plan to Close the Gap

Based on the fact that we are in need of more staff, we will have identified a shortfall. Therefore we will need to consider how to obtain the resource needed to fill this shortfall. As the shortfall is likely to be large, we can no longer fill the gap using overtime. Therefore, there will be a need to recruit new members from external sources. The cost and effectiveness of this will be determined by the availability of external resources.

One consideration that the senior managers should consider is the skill level that should be recruited. On the one hand, it may be more beneficial to recruit trainees and train them in house than qualified employees. On the other hand, experienced and highly qualified workers can bring in new ideas and skills that can improve our performance.

Wherever possible we should consider internal promotions before recruiting externally. This is because advancement and recognition are considered to increase motivation and commitment to the business.

Monitor and Review

The first action will be to close the gap between supply and demand. The HRP is an ongoing plan and the key to its success is constantly monitoring, measuring and reporting on progress as well as responding to changing circumstances.

We currently employ 165 people, all of whom will have to be trained and developed as the need for new skills and the demands of changes in technology arises. In addition, staff will leave Mavis Venderby, the reasons for which should be ascertained and analyzed.

Many thanks!

Management Accountants Assistant
Mavis Venderby

Section 3

From: Management Accountant Assistant
To: Pene Lopez, Finance Director
Subject: Hive cutting department variance report and working capital

Variance Report

Box Cedar

Only experienced labour was used to manufacture box cedar hives, which has possibly contributed to the labour efficiency here; experienced staff need less time than trainees to complete the work. In addition, the reject rate was lower than budget, indicating that much of the production was good.

Box Pine

The mix variance indicates that less of the cheaper trainee labour, and therefore more of the expensive skilled labour, was used than standard. The overall effect of this is an adverse mix variance. As trainees are not allowed to work overtime, the mix variance might have been caused by the need for experienced workers having to work extra hours to try to achieve an acceptable volume of output.

During the month, less hives were produced than budgeted. The possibility of the trainee labour being used to manufacture these hives was little. The reject rate was higher than expected and this has contributed towards the adverse labour yield variance. It was also possible that the amount of hours spent on producing the actual number of box hives was more than expected. As Ron put the less able of the trainees to work on this product line, it was probable that they reduced every worker's efficiency.

The reject rate at 12% far exceeds the expected 7. 5% which is, once again, a reflection of the trainees' lack of competence. In addition, the new operational standards that we set may not be accurate.

Slatted Cedar

Less hives were produced than budgeted. This was probably due to a fault with one of the cutting machines that stopped production. The downtime caused by this stoppage caused the idle time variance as 50 labour hours were lost. Thus we had to pay workers while, through no fault of their own, they were unable to work.

Despite a higher than expected reject rate, there was a favourable labour efficiency variance which must be explained by efficient working. This indicates that the experienced and competent staff on this production line worked quicker than standard.

The proportion of rejected hives was, at 6%, higher than standard. This may be due to the fact that the work flow had been disrupted and it is also likely that some of the hives produced before the breakdown were spoiled due to the machine fault.

Slatted Pine

The mix variance shows that a small number of hours more were worked by the expensive skilled workers compared to the standard mix. This suggests that there was less need for the skilled workers to work longer to rectify trainee's errors or increase volume (unlike box pine hives).

The trainees manufacturing this product is more able than the trainees making the box hives and the yield variance shows a relatively small adverse variance. This indicates that the trainees must be working close to the efficiency that is expected of them. As the reject rate is expected as the slight inefficiency must be due to workers working slower than standard.

Working Capitial

The Working Capital Cycle

The working capital cycle is calculated as receivable days plus inventory days less payable days. If the working capital cycle has increased, this is likely to mean a combination of increasing receivable and inventory days and decreasing payable days.

As UCP is such an important customer, we have allowed them credit terms that are more favourable than our usual ones. Our commercial beekeeper customers have traditionally been allowed 30 days but UCP have 45 days to pay. As UCP is our largest customer, the impact of this is to increase our receivables balance as well as receivables days. The increase is compounded by the fact that UCP are taking even longer than 45 days to pay.

Work-in-progress inventory will be increasing our production costs for staff wages and power cost increases will be valued in the inventory. The mix of raw materials ordered will also affect the working capital cycle. For example, Tracey will be placing larger orders for cedar, as all of the UCP products are made of cedar, this will be held in stores for 6 months, longer than any other material used.

It is likely that payable days has fallen. At Mavis Venderby, we have enjoyed excellent credit terms with our wood supplier for years. It is unlikely that any new supplier (for example the specialist mesh supplier) would offer such attractive terms. Similarly as we are new to the specialist mesh supplier, it is likely that our credit is capped until we prove ourselves to be good payers.

The danger of increasing our working capital cycle is that it will reduce our liquidity, this is particularly true during a time of rapid expansion. At an extreme point, we risk running out of cash and being unable to pay for the day-to-day transaction in our business.

Measures to Minimise the Risk that UCP do not Pay

We should ensure that all of our credit control processes are followed rigorously. Statements must be sent regularly and any overdue debts requested in a timely manner. We must be aware of any changes in the industry, which might suggest that UCP are unable to pay. We should track payment history regularly and even be prepared to stop supply if payments are excessively late.

If we consider the risk is too much for us to take, we might consider a without recourse factoring arrangement. The factor would take over control of our credit control department and bear the cost of any irrecoverable debt. Of course, this option would be quite expensive.

The risk that a debt becomes irrecoverable increases with the age of the debt. If we offer a prompt payment discount to UCP, we can reduce the risk, although once again this will reduce the value of the monies owed.

One other method that we could use to reduce the risk of UCP failing to pay us, would be the use of credit insurance. This would probably be preferable to factoring as we will get the benefit of the transfer of risk while maintaining control of our credit control function.

Many thanks!

Management Accountants Assistant
Mavis Venderby

Section 4

Cost of Quality and Accounting Treatment—Brief Notes

Cost of Quality

Prevention

The regular servicing of the machinery by Tracey's maintenance staff would help to prevent disasters, like the recent cutting machine breakdown occurring. Hence the costs associated with this are a prevention cost as they are incurred to prevent bad quality. This does come at a price—known as the cost of conformance.

The costs of this are easily ascertained. All maintenance parts ordered for this purpose can be coded via the purchase ledger and the time spent on maintenance recorded through the maintenance workers timesheets.

Appraisal

This is also a cost of conformance as we check that whether the quality of our output is sufficient to be used in the downstream process.

The cost of the quality checks that you propose to introduce to the production processes will be categorised here. So for example, if any wood is issued from stores, a check that it has the required level of moisture will ensure that further production costs are not incurred on material that will never produce a quality product.

The costs here are also easy to ascertain as we will either code a salary or a proportion of a salary from the person doing the checks.

Internal Failure

This is a cost of non-conformance and it is incurred as a result of producing items that are not of sufficient quality. The breakdown of the machine is an internal failure as it produced hives that we had to scrap and prevented us from producing good-quality hives for the duration of its repair. The cost associated with this failure is the wastage incurred as well as the costs to repair the machine.

As we have detailed costings for our hives, we can ascertain the costs incurred in producing the hives up until the stage that they were scrapped. For example, if they were half way through the cutting process, we could cost the scrap as 100% of the standard drying cost and 50% of the standard cutting cost.

The cost to repair the machine is easy to calculate, as the invoice for the part and the courier can be coded/recorded when the invoice is received. Likewise the extra overtime worked can be recorded on the time sheets.

External Failure

This is a cost of non-conformance as well. The difference here is that our poor quality effects on our customer. The complaint that we received from the Middletown Beekeeping Association is an evidence of the external failure.

The cost of this quality failure can be ascertained up to a point. We can cost a proportion of Jacinta's salary to represent the two hours that she spend in dealing with the complaint, we can also code/record the courier invoice and the cost of the frames and foundation.

However, the loss of customer goodwill and the damage to our brand name is impossible to cost accurately.

Accounting Treatment of New Production Facility Costs

IAS 16: Property, PPE states that expenditure associated with an item of PPE can be capitalised If it is either part of the purchase price (including import duties) or it can be directly attributable to getting the asset ready for its intended use.

From the schedule, the purchase price of the new plant and equipment, import duties and building contractor's cost all into this first category.

The costs that are directly attributable costs include: the architects fees, the site preparation costs, and the installation of the plant and equipment. All of these costs are necessary to build and to ensure that the machines work correctly.

The interest costs are dealt with in IAS 23: Borrowing costs. IAS 23 states that where an asset is constructed over a substantial period of time, any borrowing costs incurred from the construction date commenced up until the point the construction is complete and the asset is ready for its intended use should be capitalised. The first issue is whether the construction of our new facility is deemed to have been carried out over a substantial period of time; we will need to check this with our auditors.

On the assumption that our construction does met the conditions of IAS 23, we will be able to capitalise the interest incurred until the date at which the new facility was deemed ready for its intended use (even if we did not actually start production straight away). We will need to check when the loan was taken out as we can only capitalise interest incurred after the start of construction activities, which might be different from the date the loan was taken out.

The training costs however cannot be capitalised as they do not meet the definition of an asset. Although the training may lead to future economic benefit for our business, we cannot control it as the staff are free to leave the business at any time.

The cost of marketing and general overhead are not likely to be directly attributable and will have to be expensed as they are incurred. The marketing is an event that bears no relation to the construction of the new facility and the overhead is an apportionment rather than directly incurred, which in accordance with IAS 16 cannot be capitalised.

试卷三　参考答案

任务一

发件人：管理会计助理

收件人：财务总监 Pene Lopez

主　题：网格短缺与全面质量管理

计划表说明

这份生产计划表使用了一种被称为限制因素分析的方法。

生产计划表呈现了我们承诺给 UCP 提供的三种产品的毛利润。由于固定成本在短期内保持不变，所以我们将毛利润而非单件产品利润设定为固定成本。因此，即使每一件产品的利润会随交易量的变化而改变，但其毛利润是恒定的。

如果没有发生网格短缺，大型鸡舍将会被认为是赚钱最多的产品而兔笼是赚钱最少的产品。然而当网格成为短缺资源时，为了达到利润最大化，我们需要使每平方米网格的毛利润最大化。从计划表中我们可以看到，我们可以从生产的每个兔笼中赚取 T\$ 110/m^2，每个中型鸡舍赚取 T\$ 75/m^2，每个大型鸡舍仅赚取 T\$ 66/m^2。

如果我们尚未做出每个产品至少生产 50 件的决定，那么我们应生产更多的中型鸡舍而不是大型鸡舍，因为这样会增加毛利润。

而考虑到最低生产限制，最佳生产计划表明 83 个中型鸡舍，50 个大型鸡舍和 100 个兔笼将为最佳产品组合。完成这些产品后，我们将耗尽几乎所有可用的网格。

需要为额外的网格支付多少钱?

如果 Tracey 能够提供额外的网格，我们应该优先制作中型鸡舍，直到满足 100 个中型鸡舍的最大需求。我们最多为这些额外的网格支付 T\$ 75，加上每平方米网格的标准价格。由影子价格可知，T\$ 75 是我们可以从额外的每平方米网格中赚取的毛利润。一旦达到中型鸡舍的最大需求，我们就应该开始生产大型鸡舍。我们获得的每个额外网格都可以赚取 T\$ 66 的毛利润。因此，我们愿意支付 T\$ 66 以及每平方米网格的标准价格。一旦我们拥有足够的网格能每种商品生产 100 件，我们将不会再以高价购买更多的网格。

由于这是我们为 UCP 提供产品的第一个月，确保过程无误十分重要。向我们的合作伙伴证明，我们是专业并且可靠的，这比注重短期利益更重要。

UCP 已经声明，他们以后会增加订单数量，这表明我们将有长期收益。如果我们让他们在第一单就感到失望，这些将不会发生。因此，几乎可以说只要能确保我们有足够的金属网格，付出任何代价都不为过。

另外我们也应该考虑到，如果让客户失望，我们的声誉会受到影响，而这可能会影响我们的品牌形象和未来蜂箱的销售。

全面质量管理

高级管理层支持

没有高级管理层的支持，全面质量管理不可能成功。在梅维斯·文德柏公司内引进全面质量管理系统需要企业文化的改变，而这种改变如果没有高级管理层的热情与支持是很难实现的。本周，我们已经看到，高级管理层面临着质量问题，而他们还会继续这样做，因为这已经变成我们企业文化的一部分。作为生产经理，Joseph 是高层管理中的关键人员，他 40 年的经验和广博的知识意味着他受到所有人的尊重。他不愿意采用全面质量管理系统这一点非常令人担忧，因为没有他的支持，任何尝试都可能会失败。

预防

全面质量管理要求所有因纠正错误而消耗的材料成本都要被消除。我们需要支付额外的资源去满足增加的网格。高级管理层和采购经理已经花费大量时间和精力去最小化由于遗忘网格订单而造成的破坏。在问题被完全解决之前，可能还有更多的工作要做。如果同样的错误再三出现，企业的长期利润将会减少。防止质量低下往往伴随着一个短语——“一次就过”，为了保证错误最小化，应该将重点放在过程和系统的设计上。

全员参与

为了保证高效高质的产出过程，全面质量管理不鼓励筒仓思维，供应链的各个方面（外部和内部）都应助力于最终产品的质量和盈利能。

我们的员工被期望能够在团队中跨职能地合作，解决质量问题。在一定程度上，网格问题这件事也展示了生产、采购和财务部门可以共同合作，保证消费者能按时收到他们的货物。

在全面质量管理中，消费者是定义质量的存在。UCP 已经指定了材料并且批准了新产品的标准。为了取悦顾客，这是我们必须达到的标准化生产。他们定义了产品每月交付的数量和时间，这也是我们需要达到的标准。我们需要与客户一起合作，达到他们要求的质量标准，否则我们的盈利能力将被削弱。

企业的供应商也包含在参与过程中。被我们的消费者认定为关键质量物品的网格无法在一周内立刻提供。在未来，我们必须保证拥有足够的资源去生产被需要的产品。

十分感谢！

梅维斯·文德柏公司

管理会计助理

任务二

发件人：管理会计助理

收件人：财务总监 Pene Lopez

主　题：成本作业法和人力资源管理

成本作业法

我们已经确定了切割部门的设备安装资金池和检查活动。为了使我们能够利用成本作业法以吸收产品费用，我们需要确定每个活动的成本发生的原因（成本驱动因素）。

设备安装成本

重置机器将导致机器安装的总成本增加或减少。因此，设备安装的数量是成本驱动因素。

为了确定设备安装总数，我们首先需要计算每种产品类型所需的批次数量，其次需要计算每个产品类型的总计安装数量。

为了降低我们向 UCP 销售的产品的成本，我们需要尝试减少每个产品使用的活动量（设备安装）。例如，关于兔窝，我们应质疑为何其批次容量如此之小？有没有好的理由可以解释，为什么一批产品中，兔窝的数量只有其他 UCP 产品的一半？如果我们可以将其批量大小增加到与其他 UCP 产品相等（假设每台设备的批次容量与现在相同），设备安装的数量将减少，这样每只兔窝的安装成本也会减少。

检查费用

检查总费用由检查总时间驱动。驱动检查总时间的因素是每批次的检查次数和每次检查期间采取的行动数的总和。这些行动乘以所需的总检查数将决定检查所用的总时间。因此，成本驱动因素是检查时间。

为了确定总检查时间，我们需要首先计算每个产品类型所需的批次数量，其次是每个产品类型所需的检验时间总量。

为了降低我们向 UCP 销售的产品的成本，我们需要确定为什么 UCP 产品需要更长的时间来检查？UCP 要求每 1/5 的产品都需要进行检查，因此，我们无法减少检查次数，但在检查期间可能进行了不必要的检查，我们可以通过减少这些检查来节省时间。

人力资源计划

制订人力资源计划，将有 5 个主要阶段。

战略分析

规划员工人数的增加或减少以及长期所需技能的组合，这些都取决于我们的业务采取的战略目标和方向。目前，我们将产品范围扩大到新的市场，尽管可以使用现有的资源和经验，这也同时可能意味着我们需要长期增加员工人数。除了木工技能，其他技能，如与客户和供应商谈判价格，也越来越重要。

还应考虑更广泛的环境因素，例如员工每周工作时长限制的立法变更。我们是季节性的业务，在旺季要经常依靠加班。

现有的人力资源储备

这是一种对已存在劳动力构成的审查，组织结构详细地列出了权利和责任。

我们关于弹性工作、加班、淡季等各方面的政策都将包含在本次审查中。

确定差距

这一阶段基于第一和第二阶段，是对我们企业当前与未来对劳动力需求之间的差异的评估。目的是确定具体领域的潜在技能短缺，例如采购部门的谈判技能需求。这将确定后续计划和管理的必要性。

制订缩小差距的计划

基于我们的情况，我们需要更多的员工，我们将确定一个缺口。所以，我们需要考虑如何获得填补这个缺口的资源。由于缺口可能会很大，我们不能再用加班填补差距。因此，需要从外部招聘新成员。其成本和效果将取决于外部资源的可用性。

高级管理人员应考虑的一个因素是应聘者的技能水平。一方面，招募实习生并在公司内部培训可能会比直接招聘合格的员工更有益。另一方面，经验丰富的高素质员工可以带来新的思想和技巧，从而提高我们的绩效。

如有可能，我们应该尽量在外部招聘之前考虑内部晋升，因为提升和认可能够增加员工对工作的动力和忠诚。

监控和审查

第一步是缩小供需之间的差距。人力资源计划是一个持续的计划，其成功的关键是不断监测、测量并汇报进展情况以及对变化的应对情况。

最近，我们雇用了165人，由于新技术的需要和科技发展带来的变化，他们都需要接受培训并得到发展。另外，员工离开梅维斯·文德柏的原因应该被确定和分析。

十分感谢！

梅维斯·文德柏公司
管理会计助理

任务三

发件人：管理会计助理

收件人：财务总监 Pene Lopez

主　题：松木切割部门差异报告和营运资本

差异报告

盒式雪松蜂箱

只有熟练的工人才能生产盒式雪松蜂箱，因为这样可能有利于提高人工效率。熟练工完成这项工作的时间要比实习生少很多。此外，废品率也比预算低，这意味着这些产品大多都是优等品。

盒式松木蜂箱

这里的混合差异表明我们缺少廉价的实习生劳动力，因此需要更多价格贵但富有经验的劳动力，但往往会超过标准。整体的影响就是造成了不利的混合差异。因为实习生不允许加班工作，因此那些熟练工就要做额外的工作以保证产量达标。

本月，较之预算，松木的生产量有所减少。实习生会去生产这些松木的可能性较小。废品率比预计的要高并由此产生了不利的人工产量差异。也有可能，生产盒式松木蜂箱的实际数量所用工时比预计的要多。因为Ron安排了更少的实习生在这个生产线工作，因此有可能他们减少了每个员工的效率。

12%的废品率远超过预计的7.5%的废品率，这也再一次反映了实习生的能力缺陷。此外，我们设置的新运营标准可能不是很精确。

板式雪松蜂箱

生产的蜂箱比预计的要少。这也许是由于其中一个切割机出现故障，停止工作造成的。故障停工导致了闲置时间差异，有 50 个工时丢失了。然而我们不得不给工人支付工资，即使他们不能工作，因为从头到尾都不是他们的错。

尽管废品率比预期的要高，但也出现了有利的人工效率差异，这是因为工作有效率。这表明，有经验和有能力的员工在生产线上工作要比标准水平更快。

松木废品率是 6%，高于标准。这是由于工程线被打断，也有可能松木由于机器故障被损坏。

板式松木蜂箱

这一混合差异表明与标准混合相比，多出的那些工时会由工资更高的熟练工人完成。这表明，没有必要让技术工人加班去纠正实习生的错误或是增加产量（与盒式松木蜂箱不同）。

让实习生生产这个产品比让他们去做盒式松木蜂箱更好，产量差异显示出相对微弱的不利差异。这表明，实习生必须缩短与预期效率的差异，正如废品率被视为效率低下正是由于工人工作比标准速度慢。

运营资本

运营资本周期

运营资本周期是由应收账款周转期 + 存货周转期 – 应付账款周转期而计算得出。如果运营资金周转期增加，则可能意味着应收账款周转期和存货周转期增加以及应付账款周转期减少。

就像 UCP 这样重要的客户，我们给他们提供的贷款周期比我们的惯例更长。商业养蜂人客户一般有 30 天的贷款日，而 UCP 有 45 天。UCP 是我们最大的客户，这样做的影响就是增加了我们的应收账款余额和应收账款周转期。这一状况由于 UCP 甚至超过 45 天后才支付而变得更加复杂。

半成品存货会增加我们的生产成本，因为员工工资和电力成本的增加会被估价在存货中。原材料混合订购也会影响运营资本周期。例如，Tracey 会为雪松安排更多订单，因为所有 UCP 的产品都由雪松制成，这些雪松会在仓库中保存 6 个月，这比其他材料的时间长很多。

也有可能应付账款周转期缩短了。这些年，梅维斯 · 文德柏公司在木材供应商那里得到极好的信用期限。而新的供应商（例如特殊金属网格供应商）就不能给我们如此有诱惑的期限了。相同的，对于特殊金属网格供应商来说我们也是新客户，直到我们证明自己是一个优秀的交款人之前，我们的信用期限都无法改变。

增加运营资本周期的风险是流动资产减少，快速扩张期间尤其如此。在一个极端的临界点，我们可能会耗尽现金，无法支付日常交易款项。

UCP 未支付的风险最小化措施

我们应该确定我们所有的信用管理程序都严格执行。必须定期发送报告，任何逾期的债务都要及时催收。我们必须警惕任何一个产业上的改变，因为也许它就暗示着 UCP 无法再支付款项了。我们应该定期追踪支付记录，甚至当付款极度延迟时应准备停止供给。

如果我们认为风险太多，也许我们应该考虑进行无追索权保理的安排。这将接替信用控制部门掌握控制权，同时承担任何不可回收债务产生的费用。当然，这个选择将会十分昂贵。

随着债务年限的增加，债务变得不可收回的风险也在提高。如果我们为 UCP 提供即时付款折扣，这种风险就会被削弱，尽管这样做我们的欠款就会贬值。

另一个可以减少 UCP 不能付款的风险的方法就是利用信贷保险。这也许能更好地加以利用，因为风险转移会带来收益，同时也能保持我们对信用管理功能的控制权。

十分感谢！

梅维斯・文德柏公司

管理会计助理

任务四

质量成本和会计处理简报

质量成本

预防

Tracey 管理的维修部员工会定期检查维修机器以预防生产故障，像最近的切割机器故障一样。因此，与此相关的成本是一种预防成本，因为它们是用来预防劣质产品的。这就产生了一定的花费——一致性成本。

这个成本很容易弄清。所有为这一目标安排的维修部分，都可以通过进货分类账和维修工人的时间表记录的维修时间进行编码。

评估

这也是一种一致性成本，因为我们要检查产品的质量是否足够被用在下游的生产过程中。

在生产过程中引入质量检查的成本可以在这里进行分类。比如，如果仓库中有些木材出现了问题，一个湿度水平检测可以确保未来的产品制造成本不会因为使用了这种无法生产出高质量产品的原材料而升高。

这里的成本也很容易弄清，因为我们要么发薪水，要么发一部分检查人员的薪水。

内部失败

这是一种非一致性成本，是一项由于生产质量没达标而产生的费用。机器故障是一种内部失败，因为用它生产的蜂箱是残次品并且阻碍我们在修理期间生产高质量的蜂箱。与这项失败相关的成本是浪费及修理机器的成本。

由于详细了解了蜂箱的成本，我们可以弄清生产蜂箱的成本直到它们报废。例如，如果进行到切割过程的一半，我们可以将报废成本定为 100% 的标准干燥成本和 50% 的标准切割成本。

修理机器的成本很好计算。因为这部分的发货单和快递员在货物被签收时会被记录或编码。同理，额外的加班时间可以在时间表上进行记录。

外部失败

这也是一种非一致性成本。不同点在于我们的低质量影响了我们的顾客。米德尔顿养蜂协会对我们的投诉就是外部失败的一个证据。

在一定程度上，质量失败成本可以弄清楚。我们可以支付 Jacinta 部分工资以代表他花费两小时处理抱怨，我们也可以对快递发票和框架、底基的成本进行记录和编码。

然而，失去信誉和损坏品牌的成本是不可能精确计算的。

新生产设备成本的会计处理

国际会计准则第 16 号：不动产、厂房和设备规定，对于与某一固定资产相关的支出来说，如果它是购买价格的一部分（包括进口关税），或可直接归属于为预期用途而准备的资产，那么它就可以资本化。

在明细表中，新的厂房和设备的购买价格，进口关税和建筑师成本都分为第一类。

成本中的直接归属成本包括：建筑费、场地准备费、厂房和设备的安装费。所有这些成本都必须建立，以保证机器正确地工作。

利息费用的处理应查询国际会计准则第 23 号：借款成本。国际会计准则第 23 号规定，当资产在相当长的一段时间里被建造，从建设日期开始的任何借款费用，直到建设完成，且资产已准备好用于其预期用途时，都应该被资本化。首先要解决的问题是新设备的建造是否会被认为在相当长的一段时间里执行；我们需要与审计人员对此进行核查。

假设我们的建造符合国际会计准则第 23 号的规定，我们能够将产生的利息资本化，直到新设备被认为达到可使用状态的那一天（即使我们并没有开始直接生产）。我们需要检查偿还贷款的时间，因为我们只能在建造活动开始之后将产生的利息资本化，这可能和偿还贷款不是同一天。

然而培训费用不能被资本化，因为它不满足资本的定义。尽管培训能给公司带来未来的经济利益，我们依然不能控制它，因为员工可以在任何时刻离开公司。

销售费用和一般的间接费用不是直接归属成本，当它们产生时，它们将被费用化。销售是一件与新设备建造无关的事情，间接费用是一种分摊而不是直接发生的费用，这也就符合了国际会计准则第 16 号中不能被资本化的规定。

Variant 3　Marking Guidance

Section number	Technical skills		Business skills		People skills		Leadership skills		Integration	Total
1	Limiting factor analysis and factors to consider in respect of the price to pay for additional resource	7	TQM principles	4	Limiting factor analysis and factors to consider in respect of the price to pay for additional resource TQM principles	6 8			25	
2	ABC cost drivers	10	HR planning	12					3	25
3	Direct labour cost variances Working capital cycle and receivables risk management	13 6					Working capital cycle and receivables risk management	6		25
4	Cost of quality reporting Capitalisation of expenditure as PPE in accordance with IAS 16	12 13								25
Total marks available for each competency		61		16		14		6	3	100

试卷三　评分指南

序号	技术技能		商业技能		人际技能		领导技能		综合	合计
1	限制因素分析以及额外资源购买价格的考虑因素	7	全面质量管理原则	4	限制因素分析以及额外资源购买价格的考虑因素 全面质量管理原则	6 8				25
2	作业成本法成本动因	10	人力资源计划	12					3	25
3	直接人工成本差异 运营资本周期和应付账款风险管理	13 6					运营资本周期和应付账款风险管理	6		25
4	质量成本报告 根据国际会计准则第16号判定的作为不动产、厂房和设备的费用资本化	12 13								25
各技能评分合计		61		16		14		6	3	100

西安外国语大学名师解惑

试卷一共有四项任务，考查了 P1、F1、E1 三门课程的知识点，具体包括限制因素分析、全面质量管理、成本驱动因素、人力资源管理、运营资本周期计算、会计处理等。该试卷考核了考生的四项能力，其中技术技能的分值占 61%，商业技能的分值占 16%，人际技能的分值占 14%，领导技能的分值占 6%，与 CGMA 管理会计能力框架的技能要求一致。

该试卷的每项任务涉及以下知识点：

任务	问题	科目	知识点
任务一	限制因素分析以及额外资源购买价格的考虑因素	P1	限制因素分析（limiting factors analysis）
	全面质量管理原则	E1	全面质量管理（TQM）
任务二	作业成本法成本动因	P1	作业成本法（ABC）
	人力资源计划	E1	人力资源管理（HRM）
任务三	直接人工成本差异	P1	差异报告
	运营资本周期和应付账款风险管理	F1	运营资本周期计算
任务四	质量成本报告	E1	质量成本（quality cost）
	根据 IAS 16 判定的作为 PPE 的费用资本化	F1	资本化

上述各项任务要求以邮件、报告或工作笔记等形式来呈现答案，对问题的描述非常明确，答题时既要注意内容的针对性，也要注意形式的规范性。

其他答题注意事项包括：(1) 能否快速识别与理解问题（英语语言问题）以及对知识点的应用能力（案例考查的真正主体）；(2) 该套试题的问题指向鲜明，考生对问题的阅读与识别压力较小，问题连续且基本由连接词第一、第二或黑点标明，不需要考生有太多关于题目问题搜寻与理解的思考，关键在于能否有效地将知识应用到答案中；(3) 对于知识掌握较为一般的考生而言则压力较大，因为对于知识点的生疏会导致在答题时无话可说，考生常用的较为宽泛的表达也相对有限，知识在应用层面基本不能展现。

对应知识点深度剖析

限制因素分析

第一部分的答题压力首先来自于考生对知识点的识别。能否识别考点为限制因素是关键，无法识别问题的考生在附录数据的应用上会存在困难。能通过邮件标题、正文内容或者附录数据有效识别问题的考生，答题压力则主要集中在对数据的解释和应用。

全面质量管理

第二部分的题目范围极为明确，同时题目也明确要求与本周出现的问题关联。部分考生仅从定义的角度回答，而不关联问题，无法达到通过本场考试的要求。

作业成本法

第一部分的题目基本为“规定动作”，考生不需要有太多发挥，只需直接回答并解决问题即可。成本动因的识别与解释，对部分考生而言难度较大，尤其题目要求针对计算进行解释，因此，附录数据的应用在答案中应有所体现。

人力资源管理

第二部分题目的答案应围绕人力资源服务于公司战略的实施与调整，尤其题目情境为 HR 计划的从无到有、从无序到规范的过程，答案除了固定知识点还必须包括题目中明确提到的现有问题的解决方案。

差异报告

第一部分针对差异进行考查，要求考生在理解题目的同时用附录数据进行解释。虽然黑体的邮件文本可能会给考生带来压力，但由于题目要求较为明确，考生应当基于产品的人工差异给予反馈。这意味着考生应当客观地陈述数据，并据此进行成因及影响的分析讨论。

运营资本周期计算

第二部分主要针对 F1 的运营资本管理部分进行考查，答题压力相对较小，考生只要熟悉运营资本周期，回答该题应该难度不大。风险控制由于延续了运营资金的话题，答案的方向也较为明确，仍然以运营资金管理的角度切入，答案也较为容易。

质量成本

该部分的读题难度稍大，信息较为复杂，考生在要点信息的把控上可能会存在一些问题，好在问题非常明确，第一、第二两部分题目指向性较强，答题方向上的难度有所降低。第一部分主要考查知识点掌握的牢固程度，涉及 P1 关于质量成本的解释与应用，熟悉知识点的考生不会有太大压力。

资本化

第二部分考查资本化的问题，在 F1 部分考生压力较大，这主要是由于考生对会计准则具体条款不熟悉，也导致其在问题解析与知识应用中存在较大困难。解决方案可以分为两步：第一步，熟悉准则的具体内容，主要以理解为主，不需要刻意地逐字式记忆；第二步，结合情境予以分析应用。这个话题较为宽泛，应具体问题具体分析，很难一概而论。

Variant 4

This examination is structured as follows：

Section number	Number of tasks	Time for section(minutes)
1	1	45
2	1	45
3	1	45
4	1	45

The time available for each section is for reading,planning and writing your answer(s).

Section 1

It is the middle of March 2017. Sales of foundation have been strong over the financial year to the end of February 2017, with Mavis Venderby selling foundation to customers In other countries for the first time. In addition, Mavis has applied for a patent for a foundation pheromone that has been developed by Toby Venger, Sales and Marketing Manager. The expanding customer base and the potential of the pheromone enhance sales, and even further the directors decided on 20 February to set up a new foundation production facility in an empty building on site. We have to get the building ready so that the facility can be set up in a few weeks.

On 15 March 2017 you receive the following email from Pene Lopez, finance director.

From: Pene Lopez, Finance Director
To: Management Accountant Assistant
Subject: Performance of the foundation business

We will be having a directors' meeting next week to discuss the performance of the business over the last financial year. I have been tasked with writing a report for the meeting to cover all aspects of performance. Cormac has already prepared the numerical information and narrative for the hive business. He has also prepared the numerical information for the foundation business, for which I would like you to draft some of the narrative.

The first section I'd like you to draft relates to the production overhead variances for foundation production. I've attached to this email Cormac's schedule of the variances and what I need is an explanation of what these variances mean in terms of the performance of the foundation production cost centre. I have had a quick look and I know that Thomas is going to be surprised that the total variance is adverse. We produced 54,000 more foundations than the 346,000 we had budgeted to produce for the year ended 28 February 2017 and therefore I know he would have expected this increased production to have led to a favourable variance overall. Also the expenditure variance looks quite alarming, although I do know that our energy costs were higher than budgeted. In your analysis of the variances in Cormac's schedule, please also address these points.

The second section I'd like you to draft relates to the working capital position for the foundation business. I've attached Cormac's schedule of working capital days. The report needs to explain what is likely to have caused the movements compared to the budget and any risk implications of these movements to our business.

Many thanks!

Pene Lopez

Finance Director

Mavis Venderby

Production Overhead Variances for Foundation Production for the Year Ended 28 February 2017

Variance	Working	T$
Total	T$ 1,312,000—T$ 1,272,000	40,000 Adverse
Expenditure	T$ 1,100,280—T$ 1,312,000	211,720 Adverse
Efficiency	(96,000 hours—92,500 hours) ×T$ 13. 25	46,375 Favourable
Capacity	(83,040 hours—92,500 hours) ×T$ 13. 25	125,345 Favourable

Notes:

(1)400,000 units of foundation were actually produced in the year to 28 February 2017; budgeted production was 346,000 units.

(2) The budgeted production overhead absorption rate for the foundation cost centre for the year to 28 February 2017 is T$ 13. 25 per direct labour hour. Each unit of foundation is budgeted to take 0. 24 direct labour hours.

Working Capital Ratios for the Foundation Business

Ratio	Actual using balances at the year ended 28 February 2017	Budget using balances at the year ended 28 February 2017
Raw materials lnventory days	52	20
Finished goods inventory days	10	22
Receivables days(for credit sales)	45	25
Payables days	49	30

Write the two draft sections requested by Pene Lopez, finance director.

Section 2

A few weeks later, you attend a meeting about the new foundation production facility where Jack Curnow, Foundation Production Manager, says the following:

"The new pheromone developed by Toby is nearly ready for production. Therefore we will be setting up the new facility with this in mind as it is going to complicate our production process. In effect, there will now be two products, foundation with pheromone (to be known as FP) and foundation without pheromone (to be known as F). We expect that 25% of our total sales of foundation will be the new FP product. The pheromone will be added to the wax at the point where it is melted and it means that FP will take longer to dry than F. In addition, because we will need to ensure the correct balance of wax and pheromone when melted, we will need to produce FP in smaller batches than F. We will need to wash out the vat and reset the production line each time we switch production and we expect that production of F and FP will give rise to the same number of set-ups. FP will also require more quality checks and a greater number of both machine and direct labour hours per batch than F."

The day after the meeting, Pene Lopez sends you the following email:

From: Pene Lopez, Finance Director

To: Management Accountant Assistant

Subject: New production facility

I had a talk with Jack Curnow and Joseph Perez after the meeting yesterday about the new facility. The plan is to move the old production line machinery (which is five years old, but well maintained and still fully functional) into an existing unused building on site. The building needs considerable work before it can be used, but it will give the foundation business the scope to expand and possibly add a second production line in the future. There will be a new stores area for foundation raw materials and finished goods within the building.

Joseph believes a new foundation facility being set up is an ideal time for the business to think about sustainability in operations. He has asked for our thoughts on the factors that team need to consider in respect of setting up a sustainable foundation operation. So that I can compile a response from the finance team, I would like you to send me four ideas of how to develop a sustainable operation.

I've also been thinking about the costing system that we use for the foundation facility and I am considering ABC. I've mentioned this to Thomas Venderby and he is keen to know how this approach will differ from what we already done. Please draft a response that I can send to Thomas, which explains how ABC differs from the traditional absorption costing approach that we've always used, using examples from the foundation pan of the business to illustrate. I've attached the workings of how we've established the foundation production overhead absorption rate for the 2017/2018 foundation budget to show the approach we've taken before.

Pene Lopez
Finance Director
Mavis Venderby

The Schedule of the Workings for the Foundation Production Overhead Absorption Rate(Year Ended 28 February 2018)

The following workings were prepared earlier in the year to support the budgeted foundation production overhead absorption rate for the year to 28 February 2018, This was prepared prior to the decision to set up a new foundation facility and the launch of the pheromone foundation(FP); the effects of both are excluded from these workings.

Total Foundation Production Overhead Cost

	T$
Specifically allocated:	
Machinery related costs	186,400
Production manager and supervisor salaries	135,000
Other specifically allocated costs	34,000
Apportioned:	
Energy	420,000
Property related costs	324,800
Other apportioned production overhead costs	66,600
Share of goods inwards & maintenance service department costs	140,000
Total foundation production overhead cost	1,306,800

Foundation Production Overhead Absorption Rate

Total foundation production overhead cost	T$ 1,306,800
Total direct labour hours	95,040 hours
Foundation production overhead absorption rate per direct labour hour	T$ 13.75

Write your response to Pene Lopez, finance director.

Section 3

A few days later, Pene Lopez calls you into her office and says:

I had a discussion yesterday with Jacinta about marketing for the new pheromone foundation product. She believes that there is a large market for the product, especially in other countries. She expects that some sales will be at the expense of our existing foundation, but not to any great extent. Whilst Jacinta is confident that it will be a success, she is worried about the level of this success, although she thinks that the more we spend on marketing the better the result will be. I guess her view is to be expected given that she is in charge of marketing.

Anyway, she gave me her estimates of sales under three different demand levels: excellent, good and moderate. She also gave me her assessment of the probability of each of the demand levels occurring based on her knowledge of the market. I've used her information to prepare a schedule of expected value, standard deviation and coefficient of variation for each campaign. I am going to present this at a meeting that we have tomorrow about marketing of the new foundation. Please can you prepare the content for a briefing paper that explains the meaning of the data in my schedule and how different attitudes to risk will affect the decision regarding which campaign to undertake.

In addition, I know that Jacinta has some ideas about how we will market the new pheromone foundation, but I would like to go to the meeting feeling prepared. Please send me explanation of four marketing techniques that you feel would be particularly effective to promote this new product, including why they would be effective.

The Schedule prepared by Pene Lopez can be found in following tables.

Campaign A(Highest Marketing Spend)

Demand	Predicted additional profit (net of marketing spend) (T$ 000)	Probability	Expected value (T$ 000)
Excellent	720	0.3	216
Good	300	0.3	90
Moderate	(60)	0.4	(24)
Expected value			282

Standard deviation for campaign A = T$323,000

Coefficient of variation for campaign A = 1.15

Campaign B(Medium Marketing Spend)

Demand	Predicted additional profit (net of marketing spend) (T$ 000)	Probability	Expected value (T$ 000)
Excellent	500	0.3	150
Good	280	0.3	84
Moderate	10	0.4	4
Expected value			238

Standard deviation for campaign B = T$205,000

Coefficient of variation for campaign B = 0.86

Campaign C(Lowest Marketing Spend)

Demand	Predicted additional profit (net of marketing spend) (T$ 000)	Probability	Expected value (T$ 000)
Excellent	360	0.3	108
Good	260	0.3	78
Moderate	100	0.4	40
Expected value			226

Standard deviation of campaign C T$110,000

Coefficient of variation for campaign C = 0.49

Write your response to Pene Lopez's requests.

Section 4

A few months later, the new facility is open and fully operational. The patent for the pheromone was granted two months ago and the launch of the new foundation has been very successful, with a number of new customers from other countries.

Pene Lopez is on annual leave and Cormac Jones is absent from work due to illness when you receive the following email from Thomas Venderby.

From: Thomas Venderby, Managing Director
To: Management Accountant Assistant
Subject: Financial and environmental reporting

I know that Pene and Cormac are both away today, but I'm sure you can help me with a couple of things.

Firstly, I have just been looking at the notes that Pene left me about things that need to happen whilst she is away and I have two queries arising from this that I'd like your help on.

- Pene asked me to make sure that a payment for B $45,000 is made to our foreign supplier of equipment for the new foundation facility. I have just contacted the bank who are going to process the payment, although they have said that this now translates to T$ 28,500, which is different from the amount that is recorded in the purchase ledger of T$ 26,000. My query is what value should we record this transaction at and how will this transaction will affect our financial statements for the year to 28 February 2018.
- Pene also asked me to make a start establishing the costs that we can capitalise as an intangible asset in respect of the development work that we've undertaken to achieve the patent that we've just been awarded. She has told me that we've met the conditions to create an intangible asset. The trouble is that I don't know what types of costs can be capitalised. Please let me know what I should be including.

Secondly, in setting up the new facility, we have tried to make the environmental awareness as a part of being a sustainable operation. I think that there is much more than we could do across our business, especially in hive production. However, I've not really got any idea of how much environmental cost we generate, or indeed the costs that we incur to prevent affecting the environment. I've read that we could use the quality framework to report all of our environmental costs. In an environmental cost report I would like to know (1) how this might be applied in our business; (2) any benefits that could gain from its implementation; (3) any difficulties we might encounter.

Many thanks!

Thomas Venderby
Managing Director
Mavis Venderby

Write a response to Thomas Venderby's requests.

试卷四

本次考试的结构如下：

序号	任务数	时间（分钟）
1	1	45
2	1	45
3	1	45
4	1	45

每个部分规定的时间可用于读题、组织和书写答案。

任务一

现在是2017年3月中旬。由于梅维斯·文德柏公司首次将蜂巢底基销售给其他国家的顾客，因此在截至2017年2月底的财政年度中，底基的销售一直十分强劲。此外，Mavis还为市场营销经理Toby Venger开发的底基信息素申请了专利。不断扩大的客户群和信息素的潜力促进了销售，甚至让经理决定2月20日要在一个空的建筑工地建造一个新的底基生产设备。我们务必将建筑工地准备好以便设备能在几周内开工。

2017年3月15日，你收到了来自财务总监Pene Lopez的邮件，内容如下。

发件人：财务总监Pene Lopez

收件人：管理会计助理

主　题：底基业务的商业绩效

下周，有一个讨论上一财年商业绩效的董事会即将召开。我的任务是写一份涵盖绩效分析所有方面的会议报告。Cormac已经针对蜂窝业务准备了数据信息及相关解析，他也为底基业务准备了一些数据信息，但需要你完成解析部分。

希望由你撰写的第一个部分是关于底基的生产间接成本差异。我附上了Cormac的差异计划书，我需要你解释一下，这些差异从底基产品成本中心的绩效角度来说意味着什么。我已经浏览过文件，我感觉Thomas对于总差异是有利的将会非常惊讶。截至今年的2月28日，我们生产了比预定计划346 000件还多54 000件的底基，因此我相信他早已料到产量的增加会导致总成本差异呈正值。同样，费用支出差异看起来相当惊人，即使我知道能源成本比预算要高。在你分析Cormac的计划成本差异时请标注出这些点。

希望由你撰写的第二个部分是底基业务的运营资本。我已经附上了Cormac计划的运营资本天数。这份报告需要解释哪些因素会造成与预算的偏差以及这些偏差给我们业务带来的任何风险。

非常感谢！

梅维斯·文德柏公司

财务总监

Pene Lopez

截至 2017 年 2 月 28 日的底基生产间接成本差异

差异	工作	金额（T$）
总计	T$ 1 312 000— T$ 1 272 000	40 000 盈余
支出	T$ 1 100 280— T$ 1 312 000	211 720 盈余
效率	（96 000 小时—92 500 小时）×T$ 13. 25	46 375 亏损
生产能力	（83 040 小时—92 500 小时）× T$ 13. 25	125 345 亏损

注：

（1）400 000 个单位的底基实际上是在 2017 年 2 月 28 日之前生产的。预计生产 346 000 个单位。

（2）底基成本中心的预计生产间接成本吸收率在 2017 年 2 月 28 日之前是每直接工时 T$ 13. 25。每一单位底基预计花费 0. 24 个直接工时。

底基业务的运营资本率

比率	截至 2017 年 2 月 28 日的实际使用余额	截至 2017 年 2 月 28 日的预计使用余额
原材料存货天数	52	20
完成品存货天数	10	22
应收账款天数	45	25
应付账款天数	49	30

请针对邮件中财务总监 Pene Lopez 提出的两个部分撰写报告草案。

任务二

几周后，你参加了一个关于新底基生产设备的会议，在会上底基生产主管 Jack Curnow 说道：

Toby 生产的新型信息素即将投入生产，因此，我们也将建造新的生产设备，这会使我们的产品生产复杂化。事实上，将会出现两种产品，有信息素的底基（称作 FP）和没有信息素的底基（称作 F）。我们预期总底基销售里的 25% 都是新的 FP 产品。我们将在蜂蜡融化的时候加入信息素，这也就意味着 FP 的烘干时间要比 F 长。另外，因为我们需要确保蜂蜡在融化的时候与信息素保持比例正确，所以相比 F，我们要更小批量地生产 FP。每次转换产品时我们都需要冲洗大桶并重新设置生产线，而且我们希望 F 和 FP 的生产可以产生相同数量的固定设置。相比 F，FP 需要更高质量的检查，每一批次生产所需的机器和人工工时也更多。

会议第二天，Pene Lopez 给你发了如下邮件：

发件人：财务总监 Pene Lopez
收件人：管理会计助理
主　题：新的生产设备

昨天会议结束后，我和 Jack Curnow 及 Joseph Perez 讨论了新设备的相关事宜。我们计划将旧的生产线机械（已经使用了 5 年，但维修及时，功能完好）转移到现在还未使用的生产基地。在这个基地投入使用之前还需要完成大量的工作，但是这个基地可以扩大底基业务的经营范围，并且在未来可能增加第二条生产线。在这个基地内将会有一个新的底基原材料和产成品的储存区域。

Joseph 认为，建造新的底基设备是企业考虑运营可持续性的理想时机。他要求我们就建立可持续性底基运营所需考虑的因素提出意见。因此，我可以从财务团队那里收集反馈，希望你能给我提供 4 个关于如何发展可持续性经营的想法。

我也在考虑底基设备所用的成本法，比如成本作业法。我跟 Thomas Venderby 提过，他非常渴望知道这个方法与之前使用的成本核算方法有何不同。请你撰写一封回信，我好发给 Thomas Venderby，解决他所提出的疑惑，并举出有关底基业务的例子进行说明。我附上了我们之前为 2017 年/2018 年的底基预算建立底基生产成本吸收率的方法，以此说明我们以前采用的成本法。

梅维斯·文德柏公司
财务总监
Penez Lopez

底基生产成本吸收率的运营计划书（截至 2018 年 2 月 28 日）

在今年早些时候，为了支持截至 2018 年 2 月 28 日的预期底基生产成本吸收率，我们制定了如下表格。这些是在决定建造一个新的底基设备并启动 FP 之前完成的，两者的影响都排除在运算外。

底基生产总间接成本

	金额（T$）
特殊分配：	
机器相关成本	186 400
生产经理和监管的工资	135 000
其他特殊分配成本	34 000
分摊：	
能源	420 000
房地产相关成本	324 800
其他生产间接成本分摊	66 600
内部货物福利 & 主要服务部门成本	140 000
底基生产间接成本总计	1 306 800

底基生产间接成本吸收率

底基生产间接成本吸收率总计	T$ 1 306 800
直接生产工时总计	95 040 小时
每直接生产工时底基生产间接成本吸收率	T$ 13. 75

请回复财务总监 Pene Lopez 的邮件。

任务三

几天后，Pene Lopez 叫你去她的办公室，说道：

昨天，我和 Jacinta 讨论了一下关于新信息素底基生产的市场营销。她相信这个产品将有很大的市场，尤其是在其他国家。她预计新底基的销售将会影响现有底基，但不会太严重。不过 Jacinta 还是相信它一定会取得成功，她只是担心这个成功的程度，尽管她认为，我们在市场营销中投入得越多，最终的结果就越好。既然她是市场营销的负责人，我认为她的观点非常值得期待。

不管怎样，她提出了在三种不同需求等级下的销售估计：极品，优秀，普通。基于她的市场经验，她也对各需求等级出现的概率进行了预估。我利用她的信息，针对每项活动准备了一份预期值、标准偏差、变异系数的明细表。我将在明天的新底基市场销售会议上呈现这些数据。请你准备一份简报，解释一下表格中各项数据的含义以及对待风险不同的态度将如何影响活动决策。

另外，我知道Jacinata关于新底基的推广有她自己的看法，但是我想做好万全准备。请给我发一份报告，说说你认为对推销新产品特别有效的四种营销技巧，并解释一下为什么它们很有效。

活动A（高等市场花费）

需求	预计附加利益 净市场花费（T$ 000）	概率	期望值 （T$ 000）
极品	720	0.2	216
优秀	300	0.3	90
普通	(60)	0.4	(24)
期望值			282

活动A的标准偏差 = T $323 000

活动A的差异系数 = 1.15

活动B（中等市场花费）

需求	预计附加利益 净市场花费（T$ 000）	概率	期望值（T$ 000）
极品	500	0.3	150
优秀	280	0.3	84
普通	10	0.4	4
期望值			238

活动B的标准偏差 = T$ 205 000

活动B的差异系数 = 0.86

活动 C（低等市场花费）

需求	预计附加利益 净市场花费（T$ 000）	概率	期望值（T$ 000）
极品	360	0.3	108
优秀	260	0.3	78
普通	100	0.4	40
期望值			226

活动 C 的标准偏差 = T$ 110 000

活动 C 的变异系数 = 0.49

请回复财务总监 Pene Lopez 的邮件。

任务四

几个月以后，新的设备正式开张，全面运营。信息素的专利已经在两个月前申请完毕，随着许多其他国家的客户出现，新的底基产品非常成功。

当你收到以下来自 Thomas Vendenry 的邮件时，Penez Lopez 在休年假，Cormac Jones 因为生病离开工作。

发件人：总经理 Thomas Venderby

收件人：管理会计助理

主　题：财务与环境报告

我知道 Penez 和 Cormac 都不在公司，但是我确定你可以帮助我完成这些事。

首先，我了解到 Penez 留下了一些需要处理的事项，对此我有两个问题需要你的帮助。

- Pene 要求我确保一笔购买新信息素设施装置的 T$ 45 000 开销要支付给外国供应商。我刚才联系了要审核这笔支付款项的银行，然而她说现在转了 T$ 28 500，而这和购货分类账中记录的 T$ 26 000 是不同的。我的疑问在于，在这笔交易中我们应该记录哪个数据以及这笔交易将如何影响我们截至 2018 年 2 月 28 日的财务报表。

■ Pene 要求我着手建立成本，作为一项可以资本化的无形资产，我们的研发工作最近已经获得了专利。她告诉我，我们已经满足了创造无形资产的条件。问题是我不知道哪些类型的成本可以被资本化。请让我知道哪些成本可以包括进去。

其次，在建造新设备时，我们曾尝试将环保意识作为可持续性战略的一部分。我认为在业务范围内，我们可以做的还有很多，尤其是蜂巢业务。然而，我不确定我们会产生多少环境成本，更准确地说是为保护环境所产生的成本。我了解到，我们可以使用质量框架来报告所有环境成本。在环境成本报告中，我希望看到以下内容（1）这是如何应用于我们的业务中的；（2）我们可以从这一措施中受益多少；（3）我们会遇到哪些困难。

非常感谢！

梅维斯·文德柏公司
总经理
Thomas Vendenry

请回复总经理 Thomas Vendenry 的邮件。

Variant 4 Suggested Answers

Section 1

Performance of Foundation Business—Draft Proposal

Production Overhead Variances

Production Overhead Total Variance

The production overhead total variance shows that we have under-absorbed T$40,000 of production overhead during the year. Usually this would be the result of producing less than budget, however this year we have produced significantly more foundation than originally budgeted(400,000 units compared to the budget of 356,000). To understand the reason why we have under-absorbed overall, we need to look at the detail of the other variances.

Production Overhead Expenditure Variance

The production overhead expenditure variance shows that we have spent T$211,T$720 more than we budgeted. This is a significant increase, however, there is a key reason for this, which is not necessarily indicative of poor performance. We know that energy costs have been higher than budget. Given that the production process uses energy to melt the wax and to run the machine(including the electrical current used to embed the wire), an increase should be expected because we have produced 54,000 more units that we planned. This highlights a flaw in the way that we currently set our budget by treating all production overhead as fixed when costs such as energy are likely to be variable with production. Indeed as well as energy there could be other overheads that are variable in nature, such as machine oil and supervisor overtime arising from the higher level of production. It will be important to look at the detail of this expenditure variance to see how much the energy relates to other variable production overheads to establish whether there are any indications of poor cost control.

Production Overhead Efficiency Variance

The production overhead efficiency variance shows that based on our actual production of 400,000 units of foundation, we should have used 96,000 direct labour hours, but actually used 92,500. Therefore our foundation production workers have been more efficient than we budgeted and have been able to produce more than we expected for the hours that they worked. This will directly correlate with the direct labour efficiency variance for foundation production and will be due to possibly a higher skill base or more efficient production processes.

Production Overhead Capacity Variance

The production overhead capacity variance shows that we have expanded the capacity beyond that budgeted, in other words the foundation production employees have worked more hours than we originally budgeted. This has been arisen due to the increase in demand for foundation and is encouraging as it shows that the workforce to be adaptable and able to meet changes.

Overall

As noted above, overall production overheads have been under-absorbed. This under-absorption has arisen because the effect of the adverse expenditure variance outweighs the effect of the favourable volume related variances.

Analysis of Working Capital Ratios

Raw Materials Inventory Days

There has been a significant increase in raw materials inventory days, meaning that at 28 February 2017 the balance is significantly higher than we had budgeted. It could be that a significant order of wax and/or wire was received just before the year end, especially given the low level of finished goods inventory. Possibly a discount for bulk purchase was available and wax and wire are being stock-piled ahead of production expansion.

There is no significant risk arising from this increase in raw material inventory, especially if it will be used in an expanded production facility shortly. Wax and wire have a long shelf life and are unlikely to deteriorate unless they are not stored correctly.

Finished Goods Inventory Days

Finished goods inventory is lower than budgeted. This could be because production has not been able to keep up with the volume of sales, given the expanding market and selling to customers in other countries. We know that we produced 54,000 more foundation during the year than we expected and given the reduction in inventory days for finished goods, it's probable that the increase in sales was even more than this.

Given that currently we only sell one foundation product, having a low level of finished goods inventory is not necessarily a risky issue as long as there are no production problems that limit what we could produce.

Receivable Days

Receivable days have increased from a budgeted 25 days to 45 days. This is likely the result of selling to customers located in other countries, which we had not budgeted for. Possibly we have offered them extended credit terms to match the credit terms available in their home markets. Alternatively, these customers are not as quick to pay as our Tucland customers, who we expected to pay on average just a little under the standard credit terms of 30 days.

The increase is slightly worrying as it could be an indication that the risk of us not receiving payment from our customers has increased. This could potentially lead to financial loss and we need to review the aged receivables report in detail to identify the specific customers that have caused this increase.

Payable Days

Payable days have increased from a budget of 30 days to 49 days. This could be linked to the increase in raw material inventory at the year end. If a significant order was received at the end of February, then we will not have paid for it yet. However, we need to be careful that we do not over-stretch our credit terms with our wax and wire suppliers, as this could damage our relationships with them.

Section 2

From: Management Accountant Assistant
To: Pene Lopez, Finance Director
Subject: New production facility

Developing a Sustainable Operation

Sustainability is about engaging in operational practices that are environmentally sound as well as socially acceptable. There are a number of ways in which the new foundation production facility could operate in a sustainable way.

Production Machinery

We need to ensure that the production machinery is efficient in terms of its energy consumption. It is already five years old, however it has been well maintained and so it's energy efficiency is unlikely to have been compromised(although we will need to check this). Another factor to consider is that whilst a new production line might be more energy efficient, the manufacture of the machinery will have incurred environmental cost and therefore our overall impact on the environment might be higher if we were to invest.

Production Processes

The production process should be as efficient as possible, so that waste is limited to the minimum. We should ensure that wax has been melted and it should be recycled into production rather than wasted.

Employees

Sustainability is as much about meeting social needs as it is environmental. It is important that employees are well looked after. The production employees should feel valued and be given opportunities to develop skills. The production process itself is fairly routine and therefore it is important that employees rotate roles to add variety to their working life.

Clearly this cannot be at the expense of quality.

Sourcing Raw Materials

To be a sustainable organisation, we need to source our supplies sustainably as well as produce sustainably. We should ensure that we source wax and wire from sustainable suppliers, who ideally are located closed by. In respect of wax, we should ensure that the supplier sources the wax responsibly so as to protect bee colonies rather than to damage them.

ABC

There are two main ways in which using ABC, they will differ from the traditional overhead absorption costing that we have always used: the pooling of cost information and the identification of different cost drivers.

Pooling of Cost Information

At the moment in our traditional absorption costing approach, any production overhead costs which specifically relate to the production cost centre are allocated (for example, the costs of running the foundation machinery and the foundation supervisor salaries). Any costs which relate to more than one cost centre (such as energy costs) are apportioned on an appropriate basis. In addition, the costs of our goods inwards and maintenance service department are re-apportioned to each production department.

Under ABC this would be different, because instead of collecting cost information on the basis of type and then allocating and apportioning, we would set up cost pools for each different type of activity undertaken. This would include support activities such as maintenance or raw materials ordering and handling, as well as production related activities such as setting up machinery or quality checks. Under ABC there would be no re-apportionment of service department costs.

Therefore, the splitting down of the overhead cost in the first table of the workings would show cost pools. For example, we could have a cost pool for foundation quality checks, in which the appropriate share of supervisor salary will be included as well as any other cost associated with quality checking. There could be a separate cost pool for foundation machinery maintenance as well. Some costs classification don't need to change; energy costs could be a separate cost pool (although for accuracy of costing, especially as foundation production will be in a new building, it would be better if the costs included here were specifically related to foundation and were not an apportionment of the energy costs for the whole business).

Cost Drivers

Cost drivers are the causes of costs. For a cost such as energy, the driver of the cost will be machine hours, because the longer the machine is operating the greater the energy cost will be. This is an example of a volume-related cost driver.

For a cost such as machinery set-up (which will be required when our two foundation products are being manufactured), the driver of the cost will be the number of set-ups rather than necessarily the volume of production. This is particularly the case for our new facility as the production run size will be smaller for FP than for F. Each time there is a change in production run and set-up is required, costs will be incurred. If we were to absorb this cost on a unit basis, it would not be fair because FP set-ups will drive just as much of the cost as F set-ups (on the assumption that there are the same number of set-ups) but will receive a lower share because fewer units are produced.

Therefore, it's difference to traditional absorption costing is that instead of just one absorption base (in this case direct labour hours), each cost pool will have a separate base, which will be its cost driver. Some of these cost drivers will be volume related (for example, energy costs and machine hours) and some will be transaction related (for example, set-up costs and the number of set-ups).

Many thanks!

Management accountant assistant
Mavis Venderby

Section 3

From: Management Accountant Assistant
To: Pene Lopez, Finance Director
Subject: Marketing campaign and marketing technique

Marketing Campaign Decision

The schedule shows for each of the levels of marketing campaign spend, the predicted profit (net of that spend) under excellent, good and moderate demand levels.

Based on estimated probabilities for the demand level, the expected value has been calculated for each campaign. The expected value summarises all the different possible outcomes by calculating a single weighted average. The standard deviation for each campaign is a measure of the possible variations of the outcomes from the expected value and is therefore used as an indication of risk. The coefficient of variation for each campaign is its standard deviation divided by its expected value and allows the risk of each campaign to be compared. From the schedule, we can see that campaign A gives the highest expected value, which corresponds to Jacinta's notion that the greater the marketing spend the better the result. However, it also has the highest standard deviation and therefore risk. This is borne out by the fact that it has the greatest spread of outcomes ranging from a positive T$720,000 to a negative T$60,000.

There are some additional problems with using the decision rule of the highest expected value in this one-off decision situation. The expected value alone gives no indication of the range of possible outcomes. It is not the most likely result, it might not even be one of the possible outcomes as can be seen from looking at the possible outcomes of the three campaigns. The expected value is the long-run average outcome if the same event was to be repeated over and over again. It should also be borne in mind that the probabilities used in the calculation of the expected value of each of the three campaigns are estimates, as are the predicted profits.

Risk Attitudes

A "Risk Seeker" is a decision maker who is interested in the best outcomes no matter how small the likelihood that they may occur. At the individual level, a risk seeker would select campaign A which has the best possible outcome: an additional profit of T$720,000. Campaign A has the highest standard deviation and is therefore the riskiest campaign (due to the range and spread of the possible outcomes).

A "Risk Neutral" decision maker will select the strategy that maximises the expected value or benefit: campaign A as discussed above. Such a decision maker will base their decision on the expected value for each campaign and will not be interested in their individual possible outcomes or the associated probabilities of those outcomes.

A "Risk Averse" decision maker will always choose the option which is given the same level of return but has the lowest level of risk. Such a decision maker will use the coefficient of variation when making a decision. Here campaign C has the lowest coefficient of variation and a risk averse decision maker would select this campaign because it has the lowest level of risk per T$ of expected value.

Marketing Techniques

Here are four examples of marketing techniques that we could adopt to promote the new pheromone foundation.

Setting up Promotions to existing Customers

We already have a wealth of customer information given our on-line and telesales operations and we should utilise this to promote the new foundations. We could directly target these customers through either an email or postal promotion, maybe offering discounts on first orders. We should especially target those customers that maybe haven't brought foundation from us for a while or at all as this will potentially be new business. Despite the fact that the existing customers might simply switch from the old foundation to the new one, there is still an indirect benefit in that by blogging or commenting positively on social media about the new foundation, they will promote it on our behalf.

Adverts

We could place adverts in beekeeping and agricultural magazines to promote the benefits of the new pheromone foundation. Because of the specialist nature of beekeeping, both hobby and commercial beekeepers are likely to subscribe to at least one relevant publication. We could also seek to place adverts in the publications of beekeeping organisations. We could also approach them to place adverts on their web pages. Jacinta has many links with these organisations and we should use these links to full effect.

Trade Stands at Regional Agricultural Events

We could directly promote and sell at regional agricultural or home style events by having trade stands at these events. Our customers often travel for many kilometres to our on-site store so that they can speak to our experts, therefore we should use this expertise in direct promotion. Toby Venger in particular, as the developer of the pheromone, should be involved.

Digital Marketing

There are many forums and internet sites where beekeepers ask questions and discuss beekeeping related issues. For example, the Honeypot Beekeepers Forum is very popular in Tucland. We should look at ways of monitoring these communications and maybe joining conversations linked to foundation. In addition, we could look to advertise on social media sites to groups linked to beekeeping. Clearly there will be a cost to this, but we could perhaps offer beekeeping workshops with our experts as prizes if the page is liked. In this way we might reach a wider audience of beekeepers.

Many thanks!

Management Accountant Assistant
Mavis Venderby

Section 4

From: Management Accountant Assistant
To: Thomas Venderby, Managing Director
Subject: Financial and environment reporting

Financial Reporting Issues

Treatment of Foreign Exchange

The accounting treatment for transactions denominated in a foreign currency is governed by IAS 21. The answer to your query is that actually both values are accounted for.

We have purchased non-current assets and therefore the key date for recognising the value of these non-current assets is the transaction date. This will be the date on the invoice that we received, which is the value as recorded in the purchase ledger of T$26,000. We do not need to adjust this for any movements in the exchange rate because it is a non-monetary asset. At the year end, the non-current assets will be recorded at their cost of T$26,000. This will be subject to depreciation charges, which will be based on the useful economic life of the assets.

The value of T$28,500 will need to be accounted as the payment, because this is amount that will actually leave our bank account today in settlement of the invoice. Clearly this means that there is a mismatch between the amount in the purchase ledger and the payment value. This difference will be treated as a difference on exchange. Because we are paying more than we thought we would have to. This means that we have a loss on exchange. This loss will have the effect of reducing profit or loss.

Capitalisation of Development Costs

We can include the following costs in the capitalised value of the intangible asset.

- Salary costs of staff included in the development. This will certainly include part of Toby Venger's salary as well as anyone else involved in the development.
- The cost of any materials and services consumed. This will include the cost of any foundation used for testing and any other materials such as wax used in the development.
- Any overhead costs that are directly incurred in respect of the development. This will include a share of the depreciation charge from equipment such as hives or other testing equipment used.
- Any other direct costs such as the costs of applying for the patent.

It should be noted though that we can only capitalise costs that have been incurred from the date that we met all of the criteria set down in IAS 38 regarding recognition of an internally generated intangible asset. Any development costs incurred before then should be expensed to profit or loss.

Environmental Cost Reporting

Application of the Quality Framework to Environmental Costs

The quality framework breaks down environmental costs into conformance costs (prevention and appraisal) and non-conformance costs(internal failure and external failure). An environmental cost report will identify and quantify these costs.

Conformance costs are those incurred to either prevent environmental costs from arising(prevention) or to establish whether our activities are adhering to environmental standards(appraisal). In our business, prevention costs could include the costs of training staff in waste management and the costs of any equipment purchased to reduce our level of emissions. Appraisal costs could include the costs of any site surveys we've had performed in respect of the new facility.

Non-conformance costs are those that mean that we have generated waste. Internal failure costs are those incurred to deal with this waste before it actually harms the environment. An example of such a cost would be the costs incurred recycling wasted wax or wire. External failure costs are the costs that arise when waste or environmental emissions are released into the environment. An example would be the emissions from using energy in our production process. Typically internal failure costs are those wholly borne by the business and external failure costs are those that are borne by the environment itself.

Benefits from Implementation of Environmental Cost Report

The key benefit of implementing this type of report is that it will allow us to understand how the business is affecting the environment and what we should do(or indeed not do) to limit this impact. In making conformance costs visible, it will be easier to see where we could potentially incur more cost in order to reduce non-conformance costs.

By becoming more environmentally-aware and doing more to prevent environmental damage, we could promote ourselves as an environmental business. Our customers are increasingly interested in the environment and being able to produce honey sustainably, which will have an effect on our sales if we are not seen as environmentally aware.

We could ultimately save cost and time in production if we develop less wasteful and more efficient production processes which harm the environment less. If we were to invest in solar panels or a windmill to generate our own power as a result of being more aware of our impact, then this would have cost saving implications in the long term as well.

Difficulties We Might Encounter

The main difficulty in implementing this approach is the measurement of some of these costs. In particular measuring external failure costs is difficult, because some of our impact on the environment will be intangible in nature. There are experts available that could be engaged at a cost.

Another difficulty is identifying all of the costs in the first place and the time it will take to monitor these costs over time. It is also difficult to know what are the appropriate targets for emissions should achieve. We are a business that prides itself on quality, but waste is part of that quality process.

Many thanks!

Management Accountant Assistant
Mavis Venderby

试卷四　参考答案

任务一

底基业务的商业绩效草案

生产间接成本差异

生产间接成本总差异

生产间接成本总差异显示这一年内我们的可吸收成本比实际生产成本少了 T$ 40 000。通常这是因为实际生产少于预计生产，然而今年我们生产了比预计数量多得多的底基（实际生产 400 000 件，预计生产 356 000 件）。为了弄清可吸收成本少于实际生产成本的原因，我们需要查看其他差异的细节。

生产间接成本支出差异

生产间接成本支出差异表明我们已经花费了 T$ 211，比预算多了 T$ 720。这是个很显著的增加，然而，主要原因在于这并不是业绩不好的重要指标。我们都知道能源成本比预算多。在产品生产过程中需要用能源融化蜡，并且需要能源去运行机器（包括将电流嵌入电线中），成本增加是可以预料到的，毕竟我们比预算多生产了 54 000 件产品。这里有一个显著的缺陷，那就是目前我们使用的预算方法是将所有的生产费用设定为固定费用，而诸多能源此类的成本是随着生产而变化的。事实上，与能源成本相似的其他成本本质上也是可变的，像机油或者更高层生产导致的主管加班费。重要的是查看费用差异的细节，看看能源和其他可变生产成本关系如何，由此确定是否有任何成本控制差的迹象。

生产间接成本效率差异

生产间接成本效率差异表明，根据我们实际生产的 400 000 个单位的底基，我们应该使用了 96 000 个直接工时，但实际上却使用了 92 500 个工时。因此，生产底基的工人比预计的要有效率，并且在我们所期望的时间内有能力生产更多的底基。这直接关系到底基生产的直接人工效率差异。这可能是由于更高的技能基础或更有效的生产流程导致的。

生产间接成本资本差异

生产间接成本资本差异表明，较之预算我们已经扩大了生产能力，也就是说，底基生产员工工作时间比我们原先预算的多。这是由于对底基的需求增加而产生的，这一现象鼓舞人心，因为它表明我们的劳动力具有适应能力，能够适应变化。

整体

如上所述，总体生产成本被低估了。由于不良支出差异的影响超过了有利支出差异的影响，才出现了这种成本吸收不足的现象。

运营资本比率分析

原材料库存天数

原材料库存天数显著增加，这意味着截至 2017 年 2 月 28 日，余额将大大高于我们的预算。这可能是在年底前收到的一份重要的蜡和（或）电线的订单，特别是在成品库存水平较低的情况下。对批量采购提供折扣是可能的，在生产扩张之前，蜡和电线将被成堆积存。

原材料库存的增加并没有带来明显的风险，特别是如果不久后它将用于扩大生产设施。蜡和电线的保质期很长，如果正确储存，它们不太可能变质。

完成品库存天数

完成品库存低于预算。这可能是由于市场不断扩大，其他国家的客户需求增长，而生产一直无法跟上。我们知道，这一年里我们比预算多生产了 54 000 个底基，并且考虑到成品库存天数的减少，很可能销售额的增长比这个还多。

鉴于目前我们只销售一种底基产品，如果没有生产问题限制我们的生产，那么低水平的成品库存并不一定有风险。

应收账款天数

应收账款天数从预算的 25 天增加到 45 天，这可能是销售给其他国家客户的结果，我们没有为此进行预算。为了配合他们国内市场的信贷条件，我们可能会给他们提供更长的信贷期限。或者，这些客户不像我们 Tucland 的客户那样支付及时，我们预计他们的平均支付期限只比标准信贷期限的 30 天低一点。

这种增长有点儿令人担忧，因为这可能表明我们没有收到客户付款的风险增加了。这可能会导致财物损失，我们需要详细审查往年的应收账款报告，以确定造成这种增长的具体客户是哪些。

未付账款天数

未付账款天数已经从预算的 30 天增加到 49 天了。这可能与年底的原材料库存增加有关。如果在 2 月底收到一份重要的订单，那么我们还没有付款。然而，我们需要注意的是，我们不要过度透支与蜡和电线供应商的信用条款，因为这会损坏我们的信用。

任务二

发件人：管理会计助理

收件人：财务总监 Pene Lope

主　题：新生产设备

发展可持续性运营

可持续性是指进行环保且社会可接受的行为。有许多方法可以使新的底基生产设施以可持续的方式运作。

生产机器

我们需要确保生产机器在能源消耗方面是有效的。它已经有 5 年的历史了，但是由于维修及时，所以它的能源效率不太可能被破坏（尽管我们需要检查一下）。另一个需要考虑的因素是，虽然新的生产线可能会更节能，但机器的制造将产生环境成本。因此，如果投资的话，我们对环境的整体影响可能会更高。

生产过程

生产过程应该尽可能的高效，这样浪费就会被限制在最低限度。我们应该确保蜡被融化并且被循环生产，而不是浪费率。

员工

可持续发展既是环保的，也能满足社会需求。重要的是员工要得到较好的待遇。生产员工应该有价值感，并能获得发展技能的机会。生产过程本身是非常常规的，因此员工轮岗以增加他们工作生活的多样性是很重要的。

显然，这不能以牺牲质量为代价。

采购原材料

要成为可持续发展的组织，我们需要可持续地满足供应，并且可持续地生产。我们应该确保我们从可持续的供应商那里获取蜡和电线，他们的理想位置应该在附近。就蜡而言，我们应该确保供应商的来源可靠，以此保护蜂群而不是伤害它们。

作业成本法

使用作业成本法有两种主要方式，她与我们一贯使用的传统的间接吸收成本不同：成本信息池和不同成本动因识别。

成本信息池

在我们传统的吸收成本计算方法中，任何与生产成本中心相关的生产成本费用都被分配（例如，运行底基机器的成本和底基主管的薪水）。任何与超过一个成本中心有关的成本（例如能源成本）都是在适当的基础上分配的。此外，我们的货物进口和维修服务部的费用将重新分配给各个生产部门。

在作业成本法下就有所不同，因为它不需要以类型为基础收集成本信息然后再分配、分摊，我们是为每个不同类型的活动设置成本池。其中包括支持活动，像维修或者原材料的采购和处理，以及生产的相关活动，像机器装配或者质检。在作业成本法下，就不需要将服务部门的成本进行再分摊。

因此，在工作的第一个表中，间接成本的分解将显示成本池。例如，我们可以有一个底基质量检查的成本池，其中包括主管工资的适当份额，以及与质量检测相关的成本（尽管为了成本的准确性，特别是在新的建筑里生产底基时，如果这里的成本与底基相关而不是整个业务的能源成本分摊，那将更好）。

成本动因

成本动因是成本的形成原因。对于像能源这样的成本，成本动因将是机器工时，因为机器的运行时间越长，能源成本就越高。这是一个与用量相关的成本动因例子。

对于机器组装的成本（两种底基产品正在生产时需要），成本动因将是组装数量而不是生产量。这对于新设备来说尤其如此，因为 FP 生产运行的规模要比 F 小。每次生产运行发生改变，需要重组设备时，成本就会产生。如果我们要在一个单元的基础上吸收这些成本，这会不公平，因为 FP 的制作将会产生像 F 一样多的成本（假设有相同数量的成本），但是这只能获得更低的份额，因为生产单位更少。

因此，它与传统成本吸收法不同的是，不同于单一吸收基数（在这种情况下是直接劳动时间），每个成本池将有一个单独的基数，这将会是它的成本动因。其中一些成本驱动将会是与量相关的（例如，配置成本和制作数量），也有一些是与次数相关的（例如，安装成本和安装次数）。

十分感谢！

梅维斯 · 文德柏公司

管理会计助理

任务三

发件人：管理会计助理

收件人：财务总监 Pene Lopez

主　题：市场营销活动和营销技巧

市场营销活动决策

计划表显示了各级营销活动的花费，以及在优秀、良好和适中的需求水平下预计的利润（花费的净值）。

根据需求水平的估计概率，计算每个活动的期望值。期望值通过计算单个加权平均数来总结所有可能的结果。每项活动的标准偏差是衡量预期可能变化的指标，因此被用作风险指标。每个活动的差异系数是它的期望值除以它的标准偏差，它使得每一个活动的风险可以进行比较。从计划表来看，A 给出了最高的期望值，这符合 Jacinata 的观点，即营销花费越大，结果越好。然而，它也有最高的标准差和风险。这正是因为它的结果变化范围最大，从成功的 $ 720 000 到失败的 $ 60 000。

在做一次性决策的情况下，使用最高期望值决策会出现一些额外的问题。仅仅一个期望值无法给出可能结果的范围。这并不是最可能出现的结果，从三个活动的可能发生的结果可以看出，它甚至可能不是其中之一。如果相同的事件重复发生，期望值就是一个长期运转的平均结果。我们还应当记住，在计算每一个活动的预期价值时所用的概率是估数，也就是预测的利润。

对待风险的态度

“风险偏好者”是一种决策者类型，这种人对最好的结果感兴趣，而不管其发生的可能性有多小。在个人层面，一个风险偏好者会选择活动 A，而其最好的结果是产生额外的 $ 720 000 的利润。活动 A 有最高的标准偏差，因此也是风险最高的活动（因为可能结果的范围和弹性大）。

“风险中立者”的决策者将选择预期或收益最大化的策略：如上所述的活动 A。这样的决策者将根据每项活动的预期价值做出决定，而不会对其个人可能的结果或这些结果的相关概率感兴趣。

“风险规避者”的决策者总是选择同样收益水平下有最低风险的选项。这样的决策者在做决策时很重视差异系数。本案例中活动 C 有最低的差异系数，规避风险的决策者将会选择这样的活动，因为它期望值的每 T$ 1 风险最低。

营销技巧

这里有四个营销技巧的例子，我们可以借鉴以推广新的信息素底基。

对现有客户开展促销活动

由于我们的在线和电话销售业务，我们已经拥有了大量的客户信息，我们应该利用这一点来推广新底基。我们可以通过电子邮件或邮政促销直接联系这些客户，或许我可以在第一批订单上提供折扣。我们可以特别针对那些一段时间内还没有从我们这里购买底基的客户，或者根本不需要这样做，因为这可能是一个新的业务。尽管现有的客户可能只是简单地从旧底基转向新底基，但这里仍然有个间接的好处，那就是通过写博客或在社交媒体上积极地评论新底基，他们将代替我们推广它。

广告

我们可以在养蜂和农业杂志上刊登广告，以宣传新的信息素底基的优点。由于养蜂的特殊性质，业余爱好者和商业养蜂人都有可能订阅至少一份相关出版物。我们可以在养蜂机构的出版物上刊登广告，也可以在他们的网页上放置广告。Jactinta 与这些组织有许多联系，我们应该充分利用这些联系。

区域农业活动贸易站

我们可以通过举办这些活动，在区域农业或家庭风格的活动中直接促进销售。我们的客户经常不远万里来到我们的现场商店，这样他们就可以和我们的专家交流，因此我们应该利用这些专业知识促进销售。作为信息素的开发者，Toby Venger 尤其应该参与进来。

数字化营销

有许多论坛和网站，养蜂人会在上面提出问题并谈论相关问题。例如，蜜罐养蜂人论坛在 Tucland 很受欢迎。我们应该研究如何监控这些通讯，并尽可能加入与底基相关的对话。另外，我们还可以在社交媒体网站上针对养蜂群体投放广告。显然，这将会产生一笔开销，但是如果网页被人喜欢，作为奖励我们可以和专家共同举办养蜂研讨会。通过这种方式，我们也许能接触到更多的养蜂人。

十分感谢!

梅维斯·文德柏公司

管理会计助理

任务四

发件人：管理会计助理

收件人：总经理 Thomas Venderby

主　题：财务和环境报告

财务报告项目

外汇项目处理

以外币计价的会计处理的交易由国际会计准则第 21 号管理规定。答复您的提问，实际上这两个值都需要被考虑。

我们已经购买了非流动资产，因此确认这些非固定资产价值的关键日期是交易日期。这将是我们收到发票的日期，也就是记录在购货分类账中价值 $26 000 的发票。我们不需要对汇率的任何变动进行调整，因为它是一种非货币性资产。在年底，非流动资产将以 $26 000 的成本记录。这将受到折旧费用的影响，它基于资产的有用经济寿命。

我们需要支付的价值是 $28 500，因为这是我们今天的银行账户在结算发票上的金额。很明显，这意味着在购买总账和支付价值之间存在不匹配。这一差异可以被视为交换差异。因为我们比我们预想的支付得还要多，这意味着在兑换上出现了损失。这一损失有助于减少利润或亏损。

资本化的开发成本

我们可以在无形资产的资本化价值中加入以下成本。

- 研发部门员工的工资。这当然包括了部分 Toby Venger 以及其他研发人员的工资。
- 消耗的任何材料和服务的成本。这将会包括用于测试的底基费用，以及开发中使用的任何其他材料，比如蜡。
- 在开发过程中直接产生的任何间接成本。这包括从蜂箱或其他设备的使用中产生的折旧费用。
- 任何其他直接成本，如申请专利的成本。

应该注意到的是，我们只能从达到国际会计准则第 38 号中所规定的内部产生的无形资产的所有标准开始，将成本资本化。在此之前发生的任何开发费用都应该是损益费用。

环境成本报告

将质量框架应用于环境成本

质量框架将环境成本分解成一致性成本（预防和评估）和非一致性成本（内部失败和外部失败）。环境成本需要识别和量化这些成本。

一致性成本是指防止环境成本产生（预防）或者确定我们的活动是否符合环境标准（评估）而产生的费用。在我们的业务中，预防费用包括培训废物处理人员的费用和为降低排放量而购买的任何设备的费用。评估费用包括我们对新设备进行的现场调查的费用。

非一致性成本意味着我们产生了浪费。内部失败成本是指我们处理那些尚未真正破坏环境的废物的费用。例如，回收废弃的蜡和电线的费用。外部失败成本是指当废物或废品已经排放到环境中而产生的环境污染成本。例如，生产过程中能源的排放。通常内部失败成本由企业承担，而外部失败成本由环境承担。

执行环境成本报告的益处

实施这个报告最主要的益处是它会让我们懂得一个公司是如何影响环境以及我们应该如何限制这种影响。在一致性成本可见的情况下，为减少非一致性成本，了解我们在哪里会产生更多的潜在成本相对而言更加容易。

通过提高环保意识并加强环境破坏预防措施，我们可以升级为环保事业。我们的顾客对环境和可持续性生产的重视日益提高，如果我们没有环保意识，那将对我们的销售产生影响。

我们可以从根本上节约成本和生产时间，如果我们研发出更少浪费、更有效率的生产过程，这将会减少对环境的伤害。如果对品牌意识更加明确，我们可以投资太阳能电池板或者风车来自己生产电力，从长远来看，这将节约成本。

我们可能会遇到的困难

实施这一方法的主要困难是成本测量。特别是外部失败成本测量，因为对环境的影响是无形的。这里还有聘请专家的费用。

另一个困难是首次确定所有成本，以及从始至终控制这些成本所花费的时间。我们很难知道合适的排放目标是什么。我们是一个以质量品质为傲的企业，而废物处理也是质量控制过程的一部分。

十分感谢！

梅维斯 · 文德柏公司
管理会计助理

Variant 4 Marking Guidance

Section number	Technical skills		Business skills		People skills		Leadership skills		Integration	Total
1	Production overhead variances Working capital ratios	11 11							3	25
2	ABC	13	Operational sustainability	12						25
3	Pay-off table (including expected value, standard deviation and coefficient of variation) in respect of marketing spend decision	12			Marketing techniques	13				25
4	Accounting for intangible assets and foreign exchange Environmental cost reporting	6 9	Environmental cost reporting	4			Accounting for intangible assets and foreign exchange	6		25
Total marks available for competency		62		16		13		6	3	100

试卷四 评分指南

选项	技术技能		商业技能		人际技能		领导技能		综合	总计
1	生产成本差异 运营资本比率	11 11							3	25
2	作业成本法	13	可持续性战略运营	12						25
3	营销成本决策的支付表（期望值、标准偏差、变异系数）	12			销售技能	13				25
4	无形资产列报和外汇 环境成本报告	6 9	环境成本报告	4			无形资产列报和外汇	6		25
有能力可获得的总分		62		16		13		6	3	100

西安外国语大学名师解惑

试卷一共有四项任务，考查了P1、F1、E1三门课程的知识点。具体包括限制成本差异、营运资本、可持续发展、作业成本法、营销技巧、财务报告分析、一致性和非一致性成本等。该试卷考核了考生的四项能力。其中技术技能的分值占62%，商业技能的分值占16%，人际技能的分值占13%，领导技能的分值占6%，与CGMA管理会计能力框架的技能要求一致。

该试卷的每项任务涉及以下知识点：

任务	问题	科目	知识点
任务一	生产成本差异	P1	差异分析（costing methods）
	营运资本比率	F1	营运资本管理（working capital management）
任务二	作业成本法	P1	作业成本法（ABC）
	可持续性战略运营	E1	可持续发展
任务三	营销成本决策的支付表（期望值、标准偏差、变异系数）	P1	衡量风险指标
	销售技能	E1	营销技巧
任务四	无形资产列报和外汇	F1	无形资产
	环境成本报告	P1	环境成本

上述各项任务要求以邮件、报告或工作笔记等形式来呈现答案，对问题的描述非常明确，答题时既要注意内容的针对性，也要注意形式的规范性。

其他答题注意事项包括：（1）本套试题难度适中，整体而言，问题指向较为明确，对知识点的掌握程度要求也不高，在题目或附录中均有提示，有答题思路的线索可循；（2）可能难点在于部分题目隐藏起来了，由于阅读信号词的缺失，部分考生在答题时可能会遗漏问题。

对应知识点深度剖析

差异分析

第一部分问题比较集中，要求解释的问题较为具体，答案必须围绕差异成因展开，因此，附录数据应当被引用以支持论证过程。差异分析在P1考纲中属于成本方法中的内容，因此考频和重要性都比较突出。但案例考试中对差异的考查主要是解释差异及建议对策，因此附录中的数据一般都必须使用。

运营资本管理

第二部分属于F1考纲中的常考知识点——运营资本管理。问题指向较为明确，在天数问题上，附录数据可给予考生一定辅助。因此，答案也应该至少围绕附录表格中的4个天数展开讨论。

可持续发展

这部分题目会让部分学生感觉略难。主要原因在于问题给定不明显，需要通过阅读搜寻，对于阅读能力相对弱的考生，能否识别全部问题是一个挑战。在识别出问题以后，第一部分的问题也相对较难，因为问题范围较为宽泛，执行层面的要求又非常具体，很容易导致考生短时间内无话可写，无思路可循。

作业成本法

第二部分的问题相对简单，多数考生对该话题都较为熟悉，回答和传统成本方法的异同应该难度不大，主要问题在于能否对附录表格中的成本分类及数据进行合适的应用。

营销技巧

这部分题目主要源于E1，包含部分P1的内容。关于市场部分的知识考查，答案的灵活性较强，考生发挥的空间较大。整体而言，整个部分的难度相对低，于考生压力不大。多数考生应该能根据商业常识回答一部分。真正影响答案质量的是对于商业情境的应用，该应用不仅指附录中的数据，更多的是市场手段与案例公司背景的匹配程度及其原因阐述。

无形资产

第一部分在F1板块中遇到的问题仍然可能成为考生较大的障碍。由于汇率变化导致账面价值的变化而产生价差，相关原因以及对报表影响的阐述要求考生对这个知识点掌握较为熟练。无形资产的考核可能会让考生压力较大，许多考生在这个知识点的掌握上存在问题。考生遭遇的问题应该主要来自对会计准则内容的不熟悉，尤其是不同会计准则在不同情境下的应用。

环境成本

第二部分属于P1板块的常见考题，话题虽简单，但想回答完整并不容易。这部分考题要求考生对知识点掌握较细，了解环境成本分类的同时能够掌握并理解环境成本在企业运营中的价值体现，只有这样才能回答环境成本报告的好处。

Variant 5

This examination is structured as follows：

Section number	Number of tasks	Time for section(minutes)
1	1	45
2	1	45
3	1	45
4	1	45

The time available for each section is for reading,planning and writing your answer(s).

Section 1

The directors of Mavis Venderby have started negotiations to buy Griggs Hives. Griggs Hives is a business currently owned by Peter Griggs, who wishes to retire and realise his investment. Griggs Hives manufactures and sells cedar beehives of a similar standard and quality as Mavis Venderby, but also has a very good reputation for breeding and selling queen bees. Griggs Hives also sells beekeeping equipment.

You arrive at work to find the following email:

From: Thomas Venderby, Managing Director
To: Management Accountant Assistant
Subject: Possible acquisition of Griggs Hives

I've just come out of a meeting with Pene, Jacinta and the directors of Griggs Hives to discuss our possible acquisition of the business and I have come away with some queries. Pene is in other meetings for the rest of the day, so she suggested that I ask you to help.

Firstly, as you can imagine Peter Griggs was very positive about his business and he gave us a copy of an extract of the operating statement for the hives business for the year to 31 December 2016. Peter commented that as a result of a major un-budgeted advertising campaign in February 2016, the number of both slatted and box hives sold were significantly higher than budgeted. He also commented that they had changed their wood suppliers pan way through the year, as a result of issues with the quality of the pan seasoned timber being supplied, resulting in a T$ 1 rise in the cost per metre of cedar to T$ 23. He said that some of this increase in cost was passed onto the customers. As a result of both of these events, Peter commented that contribution was higher than budgeted, although he did note that overall, net profit was slightly lower than budget due to the cost of the advertising campaign.

Firstly, I would like you to have a look at the extract of the operating statement and let me know whether it supports Peter's comments about the advertising campaign and the wood supplier issue. If so, please explain how.

Secondly, it has struck me that we have a choice regarding how we acquire the Griggs Hives business. We could either buy 100% of its share capital out-right, or we could buy the net assets of the business. Either way we will be paying a premium for the business because of its goodwill. I have two questions:

(1) What factors influence the value of the goodwill in Griggs Hives?

(2) For both methods of acquiring Griggs Hives, how will this goodwill be recorded in our financial statements?

Please send me an email on both the variances and goodwill questions.

Thank you!

Thomas Venderby, Managing Director

Mavis Venderby

Extract of operating statement for the cedar hives business of Griggs Hives for the year to 31 December 2016:

	T$	T$
Budgeted contribution		2,117,535
Sales mix contribution variances:		
Box	(51,517)	
Slatted	65,892	
Total sales mix contribution variance		14,375
Sales quantity contribution variance		241,989
Budgeted contribution from actual sales		2,373,899
Selling price variances:		
Box	0	
Slatted	106,000	
Total selling price variance		106,000
Actual sales less standard variable cost of sales		2,479,899
Variable cost variances:		
Materials price	(38,627)	
Materials quantity	(77,758)	
Labour rate	(46,050)	

（续表）

	T$	T$
Labour efficiency	(53,640)	
Variable overhead expenditure	16,092	
Variable overhead efficiency	(18,732)	
Total variable cost variance		(218,715)
Actual contribution		2,261,184

Notes:

(1) Griggs Hives uses marginal costing and the budgeted contribution for a box hive was T$ 180.13 and for a slatted hive was T$ 230.39.

(2) The sales mix contribution variances are calculated using the individual units method.

(3) Griggs Hives uses direct labour hours to charge variable overheads to production.

Write the email requested by Thomas Venderby, managing director.

Section 2

The net assets of Griggs Hives were acquired six weeks ago. All of the staff employed by Griggs Hives were offered employment with Mavis Venderby and 70% agreed to relocate (none of which are finance staff). Over the past two weeks, staff inventory and equipment have gradually been moved to the Mavis Venderby site, where a new production facility has been set up in a previously unused barn. The aim is that Mavis Venderby's existing production facility will be used for all pine hive production and the new facility, With the Griggs Hives plant and machinery, for cedar hive production. This is to develop workers that specialise in working with either pine or cedar as it is thought that this will reduce wastage.

Two days ago, whilst in transit a number of Griggs Hives cutting machines were damaged as a result of a road accident. The machines are now on site but are damaged and it will take at least a month to repair, as specialist pans need to be imported and then fitted.

Pene Lopez, finance director, calls you into her office and says:

I had a meeting this morning with Joseph about the lack of cutting machines for the new cedar hive facility. He thinks that we should use a sub-contractor to cover the shortfall in production and gave me the figures for what this would cost for each type of hive. Joseph cannot decide whether to outsource the cutting of slatted hives or box hives. Cormac has pulled some numbers together in respect of this decision. I've had a quick look and his calculations are correct. Please could you prepare content for a briefing note which explains the schedule, states the decision arising from the schedule in terms of which type of hive to produce in-house and includes a summary of other factors that we need to consider before finalising the decision to use a sub-contractor.

Also, whilst I've got you here, there is something else I'd like you to do for me. Griggs Hives have always had a policy of extending 30 days credit to both hobby beekeepers and commercial beekeepers. Thomas is keen that this policy is continued and indeed extended to our hobby beekeepers, especially as we are going to start selling beekeeping equipment as well as hives to them and foundation. I'm not so sure that giving credit to hobby beekeepers is a good idea due to the significant risk that they won't pay us. I have been in touch with a factoring business which has said that it would take over all of our receivables ledger function (from both the Mavis Venderby and previous Griggs Hives customers) on a non-recourse basis for a fee of 2% of the value of invoices raised. The factor will advance 75% of the value of invoices when raised and will charge us a finance fee of 8%. Thomas has asked for a briefing paper on the potential benefits and drawbacks that might arise from accepting the arrangement. Please prepare the content of this briefing paper for me.

Please just send me one email that addresses both of my requests.

Schedule of the decision to sub-contract for the month:

	Production required in units	Machine hours required in hours
Box	1,600	1,320
Slatted	1,200	1,110
Total	2,800	2,430

There are a total of 1,000 machine hours available, resulting in a shortfall of 1,430 machine hours for the month.

A sub-contractor can carry out all of the same work as our cutting department, for us to then pack, at a set fee per unit.

	Box hive per unit	Slatted hive per unit
Cost of sub-contractor cutting	T$ 62.00	T$ 73.00
Variable cost of cutting in-house	T$ 51.00	T$ 61.20
Cost saving from cutting in-house	T$ 11.00	T$ 11.80
Machine hours used by cutting in-house	0.825	0.925
Cost saving of cutting in-house per machine hour used	T$ 13.33	T$ 12.76

Write the email requested by Pene Lopez, finance director.

Section 3

A few weeks later, Pene Lopez, finance director is on annual leave and you receive the following email.

From: Thomas Venderby, Managing Director
To: Management Accountant Assistant
Subject: Queen rearing business

Now that we have the hive production issues under control, myself and the other directors have turned our attention to the queen rearing business. We've successfully managed to move all of the hives, together with Percy Gambon, the queen rearing expert and his team to our premises, albeit reluctantly in respect of Percy. I really excited by this new pan of the business as it's a great extension to what we already do.

The rearing of queen bees is highly skilled and Percy, in particular, has a reputation for producing queens with an excellent temperament. We are lucky to have him and it's important that we continue to keep hold of him. We have already agreed to pay Percy a good salary (which is above that of equivalent managers in the business), but I think we need to do more. I am about to go into meetings for the rest of the day, but would appreciate your thoughts on what we could do to incentivise Percy to stay at Mavis Venderby.

Also, I was having a chat yesterday with Percy about plans for the queen rearing business. He mentioned that in the past they have always managed to sell all of the queens reared and indeed often had to disappoint customers. It got me thinking that we could expand this pan of the business. However, I've no idea how big the market might be and therefore the scale of any expansion.

Percy says that he has statistics from the Tucland Beekeepers Association about how many queen bees have been purchased in the country over the last 10 years, and has been told that it can be used to create a time series, I don't know much about time series, but I seem to recall that there are four components to it. I would like to know what the four components of a time series are and how the demand for queen bees is likely to be influenced by each of these components.

One email in respect of both the incentive scheme and the time series is fine.

Many thanks!

Thomas Venderby, Managing Director
Mavis Venderby

Write the email requested by Thomas Venderby, managing director.

Section 4

Two weeks later you arrive at work in the morning and read the following email:

From: Pene Lopez, Finance Director
To: Management Accountant Assistant
Subject: Expansion of queen rearing business

Yesterday I had a quick meeting with the other directors about the queen rearing business and possible expansion. There is spare capacity to rear more queens in terms of hives. However to increase production and therefore sales, more staff and more equipment would be needed. This equipment usually lasts a year. At the meeting a number of issues were raised towards the end which we didn't have a chance to explore.

- Thomas raised the question of whether we should retain the Griggs name and continue to sell queens under that name or to sell them under our Mavis Venderby name. I can see pros and cons either way.

- Joseph raised the idea of importing queens from Bucland, rather than incurring the additional annual costs of staff and equipment. He said that queens in Bucland were a lot cheaper to buy than the queens in Tucland. Jacinta commented that there were two possible suppliers that we could use, one of which would give us a discount the more we bought from them. Joseph suggested that we could still continue to market the queen bees as we'd reared them and no-one would need to know! I think he has a possible point regarding saving the investment in equipment and staff, so last night Cormac drew up a decision tree on the basis that our sales will be at a low, medium or high level (there is some uncertainty over this). However, I'm not so sure about selling the imported queen bees as our bees, as there is a consumer protection law in Tucland which states that the origin of any goods which are sold to consumers need to be declared.

We are going to have another meeting on the whole expansion idea tomorrow and I've been asked to take along a report which addresses the above points. As Cormac is out of the office today, I'd like you to help me by drafting sections for the report, which covers the following:

- The benefits of retaining the Griggs Hives name.
- An explanation of the decision tree that Cormac created and the resulting decision.
- An explanation of the appropriateness of using this decision tree when assessing whether it is financially beneficial to import queen bees.
- Any corporate social responsibility issues arising from selling imported bees under our own label.

Many thanks!

Pene Lopez, Finance Director
Mavis Venderby

Notes on preparation:

(1) All T$ amounts (other than the fixed costs of T$74,500) represent contribution for a period of a year.

(2) The three lines arised for each outcome represent demand for queen bees being

low, medium or high. For all outcomes, there is a 20% chance of demand being low, 50% chance of being medium and 30% chance of being high.

(3) The fixed costs of T$74,500 are the annual costs of staff and annually replaced equipment. If we were to rear all of the queen bees in-house, the expected value of the contribution would be T$237,500. After deducting fixed costs, there would be a net expected value of T$163,000.

(4) The price charged by supplier 1 reduces as the volume of bees increases. The price charged by supplier 2 is fixed. Mavis Venderby will charge the same price for the queen bees irrespective of which supplier is used.

(5) The expected values of contribution at A and B are T$165,500 and T$150,000 respectively.

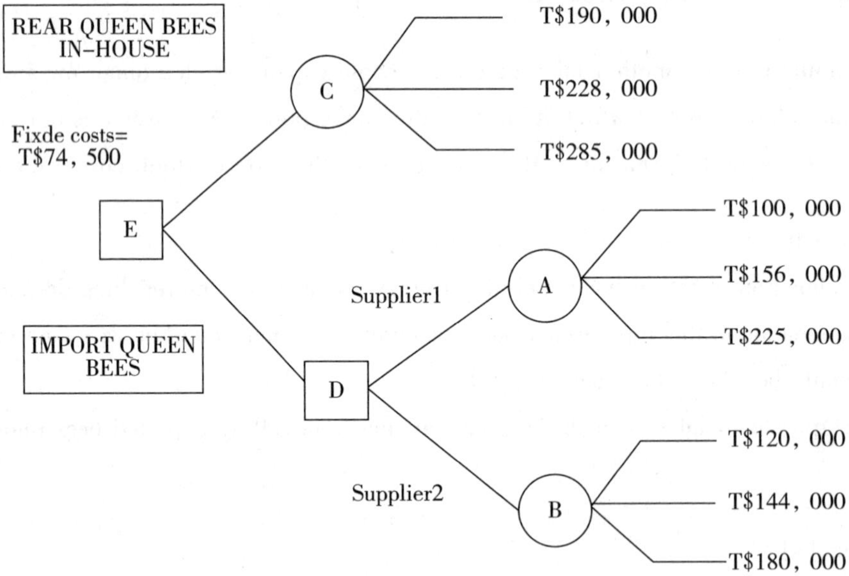

Write the sections of report for Pene Lopez, finance director.

试卷五

本次考试的构成如下：

序号	任务数	时间（分钟）
1	1	45
2	1	45
3	1	45
4	1	45

每个部分规定的时间可用于读题、组织和书写答案。

任务一

梅维斯·文德柏公司的管理者已经开始就收购格里格斯·海夫斯公司（格里格斯蜂巢）进行谈判。Peter Griggs（彼得·格里格斯）目前拥有格里格斯·海夫斯公司这家公司，他希望退休并变卖他的资产。格里格斯·海夫斯公司生产并销售与梅维斯·文德柏公司的标准和质量相似的雪松蜂箱，同时还因培育和售卖蜂王而名声大噪。格里格斯·海夫斯公司还销售养蜂的配套设施。

你收到一封邮件：

发件人：总经理 Thomas Venderby

收件人：管理会计助理

主　题：收购格里格斯·海夫斯公司的可能性

我刚刚与 Pene ，Jacinta 以及格里格斯·海夫斯公司 的总经理开完会，会上讨论了我们收购 Griggs Hives 的可能性，但我还有一些疑问。可 Pene 今天还要开其他会议，所以她建议我向你寻求帮助。

首先，像你想象的那样 Peter Griggs 对他的公司十分看好，并且他向我们提供了一份截至 2016 年 12 月份的营业报表摘录的副本。Peter 表示，由于 2016 年 2 月的一场大型的未预算的宣传活动，板式和盒型的蜂箱销售数量都明显高于预算。他也解释了他们这一年改变了木材供应商的部分渠道，以确保获得有品质保证的木材，这导致每米雪松的成本从 1T$ 涨到了 23T$ 。他说一部分增长的成本被转移到了顾客身上 。由于这些事件的结果，Peter 认为贡献高于预算，尽管他注意到了全方面的情况，但实际上宣传活动的成本导致净利润比预算的要稍微低一点。

第一，我想让你看一下营业报表的摘录，让我知道它是否支持 Peter 关于宣传活动和木材供应商问题的解释。如果是，请解释它是怎样支持的。

第二，我想到我们有一个选择，关于如何收购格里格斯·海夫斯公司。我们要么购买其 100% 的股权，要么购买它的净资产。无论哪种方式，我们都要给他们一个关于商誉的附加费。现在我有两个问题：

（1）什么因素影响了格里格斯·海夫斯公司的商誉价值?

（2）对于收购格里格斯·海夫斯公司的两种方法，怎样将商誉体现在我们的财务报表中?

请发给我一封关于所有差异商誉问题的邮件。

谢谢！

梅维斯·文德柏公司

总经理

Thomas Venderby

格里格斯·海夫斯公司截至2016年12月31号的雪松蜂箱的营业报表摘录：

	T$	T$
预计贡献		2 117 535
销售组合贡献差异：		
盒型	(51 517)	
板式	65 892	
销售组合贡献差异总和		14 375
销售量贡献差异		241 989
实际销售和预计贡献差异		2 373 899
销售价格差异：		
盒型	0	
板式	106 000	
销售价格差异总和		106 000
实际销售少于标准变动成本		2 479 899
变动成本差异：		
原材料价格	(38 627)	
原材料数量	(77 758)	
劳动率	(46 050)	
人工效率	(53 640)	

（续表）

	T$	T$
变动间接费用开支	16 092	
变动间接费用效率	（18 732）	
变动成本差异总和		（218 715）
实际贡献		2 261 184

注：

（1）格里格斯·海夫斯公司采用边际成本法，并且一个盒型蜂箱的预算贡献是 T$ 180.13，一个板式蜂箱的预算贡献是 T$ 230.39。

（2）销售组合贡献差异的计算采用独立单位计算法。

（3）格里格斯·海夫斯公司使用直接劳动时间将变动成本控制在生产上。

请根据总经理 Thomas Venderby 的要求撰写邮件。

任务二

格里格斯·海夫斯公司在 6 周前被收购，所有受雇于格里格斯·海夫斯公司的员工被梅维斯·文德柏公司雇佣，并且 70% 的人同意调动（不包括财务人员）。在过去的两周里，员工、存货和设备已经逐渐被转移至梅维斯·文德柏公司的一个安装了新生产设备、在先前未使用过的仓库。目的是将梅维斯·文德柏公司的现有生产设备用于所有松树蜂巢的生产，新设备和格里格斯·海夫斯公司的厂房以及机器设备用于雪松蜂箱的生产。这是为了使工人精通松树蜂箱或雪松蜂箱的生产，以便减少浪费。

两天以前，格里格斯·海夫斯公司的切割机器在运输期间由于道路事故损毁。这些机器目前在当地但是被损坏了，修理将会花去至少一个月的时间，因为专业零件需要进口然后才能安装。

财务主任 Pene Lopez 叫你去她的办公室，并且说：

我今天早上和 Joseph 开了一个关于新雪松蜂巢工厂缺乏切割机器的会议。他认为我们应该找一个分包商来弥补在生产上的短缺，并且给我提供了一份每种类型蜂箱的成本数据。Joseph 不能决定是外包板式蜂箱还是盒型蜂箱的切割工作。Cormac 已经就这个决定收集了一些数据，我已经快速地浏览了，他的估算是正确的。请你准备一份关于这个清单的简要说明，其中包括对明细表的解释，对根据明细表产生的在内部生产哪种蜂箱的决定的说明以及我们在决定使用分包商之前需要考虑的其他因素的总结。

并且，我让你来这儿，是我还想让你为我做一些别的事情。格里格斯·海夫斯公司一直有一个延长30天信用期限给业余养蜂人和商业养蜂人的政策。Thomas非常希望这个政策能继续施行并扩大我们的业余养蜂人的群体，特别是当我们准备开始销售养蜂设备和蜂箱给他们和基地时。我不认为给业余养蜂人延长信用期限是一个好主意，因为他们不会给我们分摊巨大的风险。我曾经接触过一个保理业务，保理人说他将在无追索权的基础上接管我们所有的应收账款的分类账功能（从Mavis Venderby和以前的Griggs Hives的客户），只收取发票金额的2%的费用。当提款时，该保理人将预付发票金额的75%，并向我们收取8%的财务费用。Thomas要求我提供一份关于接受这个计划的潜在收益和劣势的简报。请给我准备这份简报。

请给我发一封邮件，内容包括我的两个要求。

当月分包决定明细表

	生产数量	机器工作小时数
盒型	1 600	1 320
板式	1 200	1 110
总计	2 800	2 430

现在可以提供1 000个小时的机器可用时间，但这个月需要1 430个小时，这导致了机器小时数的短缺。

一个分包商能够执行所有和我们切割部门相同的工作，并可以给我们的产品进行打包，每单位都有一个固定的费用。

	盒型/每单位	板式/每单位
分包的切割成本	T$ 62	T$ 73
内部切割的可变成本	T$ 51	T$ 61. 2
内部切割的节约成本	T$ 11	T$ 11. 8
内部切割的机器使用时间	0. 825	0. 925
内部切割时每个机器每小时的节约成本	T$ 13. 33	T$ 12. 76

请根据财务总监Pene Lopez的要求撰写邮件。

任务三

几周以后，财务总监 Pene Lopez 正在休年假，然后你收到了下面的邮件。

发件人：总经理 Thomas Venderby
收件人：管理会计助理
主　题：蜂王饲养生意

蜂房生产问题既然已经在我们的控制之中，我和其他董事就把注意力转向了蜂王养殖业务。我们已经成功地管理了所有的蜂房，并将蜂王养殖专家 Percy Gambon（珀西·冈邦）和他的团队归属到了我们的公司，即使 Percy 不是很愿意。我对于这个新业务非常开心，因为它是我们所做的一个极好的拓展。

蜂王的养殖是有很高的技术要求的，尤其是 Percy，因能够在极好的温度下生产蜂王而享有盛誉。我们很荣幸拥有他，并且继续拥有他对我们来说是非常重要的。我们已经同意支付 Percy 一份不错的薪水（高于同行经理的薪水），但是我认为我们需要做的更多。我今天还要参加其他会议，所以希望你能考虑我们能做些什么来激励 Percy 更好地待在梅维斯·文德柏公司。

另外，我昨天和 Percy 就蜂王养殖生意计划进行了谈话。他提到，在过去他们总是售卖所有被养殖的蜂王，并且常常使顾客失望。这让我想到我们可以扩大这部分业务，但是，关于这个生意可能有多大的市场和扩张的规模，我并没有主意。

Percy 说他已经从 Tucland 养蜂协会统计了这个国家在过去十年里蜂王被购买的数量，并且他说他能使用这些数据创建一个时间序列。我对时间序列不太了解，但是我能想起来它有四个组成部分。我想知道时间序列的四个组成部分是什么和每一个部分是怎样影响蜂王的需求的。

请回复一份关于奖励机制和时间序列的邮件。

非常感谢！

梅维斯·文德柏公司
总经理
Thomas Venderby

请根据总经理 Thomas Venderby 的要求撰写邮件。

任务四

两周后你在早上收到以下邮件：

发件人：财务总监 Pene Lopez
收件人：管理会计助理
主　题：蜂王饲养业务的扩张

昨天，我和其他董事举行了一个关于蜂王养殖生意和扩张的可能性的会议。现在我们有闲置生产能力来饲养更多的蜂王，但是为了增加生产和销售，将需要更多的员工和设备。这种设备通常能使用一年。在这个会议中一些问题被提出，但是直到结束我们也没有机会去进一步的探讨。

- Thomas 提出的问题是：我们是以 Griggs 的商标继续销售蜂王，还是用梅维斯·文德柏公司的商标来售卖蜂王。这两种方式各有利弊。
- Joseph 提出从 Bucland 进口蜂王，以代替产生每年额外的员工和设备的成本，他说 Bucland 的蜂王比 Tucland 的蜂王更便宜。Jacinta 说这里有我们可以用到的两个供应商，他们中的一个表明如果我们从他那里买的越多，他将给我们更多的折扣。Joseph 建议我们继续出售进口的蜂王，就像是我们饲养的一样，没有人会知道。我认为在设备和员工上节省投资是一个可以考虑的点，所以昨天晚上 Cormac 草拟了一个决策树，基于我们低，中，高水平的销售（这有一些不确定性）。但是，我不认同将进口蜂王作为我们的蜜蜂进行销售，因为 Tucland 有一个消费者权益法案，它要求任何出售给消费者的商品的原产地都需要被公布。

明天我们将要举行另一个关于扩张计划的会议，我被要求带着一份阐述以上要点的报告。因为 Cormac 今天不在办公室，所以我想让你帮我草拟这个报告的部分内容，包括以下几方面：

- 保留格里格斯·海夫斯公司的商标的益处。
- 对 Cormac 创建的决策树的解释和最终决定的解释。
- 解释在评估进口蜂王是否在经济上有益时，使用这个决策树的合理性。

■ 以我们的商标销售进口蜜蜂所产生的任何企业社会责任问题。

非常感谢！

梅维斯·文德柏公司
财务总监
Pene Lopez

笔记的制备：

（1）所有 T$ 的数量（除固定成本 T$ 74 500 外）代表一年的毛利润。

（2）每一个结果产生的三条线代表对蜂王的低、中、高的需求。对于所有结果来说，低需求的概率是 20% 中等需求的概率是 50%，高等需求的概率是 30%。

（3）T$ 74 500 的固定成本是每年的员工成本和每年更换设备的成本。如果我们打算在内部饲养所有的蜂王，这个贡献的期望值将是 T$ 237 500。扣除固定成本后，净期望值是 T$ 163 000。

（4）供应商 1 的价格费用会随着蜜蜂数量的增加而降低。供应商 2 的价格费用是固定的。无论选择哪个供应商，梅维斯·文德柏公司对蜂王都会收取相同的价格。

（5）A 和 B 的平均贡献期望值分别是 T$ 165 500 和 T$ 150 000。

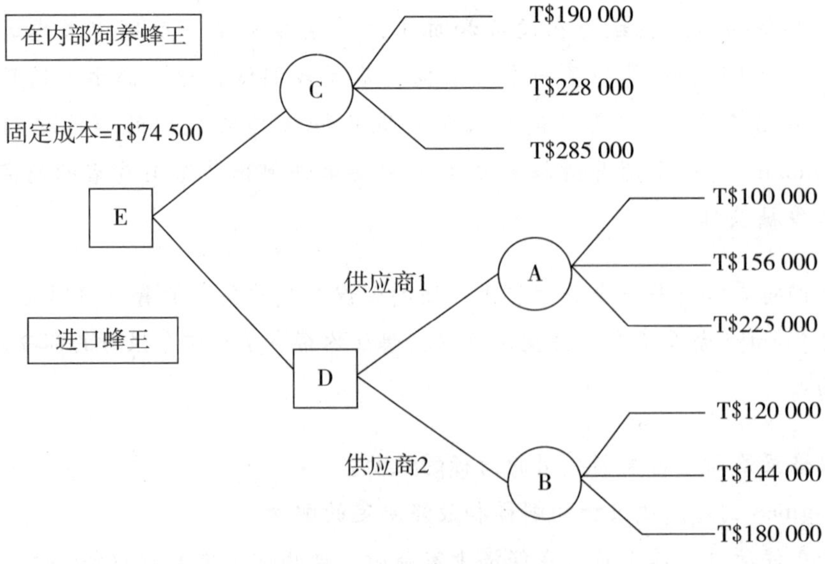

请根据财务总监 Pene Lopez 的要求撰写部分报告。

Variant 5　Suggested Answers

Section 1

From: Management Accountant Assistant

To: Thomas Venderby, Managing Director

Subject: Possible acquisition of Griggs Hives

Impact of the Advertising Campaign

Peter's comment about the advertising campaign increasing the number of hives sold is supported by the sales variances.

The sales mix variances indicate that the mix of hives sold was different to that budgeted. Looking at the split of the mix variance we can see that the slatted hives variance is favourable, meaning that a greater proportion than budgeted of the total number of hives sold were slatted. Slatted hives have the higher contribution of the two types and therefore this has resulted in a favourable total mix variance. A greater proportion of the hives sold were at a budgeted contribution of T$230. 39 rather than T$180. 13, leading to an increase in total contribution as a result of the change in mix. The mix variances in themselves do not tell us whether the advertising campaign has been successful overall, although they do indicate that perhaps the campaign was more successful for slatted hives than box hives.

The favourable sales quantity variance tells us that over the year a greater number of hives were sold than budgeted. Indeed, this variance is significant in value (at T$241,989) compared to the budgeted contribution of T$2,117,535 and indicates that the advertising campaign was indeed very successful in generating additional sales volume.

Peter's comment about the cost of the advertising campaign reducing overall profit cannot be evidenced from the extract of the operating statement that we have. Marketing costs are not a cost of production and hence will not impact contribution. Instead this un – budgeted marketing expenditure will adversely impact operating profit which is not shown in the schedule.

Impact of the Wood Supplier Issue

The impact of the wood supplier issue on performance is supported by a number of variances within the extract.

Most obviously, there is an adverse materials price variance of T$38,627, which demonstrates that across all materials, a greater price was paid for the quantity used compared to budget. Part of this will have been the T$1 increase in cedar price per metre.

However the impact of this issue has possibly extended beyond just price. There is an adverse materials quantity variance which could be the result of having to scrap production due to the poor quality of the cedar. In addition there are adverse labour rate and efficiency variances, perhaps indicating that as a result of the quality issues, a greater number of hours had to be worked at a premium rate. The increased labour hours is also reflected in the variable overhead efficiency variance.

Peter's comment about passing the cedar price increase onto customers is partly supported by the extract. There is a favourable sales price variance of T$106,000 in respect of slatted hives, indicating an increase in the selling price. However, there was no such rise in the price of box hives as the sales price variance is nil.

Accounting For the Possible Acquisition of Griggs Hives

Factors Affecting the Value of the Goodwill to Be Acquired

The value of the goodwill in respect of Griggs Hives will be determined by the difference between the amount that we pay for the business and the value of the net assets that we acquire. Therefore to some extent the value of the goodwill is down to us in terms of how much we are willing to pay for the business.

The factors that will influence this include:

(1) The strength of Griggs Hives' customer loyalty. Our business depends a lot on repeat orders from our customers and it will be the same for Griggs Hives. We will need to understand the nature of the Griggs Hives' customers and the amount of repeat orders there are.

(2) The reputation for quality of product (and service). Griggs Hives is the second largest manufacturer and retailer of wooden hives in Tucland (behind us). We know that it has a similar quality profile to us as well.

(3) In addition we know that it has an excellent reputation and is the country's leading

supplier of queen bees. This is a business, in which we have no experience and therefore buying in this experience is valuable to us.

Impact of the Goodwill on Our Financial Statements of the Different Acquisition Methods

If we acquire the equity share capital of Griggs Hives, then in essence we will have acquired an investment in another entity. Indeed we will have acquired an investment in a subsidiary as we are able to control the entity with 100% of its equity shares.

In our own Mavis Venderby financial statements, this will lead to a simple accounting entry. Assuming that we pay cash, the entry will be to reduce cash and create an investment which will be shown as a part of non-current assets on the statement of financial position. The goodwill will not be separated out from the value of the investment.

However, because we will control the entity Griggs Hives, we need to prepare group financial statements as well as our own financial statements. The goodwill in relation to Griggs Hives will appear in the group financial statements as an intangible asset within non-current assets. This will be subject to impairment reviews, but will not be amortised.

If we acquire the net assets of the business, the goodwill in Griggs Hives in effect crystallises in value because we will have paid an amount above the value of the net assets. We therefore will have purchased an intangible asset and record this in our statement of financial position at its value at the date of acquisition.

Post-acquisition it is not possible to revalue the intangible asset upwards because there is no active market in which to determine a reliable value. Instead it will be subject to annual impairment reviews, with any impairment loss taken to profit or loss.

Many thanks!

Management Accountant Assistant
Mavis Venderby

Section 2

From: Management Accountant Assistant

To: Pene Lopez, Finance Director

Subject: Subcontractor and factoring arrangement

USING A SUB-CONTRACTOR

The Schedule

The schedule shows us that cutting box hives in-house, compared to using the sub-contractor, will save us T$11.00 a hive. Cutting slatted hives in-house, compared to using the sub-contractor, will save us T$11.80 a hive.

Therefore it might appear that it would be beneficial to focus on cutting slatted hives in-house first as this would give us the greatest saving.

However, this does not take into account the number of machine hours that each type of hive uses. A box hive uses 0.825 hours, compared to a slatted hive which uses 0.925 hours.

Given that machine hours are the scarce resource and limited to 1,000 hours for the month, we need to base the decision on the costs that we would save from cutting in-house for each hour of machine time used. For box hives this is T$13.33 a hive and for slatted hives T$12.76 a hive.

Based on this, the decision should be to use the 1,000 machine hours available to cut box hives (because this would give us the greatest cost saving) and use the sub-contractor for the rest of the box hives and all of the slatted hives.

Summary of other Factors to Consider

There are a number of factors that need to be considered before a decision regarding what to sub-contract and indeed whether to sub-contract at all, is made.

We need to ensure that the data used in the schedule is reliable in the context of making this decision. Are the variable costs of cutting in-house completely variable? Are our standard machine hours accurate?

Also, we should consider whether there are any alternatives to using a sub-contractor. We should look at the scheduling of production to see if we could possibly reduce the amount of production this month? Alternatively, could some of the cutting of cedar be done in the new pine only facility temporarily? This is a peak time of year for production, however, inventory levels could potentially be allowed to fall a little to accommodate this short term problem.

We will need to consider how reliable the sub-contractor are. Will they be able to deliver on time and will the quality of cutting be high enough?

Factoring Arrangement

Benefits of the Factoring Arrangement

A key benefit of this arrangement is that it is non-recourse, meaning that the factor will be responsible for any irrecoverable debts that arise from our customers. Effectively this gives us insurance against any of our customers not paying us. We will have confidence that we don't incur any losses in respect of non-payment.

In addition the arrangement means that we receive 75% of the value of sales immediately. This will mean that the combined business (Mavis Venderby and Griggs Hives) potentially receives cash more quickly than without the arrangement. Currently, all sales to Griggs Hives' customers and Mavis Venderby's commercial beekeeper customers are on credit terms of 30 days. There would be a cash flow advantage for these customers. Mavis Venderby' s hobby beekeepers however currently pay up front, so there is no cash flow advantage here, although in the future, if credit is extended to them, this will be beneficial.

Another benefit is that the factor is an expert in credit control and will be efficient at sending out invoices and managing the receivables ledger. This is potentially very beneficial for us because we potentially do not have the resource in-house to do this. None of the finance staff have transferred from Griggs Hives and our own team would be extremely stretched to cope with the increased workload arising from combining the two businesses: that's without extending the workload in respect of the receivables ledger by offering credit to our hobby beekeepers. We will potentially need to take on more finance staff anyway; by factoring we can at least transfer responsibility for the receivables ledger.

Drawbacks with the Factoring Arrangement

A key drawback associated with factoring is it's cost. We will be paying 2% of the value of our sales to the factor as an administrative fee. This will directly affect our gross margin by an equivalent 2%. In addition we will need to pay finance charges on the 75% of sales advanced each month at 8%. This rate is likely to be higher than the rate that we could secure from a bank and is an expensive form of finance.

Another drawback is that because the arrangement is non – recourse, it means that we lose control over our receivables ledger. The factor will decide on who receives credit and how any overdue accounts are chased. It is likely that a factor will be reasonably aggressive when chasing for payment, which means that we could lose customers.

Linked to that, our customers will know that we are using a factor because correspondence is with them. This could have an impact on our reputation within the market, as the fact we are using a factor could be seen as a sign that we have cash flow issues. Similarly, we have a good relationship with our customers (especially our hobby bee-keepers who value the advice that we give). This could be damaged if they do not continue to have direct contact with us for payment.

Many thanks!

Management Accountant Assistant
Mavis Venderby

Section 3

From: Management Accountant Assistant
To: Thomas Venderby, Managing Director
Subject: Queen rearing business

Incentivising Percy Gambon

To incentivise Percy to stay with us, we could consider giving him additional rewards for his work on top of his salary (both financial and non-financial rewards). We should also ensure that he is happy with his work environment and position within the business.

Rewards

We could offer Percy performance related pay as a bonus on top of his salary. To be effective, this would need to be linked to a measure that Percy has control or influence over such as the number of queen bees successfully reared or the number of queen bees sold.

We could offer non-financial rewards on top of his salary. Such rewards need to have value to Percy in terms of meeting his needs and desires and should be tailored to him specifically. For example, he might appreciate membership fees of beekeeping organisations being paid for. Alternatively he might appreciate more standard non-financial rewards such as private health care, gym membership or a mobile phone contract.

Regarding rewarding Percy, we need to be careful that we do not upset other members of staff, who might perceive that a special case is being made for one person.

Work Environment and Position

As well as rewarding Percy, we need to ensure that he feels valued and to feel that the queen rearing business is important to Mavis Venderby. He needs to feel empowered to make decisions regarding queen rearing with autonomy given that he is the expert. We should involve him in management meetings and ensure that we listen to him in other aspects of the business as well.

Even though he is an expert, we could still give Percy opportunities to develop his skills and to cement his reputation within Tucland as an expert in the field. We should allow him to attend courses and conferences linked to his field of expertise.

We could offer Percy flexible working. There might be certain times that are better than others for him to work in respect of when the bees need most attention.

We must ensure that he has sufficient resources to carrying out his work. This includes an appropriate space on site, sufficient equipment and enough staff in his team.

Forecasting Potential Future Sales of Queen Bees

Creating a Time Series

A time series is simply a series of figures recorded over time. In this instance, the time series will be the numbers of queen bees purchased in Tucland every quarter over the past 10 years. This can be presented as a graph, however on its own it means little because the demand for bees will be affected by the general trend over the period as well as seasonal, cyclical and random variations. To be useful, each of these elements needs to be looked at in isolation.

The Trend

The trend is the underlying long term movement in the demand for queen bees. Given that there is 10 years of data, then we should be able to establish the trend quite easily. Given the growth in both commercial and hobby beekeeping in Tucland in recent years, we can expect this long term trend to be upwards.

Seasonal Variations

Seasonal variations are fluctuations in the trend specific to a period of time, and here seasonal variations will relate to specific times of year. Beekeeping and honey production is very seasonal: bees mostly produce honey in late spring and during the summer, when there are many flowering plants producing the nectar that the bees need. We see this affecting our bee hive sales which peak during the months of March to July. It is highly likely that this same seasonality applies to queen bee sales. Indeed, the seasonality variation could be even more marked than for hive production because new queens are more likely to be needed at the start of the honey production season.

Cyclical Variations

Cyclical variations are fluctuations in the trend that are medium term in nature and are caused by events that repeat in cycles. A typical cycle would be an economic boom and bust cycle. We know that beekeeping is thriving in Tucland at the moment despite the fact that the country is in the middle of an economic downturn, so it's possible that the economic cycle does not affect demand for queen bees. There could be other cycles that affect demand though such as disease cycles.

Random Variations

Random variations are fluctuations in the trend that are caused by unforeseen factors. For queen bee demand, this could be a major disease killing bees (which would potentially increase demand in the short term) or particularly bad weather in a season affecting the population. Luckily in Tucland our native bees seem to be resistant to many diseases affecting bee colonies in other countries.

Many thanks!

Management Accountant Assistant
Mavis Venderby

Section 4

The Benefits of Retaining the Griggs Hives Name

The key benefit of retaining the Griggs Hives name is that it is already well established in the market place. Not only that, Griggs Hives has an excellent reputation for rearing queen bees that are of a high quality. The name of Griggs Hives already differentiates the business from other queen bee suppliers because of this quality.

If we were to change the branding to Mavis Venderby, then certainly in the short term, there is likely to be a drop in demand. This is because beekeepers will not necessarily know that we have taken over the business. They might believe that we entered into the market with no experience and little expertise as we have never sold live bees before.

Retaining the Griggs Hive name will enhance the impact of any advertising that we undertake in respect of this business. Griggs Hives bees already have a strong brand identity linked to quality and hence it might actually reduce the amount of advertising that is required as building the Mavis Venderby brand for queen bees from scratch will be expensive.

We also need to think about the customers. Beekeepers are typically loyal to their suppliers and value the additional services that we provide. This is certainly true for Mavis Venderby in terms of our customers being able to talk to our in-house experts about hives. The same is probably true for Griggs Hives in terms of the queen bee rearing experts. If we change the name, even though we have a fantastic reputation for hives, customers might perceive a reduction in the quality of advice to be had.

Analysis of the Decision Tree

The decision tree shows that we are facing two decisions. Firstly, whether to expand our own queen rearing business, or whether to import bees to sell on. Secondly, if we decide to import bees, which supplier we should use: supplier 1 or supplier 2.

In order to use the decision tree we must work from right to left and start with the second decision. We can see that supplier 2 offers a lower price per queen than supplier 1 at low levels of demand (because contribution is higher at this level), whilst supplier 1 has the lower price at higher levels of demand. Because there is uncertainty in terms of what our demand will be, we need to calculate and compare the expected values for each outcome (where the outcome is either using supplier 1 or supplier 2). An expected value is essentially the average position taking the probabilities of the expected outcomes into account.

We can see that at point A the expected value is T$165,500 and at point B is

T$150,000. Therefore because point A is higher we should accept supplier 1.

Now we can work backwards to the decision about whether to import queen bees at all. At point D we know that the decision is to use supplier 1 with an expected value of T$165,500. We need to compare this to the expected value of rearing bees in-house, which from the notes is a net of T$163,000.

Therefore based on the information in the decision tree, the most financially beneficial decision is to import the bees rather than rear in-house.

Appropriateness of Using This Decision Tree

A decision tree approach to decision making is based on expected values. An expected value is a weighted average of all the possible outcomes, weighted according to the probability of those outcomes occurring. So, in this case the expected value at point C on the decision tree is the sum of each of the outcomes (T$190,000, T$228,000 and T$285,000) multiplied by their respective probabilities (20%, 50% and 30%).

If we were to just take this activity of rearing in-house as a one-off then the actual outcome will be one of the possibilities. However, were we to repeat this activity over and over again, then we would expect the average of all of the outcomes to be T$236,000. Therefore using expected value to make a decision is only valid where that decision can be repeated. Because this is an activity that potentially could be repeated year after year then the use of expected values is appropriate.

However, there are some limitations of using a decision tree to make a decision such as this, including:

- The data used in the decision tree to calculate contributions and expected values is estimated. Whilst we can have some confidence regarding the price that supplier 1 and supplier 2 will charge and we should know enough from the existing business to support the variable costs of rearing in-house, the level of demand is uncertain. The probabilities assigned to each possible outcome are estimates as well.
- The decision tree uses expected values which assume that the decision maker is risk neutral. This means that the range of possible outcomes and their probabilities are ignored. For example, at a higher level of demand using supplier 1 gives a contribution of T$225,000 which even without doing any calculations is higher than the outcome for in-house which is T$285,000 less T$90,000 fixed costs. If we were to

take a risk seeking approach, we might prefer the option of supplier 1 because of this potential for higher contribution, and this is not dependent on the expected values.

- The decision tree analysis ignores non-financial factors such as the impact to the business of Percy Gambon deciding to leave as a result of importing bees. In addition we should consider the effect that the decision would have on our reputation.

CSR Issues Arising From Selling Imported Bees Under Our Own Label

If we were to sell imported bees as Mavis Venderby or Griggs Hives queen bees, without declaring that we had not reared them, this would be a breach of our corporate social responsibilities in two main ways.

Firstly, there will be a breach of our legal responsibility. If we do not declare the bees have been imported, then we will not be adhering to the consumer protection law that requires such declarations. It's possible that we therefore expose the business to the risk of not only fines but also bad publicity as a result of breaking the law.

Secondly, there will be a breach of our ethical responsibility. To meet our ethical responsibilities we must act with integrity and in a just and fair way. Misleading our customers will not be acting with integrity because we are not telling the truth about the origin of the bees. The impact of this will be compounded because we are selling bees that we potentially know little about in terms of their ability to cope with our Tucland climate and their temperament. If we act this way and are then subsequently found out, this will again damage our reputation as an ethical and moral business.

试卷五　参考答案

任务一

发件人：管理会计助理

收件人：总经理 Thomas Venderby

主　题：收购格里格斯·海夫斯公司的可能性

宣传活动的影响

Peter 关于宣传活动增加了蜂箱的销售量的言论通过销售差异可以看出是真实的。

销售组合差异表明蜂箱的组合销售与预算是不同的。通过分割组合差异，我们可以看到板式蜂箱的差异是有利的，这意味着在蜂箱的总销售量中板式蜂箱比预算卖的更多。在这两种类型的蜂箱中，板式有一个更高的贡献率，因此导致了一个有利的总组合差异。出售的大部分蜂箱是按预算贡献 T$ 230. 39 计算的，而不是按 T$ 180. 13 计算，这使得组合的变化造成了总贡献的增加。虽然宣传活动的确表明在销量上板式蜂箱比盒型更为成功，但是他们公司的组合差异本身并没有告诉我们宣传活动是否是完全成功的。

有利的销售量差异告诉我们，这一年蜂箱的销量比预算的要多。的确，相比较预算的 T$ 2 117 535 贡献率，实际贡献率是 T$ 241 989 的有利差异是显著的，这表明广告宣传活动确实非常成功地增加了销售量。

Peter 关于增加广告宣传的成本导致总利润减少了的言论，从他给我们的营运报表的摘录中无法得到证明。营销成本不是生产成本，因此不会影响贡献率。相反，这种未编入预算的营销费用将对营运利润产生不利影响，而营运利润并未被列在明细表中。

木材供应商问题的影响

通过这份报表摘录中的一系列差异，我们能看出木材供应商对绩效表现产生的影响。

最明显的是，不良材料的价格差异为 T$ 38 627，这表明在所有材料中，所使用的数量与预算相比要支付更多。部分原因是雪松价格每米上涨了 T$ 1。

但是这个问题不仅会影响价格，还会影响其他方面。不利的原材料差异，可能是由于雪松的质量较差导致有报废的产品造成的。另外这些不利的劳工率和效率差异，也许表明了由于质量问题，必须以较高的劳工率工作更多的时间。而工时的增加也会反映在变动间接效率差异上。

Peter 关于将增加的雪松成本分摊到消费者身上的说法，从报表摘录中也可以看出来。在板式蜂箱上有一个有利的销售价格差异 T$ 106 000，这表明销售价格有所上涨。但是，因为盒型蜂箱的销售价格差异为 0，所以盒型蜂箱的价格并没有增加。

收购格里格斯·海夫斯公司的可能性的说明

影响获取商誉价值的因素

格里格斯·海夫斯公司的商誉价值将由我们收购该公司所支付的金额与我们获得的该公司的净资产价值之间的差额决定。因此，在某种程度上，该公司的商誉价值取决于我们收购该公司愿意支付的金额。

影响因素包括以下几点。

（1）格里格斯·海夫斯公司顾客的忠诚度。我们的业务在很大程度上依赖于顾客重复的订单，同样，格里格斯·海夫斯公司也是如此。我们需要去了解格里格斯·海夫斯公司的顾客类型和他们的重复订单的数量。

（2）产品（和服务）质量的声誉。格里格斯·海夫斯公司在 Tucland 是第二大木质蜂箱的制造商和零售商（仅次于我们）。我们清楚它有着和我们一样好的品质表现。

（3）此外，我们也知道该公司有一个极好的声誉，是全国领先的蜂王供应商。这是一个我们没有经验的行业，因此购买这种经验对我们来说是很有价值的。

商誉在不同的收购方法下对资产负债表的影响

如果我们收购格里格斯·海夫斯公司的股本，那么本质上我们将获得对另一个实体的投资。事实上，我们获得的是对子公司的投资，因为我们将能够以 100% 的股权来控制该实体。在我们梅维斯·文德柏公司的财务报表中，它将会有一个简单的会计分录。假如我们支付现金，这个分录将减少现金，并创造一项投资，这个投资将会在资产负债表中作为固定资产的一部分出现。商誉不会与投资的价值分开。

但是，因为我们将控制格里格斯·海夫斯公司这个主体，我们就需要准备集团的财务报表和我们自己的财务报表。格里格斯·海夫斯公司的商誉将会作为一个无形的固定资产出现在集团的财务报表中，接受减值评估，但不会被分摊。

如果我们收购了这个公司的净资产，格里格斯·海夫斯公司的商誉在实际上就是有价值的，因为我们要支付一个超过净资产价值的金额。因此，我们是购买了一项无形资产，且在收购之日需将其价值记录在资产负债表中。

并购后无形资产是不可能升值的，因为没有一个活跃的市场来决定其价值的可靠性。相反，它将接受每年的减值评估，任何的减值损失都会被记录在损益表中。

十分感谢！

梅维斯·文德柏公司
管理会计助理

任务二

发件人：管理会计助理
收件人：财务总监 Pene Lopez
主　题：分包商和保理安排

使用分包商

明细表

明细表显示，与使用分包商相比，在内部切割盒型蜂箱，一个蜂箱将会给我们节省T$ 11.00。而相比较使用分包商，在内部切割板式蜂箱，一个蜂箱将会给我们节省T$ 11.80。

因此，首先关注在内部切割板式蜂箱是有益的，因为这样可以最大限度地节省开支。

但是，这并没有考虑到每种类型的蜂箱使用的机器小时数。一个盒型蜂箱需使用0.825 小时，而一个板式蜂箱使用0.925 小时。

鉴于机器时间是稀缺的资源，本月的工作时间又限于1 000 个小时，我们需要根据每使用1 小时的机器工作时间而节省的成本来进行决策。每个盒型蜂箱是T$ 13.33，每个板式蜂箱是T$ 12.76.

在此基础上，这个决策应该是使用1 000 个机器工时去切割盒型蜂箱（因为这将使我们最大限度地节约成本），使用分包商去生产剩下的盒型蜂箱和所有的板式蜂箱。

总结其他需要考虑的因素

在决定分包的工作以及是否分包之前，有很多因素需要考虑。

我们需要确保在制定决策时，明细表中的数据是真实可靠的。内部切割的可变成本是完全可变的吗？我们的标准机器工时是精确的吗？

并且，我们也要考虑到除了使用分包商外还有其他的选择吗？我们应该去看看产品的生产进度以了解我们是否能减少本月的生产数量？或者，雪松的一部分切割工作能在新的松木设备中暂时的完成吗？然而，这是一年中生产的高峰期，库存水平将会被允许适当地下降以适应这个短期的问题。

我们还需要考虑分包商的可靠性。他们是否会按时的交货，并且切割的质量足够高吗？

保理协议

保理协议的益处

这种安排的一个主要好处是无追索权，这意味着保理人将对我们客户产生的任何不可收回的债务负责。而这实际上就确保了不会有客户不给我们付款，我们就有信心不会因客户未付款而蒙受任何损失。

另外，这个协议意味着我们会立即收到销售额的 75%，这也意味着合并后的公司将有可能更快地收到现金。目前，格里格斯 · 海夫斯公司的客户和梅维斯 · 文德柏公司的商业养蜂客户的销售都有 30 天的信用期限，这些顾客将有一个现金流的优势。然而，梅维斯 · 文德柏公司的业余养蜂人目前是提前付款的，所以没有一个现金流的优势，尽管在未来，如果向他们提供信用期限，也是有益的。

另一个益处是保理人是信贷控制的专家，并且在发送发票和管理应收账款账户方面是高效的。这对我们来说有很大潜在的益处，因为我们内部可能没有资源去完成这项工作。格里格斯 · 海夫斯公司的财务人员没有一个被调过来，因此我们自己的团队要非常努力以成功地应对由于两个公司合并所增加的工作量：这是通过向我们的业余养蜂人提供信用期，没有增加应收账款账户的工作量的情况下。不论如何我们都可能需要招聘更多的财务人员，通过保理，我们至少可以转移对于应收账户的责任。

保理协议的弊端

一个很明显的弊端是保理的成本。我们将支付 2% 的销售额作为管理费，这将直接影响我们 2% 的毛利润。另外，我们还需要每月支付 8% 的财务费用给那 75% 的预付款。这个利率可能会高于我们从银行获得的利率，是一种昂贵的金融形式。

另一个缺点是，由于协议规定的是无追索权，这意味着我们失去了对应收账款总账的控制权。保理人将决定哪些人获得信贷，以及如何追讨逾期账户。追讨款项时，可能会有一个保理人相当激进，这意味着我们可能会失去客户。

与此相关的是，我们的客户将知道我们正在使用一个保理人，因为保理人将直接联系他们。这可能会对我们在市场上的声誉产生影响，因为我们使用保理人可能会被视为我们有现金流问题的迹象。同样，我们需要与客户（特别是我们的业余养蜂人，他们重视我们的建议）保持很好的关系，但如果他们不能继续直接与我们联系和付款，这种关系就可能会被损坏。

十分感谢！

梅维斯·文德柏公司
管理会计助理

任务三

发件人：管理会计助理
收件人：总经理 Thomas Venderby
主　题：蜂王饲养生意

激励 Percy Gambon

为了激励 Percy 为我们效力，我们可以考虑在他的最高工资的基础上再给他额外的奖赏（包括经济上的和非经济上的奖赏）。我们也应该确保他对他的工作环境和工作岗位很满意。

奖赏

我们可以在 Percy 最高工资的基石上再用绩效报酬作为奖金。为了有效，这需要与 Percy 实施的具有控制或影响力的措施相关联来衡量，例如，成功饲养的蜂王的数量或出售的蜂王的数量。

我们也可以在他的薪水之外提供非经济奖励。在满足他的需求和愿望方面，这样的奖励需要对 Percy 有价值，应该专门为他量身定做。例如，他可能会感激为他支付养蜂组织的会员费用，并且他可能会感激更标准的非财务奖赏，如私人医疗保险，健身会员，或者手机合约。

关于奖励 Percy 这件事，我们需要谨慎一些，因为我们不能让其他的员工因此感到沮丧，他们可能会认为这是针对 Percy 的特例。

工作环境和职位

在激励 Percy 的同时，我们需要确保他能感到他有价值，并且感受到蜂王培育业务对梅维斯·文德柏公司的重要性。考虑到他是专家，他需要感受到自己被赋予权力能够自主定夺养殖蜂王方面的决策。我们应该让他参与进管理层会议中，并且确保我们在业务的其他方面也听取他的意见。

尽管他已经是一个专家，我们仍然可以给 Percy 去提高他技能的机会，以巩固他在 Tucland 地区作为领域专家的声誉。我们也应该允许他参加一些有关他专业领域的课程和会议。

我们也可以提供给 Percy 弹性工作制。因为在蜜蜂最需要照料的时候，没有比他更适合在这个工作段工作的人选了。

我们必须确保他有充足的资源来开展他的工作。这包括在一个适当的场地，充足的设备以及足够的团队成员。

预测蜂王未来潜在的销售量

创建一个时间序列

时间序列是对一段时间内一系列数字的简单记录。在这种情况下，时间序列是过去十年内每一季度在 Tucland 购买蜂王的数量。这能用图表来表示，但是就其本身而言并没有什么意义，因为对蜜蜂的需求将会受到这一时期的总体趋势和季节，周期，随机变化的影响。要使这些元素都有用，就需要分别看待它们。

趋势

这种趋势是蜂王需求的长期潜在变化。因为有十年的数据，我们应该能够很容易地建立这个趋势图。鉴于近几年 Tucland 地区的商业和业余养蜂都有所增长，我们能够预计这一长期趋势将是上升的。

季节性变动

季节性变动是一段特定时间内的趋势的波动。这里的季节性变动涉及一年中的特定时期。养蜂和蜂蜜生产是非常季节性的：蜜蜂大多是在春末和夏季产蜜，那时有大量开花植物生产蜜蜂所需要的花蜜。我们能够看出这会影响我们蜂箱的销售，带来了 3 月到 7 月的销售高峰。这个季节性很可能同样适用于蜂王的销售。事实上，蜂王的季节性变动甚至要比蜂箱生产更加明显，因为到蜂蜜开始生产的季节时更加需要新的蜂王。

周期性变动

周期性变化是中期性质的趋势中的波动，是由周期中重复发生的事件引起的。一个典型的周期是经济的盛衰周期。我们都知道尽管 Tucland 的经济处在低迷时期，养蜂业依旧在蓬勃发展，所以整个经济周期不太可能会影响蜂王的需求。但是可能会有像疾病周期一样的一些其他周期影响蜂王的需求。

随机变动

随机变动是由不可预见的因素引起的趋势波动。对于蜂王的需求来说，这可能是由于一个主要的疾病灾害造成了蜜蜂的死亡（在短期内会潜在地增加需求），或者在某个季节中出现了极端的恶劣天气灾害影响了蜂王的数量。幸运的是，在 Tucland，我们本土的蜜蜂似乎能够抵抗许多影响其他地区蜜蜂群体的疾病。

十分感谢！

梅维斯·文德柏公司
管理会计助理

任务四

保留格里格斯·海夫斯公司商标的益处

保留格里格斯·海夫斯公司商标的一个关键益处是这个商标在市场中已经占有一席之地。除此之外，该公司在饲养高质量蜂王方面也有一个极好的声誉。Griggs hives 的商标因为优秀的质量，已经使该业务很好地与其他供应商区别开来了。

如果我们想把这个品牌改为梅维斯·文德柏公司，那么在短期内可以确定的是，需求上会有一个下滑。这是因为养蜂者可能不知道我们收购了这家公司，他们可能因为我们之前没有售卖过活蜂，而觉得我们进入这个市场是没有经验和专业知识的。

保留格里格斯·海夫斯公司的商标将会增强相关业务的宣传力度。格里格斯·海夫斯公司的高质量的蜜蜂使得他们在市场上有很强的品牌认可度，因此它实际上可能会减少所需要的宣传活动量，而再建立蜂王的梅维斯·文德柏公司品牌的费用是很高的。

我们也需要考虑到顾客。养蜂人通常对他们的供应商是非常忠诚的，并且很珍惜我们给他们提供的额外服务。这对于 Mavis Venderby 公司来说无疑是正确的，因为我们的客户能够与我们的内部专家讨论蜂箱。从蜂王饲养专家的角度来看，Griggs Hives 的蜂王可能也是如此。如果我们改变了商标名称，即使我们在蜂箱方面有很好的声誉，顾客也可能会觉得建议的质量有所下降。

决策树分析

决策树显示我们面临两种决策。首先，是否扩大我们的蜂王养殖生意，或者是否进口蜜蜂来销售。其次，如果我们决定进口蜜蜂，那么我们应该选择供应商 1 还是供应商 2。

使用决策树，我们必须从右往左看，然后开始于第二个决定。我们能看出，在一个低水平的需求量上，对于每个蜂王供应商 2 能比供应商 1 提供一个更低的价格。（因为在这个水平上的贡献率是更高的），而在高水平的需求量上供应商 1 提供了更低的价格。因为我们的需求量是不确定的，所以要计算并且比较每一个结果的期望值（这个结果要么是使用供应商 1，要么是使用供应商 2）。期望值实质上是将预期结果的概率纳入计算的平均值。

我们能看到点 A 的期望值是 T$ 165 500，点 B 是 T$ 150 000。因此由于点 A 更高，我们应该选择供应商 1。

现在我们再回到关于是否进口蜂王这个决策上来。由点 D 我们知道这个决策是使用供应商 1，他有一个 T165 500 的期望值。然后我们需要将其与内部饲养蜂王的期望值进行比较，注释中写到内部养蜂的期望值是 T163 000。

因此基于以上决策树的信息，财务收益最多的决策是进口蜜蜂而不是内部饲养。

使用决策树的合理性

决策树方法是指决策的制定基于期望值。期望值是所有可能发生的结果的加权平均，加权是根据结果发生的概率计算的。所以，在这种情况下，决策树中点 C 的期望值是每一种结果（T$ 190 000，T$ 228 000，T$ 285 000）乘以它们各自的概率（20%，50%，30%）的总和。

如果我们在室内饲养蜜蜂是一次性的活动，那么实际的结果将是其中一种可能性。但是如果我们一次又一次地重复这个活动，那么我们将会期望所有结果的平均值是 T$ 236 000。因此，只有在决策可以重复的情况下，才能使用期望值进行决策。因为只有这个活动能够一年又一年地不断被重复，这个期望值的使用才会更加近似和恰当。

但是，使用决策树制定决策有一些限制因素：

- 用决策树中使用的数据计算的贡献率和期望值是估计值。虽然对于供应商 1 和供应商 2 的价格我们已经有相对的了解，并且我们已足够了解公司对内部饲养的可变成本的支持，但是需求量是不确定的。分配给每个可能结果的概率也是估计值。
- 决策树使用期望值是假定决策制定者是风险中立的。这意味着可能结果的范围和他们发生的概率被忽略了。例如，在较高需求的水平下，使用供应商 1 可提供一个 T$ 225 000 的贡献率，即使不做任何计算，也比在室内养殖的 T$ 285 000 减去 T$ 90 000 的固定成本要高。如果我们采取风险寻求方法，我们可能更倾向于选择供应商1，因为它提供了一个潜在的更高的贡献率，与期望值无关。

决策树分析忽略了非财务因素，如由于进口蜜蜂，Percy Gambon 决定离开公司所产生的影响。此外，我们还要考虑到决策会对我们的声誉产生的影响。

在我们的商标下售卖进口蜜蜂所产生的企业社会责任问题。如果我们把进口蜜蜂作为梅维斯·文德柏公司或者格里格斯·海夫斯公司的蜂王来售卖，也不去宣布它不是由我们饲养的，那么我们将会违反企业社会责任的两个主要方面：

第一，这将违反我们的法律责任。如果我们没有宣布这个蜜蜂是进口的，那么我们就没有遵守消费者保护法的要求。因此，我们可能会面临罚单还有违反法律所需承担的不好的公众声誉的风险。

第二，这也将违反我们的企业道德责任。为了履行我们的道德责任，我们的行动必须是公平、客观、公正的。误导我们的顾客就违反了我们行为的正直性，因为我们没有告诉他们蜜蜂来源的真相。这也是妥协的结果，因为我们几乎不了解我们售卖的这种蜜对我们当地气候的适应能力。如果我们直接售卖，结果显而易见，它将再一次损害我们作为一个有道德的公司的声誉。

Variant 5　Marking Guidance

Section number	Technical skills		Business skills		People skills		Leadership skills		Integration	Total
1	Variance analysis Factors affecting the value of goodwill and accounting for goodwill on acquisition	13 12								25
2	Make or buy decision Factoring	3 13	Make or buy decision	3	Make or buy decision	3			3	25
3	Time series analysis	13			Incentives for retention of staff	6	Incentives for retention of staff	6		25
4	Short-term decision making using a decision tree	7	Branding and CSR issue	13	Short-term decision making using a decision tree	5				25
Total marks available for competency		61		16		14		6	3	100

试卷五　评分指南

部分	技术技能		商业技能		人际技能		领导技能		综合	总计
1	差异分析 影响商誉价值的因素以及收购商誉的会计核算	13 12								25
2	做或买的决策 代理商	3 13	做或买的决策	3	做或买的决策	3			3	25
3	时间序列分析	13			留住员工的激励措施	6	留住员工的激励措施	6		25
4	用决策树进行短期决策	7	商标和企业社会责任问题	13	用决策树进行短期决策	5				25
可用能力的全部分值		61		16		14		6	3	100

西安外国语大学名师解惑

试卷一共有四项任务，考查了 P1、F1、E1 三门课程的知识点。具体包括差异分析、时间序列分析、员工激励、决策树、企业社会责任等。该试卷考核了考生的四项能力。其中技术技能的分值占 61%，商业技能的分值占 16%，人际技能的分值占 14%，领导技能的分值占 6%，与 CGMA 管理会计能力框架的技能要求一致。

该试卷的每项任务涉及以下知识点：

任务	问题	科目	知识点
任务一	差异分析	P1	差异分析
	影响商誉价值的因素以及收购商誉的会计核算	F1	商誉（goodwill）
任务二	决定做还是买	P1	自制还是外购（do or buy）
	代理商	F1	保理问题
任务三	时间序列分析	P1	时间序列（time series）
	留住员工的激励措施	P1	激励机制（incentive scheme）
任务四	用决策树进行短期决策	P1	决策树
	商标和企业社会责任问题	E1	企业社会责任（CSR）

上述各项任务要求以邮件、报告或工作笔记等形式来呈现答案，对问题的描述非常明确，答题时既要注意内容的针对性，也要注意形式的规范性。

其他答题注意事项包括：（1）本套试题相对较难，原因是考查了考生在复习中容易忽视的知识点，同时也考查了在运营级别的课程中相对难理解的话题内容。（2）整体而言，本套试题需要考生在知识点的熟悉和掌握程度上有较好的表现，否则会让部分习惯侧重复习高频考点的同学遭遇挫败。

考生注意事项

（1）关于如何更好地激励 Percy，给予他无特权化的奖励。（E1 人力资源管理奖励机制部分）

（2）怎样平衡蜜蜂需求量和供应量间的关系。（C04 供需平衡点部分）

（3）运用时间序列预估蜂王的需求数量来确定蜂王的生产量。（C03，P1 时间序列部分）

对应知识点的深度剖析

差异分析

第一部分的问题容易让考生陷入思维的混乱，因为可能从题目的表述上，不容易发现答案的切入点是差异分析。但是如果考生能够观察到附录数据，再结合题目的表达，就可以发现营业报表的主要侧重的就是差异。

商誉

第二部分的问题明确指向了F1板块中在并购时出现的商誉估值问题，这本身就是一个难点，同时还要求考生针对该知识进行情境分析与应用，导致整体难度上升。

自制还是外购

第一部分的题目容易使英语阅读能力偏弱的同学陷入外包的好处与坏处的讨论误区。通过附录数据，考生可以发现外包的决策依据源自自制还是外购的决策。因此明确答题的主体方向非常重要。

保理问题

第二部分考查到了F1板块中的保理问题，知识点考查较细，要求考生对该部分的知识掌握较好。对于熟悉话题的考生而言，考试压力不会太大，但是对于不熟悉话题的考生而言，可能会无从下手。

激励机制

整个部分都在围绕P1板块的知识进行考查。两个主要问题的指向都较为明确，在邮件最后有非常明确的提及。第一部分的题目主要考查情境的分析与应用，对激励计划的解释并不关键。

时间序列

第二部分的题目要求非常明确，总体要对时间序列分析进行解释，尤其要求对四个变量进行解释。这一题目对考生而言，应该相对熟悉，时间序列属于重点内容，因此考生的答题压力不大。整个部分的主要压力均来自工具在情境中的应用。

企业社会责任

整个部分的题目涉及P1和E1两部分内容，数量较多，因此考生答题的时间压力非常大。第一个问题相对宽泛，考生答题的自由度相对较高。第二、三题主要考查决策树，附录中也明确给出了决策树的具体信息，因此考生在给出答案时必须应用数据进行分析解释。这一部分的问题容易让考生耗费大量的时间，因此回答第四题就存在一定的时间压力。但第四题的难度相对较低，企业社会责任的考查也较为简单，主要问题是能否在规定时间将题目有效完成。

附录　CGMA 管理会计能力框架

CGMA 管理会计能力框架由 4 个知识领域构成：

- 技术技能；
- 商业技能；
- 人际技能；
- 领导技能。

这些知识领域由道德、诚信和专业精神加以支持。

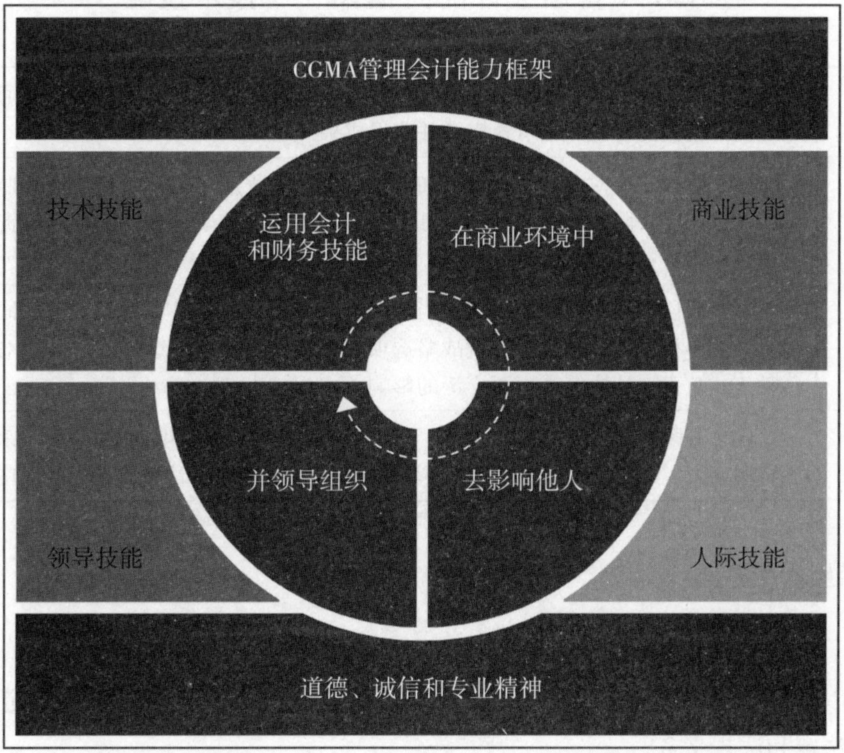

CGMA 管理会计能力框架——学习阶段

基　础	这个阶段要求对企业结构、运营和财务业绩具备基本的了解，也需要通过自身的行动而非他人的行动，来负责实施并获得成果
中　级	这个阶段需要对总体业务运营和衡量具备中等程度的了解，包括负责监督战略的实施，也需要有限或非正式地对同事负责，和/或需要有限或非正式地负责考虑广泛方式或后果
高　级	这个阶段需要对组织的环境、当前战略地位和方向具备深入的了解，同时要具备强有力的分析技巧，并且能够就战略选项为企业提供建议。这一阶段需要对同事及其行动正式负责，让决策产生更广泛的影响
专家级	这个阶段需要具备专家级知识，从而制定战略愿景，为组织的总体方向和成功提供独特洞察力。这一阶段需要对业务领域正式负责，让行动和决策具备高层战略影响力

CGMA 管理会计能力框架——技术技能

基　础	这个阶段要求对企业结构、运营和财务业绩具备基本的了解，也需要通过自身的行动而非他人的行动，来负责实施并获得成果
中　级	这个阶段需要对总体业务运营和衡量具备中等程度的了解，包括负责监督战略的实施，也需要有限或非正式地对同事负责，和/或需要有限或非正式地负责考虑广泛方式或后果
高　级	这个阶段需要对组织的环境、当前战略地位和方向具备深入的了解，同时要具备强有力的分析技巧，并且能够就战略选项为企业提供建议。这一阶段需要对同事及其行动正式负责，让决策产生更广泛的影响
专家级	这个阶段需要具备专家级知识，从而制定战略愿景，为组织的总体方向和成功提供独特洞察力。这一阶段需要对业务领域正式负责，让行动和决策具备高层战略影响力

财务会计与报告

会计准则

这可以确保组织根据会计准则（国内和/或国际准则，根据商业模式而定）执行运营，履行法定和法规义务。

基　础	■ 表现出对会计准则的认知度和了解 ■ 运用这些准则，准确地记录财务交易，创建适当的支持文档
中　级	■ 审核所记录的财务交易和相关报告的准确性和合理性 ■ 协助制定与实施新会计和报告公告，并确定因此而产生的影响 ■ 为具体交易建议适当的会计和报告处理方法
高　级	■ 表现出对会计准则的高层次理解 ■ 为实施新的或更新会计和报告公告而制订、管理和执行计划 ■ 辨别与不寻常或复杂交易有关的潜在问题，审核并批准适当的处理方法
专家级	■ 监督组织选择和实施的会计准则 ■ 辨别与所建议的会计和报告规则有关的潜在问题

交易会计与关账流程

这是根据会计准则对财务交易和事件进行记录、调整和对账的流程。

基　础	■ 执行应收账款流程中的各类活动；运用适当的方法，计算非复杂性备抵；辨别坏账风险 ■ 执行应付账款流程中的各类活动 ■ 执行月末关账活动，及时提供准确的、需提交的财务资料 ■ 根据总账对分类账进行对账，并执行其他相关的对账工作；评估账目的合理性和验证结余 ■ 了解组织账目一览表中的不同组成部分及其相关性
中　级	■ 监督应收账款流程；辨别降低债务相关风险的途径；计算债务人对财务比率的影响；计算非常规性备抵 ■ 监督应付账款流程；计算债权人对财务比率的影响 ■ 监督所有月末关账流程与活动 ■ 对来自非整合系统、涉及不一致数据的复杂账目进行对账 ■ 定义新总账账目，确保适当维护了组织的账目一览表
高　级	■ 解决应收账款流程中的异常情况；计算复杂拨备；就债务人风险缓解方法提供建议 ■ 管理中央化复杂账目应付账款流程；就债权人概况对商业业绩的意义及与应付账款有关的备选流程提供建议 ■ 简化、改进与调和现有复杂的对账与月末关账流程与系统 ■ 定义与设计有效的账目一览表 ■ 确保有效的会计流程，实施与最佳实践保持一致的变革

（续表）

专家级	■ 根据最佳实践，设计应收账款与应付账款流程及相关策略 ■ 为会计运营制定方针与政策；制定坏账避险策略 ■ 就流程改进、治理与异常情况提供建议 ■ 根据最佳实践，战略性地领导组织账目一览表的设计与功能实施 ■ 根据最佳实践，设计流程与相关策略，并制定有关备抵的企业方针

财务报告与合规

这个流程是运用适当的会计和/或法规要求，为具体的实体或集团创建内部和外部财务报告。

基　础	■ 理解并描述财务报表与报告的主要要素 ■ 理解总体合规要求，提供准确及时的财务资料
中　级	■ 编制财务报表与报告，确保其准确性、完整性及合规性 ■ 辨别潜在的合规问题，并向管理高层建议解决方案；确保及时履行财务报告要求
高　级	■ 确保财务报表的完整性、准确性和完备性；讨论适当披露的需求和性质 ■ 实施与最佳实践保持一致的高效流程变革；创造注重合规和共担责任的企业文化
专家级	■ 就相关会计政策与估计的道德选择和调整提供建议 ■ 确保组织充分合规

成本会计与管理

成本会计

这个流程用于记录成本与生产中的相关动因，对其进行分析，并在组织决策中运用相关信息。

基　础	■ 理解并运用成本会计的基本概念，支持企业的运营和财务要求 ■ 展现能够有效辨别并在必要情况下更新产品成本的知识
中　级	■ 细分关键业务流程，通过已经确定的标准化方式分配成本和收入，辨别绩效问题 ■ 运用标准成本法、边际成本法和吸收成本法等各种成本核算方法，并解释相应的优劣点 ■ 诠释原料、劳动力、变动/固定成本及相关变化

（续表）

高　级	■ 实施并运用先进的成本核算方法，判断组织运用的成本核算方法是否适当 ■ 就质量成本核算的作用和分类提供建议，包括预防、评估和内部/外部失败成本 ■ 就新产品/服务和选定产品/服务的创建提供建议，包括相应的销售价格对企业的影响
专家级	■ 就可持续性和环境成本会计的作用及其对改善环境、社会和财务业绩的贡献进行分析 ■ 批准新产品和新服务上市，就备选定价策略及其财务后果提供建议

成本管理

这个流程用于分析、规划与管理成本（包括产品定价与供应链分析），从而支持组织战略的实施。

基　础	■ 表现出对分析和管理成本的方法的基本了解
中　级	■ 运用目标成本、价值分析、生命周期等各种方法，并讨论其意义 ■ 编制分析与报告，让企业管理层能够有效地质询成本，为决策提供信息 ■ 参与企业的消除浪费行动，以便了解关键动因和成本削减机会
高　级	■ 管理成本质询流程，与企业密切合作，确保关键绩效指标是适当的指标 ■ 讨论并推荐转让定价系统，评估转让价格的影响 ■ 就成本控制和报告问题，为团队成员提供领导和辅导
专家级	■ 就战略成本转型提供建议，包括减少浪费，同时保持或加强价值创造 ■ 在战略、设计与工作实施方面领导企业

业务规划

规划、预测与预算编制

这个流程是为预先定义的时间长度评估与量化具有战略匹配度的计划，可能包括计划销量和销售额、资源数量、成本与费用、资产、负债、现金流及非财务指标。

基　础	■ 为业务规划、预算编制和开支预测流程做出贡献 ■ 运用基本的建模、预测和规划方法，制定成本预测，并辨别与解释成本动因

（续表）

中　级	■ 领导规划流程，包括设定目标、传达假设、协调预算编制、质询提交，以及在合并时寻求协作效应 ■ 为企业提供相关的财务支持，以实现有效规划，同时运用中级预算编制和预测方法 ■ 根据成本、时间和质量，为建模、规划和预测提供合理建议，其中可能包括对组织战略方向部分领域的理解
高　级	■ 将企业战略诠释为财务目标和战术方案，以经过控制的风险和奖励方式支持执行 ■ 运用标杆比较、趋势及其他规划和预测方法，诠释管理层决策并实现其有效性；制订并实施对规划流程的改进方案 ■ 在各个业务单元中建立并确保有效一致的建模、规划与预测，在这些流程中辨别与实施最佳实践
专家级	■ 为业务规划和开支预测流程提供关键信息；通过创新，加强目标设定、规划和预算编制对业务的影响 ■ 设定并定义组织目标和目的框架；领导整个组织的战略、规划、设计与实施工作 ■ 为趋势、行业、市场因素、消费者行为及影响组织的其他成本动因提供独特见解和战略建议

资本性支出与投资评估

这个流程是根据战略、承受能力、可接受收益率和选项优先顺序划分对投资进行评估的流程。

基　础	■ 运用投资评估方法 ■ 执行投资后再次评估
中　级	■ 传达和运用投资决策标准
高　级	■ 评估大型和复杂投资、资本性支出和融资项目 ■ 审核投资评估，提供指导与建议
专家级	■ 批准投资提案 ■ 预期组织的未来需求，包括资产组合行动

管理报告与分析

财务分析

这个流程是分析财务报表与数据，为组织随着时间变化及与其他组织相比较的财务业绩和状况提供洞察力。

基　础	■ 运用财务比率，分析、评估组织的绩效、财务状况、流动资金运用有效性及信誉度 ■ 运用现金流折现法（DCF），评估商业和财务决策；确定并质疑推动商业决策的假设 ■ 编制损益、经济附加值和现金流分析，以便做出决策；评估账目结余的变动，辨别需要逐级上报的项目
中　级	■ 运用现金流折现法和在险值（VAR）等常用量化方法，为典型经济活动或标准财务结构和工具的经济、财政及会计影响建模 ■ 提供分析，支持决策，包括展示经济成果，辨别关键价值动因、效益、敏感性和风险、会计和财政意义 ■ 运用敏感性分析和其他方法，准备与分析问题；审核差异分析与对账，并辨别需要管理高层关注的重要项目
高　级	■ 评估财务和现金流分析的结果，建立观点，指导管理层；解决实质性的报告差异，或在必要时建议采取纠正行动 ■ 批准财务报表与分析，并向企业高层展示，提供改进建议 ■ 设计报告与监督机制，根据企业目标跟踪绩效 ■ 运用先进的量化分析，辨别不同行动计划对组织的业务、商业和财务的影响；就改进所建模结果的行动或选项提供建议
专家级	■ 解释和诠释财务报表，推动战略性和成功的商业决策与增长；运用现金流分析中的最佳实践，为企业提供指导 ■ 向首席执行官、董事会和外部相关方传达财务业绩 ■ 评估和量化分析领域的最新进展，将相关进展融入组织的方法中 ■ 为商业分析设定标准，支持战略方向与比较；为复杂和高价值的商业决策制订与实施财务解决方案，包括非技术性风险和业务交付的各个方面

管理报告

这个流程是对组织的运营与财务状况进行提交、讨论和报告（包括质量和可持续性报告、客户盈利能力）。

基　础	■ 提取与交付明确的管理信息报告 ■ 在适当情况下编制与提供准确及时的财务数据，以便将其包含在财务控制流程中
中　级	■ 提交质量管理信息 ■ 为管理、项目或绩效报告开发业务单元报告体系，并实施流程；根据报告周期提交管理信息

（续表）

高　级	■ 评估、生成与实施优化管理信息及向多职能团队提交的创意 ■ 针对管理报告或绩效报告，领导职能报告体系的开发 ■ 质疑并实施根本性变革，解决管理信息和报告质量/正确性问题的根本原因
专家级	■ 制定在质量信息和低成本/高价值解决方案中为业务提供高质量管理信息的新策略、新流程和新系统 ■ 为企业管理报告与规定信息系统设定标准，从而支持其实施 ■ 在整个组织和更广泛的行业范围内辨别与实施最佳实践管理报告，并就报告内容提供战略性见解

绩效管理

这个流程是为了衡量与监督绩效，确保始终一致地实现组织和个人目标。

基　础	■ 诠释和提供对管理信息的基本分析，将其与业务单元战略和运营绩效相关联 ■ 分析业绩，辨别学习重点，协助并通过组织进行传达 ■ 辨别对绩效产生影响的内部和外部因素，分析市场与竞争者行为
中　级	■ 根据可靠的商业理解，为新交易或执行业务的新方式提供建议 ■ 建立、准备和领导实现有效监控，改进业绩的评估 ■ 协助基层管理人员为所辨别的改进领域制订行动计划；负责并推动关键绩效指标的运用，以及准确、及时、前瞻性地管理信息的运用
高　级	■ 在商业评估中负责、选择并运用财务和非财务关键绩效指标；在财务报告中诠释趋势，推断和评估复杂情境中的风险 ■ 在外部环境和商业目标的背景下诠释与分析管理信息，为决策者提供建议 ■ 辨别与管理在追求商机、提供产品或服务时出现的非技术性风险 ■ 评估关键资产组合决策将对成本和其他关键绩效指标产生的影响，并整合其对长期绩效管理和评估的影响
专家级	■ 开发、建立并持续改进绩效管理框架与评估方法 ■ 在企业高管层面为有效绩效管理提供建议 ■ 就财务资源的最优运用提供建议，如流动资金、信贷和风险管理 ■ 就选择适当的财务和运用指标，为企业决策者提供建议

差异分析

这个流程是运用分析来辨别差异和根本原因，并为其准备富有创造力的解决方案。

基 础	■ 评估管理报告，包括辨别与知晓业务差异的关键原因
中 级	■ 诠释财务报告与账目，辨别与评估风险和机会，在监督的同时运用适当必要的避险措施 ■ 诠释管理报告的内容，辨别业务差异的关键原因
高 级	■ 就业绩报告的内容和差异原因提供建议和指导 ■ 设计报告结构，根据企业目标和目的评估实现情况
专家级	■ 针对业务报告的内容提供战略性洞察力

标杆管理

这个流程是将组织流程和绩效与其他组织及行业最佳实践进行比较。

基 础	■ 表现出对影响绩效的内部和外部因素的基本了解
中 级	■ 在内部和外部对业绩进行标杆比较；针对具体需求，提供标杆管理信息，以便做出推动绩效的决策
高 级	■ 根据标杆数据，评估竞争对手的未来趋势与战略，为组织自身的业务辨别关键机会与威胁
专家级	■ 领导标杆比较或流程改进计划，改进控制，令流程更为高效或有效和/或缩短周期

公司财务与财资管理

现金管理

这个流程可以确定如何平衡组织的现金需求，其目的是优化现金结余，同时管理客户、供应商和投资者的需求，从而确定流动资金的最优融资途径。

基 础	■ 辨别融资需求，运用标准信用模型，评估信用评级，并实施适当的标准企业融资解决方案 ■ 执行标准现金管理解决方案
中 级	■ 为市场中可用的备选现金管理解决方案进行谈判，实施并提供长期一线支持 ■ 完成外汇现金流的企业报告，执行远期合约
高 级	■ 针对复杂或不寻常的商业要求，设计、谈判、实施和执行现金管理解决方案 ■ 管理标准现金管理解决方案合同，监督有关外汇现金流的企业报告
专家级	■ 辨别并利用技术和市场趋势，定义现金管理解决方案中的最佳未来实践，从而满足企业需求

兼并和合并

这是兼并与收购其他组织的流程。

基　础	■ 对兼并、收购和剥离前景执行有限分析 ■ 参与尽职调查任务
中　级	■ 相对内部增长，评估兼并、收购和剥离对组织的吸引力 ■ 为兼并、收购和剥离交易的估值、交易经济状况、交易结构、交易方动机及总体财务和结构方面提供独立观点和分析 ■ 管理尽职调查流程，包括与交易谈判团队的互动，从范围定义到分析结果诠释
高　级	■ 分析并传达兼并、收购和剥离对企业战略和资产组合管理的影响，并与内部增长选项进行比较 ■ 为大型多专业兼并、收购和剥离交易担任财务领导者，对所选择的商业交易领导实施后进行评估
专家级	■ 为最重要、最复杂的兼并、收购和剥离交易担任财务领导者 ■ 评估兼并、收购和剥离政策和流程领域的进展，并将相关进展融入组织战略中

资金政策与资金风险管理

这个流程用于实施政策，评估与管理与组织投资、融资活动、收款与支出有关的风险。

基　础	■ 评估并了解与所在业务单元有关的基本企业资金政策，实施适当的标准资金风险管理解决方案 ■ 运用信用模型，评估交易方的信用风险，制定中短期的基本现金流预测，并就适当的行动提供建议
中　级	■ 分析与业务领域有关的企业资金政策 ■ 评估常见的资金风险和财务工具，包括支持定价的金融数学
高　级	■ 根据企业资金政策的实施、执行和分析为业务单元提供建议，评估关键运营资金风险，设计与实施基于风险的避险措施 ■ 在适当情况下，为另类或非标准风险管理解决方案进行谈判，实施并提供持续的基层支持
专家级	■ 为企业资金政策的实施和执行担任领导者，并进行战略监督 ■ 为企业高管提供有关政策、实践和报告的见解，建立并领导风险管理文化

公司估值

这是估算某个业务单元或公司价值的流程。

基　础	■ 为企业的基本估值建模
中　级	■ 能够在尽职调查流程中分析、诠释和展示知识
高　级	■ 在分析和诠释估值决策中展示扎实的知识
专家级	■ 展现经验和高端分析能力，战略性地确定估值决策的有效性和适宜性

企业融资

这个流程用于获取或募集资金，以便实现组织目标与目的。

基　础	■ 了解基本的企业融资安排
中　级	■ 支持融资安排，协调债务评级流程
高　级	■ 将公司财务和融资方法的基本原理应用于复杂和不同寻常的情境中 ■ 对融资安排进行谈判，包括企业信贷额度、公开融资和私募安排，并尽可能降低资金总成本
专家级	■ 监督银行关系，与评级机构和投资银行保持外部沟通 ■ 评估与建议最优资本结构，开发与质疑股东模型，并将其与经济模型相关联

风险管理与内部控制

风险管理政策与程序

这个流程是为了了解并运用组织政策或程序，管理和控制组织可能面临的财务和非财务风险。

基　础	■ 获得对组织风险管理政策应用的基本了解
中　级	■ 针对不复杂的商业问题运用相关风险监管、政策与程序
高　级	■ 开发创新模式，有效且高效地管理实质性的商业风险 ■ 领导实施、执行与监控活动 ■ 就最佳解决方案提供建议，预测变革对不复杂和日益复杂的商业问题的监管、政策和程序产生的影响
专家级	■ 在整个组织范围内推动风险管理流程的整合与标准化 ■ 就组织的风险管理政策、行业最佳实践的应用提供建议，并制定组织方针 ■ 分析风险管理和内部控制领域的趋势，评估意义，并制订与实施整个组织范围内的响应计划

风险识别与评估

这个流程用于检测与评估可能会对组织战略实施产生不利影响的风险因素。

基　础	■ 表现出对企业的风险组成部分和组织控制的基本了解
中　级	■ 参与风险评估与识别工作 ■ 识别与评估风险对实现企业目标的影响，监控风险环境的变化
高　级	■ 分析企业所面临的实质性的、不同寻常的和新兴的风险
专家级	■ 就风险识别与评估的适用方面提供建议

风险反馈与报告

这个流程用于制定与实施程序，以便降低所辨别的风险或风险敞口，并向内部和外部相关方披露风险信息。

基　础	■ 了解管理具体风险的有效控制与避险选项，在必要时求助于专家
中　级	■ 对管理所识别的风险的行动有效性进行监控，并在适当时加以干涉 ■ 理解并解释避险措施的目的 ■ 理解、开发与编制风险报告
高　级	■ 为企业所面临的实质性和不同寻常的风险制定并实施适当的避险措施 ■ 为业务连续性管理机制提供建议，为合理可预见的紧急情境和事件定义适当的风险响应 ■ 设计与实施风险报告系统，并向管理高层传达风险流程和结果，包括改进建议
专家级	■ 为管理整个组织范围内的实质性商业风险开发创新和战略性模式 ■ 诠释风险报告，根据高层次的理解和专业知识，做出有效决策

内部控制

这个流程用于实施控制框架，以确保运营、财务和会计实践的完整性。

基　础	■ 了解内部控制框架和需要降低的风险类型 ■ 辨别、诠释和运用有关具体治理问题的控制方针和要求 ■ 积极促进运用风险管理和基于风险的内部控制模式 ■ 操作财务控制措施、具体的用户访问和/或数据完整性控制措施；定期执行审核，辨别职责分离冲突

（续表）

中　级	■ 协助开发和实施治理框架及恰当的财务控制措施 ■ 建立流程，根据组织的方法监控财务控制的合规性和有效性；辨别、开发与实施必要的流程改进 ■ 实施数据完整性和用户访问控制措施，从而降低与具体流程有关的风险 ■ 评估职责分离冲突的潜在影响；辨别与实施补救措施和/或薪酬控制措施
高　级	■ 担任监护人，维护企业治理和控制框架的完整性和一致性 ■ 特别改进与监控基于风险的财务控制系统；为现有控制措施的有效性制订解决方案，从而管理商业风险 ■ 管理、补救与加强合规性程序；定义和实施端对端用户访问管理流程与标准，涵盖角色设计、访问权开通、监控和补救 ■ 对系统控制措施和可用 IT 解决方案进行最优运用，推动基于风险的用户访问控制流程的标准化与整合
专家级	■ 定义恰当的控制框架，并确保控制政策在整个组织内的实施与充分合规 ■ 评估与治理和财务控制有关的监管及最佳实践的变革意义；推动整个组织范围内的响应实施 ■ 创建基于风险的治理框架，应对复杂和不同寻常的商业活动与问题 ■ 领导标杆比较或了解流程改进计划，从而改进控制

内部审计

这个流程可以检验、分析组织运营的有效性，并提供独立客观的意见。

基　础	■ 执行审计，从而提供独立客观的保证，包括运用企业内部审计方法，编制审计报告草案和审计工作计划的各个部分 ■ 维护具体领域的权限手册；管理与支持管理层自我评估的具体保证活动；辨别完成一次审计所需的资源
中　级	■ 为每次审计准备审计工作计划；开发有效且高效的保证活动 ■ 审核保证计划和审计计划，确保适当的覆盖范围
高　级	■ 确保所述的审计工作计划聚焦于所审计领域的实质性风险，并且符合所有相关的内部和外部标准 ■ 解决与审计计划有关的重大、复杂和非常规性问题，并就如何执行审计评估为他人提供建议
专家级	■ 辨别与监督最佳实践，推动审计实践的创新和战略性变革

会计信息系统

信息系统环境

这个流程可以创建IT环境，了解各个组成部分和系统之间的相关性，包括数据通过系统的工作流。

基　础	■ 获得组织信息系统环境的实际知识（硬件、软件与网络）
中　级	■ 监督组织信息系统的应用与有效性
高　级	■ 积极主动地在企业中分享知识，从而简化系统
专家级	■ 就财务系统和支持技术制定并传达战略愿景

会计应用程序

这个流程是根据政策和方针，定义并构建会计系统。

基　础	■ 表现出对会计系统和功能的了解
中　级	■ 针对内部会计流程和程序有效性及效率至关重要的应用程序，开发与维护计算机的能力
高　级	■ 确保对功能具备深入的了解（即知道什么是正确答案，数据应如何流动）
专家级	■ 确保会计信息系统采用的是最恰当的技术

技术开发与IT解决方案

这个流程用于采用和整合新技术及改进技术解决方案，从而支持组织目标。

基　础	■ 了解新型和改进后的IT开发和解决方案的适用性 ■ 展示辨别潜在升级、增强新产品及其影响的能力
中　级	■ 监督近期的技术进展，推荐实用的实施方案 ■ 发起提高生产力的技术解决方案，满足商业需求 ■ 参与会计领域中新IT解决方案的功能与规格开发
高　级	■ 领导技术升级、增强的实施 ■ 分析外部IT开发的数据完整性和访问控制管理 ■ 推荐新系统，从而实现现有流程的自动化，并设法对业务流程进行重新设计，以便有效运用新技术
专家级	■ 适应新技术和解决方案，开发整个组织范围内的有效方式和最佳实践 ■ 领导与指导新IT解决方案的定义与开发，从而改进财务控制系统的效率 ■ 与IT部门合作，确保组织具备适当的资源来实施新技术

税收策略、筹划与合规

税法

这确保组织会根据适用于组织及其业务线的法定法规和普通法规理解税法并执行运营。

基　础	■ 表现出对营业税基本原则和应用的理解
中　级	■ 根据明确的方针，了解并讨论常规税收事务，如所得税、间接税、公司税等 ■ 评估具备合理复杂性的技术性税务问题（在专业领域中）
高　级	■ 提供税务建议，创造性地解决非常规性和/或复杂的技术性税务问题 ■ 诠释新立法，评估其对组织的意义，和/或就现有立法对新情况的应用提供建议
专家级	■ 辨别具备最高复杂性和重要性的非常规性税务问题，创建解决方案并提供建议

报税与审核

这个流程是根据适用的企业税法评估与编制报税，包括所得税、财产税、消费税、增值税。

基　础	■ 在专业领域中编制基本报税
中　级	■ 审核报税，确保其准确性、完整性及合规性；为具体的企业税务问题提供解决方案
高　级	■ 批准报税，确保其准确性、完整性和法定合规性；在专业领域中为员工提供技术性指导
专家级	■ 评估税法修正案的影响

税务会计

这个流程是根据税法的规定，基于税务目的维护财务记录。

基　础	■ 运用基本税务会计原则，适当记录税务
中　级	■ 运用企业和国际税务会计准则，适当报告组织交易的税务意义 ■ 辨别与实施税务部门中的税务会计和报告流程改进，突出最新国际准则和公认会计准则（GAAP）与税务会计有关的意义
高　级	■ 根据适用会计准则，设定组织税务会计准则，解决非常规和复杂的税务会计问题 ■ 为税务部门中的税务会计流程改进提供建议
专家级	■ 分析税务会计领域中的趋势，确保组织运用的是税务会计原则和准则中的最佳实践

税务监察

这个流程可以检验组织的报税和合规性状况。

基　础	■ 对来自税务部门的信息要求做出答复
中　级	■ 对税务监察和争议进行内部解决提出建议
高　级	■ 从内部和外部角度，就重大税务监察或争议的解决提出建议并进行谈判
专家级	■ 批准对重大税务监察或争议的解决方案

税务筹划

这个流程会从税务角度检验组织的财务状况或计划（包括国际税务和转让定价）。

基　础	■ 表现出对税收策略的基本理解
中　级	■ 提供税务支持，包括范围划分到特定项目交易后的实施
高　级	■ 创新、战略性地管理企业税务事务；为影响超出一个管辖区域的复杂税务项目或交易提供解决方案和建议
专家级	■ 为组织制定税务政策、策略、标准和方针

CGMA 管理会计能力框架——商业技能

基　础	这个阶段要求对企业结构、运营和财务业绩具备基本的了解，也需要通过自身的行动而非他人的行动，来负责实施并获得成果
中　级	这个阶段需要对总体业务运营和衡量具备中等程度的了解，包括负责监督战略的实施，也需要有限或非正式地对同事负责，和/或需要有限或非正式地负责考虑广泛方式或后果
高　级	这个阶段需要对组织的环境、当前战略地位和方向具备深入的了解，同时要具备强有力的分析技巧，并且能够就战略选项为企业提供建议。这一阶段需要对同事及其行动正式负责，让决策产生更广泛的影响
专家级	这个阶段需要专家级知识，从而制定战略愿景，为组织的总体方向和成功提供独特洞察力。这一阶段需要对业务领域正式负责，让行动和决策具备高层战略影响力

战略

这个流程要清晰地阐述组织的总体认同感和方向，概括组织为什么存在、为谁存在及相关方的要求。

基　础	■ 知晓组织的商业计划、直接环境及事件和活动可能会对组织产生的影响；相对执行商业计划而言，了解当前角色 ■ 观察并关注不同寻常的事件，加以关联，得出结论，并向高层财务人员提供思路和观察结果 ■ 了解组织的战略方向，突出潜在价值或风险领域
中　级	■ 分析组织所面对的更广泛的环境，就事件和活动的影响得出结论；引导团队制订可以为商业和财务计划提供价值的解决方案 ■ 关联思路或事件，运用洞察力，构建管理者的观点，并为高层财务人员提供洞察力和观察结果，从而对商业决策产生影响 ■ 了解实现企业长期战略的步骤，辨别对企业的直接威胁或机会，并相应地加以解决或逐级上报
高　级	■ 评估组织更为广泛的环境，根据对企业的了解提供洞察力，影响战术、团队和个人层面的变革，并制定有理有据的商业决策和战略 ■ 向他人介绍组织的战略方向；制订划分优先顺序的财务计划，满足企业需求，并且与整体财务职能战略和商业计划保持一致 ■ 确保团队聚焦于所辨别的首要任务；在运营层面制订和实施解决方案，根据洞察力采取行动，减少关键风险或充分利用机会
专家级	■ 根据对政治、社会、商业、市场和金融趋势的深入理解，提供独特见解；运用洞察力，在整个组织的战略、战术、团队和个人层面领导和影响变革 ■ 制定与组织长期计划保持一致的财务战略，预期与支持商业需求，确保分配了适当的资源，并加以有效实现，包括扩大产能、提高生产力、超越行业标杆的目标 ■ 辨别并聚焦于组织的未来关键领域，制定战略，尽可能扩大机会，降低风险

市场与法规环境

这个流程是为了了解企业所运作的市场和行业，包括辨别风险与机会，同时确保对法规义务的合规。

基　础	■ 了解组织的产品与服务及所销售的市场；了解关键行业结构及组织在其中的地位 ■ 掌握组织客户和竞争者的实际知识；了解组织和行业监管部门及其他关键相关方之间的关系 ■ 表现出对外部和全局因素及其对组织绩效潜在影响的认知度
中　级	■ 将对组织产品和服务及其市场的了解运用于自身的活动中，包括监管环境和日常角色 ■ 运用对组织客户和竞争者的了解，分析与质疑商业案例；运用对法规的理解，支持报告要求和投资融资决策 ■ 针对外部因素对组织绩效的影响，基于理解构思短期战术响应
高　级	■ 运用对组织商业业务和市场的了解，为当前和未来的需求定制产品和服务，包括外部因素的影响，从而影响企业战略 ■ 设计信息报告工具，协助相关方理解法规；与内部相关方合作，支持监管机构的需求 ■ 评估并理解客户和竞争者的优势和局限性，运用洞察力，影响商业决策
专家级	■ 运用对组织产品和市场的深入了解，构建战略；建立与外部相关方的关系，设定未来法规框架的战略方向 ■ 监督和预测消费者和竞争者行为的变化，制定适当的组织响应；确定新兴商业模式的影响，发起行动，做出最优响应 ■ 就监管机制为他人提供建议，包括融资来源和监管标杆

流程管理

这项流程用于规划与监督产生具体服务或产品的结构性活动或运营。

基　础	■ 知晓与每项业务有关的、与工作领域相关的关键业务流程和关键指标 ■ 遵守相关流程和运营程序，关注阻碍流程合规的问题 ■ 为流程改进活动做出贡献，提出建议
中　级	■ 运作所分配的关键业务流程部分；了解构成每个流程的要素以及可运用的指标；积极辨别流程改进机会 ■ 实施最佳实践与行业趋势；管理他人，确保他们遵守既定的流程和运营程序，从而实现成果 ■ 确保对所有流程运用标准化——创建、制定、改进并遵守标准

（续表）

高　级	■ 建立业务流程，获得成果，评估其有效性及与每一项有关的绩效指标 ■ 辨别流程协作和整合机会，影响他人，辨别更多高效可持续的流程 ■ 为流程改进设定要求严格、具有现实意义的目标，并确保以系统化、符合逻辑的方式执行对现有流程的变革
专家级	■ 根据外部指标，对内部绩效进行标杆比较，并为企业运用最佳实践 ■ 定义流程改进，实现业务绩效；端对端管理关键业务流程，使其为企业增加价值 ■ 抓住对系统和流程进行整合、标准化和简化的机会

商业关系

这个流程用于建立及管理内部和外部关系，实现组织目标和治理责任。

基　础	■ 了解组织关键相关方的利益和概况 ■ 了解业务单元中所用的典型合同和法律协议；确保合同的执行符合所述条款，并报告合同履行 ■ 了解合同创建和完成、变更控制及变动的工具和系统，并创建适当的合同文档
中　级	■ 分析相关方概况，突出实现和改进联合效率的领域 ■ 充分了解合同条款及其商业意义；运用现有程序，协助团队成功运作合同，并报告绩效 ■ 运用所需的系统，管理合同变更控制、变动、付款和最终账目流程
高　级	■ 配合相关方，开发与推动潜在效率改进 ■ 通过来自律师的支持，起草和谈判简单的合同或修正案；分析与解释关键合同条款与风险 ■ 就成功运作合同的正确程序提供指导；管理报告程序，以便对问题做出立即响应；审核与评估正式变更控制请求，以便检查一致性和合理性
专家级	■ 辨别核心竞争力，与相关方建立战略联盟，弥合差距 ■ 辨别和实施机会，改进成功运作合同的程序 ■ 领导组织和第三方之间有关合同条款的关键决策；谈判并制定复杂的合同和/或协议

项目管理

这个流程用于整合项目的各个方面，确保适当的知识和资源在需要的时间和地点可用，更重要的是，确保以具有成本效益、质量控制的及时方式，获得预期的成果。

基　础	■ 运用对项目计划的了解，参与项目计划的制订（即行动、所需资源和时间表） ■ 执行部分项目，监督自身进度，辨别障碍，并采取纠正行动 ■ 传达项目成果
中　级	■ 制订简单的项目计划，包括商业案例、应急预案、关键路径，并运用项目管理工具与方法 ■ 管理与监督多个项目计划的实施，有效应对障碍 ■ 传达项目计划与成果
高　级	■ 领导制订和实施复杂的项目计划，对各个业务单元或整个组织产生影响 ■ 辨别实现所需项目成果的新颖和创新途径 ■ 评估与传达项目相依性的影响
专家级	■ 辨别推动价值创造的项目，使其与组织战略保持一致 ■ 调整与影响所有关键相关方，发起对整个组织具有广泛意义的项目

宏观经济分析

这个流程是为了了解与诠释外部因素对组织的影响，诸如市场或行业趋势、地理趋势、文化需求、相关方与消费者。

基　础	■ 了解国内和全球经济的基本面数据 ■ 对基本的宏观经济指标有所了解，并且综合了解其影响
中　级	■ 了解国内和全球经济中涉及的行为与问题的影响（负面、正面） ■ 分析各种经济指标及其对组织目标、战略、产品与服务的影响
高　级	■ 提供宏观经济分析建议，评估与适当诠释外部环境对组织的影响 ■ 辨别关键环境动因，了解其对企业战略与决策的影响
专家级	■ 预测未来的经济状态及经济状况，并就如何降低对组织整体的影响提供战略见解 ■ 了解宏观经济行为背后的潜在原理，并将其运用于组织的各个层面

CGMA 管理会计能力框架——人际技能

基　础	这个阶段要求对企业结构、运营和财务业绩具备基本的了解，也需要通过自身的行动而非他人的行动，来负责实施并获得成果
中　级	这个阶段需要对总体业务运营和衡量具备中等程度的了解，包括负责监督战略的实施，也需要有限或非正式地对同事负责，和/或需要有限或非正式地负责考虑广泛方式或后果
高　级	这个阶段需要对组织的环境、当前战略地位和方向具备深入的了解，同时要具备强有力的分析技巧，并且能够就战略选项为企业提供建议。这一阶段需要对同事及其行动正式负责，让决策产生更广泛的影响
专家级	这个阶段需要专家级知识，从而制定战略愿景，为组织的总体方向和成功提供独特洞察力。这一阶段需要对业务领域正式负责，让行动和决策具备高层战略影响力

影响力

这是可以对人员、关系、流程和产品产生影响的能力，同时可以在国内或国际交易中推动业绩。

基　础	■ 调整自身的个人风格，使之适用于不同人员与情况 ■ 倾听他人的观点和价值观，并对此保持敏感性 ■ 以开放、友好、专业的方式，理解来自不同文化背景的他人并与之产生联系，包括同事和客户
中　级	■ 将自身的想法和议程与他人的需求和目标关联起来，并说服他人接受 ■ 在选择所采用的方式时，预期他人的反应 ■ 在棘手情况下依然保持专业性，表现出同理心，理解他人的感受和行为，并以减少误解、促进接受的方式传达难以传达的讯息
高　级	■ 结合逻辑、个人热情、信念和人际关系技巧，对他人产生影响 ■ 关联、开发和利用组织内外的广泛关键关系网络，对他人产生影响 ■ 通过游说，为想法和计划建立幕后支持，寻求他人的参与，建立主人翁精神和接受度

（续表）

专家级	■ 对来自不同文化的组织产生影响，并建立有效合作 ■ 通过预期和管理异议和质疑，有效地实施高层谈判 ■ 在高风险情境下有效自信地沟通，解决复杂和/或敏感问题，建立共识

谈判与决策

这是适当地运用影响力技巧的能力，并由此获得积极成果，做出与组织战略方向相匹配的决策。

基　础	■ 辨别各方不同的谈判风格，并相应地调整自身的风格 ■ 提供信息并成为团队的一员，支持谈判 ■ 了解特定情况下的关键相关方，并且能够传达具体要求 ■ 根据事实、尝试、以往经验做出决策，权衡利弊，并解释决策背后的推断 ■ 与合作第三方建立工作层面的关系，解决常规问题
中　级	■ 理解相关方的立场和议价力，能够在获得一些支持的情况下进行谈判和/或参与谈判 ■ 在谈判之前和期间，管理内部相关方的接受度，赢得信任 ■ 管理内部期望值，让各方了解进展；在准备、接洽、战略、战术和风格方面确保最佳谈判实践 ■ 研究并运用各种来源的数据，做出基于事实的稳健决策；让相关方明确且简单地了解可用选择 ■ 评估决策的直接结果、广泛意义和意外后果
高　级	■ 在棘手的情况下与外部和内部相关方谈判；表现出自信以及对良好实践的精通，并在第三方关键决策者中保持可信度 ■ 如果情况发生有利或不利的变化，迅速调整个人立场和风格，做出让步，从而确保不会损害与相关方的关系 ■ 有效管理谈判团队，确保每位成员对谈判做好充分准备，始终确保可以从谈判中获得积极成果 ■ 在高风险情况下评估并领导基于事实的决策，相应地辅导他人，并对最终决策结果负责

（续表）

专家级	■ 表现出直接而富于外交技巧的风格；质疑信息，从而辨别推断中的缺陷 ■ 表现出卓越的时机感，迅速获得所有其他各方对谈判的信任和尊重 ■ 领导最复杂的谈判，表现出专业的成交技巧及卓越的政治和文化敏感性 ■ 为长期战略性问题领导基于事实的决策；在决策时分析更为广泛的商业和政治意义，包括结果的有效性 ■ 分享战略见解与知识，协助他人做出可靠决策

沟通

这是向组织内部和外部的各个层面有效诠释和传达财务和非财务信息的能力。

基　础	■ 积极地倾听他人，认可不同观点，并适当地对非口头暗示做出反应 ■ 以明确简洁的方式开发和传达口头信息，根据受众的需求度身定制 ■ 开发明确、简洁、准确、语法正确的书面材料；运用适当的语言和语气，并根据受众的需求定制信息 ■ 根据要求，为他人提供基于事实的信息；适当及时地运用沟通工具
中　级	■ 倾听并运用非口头暗示，了解整体情况 ■ 在小组和目标群体环境中让受众参与互动沟通，预期需求或问题，并做出适当响应 ■ 开发易于理解的书面材料，对商业合作伙伴和管理层产生影响力；有效响应即兴问题，并简化复杂信息，从而确保对方可以理解 ■ 为分享的信息确定适当的受众，并以平衡及时的方式，积极主动地分享基于事实的适当信息
高　级	■ 有效倾听并提炼信息的总体含义，包括他人通常忽略的信息 ■ 自信地向管理高层进行演示，并且在商业问题的答案未知时愿意对此加以承认 ■ 分享基于事实的、重要的有用信息；简化复杂的书面沟通，为组织的各个层面调整风格与内容 ■ 鼓励分享创意和最佳实践，确保理解并实现最佳成果；鼓励他人表达想法，运用同理心进行倾听，以便理解真正的动机和情绪
专家级	■ 领导组织论坛，获得广泛的思路和观点 ■ 创建论坛、系统和程序，积极获取、倾听和分享多样化观点，从而加强理解 ■ 自信地向组织的各个层面展示存在争议和/或复杂的信息 ■ 在复杂的情况下，领导书面信息的形成

协作与合作

这是建立关系和跨职能合作的能力，通过展示诚信，为企业创造价值。

基 础	■ 与商业合作伙伴建立良好关系和信任 ■ 分析商业合作伙伴的需求 ■ 认可财务部门和商业合作伙伴之间的不同优先顺序
中 级	■ 通过展示诚信，保持和加强有效的跨职能业务合作关系 ■ 影响结果，运用基于事实的数据进行适当质疑 ■ 辨别与解决商业合作伙伴的其他需求，指导他们进行价值创造和会计核算
高 级	■ 领导跨职能业务计划，鼓励团队在整个企业范围内培养关系 ■ 在多重相关方中推动协作文化和联合负责机制 ■ 积极指导和挑战可能解决方案的局限性
专家级	■ 在整个企业范围内推动创造价值的跨职能计划 ■ 在企业和外部充分发挥更广泛的网络作用

CGMA 管理会计能力框架——领导技能

基 础	这个阶段要求对企业结构、运营和财务业绩具备基本的了解，也需要通过自身的行动而非他人的行动，来负责实施并获得成果
中 级	这个阶段需要对总体业务运营和衡量具备中等程度的了解，包括负责监督战略的实施，也需要有限或非正式地对同事负责，和/或需要有限或非正式地负责考虑广泛方式或后果
高 级	这个阶段需要对组织的环境、当前战略地位和方向具备深入的了解，同时要具备强有力的分析技巧，并且能够就战略选项为企业提供建议。这一阶段需要对同事及其行动正式负责，让决策产生更广泛的影响
专家级	这个阶段需要专家级知识，从而制定战略愿景，为组织的总体方向和成功提供独特洞察力。这一阶段需要对业务领域正式负责，让行动和决策具备高层战略影响力

团队建设

这是推动团队绩效提升的能力，通过促进和鼓励参与，分享与组织战略保持一致的理念，尽可能扩大目标的实现。

基　础	■ 积极倾听、思考和采纳不同的思路和风格 ■ 与所有员工有效互动，参与团队和小组，与他人合作 ■ 有效运用对可用资源的了解
中　级	■ 在招聘、团队构建和/或制订计划和方案时，促进员工对多样化的环境的重视 ■ 让团队成员参与讨论，让他们能够贡献创意，参与设定团队目标，并在对其产生影响的问题中体验到参与感 ■ 辨别、管理团队的优势和劣势，解决问题，实现共同目标；促进信任、开诚布公、尊重他人；引导与激励团队 ■ 预期额外要求，并适当运用可用资源
高　级	■ 招聘并保留不同背景的员工，确保资源可用，协助他们在组织中获得成功 ■ 促进团队开发新创意，比原有的个人创意更加有力；消除部门内部的低价值活动 ■ 有效管理全球化团队，调整风格，适应文化差异；鼓励跨职能、跨国工作，解决利益冲突 ■ 充分利用团队的集体力量，实现商业成功；为团队创造机会，构建内部关系网络，分享知识和最佳实践
专家级	■ 倡导并成功实现多样化，在整个组织范围内充分发挥组织优势 ■ 创造出促进合作和整合的文化，取代内部竞争；积极辨别与重新调整资源，以便满足战略业务的首要任务 ■ 持续鼓励他人充分利用和发挥所有团队成员的技能、经验和专业知识；提供资源，消除障碍，从而支持跨职能、地域分散的团队 ■ 创建共同目标与氛围，让员工感到自己是整体团队的一分子，而不是去追求自身的个人成功或小团队的成功

辅导与指导

这是为他人提供培训和建议的能力，针对如何产生最佳成果，实现绩效、改进和成功。

基　础	■ 征求、提供反馈，并成功将反馈融入未来的行为中 ■ 为新雇员提供入职培训；了解自身和他人的培训需求与价值 ■ 对自身职业采取主人翁态度；实施与绩效评估保持一致的开发计划；与管理者合作，辨别优势和机会
中　级	■ 积极寻求反馈，衡量与监督进度，更新开发计划，促进持续的自我改进 ■ 参与财务员工和商业合作伙伴的培训开发与交付；运用相关培训课程和计划，培养他人的技能 ■ 为团队成员和管理层提供定期、及时、有建设性、可执行的反馈；积极主动辨别潜在员工的人才开发机会
高　级	■ 创建团队环境，其中包括团队成员能够定期及在充满挑战的情况下为彼此提供有建设性的反馈 ■ 辨别并传达他人的优势和待开发领域；确保开发计划得到实施；对所有团队成员进行赋能并给予其充分发挥才能的机会 ■ 平衡组织需求和个人的职业需求；领导部门的人才管理流程；负责培训解决方案
专家级	■ 推动战略性培训计划，加强整个组织的优势；领导并影响更为广泛的开发规划流程 ■ 积极地在其他职能领域或业务单元中安排开发或挑战性任务，从而让组织和个人获益 ■ 发起高潜力、高绩效个人的聘用、开发和保留；为辅导、指导和反馈留出时间

推动绩效

这是支持、实施和监督有效绩效管理流程、实现目标的能力。

基　础	■ 运用了解，参与绩效管理流程 ■ 建立并接受设定目标，对所委派的任务采取主人翁精神，贯彻责任，主动采取行动 ■ 始终如一地准时交付高质量工作，履行承诺 ■ 为团队和业务单元目标的实现做出贡献；支持同事，协助他们实现目标
中　级	■ 与高层管理人员和团队成员合作，为具体的任务调整个人和团队目标 ■ 确保目标与关键部门指标保持一致；理解成果实现和盈亏财务影响之间的关系 ■ 制造紧迫感，根据适当的高标准和指标，让团队聚焦于交付和获得成果 ■ 监督团队绩效和挑战，应对糟糕绩效；贯彻自身和团队的承诺

（续表）

高 级	■ 管理与传达绩效管理流程的各个方面，确保其与开发计划保持一致 ■ 在团队中承担责任，设定挑战性目标；推动具有挑战性的目标，并根据这些目标评估职能部门绩效 ■ 创造团队和个人享受实现成果的环境；充分发挥额外的资源能力，实现成果 ■ 将非凡绩效的期望值作为规范加以推广；寻找改进绩效、实现价值的新途径
专家级	■ 在整个组织中领导、推动、加强绩效管理 ■ 建立并推动实现商业计划所需的战略与标准；将内部和外部分析转化为战略与行动 ■ 为最佳实践和外包服务交付设定并建立标准；创建推动和奖励成果的计划与行动 ■ 成立并构建业务单元，使其有能力实现战略目标

激励与鼓舞

这是创造员工可以得到鼓舞、鼓励和重视的工作环境的能力。

基 础	■ 展示出“永不言败”的积极态度，在压力时期采用始终如一的积极方式 ■ 认可其他团队成员和同事的贡献和努力 ■ 协助、支持与庆祝同事的成就
中 级	■ 在必要时，以自信的方式及时做出决策，并在得到质疑时，自信地解释和保持自身的立场或决策 ■ 在设定团队方向与目标时，让团队成员参与，建立承诺；协助他们了解他们将如何为团队和组织成功做出贡献 ■ 宣传和庆祝团队或个人成就与成功；评估他人的优势和需求，充分发挥其力量；在他人遭遇挫折后加以安慰，讨论存在的问题和预防再次发生的途径
高 级	■ 亲自建立他人对自身成功或团队、部门或组织未来成功的信心；提供指导、支持和激励机制，鼓励他人 ■ 发布声明，让他人产生希望、乐观精神、兴奋和热情；表彰并奖励团队和个人贡献与成就 ■ 表现出对具体计划或策略成功的信念和高度期望
专家级	■ 创建流程或方法，促进内部或外部相关方对所在团队、部门或组织的当前和未来成功及自身成功的信心 ■ 建立集体企业识别，传达共同目的，从而激发超凡表现 ■ 创造员工因为感到受重视而发挥最佳表现的激励文化；创建策略，表彰、奖励和庆祝贡献与成就

变革管理

这是认可变革需求，采用与商业目标和财务指标相匹配的新思维模式和新工作模式的能力。

基　础	■ 了解业务需求、方向与管理变革 ■ 评估管理变革如何影响当前角色与职责 ■ 支持组织变革的事实，协助实现管理团队的目标与目的
中　级	■ 了解业务目标及变革管理如何与业务单元的绩效和业绩相关联 ■ 诠释、传达与促进变革管理的实施流程 ■ 有效管理存在潜在冲突的变革，尽可能提高接受度与达成合作，实现商业目标
高　级	■ 就变革管理提供建议和影响力，并参与组织变革的规划与实施 ■ 监督变革管理成果，根据商业目标对其加以衡量 ■ 处理组织变革管理中的敏感性问题
专家级	■ 对组织变革的选择和实施进行战略性设计，推动和超越商业目标 ■ 担任变革倡导者